THEORIES OF
Counseling and
Psychotherapy

Second Edition

This book is dedicated to Elisha Yeshua Smith. May the future hold great promise, good health, and good fortune in all that the two of you endeavor and may God's blessings surround and protect you.

THEORIES OF
Counseling and Psychotherapy
An Integrative Approach

Second Edition

Elsie Jones-Smith
Diplomate in Counseling Psychology,
American Board of Professional Psychology

Los Angeles | London | New Delhi
Singapore | Washington DC

Los Angeles | London | New Delhi
Singapore | Washington DC

FOR INFORMATION:

SAGE Publications, Inc.

2455 Teller Road

Thousand Oaks, California 91320

E-mail: order@sagepub.com

SAGE Publications Ltd.

1 Oliver's Yard

55 City Road

London, EC1Y 1SP

United Kingdom

SAGE Publications India Pvt. Ltd.

B 1/I 1 Mohan Cooperative Industrial Area

Mathura Road, New Delhi 110 044

India

SAGE Publications Asia-Pacific Pte. Ltd.

3 Church Street

#10–04 Samsung Hub

Singapore 049483

Publisher: Kassie Graves

Editorial Assistant: Carrie Baarns

Production Editor: David C. Felts

Copy Editor: QuADS Prepress (P) Ltd.

Typesetter: C&M Digitals (P) Ltd.

Proofreaders: Kristin Bergstad, Wendy Jo Dymond, Pam Suwinsky

Indexer: Diggs Publication Services

Cover Designer: Michael Dubowe

Marketing Manager: Shari Countryman

Printed in the United States of America.

Library of Congress Cataloging-in-Publication Data

Jones-Smith, Elsie.

Theories of counseling and psychotherapy: an integrative approach / Elsie Jones-Smith.—Second edition.

pages cm
Includes bibliographical references and index.

ISBN 978-1-4833-5198-8 (hardcover: alk. paper)

1. Counseling. 2. Psychotherapy. 3. Counseling—Case studies. 4. Psychotherapy—Case studies. I. Title.

BF636.6.J66 2016
158.3—dc23   2014031178

14 15 16 17 18 10 9 8 7 6 5 4 3 2 1

BRIEF CONTENTS

PART I

The First Force in Psychotherapy: Psychoanalysis and Psychodynamic Theories   25

PART II

The Second Force in Psychotherapy: Behavior Therapy and Cognitive Therapy   113

PART V

The Fifth Force in Psychotherapy: Neuroscience and Theories of Psychotherapy   627

DETAILED CONTENTS

PART I

The First Force in Psychotherapy: Psychoanalysis and Psychodynamic Theories   25

CHAPTER 2

CHAPTER 3

PART II

The Second Force in Psychotherapy: Behavior Therapy and Cognitive Therapy   113

CHAPTER 4

CHAPTER 5

CHAPTER 6

PART III

The Third Force in Psychotherapy: Existential and Humanistic Theories 229

CHAPTER 7

CHAPTER 8

CHAPTER 9

CHAPTER 10

CHAPTER 11

The Expressive Arts Therapies 345

PART IV

The Fourth Force in Psychotherapy: Social Constructivism and Postmodernism 373

CHAPTER 12

Multicultural Psychotherapy Theories 381

CHAPTER 13

CHAPTER 14

CHAPTER 15

Solution-Focused Therapy   485

CHAPTER 16

Narrative Therapy   509

CHAPTER 17

CHAPTER 18

CHAPTER 19

PART V

The Fifth Force in Psychotherapy: Neuroscience and Theories of Psychotherapy 627

CHAPTER 20

Neuroscience, Psychotherapy, and Neuropsychotherapy 635

CHAPTER 21

Comparing and Contrasting the Theories of Psychotherapy   667

CHAPTER 22

Integrative Psychotherapy: Constructing Your Own Integrative Approach to Therapy   695

PREFACE

Life is an echo, what you send out comes back.

—Chinese Proverb

Bridges are meant to be crossed.

The wisdom of building bridges is that both sides become known.

BUILDING BRIDGES BETWEEN THE PAST AND THE FUTURE

Intention is important in writing any book. I began writing this second edition of *Theories of Counseling and Psychotherapy: An Integrative Approach* with the deep intention of providing a book on theories of psychotherapy that will be truly helpful to professors teaching a course on counseling theory and that will provide a basis for students to develop their own integrative approach to psychotherapy. My overall intention was not only to examine the so-called traditional theories of counseling but also to present newer approaches to counseling and to do so in a manner that would be interesting and helpful to students. From my perspective, too many counseling theory books deal primarily with the past—with what was the prevailing view or zeitgeist about psychotherapy. One consequence of this past orientation is that the majority of the counseling theories presented in theory texts were created during the 1940s, 1950s, and 1960s—that is, theories that were developed well over a half-century ago.

Clearly, there are aspects of these counseling theories that are relevant today—otherwise, they would not be included in this second edition. Yet if we present to our students only counseling theories that represent the zeitgeist of an earlier period, then we shortchange and limit their learning. We need to move forward—to build a bridge between what was known 50 or 60 years ago, and what we now know about helping people deal with challenging life issues.

My intention in writing this second edition of *Theories of Counseling and Psychotherapy* is to build a bridge between the knowledge contained in theories of psychotherapy 50 years ago and the discoveries that researchers have made during the latter part of the 20th century and during the 21st century about the brain, the mind, the factors that bring about change in people, and the impact culture has on a therapeutic relationship. The echo that I want to send out is that it is time to move forward and to be more inclusive regarding what material we present in our theories of counseling textbooks.

This second edition of my book is all about building bridges between the past and the present and between the different cultures of the world and the theories of psychotherapy they have developed. It is time that we take into account the new age that we are living in, and that is the age of neuroscience and brain research and sophisticated technology that allows us to monitor brain changes as they occur during a therapeutic relationship. For instance, Carl Rogers could only theorize about what was going on in a person's head during psychotherapy. We now have brain imaging technology that will allow us to see which parts of the brain reflect activity during a counseling relationship. Based on the current research in cognitive neuroscience, we can state with some measure of assurance that Carl Rogers was right; the therapeutic relationship is extremely important. Neuroscience research on mirror neurons provides the bridge between what Rogers felt intuitively as he worked with clients and what we currently know about the human brain. Thus, current research in neuroscience builds a bridge for many theories. Studies can now be constructed that can examine the effectiveness of a psychotherapeutic approach during the actual therapeutic session.

The second edition of *Theories of Counseling and Psychotherapy* maintains that it is also time to build bridges between American and European psychotherapeutic approaches and those developed by different cultures within the world. Our counseling theory textbooks are largely Eurocentric. Yet we are living in a global culture, where within a matter of seconds, we can make contact with people throughout the world with our smart telephones. I maintain that there is nothing wrong with learning about European approaches to psychotherapy, unless those are the only approaches that are given any validity. Because we are living in a global culture, our textbooks should make an effort to include the psychotherapeutic methods that people from other cultures have developed. We need to learn, for example, how other cultures have dealt with psychological problems and pain. In reality, there has already been some movement toward this end with some American theorists' integration of Chinese concepts of mindfulness into their approaches to psychotherapy. For instance, mindfulness practices have been incorporated into at least three American cognitive-behavioral approaches to psychotherapy—dialectical behavior therapy (Linehan, 1995), acceptance and commitment therapy (Hayes, 2004), and mindfulness-based cognitive therapy (Segal, Williams, & Teasdale, 2002).

GOALS OF THE BOOK

Theories of Counseling and Psychotherapy: An Integrative Approach is intended for use in courses that teach students theoretical approaches to psychotherapy and counseling at both the undergraduate and graduate levels. While this second edition of the book retains many of the goals articulated in the first edition, it also puts forth additional new

goals. A major goal of the second edition is to build a bridge from the older, more established theories of counseling to the newer approaches represented by motivational interviewing, dialectical behavior therapy, acceptance and commitment therapy, mindfulness-based cognitive therapy, integrated psychopharmacology, cognitive neuroscience, and five relatively new approaches in neuroscience and neuropsychotherapy. For the college or university professor who has been teaching the same 10 or 12 counseling theories for the past several years, the second edition of *Theories of Counseling and Psychotherapy* should provide a source of new energy for teaching and engaging students. The book makes an effort to review new technology that can be used in psychotherapy.

The second major goal was to present a section on multicultural positives and multicultural blind spots for each theoretical approach. Each chapter has an expanded discussion of its goodness-of-fit with culturally diverse clients. I discuss where the counseling approach appears to offer many advantages for counseling culturally diverse clients, and where it has some limitations.

The third goal was to review each psychotherapy approach in terms of the recent emphasis on evidence-based practice. What is the evidence to support each theoretical approach? Where does the field seem to be moving in terms of each specific theory of psychotherapy? Are there new developments within the psychotherapy approach, and if so what are they? Or, is the theory of psychotherapy under review dying a slow, natural death?

The fourth goal was to make room for the more recent approaches to psychotherapy by reducing the discussion on the lives of theorists and by moving some of the exercises at the end of each chapter to the student website. In the place of the exercises, I provide five (usually new) discussion questions.

The fifth goal was to make the book more reader friendly for students who are more visually oriented in their learning style. Thus, I have included at least 10 new charts that serve as easy references for students after they have read various parts of a chapter.

The sixth goal was that I wanted to continue infusing multicultural perspectives throughout the book and to provide an opportunity for the reader to get to know some of the scholars who specialize in multicultural counseling and research. To achieve this goal, I have included brief autobiographical descriptions of some of the individuals who have developed various theoretical perspectives related to multicultural counseling. The reader will find what I believe is a fascinating discussion on cultural issues in psychopharmacology in Chapter 4, Behavioral Therapy and Integrated Psychopharmacology and an interesting new section on cultural neuroscience in Chapter 20—Neuroscience, Psychotherapy, and Neuropsychotherapy.

OVERVIEW OF THE BOOK

The second edition of *Theories of Counseling and Psychotherapy: An Integrative Approach* also breaks new ground in outlining the criteria for what I believe is the "fifth force" in psychology and psychotherapy—neuroscience. I would like to know what my readers think about these criteria. In your opinion, is neuroscience the *fifth force* in psychology and psychotherapy? E-mail me with your thoughts.

The other four remaining forces discussed in the book have been expanded and updated. To review them briefly, Part I, presents "The First Force in Psychotherapy: Psychoanalysis and Psychodynamic Theories." It examines the work of Sigmund Freud, Carl Jung, Anna Freud, Erik Erikson, Donald Winnicott, and Alfred Adler. Part II, "The Second Force in Psychotherapy: Behavior Therapy and Cognitive Therapy," considers the theories of John Watson, B. F. Skinner, Joseph Wolpe, Albert Ellis, Albert Bandura, and William Glasser, Marsha Linehan, Steven C. Hayes, and others.

Part III, "The Third Force in Psychotherapy: Existential and Humanistic Theories," discusses the existentialists and a core group of humanists: Rollo May and Viktor Frankl, Carl Rogers, Fritz Perls, William R. Miller, and other researchers connected to expressive arts therapies.

Part IV, "The Fourth Force in Psychotherapy: Social Constructivism and Postmodernism,"

examines the more recent theoretical contributions to theories of psychotherapy. The "fourth force" marks the beginning of a new paradigm in psychotherapy, one that does not emphasize the medical model or the problem-centered approach to therapy. Rather, the psychotherapy approaches discussed in Part IV emphasize how individuals construct meaning in their day-to-day lives.

WHAT'S NEW IN THE SECOND EDITION?

A wealth of new changes have been made in this second edition that I am hoping will make it easier for professors to teach a course on counseling theory and for students to become engaged in learning theories of psychotherapy. Because I have already mentioned some of the new additions to my book, I will only summarize them here.

- This is the first major counseling theory textbook to include a *chapter on neuroscience* as the *fifth force in psychotherapy*. Five different neuroscience approaches to psychotherapy are presented.
- An all-new chapter is included on *motivational interviewing*, one of the most evidence-based therapies in existence.
- A *new chapter on the expressive arts* demonstrates how to incorporate music, art, and play therapies into counseling and private practice.
- The Cognitive Approaches chapter includes new sections on dialectical behavior therapy, acceptance and commitment therapy, and mindfulness-based cognitive therapy.
- The Cognitive Approaches chapter also includes a new section on *cognitive neuroscience*, a field of study that the Nobel Laureate Eric Kandel says "will come to represent all neurosciences in the 21st century."
- The Behavior Therapy chapter includes a new section on *integrated psychopharmacology* that contains a part on cultural issues in psychopharmacology.
- Chapter 2 on psychoanalytic and psychodynamic theories contains expanded coverage of self psychology, a new section on attachment, and new charts that compare psychoanalytic

theory with ego psychology, object relations, and self psychology.

- Each chapter has expanded sections on the multicultural positives and multicultural blind spots of the theory.
- Each chapter has *new sections on empirical evidence* for each theory of psychotherapy.
- The strengths-based therapy chapter has a new section on compassionate therapeutic communication.
- *New Inner Reflections* have been incorporated into several of the chapters.

THE CASE OF JUSTIN

People who bought the first edition of *Theories of Counseling and Psychotherapy* sometimes e-mailed me to say how much they enjoyed Justin. And to all those folks, I want to say thank you and provide a few comments about Justin and the case analyses. Running through every case analysis with Justin is an underlying theme about the power of the therapeutic relationship. Therapeutic relationships trump therapy techniques most days of the week. It did not matter that I was approaching Justin from a psychodynamic or a cognitive-behavioral perspective or any other theoretical perspective examined in the book. What matters most in the case analyses was the relationship between a middle-aged, White male therapist and a 12-year old biracial boy (I like to say bi-ethnic because there is only one race and that's the human race).

I purposefully chose a White, middle-aged man who had very little contact with African Americans or biracial young people to work with Justin. The White therapist is just himself. He does not try to convince Justin that he likes Black people or that he is liberal in any kind of way. He is just himself. He is not even hip. He is middle aged, but still he is cool in a quiet sort of way. I did not choose an African American therapist or even a young person, but rather one who would face numerous challenges in crossing the bridge of human differences to work with Justin.

Both the therapist and Justin face challenges during counseling, some of which are multicultural in nature. The challenge of the White therapist was to reach out across the divide of several hundreds of years of distrust and mistrust between Whites and Blacks in America to help a young biracial boy. Age difference is another divide that he must somehow deal with successfully to work with Justin.

The challenge for Justin was "Could he get past his anger and stereotyping of some White people (even though he himself has a White mother) to accept the insight and help of his White therapist?" "Could he get past the inner city and the influence of his negative peers, poverty, and so many other issues?" Sometimes, Justin and his therapist struggle with the issues of race, injustice, economic inequality, and plain old fear of the unknown, but somehow the strength of their therapeutic relationship helps them go beyond these issues to deal with what brought Justin to counseling.

In keeping with the multicultural framework of my book, I demonstrate that we can cross our racial, cultural, and age divides for the purpose of working together to solve our very human problems. Race does matter in Justin's relationship with his therapist, but it does not dominate their relationship. Race is not swept under the rug and ignored as if it is not there in the therapy room. "I really didn't even notice that you're Black and that I'm White."

I enjoyed writing the case analyses involving Justin. Sometimes I wondered, "Where am I getting this stuff?" Justin's therapist is a composite of so many people whom I have met who are truly interested in working with young people. Justin represents many of what I call "our throwaway youth," similar to the youth who sometimes used to stop me on the street and ask for money—youth who can be helped if someone takes the time to listen to them, to show them some respect, and to help them redirect their lives.

What's new in the second edition of my book is a case analysis of Justin from a neuroscience perspective. I hope that you will enjoy reading and discussing Justin's treatment from a neuroscience framework.

FOR STUDENTS AND INSTRUCTORS _____

Theories of Counseling and Psychotherapy: An Integrative Approach is rich with instructor and student aids. Instructors will not have to create handouts or search for related materials for a given psychotherapy approach. The end of each chapter presents each of the following:

- Discussion questions and exercises designed to assist instructors in promoting classroom discussion about the different theories of counseling
- A glossary of key terms used in the chapter

The SAGE website, at https://study.sagepub .com/jonessmith2e, contains a wealth of instructor and student aids:

- PowerPoint presentations that the instructor or the student can use to review each psychotherapy model
- Additional discussion questions and exercises for most of the chapters
- The Theoretical Orientation Scale developed by the author of the text to help students determine their own counseling orientations
- A therapist disclosure statement for students to use in formulating their own professional disclosure statements
- A discussion of ethical issues related to counseling theory

ACKNOWLEDGMENTS

A number of people were important in writing this second edition of *Theories of Counseling and Psychotherapy*. When I consider the contributions of Kassie Graves (Publisher for Human Services at SAGE), I think about people who have helped create turning points in my life. Turning points have to do with making decisions at different periods in our lives—about seizing an opportunity and about making changes in our lives that we may not have anticipated. Sometimes when we miss the turning point moment, we don't get a second chance. More often than not, we only recognize turning point moments in retrospect, during quiet times when we reflect on what brought us to the life space moment we are now living.

A turning point for me occurred when Kassie and I began to talk about doing a second edition of our counseling theory book and about what we wanted to include in it. Two reviewers had suggested that I include a section on neuroscience, and another had recommended that I include a section on psychopharmacology. For the past 3 years, I had been reviewing research on the brain, and therefore, I jumped at the opportunity to write about neuroscience and psychotherapy. The challenge was to write something meaningful that students could use in their study of counseling theory. The more I studied neuroscience, the more I became convinced that we had entered a *fifth force* in psychotherapy and that force was going to have an amazing influence on what we knew about how psychotherapy affects people and about which psychotherapy approaches appear to have the most treatment efficacy.

I am grateful that Kassie gave me the opportunity to write about neuroscience as the *fifth force* in psychology and in psychotherapy. It took courage on her part and confidence in my ability to permit me to undertake the writing of a chapter on neuroscience and neuropsychotherapy. In suggesting that I write about neuroscience, Kassie has helped generate a turning point in my research efforts. Neuroscience will forever be a part of my life going forward. I cannot go back to what was. I now see the world and counseling research differently.

In addition, I also want to acknowledge Kassie for the work that she did in the early editing of this second edition, especially her freeing up of much space used in the first edition of the book so that I could include two other new chapters, one on motivational interviewing and the stages of change theory, and the other on expressive arts therapy, including art therapy, music therapy, and play therapy. Although we have retained the core part of the first edition that professors and students told us they liked, we have also branched out to embrace new areas. Clearly, Kassie is moving SAGE into a greater position of publishing leadership in the world.

Three other people at SAGE merit mentioning for their contributions to the second edition of *Theories of Counseling and Psychotherapy*. The contributions of Rajasree Ghosh (along with her team from QuADS), the copy editor for the second edition, are outstanding because of her relentless focus on the details of the written text. The author queries that Rajasree sent to me challenged me to do my very best, and therefore, I am grateful for her assistance. Every book publishing should be so lucky and fortunate as to have a Rajasree working for it. I acknowledge David Felts for monitoring the entire production process for the second edition and for making sure that things were running smoothly and on time. I credit him with the good foresight to hire Rajasree. I also want to acknowledge David's leadership and his overall positive, problem-solving attitude in getting our book to final production. Special thanks go to the following proofreaders who did a wonderful job proofreading this book: Kristin Bergstad, Wendy Jo Dymond, and Pam Suwinsky.

Much gratitude is also sent to William R. Miller, the psychologist who created *Motivational Interviewing* and who provided me with so much of the material I used in writing the chapter on his theory. His e-mails encouraged me to continue writing, and they let me know that not everyone gets a chance to write a second edition of a book.

Moreover, I wish to acknowledge the following reviewers for the second edition of my book: Virginia S. Dansby, Middle Tennessee State University; Charles Timothy (Tim) Dickel, Creighton University; Janet Newbury, University of Victoria; Robert C. Palmer, Evangelical Theological Seminary; and Cristen Wathen, Montana State University. The reviewers' comments were critical in adding new content to the second edition.

I also want to thank the number of students and professors who wrote spontaneously to me, informing me that they liked my counseling theory book. Their comments and compliments made me feel that all the days and nights I spent alone in my office drinking coffee and sipping soft drinks were well worth the sacrifice. I am also appreciative of the fact that many readers took the time to write to Kassie and tell her how much they enjoyed the book. When I was writing the second edition, I thought about their encouraging e-mails. Their supportive comments sustained me as I worked during the late night hour.

On a personal level, I want to thank my son, Travis, for his encouragement and continual support of my research. In his eyes, I saw love and concern for me. Seeing and feeling his love was enough for me to continue writing another page, another chapter—the rest of the book. It is simply amazing what love can do in a person's life. Thank you, Travis.

Two dear friends—Carolyn Phillips and Barbara Hughes—provided the spiritual support I needed to complete this project.

Finally, I thank God, who is the source of my strength and who has given me the gifts to write this book. It was simply amazing for me to observe the number of times when I felt stuck writing a particular passage or I was looking for a specific reference, and it would suddenly be right next to me—on the floor next to my foot or on a window sill. At times I wondered, "How did that get there at this very moment?" And I would look around the room for some sort of reasonable explanation for the reference's appearance—an explanation that was not forthcoming. Near the end, I just got used to thanking the Holy Spirit for helping me.

ABOUT THE AUTHOR

Elsie Jones-Smith is a clinical psychologist, a licensed psychologist, a counselor educator, and the president of the Strengths-Based Institute, which provides consultation to schools and organizations dealing with youth experiencing challenges with violence, lack of a sense of purpose, and drug addiction. She is the developer of two theories in psychology: strengths-based therapy (SBT) and ethnic identity development; an article about this theory was featured as a major contribution to psychological research by *The Counseling Psychologist* in 1985. She is a member of the American Academy of Counseling Psychology, and a fellow in two divisions of the American Psychological Association, including Division 17 Counseling Psychology. She holds dual PhDs in clinical psychology and counselor education. She is the author of *Strengths-Based Therapy*: *Connecting Theory, Practice, and Skills*; *Spotlighting the Strengths of Every Single Student*, and *Nurturing Nonviolent Children*. Previously a professor at Temple University, Michigan State University, and Boston University, she has served on numerous editorial boards.

CHAPTER 1

Introduction

Journey Toward Theory Integration

There is nothing so practical as a good theory.

—Kurt Lewin

A journey of a thousand miles must begin with a single step.

—Lao Tzu, Chinese Taoist philosopher,
founder of Taoism

There are three truths: my truth, your truth, and the truth.

—Chinese proverb

Most graduate-level students are required to develop knowledge of the theories of therapy as part of their educational and professional development. Typically, they are introduced to at least 10 theories from the major schools of psychotherapy, such as psychoanalysis, behavior, cognitive, learning, or client-centered therapy. The heart of this book is about choosing a theoretical orientation—meaning either a single theory or an integrated psychotherapy approach. A therapist without a theoretical approach to psychotherapy is like Alice in Wonderland asking the Cheshire cat which way she should go.

> Alice came to a fork in the road. "Which road do I take?" she asked.
> "Where do you want to go?" responded the Cheshire cat.
> "I don't know," Alice answered.
> "Then," said the cat, "it doesn't matter."
>
> —Lewis Carroll,
> *Alice in Wonderland*

Theories of psychotherapy are like the Cheshire cat. They provide a road map for us when we work with clients. Without such a map, therapists are only winging it. They're like Alice, wanting to go somewhere but not knowing where they want to go with a client. Effective therapists establish theoretical road maps or treatment plans for their clients.

Inner Reflections

Do you see any similarities between you and Alice? Any differences?

Would you be able to tell the Cheshire cat where you are going? Where would that be?

GOALS OF THE BOOK

One of the goals of this text is to help you learn the basics of major psychotherapy approaches and to assist you in applying such theories. I include chapters on psychoanalytic and psychodynamic approaches, behavioral and cognitive approaches,

1

as well as some of the newer forms of therapy, including counseling for gay and lesbian students, strengths-based therapy, spiritual counseling, solution-focused therapy, and narrative therapy.

A second goal of this book is to help you to construct your own integrated approach to psychotherapy (Norcross & Goldfried, 2005). Research studies have established clearly that few psychotherapists and counselors have adopted a single theoretical approach to therapy (Norcross & Goldfried, 2005; Norcross, Hedges, & Prochaska, 2002). I take the position that effective therapists need to become familiar with and skilled in the conceptual frameworks, techniques, and knowledge base of multiple theories if they are to help diverse clients from different backgrounds who have various presenting issues. It is important for therapists to develop a broad range of therapeutic expertise to meet the needs of a culturally diverse clientele.

In each chapter of the book, I ask you to consider what, if any, parts of the theory presented would you consider integrating into your own psychotherapy frameworks. Moreover, to arrive at a carefully thought-out integrative theory of your own, you are encouraged to consider what you subscribe to from the various theories, including identifying your views of human nature as well as your beliefs about what brings about behavioral change in people who are hurting, in distress, or dissatisfied with some aspect of their lives. Formulating an integrative theory of therapy is a journey that each therapist has to take for himself or herself. Moreover, your integrated theory will change over time, depending on what you find helps people make meaningful changes in their lives.

A third goal is to depart from the traditional therapy theory texts by presenting a framework for integrating theories of psychotherapy (Brooks-Harris, 2008). For instance, what does an integrated psychotherapy theory based on psychoanalysis, behaviorism, or cognitive theory look like? How does the practitioner integrate what appears to be contradictory views of human nature and conflicting philosophical systems? How might a beginning practitioner integrate concepts from cognitive theory with elements of self theory or psychodynamic

theory? The goal is to help you get a sense of what is involved in psychotherapy integration.

Most textbooks on counseling theories omit spiritual approaches to counseling (Plante, 2009). A fourth goal of this book is to deal with some of the spiritual approaches to psychotherapy. I examine issues surrounding spirituality and the therapeutic process. In particular, I examine mindfulness, which has been adapted from Chinese Buddhist practices. Rather than teach therapists a formalized theory of spirituality and therapy, this chapter deals with such issues as assessment and spirituality, consultation with religious professionals, and best practices in spiritual approaches to therapy.

A fifth goal is to infuse multicultural concepts throughout the book (Pedersen, 2003). I examine each psychotherapy approach under consideration in terms of multicultural issues. The chapters focus not only on Western multicultural approaches to psychotherapy but also on Eastern approaches. For instance, I include Naikan therapy, Morita therapy, mindfulness therapy, Arab Muslim approaches to psychotherapy, and one African approach to psychotherapy (Ma'at). Although many counseling theory texts examine the traditional psychotherapy theories from a multicultural perspective, few deal with multicultural theories, and still fewer present Eastern approaches to psychotherapy.

A sixth goal is to present a case study throughout the book that deals with issues that reflect some of the dilemmas of present-day America. Most counseling theory textbooks present case studies dealing with adults. However, increasingly, the typical client seen at agencies is a youth who has been referred to counseling by the courts or by a school guidance counselor or a school social worker. Throughout the book, I present the case study of Justin, a 12-year-old boy of mixed parental heritage (mother, White; father, African American) who has moved from the inner city of Chicago to Utah to escape the gangs. Justin is very real, and so are the issues that he faces in living with a single mother in a school struggling to deal with multicultural conflicts and situations. The case study is presented in each chapter so that it is viewed from each of the major theoretical perspectives discussed within this text.

This book represents a step forward from the traditional text on counseling theories. I've made a concerted effort to bridge the traditional approaches to psychotherapy with the newer approaches—to make the study of counseling theories more than just the study of what was and has been but also the study of what is current and relevant—solution-focused therapy, narrative therapy, and strengths-based therapy, to neuroscience and neuropsychotherapy, to name just a few. I also endeavor to engage the reader in making a critical analysis of the theories that are studied in most graduate-level school programs with neuroscience, which is not taught in most counseling and social work graduate programs of study. This is the first counseling theory book that presents an entire chapter on neuroscience and neuropsychotherapy—the fifth major paradigm shift in psychotherapy and counseling. Neuroscience developments hold the possibility of revolutionizing many of the major theories of psychotherapy. Students will be introduced to some of the outstanding developments in neuroscience, including new psychotherapy approaches based heavily on neuroscience. They will be introduced to the concept that counseling and psychotherapy build new brain networks in their clients (the concept of neuroplasticity), that therapists and counselors can influence their clients through the practice of engaging mirror neurons, that therapy is primarily a process of right brain to right brain engagement, and that a client's attachment history has a significant influence on his or her brain development as well as his or her mind development. The chapter on neuroscience is truly an exciting and informative chapter.

ORGANIZATION OF THE BOOK

The book groups theories of psychotherapy under the headings of five major forces in psychology and in psychotherapy: the first force, which includes psychoanalytic and psychodynamic theories; the second force, which contains behavior and cognitive therapy theories; the third force, which includes existential-humanistic theories; the fourth force, which includes social constructivist, postmodern, and integrative approaches to therapy; and the fifth force, which includes neuroscience and psychopharmacology (which is not included in this book). This introductory chapter presents a number of definitions and concepts and it proposes questions that will help guide students in forming their own integrative focuses.

Part I of the book, "The First Force in Psychotherapy," contains Chapters 2 and 3. Chapter 2 discusses the theoretical contributions of Sigmund Freud, Carl Jung, Anna Freud, Erik Erikson, and Donald Winnicott (object relations and the good-enough mother) and self psychologists (Heinz Kohut—the narcissistic personality). This second edition of my book contains an expanded section on self psychology and a new section on attachment and another section on evidence-based research for psychodynamic approaches to psychotherapy. Chapter 3 explores the contributions of Alfred Adler, an individual who has had a profound influence on psychology; many of his ideas have been incorporated into other theoretical approaches such as solution-focused brief therapy. The section on evidence-based research for Adlerian psychotherapy presents the evidence for and against the theory's demise.

Part II, "The Second Force in Psychotherapy," includes Chapters 4, 5, and 6. Chapter 4 presents in detail the contributions of John Watson, B. F. Skinner, and Joseph Wolpe. Because the behavioral movement has now merged with the cognitive approach to psychotherapy, two chapters are devoted to the cognitive movement in psychology. Chapter 5 discusses Albert Ellis's rationale emotive behavior therapy and Aaron Beck's cognitive therapy. Also covered in this chapter is Albert Bandura, who did not provide a theory of therapy but whose research findings on observational learning and self-efficacy were so great that they influenced theorists who did develop a specific approach to therapy.

What's new to this second edition is a rather sizable section on what is being called the "third-wave cognitive-behavioral therapies"—those cognitive-behavioral theoretical approaches that have incorporated Eastern perspectives and the mindfulness. Three new cognitive-behavioral approaches to psychotherapy are presented in Chapter 5, and these include dialectical behavior therapy, acceptance and commitment therapy, and mindfulness-based cognitive therapy. Chapter 5 shows the development of the cognitive school of psychotherapy—from the second-wave approaches of Ellis and Beck to the third-wave theories of Linehan and Steven C. Hayes. Chapter 6 focuses on William Glasser's reality therapy; however, it contains expanded sections on multicultural impact and evidence-based research.

Part III, "The Third Force in Psychotherapy," contains Chapters 7, 8, 9, 10, and 11. Chapter 7 presents the existential-humanistic theories of Rollo May and Viktor Frankl. Chapter 8 provides in-depth coverage of Carl Rogers and his contribution of client-centered/person-centered therapy. Chapter 9 features Fritz Perls and Gestalt therapy. Two important chapters have been added to the third force in psychotherapy: (1) Chapter 10 on William R. Miller's motivational interviewing and (2) Chapter 11 on expressive arts therapies, including art therapy, music therapy, and play therapy. Miller is placed in the humanistic third force section because he told me personally that he belonged in that section and because his theory is based partly on the work of Carl Rogers. To the best of my knowledge, this is the first textbook on counseling and psychotherapy theories that contains a section on play therapy—a therapeutic approach that has been used with children and adolescents for well over a half-century.

Part IV, "The Fourth Force in Psychotherapy," is conceptualized as the "postmodern and social constructivist movement." Others have termed the *fourth force* as the multicultural movement; however, I maintain that multiculturalism is subsumed under the heading of social constructivist. Although multiculturalism is not conceptualized as the fourth force, its influence on psychology has been profound and widespread.

Part IV is the longest and most varied part of the book. Chapters 12, 13, and 14 constitute a trilogy that deals specifically with multiculturalism.

To my knowledge, there is no other text that offers such a concerted focus on multicultural approaches to psychotherapy. In using this text, instructors will find that they no longer have to supplement their presentations with outside material on cultural diversity. Much of what you might desire to present to students is contained within these three chapters. Chapter 12, on multicultural psychotherapy theories, presents an in-depth analysis of five theoretical approaches to multicultural identity and psychotherapy. Most of the multicultural theories discussed in Chapter 12 have been put forth by Americans.

Chapter 13, titled "Transcultural Psychotherapy: Bridges to Asia, Africa, and the Middle East," examines the international contribution to cultural diversity in psychotherapy. This chapter contains a description of Naikan therapy and Morita therapy—two Japanese approaches. The chapter also reviews mindfulness, which is the Chinese approach to psychotherapy. Currently, mindfulness has been integrated with a number of theoretical approaches to psychotherapy, including cognitive-behavioral therapy, dialectical therapy, and so on. Within the past few years, more than 40 books have been written on mindfulness, integrating it with other theories. Ma'at, an African approach to psychotherapy, is reviewed briefly. The chapter also presents Arab Muslim views on psychotherapy. Typically, even though this population numbers about 1.5 billion strong throughout the world, it is excluded from most counseling theory textbooks. The Arab Muslim view of psychotherapy should be presented along with the contributions of Japanese and Chinese.

> ## Inner Reflections
>
> Do you think therapists should try to integrate theories of psychotherapy from the East and the West?
>
> To what extent is it feasible to use Buddhist concepts in therapy for the average American?
>
> Are the theories that we study in counseling theory courses culturally bound and Eurocentric?

The trilogy on multiculturalism is rounded out with Chapter 14 on feminist therapy and lesbian and gay therapy. While some counseling theory textbooks contain a chapter or a section on feminist therapy, very few deal with lesbian and gay issues in therapy. This textbook is a trailblazer in dealing forthrightly with challenges that face the gay and lesbian population. It explores such critical issues as gay and lesbian identity development, issues related to coming out, and therapist bias and heterosexism.

Next, this section moves to some of the newer social constructivist theories. Chapter 15 reviews solution-focused therapy and the contributions primarily of Insoo Kim Berg and her husband, Steve de Shazer. Chapter 16 focuses on narrative therapy and the major theoretical offerings of Michael White and David Epston. These theorists maintain that throughout our lives we construct stories about our lives, about who we are and where we either are going or not going. A therapist listens to our stories and helps us rewrite and renarrate them so that we can live more fulfilling lives.

The book next navigates to include spiritual therapy. Chapter 17 is titled "Integrating Religious/Spiritual Issues During Psychotherapy." Again, the inclusion of a separate chapter on spirituality and psychotherapy in a counseling theory book is a major milestone. An important theme of this chapter is taken from Steven Covey's quotation: "We are not human beings on a spiritual journey. We are spiritual beings on a human journey." In keeping with the theme of psychotherapy integration, this chapter explores how a therapist might integrate spiritual issues into therapy. There's a brief section on "listening for clients' spiritual language." The chapter also provides a section on clinical assessment and questions to bring forth clients' spiritual life: (1) questions designed to evoke clients' past spirituality, (2) questions designed to elicit clients' present or current spirituality, and (3) questions related to clients' future spirituality. In addition, the chapter presents a client intake form that focuses on clients' spirituality.

Chapter 18 is devoted to my theory of strengths-based therapy, emanating from the highly popular article "Strength-Based Counseling" that was published in 2006 in *The Counseling Psychologist*. Strengths-based therapy is an integrative approach that can be traced to several theories, including research on brain development and strength, needs theory, and logotherapy. Also included in this chapter are the contributions of a number of strengths-based therapists, including the seminal work of Dennis Saleebey from social work and positive psychology. Most therapists acknowledge that therapy should emphasize a client's strengths. Yet many find themselves challenged when implementing a strengths-based practice. Chapter 18 not only provides one of the few theoretical approaches to strengths-based therapy but also offers practical steps and exercises a therapist might use in working with clients.

Chapter 19 deals with several theories from family therapy. My rationale in including family therapy in the postmodern, social constructivist part of this text rests on the fact that theories related to family therapy have been constructed from a number of theoretical approaches, including general systems therapy, psychoanalytic and psychodynamic theory, as well as experiential theory. I review the theoretical approaches of Alfred Adler, Murray Bowen and Bowenian family therapy, Virginia Satir and Carl Whitaker (experiential family therapists), Salvador Minuchin and structural family therapy, and Jay Haley and strategic family therapy.

Part V, "The Fifth Force in Psychotherapy" is made up of Chapters 20, 21, and 22. During the past several decades, an explosion of knowledge has been witnessed in the field of neuroscience. Neuroscience has changed our knowledge about the human brain, mind, nervous system, and psychotherapy. I maintain that the developments in neuroscience as they relate to psychotherapy are revolutionary and that neuroscience changes the current cognitive-behavioral paradigm in psychology and psychotherapy such that it creates a fifth force. Neuroscience is helping scientists and practitioners to understand the human attachment and motivational systems. Neuroscientists assert that human emotions and motivations develop from distinct systems of neural activity. Why should knowing and learning neuroscience matter to psychologists and helping professionals? According to Cozolino (2010),

> On a practical level, adding a neuroscientific perspective to our clinical thinking allows us to talk with clients about the shortcomings of our brains instead of the problems with theirs. The truth appears to be that many human struggles, from phobias to obesity, are consequences of brain evolution and not deficiencies of character. (p. 356)

The book's introduction to the fifth force in psychotherapy presents six criteria for arriving at the conclusion that neuroscience is this new major force. Chapter 20 examines the latest developments in neuroscience and neuropsychotherapy. It reviews several approaches to neuropsychotherapy, including brainspotting (Grand, 2013), eye movement desensitization and reprocessing (EMDR; Shapiro, 2001), and coherence theory (Ecker, Ticic, & Hulley 2012). In addition, the neuropsychotherapeutic approaches of Daniel Siegel (2010) and Rick Hanson (2013) are also discussed briefly. To the best of my knowledge, this is the first time that a textbook on theories of counseling and psychotherapy has included a full chapter—not a brief mentioning, but an entire chapter on neuroscience and neuropsychotherapy.

Chapter 21, titled "Comparing and Contrasting the Theories of Psychotherapy," reviews all the theories using a consistent set of dimensions, such as worldview, key concepts, goals of therapy, role of the therapist, and techniques of therapy. This chapter is, however, much more than just a comparison of key points among the counseling theories. This chapter includes a section that provides a multicultural conceptualization framework for clients that is based on the theories examined throughout the book.

The future outlook of theoretical approaches to psychotherapy is analyzed within the evidence-based movement. For instance, what impact will the evidence-based movement have on theories that are not supported with empirical research? Will managed care demand that therapists use only those psychotherapy theories that have empirical research evidence?

Chapter 21 includes a reference to the Theoretical Orientation Scale (TOS) so that students can get some objective determination of their own theoretical leanings. In an effort to save space for the new theories, the TOS is now online in the student resource section. The TOS helps determine a student's theoretical orientation and provides a fitting closing activity after the review of all the counseling theories.

Many instructors at some point during a course assign students a written paper on counseling theories. Chapter 21 will make it a great deal easier for students who might feel overwhelmed after reading the theories to complete such an assignment. This chapter supports students' critical thinking about what theories they might incorporate into their own practice.

Throughout the book, in each chapter, I asked readers to consider what, if any, parts of the theory presented they would integrate into their own psychotherapy framework. Chapter 22 is titled "Integrative Psychotherapy: Constructing Your Own Integrative Approach to Therapy." It offers a wealth of information and a new approach to theoretical integration. After tracing psychology's emphasis on a single approach to psychotherapy, I direct the readers' attention toward multitheoretical models to psychotherapy integration. Jeff Brooks-Harris's (2008) multitheoretical psychotherapy framework is offered as a model that students might use in developing their own approaches to psychotherapy. In contrast to the Brooks-Harris model, I include the components of spirituality. After reading this chapter, students will be able to construct their own integrative approach to psychotherapy using either the Brooks-Harris multicultural dimensions or the framework that I propose that includes a spiritual dimension.

Because I have chosen to discuss each of the theories in terms of the forces that they represent, the order of the chapters here is not the same as one finds in typical textbooks on theories of psychotherapy. Most such textbooks present the existential and humanistic school right after the psychoanalytic and psychodynamic theories. The world was talking first about B. F. Skinner and then about Carl Rogers. Clearly, the behavioral school had developed approaches to therapy long before the existential-humanist theorists had made their mark on the world. Therefore, this book presents the cognitive-behavioral school immediately following the psychoanalytic and psychodynamic schools. I hope that my presentation of the theories will motivate people to discuss theories in terms of the forces that they represent in psychotherapy. And in presenting some of the more recent theories of psychotherapy, I hope to make my psychotherapy text more relevant to the lives of people living in the 21st century.

DEFINITIONS OF COUNSELING AND PSYCHOTHERAPY _____

Counseling and psychotherapy may be conceptualized as overlapping areas of professional competence. Typically, counseling is conceived as a process concerned with helping normally functioning or healthy people to achieve their goals or to function more appropriately. In contrast, psychotherapy is usually described as reconstructive, remedial, in-depth work with individuals who suffer from mental disorders or who evidence serious coping deficiencies.

Historically, counseling has tended to have an educational, situational, developmental, and problem-solving focus. The helping professional concentrates on the present and what exists in the client's conscious awareness. Counseling may help people put into words why they are seeking help, encourage people to develop more options for their lives, and help them practice new ways of acting and being-in-the-world. Therapy is more a process of enabling a person to grow in the directions that he or she chooses.

In comparison to counseling, psychotherapy is considered a more long-term, more intense process that assists individuals who have severe problems in living. A significant part of the helping process is directed toward uncovering the past. Typically, counseling is focused on preventive mental health, while psychotherapy is directed toward reparative change in a person's life. Whereas the goals of counseling are focused on developmental and educational issues, the goals of psychotherapy are more remedial—that is, directed toward some significantly damaged part of the individual. In general, counseling denotes a relatively brief treatment that is focused most on behavior. It is designed to target a specific problematic situation. Psychotherapy focuses more on gaining insight into chronic physical and emotional problems.

Usually, psychotherapy requires more skill than simple counseling. It is conducted by a psychiatrist, trained therapist, social worker, or psychologist. While a psychotherapist is qualified to provide therapy, a counselor may or may not possess the necessary training and skills to provide psychotherapy. Throughout this book, the terms *counselor*, *psychotherapist*, *helper*, *clinician*, and *mental health therapist* are used interchangeably; I acknowledge at the outset that there are differences among these terms.

THE ROLE OF THEORIES OF PSYCHOTHERAPY _____

A *theory* may be defined as a set of statements one uses to explain data for a given issue. Theories help people make sense out of the events that they observe. A theory provides the means by which predictions can be made, and it points out the relationships between concepts and techniques. A psychotherapy theory supplies a framework that helps therapists understand what they are doing (Mikulas, 2002). It is a systematic way of viewing therapy and of outlining therapeutic methods to intervene to help others. It provides the basis for a therapist's deciding what the client's problem is, what can be done to help the client correct the problem, and how the relationship between the therapist and the client can be used to bring about the desired or agreed-on client change.

In psychotherapy, a theory provides a consistent framework for viewing human behavior, psychopathology, and therapeutic change. It supplies a means for therapists to deal with the impressions and information they form about a client during a therapy session. A psychotherapy theory helps therapists describe the clinical phenomena they experience, and it helps them to organize and to integrate the information they receive into a coherent body of knowledge that informs their therapy (Prochaska & Norcross, 2003).

A theory influences which human capacities will be examined and which will be ignored or reduced in importance. Therapists develop treatment interventions based on their underlying conceptions of pathology, mental and physical health, reality, and the therapeutic process (Mikulas, 2002). A psychotherapy theory deals, either explicitly or implicitly, with the theorist's view of the nature of people, human motivation, learning, and behavioral change. Does the theorist believe that people are basically good or evil?

Theories may be measured against several criteria. The first criterion is clarity. Is the theorist clear in his or her outline of the basic assumptions that underlie the theory? Second, the various parts of a theory should be internally consistent and not contradict one another. Third, a theory should be comprehensive and explain as many events as possible. It should be precise, parsimonious, and contain testable hypotheses or propositions. Fourth, a theory should be heuristic and serve to promote further research. As additional research evidence is accumulated, the theory is further substantiated, revised, or rejected. As you review the theories presented in this text, evaluate how well each adheres to these criteria.

A sample of how theory works in therapy can be illustrated by examining a therapy interview. A client comes to a therapist for assistance in dealing with a problem. The therapist begins the interview with some observations and thoughts about the client's problem and some possible interventions that might help to resolve the client's issues. The therapist's initial thinking or hunches serve as a hypothesis about what goals, interventions, and outcomes may reduce the client's symptoms. The therapist's hypothesis about the client's issues and needs is supported or rejected by his or her experience with the client.

The therapist's next step in theorizing is to have additional sessions with the client during which he or she observes what takes place in the interactions with the client. Based on his or her observations, the therapist formulates hypotheses about what is happening with the client. These hypotheses form part of the therapist's theory. For instance, a therapist may observe that it is important to use the first session to establish a working alliance with the client rather than to ask too many questions. That is, he or she observes the various conditions under which the client responds positively or negatively, and from such observations, he or she formulates generalizations that result in mini-theories about what is working with the client.

Inner Reflections

List three ways that a theory of psychotherapy might be useful to you in your work with clients.

In the best of all possible worlds, how do you see yourself using a theory of psychotherapy?

THE THEORY BATTLES IN PSYCHOTHERAPY

For decades, theorists engaged in a battle over which theory was right or wrong and what approach to therapy and psychotherapy produced the most positive change in clients (Fiedler, 1950, 1951; Gelso & Carter, 1985). Various theorists argued that their particular approaches produced distinguishing outcomes. In the early days of therapy, graduate schools advocated specific therapy and psychotherapy approaches. Currently, many graduate schools emphasize helping students achieve their own integrative therapy theories after they have reviewed the major therapists. This position is taken because past research has demonstrated that no one therapy theory has produced consistently positive therapeutic results. Repeatedly, studies have reported that there is more than one road to effective psychotherapy and that therapists are remarkably similar in what they do regardless of their theoretical orientation. For instance, during the 1950s, Fiedler (1951) observed that therapists of varying orientations were very similar in their views of the "ideal therapy." Sundland and Barker (1962) followed up with a study that showed that more experienced therapists were similar in their approaches to therapy, regardless of their theoretical orientations.

Some 25 years later, Gelso and Carter (1985) concluded in an extensive review of the literature that "most clients will profit about equally, but in different ways, from the different therapies" (p. 234). Similarly, Stiles, Shapiro, and Elliott (1986) concluded that psychotherapies share common features that underlie or override differences in therapists' treatment and that these common features are responsible for the similar equivalence in effectiveness of therapies.

During the past four decades, psychotherapy has witnessed dramatic increases in the numbers of psychotherapies. Since the 1960s, the number of psychotherapy schools and theories has grown approximately 600% (Hubble, Duncan, & Miller, 1999). In 1966, about 36 distinct systems of psychotherapy were identified. In 1976, Parloff reported more than 130 therapies. Currently, it is estimated that there are now more than 250 therapy models, and the techniques associated with these models exceed 400 (Wampold, 2001). Because of the meteoric growth, Garfield (1987) exclaimed, "I am inclined to predict that sometime in the next century there will be one form of psychotherapy for every adult in the Western world" (p. 98).

Managed Care and the Psychotherapy Theory Battles

The problem with so many different therapies is that the public has become confused and angered over the proliferation of therapies and lack of clarity about what really works. Each therapy system has produced rival claims of being differentially effective and uniquely different from the others. Yet empirical results have not supported their individual claims. A once healthy diversity of therapeutic models has now deteriorated into an unhealthy Babel land (Miller, Duncan, & Hubble, 1997). As a consequence of the proliferation of therapies and unsupported claims, a managed health care and public environment that used to be receptive to such therapies as primal screams, rebirthing, long-term hospitalizations, and past-life regressions has now put the brakes on reimbursement for mental health services.

Presently, managed mental health care companies regulate such features of therapy as the frequency and number of sessions, whether therapy will be individual, group, marital, or family (mode), and the setting for therapy (inpatient or outpatient) (Prochaska & Norcross, 2003). Health care companies have been largely responsible for the shift toward short-term treatment, or brief therapy, which is one of the strongest trends in psychotherapy in recent years. Instead of spending years in treatment, clients may be given treatment over the course of a few weeks or months.

Health maintenance organizations limit the number of therapy sessions they will reimburse during a year for each insured person. While some managed care firms permit 20 sessions each year, some allow as few as eight sessions per year. Health care companies are seeking to gain greater influence over the therapist's treatment philosophy and technique (Hubble et al., 1999). Presently in health maintenance organizations, it is no longer the therapist who decides how many sessions a client will be seen in therapy. The typical managed care firm has case reviewers who decide on how many sessions of therapy each person should be given. On average, a case reviewer will initially authorize only a small number of sessions. If the therapist and the client want to continue beyond the initially permitted number of sessions, he or she must get approval from the case reviewer. If the client desires to go beyond the maximum number of allotted sessions, he or she must pay the full cost of therapy.

Moreover, managed care may have a greater influence on a therapist's practice of psychotherapy than the theoretical school to which he or she subscribes (Shueman, Troy, & Mayhugh, 1994). Managed care organizations have begun to develop specific protocols for treatment of the different types of problems people bring to therapy. They are spearheading evidence-based treatment. Evidence-based (or empirically validated) therapies are treatments that have been studied by researchers in controlled experiments and found to be helpful in comparison with no treatment or with some other treatment. Managed care organizations assert that psychotherapists have a responsibility to learn what treatment, person, and problem matches are supported by research evidence and to provide clients with the best one—or refer the client.

Cummings (2002) has predicted that **evidence-based therapies (EBTs)** will soon be mandatory for third-party reimbursement. He has stated,

> EBT's are defensible both legally and morally.... This emphasis on the use of empirically tested procedures fits well with the requirements of managed care mental health programs. Restricting payments to EBT's would reduce much of what managed care regards as run-away, questionable or needlessly long-term psychotherapy. (p. 4)

Therapists have received a wake-up call from both the public and the managed health care system. If they want to be reimbursed for their services, increasingly they must show evidence of the effectiveness of their treatment (Ogles, Anderson, & Lunnen, 1999; Shueman et al., 1994). For a number of reasons, then, the boundaries separating theories of psychotherapy have become more permeable. Bergin and Garfield (1994) have stated,

> A decisive shift in opinion has quietly occurred; and it has created an irreversible change in professional attitudes about psychotherapy and change. The new view is that the long-term dominance of the major theories is over and that an eclectic position has taken precedence. (p. 7)

This book subscribes to the prevailing view that no one therapy

---

Inner Reflection

From what you know about theories of psychotherapy, do you believe that "the long-term dominance of major theories is over"?

theory has a stronghold. Instead, there are many roads to client change.

CHOOSING A THEORETICAL ORIENTATION TO THERAPY

The reasons that therapists choose to follow one theoretical psychotherapy orientation over another are complex. Studies of therapists' choices of theories of psychotherapy have been sparse, with some of the most enlightening ones conducted more than a decade ago. Feltham (1997) has listed 15 items that underlie a therapist's choice of a psychotherapy orientation, including original training, truth appeal, selecting the best, accepting research evidence, clinical experience, retraining, **eclecticism**, certitude, respect, and atheoretical or diagnostic stance.

Cummings and Lucchese (1978) have pointed out the role of the inadvertent and have suggested that although the choice of a theoretical orientation is a complex process, it is also influenced by the whims of fate. Mahoney and Craine's (1991) study showed widespread and significant changes in beliefs about psychological change and the ingredients of optimal therapeutic practice. As therapists develop professionally, they experience an evolving process of personal integration. Therapists' journeys toward psychotherapy integration may represent their efforts to join up the discontinuities in their educational training and professional lives.

Quenk and Quenk (1996) reviewed studies of therapists' preferred models of therapy using the Myers-Briggs Type Indicator. They found no significant relationship between personality and theoretical orientation, but there were clear associations between therapists' preferences and specific dimensions. Therapists who were more of the "feeling types" tended to gravitate toward humanistic approaches. In contrast, therapists who evidenced a preference for thinking tended to be associated with more cognitive-behavioral approaches that stressed logical and analytic processes.

Poznanski and McLennan (1995) have proposed that a therapist's choice of theoretical orientation is made up of four multifaceted and hierarchical components: (1) personal therapeutic belief systems; (2) theoretical school affiliation, which is the therapist's self-reported adherence to one or more theoretical schools; (3) espoused theory, or what the therapist says he or she does; the self-reported use of theoretical concepts and therapeutic operations that does not necessarily reflect the therapist's theory-in-action; and (4) theory-in-action, what is inferred by people observing the therapist's behavior when working with clients. Poznanski and McLennan found that a therapist's endorsing of a therapeutic school may not reflect accurately his or her theory-in-action or what he or she actually does in therapy.

Moreover, a therapist's activity level during the process of therapy is an important consideration when choosing a theoretical approach. Some therapists find it uncomfortable to remain "a blank screen" for transference during therapy. Others feel at ease actively disputing a client's irrational thoughts in the same way as did Ellis. Still other therapists find it too confining to continue making statements of reflection like "You're really feeling angry" to clients. Some clients have responded, "Why do you keep repeating everything I say and shaking your head with an 'Uh huh'?"

The underlying values about people espoused by a theory of psychotherapy are another factor. To what extent does the theory espouse values with which you are comfortable? Each theory makes certain assumptions about people and the primary motives of human behavior. To what extent do you feel comfortable or uncomfortable with the way in which the theorist has conceptualized what motivates people?

There are ample reasons to examine your theoretical orientation in terms of ethical issues. In fact, if the shift toward evidence-based and manualized treatment (treatment following a psychotherapy manual) continues, clients may soon begin to sue their therapists on ethical grounds of failing to provide a basic standard of care because they failed to use the treatment approach that has been found empirically to be the most efficacious. Moreover, ethical codes transcend the various theoretical schools. You cannot just dismiss a standard of professional practice because your theoretical school endorses a certain practice. Ethical codes not only provide guidelines but also establish consequences for therapists' and psychologists' behavior.

THERAPIST BELIEFS AND VALUES: RELATIONSHIP TO CHOOSING A THEORY _____

Therapists need to understand their beliefs, attitudes, and values prior to the end of their formal training. A *belief* can be defined as a judgment of relationship between an object and some characteristic of the object. Beliefs are cognitive constructs that can be distinguished from *attitudes* (positive or negative feelings toward an object) and *behavior* (action toward an object). Furthermore, beliefs can be distinguished from *values* because beliefs merely represent how an individual perceives the world. In contrast, values contain propositions about what should be.

Therapists do not simply abandon their own values during the therapeutic process. It is impossible to work value-free with clients. Moreover, value clashes may occur when there are recognized cultural differences intruding in the therapy relationship. Values that have a potentially negative impact on the therapy relationship are those that deal with clients' and therapists' morality, ethics, and lifestyles.

Therapy is characterized by the values that permeate the therapy process. The therapy relationship between the client and the therapist is the means by which values are expressed. A national survey of therapists and mental health practitioners found

Inner Reflections

It is not easy choosing a single therapy orientation, let alone an integrative therapy approach.

What, if any, concerns do you have about finding a personal theory approach that works for you?

How do you plan to deal with those concerns?

that certain values are held widely by practitioners. These values include assuming responsibility for one's actions; having a deepened sense of self-awareness; having job satisfaction; demonstrating the ability to give and receive affection; having a purpose for living; being open, honest, and genuine; and developing appropriate coping strategies for stressful life situations (Richards & Bergin, 2005).

Therapists' values influence clients' values during the course of the therapy process. It takes time for a therapist to become aware of his or her values (Richards & Bergin, 2005). The therapist's therapeutic task is to create a climate in which clients feel free to explore their thoughts, feelings, and behavior and arrive at decisions that are right for them. Values, however, must be placed into a broader framework of culture. Values are based on one's relationship with culture. Culture represents shared beliefs, assumptions, and values that influence patterns of behavior for a given group.

Individuals within any given culture may differ widely even though they are influenced by some of the same cultural assumptions, values, and beliefs. Individuals create their own interests, values, and activities, thereby creating their own personal cultures. For instance, Elena shares many cultural characteristics and values of her family; yet she also differs from her parents, siblings, and other family members as well as from others in the culture to which she belongs.

One value that most therapists share is a respect for their clients. The therapist seeks to do no harm. Therapy is not a neutral process. It is for better or for worse. Moreover, therapists do not look down on their clients because their clients have problems. They respect their clients as human beings who are searching for solutions to their problems and pain. Psychotherapy involves a basic acceptance of the client's perceptions and feelings, even if they are at odds with the therapist's values. You must first accept the client where he or she is before you can contemplate who the client might become.

Therapists do not rush to judgment about people and their issues. You are not there to judge your clients or to give them your values. Instead, you are there to help them identify, explore, and find solutions to the values they have adopted. As a therapist, you neither judge nor condone a client's values; instead, you understand the client's point of view and let him or her know that you understand his or her point of view (Egan, 2002). Good therapists challenge clients to clarify their values and to make reasonable choices based on them. When you respect your clients, you are willing to enter their worlds to help them with their presenting issues.

Another psychotherapy value is that the therapist is competent and committed to helping the client. Ethical standards of mental health professionals require high standards of competence. Egan (2002) has asserted that competence refers to whether the therapist has the necessary *information*, *knowledge*, and *skills* to be of help to the client. Therapist competency is determined by the outcomes of therapy. Therapists take responsibility for their own growth, and they strive for excellence in their personal behavior. They become good at whatever theoretical models they use. Having respect for clients is not enough. There is no room in therapy for the caring but incompetent therapist. Therapists adopt a value of getting the help they need in working with clients if they discover that they are not being effective during the helping process.

Therapists also have a value of adopting a neutral posture. Being a therapist suggests that one has a dedication to helping other people without having a vested interest in the directions they choose to take. Therapists work toward helping clients make decisions without having investments in

Inner Reflections

Imagine that you were told that you were going to be of the lucky ones to build a 21st-century Walden Pond. The problem is that you can only take three of your values with you to this new community.

What three values would you take and why?

How might these three values influence your practice of psychotherapy?

those decisions. They devise ways to avoid thinking about client problems during the times they are not in session with their clients.

The value of being neutral in the helping process allows therapists to establish boundaries between themselves and their clients. In learning to become a therapist, you learn how to become comfortable in the presence of others' discomfort. Clients may come to the therapy session full of rage and hurt. They may cry and scream. Therapists learn how to step back and assume a neutral posture, all the while taking the full force of the client's emotional energy. As helping professionals adopt a neutral position, they avoid getting caught up in the client's behaviors and dysfunctional communication patterns. Therapists who are neutral do not allow themselves to be manipulated by clients who try to get them to rescue them. Moreover, providing therapy to individuals from different ethnic, gender, and socioeconomic backgrounds requires therapists to transcend their internalized cultures.

STAGES IN CHOOSING A THEORETICAL ORIENTATION

The process of deciding on a theory of psychotherapy can be overwhelming for a graduate student. It involves a great deal of soul searching, reading, "trying on of new clothes," and then trying to find yourself underneath it all. You don't have to decide at this point in your life on a psychotherapy theory that will guide your practice from here on out—even though you might be required to write a paper at the end of a course on "your personal theory of psychotherapy." It is, however, very important to construct your personal approach to psychotherapy out of your training, your reading, your clinical experiences, and your soul searching. Having your own approach to psychotherapy can be compared to having constructed a compass that will lead you and your client out of the woods.

Why are there so many theories of psychotherapy? Which theorist has the right answer? Is there any right answer in psychotherapy? Perhaps the answer lies in the proverbial phrase "It all depends on your perspective." The Indian parable of the five blind men and the elephant provides some insight why there are so many theories of psychotherapy (Das, 1996):

> Five men from India, who were blind from birth met one day and spent their time telling each other amusing stories. While sharing their stories, they heard a rustling in the bushes. Unknown to them, an elephant had wandered in the bushes nearby. Believing that the sounds of the rustling bushes came from a harmless source, the blind men approached the elephant and began touching different parts of its body to determine what was in their midst. The blind men began to disagree vociferously with each other regarding what they had found. The first blind man felt the elephant's body and believed that he had touched a mud wall. The second blind man touched the elephant's tusk, and pronounced it to be an ivory spear. The third blind man felt the elephant's moving trunk and interpreted it to be a python hanging from a tree. The fourth blind man grabbed the elephant's tail and said it was a rope. The fifth blind man reached around the elephant's leg and said that it was a palm tree.
>
> Just then, a small boy walked by and asked why they were all touching the elephant. Instead of responding to the boy, the men felt foolish and ashamed at having so boldly stated their limited interpretations of what they felt as the whole truth. Embarrassed at their mistakes, the fourth blind man said: "It might have been better if we had been still and said nothing." The fifth man claimed that it is best to learn the truth from one who directly knows it.

No one theorist has a monopoly on the truth for what works in psychotherapy. No one therapist has claimed that he or she can work effectively with all clients and with all types of presenting problems. Perhaps the best that theorists can do is to find one small snip of the truth. As you read the various theories of psychotherapy, ask yourself, "Do I believe this theory represents truth, or is the theorist like one of the five blind men who mistook an elephant's tail for a rope?" Your journey as a therapist will consist of truth seeking and truth determination about what techniques seem to work with what client with what problem. What might your journey as a therapist look like? After taking a course on counseling theories, will you be able to choose a theory or an integrated theory consisting of several theories? One hopes that the answer is a resounding "yes."

The Theory Orientation Journey According to Watts

Watts (1993) has conceptualized a graduate student's personal theory development as a process involving four steps or stages. Watts calls Stage 1 as "exploration stage." During this stage, you are encouraged to conduct an internal inventory of your values and beliefs. You explore your personal values and convictions about people and about life in general. How are these values informed by your family, ethnicity, cultural background, and religion? Do not be hesitant to examine your personal values closely. Any belief that you have that is worth having should be able to withstand critical scrutiny. From this foundation of awareness, you strengthen your position to explore the major theories of psychotherapy.

During the exploration stage, you explore the major theories of counseling and psychotherapy. You can learn a great deal about the major theories through classroom study, films consultation, talking with practitioners, and from your own personal experiences. A major goal of the exploration stage is to compare and contrast your beliefs and values with those represented in the various theories.

Watts (1993) labels the second stage the "examination stage." After reviewing all the theories, you select the one or two that most closely resemble your own values and beliefs. The theories that you choose become your first approximation, your base. Once you have made your first choices of psychotherapy theories, immerse yourself in primary reading about the theory. Read about your chosen theory in depth. Consider taking training workshops to get supervised practice with the theory's techniques.

Make sure you understand what draws you to this theory and why. Write down your areas of disagreement with the theory and your reasons for disagreement. If you discover that you have more points of disagreement than agreement, recognize that there is not a "goodness of fit" between who you are as a person and the psychotherapy theory that you have chosen. Even though you might feel frustrated and discouraged, remember that your time was not wasted. You learned a lot about who you are, what values are important to you, and the basic tenets of a major theory of psychotherapy. The better you are able to integrate your own values and those espoused by the therapy theory, the better the theory has a goodness of fit for you. When there is not a goodness of fit between you and your chosen theory, start the process all over from the very beginning—that is, go back to Stage 1, the exploration stage. Revisit your values and review your understanding of the theories.

If, however, you resonate with your chosen theory of psychotherapy, then continue with the examination stage by learning how to apply the theory with clients under supervision in a pre-practicum or practicum course. Apply what you have learned about the theory in your work with clients. Evaluate how well this therapy approach works for you in a clinical setting. If your application of the theory leaves you feeling uncomfortable or ineffective in working with clients, this might be a signal that you need to study the theory and its applications more thoroughly. Feelings of discomfort with your application of the theory could also mean that you might be discovering your therapy limitations or might be identifying those situations in which the theory does not work well. Extreme feelings of discomfort with using a particular theory of psychotherapy should be taken as a signal to go back to the beginning and start the process of exploration all over again.

If you have found a goodness of fit with your own values and the theory of psychotherapy, you enter the third stage, which is labeled the "integration stage." Integration takes place when your chosen theory becomes an intimate part of who you are. You make a commitment to refining, expanding, and clarifying your personal values and their relationship to the process of therapy. You might consider this stage an immersion into your base or "anchor" theory. Also during the integration stage, you incorporate techniques from other counseling theories into your personal approach to therapy, a process known as **technical eclecticism**. Some therapists never reach the integration stage because they do not develop a sufficient level of self-understanding. Therapist self-understanding is critical to the practice of effective psychotherapy. The effective therapist is a reflective practitioner who spends time thinking about what he or she is good at in therapy and on what he or she needs additional practice, reading, or understanding.

Watts (1993) labeled the fourth stage as the "personalization stage." During this stage, you make a lifelong commitment to clarifying, refining, and expanding your values and their relationship to your personal theory of counseling. It is recommended that you identify those situations in which your chosen theory does not work for you. During this stage, you also take a good hard look at other theories of psychotherapy. Do any of the other theories offer a technique that fits well with your chosen theoretical anchor base? Do any of the other theories provide any explanatory concepts that are philosophically consistent with your anchor or base theory? Do concepts from these theories blend well with your values and beliefs?

Whereas the first two stages (exploration and examination) of Watts's (1993) stage model of personal theory development can be mastered by the work you complete in your graduate program of study, the latter two stages (integration and personalization) rely on your investment of time in becoming a competent therapist. At this stage of development, it is critical that you explore yourself and the goodness of fit with the theory you are considering.

Inner Reflections

Looking at your life now, where would you place yourself in the journey toward finding your personal theory of therapy?

Among the stages that Watts has described for choosing a therapy orientation, where would you locate yourself?

It is important to remember that the process that Watts (1993) has described never quite ends. As new approaches to psychotherapy are constructed, you might examine them and integrate them within your theoretical base. You will not gain the knowledge and experience required to integrate meaningfully different theories of psychotherapy merely by completing a beginning course in theories of psychotherapy. The process of psychotherapy integration usually takes years of study, training, and practical experience.

INTEGRATIVE PSYCHOTHERAPY: THE FOCUS OF THIS BOOK _____

A major contribution of this text is that it acknowledges from the beginning that the average practitioner will probably pick and choose from the various therapies what works for her or him. Oftentimes, however, a therapist might evidence scant theoretical rationale for selecting certain elements of a particular theory. There are pathways to psychotherapy integration; the picking and choosing that practitioners engage in does not have to be haphazard. To develop an integrated therapy perspective, one must have an in-depth knowledge of psychotherapy theories; a therapist cannot integrate what he or she does not know.

There has been a recurrent, 40-year finding that therapy theories and their related techniques have a limited influence on therapy outcome (Lambert, 1992). The majority of client improvement is attributable to factors common to the various psychotherapeutic approaches and not to factors specific to individual therapy theories. There is also a large body of research that shows that the personal qualities of the therapist contributed almost three times more to the variance of psychotherapy outcome than did the therapy theory framework used (Luborsky, Crits-Christoph, Mintz, & Auerbach, 1988).

This book provides guidelines for constructing an integrative psychotherapy practice. It encourages the therapist to ask certain questions of himself or herself, such as What have I learned about my own values, my own culture and its influence on my behavior? How might my attitudes and beliefs promote or retard the establishing of an effective therapy relationship? The ensuing sections of this chapter examine psychotherapy integration: what it is and what it is not. It begins with a definition of integrative psychotherapy and a brief history of key people and developments in the movement.

Definition of Integrative Psychotherapy

What is integrative psychotherapy? Integrative psychotherapy involves an attitude toward the practice of psychotherapy that affirms the underlying factors of different theoretical approaches to therapy (Stricker, 2001). Integrative psychotherapy takes into consideration many views of human functioning, including the psychodynamic, client-centered, behavior, cognitive, family therapy, Gestalt therapy, object relations, and psychoanalytic therapy. Therapists subscribe to the view that each theory is enhanced when integrated with another.

Psychotherapy integration has been conceptualized as an attempt to look beyond the confines of single-therapy approaches for the purpose of seeing what can be learned from other theoretical therapy schools (Stricker, 2001). It represents openness to different ways of integrating diverse therapy theories and techniques. Psychotherapy integration is not a particular combination of therapy theories; rather, it consists of a framework for developing an integration of theories that you find most appealing and useful.

Moreover, psychotherapy integration is based on several key beliefs. First, all theoretical therapy and personality models have limited applicability to clients in therapy. Second, the therapeutic relationship is much more important than any specific expert therapy or theoretical technique. Third, what clients think, feel, believe, and desire is more significant to therapy outcome than any academic or theoretical conceptualization (Hubble et al., 1999).

Psychotherapy integration is a process to which therapists must decide whether or not they want to commit themselves. This approach to therapy emphasizes the personal integration of theories of psychotherapy. Integrative psychotherapists maintain that there is an ethical obligation to dialogue with colleagues of diverse theoretical orientations and to remain informed of the developments in the field.

Psychotherapy integration is based on the belief that no one theory of psychotherapy has all the answers for all clients. Each theory conceptualizes human motivation and development with its own particular slant. Dattilio and Norcross (2006) maintain that most clinicians currently acknowledge the limitations of basing their practices on a single theoretical system and are open to integrating several theories. Practitioners may find that several theories play crucial roles in their therapeutic approaches. As therapists accept that each theory has strengths and limitations, they become open to integrating different theoretical approaches into their clinical practices. To construct an integrative approach to therapy, you need to be very familiar with several theories and open to the idea that you can unify them in some kind of meaningful way. It is important to recognize that an integrative perspective to therapy requires a great deal of reading, research, clinical practice, and theorizing.

The Need for Cultural Diversity and Psychotherapy Integration

I advocate taking an integrative perspective for theories of psychotherapy for other reasons. The world is changing rapidly. We have moved toward a global economy and a global workforce. Many countries in the world have experienced an influx of people from diverse nations. The United States, for instance, is becoming increasingly diverse, with citizens who have immigrated from all over the world. Understanding cultural differences is not just politically correct. It is absolutely necessary if therapists are going to be able to work with all Americans and not just those whose origin is Western countries.

For the most part, theories of psychotherapy are based on a Western view of life. It is only relatively recently that non-Western healing methods have been explored for the purpose of integrating them into Western psychotherapy. Moodley and West (2005) provide a rich description of a large number of psychotherapeutic healing methods from culturally diverse contexts that can be integrated into the current largely Western theories of psychotherapy. They contend, in part, that their review of non-Western healing approaches is necessary because Western psychology and psychotherapy have failed to address the needs of culturally diverse clients. They recommend that various culturally diverse approaches to healing be integrated into Western psychotherapy. Similarly, Wong and Wong (2006) discuss a number of culturally diverse approaches to be taken into account when managing stress.

While the broader world is moving toward psychotherapy integration, most textbooks on counseling theory are still stuck in the past. There have been at least 40 books published on Buddhist mindfulness; yet few psychotherapy theory textbooks contain a section on mindfulness therapy. Practicing therapists have made a clarion call to integrate Buddhist mindfulness with different theoretical approaches to psychotherapy. For instance, Epstein (1995) integrated mindfulness with Western psychodynamic theory. Likewise, Segal, Williams, and Teasdale (2002) have integrated mindfulness with cognitive therapy to deal with issues relating to relapse from depression. McQuaid and Carmona (2004) have integrated mindfulness and cognitive-behavioral psychology to help clients suffering from depression. Hayes, Follette, and Linehan (2004) offer a series of articles that seek to widen the field of cognitive-behavioral therapy by integrating concepts from mindfulness and acceptance. Brantley (2003) has used mindfulness and compassion in his integrative approach for dealing with client problems such as anxiety, fear, and panic.

Clearly, the Western paradigm in psychotherapy is inadequate in addressing the needs of a culturally diverse population. The Western paradigm in psychotherapy is ethnocentric because it restricts the field to only those approaches that it defines as part of the helping profession. It eliminates most non-Western approaches by labeling them as belonging in the realm of the spiritual, philosophy, or superstition. Non-Western approaches are considered to be unscientific.

The major challenge is to find areas of commonality between Western psychotherapy and non-Western approaches. According to Santee (2007), the teachings of Buddhism, Daoism, and Confucianism are basically stress management programs. The Chinese believe, as do many Western therapists, that psychological disorders are caused by the chronic and repeated activation of the stress response. Given that the point of commonality between Western and Chinese approaches is stress management, there is room to integrate the culturally different approaches to healing. As Santee (2007) has stated,

> Once the commonality is established, theory and practice from non-Western approaches can be integrated for the purpose of informing, enhancing, and expanding the Western paradigm of counseling and psychotherapy. This being the case, it is necessary to build a bridge, if you will, between Western counseling and psychotherapy and non-Western approaches to allow for the transference of theory and technique. This bridge will allow for a solution to the previously noted problems of (1) the restrictive paradigm in Western counseling and psychotherapy and (2) the removal of ethnocentric bias. (p. 3)

Even though most counseling theory textbooks endorse multicultural competencies, very few consider non-Western approaches to psychotherapy. It might be more accurate to label such texts as describing Western approaches to psychotherapy (Ishii, 2000; Maeshiro, 2005; Yoshimoto, 1983). Your need to integrate theories of psychotherapy goes beyond just integrating Western theories. Consideration must also be given to integrating Eastern and Western approaches to psychotherapy.

Integrative psychotherapists maintain that there is an ethical obligation to dialogue with colleagues of diverse theoretical orientations and to remain informed of the developments in the field. Psychotherapy integration is usually the end point of therapist training. To reiterate, before you can integrate your own therapy theory, you must know yourself as a therapist and understand your values, beliefs, and culture, as well as the cultures of others.

Psychotherapy Integration: Position or Process?

A therapist who is on an integrationist journey is confronted eventually with the question of whether or not psychotherapy integration is a position, process, or a combination of the two. Therapists who see psychotherapy integration primarily as a position to be arrived at tend to emphasize bringing together two or more theoretical approaches to produce a new integrative theory that stands on its own. Some individuals who advocate that psychotherapy integration is primarily a position may even push for a single paradigm that will define the psychotherapy profession.

The average integrationist will take the route of bringing together two or more existing approaches to create new integrative models. This approach to psychotherapy integration is open to criticism because it proliferates therapy approaches, and it does little to eliminate or reduce the number of therapies that already exist. Therapists who view integration as primarily a process view it as a quest that does not end. It is viewed as an ongoing process in a continual state of development and evolution.

Questions to Consider in Developing Your Own Integrative Theory of Psychotherapy

In developing your own integrative psychotherapy practice, you work to achieve a balance between knowledge of the particular theories from which you will draw and a thorough description of why each theory is important and relevant to you as a therapist. You should be able to explain in depth your reason for choosing your theories and their basic tenets. What are the core ideas or central themes that run through your integrated theory of therapy?

This section poses five categories of questions that I hope you'll ask of yourself in formulating your own personal integrated theory of psychotherapy. You may decide to select theories to form your integrated theory based on how closely they resemble the views you adhere to for each of the categories.

The first category of questions deals with your personal belief system, your worldview, or your way of understanding the world and the people around you. The second category relates to your understanding or views on human development, including the establishment of healthy and unhealthy behavior. The third addresses the therapist as a person; the fourth, views of your client's world; and the fifth category elaborates on the therapy process, including your therapeutic interventions.

1. *Worldview and way of understanding the world:* The term **worldview** refers to the manner in which you construct meaning in the world. Your worldview includes your beliefs, values, and biases that you have developed as a result of having been brought up in a particular culture or cultures. For instance, individuals who are monocultural (meaning having been raised in only one cultural framework) have a worldview different from those who are bicultural. Each one of us experiences cultural conditioning, which in turn affects the way we see ourselves and others. Our worldview also influences our views on what constitutes mental health, adaptive behavior, and appropriate coping and healing.

Each theory of psychotherapy presents a worldview. For example, the existential-humanistic worldview tries to understand how the client makes sense of his or her world. These theorists take the position that clients will eventually find their own answers to life's issues. The psychodynamic worldview emphasizes that the past is a window to the present and the future. Psychodynamic therapists tend to believe that for change to be long-lasting, clients need to understand how their present situation relates to their past life experiences. In contrast to both the existential-humanistic and the psychodynamic worldviews, the cognitive worldview is oriented toward action and observable behavioral change. A multicultural perspective uses the therapeutic process to examine how culture and social processes have influenced individuals.

In choosing a theoretical orientation, give careful attention to the worldview that the theory espouses, for it may or may not be compatible with your own. You might also consider how relevant your theoretical worldview is for helping your clients. Is your theoretical worldview compatible with your clients' ways of construing the world?

Most therapy theories have a Eurocentric worldview rather than an Afrocentric, Latino, or Native American perspective. For instance, Western, Eurocentric therapy worldviews emphasize individuality, autonomy, and self-actualization, overemphasizing individual, intrapsychic features in the therapeutic setting while sometimes failing to attend sufficiently to social issues and social changes that might lead to positive outcomes for individuals from minority backgrounds (Smith, 1991). It has been found that 50% of minority individuals do not return for a second therapy interview (Sue & Sue, 2008).

In developing your theoretical framework, consider asking yourself the following:

- What is your worldview, including your view of human nature?
- What are some of your basic assumptions about people, their nature, and their ability to change?
- To what extent do people orchestrate their own lives? Are they governed by forces out of their unconscious awareness (free will or determinism)?
- To what degree are people influenced by their environment or by heredity (nature vs. nurture)?
- What role does the past or the present play in individuals' lives (past or present orientation)?
- Are people controlled by the early events in their lives, or can they change and move beyond whatever happened to them when they were young?

In terms of your own cultural identity, consider asking yourself the following:

- How do you describe yourself culturally?
- Which ethnic or cultural group other than your own do you think you understand the best?
- In what ways do your cultural values and attitude influence your therapeutic approach?
- What is your knowledge of other cultures, your knowledge and awareness of your culture, and what skills do you have to assist diverse clients?
- What is your level of self-awareness of the influence of cultural factors in the therapy relationship?
- What are your ethnic attitudes toward others, and how do you communicate these to clients?

2. *Views of human development:* Your outlook on human development also influences your therapeutic orientation. What is your view of human development? What is the theory's concept of personality? Does the theory focus on interpersonal functioning? This orientation suggests that therapy is inclined to work primarily with the individual because the basic problem is assumed to lie within him or her. Conversely, a theory might stress the sociopolitical nature of most problems or how problems are connected to the sociopolitical system in which the individual finds himself or herself.

- What, if any, do you believe are the critical periods in personality and behavior development?
- How do people develop mental disorders?
- What constitutes healthy and unhealthy personality development?
- What are your beliefs about change and people's ability to make changes in their lives?
- How is behavior changed?
- What motivates people?
- What is the relationship among cognition, affect, and behavior?

3. *Views of the therapist as a person:* The therapist as a person is extremely critical in therapy.

- What are your key values and how do these values affect how you see yourself as a therapist? For instance, if a client came to you expressing ambivalent feelings about coming out, what influence might your values have on therapy with the person?

- How would you describe your personality? How would you describe yourself to another person?
- What in your background or in your personality resonates with a certain theory or theories?
- How have your experiences and personal history contributed to your integrated theory of therapy?

4. *Views of your client's world:* How you think about your client's world is highly significant for therapy. Therapists need to understand how their own worldviews affect the manner in which they work with clients, and they need to understand how their clients think about their own worlds. Theories of psychotherapy help you work with clients from varying perspectives. Sometimes you may have to integrate theories to meet your clients' needs. If you can meaningfully enter your client's world, understand life from her or his perspective, walk with her or him on the journey for understanding, you will have made a contribution to this world.

- What is the client's worldview?
- How does your client view his or her problem?
- What does the client say were the first signs of the problem?
- What efforts has the client made to resolve his or her problem?
- How does the client's worldview influence the steps he or she has taken to deal with the presenting issue?
- How successful has the client been in resolving the presenting issues?
- What does the client believe is the ideal way to resolve the presenting issue?
- What, if any, control does the client believe he or she has over the presenting issue?

5. *Views on the process of psychotherapy and ways of intervening:* Your integrative theory of psychotherapy must deal with your understanding of the therapy process and your views on ways of intervening during therapy.

- What are your goals of therapy?
- What is the role of the therapist and the client in establishing therapy goals?
- How does your integrative theory conceptualize what constitutes a problem in therapy?
- What is the nature of the therapy relationship?
- What is the assessment process during therapy?
- What role does diagnosis have in your integrated theory?
- What are some of the strengths and weaknesses of the theories you have chosen to integrate?
- What therapy intervention techniques do you believe are essential to you in your practice?

Forming an integrative theory of psychotherapy is not an easy task. For most therapists, it takes years to become comfortable with an integrative way of providing therapy services. In developing such a perspective, it is important that you understand your own worldview, the worldviews of your clients, human development, characteristics of effective therapists, and your views on the process of psychotherapy and ways of intervening. Each theory presents a different perspective from which to look at human behavior. If you are currently a student, it will take a while for you to develop a well-defined integrative theoretical model. This goal can be accomplished with much experience, reading, and studying. Your first challenge is to master one or two theories of psychotherapy that resonate with you and that meet the needs of those with whom you work.

CASE STUDY

Justin

Justin is currently under PINS (Persons in Need of Supervision) with the Utah District Family Court because he has repeatedly gotten into trouble at school and because he was with some boys who stole items from the local Walmart. Justin denied that he stole anything; but because he was with the boys who did steal, he was given a citation for appearance in family court. The court has informed Justin that he must meet with it periodically and that he must not get into any more trouble; otherwise, he may be placed in a residential treatment facility that has a school for young boys. The family court judge has specifically stated that Justin must improve his grades in school and that he must not get into any more fights in school. The judge will obtain periodic reports from his school to see whether Justin is acting responsibly.

The judge has also indicated that if the school and Justin's mom, Sandy, can come up with a workable plan to improve Justin's grades, this will serve as a mitigating factor in the judge's decision to let Justin remain at home or to send him to a residential treatment facility. Furthermore, Justin must be on time for all court appearances, because he was late for the past two appearances. The court has also assigned Justin a probation officer who will gather the material from his school and mother for the purposes of reporting back to the judge and giving his recommendations for Justin. The judge has placed the question on his file: What will it take to save Justin? Can he be helped?

Justin could achieve much higher than what he has performed academically in school. He complains that he can't seem to remember all that he reads and that he can't focus his attention on reading an entire chapter. Justin has asked for a tutor, but his school has been unable to provide one for him on a personal basis. Justin sometimes acts up in his class. While everyone else is reading or working on an assignment in class, Justin gets up and starts walking around the classroom. Sometimes he pokes a student or makes fun of one of the smarter students in the class. He has gotten into several fights at school and has been suspended for fighting at least three times. The principal has indicated that if he gets into another fight in school, he may be expelled.

Despite these observations, Justin's art teacher seems to believe in him. She has indicated that Justin has a lot of raw talent for painting. Despite his considerable talents in painting, Justin paints very little. Last year, he won the school's artistic award for painting.

Except for standardized tests, Justin has not been tested in school. He has met the guidance therapist and psychologist on only two occasions. This semester he has received three Ds and two Cs; he is in a regular seventh-grade class. Justin told his mother that he did not like the psychologist or the guidance therapist because they seemed to act like they thought he was crazy or retarded. Both the psychologist and the guidance therapist read the riot act to Justin, and they tried to impress on him the seriousness of his behavior. Also, they informed him that if he ever wanted to talk about what was going on, their doors would be open. Neither the guidance therapist nor the psychologist has contacted his mother. Justin's teachers have called her at home about his acting-out behavior in class and his dismal academic performance. Sandy has visited the school about Justin on at least three occasions, but each time, she felt unwelcome.

Justin believes that, for the most part, he is on his own—that is, except for his brother, mother, and "home boys." According to his philosophy, you have to get someone before he gets you. He was glad that he had his home boys to back him up. His home boys were his real family. He could trust them because they would not leave him and they would fight for him if anyone tried to jump him.

Although Justin is biracial, he hangs out primarily with African American kids. He does have a few White friends, but two of these individuals shy away from him because they are performing reasonably well in school, and Justin gets into so much trouble that the two do not want to be associated with him. Justin hangs out with kids older than he is. For instance, the third White kid he hangs out with is 16 years old, and he is a member of a gang.

Justin's older brother, James, has been in repeated trouble with the law. Just this past semester, he dropped out of school after completing the 10th grade. James smokes pot on a regular basis. Most of James's friends are in a gang. Justin looks up to his older brother. In a surprising admission, James said that he wanted things to be better for Justin than what he has experienced in his life. Sometimes James makes Justin complete his homework. It's clear that there is a strong bond between Justin and James.

(Continued)

(Continued)

For the most part, Justin hangs around with a small group of people who seem to look up to him for leadership. Justin "gets over" in part because of his good looks. He has brown curly hair, green eyes, and his skin color is of a caramel hue. He is slender and agile. Justin has evidenced only passing interest in girls.

Justin suffers from feelings of inferiority because of his mixed racial parents. Students at school sometime refer to him as half-breed, and that is one of the reasons that he got into a fight. People at the mall and other places ask him where his mom is, even when she is near him. When he points to his White mother, they say something like, "Oh, I'm sorry. I didn't know that she was your mother."

In addition, Justin has inferiority feelings about the low grades he has received in his courses. Sometimes, he feels just like hauling off and hitting a couple of the bright kids—just because they think that they are all that much. On his standardized IQ test, Justin scores within an average range; however, his performance IQ component score is higher than his verbal IQ score. Except for art class, many of the so-called bright students mock him in class—not so much with words, but by their looks to each other whenever he is called on by the teacher. They expect that he either won't have the right answer or that he will say something really stupid. Justin won an award for having the best art work for a seventh grader.

Justin's relationship with his mother is tumultuous. One day he loves her, and the next day he is cursing and yelling at her, especially if she disciplines him. Sandy loves Justin very deeply; she calls him her baby. When Sandy becomes angry with Justin, she curses him out and sometimes hits him. Sandy has said that Justin is all that she has left. In addition, Sandy needs some training in parenting because sometimes she hosts pot parties in her home with Justin and James present. She excuses this with the explanation that pot helps her to cope and her kids should do as she says, not as she does.

Sandy can't seem to get a handle on understanding Justin and his needs. One minute he is smoking like an adult and cursing, and the next minute he is crying like a little baby. For instance, he cried in court and in the car on the way home because the judge told him that if his behavior did not change he was going to send him to the county's residential treatment center for wayward and out of control boys. As if to encourage him, the judge did praise the residential treatment center and noted that several of the boys he sent there to get their lives straight came out and did well. These boys completed college and obtained good jobs.

Justin's mother has attended 1 year of community college. She said that she breast-fed Justin and that she used to read stories to him at night. At best, however, Sandy belongs to a lower socioeconomic group. She says that as soon as the court gets out of her life, she is going to get a full-time job. She keeps a neat house, but she is challenged in doing so. Justin and James provide little assistance in keeping the house clean and organized. In addition, Sandy is challenged when setting up structure for her children to follow. For instance, Justin and James eat whenever they want, with no set time for dinner or for getting up and completing homework or chores.

Justin's response to the court has been mixed. He has arrived more than 20 minutes late on two occasions. His mother has to call him repeatedly to get out of bed so that he wouldn't be late for court. Justin has struck up a positive relationship with his probation officer. For the most part, Bob, the probation officer, has given encouraging reports to the presiding judge. One consequence of these reports is that they have kept Justin from being sent to the residential treatment facility. Bob is concerned, however, that Justin is not going to make it. He points to Justin's brother, James, and the life of crime he has lived.

Justin is terrified that the court will take him away from his mother and place him in the residential treatment facility for boys. Most of the time, he covers up this fear with a great deal of posturing and bravado. Justin says that he is going to do better in school; but thus far, he has not achieved very much. Moreover, he and his mother have failed to come up with a workable plan for the improvement that the judge indicated he would consider a favorable action in Justin's case. Every time Sandy mentions creating a plan, Justin says that he will do it tomorrow. The truth of the matter is that Sandy has few clues regarding how to go about creating a plan for helping Justin to deal successfully with his issues at home and at school.

When the therapist asked Justin about his earliest memories, he first said that he couldn't remember anything when he was very young. "It's all kind of like nothing is there. It's as if my entire life did not happen when I lived in Chicago. I keep trying to remember what my house looked like, but I can't remember anything." The therapist paused for a few moments.

"Tell me about your father. What do you remember about your father?"

Justin's eyes began to fill with tears, and he began fidgeting in his chair, signaling that he was uncomfortable with the therapist's line of questioning. The therapist reached over and handed Justin a tissue to wipe his watery eyes. "My question has resulted in your tears, Justin. Can you tell me about those tears? What are they saying to you? "

"Tears can't talk, you know that."

"But sometimes they provide a signal to us that we are experiencing pain. I sometimes cry when I am sad. I also cry sometimes when I am very, very happy."

In response to his therapist, Justin added, "My mom cries when my brother and I get into trouble. She says that we are trying to send her to the crazy house."

"We laugh at her. She's supposed to be a grown-up, but she cries when things don't go the way that she wants them to be."

"So, how do you feel Justin, about your tears as we are talking together?"

"Embarrassed . . . like I'm a baby or something. I'm no baby. I know how to take care of myself."

Justin went on to discuss his relationship with his father, whom he barely remembered. His earliest memory of his father was with his mother and father arguing loudly in the kitchen. Justin tried to get in between his parents with a plea that they not fight any more. First, his father knocked him to the floor, but when he began crying his father picked him up and said, "Hey Champ, big boys don't cry." Then, seemingly catching himself from this outburst of anger, he said, "Come on," cajoling Justin, who was still crying, and he took his fist and he playfully touched him a couple of times with fake punches.

Justin said that this was his last memory of his father—asking him to be strong when he really just wanted to be comforted by his father. For Justin, the memory of his father was both positive and negative. He could never understand why his father was not like the fathers he had seen on television. Justin's family was at war then, much in the same way that it is now embroiled in turmoil.

SUMMARY

This chapter has introduced you to the concept of theories in psychotherapy. A theory can be a good thing if it provides a well-thought-out, organized way of conceptualizing human development and behavior.

Emphasis was placed on the idea that therapists must consider integrating Eastern and Western approaches to psychotherapy. Currently, there is evidence of a movement to incorporate Eastern approaches to psychotherapy as evidenced by the fact that three relatively new cognitive-behavioral therapies (dialectical-behavior therapy, acceptance and commitment therapy, and mindfulness-based cognitive therapy) have incorporated mindfulness and other Asian approaches to psychotherapy. The process of choosing a theory can be described as a long process, and for some individuals, a lifelong process that involves continually evaluating, incorporating, and fine-tuning one's practice to conducting psychotherapy. Psychotherapy integration has become the norm rather than the exception. Most therapists are choosing to incorporate aspects of several theoretical models in their therapy practice.

SUPPLEMENTAL AIDS _____

Discussion Questions

1. *"Why I want to become a therapist"*: Divide into groups of four or five people. Designate one person as the group recorder. Each student writes down and describes three reasons why he or she wants to become a counselor or a therapist. The group's recorder keeps track of these reasons. What common themes came forth from the group? What differences did you find in the reasons that people gave for wanting to choose the helping profession? Each group reports back to the class as a whole so that students will be able to examine their own reasons for becoming a counselor or a therapist as well as the reasons that their classmates give.

2. Discuss five values you have that might have an impact on how you would approach psychotherapy with a client.

3. Discuss three reasons why you either would or would not choose to enter psychotherapy for yourself before conducting psychotherapy with a client.

4. What factors are important in choosing a theoretical orientation? Discuss at least three factors that you will take into consideration when you choose your own integrative approach to psychotherapy?

5. Discuss the level of activity you think you would be comfortable with in conducting therapy: high, medium, or low activity in counseling? Explain.

Glossary of Key Terms

eclecticism   Process that involves a therapist choosing certain features of a theory of psychotherapy. An eclectic approach does not necessarily seek a meaningful integration of assumptions and critical concepts but rather usually focuses on using techniques from different theoretical schools.

evidence-based therapy (EBT)   Practice based on the belief that solid, empirical research as well as clinical experience should inform therapy and professional decision making regarding interventions to use.

psychotherapy integration   Approach to psychotherapy that integrates in a meaningful way two or more theories of psychotherapy for the expressed purpose of meeting the needs of a therapist and his or her clients.

technical eclecticism   Most common approach to psychotherapy integration for therapists who regard themselves as eclectic. In this approach, the therapist chooses interventions from a variety of schools to work with his or her clients. This integration approach lacks any unifying theoretical understanding of the various schools from which it draws therapy intervention techniques.

worldview   A person's worldview may be defined as the way in which he or she constructs meaning in the world. A worldview contains the different beliefs, values, and biases a person develops as a result of having been raised in a given culture.

Website Materials

Additional exercises, journals, annotated bibliography, and more are available on the open 1 access website at https://study.sagepub.com/jonessmith2e.

PART I

The First Force in Psychotherapy
Psychoanalysis and Psychodynamic Theories

Chapter 2

Psychoanalytic and Psychodynamic Theories

Chapter 3

Adlerian Psychotherapy

PSYCHOLOGY'S INDEBTEDNESS TO SIGMUND FREUD

Psychology is deeply indebted to psychoanalysis and to Sigmund Freud for ushering in the development of a psychotherapeutic treatment known as the "talking cure," and it is this treatment approach and conceptual model that constitutes the "first force" in psychotherapy. Freud popularized the talking cure. Most of psychotherapy is based on the treatment approach that Freud developed. Psychoanalysis consists of a number of theoretical approaches to psychotherapy. Some of the prominent theorists that emerged out of Freud's early work include Carl Jung, Erik Erikson, members of the object relations school, the self psychologists, and Alfred Adler. Chapters 2 and 3 discuss these theorists and their work.

Psychoanalytic theories are those that posit unconscious processes, psychosexual stages of development, and a tripartite personality structure labeled the *id*, *ego*, and *superego*. Psychoanalytically oriented therapies adopt many of Freud's treatment techniques, such as free association and interpretation. Psychoanalysis is generally considered to be a depth psychology, and therapists who subscribe to this theoretical school maintain that human behavior is mainly influenced by what takes place in the unconscious mind. Sessions may take place three to five times a week, and it is long term rather than short term. Psychoanalysis proper is usually conducted with the analyst sitting behind the client, who reclines on a couch. What is often called psychoanalytic therapy is, in reality, psychoanalytically oriented therapy instead of analysis proper.

SOME DISTINCTIONS BETWEEN PSYCHOANALYSIS AND PSYCHODYNAMIC THEORIES

The line of demarcation between psychoanalytic and psychodynamic theory is fuzzy at best. In general, however, psychodynamic therapy has come to signal a much broader view of treatment. It includes psychoanalysis as well as object relations theory and psychoanalytic self psychology. There are some fruitful ways of comparing a classical psychoanalytic (Freudian) approach and a psychodynamic one.

Classical psychoanalysis emphasizes the id (or what is commonly referred to as "drive theory"). In contrast, the psychodynamic school highlights the ego instead of the id. The ego psychologists are the leaders within the psychodynamic school in underscoring the importance of the ego. Whereas Freud was concerned primarily with intrapsychic conflicts (psychological conflicts within an individual), psychodynamic therapists focus on interpersonal conflicts or conflicts between individuals. The object relations schools continue the interpersonal focus of psychodynamic theory by proposing the concept of objects or significant people in a person's life. Psychodynamic therapy helps clients describe and put into words feelings that are troubling, threatening, or contradictory. Psychodynamic approaches help clients identify and explore recurring themes and patterns in their lives. Therapy focuses on past experiences and on the therapy relationship.

INTEGRATION OF FREUDIAN CONCEPTS: THE UNCONSCIOUS AND TRANSFERENCE

In Chapter 2, I focus first on Sigmund Freud's psychoanalytic approach to therapy. Freud's writings are prolific; therefore, I review only some of his essential concepts, including Freud's theory of personality, his psychosexual stages, and phases of psychotherapy. Next, I examine the contributions of Carl Jung, who was Freud's chosen successor (once called the "crown prince" of psychoanalysis) and heir apparent to lead the psychoanalytic movement. Carl Jung adopted Freud's emphasis on the unconscious and the use of dream interpretation during therapy. He also proposed his own analytic psychology, which he put forth when he could no longer accept Freud's all-embracing concept of the libido.

Jung is remembered most for his concepts of the collective unconscious and archetypal patterns and images that are associated with it. For instance, he proposed the archetype of the Wise Old Man, the Great Mother, and the lion. Jung maintained that archetypal images are universal and that they can be found in the religions and mythologies of diverse cultures. Jung also stressed the persona, the social role, or mask that individuals assume and wear; the anima–animus (which is the unconscious opposite or other sex side of a man's or woman's personality and a concept that was later incorporated in Sandra Bem's sex role, feminist theory); the shadow (the unconscious features of our personality that we reject); and the self (which Jung saw as the center of an individual's personality). Some of Jung's concepts, such as his constructions of personality types (introversion–extraversion, thinking–feeling, and sensing–intuiting), have been widely accepted.

NEW FORMS OF PSYCHOANALYSIS

Other followers of Freud such as Anna Freud (ego defense mechanisms) and Erik Erikson (psychosocial stages of development) have emphasized the role of the ego more so than the id, and they have highlighted the role of social factors. The impact of Anna Freud and her list of ego defense mechanisms has been widespread. Most therapists acknowledge in some form that people adopt various strategies to protect the ego or the self. Individuals use a number of defense mechanisms to protect the ego, including regression and denial.

Erikson's theory of psychosocial development is currently taught in most child development courses across the world. In contrast with Freud, he considered the social factors that influence a person's development and a person's interpersonal interactions within a given culture. Erikson, himself, however, had his own identity issues as an adopted child.

Object relations theory (proposed by Donald Winnicott) is a newer form of psychoanalytic therapy that explores a person's internal, unconscious identifications and internalizations of external objects, usually described as significant people in their lives. For instance, individuals internalize a view of their mothers (mother object) and fathers (father object). Object relations theorists have focused on early childhood development, the way that young children relate to their mothers, and how disruptions in the mother–child relationship can lead to later childhood and adult psychological disorder. The basic task of human development is conceptualized as one of differentiation and integration with the final emergence of a sense of identity.

Clients who are experiencing issues with separation and individuation or dependency versus independency may find the work of ego psychologists and object relations theorists quite useful. Self psychologists such as Heinz Kohut have also provided significant contributions to psychotherapy, primarily in terms of treatment of specific disorders, such as narcissism.

Relational analysis is one of the newer derivatives of the psychoanalytic school. Theorists within this school emphasize the importance of the therapeutic relationship within an analytic framework. Adherents of this approach renounce the role of the therapist as a blank screen, and they offer a brief form of psychoanalytic/psychodynamic therapy. Relational analysis is based on the fundamental human desire for and defenses against deep emotional connection with others, rather than on the classical psychoanalytic emphasis on conflicts regarding infantile drives for sex and aggression. The relational analyst engages the client as an active co-participant in the therapeutic process. Hence, a client's experience in a relational analysis is quite different from being in a classical Freudian analysis, in which the therapist seeks to function as a blank screen onto which the client projects.

Currently, some practicing psychoanalysts and psychodynamic therapists continue to use many of Freud's concepts, all the while incorporating concepts of later theorists. For instance, some theorists make use of Freud's constructs of conscious and unconscious, and others use his personality constructs of id, ego, and superego. Other pivotal concepts in psychotherapy, such as transference and countertransference, have been adopted across many theoretical lines. Freud's conceptualization of psychosexual stages—oral, anal, phallic, latency, and genital—are not so widely accepted. Psychoanalysis continues to reformulate and re-create itself using concepts from the offshoots of classical analysis.

Chapter 3 is entirely focused on Alfred Adler because of his profound influence on psychotherapy. Most of Adler's ideas have been relabeled and incorporated in many other theories of psychotherapy. For instance, Adler proposed an early form of the "miracle question" long before solution-focused therapy ever arrived on the scene. Adlerian concepts such as inferiority and superiority complexes, mistaken goals of children (negative attention getting), and the power of helping others in reducing psychological problems (social interest) have been widely adopted without acknowledging the early contributions of Adler. Adler conducted seminal work on the family, the family constellation, and birth order research, and his child guidance clinics may be considered an early forerunner of family therapy.

As can be gleaned from examining some of the contributions of the leading psychoanalytic and psychodynamic theorists presented in Chapters 2 and 3, the first force in psychotherapy has had a powerful influence on psychotherapy.

CHAPTER 2

Psychoanalytic and Psychodynamic Theories

BRIEF OVERVIEW

The primary focus of this chapter is on Freud's contributions to psychoanalysis. Freud's view of human nature, the structure of personality that he proposed, and his pivotal contribution about the conscious and unconscious are examined. Levels of consciousness and psychosexual phases are also covered. I present in brief summary the contributions of some of the offshoots of Freud and psychoanalytic theory. The work of Carl Jung, one of Freud's important disciples, is reviewed. I discuss ego psychologists (Anna Freud and Erik Erikson), object relations psychologists (Donald Winnicott), self psychologists (Heinz Kohut), and relational psychoanalysis.

Inner Reflections

Would you ever consider integrating psychoanalytic therapy into your integrative approach?

If yes, what parts of this theoretical approach would you choose to integrate?

PSYCHOANALYTIC THERAPY

Major Contributor: Sigmund Freud (1856–1939)

Sigmund Freud

The great question that has never been answered, and which I have not yet been able to answer, despite my thirty years of research into the feminine soul, is "What does a woman want?"

Love and work . . . work and love, that's all there is.

—Sigmund Freud

29

Brief Biography

Sigmund Freud was born on May 6, 1856, in the village of Freiburg, Moravia, a small town at the time in Austria and now a part of Czechoslovakia. His father, Jakob, was a wool merchant; his mother was half his father's age. Because Freud's great grandfather was a rabbi, Sigmund was raised in the traditions and beliefs of the Jewish religion. The family traveled to Vienna when Freud was 4 years old, where they lived for most of his life. Sigmund, born into a lower-class Jewish family, was treated by his parents as a "golden child." He graduated from high school with honors, and he was proficient in eight languages: German, French, English, Italian, Spanish, Hebrew, Latin, and Greek (Jones, 1955).

Initially, Freud considered a career in law, but he later switched to medicine. At the age of 25, he earned his medical degree at the University of Vienna (Gay, 1988). Subsequently, he practiced medicine at Vienna's General Hospital, where he focused on organic diseases of the nervous system. In 1886, he married Martha Bernays; together they had six children, three boys and three girls. (Anna, the youngest, later became a famous psychoanalyst who specialized in the treatment of children and who developed the concepts of defense mechanisms.) Sigmund Freud found the practice of medicine and research to be too restricted, with limited opportunities for Jews. As a consequence, he supported his family through his private practice in psychiatry.

Early on in his practice, Freud used the conventional treatments of his day, including baths, massage, electrotherapy, and rest cures. Later, he became less interested in the physical aspects of the nervous system and more interested in its psychological connections. He devoted full-time study to the psychological causes of neuroses (Gay, 1988). He maintained that the basis of **neurosis** was sexual conflict between one's instinctive desires and society's punishment for an individual's direct expression of those wishes.

At the beginning of his private practice, Freud used hypnosis and his colleague Joseph Breuer's cathartic method to help clients with neuroses (Fine, 1979). In the cathartic method, the client expresses and discharges emotions through the process of free association and client talk. In 1895, Breuer and Freud published *Studies on Hysteria*, in which they proposed that symptoms of hysteria arose from a combination of very painful memories and unexpressed emotions. The psychiatrist's task was to help the client recollect forgotten events and the emotional expression of those events. Freud believed that the traumatic events that produced hysteria were caused by sexual conflicts developed in the client's childhood. He soon discovered, however, that clients resisted his suggestions and hypnotic techniques. As a result, he turned to another concentration technique that involved clients lying on a couch with their eyes closed for the purpose of recalling all memories of the symptom without censoring any of their thoughts. Subsequently, Freud used the technique of free association: asking his clients to report whatever came to their minds (Freud, 1933). His treatment approach became known as the talking cure; the ultimate goal of talking was to release the patient's emotional energy that was being held captive in his or her unconscious. Anna O, a client who was treated by Joseph Breuer, coined the term *talking cure* (Fine, 1979).

In 1897, Freud entered a 3-year process of performing psychoanalysis on himself. He came to understand that he felt intense hostility toward his father and that he had sexual feelings for his mother, who was very attractive. By 1900, Freud had emerged much healthier. Shortly thereafter, he wrote about the conflict between the conscious and the unconscious features of an individual's personality. In 1900, he published *The Interpretation of Dreams*, which was based on his observations of his own dreams and those of his clients.

It was not until the early 1900s that Freud's brilliance was recognized by the medical and psychology professions, and he began to attract followers who were interested in his ideas. In the beginning, the followers met at his home, and the group was called the Wednesday Psychological Society. During this time, Freud published *The Psychopathology of Everyday Life* (1901), *Jokes and Their Relation to the Unconscious* (1905a), and *Three Essays on Sexuality* (1905b). In 1908, he was joined by a group of outstanding colleagues, and the Wednesday group was renamed the Vienna Psychoanalytic Society.

Freud received American recognition for his works when G. Stanley Hall, one of the founders of Clark University in Worcester, Massachusetts, and the American Psychological Association, of which he was the first president, invited him to lecture at Clark University in 1909 (Jones, 1955). After this lecture, Freud further developed his views on the libido, the driving force of an individual's personality, which contains sexual energy. He distinguished between an individual's sexual energies that were directed toward the self and those that were directed outward toward objects represented in his or her external world. According to Freud, **narcissism** resulted when a person withdrew energy from others and directed it toward himself or herself. Freud's work on infant relationships and narcissism formed the foundation for later object relation and self psychology theorists—two major branches of the psychoanalytic school. Freud published his *Introductory Lectures on Psychoanalysis* (1917) and *The Ego and the Id* (1923), which presented his theory of personality.

Freud did not tolerate dissent or differences from his small circle of followers. Freud insisted that he alone, as the founder of psychoanalysis, had the right to decide what would be included under the rubric of psychoanalysis. He expelled from the group those who disagreed with him. Ernest Jones, Hans Sachs, Alfred Adler, Carl Jung, and Otto Rank all broke their ties with him and developed their own theories of psychotherapy. Subsequent disciples who also broke ties with Freud are known as "neo-Freudians," because they focused more on social and cultural factors than they did on Freud's biological determinants of behavior. Karen Horney (1926, 1937) objected to Freud's views on female sexuality, especially his views on penis envy (discussed later in the chapter).

Freud dedicated most of his life to developing and revising his theory of psychoanalysis. He was very productive, and his collected works comprise 24 volumes. Frequently, he put in 18-hour days writing. In 1932, he was awarded the Goethe Prize to honor his contributions to psychology as well as to German literary culture. Yet, just 1 year later, when the Nazis took control of Germany, they burned Freud's books (Gay, 1988). The Nazis murdered all of Freud's sisters. In March 1938, Germany annexed Austria, and in June that year, Freud fled to London.

> **Inner Reflections**
>
> What family factors, experiences, or cultural factors within his own life led to Freud's development of psychoanalysis?

KEY CONCEPTS OF SIGMUND FREUD

View of Human Nature

The Freudian outlook on human nature is deterministic. It maintains that an individual's personality is fixed largely by the age of 6 (Freud, 1923). People do not have free will; rather their behavior is determined by innate drives that have to do with sex and aggression or love and death. A great deal of Freud's determinism also deals with how one is raised by one's parents.

The first part of Freud's determinism maintains that human behavior is determined by forces that might be described appropriately as "drives," "biological forces," or "instinctual forces." In the German language, the word *drive* is *trieb*, which is usually translated incorrectly as "instinct." (The terms *instincts* and *drives* are used interchangeably in this chapter.)

Freud used the word *drive* to convey the belief that bodily forces make demands on one's mental life. A drive is a state of central excitation in response to a stimulus (Freud, 1923). Each drive has a source (bodily needs that arise from the **erogenous zones**), an internal aim (e.g., the temporary removal of the bodily need), an external aim (the steps taken to reach the final goal of the internal aim), and an object. Drives lead to the rise of energy that forms the foundation for all psychological activity.

Individuals never experience the drive itself; instead, we experience its representation or idea in our minds. For instance, sexual and aggressive urges take place within most people; however, the free expression of these urges is in conflict with society. Most societies demand that we control our basic urges.

Death instincts (*Thanatos*) were described in Freud's book, *Beyond the Pleasure Principle* (1920). Freud proposed that "the goal of all life is death." He postulated that people hold an unconscious desire to die but that this wish is largely tempered by the life instincts. In his view, self-destructive behavior is an expression of the energy created by the death instincts. When this energy is directed outward onto others, it is expressed as aggression and violence. When it is expressed inward, the end result may be suicide.

Theory of Personality

Freud's theory of personality can be viewed in terms of his views on levels of consciousness and his tripartite structure of the id, ego, and superego. I begin with levels of awareness because awareness comes first, and out of one's awareness the structure of one's personality is formed.

Freud's Levels of Consciousness

Freud proposed three levels of consciousness: (1) the conscious level, (2) the preconscious level, and (3) the unconscious level. Our thought processes operate on the conscious level (Freud, 1905a). The mind can be compared to an iceberg, where only the tip of the iceberg (our consciousness) is visible. All that we think, perceive, or understand rests within our conscious level of awareness. The *conscious level* is the level on which all of our thought processes operate (Freud, 1905a). Everything we are aware of is stored in our **conscious**; however, our conscious makes up a very small part of who we are. At any given time, we are aware only of a very small part of what makes up our personality; most of who we are is buried and inaccessible to us. Only 10% of an iceberg is visible (conscious), while the other 90% is beneath the water (preconscious and unconscious).

Just under the water line is our *preconscious level*, which contains our memories and thoughts that are not at the conscious level but that may threaten to break into the conscious level at any moment. At the **preconscious** level, events, thoughts, and feelings are easily recalled. Sometimes, parts of the iceberg may break off and float to the surface if our memories are jogged. The preconscious is usually allotted about 10% to 15% of the iceberg of the mind. Material can pass easily back and forth between the conscious and the preconscious. Likewise, material from these two areas can slip into the unconscious. For instance, at one time in our lives, we were totally aware of what our parents said to us. As we age, this material gradually slips into the unconscious. On our own, we cannot access our unconscious material. According to Freud, we need a psychoanalyst to help us retrieve material from our unconscious level.

The **unconscious** is the lowest and deepest level of awareness or, perhaps more accurately, unawareness. The vast part of the iceberg contains our unconscious, which holds the bulk of our past experiences, including all the impulses and memories that threaten to debilitate or destabilize our minds. Typically, the unconscious is said to constitute an overwhelming 75% to 80% of the mind.

Freud's Theory of Personality

Freud (1901, 1923) described personality as "the scaffold of the mind." He divided the mind into three components: (1) the *id*, which represents the biological self in one's personality; (2) the *ego*, which is the psychological center of one's personality; and (3) the *superego*, which is the social controller (our parents usually) that brings behavior within socially acceptable limits (see Figure 2.1). Freud maintained that the basic dynamic forces motivating personality were *Eros* (life and sex) and *Thanatos* (death and aggression). People continually desire immediate gratification of their sexual and aggressive impulses.

The **id** is the most basic of the three personality structures. The id contains our instincts, needs, and wishes. The id participates in **primary process** thinking, which can be compared to that of a newborn baby who instinctually grasps, sucks at a mother's breasts, and eliminates when it feels the

Figure 2.1   Freud's Structural and Topographical View of Personality Structure

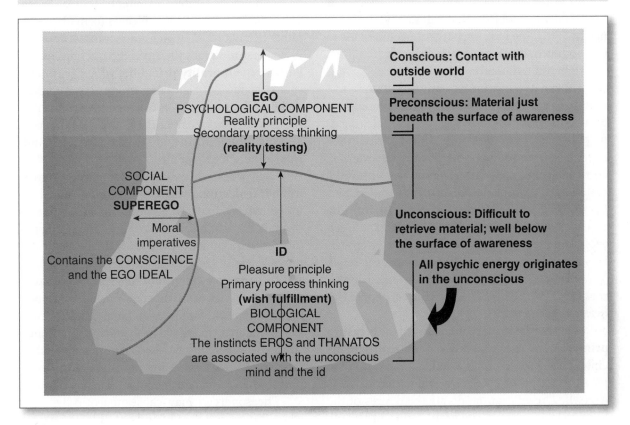

need to do so. The id is usually preoccupied with its own needs and desires. As a consequence, it is self-centered. Primary process can be described as the preverbal and dreamlike original, irrational state of libido (Freud, 1920). It lives in the immediate present and finds it extremely difficult to defer pleasure. An infant's primary process produces a memory image of an object needed for gratification so that he or she can reduce the frustration of not having yet been gratified. The primary process sets into operation a means for forming an image of something that helps reduce a drive. The infant may form the image of a mother's breast to reduce hunger and thirst. Freud called this process primary because it comes first in human development.

A young infant is all id. The id is governed by the pleasure principle, and it is illogical, amoral, and driven to satisfy its instinctual needs and desires. The id is largely out of the person's conscious awareness. The infant or child *cathects* or *invests energy* in objects that will satisfy his or her needs. When the id is in charge, a person tends to eat too much, drink too much, have sex too often, and fight too frequently.

The **ego** develops most clearly from about 6 to 8 months of age. Often called the "I," the ego develops to help the id satisfy its physical and social needs without harming others. Freud (1926) described the ego as "a kind of façade of the id . . . an external, cortical layer of it" (p. 18). The ego lies within the realms of the conscious, preconscious, and unconscious. The ego is *rational*, capable of forming realistic plans, and it functions as a liaison between the id and the superego. The ego can be conceptualized as a mediator between the id and the superego. The behavior of the ego is reality oriented, and it seeks to protect the self—hence the concept of ego defense mechanisms.

Whereas the id is oriented toward the **pleasure principle**, the ego leans toward the **reality principle**. The ego determines whether it can satisfy the pleasures that the id seeks without harming others or itself. The ego can moderate the desires of the id by delaying immediate gratification of the id's impulses. For instance, a child might say that he or she is hungry (Freud, 1920). The child responds

to the mother that he or she can wait. The ego's ability to exercise control or restraint over the id is referred to as *anticathexis*. In this manner, the ego functions to keep us from crying or throwing a tantrum when we do not get our way. According to Freud (1923, p. 15), "Like a man on horseback, [the ego] has to hold in check the superior strength of the horse."

While the id is engaged in primary process thinking, the ego participates in **secondary process** thinking, that is, thinking directed toward problem solving and self-preservation. The ego has the capacity for rational decision making and decides when not to satisfy the urgings of the id. A person may become anxious as the ego reacts to threatening urges from the id.

The **superego** is the third component of an individual's personality; it represents parental values and societal standards. As a child develops, he or she incorporates the parents' values (Freud, 1923). As a result, the ego ideal is formed; it contains behaviors of which the parents approve. According to Freud, the superego operates on the basis of the **morality principle**, which represents society's views of right and wrong. The superego seeks perfection, and it is oriented toward the past rather than the present or the future. The superego seeks to inhibit the id and the ego, and it demands rigid adherence to an ideal.

Each of us develops content for our superego by using **introjection**, which involves a process of the individual's incorporating the norms and standards of a culture into his or her culture. The process of introjecting is aided by the individual's identification with significant adults during childhood (Fine, 1979). The major significant role models who provide content for one's superego include a diverse group—parents, family members, teachers, and clergy. Parents are critical in the formation of their children's superego because they offer love when their children are good and punishment or disapproval when the parents' standards are not followed.

The superego may cause neurotic behavior when it demands that id and ego abide by parental or societal wishes. An overly strong superego can lock a person into rigid moral patterns that suffocate rather than liberate. Individuals who are perfectionists tend to have an overactive or dominant superego. When the id has too much control, we become impulsive or self-indulgent. When the superego is too dominant, we set unrealistically high or perfectionist goals for ourselves.

Anxiety is a state of tension within us that pushes us to do or not to do something. There are three kinds of anxiety: realistic, neurotic, and moral (Freud, 1926). *Realistic anxiety* represents fear of danger from the external world, and the degree of anxiety must be in keeping to the degree of harm. Neurotic and moral anxieties develop as a result of the conflict among the id, ego, and superego. *Neurotic anxiety* takes place when individuals fear that their instincts or the desires of their id will get out of control and cause them to do something that they will regret. *Moral anxiety* takes place when one does something against one's own **conscience** or when one fears excessively criticism

Inner Reflection

Using Freud's theory of personality structure, which part of the structure seems to have the strongest hold on your personality and behavior—id, ego, or superego?

and demands from one's parents or society (Freud, 1926). An overly active superego produces an individual who suffers from strong feelings of guilt and inferiority.

Freud's theory of drives changed throughout his life. He determined that all instincts fall into one of two major classes: (1) the life instincts or (2) the death instincts. Life instincts were given the label "Eros." The life instincts are those that deal with basic survival, pleasure, and reproduction, and they are sometimes referred to as "sexual instincts." These instincts are important for sustaining the life of the individual as well as the continuation of the species. They also include thirst, hunger, and pain avoidance. The energy created by the life instincts is also known as the **libido**. From a positive perspective, behaviors commonly associated with the life instinct include love, cooperation, and other prosocial actions.

Psychosexual Phases of Development

The pleasure principle dominates Freud's theory of personality. Freud proposed five **psychosexual phases** of development, each phase characterized by a pleasure zone or area of the body through which the child or youth seeks gratification. Freud believed that it would be a mistake to conclude that each of these phases succeeds one another in a clear-cut fashion. The phases may overlap, and/or they may be present alongside one another (Fine, 1979). Most people pass through these phases without too much difficulty; however, sometimes people become stuck at a particular phase rather than proceeding smoothly through the entire five phases of development. Freud used the term **fixation** to describe what happens when a person becomes stuck at a particular phase. Fixation is generally a defense against anxiety. Both frustration and overindulgence may lock some amount of the child's libido into the phase at which such circumstances occur.

Conversely, if a child progresses normally through the phases, resolving each conflict and moving on to the next phase, then little libido is left invested in each phase of development. But if the person fixates at a particular phase, his or her method of obtaining satisfaction that characterized the phase of fixation will dominate and influence his or her adult personality.

Oral Phase

Freud described the earliest phase of development as the oral phase. This stage takes place from birth to about 18 months. During the oral phase, the infant's chief source of libidinal gratification centers around feeding and the body organs associated with this function—namely, the mouth, lips, and tongue, along with the infant's feelings of security that occur as a result of his or her being held. When the infant's oral needs are satisfied (a state of satiety), the tension is reduced, and he or she may fall asleep.

Psychoanalysts have made a number of hypotheses about the oral phase of development and people's subsequent character traits, which are often referred to as *oral incorporation traits*. According to Abraham (1927), fixation due to either deprivation or overindulgence leads to the development of an **oral personality** that may have some of the following characteristics: pessimism/optimism, suspiciousness/gullibility, self-belittlement/cockiness, and passivity/manipulativeness. Deprivation during this stage is likely to result in pessimism that one's needs will not be met. A child's biting and spitting during the oral stage have been related to oral aggressiveness characteristics that include sarcasm, cynicism, and argumentativeness.

Dependency has often been associated with the oral stage. If a child is overindulged by breast feeding and nursing, the child tends to turn into an adult who is gullible and full of admiration for others around him or her (Fine, 1979). For instance, children who depend overly on their mothers during the oral phase may fixate at this stage and become too dependent during adult life. Conversely, children who experience anxiety during feeding may become anxious during their adult years. Individuals who are fixated at the oral stage often find themselves dealing with separation anxiety during adulthood.

Anal Phase

Between the ages of 18 months and 3 years, the anal area becomes the main source of pleasure for children (Freud, 1923). Children explore their bodily functions, which may include touching and playing with feces. When adults respond with disgust to children during their play with these activities, children may develop low self-esteem and a type of stubborn assertiveness and rebelliousness to be in control. The anal phase involves power struggles that seem to become exacerbated during the "terrible twos." Children become fixated at the anal phase if their caretakers are too demanding or overindulgent (Fenichel, 1945; Freud, 1925). The over-demanding or over-controlling parent who forces toilet training too quickly or too harshly tends to produce an adult who exhibits an **anal personality**, meaning one who is dominated by

a tendency to hold onto or to retain. Such anal personality types hold on to money (stinginess), their feelings (constrictedness), and their own way of doing things (stubbornness). When children are toilet trained harshly, they learn that they will be punished if they are not meticulous, neat, and punctual.

Overindulgent parents who are lackadaisical about toilet training encourage children to do whatever they want when they feel pressure. They produce children and adults who are inclined to be wasteful about spending their money and to let go of their feelings (become explosive). If parents are too lenient, and the child gets pleasure from expulsion of feces, such parenting will result in the formation of an anal expulsive character, who is generally messy, disorganized, reckless, careless, and defiant (Freud, 1925).

Phallic Phase

The phallic phase is the setting for the most crucial sexual conflict in Freud's psychosexual stages of development. It lasts from about age 3 until 5 or 6 years. The source of gratification shifts from the anal region to the genital area. During this phase, children play doctor games to clarify their own curiosity about the genitalia of boys and girls.

The major conflict that children experience during this phase is over the object of their sexual desire. For a boy, the object of sexual desire is his mother, and for a girl, her father. The phallic phase is noteworthy for the occurrence of the **oedipal complex** (from the Greek play, *Oedipus Rex*, in which Oedipus kills his father and marries his mother, although he did not know he had done so when he engaged in these acts. When Oedipus discovers the truth of his acts, he is distraught and gouges out his eyes with his mother's brooch. Freud suggested that "the guilt of Oedipus was not palliated by the fact that he incurred it without his knowledge and even against his intention" [Hartocollis, 2005, p. 315]. Oedipus punished himself out of guilt feelings generated from the superego).

To deal with his anxiety and fear of penis castration, the boy learns to identify with his father and to move from sexual to nonsexual love for the mother. Although Freud proposed initially that girls suffered from an **Electra complex**, wherein they desired their fathers, he dropped this idea in his later writings. Freud theorized that girls suffer **penis envy** during this phase of development.

Psychoanalysts have questioned Freud's theory of penis envy. Karen Horney (1926) challenged Freud's claim that motherhood was a woman's way of compensating for her "organ inferiority." According to Horney, Freud's image of women was biased because he based it on the observations of neurotic women. Others have criticized penis envy as a symbolic reflection of men's superior economic and cultural advantage. The anthropologist Margaret Mead (1974) theorized that when boys accept the fact that they cannot bear children, they compensate for this inferiority by choosing to place a high value on achievement. More recent psychoanalysts have agreed with Mead and emphasize boys' fascination with childbirth and mothers' ability to have children.

What allows both boys and girls to successfully complete this phase is identification with the same-sex parent, which reduces the child's anxiety over his or her sexual desires for the parent. Such identification is believed to foster the beginning of the superego, the moral part of a person's personality. People who experience difficulty with the phallic phase may experience later sexual identity problems. Parents are encouraged not to overreact or to overindulge their children's fantasies of replacing the other parent.

Fixation at the phallic phase results in the development of a phallic personality, one who is reckless, narcissistic, and excessively vain and proud. People who fail to resolve the conflict successfully are said to be afraid or incapable of close love. Freud theorized that such fixation could be a major cause of homosexuality.

Latency Phase

The resolution of the phallic phase leads to the latency phase, which is a period in which the young child's sexual drive lies dormant. Freud believed that latency was a period of unparalleled repression of sexual desires. The latency period is a relatively quiet stage of development that lasts from the ages of 6 to 12 years (or puberty). During latency, children repress their sexual energy and channel it into school, their friends, sports, and hobbies; they direct their attention to the larger world. The changes that take place during this phase are crucial in establishing an adult identity. Latency was conceptualized as a quiet time between the conflicted, pregenital time and the storm that would begin during adolescence. Latency is a time for ego development and for learning the rules of society. This phase prepares a child to enter the genital phase during adolescence (Freud, 1923).

Genital Phase

The genital phase signals the onset of adolescence, and it begins around the age of 13. Young people focus their sexual energy (libido) toward people of the opposite sex (if heterosexual) or toward the same sex (if homosexual). The less energy the child has invested in unresolved psychosexual developments, the greater will be his or her capacity to develop normal relationships with the opposite sex. Freud (1923) maintained that no one becomes a mature genital character without undergoing a successful **analysis**. The genital phase can be contrasted with the first three phases because it is more altruistic and less selfish than the others. Psychoanalytic theory suggests that people unable to make psychological attachments during adolescence and young adulthood will manifest abnormal personality patterns.

> ### Inner Reflection
>
> Your client smokes, seems to be overly dependent on others' approval, and has difficulty making decisions on her own. In what phase of psychosexual development might you consider placing her?

Theory of Maladaptive Behavior

Psychoanalytic thought suggests that we are all "a little neurotic" (Freud, 1901). The conflicts of childhood form the core of neurotic disorders. Maladaptive behavior occurs because we all experience conflicts and fixations during our early years. No one goes through each developmental stage without experiencing some problems. We experience symptoms of abnormality depending on the psychosexual stage in which the conflicts and fixations first developed and the defense mechanisms used to deal with the conflicts. Typically, childhood neurosis takes the form of general apprehensiveness, nightmares, phobias, tics, or mannerisms. Phobia is the most frequent example of childhood neurosis.

Freud maintained that anxiety is at the core of all maladaptive behavior. Neuroses develop in adults because of the pressures between drives and the defensive forces of the ego are out of alignment. A great deal depends on how the ego manages anxiety. When the ego manages anxiety effectively, it blocks the emergence of the dangerous id impulses. Anxiety is less likely to develop when the ego is able to negotiate successfully the dictates of the superego with the desires of the id (Freud, 1926).

When a client has a weakened ego, he or she spends a great deal of psychic energy struggling with the demands of the superego and id. As the id takes over, clients may regress to an earlier stage or point of fixation, and their behavior may become childish, narcissistic, or destructive. A weakened ego may also be damaged by the pleasure demands of the id. In such instances, the ego fails to rein in the id, and it becomes a destructive force in an individual's life. People become anxious when the conflict they are experiencing emerges into consciousness and can no longer be denied.

THE THERAPEUTIC PROCESS

Psychoanalysis is the orthodox application of Freudian theory (Freud, 1933). In contrast, psychoanalytically oriented therapy makes use of some of Freud's concepts, but these concepts are applied flexibly. Psychoanalytical training is long term and intense, usually comprising at least 5 years. Students preparing for careers as therapists or counselors may be required to undergo psychoanalytic therapy. In a letter to his friend Wilhelm, Freud commented on his own painful struggles with self-analysis and stated,

> My dear Wilhelm, My self-analysis is the most important thing I have in hand, and promises to be of the greatest value to me, when it is finished. When I was in the very midst of it, it suddenly broke down for three days, and I had the feeling of inner binding about which my patients complain so much, and I was inconsolable. . . .
>
> It is no easy matter. Being entirely honest with oneself is a good exercise. Only one idea of general value has occurred to me. I have found love of the mother and jealousy of the father in my own case too, and now believe it to be a general phenomenon of early childhood. (Freud, 1954, pp. 221, 223)

Typically, the psychoanalytic approach to therapy begins with asking the person to lie down on the couch, looking away from the therapist (Davidson, 1987). Next, the person expresses whatever thoughts, feelings, or images come to mind, without censoring, suppressing, or prejudging them. The therapist sits behind the couch and listens in a nonjudgmental manner to the client. Periodically, the therapist interrupts the client's associations, helping him or her to reflect on the possible connections and significance of his or her associations. As the therapist intervenes, her or his role changes from a passive observer to an active observer and interpreter.

The underlying theory is that the client's thoughts and associations come primarily from persistent dynamic internal drives that are organized unconsciously within (Freud, 1933). The therapist's goal is to make the unconscious conscious, to interpret transferences, to work through and resolve such transferences, and to strengthen the client's ego so that the behavior is based more on reality and less on libidinal urges or irrational guilt. Childhood experiences are reconstructed, interpreted, and analyzed. Analytic therapy is directed toward achieving insight and self-understanding.

The Therapeutic Relationship

Freud originally discussed the importance of the therapeutic relationship in his early theoretical papers on transference. Although Freud first discussed the significance of making a patient a collaborator in his *Studies of Hysteria* (1885/1955), he was primarily concerned with the transferential aspects of the relationship and the importance of transference analysis. In the psychoanalytic approach to psychotherapy, the client–therapist relationship revolves around induced transference neurosis. The client resurrects and relives the highly emotional conflicts that took place with significant others in early childhood; these emotions are then transferred to the therapist. The feelings directed toward the therapist are usually intense. As a result, the therapeutic alliance must be strong enough to withstand a high level of emotional intensity.

Traditionally, two general approaches toward the alliance in the psychoanalytic school have existed. Practitioners of *classical* or *drive-conflict* theories have tended to view the alliance as a necessary but not sufficient condition for therapeutic change. Conversely, therapists who practice *interpersonal* and *relational psychoanalysis* have been inclined to view the negotiation of the therapeutic alliance as being at the heart of the change process.

Goals of Therapy

Psychoanalysis is designed to bring about changes in an individual's personality and character structure. According to Freud, psychoanalysis offered the hope of helping those who are willing and able to participate in a lengthy and often painful process to achieve a resolution of some intrapsychic conflicts so that they might experience life in a mature manner. Other therapist goals are to help clients achieve self-awareness, honesty, and more effective interpersonal relationships and gain better control over their irrational and id impulses. The ultimate goal of psychoanalysis

is reorganization that promotes the integration of dissociated psychic material and results in a fundamentally changed, firmly established new structure of personality. The therapist seeks to promote the psychoanalytic approach to therapy, teaching the process of free association, strengthening ego so that behavior is more reality based, and helping the client gain insight into and work through the transference process.

Role of the Therapist

The therapist begins by evaluating whether the client is a suitable client for psychoanalysis. As Greenson (1967) has stated, "People who do not dare regress from reality and those who cannot return readily to reality are poor risks for psychoanalysis" (p. 34). Clients who have been diagnosed as schizophrenic, manic-depressive, schizoid, or borderline personalities are believed to be poor risks for psychoanalysis. Freud maintained that compassionate neutrality was the appropriate attitude for the therapist to convey during psychotherapy. The therapist does not offer advice or extend sympathy. Usually, the therapist is seen as very passive and detached. Psychoanalysis focuses on intrapersonal conflicts in therapy. The ideal client is one who is capable of pregenital fixations. The genital personality is the ideal (Kramer, 2006).

As noted, classical analysts use what has been called the **blank screen** approach. They permit very little, if any, self-disclosure. If therapists say very little about themselves, they maintain that whatever the client says is the result of past conflicts. Modern-day analysts sometimes dispense with the couch and develop a less neutral role with their clients. Whereas a classic psychoanalyst focuses on lifting repressions and resolving internal conflicts, relational analysts might concentrate on conflicts in the present.

Role of the Client

Clients in psychotherapy must commit to long-term and intensive therapy. They agree to talk and to free associate because talk is at the heart of the therapeutic process. Clients terminate psychoanalysis when they and their analyst agree that they understand the historical roots of their difficulties. At the end of therapy, successful clients have worked through their childhood conflicts. Freud restricted treatment to clients of normal intelligence who had a certain degree of ethical development and who were under the age of 50. He believed that after the age of 50, a person was less able to benefit from undoing psychic conflicts.

Assessment

During psychoanalysis, the process of assessing clients' family history, dreams, and other material continues throughout the course of therapy. Some therapists use a very structured approach in the initial sessions by taking a family and social history, while others may use assessment during the first few weeks of therapy. To assess clients, therapists listen for unconscious motivations, early childhood relationship issues, defenses, and related material.

Both Freudian and neo-Freudian psychology highlight the importance of understanding clients' unconscious material and averting their strong defense mechanisms to help them with presenting issues. Information is often hidden from clients in their unconscious. Freud described *projection* as a common defense mechanism of clients. Psychoanalysts use the concept of defense mechanisms in clinical assessment by using projective tests. The goal is to give clients neutral and non-threatening stimuli and to ask them to interpret ambiguous pictures, fill in the blanks, make associations, or tell stories. According to the theory of projection, clients will project their own unconscious material onto the nonthreatening stimuli, permitting the clinician to interpret and move the client toward insight.

Inner Reflections

In your opinion, what type of client would be a good candidate for psychoanalytic therapy? Why?

If you have clients with whom you are working, would you consider using psychoanalytic techniques with them?

Inner Reflections

If you could be granted training in only one of the projective tests, which one would it be and why?

Does your program of psychotherapy provide such training?

Phases of Therapy

Classical psychoanalysis can be subdivided into four phases: (1) the opening phase, (2) development of transference, (3) working through, and (4) resolution of transference (Arlow & Brenner, 1990).

1. *Opening phase:* The opening phase consists of the therapist's first contact with the client and lasts from 3 to 6 weeks (Freud, 1919). The therapist notes everything that the client says and does for possible later use in treatment. The therapist assesses the nature of clients' problems, including their current life situations, what brought them to therapy, their manner of relating to others, their family background, and child development. Psychoanalysts frown on formal history taking that uses a prescribed form. Instead, they maintain that clients should set the priorities of the psychoanalytic session (Arlow & Brenner, 1990). The therapist describes the process of psychoanalysis and the client's obligations.

The next part of the opening phase involves introducing clients to the couch and the techniques of psychoanalysis, such as free association. The analyst probes gently to understand the nature of the client's unconscious conflicts. Eventually, the therapist detects themes from the client's childhood that remain dynamically active in the client's present life in distorted and unconscious fantasies. The therapist focuses primarily on conflicts that are readily accessible to the client's consciousness.

2. *Development of transference:* The development of **transference** constitutes the second phase of psychoanalysis. Transference and working through (Phase 3) form the major portion of psychoanalytic counseling. Freud believed that in transference, the client was unconsciously reenacting forgotten childhood memories and repressed unconscious fantasies. Transference prevents us from seeing others entirely objectively; rather we "transfer" onto them qualities of other important figures in our earlier life. Transference leads to distortions in our relationships with others. Psychoanalytic treatment is designed to magnify transference phenomena so that they can be examined and untangled from the client's present-day relationships. Transference was conceptualized as a form of memory in which the client repeats in therapy conflicts from his or her early childhood as if they currently existed. There is some theory that the beginning stages of transference take place as soon as the client makes the telephone call for a therapeutic appointment. In anticipation of help, the client may find that unconscious wishes and conflicts may come quickly to the surface. One benefit of transference analysis is that it helps clients distinguish fantasy from reality and the past from the present. The psychoanalyst and the client create a relationship wherein all the client's transference experiences become part of the psychoanalytic setting and can be examined and understood. Transference also reveals to clients the force of their unconscious, childhood fantasy wishes. Moreover, the therapists' transference analysis helps clients see how they misperceive, misinterpret, and relate to people in the present according to their interactions with people in their past—usually their parents. Clients are able to evaluate the unrealistic nature of their impulses and anxieties, to make appropriate decisions based on reality rather than on distorted fantasies, and to restore the dynamic equilibrium between their impulse and conflict—a balance that will ultimately lead to life satisfaction and happiness.

3. *Working-through phase:* The analysis of transference is continued in the **working-through** phase. "Working through" might be defined as a slow, gradual process of working again and again with the insights that have emanated from the therapist's interpretations of resistance and transference (Freud, 1949). The working-through phase entails clients' gaining insights to their issues as a result of transference analysis. Typically, a successful transference analysis leads to a client's ability to recall crucial childhood experiences. The therapist helps the client work through the forgotten or repressed memories and see how they are affecting the client in the present by analyzing their transference onto the therapist. Typically, clients become aware of their many defensive maneuvers, the impulses they have tried to defend against, and the many ways in which they are currently manifesting their symptoms.

One of the benefits of the working-through process is that clients come to understand that they do not have to fear their impulses as they did when they were children, because in the transference relationship, they expressed those same impulses in intense words and were not castrated, rejected, or abandoned (Freud, 1949). Gradually, clients become aware that they can choose more mature ways of dealing with their impulses. As clients increase their conscious awareness of their behavior and defenses, they make structural changes in their personalities. Energies that were once bound up in pregenital conflicts are now at the service of the mature adult ego.

4. *Resolution of transference:* The resolution of transference constitutes the termination phase of treatment. As soon as the client and the analyst believe that the major goals of analysis have been achieved and that the transference is well understood, they set a date for ending therapy. Both the analyst and the client must resolve any remaining attachment issues the client has with the therapist. Sometimes, clients do not want to leave therapy

because they feel safe, and they have found a gratifying human relationship. A therapist helps clients examine their fantasies about what life will be like at the end of treatment. Failure to prepare clients adequately for termination may lead to a relapse.

Therapy Techniques

Freud's major techniques of analysis were (1) free association, (2) dream analysis, (3) analysis of resistance, and (4) analysis of transference.

1. *Free association:* **Free association** is the cardinal technique of psychoanalysis that allows clients to say anything and everything that comes to mind regardless of how silly, painful, or meaningless it seems. It is founded on the belief that one association leads to another that is deeper in the unconscious. Free association permits clients to abandon their usual ways of censoring or editing thoughts. Slips of tongue are analyzed for what they reveal about clients' feelings.

2. *Dream analysis:* Freud considered dream analysis to be the pathway to the unconscious (Abrams, 1992). When people sleep, the ego releases its control over unconscious material. **Dreams** are said to have two levels of content: a manifest and a latent content (Freud, 1953a). The **manifest content** of a dream is the surface meaning of the dream. You dream that you are running and running, and when you look back, no one is there.

The **latent content** of a dream contains the deeper, hidden, and symbolic meaning. Because the impulses underlying the dream are so threatening (unconscious sexual and aggressive impulses), these impulses are translated into the acceptable manifest content—that is, as the dream appears to the dreamer on the surface (Freud, 1953a). The process by which the latent content of a dream is transformed into the less threatening manifest content is called *dreamwork*. You dig deeper and you discover that the dream is telling you that you feel overwhelmed by circumstances and that you would like to run away from your responsibilities.

The therapist's task is to help the client uncover disguised meanings by studying the symbols in the manifest content of the dream (Freud, 1953b).

3. *Analysis of resistance:* In psychoanalysis, **resistance** is said to exist when client behaviors interfere with or hinder the analytical process. As clients begin to experience uncomfortable thoughts and feelings (as they become conscious), they will resist the self-exploration that would bring them fully into awareness. Resistance prevents the client from producing unconscious material. Some common client resistances include not attending sessions, arriving late, complaining about or refusing to make payments for service, censoring thoughts, disrupting the free association process, or refusing to report dreams.

During therapy, resistance is the client's reluctance to bring to the surface of awareness unconscious material that has been repressed. For instance, during free association, the client may manifest an unwillingness to relate certain thoughts or feelings. Freud (1919) viewed resistance as an unconscious situation clients use to defend against anxiety.

Psychoanalysts view client resistance as an opportunity to gain insight into their clients' unconscious motivations or defensive mechanisms. As clients progress through therapy, their resistance increases to free association, discussing past events, and dealing with their transference onto their therapist. Some clients may consciously want change but unconsciously resist it. Resistance helps keep the unconscious conflict intact; it thwarts the therapist's attempts to get at the real causes of personality issues.

The therapist's analysis of resistance is designed to help clients become aware of the reasons for resistance so that they can confront them. Because client resistance forms a line of defense for the self against anxiety, it is extremely important that therapists respect clients' resistances. The goal should not be to strip clients completely of their resistances because such stripping may leave them without adequate defenses. As analysis continues, clients may begin to feel less threatened and more capable of facing the painful things that caused them to resist treatment. They begin to overcome their resistance.

4. *Analysis of transference:* Initially, Freud viewed transference as an impediment to therapy. Gradually, he realized that transference made treatment and the cure possible. Free association brings to the surface childhood remembrances and feelings (Freud, 1919). Clients reexperience their early conflicts and in transference identify the therapist as a substitute for their parents. Their love and hate for therapists can become intense and block therapeutic efforts.

Therapists interpret the distorted displacements of significant relationships clients experience during their transference onto the therapist. Therapists interpret clients' buried feelings, traumatic conflicts, and unconscious fixations of early childhood. Analysis of transference helps clients gain insight into the influence of their past on their present lives. During the interpretation of transference, clients learn how to work through old conflicts that hindered their psychological growth (Freud, 1919).

> ### Inner Reflections
>
> Have you ever had a recurring dream? If so, what was the manifest and the latent content of the dream?
>
> Did you resolve the issues in your recurring dream?
>
> How did you resolve the issues in your dream?

Countertransference

Freud emphasized that countertransference was a reaction to the transference of a client. For instance, if a female client becomes angry with the therapist because the therapist reminds her of her mother, and the therapist becomes angry with the client, this would be an example of countertransference. **Countertransference** is any unconscious attitude or behavior on the part of the therapist that is prompted by the therapist's needs rather than the client's needs. Sometimes, therapists have personality and developmental issues that bring on countertransference issues. For instance, a therapist may have difficulty working with angry clients because as a child she was punished for being angry. Psychotherapists must consider the types of strong feelings, preferences, assumptions, and expectations they bring to the therapeutic relationship that impede their effectiveness with clients.

THE MOVEMENT TOWARD CONTEMPORARY PSYCHODYNAMIC THERAPY

After Freud's death in 1933, psychoanalysis continued to undergo the many revisions that had begun with the rebellion and departure of many of his early disciples, including the departure of Carl Jung and Alfred Adler. Gradually, theorists and practitioners of psychoanalysis started using the term psychodynamic therapy to describe their work instead of the term psychoanalysis. The term *psychodynamic* refers not only to the psychoanalytic therapy developed by Freud but also to the separate theories developed by Jung (analytic psychology [1954] and Adler (individual psychology [1959]), as well as the work of the ego psychologists (Anna Freud [1936] and Erik Erikson [1950]), object relations therapy (Melanie Klein [1932] and Donald Winnicott [1953], two prominent contributors), the development of self psychology by Heinz Kohut (1971, 1977), relational analysis (Mitchell, 1988), and brief psychodynamic therapy (BPT; Messer & Warren, 2001).

Freud himself was the first one to use the term *psychodynamic*. Freud was influenced by the theory of thermodynamics and used the term *psychodynamic* to describe the processes of the mind as flows of psychological energy from the libido to one's brain. Currently, some therapists use psychodynamic therapy interchangeably with psychoanalytic therapy. This situation exists because of the commonalities that exist between the two theoretical approaches (i.e., focus on the unconscious, uncovering).

While psychoanalytic and psychodynamic therapeutic approaches have a common origin with Freud, there are some basic differences between them. In general, the term *psychodynamic* refers to using some principles of psychoanalysis, while using fewer frequent meetings and having more of a focus on exploring only the past that is relevant to the presenting issue. According to Shedler (2010), "The essence of psychodynamic therapy is exploring those aspects of self that are not fully influenced in the therapy relationship" (p. 98). Furthermore, Shedler (2010) has outlined seven features of psychodynamic therapy that "reliably distinguished psychodynamic therapy from other therapies, as determined by empirical examination of actual session recordings and transcripts" (pp. 98–99). The seven features of psychodynamic therapy Shedler listed are as follows:

1. *Focus on affect and expression of emotion:* The therapist helps the client put into words contradictory feelings, feelings that are troubling or threatening, and feelings the client may be unable to recognize (unconscious) or acknowledge. Shedler (2010) notes that the psychodynamic focus on feelings is in contrast to a cognitive focus, "where the greater emphasis is on thoughts and beliefs" (p. 99). The therapist recognizes that intellectual insight is not the same as emotional insight, which operates at a deep level and produces behavioral change.

2. *Exploration of attempts to avoid distressing thoughts and feelings:* This feature of psychodynamic therapy refers to the therapist's use of the concepts of client defense and resistance. Shedler (2010) states that client avoidance or resistance in psychodynamic therapy may take such courses as missing sessions, arriving late, being evasive, subtle shifts of topic when certain ideas come up, focusing on minor aspects of an experience instead of on what is psychologically meaningful, or focusing on external circumstances rather than on one's own role in creating events. Psychodynamic therapists focus on and explore client avoidances.

3. *Identification of recurring themes and patterns:* Psychodynamic therapists help clients identify and explore recurring themes and patterns in client's thoughts, feelings, self-concepts, relationships, and life experiences.

4. *Discussion of past experience (developmental focus):* The therapist may explore early attachment experiences and past relationships. According to Shedler (2010),

> Psychodynamic therapists explore early experiences, the relation between past and present, and the ways in which the past tends to "live on" in the present. The focus is not on the past for its own sake, but rather on how the past sheds light on current psychological difficulties. The goal is to help patients free themselves from the bonds of past experience in order to live more fully in the present. (p. 99)

5. *Focus on interpersonal relations:* Psychodynamic therapy puts a strong emphasis on clients' relations and interpersonal experiences (in theoretical terms, object relations, and attachment).

6. *Focus on the therapy relationship:* The psychodynamic therapist focuses on transference and countertransference issues. The therapeutic goal is to help the client gain greater flexibility in interpersonal relationships, instead of transferring onto them unresolved issues of their past.

7. *Exploration of fantasy life:* In contrast to other therapies that may structure sessions or follow a predetermined manual format, psychodynamic therapy encourages clients to speak freely about whatever is on their minds—including their fantasies. "The goals of psychodynamic therapy include, but extend beyond, symptom remission. Successful treatment should not only relieve symptoms (get rid of something) but also foster the positive presence of psychological capacities and resources" (Shedler, 2010, p. 100).

The term *psychodynamic* is not just one theory. It is a set of theories: (1) psychoanalytic therapy, (2) ego psychology, (3) object relations, and (4) self psychology theory. These set of theories describes the inner energies that motivate and control a person's behavior. Ego psychologists examine how a person's ego functions. They focus on such issues as reality testing, judgment, sense of reality of the world and the self. An important question for ego psychologists is, "How does the person modulate and control drives, affects, and impulses?" Object relations theorists examine the early formation and differentiation of psychological structures (the inner images of the self and the other, or the object).

EGO PSYCHOLOGY

Classical psychoanalysis was founded primarily on id psychology, in which our instincts and conflicts over such instincts were viewed as the main movers of personality and psychotherapy. Classical psychoanalytic theory maintains that the ego derives all of its energies from the id. Freud once said, "Where there is id, ego shall be." During the 1920s, Freud moved beyond the id and focused his attention on the analysis of the ego.

Freud's followers found ways to incorporate the psychosexual drives of the id with social and nondrive motives (ego). **Ego psychology** maintains that a major function of the ego is to adapt to and master an objective reality. Although ego psychologists do not deny that conflicts over impulses striving for immediate gratification are significant influences on development, they assert that the ego has a separate striving for adaption and mastery. The ego develops as young people develop a desire for effectiveness and competence (Freud, 1936).

Young people can be motivated to learn their times tables, colors, and other language skills independent of any longings for sexual or aggressive gratification. The ego has its own energies, and it becomes a major force in the development of a personality that is adaptive and competent. When individuals fail to develop such ego processes as judgment and moral reasoning, they may begin the development of psychopathology. Individuals who have poor ego development are inadequately prepared to adapt to reality.

Critical areas of therapy for ego psychologists involve achieving identity, intimacy, and ego integrity (Eagle, 1997). Psychotherapy travels back into clients' history only to analyze the unresolved conflicts that are interfering with their lives. While ego psychoanalysts are in agreement with Freudian analysts in their use of long-term intensive therapy, free association, transference, and interpretation of resistance, they tend to be more flexible in their use of psychodynamic therapy (Eagle, 1997).

Ego psychologists maintain that because the ego has its own energies, much more is involved in individuals' development than just the resolution of conflicts over sex and aggression (Friedman, 1999). Hence, the psychosexual stages of Freud do not provide sufficient explanations for all of personality and psychopathology. Whereas Freud placed emphasis on psychosexual development, ego psychologists stress the importance of psychosocial development. While Freud conceptualized the ego as serving the demands of the id and superego, ego psychologists portrayed the ego as striving for relationship with the outside world, especially other people (Coles, 2000).

Moreover, because the ego strives for adaptability, competency, and mastery well beyond the first 5 years of life, later stages are required to explain personality development and psychopathology. Ego psychologists attempt to build ego strength—the capacity of the ego to pursue its healthy goals—despite perceived threat and stress. Ego psychologists have broadened the goals of psychoanalytically oriented therapy. Ego psychology emphasizes improved reality testing and judgment (Coles, 2000).

Therefore, one therapeutic goal might be helping a client see the outside world as it

Inner Reflections

Suppose that you were a client who desired to see a therapist for one of your real personal issues; from which one of the theoretical orientations presented in this chapter would you select (psychoanalytic, psychodynamic, ego, object relations, or self psychology) a therapist?

What benefits might there be in your seeing a therapist from the theoretical orientation you have chosen? Why?

is without much distortion from inner conflicts. In addition, ego psychologists place major importance on analyzing clients' defense mechanisms, especially those that are rigidly used. Two of the best-known ego psychologists are Anna Freud and Erik Erikson (Eagle, 1997). Freud's daughter Anna made important revisions to Freudian psychoanalysis by emphasizing ego development and defense mechanisms in people. Her student, Erik Erikson, developed the psychosocial stages of development that unfolded over a person's life span. Anna Freud's (1936) and Erikson's (1950, 1968) work form the foundation of ego psychology.

Major Contributor: Anna Freud

Photo courtesy of Library of Congress.

Anna Freud

I was always looking outside myself for strength, but it comes from within. It is there all the time.

—Anna Freud

Anna Freud (1895–1982) applied psychoanalysis to the treatment of children. She also further developed the concept of ego defense mechanisms. Her father, Sigmund Freud, first described defensive operations in *The Neuro-Psychoses of Defense* (1894/1984). Although Freud later pointed out that his theory of repression or defense was at the

heart of psychoanalysis, he never fully systematized knowledge about defenses.

Anna Freud treated nursery school children at her Hampstead Clinic in London. She studied measures of child maturation, such as moving from dependence to self-mastery. According to her, both the id and the ego should be the focus of psychoanalytic treatment. In her book, *The Ego and the Mechanisms of Defense* (1936), Anna Freud delineated 10 defense mechanisms, and she pointed out both the adaptive and maladaptive means of using defense mechanisms.

In psychoanalytic theory, **ego defense mechanisms** are psychological strategies individuals use to cope with reality and to maintain their self-images. The purpose of ego defense mechanisms is to protect one's mind/self/ego from anxiety, social sanctions, or to provide refuge from situations that tax one's ability to cope. They are described as ego defense mechanisms because they occur when id impulses conflict with superego values and beliefs and when an external threat is posed to the ego.

Ego defense mechanisms work by distorting the id impulses into acceptable impulses or by unconscious or conscious blockage of these impulses. Healthy persons use different defenses throughout life. An ego defense mechanism becomes pathological only if it involves persistent use that leads to maladaptive behavior. The ego marshals an individual's favorite defense mechanism to combat anxiety (Blanck & Blanck, 1986). Defense mechanisms have two common characteristics: (1) they either deny or distort reality and (2) they operate at the unconscious level of awareness (Freud, 1936). Common defense mechanisms include the following:

- *Projection:* You attribute to others your own characteristic ways of being. For instance, an overcontrolling person might see everyone else as striving to control him or her. Generally, projection is shifting one's unacceptable thoughts, feelings, and motivations within oneself onto others, so these behaviors are perceived as being possessed by the other. A common projection among men who have been rejected by a woman might be, "She wants me."

• *Repression:* Repression is a defense mechanism that excludes threatening or painful thoughts from awareness. Although it is believed that most of the painful events of the first 5 years of life are buried, these events still influence individuals' behavior. For instance, an adult may have experienced terrible child abuse in early years. If anger toward the abusing parent is repressed, the adult may not experience any conscious memory of the events. However, the person may seek conscious expression of the abuse through anger toward some authority or parent-like figure (Freud, 1936).

• *Regression:* Regression is a method of reducing anxiety by retreating to an earlier period of life that was more pleasant and safe. Childish behaviors—throwing a temper tantrum and pouting—are often associated with regression. One adult female would suck her thumb whenever anxiety threatened her.

• *Intellectualization:* The individual escapes his or her emotions by focusing on intellectual concepts or insignificant details. An example of intellectualization is a person who experiences a painful breakup with his spouse of 10 years and who chooses to discuss the breakup devoid of any emotion and primarily in abstract, intellectual terms (Freud, 1936).

• *Denial:* Denial is a way of distorting what a person thinks, feels, or perceives in a given situation. A person defends against anxiety by "closing his or her eyes" to a threatening reality. One denies that his mate is cheating because facing that reality would be too anxiety provoking. Denial protects the self from any unpleasant reality by refusing to even perceive it.

• *Rationalization:* This defense mechanism is sometimes referred to as "sour grapes" because it is based partially on the Aesop fable of the fox who tried repeatedly without success to reach a bunch of grapes. After trying several times, the fox finally gave up, rationalizing that he really did not want the grapes anyway.

• *Reaction formation:* Sometimes, individuals defend against the expression of a forbidden impulse by expressing its opposite. **Reaction formation** contains two steps: (1) individuals deny the unacceptable id impulse and (2) the opposite is expressed on a conscious level. A person may experience extreme hostility toward a person, but instead of expressing this hostility, he or she responds with great kindness.

• *Sublimation:* Individuals transform negative emotions or impulses into positive actions, behavior, or emotion. According to Anna Freud, sublimation is the only healthy way to cope with objectionable impulses because it permits the ego to convert them into socially acceptable forms. A person may sublimate anger by working late in the garage to build something (Freud, 1936).

• *Displacement:* This process shifts sexual or aggressive impulses to a more acceptable or less threatening object. It redirects emotion to a safer object. For instance, a mother may yell at her child because she is angry with her husband, and the child then kicks the dog because he is angry with his mother.

• *Introjection:* This defense mechanism involves taking in and absorbing the values and standards of others—usually to avoid some unacceptable consequence. For instance, during war times, prisoners may identify with the aggressor to survive the prison experience.

Inner Reflections

Both the psychoanalytic and the psychodynamic approaches to therapy underscore the importance of the first 5 years of a person's life.

Do you believe that a person's current problems can be traced back to what happened to him or her at age 3 or 5?

What connections, if any, do you see about your own childhood experiences and your present personality?

A positive example of introjections entails taking in the values of one's parents.

Major Contributor: Erik Erikson

Erik Erikson

Children love and want to be loved and they very much prefer the joy of accomplishment to the triumph of hateful failure.

Hope is both the earliest and the most indispensable virtue inherent in the state of being alive. If life is to be sustained hope must remain, even where confidence is wounded, trust impaired.

—Erik Erikson

Eric Erikson (1902–1994) was a Danish-German-American developmental psychologist and psychoanalyst who developed a theory of social development for people. His interest in the psychology of identity can be traced to the circumstances of his childhood (Coles, 1970, 2000; Stevens, 2008). He was born in Frankfurt to Danish parents. Erik was conceived as a result of his mother's extramarital affair; Karla Abrahamsen, his mother and the daughter of a prominent Jewish family in Copenhagen, concealed the circumstances of Erik's birth from him during his early childhood (Stevens, 2008). Little information is provided about Erik's biological father, other than that his name was Erik.

There were rumors that he also was married at the time of Erikson's conception.

Karla Abrahamsen was married to Jewish stockbroker Valdemar Isidor Salomonsen at the time of Erikson's birth. Initially, Erik was registered as Erik Salomonsen. After Erik's birth, Karla moved to Karlsruhe, and in 1904, married a Jewish pediatrician named Theodor Homburger. In 1911, Erik was adopted by his stepfather (Stevens, 2008).

Erikson's concern with the development of a person's identity was a concern in his own life. For most of his childhood and early adulthood, he was known as Erik Homburger (Stevens, 2008). He was a tall, blond, blue-eyed boy who was reared within the Hebrew or Jewish tradition. When he was at temple, the kids teased him for being Nordic; and when he was at his grammar school, kids teased him for being Jewish. He searched first for his own identity and in his later work helped others achieve theirs.

Initially, Erikson was not interested in becoming an analyst. He was an artist, a painter who did portraits of children. At a Vienna school for psychoanalytic treatment of children, Erikson was hired to paint the portraits of four children. During 1927, Anna Freud became his analyst. Following a short period as a tutor and painter, Erikson was asked if he would consider becoming a child analyst—a profession about which he knew little. He was trained in psychoanalysis at the Vienna Psychoanalytic Institute, and he studied the Montessori method of education for children. He graduated from the institute in 1933 (Stevens, 2008). During his work at the institute, he met his wife, Joan Serson, a Canadian.

Because of the rise of Nazism in Germany, Erikson emigrated with his wife first to Denmark and then to United States, and he became the first child psychologist in Boston. He held positions at Massachusetts General Hospital, the Judge Baker Guidance Center, and the Harvard Medical School (Friedman, 1999).

In 1936, Erikson accepted a position at Yale University, where he taught at the medical school. Thereafter, he spent a year observing children on a Sioux reservation in South Dakota. He moved to California and joined the faculty of the University of California at Berkeley (Friedman, 1999). During his stay in California, he studied children of the Yurok Native American tribe. It was also during this period that he became an American citizen and changed his name from Erik Homburger to Erik Erikson. In 1950, Erikson published the book for which he is best known, *Childhood and Society*. He left the University of California because he refused to sign a loyalty oath (required by President Harry S. Truman of persons who were suspect of holding party membership in Communist or anti-democratic organizations) and returned to Massachusetts, where he spent 10 years working with troubled young people and teaching at the Austen Riggs Center, a prominent psychiatric treatment facility in Stockbridge, Massachusetts. While at the Austen Riggs Center, Erikson emphasized the universal process of resolution of identity conflicts, and he wrote a study on the youthful Martin Luther (*Young Man Luther*, 1958).

During the 1960s, Erikson returned to Harvard University as a professor of human development, and he stayed there until his retirement in 1970. In 1969, he published *Gandhi's Truth*, which explored the evolution of a passionate commitment in maturity to a humane goal and on the inner factors of Gandhi's nonviolent strategy to achieve this goal (Friedman, 1999). This book won a Pulitzer Prize and a U.S. National Book Award.

Erikson died in 1994 on Cape Cod, Massachusetts. His advice to educators about children still remains: "Do not mistake a child for his symptom."

Erikson was an ego psychologist who extended Freud's theory by emphasizing the psychosocial aspects of development beyond childhood (Brenman-Gibson, 1997). He believed that Freud gave insufficient attention to the role of the ego in personality development and did not give sufficient emphasis to social influences throughout the life span. According to ego psychologists, current problems cannot simply be reduced to repetitions of unconscious conflicts with id impulses from early childhood.

Erikson (1968) deals with issues such as identity, intimacy, competency, and integrity, in addition to the Freudian concepts of sex and aggression. He proposed eight **psychosocial stages** (1950) that focus on crises that must be negotiated at different stages in life: (1) trust versus mistrust, (2) autonomy versus shame and doubt, (3) initiative versus guilt, (4) industry versus inferiority, (5) identity versus role confusion, (6) intimacy versus isolation, (7) generativity versus stagnation, and (8) ego integrity versus despair. He broadened the concept of life stages into adulthood and proposed social and nonsexual reasons for adult development. His widow, Joan Serson Erikson, proposed a ninth stage (old age) to take into consideration individuals' increasing life expectancy (Friedman, 1999). One primary element of Erikson's psychosocial stage theory is the development of ego identity (1968). Erikson proposed that our ego identity is continually changing due to the experiences that we acquire daily. He coined the term **identity crisis** to represent a developmental challenge that takes place during adolescence, whereby the youth attempts to define his or her place in life with regard to sexual, personal, and career identity, making a vocational choice. Besides ego identity, Erikson maintained that a sense of competence also motivates our behaviors and actions. Hence, each stage in his theory involves becoming competent in an area of life. If the person handles the psychosocial stage successfully, he or she develops a sense of mastery or ego strength. If the person negotiates the psychosocial stages unsuccessfully, he or she develops a sense of inadequacy.

In each stage, Erikson asserted that people experience a conflict that serves as a turning point in development. The resolution of each stage ends in a person's either developing a psychological quality or failing to develop that characteristic (Erikson, 1968). Erikson's primary contribution to psychology and psychotherapy was that his psychosocial stages covered the entire life span (Mishne, 1993).

Erikson's psychosocial stages are presented with Freud's stages in Table 2.1

Table 2.1 Erikson's Stages of Personality Development

Stage	Basic Conflict	Important Events	Outcome
Infancy (birth to 18 months)	Trust versus mistrust	Feeding	Children develop a sense of trust when caregivers provide reliability, care, and affection. A lack of this will lead to mistrust.
Early childhood (2–3 years)	Autonomy versus shame and doubt	Toilet training	Children need to develop a sense of personal control over physical skills and a sense of independence. Success leads to feelings of autonomy; failure results in feelings of shame and doubt.
Preschool (3–5 years)	Initiative versus guilt	Exploration	Children need to begin asserting control and power over the environment. Success in this stage leads to a sense of purpose. Children who try to exert too much power experience disapproval, resulting in a sense of guilt.
School age (6–11 years)	Industry versus inferiority	School	Children need to cope with new social and academic demands. Success leads to a sense of competence, while failure results in feelings of inferiority.
Adolescence (12–18 years)	Identity versus role confusion	Social relationships	Teens need to develop a sense of self and personal identity. Success leads to an ability to stay true to oneself, while failure leads to role confusion and a weak sense of self.
Young adulthood (19–40 years)	Intimacy versus isolation	Relationships	Young adults need to form intimate, loving relationships with other people. Success leads to strong relationships, while failure results in loneliness and isolation.
Middle adulthood (40–65 years)	Generativity versus stagnation	Work and parenthood	Adults need to create or nurture things that will outlast them, often by having children or creating a positive change that benefits other people. Success leads to feelings of usefulness and accomplishment, while failure results in shallow involvement in the world.
Maturity (65 to death)	Ego integrity versus despair	Reflection on life	Older adults need to look back on life and feel a sense of fulfillment. Success at this stage leads to feelings of wisdom, while failure results in regret, bitterness, and despair.

OBJECT RELATIONS THEORY

Object relations theory is a newer form of psychoanalytic therapy that entails exploring clients' internal, unconscious identifications and internalizations of external objects. The term originated from Freudian theorists who wanted to point out that at certain points for infants, other people are merely objects for gratifying needs. Object relations is a theory that emphasizes interpersonal relations, primarily in the family and particularly between mother and child. It conceptualizes the relationship between self and objects as the organizing principle of the psyche. Donald Winnicott, one of the foremost practitioners of object relations, believed that the central feature of healthy development

Inner Reflections

Using Erikson's theory of psychosocial stages, in what stage would you place yourself?

In what stage did you meet Erikson's criteria most successfully?

was rooted in relationship (Winnicott, 1953).

Object relations theorists examine the early formation and differentiation of psychological structures (inner images of the self and the other, or object) and how these inner structures are manifested in a person's interpersonal situations. These theorists focus on the relationships of early life that leave a lasting impression—that is, a residue or remnant within the psyche of the individual. These residues of past relationships or inner object relations shape a person's perceptions of other people as well as his or her relationships with other individuals. Individuals interact not only with an actual other person but also with an internal other, a psychic representation that may be an accurate representation of another person or a distorted version of some actual person.

In object relations theory, **objects** are usually persons, parts of persons, or symbols of one of these. An object is that to which a person relates. An object is mental representation of other people or put in an alternate way, interpersonal relations that are represented within a person's psyche. Such objects are considered to be features of significant people in their lives, such as a mother or father.

Representation refers to the manner in which the person has or possesses an object. An object representation is the mental representation of an object. These object representations of significant others should not be confused with the actual persons, who may or may not be represented accurately. Object relations theory takes into account both internal and external objects. An *external object* is an actual person, place, or thing that a person has invested with emotional energy. In contrast, an *internal object* is an individual's representation of another, for instance, a reflection of the child's way of relating to the mother. It is a memory, idea, or fantasy about another person, place, or

thing. The self is an internal image that consists of conscious and unconscious mental representations of oneself, especially as experienced in relationship to significant others. The term **self-object** is used to refer to a loss of boundaries, such that the self and object are blurred, and the distinction between self and external object is unclear.

Object constancy refers to maintaining a lasting relationship with a specific object or rejecting any substitute for that object. For instance, one may reject mothering from anyone except one's own mother. Mahler (1968) defined object constancy as the capacity to recognize and tolerate loving and hostile feelings toward the same object, the capacity to keep feelings focused on a specific object, and the capacity to value an object for characteristics other than its function of satisfying needs.

Object relations is primarily a stage theory that focuses on the process of becoming an independent person and viewing other people as stable, complex, and real. Theorists place the most importance on the first 3 years of life, during which time children evolve from fusion with their mothers (no psychological awareness of separateness) to total dependence, to limited self-directed exploration, and finally to separation and individuation. The images of self and others are introjected; that is, children mentally and emotionally accept these images as real. The introjected images may not be accurate images of the actual people. According to Bornstein (1993), "Parental introjects must by definition be personalized, idiosyncratic, and distorted" (p. 7) because they are created from the viewpoints of children under the age of 3.

Object relations theory developed almost entirely

Inner Reflections

Which person in your life has helped you most to shape who you are today?

Looking back on your life, what object relations have you introjected into your personality?

Do you ever find yourself repeating similar elements of your object relations that you established early with your mother or father with other people in your life?

within the context of families that had newly relocated. None of these theorists studied extended family systems in which there were multiple mothering and fathering figures, in the form of aunts, uncles, and grandparents who related to the infant in early life, with any examination of how the developmental process may vary under such circumstances. Moreover, this branch of psychology does not take into account the social system that creates pathology. On the contrary, object relations theory is an interpersonal approach that focuses extensively on the dyadic relationship between mother and infant.

Major Contributor: Donald Winnicott (1896–1971)

Donald Winnicott

Donald Winnicott (1896–1971) was a London pediatrician who studied psychoanalysis with Melanie Klein (1932), one of the founders of object relations theory. He believed that the central feature of healthy development was rooted in relationship (Winnicott, 1953). From his work with psychologically disturbed children and their mothers, Winnicott developed some of his important theoretical concepts, including the holding environment, the transitional object, the good-enough mothers, and the transitional experience. According to Winnicott, an infant child exists in a stream of unintegrated, unconnected moments (Rodman, 2003). Such an existence is pleasant and

not frightening for the child. Winnicott theorized that the person responsible for providing the child's framework is the mother. Gradually, the infant progresses from a state of unintegrated drift into the capability to identify environmental objects.

Winnicott proposed the concept of the holding environment to describe part of an infant's early development. He maintained that for an infant to have healthy development, it is critical that the mother is there when needed. A **holding environment** is a psychical and physical space within which an infant is protected without knowing that he or she is protected (Rodman, 2003). Soon after a child is born, the mother is much occupied with the child. Gradually, the mother moves away from this state of maternal preoccupation and provides an environment in which the child moves about and learns from experience. These experiences help the child understand that there is an outside world (objective reality) that does not always exist to satisfy his or her wants. If the mother does not provide a healthy holding environment, a child may become traumatized. During objective reality, the child learns that the objects he or she relates to, mainly his or her mother, are separate and not under his or her control.

One of Winnicott's most important concepts involves the transitional experience and the transitional object (Winnicott, 1953). The *transitional experience* is the middle ground between objective reality (also labeled the "not-me") and subjective omnipotence (the "me"). The *transitional object* inhabits the transitional zone. The transitional object is children's first "not-me" possession, such as a teddy bear or a blanket. This object helps the child ward off anxiety and permits him or her to maintain a connection to the mother while she gradually distances herself from the child. Transitional objects help children separate from the mother.

Winnicott also developed the concept of the **good-enough mother**. The good-enough mother adjusts to her baby appropriately at differing stages of infancy, thereby permitting an optimal environment for the healthy development of a separate child, eventually capable of establishing object relations.

According to Winnicott, the good-enough mother begins by adapting almost completely to her infant's needs and as time goes on adapts less and less according to the infant's growing ability to deal with her failures.

The good-enough mother's failure to satisfy the infant's needs immediately causes the latter to compensate for the temporary deprivation by his or her own mental activity and by understanding. Hence, the infant learns to tolerate his or her ego needs and instinctual tensions for increasingly longer periods of time. The good-enough mother must not be perfect in her tasks related to meeting her infant's needs because the infant needs to feel frustration and learn to trust that help will come. When the child is between 18 and 36 months old, the mother must learn how to balance between physically serving a child's needs and being available as the child becomes more independent.

An important task for the good-enough mother is to give her child a sense of a loosening rather than the shock of suddenly being dropped by the mother. During the transitional period of loosening or letting go in small steps, a transitional object may play a highly significant role. In contrast to the good-enough mother, the perfect mother satisfies all the infant's needs on the spot, thereby preventing him or her from developing. By the age of 3, Winnicott asserted, if all goes well, the child learns that he or she and the mother are separate people who are closely related and reliably loving.

Winnicott proposed a true self and a false self. The *true self* is the part of the infant that feels creative, spontaneous, and real. A true self has a sense of integrity, of connected wholeness. The infant's true self flourishes primarily in response to the mother's optimal responsiveness to his or her spontaneous expressions. With good-enough mothering or care, the infant's true self can emerge. Without such care, the false self develops.

The **false self** is one that is based on compliance with parental wishes. When a child has to comply with external rules, such as being polite or following social rules, a false self develops. The false self is a mask, a false persona that continually seeks to anticipate demands of others for the purpose of

maintaining that relationship. On an unconscious basis, the false self protects the true self from threat, wounding, or destruction. At some point, the false self may come to be mistaken for the self to others, and even to the self. When individuals who have achieved great success say that there is a certain sense of unreality about themselves, of not being really alive, the false self is said to exist.

Winnicott believed that during our lives, we repeat unconscious early object relationships in one form or another (Winnicott, 1969). When a good-enough mother has been responsive so that she has supported the natural process of individuation, the result is an adult who has a stable image of himself or herself and who views other people realistically. Such a person sees self and others as having identities that are continuous and that are both positive and negative, instead of being just all positive or all negative.

For Winnicott, the therapist's main task is to provide a holding environment for clients so that they have an opportunity to satisfy neglected ego needs and to permit their true selves to come forth and to achieve creative and joyous understanding. It is the client who has the answers. Winnicott believed that patience is a critical therapist skill (1969) to allow clients this full opportunity.

Inner Reflections

Winnicott talked about a "holding environment," which may be defined as a psychological space that a person feels is both safe and comfortable. A good holding environment is a reliable one in which one feels loved, understood, and protected. Therapy is also a type of holding environment.

Describe the holding environment of one of your clients.

What kind of holding environment do you want to have for your clients? Winnicott defined patience as a critical therapist variable. How do you rate yourself on patience with others, with clients?

How would you describe the early holding environment in which you grew up?

SELF PSYCHOLOGY

Major Contributor: Heinz Kohut (1913–1981)

Heinz Kohut

Heinz Kohut (1971, 1977, and 1984), considered the father of self psychology, incorporated important concepts from object relations into his theory. He believed that the self is at the center of an individual's personality. Heinz Kohut (1913–1981) is the author of books such as *The Analysis of the Self* (1971), *The Restoration of the Self* (1977), and *How Does Analysis Cure?* (1984). The cornerstones of Kohut's self theory involve the concepts of self, object, and self-object. Kohut arrived at his self theory as a result of his empathic attempts to understand his clients (St. Clair, 2000). He conceptualized the self as the center of a person's personality.

The cornerstones of Kohut's self theory involve the concepts of self, object, and self-object. Kohut based his theory on his work with people who had narcissistic personality disorders. Kohut used the term *self* to denote the center of an individual's psychological universe (St. Clair, 1996). Kohut asserted that from the very beginning—from birth—children have needs for a psychological relationship in addition to having their physical needs met or satisfied. He focused on these needs in terms of the role of narcissism in child development. Kohut labeled these needs as normal narcissistic needs, and he outlined three different situations that must be met for normal childhood development to proceed. The *first need* is for an adequate **mirroring**, or confirming response from a mother or a primary caretaker. The *second need* is to "idealize" or merge with a calm, soothing, and idealized other, and the *third need* is to feel a sense of *belonging* and of being like others, which is the *alter ego need*. If primary caregivers respond to these three needs sufficiently, then the person develops a sense of "self." According to Kohut (1971), the self is part of the personality that is cohesive in space, enduring in time, and the center of a person's initiative.

Kohut (1971, 1977, and 1984) used the term *self-object needs* to describe children's needs. Kohut and Wolf (1978) have stated,

> *Selfobjects* are objects which we experience as part of our self; the expected control over them is, therefore, closer to the concept of control which a grown-up expects to have over his own body and mind than to the concept of the control which he expects to have over others. There are two kinds of selfobjects: those who respond to and confirm the child's innate sense of vigor, greatness and perfection; and those to whom the child can look up and with whom he can merge as an image of calmness, infallibility and omnipotence. The first type is referred to as the mirroring self object, the second as an idealized parent image. (p. 414)

The first need for the infant is the grandiose-exhibitionistic or mirroring need. To have this need satisfied, children need to receive the strong message that their parents love and delight in them. The second self-object need is the idealizing need or the need for an "idealized parental image." If children have enough experiences of perceiving that one or more of their caretakers are strong, calm, and competent, then this need is satisfied. The third self-object need for developing children is the need to be like others, what Kohut described as the "alter ego" or the "twinship" need. Children need to feel that they are like their caretakers, and when this need is met, they develop a feeling of belonging.

At some point, most caretakers fail to provide an adequate response to one of these three needs that children have. If these experiences are not too frequent and not too traumatic, and if they take place within an environment of parents' having satisfied most of the needs most of the time, then children learn from these experiences, and they become developmental opportunities. During these occasions, children learn to take on or to perform each of these self-object functions for themselves. Kohut termed the process of external object relations becoming an inner relational structure as **transmuting internalization**. These experiences promote the development of children's confidence about coping with the external world and with internal conflicts and pressures. Children build features of a strong, cohesive self from their optimal experiencing of gratification and frustration of their needs. From Kohut's (1971) perspective, healthy childhood development takes place when both gratification and frustration of needs are optimal for children.

Children who have been sufficiently mirrored learn from their optimal frustration experiences that they are acceptable, and they tend to be less concerned with eliciting confirmation of their acceptability from others. Likewise, children whose idealizing needs have been met learn to feel confident about their own ability to cope with not only their external world but also with their own internal conflicts and pressures. Such children develop the ability to become self-soothing. When children's need to be like others is responded to sufficiently, they develop a sense of belonging. People experience self-object needs throughout their lives; therefore, the process of building a person's self-structure is never completely finished.

In contrast, if children receive insufficient positive responses to any of these three needs, the self-object need may become traumatically frustrated. In such instances, the unsatisfied need may become denied or repressed and will remain in primitive form and not become integrated into the self. Such failure to become integrated into the self may result in the person's experiencing of problems or disorders of the self during both childhood and adulthood (Kohut, 1971, 1977). For instance, traumatic frustration may result in an adult who feels insecure and who lacks self-worth and who, therefore, takes on a sense of grandiosity or boastfulness in an effort to obtain gratification of these unsatisfied needs. Traumatic frustration of mirroring needs can lead to a lack of vitality and joyfulness. Frustration of children's alter ego needs results in people who feel different from other people.

Children are often faced with choosing between a grandiose self, which is the self that says, "I deserve to get what I want," and the self that wants to do what his or her parents say (the idealized self-object). When children do not get what they want, they may engage in temper tantrums or what Kohut called "narcissistic rage."

From Kohut's perspective (1971), the ideal type of identity is an autonomous self that is characterized by self-esteem and self-confidence. As children develop, the ideal situation is for them to have both their needs to be mirrored and their needs to idealize satisfied by their interactions with their parents. Kohut makes it clear that he does not believe that poor child rearing stems from a parent's occasional mistakes, but rather it takes place within a home environment that is chronically not meeting the child's needs. Kohut (1978) discusses two instances in which self-objects will fail to provide the child with adequate responding to his or her needs. The first instance takes place when a child excitedly relates to the mother some great success, and instead of listening to the child with pride, the mother deflects the conversation from the child to herself. The second example takes place when a little boy wants to idealize his father, expecting that he will tell him about his success in life, but instead, the father responds with embarrassment, leaves the home, and drinks with friends (Kohut, 1978). Kohut maintained that some parents are inadequately sensitive to the needs of their children and that, as a result, they respond to the child out of their own insecurely established self (Kohut, 1978). A parent's traumatic failures to provide a child with adequate mirroring and self-object idealization tend to result in the child's excessive demands to be mirrored as well as to find others to idealize.

Kohut focused on the narcissistic disorder, and he described several different types of narcissistic personalities that develop from insufficient mirroring or idealizing. For instance, mirror-hungry people crave admiration and appreciation. Children who continually seek to be at the center of attention are mirror hungry. In contrast, ideal-hungry people continually search for others whom they can admire for their prestige or power. They feel a sense of worth from looking up to other people.

Kohut's (1971, 1978) concepts of mirroring, self-object idealization, and optimal frustration are important concepts that provide a means to evaluate healthy and unhealthy development of the self. Furthermore, his understanding of narcissistically based behavior as a means to satisfy unmet developmental needs by seeking an ideal self-object provides another way of conceptualizing narcissism.

The self psychologist supplies a corrective emotional experience that heals the fragmented parts of the self. Therapy using self psychology involves the therapist to interact emotionally with a client, similar to the relationship of a parent and a child. The therapist does not treat the client as a child. Instead, the therapist is very sensitive to the emotional needs of the client. For instance, the client may have a need to have someone reflect pride in what he or she has done well. The therapist provides the unmet emotional need in an appropriate manner.

According to Kohut, traditional psychoanalysis is inappropriate for narcissistic personalities because people with self disorders cannot project emotions toward others onto the therapist. Traditional psychoanalysis relies on clients' transference onto the therapist and the therapist's interpretation of these transference relations. Clients with narcissistic personality disorders are not good candidates for transference. Instead, the therapist must "mirror" them, and they must be permitted to idealize the therapist. That is, the therapist must meet the needs of their narcissistic clients. As McLean (2007) has asserted,

> Using Heinz Kohut's self psychology model, the goal of therapy is to allow the patient to

incorporate the missing self objection functions that he needs into his internal psychic structure. Kohut calls this process transmuting internalization. In this sense, these patients' psyches are "under construction" and therapy is a building time. In order to achieve this goal, a therapist does not just try to imagine what feelings a certain situation might evoke, but rather can feel what the patient felt in that situation. This has been referred to as "temporary indwelling." This empathy has been credited with being one of the vehicles for making lasting changes in therapy. Without it, the patient, whose self is too weak to tolerate more aggressive interpretation would not benefit from therapy and in fact may suffer more damage.

Self psychology does not endorse using interpretations early in the therapy. Instead, self psychology asserts that allowing the transferences to unfold completely is the vehicle to helping the patient gain insight. (Retrieved from http://www.ncbi.nlm.nih.gov/pmc/articles/PMC2860525)

COMPARISON AND CONTRAST OF PSYCHOANALYTIC AND PSYCHODYNAMIC THEORIES

Psychodynamic therapy shares many roots with psychoanalytic therapy in that it generally embraces many of Freud's principles involving the unconscious and the conscious; however, there are important differences regarding what constitutes the focus of treatment and the length of treatment. Whereas classical psychoanalysis emphasized that people are driven by instincts and needs for sex and power, psychodynamic theories stress that people are driven by a need for attachment and relationships and that mental health problems occur when these needs are not met.

The traditional Freudian model understands psychological disturbance as conflict between a person's instinctual drives and the demands of reality, which often results in conflict among the id, the ego, and the superego. The unresolved conflicts of childhood, especially unfinished oedipal conflicts, tend to continue unconsciously and to reemerge during adulthood. When the individual's ego responds defensively to threatening thoughts and libidinal feelings, a neurotic compromise is reached that manifests itself in neurotic symptoms. The classical psychoanalyst will endeavor to uncover such conflicts and will seek the unconscious causes of the neurotic symptoms.

In contrast to Freud's emphasis on psychological problems associated with the oedipal complex, theories of object relations and self psychology focus on *earlier, preoedipal development*. For object relations therapists, psychological disturbance entails damage to the self and the structures of the psyche. Object relations therapists and self psychology therapists also view mental illness or psychological disturbance *in terms of a person's developmental arrest* rather than as structural conflicts with basic drives. Early developmental deficits hinder building a cohesive self and prevent the integration of psychic structures. These preoedipal developmental deficits can result in narcissistic and borderline personalities, which are more serious disturbances than the classical neurosis. Developmental arrests (a) have an impact on object formation, transitional objects, and self structure; and (b) result in unfinished and unintegrated structures of an individual's personality. In general, object relations and self psychology therapists view psychological disturbance as significant damage to the object relationships of the person or to the structures of the self.

Moreover, while Freud focused on repression and the neurotic personality, object relations theorists and self psychologists tend to highlight problems in the structure of personality that manifest themselves in serious difficulties in relationships. For instance, Kohut describes narcissistic personality disorders where there are deficits in the structure of the self. The narcissistic personality's disturbed relationships reflect the unfinished, archaic self-seeking fulfillment of infantile needs.

Another area of controversy between object relations theorists and Freud is related to the role of aggression. For Freud, aggression was fueled by an instinctual drive. Object relations theorists and self psychologists regard aggression not so much as an instinct but rather as a reaction to a pathological environment or situation. Early developmental deficits and early frustrations in relationships produce aggression. Kohut sees narcissistic rage as a response of the archaic self to not getting what it needs.

The time frame for classical psychoanalytic therapy is usually two to three times a week for 3 to 6 years. Psychodynamic therapy is usually shorter than classical psychoanalysis—6 months to a year. Therapy focuses on the here-and-now as well as on the client's personal history. The focus of treatment for psychodynamic approaches to therapy is usually much more specific, more immediate, and limited than dealing with a person's overall personality as is the case in classical psychoanalysis. The time for treatment for ego psychology is usually limited to one session per week for 6 months to a year. Practitioners believe that an initial short intervention will begin a process of change that does not require the constant involvement of the therapist (see Table 2.2).

OTHER THEORISTS AND THERAPY APPROACHES

Attachment Theory: John Bowlby and Mary Ainsworth

John Bowlby is considered to be the father of the **attachment theory**. Bowlby, an English

Table 2.2 Similarities and Differences Between Psychoanalysis, Ego Psychology, Object Relations, and Self Psychology

	Psychoanalysis	Ego Psychology	Object Relations	Self Psychology
Similarities				
Past Emphasis	Examines the ways in which individuals' past influences their present behavior and relationships	Examines the ways in which individuals' past influences their present behavior and relationships	Examines the ways in which individuals' past influences their present behavior and relationships	Examines the ways in which individuals' past influences their present behavior and relationships
Focus on Unconscious	Emphasis on the unconscious and conscious	Emphasis on the unconscious and conscious	Emphasis on the unconscious and conscious	Emphasis on the unconscious and conscious
Focus on Client's Inner World	Theorists and therapists are interested in the person's inner world; however, they explain that inner world differently and emphasize different features because of their theoretical orientation	Theorists and therapists are interested in the person's inner world; however, they explain that inner world differently and emphasize different features because of their theoretical orientation	Theorists and therapists are interested in the person's inner world; however, they explain that inner world differently and emphasize different features because of their theoretical orientation	Theorists and therapists are interested in the person's inner world; however, they explain that inner world differently and emphasize different features because of their theoretical orientation
Differences				
	Instinctual Drives	**Relationships**	**Relationships**	**Relationships**
	Emphasis on the concept of instinctual drives	Share a common concern about the primacy of relationships over innate instinctual drives	Share a common concern about the primacy of relationships over innate instinctual drives	Share a common concern about the primacy of relationships over innate instinctual drives
	No Environment	**Yes Environment**	**Yes Environment**	**Yes Environment**
	Does not place great weight on the influence of the environment in shaping a person's personality	Tends to give greater weight to the influence of the environment in shaping personality than did Freud	Tends to give greater weight to the influence of the environment in shaping personality than did Freud	Tends to give greater weight to the influence of the environment in shaping personality than did Freud

	Psychoanalysis	Ego Psychology	Object Relations	Self Psychology
	Emphasis on Tripartite Structure of Personality	Emphasis on the Ego and Its Adaptive Functioning	Emphasis on Early Object Relations, With Focus on How an Individual Develops a Self Through Relationships Within a Family	Emphasis on Self Involvement
	Investigates the structure of an individual's personality in terms of the id, the ego, and the superego conflicts		Shifts from Freud's views on notions of objects. In Freud's theory, drives precede the object and even create the object	Critical issue in self psychology is the nature and kind of emotional involvement in the self. Kohut speaks of narcissistic investment, whereas Freud emphasizes libidinal investment
Human Development	Views human development in terms of instincts, with the greatest developmental challenge being the oedipal crisis. Instinctual drives serve as the basic human motivation, and they determine the quality of relationships. Freud's developmental model focuses on the continual appearance of instinctual energy in bodily zones that take place during the oral, anal, and genital stages.	Individual passes through various psychosocial stages instead of psychosexual stages of development. The focus is on the development of the ego. Freud ends his conceptual of human development at the conclusion of the genital period, whereas ego psychologists such as Erikson consider developmental stages throughout old age.	Views human development as developmental stages in relationships with others. The drive that a person has is for a relationship and not for the satisfaction of biological instincts. Object relations theories are developmental theories that investigate developmental processes and relationships that took place prior to the oedipal period.	Kohut's concerns are for the formation of a cohesive self that takes place by transmuting internalizations, which is a process whereby the self gradually withdraws narcissistic investment from objects that performed functions for the self for which the self is now capable of performing. The self engages in reality testing and in regulating self-esteem.

(Continued)

Table 2.2   (Continued)

	Psychoanalysis	Ego Psychology	Object Relations	Self Psychology
			The self emerges with the increasing maturity of relationships with objects.	
Narcissism	Narcissism is a stage through which the normal person passes through as he or she grows older.	Narcissism is an early stage that diminishes as the ego grows stronger and more in touch with society's influence.	Adopts the Freudian view of narcissism with notation that a child introjects a distorted view of self because he or she did not get sufficient attention from parents.	Narcissism has its own separate development and its own form of pathology requiring special treatment. The cause of narcissistic disorders is the failure to develop positive feelings about the self because of disruptive or inadequate parenting.
Psychological Disturbance	Mental illness occurs because of conflicts between the different parts or structures of the personality, such as between sexual instincts and the demands of the ego. The unconscious and unresolved conflicts of childhood, particularly unfinished oedipal conflicts, emerge throughout one's life and into adulthood. When a person's ego responds to threatening thoughts and libidinal urges, a neurotic compromise is reached that shows itself in neurotic symptoms.	Ego psychologists deal with client's anxiety when ego defense mechanisms have become inadequate or when a client's reality testing is insufficient. Client fails to proceed adequately through psychosocial stages of development.	Object relations theorists state that psychological disturbance involves damage to the self and the structures of the psyche. They focus on problems in a person's personality that manifest themselves in serious difficulties in relationships. Relationships cause pathology.	Self psychologists state that psychological disturbance involves damage to the self and the structures of the psyche. They focus on problems in a person's personality that manifest themselves in serious difficulties in relationships. Kohut maintains that narcissistic disorders are deficits in the structure of the self.

	Psychoanalysis	Ego Psychology	Object Relations	Self Psychology
Treatment Focus	The Freudian psychoanalyst works to uncover the conflicts and analyzes the unconscious causes of the client's neurotic symptoms.	Examines the functioning of the client's ego and defense mechanisms. Considers adaptive functioning of client.	Investigates childhood relationship with mother, individuation, transitional object, good-enough mother, and true and false self.	Examines narcissism, self-object, grandiosity, and idealized parent.
Goals of Therapy	Change in client's personality structure, resolve client's conflicts, and reinterpret childhood experiences	Help client understand his or her ego defenses and increase adaptation to the external world. Strengthen ego and work toward ego mastery Assist client in passing through identified psychosocial stage.	Explore introjected objects in client's life. Explore and resolve separation and individual issues	Help client resolve issues dealing with self-absorption and idealized parents.

psychiatrist who trained initially as a Freudian psychoanalyst, wrote in 1969 the first of the three influential books on attachment and loss. He believed that attachment begins at infancy and continues throughout a person's life. Attachment can be defined as a psychological connection between two people that allows them to have relational significance to each other. It is an affectionate bond between two people that endures through time. Mothers typically have some kind of bond for their child after having carried him or her for 9 months. Even before birth, the umbilical cord provides the foundation for the bond between a mother and her child. Research shows that babies in the womb have emotional and intuitive capabilities to sense their mother's love.

What are bonding acts between a mother and a child? Bonding experiences include holding, rocking, feeding, singing, gazing, kissing, and other nurturing behaviors that occur as a part of caring for infants and children. Factors critical to bonding include the time the caregiver and child spend together, face-to-face interactions, eye contact, physical proximity, and touch.

According to Bowlby (1969, 1988), the mother–infant attachment relationship provides the basis for the emergence of a biological control system that functions in the infant's state of arousal. This early learning then becomes internalized. Bowlby (1969) maintained that the capacity of an infant to cope with stress is connected to early attachment behaviors that are recorded in the child's brain and neuropsychological structure. He termed the manner in which a child begins to understand his or her surroundings as the child's "inner working models." The inner working model that a child develops influences his perceptions about himself and others well into early childhood and well into adulthood. Attachments are "neither subordinate to nor derivative from food and sex. . . . Instead the capacity to make intimate emotional bonds . . . is regarded as a principal feature of effective personality functioning" (Bowlby, 1988, p. 121).

Bowlby (1969, pp. 319–323) outlined the development of attachment in four phases:

- *Phase 1:* orientation and signals without discrimination (from birth to 3 months): The infant will respond to any person in his or her vicinity by orienting toward them and by exhibiting behaviors such as eye tracking, grasping and reaching, smiling and babbling.

- *Phase 2:* orientation and signals directed toward one (or more) discriminated figure(s) (approximately 3 to 6 months): The infant begins to focus more attention on familiar rather than unfamiliar people.

- *Phase 3:* maintenance of proximity to a discriminated figure by means of locomotion as well as signals (from 6 months to 3 years): The infant actively seeks to maintain contact with the mother or the primary caregiver. The infant begins to follow a departing mother, greet her on her return, and use her as a base from which to explore. The friendly and rather undiscriminating responses to everyone else declines such that strangers become treated with increasing caution and are likely to evoke alarm and withdrawal.

- *Phase 4:* formation of a goal-corrected partnership (3 years and older): By observing the behavior of the mother figure and what influences it, the child begins to gain insight into her feelings and motives. This understanding brings about a much more complex relationship between the mother and the child, which Bowlby calls "partnership." During this phase, the child increasingly tolerates separation from the mother figure and forms other close bonds.

Attachment and the Role of the Right Hemisphere of the Brain

There is a connection between the right hemisphere of the brain and attachment. During early infant development, the right hemisphere of the brain connects into both the limbic system and the autonomic nervous system. The right hemisphere is critical for the control of vital functions that support survival and that help the infant to cope with stresses and challenges (Schore, 2000). It is also specialized for inhibitory control and feelings of violence that can develop later on in life. The right hemisphere is also dominant for unconscious processes. It weighs on a moment-to-moment basis the threat of external stimuli.

In growth-facilitating environments, children's positive contact with the mother causes a burst of mature connections within the limbic system. Conversely, in growth-inhibiting environments, early inadequate caregiving experiences have major effects on the neurochemicals released by children. When children have severely compromised attachment relationships with their primary caregivers, their brain development may become inefficient in regulating their affective states related to anger and self-control (Schore, 2000).

Why Is Attachment So Important?

Children's attachment to a primary caregiver is absolutely critical for their development of a healthy personality. The parent–child bond is instrumental for later bonding with society and the social institutions within a society. Attachment also helps one to be able to handle fear and worry, and to cope with stress and frustration. Poor attachment militates against children's commitment to long-term goals.

When a parent responds to a child's cry for food or for a dry diaper with "shut up" or worse yet, by slapping the child, she is quieted by the caregiver's slap. Hence, at the height of the child's emotional state, she has learned that her needs are fulfilled by abuse (Bowlby, 1988). Abuse has replaced loving care, and if the abuse is severe, the child may use such abuse as a source of gratification. For instance, some children may respond to a caregiver's slap by banging their heads on the floor, by pulling out their hair, or by some other method of self-abusive behavior. They feel secure in their anger and in their own self-abusive behavior.

Attachment is important because it is necessary for an individual to develop a conscience (Figure 2.2). A child's lack of conscience may be caused by his lack of trust in others. Positive attachment also helps children to cope with stress, to handle perceived threats to the self, to form intimate adult relationships, and to later parent their own children. Children's positive attachment to a primary caregiver has the following benefits (Bowlby, 1988):

1. Infants and children learn basic trust and reciprocity, which serves as a guide for all future relationships.

2. Securely attached infants explore the environment with feelings of safety and security (secure base), which leads to their positive mental and cognitive development.

3. They develop the ability to self-regulate, which results in their effective management of impulses and anger.

4. They form a personal identity that includes a sense of competency, dependence, and autonomy.

5. They establish a prosocial moral framework that includes empathy and compassion for other.

6. They develop a core belief system that contains appropriate cognitive appraisals of themselves, their caregivers, and the others who come into contact with them.

7. They develop a defense against stress and trauma and are resilient.

Ainsworth's Patterns of Attachments

Mary Ainsworth (1969, 1979) outlined different patterns of attachment using the research method called "Strange Situation," which was a laboratory experiment that recorded the interaction between mothers and their children prior to, during, and after a brief separation. The Strange Situation is a widely used laboratory procedure for

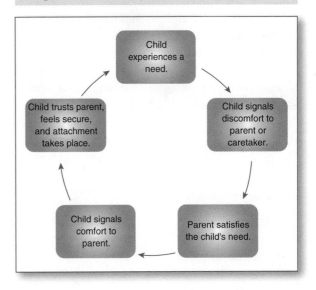

Figure 2.2 The Cycle of Attachment

assessing the quality of attachment for children between 1 and 2 years of age. It takes the baby through eight short episodes in which brief separations from and reunions with the parent take place. Ainsworth and her colleagues reasoned that securely attached infants and toddlers would use the parent as a secure base from which to explore an unfamiliar playroom, and that when a parent leaves, an unfamiliar adult would be less comforting than the parent. Ainsworth identified the following three categories:

- *Secure attachment:* The child protested when the mother left the room, and looked for her when she was gone. She greeted the mother with delight when the mother returned, and she explored more when the mother was present.
- *Anxious attachment:* The child protested when the mother left and showed little relief when reunited with the mother. The child was not inclined to explore her environment, even when the mother was present.
- *Avoidant attachment:* The child was relatively indifferent to the mother, rarely cried when she left, and showed little positive response on her return to the room. The child's curiosity was unaffected by the mother's presence.

Attachment theory forms the foundation for much of the current neuroscience investigations regarding the brain and psychological functioning. It has been theorized that a child's early attachment relationships affect the therapeutic relationship either positively or negatively. Therapy has been conceptualized as creating therapeutic attachments for clients (Hanson, 2013).

Relational Analysis

The most recent offshoot of Freudian psychoanalysis has been relational psychoanalysis, which stresses the importance of the relationships in a person's life, including the person's relationship with his or her therapist. It is represented by works such as Mitchell's (1988) *Relational Concepts in Psychoanalysis* and Mitchell and Lewis's (1999) *Relational Psychoanalysis: The Emergence of a Tradition*. **Relational analysis** stresses the importance of real and imagined relationships with others in mental disorder and in psychotherapy. It began in the 1980s with object relations theory and interpersonal relations theory. Relational analysts maintain that personality develops from early relationships with parents and other significant figures in our environment. Relational analysts maintain that the major motivation of the psyche is to be in relationships with others. Individuals attempt to re-create the early relationships they learned in their families.

Relational psychoanalysts argue that desires and urges cannot be separated from the relational contexts in which they arise. When treating clients, they stress the importance of creating a lively, genuine relationship with them. Relational analysts maintain that psychotherapy works best when the therapist concentrates on establishing a healing relationship with clients.

BRIEF PSYCHODYNAMIC THERAPY _____

Perhaps the area that has the greatest potential for growth includes practitioners who work with **brief psychodynamic therapy (BPT)**. Messer and Warren (2001) use psychodynamic principles to treat selective disorders within a preestablished time limit of 10 to 25 sessions. In contrast to psychoanalytic therapy, most forms of BPT require the therapist to use an active and directive role in formulating a treatment plan. Messer and Warren have asserted that the objective of BPT is "to understand and treat people's problems in the context of their current situation and earlier life experience" (p. 83). Prochaska and Norcross (2003) maintain that BPT shares the following common characteristics:

- BPT approaches establish a time limitation.
- BPT therapy identifies a specific interpersonal problem during the initial session.
- Therapists take a less neutral therapeutic stance than traditional analysts.
- BPT therapists use interpretation relatively early in the therapy relationship.

Major Contributor: Carl Gustav Jung (1875–1961)

Photo courtesy of Library of Congress

Carl Gustav Jung

I have treated many hundreds of patients. Among those in the second half of life— that is to say, over 35—there has not been one whose problem in the last resort was not that of finding a religious outlook on life.

The greatest and most important problems of life are all fundamentally insoluble. They can never be solved but only outgrown.

—Carl Gustav Jung

Brief Biography

Carl Gustav Jung was a Swiss psychiatrist who was one of the first to say that the human psyche is by nature religious, and he is perhaps best known for his emphasis on the spiritual and the religious. He was a pioneer in dream analysis and spent a great deal of his life exploring Eastern and Western philosophies (Casement, 2001). His therapeutic approach highlights the importance of helping clients become aware of their unconscious aspects via dreams and fantasy material. Jung studied symbols that all humans have in common, for which he used the term *archetypes*. Jung stressed the importance of the individual's social role—the persona and the *anima–animus* (the unconscious other-sex side of a man's or woman's personality).

Jung was born on July 26, 1875, at Kesswil by Lake Constance in Switzerland (Casement, 2001). Family legend held that Jung's grandfather was the natural son of Johann Wolfgang von Goethe, the great writer of *Faust*. Carl's father, Paul Achilles Jung, was a parson of the Basel Reformed Church, and his mother, Emilie Preiswerk, was the daughter of Paul Jung's Hebrew teacher (Jung, 1961). Prior to Carl's birth, two elder brothers died during infancy. Jung was an only child for 9 years; then Gertrude, a younger sister, was born (Casement, 2001). Eventually, Jung's mother Emilie, an eccentric and depressed woman, retreated to her own separate bedroom, saying that spirits visited her at night. One night, Jung claimed that he saw a faintly luminous and indefinite figure coming from his mother's room, with a head detached from the neck and floating in the air in front of the body (Jung, 1961, p. 18).

Jung has described his mother as "enigmatic" because she had unpredictable moods (Jung, 1961). When Jung was a young child, his mother spent a few months in a mental hospital. As a consequence, he felt abandoned by her, and the relationship between Jung and his mother was challenged throughout his life. In his autobiography, *Memories, Dreams, and Reflections* (Jung, 1961, p. 8), as cited by Dunne (2002), Jung wrote,

> My illness in 1878 must have been connected to a temporary separation of my parents. My mother spent several months in a hospital in Basel and presumably her illness had something to do with the difficulty in the marriage. An aunt of mine, who was a spinster and some twenty years older than my mother, took care of me. From then on, I always felt deeply distrustful when the word "love" was spoken. The feeling I associated with "woman" was for a long time that of innate unreliability. "Father," on the other hand meant reliability and powerlessness. That is the handicap I started off with. Later these early impressions were revised. (p. 5)

Jung loved nature, and he played alone deliberately, almost as if he were avoiding making friends so that he would not be disappointed or judged by others. Dunne (2002) cites a quotation of Jung regarding his playing alone:

> I played alone, and in my own way. Unfortunately I cannot remember what I played. I can recall only that I did not want to be disturbed. I was deeply absorbed in my own games and could not endure being watched or judged while I played them.

Jung's early student years were difficult. At age 12, he was pushed to the ground by another boy and hit his head on a curbstone; he was unconscious for a brief time (Casement, 2001). During this experience, Jung claimed that he heard an inner voice telling him that he would no longer have to go to school. For some time, Jung had fainting spells whenever he had to go to school. His reluctance to attend school may have indicated the presence of a larger issue, such as an anxiety disorder, depression, sleep disorder, separation anxiety, or panic disorder. Jung conquered his school refusal problem when he overheard his father questioning what would become of him if he could not earn his own living (Casement, 2001). Following graduation from the Humanistisches Gymnasium (sometime between 1891 and 1893), Jung decided to study medicine. Because of his family's dire finances, he applied to the university for a stipend.

Jung studied medicine at the University of Basel and earned his medical degree as a psychiatrist in 1900. In 1902, he received a Ph.D. from the University of Zurich. In addition, he worked with severely disturbed mental patients at Burghölzli, a psychiatric hospital in Zurich. In 1903, Jung married Emma Rauschenback, who worked with him as an analyst. From 1932 to 1940, he was professor of psychology at the University of Zurich, and from 1944 to 1945, he worked in medical psychology at his alma mater, the University of Basel.

Despite his professional success, Jung's personal life was turbulent. He was actively involved in a number of affairs. It has been said that his wife had to tolerate one such woman, Toni Wolf, as a regular guest at Sunday dinner (Donne, 2002).

Carl Jung died on June 6, 1961, at the age of 85 in Kussnacht, Switzerland. Prior to his death, he had reported a number of dreams portending a transition to a tower bathed in light on the "other side of the lake" (Dunne, 2002). The cause of his death was unspecified.

Jung and Freud

Jung was once considered Freud's heir apparent, although the two later parted ways. After publishing *Studies in Word Association* (1904–1907), Jung (then 30 years of age) sent a copy of the book to Sigmund Freud (age 50); a close friendship developed between the two men and lasted for about 6 years. Jung and Freud's relationship became strained, however, when Jung began to reduce the importance of sexuality in psychoanalysis and to be interested in parapsychology and the occult (Charat, 2000). During 1911, Jung wrote *Symbols of Transformation* (1911/1956), in which he described the Oedipus complex not as sexual attraction but rather as an expression of spiritual or psychological needs and bonds. In response, in 1913, Freud wrote Jung a letter stating, "I propose that we abandon our personal relations entirely" (McGuire, 1974, p. 539). Jung resigned as president of the International Psychoanalytic Association and from his editorship of the *Psychoanalytic Yearbook*.

As a result of Freud's and Jung's estrangement, Jung endured 6 years of mental suffering (1913–1919). Even though Jung would give credit to Freud for many of his ideas, the two never saw each other again. Jung (1961) has described the devastation that the breakup with Freud had on his life. "When I parted from Freud, I knew that I was plunging into the unknown. Beyond Freud, after all, I knew nothing; but I had taken the step into darkness" (p. 199). During this time, Jung saw visions and heard voices. At times, he wondered if he suffered from a psychosis or schizophrenia. Jung wrote about his visions in a red leather-bound book that has been called the "Red Book." After scholars pleaded with the Jung family to release the Red Book, his grandson published it in 2007 (Jung, 2007).

Jung's Legacy

Jung's collected works are contained in 19 volumes. His most popular works are *Psychology of*

Inner Reflections

As you read about Jung's life, consider how his family background and early life experiences influenced the development of Jungian psychotherapy.

Suppose that you become a famous psychotherapy theorist. What factors in your family background and life experiences might contribute to your theory?

What name or label would you give to your theory of psychotherapy?

On a scale of 1 to 10, how would you rate Jung's professional reputation?

the Unconscious (1971, first published in 1912) and *Psychological Types* (1921). Although his theories have received limited acceptance in mainstream psychology, Jung was awarded honorary degrees from Harvard and Oxford. He is also credited with developing the following:

- The concept of introversion and extraversion as two personality types
- The concept of the complex
- The concept of the archetypes and the collective unconscious
- The influence of spirituality in psychotherapy

The Myers-Briggs Type Indicator (Myers, McCaulley, Quenk, & Hammer, 1998) is based on concepts from Jung.

KEY CONCEPTS OF CARL JUNG___

Levels of Consciousness and the Collective Unconscious

Jung proposed three levels of consciousness: (1) the conscious, (2) the personal unconscious, and (3) the collective unconscious. Consciousness is always in a process of being developed (Stevens, 1994). The ego is at the center of consciousness. Under the conscious realm resides the unconscious. From Jung's perspective, the unconscious level of awareness dominates the awareness of people in primitive cultures. The personal unconscious contains experiences, thoughts, feelings, and perceptions that the ego refuses to admit. Although materials stored in personal unconscious are usually trivial, the unconscious also contains personal conflicts, unresolved moral concerns, and emotionally charged repressed thoughts (Stevens, 1994).

Deeper within the human psyche, beneath the layers of the personal unconscious, resides our prehuman evolutionary experience. Jung labeled this layer of experience as the **collective unconscious**. Jung used the term *collective* to suggest that these materials are found within all people (Hopcke, 1999). The collective unconscious is our psychic inheritance. It constitutes the reservoir of our experiences as human beings. It is a type of knowledge with which we are all born but that lies in our unconscious. The collective unconscious contains images and concepts that are independent of a person's consciousness. According to Jung, the collective unconscious refers to "an inherited tendency of the human mind to form representations of mythological motifs—representations that vary a great deal without losing their basic pattern" (Jung, 1970, p. 228). Although Jung did not believe that specific memories or conscious images were inherited, he did believe that each of us has a predisposition for certain thoughts. Jung considered the experiences of love at first sight, of déjà vu (the feeling that you have been there before), and the immediate recognition of some symbols as part of the collective unconscious (Hopcke, 1999).

The near-death experience has been discussed as part of our collective unconscious. People from diverse cultural backgrounds have described the near-death experience as one of leaving their bodies, seeing other bodies, being pulled toward a white light, or of seeing relatives who preceded them in death. Jung would say that we are all built to experience death in this way (Hopcke, 1999).

Archetypes

Archetypes may be conceptualized as ways of perceiving and structuring experiences (Jung, 1961). They have form but no content. Archetypes are the inherited part of the psyche that produces patterned tendencies of thought (Casement, 2001). The term **archetype** may be broken into *arche*, which means "original" or "master copy," and *typos*, which means "stamp." All of us inherit the same archetypes, the same invisible patterns or emotions that are built into the structure of the human psyche. Different cultures give their own special interpretations or stamps on various archetypes. Examples of archetypes include the hero, the divine child, the great mother, death, and rebirth.

The most important archetypes are the shadow, anima–animus, wise old man/wise woman, and the self. Archetypes manifest themselves in myths, dreams, tribal lore, fairy tales, visions, religions, and historical developments. According to Casement (2001), bipolarity is inherent in the archetypes. To illustrate this point, there is the archetype of the hero/heroine. When archetypes are activated, they show that a person's problem is a basic human problem rather than an isolated difficulty.

An archetype can also be conceptualized as an organizing principle and a system of readiness (Douglas, 2011). It is analogous to the "circuitry pattern in the brain that orders and structures reality; as a system of readiness, it parallels animals' instincts; as a dynamic nucleus of energy, it propels a person's actions and reactions in a patterned way" (p. 97). Moreover, archetypes can be likened to "pathways along whose course energy flows from the collective unconscious into consciousness and action" (p. 97). According to Jung, there are as many archetypal images in the collective unconscious as there are typical situations in life—for instance, the inner child is often viewed as the childlike part of an individual's personality, the maiden, the heroic quest, the divine child (Douglas, 2011).

The mother archetype is our built-in ability to recognize a relationship of mothering. We tend to personify an archetype, even when there is no real person available. We turn our mother archetype into a storybook character. Jung suggested that the mother archetype is represented by the primordial mother or "earth mother" of mythology, by Eve and Mary, and by institutions such as the church or a nation. Jung believed that when someone's own mother failed to satisfy the demands of his or her archetype, that person would spend his or her life seeking comfort in a church or in identification with the motherland. Other archetypes include the hero represented in movies by people such as Luke Skywalker in the *Star Wars* films. Also, in *Star Wars*, the wise old man is represented by Obi Wan Kenobi, and later, Yoda. Not only do they teach Luke Skywalker about the Force, but as Luke matures, they die and form a part of him.

The Shadow Archetype

Sex and the life instincts are represented in Jung's system as part of an archetype labeled the **shadow**. This archetype comes from our prehuman, animal past. The dark side of the ego is stored in the shadow. The shadow is the negative or inferior (undeveloped) side of one's personality (Hopcke, 1999). It includes all of the negative or reprehensible characteristics that each of us has but wants to deny. If we are unaware of our shadow, it becomes blacker and denser. If we disassociate the shadow parts of ourselves from conscious life, it will become a compensatory demonic dynamism. We often project the shadow parts of ourselves outward onto other individuals or groups who then are believed to embody the immature, evil, or repressed parts of our own psyche. Some symbols of the shadow include the snake (as in the Garden of Eden) or dragons and monsters that guard the mouth of a cave (the collective unconscious). Dreams about wrestling with the devil may symbolize your wrestling with yourself (Stevens, 1994).

Complexes

Whereas the collective unconscious manifests itself to an individual by way of archetypal images, the personal unconscious reveals itself through complexes. Archetypal images gravitate from the collective unconscious into the personal unconscious by means of a **complex**, which is a cluster of emotionally charged associations at the unconscious level that are gathered around an archetypal center. Complexes form the contents of the personal unconscious, while archetypes are located in and form the collective unconscious. A complex is a sensitive, energy-charged cluster of emotions, such as an attitude toward one's mother. Complexes are usually repressed because they are so emotionally charged. They can cause psychological disturbances and symptoms of neuroses. During analysis, therapists can help make clients' complexes become conscious and greatly reduced in their negative pull.

Persona

The term **persona** represents the aspect of a person that is in relation to the outer world. It is derived from the Greek word for "mask" and connotes that Greek actors wore masks in performing comic and tragic parts in plays (O'Connor, 1985). People hide the less acceptable parts of their personalities behind the persona. Your persona represents your public image. It is the mask that you put on before you show yourself to the outside world. When viewed from the most positive perspective, our persona is the "good impression" that we want to present to others. A negative connotation of persona can be seen as our desire to give a "false impression" so that we can manipulate people's views of us. Sometimes, we can mistake our own persona as our true selves. That is, we begin to believe that we are who we pretend to be (O'Connor, 1985).

The Self

The self is the most important archetype. It represents the ultimate unity of an individual's personality and is symbolized by the circle, the cross, and the mandala, which is a drawing that draws a person's focus back to the center. A child begins in a state of unitary wholeness. Gradually, the process of living and socialization causes the child to fragment into subsystems (Douglas, 2011). Our conscious understanding of who we are derives from two sources: first, from our contact and interactions with others—what others tell us about ourselves—and second, from our own self-observations. If others agree with our view of ourselves, we see ourselves as normal. If there is disagreement, we tend to see ourselves as abnormal.

The goal of life is to realize the development of the self. The self is an archetype that is supposed to transcend all opposites within one's personality in order to allow every aspect of that personality to be expressed equally. As we age, we focus more on the self. The self-realized person is mature and less selfish than he or she was during youth. The most important part of the self is the ego, which begins when the child recognizes himself or herself as distinct from others. The child's ego becomes the "I" (Douglas, 2011).

Spiritual Self

Jung's early exposure to spiritual issues provided him with a different outlook on life than Freud's. Whereas Freud stressed the physical or animal nature as the primal driving force of people, Jung emphasized the spiritual self and the transcendent soul as the more important force in a person's life. According to Jung, the spiritual self and our drives arising from it create our needs to grow, to experiment, and to achieve higher levels of purpose (Hopcke, 1999).

Anima and Animus

Our sex role constitutes part of our persona. We learn the role of male or female that we are supposed to assume in a given society. Jung felt that we are bisexual in nature. Our lives as fetuses begin with undifferentiated sex organs that become male or female under the influence of hormones. The expectations differ for men and women. The **anima** constitutes the female aspect present in the collective unconscious of men, while the **animus** represents the male aspect present in the collective unconscious of women (Stevens, 1994). The anima or animus is the archetype that is responsible for much of our love lives. Jung believed that both men and women contained anima and animus.

Jung's Theory of Personality

Jung's theory of personality is based on the concept of a dynamic unity of all parts of an individual (Casement, 2001). Throughout our lives, we strive to achieve wholeness. The self is the center of our personality. It is conceptualized as an individual's midpoint that serves as a center between consciousness and unconsciousness. The self represents the harmony and balance between the opposing qualities that make up our psyche. Jungian theory proposed that our self unifies our personality (Stevens, 1994). According to Jung, the major task of the first part of life involves strengthening the ego and assuming one's place in the world with others. The second half of life is to reclaim the undeveloped parts of oneself (Douglas, 2011). Jung labeled this second process as **individuation**, which implies becoming one's own self—something of "I did it my own way," or "I'm my own woman or man." Fordham (1996) has argued that individuation does not have to wait as late as middle age. The process of individuation involves an individual's attempt at completion and wholeness—of reclaiming previously discarded parts of oneself. The goal of individuation is to rid the self of the false trappings of the personal.

Jung proposed that individuation takes place in two stages: youth and middle age. Youth takes place from birth through the late 20s and early 30s. Middle age occurs sometime between 35 and 40 years of age. Jung maintained that the major task of the first part of life is to strengthen our egos, take our places in the world with others, and to fulfill our obligations to society (Douglas, 2011). The task of the second half of life is to reunite and to reconnect undeveloped or previously discarded parts of ourselves. Oftentimes, individuals come to therapy because of dealing with the task of individuation. During this time period, people begin to reexamine their values and to appreciate the opposites of their earlier ideals. While the first stage is marked by an extroverted attitude (directed outward toward material things, marriage, and a career), the second stage of individuation is characterized by introversion, with a focus on the person's inner world (Hopcke, 1999).

Personality Types

In *Psychological Types* (1921/1971), Jung outlined the different ways people habitually respond to the world. He developed a personality topology that is currently being used in the Myers-Briggs Type Indicator. According to Jung, people are either introverts or extroverts. **Introverts** are those who prefer their own internal world of thoughts, feelings, dreams, and so on to the company of others. In contrast, **extroverts** are those who prefer the external world of things, people, and activities. For the introvert, energy flows inward, whereas for the extrovert, energy flows outward. Jung theorized

that nations also are either introverted or extroverted. He saw Switzerland as introverted, while he viewed the United States as extroverted.

In addition, Jung (1921/1971) classified people's tendency to perceive reality through one of four mental functions: thinking, feeling, sensation, and intuition. Jung outlined a pair of types that he labeled as "sensing" and "intuiting." These are two different modes of encountering the world. *Sensing* refers to getting information from our senses. A sensing person has good skills involving looking, listening, and taking in the world. Sensing people are usually those who are detailed, concrete, and present. In contrast, an *intuiting* person uses sensing that comes from the complex integration of large amounts of information, instead of just seeing or hearing. Intuiting people see multiple possibilities in situations; they go with their hunches; they may be considered impractical; and they sometimes become impatient with details.

The next pair involves thinking and feeling. *Thinking* refers to evaluating information or ideas rationally or logically. Jung labeled this a rational function because it involves decision making. People who are categorized as thinking are viewed as logical; they see cause-and-effect relations; and they may be described as cool, distant, frank, and questioning. Although *feeling* also involves evaluating information, it is completed by weighing one's overall emotional response to a situation (Stevens, 1994). Individuals who use the feeling function tend to be creative, warm, and intimate. Under ideal situations, we should develop equally the two attitudes of extroversion and introversion as well as the four functions of sensing and intuiting, thinking and feeling.

Jungian Psychotherapy

Jungian or analytic psychotherapy has four basic tenets: (1) the human psyche is a self-regulating system, (2) the unconscious has a creative and compensatory component, (3) the therapist–client relationship is important in facilitating individuation and healing, and (4) personality growth occurs during many stages over one's life span (Douglas, 2011).

Jung theorized that people develop neuroses when they fail to accomplish some important developmental task. When people experience a neurosis, their equilibrium is disturbed. Jungian analysis focuses on bringing unconscious material into consciousness. Therapists make active use of clients' dreams. They engage in word–association tests to assess clients' complexes.

RESEARCH AND EVALUATION

Multicultural Positives

Psychoanalytic and psychodynamic approaches to psychotherapy can be used effectively with clients from ethnic minority backgrounds because all people have a background of childhood experiences that may have a bearing on the current issues that bring them to therapy. Such childhood experiences must be examined in terms of a client's cultural background. Psychodynamic theories are useful because they point out that a client's presentation of an issue may not be the critical issue underlying the problem. As theorists from Freud to Bowlby have indicated, the unconscious is extremely powerful. All people undergo an attachment process that becomes a critical force in their later development. Psychodynamic theorists' emphasis on the unconscious has been adopted and integrated by most theories of psychotherapy.

Leong, Wagner, and Tata (1995) suggest that the modern psychodynamic approach can deal with multicultural issues effectively. These researchers use multicultural factors as part of the free association and insight part of therapy. According to Leong et al., the therapist's prejudice will show in analysis of countertransference. Similarly, Taub-Bynum (1999) proposes a construct called the "family unconscious." Each member of a family is a part of the family unconscious.

The work of the ego psychologists seems to have solid relevance for individuals from ethnic minority backgrounds. The stages of development outlined by Erikson take into consideration psychosocial factors that can either impede or facilitate a client's forward movement.

Multicultural Blind Spots

In general, researchers from a multicultural perspective have heeded caution in using psychoanalytic, and to some extent, psychodynamic approaches with ethnic minority clients. In an article on ethnic minority clients who are borderline, Comas-Diaz and Minrath (1985) point out that ethnic and cultural identity problems may be complicated when a person occupies a minority status within a society. Ethnic minority clients, especially those from mixed races, may suffer inner instability (borderline) and a sense of instability within the broader culture. Moreover, therapists may experience a type of countertransference with ethnic minority clients who are racially or ethnically identified. The working alliance between the therapist and the client may be difficult to establish because of cultural and ethnic mistrust on both sides.

Psychodynamic approaches have been criticized as irrelevant for anyone not coming from a verbal middle-class background. Feminist theorists (Brown, 1994; Hill & Ballou, 2005) contend that by continuing to emphasize individualistic approaches to therapy (as opposed to viewing women in society), psychodynamic theories perpetuate forms of patriarchy and male domination that are harmful to women's mental health. Both feminists and multiculturalists note that a major limitation of psychodynamic theories is that they focus on the individual rather than the family or elements of one's environment.

Multiculturalists hold that both psychoanalytical and psychodynamic therapies are insufficient because they do not deal adequately with present concerns or with issues related to oppression and domination. There is a need for therapists to take into account external sources of a client's problems. More consideration needs to be made for the social, cultural, and political issues that contaminate a client's problems.

Cost or affordability is another issue with classical psychoanalysis. For the most part, classic psychoanalysis is very costly and is usually only affordable to those with a substantial income. Moreover, Freud's emphasis on psychosexual stages has been criticized as applying only to some cultures—mainly those that are Eurocentric in outlook.

Contributions and Limitations of Psychoanalytic and Psychodynamic Approaches

The major contribution of the psychoanalytic school and its modern derivatives is its emphasis on the unconscious. Things are not what they appear to be on the surface. Hence, **psychodynamic theory** provides a useful framework for conceptualizing clients and their issues. The psychodynamic approach can be very effective if it is coordinated with other counseling approaches that emphasize change. Most dynamic approaches stress the importance of insight rather than behavior change. Other writers have challenged the role of insight in psychodynamic approaches. Sue and Sue (1999) have indicated that insight is not valued highly in Asian American culture. The esteemed value is to think about the family rather than oneself.

The concept of transference and counter-transference constitutes two major contributions that psychoanalytically oriented approaches have provided to the field. It is highly probable that most clients transfer their past history of interpersonal relationships onto the therapist. Therapist awareness of clients' transferential patterns is critical to the counseling process. Likewise, it is important that therapists become aware of their own countertransference relations with clients.

A frequent criticism of psychodynamic approaches is the amount of time they take. Because of their emphasis on long-term therapy, psychoanalytic and psychodynamic therapies have been criticized as therapy for the wealthy. Feminists have criticized this school on the grounds that it is sexist because of such concepts as penis envy. Currently, most insurance companies will reimburse people for only 10 to 16 sessions. Sometimes, psychodynamic therapy can take several years. Hence, only those who earn a good salary will be able to afford psychodynamic-oriented therapy. Another objection is that psychodynamic approaches require extensive study and supervised practice from carefully trained individuals. The number of colleges and universities that offer a psychoanalytic or psychodynamic approach has declined. Therefore, there is a smaller number of people available to supervise practitioners who subscribe to a psychodynamic orientation.

Psychodynamic theories continue to grow well beyond the original theory of Sigmund Freud. Although contemporary psychodynamic therapy has branched out from the original Freudian emphasis on drives, most therapists who subscribe to a psychodynamic model of therapy still adhere to such basic Freudian concepts as unconscious motivation, transference, countertransference, and resistance. On the other hand, analysts have become more directive in their assessments and therapeutic interventions, and they have continued to adapt to change. For instance, one adaptation involves setting a limit on the number of sessions as contrasted with engaging in open-ended therapy, making interpersonal problems more central in therapy, becoming more active and less of a blank slate for transference, and establishing a strong working alliance.

> **Inner Reflections**
>
> Imagine that you have developed a famous integrative theory of psychotherapy.
>
> Whom would you want for professional associates?
>
> What rules would you develop in order for your associates to continue to be affiliated with your integrative theory?

Evidence-Based Research

Shedler (2010) investigated the efficacy of psychodynamic psychotherapy, in part to quiet the claim that psychodynamic approaches lack empirical evidence. After reviewing a number of meta-analytic studies investigating the effectiveness of psychodynamic therapy, Shedler concluded that "the effect sizes for psychodynamic therapy are as large as those reported for other therapies that have been actively promoted as 'empirically supported' and 'evidence based'" (p. 98). Moreover, clients who are given psychodynamic therapy maintain their therapeutic gains and seem to continue to improve after treatment is terminated. Pointing out that most therapies tend to borrow from each other such that no approach is actually free from being influenced by another, Shedler (2010) concluded his review of psychodynamic studies by asserting,

> Finally, nonpsychodynamic therapies may be effective in part because the more skilled practitioners utilize techniques that have long been central to psychodynamic theory and practice. The perception that psychodynamic approaches lack empirical support does not accord with available scientific evidence and may reflect selective dissemination of research findings. (p. 98)

Shedler's conclusions are supported by a number of other meta-analyses of studies investigating the efficacy of psychodynamic therapy. For instance, the Cochrane Library (more widely known in medicine for promoting evidence-based research) published a study by Abbass, Hancock, Henderson, and Kisely (2006) who had examined 23 randomized controlled trials involving 1,431 clients. The studies compared clients with a range of disorders (nonbipolar depressive disorders, anxiety disorders, somatoform, and personality disorders) who received short-term (fewer than 40 hours) psychodynamic therapy with controls, and they yielded an overall effect size of 0.97 for general symptom improvement. The effect size increased to 1.51 when the clients were assessed in a 9-month posttreatment session.

Leichsenring, Rabung, and Leibing (2004) conducted a meta-analysis of 17 high-quality randomized controlled trials of short-term (average 21 sessions) psychodynamic therapy compared with controls. The researchers reported a pretreatment to posttreatment effect size of 1.39, which increased to 1.57 at a long-term 13 months posttreatment follow-up session.

Abbass, Kisley, and Kroenke (2009) conducted a meta-analysis that examined the efficacy of short-term psychodynamic therapy for somatic disorders. The meta-analysis contained 23 studies that involved 1,870 clients who suffered from dermatological, neurological, cardiovascular, respiratory, gastrointestinal, and other problems. The study reported effect sizes of 0.69 for improvement in clients' general psychiatric symptoms and 0.59 for improvement in somatic symptoms.

The efficacy of psychodynamic therapy was also supported in randomized controlled trials for depression, anxiety, panic, somatoform disorders, eating disorders, substance disorders, and personality disorders (Leichsenring, 2005; Milrod et al., 2007). A study of clients with borderline personality disorder (Clarkin, Levey, Lensenweger, & Kernberg, 2007) found treatment benefits for psychodynamic therapy that equaled or exceeded those of another evidence-based treatment—dialectical behavior therapy (Linehan, 1993). Clearly, psychodynamic therapy does help clients improve the psychological symptoms that brought them to therapy.

CASE ANALYSIS

Psychoanalytic and Psychodynamic Therapy Applied to Justin

Every case conceptualization contains the following parts: (a) assessment, or the development of critical information related to the client; (b) theory, or the placement of the client's problem within a theoretical context; (c) treatment, or development of a change strategy; and (d) evaluation of the success or limitations of the treatment. Justin's case is examined using this four-part strategy.

(Continued)

(Continued)

The primary approach used with Justin in this case analysis is psychodynamic therapy. To help you review Justin's issues, refer to his case study in Chapter 1. Justin is working with a 45-year-old White male therapist. One of Justin's goals is that he wants to get in control of his behavior in school and at home. Second and third goals are that he wants to get along with his mother and doesn't want to get in any more fights at school. Otherwise, he will risk expulsion from school and may be forced to go to a residential treatment facility located about 150 miles from his home for 2 years.

The psychodynamic approach focuses on the unconscious forces that are operating in the present on Justin's behavior and emotions. Emphasis is placed on Justin's anger, especially as displayed against his mother and classmates. The therapist has some hunches that Justin's anger may be related to the loss of his father. He theorizes that quite possibly Justin's anger toward his mother is because he blames her for the loss of his father.

At the onset, Justin presents certain challenges to the therapist. Justin views his therapist with suspicion because he seems to him primarily a White male who can't possibly understand how he feels. From his viewpoint, White males are implicated in some of his problems. Furthermore, he believes that Whites treat African Americans unfairly in Utah and that they look down on him because he is poor and lives in a deteriorating section of the city. All the people who have any ability to take him away from his mother and brother are members of the majority group. The judge is White, the lawyers are White, and so are his probation officer and the police officer who took him into custody for stealing. Justin believes that his world is controlled by White people who don't like him because of his race and who don't care to understand him.

Other issues also exist that have the potential of derailing the therapeutic relationship. Justin is a resistant client who has been directed by the court to engage in counseling as one of his conditions of temporary probation. He does not want to be in counseling. Moreover, he has negative views about counseling. Counseling is for people who are mentally ill, and he believes that there is nothing wrong with him.

Furthermore, Justin has been raised in a family in which there is an unspoken rule that family members don't talk about their business with strangers. Instinctively, he senses that the therapist is going to try to make his mother out to be a bad mother, and he has decided to defend her at all costs.

Justin's age presents certain hurdles for the therapist. The therapist cannot ask Justin to free associate and to lie on a couch because Justin may be too young to respond to such requests. Psychodynamic therapy works better with adults who are highly verbal rather than with young children. Justin may tire of talking about his problems; hence, the therapist might consider some modified form of play therapy. Thus, it might be more beneficial for the therapist to use parts of ego psychology (Erikson), object relations (Winnicott), and self psychology (Kohut).

The psychodynamic approach focuses on the unconscious basis of Justin's behavior. A critical component is Justin's relationship with his mother (Sandy). From an object relations approach, the therapist might assess the type of object introject that Justin has related to his mother. The therapist might ask, "What's the first thing that comes to your mind when you think about your mother? Anything? There is no right or wrong answer, just anything that comes to mind." This series of questions is a modified way of asking Justin to free associate.

The therapist might also have several sessions with Sandy asking her to describe the type of pregnancy that she had (whether it was difficult or easy), how she felt about being pregnant, any complications that she had during the delivery process, and so on. Such questions are designed to get at the mother's mindset and feelings during and immediately after pregnancy. In addition, assessment questions focus on the early type of relationship that Sandy established with Justin. The therapist might assess the holding environment (Winnicott) that she created for Justin and whether she strove to be a "good-enough mother" or a "perfect mother." What does she think were the outcomes of her efforts on Justin?

Moreover, assessment inquiries ask how Sandy would describe Justin in each of Erikson's psychosocial stages. In each stage, the therapist asks Sandy to focus on the type of relationship that she attempted to establish with Justin and the outcome of her efforts on Justin and herself.

Another critical area of assessment involves Sandy's relationship with and knowledge about Justin's father. How would she describe Justin's father's relationship with both her and Justin? What was Justin's reaction when his father left? Does Justin ever mention his father? The purpose of such inquiries is to construct Justin's object relations with both his mother and father, and how these early object relationships might be affecting his current relationships with his teachers and classmates.

After the initial assessment stage, which includes meeting with Justin's mother and teachers, as well as having a session with Justin, the therapist is in a position to frame a theory of the case. He places Justin's behavior and the other information that he has gathered into a clear theoretical framework. For instance, he might use Erikson's psychosocial theory as an overall framework. Within each of the stages (infancy vs. trust, autonomy vs. shame and doubt, initiative vs. guilt, and industry vs. inferiority), the therapist establishes tentative hypotheses about Justin's interpersonal relationships.

A key strategy is to trace the origin of Justin's anger. How did the key figures in his life (mother, father, and brother) handle anger? What influence has the brother's run-ins with the law had on Justin? What techniques has Justin learned for controlling his emotions? How does Justin self-regulate?

The therapist might form some beginning hypotheses, such as that Justin's anger is displaced on others. He is angry with both his mother and father for their failure to provide adequately for his needs of love and belonging. The therapist would note whether Justin had passed successfully through Erikson's first four psychosocial stages. If not, what kept him from making a successful stage completion? What introjects dominate Justin's current interpersonal relationships, both at home and at school?

After assessing Justin's case and placing it within a theoretical context, the therapist develops a treatment plan and a change strategy. The therapist uses strategies developed from relational analysis to establish a working alliance with Justin. Trust has to be developed between the therapist and Justin. In addition, the therapist must develop a change strategy for Justin. How can therapy help Justin to bring about the change that he desires—anger control, staying out of the residential treatment facility, not fighting in school, and achieving academically?

The therapist believes that Justin needs to gain better ego strength. Justin's weak ego strength has gotten him into trouble at school (fighting) and with the police (stealing). He allows others in his environment to provoke him because of their words or because he attributes to them negative intentions. Justin also needs to learn how to draw better boundary lines to separate himself from the negative influences in his environment, notably that of his older brother and friends. How is he negotiating the issue of separation and individuation from his mother? Has his brother taken on the role of his father?

The therapist investigates how Justin's unconscious forces are influencing his behavior. What are the kinds of defense mechanisms Justin uses to deal with anxiety? Are such defenses appropriate or are they in need of change?

The therapist focuses on Justin's transference relationships during therapy. The therapist is careful to examine any countertransference taking place between Justin and himself. The mechanism for change or strategy for achieving these goals is the therapeutic alliance. The belief is that Justin will eventually relate to the therapist as he does to his mother and quite possibly to his father. The goal would be to help Justin understand better some of the dynamics of his behavior.

The greatest threats to Justin are environmental challenges: poverty, gangs in the neighborhood, and an ineffectual mother. The therapist has to take these factors into consideration when making recommendations for Justin.

(Continued)

Should Justin be placed in residential treatment so that he can get away from the environmental challenges, or should he remain at home with his mother, who loves him but who has her own share of psychological issues (smoking pot in front of her children)?

To evaluate Justin, the therapist gathers all relevant data collected during the assessment process. Although all children are oppositional at one time or another in their lives, a tentative diagnosis of oppositional defiant disorder is made based on the assessment. Children who are given a diagnosis of oppositional defiant disorder may argue, talk back, disobey, and defy parents, teachers, and other adults. Although oppositional behavior is often a normal part of development for 2- to 3-year-olds and early adolescents, it becomes maladaptive when it is so frequent and consistent that it stands out in comparison with the behavior of children of the same age and developmental level and when it seriously impairs the young person's life. Justin's frequent temper tantrums, his excessive arguing with his mother and some teachers, his active defiance of school rules, and his frequent anger and resentment are all symptoms that suggest a tentative diagnosis of oppositional defiant disorder. Some children who have a diagnosed oppositional defiant disorder may proceed to develop a conduct disorder, which usually leads to contact with law enforcement officials and to an adult diagnosis of antisocial personality disorder. Justin appears headed in that direction, and the court's threat of residential treatment is designed to prevent his full-blown development of a conduct disorder.

If the therapist's tentative evaluation of Justin is one of oppositional defiant disorder, it is important for the therapist to prepare a comprehensive evaluation and to look for other disorders that might be present, such as attention-deficit/hyperactivity disorder, learning disabilities, mood disorders (depression and bipolar), and anxiety disorders. It is recommended that Justin's mother participate in parent management training and that he receive individual psychotherapy to help manage his anger. Justin also needs therapy to help him develop greater ego strength or self-regulatory behavior.

SUMMARY

Psychoanalytic therapy represents the first powerful force in psychology. Currently, many therapists use Freud's basic personality constructs of the id, the ego, and the superego. His theory about the unconscious remains a dominant force in psychology. However, few psychologists practicing today accept unquestionably Freud's theory of psychosexual stages and conflicts.

Freud's disciples have made important contributions to both the psychoanalytic and the psychodynamic traditions. Ego psychologists continue to make important contributions to psychodynamic theory. Anna Freud's primary contributions were with children and in understanding defense mechanisms. Erik Erikson's theory about psychosocial development throughout the entire life span has had a lasting effect on personality theory.

Object relations therapists have been concerned with childhood development before the age of 3, the manner in which infants relate to people around them, especially their mothers, and how the disruptions in early relationships influence their later development. Self psychologists have focused on the development of the ego within an object relations framework. Relational psychoanalysts have bridged the gap between humanists and analysts.

Despite the fact that the death of psychoanalysis has been repeatedly predicted, it continues to live on and may be experiencing a resurgence under the banner of brief analytic therapy and relational analysis. The psychoanalytic influence on psychology and psychotherapy continues despite numerous objections regarding its lack of relevancy for women and members of ethnic minorities.

SUPPLEMENTAL AIDS _____

Discussion Questions

1. Describe three psychoanalytic concepts that you would incorporate into your integrative theory of psychotherapy. Provide the rationale for incorporating these concepts into your approach.

2. Each one of us uses coping mechanisms to get through the everyday issues confronting our lives. From the list below, choose the coping mechanism you use and indicate how it has helped and hindered you in life.

- Projection
- Reaction formation
- Sublimation
- Regression
- Intellectualization
- Displacement
- Introjection
- Denial

3. In groups of four, choose a famous celebrity, fictional character, or literary character and analyze his or her core issues from a Freudian, Jungian, or Eriksonian viewpoint. What are the person's core issues? What developmental issues or phases have had an impact on the person's life? Discuss two treatment strategies you would use as the person's therapist.

4. Imagine that each of the theorists discussed in this chapter was miraculously available to you for the purpose of answering any questions about his or her own personal life or theory. Discuss one question you would like to ask him or her about his or her private life and one question you would like to ask about his or her theory.

5. Discuss two psychoanalytic or two psychodynamic approaches you might consider integrating as a therapist. What two theories would you integrate? Are there any points of incompatibility that would work against your integrating the theories? What would be the advantage of integrating the two theoretical approaches?

Glossary of Key Terms

anal personality   A person who is fixated at the anal level of Freud's psychosexual stage of development. The anus is charged with energy. In general, people who are fixated at this stage tend to be parsimonious, stubborn, hoarding, and perfectionistic.

analysis   Therapeutic strategy used for the purpose of giving a person's ego more control over id impulses.

anima   The female component present in the collective unconscious of men.

animus   The male component of the unconscious female psyche.

anxiety   Three types: (1) reality (anxiety about the external world), (2) normal or moral (anxiety about the superego's [parents'] shoulds and wants), and (3) neurotic anxiety (anxiety that a suppressed sexual wish might surface). Anxiety is felt only by the ego. Freud described anxiety as a warning signal.

archetype   The contents of the collective unconscious. Archetypes point to the fact that all human beings share a common physiology and a common way of perceiving the world through our senses. Some examples of archetypes include the mother, the wise old man, and the innocent child. These archetypes are inherited at birth and point to the belief that human beings share similar longings and perceptions. See also **collective unconscious**.

attachment theory   A theory developed first by John Bowlby that described the bonding relationship between an infant and his or her mother.

blank screen   The therapist's stance or position that is assumed during therapy. Classical therapists use it to promote client transference.

brief psychodynamic therapy (BPT)   A time-limited and shortened approach to therapy that uses psychoanalytic principles.

collective unconscious   The source of innumerable archetypes that influence our longings and relationships. Even though each of us grows up influenced by his or her parents and family, there is another level at which we are unconsciously driven or influenced by deep archetypal images. See also **archetype.**

complex   A cluster of emotionally charged associations that are usually unconscious and gathered around an archetypal center. A complex can be conceptualized as repressed emotional themes. Both troubled and healthy people have complexes. Complexes first originate in childhood, and they are always either the cause or the effect of a conflict or a clash between the need to adapt and a person's inability to meet that challenge.

conscience   One of two components that make up the superego. It is often used to refer to an internalized critical parent.

conscious   (or consciousness) As defined by Freud, it is that part of the mind or mental functioning of which individuals are aware, such as sensations, feelings, and experiences.

countertransference   The therapist's transference projections. The therapist enacts old conflicts from the family of origin onto the client. It is a type of inappropriate therapist projection unto the client. See also **relational analysis** and **transference.**

dreams   Symbolic expressions of the unconscious. Psychoanalysts analyze dreams as a means to get to clients' unconscious.

ego   Refers to the "I" that develops out of the id. The ego is formed by the child's identifications. Ego exists primarily at the conscious level. It has been described as the conscious self. The ego is often viewed as a mediator between the id and the superego. See also **relational analysis, id,** and **superego.**

ego defense mechanisms   Intrapsychic processes that serve to protect a person from anxiety-provoking thoughts or threats to the self.

ego psychology   That branch of psychology that is considered an offshoot of the psychoanalytic school and that focuses on the development of the ego or the self at various stages of development.

Electra complex   A term Freud used to represent the feminine equivalent of the male oedipal complex.

erogenous zones   Those areas of the body that provide sexual stimulation during various psychosexual stages of development, namely, the mouth, anus, and penis, although Freud regarded the entire body as an erogenous zone.

extrovert   A personality typology developed by Jung that asserts that extroverts are people who prefer the external world of things, being with people, and participating in actions. See also **introvert.**

false self   When an infant does not have good-enough mothering, the child adopts the mother's self instead of developing his or her own self. It is used in contrast with the *true self.*

fixation   The state of being stuck at one of Freud's psychosexual stages of development. One can become, for instance, fixated at the oral or the anal stage.

free association   A major psychoanalytic technique that therapists use to get the spontaneous and uncensored thoughts of a client. The therapist asks, "What does that bring to mind?" The client's responses are *free* because they are uncensored thoughts about a particular situation.

good-enough mother   A term Winnicott used to describe a mother who responds adequately to her child's needs during early infancy and who gradually helps the child develop independence.

holding environment   A holding environment may be defined as a space or setting that is psychologically safe for the infant. A good holding environment is a reliable one that makes one feel protected, understood, and loved. Therapists can provide a holding environment for clients.

id   That part of a person's personality structure that is present at birth that functions to discharge tension and then to return to a state of equilibrium. From the id (the "it") originates all drives that propel psychic life. The id is sometimes referred to as the amoral beast within us that seeks only its own gratification through tension discharge. One task of the ego is to dominate the id. See also **ego** and **superego.**

identity crisis   Term coined by Erikson to represent a developmental challenge that takes place during adolescence, whereby the youth attempts to define his or her place in life with regard to sexual, personal, and career identity, making a vocational choice.

individuation   The process by which a person integrates unconscious material into consciousness, with the result being that he or she becomes a psychologically whole person. Jung used the term to represent self-realization. Individuation is the human expression of our urge toward growth.

introjection   A psychological term that indicates a psychological action by which a person is internalized and made a part of his or her own psyche. The term is often used by object relations and self theorists.

introvert   Jung's term to refer to people who prefer the internal world of their own thoughts, feelings, dreams, and so on. See also **extrovert**.

latent content   Term used to represent the disguised and repressed part of a dream. See also **manifest content**.

libido   The psychosexual energy that originates in the id. The libido contains the instinctual drives of the id. It is a source of psychic energy. See also **id**.

manifest content   What a dream represents on the surface level. Freud viewed the manifest content of dreams as a disguise of the true latent dream material. See also **latent content**.

mirroring   When the parent or primary caretaker indicates that he or she is happy with the child, the child's grandiose self is supported. The caretaker mirrors or reflects the child's view of himself or herself.

morality principle   The principles of right and wrong that are accepted by an individual or a social group. The superego governs the morality principle.

narcissism   The investment of libido into oneself. Narcissism is believed to be extreme self-love in contrast to loving others. A narcissistic personality has a grandiose and exaggerated sense of self. He or she tends to display an exploitative attitude toward others; such an attitude hides a poor self-concept.

neurosis   A conflict between the id and the ego that produces anxiety or symptoms of discomfort. The anxiety may not be conscious.

object   A term used in psychoanalytic theory to refer to a significant person in a child's life.

object relations theory   A relatively recent school of psychoanalytic thought that emphasizes the self in relation to others.

oedipal complex   A boy's tendency (largely unconscious), usually occurring around the age of 5, to have sexual strivings toward his mother and to want to replace the father in her affections.

oral personality   Person fixated at the oral stage of psychosexual development. One who has an oral personality wants to suck and to take in. Oral personalities are viewed as needy and forever hungry for approval.

penis envy   The supposed envy of women toward males. Freud maintained that women blamed their mother for leaving them without a penis.

persona   The socially acceptable mask that we wear to deal with the outer world; one's public image. Viewed positively, it is the "good impression" that we wish to make on others. From a negative perspective, persona suggests a type of falseness about a person—deceit.

pleasure principle   Principle that represents our striving toward pleasure and movement away from pain. We feel pleasure when tension is relieved. The id operates on the pleasure principle.

preconscious   One of Freud's three topographical divisions of the psyche. It includes those thoughts and memories that are not conscious but that may be brought into conscious by the client's or the therapist's efforts.

primary process   In Freud's psychoanalytic theory of personality, resolves tension created by the pleasure principle. Instead of acting on the dangerous or unacceptable urges, the id forms a mental image of a desired object to substitute for an urge in order to diffuse tension and anxiety.

psychodynamic theory A theoretical school that includes Freud's contributions as well as those of his followers. It maintains that (a) a therapist must take into account the unconscious factors in a client's life, (b) individuals use ego defense mechanisms to deal with anxiety, and (c) one's early upbringing in the family is the source of many difficulties presented in therapy.

psychosexual phases Freud's conception of life phases that individuals go through. Each phase has an erogenous zone, or an area of the body where people find sexual pleasure—the mouth, oral pleasure, and so on.

psychosocial stages The stages that Erikson identified from infancy to old age. Each stage contains psychological and social tasks to be mastered if the individual is to develop in a mature fashion.

reaction formation An ego defense against impulse that one views as threatening wherein one expresses the direct opposite of the impulse. This principle governs the pleasure principle.

reality principle The ego's sense of realistic and rational adaptation to life's issues.

relational analysis A relatively recent branch of psychodynamic therapy founded on the belief that it is the relationship between the therapist and the client that is most important. The therapist's countertransference during therapy is recognized and analyzed for what it says for the therapist's and the client's relationship. See also **countertransference**.

resistance The client's reluctance to deal with threatening unconscious material that usually has been repressed.

secondary process In Freud's psychoanalytic theory, process that discharges the tension between the ego and the id that is brought on by libidinal urges or unmet needs.

self-object Patterns of unconscious thoughts, images, or representations of another person within an individual; and this representation may influence a person's self-esteem.

shadow A Jungian archetype that represents the dark side of the ego; the evil that we are potentially capable of is stored there. The shadow represents those parts of ourselves that we can't quite accept. Symbols of the shadow are the snake, the dragon, and demons.

superego That part of an individual's personality that represents one's moral training. It strives for perfection and is usually associated with the teachings of one's parents. See also **ego** and **id**.

transference The client's unconscious projection onto the therapist feelings and fantasies that are displacements based on reactions to significant others in the client's past, especially parents, siblings, and significant relationships. See also **countertransference**.

transmuting internalization Representations of interactions with others that gradually form a personality structure for the child. Children learn that they cannot always get what they want and that their parents make mistakes and are not perfect.

unconscious That feature of a person's psychological function that contains experiences, wishes, impulses, and memories that are not within his or her awareness because they may provoke anxiety.

working-through A phase of psychoanalytic therapy that entails resolving clients' basic conflicts. During this phase, the therapist interprets the client's transference and resistance.

Website Materials

Additional exercises, journals, annotated bibliography, and more are available on the open-access website at https://study.sagepub .com/jonessmith2e.

CHAPTER 3

Adlerian Psychotherapy

Alfred Adler

A simple rule in dealing with those who are hard to get along with is to remember that this person is striving to assert his superiority; and you must deal with him from that point of view.

It is easier to fight for one's principles than to live up to them.

Meanings are not determined by situations, but we determine ourselves by the meanings we give to situations.

—Alfred Adler

BRIEF OVERVIEW

Although Freud's theory of psychoanalysis provides the primary general foundation for the psychodynamic school of thought, his early protégés (Jung and Adler) have also had a major impact of their own. Clearly, Adler belongs to the psychodynamic school of theorists. This chapter focuses on the contributions of Alfred Adler who developed individual psychology, which is commonly called Adlerian therapy. Adler is often credited with helping make the shift from psychoanalysis to ego psychology. According to Ellenberger (1970), the shift of psychoanalysis to ego psychology reflected Adler's original thinking.

Adler's ideas have permeated so much of psychological thought that they are often just generally accepted and not traced back directly to him (Stein & Edwards, 1998). For instance, Adler's belief that "human beings live in the realm of meanings" is similar to the social constructivist view of human behavior (Stein & Edwards, 1998). Adler was an early feminist who maintained that both men and women suffered from our society's overvaluing of men and undervaluing of women—a key construct within current feminist theory. In his early works, he also argued for the unity of mind and body. Thus, wellness and even some of the constructs in neuroscience that emphasize the interrelationship of the mind and health were early Adlerian principles. As Stein and Edwards (1998) have asserted, Adler caused, in part, a paradigm shift because he

81

created "an integrated, holistic theory of human nature and psychopathology, a set of principles and techniques of psychotherapy, a world view, and a philosophy of living."

This chapter provides a brief biographical sketch of Adler, and it also describes his view of the human condition, his ideas related to personality development, and his explanation of what happens to cause psychopathology. Moreover, Adlerian levels of psychotherapy intervention, the therapeutic process, role of the therapist and client, and therapy techniques are also presented. The chapter begins with his basic concepts.

MAJOR CONTRIBUTOR: ALFRED ADLER (1870–1937)

Alfred Adler was raised in Vienna, Austria, in a middle-class, Jewish grain merchant family. He was the second of six children (four boys and two girls). Adler experienced a number of traumatic events while growing up. One of his brothers died lying next to him. During his early years, Adler was his mother's favorite because he was quite sickly. He suffered from rickets, which kept him from walking until he was 4 years old. The third child dethroned Adler as his mother's favorite, and thereafter, he turned to his father for support. Father and son remained close for most of Adler's life (Watts, 2003).

When Adler was 5 years old, he nearly died of pneumonia. During the doctor's visit, Adler heard the doctor tell his father that "Alfred is lost." It was because of this near-death experience that Adler decided that he wanted to become a medical doctor.

Many of the ideas and concepts that make up current psychotherapy can be traced directly to Adler's views of his early childhood experiences. Adler's earliest memories were of sibling rivalry, jealousy, and sickness. He was known for his competitive spirit toward his older brother Sigmund, whom he viewed as a strong rival. Adler's early childhood experiences with illnesses and trauma provided the basis for his theory of **organ inferiority** and **inferiority feelings**. According to Adler, each person has a weak area in his or her body

(organ inferiority) that tends to be the area where illness takes place—the stomach, head, or heart. Adler (1917) wrote psychoanalytic articles on organ inferiority. He was one of the first theorists to propose that feelings of inferiority could stimulate a striving for superiority.

To compensate for his physical limitations, he developed his leadership abilities (Watts, 2003). During secondary school, he failed in mathematics. The teacher recommended that he be removed from school and become apprenticed as a shoemaker. Despite this recommendation, Adler persisted, studied at home, and thereafter went to the head of his class in mathematics.

As Adler grew older, his health improved. Adler's father encouraged him to attend medical school. In 1895, he began his practice as an ophthalmologist. Later, he switched to a general practice. Next, he began to study psychiatry in order to understand his patients psychologically. Adler maintained that he was interested in the development of the whole person, and this philosophy would govern his practice in psychiatry. In 1897, Adler married Raissa Epstein, a Russian, and both became devoted to socialism.

In 1902, Sigmund Freud invited Adler to join his select Wednesday evening psychoanalytic discussion circle. Initially, Adler was receptive to many of Freud's views. Yet, increasingly, the two men differed in their views. Although both believed that individuals' personalities are formed by the age of 6, they differed substantially about the essential conflicts people face in their development. Adler criticized Freud for what he called an overemphasis on sexuality. They disagreed on the role of the unconscious, the importance of social issues, and the role of drive theory. Freud maintained that Adler gave too much credit to conscious processes.

Although Adler was president of the Vienna Psychoanalytic Society in 1911, he resigned this position and left with 9 of the 23 members. Adler established himself as the leader for a new system of psychotherapy that he labeled **individual psychology** to highlight that he was studying the whole individual. In 1912, he formed the Society of the Individual Psychology.

During World War I, Adler served as a physician in the Austrian army. Shortly after the war, he established the first of 30 child guidance clinics in the Viennese school system. During his lifetime, 39 Adlerian societies were established. Although he had been raised as a Jew, at this time, Adler converted to Protestantism. During the early 1930s, most of his Austrian clinics were closed because of his Jewish heritage (even though he had converted to Christianity). With the rise of Nazism in Europe, Adler and his wife moved to the United States in 1935. Adler continued his private practice in the United States, and he was appointed to the chair of medical psychology at the Long Island School of Medicine.

Adler lived a life of hard work. Unfortunately, he ignored his friends' admonitions to slow down. He loved walking before lectures. During a long walk before a scheduled lecture in Aberdeen, Scotland, Adler collapsed and died of a massive heart attack. Two of his children, Kurt and Alexandra, spread Adler's work throughout the United States. Rudolf Dreikurs, perhaps Adler's most famous disciple, moved from Austria to the United States and established child guidance clinics in Chicago. Since the 1990s, there has been a resurgence of interest in Adlerian therapy in the United States (Hoffman, 1994).

Alfred Adler had a major impact on psychology. He influenced Karen Horney on social factors in her theory of personality and Gordon Allport on the unity of personality. Other notable psychologists whom he influenced were E. C. Tolman (purpose), Julian Rotter (expectancies), and Abraham Maslow (self-actualization). Maslow, Rollo May, and Carl Rogers studied under Adler and noted that he had a major impact on their thinking.

One of Adler's primary contributions to psychology is his theory that human personality and behavior are inherently goal directed, driven by some inner force that deals with overcoming inferiority feelings, and that very early in life we construct goals that we strive to achieve throughout our lives. He had a great impact on what is commonly regarded as good parenting and child management. Although Adler was an excellent therapist, his primary interests were in preventive psychology and in the interaction of families. He was one of the first to advocate democratic parenting, and he outlined two types of parenting that led to later problems: (1) pampering or overprotecting a child and (2) neglecting a child.

KEY CONCEPTS

View of Human Nature

Adler's concept of humanity was that people are basically self-determined and that they forge their personalities from the meaning they give to their life experiences. People create their own lives by using their creative power. Although heredity provides individuals with certain abilities and the environment gives them opportunities to realize those abilities, it is the individual himself or herself who must ultimately be responsible for making good use of those abilities.

Adler highlighted the importance of an individual's subjective experiences. He believed that a person's interpretation of his or her experiences is far more important than the actual experiences. Departing from Feud's deterministic position, Adler asserted that people are motivated by their present perceptions of the past and by their present expectations of the future. According to Adler, people do not determine meanings by situations, but they determine themselves by the meanings they give to situations. People create their own personalities, and they can change their personality by developing new attitudes. Ultimately, people are responsible for developing their own personalities. Their creative power can transform their feelings of inadequacies into social interest. People can then choose between psychological health and maladaptive behavior. Mentally healthy people evidence a high level of social interest, but they have the freedom to accept or reject social interest and to become what they want to become.

Adler's view of human nature was essentially optimistic. People are forward moving, and they are motivated by their striving to achieve their goals rather than by innate instincts or causal forces. He maintained that people are capable of living together in cooperation with one another where they strive for self-improvement, self-fulfillment, and contribute to the common good of the society in which they live. Adler predicted that if we did not learn to cooperate with one another, then we might eventually annihilate one another. The core problem that human beings face on this earth is how to live on earth in cooperation with one another.

Adler's view of human nature is holistic and phenomenological in orientation. He emphasizes that individuals' perceptions of their early childhood events have an important influence on the rest of their lives. Human behavior is developed within a social context, and therefore, therapy should take into consideration that context. Furthermore, all human conflicts are social conflicts. Because the basic desire of people is to belong, they can fulfill themselves and become significant only within a group context.

Adler's concept of the nature of people differed sharply from that of Freud, who saw people as driven primarily by instincts that had to be controlled or transformed into socially acceptable behavior. In contrast, Adler (1907, 1926/1964) asserted that human behavior was primarily learned rather than instinctual and that people are in control of their behavior and the situations they encounter.

Adler believed people to be more conscious than unconscious. What we are and how we relate to the world is a conscious choice, not one that should be blamed on unconscious influences.

The fundamental nature of people is social. Moreover, Adlerians believe that dividing up individuals into parts or forces (i.e., Freud's id, ego, and superego) was counterproductive because it was mechanistic. Human beings are creative,

Inner Reflections

How would you compare Adler's views on human nature with Freud's?

What, if any, part of Adler's views on the nature of people do you agree with? Which do you disagree with?

self-determined decision makers who are free to choose their life goals. We construct our reality based on our ways of viewing the world (Mosak, 2005).

From Adler's perspective, people are neither inherently good nor bad, but based on their appraisal of an immediate situation and its payoff, they may choose to be good or bad. Individuals have an innate human potential for social interest. Children enter the world with an innate response pattern of love and affection. Adler described **social interest** as the ability to participate and the willingness to contribute to society. To function adequately in life, people must develop sufficient social interest; otherwise, deficiency and maladjustment occur. Our desire to belong is a lifelong pursuit and is marked by our efforts to find our "place in life."

Individuals' development of feelings of inferiority is considered to be part of the human condition and inevitable. All of us at some point (usually in early childhood) experience evaluations of inferiority, which may lead to feelings of inferiority. It is the nature of people to try to overcome feelings of inferiority developed in childhood by striving to become superior in self-selected areas. Adler believed that feelings of inferiority are not necessarily negative; they provide the motivations for subsequent adolescent and adult achievement in life.

Inner Reflections

Oftentimes clients come to therapy because they are experiencing inferiority feelings.

How would you assess for inferiority or superiority feelings?

What Adlerian therapeutic techniques would you use for working with clients who have feelings of inferiority?

Theory of Personality

Whereas Freud stressed the role of psychosexual development and the oedipal complex, Adler emphasized the effects of children's perceptions of their family constellations and their struggles to find their own significant niches within them. Adler argued that one's personality is a complete unity—the principle of **holism** (Mosak, 2005). Whereas Freud said that there was a conflict between his three proposed parts of one's personality (id, ego, and superego), Adler maintained that there was no internal war or conflict and that the individual moves only in one direction. Clients should not be analyzed from the perspective of urges and drives but rather from the perspective of the total fields in which they operate. The Adlerian concept of the unity of behavior is similar to Gestalt psychologists' view of behavior. A person is an indivisible unity. The Adlerian concept of personality development is founded on the following nine concepts: (1) social interest, (2) masculine protest, (3) lifestyle, (4) goal-directed and purposeful behavior, (5) feelings of inferiority, (6) striving for superiority, (7) fictional finalism, (8) family constellation, and (9) birth order (Mosak, 2005).

Social Interest

Social interest is an Adlerian concept that refers to individuals' sense of being part of the human community and their attitudes toward others. Adler maintained that society was important in the development of one's individual character and one's emotion. Children seek to find their places in society; they also develop a sense of belonging and of contributing. Adler described social interest as an individual's ability to empathize with others: "to see with the eyes of another, to hear with the ears of another, to feel with the heart of another" (as cited in Ansbacher & Ansbacher, 1979, p. 42). People show or demonstrate their social interest. Adler presumed an innate potential for social interest.

When our social interest has been developed adequately, we find solutions to problems and feel at home in the world. Adlerians believe that to have solid mental health, one must have adequate social interest. At the affective level, social interest is an individual's deep feeling of belonging to the human race and empathy with fellow men and women. At the cognitive level, social interest is a person's recognition of interdependence with others, that is, that the welfare of any one individual ultimately depends on the welfare of everyone. At the behavioral level, a person's social interest can be conceptualized as actions aimed at self-development as well as cooperative and helpful movements directed toward others. The person whose social interest is developed tends to find solutions to problems, feels at home in the world, and sees things more clearly.

The person not interested in his or her fellow or community faces the greatest difficulties in life and creates the greatest injury to others. Lifestyles that do not evidence an interest and concern for the welfare of others are considered pathogenic. Pathological lifestyles are marked by strivings that are self-centered, exploitive, demanding, uncaring, and aggressive. Criminal behavior frequently results from pathological lifestyles. The development of social interest is, therefore, critical to the prevention of antisocial behavior. Adler proposed that social interest could be used to change the behavior of antisocial and criminal people. Social interest provides us with a basically positive outlook on life and an interest in developing the welfare of others (Adler, 1926/1964).

Inner Reflections

Schools have emphasized the importance of social interest by constructing graduation requirements that require service projects.

In working with your clients, would you ever consider asking them to become involved in social service projects? Is recommending that your client become involved in a service program really therapy? If so, why? If not, why not? What is appropriate material for therapy?

Masculine Protest

Adler was an early supporter of women's rights. Repeatedly, he argued that only if women were given the same opportunities as men could they deal successfully with their sense of inferiority (Worell & Remer, 2003). As a result of his commitment to equal rights, Adler developed the concept of the *masculine protest*, which was defined as the desire to be a "real man": a desire to be superior, to strive to be perfect. He explained that men carefully hide their feminine traits through exaggerated masculine wishes and efforts. These exaggerated protestations of masculinity result in men's overcompensation and their denial of their feminine sides. The masculine protest can lead to men setting high, almost unattainable goals for themselves. Men who suffer from strong masculine protests tend to develop pathological fantasies of grandeur. In contrast, the masculine protest in a woman reveals itself in a repressed wish to become transformed into a man. One positive consequence of the masculine protest in women is that some women may strive very hard for superiority in their professional fields, especially if such professions are dominated by males.

Lifestyle

Adlerians maintain that behavior is lawfully organized and that each person develops a generalized pattern of responses to most situations—a **lifestyle** (Oberst & Stewart, 2003). All behavior is organized around lifestyle, which is defined as a habitual pattern of behavior unique to each person. Lifestyle provides a theme that unifies our lives. It gives consistency to the way we live. According to Ansbacher and Ansbacher (1964, p. 332), lifestyle can be compared to the melody of a song. "We can begin wherever we choose: every expression will lead us in the same direction—toward the one motive, the one melody, around which the personality is built." Our lifestyle is considered a major key to our behavior. Lifestyle includes our goals, our opinions of ourselves and the world, and the habitual behaviors we use for achieving desired outcomes. Children create their own lifestyles by the age of 5; thereafter, it becomes difficult for them to change their approaches to the world.

Lifestyle consists of our interpretation of events, rather than the events themselves, that

deeply affect our personalities. Our individual views about ourselves, others, and the universe form a personal filter for all future experiences. We can make faulty interpretations of events, which may lead to mistaken beliefs in our own **private logic**—the reasoning we invent to stimulate and justify our lifestyles. (By contrast, common sense represents society's cumulative, consensual reasoning that recognizes the wisdom of mutual benefit.) Our mistaken beliefs can influence current behavior. Therapy helps us become aware of our mistaken beliefs or faulty interpretations of events and, hence, the errors in our private logic. Adlerian therapists assist clients in reframing events that took place during childhood so that clients consciously create a new lifestyle or a new way of organizing their lives.

During the process of developing their lifestyles, children construct statements about the conditions, personal or social, that are necessary for them to feel secure (Mosak, 2005). Such statements are termed our **lifestyle convictions**. When there is conflict between one's self-concept and one's ideal self, one develops inferiority feelings. When a person begins to act inferior rather than just to feel inferior, he or she actively engages in "discouragement" or the inferiority complex. Adlerian theory suggests that a person has four lifestyle convictions (Mosak, 2005):

1. *The self-concept:* The convictions I have about who I am

2. *The self-ideal:* The convictions that pertain to what I should be or am obligated to be in order to have a place in the world

3. *The* Weltbild, *or "Picture of the world":* The convictions about the not-self (e.g., world, people, nature, etc.) and what the world demands of me

4. *The ethical convictions:* The individual's development of a personal code of right and wrong

Four Lifestyles. Adler outlined four basic lifestyles (Boldt & Mosak, 1997). The first, the socially useful type, consists of people who have a high social interest and who use high activity to achieve goals. People who fall into the socially useful category tend to be mature, positive, well adjusted, and courteous and considerate of others. They do not strive for personal superiority over others. Instead, they seek to solve problems in ways that are helpful to others. Socially useful types help others in their families, and they work for social or political change (Adler, 1929).

The second lifestyle category is called the *ruling type*. Individuals in this category have little social interest and are active in seeking control over others. They try to prove their personal superiority by ruling others. The ruling type takes a dominating and antisocial approach to society. Some of their activities may be asocial, for example, the activities of thieves, con artists, substance abusers, and so on. Frequently, juvenile delinquents and criminals fall within this category (Adler, 1929).

The third lifestyle is labeled the *getting type*. People in this lifestyle category desire to get everything from others without any personal effort or struggle. They have both low social interest and low activity levels. They selfishly take without giving back. Everybody owes them something, but they owe nothing to anyone.

The fourth lifestyle type is called the *avoiding type*. People in this category evidence low social interest and low activity levels. They avoid failure by avoiding involvement with work, friends, or society in general. They are likely to have low social contact for fear of rejection or defeat in any way. Three factors interfere with development of social interest: (1) organ inferiorities, (2) parental pampering (why should I love my neighbor when he has not done anything for me?), and (3) neglect of a child (society owes me).

Goal-Directed and Purposeful Behavior

All behavior is purposeful and goal directed. Thus, when we act, our actions are based on a goal we are trying to attain. If counselors want to understand their clients, they must first understand their clients' goals. For instance, one goal of a misbehaving child might be to get attention from a parent or a teacher. Acting out allows a child to achieve his or her goal of attention.

Children set two types of goals: immediate and long range. *Immediate goals* are the easier ones to work with, and they are generally observable in day-to-day functioning of children. Children may have several immediate goals at once; these goals are more amenable to change and short-term counseling, if necessary. In contrast, *long-range goals* indicate children's private, inner logic and form their basic outlooks on life. Long-range goals are established early in life; they are more rigid and less susceptible to change (Dreikurs, 1949).

Children's perceptions of their interactions within their families are pivotal in their establishment of long-range goals. For instance, if a child believes that he or she is rejected or not loved by a parent, his or her basic goal in life might be to obtain love from others—regardless of the cost. Another reaction might be a child who establishes a long-range goal of punishing his or her parents. This behavior is predominant in angry children, delinquents, and others who may seek to harm their parents by harming themselves (Dinkmeyer, Dinkmeyer, & Sperry, 1990).

All human behavior has a purpose, which is usually of a social nature. We establish both immediate and long-range goals, and we may not be consciously aware that we have set such goals for ourselves. We set goals to find and secure our places in life. The movement toward a goal is always in relationship to ourselves and others. All behavior has its own private logic, which is usually located at the unconscious level. Our private logic affects the way we think and feel about our purpose in

Inner Reflections

Think back on your life as you were growing up.

How would you analyze your own lifestyle?

What factors led to the development of your lifestyle?

Can you think of any lifestyle convictions that you have?

Of the four lifestyles that Adler outlines, which is your current one?

life and the manner in which we seek to achieve our fictional goals (Adler, 1959a).

Healthy human development takes place when we become more conscious of our own private logic and the unique ways in which we have unconsciously constructed meaning of the world. Most times, we are unaware of the inner private logic that guides our behavior. When counselors help clients analyze their goals and private logic, they are taking important steps to helping them lead more productive lives.

Feelings of Inferiority

According to Adler, all humans begin their psychological life with feelings of inferiority. When we are born, we are totally dependent on others for our survival. Hence, we become aware of strong general feelings of inferiority very early in our lives, especially in relationship to our parents.

From Adler's perspective, an **inferiority complex** is "the presentation of the person to himself and others that he is not strong enough to solve a given problem in a socially useful way" (Ansbacher & Ansbacher, 1956, p. 258). An inferiority complex is a pervasive feeling that one's abilities and characteristics are inferior to those of other people. For instance, while some people view themselves as less intelligent, others may see themselves as less attractive or less athletic than those around them.

Adler conceptualized feelings of inferiority as much more than a sense of inadequacy. These feelings provide the motivating force behind all growth and development. They constitute a *minus state* that we seek to overcome. All our strivings are attempts to overcome or to compensate for feelings of inferiority. Adler maintained that our innate sense of inferiority helps humans survive while other species become extinct. He characterized feelings of inferiority as inevitable, universal, and normal (Adler, 1926/1972).

Striving for Superiority

People seek to compensate for feelings of inferiority by striving for superiority, which is a concept Adler used to explain our drive to master external obstacles, to gain power and status, and to arrive at a positive state. Because we cannot ever completely rid ourselves of feelings of inferiority, striving for superiority becomes a dominant theme in our lives (Adler, 1926/1972).

It is important to understand the differences between striving for superiority and a superiority complex. In using the term *superiority*, Adler did not emphasize being superior to others. An individual who has a superiority complex inflates his or her own self-importance to overcome feelings of inferiority. When one has a **superiority complex**, one has a negative impact on others. We put others down to mask our own negative feelings about ourselves.

Striving for superiority is a positive striving for perfection (Schultz & Schultz, 2001). Healthy people strive for superiority; however, they do not develop a superiority complex to mask true feelings of inferiority. Throughout our lives, we struggle to achieve our places in life, and we strive for perfection in achieving our goals. Our striving for superiority contributes to the development of the human community because it pushes us to make positive contributions in science, technology, and in the arts (Adler, 1926/1972).

Fictional Finalism

Adler was influenced by the philosopher Hans Vaihinger, whose book *The Psychology of the "As If"* was originally published in 1924. According to Vaihinger, people live by many fictional ideals that have no relationship to reality and that cannot be tested and confirmed. Some examples of such fictionalisms include "Honesty is the best policy," "All men are created equal," and "The end justifies the means." Any ideal or an absolute is usually a fiction. Fictionalisms can help us deal more effectively with reality, or they may block our attempts to accept reality. If we believe there are a heaven and a hell, such beliefs will influence how we live.

Adler believed that fictional goals develop during individuals' early childhood, and they exist primarily at the unconscious level of awareness throughout one's life. Our fictional goals influence the way we think, feel, and act throughout our lives. Ansbacher (1968) indicates there are five points to Adler's understanding of **fictional finalism**. A fictional goal has the following features:

1. Provides for the internal, subjective causation of a psychological event

2. Represents a creation of the person and is primarily subconscious

3. Becomes the principle of unity and self-consistency of one's personality

4. Forms the basis for a person's orientation in the world

5. Supplies one way of compensating for feelings of inferiority

Family Constellation

Adler made important contributions regarding the functioning of families. He used the term **family constellation** to describe the composition of a family and one's position within that system (Adler, 1937). According to Gilliland and James (1998),

> The family constellation mediates the genetic and constitution factors the child brings into it and the cultural factors the child learns from it. The personality characteristics of each family member, the sex of the siblings, family size, and the birth order of the children all influence how individuals find their niche in life. (p. 49)

Each of us engages in creative and subjective interpretations of our place within our families. We live in our own unique private worlds created by our own perceptions. It is not *what* we are that determines our behavior, but rather, it is what *we think* we are that has the most impact on us. We develop expectations that become self-fulfilling prophecies because we enact in our lives what we believe about ourselves and other people.

Birth Order

Adler (1929) attributed a great deal of importance to our ordinal position within our families, which he believed influenced our relationships with our parents, our interactions with other family members, and the specific feelings of inferiority we experienced in life. **Birth order** refers to the placement of siblings within the family. Five ordinal positions within a family constellation are identified in the literature: (1) the firstborn, (2) the second born, (3) the middle child, (4) the youngest child, and (5) the only child. There is potentially a favorable or an unfavorable outcome based on each birth order place. Our birth order may present us with special challenges and encourage us to form complex rivalries and alliances within our families. Adler (1929) posited that birth order was one of the major childhood social influences from which the child creates a lifestyle.

The Firstborn. Many parents lavish a great deal of time and attention on their firstborn (Adler, 1937). As a result, the child may hold a secure position within the family. Adler referred to the firstborn as the "reigning monarch" who is given undivided attention. With the arrival of the second child, the monarch is dethroned because parents must share their time with the new arrival. One consequence is that the former monarch waits to be served. He or she builds resentment, and the battle is begun to regain the monarch position.

Adler theorized that all firstborns suffer the loss of the privileged position, but only those who have been pampered excessively by their parents feel great resentment, discouragement, and hatred toward the new sibling. A number of factors moderate the firstborn's degree of discouragement, including the age when displaced and the amount of parental preparation for the new arrival. Yet the fact is abundantly clear: The firstborn's place in the family is no longer the same. The new arrival makes the former little monarch the older child who is given high expectations of responsibility and cooperation.

Adler stated that of all the children within a family, the firstborn best understands the significance of power and the exercise of it (Dinkmeyer & Sperry, 2000). Some other characteristics of firstborns are that they become conservative in outlook, they nostalgically look to the past, and they are disproportionately interested in organization and the maintenance of the status quo. Firstborns tend to become highly organized, responsible, and conscientious. When they are deficient in social interest, they are inclined to be very insecure, suspicious, and hostile toward others and society in general. A favorable outcome of being the oldest child is that one feels a sense of responsibility and takes care of others. In contrast, an unfavorable outcome might be that one feels insecure and becomes overly reliant on rules.

The Second Born. The second-born child grows up knowing that he or she has to share parental time and attention (Adler, 1937). Because second-born children are not concerned about the loss of power and authority, they tend to be optimistic, competitive, and ambitious. If the firstborn encourages the second born to "catch up," the latter's development tends to be positive and healthy. Conversely, if the older sibling expresses strong resentment against the second child and excels in virtually every area, the second child might set high goals that eventually lead to failure. In most instances, the second child strives in directions different from the firstborn. A great deal depends on the second-born child's interpretations of how he or she is treated within the family.

The Middle Child. The middle child must share from the very beginning. Such children often feel as if they are in a difficult and an unfair position (Adler, 1937). Middle children may feel defeated by their older and younger siblings, or they may surpass them. They learn the skills of manipulation and negotiation from the family politics in which they find themselves. Middle children strive in areas different from those of the oldest child. One potential favorable outcome for middle children is that they are ambitious and develop a strong social interest. Unfavorable outcomes are that they are rebellious and envious, and they often experience difficulty being a follower.

The Youngest Child. The youngest child tends to be pampered within the family constellation. The youngest children often have older siblings to look after them. They may become "family pets" and be considered cute (Adler, 1937). Because there are so many role models within the family constellation, youngest children may excel over all others to establish their place within the family. Many youngest children develop a competitive orientation, and they become high achievers at whatever they undertake. Youngest children who are spoiled and pampered expect that others will take care of them. As adults, they may find adult responsibilities too much to bear, or they become dependent on using their charm to get others to meet their needs. One favorable consequence of being the youngest child is that one gets much stimulation and loads of opportunities to compete. A potential unfavorable result is that one feels inferior to everyone.

The Only Child. Similar to the youngest child, the only child is usually pampered. Adler (1937) suggested that the only child is not likely to develop a competitive spirit. Instead such children develop exaggerated views of their own importance. Because only children spend a great deal of time alone, they may develop rich imaginations. Without models or competitors, they seldom learn to share or to compete for attention. Only children may develop lifestyles that are characterized by timidity and overdependence on others. They are likely to be deficient in social interest.

Adler (1937) believed that a person's perceived role within a family constellation was more important than the birth order itself. Adlerians examine the number of years between siblings and claim that such distance may take on the role of birth place. For instance, if there are three siblings, with the oldest being 10 years of age, the second 8 years, and the third 1 year old, this family constellation resembles a family with an older and younger sibling (first two children), and the youngest child as being more akin to that of an only child.

Research on Adlerian birth order theory is mixed. Although Adler claimed that the second borns were the highest achievers, research has found that the firstborns achieve the most and are often more intelligent than the other siblings. Of the 23 American astronauts sent into outer space, 21 were firstborns, and the other 2 were only children. Firstborns are also overrepresented at Harvard, Yale, and Princeton universities (Sulloway, 1997).

A major contribution of birth order research is that it has helped psychologists understand why brothers and sisters within the same family are no more similar in personality than are those from different families. According to Sulloway (1997), the family is not a shared environment but a set of niches that provide siblings with different outlooks on life. The personalities of siblings vary within the same family because they adopt different strategies to achieve parental favor. Adlerians believe that independence training for children is critical. Never do for your children what they can do for themselves. Children who are dependent are demanding.

Does birth order make any difference in how we develop as individuals? In general, the answer is yes. An individual's birth order position within the family has been linked to differences in achievement, intelligence, attitudes, and such behaviors as juvenile delinquency, mental illness, and success or failure in marriage (Sulloway, 1997). One research study reported that firstborn individuals are overrepresented in the college population compared with their siblings (Maddi, 1996). Belmont and Marolla (1973) studied nearly 400,000 young men from the Netherlands and found a positive relationship between birth order and nonverbal intellectual aptitude. Likewise, Zweigenhaft's (1975) study found that firstborns were overrepresented as members of the U.S. Congress.

Inner Reflections

In working with clients, how important is it for you to assess the ramifications of their birth order?

Make two arguments for and two arguments against examining a client's birth order position.

Adler's Theory of Life Tasks

Adler (1963) considered the desire to experience a heightened sense of belongingness with other people as a universal drive. Our drive for belongingness motivates us to become involved in a series of **life tasks** that are central to our psychological development and mental health (Adler, 1959a). Three life tasks contained in Adler's theory of individual psychology are as follows:

1. Developing friendships with others

2. Realizing a loving relationship with another person

3. Working in a satisfying and meaningful occupation

Theory of Healthy Mental Development

Adlerians postulate that children feel they have to stake out territory that will allow them to excel, to become popular, or to be a real man or a real woman. If children evaluate their own abilities and believe that they can achieve their desired places, they will pursue positive behaviors and have positive mental health. Conversely, if they feel that they cannot find their places, they will become discouraged and may engage in disturbing behavior in an effort to find their place. The maladjusted child is not "sick" but rather discouraged. Dreikurs (1957) placed the goals of the misbehaving child into four categories: (1) attention getting, (2) power seeking, (3) revenge taking, and (4) declaring deficiency or defeat.

Adlerians observe that individuals' health is significantly influenced by their ability to form and maintain friendships and meaningful relationships with others. People who experience difficulty establishing and maintaining meaningful friendships are often at risk for depression, frustration, anger, and social alienation. Mental health is also linked with encouragement; whereas poor mental functioning is associated with discouragement. Adler observed that we cling to the mental, emotional, and behavior habits we developed in childhood to cope with feelings of inferiority. Because we interpret our experiences in terms of our lifestyles (or habitual ways of viewing the world), we invent excuses to support our world perceptions. Common excuses are "Nothing ever works out for me," or "Nobody ever really loved me."

Theory of Maladaptive Behavior

Adlerian psychotherapy posits that people seeking therapy should not be considered sick, but rather they are discouraged, and therefore, they need to be encouraged to develop more social interests and a more effective lifestyle. According to Adler (1959a), an individual's underdeveloped social interest is the one factor that underlies all types of psychological maladjustments. Adlerian psychology conceptualized maladjustment as the individual's development of exaggerated feelings of inferiority and exaggerated striving for superiority (Adler, 1930). Adler equated psychopathology with a feeling of discouragement, a feeling of hopelessness, and the belief that one's world is not going to change for the better. Maladaptive behavior develops when individuals become discouraged or when they encounter disappointing circumstances. When people lose the courage to face demanding life situations, they move from a position of inferiority to inferiority complex (Adler, 1926/1972). They become unconsciously convinced of their inferiority, and as a consequence, they develop abnormal behavior to divert attention from their difficulties (Ansbacher, 1992).

Individuals develop maladjusted or disordered behavior primarily because (1) they have greater numbers of feelings of inferiority than are present in the average population and (2) they develop accompanying sets of inappropriate compensatory responses to offset their deep-seated feelings of inferiority. Although both the normal and the maladjusted person manifest feelings of inferiority, these feelings are exaggerated in the maladjusted individual. Adler believed that poor mental health results only when people *behave* as if they are inferior.

The seeds for psychopathology are sown early in life, especially within the family and within our sibling relationships. Developing adequate social interest is critical to individuals' positive mental health. Adler considered the mother as the primary person for teaching children social interest. A mother demonstrates nurturing, cooperation, and social interest in general when she nurses the baby at her breast (Adler, 1926/1964). Mothers help their children extend positive relationships to the father and to others within the family. Mothers who fail to show sufficient social interest while parenting their children risk raising young people who become maladaptive in their interpersonal relationships because they lack sufficient social interest.

An important physical deficiency or a severe illness, especially when one is young, may also bring out strong feelings of helplessness. Problems occur when such children are not able to compensate adequately for inferiority feelings. Abnormal behavior results when individuals develop a massive sense of inferiority in early childhood such that they become discouraged about life. In an effort to compensate, they develop inappropriate patterns of behavior, show an unrealistic striving for superiority over others, develop a superiority complex, or create an exaggerated opinion of their own abilities and accomplishments.

Adler used a number of characteristics to describe the maladjusted or neurotic individual (Ansbacher & Ansbacher, 1956). The neurotic person overcompensates for feeling insecure. For instance, the overindulged child may become self-centered; the neglected child may seek revenge against society. Neurotic approaches to life include a distancing attitude and a hesitating attitude. A person who uses a distancing attitude attempts to protect himself or herself by keeping others at bay, perhaps even becoming overly formal in conversations. An individual who develops a neurotic hesitating attitude is never quite sure of himself or herself; therefore, he or she hesitates in making important decisions about life in an effort to avoid any feelings of inferiority.

Safeguarding Tendencies

The neurotic individual is inclined to be rigid in thought, to see life in dichotomous black-and-white terms, to have excessive fears, to vacillate, and to be dependent rather than independent. What distinguished one maladjusted person from another was the safeguarding tendencies each individual acquired to protect himself or herself from feelings of inferiority. Adler used the term *safeguarding tendencies* to describe his belief that people create patterns of behavior to protect their exaggerated feelings of self-esteem against public disgrace. His concept of safeguarding tendencies is similar to Freud's concept of defense mechanisms. Whereas Freud maintained that defense mechanisms operate unconsciously to protect the ego against anxiety, Adler asserted that safeguarding tendencies are primarily conscious. The type of safeguarding tendency chosen differentiated the type of disorder the individual developed. Adler considered an individual's selection of a safeguarding tendency as a creative act. Some common safeguarding tendencies are excuses, aggression, and withdrawal.

Excuses form the most common type of safeguarding tendency. Typically, people express excuses with phrases such as "Yes, but" or "If only." In the "Yes, but" excuse, people initially state what they claim they would like to do—"I would like to go back to complete my degree"—and then they follow this that sounds good with an excuse—"but I don't have the time, enough money," and so on. The "If only" excuse is similar to the "Yes, but" one; however, the person usually blames someone else for his or her not completing the desired act.

Aggression is another common safeguarding tendency. According to Adler (1959a), people use aggression to safeguard their exaggerated superiority complexes. Safeguarding by aggression may take the form of depreciation or accusation. Depreciation is the tendency to undervalue another person's accomplishments while overvaluing one's own. Criticism and gossip are aggressive behaviors: "The only reason, Jennifer got the promotion is that she slept with the boss."

Withdrawal is another safeguarding tendency. An individual may safeguard himself or herself from another by putting distance between the two. Adler (1959a) outlined four types of safeguarding using withdrawal: (1) moving backward (the tendency to safeguard one's fictional goal of superiority by reverting to a more secure period of life), (2) standing still (people who stand still do not move in any direction, and they insulate themselves against any threat of failure), (3) hesitating when faced with difficult problems (procrastinations give them the excuse, "It's too late now"), and (4) constructing obstacles (building a straw house to show that one can knock it down).

Everyone develops some form of safeguarding tendency. Safeguarding tendencies can become neurotic or self-defeating because their goals of self-protection and personal superiority block them from obtaining authentic feelings of self-esteem. Adler was convinced that most compulsive behaviors are attempts to waste time. He considered compulsive hand washing, retracing one's steps, behaving in an obsessive orderly fashion, and leaving work incomplete as examples of hesitation. He believed that people construct straw houses to protect their self-esteem and prestige.

THE THERAPEUTIC PROCESS

The therapeutic process for Adlerian psychotherapy is usually time-limited, supportive therapy focused on specific problems. It is designed to bring about moderate insight, attitude change, and behavioral change. Adlerian counseling may focus on parenting, marital relationships, and career choice and development. Adlerian therapy helps clients understand how they have had a role in creating their problems and how they can take responsibility for creating change. When mistaken goals are identified, clients can choose to pursue more appropriate goals. The overall goal of Adlerian psychotherapy is to help a person develop from a partially functioning person into a person who lives life more cooperatively, more courageously, and with a greater sense of contribution to his or her community. Put in an alternate fashion, the overall goal of Adlerian therapy is to increase the individual's feeling of community.

The Therapeutic Relationship

A major goal of therapy is to encourage clients and to help them feel that change is possible. Adlerian therapists view the therapeutic process as a collaborative partnership based on respect, parity, trust, and cooperation. The first principle of Adlerian therapy is to establish and maintain an accepting, caring, and cooperative relationship with the client. The therapeutic relationship is established by reflecting accurately clients' feelings and by communicating a deep understanding of the clients' lifestyles. Clients learn that their life goals and their lifestyles are understandable. Therapists encourage clients to develop social interest or an active concern for the well-being of others (Dinkmeyer et al., 1990).

To symbolize that their relationship is one of equals, the Adlerian therapist and the client sit facing each other with their chairs at the same level. The therapist informs the client that people actively create their own problems based on their faulty perceptions or their inadequate learning. What has been learned can be unlearned; the therapist imparts the strong belief that the client is capable of change. Despite the egalitarian focus, Adlerian therapy also takes on a psychoeducational atmosphere. Adler accepted advice giving under certain conditions.

Goals of Therapy

The goals of Adlerian counseling are centered on helping clients develop healthy lifestyles. The therapist talks about what a healthy lifestyle is and assists clients to overcome feelings of inferiority (Oberst & Stewart, 2003). An unhealthy lifestyle is self-centered and based on mistaken goals. Adlerian psychotherapy has four major goals: (1) establishing and maintaining a good client–therapist relationship; (2) uncovering the client's dynamics, which include his or her lifestyle, goals,

the dynamics of his or her family constellations, childhood illnesses, and the basic mistakes included in his or her lifestyle; (3) developing interpretations that culminate in client insight; and (4) reorientating the client (Oberst & Stewart, 2003).

Adler declared that people can change their lifestyles and rid themselves of mistaken beliefs. He underscored again and again that individuals' interpretations of facts were far more important than the facts themselves. Adler used three entrance gates to an individual's mental life: (1) his or her birth order position in the family of origin, (2) his or her first childhood memory, and (3) his or her dreams.

Role of the Therapist

Adlerian therapists establish a friendly relationship between equals. Adler believed that the client and the therapist should collaborate to bring about change. To demonstrate client and therapist equality, Adler was one of the first therapists to leave the couch and to face the client directly. Moreover, Adlerian therapists are often considered to be educators. They encourage their clients to use their talents to help others—to develop a social interest. Believing that their clients are discouraged when they begin therapy, Adlerians strive to create a supportive and encouraging therapeutic relationship. Unlike Freudians, Adlerian counselors tend to be talkative and active in therapy. They try to assess the reasons clients have their particular ways of thinking and behaving. They strive to develop and broaden their understanding of their clients' lifestyles. Therapists discuss clients' basic beliefs and how such beliefs have influenced their lifestyles. Even though Adlerian counselors are empathic and caring, they confront clients with their basic mistakes, misplaced goals, and self-defeating behaviors (Watts, 2003a). Such confrontations help clients deal with the contradictions in their lives and to replace mistaken goals. In their role as educators and collaborators, Adlerian therapists encourage clients to develop new alternatives for reaching their revised goals.

Adlerian therapists take a nonpathological view of clients' difficulties. They avoid labeling clients with the traditional medical model's diagnoses. Instead, they help them better understand and to modify their life stories. As Disque and Bitter (1998) point out, "when individuals develop a life story that they find limiting and problem saturated, the goal is to free them from that story in favor of a preferred and equally viable alternative story" (p. 434).

Role of the Client

The client's role is one of equal collaborator in discovering mistaken goals, inferiority feelings, and superiority feelings (Watts, 2003a). Clients work to become more courageous and self-confident in their lives and believe that solutions can be found to life's challenges. Clients seek actively to find solutions to their presenting problems. They understand that the true solutions to their issues reside within themselves rather than within the therapist. Clients may be given simple homework assignments to complete and to bring to therapy (Watts, 2003a).

Phases of Therapy

Adlerian therapists are concerned with understanding the unique, private beliefs and strategies that reveal our private logic and mistaken beliefs. Counseling can be short-term, intensive work to increase social interest, to encourage a greater sense of responsibility for our behavior, and to support behavioral change. Adlerian counseling helps individuals correct mistakes in perception and private logic that they make in their attempts to fit into social relations and to overcome feelings of inferiority (Watts, 2003b). Once individuals have adopted "mistaken goals," they construct other misconceptions to support the "faulty logic."

Phase 1: Establishing the Therapeutic Relationship

During the beginning phase of therapy, clinicians work to establish a positive therapeutic relationship. They may use humor and small talk to establish a therapeutic alliance. The first therapeutic goal is to help the client become a more cooperative person, which starts with his or her learning how to cooperate in therapy. If the client's cooperation is lacking, the therapist can point tactfully to this. In the beginning, the client may need to express a great deal of distress with minimal amount of interruption from the therapist. In response, the therapist offers genuine warmth, empathy, acceptance, and understanding. The therapist must be able to feel the client's distress (e.g., hopelessness) without feeling sorry for the client. The therapist must not only be able to empathize with the client but also be able to remain neutral in order to discuss possible improvements in their situations.

Phase 2: Uncovering the Client's Dynamics

Assessment and Diagnosis. An assessment of the client's functioning is divided into two parts. First, the therapist assesses the client's lifestyle. Second, the therapist assesses and interprets the client's **early recollections**. This search for clinical understanding of clients is called a lifestyle investigation or lifestyle assessment, and it usually involves both individualized and structured exercises. Adlerian therapists begin by asking clients to tell their life stories. Because we can never fully capture our entire life story, the events and people we choose to mention in our brief summary are those who have become significant in our lives. The therapist listens for themes in clients' life stories, such as themes of achievement or failure.

Adlerian therapists make a comprehensive assessment of clients' functioning. Using an interview questionnaire, therapists gather information about clients' family constellations and lifestyles. After analyzing and summarizing this information, the therapist gains an understanding of the client's early life. Adler used a structured interview to assess clients. In his book *Social Interest: A Challenge to*

Mankind (1938), Adler provided the following outline for an interview:

1. What are your complaints?

2. What was your situation when you first noticed your symptoms?

3. What is your situation now?

4. What is your occupation?

5. From your perspective, describe your parents' character and their health. If not alive, what illness caused their death? What was their relation to you?

6. How many brothers and sisters have you? What is your position in the birth order? What is their attitude toward you? How do they get along in life? Do they also have any illness?

7. Who was your father's or your mother's favorite child? What kind of up-bringing did you have?

8. Inquire for signs of pampering in childhood (timidity, shyness, difficulties in forming friendships, disorderliness).

9. What illnesses did you have in childhood and what was your attitude to them?

10. What are your earliest childhood recollections?

11. What do you fear, or what did you fear the most?

12. What is your attitude toward the opposite sex? What was it in childhood and later years?

13. What occupation would have interested you the most, and if you did not adopt it, why not?

14. Is the patient ambitious, sensitive, and inclined to outburst of temper, pedantic, domineering, shy, or impatient?

15. What sort of persons are around you at present? Are they impatient, bad-tempered, or affectionate?

16. How do you sleep?

17. What dreams do you have? (Of falling, flying, recurrent dreams, prophetic, about examinations, missing a train?)

18. What illnesses are there in your family background? (pp. 408–409)

Analysis of Clients' Basic Mistakes. After Adlerian therapists have obtained a summary of their client's early recollections and lifestyle, they can examine the client's basic mistakes. As noted earlier, most of us develop basic mistakes as we develop our lifestyles. During childhood, we construct reasons and principles regarding what we experience; these principles may be purely or partly fictional. Mosak (2005) lists five basic mistakes that people commonly make:

1. *Overgeneralizations:* "People are no good." "You have to be careful of not getting too close to people."

2. *False or impossible goals of security:* "I must please everyone, if I am to be loved."

3. *Misperceptions of life and life's demands:* "I never get any breaks."

4. *Minimization or denial of one's worth:* "I'm stupid."

5. *Faulty values:* "I must be first, regardless of who gets hurt in the process."

Early Recollections as an Assessment Technique. Adlerians also use clients' earliest memories as a major assessment tool. The therapist asks the client to recall his or her earliest memories, the age at which the event was remembered, and the feelings connected with the recollections. According to Adler, we select memories that coincide with our basic beliefs about ourselves and the rest of the world. It makes little difference whether or not these memories are real events or fantasies. Our adult

> ### Inner Reflections
>
> According to Adler, we all have mistaken beliefs about life and ourselves.
>
> What basic beliefs do you have?
>
> What impact have they had on your life, or on relating to others, and on your self-fulfillment?

Think of a headline that captures the spirit of your earliest memory—for example, "Talented Child Makes Her Mark."

What would your headline say? How do you feel about this headline?

lives revolve around what we perceived as having happened. Our earliest memories provide the therapist with an understanding of our mistaken beliefs, social interests, and future actions.

Questions used to reveal earliest recollections include "Think back as far as you can and tell me your earliest childhood memory." After surfacing a memory, the counselor searches for additional information about the memory by asking questions such as the following:

- What part of the memory stands out most in your mind?
- What are you feeling as you recall this memory?
- Where is this feeling located in your body?
- Are you an observer or an active participant in the memory?
- What are you trying to convey to the world with this memory?

Additional questions related to early recollections include the following:

- Who is not present?
- How are different people portrayed?
- What is the world like (e.g., friendly, hostile, cooperative, sad)?
- How would you describe your role (helping, passive, angry, and dependent)?
- What outcomes take place in the memory?
- How would you describe your primary social attitude ("I" or "we")?
- Describe in a single sentence the underlying theme in your memory ("Life is . . .").

Memories of danger or punishment suggest a tendency toward hostility, and memories of a sibling's birth indicate dethronement issues.

Analysis of Clients' Dreams. Adler believed that dreams were a way of dealing with our insecurities. Our dreams help us try out strategies for overcoming our limitations, or they may represent a type of wish fulfillment. Dreams can serve as a bridge to what we want. Adler believed that there is a correlation between the number of dreams you have and the problems in your daily life. The more problems you have, the more dreams you are likely to have. Conversely, the fewer dreams you have, the fewer problems you have and the more psychologically healthy you are (Watts, 2003a).

Adlerian dream analysis involves examining the parts of a dream and analyzing what problems or inferiorities they might represent. For example, a dream about falling could symbolize a fear of flying, especially if the dreamer is soon to fly or climb a mountain. The dream could also represent a "fall from grace" or loss of face and social standing. If the person is caught by an angel, it might have religious or spiritual meaning or simply refer to trusting and relying on one special person. By revealing to us our innermost fears and our preferred strategies for dealing with problems, dreams reveal a great deal about our personality and style of life.

Adler asserted that control, power, and motivation drives behavior. From his perspective, our striving for perfection and need for control cause us to do the things we do. Adler believed that dreams are a way of overcompensating for the shortcomings in our waking lives. For example, if you are unable to stand up to your boss during the day at work, you may find it easier to lash out at him within the comfort and safety of your dream. Dreams offer satisfaction that is more socially acceptable.

From the Adlerian perspective, dreaming is purposive. Adlerians insist that dreams prepare clients to solve their current problems or to overcome their present circumstances by rehearsing them for potential future actions. The dream function is to connect present problems or conflicts to future goal attainment (Mosak, 2005).

Adler admonished therapists not to become too involved in uncovering common symbols when interpreting dream material, because the symbols of one client's dreams may represent entirely different things from the same symbols in another client's dreams. He did, however, refer to a few common dream symbols, such as flying (moving or striving from below to above), falling (moving or striving from above to below), being chased (an expression of inferiority or weakness in relation to others), and being unclothed in public (fear of disclosure or being found out). The emotional tone of a dream is highly significant, perhaps more so than the symbols.

Integration and Summary of Adlerian Uncovering and Assessment. Once the therapist has developed materials from the client questionnaire and interview, he or she prepares integrated summaries of the information that contain the client's subjective experience and life story; a summary of family constellation and developmental data; and a summary of early recollections, personal strengths, basic mistakes, and coping strategies (Oberst & Stewart, 2003). The therapist gives the client copies of these summaries, and they are discussed in the session with the client having the right to modify different points.

Phase 3: Client Insight and Self-Understanding

The third phase of counseling is the insight and self-understanding phase. Insight represents the client's understanding of the purposive nature of his or her behavior and the mistaken beliefs that sustained it. Therapists promote client insight by ordinary communications, dreams, fantasies, behavior, symptoms, or the client–therapist interactions. During interpretations, the emphasis is on discovering purpose rather than the cause of a client behavior or action. Adlerians posit that self-understanding results when therapists help clients make conscious hidden lifestyles and goals. The therapist and client together build interpretations from information presented during assessment. These collaborative interpretive efforts give clients insight to their issues.

To help make an interpretation acceptable to the client, the therapist usually presents it only as a possibility to be considered rather than as a fact (Slavik & King, 2007). The therapist might say, "Is it possible that . . . ?" or, "Do you think it might be . . . ?" When the interpretation is on target, clients are encouraged to view their behavior from a different perspective. They may accept the validity of the interpretation, deny it, or suggest an alternative interpretation. A client's responses to accurate interpretations of behavior may take place with a reflexive quick smile, glance, or nod of the head or a verbal statement, such as "Exactly" or "You got it."

Good interpretations provide clues regarding the purpose of a client's behavior. They should help a client answer the following questions: "What life task is my symptom allowing me to avoid?" And "What price am I paying for this symptom?" Adler was convinced that clients' symptoms had an underlying purpose. Client insight may also entail an analysis of the client's basic mistakes and how they are affecting his or her life. Adler believed that insight alone was insufficient for successful therapy. There must be some change in client behavior.

Phase 4: Reorientation

The final phase of Adlerian therapy is called *reorientation* (Carlson, Watts, & Maniacci, 2005). The purpose of the reorientation phase of therapy is to help the client gain or regain the courage to face life's challenges—to put insight into action and to redirect goals. The majority of the counseling techniques are used during the reorientation phase. For instance, a client may discover that it is exciting rather than threatening to take risks. With the collaboration of the therapist, the client decides what behaviors she will keep to help her reach her goals and which she will discard. During the reorientation phase, the client is encouraged to develop more social interest in others. Throughout this phase of counseling, the dominant technique used is encouragement. The client has learned to feel and function better.

Therapy Techniques

Adlerian therapists use a number of techniques in working with their clients. Some of the more popular techniques include encouragement, the question, the push button, behaving "as if," catching yourself, task setting, and others.

Adlerians maintain that time limits must be set with clients. Sessions with children usually last for 30 minutes, while those with adults last for 45 to 50 minutes. Near the end of the session, therapists do not bring up any new material. Instead, they may summarize the interview with the client's assistance (Slavik & King, 2007). Homework assignments are usually made near the end of the therapy session.

Offering Encouragement

Encouragement is both a principle and a technique that pervades all of Adlerian therapy; however, it is particularly important when working with children. Adlerians assert that encouragement is necessary for children's healthy development. Children become what they are encouraged to become (Dinkmeyer & Dreikurs, 2000). Therapists use encouragement in working with clients when they express faith and belief in them. The encouraging therapist does the following:

- Values the client as he or she is
- Demonstrates faith in the client
- Tries to build a positive self-concept within the client
- Gives the client recognition for his or her efforts
- Concentrates on the strengths and assets of the client

Asking "The Question"

Adler proposed asking clients **The Question**, which may be paraphrased as "If I could magically eliminate your symptom immediately, what would be different in your life?" Or "What would be different if you were well?" Questions such as these help clients get to the heart of what they would like to see changed in their lives. For instance, a client might reply, "I would be a wife who spent more time with her husband," or "I would quit my job and start my own small business." Typically, clients are asked this question at the beginning of counseling. Solution-focused therapists have relabeled this technique the "miracle question" (Carlson et al., 2005).

Acting "As If"

Clients who state that they would do thus and so if only they possessed certain qualities are encouraged to act for a short period of time *as if* they possessed the qualities they believe they lack. They are instructed to behave **as if** they possess a certain behavior, and they are encouraged to try on new behaviors and new roles. A therapist might tell a client to act as if it is impossible to fail in her new business (Oberst & Stewart, 2003). A male client who was afraid of asking a woman out might be instructed to act as if he possessed the confidence necessary to ask a woman out for a date and to further ask two women out for dinner. The "as if" technique is based on the belief that clients must change their behaviors to elicit different responses from others.

Using the Push-Button Technique

Adler would ask clients to imagine pushing a button. Then he directed them to picture a pleasant experience in as much detail and vividness as possible. Next, Adler requested clients to make note of the pleasant memory that made them feel good as they engaged in the imaginary push-button exercise. Finally, Adler would give the same directions—only this time asking clients to imagine a negative experience in as much detail as possible. After repeating this technique several times with pleasant and negative experiences (Carlson et al., 2005), Adler told clients that they can exercise inner control regarding how they feel at any moment by controlling what they think about.

Catching Oneself

Catching oneself permits clients to become aware of their self-destructive behaviors or thoughts without feeling guilty about them. For instance, when trying to change nonfunctional behavior, some clients may revert back to their old behavior out of sheer habit. Clients are told to "catch themselves" when they are just about ready to revert back to their old ways and to substitute the new behavior. If a client blows up at his wife when she spends money on gifts, he catches himself in the angry mode and chooses a different response. The goal is to help clients change maladaptive old habits.

The Midas Technique

This technique entails exaggerating the client's irrational demands. Based on the myth of King Midas, who was granted his wish that everything he touched would turn to gold, the Midas technique helps clients see that their wishes, when taken to their logical extreme, can be absurd. Clients laugh at their own wishes and positions taken.

Pleasing Someone

This technique is designed to increase clients' social interest. The therapist suggests that the client do something nice for someone else. Adler believed that clients spent too much time obsessing about their own problems. Clients can become stuck in their own "selfness." The therapist might recommend that a client volunteer his or her service and have no expectation of a reward other than that which comes from serving another person. The technique of pleasing someone helps put the client back into society.

Socratic Questioning

Adler used the Socratic method of leading an individual to insight through a series of questions (Stein & Edwards, 1998). During the early phases of psychotherapy, the therapist uses questions to collect relevant information, clarify client meaning, and verify client feelings. In the middle phase of therapy, the questions become more penetrating because they seek to uncover the deeper structures of the client's private logic, hidden feelings, and unconscious goals. In the latter phase of therapy, the Socratic method is used to evaluate the impact of the client's new direction. The Socratic style makes the client responsible for his or her own conclusions.

Task Setting

Adlerian therapists give homework assignments to give clients practice with a behavior. By using this technique, the client finds threatening situations less and less frightening. A therapist might give a depressed client the task of doing something pleasant each day on a "pleasant event" schedule. To promote clients' social interest, therapists often assign community service homework, such as volunteering at a homeless shelter. The tasks tend to be relatively simple and are set at a level at which clients cannot fail.

Creating Images

Adler used to describe clients with a single phrase, such as the beggar as king. Currently, Adlerians use images to describe clients. The client is informed of the image such as the woman with buried treasure, the complainer, the excuse maker, and so forth. In describing the creating images technique, Mosak and Maniacci (2011) relate the story of a client who came to therapy because he was impotent sexually. The therapist commented that he had never seen an impotent dog. The client responded that "The dog just does what he's supposed to do without worrying about whether he'll be able to perform." "The therapist suggested that at his next attempt at sexual intercourse, before he made any advances, he should smile and say inwardly, "Bow wow." The following week, the patient informed the members of his group, "I bow wowed" (Mosak & Maniacci, 2011, p. 92).

Brainstorming

After helping the client identify mistakes in thinking, Adlerian counselors brainstorm with clients' alternative beliefs and convictions. For example, in place of "I never get what I want," a client might substitute "Sometimes I get what I want." The latter conviction promotes healthy development.

"Spitting in the Client's Soup"

Adler partially borrowed the underlying concept of this technique after he had observed boys in a private school dining hall. The boys would spit in their neighbor's soup because the person would refuse to eat the soup after someone spat in it. Adler's intent in using this technique is to spit in the client's soup of excuses and hidden goals. When therapists reveal the hidden purpose of a client's symptom or behavior, they deprive him or her of the secondary gains that the symptoms provide. Similar to the boys in the dining hall, clients may decide not to eat the soup after the therapist has revealed the hidden purposes behind their behaviors. A mother who enjoys making her daughter feel inferior may continue to do so even after the behavior is pointed out; however, the reward for the mother's behavior has diminished considerably.

Paradoxical Intention

Even though paradox (a seemingly contradictory statement or situation) has been a part of human condition since time immemorial, it is only relatively recently that paradoxical interventions have been applied to therapy. Adler is usually considered to be the first theorist in Western civilization to write about paradoxical strategies and to use them during individual therapy (Mozdzierz, Machitelli, & Lisiecki, 1976). Adler believed that the therapist should use strategies to overcome the opposition of the neurotic patient, whom he conceptualized as always ready to pick a fight. The therapist actually helps the client overcome his own opposition by encouraging him to do that which he is complaining about. A client tried to undermine Adler's efforts as a therapist by asking him if any of his clients ever died while he was working with them. Relating this incident, Ansbacher and Ansbacher (1956) quote Adler's meeting with the client: "A patient once asked me, smiling, 'Has anyone ever taken his life while being treated by you?' I answered him, "Not yet, but I am prepared for this to happen at any time" (p. 339).

Adler's therapeutic tactics can be considered paradoxical because they were unexpected and contrary to the client's expectations about the nature of psychotherapy—specifically that therapists work to change clients. Some of the specific paradoxical strategies Adler used were statements such as "never do anything you don't like" or "don't stop worrying." In other words, paradoxical interventions can be used to encourage a client symptom or to give him permission to do something. For instance, a client might come to an Adlerian to get rid of his stammering. Instead, the therapist would paradoxically encourage the client to stammer when the therapist told him to do so as a method of cure. The client practices stammering under the therapist's direction and the therapist should explain that stammering not only is not defective speech and is not deplorable but rather that it is a necessary accomplishment. Adler believed in asking clients to exaggerate or to amplify the target behavior to show the client how ridiculous the behavior is.

> ### Inner Reflection
>
> What parts of Adlerian therapy, if any, would you like to integrate into your own approach to psychotherapy?

Adler and Parenting Style

Adler's theory of personality and therapy had an important impact on the development of good parenting skills. As discussed earlier, he identified two parenting styles—pampering and neglect—that were destined to cause problems in adulthood (Dinkmeyer, McKay, Dinkmeyer, & McKay, 1997). Pampering—overprotecting children, giving them too much attention, and protecting them from the harsh difficulties of life—results in children who are poorly prepared to deal with the realities of everyday living, are highly dependent, and are apt to find it hard to make decisions on their own. They may think that things should be given to them, and they may not develop a strong desire to be independent and to overcome inferiorities. Pampered children may not learn self-reliance; they approach life, work, and marriage from a self-centered orientation. They grow up to be adults who try to resolve their problems by making unrealistic demands on other people and by expecting everyone to respond positively to their desires (Stone, 1993).

The neglected child as an adult becomes the opposite of the pampered child. The neglected child (one who was given very little support) grows up fearing the world, distrusting others, and experiencing difficulty in forming close interpersonal relationships (Dinkmeyer et al., 1997). When parents fail to provide sufficient love and care for their children, the net result is that such children view adults negatively. Their inferiority gets manifested by suspicious behavior, isolation, and maliciousness (Adler, 1958a). Although both the pampered and the neglected child received different kinds of parental treatment, the end results of the treatment may be the same: children's feelings of inadequacy.

Many of Adler's ideas about good parenting techniques have become commonplace knowledge. Successful parenting is based on the following aspects:

- *Mutual respect:* Parents who show respect for children teach them to respect themselves and others.

- *Encouragement:* Encouragement suggests faith in and respect for children as they are, rather than as we want them to be.
- *Natural and logical consequences:* Consequences permit the child to experience and learn from the results of his or her own behavior. For instance, a child refuses to wear a coat while it is raining; he gets wet.
- *Setting freedom and limits for children:* Adlerians maintain that children need and want limits and that those limits should be expanded as the child ages. Part of the role of parents is to filter out negative influences in their children's lives. Reasonable limits make a child feel protected by his or her parents. Children accept limits better when they help make the rules through a process of discussion that includes a statement containing the reasons for the rules or limits (e.g., safety). Parents must enforce limits consistently.

RESEARCH AND EVALUATION
Multicultural Positives

If Adler were alive today, most likely he would garner a great deal of support from multiculturalists. He stressed the importance of the social world of the client, and he placed a great deal of emphasis on the positive benefits of creating social interest in individuals. In fact, he postulated that without sufficient social interests, most people would have impaired or unhealthy development. A number of Adler's other concepts have found significant support in the multicultural literature, including (1) the importance of the cultural context of clients' lives, (2) the focus on trying to understand individuals in terms of their core goals and lifestyles, and (3) the emphasis on prevention and on helping clients develop their strengths or assets. Adlerian therapy is based on understanding a client's culture and worldview rather than trying to fit the client into the diagnostic categories of the medical model.

Adlerian therapy has a strong multicultural foundation because it stresses the importance of encouragement and empowerment of client. Adlerians oftentimes have clinical success with populations that are difficult to reach. For instance,

Sapp (2010) observed that Adlerian therapy represents a strengths-based model—this is effective with at-risk youth. Moreover, the Adlerian focus on social interest with an emphasis on helping others, belonging, and the collective spirit resonate with the traditional value systems of ethnic minority groups that are more group than individual oriented. Adler's emphasis on the equality of women can be compared with the thrust of contemporary multicultural, feminist, and social justice counseling advocates.

Furthermore, multiculturalism involves an appreciation of the role of religion or spirituality in the lives of clients (Mosak, 2005). Whereas most psychotherapy schools have not given much attention to religion or spirituality in clinical practice, Adlerian therapy has been receptive to religious and spiritual issues. Adler believed that religion was a manifestation of a person's social interest, and he gave his support to religions that stressed people's responsibility to one another. Contemporary Adlerians also view spirituality as one of the major life tasks because "each of us must deal with the problems of defining the nature of the universe, the existence, and nature of God, and how to relate to these concepts" (Mosak, 2005, p. 55).

After analyzing various theories of counseling, Arciniega and Newlon (1999) concluded that Adlerian theory has the most promise for addressing multicultural issues. According to them, Adlerian counseling is compatible with the values of many racial, cultural, and ethnic groups because it stresses the importance of understanding the individual in a familial and sociocultural context. Adlerian assessment is heavily concentrated on the structure and dynamics of clients' families. Moreover, Adlerian counselors endeavor to be sensitive to lifestyle and gender differences. Adler was one of the first psychologists to advocate for women's equality. The Adlerian approach is democratic and honors the belief that all people are created equal.

Multicultural Blind Spots

In spite of its early multicultural focus, Adlerian therapy does have some cultural blind spots, which include the theory's emphasis on individual choice, which may be offensive to individuals who come from cultures that are oriented toward the group rather than the individual. Likewise, its egalitarian relationship between the therapist and the client may cause difficulties with clients from cultures that view therapists as the experts. Some non-Western cultures view the therapist as an expert, and they may desire to be instructed what to do or how to remedy their situation.

Similar to other Western theories of psychotherapy, Adlerians place the focus of change and responsibility on the self—on the individual. Cultures that have a group orientation or a collectivist orientation may consider such a "self" focus as being inappropriate for their group. Native American culture, African American culture, Latino culture, and Asian culture tend to value collectivism over individualism (Paniagua, 2001). Therefore, when a therapist emphasizes the self, it may create internal conflict that cannot be easily understood by those who have been raised in individualist cultures—primarily European cultures. For instance, it is easier for members of the majority White American culture to focus on the self because they have been socialized to practice being individuals. It is a complex process to deal with modifying collective values and beliefs and to adjust to a way of balancing one's self desires with collective values. Moreover, another limitation of Adlerian theory is that its emphasis on individual responsibility may militate against the notion of environmental constraints, which is sometimes the case for members of oppressed minority groups. One cannot accept responsibility for the effects on one's life because of another person's racism or sexism.

In addition, some cultures (e.g., Latino, African American) have prohibitions about revealing personal information and data that might be gathered when the Adlerian therapist engages in conducting a lifestyle assessment. A therapist who tries to collect too much information about a Latino family may be viewed as threatening and suspect (Paniagua, 2001).

Contributions of Adlerian Therapy

Adler once stated that he was more concerned that his theory would survive than he was concerned about whether or not his name would be linked with the theory. To a certain extent, Adler prophesized somewhat the future of his own theory of psychotherapy in that bits and pieces of his theory have been incorporated by the various schools of psychotherapy. Commenting on Adler's influence on contemporary schools of psychotherapy, Henri Ellenberger (1970) asserted, "It would not be easy to find another author from which so much has been borrowed from all sides without acknowledgement than Adler" (p. 645). Some psychotherapy theorists have, however, credited Adler with contributing to and influencing their work. For instance, Karen Horney wrote about "neurotic ambition" and the "need for perfection"—basic concepts articulated by Adler. Fritz Wittels (1939) once wrote that neo-Freudians should more properly be called "neo-Adlerians."

Adlerian concepts or principles can also be found in the humanistic writings of Carl Rogers who like Adler proposed that people are self-consistent, creative, and capable of change. Rogers (1951) posited that the organism reacts as an organized whole to the phenomenal field, that the best vantage point for understanding a person's behavior is from that person's internal frame of reference, and that, further, the organism has one basic tendency and striving—to actualized and maintain the experiencing organism.

Furthermore, Albert Ellis acknowledged his indebtedness to Adler. What Adler called basic mistakes, Ellis renamed irrational beliefs or attitudes. Both Alder and Ellis put forth the idea that our emotions are created and maintained by our thoughts. Both Adler and Ellis used intervention tactics that encouraged clients to assume responsibility for their own lives. Ellis (1957) wrote about the major difference between Adlerian therapy and his rational emotive therapy. He asserted,

> Where Adler writes, therefore, that "all my efforts are devoted towards increasing the social interest of the patient," the rational therapist would prefer to say, "Most of my efforts are devoted towards increasing the self-interest of the patient." He assumes that if the individual possesses rational self-interest he will, on both biological and logical grounds, almost invariably tend to have a high degree of social interest as well. (p. 43)

Adler's contributions have also been acknowledged for building the foundation of humanistic psychology. Albert Ellis (1970) proclaimed that Adler was "one of the first humanistic psychologists" (p. 32). Rollo May (1970) expressed his gratitude to Adler by stating,

> I appreciate Adler more and more. . . . Adler's thoughts as I learned them in studying with him in Vienna in the summers of 1932 and 1933 led me indirectly into psychology, and were very influential in the later work in this country of Sullivan and William Alanson White, etc. (p. 39)

Another humanist, Abraham Maslow (1970b) also credited Adler with influencing his views. Maslow (1970b) stated,

> For me Alfred Adler becomes more and more correct year by year. As the facts come in, they give stronger and stronger support to his image of man. I should say that in one respect especially the times have not yet caught up with him. I refer to his holistic emphasis. (p. 30)

Even cognitive therapies have borrowed from or based their theory on part of the foundation that Adler built. Beck and Weishaar (2005) have acknowledged similarities between Adler's statements about the importance of the way that people view the world. Whereas Beck and Weishaar (2005) speak about cognitive distortions, Adler emphasized the client's basic mistakes in thinking. Cognitive therapy incorporated part of what Adler labeled as Socratic questioning. Beck and Weishaar have described cognitive therapy as "collaborative empiricism, Socratic dialogue, and guided discovery."

Furthermore, as noted, solution-focused therapy changed Adler's technique of "the question" to "the miracle question." It seems clear that some of the basic tenets of Adlerian psychotherapy will continue to be mainstreamed into contemporary theories. Adlerian constructs are evident in both the strengths-based therapy approach and in the positive psychology movement. For instance, strengths-based therapy has incorporated encouragement and hope as key features of its theoretical approach. Clients come to therapy with varying degrees of hope—from being completely hopeless to expecting an overnight miracle. Clients who are encouraged by their therapists are likely to feel hopeful about their future. Likewise, the positive psychology movement aims to put less emphasis on psychopathology and more attention on an individual's positive strivings in life. Even realty theory's emphasis on client responsibility can be traced to Adler's earlier emphasis on clients owning their own basic mistakes and taking responsibility for them. The therapist's Socratic questioning was designed to help the client gradually assume responsibility for his or her life.

Adler was a strong forerunner of parent education in his child guidance clinics. He emphasized understanding the purpose of a child's misbehavior, helping children accept the logical and natural consequences of their actions, holding family meetings, and using encouragement rather than punishment to change poor behavior. In the United States, two leading parent education programs are based on Adlerian principles: the STEP (Systematic Training for Effective Parenting) Program (Dinkmeyer et al., 1997) and Active Parenting (Popkin, 1993). Some well-known contributions of Adler include the following:

- Coined phrases: inferiority/superiority complex
- Birth order importance
- Lifestyle, worldview
- Behavior goal directed and purposeful
- Early recollections

Moreover, Adler had a great deal of influence on humanistic and existential psychology (Frankl, 1970; Maslow, 1970b). Maslow incorporated Adler's emphasis on the creative power of individuals to shape their own destinies and on the importance of future goals. Similarly, Carl Rogers's (1961) key construct of empathy is a direct influence of Adlerian therapy.

Another strength of Adlerian therapy is its emphasis on an egalitarian relationship between therapists and client. Adler's theory of personality and therapy was ahead of its time. His concepts relating to organ inferiority are pivotal in counseling individuals with disabilities. The therapist focuses on how the client's lifestyle and goals influence his or her response to disability.

Limitations of the Adlerian Approach

One major limitation of Adlerian therapy is that contemporary Adlerians have simply failed to update Adler's concepts into present-day terms and relationships, and this failure may be a major contributing factor to this theory's decline. Hence, the most challenging limitation of Adlerian therapy is the stagnation of thinking and theory building that currently surrounds the theory. History has shown that the older theories of psychotherapy do not just fade away, but rather, they are incorporated into what appear to be new theoretical approaches. For instance, Adlerian therapy preceded and strongly influenced rational emotive behavior therapy (Ellis & Ellis, 2011), which contributed to cognitive-behavioral therapies. Despite the fact that Adlerian ideas are alive in other theoretical approaches, the question has arisen about whether or not Adlerian therapy can continue to be a stand-alone, viable therapy approach. If the Adlerian approach to therapy is to survive, it must look for ways to make itself relevant in a modern, contemporary world. One approach would be to broaden the theory so that it includes the modern concepts that are involved in theories that have to do with social justice, multicultural issues, and feminism. Another avenue might be to seek formal incorporation into some of the newer existing psychotherapies, such as strengths-based therapy or reality therapy. Similarities exist with both of these newer approaches to psychotherapy and Adlerian therapy. For instance, similar to Adlerian theory, strengths-based therapy focuses on encouragement as a part of its therapeutic practice, while reality theory deals with responsibility and choice.

Another limitation of Adlerian theory is that Adler failed to systematize his thoughts so that they could be easily understood. Adler chose to spend more time teaching the principles of his theory than on organizing and presenting a well-defined and systematic theory. His writings can be difficult to understand and to follow. In addition, Adlerian therapy faces the challenge of adapting the theory for brief and short-term therapy. The Adlerian model of psychotherapy is most suited to long-term therapy; however, relatively recently it has been adapted for effective brief therapy (Carlson & Sperry, 1998). Manaster (1989) has suggested that Adlerians focus on limiting time instead of limiting goals. "Adlerian therapists attempt full and complete therapy in whatever time is available and in the shortest time possible" (p. 245).

Evidence-Based Research

A major criticism of Adlerian therapy is that it has not produced evidence-based studies to demonstrate the efficacy of its therapy. There is much truth to this criticism. A paucity of empirical research exists on the theory's basic concepts, such as birth order, earliest childhood memories, and social interest. The research completed on these concepts has revealed mixed results. Furthermore, little empirical research has been conducted on the effectiveness of Adlerian therapy with either adults or children (Rule & Bishop, 2006).

Adler himself was against group studies or the nomothetic. Instead of focusing on the efficacy of Adlerian therapy, studies have examined key Adlerian concepts. The Adlerian concepts that have been the most researched are those of birth order and social interest. Several studies have found that individuals' birth order can help influence their personality, affect their goal-setting process, influence how they solve problems, and determine how they behave socially (Carette, Anseel, & Van Yperen, 2011; Courtiol, Raymond, & Faurie, 2009;

Dixon, Reyes, Leppert, & Pappas, 2008; Pollet, Dijkstra, Barelds, & Buunk, 2010; Skinner & Fox-Francoeur, 2010). Despite the numerous studies that have been conducted on birth order, only mixed results have been found linking birth order and personality traits.

Adler believed that people with social interest value something outside of themselves. Social interest entails a sense of social feeling toward humankind. People with social interest have an absence of self-centeredness, egocentricity, and self-absorption. They are the opposite of Kohut's narcissistic individuals. To have social interest, one must identify with others and transcend one's own interests, resulting in a genuine concern for and striving for community and human welfare. Adler's theory asserted that social interest has important implications for both personal adjustment and the well-being of a society. Social interest was conceptualized as the foundation of mental health, and Adler maintained that many intrapersonal and interpersonal difficulties could be traced to an absence of social interest and community feeling.

During the past several decades, researchers have reported that individuals with relatively high levels of social interest, as assessed by a variety of instruments, possess common personality traits, such as friendliness, empathy, cooperation, tolerance, nurturance, and constructive independence (e.g., Crandall, 1981; Leak, Millard, Perry, & Williams, 1985; see also Watkins, 1994). Individuals have also been found to have higher levels of marital satisfaction (e.g., Markowski & Greenwood, 1984), faith development, and spiritual maturity (Leak, 1992) and to have fewer symptoms of neuroticism, such as anxiety, hostility, and depression.

Leak and Leak (2006) have pointed out the similarity of concepts in Adlerian therapy and in positive psychology, especially in the relationship between prosocialness and social interest. Leak and Leak found a positive correlation between a measure of social interest (Greever, Tseng, & Friedland, 1973) and some measures of positive psychological functioning; the researchers proposed the integration of social interest into positive psychology. Some Adlerian authors have highlighted the positive outcomes of social interest for general health and mental health (Nikelly, 2005) and that lacking social interest is related to an increased risk of physical and/or psychological disorder (Rareshide & Kern, 1991).

There is some evidence that Adler's concepts may be influencing schools. The Ready to Learn program, a prekindergarten through first-grade program is indicating some positive empirical support. In addition, there are a few parenting programs based on Adlerian concepts (STEP) that has also reported positive results (Gibson, 1999). This monograph was written for the American Guidance Services, Inc. It summarizes research related to the use and efficacy of the systematic training and effective parenting program (1976–1999).

Despite the use of Adler's concepts, there is only sparse empirical research attesting to the efficacy of Adlerian therapy. As noted, Adler believed that nomothetic research that compares group outcomes to be of little value. The primary focus of Adlerian studies has been ideographic in the form of case studies. A recent Delphi Poll (Norcross, Hedges, & Prochaska, 2002) has predicted that Adlerian therapy will decline over the next decade. It may very well be that part of this decline can be attributed to the absence of empirical studies that compare groups of individuals to determine the efficacy of this theoretical approach.

CASE ANALYSIS

Justin Working With an Adlerian Therapist

The goals of Adlerian counseling focus on helping clients develop healthy lifestyles, to assist them with dealing effectively with feelings of inferiority, and to create healthy social interest. The counselor sets up the four stages of Adlerian counseling: (1) establishing and maintaining a therapeutic alliance with Justin, (2) exploring Justin's dynamics, (3) encouraging Justin to develop insight and self-understanding, and (4) helping Justin consider new alternative behaviors and to make good choices.

To develop trust with Justin, the therapist had some art tools and material for him to use while he waited in the counselor's office. The therapist began by asking Justin about his paintings and about his artistic talent and the awards he had won for his artwork. During the initial setting, Justin is prepared to reject his counselor. He knows he can't trust the counselor because he is White, lives on the other side of town, and is old looking. Sensing Justin's uncomfortableness with him, the counselor mentions the issue of trust between the two of them. Intuitively, the counselor asked, "You probably don't trust me, do you Justin?"

Without waiting for an answer from Justin, he continued, "Maybe if I were you, I wouldn't trust me either, Justin. Most likely from your perspective, I'm an old White man (although I'm not that old . . . [laughter]), and you're a young boy who has a White mother and an African American father, but I am hoping that somehow we can reach out to each other." The counselor paused for a moment, hoping for a response from Justin, but he only gave a nervous smile that acknowledged part of what the counselor had said. Justin responded, "Well, old . . . but not old as my grandmother."

Feeling good about the exchange with Justin, the counselor used the rest of the session to establish a therapeutic relationship. He began to explore on a surface level Justin's feelings about being a son of a biracial relationship. Trying to put himself in Justin's shoes, the counselor said, "I would imagine that it probably hasn't been easy for you to deal with those two parts of you—one Black and the other White." The rest of the session focused on the court's mandated counseling. The counselor asked Justin what goals he would like to construct for the time they were to spend in a counseling relationship.

(Continued)

(Continued)

The second phase of Adlerian counseling with Justin involves exploring Justin's dynamics. Observation of the child is extremely important in Adlerian counseling. During the observation period, the counselor seeks to do the following:

- Understand the subjective field in which Justin's behavior takes place; to achieve this end, the counselor must attempt to see the situation through Justin's eyes
- Look for the purposes and goals of Justin's behavior
- Record classroom observation of Justin's behavior
- Recognize that Justin's behavior is a creative act designed to help him find his place in life
- Look for recurring patterns of behavior under different situations—at home and school
- Take into consideration Justin's stage of development

In the next couple of sessions, the counselor conducted a lifestyle assessment of Justin. The lifestyle assessment questionnaire dealt with Justin's family constellation, including his birth order and sibling description. The therapist asked questions regarding how socially useful Justin feels and inquired whether he had any feelings of inadequacy or inferiority. Some questions the counselor asked relating to Justin's early recollections included the following:

- What kind of person is your mother?
- Tell me something about her attitude and behavior toward you?
- How do you feel about her?
- What kind of person was your father?
- How do you feel about him?
- How did your parents get along?
- What were you like as a child?
- Describe your favorite childhood story, fantasy, or recurring dreams?
- How many siblings do you have?
- What are their ages?

The treatment plan for Justin involves helping him understand the goals of his misbehavior and encouraging him to do better. Adlerian counselors maintain that the fundamental desire for each child is to find a place in the group and to feel that he belongs. A well-behaved and well-adjusted child has been able to find social acceptance by conforming to the requirements of a particular group and by making meaningful contributions to it. The underlying assumption of the misbehaving child is that his or her actions will provide a sense of importance or social status within a group. The misbehaving child is a discouraged child who does not see the possibility of ever solving his or her problems or moving toward potential solutions.

Discouraged children have little or no confidence in their own abilities; they have negative expectations about life. They fear being failures or being proven inadequate or humiliated in some way. One way to help discouraged children is to change their expectations about themselves and life. To help a discouraged child, such as Justin, one has to first learn how to encourage him.

To pinpoint Justin's areas of discouragement, the counselor might consider administering an encouragement scale to measure the degree to which Justin feels discouraged at school and at home. According to Adlerian counselors, encouragement is the process of helping a child develop his inner resources and providing courage so that he makes positive choices. The counselor actively encourages Justin by using such phrases as, "I think you can do it," "You have what it takes," "You put a lot of effort into your work." Adlerian counselors believe that children's misbehavior cannot be corrected without encouragement. Yet children who misbehave, such as Justin, are the least likely to receive encouragement. The counselor conveys a feeling of anticipated success for Justin rather than failure. The counselor encourages Justin by the following ways:

- Valuing him as he is
- Demonstrating faith in him
- Building his self-concept
- Giving him recognition for his efforts
- Concentrating on his strengths and assets

The Adlerian counselor consults with Justin's mother and older brother. He would invite the entire family into consultation for the purpose of helping Justin. A key issue in working with the family is teaching it the process of encouragement. Justin's mother is inconsistent in her behavior toward him. She curses at him when she is angry or when he misbehaves. The counselor teaches her the principle of logical consequences in disciplining Justin. Moreover, Justin's mother's behavior is inappropriate when she engages in the pot parties held at her home. The counselor suggests that she eliminate the pot parties at her home.

In working with Justin's family, the Adlerian counselor elicits the family members' assistance in discovering the goals of Justin's misbehavior. The family also works cooperatively with the therapist to establish a viable treatment plan for both Justin and the family. In addition, the family and the therapist evaluate the success or failure of the treatment plan for Justin. Positive outcome evaluation for therapy for Justin and his family focuses on (1) the repair of the disturbed family relationships, (2) Justin's improved behavior at school, and (3) his involvement in positive social interest activities within his family, community, and at school. Emphasis is placed on helping Justin not only gain insight into his behavior but also substitute positive goals for his future interactions at school and within the community.

SUMMARY

Alfred Adler labeled his therapeutic approach individual psychology to stress his focus on the unity of the individual. Adler's approach can be described as social, teleological, phenomenological, holistic, and humanistic. The underlying assumptions of this theoretical approach is that each person is unique and self-consistent and that the individual is responsible for creating his or her life—that within certain constrictions, people can control their own destinies. Adlerians maintain that all human behavior is goal-directed and embedded within a society. The individual seeks to find his or her place within the world. Birth order (the order in which one was born in relation to one's siblings)

is a factor that influences one's psychological development. Adlerian psychology postulates that people must be considered holistically, within a social context.

Adlerian psychotherapy puts forth the idea that people who seek therapy are not sick, but rather, they are discouraged and that the goal of therapy is to encourage them to develop social interests and a more effective lifestyle so that they achieve success in the tasks of life.

Adler's early personal experiences with illness contributed to his theoretical focus on inferiority and superiority complexes. According to Adler, every person experiences a sense of inferiority, and he or she strives to overcome such feelings. Adler defined inferiority feelings as the source of human striving and as the normal condition of all people. A person can develop an inferiority complex, a condition that grows when the person is unable to compensate for normal inferiority feelings. Discouragement is the dominant theme in the development of an inferiority complex.

Adler believed that social interest (an intrinsic concern for others) is central in the development of positive mental health. Conversely, maladaptive behavior stems from discouraging or disappointing experiences that can be traced to the family of origin relationships. Both the pampered and the neglected child evidence maladaptive behavior because the child attempts to compensate by developing unrealistic striving for superiority in life.

Adlerian personality theory centers on the notion of lifestyle, which is a system of subjective conviction the individual holds that reflects his or her self view and view of the world. An individual develops **basic mistakes** (self-defeating attitudes and beliefs) and has basic life tasks that contain the questions and challenges of life that have influenced his or her development.

Adlerian therapists establish a warm, collaborative therapeutic relationship with clients. Frequently, they function as educators who encourage clients to use their strengths in dealing with life challenges. Adlerians do not use the medical model to deal with clients. They view clients' displays of maladaptive behavior as signs of their discouragement. The Adlerian theory of therapeutic change maintains that all people are in the process of becoming and that therapy is not about curing a client, but rather, it should be about encouraging a client's growth and development. Adlerians point out clients' mistaken goals so that they achieve insight and subsequently change their goals. The therapist uses an egalitarian approach where therapy is between two equals.

Adler was one of the first to posit the relationship between thinking and feeling. The individual acts as if his convictions are true and uses his lifestyle as a way to explore and live life. A person can only be understood within his or her social context.

The goal of therapy is to decrease clients' feelings of inferiority and to increase their social interest. Therapy proceeds through four phases: (1) establishing the therapeutic relationship, (2) investigating and assessing client dynamics, (3) encouraging insight and interpretation, and (4) helping with reorientation. Some common counseling techniques include investigating clients' lifestyles and analyzing their earliest recollections and birth order. Adlerian concepts have been adopted broadly in psychology and especially in educational clinics for children and families. The ultimate goal of psychotherapy is to increase and release clients' social interest so that they cooperate with their fellow human beings. Finally, Adler had a major influence on a number of schools of psychology, including ego psychology, humanistic psychology, rational emotive therapy, and cognitive therapy. Despite his influence, a major criticism of Adlerian psychotherapy is that there are insufficient numbers of empirical studies supporting the efficacy of this approach. Adlerians have tended to use case studies to examine the efficacy of their theoretical approach.

SUPPLEMENTAL AIDS _____

Discussion Questions

1. *Family constellation and birth order:* Analyze your own family in terms of Adler's family constellation with regard to birth order. List each of your siblings and indicate the most outstanding characteristic that each has manifested in life. Choose three words that capture the essence of each one of your siblings. Which sibling is closest to you and why? Which sibling is the most different from you? Was there any evidence of sibling rivalry in your family? If so, who were the major players in the rivalry scenes?

2. *Early recollections:* Form groups of four or five people in your class. Using a simple go-around technique, let each person describe his or her earliest memory and why the memory stands out for him or her. What feelings are connected to your earliest memory? To what extent does this earliest memory represent a significant issue in your life? Are there any themes that reoccur in your earliest

memories, and are these themes still of concern for you today?

3. *Lifestyle assessment:* Each person in the class conducts a lifestyle assessment of one of the following individuals: (1) yourself; (2) someone in your family; (3) a mate, friend, or lover; or (4) a famous literary or fictional character. In conducting this lifestyle summary, provide a brief description of the person's family constellation, a summary of his or her early recollections, a summary of his or her basic mistakes; a description or summary of his or her basic life goals and social interest.

4. *Basic mistakes:* Do you believe that Adler's concept of "basic mistakes" actually exists? If so, how would you characterize your basic mistakes?

5. *Birth order:* What do you think about Adler's views on birth order? What was your birth order, and describe the extent to which you believe your birth order has had an impact on your life.

Glossary of Key Terms

as if   A therapeutic technique in which the therapist asks the client to act "as if" there were no barriers to achieving his or her goal.

basic mistakes   False, self-defeating attitudes, perceptions, and beliefs that individuals form about life, usually early during their childhood. Examples of basic mistakes include overgeneralization and misperceptions of life and life's demands.

birth order   Ordinal position or birth placement within a family. Adler posited that individuals' birth order within the family increases the probability that certain behavior patterns would develop.

early recollections   A person's early childhood memories (before age 9) that Adlerians use to understand a person's lifestyle, social interest, and mistaken beliefs.

encouragement   A technique Adlerians use to increase clients' ability to deal with life tasks. Adlerians use encouragement to combat discouragement and to help clients work toward their goals.

family constellation   The structure of the system, which includes elements such as birth order, the person's perception of self, and sibling and parental relationships.

fictional finalism   An imagined final goal that provides direction to one's life and behavior.

holism   An approach that says people should be treated as integrative wholes rather than as individual parts of the psyche.

individual psychology   Adlerian approach to psychotherapy that views each person as a unique, whole entity whose development can be best understood within the context of a community.

inferiority complex   A pervasive feeling that one's abilities and characteristics are inferior to those of other people. Exaggerated feelings of inferiority and insecurity lead to neurotic behavior. Whereas inferiority feelings are normal, an inferiority complex is abnormal. See also **superiority complex**.

inferiority feelings   Viewing oneself as inadequate or incompetent in comparison with others or with one's ideal self. Most people have inferiority feelings. Feelings of inferiority begin with individuals' perception and self-evaluation of situation events in which they feel inadequate; a minus state that people seek to overcome.

life tasks   The basic challenges and obligations of life.

lifestyle   The internal organizer of an individual's behavior. Lifestyle helps an individual achieve what one might designate as internal consistency of thoughts, feelings, and behaviors.

lifestyle convictions   The conclusions a person reaches based on life experiences and the interpretation of those experiences.

organ inferiority   Perceived or actual congenital defects in an individual's biological organ systems, which Adler thought led to the individual's compensatory striving to overcome these deficits.

private logic   The reasoning an individual invents to stimulate and justify a style of life.

The Question   A question an Adlerian therapist uses to discover the purpose that symptoms or behavior have in a person's life: "How would your life be different, and what would you do differently, if you did not have this symptom or problem?"

social interest   A person's feeling of being part of a community or society; one's need and willingness to contribute to the general welfare of a society.

striving for superiority   An individual's striving to become competent.

superiority complex   A false feeling of power and security that invariably conceals an underlying inferiority complex. A superiority complex develops from an attempt to evade one's problems rather than to face them. See also **inferiority complex**.

Website Materials

Additional exercises, Lifestyle Assessment, journals, annotated bibliography, and more are available on the open-access website at https://study .sagepub.com/jonessmith2e.

PART II

The Second Force in Psychotherapy

Behavior Therapy and Cognitive Therapy

The second force in psychotherapy involves behavior therapy and cognitive therapy, two overlapping approaches to psychotherapy. Each of these approaches has become inextricably intertwined with the other, so that most therapists now use the two within the same reference—cognitive-behavioral. This second cognitive-behavioral force in psychotherapy has become a dominant theoretical perspective in psychotherapy—if not the most dominant force in psychotherapy.

DEFINITION OF BEHAVIOR THERAPY

What is behavior therapy? **Behavior therapy** is a form of psychotherapy that is based on the principles of behaviorism. It is designed to help individuals understand how changing their behavior can lead to changes in how they are feeling. The ultimate goal of behavior therapy is usually to increase the client's engagement in positive or socially reinforcing behavior and to decrease or eliminate unwanted or maladaptive behaviors. It is a structured clinical approach that measures carefully the client's behavior and then designs techniques to either increase positive behavior or to eliminate negative behavior. The techniques in behavior therapy are based on the theories of classical conditioning and operant conditioning.

Behaviorism maintains that psychological disorders are a result of maladaptive learning. It assumes that all behavior is learned from individuals' environment and that a person develops symptoms through classical conditioning and operant conditioning. Whereas classical conditioning involves learning by association (as is the case with most phobias), operant conditioning involves learning by reinforcement (e.g., rewards) and punishment. Learning is a critical component of behavior therapy. Behaviorists believe that if a behavior has been learned, it can also be unlearned. The therapist unravels for the client the learning process that took place to get the maladaptive behavior for the purpose of extinguishing it. The goal is to help clients learn new behaviors. Behavior therapy differs from insight-oriented therapies such as psychoanalytic and humanistic approaches in that it is action based.

BRIEF HISTORICAL OVERVIEW OF BEHAVIOR THERAPY AND COGNITIVE THERAPY

Behavior therapy has had a robust history. Of the two theoretical approaches, behavioral psychology and psychotherapy developed much earlier. Ivan Pavlov's work with classical conditioning used rigid laboratory controls that were empirically observable and quantifiable and that subsequently gave rise to an academic psychology in the United States led by John Watson. Initially, the first force excluded the subjective data of consciousness and human personality development. Watson reacted to the prevalent "introspectionistic" theories, which maintained that to understand human behavior, psychologists needed to look inside the individual. In contrast to this position, Watson viewed human behavior as caused by environmental factors.

Experimental research on learning was an important event that promoted the development of behavior therapy and the resultant principles of classical and instrumental conditioning, which was spearheaded by B. F. Skinner. During the 1930s, O. Hobart Mowrer and W. M. Mowrer (1938) used conditioning procedures (which are currently being used) to treat bed-wetting problems in children.

Yet it was not until Joseph Wolpe (1958) wrote his book *Psychotherapy by Reciprocal Inhibition* that therapists were given a set of techniques to use in behavior therapy. Prior to his work, therapists did not have a set of techniques that helped them apply conditioning principles to their work with clients. Working in his clinic in South Africa, Wolpe maintained that most human problems were caused by anxiety. To this extent, Wolpe echoed the position of psychoanalysts. However, Wolpe distinguished the behavioral school from psychoanalysis by applying a combination of classical conditioning theory and **learning theory** to the treatment of anxiety. Wolpe asserted that anxiety was learned as a result of conditioned autonomic reactions, and he devised the technique of systematic desensitization to treat adult neurotic clients.

Following Wolpe's success in treating anxiety disorders with desensitization techniques, behavior therapists began to branch out to using different types of therapy. Albert Bandura became a leading social learning theorist of the 1960s and 1970s. He stressed the importance of observational learning. Observational learning takes place when one learns simply from observing the behavior and consequences of behavior related to another person. Albert Bandura wrote *Principles of Behavior Modification* (1969) and introduced the concepts of vicarious reinforcement, modeling, and behavior rehearsal. Observational learning takes place via the process of vicarious reinforcement (being influenced by observing another person getting reinforced), modeling (learning by watching another person perform a behavior), and behavior rehearsal (acting out a behavior to learn it and to hone it as a skill). Also, Donald Meichenbaum (1985, 1991) was one of the leading figures who nudged behavior therapy to the cognitive movement with his concepts of self-management, self-instructional learning, and stress inoculation.

THE THREE WAVES OF BEHAVIOR THERAPY

Recently researchers have begun to discuss the development of behavior therapy in terms of the three waves of behavior therapy (Hayes, 2004; Hayes, Masuda, & De Mey, 2003). During *the first wave*, behavior therapists questioned the conventional belief that inner experience was central to understanding human behavior. Included in the first wave of theorists would be Watson, Skinner, Wolpe, and Meichenbaum. As a result, behaviorists during the first wave used classical and operant conditioning principles to explain behavior without referring to events inside the person's head—his or her emotions. The focus was on the development of treatments that emphasized modifying behavior through stimulus control and contingency management. Observable behavior was the mantra and the focus of attention.

The cognitive revolution during the 1970s brought about *the second wave* of behavior therapy. As Sperry (1993) stated in his article "The Impact and Promise of the Cognitive Revolution,"

> During APA's [American Psychological Association] first hundred years, psychology is said to have gone through three major revolutions. In addition to the recent shift to cognitivism, there were two earlier revolts, which were associated with J. B. Watson and Sigmund Freud. I believe that, of the three, the current so-called cognitive, mentalist, or consciousness revolution is the most radical turnaround—the most revisionary and transformative. (p. 878)

The cognitive revolution stressed the significance of mediating variables in explaining and changing behavior. The cognitive revolution contradicted the prior belief that science has no use for consciousness to explain brain function. Again, commenting on the cognitive revolution in psychology, Sperry (1993) has maintained,

> Subjective mental states as emergent interactive properties of brain activity become irreducible and indispensable for explaining conscious behavior and its evolution and get primacy in determining what a person is and does. Dualistic unembodied consciousness is excluded. A modified two-way model of interlevel causal determinism introduces new principles of downward holistic and subjective causation. The prior belief that cognitive variables were irrelevant to understanding human behavior was modified and paved the way for "cognitive-behavioral theories." (p. 878)

The cognitive revolution produced a more comprehensive and accurate conceptual foundation for understanding human behavior. It signaled a diametric turn away from the centuries-old dualistic treatment of the mind and consciousness in science. Within that revolution, the content of mental consciousness made a dramatic comeback from Freud's earlier emphasis on the unconscious. The cognitive-consciousness revolution represents a revolt from the microdeterministic views of personhood and the physical worldviews of personhood and the physical world to a more wholistic, top-down view in which the mental, social, and other forces gain their due recognition in psychology. The new cognitive position is mentalistic, maintaining that behavior is mentally and subjectively driven.

> In the new synthesis, mental states, as dynamic emergent properties of brain activity, become inseparably interfused with and tied to the brain activity of which they are an emergent property. Consciousness in this view cannot exist apart from the functioning brain. (Sperry, 1993, p. 879)

The cognitive approach freed behaviorism from the yoke of theoretical and applied behaviorism. Three theorists dominated the cognitive revolution, Albert Ellis, Aaron Beck, and Albert Bandura. In 1962, Albert Ellis published *Reason and Emotion in Psychotherapy*, in which he contended that our cognitions—what we think and say to ourselves—cause our psychological unhappiness and disturbance. Other cognitive approaches to psychology soon followed. Soon concepts such as irrational beliefs, schemas, and self-efficacy began to dominate the field.

The popularity of the cognitive school led to its incorporation within behavioral psychotherapy approaches. Initially, Albert Bandura (1969) was one of the leading proponents promoting the integration of behavioral and cognitive theories. Currently, the behavioral and cognitive perspectives have been merged or integrated more successfully than any other combination of theoretical approaches.

The *second wave of behavior therapy* challenged the conventional wisdom of prior behaviorists who asserted that cognitive variables were irrelevant to understanding a person's behavior (Hergenhahn, 1994). On the contrary, the then new cognitive-behavioral theories emphasized the importance of mediating variables in explaining and modifying behavior. As Storaasli, Kraushaar, and Emrick (2007) have stated,

> Representing a more sophisticated instantiation of early Greek Stoicism or folk psychological notions on the causes of behavior (cf. O'Donohue, Callaghan, & Ruckstuhl, 1998), the cognitive approach liberated theoretical and applied behaviorism over the next few decades. In the clinical area, the dialogue was dominated by the likes of Albert Ellis's rationale-emotive therapy (RET, 1974) and Aaron T. Beck's (Beck, Rush, Shaw, & Emery, 1979) cognitive therapy, and such concepts as irrational beliefs, schemas, and self-efficacy expectations entered the behavior therapist's lexicon. Along the way, second-wave therapies realized great success in clinical trials, expanded the clinical armamentarium of behavior therapists, and made behavior therapy accessible to new generations of behavior therapists. (p. 150)

The cognitive and behavioral approaches have become more than *just the second force in psychotherapy*. These two schools have become the dominant psychotherapy orientation in therapy—primarily because they emphasize brief therapy and the person–environment interaction. Research studies have tended to report that cognitive-behavioral therapy has the most evidence-based research of all the theoretical approaches. In fact, most therapists report that they have adopted some techniques from this school. As Storaasli et al. (2007) have explained, "Along the way, second-wave therapies realized great success in clinical trials, expanded the clinical armamentarium of behavior therapists, and made behavior therapy accessible to new generations of behavior therapists" (p. 150).

Currently, the field is experiencing the emergence of a *third generation or a third wave of behavior therapists*. The third wave of cognitive-behavior therapists draws from Eastern traditions such as the mindfulness therapy approach of the Chinese and less empirically oriented therapeutic approaches. The third-wave movement has redefined the behavioral therapeutic landscape. Storaasli et al. (2007) have stated,

> We are now witnessing the emergence of a third generation of behavior therapists, and the conventional wisdom of the second wave is being questioned. Drawn from basic and applied behavior analysis of language (see, e.g., Hayes, Barnes-Holmes, & Roche, 2001), Eastern mystic traditions and less empirically oriented therapeutic approaches (see Hayes, 1984, 2002), the third-wave movement is redefining the behavioral therapeutic landscape. Examples include Acceptance and Commitment Therapy (ACT; Hayes & Strosahl, 2005; Hayes, Strosahl, & Wilson, 1999), Dialectical Behavior Therapy (DBT; Linehan, 1993), Functional Analytic Psychotherapy (FAP; Kohlenberg & Tsai, 1991), Mindfulness-Based Cognitive Therapy (MBCT, Segal, Williams, & Teasdale, 2002), and Integrative Behavioral Couples Therapy (IBCT; Jacobson, Christensen, Prince, Cordova, & Eldridge, 2000), among others. . . .
>
> Although the factors that unite these approaches cannot be easily characterized, at their core, they suggest that to behave differently (vis., live well), it is not necessary that one must first feel good or think differently. Philosophically, they tend to be more contextually and experientially based—emphasizing such issues as acceptance, mindfulness, cognitive defusion, dialectics, spirituality and values (Hayes, 2004; Hayes et al., 2003) and tend away from second-wave theories that emphasize behavioral modification via cognitive change (e.g. J. Beck, 1995; Ellis, 1974; Meichenbaum, 1977). (pp. 150–151)

What was originally called behavior therapy has changed enormously. In this second edition of *Theories of Counseling and Psychotherapy: An Integrative Approach*, I have made a concerted effort not only to reflect the first and second waves of behavior therapy but also to present the third wave of cognitive-behavioral theory development. Behavior therapy is no longer simply focusing on behavior. It is much more contextual, and it has even begun to adopt the theoretical framework and principles of therapeutic practices in Eastern cultures. From my perspective, the biggest development in the new theoretical approaches to psychotherapy is the impact of mindfulness and other Eastern approaches on psychotherapy. All three third-wave cognitive-behavioral approaches presented in Chapter 5 of this text— dialectical behavioral therapy (DBT, Linehan, 1993), acceptance and commitment therapy (ACT, Hayes, 2004), and mindfulness-based cognitive therapy (MBCT, Segal, Williams, & Teasdale, 2002)—have adopted a large component involving Chinese mindfulness philosophy and techniques.

It appears that we are witnessing a cross-cultural integration of Chinese and American theoretical approaches to psychotherapy. To this extent, all the third-wave cognitive-behavioral approaches discussed in Chapter 5 (DBT, ACT, and MBCT) are by definition integrative and multicultural psychotherapies. It appears that a multicultural revolution in counseling theories is beginning to take place. Because American theorists are now integrating Eastern and Western cultures in their theories of psychotherapy, such therapies are no longer solely Eurocentric. In some respects, the third-wave cognitive-behavior therapies discussed herein can best be described as partially integrated Euro-Asian approaches to psychotherapy.

Outline of Chapters on the Second Force. Chapter 4 on behaviorism emphasizes the contributions of behaviorists in the first wave, with two major exceptions, which include applied behavioral analysis, which is currently being used extensively in working with children diagnosed with autism and other childhood behavioral disorders, and the rapidly growing field of behavioral pharmacology. The second-wave theorists (e.g., Albert Ellis, Albert Bandura, and Aaron Beck) are presented in detailed fashion in the first half of Chapter 5 on cognitive-behavioral psychotherapy. Also contained in Chapter 5 is a more abbreviated section describing three third-wave behaviorists (Marsha Linehan, 1993 [DBT]; Hayes & Strosahl, 2005 [ACT]; Segal, Williams, & Teasdale, 2002 [MBCT]). Finally, Chapter 6 presents reality/choice therapy developed by William Glasser (1985), who is on the cusp between the second- and the third-wave cognitive behaviorists.

CHAPTER 4

Behavior Therapy and Integrated Psychopharmacology

BRIEF OVERVIEW

Behavior therapy (along with cognitive therapy) constitutes the second major force in the fields of psychology and psychotherapy. Behavior therapy has had an enormous impact on the field of psychotherapy. Begun during the late 1950s, behavior therapy approaches were founded on Pavlov's concept of classical conditioning and Skinner's research on operant conditioning. Subsequent developments in behavior therapy include Wolpe's work on anxiety hierarchies, relaxation, and desensitization, along with Meichenbaum's development of self-instructional learning and stress inoculation. During the early years, behavior therapy was a radical minority movement that challenged the then dominant psychoanalytic school of psychotherapy. It has come a long way since then.

Significant differences exist between behavioral therapies and other psychotherapies examined in this book. Behavior therapies were constructed from discoveries made on animals in experimental psychology and physiology laboratories. Psychodynamic and existential-humanistic therapies were developed primarily from the clinical efforts of therapists working with clients. Although all psychotherapies rely on client learning, a defining feature of behavioral approaches to therapy is that they emphasize learning principles.

How did the radical minority consisting of behavior therapists assume such prominence in the field of psychotherapy? Much of the American shift from psychoanalysis toward behavior therapy can be attributed to the changing focus of prominent graduate training programs in clinical psychology. During the 1960s in the United States, several prominent graduate clinical programs in distinguished universities announced that the primary training model would be in behavior therapy. Sayette and Mayne (1990) conducted a study of the orientations of faculty in doctoral programs accredited by the American Psychological Association and found that 14% described themselves as having an applied behavioral or radical behavioral approach, while another 42% emphasized cognitive-behavioral or social learning approaches.

Perhaps one of the most significant developments in behavior therapy was its movement to include cognitive influences. The former behavioral school of psychotherapy has now become identified as the cognitive-behavioral school. In general, behavior therapists are now inclined to identify themselves as cognitive-behavioral therapists rather than as simply behavioral therapists. This change was solidified in 2005 when a decision was made to change the name of the Association for Advancement of Behavioral Therapy (AABT) to the Association for Behavioral and Cognitive Therapies (ABCT). It remains to be seen if behavior therapy will continue to be practiced as a pure behavioral approach to therapy, or if it will gradually be incorporated under the general rubric of cognitive-behavioral therapy.

It seems reasonable to me that behavior therapy may become a major footnote in the development of cognitive-behavioral therapy and that future textbooks in counseling theory will simply present cognitive-behavioral therapy instead of their current tendency to present both approaches. Reality demands that we move on from the past—much as psychoanalytic therapy was forced to move forward with ego psychology, object relations, self psychology, and now relational analysis.

Focus of This Chapter. This chapter begins with a review of the contributions of John Watson, B. F. Skinner, Joseph Wolpe, and Donald Meichenbaum. Next, key concepts involved in behavior therapy are defined, including classical conditioning, operant conditioning, reinforcement, shaping, and others. The behaviorist's view of human nature and therapeutic processes, including the goals of the therapist, the role of the therapist, and intervention techniques, are also considered. A new section on evidence-based behavioral therapy is provided. In keeping with this book's emphasis on working with youth, I present a case study of Justin from a behavior therapy perspective. The next section provides information on the early major contributors to behavior therapy.

BEHAVIOR THERAPY

Major Contributor: John Watson (1878–1958)

Source: ©Underwood & Underwood/CORBIS.

John Watson

John B. Watson was a major proponent of the behavioral school. According to Watson, behaviorists study observable animal and human behaviors, instead of states of consciousness, which are difficult to verify (Watson, 1924/1925). One of Watson's best-known experiments was with his graduate assistant, Rayner, and an 11-month-old child named Albert B ("Little Albert"). He and Rayner conditioned the

child to fear rats and other furry animals. They placed a white rat by Little Albert, and when he reached for it, they frightened him with a loud noise. Several times, they repeated this sequence of actions, thereby conditioning Albert to cry each time he saw the rat. As a consequence of conditioning, Albert began to associate the scary noise with any furry thing, including dogs, rabbits, fur coats, and cotton balls. Watson and Rayner's (1920) work demonstrated that human emotions are learned and can be generalized. Little Albert generalized his fear of rats to white, furry objects. The ethics of the experiment are often criticized today, especially because Albert's fear was never deconditioned.

Despite Watson's contributions, behaviorism is associated primarily with the name of B. F. Skinner, who made his reputation by testing Watson's theories in the laboratory. Skinner's studies led him to reject Watson's almost exclusive emphasis on reflexes and conditioning. The ensuing sections discuss the work of three psychologists: B. F. Skinner, Joseph Wolpe, and Donald Meichenbaum.

Major Contributor: B. F. Skinner (1904–1990)

B. F. Skinner

Burrhus Frederic Skinner was born on March 20, 1904, in Susquehanna, a small Pennsylvania railroad town located close to the border of New York. He was the elder son of William Arthur Skinner and Grace Madge (Burrhus) Skinner.

He had one brother, 2 years his junior, who died suddenly at age 16. Skinner's father was a lawyer, and his mother was rigid with high moral standards. His parents rarely punished him physically (except for washing his mouth out with soap when he cursed). Skinner believed that his parents' disciplinary techniques were effective and fair.

As a young boy, Skinner was mechanically inclined, spending much of his time constructing a roller skate scooter, steering mechanisms for wagons and carts, and kites, to name a few (Skinner, 1976). Skinner wanted to become a writer, and he majored in English at Hamilton College, a small private school near Albany, New York. Following graduation in 1926, he wrote short stories. Robert Frost, the great American poet, gave a positive critique of three of Skinner's short stories (Nye, 1992).

Skinner invented what became known as the "Skinner box," in which a rat learns to obtain food by pressing a lever. He is also famous for his research on operant conditioning and negative reinforcement. He developed a device called the "cumulative recorder," which showed rates of responding as a sloped line. Using this equipment, he found that behavior did not depend on the preceding stimulus as Watson and Pavlov maintained. Skinner found that behaviors were dependent on what happens *after* the response, which he called *operant behavior*.

Skinner developed the theory of **operant conditioning**, the idea that behavior is determined by its consequence—reinforcements or punishments that make it more or less likely that the behavior will occur again. Principles of operant conditioning are still incorporated within treatments of phobias, addictive behaviors, and in computer-based instruction. Skinner asserted that the only scientific approach to psychology was one that studied human behaviors instead of internal (subjective) mental processes. Similar to Watson, Skinner denied that the mind or feelings play any part in determining human behavior. Instead, our experience of reinforcements determines our behavior. Skinner maintained that operant conditioning could explain even the most complex of human behaviors. His theory became known as *radical behaviorism* because he focused on the functional analysis of behavior—the relationship between environmental events and a particular response. Radical behaviorism makes no allowance for cognitive processes.

During Skinner's lifetime, there were rumors that he put his daughter Deborah in a Skinner box, which led to her lifelong mental illness and a bitter resentment toward her father. Skinner's daughter said that there was no truth to this rumor and that she was not a lab rat in an experiment created by her father. These rumors were promoted because of the stance Skinner (1971) took in his classic book *Beyond Freedom and Dignity*.

Skinner's work resulted in his receiving numerous awards, including the National Medal of Science from President Lyndon B. Johnson in 1968. In 1971, the American Psychological Association awarded him the Gold Medal of the American Psychological Foundation. Eight days before his death, the American Psychological Association awarded him the first Citation for Outstanding Lifetime Contribution to Psychology (Epstein, 1997). Skinner died on August 18, 1990, from leukemia.

Major Contributor: Joseph Wolpe (1915–1998)

Born in Johannesburg, South Africa, on April 20, 1915, Joseph Wolpe was the son of Michael Salmon and Sarah Millner Wolpe. Later in his life, he became an American citizen. One of Wolpe's primary contributions was that he developed the

> ### Inner Reflections
>
> What has had the most important impact on your life—rewards or punishment?
>
> What similarities do you see between Skinner's preference for positive reinforcement and Adler's emphasis on encouragement as a primary motivator for people?

behavioral technique of **systematic desensitization**, which involved developing a **hierarchy** of anxiety-provoking situations and learning relaxation techniques and then learning to associate a previously anxiety-provoking situation with relaxation. In the beginning, his experiments were with cats that were given mild electric shocks accompanied by specific sounds and visual stimuli. Once the cats equated the unpleasant shock with these images or sounds, the signals created a feeling of fear. Wolpe wanted to prove that we could unlearn our fears. He gradually exposed the cats to these same sights and sounds, only this time providing them with food instead of shocks. The cats gradually "unlearned" their fear of these sights and sounds when they were paired with food.

Wolpe felt that his experiment with cats could also be used with people. People could unlearn their fears. Wolpe maintained that he could teach clients relaxation techniques and that he could reduce their fears by having them gradually rehearse fearful or stressful situations until they were able to handle the fear-producing objects. One major contribution of Wolpe's research was that it led to assertiveness training. Wolpe demonstrated that effective, compassionate therapy could be combined with empirical methods in a way that used both to their best advantage. Wolpe's books, *Psychotherapy by Reciprocal Inhibition* (1958) and *The Practice of Behavior Therapy* (1969), are considered classics in behavior therapy studies.

Major Contributor: Donald Meichenbaum

Meichenbaum (1985, 1991, 1993, 1994, and 2003) is one of the primary figures who has helped push behavior therapy to its current cognitive-behavioral perspective. He (1985, 1996) is credited with developing the concepts of self-management, self-instructional learning, and stress inoculation. He conceptualized self-instructional training as a means by which people could teach themselves how to deal effectively with situations that had caused problems in prior situations. Self-instructional training has been used to deal with

anxiety, anger, eating problems, addiction, and creative blocks. It also has been applied to **assertiveness training**. For instance, one woman complained that her husband often let his family members borrow her personal items. In therapy, the counselor modeled an assertive position: "Please do not give my personal items to Ericka without first asking my permission." The client was given written statements she could use to practice assertive behavior. Clients are asked to keep records to demonstrate their progress in self-management.

KEY CONCEPTS OF BEHAVIOR THERAPY

View of Human Nature

From the behavioral perspective, people are basically neutral at birth; they are neither good nor bad. The laws of learning suggest that people are influenced by what happens to them and by what they learn. Therefore, behavior therapists are less inclined to highlight stages of development than are some of the psychoanalytic and psychodynamic therapists. Behaviorists maintain that learning can result in the development of any pattern of human behavior, provided that the person has a certain learning history and biological capability.

The behavioral concept of human nature includes both personal and environmental determinants of human behavior. Behaviorists argue that intrapsychic conceptions of personality underuse the pervasive effect of learning and external events on individuals. In contrast, clients' overt behavior is of interest only to the extent that their behavior is representative of deep-seated personality traits. Hence, from a psychodynamic perspective, behavior cannot be taken at face value but instead must be interpreted symbolically.

Freud's case of "Little Hans" demonstrates the difference between psychodynamic and behavioral approaches in the conceptualization of human nature. Little Hans developed a phobia for horses, which Freud attributed to Little Hans' issues of oedipal and castration anxiety. Reinterpreting this case, Wolpe and Rachman (1960) contended that Little Hans had recently experienced four incidents in which horses were associated with fear-producing events that might have created a classically conditioned phobic reaction. For instance, on one occasion, he witnessed a horse that was pulling a loaded cart knocked down and killed.

Psychodynamic theorists claim that the external stimuli that Little Hans saw had very little effect on the phobia. Instead, Little Hans's fear of horses was not as significant as the underlying conflict. A conditioning explanation points out that a specific stimulus element accounted for Little Hans's fear of horses. In short, behavior theorists see humans as hedonistic in nature. The nature of people is to reduce suffering and to increase pleasure.

Inner Reflections

How do you view one's personality? Does an individual's personality actually exist, or is it a construction that people have created (Skinner's view) to explain another's behavior?

Is an individual's personality pretty much formed by age 5 or 6, or is it continually within a state of flux?

How would you describe your own personality? What theoretical school do you use to describe your own "personality"?

Theory of Personality

In contrast to other theories presented in this book, behavior therapy does not have a comprehensive personality theory from which it is derived (Liebert & Liebert, 1998). The behavioral theory of personality is based on a theory of learning that states that all behaviors are acquired through learning and conditioning. Unlike psychoanalytic and psychodynamic theorists of personality, behaviorists are reluctant to provide accounts of an individual's "personality." In the absence of data, behaviorists are reluctant to speculate how a specific behavior pattern was acquired. Behaviorists are hesitant to attribute explanatory or causal status to a person's so-called mental or intrapsychic working. For instance, Skinner (1974) argued that "a self or personality is at best a repertoire of behavior imparted by an organized set of contingencies" (p. 149). Behaviorists consider personality an individual's particular series of reactions to specific stimuli. More recently, another behaviorist, Staats (1993), stated that "personality is composed of specifiable, learned behaviors" (p. 10).

Behavioral definitions of personality maintain that personality consists of behavior–environment contingencies that are subject to control and modification by the environment and heredity. The terms *personality* and *self* are conceptualized as behaviors that need to be identified and explained in terms of their causal variables. From the behavioral perspective, personality is highly consistent, but still malleable, within the limits imposed by the person's environment and heredity. Behaviorists view personality as being in a state of flux, as something that is stable yet changing depending on the contingencies in one's environment. As Pronko (1980) has stated, "Everything is in a state of flux; so is personality. An inventory of one's personality would stop only with the death of the individual" (p. 201).

Classical Conditioning

Ivan Pavlov, the Russian physiologist, first conducted experiments and described **classical conditioning**. Pavlov observed that dogs automatically salivated at the sight of food, a response that he believed was hardwired into many animals for the purpose of promoting digestion. In Pavlov's experiment, the food was the **unconditioned** stimulus (UCS), and the behavior of salivation was the **unconditioned response** (UCR). The sight of the food (UCS) automatically triggered the salivation (UCR) of the dogs. Pavlov observed that when he presented or paired some other stimulus such as a sound with the presentation of the food (the UCS), over time, this new stimulus (the sound of the bell ringing) produced the same response (dogs' salivation) as the UCS (the presentation of the food itself). Pavlov labeled the new stimulus (the bell ringing) a conditioned stimulus (CS) because the ringing of the bell prior to the presentation of the food conditioned the dog to salivate. He labeled the dogs' salivation at the sound of the ringing bell as a **conditioned response** (CR). When a dog salivates because it sees a dog bone or steak, the steak is the UCS and its salivation is the UCR. That is, dogs automatically salivate at the sight of a ribeye steak or a juicy dog bone. Dogs do not usually salivate at the sound of a ringing bell. If one continually rings a bell every time that a steak is placed in front of a dog, the dog subsequently learns to salivate after hearing the bell, even if the steak is not presented. Classical conditioning is a type of associative learning. That is, if the CS and the UCS are repeatedly paired, the two stimuli become associated, and the person or animal gives a behavioral response to the CS. In the latter instance, the bell is the CS because it signals to the dog that food is coming, and the dog's salivation at the sound of the bell is the CR.

Operant Conditioning

The concept of operant conditioning is associated with two American psychologists, Edward Thorndike and B. F. Skinner. Thorndike (1911) conducted experiments to study learning around the same time period as Pavlov completed his famous studies. Unlike Pavlov, Thorndike used cats in his experiments. He placed food outside a cage and then observed how a cat would try to escape and find the food by releasing a latch. The cat used trial and error to engineer its first escape from the cage. As the experiment was repeated, the cat was able to escape more quickly. Thorndike plotted a

learning curve that recorded the time taken to press the latch. On the basis of his experiments, Thorndike developed the law of effect: "Consequences that follow behavior help learning" (Kazdin, 2001, p. 17).

Although Thorndike's studies on learning were quite important, it is Skinner's name that is most often associated with operant conditioning. Operant conditioning is a form of learning in which behavior is changed by systematically changing the consequences. Skinner placed pigeons in a cage that became known as a Skinner box, which was a small chamber in which the pigeon pecked at a lighted key. The experimenter controlled the amount of food pellets that the pigeon was given (reinforcement), and the pigeon's pecks were automatically recorded. In the Skinner studies, the experimenter reinforced the pigeon with food pellets when the light was green rather than red. Gradually, the pigeon learned to peck at the green light rather than the red light.

One definition of operant conditioning is that it occurs when a behavior is followed by a consequence, and the nature of the consequence changes a person's or an organism's tendency to repeat the behavior in the future. The idea is that we are rewarded or punished for actions and that we learn to discriminate between behaviors that bring rewards and those that do not. We are more likely to increase behavior that is rewarded and to decrease behavior that is either punished or not reinforced. The theory is that we do not shape our environments as much as we are shaped by them. The consequences of a behavior determine if that behavior will be learned or repeated.

Reinforcement

In behavior therapy, the term **reinforcement** means to strengthen some behavior. It refers to any stimulus that strengthens or increases the likelihood of a specific response from a person. Reinforcement is used to help increase the likelihood that a specific behavior will take place in the future by delivering a stimulus immediately after a response or behavior is made. There are three basic types of reinforcement: positive, negative, and punishment. **Positive reinforcement** can be thought of as adding something to increase a response. For instance, if a man is praised for the excellent grass cutting job he does, then he is likely to continue cutting the grass. The most common types of positive reinforcement involve praise and rewards. We recognize children for getting grades with both praise and sometimes rewards, such as a new bike or a cell phone. It is through the process of positive reinforcement that most of our pleasurable learning takes place.

In contrast, **negative reinforcement** takes place when a certain stimulus (usually an aversive stimulus) is removed after a specific behavior is exhibited. It involves taking something away to increase a response. The likelihood of a behavior taking place again in the future is increased because of removing/avoiding the negative consequence. Negative reinforcement should not be confused with a punishment procedure. With negative reinforcement, one is increasing the likelihood of the occurrence of a behavior, whereas with punishment, you are decreasing the likelihood that a person will exhibit a specific behavior. Remember that the end result of reinforcement is to try to increase the behavior. Some examples of negative reinforcement include a person washing the dishes (behavior) to avoid his parents' nagging (negative stimulus). A man puts the garbage out to keep his wife from nagging him. The nagging has become an aversive stimulus. The removal of the wife's nagging is reinforcing and will most likely increase the chances of his putting out the garbage again. Other examples of negative reinforcement are learning to carry your gloves on a cold day, going a different way to avoid the traffic jam you experienced the previous day.

When thinking about reinforcement, remember that the goal is always to increase the behavior, whereas punishment procedures are used to decrease target behavior. For positive reinforcement, we add something positive (praise, reward) to increase a desired response (wash the dishes, earn good grades). Negative reinforcement involves taking something negative away to increase a desired response. Praise and encouragement are usually viewed as positive reinforcers, while criticism is a negative reinforce.

To reiterate, **punishment** involves adding something aversive for the purpose of decreasing a behavior. A common type of punishment is spanking a child who has run out into the street. The child does not like to be spanked; therefore, he or she is less likely to run out into the street again because of the spanking. With punishment, we learn to inhibit behavior. The child seeks to avoid the punishment. Reinforcement serves to increase a behavior, while punishment helps decrease a behavior.

Reinforcers and punishers are different types of consequences that a person might experience as a result of some behavior. Moreover, a reinforcer may be either primary or secondary. A primary reinforcer is one that a person values intrinsically, such as food. A primary punisher could be pain or freezing temperatures—things that are naturally unpleasant. A secondary reinforcer (e.g., money, fast cars, and good grades) acquires its value from being associated with a primary reinforcer. A secondary punisher can be failing grades or parental disapproval. Secondary reinforcers and punishers are labeled conditioned reinforcers and punishers because they are learned. In behavior therapy, clients determine what reinforcers are the best for them.

Extinction

Extinction takes place when reinforcers are withdrawn or unavailable, and people stop demonstrating a behavior. It may be defined as the process of removing an unwanted response by not reinforcing it. A child acts out in class because he wants to obtain attention from his teacher and class members. When he receives their attention, the child is reinforced. Soon the class and teacher ignore the acting-out child each time he demonstrates a negative attention-getting behavior. Without the reinforcement of the class's attention, the child eventually stops the acting-out behavior. *Asking a child to stop doing something is far less effective than* *if the parent or teacher stops reinforcing the behavior with whatever the child decides is a reward.*

Generalization

When behavior is reinforced on a consistent basis, it may become generalized to other situations. A father praises his daughter for her excellent grade in math. The child perceives the praise as reinforcing, and she begins to generalize the behavior to her other subjects. If children are reinforced for whining with gifts, they will continue to whine to get the reward or reinforcer. The important task is to learn how to generalize appropriate behavior to similar situations. We can make both negative and positive **generalizations** for situations in our lives. We can also overgeneralize. For instance, a woman finds that her boyfriend has cheated on her. She overgeneralizes and begins to view all men as "cheaters." Ethnic or racial stereotypes are also overgeneralizations that we make to deal with members of specific ethnic/racial groups.

Discrimination

Just as we must learn how to generalize our behavior to appropriate similar situations, we must also learn how to respond differently to stimuli, depending on the situation with which we are presented. The pigeons in the Skinner experiment had to learn how to discriminate between the red and green light to get the food pellets. Pecking at the red light did not produce food pellets, while pecking at the green light did result in food.

Shaping

Shaping is defined as behavior that is learned gradually in steps by successive approximation. It entails a gradual movement from the original behavior to the desired behavior by reinforcing approximations of the desired behavior. Shaping takes place when a person actually practices a behavior. When clients are learning new skills, counselors break down behavior into manageable units. They help shape a client's behavior by the use of reinforcement, extinction, generalization, and discrimination. For instance, a client desires to become more assertive in her or his work with others. The counselor gives homework assignments that require the client to practice the skill in diverse settings. Each time the client demonstrates a reasonable approximation of assertiveness, the therapist reinforces him or her. As the client reaches each target behavior, the counselor stops giving praise for reaching the previous target. The therapist has shaped the client's behavior so that it is now assertive (Table 4.1).

Counterconditioning

Counterconditioning is a technique in which a second CR (approaching a snake) is introduced for the expressed purpose of counteracting or nullifying a previously conditioned or learned response (e.g., fear of snakes). **Desensitization** is a specific type of counterconditioning technique that is discussed in more detail in the section on Wolpe. The basic premise is that because anxiety can be learned through conditioning, it can be unlearned by a process of counterconditioning. Wolpe (1973) concluded that for counterconditioning to take place, (a) the therapist must find a response that is incompatible with anxiety and that can be paired with the stimuli that evoke anxiety and (b) "if a response-inhibiting anxiety can be made to occur in the presence of anxiety-evoking stimuli, it will weaken the bond between these stimuli and anxiety" (p. 17). The underlying premise is to do

Table 4.1 Chart for Positive Reinforcement, Negative Reinforcement, Punishment, and Shaping

Positive Reinforcement	Common Types of Positive Reinforcement	Example 1	Example 2
Strengthens some behavior	Praise	A mother praises (positive stimulus) her daughter for completing homework (behavior)	A boy earns $10.00 (positive stimulus) for every A (behavior) he receives on his report card
Increases the likelihood of a specific response from a person	Rewards		
Adding something that will motivate a person to increase the likelihood the person will engage in that behavior again			
A person presents a motivating/reinforcing stimulus to another person after the desired behavior is exhibited making the behavior more likely to occur again			
Negative Reinforcement	**Common Types of Negative Reinforcement**	**Example 1**	**Example 2**
A stimulus is removed (usually an aversive stimulus) after a specific behavior is exhibited	Removal/avoidance of aversive stimuli	Removing a stone that has lodged inside your shoe while walking	Leaving a movie theater if the movie is really bad
Likelihood of the behavior occurring again in the future is increased because of removing/avoiding the negative consequence	Taking something away to increase the likelihood of a response		
Punishment	**Common Types of Punishment**	**Example 1**	**Example 2**
An aversive event likely to terminate any behavior that it follows	The end result is to decrease the undesirable behavior by applying a negative consequence after the behavior is exhibited	A child hits another child and is sent to the "time out" corner	Siblings fight over who gets the biggest piece of cake, and mother gives the cake away to homeless

(Continued)

Table 4.1 (Continued)

Punishment	Common Types of Punishment	Example 1	Example 2
A process whereby a consequence immediately follows a behavior, which decreases the future tendency of that behavior			

Shaping	Common Types of Shaping	Example 1	Example 2
Shaping modifies behaviors by reinforcing behaviors that progressively approximate the target behavior	Successive approximation	A boy has difficulty handing in his homework and the teacher rewards each approximation of his completing his homework	To teach a child to learn how to write her name, the teacher initially praises her for writing the first letter of her name. After the child has mastered the first letter of her name, the teacher praises letter by letter until the child masters writing her entire name
	Can assist in changing a negative behavior or in creating an appropriate behavior that is not yet in the person's repertoire of behavior		

the opposite of the anxiety-provoking problem and the anxiety will lessen. The therapist pairs the anxiety situation with relaxation, assertion, and exercise.

Counselors are cautioned to use baby steps in counterconditioning. Otherwise, they may substantially increase a client's anxiety. As the therapist increases the pairings of the anxiety-inhibiting response with anxiety-evoking stimuli, the client develops a new, more adaptive response that is substituted for his or her prior maladaptive anxiety.

Token Economies

Counselors use **token economies** to shape client behavior when approval and other reinforcers do not work. When clients demonstrate a target behavior, the counselor reinforces them with "tokens" that can be exchanged for desired objects or privileges. For example, a mother established a token economy to deal with her daughter's disruptive behavior in class. Together, she and her child had bought some items that were desired. The mother assigned points to the toys and candy based on her perception of what is rewarding to the child. The greatest reward (reinforcer) was given the highest number of points. The teacher provided daily reports of the daughter's behavior. Each day that there were no negative reports, the daughter received a given number of points that were additive in nature. The daughter also received points when she demonstrated positive behavior. Gradually, the daughter changed her classroom behavior.

Token economies provide a concrete measure of a person's motivation to change specific behaviors. An advantage of using a token economy is that individuals decide how to use their tokens, thereby giving them a sense of control over their lives.

Theory of Maladaptive Behavior

Behavior therapy is based on the principle that mental disorders are learned behaviors that eventually result with a symptom of the disorder. Behavior therapists argue that maladaptive behavior is not caused by unconscious conflict, lack of insight, lack of positive regard, or any other concept outlined in psychodynamic or humanistic therapies. Instead, the client's maladaptive behavior constitutes the disorder. Whereas psychodynamic and existential-humanistic clinicians emphasize a client's need for insight regarding what "lies behind" his or her maladaptive behavior, behavior therapists argue that insight is not necessary for behavior change to take place. Behavior therapists focus on helping clients unlearn maladaptive behaviors and replace them with newly learned adaptive behaviors.

Behaviorists believe that both adaptive and maladaptive behaviors are controlled by their consequences. The same learning principles that govern adaptive human behavior also influence maladaptive behavior. Maladaptive responses increase in their frequency if they are followed by reinforcements, such as special attention. Conversely, maladaptive responses tend to decrease if they are followed by punishments or if they go consistently unrewarded (extinction).

Maladaptive behavior is sustained by a stimulus situation that sets up the occasion for the behavior. For instance, a person is able to refrain from drugs while attending a rehabilitation center, but he relapses very quickly when he returns to his neighborhood because it contains stimuli (the building in which he shot up or familiar faces that signal former drug use) that signal drug use for him. If the same person is relocated in a different neighborhood, he stands a greater chance of avoiding a relapse into drug use because the new neighborhood lacks the same discriminative stimuli. The old environment is said to have stimulus control over the drug addict.

Likewise, stimuli may also signal that reinforcement will not follow a behavior made under different stimulus situations. Hence, the corporate executive beats his wife at home but never in a public place. Aggressive behavior and drug use are reinforced in one situation but not in another. In fact, punishment may result when the corporate executive hits his wife in public or when an addict shoots up in a different neighborhood.

Behaviorists conceptualize psychopathology as behavior that is disadvantageous or dangerous to the person and/or to other people. Specific environmental circumstances help shape the development of maladaptive behavior. For instance, children who are raised in neglectful or abusive home environments may have had their aggressive behavior reinforced in interpersonal relationships. A parent might instruct a child to "fight back or I'll handle you when you get home." Insufficient reinforcement may also contribute to maladaptive behavior as is the case when a child is only infrequently reinforced for completing homework.

In addition, maladaptive behavior also results when we use a single reinforcer in a negative or destructive way, such as when we overeat and become obese. Addictive behaviors usually emphasize a single reinforcer in a negative way—smoking, drinking, using cocaine, and so on. Krumboltz and Thoresen (1976) have pointed out that excessive punishment to control a child's behavior can lead to the child's subsequent development of maladaptive behavior.

Maladaptive behavior can also emanate from insufficient cues to predict consequences of our behavior. We may not be aware of the effects of our behavior on others. The behavior may have been tolerated at home, and we generalized inappropriately the behavior to other situations.

THE THERAPEUTIC PROCESS ___

Behavior therapy rests on two cornerstones. First, it is a psychological model that departed significantly from psychoanalytic and psychodynamic therapies. Second, it uses the scientific method in working with clients and in investigating the efficacy of its approach (Wilson, 2011). Behavior therapy emphasizes modifying and gaining control over unwanted behaviors. Oftentimes, people who seek behavior therapy have a deficit or an excess of a given behavior that they want to increase or decrease. Behavior therapy is the treatment of choice for clients who are unable to participate effectively in insight-oriented or cognitive therapies. The behavioral theorist's worldview is characterized by the following perspectives:

- Counseling and psychotherapy should focus on clients' observable behavior and their life responses, not on their unresolved, unconscious conflicts, which behaviorists maintain cannot be effectively studied or defined.
- Learning is a central principle for understanding and changing a client's behavior. A client's learning in behavior therapy is carefully structured. In contrast to other psychotherapists, behavior therapists often ask clients to do something such as practicing relaxation training, monitoring one's caloric intake, refraining from engaging in compulsive rituals, or confronting anxiety-provoking situations (Wilson, 2011).
- Clients' changes in behavior are governed by the law of effect, which Thorndike (1911) defined as "behavior that is followed by satisfying consequences will be more likely to be repeated and behavior that is followed by unsatisfying consequences will be less likely to be repeated" (p. 74).
- Learning is also governed by contingencies. Clients change their behaviors as they discover relationships between sequences of events and their behaviors—a process known as associate learning (Wolpe, 1990). In contrast to psychodynamic therapists, behavior therapists put a premium on the client's activities in the real world outside of therapy.
- Behavior therapy is an individual-focused approach. It is usually tailored for a specific client who comes to counseling with specific presenting concerns.
- Behavior therapy takes a nonpathological approach to what other schools of thought label as mental illness. Instead of viewing anxiety, sexual, and conduct disorders as mental illness, behaviorists conceptualize these challenges as problems in living.
- Most abnormal behavior is assumed to be acquired through learning and maintained in the same manner as normal behavior.
- Instead of focusing on the past, behavioral assessment examines the current determinants of behavior. As Wilson (2011) has stated, "Specificity is the hallmark of behavioral assessment and treatment, and it is assumed that the person is best understood and described by what the person does in a particular situation" (p. 237).
- To conduct treatment in psychotherapy, the therapist conducts a prior analysis of the problem into its components or subparts. Clinical procedures are then systematically targeted at the specific components of the client's problems or issues.
- The behavior therapist develops treatment strategies that are individually tailored for each client, depending on the issue for which they request assistance.
- It is not essential for a behavior therapist to understand the origins of a psychological problem in order to produce positive client behavioral change. A client's past experiences are significant only to the extent that they contribute to the client's current distress or presenting problem.

- Behavior therapists must commit to the scientific method in their work with clients.

  This includes an explicit, testable conceptual framework; treatment derived from or at least consistent with the content and method of experimental-clinical psychology; therapeutic techniques that have measurable outcomes and can be replicated; the experimental evaluation of treatment methods and concepts; and emphasis on innovative research strategies that allow rigorous evaluation of specific methods applied to particular problems instead of global assessment of ill-defined procedures applied to heterogeneous problems. (Wilson, 2011, p. 237)

The process of behavior therapy begins with problem identification and assessment. That is, the therapist's first task is to identify and understand the client's presenting issues. The therapist investigates the specific dimensions of a client's presenting issues and asks questions such as the following: When did the problem first occur? What was the severity and the frequency of the problem? How does the client think and feel about the problem and what has he or she done in the past to cope with the problem? After gaining the information described herein, the therapist proceeds to conduct a functional analysis of the client's presenting issue, which usually involves identifying specific environmental and person variables that seem to maintain the maladaptive thoughts, feelings, or behavior.

The Therapeutic Relationship

Despite what some people believe, behaviorists establish a warm and empathic relationship with their clients. More than three decades ago, Sloane, Staples, Cristol, Yorkston, and Whipple (1975) found that in a study of 94 clients with different problems, clients who were given behavior therapy rated their counselors higher on accurate empathy, self-congruence, and interpersonal contact than did clients who received psychoanalytical, insight-oriented therapy. This finding was surprising to many because they thought behaviorists would be rated as cold because of their emphasis on observable and measurable behavior.

The therapeutic relationship is central in behavior therapy because the therapists must be able to get clients to trust them in such sensitive issues as dealing with their deepest fears. Behavior therapy is based on a collaborative relationship between the therapist and the client. The majority of behavioral practitioners assert that factors such as warmth, empathy, authenticity, and acceptance are necessary but not sufficient for behavior change to take place. In contrast to the experiential schools of psychotherapy, behavioral clinicians believe that clients make progress in therapy primarily because of the specific behavioral techniques that they use rather than because of their relationship with the client. Clients learn self-control and self-management techniques so that they, rather than the therapist, are in control of their lives. Behavior therapists are more directive than therapists who subscribe to the psychodynamic or existential-humanistic schools. As Wilson (2005) has stated,

> **Inner Reflections**
>
> What are your thoughts and feelings about behavior therapists and the therapeutic relationship?
>
> In your mind's eye, can you see yourself functioning effectively as a behavioral therapist?

Both behavioral and psychodynamic treatments attempt to modify underlying causes of behavior. The difference is what proponents of each approach regard as causes. Behavior analysts look for current variables and conditions that control behavior. Some psychodynamic approaches (e.g., psychoanalysis) ask, "What is this person trying to achieve?" Others (e.g., Adlerian psychotherapy) ask, "What is the purpose of this person's behavior?" Behavioral approaches ask, "What is causing this person to behave in this way right now, and what can we do right now to change that behavior?" (p. 214)

Goals of Therapy

The goals of the behavior therapist emphasize modifying or eliminating the maladaptive behavior the client manifests and on helping him or her develop healthy, constructive ways of acting. Unproductive actions are replaced with productive ways of responding. At the beginning of the therapeutic process, the client, with the assistance of the therapist, outlines specific goals. The goals must be clear, concrete, and agreed on by the client and the therapist. These goals then form the basis of a contract that directs the therapeutic process. Behavior treatment goals are stated in measurable terms so that clients can assess their progress in goal accomplishment. During psychotherapy, goals may be changed depending on client learning and need. Cormier and Nurius (2003) have outlined the following goal-setting process in behavior therapy:

- The counselor informs the client about the need for goals, the role that they play in therapy, and the client's involvement in the goal-setting process.
- Next, the client indicates the positive changes he or she desires from therapy. Emphasis is placed on what the client wants rather than what he or she does not want.
- The therapist highlights that change can only come from the client and the fact that the client must accept responsibility for the desired change in behavior.
- Throughout the therapy process, the client and the therapist work on identified goals, revising them as the need arises. A plan of action is developed to achieve the identified goals.

Role of the Therapist

Behavior therapists function as consultants in producing behavioral change. During the change process, therapists not only motivate and support clients but also help redesign goals and procedures when appropriate. Therapists continually assess and reassess the effectiveness of therapy. Typically, behavior therapists are active and directive during counseling. They set up learning experiences for clients and determine the best clinical methods for client change. For instance, if a client wants to learn how to control his anger, he must first define what becoming angry means for him. Small incremental steps are outlined that will help the client control his anger in specific situations. In addition, behavioral therapists perform a number of other functions (Miltenberger, 2004), including the following:

- Conduct a complete functional assessment to identify the variables that maintain the conditions about which the client complains. Psychotherapists take detailed notes on the situational antecedents that produced the undesirable behavior, as well as the components and consequences of it on the client.
- Generate initial treatment goals and construct a treatment plan to achieve these goals.
- Teach concrete skills to the client by instruction, **modeling**, and performance feedback.
- Use therapy techniques to promote maintenance of behavior change.
- Measure the effectiveness of treatment procedures.
- Complete follow-up assessments.

Role of the Client

Behavior therapy adopts an active role for both the therapist and the client. The client participates in therapy by agreeing to perform homework assignments and by engaging in behavioral rehearsal until skills are learned. Behavior therapy rests on the assumption that the clients who come for therapy are motivated to change. Therapists encourage clients to experiment and to enlarge their repertoire of adaptive behaviors. Clients are expected to do more than just gain insights about their behavior. They understand that the goal is behavioral change. Clients engage in role play, role rehearsal, relaxation training, and assertion training as well as other behaviors that the therapist may outline.

Behavior Therapy Techniques

Behavior therapists design counseling procedures for a particular client, and they can become creative in using the techniques. Lazarus, one of the pioneers in contemporary clinical behavior therapy (1997, 2000), maintains that behavioral clinicians can incorporate into their treatment plans any technique that can be shown to change behavior effectively. The following sections discuss a number of behavioral counseling techniques, including relaxation training, reciprocal inhibition, systematic desensitization training, flooding, and in vivo exposure.

Relaxation Training Techniques

The relaxation technique has been mentioned several times in this chapter because of its importance in behavioral counseling. This section differs from early descriptions in that it provides detailed steps for using this technique. Jacobson (1938) was the first to develop the **progressive relaxation** procedure, which requires therapists to teach clients how to relax the muscles throughout their bodies. The underlying premise of progressive relaxation training is that muscle tension increases anxiety. Therapists teach clients how to discriminate between when their muscles are tensely contracted and when they are fully relaxed. When clients learn how to discriminate between tense and relaxed muscle groups and to relax muscles on cue, they reduce tension in their bodies. They begin to have a better understanding of what tension is and how they can control it.

Steps in Using the Relaxation Technique. The steps in using the relaxation technique are quite simple. The therapist asks the client to be seated comfortably in a reclining chair or lie on the floor.

- *Step 1:* The therapist suggests that the client close his or her eyes, take a few deep breaths, and slowly exhale SA: to the count of five.
- *Step 2:* The therapist tells the client,

  "We will be participating in a systematic relaxation exercise. This exercise is designed to help you learn how to relax your body when you feel tense. We will be tensing and relaxing different muscle groups within your body. I want you to notice how you feel when you tense your muscles and when you relax them." The therapist might ask the client where the most tension exists in his or her body and begin there. Another approach might be that the therapist begins with the head first (specifically the back of the neck) and then proceeds to the rest of the body muscle groups, ending with the feet. The clinician states, "First, I would like you to tighten the back of your neck and to hold it tight for about 5 seconds—one, two, three, four, and five. Now let the tension go, and as you do, exhale slowly. How does that feel? Notice the difference between the relaxation and tension in your neck as you tighten and relax your neck muscles. We will be alternatively tightening and letting go of each muscle group."

- *Step 3:* The practitioner continues by having the client tighten and relax all muscle groups within his or her body. The practitioner has the client (a) tighten the muscle group, (b) hold the tension for about 5 seconds, (c) let the tension go, and (d) notice the difference between tension and relaxation.

- *Step 4:* When all muscle groups have been tensed and relaxed, the therapist suggests that the client continue to sit or to lie still, enjoying the feelings of relaxation and self-control in bringing such feelings to pass. The clinician states, "Now whenever you feel comfortable returning back to the here and now, I want you to slowly open your eyes, feeling a greater sense of relaxation."

In using relaxation training, counselors must understand that some clients have developed a chronic state of muscular tension that may not go away after one or two muscle relaxation exercises. The successful use of relaxation training should be individualized for each client.

Reciprocal Inhibition and Systematic Desensitization

As noted earlier, Wolpe (1958, 1982) developed the behavioral concepts of reciprocal inhibition and systematic desensitization using the learning principles of classical conditioning. Reciprocal inhibition is a behavioral technique that is based on the inhibition of responses by the occurrence of another response that is incompatible with it. Relaxation training uses principles of reciprocal inhibition when clients are instructed to use deep breathing and muscle relaxation techniques in response to anxiety-provoking and fearful situations.

Systematic desensitization may be defined as the pairing of a neutral event or stimulus with a stimulus that already elicits fear. Key components of desensitization include counterconditioning, reciprocal inhibition, and substitution of one type of response for another to gradually lower a client's level of fear. Systematic desensitization techniques are used with clients who experience a variety of phobias, such as irrational fear of heights, objects, or animals, and feel a heightened sense of anxiety and stress in social situations.

Systematic desensitization is composed of three primary steps: (1) training in deep muscle relaxation, (2) construction of anxiety hierarchies, and (3) matching specific anxiety situations from the hierarchies with relaxation training. The technique is based on the fact that it is impossible to be relaxed and anxious at the same time. A major purpose of systematic desensitization is to train the client to have an automatic relaxation response when the previously feared object appears.

Students who take examinations sometimes experience test anxiety. Initially, a counselor trains them in systematic desensitization. Next, the counselor engages in a collaborative applied behavioral analysis of the antecedents, resultant behavior, and consequences related to the students' examination anxiety. An **anxiety hierarchy** is constructed that represents a scale of the clients' fears about test taking. Wolpe and Lazarus (1966) have provided some directions in constructing an anxiety scale:

> Think of the worst anxiety you have ever experienced or can imagine experiencing, and assign to this the number 100. Now think of the state of being absolutely calm, and call this 0. On this scale how do you rate yourself at this moment? (p. 73)

The situations in an anxiety hierarchy should represent a well-designed progression of anxiety. One way to achieve this goal is to first generate about 10 to 15 items. Write each item on your anxiety hierarchy on its own separate 3- by 5-inch card. For instance, if one has a fear of flying, the following hierarchy might be constructed:

- Making plane reservations
- Packing luggage
- Driving to the airport
- Standing in a long line at a crowded ticket counter to have luggage checked
- Waiting for boarding
- Boarding the airplane
- Taxiing of the airplane on the runway
- Hearing the flight attendant give directions about what to do in an emergency
- Climbing to a cruising altitude
- Ears popping as the airplane ascends
- Turbulence throughout the airplane so that it rocks back and forth
- Descending and taxiing on the runway
- Landing of the airplane and hearing the plane's wheel come down on the ground
- Lining up and waiting for deplaning on arrival
- Deplaning the airplane

Next, grade the anxiety of each item by assigning it a number on a scale from 0 to 100, where 100 is the highest level of anxiety imaginable and 0 represents no anxiety or complete relaxation. A potential grading category is provided for your consideration. Place each item generated for the anxiety hierarchy above on a separate card. Then sort the items in one of the anxiety piles listed on the next page.

Anxiety Hierarchy Pile	Anxiety Grade
Low anxiety	1–19
Medium–low anxiety	20–39
Medium anxiety	40–59
Medium–high anxiety	60–79
High anxiety	80–100

Clients' systematic desensitization sessions should not exceed 30 minutes, and therapists should try not to have them desensitize more than three of the anxiety hierarchy items per counseling session. Begin each new session with the last item desensitized. If possible, have the client practice desensitization once a day five times each week. Research studies have found that systematic desensitization can be effective for most phobias with the following considerations:

- Systematic desensitization is more effective for specific phobias than for disorders that involve "free-floating" anxiety, such as social phobia or agoraphobia.
- Systematic desensitization tends to be more successful if skill deficits are not the cause of anxiety. For instance, if a person is anxious to take an exam because she has not studied for it, then systematic desensitization will not be effective. However, if a student has studied and knows the material like the back of her hand but freezes up when taking tests, then desensitization might be used to desensitize her to performance fears.

Stress Inoculation Training

Meichenbaum (1985) also developed stress inoculation training, which was designed to help inoculate people against collapse as they experienced stress. The primary goal in stress inoculation was to change individuals' beliefs about the behaviors and statements they make to themselves regarding how they deal with stress (e.g., "I come apart under stress" or "I'm at my best when I am under stress"). He outlined three phases of stress inoculation: (1) the conceptual phase, (2) the skills acquisition phase, and (3) the application phase. Stress inoculation training helps clients to induce a relaxation response, engage in cognitive restructuring, and perform effective problem-solving skills. Treatment can be directed toward changing client behavior by imagining fearful or anxious situations or by confronting them in a real-life situation.

During the conceptual phase of stress inoculation, the therapist and client gather information about how to conceptualize the client's challenge. Clients describe different situations that produce stress in their lives. In response to a client's descriptions of stressful situations, the therapist points out that the client's cognitions and emotions maintain the stress felt. The therapist asks the client to pay attention to the self statements that he or she makes about the anxiety-provoking situation and to keep a log or a diary of these statements.

During the skills acquisition phase of stress inoculation training, the therapist teaches a number of skills to the client, including relaxation training, cognitive restructuring, problem-solving skills, and positive self talk and affirmations. For instance, the client might be taught the following: "Whenever I become angry, I take a deep breath, and I count to ten. I focus on responding rather than reacting to the situation at hand."

The application phase of stress inoculation training helps clients to put their newly learned stress reduction skills to use. The woman who is afraid of dogs is asked to visualize herself walking past a dog without fearing. After the client's visualization is over, the therapist gives homework assignments to practice quieting the client's fears of dogs.

Exposure Therapies

Exposure therapies are a general category of behavior techniques that are designed to treat phobias and a wide range of other behaviors. Therapists introduce clients to the situations that have contributed to their problems. The ensuing paragraphs discuss three types of exposure techniques: flooding, in vivo exposure, and implosive therapy.

Flooding. Flooding therapy constitutes either an in vivo or imaginal exposure to anxiety-evoking

Inner Reflections

What behavioral techniques do you feel the most comfortable using?

Is behavior therapy an approach that you would like to include in an integrative approach to therapy? If so, why? If not, why?

stimuli for a prolonged period of time. The principles underlying **flooding** are similar to those for desensitization. When clients avoid exposure to a fear situation, they are reinforced by their relief of not facing it. Flooding maintains that anxiety cannot be sustained with prolonged or repeated exposure to a situation, when no actual aversive consequences take place from such exposure. In flooding therapy, the therapist exposes the client to a safe version of the fearsome stimulus at maximum intensity. As a consequence of the flooding or high exposure to the stimuli, the client's anxiety reaction burns out, and extinction occurs after that. Time exposure is critical in exposure therapies. If the exposure is long enough, extinction takes place. Wolpe (1990) gives an example of flooding:

[Dr. E., a dentist suffered from two disabling neurotic fears]: an inability to give dental injections because of a fear of the patient dying in the chair, and an extravagant fear of ridicule. Since attempts to desensitize to these were making painfully slow progress, I decided to try flooding. Under light hypnosis, he was asked to imagine giving a patient a mandibular block, then, withdrawing the syringe, standing back and seeing the patient slump forward, dead. Dr. E. became profoundly disturbed, sweating, weeping, and wringing his hands. After a minute or so, noticing that the reaction was growing weaker, I terminated the scene and told him to relax. Two or three minutes later, the same sequence evoked a similar, but weaker reaction. The sequence was given three more times, at the last of which no further reaction was observed. Dr. E. said that he felt he had been through a wringer—exhausted, but at ease. At the next session, the fear of ridicule was introduced. Dr. E. imagined that he was walking down the middle of a brilliantly lighted ballroom with people on both sides pointing their fingers at

him and laughing derisively. At the fifth flooding session, it was clear that nothing remained to be treated. Four years later, at an interview, Dr. E. stated that his recovery had been fully maintained. The same was true 23 years later. (p. 223)

In Vivo. Although Dr. E.'s flooding treatment was imaginal, flooding can also be completed **in vivo**—for instance, sitting in a room with harmless spiders in a corner of the room. The term *in vivo* refers to procedures that take place in the client's actual environment. In a flooding experience, the client's anxiety reaches a peak, decreases to a plateau, and then decreases steadily thereafter (Foa & Kozak, 1986). John had tried to quit smoking on numerous occasions, but he always reverted back to smoking. One day, he began smoking one cigarette after another until he almost became sick from smoking. From that point on, he no longer felt the need to sneak to the garage to smoke.

It is recommended that therapists use a graduated approach to reducing fears. If the client becomes tense, the therapist might use a progressive relaxation technique to reduce his or her anxiety. Usually, clients who are exposed to in vivo approaches reduce their anxiety or discomfort much more quickly than do those exposed to imaginable flooding. Flooding has been used in the treatment of anxiety, including some favorable initial results with obsessive compulsive neurosis.

Implosive Therapy. Implosive therapy is a variation of flooding therapy that uses exaggerated imagined scenes that often draw on hypothesized, psychoanalytic sources of anxiety. **Implosive therapy** was developed by Stampfl (1970). Implosive therapy may be conceptualized as having the following characteristics: (a) The client imagines all anxiety situations, (b) the imagined anxiety scenes are exaggerated to elicit as much anxiety as possible, and (c) the imagined scenes are based on hypothesized sources of anxiety, which are psychodynamic in nature. The hypothesized sources of anxiety focus on hostility toward parental figures, rejection, sex, and dynamic concepts such as the oedipal complex.

Implosive therapists assert that some situations are fearful not so much because they are linked with an identifiable negative event but rather because the situation evokes inner stimuli associated with sex and aggression (i.e., fear of castration, penis envy, etc.). Both flooding and implosive therapy form part of the treatment of choice for posttraumatic stress disorder and from trauma such as rape, natural disasters, and wartime horrors (Foa & Meadows, 1997).

CURRENT TRENDS IN BEHAVIOR THERAPY

Prior to the 1960s, behaviorists were regarded as mechanistic and experimentally oriented with animals. Since the 1970s, however, behavior therapy has undergone a renaissance in the field of psychology. Virtually all areas of American life have adopted behavioral techniques or concepts, including child raising, business and industry, education, counseling and psychotherapy, sports psychology, and advertising. During the past 50 years, behavior therapy has been pivotal in changing psychotherapy by developing new treatment strategies and by influencing how we measure treatment effectiveness.

There are two major trends in behavior therapy that merit mentioning: (1) applied behavioral analysis as a field of study and (2) behavioral pharmacology. This section provides a brief summary of each of these trends and references are provided that might be helpful in learning more about these two burgeoning areas within behavior therapy.

APPLIED BEHAVIORAL ANALYSIS

Applied behavioral analysis is the application of operant (system of rewards and consequences) and classical conditioning to modify human behavior or the application to teach an individual new skills while replacing undesirable behavior with desirable behavior. It has been used quite successfully to help children diagnosed with autism spectrum disorder. In some states, the department of mental health requires behavior specialists to obtain certification by the Behavior Analyst Certification Board. Some colleges are now offering a certificate specializing in applied behavior analysis—for instance, St. Joseph's University and Drexel University. Although applied behavior analysis is often used to work with children who have been diagnosed with autism spectrum disorder, it has also been applied to work with a broad section of issues, including severe mental disorders, parenting, and health and exercise (De Luca & Holborn, 1992; Kuhn, Lerman, & Vorndran, 2003; Wong et al., 1993). Applied behavior analysts identify the observable relationship of a person's behavior to his or her environment, and they point out the antecedents and consequences of a particular behavior. The dimensions of a functional behavior assessment must be accountable, public (meaning must be completely visible and public), doable (a wide variety of individuals can implement applied behavior procedures) and optimistic (Heward et al., 2005). The ensuing section examines what goes into making a functional behavioral assessment.

Behavioral Assessment: The Functional Assessment Model

Applied behavioral analysis is a key type of assessment that behavioral clinicians use. It is defined as a systematical method of collaboratively investigating the client and his or her environment to develop specific techniques for addressing the client's problems. In a functional analysis, the therapist engages in examining the ABCs of behavior, which is the study of the antecedent events (A), the resultant behavior (B), and the consequences of that behavior (C). The behavior therapist seeks to find out what happens just prior to a specific behavior, how the specific behavior manifested itself, and what the result or consequence of that behavior was on the client. In Chapter 5, I explore Albert Ellis's cognitive-behavioral counseling theory that uses the ABCs for inner thoughts and feelings.

In the first part of behavioral assessment, the clinician identifies the client's presenting problems. For instance, a woman comes to therapy complaining of depression and crying episodes at home. The clinician seeks detailed information about the specific dimensions of the woman's depression, such as what does the woman mean when she says she is depressed. For instance, the clinician might ask, "How do you know when you are depressed?" The woman might respond, "I know I am depressed when I start sleeping all day" or when "I get this confused feeling in my head." The clinician wants to get a clear understanding of what depression feels like for the client and how it manifests itself behaviorally in her life.

After the clinician gains an understanding of what depression feels like and how it shows itself in the woman's life, he can then collect such information as (a) when the behavior occurs, (b) how frequently it takes place, (c) what usually comes before and after the behavior, (d) what the client thinks and feels during the behavior, and (e) what the client has already tried to do to resolve the problem. Prochaska and Norcross (2003) point out that most behavior problems can be placed into one of three categories of excess, deficit, and inappropriateness. Examples of problems of excess occur when individuals do too much of something, such as eating, sleeping, or drinking too much. Deficit-oriented problems are those that involve not doing enough of something, such as not speaking up for oneself or not being able to say no to loved ones. Examples of inappropriate behavior might include a child's display of sexual behavior far in advance of his or her age or a child using baby talk to get what he or she wants.

During the second phase of assessment, the clinician conducts a functional analysis of the client's problem, identifies specific environmental and person variables that maintain the problem behavior, and refrains from asking why questions (e.g., "Why do you become depressed?"). Instead, the clinician focuses on using how, when, where, and what questions.

Another important part of performing a functional analysis involves learning how the behavior develops and maintains itself via a system of rewards or reinforcers and punishments. The underlying principle is that what follows a particular behavior will increase the likelihood of it taking place again. With both children and adults, therapists must examine patterns of attention that people gain from displaying their behavior. For instance, do you gain more attention when you are depressed than when you do not show depression? In the book *Games People Play*, Eric Berne (1964) discusses the payoff or reward for playing "wooden leg" or "woe is me." Playing wooden leg brings the sympathy, attention, and help of others.

Applied behavior analysis helps clients to work more quickly toward resolving problems than some psychodynamic approaches because it breaks down an amorphous idea of depression into manageable behavioral units. As the therapist focuses on the behavior, the client demonstrates when she is depressed, and the client is better able to take small steps in ending the depression. This situation takes place because the therapist places a high priority on the client's acting or doing something about the depression. For instance, when the client analyzes her depression signals, she learns that certain thoughts or specific comments from others (disapproval and criticism) bring on the depression. She is taught how to combat criticism.

A client might learn to say, "Jennifer's comments have nothing to do with how I feel about me. She's entitled to her opinion. I do not agree with her opinion of me. I dismiss her negative comments."

Functional behavioral assessments have become quite popular in schools, and they are usually used for dealing with student problem behavior. A functional behavioral assessment is a systematic method to gather data, to examine the environment, and to look for relationships that help the counselor identify variables that influence student behaviors. The basic premise of functional behavioral assessment is that behavior serves a purpose, and behavior is related to the environment in which it occurs. When counselors understand what influences students' behavior, they are in a better position to determine how those variables can be changed to promote positive behavior. The counselor tries to identify what takes place prior to (antecedents to) the student's display of problem behavior and what occurs after (consequences of) problem behavior. Table 4.2 is an example of an ABC observation form.

Table 4.2 ABC Observation Form

Student Name: _____	Teacher Name: _____	Observation Date: _____
Observer: _____	Classroom: _____	Time: _____
Activity: _____	Referred by: _____	Class Period: _____
ANTECEDENT	**BEHAVIOR**	**CONSEQUENCE**

Source: © Elsie Jones-Smith (2012).

Inner Reflections

Sometimes fights take place because family members fail to understand what contributes to an angry outburst or tears.

Think about your most recent family conflict. Conduct a behavioral assessment of the family members involved in the conflict or heated discussion.

What were the antecedent events that seemed to spark the conflict? What behavior did the individuals display? What were the consequences of the behavior?

A major problem with traditional teacher disciplinary techniques is that teachers often address problem behavior by manipulating events that follow the misbehavior (e.g., verbal reprimands, isolation, detention, suspension). Such an approach fails to teach the student acceptable replacement behaviors. Two students may curse at a teacher; however, the first student curses to gain peer approval, while the second curses because he is attempting to escape an aversive teacher–pupil interaction. A functional behavioral assessment helps individualized education program teams to understand the function that the problem behavior serves for the students and results in interventions that reduce or eliminate problem behavior by replacing it with behavior that serves the same function for the student but is more socially acceptable. If Charles curses at the teacher because he wants peer attention, a functional behavioral analysis would teach Charles replacement behaviors or more socially acceptable ways to gain attention.

Functional behavioral assessments are usually reserved for serious, recurring student disciplinary problems that are not responsive to usual discipline strategies. Questions a counselor might ask prior to a functional behavioral assessment are the following: Does the student's behavior differ significantly from that of his or her classmates? Does the student's behavior reduce the possibility of successful learning for the student and classmates? Does the student's behavior represent a behavioral deficit or excess, rather than a cultural difference? If the behavior persists, is some disciplinary action likely to take place?

Functional Assessment Interview Form

Interviewer(s) _____ Date _____

Student(s) _____

Respondent(s) _____ Title _____

1. Describe the behavior of concern. _____
   _____
   _____

2. How often does the behavior occur? _____
   _____

3. How long does it last? _____

4. How intense is the behavior? _____

5. What is happening when the behavior occurs? _____
   _____
   _____

6. When/where is the behavior most/least likely to occur? _____
   _____
   _____

7. With whom is the behavior most/least likely to occur? _____
   _____

8. What conditions are most likely to precipitate (set off) the behavior? _____
   _____

9. How can you tell the behavior is about to start? _____
   _____

10. What usually happens after the behavior? Describe what happens according to adult(s), peers, and student responses. _____
    _____

11. What is the likely function (intent) of the behavior—that is, why do you think the student behaves this way? What does the student get or avoid? _____
    _____
    _____

12. What behaviors might serve the same function for the student that is appropriate within the social/environmental context? _____

13. What other information might contribute to creating an effective intervention? _____

14. Who should be involved in planning and implementing the intervention plan? _____
    _____

Source: © Elsie Jones-Smith (2012).

INTEGRATED PSYCHOPHARMACOLOGY

Brief Overview

The integration of psychotherapy with pharmacology appears to be one of the major current trends in psychotherapy. Behavioral psychopharmacology is a branch of psychology that studies the effects of behavior-altering drugs (Preston & Johnson, 2014). Most of the drugs studied are psychoactive or mind-altering drugs that bring about change in an individual's perception, mood, thought patterns, and behavior. The American Society for Pharmacology and Experimental Therapeutics (ASPET) is a 4,800-member scientific society whose members conduct pharmacological research. This organization's website states the following:

> The Division of Behavioral Pharmacology serves members interested in research on the behavioral effects of drugs. These interests range from behavioral approaches to the study of CNS pharmacology to investigations of how drugs alter behavior and encompass perspectives that range from descriptive to mechanistic. Most often, behavioral pharmacologists examine drugs with an emphasis on effects in the whole organism, and with an appreciation of the considerable influence of environmental variables on drug action. (http://www.aspet.org/Behavioral_Pharmacology/Home/)

Drugs are an ever-present part of the current mental health environment (Grayson, Schwartz, & Commerford, 1997). A large percentage of psychotherapy clients have either taken or have been prescribed a pill to feel less anxious or depressed. Psychotropic drugs are now being widely prescribed for children. The American Psychological Association (2008) has reported that

> The number of prescriptions dispensed in the United States for antidepressant, anti-anxiety, analeptic and antipsychotic medications grew significantly from 2002 to 2006, according to projections prepared by IMS Health, a health-care case information company that tracks prescription sales

nationwide. Antidepressant prescriptions grew by 12 percent, anxiety medications by 16 percent, antipsychotics by 35 percent, and drugs used to treat attention deficit hyperactivity disorder by 37 percent. (p. 52)

According to Dr. Axe (a physician who is the creator of a leading natural health website), psychotropic drugs are the most widely prescribed drugs in the United States. Prescription drugs are a multibillion dollar business, bringing in $643 billion worldwide, with the United States accounting for more than half of this market (see http://draxe.com/brainwashed-by-psychotropic-drugs/). Oftentimes, young people who are diagnosed with attention deficit disorder are given drugs to make them more compliant in class and at home for their parents. Children who are labeled ADHD (attention-deficit/hyperactivity disorder) and bipolar disorder are often drugged and made into lifelong customers of the pharmaceutical industry. In 2008, the pharmaceutical industry made 4.8 billion dollars off ADHD medications in the United States.

It is highly likely that the average master level practitioner will, at some point in his or her career, come into contact with clients who are either on medications designed to reduce anxiety or on psychotropic drugs that reduce behavioral and mood disorders (Kaut & Dickinson, 2007). It is important, therefore, for him or her to learn about the brain, neurons, neurotransmitters, pre- and post-synaptic receptors, and medications that target different parts of the brain because changes in neurotransmitters and/or their receptors are responsible for the therapeutic effects of many drugs. Medication may be critical for clients' functioning and clinicians' knowledge of the brain, and neurotransmitters will help them comprehend how different treatments work with their clients.

Although many master level clinicians have not had specific training in psychopharmacology, nearly 90% of them report having clients who take psychotropic medications (Ingersoll & Brennan, 2001; Scovel, Christensen, & England, 2002). Psychotherapy integrated with psychopharmacology is quite common in mental health practice

(Kaut & Dickinson, 2007). Clinicians and clients should endeavor to gain an informed understanding regarding what psychopharmacology integrated with psychotherapy can provide.

Role of the Therapist in Integrated Behavioral Psychopharmacology

There are three main roles that a practitioner might assume in integrated behavioral psychopharmacology. First, practitioners may serve as mental health consultants within the health care system—especially with medical providers. This situation exists because counselors will most likely consult with members of the medical establishment, and it is helpful for them to recognize the roles that psychiatrists, general practitioners, pediatricians, and other specialists assume. As a consultant, a mental health clinician might be asked to contribute information about a client's overall assessment or to address concerns from physicians about a client's need for medication. As Kaut and Dickinson (2007) asserted,

> The counselor as consultant should be able to discuss a client's relevant behaviors with a physician, including any past history or contextual circumstances that might be an important part of a medication decision-making process. More specifically, physicians should be encouraged to clarify the rationale for a medication, coupled with even a brief mention of the expected benefits of the drug and any issues regarding the time-course of treatment. Regarding the course of treatment, a counselor might inquire about any potential delay between initiation of drug therapy and the emergence of therapeutic effects (e.g., some drugs may be on the order of week). (p. 213)

The second role for a practitioner is that of an information broker. Kaut and Dickinson (2007) maintain that even though mental health clinicians are not in the business of prescribing medications, they should at least be aware of the rationale for a drug, and be able to communicate the rationale to

clients. To address client concerns or therapeutic issues, clinicians need to have a familiarity with current drug manuals (e.g., *Physician's Desk Reference* [PDR Network, 2014]; *Physicians Drug Handbook* [PDH, 2007], as well as online resources).

The third role for a practitioner is progress monitoring for clients' medications (Julien, 2001; Julien & Lange, 2001; King & Anderson, 2004). As Mantell, Ortiz, and Planthara (2004) have pointed out, a client's beliefs and preconceived notions of what drugs can do or what they represent can shape a client's experiences with medications. The mental health practitioner may be the only health care professional to have sustained contact with a client over extended periods of time. The practitioner makes simple inquiries about a client's physical condition, symptoms, and relevant social developments.

A Framework for Integrating Psychotherapy With Behavioral Psychopharmacology

An integrated perspective is needed for the mental health treatment of clients on various medications and drugs. It is important for practitioners to recognize that medication may be critical to a client's mental health and that a balanced perspective regarding the role of psychotherapy and psychopharmacology is needed. Kaut and Dickinson (2007) have provided a useful framework for clinicians to consider when integrating psychotherapy and psychopharmacology (Table 4.3).

Major Classes of Medications for Anxiety, Depression, and Behavioral and Mood Disorders

This section reviews briefly the following categories of medications: (1) anti-anxiety medications, (2) antidepressants, (3) bipolar medications, (4) stimulants, (5) antipsychotic medications, and (6) over-the-counter medications for anxiety and depression.

Table 4.3   Questions and Issues to Consider in Psychopharmacology

---

Client's Observable Behavior

What is the rationale for the medication being prescribed?

How does the drug deal with the client's presenting concerns?

What are the anticipated behavioral, emotional, or cognitive changes as a result of the prescribed medication?

What is the expected time course for therapeutic effect?

Drug Properties

What is the drug's pharmacological and therapeutic classification?

What is the known (or proposed) mechanism of action?

What neurotransmitters are involved with the medication?

What is the drug's receptor activity?

How is this drug metabolized and eliminated from the body?

What precautions or contraindications are important for this specific client?

Side Effects Issues and Questions

How does the medication interact with other medications (e.g., alcohol, over-the-counter drugs)?

What are the client's knowledge and expectations about the drug?

What is the client's understanding of his or her current condition?

Has the client been informed of the medical and psychosocial basis for the prescription medication?

Does the client understand the nature of the drug and its effects (i.e., therapeutic implications)?

Are there important side effects of the medication, such as lower sex drive?

What expectations or biases might the client have concerning the drug?

In general, are there specific needs for client education or clarification?

Issues Related to Monitoring of Client's Progress

Is the client adhering to the prescription regimen as outlined?

Has the client experienced any behavioral changes (i.e., intended or problematic) since drug inception?

Is there a need for the counselor to consult with the prescribing physician?

Should the dosage of the medication be adjusted?

Should the medication for the client be discontinued?

Are there suitable alternative considerations (i.e., other medications or therapies)?

Anti-Anxiety Medications

As noted earlier, a large percentage of medications are prescribed for anxiety and behavioral and mood disorders. Anxiety steals the joy out of a person's life. Typically, anxiety begins with a person's random encounter with harmless emotional discomfort over small things. Over a period of time, however, what once was a small upset or irritation, gradually turns into a pathological condition, sometimes resulting in panic attacks. Clinical anxiety disorder usually consists of four components: (1) mental apprehension, (2) physical tension, (3) dissociative anxiety, and (4) physical anxiety symptoms. The following information is compiled from several sources (Preston & Johnson, 2014), including John Preston's "Quick Reference to Psychotropic Medications" available at http://psyd-fx.com/quick_reference.pdf.

Anti-anxiety medications or anxiolytics (commonly called tranquilizers) are prescribed for a variety of anxiety disorders and panic attacks. The most common categories of anti-anxiety drugs are benzodiazepine and beta blockers. Below is a description of the medication and its intended medical effect. Typically, people are prescribed anti-anxiety drugs for only a few weeks because they can become highly addictive. If clients attempt to immediately discontinue usage of anti-anxiety medications, they can become restless and even more anxious than before. Two types of anti-anxiety medications are reviewed in this section: (1) benzodiazepines and (2) beta blockers.

Benzodiazepine: Benzodiazepine is extremely effective in increasing the effects of the primary inhibitory neurotransmitter, GABA (gamma aminobutyric acid). This medication produces a calming effect, often inducing sleep and relieving the client's anxiety. It is effecting in reducing phobic symptoms and decreasing or preventing panic attacks. The enhanced GABA activity also functions as a muscle relaxer. Some of the well-known anxiety medications are as follows:

Generic Name	Brand Name
Diazepam	Valium
Alprazolam	Xanax
Lorazepam	Ativan
Clonazepam	Klonopin
Chlordiazepoxide	Librium

Beta blockers: Typically beta blockers are used to handle situations of cardiac arrhythmia (abnormality in the electric conduction system of the heart), hypertension, and heart attack (myocardial infarction). In addition, beta blocker medication is effective in dealing with anxiety symptoms, such as increased heart palpitation and increased blood pressure, and stopping or slowing down the

stress-inducing effects of adrenaline. This medication is used to reduce performance anxiety, social phobia, and panic associated with stage fright and public interaction. Anti-anxiety medications under this category include the following:

Generic Name	Brand Name
Propranolol	Inderal
Atenolol	Tenormin

Antidepressants

Anti-depressants have been linked with neurotransmitters in the brain. Researchers believe that the benefits of antidepressants come from how they affect the brain circuits and the chemicals (called neurotransmitters) that pass signals from one nerve cell to another in the brain. These chemicals include serotonin, dopamine, and norepinephrine. It is believed that different antidepressants affect how these neurotransmitters respond. This section reviews three types of antidepressants: (1) tricyclic antidepressants, (2) monoamine oxidase inhibitors (MAO), and (3) selective serotonin reuptake inhibitors (SSRIs).

Tricyclic antidepressants: Tricyclic antidepressants, also called cyclic antidepressants, were the earliest depressants, but they have generally been replaced by antidepressants that cause fewer side effects. Tricyclic and tetracyclic antidepressants ease depression by affecting neurotransmitters that are used to communicate between brain cells. These medications are usually used in the treatment of clinical depression. Sometimes these antidepressants are used to treat anxiety disorders. Some medications under this category include the following:

Generic Name	Brand Name
Venlafaxine	Effexor
Imipramine	Tofranil
Clomipramine	Anafranil
Desipramine	Norpramin
Duloxetine	Cymbalta
Amitriptyline	Elavil

Monoamine oxidase inhibitors (MAO): This medication functions as a type of antidepressant. Medications under this category include the following:

Generic Name	Brand Name
Tranylcypromine	Parnate
Phenelzine	Nardil

Selective serotonin reuptake inhibitors: SSRIs are commonly prescribed antidepressants. Drugs in this category control anxiety disorder by inhibiting the reuptake of serotonin, a neurotransmitter that is associated with feelings of well-being and euphoria, into the presynaptic cell by heightening the former's extracellular level. This process increases serotonin level in the synaptic cleft, which allows it to bind to the postsynaptic receptor. SSRIs include Celexa, Lexapro, Paxil, Prozac, and Zoloft. Abilify and Seroquel have been FDA approved as add-on drug therapy for treatment of resistant depression. Serotonin and norepinephrine reuptake inhibitors (SNRIs) form the more recent types of antidepressants. They block the reuptake of both serotonin and norepinephrine and include drugs such as Cymbalta and Effexor. Some SSRI medications include the following:

Generic Name	Brand Name
Paroxetine	Paxil
Fluoxetine	Prozac
Sertraline	Zoloft
Fluvoxamine	Luvox
Venalafaxine	Effexor (also treats bipolar disorder)
Citalopram	Celexa
Escitalopram	Lexapro
Duloxetine	Cymbalta

Bipolar Disorder Medications

Mood stabilizers balance neurotransmitters that control emotional states and behavior. They are used to treat mania and to prevent the return of both manic and depressive episodes in bipolar disorder. Mood stabilizers such as lithium and carbamazepine may provide relief from acute episodes of mania or depression and can help prevent them from recurring.

Generic Name	Brand Name
Lithium carbonate olanzapine	Eskalith, Lithonate
Carbamazepine	Tegretol, Equetro

Stimulants

These psychotropic medications stimulate the central nervous system by increasing the release of certain chemicals in the brain. Stimulants increase the levels of dopamine in the brain, a neurotransmitter that is related to concentration, attention, and feelings of reward and pleasure. Some stimulant drugs also increase the level of glutamate, a neurotransmitter associated with behavioral control and inhibition. People with attention deficit disorder often have low levels of glutamate. Most prescriptions for stimulants are written for attention deficit disorder in children and adults.

Generic Name	Brand Name
Methylphenidate	Ritalin
d-and l-amphetamine	Adderall

Antipsychotic Medications

Antipsychotic medications are prescribed to decrease symptoms such as hallucinations, paranoia, extreme agitation, and aggression. Antipsychotics with high potency can produce movement disorders in clients. Newer antipsychotics such as Risperdal, Seroquel, and Abilify do not cause movement disorders.

Low Potency:

Generic Name	Brand Name
Chlorpromazine	Thorazine
Thioridazine	Mellaril
Quetiapine	Seroquel

High Potency:

Generic Name	Brand Name
Trifluoperazine	Stelazine
Fluphenazine	Prolixin

- Haloperidol   Haldol
- Risperidone   Risperdal
- Aripiprazole   Abilify

Anxiety and Depression
Medication Herbal and Over the Counter

For years, different countries have used certain herbal and natural remedies for ameliorating anxiety and stress. Some over-the-counter medications include the following:

- Chamomile   Treats anxiety
- St. John's wort   Treats depression and anxiety
- SAM-e   Treats depression
- L-Theanine   Treats anxiety, ADHD
- Benadryl   Treats anxiety

Benadryl is one of the most abused drugs and regular use without medical supervision may develop drug dependency.

Cultural Issues in Psychopharmacology

Although psychotropic drugs have been used throughout the world, only relatively recently studies have begun to investigate variations in clients' treatment responses across ethnic and cultural populations (Lin, 2010). For instance, what is the effectiveness of medications with different ethnic groups? What kinds of dosing strategies should be used with clients from different cultures, and what has been learned about the adverse effects of some drugs with clients from various cultures?

For the most part, psychopharmacological research has been conducted primarily in North America and Western Europe and has seldom included persons of ethnic minority or cross-cultural backgrounds (Chen & Davis, 2001). According to Lin (2010), this situation

> reflects the asymmetrical distribution of resources and the "Eurocentric" slant of the research establishment. Responsibility for such biases also lies in deeply rooted beliefs and assumptions that suggest that treatment responses are predominantly determined by biological mechanisms and that biological processes are universally applicable and thus color- and culture-free. (para. 2)

Lin (2010) also points out that there are important differences within ethnic minority and majority groups, and therefore, one should be mindful of cultural stereotyping of people. Not all members of an ethnic or cultural group will respond in the same manner to a specific medication. He notes, for example, that "there are substantive ethnic variations in haloperidol metabolism between Asians and whites. At the same time, equally extensive interindividual variations within each of the ethnic groups also have been seen, resulting in significant overlap between the two groups" (para. 5).

Culture has a profound impact on how individuals respond to medications. For instance, in Native American culture, the body, mind, and spirit are viewed holistically and perceived as connected to all things in the universe. Thus, some individuals from Native American culture may not respond positively to a drug for depression because the desired symptom relief would not address his or her life in a more holistic sense. Likewise, for some Chinese who have a traditional view of medicine, using techniques that stress different energy systems in the body might make more sense for treating depression than a medication designed to change one's mood. Individuals who adopt a traditional Chinese perspective might be more predisposed to using a naturally occurring plant that might have an impact on the energy systems related to depression.

Differences in responses to various medications may also be caused by cultural dietary practices and the use of medicinal herbs across cultural groups. For instance, the metabolism of drugs such as antipyrine and clomipramine is significantly slower in Sudanese people and South Indians when they live in their native countries; however, when they immigrate to Western countries and gradually adapt to the diet of the host society, their metabolism of these drugs speeds up and matches the levels found in White populations (Ajir et al., 1997; Branch, Salih, & Homeida, 1978; Lewis, Rack, Vaddadi, & Allen, 1980).

Although culture and biology are often portrayed as distinctly different forces in most European societies, they often interact with and influence each other. The existing belief systems within a culture affect a person's interpretation and responses to various drugs and medications. Each culture creates symbolic effects of healing related to drugs and medications. In addition, the healing practices of each culture promote hope and expectations of recovery. Thus, cultural beliefs about healing and various medications may function in a manner similar to a placebo. Cultural beliefs alone may help a client become better, even without actual medication.

It is important that therapists and clients share a general agreement about the efficacy of drugs or cultural practices in healing. As Lin (2010) has stated,

> Where health beliefs diverge—as often is the case between Western-trained clinicians and patients imbued with traditional concepts of health and illness (which are surprisingly common and tenacious, even among the highly educated)—the treatment offered is not likely to be useful, no matter how powerful the instrumental effects are of a medication. (para. 12)

Cultural differences between therapists and clients often lead to medication nonadherence. For members of ethnic minority groups within a given society, failure in medication adherence is often the norm rather than the exception. In contrast to medical healing, cultural healing practices are predominantly mediated by symbolic factors.

Recent research in medical anthropology and cultural psychiatry has resulted in the development of specific approaches to reduce noncompliance brought on by a difference in the client's and the therapist's belief systems. Lin (2010) recommends that clinicians make a concerted effort to understand clients' personal, cultural, and social world—that is, the context within which mental and behavior problems develop. From this perspective, clinical assessments of clients should include the elicitation of a client's perspectives on the following:

- The possible causes of the illness
- Modes of onset
- Illness course
- Beliefs about the outcome
- Name or label for the problem(s)
- Range of available treatment approaches and the client's expectations about the effectiveness of both biomedical and indigenous interventions.

RESEARCH AND EVALUATION __
Multicultural Positives

Because of its emphasis on tailoring therapy to the specific individual, behavior therapy has the potential to address the needs of members of ethnic minority groups. One cross-cultural benefit of behavior therapy is that assessment data are gathered from multiple sources, including questionnaires, in an approach that recognizes the diversity of environmental influences and pathways that offer the potentiality of symptom reduction. The behavioral approach to therapy emphasizes a complete assessment of a client's life situation for the purpose of determining the conditions that contribute to the client's problems and to discern if these conditions are amenable to change and therapeutic intervention. The assessment involves examining the environmental conditions that influence a client's problems—including factors such as discrimination, economic forces, and cultural issues. A behaviorist approach can help therapists avoid a judgmental perspective toward client differences. The emphasis is on problem solving, and clients who are seeking concrete action plans may be inclined to cooperate with this approach because of its nonjudgmental stance.

Moreover, behavioral therapists are mindful of their clients' culture in that the approach emphasizes the collaborative nature of treatment. Although the therapist is the expert on developing a treatment plan, the client is the expert on himself or herself and his or her problems. For instance, in behavioral parent training, therapists provide parents with a package of skills to facilitate change in their children (Briesmeister & Schafer, 1998). The therapist and parents collaborate to share their expertise for the benefit of the child. Likewise, therapists who conduct behavioral couple therapy establish a collaborative therapeutic relationship, where the therapist and couple share their conceptualizations of the problems and discuss the rationale for instituting specific behavioral principles and the types of interventions that will be made (Sayers & Heyman, 2003).

Behavioral therapy is responsive to cultural diversity in that it focuses on changing specific client behavior instead of changing clients' feelings and on their sharing of their personal concerns with the therapist. Members from Latino, African American, and Asian American cultures may find the emphasis on changing behavior more acceptable than other approaches that rely on taking long client histories that delve into their family backgrounds. Clients from ethnic minority cultures may prefer the present-versus-past orientation of behavior therapy, its specificity, and its task and action orientation. Moreover, from the beginning, behavior therapy has advocated an individualized approach where the therapist endeavors to understand the individual's problems in light of the client's worldview and interpersonal context. Oftentimes, clients from diverse cultures are searching for a therapist who is directive, who will outline the progress of therapy, and who is goal oriented. There is a tendency for ethnic minorities from Latino, Asian American, and African American backgrounds to prefer time-limited therapy, as is the usual case with behavior therapy.

Researchers have observed that Chinese people prefer treatment that is directive, structured, and short term because this type of therapeutic approach conforms to the expectations of professionals as authoritative experts. For instance, Chu (1999) found that the behavioral style of psychotherapy was more effective in treatment outcome with Chinese people than that of a nondirective person-centered approach. Behavioral therapy is an evidence-based, structured, and problem-focused short-term psychotherapy. The principles and practice of behavioral therapy would appear to be compatible with the expectations preferred by Chinese people because it encourages self-help, is psycho-educational, and teaches new coping skills to manage distressing emotional problems. The conceptual behavioral framework is well suited to take into consideration the idiographic nature of the client's problems in terms of cultural factors and the influence of immigration, somatic complaints, interpersonal relationships, and other areas of importance that influence a client's psychological well-being.

It is important to consider the impact of similar expectations for therapy on the client's responsiveness to therapy. I maintain that a match in ethnic minorities' expectations of treatment increases the appeal of the therapy (and in this case, behavioral therapy) not only for Chinese people but also for ethnic minorities who have a collective orientation worldview. Zane et al. (2005) found that even when the therapist and the client were not ethnically matched, significant therapeutic achievements resulted if the therapist and the client shared similar perceptions of the presenting problem and if the therapist understood the client's coping style and expectations about treatment goals. A positive therapist–client "cognitive match" was significantly related to clients' positive attitudes toward the therapy sessions, a reduction in avoidant coping behaviors, and an improvement in client's psychosocial functioning.

Similarly, the cultural match theory suggests that Hispanic/Latino clients are inclined to adhere to and benefit more frequently from treatment interventions that agree with their beliefs. Conversely, Latinos often reject those mental health services (e.g., traditional medical model) that do not embrace their cultural values. Behavior therapy has been found to be effective for Latino clients (González-Prendes, Hindo, & Pardo, 2011).

Behavior therapy has also been found effective for African American women (McNair, 1996). McNair pointed out specific aspects of behavior theory that are compatible with assessing culturally relevant variables, which include a focus within behavior assessment on environmental, social, and cultural factors that influence learning. Neal-Barnett and Smith (1996) have acknowledged that little literature exists on behavior therapy with African American children. The authors discuss the concept of Radical Black Behaviorism and using an Afrocentric approach within behavior therapy.

Behavior therapy has been used with clients from ethnic minority cultures. The predominant emphasis has been on modifying the behavioral approach by adding culturally specific knowledge about and pointing to goodness of fit with behavior therapy and the worldviews of various ethnic minority groups. Behavior therapy is well suited to deal with multicultural issues. It does not place an emphasis on catharsis or on expressing one's emotions. The emphasis in behavioral counseling is on changing behaviors, and such change can take place within one's own cultural framework. One strong point of behavioral counseling is that it takes into account the social and cultural dimensions of a client's life. As Tanaka-Matsumi, Higginbotham, and Chang (2002) have pointed out, the behavioral approach takes into consideration the client's cultural conception of problem behaviors, and it uses appropriate social influence agents.

Multicultural Blind Spots

Although behavior therapy has many pluses for working with members of ethnic minority groups, it also has some limitations. Historically, behavior therapy has evidence of a lack of attention to diversity issues; however, things have begun to change as the world is witnessing a multicultural revolution. As Iwamasa (1997) pointed out some time ago, there are some positive signs of behavior therapists' establishing a commitment to diversity in behavioral research—especially as behavior therapy continues its movement toward cognitive-behavioral therapy. Spiegler and Guevremont (2010) have pointed out that behavior therapy might consider developing empirically based recommendations related to how this approach can best serve culturally different clients. Behavior therapists can also take into consideration a host of environmental factors that affect the lives of ethnic minority clients. Behavior therapists should become more acquainted with the cultural values of clients with whom they work. It is important that behavior therapists conduct cultural assessments related to how a client's culture is influencing his or her difficulties. Currently, many behavior therapists are not trained to conduct cultural assessments related to their clients' issues.

Contributions and Criticisms of Behavior Therapy

Behavior therapy has made a number of contributions. It is one of the most evidence-based therapies in existence. This situation exists because behaviorists conduct well-controlled research studies; therefore, good research exists on how behavioral techniques affect the process of counseling. Another contribution of behavior therapy is that it has demystified the process of psychotherapy and made it possible for clients and evaluators to assess in a measurable way its level of accountability. A third contribution of the behavioral school is that it has led to the development of a strong self-management focus in therapy.

A fourth contribution is that behavior therapy has been used to treat a wide range of psychological conditions, including, but not limited to, depression, attention deficit disorder, compulsive disorder, insomnia, chronic fatigue, anxiety disorders, and phobias. Behavior therapy has even been used for the treatment of obesity. Behavioral techniques have been used in more areas of human functioning than have any of the therapeutic approaches discussed in this book (Kazdin, 2001). It is involved in medicine, geriatrics, rehabilitation programs, and stress management programs. **Behavior modification** techniques have been used in schools and parenting classes, and they have helped individuals cope with pain.

One challenge that behavior therapists face is to develop more effective treatments for a broader variety of problems than those listed in the contributions section. Moreover, behavior therapy has been criticized because it involves control and manipulation by the therapist, treats symptoms rather than causes, and ignores relational factors in therapy and does not produce client insight. In response to these criticisms, behaviorists point out that there is no evidence that clients undergo symptom substitution as some have charged, that a change in behavior oftentimes results in an increase in self-insight, and that they, too, believe in the importance of the therapeutic relationship. While they acknowledge that a good therapeutic relationship is important in therapy, they do not place primary weight on it. More research needs to be completed on the brain and clinical disorders if behavior therapies are to make continuing contributions to psychotherapy.

Several researchers (Kazdin, 2001; Miltenberger, 2004; Spiegler & Guevremont, 2003) have summarized the contributions of behavior therapy as follows:

1. Behavior modification studies produced a high number of cases reported (Wedding & Corsini, 1989). Many of the treatments that work in psychotherapy are behavioral or cognitive-behavioral in orientation (Nathan & Gorman, 2002). Behavioral approaches dominate the number of empirically supported treatments. Such approaches tend to use careful measurement and assessment techniques, and they clearly define treatments. As a result, many behavioral treatments are reported

in manuals that give a step-by-step approach that can be used by other therapists.

2. Behavior therapy focuses on the clients' current problems and the forces influencing them. Less attention is given to completing a historical analysis of clients' issues, although behaviorists may investigate how environmental events contribute to current problem behaviors. Client relief from symptoms is much quicker than with other therapies.

3. Behavior therapy advocates a self-control approach that helps clients learn self-management strategies. Clients are empowered to take control of therapy by accepting responsibility for changes in their lives.

Evidence-Based Research

According to Wilson (2011), "The efficacy and effectiveness of behavior therapy has been studied more intensively than in any other form of psychological treatment" (p. 266). This statement may need to be modified in light of the phenomenal growth of cognitive-behavioral psychology and its related studies. Behavior therapy has been reviewed favorably in the NICE (National Institute for Clinical Excellence) evaluations for a variety of clinical disorders. The NICE (2004) report for behavior therapy has given it an A rating for the treatment of specific mood and anxiety disorders, and it has been evaluated equally as effective as pharmacological therapy. Fairburn, Cooper, and Shafran (2008) found that behavior therapy was even more effective than medication. Division 12 (Clinical Psychology) of the American Psychological Association has reported that behavioral treatments dominate the list of empirically supported therapies (Woody, Weisz, & McLean, 2005). Clearly, one needs to examine the effectiveness of behavior therapy for specific disorders. Much of the evidence-based research on behavior therapy now examines the cognitive-behavioral approach to therapy.

Justin Working With a Behavioral Therapist

When working with Justin from a behavioral perspective, the therapist first listens to Justin to see how he conceptualizes his challenges and problems. The therapist's goal is to establish a relationship with Justin. Next, the therapist conducts a functional behavioral assessment. To complete the functional behavioral assessment, the clinician also meets with Justin's mother, his teacher, his counselor, and his probation officer.

The therapist uses an ABC observation form as a method for conducting a preliminary assessment of Justin's behavior. The ABC observation form requires the therapist to note the classroom, teacher, time of day, any antecedent that preceded problematic behavior, the behavior itself, and the consequence of the behavior in the classroom setting.

After informing Justin that he would be visiting him in his class to see if he could help eliminate some of the problems that both Justin and the court identified, the therapist comes to Justin's class. It is important that the therapist lets Justin know ahead of time that he will be visiting him in class and taking notes. The therapist informs Justin that at the appropriate moment, he will share his observations with Justin for the purpose of getting feedback from him and to compare how both of them viewed what happened during the visit.

In addition, the therapist uses a functional assessment form that requires the therapist to assess the behavior of concern, how often the behavior occurs, its intensity, and what takes place before and after the behavior is displayed. The therapist also asks the teachers and Justin's mother, Sandy, to complete the same functional assessment form for Justin. The therapist takes these completed forms from mother, teachers, and probation officer and combines them with his to arrive at a view of Justin's behavior. Multiple observations of Justin's behavior increase the likelihood that the therapist will be able to accurately assess relevant dimensions of his behavior and that he will be able to write accurate behavior intervention plans. Therefore, information is collected on the following:

- Times when the behavior does/does not occur (e.g., just before lunch, during a particular course or activity)
- Location of the behavior (e.g., classroom, playground, and home)
- Conditions when the behavior does/does not take place (e.g., when working in small groups, structured or unstructured time)
- Individuals present when the problem behavior is most/least likely to take place (e.g., when there is a substitute teacher or with certain other students)
- Events or conditions that usually take place after the behavior (e.g., student is sent to the principal's office)
- Additional behaviors associated with Justin's problem behavior (e.g., a series of negative peer interactions)

Once Justin's problem behavior has been adequately identified, the therapist makes a detailed description of it. For instance, one observation might be that Justin gets angry and curses when a student laughs or makes fun of him when he is asked to read aloud in class. An appropriate comment might be, "When Justin is asked to read, he looks around the room to gauge his classmates' opinion of his reading, and then he makes irrelevant and inappropriate comments just before he begins reading or after having read only a few sentences." The therapist observes any hyperactive behavior because Justin has complained that he is not able to focus his complete attention when

(Continued)

(Continued)

reading. The therapist notes, "Justin leaves his assigned seat without permission, walks around the class, and blurts out answers without raising his hand."

Following this in-depth problem definition, the therapist collects information about possible functions of Justin's problem behavior. He gathers information about Justin's behavior in terms of antecedent and consequence events (events preceding or following the behavior) because they help him predict when, where, with whom, and under what conditions Justin's problem behavior is likely to occur. The therapist also asks Justin's mother and teachers what they think the function of his behavior is. Some possible functions of Justin's behavior are as follows:

- Attention from peer(s)?
- Attention from teacher or other adult(s)?
- Escape or avoid a task?
- Escape or avoid a social situation or conflicts with other people?
- Sensory stimulation?
- Obtains some tangible object (e.g., gets food or money following bullying or throwing tantrums)?
- Obtains opportunity to continue with or to begin a preferred activity?

The therapist is especially interested in talking with and gaining the observations of Justin's art teacher, who indicated that Justin had special talent in art. He also spends time talking with Justin about his feelings about art. A major purpose of this session is to see if participating in art could be used as part of a reward system for Justin. The therapist looks for ways to categorize Justin's behavior for the purposes of behavioral intervention. Is Justin's behavior designed to get something that is positively reinforcing for him, such as peer attention or to avoid or escape something that is aversive to him (e.g., academic assignments that are too demanding, interactions with specific classmates)? Does Justin make wisecracks during class because he finds the laughter of his classmates rewarding? Justin's wisecracks may serve to draw attention away from the fact that he has difficulty reading.

Moreover, the therapist must distinguish between Justin's behaviors that emanate from a skill deficit and those that result from a performance deficit. Justin is examined for a possible attention deficit disorder. Such a diagnosis might explain his problems in reading, even though he is average to above average in intelligence. Skills deficits indicate that Justin may not be able to perform the appropriate behavior. Justin may manifest performance deficits when he knows how to do something, but he chooses an inappropriate way of implementing the task.

From the functional behavioral assessment of Justin's behavior, the therapist sets up a behavior modification plan. He asks Justin to indicate his agreement or disagreement with the plan, to modify it, and to agree to a behavioral contract. The behavioral plan establishes both short-term and long-term goals for Justin. It focuses on the extinction of problem behaviors that the court indicated Justin would have to correct if he were to escape being sent to a residential treatment center. Justin's behavioral plan also clearly outlines replacement behaviors. The following list contains some possible teaching and reinforcing replacement behaviors for Justin:

- Teaching a way to ask appropriately for help, a break, or feedback
- Teaching a way to express one's opinions appropriately
- Teaching a way to get attention from peers appropriately
- Teaching a way to get adult attention appropriately
- Teaching conflict resolution, mediation, or negotiating skills to avoid fights
- Teaching coping or relaxation techniques

- Teaching academic skills (reading) related to the area of behavior concern
- Teaching study or organizational skills
- Teaching self-management and self-regulatory skills

The plan also includes measures of the effects of the interventions that Justin and the therapist discuss. Some measures of Justin's effectiveness will come from teacher/staff ratings of his progress, records of direct observation of Justin's behavior, records of direct observation of Justin's behavior kept by the teacher and Justin's mother, and Justin's own self-monitoring records that he keeps on a daily basis to record his progress.

The therapist also works with Justin's teachers and with his mother to help him complete his behavior modification plan successfully. He asks Justin's teachers and his mother to "catch him doing something good" and reward him verbally on such occasions. Low self-esteem is a critical issue for Justin; therefore, his mother and teachers are asked to be allies in rebuilding his self-esteem. Whenever possible, Justin's mother and his teachers are asked to emphasize his strengths and to minimize his weaknesses whenever possible. His teachers reinforce Justin positively for displaying agreed-on behaviors in the classroom. Justin is encouraged to monitor his behavior. A teacher might catch Justin being good and say to him, "What is really great about what you're doing now, Justin?"

Justin's mother is encouraged and taught how to establish routines for him rather than the catch-as-catch-can environment in which she has maintained her household. Young people who have behavioral problems benefit from having clearly established family routines. Moreover, his mother helps him to change the reward system that Justin has established for himself. He is mandated to stop associating with boys much older than he is, and he can no longer associate with boys who are gang members. A reward system is presently being established that focuses on his artistic ability. Justin has been encouraged to enter some of his artwork in a local contest. A schoolwide student art show also includes Justin's art.

Justin's mother is asked to consider becoming involved in therapy herself so that she can be of greater assistance to Justin during his behavioral adjustment period. She is informed that she must eliminate the pot parties or risk having Justin taken away from her and being prosecuted by the law. Efforts are made to involve James, Justin's older brother, in Justin's behavior modification plans since he has expressed the sentiment that he does not want Justin to grow up like him.

The goal of therapy for Justin is to extinguish the behavior that has brought him to the attention of the court and of his school principal. Extinction means changing Justin's environment so that his problem behavior is no longer followed by what reinforced it previously. The therapist does not explore Justin's early childhood experiences but rather focuses on the current behaviors that are problematic. By learning more appropriate replacement behaviors, Justin stands a chance of remaining at home with his family and of not being placed in the residential treatment facility for young boys. Justin is given positive behavioral supports from his therapist, mother, and teachers.

SUMMARY

Behavior therapy grew out of the contributions of several individuals: John Watson, B. F. Skinner, and John Wolpe. Donald Meichenbaum's contributions straddled the lines between behaviorism and cognitive therapy. Brief histories of the contributions of these leading figures were presented. Major concepts linked with behaviorists were discussed, including operant conditioning, shaping, reinforcement, extinction, generalization, and counterconditioning. Learning is a key component of the behavioral school. In fact, behaviorists maintain that all behavior, adaptive or maladaptive, is learned and that therapy should consist of unlearning dysfunctional behaviors, extinguishing them, and replacing them with positive adaptive behavior that allows the individual to lead a productive and meaningful life.

Behaviorists see people as products of their environments and experiences. They are neither inherently good nor bad. Behaviorists do tend to see human nature as being hedonistic in nature—that is, responsive to positive reinforcement that satisfies basic needs and pleasure. Unlike some of the other theorists, they do not espouse a model of human nature to which we should aspire. Psychopathology or maladaptive behavior develops from learned behavior and from insufficient cues to predict reinforcement or from inadequate reinforcement.

Behavior therapists use conditioning procedures to change problem behaviors. From their perspective, conditional emotional responses are often associated with maladaptive behavior. A conditioned emotional response takes place when a person associates a stimulus with an emotional response. For instance, if a person has suffered an accident on an escalator, she or he may become anxious each time she or he goes near an escalator.

Although behavior therapists believe that the therapeutic relationship is important in counseling, they do not believe that it alone is sufficient to bring about change. One must work with the client to change specific behaviors. Insight is not valued above behavior change. Behaviorists assert that insight comes from behavior change. The behavior therapist is very active in counseling, functioning as a consultant, supporter, and model.

All behavior therapies are, for all practical purposes, extinction therapies. The primary goal of therapy is to extinguish undesirable or unwanted behavior and to introduce adaptive behavior that replaces what was maladaptive. Desensitization is a therapy designed to eliminate unwanted emotional responses. In the classical example of desensitization, clients imagine gradually more fearful situations, while they are fully relaxed, until they are sufficiently strong emotionally to tolerate the most frightening images.

Learning is a key element in the counseling process. The therapist and the client work collaboratively to develop an individualized treatment program that highlights the behavior to be changed, increased, or eliminated. Some common counseling techniques include token economies, functional behavioral assessments, desensitization, relaxation training, flooding, and positive reinforcement.

Behavioral assessment and behavioral pharmacology/psychopharmacology are two of the current trends in behavior therapy. Some colleges and universities are now offering behavioral assessment certificates for individuals who wish to work with young people diagnosed with autism and other behavioral disorders. Most therapists and clinicians will one day find themselves working with individuals who are on some form of anxiety or psychotropic medication. Psychotropic medications are here to stay, as newer and more targeted medications are currently being developed. Debate is also likely to continue about the ethics and utility of medications.

Currently, behavior therapy has, for all practical purposes, merged with the cognitive school, and most people use the term *cognitive-behavioral* to indicate this merger of the schools. Research has indicated that the behavioral school has been able to develop evidence-based treatments. The behavioral school has affected more professional fields than most of the other therapies, including medicine, sports, advertising, business, and schools. Behavior modification holds great promise for schools.

SUPPLEMENTAL AIDS _____
Discussion Questions

1. Imagine that you have been asked to participate voluntarily in a self-management program where you are given the opportunity to change a behavior that you have been wanting to change on and off. Choose some two behaviors you would like to change (e.g., excessive eating, smoking, drinking). Develop a behavior treatment plan, implement the plan, and then evaluate it. In constructing your plan, please outline or state clearly

the following: (a) the two specific behaviors you want to change, (b) the actions that you are willing to take to make that change, (c) the system of rewards as you work toward achieving the desired behavior, (d) the recordkeeping or **self-monitoring** procedures you will use, and (e) evaluation of the success or failure of your treatment plan with explanation. You are to complete your treatment plan individually and report the results of it to your assigned small group.

2. You have decided to participate in progressive relaxation in order to unwind at night. You also want to pay closer attention to your emotional states, such as becoming uptight or anxious. Review the progressive relaxation outlined in this chapter, and then participate in it at least once a day. Keep a journal of your response to the progressive relaxation exercise.

3. A local middle school is having disciplinary problems in several different areas: truancy, fighting, and failure to complete teacher-assigned homework in a timely fashion. You are a newly hired guidance counselor in that school system. Your job is to develop a token economy to deal with the three disciplinary problems mentioned. Token systems can be used in an individual or a group format.

4. You are working in an agency with clients who suffer from alcohol and drug addiction. Your supervisor has just indicated in a group meeting that she wants to institute a voucher program (**contingency management** program—similar to token economy) for the clients in the program. In voucher-based contingency management, clients earn vouchers that are exchangeable for retail items contingent on objectively verified abstinence from recent drug use or compliance with other behavior change targets. Originally, this voucher form of contingency management was introduced in the early 1990s as a treatment for cocaine dependence. Studies have reported that this approach is reliably the most effective method for producing cocaine abstinence in clinical trials. Your assignment is to organize a small group that works on a voucher program for cocaine addiction. In small groups of four or five people, develop a voucher plan for cocaine addiction.

5. This assignment deals with avoidance behaviors. Most of us have developed avoidance behaviors. The goal of this assignment is to help you overcome your avoidance and face the things you fear. To cope with stressful situations, you must accept and face some anxiety. Only you know what triggers your anxiety and avoidance. The things that you avoid indicate what you should expose yourself to. Write down two things that you avoid to reduce your anxiety. They could be something as simple as speaking in public or confronting a friend who has betrayed you or something more difficult such as fear of spiders. Arrange your exposure tasks in order of difficulty (another way of saying establish a hierarchy of anxiety). Consider taking direct behavioral action to eliminate your avoidance behavior. The general rule for dealing with your avoidance behavior is to establish 2-hour homework sessions every day. This can be broken down into two 1-hour sessions. During this time, stop all social anxiety avoidance behaviors. Decide which goals you are going to achieve in each session every day for a full week. Be specific about your goals. Write a brief report (no more than two pages) of your experience and what you achieved in reducing your avoidance anxiety.

GLOSSARY OF KEY TERMS

anxiety hierarchy   A hierarchy of situations that bring on anxiety from the least to the most anxiety-producing triggers. Therapists work with clients to create an anxiety hierarchy as part of a behavior therapy technique known as systematic desensitization. If a client has anxiety triggers whenever she is asked to engage in public speaking, the therapist might first ask her to speak at a family dinner, then to a group at her work setting, and finally in front of a large business group.

assertiveness training   A form of behavior therapy designed to help people stand up for themselves. Originally, the approach was used during the 1970s to encourage women to stand up for themselves appropriately. Assertiveness training is designed to help clients maintain an appropriate balance between passivity and aggression.

behavior modification   Seeks to extinguish or inhibit abnormal or maladaptive behavior by reinforcing desired behavior and extinguishing undesired behavior.

behavior therapy   Psychotherapy where the therapist's goal is to extinguish or inhibit abnormal or maladaptive behavior by reinforcing desired behavior and extinguishing undesired behavior.

behaviorism   A psychotherapeutic treatment approach that emphasizes only actual behavior that is appropriate for therapy and scientific study.

classical conditioning   A form of associative learning, also referred to as Pavlovian or respondent conditioning, that was first demonstrated by Ivan Pavlov. The scientist presents a neutral stimulus along with a stimulus of some significance. Pavlov referred to this as a conditioned stimulus (CS). If the CS and the unconditioned stimulus (UCS) are repeatedly paired, eventually the two stimuli become associated, and the person or animal begins to produce a behavioral response to the CS. Pavlov called this the conditioned response (CR). Classical conditioning takes place when your father gives you a credit card at the end of your first year in college because you did so well. Because you want to continue receiving the financial reward from your father, your grades continue to get better in your second year.

conditioned response   The learned response that a person or animal gives to the previously neutral stimulus. In Pavlov's experiment, the dog learned to salivate at the sound of the bell, which was a previously neutral stimulus.

contingency management   A plan in which a person's access to a high-probability behavior (one that is likely to occur) is made contingent on a low-probability behavior (one that is unlikely to occur). The person learns that participating in a desired activity depends on completing an undesirable

task. Sometimes parents state, "Complete your homework and you can go to the movies." In this example, the undesirable activity is completing homework, while the desired activity is going to the movies. Contingency management is sometimes referred to as the Premack principle. When the contingency management plan is written down, it becomes a behavior contract.

counterconditioning   Occurs when a group of conditioning techniques is used to replace a negative conditioned response to a stimulus with a positive response. It is a technique of changing an undesirable response of an animal or a person to a stimulus by engaging the animal/person in another response that is incompatible with the first.

desensitization   A technique used in behavior therapy to treat phobias and other behavior problems that generate anxiety. A client is exposed to the threatening situation under relaxed conditions until the anxiety reaction is extinguished.

extinction   Conditioning phenomenon in which a previously learned response to a cue is reduced when the cue is presented in the absence of the previously paired aversive stimulus. When the conditioned stimulus (CS) is presented without the aversive unconditioned stimulus (UCS), the animal/person gradually "unlearns" the CS–UCS association.

flooding   Involves forced, prolonged exposure to the actual stimulus that provoked the original trauma. In real practice, flooding can be difficult to enact. It isn't really practical to fill a room with snakes and spiders, for example, and force someone to sit in it for hours. Flooding uses relaxation skills to help a client face the most anxiety-provoking situation. In comparison with flooding, systematic desensitization is the preferred technique of the two.

generalization   Also referred to as stimulus generalization. A client or animal perceives similarity or a relationship between different stimuli. The person/animal responds to the stimulus in a similar way. In classical conditioning, stimulus generalization is the tendency for the conditioned stimulus to evoke similar responses after the response has been conditioned. For instance, if Little Albert has been conditioned to fear a stuffed white rabbit, he will exhibit fear of objects similar to the conditioned stimulus.

hierarchy　A list of stimuli on a specific topic that are ranked according to the amount of anxiety they elicit. A therapist uses a hierarchy as a graded set of anxiety-producing stimuli so that the client is exposed to the least anxiety-producing stimuli first.

implosive therapy　May be defined as a type of intensive and prolonged exposure therapy in which the therapist asks the client to imagine increasingly anxiety-provoking scenes about the feared stimuli, such as imagining spiders getting closer and closer to the client.

in vivo　A form of exposure treatment that is used in behavior therapy. Exposure treatment is used for a variety of anxiety disorders. Usually, exposure treatment involves presenting a client with anxiety-provoking material for a long enough time to decrease the intensity of the client's emotional reaction. Exposure treatment can be conducted in real-life situations, which is labeled *in vivo exposure*, or it can be done through imagination, which is called *imaginal exposure.*

learning theory　The theory that behavior can be best understood in terms of how people and animals learn to respond to a stimulus. It includes learning by rewards and punishments (operant conditioning) and learning by association (classical conditioning).

modeling　Involves having an individual demonstrate behavior that is to be learned. Role playing is a frequent way in which modeling is completed. Albert Bandura introduced the concepts of *modeling* and *behavior rehearsal* to behavior therapists. He also emphasized *observational learning* and *modeling* (learning by watching another person perform a behavior), as well as *behavior rehearsal* (acting out a behavior to learn it and refine it as a skill).

negative reinforcement　When a specific behavior is strengthened by the consequence of stopping or avoiding a negative condition. In an attempt to increase the likelihood of a behavior occurring in the future, an operant response is followed by the removal of an aversive stimulus. For example, a rat is placed in a cage and immediately receives a mild electrical shock on its feet. The shock is a negative condition for the rat. The rat presses a bar and the shock stops. The rat receives another shock, presses the bar again, and again the shock stops. The rat's behavior of pressing the bar is strengthened by the consequence of stopping the shock.

operant conditioning　Term used by B. F. Skinner to describe the effects of the consequences of a particular behavior on the future occurrence of that behavior. Skinner outlined four types of operant conditioning: positive reinforcement, negative reinforcement, punishment, and extinction. Both positive and negative reinforcements strengthen behavior while both punishment and extinction weaken behavior.

positive reinforcement　When a specific behavior is strengthened by the consequence of experiencing a positive condition. For instance, a hungry rat presses a bar in its cage and receives food. The food is a positive reinforcer for the hungry rat. The rat presses the bar again and again receives food. The rat's behavior of pressing the bar is strengthened by the consequence of receiving food.

progressive relaxation　Progressive muscle relaxation (PMR) technique developed by Edmund Jacobson in 1938. The PMR procedure teaches you to relax your muscles through a two-step process. First you deliberately apply tension to certain muscle groups, and then you stop the tension and turn your attention to noticing how the muscles relax as the tension flows away. Through repetitive practice, you quickly learn to recognize—and distinguish—the associated feelings of a tensed muscle and a completely relaxed muscle. With this simple knowledge, you can then induce physical muscular relaxation at the first signs of the tension that accompanies anxiety. And with physical relaxation comes mental calmness—in any situation.

punishment   Technique used to weaken a specific behavior as a consequence of the person/animal experiencing a negative condition. For example, a rat presses a bar in its cage and receives a mild electrical shock on its feet. The shock is a negative condition for the rat. The rat presses the bar again and again receives a shock. The rat's behavior of pressing the bar is weakened by the consequence of receiving a shock.

reinforcement   Defined as a consequence that follows an operant response that increases (or attempts to increase) the likelihood of that response occurring in the future.

self-monitoring   A procedure developed by Meichenbaum and others where clients learn to observe their own behavior patterns and their interactions with others.

shaping   Involves first reinforcing a behavior similar to the one desired. Once that is established, you look out for variations on the behavior that come a little closer to what you want.

systematic desensitization   A step-by-step treatment procedure to help clients replace anxiety with relaxation while gradually exposing clients to an anxiety-producing situation.

token economy   A program usually established for young people that gives clients short-term reinforcement for specific behaviors by giving them tokens (poker chips or points) that are exchanged for privileges or desired objects.

unconditioned response   The unlearned response that occurs naturally in response to the unconditioned stimulus. For example, the smell of food is the unconditioned stimulus, and the feeling of hunger in response to the smell of food is the unconditioned response.

unconditioned stimulus   A stimulus that naturally and automatically triggers a response. For example, the smell of food is an unconditioned stimulus.

Website Materials

Additional exercises, journals, annotated bibliography, and more are available on the open-access website at https://study.sagepub.com/jonessmith2e.

Cognitive Approaches to Psychotherapy

BRIEF OVERVIEW_____

The **cognitive** school is part of the second force in psychotherapy. The beginnings of cognitive-behavioral therapy (CBT) can be traced to the development of behavior therapy during the early part of the 20th century, to the creation of cognitive therapy during the 1950s and 1960s, and to the subsequent merger of these two schools during the 1980s and 1990s. There is no easy line of demarcation between the history of behavior therapy and cognitive therapy. What was once labeled separately as behavioral and as cognitive has now become irretrievably linked together as cognitive-behavioral. The terms **cognitive-behavioral therapy** and **cognitive therapy** are used interchangeably in this chapter to indicate that they are one and the same.

By 1971, it had become clear that a significant proportion of psychologists had come to recognize that their discipline was in the process of undergoing a major paradigm shift, in which behaviorism was being replaced by an opposing new mentalism or cognitivism (Sperry, 1993). The cognitive paradigm shift from behavior therapy brought to science a "higher role and level of meaning, one that uses the emergent properties of specialized brain processes to offer new beliefs and value systems for the 21st century" (Sperry, 1993, p. 884).

Similarities and Differences Between and Among Cognitive Therapies

There is no one father of the cognitive-behavioral school. At least 20 different therapies have been categorized as cognitive or "cognitive-behavioral," including rational emotive behavior therapy (REBT), cognitive therapy, and multimodal therapy (Lazarus, 1989); schema-focused therapy (Young, Klosko, & Weishaar, 2003); dialectical behavior therapy (DBT; Dattilio, 2000; Dattilio & Padesky, 1990; Linehan, 1993; Mahoney & Lyddon, 1988); acceptance and commitment therapy (ACT; Hayes, 2004); and mindfulness-based cognitive therapy (MBCT; Segal, Williams, & Teasdale, 2002).

Although each cognitive-theoretical approach has its own developmental history and its own major contributors, there are similarities and differences among them. According to Dobson and Dozois (2010), current cognitive approaches to psychotherapy have in common three basic propositions. The *first proposition* is the mediational role of cognition, which maintains that there is almost always a cognitive processing and appraisal of internal and external events that can influence a person's response to life events; the *second proposition* asserts that cognitive activity may be monitored, assessed, and measured; and *the third proposition* is that behavior change may be an indirect sign of cognitive change. A defining characteristic of cognitive therapy is the principle that symptoms and dysfunctional behaviors are cognitively mediated, and therefore, a therapist helps a client improve by assisting him or her to modify dysfunctional thinking and beliefs.

Additional similarities between cognitive theories of psychotherapy are that most cognitive therapies are time limited, with many treatment manuals recommending 12 to 16 sessions for depression and anxiety and much longer time—1 to 2 years—for personality disorders and other chronic disorders. Second, virtually all cognitive therapies focus on specific problems or disorders, a defining feature that reflects their behavior therapy heritage. The problem-focused nature of cognitive therapy helps researchers and clinicians document therapeutic effects and identify the most efficacious therapy for a specific problem. Third, cognitive therapies emphasize that the client is an active agent during his or her treatment. Fourth, many cognitive therapies are explicitly or implicitly educative in nature, with the therapeutic model often being taught and the rationale for intervention communicated to the client. Clients learn therapeutic skills that they themselves can subsequently apply to different problems in their own lives.

Focus of This Chapter

This chapter is divided into three sections. The first part focuses on the three major early contributors to CBT: Albert Ellis, Albert Bandura, and Aaron Beck. Ellis and Beck are two theorists associated with a therapeutic approach, whereas Bandura is more of a bridge between behaviorism and cognitive therapy. Bandura did not create a formal therapeutic approach. Instead, his studies on role modeling and self-efficacy form an important part of cognitive counseling techniques, and he represents an important bridge between the behavior and cognitive schools. As you read this chapter, you will discover that although Ellis and Beck hold similar views about the important role that cognitions play in the development of mental disorders, they differ in how they believe a therapist should treat irrational or maladaptive cognitions. On the whole, REBT is more challenging and confrontative with the therapist pointing out a client's **irrational beliefs** to which many people fall victim. In contrast, Beck uses a supportive Socratic questioning method that helps a client determine the accuracy of his or her beliefs. Whereas Ellis points out a client's irrational beliefs, Beck works to get clients to examine the accuracy of their beliefs. Both Ellis and Beck focus on specific issues in clients' lives instead of trying to help them with personality revision or long-standing issues. Clients are encouraged to study their own thought processes and the consequences of their thinking on how they feel.

The second major part of this chapter deals with current trends in cognitive therapies and introduces the third wave of cognitive theories, specifically DBT (Linehan, 1993), ACT (Hayes, 2004; Hayes, Strosahl, & Wilson, 1999), and MBCT (Segal et al., 2002). These therapies have established mindfulness practices as a core component of their theoretical approaches.

The chapter begins with an in-depth discussion of the contributions of Ellis. Next, a brief discussion of Bandura's contributions and then Beck's theory of cognitive therapy are presented. Key concepts in each of these differing cognitive-theoretical approaches are examined. The chapter concludes with a brief review of the third wave of cognitive-behavioral approaches to psychotherapy—namely, DBT (Linehan, 1993), ACT (Hayes & Strosahl, 2005; Hayes, Strosahl & Wilson, 1999), and MBCT (Segal et al., 2002), and the case of Justin using a cognitive approach. Because of space limitations, this chapter's presentation of the DBT, ACT, and MBCT is in summary rather than in detailed form.

The third part of this chapter presents the multicultural positives and blind spots of the CBTs. In addition, empirical research is reviewed for CBTs across the board. Next, I present a case analysis of Justin from a cognitive-behavioral perspective. This case analysis is followed by a summary and discussion questions.

RATIONAL EMOTIVE BEHAVIOR THERAPY_____

Major Contributor: Albert Ellis (1913–2007)

Albert Ellis

I get people to truly accept themselves unconditionally, whether or not their therapist or anyone loves them.

The best years of your life are the ones in which you decide your problems are your own. You do not blame them on your mother, the ecology, or the president. You realize that you control your own destiny.

We teach people that they upset themselves. We can't change the past, so we change how people are thinking, feeling and behaving today.

—Albert Ellis

Born of Jewish parents on September 17, 1913, in Pittsburgh, Pennsylvania, Albert Ellis was the eldest of three children. He had a brother who was 2 years younger and a sister, 4 years younger. When he was 4 years old, the family moved to the Bronx in New York. Ellis has described his father as a businessman who experienced minimal success, who showed a modicum of affection to his children, and who was often away from home on business trips during Ellis's early years (REBT Network,

2006). Ellis described his mother as a self-absorbed woman of bipolar affect. Similar to his father, Ellis's mother was emotionally distant from her children. When Ellis was 5 years old, he was hospitalized with a kidney ailment. Subsequently, he was hospitalized eight times between ages 5 and 7, with one hospitalization lasting almost a year. Ellis stated that his illnesses taught him how to confront his feelings of inferiority because his parents provided him with little emotional support during this time. His parents divorced when he was 12 years old.

In 1942, Ellis entered the clinical psychology program at Columbia University. In 1947, Ellis convinced associates of Karen Horney to work with him, even though he did not have a medical degree. Ellis finished a complete analysis and began to practice psychoanalysis. In 1952, Ellis expanded his private practice to full time. His reputation as a therapist and a sexologist grew after the publication of his books, *The Folklore of Sex* (1951), *The American Sexual Tragedy* (1954), and *Sex Without Guilt* (1958). Ellis's recognition as an advocate for sexual freedom cost him dearly. Both his undergraduate school, City College of New York, and his graduate school, Teachers College, Columbia, refused to give him teaching positions because of his "controversial" sex writings. Moreover, many psychology departments banned or canceled presentations by Ellis because of his abrasive style of presentation and his views on sex. In 1951, Ellis became the American editor of the *International Journal of Sexology*, and he began publishing a number of articles advocating sexual liberation. During his early career, Ellis married twice; the first ended in an annulment, and the other ended after about 3 years. None of his marriages resulted in children.

Ellis developed the first intentionally therapeutic approach to cognitive-behavioral psychotherapy, and he initially called it rational emotive therapy (RET). He constructed this therapeutic approach partly because he found psychoanalysis to be inefficient and ineffectual. The philosophic origins of RET can be traced back to the Stoic philosophers, including Epictetus and Marcus Aurelius. In *The Enchiridion*, Epictetus wrote, "Men are not disturbed by things, but by the view they take of them" (www.brainyquote.com/quotes/quotes/e/epictetus 149127.html). Ellis believed that all extreme, disturbing, or neurotic emotions are a result of a person's view of the situation, not the situation itself. During the 1980s, Ellis revised RET by inserting the word *behavior* in his theoretical approach. RET became REBT, and a primary goal was to modify client's **self talk**. In addition, REBT became closely linked with the cognitive-theoretical school because it sought to change the way people think and reason about the events of their lives.

Ellis was designated a diplomate in Clinical Psychology of the American Board of Professional Psychology and of the American Board of Sexology. He published well over 54 books and hundreds of articles on the theory and applications of REBT. Some of the books he authored include *Reason and Emotion in Psychotherapy* (1962); *Better, Deeper, and More Enduring Brief Therapy* (1996); and *Rational Emotive Behavior Therapy: It Works for Me—It Can Work for You* (2004). After a long illness, Albert Ellis died on July 24, 2007.

Theoretical Influences of REBT

The origin of Ellis's REBT comes from several sources. He borrowed a great deal from the Greek Stoics, who stressed the importance of our thoughts on our behavior. The Greek influence led Ellis to conclude that his clients' unhappiness and dysfunctional behavior often stemmed from irrational thoughts. Marcus Aurelius's statement that people are stressed by the view that they take of things rather than by the situations themselves became the underlying premise of REBT. Ellis asserted that people create their psychological problems by the way they respond to and interpret events in their lives (Ellis, 1962, 1976, 1994, 1996, 1998, 2000a, 2001a, 2001b, 2002). People's cognitions, emotions, and behaviors interact to produce a life that is filled with unhappiness.

Ellis combined the Greek influence on the power of our thoughts with learning theory, which was a dominant theoretical perspective during the 1950s. He asserted that people learned maladaptive behavior, and hence, they could unlearn such behavior by changing their thoughts. Clients need a therapist to be involved in changing dysfunctional cognitions, emotions, and behaviors (Ellis & Dryden, 1997).

Ellis borrowed a great deal of his RET from several theorists, including Karen Horney and Alfred Adler. He took Karen Horney's concept of the tyranny of the "shoulds" and made it a focal part of his 11 irrational beliefs. Horney had said that people suffer psychologically because of "should pressures": I should be loved; I should be this or that. According to Horney, the pressures of the "shoulds" came from the demands of the superego—our parents. Ellis developed 11 irrational beliefs based on Horney's concept of the tyranny of the "shoulds."

Adler also had a profound influence on Ellis's REBT theory. He asserted that our lifestyle and goals in life are determined by our basic beliefs about ourselves and about life. According to Adler (1964), our behavior often comes from our mistaken ideals. The individual relates himself or herself to the rest of the world based on that person's interpretation of himself or herself and on his or her presenting problem. Adler asserted that it is our attitude toward life that determines our relationship to the outside world. In his book on individual psychology, Adler's motto was *Omnia ex opinione suspense sunt* (Everything depends on opinion).

Moreover, Adler (1931) offered an early version of the A-B-C system or S-O-R (stimulus–organism–response). According to Adler, we do not suffer from the shock of our experiences or the trauma that we experience. Rather, we suffer from what we make out of our trauma, and we choose to conclude just what suits our purposes (Ellis, 2005). Other similarities also exist with Adlerian individual psychology and REBT. For instance, Adler (1931) proposed that people have fictional premises and goals, and they operate their lives on the basis of such false hypotheses. REBT maintains that people are disturbed because they hold irrational beliefs, and they make illogical deductions or conclusions based on their faulty beliefs. Although REBT has adopted some premises of Adlerian theory, it has declined to stress the Adlerian emphasis on the importance of early childhood memories and social interest. Ellis does contend that we are happiest when we help others.

To some extent, REBT has also adopted basic tenets of existential, phenomenologically oriented therapy because it focuses on helping clients define their own freedom, cultivate their own individual identity, and be fully present in the immediacy of the moment (Ellis, 2001a, 2002). Ellis has cautioned that many so-called existential humanistic therapists are anti-intellectual and use few clearly defined psychotherapeutic techniques.

Ellis (2005) placed REBT closer to cognitive theory than to behavior theory. From his perspective, REBT has a close affinity with cognitive and multimodal theories, such as those of Aaron Beck, Arnold Lazarus, and Donald Meichenbaum. Ellis considered REBT cognitive because he believed that our emotional dysfunctions are caused by negative self talk, which was his label for the way a person's inner voice operates. According to Ellis, there are important differences between Beck's cognitive therapy and his REBT. First, Ellis stated that REBT disputes irrational beliefs much more actively than does Beck's cognitive therapy, and furthermore, REBT stresses that most irrational beliefs stem from clients' adoption of several "shoulds." REBT uses shame-attacking exercises, and it also uses penalties in addition to reinforcements.

In comparing REBT with other psychotherapeutic approaches, Ellis has been most critical of psychoanalysis. REBT differs most from psychoanalysis in that it places little emphasis on free association, working with dreams, focusing on clients' past history, or discussing at great length clients' feelings. Ellis (2000b) has labeled therapeutic approaches that use such techniques as *indulgence therapy* that produce few observable results.

KEY CONCEPTS OF REBT

View of Human Nature

REBT is based on the belief that people are born with a potential for irrational or rational thinking. Ellis maintained that human beings have predispositions for self-preservation, happiness,

and growth actualization. We also have leanings toward self-destruction, repetition of past mistakes, self-blame, and avoidance of self-actualization. We contaminate our positive growth potential when we use negative self talk and when we make unrealistic demands on ourselves for perfection (Ellis, 2005; Ellis & Dryden, 1997).

Moreover, REBT posits that people are constructivists and have a great deal of resources for human growth. At birth, we are born with the choice of changing our behaviors. We are quite capable of changing our destinies (Ellis, 2001b). We have an innate tendency to want, to "need," and to condemn ourselves, others, and the world when we do not get what we think we need. We defeat ourselves by our inborn and acquired self-sabotaging ways (Ellis, 2005). Although we are born with a great deal of demandingness regarding life, we can change from this position to *only desiring* rather than demanding.

Inner Reflections

Do any of Ellis's 11 irrational beliefs apply to you? If so, which ones?

What events tend to activate irrational beliefs on your part?

Theory of Personality: Rational Emotive A-B-C

REBT emphasizes the A-B-C model of personality (Ellis, 2004). *A* stands for an activating event or experiences, such as family problems or early childhood trauma, that trigger stress or worry. *B* stands for "belief system"—the cognitive component in our reaction to events. Especially important are irrational, self-defeating beliefs that form the source of our unhappiness. *C* is for consequences (the neurotic symptoms and negative emotions, such as depression, anger, and rage) that come from our beliefs. Irrational beliefs produce negative consequences for people. A person who is continually saying to herself "I can't take this" may talk herself into feeling helpless and worthless. Ellis labeled this kind of repetitive negative thought as *rumination* (Ellis, 2004).

A = Activating event	
B = Belief system	
C = Emotional consequences of A and B	
D = Disputing irrational thoughts and beliefs	
E = Cognitive and emotional effects of revised beliefs	

Although our activating experiences may be very real and cause excruciating pain, our irrational beliefs actually create maladaptive behavior. Ellis added *D* and *E* to the A-B-C formula. The therapist helps the client *dispute* (*D*) the irrational beliefs for the client to enjoy the positive psychological *effects* (*E*) of ridding himself or herself of irrational beliefs (Table 5.1). If a person experiences depression after a marital or partnership breakup, it is probably caused by what the person is telling himself or herself about the breakup (Ellis, 2004). People

Table 5.1   ABCDE Chart for Rational Emotive Behavior Therapy

A = Activating Event	B = Beliefs About Activating Event	C = Consequences of Activating Event	D = Disputes for Each Irrational Belief	E = Effective New Thinking
A = Wife became angry because husband was late for dinner. A = Mother became upset because daughter failed to wash the dishes. A = Man became upset because he is stuck in traffic.) What do you think happened? What was happening at the time you became upset/stressed/angry/depressed? Ask yourself: What would a camera see? Where were you? Who was there? What was taking place?	"Ain't it awful that John is late again for dinner, that Mary did not wash the dishes, that I am stuck in traffic?" A common belief is that we should become angry about someone else's behavior. People don't make us angry. We feel angry about another person's behavior. REBT theory says that it is usually irrational and self-defeating to get all worked up about someone else's behavior.	"I feel angry that John was late for dinner again." "I feel angry when Mary does not wash the dinner dishes." "I am angry because I am stuck in traffic."	It is irrational for me to become angry about John's lateness. Maybe there is a good reason for his lateness. It is irrational for me to become angry about Mary's not washing the dishes. It is better to focus on how this problem behavior can be resolved. It is irrational for me to become angry over being stuck in traffic. My anger will not resolve the traffic jam. Change your thinking about the situation. Change the irrational demand to a preference. Once you downgrade a demand to preference, you are better able to cope with situation.	People are late for dinner. I will choose not to upset myself over John's lateness. I will schedule dinner an hour later. (I am calm.) Mary and I will establish a reward system for her to do dishes on a timely basis. (I am calm.) It is better that I use my GPS (Global Positioning System) to find another route or to leave for the appointment in sufficient time to deal with traffic I have found a new route to avoid the traffic delays. (I am calm.)

are responsible for creating their own emotional reactions and disturbances.

There are three elements of the *disputing process:* detecting, debating, and discriminating. Therapists teach clients how to detect their irrational beliefs, especially their absolutist "shoulds" and "musts," their "awfulizing," and their "self-downing." Next, clients debate their dysfunctional beliefs by learning how to challenge their irrational beliefs. Last, clients learn how to discriminate irrational (self-defeating) beliefs from rational beliefs (Ellis, 1994). During his prime, Ellis cussed, interrupted, shouted, and focused on clients' irrational thoughts. His goal was to help clients replace negative, unrealistic thinking with a more realistic and adaptive appraisal of difficult situations. REBT seeks to replace irrational self talk with adaptive self talk.

After clients are taught to distinguish their irrational beliefs from their rational ones, they are helped to develop *E*, an effective philosophy. *E* stands for the effects of people changing their interpretation of the situation. Ellis found that when he encouraged clients to give up their basic irrational ideas, they often resisted. Such resistance was not as the Freudians had postulated, because they hated the therapist or were resisting parental dictates, but rather because they tended to musturbate. They demanded that they must do well and win others' approval, that people must act considerately and fairly, and that environmental conditions must not be frustrating (Ellis, 2005). Ellis theorized that human beings are self-talking, self-evaluating, and self-construing. They have strong desires for love, approval, and success and misleadingly define these preferences as needs.

Ellis maintained that passive, nondirective therapeutic methods, such as reflection of feeling and free association, do not work in therapy. Although catharsis helps clients feel better, it reinforces their demands that the world be as they desire. Therapy is effective when clinicians engage in an active–directive, cognitive–emotive–behavioral attack on major self-defeating "musts" and demands. According to REBT, effective therapy involves a tolerance of oneself and of others as people, combined with a campaign against one's self-defeating, irrational ideas (Ellis, 2005).

REBT therapists teach clients the process of **cognitive restructuring** or thought changing. In REBT, cognitive restructuring is the process of learning how to refute irrational beliefs or cognitive distortions by replacing one's irrational beliefs with more accurate and beneficial ones. Cognitive restructuring takes place when people are able to gain awareness of negative thought habits, when they learn how to challenge such habits, and when they substitute life-enhancing thoughts and beliefs. Cognitive restructuring is an active effort to change maladaptive thought patterns and to replace them with more adaptive cognitions.

Healthy Psychological Development

To have a healthy psychological development, we must develop a positive thought life, focus on our own self-respect rather than on other people's approval, and rid ourselves of irrational beliefs. When we have healthy development, we learn to modify our perspective on life events. We arrive at the understanding that most human unhappiness is caused by the view that people take of the situations in which they find themselves. If it is impossible to change negative events, it is better to quit telling oneself about how awful things are.

Do you see any similarities between Adler's emphasis on social interest and service to others and Ellis's belief that healthy absorption helps people deal with their own issues?

To live rationally, you should plan your life so that you have more growth-enhancing experiences in your life (Ellis, 2004). Ellis has maintained that most people are happiest when engaged in some activity that draws them outside of themselves. The three major forms of healthy absorption include (1) loving, or feeling absorbed in other people; (2) creating or getting absorbed in things; and (3) philosophizing or being involved in ideas. Living healthy means doing, acting, loving, creating, and thinking.

Theory of Maladaptive Behavior

Ellis and Harper (1997) listed 11 irrational ideas that cause people to develop maladaptive behavior. These irrational ideas constitute the major causes of emotional problems and maladaptive behavior. In addition, they carry a sense of self-blame and blame of others. Although these irrational beliefs were quite controversial when Ellis first offered them, the cognitive-behavioral school has incorporated them as part of its general foundation.

Irrational Belief 1 is the idea that you must have love or approval from all the people you find significant. Although most people experience love, affection, and approval, it is not absolutely necessary to have such to be happy. Moreover, you can harm yourself psychologically if you seek the impossible goal of having everybody love you. Ellis posited that emotional disturbance takes place when you care too much about what others think and when you believe you can accept yourself *only if* others think well of you. Under such circumstances, we increase our desire for others' approval into such an absolute need that we become anxious and prone to depression when it is withheld (Ellis, 2005). It is our tendency to exaggerate the importance of others' acceptance that brings on self-denigration and

maladaptive behavior (Ellis, 1962; Ellis & Harper, 1975, 1997).

Irrational Belief 2 is "I must not fail" or, as Ellis and Harper (1975, 1997) have stated, the ideal that you must be thoroughly competent, adequate, and achieving. This belief is irrational because nobody is good at everything, and people do fail sometimes. Ellis discovered that clients often engaged in what he labeled **musterbating**—that is, saying one "must" do something, simply because it is expected or demanded by another person.

Irrational Belief 3 is related to the concept of damning. This belief states that when people act obnoxiously and unfairly, you should blame and damn them and see them as bad, wicked, or horrible people. For instance, a woman whose husband is leaving her spends the first part of therapy detailing his marital infidelities, how he disrespected her and the kids, and on and on. While all of the woman's complaints might be true, Ellis would say that the woman is engaged in *damning*. Ellis points out that when a marriage fails, all blame cannot be put on one person. He would then redirect the woman's thinking to ways of learning from the experience or of moving forward rather than being stuck in the past.

Irrational Belief 4 deals with *awfulizing*, which is the belief that you have to see things as awful, terrible, and horrible when things go wrong. When people say to themselves that they can't stand or tolerate something, eventually they can't. It is better to say, "This bothers the heck out of me, but I will survive it."

Irrational Belief 5 is the idea that emotional unhappiness stems from external pressures and that you have little capacity to control or to change your feelings. Ellis encouraged his clients to take control of their destinies by taking responsibility for how they interpret and react to events. Some people believe that they are shaped by other people and that if they could only change those people and circumstances, they would be happy. We determine whether or not we are happy or sad because we have ultimate control over our emotions.

Irrational Belief 6 is often called the **catastrophizing** belief. It is awful and catastrophic when your life's conditions are not the way you would like them to be. Ellis pointed out to his clients that no situation is entirely perfect. When you respond to an event as catastrophic, your response will not change that event. Mature people learn how to adjust and to accept the things that they cannot control. Time spent catastrophizing is wasted time.

Irrational Belief 7 is the notion that avoiding life's challenges is more rewarding than seeking challenges. The best route is to try to resolve the matter without upsetting ourselves unnecessarily (Ellis & Harper, 1997). We all want to feel safe, but not at the expense of postponing the realization of our dreams. We cheat ourselves when we procrastinate.

Irrational Belief 8 is the idea that you need to be dependent on someone stronger than yourself. To some extent, all of us depend on someone else at one time or another; however, overdependency results in a loss of our independence, individualism, and self-expression. People who are self-reliant feel better about themselves than do those who are dependent largely on others. Albert Bandura picks up on the significance of this irrational belief in his experiments on self-efficacy. People who feel competent or feel that they can do things for themselves rather than depending on others have high self-efficacy abilities.

Irrational Belief 9 is the notion that past events in our lives determine our destinies and that because an event once had a strong influence on our lives, it will continue to do so. Things continue to affect our lives primarily because we allow them to influence our behavior. Focusing on the past provides us with a convenient excuse not to do anything about our lives. The more healthy response is for us to learn from past experiences.

Irrational Belief 10 states that it is irrational for us to become unduly upset about other people's problems (Ellis & Harper, 1997). If you worry too much about other people's problems, they become your difficulties. A more rational approach to take is to say to yourself that your friends or family members must first change themselves and that putting too much pressure on others to change may have the opposite effect.

Irrational Belief 11 states that it is irrational for you to believe that there is always a right, precise, and perfect solution to human problems, and it is catastrophic if this perfect solution is not found. Our search for the definitive solution generates only anxiety and leaves us feeling empty and dissatisfied.

Ellis's two most common irrational beliefs center on *approval from others* (e.g., "If I am not liked and approved by others, that is awful, and I am no good") and *perfection* ("If I don't always do a good job, then I am worthless"). To maintain a mental disorder, we must continually indoctrinate ourselves with the negative messages about ourselves or about how horrible an event was in our lives. Mental disorders are sustained by our disordered or irrational thoughts. Ellis and Harper (1975) have stated,

> No matter what a person's past history may be, or how his parents, teachers, and other early associates may have helped him to become emotionally disturbed, he only remains disturbed because he still believes some of the unrealistic and illogical thoughts which he originally imbibed. (p. 50)

THE THERAPEUTIC PROCESS AND REBT

REBT is designed to help clients gain a more realistic, rational philosophy of life. REBT practitioners do not devote a great deal of time listening to clients' histories or their long tales of distress. Although such therapists are deeply interested in understanding their clients and their views, they keep their reflection of feelings and other techniques relatively short in comparison with some of the other therapeutic techniques because they consider such long-winded dialogues to be a form of indulgence therapy, that is, therapy that helps clients feel better but rarely get better (Ellis, 2001a). The therapist does not devote much time to examining the morbid details of the client's life, of who did what to whom. These items are viewed as a smokescreen that obscures the real issue of irrational thinking. The REBT therapist often challenges clients' irrational beliefs in the first few sessions.

REBT is intended to be brief therapy. Clients who come to REBT on a short-term basis usually stay for 1 to 10 sessions. Within this timeframe, clients can usually learn the A-B-C method of understanding emotional problems, gain a handle on their dominant philosophic position, and begin to change basic disturbance-creating irrational beliefs (Ellis, 2001a). Clients with severe disturbances are encouraged to come to individual and/or group sessions for at least 6 months.

The therapeutic process can be sped up using two techniques. The first approach is to tape the entire session. Clients then listen to the recordings several times so they can ascertain their problems and the REBT way of handling them (Ellis, 2005). The second device is to give an REBT Self-Help Form to teach clients how to use the method when they experience emotional problems between therapeutic sessions. For instance, clients are asked to briefly summarize the situation about which they are disturbed. Other questions are designed to get at the nature of the A, the activating event. Is the event internal or external, real or imagined? Is the event in the past, present, or future?

Next, clients are asked to list the irrational beliefs that support their emotional disturbance. Clients look for dogmatic demands (musts, absolutes, and shoulds), awfulizing (It's awful, terrible, and horrible), and low frustration tolerance ("I can't stand it."). Following this, clients are required to list their disputing of the irrational beliefs. For instance, the client asks,

> Where is holding this belief getting me? Where is the evidence to support the existence of my irrational belief? Is it consistent with social reality? What are the consequences of my negative emotions and self-defeating behaviors? What healthy emotions might I substitute for the unhealthy ones?

The Therapeutic Relationship

The therapeutic relationship in REBT is one of therapist/collaborator/teacher. Unlike some other therapeutic schools, rational emotive behavior therapists do not believe that a warm relationship between a client and a therapist is either a necessary or a sufficient condition for effective therapy or for client personality change. A warm client–therapist relationship is desirable but not necessarily sufficient in the therapeutic process. Although REBT therapists do emphasize unconditional acceptance and close collaboration with clients, they encourage clients to accept themselves unconditionally.

REBT is not just geared toward symptom removal but rather is designed to help clients examine and change some of their basic values that keep them disturbed. Ellis proposed two types of REBT: (1) general REBT, which is very similar to CBT; and (2) preferential REBT, which stresses a deep philosophical change in the client's life and way of relating to people. The goal is to empower people. Moreover, REBT provides clients with three powerful insights. **Insight Number 1** points out that a person's self-defeating behavior usually stems from the interaction of A (adversity) and B (belief about the adversity). Disturbed consequences C follow the interaction of A and B, such that A + B = C.

Insight Number 2 is the understanding that people have made themselves emotionally disturbed because they keep indoctrinating themselves with similar irrational beliefs. These beliefs have become a conditioned response and, therefore, automatic in clients' lives. Until clients admit and face their responsibilities for the continuation of dysfunctional beliefs in their lives, such beliefs will likely remain.

Insight Number 3 is that clients recognize that only hard work and practice will correct irrational beliefs. Therefore, Insights 1 and 2 alone are insufficient. Clients must commit themselves to repeated challenging of irrational thoughts until they are fully extinguished (Ellis, 2004).

Role of the REBT Therapist

REBT therapists must understand belief systems and how to distinguish rational and irrational beliefs. The therapist's primary role is to focus on the main irrational ideas that lie behind the feelings clients have expressed in therapy, especially their ideas that it is awful the way in which people have treated them. The therapist is active and contradicts clients' irrational ideas by using evidence from the clients' own lives and from the therapist's knowledge of people in general. The therapist helps clients admit and acknowledge "shoulds" and "musts" in their lives and then dispute them. Instead of merely telling clients that their ideas are irrational, the therapist keeps trying to get clients to see this for themselves. The therapist's encouraging insistence that clients can feel something other than anxiety and depression helps them move toward constructive and positive behavior.

REBT consists of three phases (Ellis, 2005). During the *cognitive phase*, the therapist presents the cognitive rationale for REBT to the client. Therapists begin by asking, "What problems have you been bothering yourself about?" The cognitive phase is devoted to clients writing down their troublesome thoughts. During the *emotive phase*, clients are instructed that they can learn to control their emotions by becoming aware of the thoughts that support such emotions and by learning to substitute alternative thoughts. During the *behavioristic phase*, clients are taught to change their behavior.

> ### Inner Reflections
>
> As you read about REBT, could you visualize yourself as an REBT therapist?
>
> What part of the role of an REBT therapist resonates with you, and what aspects turn you off?

Role of the Client

Ellis did not claim that he could treat all clients successfully (Ellis & Harper, 1997). He noted that individuals who are out of contact with reality, in a highly manic state, seriously autistic or brain injured, and in the lower ranges of mental deficiency are not good candidates for REBT. Instead, such clients should be referred for medical treatment or for behavior therapy coupled with operant conditioning (Ellis & Dryden, 1997).

REBT is more effective with clients who have a single major symptom, such as depression, than with clients with serious disorders. Clients are instructed that part of their role is to engage in a reeducation process that helps them apply rational thoughts to their everyday issues (Ellis & Dryden, 1997). They are instructed to focus on the present rather than on the past, and they are expected to participate actively in the therapeutic process and to complete assignments. Near the end of therapy, clients reexamine their programs and identify strategies for continual disputing of their irrational beliefs.

REBT Counseling Techniques

REBT uses a variety of therapeutic techniques, including didactic discussion, bibliotherapy, role-playing, assertion training, operant conditioning, and activity-oriented homework assignments. One technique used is called *changing one's language*. REBT maintains that imprecise language contributes to distorted thinking. Clients learn how to change their "musts" to "preferences." Instead of saying, "It is horrible that she treats me this way," clients learn to say, "It would be preferable if she did not treat me this way."

REBT therapists use humor to help clients deal with their irrational beliefs. According to them, emotional disturbance comes from taking oneself too seriously (Ellis, Gordon, Neenah, & Palmer, 1997). The Institute for Rational Emotive Behavior Therapy has written an RET songbook and cassette recording that features songs sung by Ellis.

Ellis (1999, 2000a) also used shame-attacking exercises to help clients reduce shame over how they have behaved. Such exercises are designed for increasing client self-acceptance. For instance, clients might be given an assignment to sing at the top of their lungs while waiting for a bus or to ask for something silly in a store. By carrying out such assignments, they learn not to feel ashamed by the judgments of others. Instead, clients learn to develop an internal reference for appraising their own behavior.

Other counseling techniques include disputing, which involves two stages. The first part entails a detailed examination sentence by sentence of any irrational belief that the client states during therapy.

The second stage consists of using three forms of disputation: cognitive, imaginal, and behavioral. Cognitive disputation attempts to persuade the client by asking direct questions. For instance, the therapist might ask, "Can you prove it? How do you know? If what you say is true, what's the worst thing that can happen to you? As long as you believe that, how will you feel?"

A second type of disputation is imaginal disputation. The therapist asks clients to imagine themselves in the situation about which they feel uncomfortable. After clients have been guided into the feelings of that moment, the therapist asks that they change their fear to mild apprehension and their anger to mild irritation. Once clients signal that they are imagining different feelings and behavior, they are instructed to notice what they are saying or thinking to themselves to produce their different emotions. If clients continue practicing rational emotive imagery, they can reach the point where they no longer feel upset over negative events (Ellis, 2001b).

> ### Inner Reflections
>
> Write an emotional control card for yourself. What four emotionally debilitating categories are on your card?
>
> Write an emotional control card that might help someone close to you.

Emotional Control Card

Sometimes, the REBT therapist uses an emotional control card (Sklare, Taylor, & Hyland, 1985). This card is wallet sized and contains four emotionally debilitating categories (anger, self-criticism, anxiety, and depression), a list of inappropriate feelings, and a parallel list of appropriate feelings. In a difficult situation, a client refers to the card for the purpose of changing his or her feelings about the situation. At the ensuing session, the counselor and the client discuss the use of the card to cognitively restructure thoughts to make them rational. For instance, the card states that the inappropriate self-destructive feeling is anger—feelings of resentment, anger, madness, fury, rage. Across from this column are the nondefeating feelings (Sklare et al., 1985). In contrast to anger, the appropriate response is irritation. The goal is to get clients to become aware of the feelings that they are using and to encourage them to rationally choose the emotions they display.

RESEARCH AND EVALUATION OF REBT _____

Contributions of REBT

Ellis's primary contribution to psychology is his insistence that psychological disturbance is maintained by distorted beliefs. Some critical points Ellis made are as follows:

1. Clients create their own emotional disturbance by distorted or irrational thinking, and they can alleviate their suffering by changing their underlying thoughts or premises.

2. If therapists are to be of help to clients, they must teach them how to monitor carefully their language for words such as *should*, *must*, *ought*, and *always*. For instance, clients catch themselves when they say, "He made me so angry." They learn that no one can make you feel anything without your consent.

3. Therapists can challenge clients' illogical thinking.

REBT is the forerunner of other cognitive-behavioral approaches, including that by Beck.

Criticisms of REBT

There have been several dominant criticisms of REBT. Critics have noted that although Ellis states that he is a scientist, he functions primarily as a philosopher and as a rationalist. Ellis has been a prolific writer on REBT, yet only a handful of his hundreds of articles and books report properly controlled, empirical experiments on its effectiveness. Even those studies that purport to have used empirical methods have been reviewed as seriously flawed. Major criticisms have been leveled at the counseling techniques and role of the therapist. Some prominent objections to REBT are the following:

- REBT places too much emphasis on thought processes to the relative exclusion of many legitimate feelings. To this extent, REBT has been said to contribute to repression and denial of feelings.

- REBT has a small range of clients with whom it is effective, primarily White middle-class individuals who are highly verbal and who have few major problems in life. REBT is less effective with clients who already have difficulties with overintellectualizing or with those who do not have the ability to reason logically (young children, schizophrenics, or clients with low intelligence).

- Some REBT therapists complain of boredom and burnout from repeatedly stating the same arguments and processes with all clients.

- REBT may be hard for some therapists to practice if they are not combative and if they do not like debate and confrontation.

- Clients undergoing REBT counseling may feel overpowered and dominated because the therapist is so verbal, active, and directive during treatment.

SOCIAL MODELING, OBSERVATIONAL LEARNING, AND SELF-EFFICACY _____

Major Contributor: Albert Bandura (1925–)

Jon Brenneis/TIME & LIFE Images/Getty images.

Albert Bandura

Albert Bandura's work bridges the gap between behaviorism and CBT. Bandura's contributions are primarily those of a researcher rather than those of a therapist, and therefore, no theory of psychotherapy is presented for him. His research laid the groundwork for much of the theoretical underpinnings of what has become known as cognitive therapy.

Born on December 4, 1925, Bandura was raised in the tiny hamlet of Mundare, which is located 50 miles from Edmonton, Canada. He was the only boy and the youngest among six children. Bandura's parents had immigrated to Canada when they were adolescents—his father from Krakow, Poland, and his mother from Ukraine. His parents were wheat farmers of Polish heritage who encouraged him to get an education so that he would have a better life than they had had.

Bandura's elementary and high school education took place at the one and only school in town that had only two teachers for the entire curriculum. The poor educational resources of the school turned out to be an enabling factor for Bandura. He would learn on his own. Despite the educational limitations of the school, almost all of the students went on to attend universities throughout the world.

Bandura took his parents' advice and enrolled as a student at the University of British Columbia. He majored in psychology because it offered classes that fit in his work schedule. Fascinated by psychology, Bandura graduated within 3 years. He continued his education in graduate school at the University of Iowa. After earning his Ph.D. in 1952, Bandura accepted a position as a lecturer at Stanford University for 1 year. Although Albert Bandura is most often described as a behaviorist or as a neo-behaviorist, he describes his work as "social cognitivism."

Influenced by Sears's research, Bandura began a program of research on social and familial antecedents of aggression with one of his graduate students, Richard Walters. Bandura and Walters (1959) found that parents of "hyper-aggressive boys were modeling very hostile attitudes. Although they would not put up with aggression in their homes, they demanded that their sons be tough and that they settle disputes with their classmates with physical strength, if necessary." Bandura and Walters (1959) published their early work in a book titled *Adolescent Aggression.* The researchers concluded that the boys modeled the aggressive attitudes of their parents. This conclusion contradicted the Freudian belief that direct parental punishment would internally inhibit boys' expression of aggressive drives.

The results from the aggression studies influenced Bandura to conduct a program of research on social modeling that involved the now-famous inflated Bobo doll. During the 1950s and 1960s, therapists subscribed to the Freudian view of catharsis that modeled violence would drain observers' aggressive drives and limit their violent behavior. Bandura challenged this belief by having children in his studies exposed to social models who demonstrated either nonviolent or violent behavior toward the rebounding 1961 Bobo dolls (Bandura, Ross, & Ross, 1961, 1963). In the experiment, Bandura made a film in which a woman was shown beating up a Bobo doll and shouting aggressive words. Subsequently, the film was shown to a group of children. Afterward, the children were allowed to play in a room that held a Bobo doll. Imitating the woman in the film, the children immediately began to beat the doll.

Bandura's hunches proved right. Children learned from simply observing others. Children who were exposed to violent adult models afterward displayed aggression toward the Bobo doll, but control children rarely did so. Bandura and his associates drew the conclusion that children could learn new patterns of behavior vicariously without actually performing them or receiving rewards. This conclusion challenged the prevailing behavioral notion that learning either took place or did

not take place as a result of rewards, reinforcement, or punishment.

Bandura's experimental study was significant because it challenged the dominant behaviorist position that said all behavior is influenced by conditioning, reinforcement, or rewards. In the Bobo doll experiment, the children received no encouragement, rewards, or reinforcement to beat up the doll. On the contrary, they were simply imitating the behavior they had observed. Bandura termed this phenomenon *observational learning* and enumerated the elements of effective observational learning as attention, retention, reciprocation, and motivation.

During the 1960s, Bandura studied children's development of self-regulatory capabilities. The question he and his colleagues raised was, How do children acquire performance standards for self-reward? Bandura and his doctoral students used a bowling game wherein children could reward themselves with candy for whatever performance level they felt they merited. Children viewed an adult or a peer model who bowled and rewarded himself or herself based on either a high or a low performance standard. The study found that when the children had an opportunity to bowl, those who had viewed a model set a high standard of self-reward adopted a more stringent performance criterion for self-reward than those who watched a model set a lax standard (Bandura & Perloff, 1967).

> ## Inner Reflections
>
> In your estimation, what is the role of self-regulation in healthy and maladaptive behavior development?
>
> Researchers are beginning to question if attention-deficit/hyperactivity disorder is a matter of the absence of self-regulation.
>
> How might you go about teaching self-regulation to your clients?

Although most psychology textbooks categorize Bandura's social learning theory with those of the behaviorists, Bandura himself noted that he never really fit well as a behaviorist. In fact, Bandura argued that reducing behavior to a stimulus–response cycle was far too simplistic. Even though he used behavioral terminology, such as *conditioning* and *reinforcement*, he conceptualized these phenomena as operating through cognitive processes. From his perspective, psychology textbooks mischaracterized his approach as behavioristic rather than as cognitive.

Bandura is also known for the concept of self-efficacy, which deals with how well people perceive that they can deal with life tasks and challenges (Bandura, 1986). People who have a strong sense of self-efficacy believe that they have the ability to accomplish important tasks. They believe that they can succeed and, therefore, have a low level of anxiety when they approach tasks. People who believe that they can bring about their desired outcomes have a greater incentive to act and to persevere in the face of adversity. A large number of empirical studies support Bandura's position that our beliefs concerning our own personal efficacy touch virtually every aspect of our lives, including how we think (pessimistically or optimistically), how well we motivate ourselves and persevere in the face of adversities, and our vulnerability to stress and depression, as well as the life choices we make.

In addition, Bandura has also noted the remarkable cultural diversity of behavior patterns. Social modeling, self-enabling beliefs, and self-regulation are pervasive across cultural contexts and domains of human functioning. In 1977, Bandura published his research on self-regulation and self-efficacy based on a triadic model of reciprocal causations. According to him,

> Perceived self-efficacy not only reduces anticipatory fears and inhibitions but, through expectations of eventual success, it affects coping efforts once they are initiated. Efficacy expectations determine how much effort people will expend, and how long they will persist in the face of obstacles and aversive experiences. The stronger the efficacy or mastery expectations, the more active the efforts. (Bandura, 1977, p. 80)

Bandura asserted that "what people think, believe, and feel affects how they behave" (p. 25).

During the 1980s, Bandura focused his attention on the impact of self-efficacy beliefs on personal goal setting and mastery. He found that students who set proximal personal goals (e.g., completing a specified number of math problems each day) developed a higher sense of self-efficacy, intrinsic interest, and competency than students who pursued only distal goals or no goals at all. Bandura concluded that feelings of self-efficacy are the foundation of human motivation and action.

During the 1990s, Bandura continued his work on self-efficacy, and he and his students discovered that students' self-efficacy beliefs about regulating their academic learning activities and writing were highly predictive of their academic goal setting and academic achievement (Zimmerman & Bandura, 1994). In 1997, Bandura published *Self-Efficacy: The Exercise of Control*, which demonstrated how the concept of self-efficacy could be applied to education, health, and the treatment of clinical problems such as depression and substance abuse, athletics, and organizational functioning.

Bandura's contributions have been enduring and important because he helped disprove the prevailing Freudian notions about aggression and the behavioral notions of reinforcement and reward as being the primary determinants of learning (Pajares, 2004). Prior to Bandura's research, many scholars adhered to the Freudian view that aggression was the product of intrapsychic forces that operated mostly at the unconscious level. Psychoanalytically oriented therapists viewed students' aggression on playgrounds as an expression of their impulses that were demanding release in negative ways. Television producers had viewers thinking that viewing violence on television was cathartic—that it allowed them to release their violent feelings without action. Bandura's Bobo doll experiments successfully disputed these claims and showed the real power of televised or filmed violence on children's aggressive tendencies. In part, the Bobo doll experiment led to the U.S. Surgeon General's commissioning of a panel to evaluate research on media violence (Comstock & Rubinstein, 1972).

Moreover, Bandura's work on moral thought and conduct has had a tremendous impact. Bandura proposed that students' moral conduct is deeply influenced by their ability to self-regulate. According to him, students monitor their conduct and the conditions under which it takes place (Pajares, 2004). They then judge their conduct in relation to their moral standards, and they regulate their behavior by the consequences they apply to themselves. All of this is done to give a person a sense of self-worth. Breakdowns in a person's moral self-regulation take place because he or she is able to disengage from the moral self-sanction. Bandura has outlined eight mechanisms of moral disengagement and displacement of moral responsibility, including moral justification, that are used to disengage moral self-sanctions. Other types of disengagement include minimizing and ignoring. Bandura has warned, "You don't have to change a person's basic codes or transform their personality; all you have to do is to create conditions for disengagement of moral control" (Stokes, 1986, p. 3).

Some of the awards Bandura has received include the Distinguished Scientific Contributions Award of the American Psychological Association (APA), the Distinguished Scientist Award from Division 12 of the APA, the William James Award of the American Psychological Society for outstanding achievements in psychological science, and the Distinguished Contribution Award from the International Society for Research in Aggression. He is the recipient of 16 honorary degrees from universities. In 2003 and 2004, Bandura received his 15th and 16th honorary degrees from the University of Athens and the University of Catania, respectively (see also Division of Educational Studies, 2004).

In August 1999, Bandura received the Thorndike Award for Distinguished Contributions of Psychology to Education from the APA. In 2001, he received the Lifetime Achievement Award from the Association for the Advancement of Behavior Therapy (see also Division of Educational Studies, 2006).

In May 2004, he was given the James McKeen Cattell Award from the American Psychological Society. In August 2004, Bandura was awarded the Outstanding Lifetime Contribution to Psychology Award from the APA.

At 89 years young, Professor Bandura continues to research and teach at Stanford University. He has been quoted as saying,

> As I reflect on my journey to this octogenarian milepost, I am reminded of the saying that it is not the miles traveled but the amount of tread remaining that is important. When I last checked, I still have too much tread left to gear down or to conclude this engaging Odyssey. (Pajares, 2004)

Bandura's Contributions to Control Therapy

Although Bandura never developed his own cognitive therapy theory, his work on self-regulation has led to self-control therapy, a recent cognitive therapy approach. According to Shapiro and Astin (1998), "One of our greatest human fears is losing control, and one of our strongest motivations is to have control over our lives" (p. ix). Self-control therapy has been successful with simple habit problems, such as smoking, overeating, and study habits. Self-observation requires clients to monitor closely their behavior, both before and after change has taken place. Records of client behavior are kept in behavioral diaries. Clients might count how many cigarettes they smoke a day in a behavioral diary.

Next, clients participate in environmental planning. After clients have maintained behavioral charts and diaries, they are in a position to engage in environmental planning or making changes to their environment. For example, clients remove or avoid some of the cues that lead to their smoking. Therefore, they put away ashtrays, remove matches from their homes, and drink tea instead of coffee. Finally, clients construct self-contracts that reward them depending on how well they have implemented and kept their nonsmoking plan. A self-control contract is written and witnessed by the client's therapist. This therapeutic approach is relatively new, and therefore, clients are cautioned to go slowly and proceed with the assistance of a therapist. Self-control therapy indicates how Bandura's work has formed a bridge between the behavioral and the cognitive schools.

COGNITIVE THERAPY AND DEPRESSION

Major Contributor: Aaron Beck (1921–)

Photo courtesy of The Beck Institute for Cognitive Therapy and Research.

Aaron Beck

Initially, Aaron Beck became famous because he developed a cognitive therapy approach to depression. Since his early work on depression, Beck has become closely allied with cognitive therapy. Born on July 18, 1921, in Providence, Rhode Island, to Russian Jewish immigrants, Aaron was the youngest of five children. From the moment of his birth, Beck was in a family marked by tragedy. Two of his elder siblings (a brother and a sister) died in 1919 during the influenza pandemic (Weishaar, 1993). The death of Beck's two siblings led his mother to become severely depressed for long periods of his childhood. His encounter with his mother's depression was to become pivotal in his research on cognitive therapy and depression. Beck considered himself a replacement child who eased his mother's sense of loss.

Two other key events influenced Beck profoundly. During his childhood, he broke his arm. His recovery in the hospital was long. Beck's extended absence from school led him to believe that he was stupid and dumb, especially when one teacher held him back for a year. Through hard work, Beck surpassed his peers. His school success was instrumental in changing his belief that he was stupid. He considered his being able to detect his teacher's anger and his mother's mood swings pivotal in developing his keen sensitivity to changes in clients' moods (Weishaar, 1993). Throughout his lifetime, Beck suffered from periods of depression, and he suffered from several anxiety phobias as a result of his early hospitalization for his injury.

In 1942, Beck graduated Phi Beta Kappa from Brown University. He completed his medical degree from Yale in 1946. In 1953, he became board certified in psychiatry and thereafter assumed a professorial position in psychiatry at the University of Pennsylvania Medical School. Beck constructed his cognitive model from research studies that he initiated to explain the psychological processes in depression. His goal was to prove Freud's theory of depression as repressed retroflexed hostility. During the process of conducting his studies, he found that instead of hostility and anger, his clients revealed a sense of defeat, failure, and loss. The themes of depressed persons were the same during dreaming and waking. Based on his research findings, Beck concluded that the symptoms of depression could be explained in cognitive terms as biased interpretations of their life events based on their activation of negative representations of the self, their personal world, and their future world.

During 1959, Beck began researching the dreams of depressed persons using concepts from psychoanalytic theories (Weishaar, 1993). This research signaled the beginning of cognitive therapy (Beck, 1963, 1964, 1967). One of Beck's research goals was to validate Freud's theory of depression, which was conceptualized as "anger turned on the self." Instead of validating Freud's theory, he found that depressed patients evidenced a negative bias in their cognitive processing. On the basis of this research, Beck developed his theory of emotional disorders and a cognitive model of depression (Beck & Weishaar, 2005).

Beck's theory of depression postulated that depressed people adopt a negative schema of the world in childhood and adolescence. They construct such schemas because of a loss of a parent, rejection by peers, or criticism from teachers or parents. When people with a depressed schema encounter a situation that resembles the original negative schema, depression ensues. Depression is supported by negative schemas about life and one's role in it.

Beck also developed theoretical concepts about suicide and its prevention. He found that suicidal risk was increased by a sense of hopelessness. His longitudinal studies of both inpatients and outpatients who evidenced suicidal ideation had a cutoff score of 9 or more on the Beck Hopelessness Scale. This score was predictive of eventual suicide (Beck, Brown, Berchick, Stewart, & Steer, 1990; Beck, Steer, Kovacs, & Garrison, 1985). Recently, studies have found that cognitive therapy reduces the frequency of subsequent suicide attempts and extends the time period before a person makes another suicide attempt. Beck's work on cognitive therapy has produced a number of other assessment scales, including the Beck Depression Inventory (Beck, Steer, & Brown, 1996), the Beck Anxiety Inventory (Beck & Steer, 1990), and the Beck Self-Concept Test (Beck, Steer, Brown, & Epstein, 1990).

Currently, Beck is the president of the nonprofit Beck Institute for Cognitive Therapy and Research and professor emeritus at the University of Pennsylvania. He is reported to be the only psychiatrist to receive research awards from both the American Psychological Association and the American Psychiatric Association. Beck has been a consultant for the review panels of the National Institute of Mental Health, has served on the editorial boards of many journals, and has been a visiting professor at Harvard, Yale, and Columbia. He has published more than 540 articles and has authored or coauthored 22 books. He has been called one of the five most influential psychotherapists of all time by *The American Psychologist* (July 1989).

KEY CONCEPTS OF BECK'S COGNITIVE THERAPY

Presently, cognitive therapy is the most frequently used therapy orientation in practice. One of the reasons for CBT's popularity is its direct interviewing procedures and clearly measurable behavioral changes. Cognitive therapists maintain that our beliefs have their origin in early childhood and that they continue developing throughout our lives. Early childhood experiences become the foundation for basic beliefs about ourselves and our world. Cognitive therapists are interested in the impact of thinking on individuals' personalities and on their behaviors.

Automatic Thoughts

The **automatic thought** is an important concept in Beck's cognitive psychotherapy. Such thoughts take place spontaneously, without any effort or choice on our part. When individuals experience psychological disorders, their automatic thoughts are frequently distorted, extreme, or inaccurate. A man has automatic negative thoughts whenever he sees an attractive woman. He tells himself that the woman would never go out with him or find him appealing. His automatic thoughts may also bring to the surface other core negative thoughts that he has about himself.

Cognitive Schemas

Human beings survive because they have an information-processing system that takes into account relevant information about the environment that synthesizes such information and then formulates a plan of action based on the synthesis. Each system that is critical in our survival—cognitive, behavioral, affective, and motivational—consists of structures known as schemas (Beck & Weishaar, 2005).

Our past experiences help us form our **cognitive schemas**. A schema is a cognitive framework or concept that helps us organize and interpret information. Cognitive schemas function as organizers of meaning about all aspects of our worldview, including relational views toward ourselves, others, and the world. Cognitive schemas are developed during childhood, and we elaborate on schemas throughout our lives. If triggered, cognitive schemas produce automatic thoughts, strong affects, and behavioral tendencies. Most people (even those who are not diagnosed with a psychiatric disorder) have problems in one or more schema areas. This is the idea underlying the identification of a client's core issue (e.g., early maladaptive schema).

There are both advantages and disadvantages to schemas. On the plus side, these mental frameworks permit us to take shortcuts in interpreting a large amount of information. Conversely, they may cause us to exclude relevant information in favor of information that confirms our preexisting beliefs and ideas. Schemas play a central role in contributing to stereotypes because they make it difficult to retain new information that does not conform to our established schemas.

Clark, Beck, and Alford (1999) have listed five types of schemas: (1) cognitive-conceptual, (2) affective, (3) physiological, (4) behavioral, and (5) motivational. Cognitive-conceptual schemas supply a method for storing, interpreting, and making meaning of our world. Core beliefs form cognitive-conceptual schemas. Affective schemas contain our negative and positive feelings. Physiological schemas consist of perceptions of physical functions, such as a panic reaction and hyperventilating. Behavioral schemas consist of actions that are taken, such as laughing when happy. Motivational schemas are those that initiate an action to achieve something, such as to avoid pain, to eat, and to play. They may be adaptive or maladaptive.

Cognitive Distortions

Our important beliefs or schemas are vulnerable to cognitive distortion. The thought processes that support schemas begin in early childhood and, therefore, contain early errors in reasoning. **Cognitive distortions** take place when our information processing is inaccurate. DeRubeis, Tang, and Beck (2001) have proposed a number of common cognitive distortions that are in existence with different psychological disorders. If cognitive distortions occur frequently, they can lead to psychological problems. When cognitive distortions are frequent, people experience depression, anxiety, and other types of disorders. Cognitive therapists search for cognitive distortions in their clients' account of their lives, and they help them learn how to make changes in their thinking.

Beck contends that people with emotional problems are inclined to commit characteristic "logical errors" that lean toward self-deprecation. Hence, cognitive therapy conceptualizes maladaptive behavior as originating from faulty thinking, making incorrect inferences on the basis of inadequate information, and failing to distinguish between fantasy and reality. Nine cognitive distortions are discussed below.

- *All-or-nothing thinking:* When we believe that things have to be exactly as we want them to be, we are participating in **all-or-nothing thinking**. A woman who says that she is a failure unless she can keep her home in perfect order is engaging in all-or-nothing thinking.
- *Selective abstraction:* It exists when we form conclusions based on an isolated detail of a situation.

We ignore other information, and we miss the significance of the total situation. People focus only on their shortcomings rather than on the totality of their behavior.

- *Overgeneralization:* It takes place when we make a rule based on a few occurrences of a situation. If we perform poorly on one or two science exams, we might overgeneralize and state that we are no good in science.
- *Mind reading:* It refers to the notion that we know what another person is thinking about. For instance, a person might state to his wife, "I know why you are looking at me that way." He is engaging in **mind reading** because he has not permitted his wife to state the reasons why she may be looking at him in a certain manner.
- *Magnification and minimization:* They involve seeing something as far more important or far less significant than it actually is. Individuals magnify imperfections, or they minimize good points. A woman views a pimple on her face as much larger than it really is. An athlete may have suffered a severe head injury, but he minimizes the concussion. **Magnification** and minimization distortions can lead to depression.
- *Personalization:* It means that a person takes an unrelated event and makes it related or causal to him or her. A person might complain, "It always rains whenever I get my hair done."
- *Negative prediction:* It occurs when an individual believes that something bad is going to happen, but there is no hard evidence to support such a conclusion. For instance, a person might say, "I know something bad is about to happen because things have been going too well in my life."
- *Labeling and mislabeling:* These are said to occur when a person describes his or her identity on the basis of imperfections and mistakes made in the past and permits such imperfections to continue to define his or her identity. For example, a woman describes herself as a klutz because she once spilled her drink on a date.
- *Catastrophizing:* It is a type of cognitive distortion that takes place when we take one event and exaggerate it so that it becomes fearful in our lives. A person might say, "I know that I am going to be just a failure at that job interview because it is so important to me."

Cognitive Theory of Personality

Cognitive therapy stresses the role of information processing in forming an individual's personality. When people perceive that a situation necessitates a response, they may set into motion a set of cognitive, emotional, motivational, and behavioral schemas. Cognitive therapy views personality as being shaped by the interaction between people's innate disposition and their environment (Beck, Freeman, & Davis, 2003). Personality attributes reflect our basic schemas or interpersonal strategies we construct in response to our environment. Personality is also shaped by our temperament and cognitive schemas. Our thoughts about ourselves, others, and the world form our personality. Our personality is flexible; it changes with the experiences and the people we meet.

Theory of Maladaptive Behavior

Cognitive therapy conceptualizes psychological distress as being caused by a number of factors, including predispositions to illness. Each person constructs a set of idiosyncratic vulnerabilities that predispose him or her to psychological distress. These schemas are reinforced by later learning experiences. The schemas people develop may be adaptive or dysfunctional. Although cognitive schemas are usually latent, they can become active if specific stressors act on us. There is an important learning component in maladaptive behavior.

Beck et al. (2003) proposed that most psychological disorders are caused by a bias in the way we engage in information processing. The beginnings of a psychological disorder usually can be traced to our schema that predisposes us to identify a situation as posing a danger or a loss. Beck (1967) developed various cognitive profiles for psychological disorders, including profiles or schemas for depression, anxiety, mania, and panic disorder.

Cognitive Model of Depression

Beck challenged the psychoanalytic view that depression results from anger turned inward. On the basis of his early research, Beck (1963) found that depression was caused by negative thinking and biased interpretation of events (DeRubeis & Beck, 1988). His cognitive model of depression consisted of a **cognitive triad** model. Depressed people have a negative view of themselves, the world, and their future. They perceive that large barriers loom to block access to the completion of their goals. For them, the world is empty of pleasure. Their perceptions of the future are pessimistic because they believe their situations will not change. In addition, depressed persons may have suicidal wishes that are geared toward their escaping from what they perceive as unbearable problems.

People who evidence a tendency toward depression often establish perfectionist goals that may be very difficult for them to achieve. They screen out successful life experiences that are not consistent with their negative views of themselves. Depressed people have cognitions that center on a sense of irreversible loss, which leads to an almost permanent sense of sadness.

Cognitive Model of Anxiety Disorders

Beck conceptualized anxiety disorders as excessive functioning or malfunctioning of normal survival mechanisms (DeRubeis et al., 2001). Both anxious and normal people have the same basic mechanisms for coping with threat, and their physiological responses prepare their bodies for escape or self-defense. What differs between normal and anxious people is that the latter's perception of danger is based on false assumptions or exaggerated signs of danger. A normal response is founded on a more accurate assessment of risk and the size of danger. Whereas normal individuals can correct their misperceptions using logic and evidence, anxious people experience difficulties recognizing cues of safety and other signs that reduce threat. In anxiety disorders, cognitive content centers on themes of danger, and the person tends to maximize the chances of harm while minimizing his or her ability to cope. Freeman and Simon (1989)

have pointed out that the significant cognitive schema of a generalized anxiety disorder is that of hypervigilance. People with this cognitive schema have a history of being alert to their environmental surroundings. They have automatic thoughts that suggest certain situations (rainy roads or the looks on others' faces) are threats to them. Less anxious people have an accurate assessment of risk and danger compared with a hypervigilant one.

Cognitive Model for Mania

The manic client's biased thinking is the direct opposite of that for individuals suffering from depression. People who experience mania selectively perceive gains in each experience, while they block out negative experience or reinterpret them to be positive. Clients with a mania disorder unrealistically expect favorable results from different situations. They may have exaggerated perceptions of their own abilities and accomplishments, which lead to feelings of euphoria. As clients experience heightened optimistic expectations about events or themselves, they become involved in one questionable enterprise after another.

Cognitive Model for Panic Disorder

Clients with panic disorder view any unexplained symptom or sensation as an indication of impending doom or catastrophe. Each client has a specific equation for focusing his or her attention on bodily or psychological experiences and then translating this information into various psychological reactions. For instance, one client associates distress in the chest with a heart attack, while another person's feelings of light headedness signal imminent unconsciousness to him (Beck & Weishaar, 2005).

Cognitive Model for
Obsessions and Compulsions

Individuals with obsessive thoughts (thoughts that cause continual worry) search out certainty of danger or problems in situations that most people believe to be relatively safe. For instance, a person who continually goes back to check if the door to his house is locked is quite different from one who goes back only once because she can't remember if she locked it or not. Beck, Freeman, and Associates (1990) have listed a number of automatic thoughts caused by obsessions and compulsions:

- "What if I forget to pack something?"
- "I better do this again to be sure I got it right."
- "I have to do this myself or it won't be done correctly." (p. 314)

People suffering from obsessions experience guilt when they do not do what they think they should do. They experience anxiety even when they are reassured that everything is okay. *Habituation training* is one specific technique used to treat obsessions. Habituation training elicits clients' obsessional thoughts on a repeated basis. The therapist makes a detailed assessment of the client's obsessional thoughts. Then he or she develops ways to get the client used to obsessional thoughts without feeling that anything needs to be done about them. Finally, the therapist asks the client (a) to deliberately evoke the thoughts (b) to write these thoughts down repeatedly, and (c) to listen to a tape of the thoughts with the client's voice (Rush & Beck, 2000). Gradually, clients habituate to the thoughts without feeling that it is necessary for them to do anything about them.

Underlying Assumptions of Cognitive Therapy

Cognitive therapy has three underlying assumptions: (1) People's internal communication is available for introspection, (2) clients' beliefs contain highly personal meanings, and (3) clients can discover the meaning of their internal communications (Weishaar, 1993). Therapists can help people by understanding what they are saying to themselves about an upsetting event (DeRubeis & Beck, 1988). A primary goal of cognitive therapy is to change the way clients think by understanding

their core schematic thoughts and changing them to become healthy.

Cognitive therapy emphasizes the present, and it usually lasts for 10 to 16 sessions. Treatment is focused on clients' current issues rather than on their past. Therapy attempts to provide some form of symptom relief for clients' most pressing problems. Clients may be taught specific strategies for handling their discomfort or problems.

Cognitive therapy stresses individuals' learning history, the influence of important life events, and the role they might have played in the development of a psychological disturbance. Psychological distress is the result of a number of interacting forces (Beck & Weishaar, 2005). For example, depression may be caused by predisposing hereditary factors, diseases that cause persistent neurochemical abnormalities, developmental traumas that make one susceptible to specific cognitive vulnerabilities, and inadequate coping skills.

THE THERAPEUTIC PROCESS

The therapeutic process for CBT is highly structured. CBT mandates a detailed analysis of a client's behavior, cognition, and emotions and a precise determination of the treatment goals for a client. It maintains that cognitive activity can be observed, measured, and changed. Furthermore, CBT asserts that a client's cognitive processes contribute to his or her dysfunctional behavior and emotional experience through focusing, selective perception, memory, and cognitive distortion. The ensuing sections describe the therapeutic process for CBT, including the therapeutic relationship, the goals of therapy, role of the therapist, phases of therapy, and therapy techniques.

The Therapeutic Relationship

In contrast to REBT, Beck's cognitive therapy emphasizes the importance of the therapeutic relationship. Whereas Ellis maintained that it was not necessary for the therapist to establish a warm relationship with clients, Beck asserted that the quality of the therapeutic relationship is critical to the practice of cognitive therapy. Beck (2005) asserted that therapists must practice empathy and positive regard for clients. To a certain extent, Beck embraced Rogers's core therapeutic conditions that posited that therapists should exemplify certain conditions for therapy to proceed, including therapists' positive regard and empathy for clients, regardless of their specific circumstances. According to Rogers, the conditions for therapy were necessary and sufficient for a positive change in client behavior. Beck differed from Rogers in that he asserted that the conditions for therapy espoused by Rogers were necessary, but not sufficient to produce positive therapeutic change. Cognitive therapists use Rogerian listening skills to identify clients' feelings and to enhance the therapeutic relationship. However, they assert that clients change because they learn how to think differently, and they act on that learning—not just because the therapist has provided certain "necessary and sufficient" conditions for therapy that Rogers presented. Beck also asserted that therapists must also have a cognitive conceptualization of a case, be active and creative in designing therapeutic homework assignments, be able to engage clients through a process of Socratic questioning, and be skilled in guiding clients in order to produce important self-discovery that leads to desired changes in a client's thinking or behavior.

In Beck's cognitive therapy, the therapeutic process is governed by three principles: (1) collaborative empiricism, (2) Socratic dialogue, and (3) guided discovery. **Collaborative empiricism** refers to the fact that both the therapist and the client jointly determine the goals for treatment and decide how feedback will take place. As coinvestigators, they review evidence to support or reject the client's cognitions. The therapist and the client also function as coinvestigators in that they examine the evidence to support or reject the client's cognitions. Gradually, the therapist helps expose the client's biased thinking and assist him or her with more healthy or adaptive thinking.

Cognitive therapists use the Socratic dialogue or method of questioning as a major therapeutic part of establishing a therapeutic relationship (Beck & Young, 1985). To facilitate new learning, the therapist carefully constructs a series of questions. Such questions are designed to (a) clarify or define the problem, (b) help in the identification of clients' thoughts and assumptions, (c) assess the meanings clients give to events, and (d) measure the consequences of clients maintaining maladaptive thoughts and behaviors.

Inner Reflections

Both Ellis and Beck used a structured approach to therapy.

Compare and contrast their two approaches.

Would you be more comfortable using Ellis's or Beck's structured approach to therapy?

The Three-Question Socratic Technique

Beck uses three questions modified from Socrates to help clients change their negative thinking. Each question challenges clients' negative thinking. The therapist asks,

1. What is the evidence for the belief?

2. How else might you interpret the situation?

3. If it is true, what are the implications?

Therapists often ask clients questions, such as "How do you know that those people are really laughing at you?" "Could it be they are laughing about something else?" Liese (1993) describes an example of a medical doctor using the three-question technique with a client suffering from AIDS:

Dr.: Jim, you told me a few minutes ago that some people will scorn you when they learn about your illness. (reflection) What is your evidence for this belief?

Jim: I don't have any evidence. I just feel that way.

Dr.: You "just feel that way." (reflection) How else could you look at the situation?

Jim: I guess my real friends wouldn't abandon me.

Dr.: If some people did, in fact, abandon you, what would the implications be?

Jim: I guess it would be tolerable, as long as my real friends didn't abandon me. (p. 83)

Beck and Young (1985) indicate that questions are not used to trap clients but rather to help the therapist understand their position. Questions are posed sensitively and compassionately. In the following section, Beck and Young indicate how questions change during the course of therapy:

> In the beginning of therapy, questions are employed to obtain a full and detailed picture of the patient's particular difficulties. They are used to obtain background and diagnostic data; to evaluate the patient's stress tolerance, capacity for introspection, coping methods and so on; to obtain information about the patient's external situation and interpersonal context; and to modify vague complaints by working with the patient to arrive at specific target problems to work on.
>
> As therapy progresses, the therapist uses questioning to explore approaches to problems, to help the patient weigh advantages and disadvantages of possible solutions, to examine the consequences of staying with particular maladaptive behaviors, to elicit automatic thoughts, and to demonstrate maladaptive assumptions and their consequences. In short, the therapist uses questioning in most cognitive therapeutic techniques. (p. 223)

Guided discovery is the third major principle that guides the therapeutic process. As a result of guided discovery, clients learn how to modify maladaptive beliefs. The therapist functions as a "guide" who clarifies errors in cognitions by constructing new experiences (behavioral experiments) that promote the development of new skills. Guided discovery suggests that the therapist does not exhort, cajole, or badger clients to adopt a new set of beliefs. On the contrary, the therapist encourages clients to use the new information they have acquired (Beck & Weishaar, 2005).

Goals of Therapy

The fundamental goal of cognitive therapy is to remove or to eliminate biases in clients' thinking that prevent them from functioning optimally. The therapist focuses on the manner in which clients process information, especially as such processing is used to maintain maladaptive feelings and behavior. In cognitive therapy, goal establishment is usually a joint venture. Therapists help clients become specific in delineating their goals as well as in prioritizing them. When clients' goals are specific and concrete, the therapist is in a better position to choose treatment techniques that will help them change their belief systems, feelings, and behaviors.

Role of the Therapist

Beck (1976) has maintained that "cognitive therapy consists of all of the approaches that alleviate psychological distress through the medium of correcting faulty conceptions and self-signals" (p. 214). The cognitive therapist helps clients learn how to identify their distorted and dysfunctional cognitions. Clients learn the influence that their cognitions have on their feelings and behaviors. Cognitive therapy assists clients to recognize, observe, and monitor their own cognitions. Cognitive-behavioral therapists learn what their clients desire out of life, and then they help them achieve their goals. The therapist's role is to listen, teach, and encourage. The client's role is to express concerns, learn, modify behavior, and implement new cognitions.

Assessment

The cognitive therapist plays a critical role in assessment. The therapist takes detailed notes in assessing clients' problems and cognitions.

Assessment focuses on clients' specific thoughts, feelings, and behaviors. Close attention is paid to the selection of therapeutic techniques that can be used to assist clients in correcting their cognitive distortions. Judith Beck (1995) has developed a Cognitive Conceptualization Diagram to organize client information. For instance, the therapist assesses relevant childhood data. Emphasis is placed on discovering the following: What experiences contributed to the development of the client's core belief(s)? What is or are the client's core belief(s)? What is the client's most central belief about himself or herself? Which positive beliefs help the client cope with his or her core beliefs? What are the negative counterparts to the core beliefs? What compensatory strategies has the client developed to deal with his or her core belief? What automatic thoughts does the client have? How are such automatic thoughts related to his or her behavior and feelings?

Cognitive therapists frequently administer brief symptom checklists, including the Beck Depression Inventory and the Beck Anxiety Inventory prior to counseling sessions to both identify clients' faulty thoughts and to provide a means to evaluate clients' progress at the end of therapy.

To ensure therapeutic collaboration, therapists elicit feedback from the client at the end of each session. The client is asked what he or she found to be helpful or not helpful. In many instances, therapists summarize the session or may ask the client to do so (Beck & Weishaar, 2005). In an effort to demystify the therapeutic process, the therapist provides the client with a rationale for each procedure used.

Phases of Therapy

Beck and Weishaar (2005) have outlined three stages of cognitive therapy: (1) initial sessions, (2) middle and later sessions, and (3) termination. During the initial sessions, the therapist is very active. For instance, he or she builds a therapeutic alliance with the client, educates the client about the cognitive model and the relationship between thinking and feelings, defines and assesses the problems, establishes client goals, and talks about

homework assignments and other techniques used during treatment.

During the middle stage of cognitive therapy, the focus is on helping the client to think and challenge automatic thoughts. The therapist also examines the client's underlying cognitive schemas. In the later sessions, the client assumes greater responsibility for identifying problems and solutions and for developing homework assignments. The therapist assumes the role of advisor rather than teacher, as in the initial sessions. Treatment ends when clients are able to use cognitive therapy to solve their problems.

Therapy Techniques

Cognitive therapists use a variety of cognitive and behavioral techniques. Some cognitive techniques include decatastrophizing, reattribution, redefining, decentering, and doing homework. Beck and Emery (1979) describe **decatastrophizing** as the "what if" technique that helps clients prepare for feared consequences. This technique is used to decrease clients' avoidance of anxiety-provoking conditions or situations.

Reattribution techniques test clients' automatic thoughts by introducing alternative causes of events. Sometimes, clients attribute responsibility for situations or conditions to themselves when, in reality, they have little responsibility for the situation. When therapists use the technique of reattribution, they help clients distribute fairly the responsibility for a condition or a situation. For instance, the person might say, "Maybe if I hadn't said anything while he was driving, we would not have had that accident." A number of conditions might have contributed to the accident, including slippery roads and poor lighting.

Decentering is a technique used in treating anxious clients who mistakenly believe that they are the focus of everyone's attention. Beck and Weishaar (2005) cite the example of a student who was afraid to speak in class because he was afraid his classmates would notice his anxiety. Treatment involved learning how to focus on things other than on his anxiety or his classmates.

Doing homework is another cognitive-behavioral technique. At the beginning of therapy, the therapist might ask clients to keep a diary of any incidents that provoke feelings of anxiety or depression, so that they can examine their thoughts about the event. Specific assignments are given to the client for collecting data on thoughts and behavior. The therapist might assign exercises designed to help clients cope with other issues. Homework takes place between sessions, and homework assignments are discussed in each session.

Another useful cognitive intervention is the thought change record. In the early phase of therapy, clients are introduced to thought recording by asking them to make a note of automatic thoughts that take place in stressful situations and to identify emotions associated with these thoughts. As the client becomes more adept with CBT, a three-column thought change record can be used in which the client (1) identifies cognitive errors in automatic thoughts, (2) generates rational alternatives, and (3) charts the outcome of making these changes.

Cognitive-behavioral therapists also use a number of behavioral techniques. For treating anxiety disorders, the therapist uses hierarchical exposure to feared stimuli, relaxation training, and breathing training. Clients are encouraged to expose themselves gradually to stimuli until their anxiety response dissipates, and they develop a greater sense of self-control and mastery.

COMPARISON OF ELLIS'S AND BECK'S APPROACH TO PSYCHOTHERAPY _____

Beck's approach to therapy has been simply labeled *cognitive therapy*. Although he developed his theory independently of Ellis, the two exchanged ideas. Both approaches are action oriented, and both focus on changing people's negative thoughts and maladaptive beliefs. A major difference between these two therapists is that cognitive therapy maintains that each disorder has its own typical content or cognitive specificity. The cognitive profiles for clients suffering from depression, anxiety, and panic disorder are quite different, and therefore, the therapist uses different techniques in treating them. Conversely, REBT does not view disorders as having cognitive themes but instead focuses on the "musts" and "shoulds" that are believed to be at the foundation for all disorders.

Moreover, the role of the therapist also differs in Ellis's REBT and Beck's cognitive therapy. In REBT, the therapist is highly directive and confrontational. Beck uses a Socratic dialogue approach with open-ended questions designed to get clients to reflect on their own actions and thoughts. Cognitive therapy encourages clients to discover their own misconceptions about their thoughts, whereas REBT therapists use a process of rational disputation. The therapist works to persuade clients that some of their beliefs are irrational and dysfunctional.

SUMMARY OF BANDURA, ELLIS, AND BECK_____
Albert Bandura

- Bridged gap between behavior theory and cognitive theory
- Pointed out that people learn a great deal from watching others (social learning)
- People learn from modeling and observational learning
- People choose behaviors to imitate based on perceived consequences
- A person stands a greater chance of imitating an act when he or she has observed positive consequences in others
- Modeling in groups, such as role-playing difficult situations, is an important tool to use in therapy
- Talked about self-control, self-efficacy, and self-regulation
- Goals can serve as guides for self-regulation when they are observable and measurable

Albert Ellis

- Emphasized cognitive restructuring and a process for discovering and disputing irrational beliefs

- Focused on having clients acknowledge their responsibility for creating their own problems
- Clients accept their ability to change
- Clients learn that their emotional problems stem from faulty or irrational thinking
- Therapist and client work to dispute irrational beliefs
- Therapist and client have continued monitoring and restructuring of client thoughts

Aaron Beck

- Began with his work on depression and discovered that depression was caused by maladaptive interpretations and conclusions
- Maintained that psychological disturbances often stem from automatic negative thoughts
- Automatic thoughts indicate habitual errors in a person's thinking
- Used "Socratic dialogue" to help clients deal with their negative automatic thoughts
- Emphasized the importance of cognitive schemas
- Developed a series of inventories, including the Beck Depression Inventory

COGNITIVE NEUROSCIENCE ____

Cognitive Neuroscience—with its concern about perception, action, memory, language and selective attention—will increasingly come to represent the central focus of all Neurosciences in the 21st century.

—Eric R. Kandel (Nobel Laureate)

Brief Overview

Although many counseling theory textbooks have a chapter on CBT, most do not have anything on cognitive neuroscience—despite the fact that this field of study has been around for almost three decades. Cognitive neuroscience is one of the fastest growing fields in the CBT school. What is this new school of thought or approach to psychotherapy? According to Gazzaniga, Ivry, and Mangun (2002),

cognitive neuroscience is an academic field of study that deals with the scientific study of biological substrates that underlie cognition, with a specific focus on the neural substrates of mental processes. It investigates how psychological and cognitive functions are produced by neural circuits in the brain. Cognitive neuroscience is a branch of both psychology and neuroscience, and it relies on theories in cognitive psychology, neuropsychology, and computational modeling. It is multidisciplinary in nature, and cognitive neuroscientists have backgrounds in areas such as neurobiology, bioengineering, psychiatry, neurology, and computer science. Cognitive neuroscience addresses how the brain creates the mind and how a certain area of the brain is connected to feelings or thoughts. It is an interdisciplinary approach for understanding the nature of thought.

> ### Inner Reflections
>
> Would you consider including cognitive theory in your integrative approach to therapy? If so, why? If not, why?
>
> What features of cognitive therapy are most attractive and least appealing to you?
>
> How well do the concepts about healthy and maladaptive development fit with your views on these topics?

The term *cognitive neuroscience* was first coined by Michael S. Gazzaniga, one of the founders of the *Journal of Cognitive Neuroscience*, and the cognitive psychologist George A. Miller as the two were on their way in the back seat of a taxi cab going to a dinner meeting at the Algonquin Hotel in New York City near the end of the 1970s (Gazzaniga, 2004; Gazzaniga et al., 2002). The dinner had been organized for scientists from Rockefeller University and Cornell University who had come together to study how the brain produces or enables the mind. From the results of the discussion during the taxi ride came the term cognitive neuroscience, which was subsequently embraced by the scientific community.

Prior to the development of cognitive neuroscience, psychologists had been investigating the details of mental processes for more than a century without knowing or, perhaps, even caring about what parts of the brain are involved with certain behaviors and thoughts. Cognitive neuroscience changed this lackadaisical approach to understanding the neural bases of mental processes. This field of study has now brought new understanding about the brain and the mind. The mind is the product of the activity taking place in the brain at the neural level. The mind is affected by a person's interpersonal relationships, cultural background, and societal experiences. The mind is affected by the neural pathways it has developed as a result of its myriad experiences.

Cognitive Neuroscience and Areas of Study

Cognitive neuroscience examines areas such as attention and brain function, emotional learning and memory, and the impact of a therapist and the therapeutic relationship on clients. Cognitive neuroscience might possibly end the turf wars between theories of psychotherapy by conducting brain imaging studies that measure the effectiveness of different theoretical approaches on clients. It has shed light on the nature of human thought and behavior, thereby contributing to our understanding of why we behave the way that we do. Cognitive neuroscience can help us understand how the brain processes a variety of information and the effects of this information processing on our emotional state and feelings. Knowing how the brain produces certain responses can possibly lead to the development of therapeutic interventions to treat mental disorders. In fact, some biological interventions are now being developed that can target specific brain areas, thereby providing hope for improving the therapeutic treatment of mental disorders.

Methods and Techniques of Cognitive Neuroscience

Cognitive neuroscience uses methods of investigation that go beyond just talk. For instance, it can use functional neuroimaging and electrophysiology. It has provided information regarding cognitive deficits due to brain lesions. Cognitive neuroscience can examine the effects of damage to the brain and subsequent changes in a person's thought processes as well as investigate a person's cognitive abilities based on brain development.

Prior to developments in cognitive neuroscience, the cognitive-behavior paradigm did not deal with the biological bases of mental disorders. It has only been relatively recently that neuroscience research has increased our knowledge about the neurobiological substrates of psychological functions and the changes that take place as a result of using therapeutic interventions (Beauregard, 2007; Frewen, Dozois, & Lanius, 2008). Brain imaging methods have now been used to investigate cognitive functioning, emotional experience, self-regulation, psychological disorders, and a host of other phenomena (Linden, 2006). Positron emission tomography and functional magnetic resonance imaging are methods now being used to measure the brain while it is at rest and then again after stimulation. During scanning, glucose or oxygen metabolism is measured in various brain regions. Metabolic activity in the brain regions that are activated by a stimulus differs from their at-rest brain measurement, and these measurements are used to infer neural activity.

As a result of functional magnetic resonance imaging methods, researchers are able to compare brain metabolic activity in individuals with and those without mental disorders and thereby identify the functional neural circuitry by which they differ. For instance, Frewen et al. (2008) have measured pre and post changes in the brain metabolic activity that take place during effective psychotherapeutic treatment. They found that using functional tasks during scanning clearly delineates specific neurobiological components of depression and how psychological treatments may or may not specifically target relevant brain regions.

Cognitive Neuroscience and Cognitive Regulation of Emotions and Behavior

Research in cognitive neuroscience has helped clarify connections between cognitive regulation of emotions and behavior and illnesses such as depression. Davidson, Putnam, and Larson (2000) found that a person's chronic inability to self-regulate the negative emotions of fear and anger contributes to clinical depression, anxiety disorders, and other mental disorders.

Cognitive neuroscience has found a way to measure the cognitive-behavior hypothesis that maintains that emotional reaction and behavior depend on an individual's cognitive processing and brain reactions to such processing. The CBT model asserts that each individual receives and process data from the environment in his or her own unique way. An individual develops an emotional response based on his or her (a) perception of the information, (b) interpretation of the importance of the information, and (c) understanding of causative relations and personal meaning ascribed to an event (Jokić-Begić, 2010). That is, events in and of themselves have no objective meaning. Each individual perceives, interprets, remembers, and evaluates events in terms of himself or herself. Cognitive psychologists maintain that for something to be perceived at all, it must be personally relevant, and that this importance is usually based on the individual's past experience.

One of the basic tenets of CBT is that one can learn how to self-regulate unpleasant emotions and thoughts (Beauregard, 2007). During therapy, a clinician might use CBT techniques such as refocusing and cognitive restructuring to reduce the effects of negative emotional states. Cognitive neuroscience is beginning to elucidate the relationship between types of information processing and activation in different parts of the brain. Two types of information processing are related to a person's cognitive thoughts and his or her emotional state: (1) bottom-up processing and (2) top-down processing. Bottom-up processing is dominated by situational cues (Clark & Beck, 2010). It is reactive to events in an almost knee-jerk way. In contrast, top-down information processing is deliberate and explicit. It is a strategic form of rational processing that uses rule-based knowledge to guide the information processing system. Neuroscience studies have found that psychotherapy influences top-down information processing and that this type of information processing takes place in the orbitofrontal cortex (Clark & Beck, 2010).

Neurobiological studies have found that CBT is associated with decreased activity in the amydalo-hippocampal subcortical region (i.e., bottom-up information processing) and increased activation in the frontal cortical regions (i.e., top-down processing) (Clark & Beck, 2010). In an article on the cognitive model of depression and its neurobiological correlates, Beck (2010) stated,

> It is now possible to sketch out possible genetic and neurochemical pathways that interact with or are parallel to cognitive variables. A hypersensitive amygdala is associated with both a genetic polymorphism and a pattern of negative cognitive biases and dysfunctional beliefs, all of which constitute risk factors for depression. Further the combination of a hyperactive amygdala and hypoactive prefrontal regions is associated with diminished cognitive appraisal and the occurrence of depression. Genetic polymorphisms also are involved in the overreaction to the stress and the hypercortisolemia in the development of depression—probably mediated by cognitive distortions. I suggest that comprehensive study of the psychological as well as biological correlates of depression can provide a new understanding of this debilitating disorder. (p. 969)

Empirical research has found that neurobiological changes take place after using CBT to treat clients with arachnophobia (Paquette et al., 2003), obsessive-compulsive disorder (Baxter et al., 1992; Schwartz & Begley, 2002), panic disorder (Prasko et al., 2004), social phobia, major depressive disorder, and chronic fatigue syndrome. Some notable findings of these studies indicated that (a) CBT treatment may lead to adaptive changes in specific brain regions with individuals with anxiety disorders; (b) effective CBT positively changes brain metabolism in individuals with panic disorder; (c) a prefronto-cortico-striato-thalamic brain system is involved in the mediation of obsessive-compulsive disorder symptoms, and CBT produced significant changes in brain activity; and (d) CBT is the method of choice in the treatment of depression.

CBT affects clinical recovery from depression by modulating the functioning of selective areas in limbic and cortical regions of the brain.

In general, the studies cited indicate that CBT interventions change brain functioning associated with problem solving, self-referential and relational processing, and affect regulation. Cognitive therapy influences top-down brain regulation; therefore, the changes that clients experience become permanent and generalized to different life areas. One of the benefits of cognitive neuroscience studies has been the discovery of a neural mirroring system in the premotor cortex and other areas of the brain. Mirror imaging may be conceptualized as the neurobiological correlate of action understanding, nonverbal communication, and empathy (Linden, 2006). As a result of the findings regarding mirror imaging, greater importance is now being given to the therapist–client relationship in the CBT approach (Fuchs, 2004). As Eric Kandel has stated, "Cognitive Neuroscience . . . will increasingly come to represent the central focus of all Neurosciences in the 21st century."

CURRENT TRENDS IN COGNITIVE THERAPIES

The best prediction about CBT is that it will continue to grow and that its principles will be integrated across a broad array of theoretical approaches. CBT has produced the most evidence-based research of all the therapeutic approaches. Moreover, such therapies have become manualized with disorder-specific treatment manuals that show step-by-step how to treat various disorders. It is expected that publication of specific manuals for various disorders will increase and that graduate schools will begin to emphasize manualized training for a wide range of maladaptive behavior. Beck's cognitive therapy stands the greatest chance of proliferating itself during the next 5 years primarily because it has integrated so many concepts and techniques from other approaches. CBT has become one of the best examples of an integrated approach to therapy.

I predict that computerized training manuals will become commonplace, as people seek a self-help approach to their issues. There are CBT sessions in which the user interacts with computer software or sometimes by a voice-activated phone service. Computerized cognitive-behavioral treatment might be useful for individuals who lack sufficient sums to pay for face-to-face therapy with a psychologist. Online counseling will expand using a cognitive-behavioral framework. Online counseling may become the treatment modality of choice for young people who have grown up communicating via a computer.

THE THIRD WAVE IN BEHAVIOR THERAPY: MINDFULNESS INTEGRATED INTO COGNITIVE-BEHAVIOR THERAPIES (DBT, ACT, AND MBCT)

Within the cognitive-behavioral school is the third wave of behavior therapy, and that wave involves the incorporation of the Chinese cultural practice of mindfulness into various cognitive therapy approaches. All the three new cognitive approaches discussed in this chapter (DBT, ACT, and MBCT) have adopted mindfulness as a major component of the theory. Thus, what we are witnessing is the inclusion of Chinese or Eastern cultural values into primary Western, Eurocentric therapies. What is positive about the incorporation of mindfulness is that we see the merger of critical components of another cultural framework—primarily the Chinese cultural worldview—for viewing life into American and European approaches for dealing with mental health and mental disorders. The downside of this phenomenon is that there is little acknowledgment within DBT, ACT, or MBCT of this practice of incorporation of the cultural values of another culture and, indeed, of another nation—namely China—although parts of mindfulness can be traced to Indian (Hindu) culture and Japanese culture as well. An important question is, "Are we witnessing the incorporation of Chinese culture worldviews into largely American psychotherapeutic approaches, or are we watching silently the usurpation of a critical component of Chinese culture with insufficient tracing of the concept to its rightful cultural origin?"

The critical point that American theorists of psychotherapy are "borrowing" from the Chinese is the cultural value of acceptance of what happens in life. For instance, DBT uses skills training to help clients develop the practice of meditation and viewing the circumstances of one's life without getting too upset about those circumstances. Likewise, a key component of ACT is helping clients learn how to accept rather than to constantly engage in a struggle with trying to master or to conquer the problem.

The next section describes DBT followed by a brief discussion of ACT and then MBCT.

Dialectical Behavior Therapy: Marsha Linehan

Marsha Linehan

Brief Overview

Dialectical behavior therapy (or DBT) developed by Marsha Linehan (1993) is part of the third wave of behavior therapy. DBT is a form of behavior therapy that was developed specifically as a treatment approach for chronically suicidal individuals who met the criteria for borderline personality disorder (Linehan, 1993). Borderline personality disorder is characterized by a client manifesting emotional dysregulation, strained interpersonal relationships, and low self-esteem. People diagnosed with a borderline personality disorder commit suicide more frequently than do individuals within the average population, and they also practice nonsuicidal self-injurious behaviors (Pompili, Girardi, & Ruberto, 2005; Linehan, 1993).

DBT can be described as an integration of three theoretical positions: (1) behavioral science, (2) dialectical philosophy, and (3) Zen practice, specifically mindfulness. It is based on the belief that (a) borderline individuals lack important interpersonal, self-regulation (including emotional regulation), and distress tolerance skills and capabilities; and (b) personal and environmental factors inhibit the use of behavioral skills the individual does have, "interfere with the development of new skills and capacities, and often reinforce inappropriate and extreme behaviors" (Linehan, 1995, p. 1; see also Linehan, Armstrong, Suarez, Allmon, & Heard, 1991)

Goals of Therapy

The goal of DBT is to help clients create and maintain consistent, stable environments, in which they are comfortable with change. The DBT therapist recognizes the dialectical tensions and balances that take place in the therapeutic relations and carefully integrates opposing strategies and therapeutic positions in each counseling interaction. A second goal of DBT is to bring out the opposites in the therapeutic situation and in the client's life and to provide him or her with the conditions for synthesis. The therapist also teaches clients dialectical reasoning.

DBT emphasizes conducting a thorough behavioral assessment of the client's current behaviors and the outlining of precise targets for treatment, orienting the client to the theory and procedures for treatment, and developing a collaborative working relationship between the therapist and the client. Some cognitive-behavioral techniques used in DBT include social skills training, contingency management, exposure techniques, cognitive restructuring, reinforcement for use of knowledge bases, and cognitive modification.

The primary dialectical strategy is the *balanced therapeutic* stance, which combines acceptance with change. Both the therapist and the client search for what is being left out in terms of the client's ordering of reality. Some strategies include use of stories, metaphor, myth, paradox, and ambiguity. Table 5.2 provides the dialectical strategies Linehan outlines in her program manual for treating borderline personality disorder.

Table 5.2 Dialectical Strategies

1. *Entering the paradox* involves highlighting the paradoxical contradictions of the client's behavior, of the therapeutic process, and of reality in general without pulling the client out of the struggle.

2. *Metaphor* entails using metaphor, analogies, anecdote, and parables teaching stories and myths to reveal new ways of thinking, feeling, and behaving.

3. *Devil's advocate technique* involves the therapist's presenting an extreme statement, asking the client if he or she believes the statement, and then playing the role of the devil's advocate (antithesis) to counter the client's counterarguments to reach a synthesis.

4. *Extending* is used when the therapist takes the client more seriously than the client is taking himself or herself to make a point.

5. *Wise mind* is a technique that pushes the client to integrate emotion and reason, accessing intuitive and spontaneous responses.

6. *Lemonade out of lemons* involves turning a problematic situation into an asset.

7. *Allowing natural change* is a technique that permits natural changes and instability into the therapy relationship.

8. *Dialectical assessment* involves continually looking for what is missing from individual or personal explanations of current behaviors and events.

Therapy does not start until (a) the client has been provided with an overview of DBT, (b) the therapist and the client have reached an agreement to work together, and (c) the client and the therapist have committed to standard agreements, which includes the client's agreement to stay in therapy for a specified period of time, attend all scheduled sessions, reduce suicidal and self-injurious behaviors, participate in skills training, and so forth.

DBT maintains that any comprehensive therapy must meet five critical functions. The therapy must (1) enhance and maintain the client's motivation to change, (2) improve the client's capabilities, (3) ensure that the client is assisted in generalizing his or her new capabilities to all relevant environments, (4) enhance the therapist's motivation and capabilities to treat clients, and (5) structure the clinical environment for therapy. It is noteworthy that the therapist's capabilities are enhanced and burnout prevented by using weekly consultation team meetings. The consultation team assists the therapist in maintaining his or her balance in working with clients.

DBT also organizes clinical treatment into stages and targets; it also adheres strictly to the order in which problems are addressed. The organizational format of DBT prevents therapy from just focusing on the crisis of the moment. Each stage of DBT has its own hierarchy for treatment targets. For instance, the outline of the behavioral targets deals with (a) behaviors that could lead to a client's death (suicide behaviors), then (b) behaviors that could lead to premature termination from therapy (therapy-interfering behaviors), followed by (c) quality of life-interfering behaviors (behaviors causing immediate crisis), and (d) increasing behavioral skills (i.e., skills currently being taught in skills training). The pretreatment stage of DBT focuses on assessment, commitment, and orientation to therapy. The targeted behaviors of each stage are brought under control before the client with borderline personality disorder can move on to the next phase. At each stage, treatment is focused on the identified targets, which are arranged in a hierarchy of relative importance. Therapists follow a detailed procedural manual. A general goal in every stage of therapy is to increase dialectical thinking. Table 5.3 provides the four stages and goals of DBT.

Standard DBT consists of three formats or models of treatment: (1) individual therapy, (2) skills-teaching group, and (3) coaching. Groups use a didactic skills-training orientation and contain four modules: (1) mindfulness, (2) distress tolerance, (3) interpersonal effectiveness, and (4) emotion regulation. Mindfulness is the core skill on which the others are based. Table 5.4 is a brief summary of DBT skills.

Evidence-Based Research and DBT

The National Institute of Mental Health and the National Institute on Drug Abuse have supported with grants two randomized controlled trials of DBT that found that DBT is more effective than treatment-as-usual in treatment of borderline personality disorder and comorbid diagnosis of substance abuse (Linehan et al., 1991). Clients who received DBT in comparison to the treatment-as-usual group were significantly less likely to drop out of therapy, were significantly less likely to engage in parasuicide, reported significantly fewer parasuicidal behaviors, and, when engaging in parasuicidal behaviors, had less medically severe behaviors. In addition, clients who received DBT were less likely to be hospitalized, had spent fewer days in the hospital, and had higher scores on global and social adjustment. DBT was also more effective than treatment-as-usual in reducing alcohol abuse. Koons et al. (2001) randomly assigned 20 women veterans diagnosed with borderline bipolar disorder to either a DBT or

Table 5.3 Stages and Goals of Dialectical Behavior Therapy

Stages	Goals
Stage 1	Focuses on client's suicidal behaviors, therapy-interfering behaviors, and behaviors that interfere with client's quality of life, plus an emphasis on developing the requisite skills to resolve these problems. The goal of stage 1 is to get the clients' behavior under control. Clients may be struggling with the threatening behaviors (e.g., cutting, suicide attempts, and excessive drinking). They may evidence treatment-interfering behaviors (e.g., premature termination or dropping out of treatment, hostility toward the therapist, coming late, or skipping therapy). They are also struggling with major life-interfering behaviors (e.g., risk of losing house, losing custody of children, and so forth).
	Progress in therapy cannot be made on the client's underlying emotional issues until the client learns the skill of managing emotions without engaging in dangerous behaviors and until the client commits to therapy. The therapist uses distress tolerance techniques.
Stage 2	The focus is on the client's emotional experiencing. For clients with a posttraumatic stress disorder, the therapist explores past trauma and maladaptive thoughts.
	The primary goal of stage 2 is to reduce traumatic stress. Stage 2 targets are worked on only after the client's behavior is under control. The client is helped to remember and accept the facts of his or her earlier traumatic events, to reduce self-blame, and to resolve dialectical tensions.
Stage 3	The primary goal of stage 3 is to solve the problems of everyday living and to improve client's general level of happiness.
Stage 4	The primary goal of stage 4 is transcendence and to help build client's capacity for joy. Clients are encouraged to take steps to make their lives more meaningful.

Table 5.4   Summary of Dialectical Behavior Therapy (DBT) Skills

Mindfulness	This is the core of DBT. Mindfulness involves the practice of nonjudgmental observation, description, and participation in a given moment of the client's life. The DBT skill of mindfulness helps clients feel more centered and be present in the moment rather than worrying about the past or the future.
Distress tolerance	The DBT skill of distress tolerance emphasizes the client learning how to improve impulse control and how to gain better tolerance of stressful or painful experiences. Distress tolerance stresses dealing with life as it is in any given moment, accepting the circumstances of one's life, and using mindfulness practices to operate within those circumstances.
Interpersonal effectiveness	This DBT skill teaches clients how to communicate better, learn to say no, and to cope with interpersonal conflict. This DBT skill helps clients improve their personal and professional relationships.
Emotion regulation	The DBT skill of emotion regulation helps clients better understand their emotions and reduce their vulnerability to those emotions.

treatment-as-usual group. Subjects who were enrolled in DBT demonstrated statistically significant reductions in suicidal ideation, depression, hopelessness, and anger compared with those who were enrolled in the treatment-as-usual group. DBT has established its effectiveness in working with individuals diagnosed with borderline personality disorders.

Acceptance and Commitment Therapy: Steven C. Hayes

Steven C. Hayes

Steven C. Hayes is credited as the founder of ACT. Currently, he is the Nevada Foundation Professor at the Department of Psychology at the University of Nevada. He is the author of 35 books and more than 500 scientific articles. His research career has focused on an analysis of the nature of human language and cognition and the application of this to psychotherapy. He has been president of Division 25 of the APA, of the American Association of Applied and Preventive Psychology, the Association for Contextual Behavioral Science, and of the Association for Behavioral and Cognitive Therapies. In 1992, he was listed by the Institute for Scientific Information as the 30th "highest impact" psychologist in the world. His work has been recognized by several awards, including the Exemplary Contributions to Basic Behavioral Research and Its Applications from Division 25 of APA, the Impact of Science on Application Award from the Society for the Advancement of Behavior Analysis, and the Lifetime Achievement Award from the Association for Behavioral and Cognitive Therapies.

Brief Overview

Although the literature on ACT dates back to the early 1980s, it has only been recently recognized widely as a therapeutic approach (Hayes, 2004). This therapeutic approach was initially called *comprehensive distancing* (Zettle, 2005). Comprehensive distancing was developed from efforts to extend Beck's work on cognitive distancing. ACT is from the third generation or the third wave of the behavioral school of psychotherapy (traditional behaviorism, the first wave; CBT, the second wave; and the third generation of contextual approaches, which has adopted the Chinese culture view of mindfulness as a core part of the theoretical approach). An important premise of Chinese mindfulness approaches is that suffering is a basic characteristic of human life and that trying to avoid the problems associated with emotional pain may actually increase the suffering one experiences. ACT adopts the perspective that suffering is an inevitable part of human life.

ACT is based partly on relational frame theory (RFT). RFT deals with the power of language and verbal behavior. The theory posits that psychopathology is the result of the human tendency to avoid negatively evaluated private events (what we think and feel). RFT can be traced to the philosophy of functional contextualism, which can be contrasted with mechanistic theories whose goal is to repair, change, or fix problems. Both RFT and ACT assert that language traps clients into attempts to wage war against their internal lives. During ACT, clients learn to recontextualize and accept the painful private experiences, to develop clarity about their personal values, and to commit to desired behavior change.

ACT uses mindfulness skills to help clients (a) develop psychological flexibility and (b) clarify value behavior. ACT therapy was created in 1986 by Steven Hayes and colleagues (Hayes, Strosahl, & Wilson, 1999). ACT is mindfulness-based behavioral therapy that challenges the ground rules of many Western psychotherapy approaches (Bach & Hayes, 2002). Most Western therapy models are geared to repair, change, or fix problems. ACT does not have as its therapeutic goal symptom reduction. On the contrary, it maintains that therapy's attempt to get rid of symptoms actually creates a clinical disorder. When private experiences are labeled as symptoms, Harris (2006) maintains that

> it immediately sets up a struggle with it because a "symptom" is by definition something "pathological"; something we should try to get rid of. In ACT, the aim is to transform our relationship with our difficult thoughts and feelings so that we no longer perceive them as "symptoms." Instead, we learn to perceive them as harmless, even if uncomfortable, transient psychological events. Ironically, it is through this process that ACT actually achieves symptom reduction—but not as a by-product and not as the goal. (p. 72)

ACT does not view clients as damaged or flawed and does not conceptualize unwanted experiences as "symptoms" or problems, but instead defines the function and the context of behavior. ACT accepts the thought simply as a thought, for example, "I'm having the thought that my life is hopeless." As Bach and Hayes (2002) have asserted,

> ACT is based on the view that many maladaptive behaviors are produced by unhealthy attempts to avoid or suppress thoughts, feelings, or bodily sensations (Hayes, Wilson, Gifford, Follette, & Strosahl, 1996). Among other components, patients are taught (a) to identify and abandon internally oriented control strategies, (b) to accept the presence of difficult thoughts or feelings; (c) to learn to "just notice" the occurrences of these private experiences, without struggling with them, arguing with them, or taking them to be literally true, and (d) to focus on overt behaviors that produce valued outcomes. (p. 1130)

Goals of ACT

ACT takes its name from one of its core messages: accept what is out of your personal control; instead commit to action that which improves and enriches your life. The goal of ACT is to help people realize their potential for a rich and meaningful life by teaching them mindfulness skills to help them clarify what is really important and meaningful to them and then to use that knowledge to motivate them to change their lives for the better. Acceptance is not the same thing as approval of how things are without any attempt to change them. It is a skill that is developed from training in mindfulness procedures.

> The goal of ACT is to create a rich and meaningful life, while accepting the pain that inevitably goes with it. "ACT" is a good abbreviation, because this therapy is about taking effective action guided by our deepest values and in which we are fully present and engaged. It is only through mindful action that we can create a meaningful life. Of course, as we attempt to create such a life, we will encounter all sorts of barriers, in the form of unpleasant and unwanted "private experiences" (thoughts, images, feelings, sensations, urges, and memories). ACT teaches mindfulness skills as an effective way to handle these private experiences. (Harris, 2006, p. 70)

ACT therapy uses the metaphor of what one should do when stuck up to one's neck in quicksand. Struggling in quicksand will only lead to drowning in quicksand. Once a person lifts one foot, all his or her weight rests on only the other foot (half the previous surface area), and as a result, the downward pressure doubles (Hayes & Smith, 2005).

European culture tends to emphasize dominance and exerting control over negative or challenging forces in one's life. The European approach to problem solving involves struggle with problem solving. ACT therapy differs from standard cognitive behavior therapy in that instead of challenging distressing thoughts by looking for evidence and coming up with a more rational response, in ACT, the thought is accepted as a thought, "I'm having a difficult time with this issue, and that's all right. I'm not going to struggle with it to make it right. I accept it as a problem, and I notice what the problem feels like in my body."

Sometimes it's best not to struggle, but rather to notice the thought and feeling that has produced the struggle or the anxiety. In quicksand, one lies flat, spread-eagled to maximize contact with the quicksand without struggling against it. As Harris (2006) has stated,

> The more time and energy we spend trying to avoid or get rid of unwanted private experiences the more

we are likely to suffer in the long term. Anxiety disorders provide a good example. . . . At the core of any anxiety disorder lies a major preoccupation with trying to avoid or get rid of anxiety. . . . Sadly, the more importance we place on avoiding anxiety, the more we develop anxiety about our anxiety—thereby exacerbating it. . . . What is a panic attack, if not anxiety about anxiety. (p. 72)

ACT, Mental Health, and Maladaptive Behavior

ACT maintains that the psychological process of a normal human mind is often destructive, and that such destruction can be traced to our use of language. A central or core conception of ACT is that psychological suffering is often caused by our experiential avoidance of pain, cognitive entanglement with words, and psychological rigidity. ACT considers that the core of many human problems may be attributed to the concepts contained in the acronym, *FEAR*:

- *F*usion with one's thoughts
- *E*valuation of one's experience
- *A*voidance of one's experiences and emotions
- *R*eason-giving for one's behavior.

The healthy alternative to *FEAR* is *ACT*, *A*ccept your reactions to events and thoughts; *C*hoose a direction based on your values; and *T*ake committed action based on your values.

ACT and Therapeutic Practice

The ACT therapist presents clients with an alternative to experiential avoidance via a number of therapeutic interventions. Clients come to psychotherapy desiring to get rid of their depression, anxiety, traumatic memories, and so forth. ACT makes no attempt to control these private experiences. Instead of learning how to reduce, suppress, or eliminate these unwanted emotional experiences, clients learn to reduce the impact and influence of such undesirable thoughts and feelings via mindfulness techniques. ACT interventions emphasize two primary processes: (1) developing an acceptance of undesirable private experiences, which are out of one's personal control; and (2) making a commitment and taking action toward living a valued life (Hayes, Strosahl, & Wilson, 2011).

Six Core ACT Therapeutic Processes

There are six core processes involved in ACT, and these are as follows (Hayes, Strosahl, & Houts, 2005):

1. Acceptance
2. Cognitive defusion
3. Contact with the present moment
4. The observing self
5. Values
6. Committed action

The majority of the skills involved in the six core processes of ACT are actually mindfulness skills, which can be divided into four categories:

- *Acceptance*—which entails making room for painful feelings, urges, and sensations and allowing them to come and go without a struggle. Here the therapist uses the metaphor of quicksand, the "struggle switch"; imagine that there is a struggle switch at the back of your head. When it is turned on, it means you are going to struggle against something, for instance, emotional or physical pain (Hayes et al., 2005). Therefore, if anxiety shows up, that's not a problem. It's unpleasant, but not a problem. Once a person's struggle switch is off, he or she can get a natural level of physical discomfort called "clean discomfort" in ACT language. All people experience clean discomfort. Once clients start struggling with an issue, their discomfort level rises and produces additional suffering, and is therefore, called "dirty discomfort" in ACT. A therapist might say, "At this very moment, you're feeling anxious. Is the struggle switch on or off?" From this point on, a therapist helps the client increase his or her flexibility in dealing with the situation. ACT can result in good symptom reduction, even though this might not be a goal. By being accepting of unwanted thoughts without judging them but with simply noticing them, a lot of behavioral exposure takes place similar to in vivo exposure therapy.
- *Cognitive defusion*—which involves distancing oneself from, letting go of, unhelpful thoughts, beliefs, and memories. The client learns that these are only transient private events. As clients defuse their thoughts, they have less of an impact on them. To engage in cognitive defusion, a therapist might have the client simply observe a thought with detachment or repeat it out loud many times until it becomes a meaningless sound, or say "thanks, mind, for such an interesting thought." In contrast to CBT, cognitive defusion techniques do not involve disputing or evaluating unwanted thoughts.
- *Contact with the present moment*—engaging fully with the here-and-now with an attitude of openness and curiosity.
- *The observing self*—being engaged in observing one's response to situations. The observing self is what ACT theorists call the "self-as-context"— the you that is always there observing and experiencing, but somehow the you that is also distinct from your thoughts, feelings, sensations, and memories. To the observing self, no thought is dangerous or threatening. The therapist asks the client to observe his or her thoughts as they are occurring without taking any particular stance toward those thoughts.

Two other core processes are *values* and *committed action* (Hayes, Follette, & Linehan, 2004). The therapist helps the client clarify what is most important, deep in his or her heart. The therapist poses questions such as the following: What kind of person do you want to be? What is most meaningful to you? Committed action entails having the client set goals that are guided by his or her values and taking effective action to accomplish those goals.

Role of the Therapist and the ACT Therapeutic Relationship

The training of ACT therapists focuses on helping therapists develop the qualities of compassion, acceptance, and empathy, while being able to withstand a client's strong emotions (Table 5.5). ACT teaches therapists that they, because of language, are in a boat similar to that of their clients. Harris (2006) has presented a sample statement of what he might say to one of his clients:

I don't want you to think I've got my life completely in order. It's more as if you're climbing your mountain over there and I'm climbing my mountain over here. It's not as if I've reached the top and I'm having a rest. It's just that from where I am on my mountain, I can see obstacles on your mountain that you can't see. So I can point those out to you, and maybe show you some alternative routes around them. (p. 76)

Evidence-Based Research and ACT

ACT is an empirically supported therapy. By 2006, ACT had been evaluated in approximately 30 controlled time-series studies or randomized clinical trials for a broad range of client problems (Hayes, Luoma, Bond, Masuda, & Lillis, 2006). Just 4 years later, Ruiz (2010) reported that the number of empirical ACT studies had approximately doubled. ACT is considered an empirically validated treatment by the American Psychological Association, with the status of "Modest Research Support" in depression and "Strong Research Support" in chronic pain. ACT is also listed as evidence-based by the Substance Abuse and Mental Health Services

Table 5.5   Acceptance and Commitment Therapy Chart

Activating Event	The Struggle or Consequence	Acceptance	Cognitive Defusion	Contact With Present Moment	The Observing Self	Values Clarification	Committed Action
What took place, where, when, with whom, outside event, or internal trigger.	"The quicksand effect"—the more one struggles, the bigger the problem becomes The struggle switch "on" or "off"—wanting to avoid the painful feeling or thought.	Accepting painful feelings, allowing them to come and go without struggle. Client experiences "clean (normal) discomfort." If acceptance does not take place, there is a struggle, which brings about additional suffering and "dirty discomfort."	Defusion involves seeing thoughts and feelings for what they are— streams of words, passing sensations— not what they say they are (dangers or facts). Notice unhelpful thoughts. Say them slowly. Write them down. Say them in your favorite cartoon voices.	Stay in the present moment with mindfulness meditation. Meditation rewires the brain's neural structures. Notice when you are in the present moment versus when you are stuck in your head in either the past or the future.	Observe your response to the activating event. What are you thinking and feeling?	What is most important in the deepest part of your heart?	Client sets goals driven by values clarification. Takes action.

Source: ©Elsie Jones-Smith.

Administration of the U.S. federal government, which used randomized trials for ACT in the areas of psychosis, work site stress, and obsessive compulsive disorder, including depression outcomes.

Research evidence indicates that ACT reduces the negative behavioral impact of undesirable thoughts and feelings. When ACT is applied to work site anxiety and stress, subjects experienced an increase in the acceptance of these emotions and the positive work behaviors suppressed by them (Bond & Bunce, 2000). An ACT acceptance position increases clients' tolerance of pain, even if the pain itself is not reduced (Hayes, Bissett, et al., 1999). Moreover, ACT appears to reduce the believability of negative private events more rapidly than direct cognitive disputation in some clinical populations (Hayes, Strosahl, & Wilson, 1999; Zettle & Hayes, 1987).

Hayes (2004) has maintained that the ACT model works across an unusually broad range of problems. For instance, research has found that ACT is efficacious for sexual abuse survivors, at-risk adolescents, and those with substance abuse or mood disorders (Wilson, Follette, Hayes, & Batten, 1996). Evidence-based studies have reported that ACT is appropriate for individuals with substance abuse issues and for those experiencing psychotic ideation. Gaudiano and Herbert (2006) found that ACT produced improvement in clients' affective symptoms, social impairment, and distress associated with hallucinations.

Moreover, ACT has been used for trauma work, as well as for those with phobias and obsessive behavior (Twohig, Hayes, & Masuda, 2006). Those who suffer from posttraumatic stress have been found to benefit from being able to accept the experience without resigning themselves to its continuing negative symptoms. ACT maintains that it is a client's unwillingness to experience pain associated with trauma that creates an internal struggle (verbal battle: "I should not be experiencing this flashback") that keeps the trauma alive.

ACT may provide a meaningful framework for dealing with survivors of childhood abuse. From an ACT perspective, the cognitions and emotions that result from a history of abuse are amenable to alteration. Whereas the second wave of cognitive behaviorists may work to dispute the negative thoughts of a client who had been sexually abused, ACT strives to change the function of the thoughts and feelings. Instead of telling a sex abuse survivor that her disturbing thoughts in situations of sexual intimacy are irrational, ACT points out the psychological function of these thoughts, which might include to paralyze the individual from enjoying or participating in sex (Wilson, Follette, Hayes, & Batten, 1996).

ACT has been used in working with couples and families. Jacobson and Christensen (1996) conducted a study that revealed that acceptance strategies increased the effectiveness of traditional behavioral marital therapy. The goal of ACT therapy is not to accept all partner behaviors but rather to effectively "generate a context where both accepting and changing will occur" (Jacobson & Christensen, 1996). ACT interventions helped couples generate greater intimacy with the conflict area, produced greater partner tolerance, and resulted in change (Jacobson & Christensen, 1996). In couples' therapy, acceptance did not necessarily mean accepting a partner's behavior, but letting go of the struggle to try to change the partner's behavior.

Mindfulness-Based Cognitive Therapy: Zindel Segal, Mark Williams, and John Teasdale

Zindel Segal

Zindel Segal is the Morgan Firestone Chair in Psychotherapy in the Department of Psychiatry at the University of Toronto and head of the Cognitive Therapy Unit at the Centre for Addiction and Mental Health.

Mark Williams

Mark Williams is professor of clinical psychology at the University of Oxford and Wellcome Trust Research Fellow, and coauthor with Drs. Segal and

Teasdale of *Mindfulness-Based Cognitive Therapy for Depression: A New Approach to Preventing Relapse.*

John Teasdale

John Teasdale has held senior research appointments in the Department of Psychiatry at the University of Oxford and in the Cognition and Brain Sciences Unit in Cambridge.

Brief Overview

MBCT is the final third-wave CBT considered in this chapter. MBCT was developed to help prevent the relapse of depression in individuals with major depressive disorder. The theory was developed by Zindel Segal, Mark Williams, and John Teasdale. In 2002, these authors published the book *Mindfulness-Based Cognitive Therapy for Depression: A New Approach to Preventing Relapse.* The theory was an outgrowth of an earlier theory of the mind developed by Barnard and Teasdale called "interacting cognitive subsystems" in 1991. The core component of interacting cognitive subsystems was metacognitive awareness, or the ability to experience negative thoughts and feelings as mental events that pass through the mind, instead of becoming part of the self. Using Barnard and Teasdale's interactive cognitive subsystems model, Teasdale subsequently worked with Segal and Williams to develop MBCT, which is partially based on the mindfulness-based stress reduction program developed by Jon Kabat-Zinn (1990, 1994). MBCT is also based on an integration of features of CBT for depression (Beck, Rush, Shaw, & Emery, 1979). In contrast to CBT, there is little emphasis in MBCT on changing the content of a client's thoughts. Features of CBT that are included in MBCT are designed to promote "decentered" views, such as "Thoughts are not facts" and "I am not my thoughts" (Teasdale et al., 2000).

Goals of Therapy

The goal of MBCT is to prevent a relapse in depression for individuals diagnosed with a major depressive disorder (Segal et al., 2002). Prevention of client relapse is achieved by teaching clients to become more aware of their thoughts and feelings and to relate to such occurrences in decentered perspective as "mental events" instead of as aspects of the self or as true reflections of reality. The theory assumes that teaching clients how to decenter their thoughts will prevent the escalation of negative thinking that is linked to depression relapse. In contrast to CBT, there is little emphasis in MBCT on changing the content or specific meanings of negative automatic thoughts (Teasdale et al., 2000). The primary goal is to change clients' awareness of their automatic negative thoughts and their relationship to such thoughts.

Therapeutic Processes

MBCT is an 8-week group treatment program based on Jon Kabat-Zinn's (1994) Mindfulness-Based Stress Reduction (Segal et al., 2002). The 8-week program teaches clients the art of meditation. During therapy, clients are helped to become liberated from their obsessive thought patterns that replay the same negative messages again and again. Instead of living in a depressed mood, a client learns how to separate himself from negative thoughts that lead to depression relapse. MBCT uses experiential learning, in-session practice, and homework assignments.

MBCT uses a manual, and it is delivered by trained instructors through the following sessions (Segal et al., 2002):

- A one-on-one orientation session
- Eight 2-hour core sessions delivered weekly in a group format with 9 to 15 participants who are either in full remission (meaning experiencing a clinically normal mood) and using no medication or in partial remission (having residual depression symptoms) and continuing use of medication
- One to four 2-hour follow-up reinforcement sessions delivered in a group format 4 to 12 months after the eight core sessions

MBCT instructors help clients improve their mindfulness meditation through practice and develop cognitive skills that help them disengage from habitual ("automatic") negative thoughts. Clients learn to recognize their depression relapse-related patterns of negative thinking, feelings, and bodily sensations and to relate to them positively by assuming a more detached response (i.e., viewing them as passing events in the mind). Learning decentering helps clients purposefully shift their mental focus away from negative thought patterns that might lead them into another relapse episode of major depression. During later core sessions, clients are given customized strategies they can use outside of the program to prevent depression relapse or recurrence (e.g., involving family members in an early warning system, keeping written suggestions to engage in activities that are helpful in interrupting relapse processes, and ferreting out habitual negative thoughts). MBCT instructors (usually cognitive therapists) are required to personally engage in mindfulness meditation and to have at least 1 year of experience working with mood disorder patients (Segal et al., 2002).

The brevity of MBCT is one of its advantages. Fresco, Flynn, Mennin, and Haigh (2011) have described the sessions involved in an MBCT program for clients:

- The first session begins by helping clients identify their negative automatic thoughts and by introducing some basic mindfulness practices.
- During Session 2, clients are taught to pay attention to the reactions they have to life experiences, and they learn more about mindfulness practices.
- Session 3 focuses on teaching breathing techniques and on how to focus on the present.
- Session 4 deals with learning to experience the moment without becoming attached to the outcomes.
- The fifth session helps clients accept what they are experiencing without holding on to such experiences.
- During Session 6, clients are taught to describe thoughts as merely thoughts and that they do not have to act on their thoughts or become upset by them.
- During Sessions 7 and 8, clients are taught how to take care of themselves to prevent depression relapse and how to apply mindfulness practices to their everyday lives.

Evidence-Based Research and MBCT

The data supporting MBCT indicate that it effectively reduces relapse rates by 50% in patients with recurrent depression. MBCT has recently been recommended by the National Institute for Clinical Excellence in the United Kingdom as an empirically supported depression prevention treatment. The empirical support for MBCT has raised awareness about the need for effective and comprehensive treatment of depression, and individuals can participate in this treatment regardless of whether they recovered from their depression via medication or talk therapy (see links for further information). Previous research has shown that MBCT is an effective treatment for mood and anxiety disorders (Hofmann, Sawyer, Witt, & Oh, 2010; Kim et al., 2009; Manicavasgar, Parker, & Perich, 2011; Teasdale et al., 2000). The success of MBCT with treatment of relapse in depression has led to its use with several other conditions including the following:

- Chronic fatigue syndrome
- Generalized anxiety disorder
- Panic disorder
- Bipolar mood disorder

DIFFERENCES BETWEEN ACT, CBT, DBT, AND MBCT _____

ACT differs from CBT, because instead of challenging distressing thoughts by looking for evidence and arriving at a more rational response (CBT), ACT accepts a thought as a thought and nothing more. There are also differences between ACT and two other third-wave cognitive-behavioral approaches, namely, DBT and MBCT. First, ACT differs from DBT and MBCT in that both DBT and MBCT are manualized treatment protocols for specific disorders. Moreover, MBCT is designed for use with groups for treatment of *stress and depression*. DBT uses a combination of group skills training and individual therapy, and it is designed primarily for treatment of borderline personality disorder. **Borderline personality disorder**, or BPD, is a serious mental illness that is grouped under the umbrella term of personality disorders. Individuals with BPD have often intense, unstable emotions and engage in risky behaviors such as overspending, unsafe sex, or abusing drugs and alcohol. Second, in contrast to the other theoretical approaches, ACT can be used with individuals, couples, and groups for a wide range of clinical populations in either brief therapy or long-term therapy. Instead of following a manualized protocol, ACT permits the therapists to create their own approach to mindfulness. Third, another difference is that ACT does not just use meditation as a way for clients to practice mindfulness.

RESEARCH AND EVALUATION OF CBTS_____

Multicultural Positives of CBTs

It has been well established that people from different cultures tend to think about different things and, when thinking, do so from a different perspective (Pedersen, Draguns, Lonner, & Trimble, 2008). The fact that people from different cultures think differently has important implications for CBT because this theoretical approach deals with a client's thoughts and thought processes. Moreover, cultural norms about what constitutes appropriate behavior can also influence cognitive therapy. A critical issue that must be addressed is what happens when the therapist's worldview, experience, and expectations about therapy and life are different from the client's—primarily because such differences may hinder a shared understanding of the client's problems and potential solutions.

Hays (1995) has identified four strengths of CBT in working with clients from ethnic minority backgrounds. The first strength Hays mentions is CBT's emphasis on the uniqueness of the individual. Hays traced the roots of CBT to the behavioral principle that therapy must be adapted to meet the needs of the individual. A multicultural perspective emphasizes cultural instead of individual differences to increase the appropriateness and effectiveness of therapy for each person. Both multicultural and cognitive-behavioral approaches are similar in that they place importance on tailoring the therapy to a client's unique life situation.

A second multicultural strength of CBT is its focus on client empowerment. As Hays (1995) has stated,

> Cognitive-behavior therapy views clients as being in control of their thoughts and emotions and thus able to make changes themselves (Dobson & Block, 1988) . . . cognitive-behavior therapy empowers clients to apply newly learned skills as independently as possible so that, in future situations, these skills can be used without the therapist. (p. 311)

Thus, CBT shows respect for a client's abilities and his or her understanding of therapeutic issues.

Third, CBT emphasizes conscious processes and specific behaviors instead of unconscious processes. Many non-Western cultures prefer to deal with conscious processes in the here-and-now than abstract, unconscious processes (Hays, 1995). Because CBT focuses on more concrete than abstract happenings, the potential for misunderstandings between the client and the therapist is less. CBT is also more action-oriented and more present-focused than other approaches (psychodynamic), and these factors may be more attractive to members of ethnic minority groups. A fourth strength that Hays (1995) points out about CBT is its integration of assessment throughout the course of therapy. According to Hays (1995), "Furthermore, the ongoing nature of cognitive-behavioral assessment demonstrates the therapist's commitment to a collaborative process, respect for the client's opinions, and consideration of financial and time constraints" (p. 311). Similar to Hays (1995), Spiegler and Guevremont (2003) have identified a number of factors that make CBT effective with ethnic minority clients, including its individualized treatment, its active nature, its emphasis on learning, reliance on empirical evidence, brevity, and its focus on the client's present behavior.

Increasingly, CBT studies are being conducted with individuals from Native American (Simms, 1999), Latino (González-Prendes et al., 2011), African American (Kelly, 2006), and Asian American backgrounds (Rathod et al., 2013). Simms (1999) has advocated using a blended counseling approach that combines an integrated relational behavioral-cognitive strategy with traditional healing approaches, including talking circles, sweats, and participation in cultural forums. In counseling Native American clients, Herring (1999) has recommended that the therapist

(1) address openly the issue of dissimilar ethnic relationships rather than pretending that no differences exist; (2) schedule appoints to allow for flexibility in ending the session; (3) be open to allowing the extended family to participate in the session; (4) allow time for trust to develop before focusing on problems; (5) respect the uses of silence; (6) demonstrate honor and respect for the [client's] culture[s] and (7) maintain the highest level of confidentiality. (pp. 55–56)

In describing how cultural values may be integrated into CBT for a Latino youth with depression, González-Prendes et al. (2011) have pointed out,

It benefits the CBT practitioner to be cognizant of the cultural difference between the therapist and the client, and to learn about the relative importance and role of the client's beliefs, emotions, and behaviors within the client's culture. Thus, cognitive therapists must recognize that beliefs, relative to self, family, and life in general, are central to one's culture, and that, when evaluated outside the context of that culture, may lead to erroneous conclusions and pathological conceptualizations, and hinder the collaborative process. (p. 377)

According to these researchers, it is important that CBT clinicians integrate the cultural values of the client into the conceptualization of the problems and that the clinician should consider Latino values such as

- *familismo* (importance of family orientation— the centrality of the family as a source of loyalty, support, and identity, and placing family interests above individual interests),
- *personalismo* (trust, warmth, and attention to the personal dimensions of a relationship—an orientation toward people and over concepts and ideas),
- *respeto* (the relative level of importance and deference given to an individual within a family— father assumes the predominant role, followed by mother, and children), and
- *machismo* (men's sense of leadership and responsibility to provide for and protect their families).

Kelly (2006) has also asserted that CBT has the potential to address African Americans' psychotherapeutic treatment needs. She pointed out the benefit of gathering assessment data from multiple sources. According to her, Black behaviorism states that "observable behavior should never be explained by unobservable mentalistic events such as motivation or intelligence but rather understood in light of its environmental consequences" (p. 103). Summarizing the benefits of using CBT with African Americans, Kelly (2006) has stated, "In summary, the advantages of CBT with African Americans include an emphasis on nonjudgmental, collaborative problem solving and empowerment of the client through skill building and strengthening of natural support systems" (p. 103).

Similarly, Asian American multiculturalists have pointed out the benefits of using CBT with Asian clients. It has been observed that Chinese people prefer treatment that is directive, structured, and short term (Yip, 2005). CBT is effective for Chinese people because there is a good cognitive match between elements of Chinese culture (regarding authority figures as knowledgeable, preferring an instructive and didactic style early in the therapeutic relationship) and cognitive therapy's educative style in teaching the elements of that theoretical approach. Williams, Foo, and Haarhoff (2006) have pointed out that CBT was successful in helping an elderly Chinese client understand the nature of her problem and guiding treatment to reduce some of her anxiety and depressive symptoms. The client gained a sense of self-efficacy in being able to control her worries.

The cognitive-behavioral approach is well suited for multicultural issues. Exploring values and core beliefs is important for therapists with this orientation. Counselors can help clients understand the cultural basis of their beliefs. For some individuals, reviewing automatic thought patterns from a multicultural or gender perspective is very enlightening. Cognitive-behavioral techniques are often accepted by minority clients because of their clarity and directedness.

Multicultural Blind Spots of CBTs

On the other hand, cognitive-behavioral theories have been criticized because of their negative view of dependency and because of their emphasis on rationality—values associated with Western cultures. Cognitive behaviorists must recognize that it is disrespectful to question the core beliefs of some cultures. Hays (2009) has recommended that therapists avoid challenging the core cultural beliefs of clients. She has also indicated that it may be counterproductive for a cognitive therapist to engage in confrontation (a core part of REBT) and that it might be beneficial to emphasize collaboration with a client whose cultural values are harmony. Similarly, Cormier, Nurius, and Osborn (2013) have suggested that therapists should not use disrespectful terms such as *irrational, maladaptive,* or *dysfunctional* when discussing a client's core beliefs. To be culturally responsive, CBT must recognize and respect clients' cultural values, which means that the client's problem must be defined in relation to his or her cultural norms (Tanaka-Matsumi & Higginbotham, 1989).

There has also been some concern that cognitive therapies place too much emphasis on counseling techniques rather than the importance of therapist attitudes, values, and beliefs. In addition, the cognitive-behavioral school has been criticized because of its focus on setting goals and making changes without taking into consideration environmental, social, and cultural factors. Multiculturalists have cautioned that there may be a basis for some automatic thoughts that minority clients have regarding race and their minority status (Kelly, 2006). Past experiences with racism and ethnic discrimination may lead to negative automatic thoughts about their ability to achieve their goals.

In addition, CBT has been relatively silent on issues related to social justice. It has not been explicit about the impact of racism and other forms of oppression on clients. Another limitation of CBT is its emphasis on rational thinking and the scientific method. Kantrowitz and Ballou (1992) have asserted that a cognitive-behavioral orientation reinforces a Euro-American and masculine view of the world and that such views might be incompatible with less linear or contextualized styles of interacting and more cooperative than confrontational styles.

Evidence-Based Research and CBT

CBT is one of the most widely researched approaches to psychotherapy. Between 1986 and 1993, more than 120 controlled clinical trials were conducted testing the efficacy of CBT (Dobson, 2001; Hollon & Beck, 1994). In 2006, there were more than 326 published outcome studies on cognitive-behavioral interventions. Research has found that CBT is effective in reducing symptoms and relapse rates, with and without medication in a broad range of psychiatric disorders. Beck applied cognitive therapy to depression, suicide, anxiety disorders and phobias, panic disorder, personality disorders, and substance abuse and found that cognitive therapy was a helpful treatment approach (Beck, 1997, 2005). The growth in outcome studies can be partially attributed to the increasing popularity of CBT for an ever wider range of disorders (Beck, 1997).

Despite the increasing number of evidence-based studies for CBT, questions remain about its differential effectiveness by disorder, the nature of the control group in which effectiveness has been established, and the degree to which its effects last after treatment is completed (Butler, Chapman, Forman, & Beck, 2006). A review of 16 meta-analyses for a wide range of psychiatric disorders was completed. The review found large effect sizes for

CBT for unipolar depression, generalized anxiety disorder, panic disorder with or without agoraphobia, social phobia, posttraumatic stress disorder, and childhood depressive and anxiety disorders. According to Butler et al. (2006),

> Effect sizes for CBT of marital distress, anger, childhood somatic disorders, and chronic pain were in the moderate range. CBT was somewhat superior to antidepressants in the treatment of adult depression. CBT was equally effective as behavior therapy in the treatment of adult depression and obsessive-compulsive disorder. Large uncontrolled effect sizes were found for bulimia nervosa and schizophrenia. The 16 meta-analyses we reviewed support the efficacy of CBT for many disorders. (p. 17)

Contributions and Criticisms of the Cognitive-Behavioral Approach

The cognitive-behavioral approach has been credited with major contributions to psychotherapy. First, there is mounting empirical evidence that CBT is effective for the treatment for a variety of other problems, including anxiety, depression, and eating disorders. A second strength of CBT is that it has demonstrated a strong commitment to empirical evaluation, revision, and openness to integrating other points of view, especially concepts in the area of the therapeutic alliance and conditions for therapy. Dattilio (2002) has proposed using cognitive-behavioral techniques within an existential framework.

A third contribution of CBT is that it recognizes that one treatment may not be appropriate for all types of psychological disorders. For instance, in psychoanalysis, the same treatment approach is used for a broad range of psychological disorders. In contrast, cognitive-behavioral therapists assert that different cognitive schemas exist for different disorders. Therapy has to be more than a one-size-fits-all approach. Consideration must be given for the type of problem the client brings to therapy.

Leahy (2002) has stated, "Over the past 20 years, the cognitive model has gained wide appeal and appears to be influencing the development of the field more than any other model" (p. 419). Leahy lists four reasons the cognitive-behavioral approach has had such a profound impact on psychotherapy:

- It works.
- It is an effective, focused, and practical treatment for specific problems.
- It is transparent and uncomplicated, and it promotes a transfer of knowledge from the therapist to the client.
- It is a short-term and cost-effective form of treatment.

One major criticism of the cognitive-behavioral treatments is that they are too structured and too manualized, so that counselors can follow the same treatment. Critics have questioned if this degree of prescriptiveness is the best way for therapy to progress. Such opponents have argued that lasting changes in personality and behavior are achieved by a much slower client pace than what therapists permit. Clients should have more of a role in determining at what pace therapy will proceed.

Another criticism of CBT is that insufficient attention is paid to early experiences and unfinished business from the past. Prochaska and Norcross (1999) have contended,

> Are we to believe that such traumatic events as being beaten by one's mother, molested by one's father, bereaved of both parents, rejected by peers, and ridiculed by teachers are less significant in producing emotional disturbances in children than are the beliefs children possess about these events? (p. 349)

From their perspective, a present-oriented treatment focus places too much responsibility on the client and blames the client rather than his or her perpetrators.

Other critics have labeled the cognitive-behavioral approach as being much too simplistic. Beck's approach has been characterized as just another version of the power of positive thinking. Ellis's challenging of irrational beliefs has been objected to as just another form of therapeutic brainwashing. It is unclear that Ellis's confrontative changes will continue after his death. One reason that Beck's cognitive therapy found a better reception among psychologists and therapists was that his approach appeared to be softer and gentler than Ellis's approach. The CBT school is a major force in psychology, and it is predicted that it will continue to dominate the therapeutic scene.

CASE ANALYSIS

Justin Working With a Cognitive Therapist

The cognitive-behavioral counselor focuses on Justin's behavior and the underlying thoughts that support such behavior. The therapist first gains an understanding of Justin's antisocial behavior because his actions have gotten him into difficulty with the police. Antisocial behavior in young people covers a wide range of acts that evidence their social rule violations and actions against others. Over the course of development, most children engage in such behaviors as fighting, lying, and stealing. Justin's behavior goes beyond the typical behavior for middle school children. He has broken the law and gotten caught doing it.

The cognitive-behavioral therapist would probably diagnose Justin's behavior as conduct disorder. Conduct disorder refers to antisocial behavior that is clinically significant and beyond normal development. The degree to which antisocial behaviors are sufficiently severe to warrant a diagnosis of conduct disorder depends on the frequency, intensity, and chronicity of behavior; whether the young person's acts are isolated or are part of a larger syndrome with other deviant behaviors; and whether they will lead to significant impairment of the young person, as evaluated by parents, teachers, and others. Conduct disorder is a frequent cause of referral to therapists for young people. In addition, the disorder has a poor long-term prognosis, and one of its characteristics is that it is transmitted across generations. Justin's brother (by fighting, membership in a gang) shows evidence of a possible conduct disorder diagnosis.

Cognitive-behavioral treatment for Justin is designed to address factors that contribute to the development of conduct disorder, including (a) inconsistent parenting (i.e., the failure to provide a consistently supportive and nurturing environment, inconsistent discipline, and an overreliance on punishment to change behavior; (b) genetic and biological factors, such as temperament, impulsivity, and attention deficit disorder; (c) poor social skills; and (d) maladaptive or negative beliefs about his personal worth (self-esteem).

Justin has experienced ineffectual and inconsistent parenting from his mother, Sandy. His relationship with his mother has been erratic and tumultuous and characterized by inconsistent love and discipline. Sandy needs help with her parenting skills, and therefore, the therapist assigns her to parent management training. As described in the case study, Sandy curses Justin and sometimes hits him when she is angry. Sandy holds pot parties in her home. She excuses her behavior with the explanation that pot helps her to cope and that her children should do as she says rather than as she does. As a mother seeking to be a role model for her children, Sandy's behavior is inexcusable.

One goal of parent management training is to work together with a therapist and other similar parents to develop a specific and systematic plan to change Justin's oppositional behavior. Justin's mother might be helped to develop plans that include the setting of specific limits and boundaries for Justin because children who are diagnosed with a conduct disorder often believe that they are entitled to behave in any way they desire.

Two other family approaches to treatment would be useful to both Justin and his mother. Sandy needs to learn more appropriate communication patterns with Justin. Functional family therapy aims to change a young person's communication and interaction styles by using various cognitive-behavioral techniques to create more positive exchanges and interactions within the family.

Another form of family therapy that I would recommend highly for Justin and Sandy is multisystemic therapy, which attempts to analyze and then correct the major environmental factors that have contributed to a child's diagnosis of conduct disorder. According to multisystemic therapy, a system is an environment or institution in which a child with conduct disorder spends a great deal of time, such as school and home environments, peer and other social groups, plus the local neighborhood. It is suggested that Justin's relationships be analyzed for the purpose of creating distance between him and deviant peers. Multisystemic strategies are needed to help Justin (a) bond better with safer, more conventional peers; (b) develop his academic and social skills; and (c) to assist Sandy in becoming a more effective parent.

Justin needs both individual and group counseling to assist him with cognitive problem solving. Repeatedly, he has made poor decisions. Even though Justin claims that he did not steal anything at Walmart, he made a poor decision to be with the wrong people. The therapist works with the school counselor to get Justin involved in an outpatient cognitive problem-solving skills training program. Such a training program would teach Justin new and better ways of thinking about and resolving difficult situations both inside and outside of school. During such training, the therapist models appropriate ways to relate to others. Justin would be reinforced and rewarded when he subsequently chose to respond according to the model.

Justin will be taught how to control his thoughts, how to increase his ability to control his impulses, and how to sit and cooperate with others. As part of his cognitive-behavior training, Justin will be helped to develop positive cognitive skills, including cognitive reframing of stressful events (e.g., helping him generate alternative, more peaceful ways of thinking about the meaning of stressful situations so that anger is not an automatic response). Justin will be required to attend small-group anger management classes so that he learns better ways to manage frustration by learning to recognize anger sensations.

In school, Justin would be required to attend a positive self-esteem group consisting of his school peers. The counselor would engage Justin in various exercises designed to help him feel more positive about his mixed ethnic/racial heritage and about his academic ability. Justin would be encouraged to focus on producing at least one major artwork that he would present to the group and to the school (along with others in the school's art show).

Each person in Justin's positive self-esteem group would be required to sign a behavioral contract that would list three ways he or she would interact positively with other classmates and with parents and siblings at home. Justin's behavioral contract describes in explicit detail what he is going to do to reduce disrespectful behaviors in his classroom and toward classmates. For instance, Justin has a habit of mumbling under his breath, talking back to the teacher, rolling his eyes, and so on. The consequences for Justin's engaging in disrespectful behavior are spelled out, as are those for more desirable alternative behaviors and the rewards that will accompany these new appropriate behaviors.

Along with the medical doctor, the school psychologist assesses Justin to determine if he does have an attentional disorder. Justin is also taught behavioral ways to focus his attention. The therapist discusses with Justin's mother, his family medical doctor, and teachers if Justin should be placed on medication (Ritalin) designed to reduce his attentional problems in class.

In addition, Justin's teachers will be given brief in-service training regarding how to deal effectively with students who have problems in attention in their classrooms. Teachers will be taught to reinforce Justin's good behavior in the classroom by giving him a positive nod, a pat on the shoulder, or other acknowledgment of appropriate behavior. They will be encouraged to be consistent about awarding praise to all students, so that Justin is not singled out for praise. In addition, teachers will be taught how to manage Justin's misbehavior, such as how to ignore his negative or inappropriate attention-getting efforts. A great idea for rewarding Justin and other students in his classes would be to give them a spot on the classroom bulletin board to display pictures of themselves, their families, and their favorite things as a reward for being "positive star students."

If Justin and his mother succeed in any of the cognitive-behavioral strategies, it is recommended that his probation officer ask the presiding judge to let him stay out of inpatient, residential treatment. Major changes will have to be made to the family situation and to Justin's conduct in school before such a recommendation can be made to the judge.

SUMMARY

Cognitive behavioral therapies integrate two different theoretical and therapeutic approaches that emanate from two different, but complementary paradigms of human nature and psychopathology (Jokić-Begić, 2010). The behavioral paradigm is based on learning theory and models of experimental psychology. Its basic underlying assumption and concept is that every behavior, either adaptive or maladaptive, has been learned. The cognitive paradigm maintains that mental disorders develop from faulty thinking processes and faulty information processing. Several cognitive-behavioral theorists were reviewed in this chapter. Cognitive behavior therapies are short-term, collaborative, and problem-focused therapeutic techniques designed to reduce a client's symptoms so that he or she may enjoy life.

Albert Ellis, a psychoanalytically trained psychologist, is credited with naming and popularizing REBT. Ellis stressed the role of irrational thoughts in psychological disturbance. Although we are born with the potential to be rational, we become irrational because of distortions developed during childhood and reinforced throughout our lives. Maladaptive behavior results from illogical ideas (e.g., "I must be loved by everyone"; "being loved and approved by everyone is necessary for happiness"). Such irrational ideas lead to our feelings of worthlessness and low self-esteem. Ellis's **A-B-C-D-E system** for examining irrational thoughts and treating clients lies at the heart of REBT.

Beck's model for cognitive therapy shares similarities with REBT; however, major differences between the two approaches can be found in the theorists' underlying philosophy and the process by which therapy takes place. Similar to Ellis, Beck's therapeutic approach examines the effect of maladaptive thinking on psychological disorders. One important cornerstone of Beck's cognitive therapy is the notion of automatic thoughts that dominate a client's belief system. Moreover, each person develops cognitive schemas (belief systems) that may be positive or negative. Beck identified cognitive distortions that influence people's feelings, thoughts, and beliefs, such as all-or-nothing thinking, overgeneralization, and catastrophizing.

Beck constructed specific cognitive procedures for treating depression and anxiety. He considers CBT to be integrative because it draws from many different types of psychotherapy. Beckian cognitive therapy is rapidly growing throughout the United States. One reason for this rapid growth is that cognitive therapy has become manualized; it is relatively brief, extensively evaluated, and problem focused.

The third-wave CBTs—dialectical behavioral therapy, ACT, and MBCT—have extended the therapeutic choices for the cognitive school. Each of the new cognitive-behavioral approaches has adopted mindfulness as a core part of the theory. Finally, cognitive neuroscience represents the newest development within the cognitive-behavioral school. This school deals with attention, perception, action, memory, language, behavior, and the effectiveness of psychotherapy. Cognitive neuroscience offers the potentiality of revolutionizing not only cognitive behavior therapy but also the other therapies discussed in this book. This new approach highlights the importance of the brain and processes such as mirror imaging, the high significance of the therapeutic relationship, and the manner in which various theoretical approaches affect the brain and behavior change.

SUPPLEMENTAL AIDS

Discussion Questions

1. Discuss three irrational beliefs that you have and identify how such beliefs have affected your life. Mention at least one way that you can challenge each irrational belief that you identified.

2. If you were a client, which cognitive approach would you prefer the therapist to use—Ellis's REBT or Beck's CBT? Explain why.

3. To what extent do you believe that if you change a person's thinking, you can change the way he or she behaves and feels? Explain.

4. Cognitive therapists emphasize the importance and impact of self talk on a person's thinking and behavior. Discuss three self talk statements that you make about you. Would you like to change these self talk statements? Why? How might you change your self talk statements?

5. Cognitive therapy is the theoretical orientation most often chosen by therapists in the United States. Do you see yourself integrating principles of CBT in your therapeutic practice. Explain. Discuss two aspects of CBT that you intend to include in your clinical practice.

Glossary of Key Terms

A-B-C-D-E system A system that Albert Ellis used as a central part of his rational behavior therapy, wherein A = activating event, B = beliefs about the activating event, C = emotional consequences of A and B, D = disputing irrational thoughts and beliefs, and E = cognitive and emotional effects of revised beliefs. The theory holds that individuals' problems do not originate from activating events but rather from their beliefs about such events. The best way to become healthy is to change one's irrational beliefs.

all-or-nothing thinking Thinking that represents a cognitive distortion. When we believe that things have to be exactly as we want them to be, we are participating in all-or-nothing thinking. "I can't be happy unless I have a man or a woman." A student who receives a C on an examination believes that he has failed.

automatic thought Thoughts based on beliefs we have about ourselves and the world in which we live. We can work to change our automatic thoughts by changing our deeply held core beliefs. An automatic thought can be demonstrated in the following example. Someone cuts us off in traffic, and we may have an automatic thought: "That is so rude and dangerous!" This thought sparks feelings of anger. Therefore, we may scream and yell in our car, catch up with the person, and "give them the finger," or take that anger home with us and yell at our loved ones. That single automatic thought initiated a chain reaction that touched off a negative

situation. We believe that our automatic thought is right, but usually, there are alternative thoughts that we might have in the same situation.

borderline personality disorder A personality disorder characterized by a person's having difficulty forming and keeping stable relationships, highly emotional or aggressive behavior, impulsivity, and rapid shifts in values, self-image, mood, and behavior.

catastrophizing A focus on the worst possible outcome or when we think a situation is unbearable or impossible when it is really only uncomfortable.

cognitive One's thinking, including the thoughts and beliefs that one holds as well as one's reasoning.

cognitive distortions Pervasive and systematic errors in our reasoning.

cognitive restructuring An active effort to change maladaptive thought patterns and to replace them with more adaptive cognitions.

cognitive schema A cognitive framework that functions to organize and interpret information. Schemas permit us to take shortcuts in interpreting a vast amount of information. Viewed from another perspective, these cognitive frameworks also cause us to exclude relevant information in favor of information that confirms our preexisting beliefs and ideas. Schemas determine what we notice, attend to, and remember of our experiences. Schemas can contribute to stereotypes and make it hard to acquire and retain new information that does not conform to our established cognitive schemas.

cognitive therapy A psychotherapeutic approach that is designed to change an individual's problematic and dysfunctional thoughts. It is an umbrella for therapy approaches that share a common theoretical foundation in behavior learning theory and cognitive psychology.

cognitive triad Beck's negative cognitive triad that explains that negative thoughts are about the self, the world, and the future. For example, if a person does poorly on an exam, he may have a negative opinion about himself and his future.

cognitive-behavioral therapy   Developed by a merger of behavior therapy with cognitive therapy. These two theoretical approaches focus on the here-and-now and symptom removal. Cognitive therapy is founded on information-processing theory, which indicates that schemas develop as part of our normal cognitive development. Information-processing theory maintains that we group experiences into categories to help us understand and organize our world. For instance, we tend to group dogs, cats, and bears as animals. Some of us categorize dogs and cats as pets. Cognitive-behavioral therapy focuses on schemas that are closely related to our emotional states.

collaborative empiricism   An approach that represents a strategy of viewing the client as a scientist capable of objective interpretation. It refers to the process in which the therapist and the client work collaboratively to phrase the client's faulty beliefs as hypotheses and where the therapist constructs homework assignments so that the client can test these hypotheses.

decatastrophizing   A technique used by Ellis to help a person change from thinking what happened is a catastrophe to what happened is unfortunate but not a catastrophe.

dialectical behavior therapy (or DBT)   A cognitive-behavioral therapy originally developed by Dr. Marsha Linehan for the treatment of borderline personality disorder (BPD). Its goal is to help persons with BPD to validate their emotions and behaviors and make a conscious and deliberate effort to bring about positive changes. DBT focuses on teaching individuals a number of different skills, including mindfulness, emotion regulation, distress tolerance, and interpersonal effectiveness skills.

Insight Number 1   Insight showing clients how and when they are irrational.

Insight Number 2   Insight to convince clients that they maintain their own emotional disturbance by reindoctrinating themselves with the same irrational ideas.

Insight Number 3   Insight leading clients to understand that they can rid themselves of their issues by challenging their irrational beliefs and by working with the therapist to develop more rational ways of thinking.

irrational belief   An unreasonable belief (REBT) that contributes to a person's emotional and behavioral upset (for insisting that people be different from what they are).

magnification   A person's tendency to exaggerate the importance of his or her problems and difficulties.

mind reading   Process in which people tell others what the others are thinking and feeling. Parents sometimes tell their children, "I know just what you are thinking, and it won't work."

musturbation   A term Albert Ellis used to describe behavior that is based on our "musts" in life. We must do this or that; "we should be perfect" in our daily interactions with others.

self talk   The conversations people have with themselves or what people say to themselves when they are thinking. It consists of individuals' internal dialogues when they are faced with certain situations.

Website Materials

Additional exercises, journals, annotated bibliography, and more are available on the open-access website at https://study.sagepub.com/jonessmith2e.

CHAPTER 6

Reality/Choice Therapy

We are driven by five genetic needs: survival, love and belonging, power, freedom, and fun.

It is almost impossible for anyone, even the most ineffective among us, to continue to choose misery after becoming aware that it is a choice.

—William Glasser

BRIEF OVERVIEW

Reality and choice theory constitutes a major cognitive therapy that was developed by William Glasser, an American psychiatrist. I devote an entire chapter to this approach because of its current widespread use in a number of settings, including schools and rehabilitation centers for youth and drug addiction. A slash is used with this theoretical approach to indicate that recently Glasser has merged reality therapy with principles that he developed for choice theory.

MAJOR CONTRIBUTOR: WILLIAM GLASSER (1925–2013) _____

Photo courtesy of The William Glasser Institute.

William Glasser

Glasser was born in Cleveland, Ohio, on May 11, 1925, as the youngest child of three siblings. For the most part, he led an early life that was rather unremarkable. He graduated from Cleveland Heights High School, where he played coronet in the band. In 1945, he earned a B.S. degree in chemical engineering at Case Western Reserve University in Ohio and an M.A. degree in clinical psychology in 1948. While a student, Glasser married Naomi Judith Silver. After graduation, he worked toward a Ph.D. degree in clinical psychology, but his advisers rejected his dissertation. Discouraged but not defeated, Glasser managed to get accepted to the medical school at Western Reserve University, where he was awarded an M.D. in 1953. Between 1954 and 1957, he completed a psychiatric residency at University of California–Los Angeles and at the Veterans Administration Hospital of Los Angeles, becoming board certified in 1961.

During his residency, Glasser became disenchanted with Freudian psychoanalysis and the poor results it was producing with his clients. Feeling disheartened by psychoanalysis' ineffectiveness with his clients and with the medical profession's approach to mental disorders, Glasser (1961) wrote *Mental Health or Mental Illness?* In this book, he warned the general public about the potential harmful effects of psychiatric approaches that focused on diagnosing a client with mental illness and then prescribing medications to treat the particular illness when, in fact, the client's symptoms may only indicate unhappiness with life rather than a psychiatric disorder. Glasser asserted that labeling clients with a medical diagnosis should only be done when it is necessary for insurance purposes. Medical diagnoses simply describe people's efforts to deal with the pain in their lives, especially their unsatisfying relationships. He argued against using drugs to treat symptoms of unhappiness and inappropriate client behavior (Glasser, 2003).

Partly as a response to his dissatisfaction with psychoanalysis and the medical profession, Glasser began experimenting with different therapeutic techniques. In 1962, he was hired at an institute for adolescent girls suffering from drug addiction in Ventura, California. His work with residential treatment was critical for his development of reality

therapy. As Glasser's success rate at the Ventura School for Girls became widespread, the California school system chose him as a major consultant. His experiences within the California school system led him to claim that reality therapy would help schools deal more positively and successfully with school discipline problems.

In 1969, Glasser wrote *Schools Without Failure*, which had an impact on schools within the United States and throughout the world. He claimed that schools did not do enough to prevent young people from developing a failure identity. According to him, schools should help students gain a sense of control over their lives, infuse them with a success-oriented philosophy, and help them become more responsible for their classroom behavior.

In 1986, Glasser wrote *Control Theory in the Classroom*, which not only continued the thrust of his earlier work on education but also introduced fundamental concepts from choice theory. **Choice theory** stressed personal choice, responsibility, and personal transformation. Thereafter, Glasser wrote two additional books for educators: *The Quality School* (1998b), which applied choice theory principles for managing schools, and *Every Student Can Succeed* (2000b), which demonstrated how teachers can use choice theory for disciplinary issues with challenging students.

Currently, reality therapy and the institute that houses it have undergone a number of revisions and name changes. For instance, in 1967, Glasser founded The Institute for Reality Therapy, which was renamed The Institute for Control Therapy, the Reality Therapy and Quality Management in 1994, and The William Glasser Institute in 1996. The institute is located in Chatsworth, California, and has branch institutes throughout the world.

Moreover, reality therapy has gravitated from its original premises to control theory and then to choice theory. The therapy's progression demonstrates the various influences on Glasser's thinking. In 1977, Glasser was influenced by William Powers's book *Behavior: The Control of Perception* (1973). Powers dealt with ways to help people make choices about their lives. Influenced by Powers's work, Glasser wrote *Stations of the Mind* (1981), which was a technical application of control theory for people. Glasser wrote another book on applying control theory to reality therapy, *Control Theory: A New Explanation of How We Control Our Lives* (1985). By 1996, he again renamed his therapeutic approach from control theory to choice theory, a designation that has remained to the present time.

Reality therapy is designed to help clients gain more effective control over their lives. It is a method of counseling that emphasizes client problem solving of problematic life issues. Reality therapy is intended to help people to (a) take an honest look at both what they want out of life and what they are doing to get what they want, (b) evaluate the effectiveness of what they are doing, and (c) use this self-evaluation as a means to make positive change in their lives.

The reality/choice school maintains that most clients have the same problem, which is they are either involved in a current unsatisfying relationship or lack a meaningful relationship in their lives. Clients' difficulties are caused by their inability to connect, to get close to others, or to have at least one significant relationship in their lives. Therapists teach clients how to behave so that they experience more satisfying relationships and connections with significant others in their lives.

Glasser has published well over 20 books on reality therapy, control theory, and choice theory. In 2000, he wrote additional books on choice theory and reality therapy, including *Counseling With Choice Theory* (2000a), *The Language of Choice Theory* (Glasser & Glasser, 1999), and *Getting Together and Staying Together* (Glasser & Glasser, 2000). These books demonstrate how choice theory can be applied to relationships and other types of problems.

Glasser turned 88 in May 2013. His lifetime accomplishments are impressive. In 1990, the University of San Francisco awarded an honorary degree to him. The American Counseling Association awarded Glasser the Professional Development Award in 2003 and the "A Legend in Counseling" award in 2004. In 2005, the American Psychotherapy Association gave him the Master Therapist award. Also in 2005, the International Center for the Study of Psychiatry and Psychology bestowed on him the Life Achievement Award. Currently, the mission of The William Glasser Institute is to teach choice theory to as many people as possible. Glasser uses his 1998 book, *Choice Theory: A New Psychology of Personal Freedom* (Glasser, 1998a), as the primary text for The William Glasser Institute.

KEY CONCEPTS

View of Human Nature

Choice theory is an internal psychology because it assumes that all behavior come from within. People choose their behavior, and they choose the best behavior for their needs at any given time. Glasser postulates that we are born with five genetic needs that drive all our needs, and these **basic needs** are survival, belonging and love, power, freedom, and fun. These needs are universal, innate, overlapping, and satisfied from moment to moment, and they conflict with other people's needs. If a person fails to meet one or more of these needs, he or she feels bad. Glasser contends that all behavior reflects our current knowledge and skills to meet one or more of our basic human needs. Our basic needs provide the general motivation for everything we do in life.

Survival needs involve taking care of ourselves, such as eating, drinking, sleeping, seeking shelter, and avoiding illness. The need for belonging involves our need to love and to be loved, to share, and to cooperate. We meet our belonging needs by forming friends and by our involvement within our families and other people. According to Glasser (2000a), the need to love and to belong is the primary need in people. Yet this need may be the most difficult to satisfy because other people's cooperation is necessary to satisfy it.

We fulfill the need for power by achieving and accomplishing our goals and by being recognized

<table>
<tr><td>

Inner Reflections

To what extent do you believe that Glasser has identified the basic needs of people?

How would you compare Glasser's basic needs with those outlined by Maslow?

</td></tr>
</table>

and respected within our families, at work, and within the general society. Sometimes our power needs may conflict with the need for love and belonging. Conflicts in interpersonal relationships, especially those involving marriage, often entail power struggles. We fulfill the need for freedom by making daily choices in our lives. The need for freedom refers to how we want to live our lives and the living conditions we are willing to accept. The need for fun involves our desire for pleasure and enjoyment. We fulfill the need for fun by laughing, participating in sports activities, reading, and performing various other activities of our lives.

We may not be fully aware of our basic needs; however, we come to understand that there are circumstances that relate to how we feel. For instance, we behave lovingly toward our children because it feels good. When people pay attention to what we say, we feel powerful. Although human needs are the same for everyone, we choose different behaviors to satisfy those needs. We are acting all the time to meet these five needs; however, we do not necessarily act effectively to satisfy our needs. If clients are experiencing distress in their lives, one basic thing to review is whether they are succeeding in meeting their basic psychological needs for survival, love and belonging, power, freedom, and fun.

Our brains continually monitor whether or not our needs are being met. As a result of their brain monitoring, people may experience a gap between their needs and what they are getting. They choose behavior to close the gap between their needs and wants.

Perceived World

Glasser (1998a) asserts that the only way we experience the real world is through our perceptual system, which first involves our sensory system: our eyes, ears, nose, mouth, and skin. Our perceptions constitute our reality. How we perceive the world around us and see ourselves forms our reality of the world at any given point in time. Moreover, the sensory sensations involved in our perception world are filtered by what Glasser labels

our *total knowledge filter*, which contains everything we know or have experienced. One of three things takes place when information passes through our total knowledge filter:

1. We decide that the information is not meaningful to us, and the perception ends here.

2. We do not immediately recognize the information, but we take the position that it may be meaningful to us; therefore, we desire to gain more information.

3. The information is meaningful to us, and hence it passes through the next filter, called the valuing filter.

As information passes through our valuing filter, we put one of three values on it. If the information is something we have learned that satisfies our needs, we place a positive value on it. If it is something that we have learned that limits our ability to satisfy our needs, we place a negative value on it. When the information neither helps nor hinders us in meeting our needs, we place little or no value on it, and therefore, the information is perceived as neutral. Because we don't all come to each situation with the same knowledge and experience, our perceptions of the world are different. As a result, we do not all live in the same "real world."

We live our lives in our **perceived worlds** (Glasser, 2000a). Our perceived worlds are (1) very subjective because they are influenced by our culture, education, experience, gender, age, and so on; (2) unique for each person; (3) under continual revision and change (new information, new experiences create new perceptions); and (4) often inaccurate.

We have to be careful of the perceptions that we choose to hold of people and situations because our perceptions of others influence our behavior and feelings toward them. For instance, a man may choose to have negative views of achieving women. The pictures in his head characterize achieving women as aggressive, manlike, and negative. As a consequence, he responds negatively to women climbing the corporate ladder. We all carry pictures

We all carry pictures in our head.

What are the pictures in your head about the good mother, the good father, son, daughter, and so on?

Are the pictures in your head about life realistic or unrealistic?

in our heads of good men and women. What do these pictures look like? Who is represented in them?

It is important for a clinician to understand clients' perceived reality and to have them evaluate and reevaluate their perceptions of the world and of themselves. To get clients to examine their perception of reality, therapists ask questions such as "Who are all of those who say that you are no good? How do you see that situation? How do you think other people see you? How would you like for them to see you?"

Our Quality World

Reality therapists teach clients to identify and satisfy frustrated needs (Wubbolding, 2000). We do not satisfy our needs directly. Instead, from birth, our brains keep track of what feels good to us, and we store this information in a special place in our brain labeled our **quality world**. Our quality world functions as a **picture album** that contains perceptions and images of the basic psychological needs that we have to fulfill. We choose to live according to the pictures in our heads or according to our perceptions of reality. Our quality world pictures supply the fuel for our motivation to achieve, to participate in activities, and to acquire worldly goods. They reflect what we see as the good life: a Ford or a Mercedes Benz, an apartment or a mansion in the suburbs.

At any one given moment in time, we are living the best life we can based on the pictures in our heads. For instance, the delinquent youth chooses the best he or she understands at the time to keep some sort of balance in life. The reality clinician explores clients' ways of meeting their needs and the current level of overall need satisfaction they are experiencing.

The quality world pictures in our heads provide clues regarding how we meet our basic needs. Whereas the basic human needs are universal, our quality worlds are unique to each of us. My quality world pictures differ from yours, and yours vary from your sister's. Our quality world pictures meet one or more of our basic needs, and they are constantly changing.

Our quality world pictures may conflict with each other, and they vary in levels of intensity and attainability. To understand more fully your quality world, ask yourself the following questions.

Questions to Determine Your Quality World

1. Who are the most important people in your life?

2. What values do you hold most deeply?

3. What traits or characteristics would you ideally have if you were to become the person you desire to be?

4. Name an accomplishment of which you are very proud.

5. What would the perfect job be for you?

6. Describe a peak experience in your life.

7. What does it mean for you to be a friend and to have a friend?

8. What brings real meaning to your life?

9. In your opinion, what makes a house a home?

For counseling to be effective, a clinician must be the kind of person that clients would want to put in their quality world (Glasser, 2000a). When therapists are able to become part of their clients' quality world, a strong therapeutic alliance has been formed. Therapists ask three questions to determine if a client is meeting his or her basic needs: (1) What do you want? (2) What are you doing to get what you want? (3) Is it working?

The Comparing Place

We often compare what we want (our quality world pictures) with what we have (our perceived world). Usually, we are quite happy and mentally healthy when our quality world pictures and our perceived world pictures match. Glasser (2000a) described the comparing place as a set of scales. When our comparing place scales are in balance, then we have what we want. Such balance between what we have and what we want causes us to experience life satisfaction; therefore, we continue doing what we have been doing. We might say to ourselves, "I'm so happy. I have everything I have dreamed about and then some." When our comparing place scales get out of balance, our brain sends a frustration signal, and we feel the urge to behave or to do something to correct the imbalance. Our brain signals to us, "I am unhappy because I don't have any of the pictures I have in my head about my good life. I'm a terrible failure."

Theory of Maladaptive Behavior

Reality therapists reject the medical model and the notion that different forms of mental illness or disorders exist. From Glasser's (1984) perspective, people choose mental illness. He discounts biology as a factor in mental illness and conceptualizes maladaptive behavior as a result of individuals' irresponsibility. Maladaptive behavior takes place when we are not taught or do not accept responsibility for our behavior. We develop a failure or negative identity when we do not accept responsibility for our behavior. Failure identities do not fulfill our need to feel worthwhile. Instead, identities put us at risk for what is traditionally labeled as mental illness and maladaptive behavior. A **success** identity has a positive impact on our lives and on our behavior. We are happier, and we achieve more when we have a success identity.

Moreover, Glasser's model of maladaptive behavior postulates that individuals create behaviors, including mentally disturbing ones, such as delusions and hallucinations, for the purpose of creating an identity for themselves that satisfies their expectations. Glasser does not use medical terms such as *depressed*, *angry*, *anxious*, or *panicky* to describe clients' behavior. Instead, he uses the verb forms of these words to emphasize that we choose certain behaviors. Clients engage in depressing and angering behavior. To show that they are depressed, clients may sleep all day or withdraw from their normal activities. A client who is angry breaks things or beats up others to demonstrate to himself or herself and to others that he or she is angry.

Moreover, clients choose what Glasser calls **paining behaviors**. Clients choose misery by developing symptoms (e.g., headaches, depressing) because at a given point in time they appear to be the best behaviors to use for survival. Glasser maintains that when clients state that they are choosing to depress rather than they are depressed, they are taking **responsibility** for their behavior. He also asserts that depressing is the most common way we use to ask for help without begging. When we show that we are suffering by depressing, others reach out to us.

Glasser (2000a) stresses the significance of choice in his work with Teresa, a 40-year-old woman who states she is very depressed. His therapeutic analysis of Teresa is that she was choosing to depress, and she could make choices other than depressing in behavior. Glasser (2000a) describes his initial contact with Teresa. He focuses on Teresa's choosing and does not accept "choosing not to" as an alternative.

I was determined not to ask Teresa to tell me her story and, especially not to ask her how she felt. I had to try to convince her that she was making ineffective choices in her life, knowing full well that my claim that she was making choices, especially choosing to depress, would be the furthest thing from her mind. If I couldn't convince her on her first visit, there was little chance of any measurable progress. (p. 129)

Glasser consistently uses choice theory to conceptualize clients' problems. Clients choose various means of coping with their environments. For instance, they adopt eating disorder behaviors, drug abuse, or anxiety as a way of avoiding taking responsibility for the challenges that they face. People who have an eating disorder diagnosis often describe their refusal to eat as a means to exercise control over their environment and bodies. Clients use what might be called mental disorders in other therapeutic approaches to exercise control over their environment.

Naomi Glasser supports Alcoholics Anonymous because members are required to take responsibility for their behavior. She asserts that bizarre behavior stops when individuals are told to repeat the same ridiculous things that they did when they were drunk. Glasser (1989) describes an addiction in the following manner: "An addiction is a behavior we choose that we can do easily, that does not depend on others, and that consistently gives us immediate pleasure, or we believe will soon give us pleasure" (p. 301).

Total Behavior

According to Glasser (1985), behavior is "all we know how to do, think, and feel" (p. 88). Glasser labels this combination our **total behavior**. Our behavioral system contains two parts: (1) organized behaviors with which we are familiar and (2) the creative component of behaviors that are constantly being reorganized. Total behavior is composed of four components: (1) acting, (2) thinking, (3) feeling, and (4) physiology. Thus, at any given moment, four things are happening for us: (1) what we are doing, (2) what we are thinking, (3) what we are feeling, and (4) what is going on in our bodies. When these four components of behaving are working in harmony, we are smiling (doing), thinking positive thoughts, and feeling content and physically relaxed. If we are upset and angry, then we may be shouting (doing), thinking angry thoughts, feeling upset, and experiencing a racing heart. If we can change any one of the four components of total behavior, we stand a good chance of changing the others. The golden rule is that if you want to change how you feel, begin by changing what you are either thinking or doing.

For instance, a client might complain that he needs to exercise to lose weight, but he is too tired when he comes home from work. If he can discipline himself even though he does not feel like it, he gains the experience of having the release of endorphins. Hence, he may have more energy after the walk and be in a better mood; therefore, he feels better. In this case, the client changed his physiology to feel better. To bring about change in clients' lives, they must do something different. Remaining the same creates a state of imbalance and a sense of frustration, which, in turn, leads to maladaptive behavior.

A great deal depends on what aspect of your total behavior you change. Change is brought about most quickly and easily by changing your thoughts. Change your thoughts and you change how you feel about a situation. However, during grief situations, it may be difficult to change how you feel by changing your thoughts. Instead, you change what you do, and thoughts will follow. For instance, some parents have been able to turn around their grief over losing a child by forming a foundation and working on that foundation for a goal they believe is worthwhile.

"Doing" is at the core of reality therapy. Talk alone in counseling is insufficient to bring about change in a client's behavior. It is very difficult to change your emotions or feelings directly without

Inner Reflections

Therapy has been labeled the talking cure. What are some ways that you might change the focus in therapy from talking to doing?

Take a moment to reflect on your own life. Do you spend more time talking about a problem or taking action about a problem?

doing something differently. Reality therapists assert that changing what you do is the key to changing how you feel and to getting what you want. They assess clients' total behaviors as they talk about their physical feelings, emotional feelings, their thoughts, and what they are doing in their everyday lives.

Control: A Key Component of Reality Therapy

Reality gives a prominent place to the issue of control. In fact, until recently, the theory forming the foundation for reality therapy was called control theory. It is now called choice theory. People need some measure of control to meet their five human needs. People seek to control in different ways. At the center of Glasser's reality/choice theory is the belief that the only person "I can really control is myself." The moment that I believe I can control others, I am leaning in the direction of possible frustration. Conversely, if an individual believes that others can control him or her, he or she is inclined to do nothing and thereby also head in the direction of frustration. Reality therapy maintains that trying to control others is a never-ending battle that alienates one from others and causes pain and frustration.

Reality therapists teach clients to focus on what is in their control and to respect the right of other people to seek means to meet their needs. Glasser contends that drug users try to control their environment by abusing alcohol or other drugs. In actuality, they lose control over both themselves and their environments. A common example of a control issue is demonstrated in the family when teenagers attempt to get control over their lives by banishing their parents from their rooms.

The 10 Axioms of Choice Theory

In traditional logic, an *axiom* or a *postulate* is a proposition that is not proved or demonstrated but considered to be self-evident. Therefore, its truth is taken for granted and serves as a starting point for deducing and inferring other (theory-dependent) truths. Greek philosophers defined an axiom as a claim that could be seen to be true without any need for proof. Glasser (1998a) asserts that choice theory is founded on the following 10 axioms:

1. The only person whose behavior we can control is our own.

2. The best a therapist or another person can do is to give information to a person.

3. All long-lasting psychological disturbances are relationship problems.

4. A person's relationship problem is always part of his or her present life.

5. Although the past may affect what we are today, we can only satisfy our basic needs in the present and plan to continue satisfying them in the future.

6. We can only satisfy our needs by satisfying the pictures in our quality world.

7. All we do is behave.

8. All behavior is total behavior and is made up of four components: acting, thinking, feeling, and physiology.

9. All total behavior is chosen, but we only have direct control over the acting and thinking components. We control our feeling and physiology indirectly through how we choose to act and think.

10. All total behavior is named by verbs and named by the most recognizable part.

Seven Deadly Habits and Seven Caring Habits

Glasser's (1992) choice theory presents seven deadly habits and seven caring habits. Most of people's unhappiness comes from unsatisfactory relationships that involve what Glasser calls the seven deadly habits. To build satisfying relationships, we need to learn how to use seven caring habits. The seven deadly habits are criticizing, blaming, complaining, nagging, threatening, punishing, and bribing/rewarding to control. Whenever you blame, bribe, complain, criticize, punish, or threaten anyone, that person will resist and argue with you. People are genetically wired to resist being coerced into doing something that they do not want to do.

Glasser recommends running a reality check to determine if you use the seven deadlies in your relationships with others. Ask yourself the following questions: How did you talk with a family member, spouse, or child this morning? Did you listen to what they were saying? Did you support them in their choices, or did you put them down?

The best way to eliminate the seven deadly habits is to replace them with the seven caring habits, which are supporting, encouraging, listening, accepting, trusting, respecting, and negotiating differences. These habits involve accepting people for who they are, listening to them, respecting them, trusting them, and encouraging and supporting them. To become a user of the seven caring habits, Glasser suggests that you envision the new you by drawing a mental picture of yourself as a person who practices the seven caring habits.

Glasser uses the seven deadly and seven caring habits to teach relationship issues in marriage and family issues. He suggests treating family members, spouses, and partners as if they are your best friends. We should stop trying to change family members and loved ones because the only person we can change is ourself.

Another Glasserian technique is to pick a role model who uses the caring habit that may be at issue for you. Then ask yourself, "What would the person you most admire do about the situation? What would this person do before reacting with one of the seven deadlies?" Clients are asked to keep a daily journal to keep track of their progress toward replacing the seven deadly habits for the seven caring ones.

Inner Reflections

Which do you use more frequently with the people you love—the seven deadly or the seven caring habits?

How did you talk with the one you love this morning?

THE THERAPEUTIC PROCESS

Glasser provides numerous examples of the therapeutic process for reality/choice theory. He describes reality/choice therapy as consisting of the therapy environment and specific procedures that produce client change. The therapist is directed to establish a friendly personal counseling relationship. Therapists are involved with clients from the beginning and create warm, supportive, and challenging relationships. As the therapeutic relationship deepens, the therapist becomes firmer. **Involvement** and concern for clients are conveyed throughout the counseling process. According to Bassin (1993), the reality therapist is friendly, warm, and optimistic. The goal is to help clients meet their basic need for belonging (Glasser, 1985). In establishing a relationship with clients, the therapist may reveal information about himself or herself (Bassin, 1993). To establish a relationship with a client, the therapist may joke when suggesting ways that the client may meet his or her needs.

Once trust is established, therapists can confront clients with reality and consequences of their actions. Therapists avoid criticizing clients, accepting their excuses, and giving up on them. Glasser (2000a) provides a case analysis of Alan, a 20-year-old Chinese American college student who lives with his parents, has friends only from his high school years, but would like to begin dating. Toward the end of the first counseling session, the therapist helps Alan put his complaints in terms of wants, needs, and perceptions. Alan wants to find a career path that will bring satisfaction. He wants real friends who care about him, and he wants to date and to feel less anxious when he dates. The therapist assesses Alan's needs-satisfying environment in terms of the five basic human needs.

Goals of Therapy

The overarching goal of reality/choice therapy is to help clients better meet their needs for love, belonging, survival, freedom, and fun. Within this framework, Glasser establishes a series of additional goals. For instance, one goal of reality therapy is to help clients learn more effective ways of satisfying all basic needs. Reality therapists begin by asking clients what they want and what brings them to counseling. From this information, the therapist establishes what the client wants to accomplish in therapy. This procedure also provides additional information for uncovering clients' needs for belonging, power, freedom, survival, and fun. The goals of reality/choice therapy are several:

- Build a satisfying relationship with the client
- Help the client learn how to satisfy his or her basic human needs
- Teach the client the tools for meeting his or her needs
- Promote client movement by helping him or her to change what he or she is doing

Therapy is designed to help clients accept personal responsibility for their behavior and to regain control of their lives. A second goal of therapy is to challenge clients to examine what they are doing, thinking, and feeling. A third goal is to teach clients to self-evaluate their behaviors and to determine what they want to change. Therapists emphasize that change is always a choice. As clients begin to understand that they can control only their own behavior, therapy is in progress. The remaining therapy sessions examine how clients can make better choices. Clients learn that there are more choices available to them than they realized. Previously, they may have been stuck in blaming, criticizing, and feeling sorry for themselves about things that happened in their past. They come to understand that things change when they make better choices. Clients learn they are not victims of their life circumstances.

Another goal of reality/choice therapy is to help clients deal with their addictions. The world presents us with the possibility of choosing either positive or negative addictions; however, what behavior we choose is left up to us. We can choose addictions that cause pain or joy (Glasser, 1976). Glasser suggests that clients choose **positive addictions** that contribute to a more satisfactory life, including activities such as jogging, meditation, or visiting with friends.

Role of the Therapist

The reality therapist is a role model who knows what life is all about and who is successful in dealing with life issues. A key reality therapist statement is that "there is no guarantee that life is fair. The only guarantee you have is related to yourself. Complaining may feel good for a brief time, but it is a completely ineffective behavior. Therefore, these behaviors are not encouraged." The therapist helps clients to change irresponsible behavior and to accept responsibility for their lives and the choices they make.

Teacher and Collaborator. The reality/choice clinician assumes part of the role of teacher and collaborator. The therapist helps clients change their awareness of responsibility and choice in their lives. In assessing clients' total behavior, the therapist (a) accepts no excuses for irresponsible client behavior; (b) does not stay in the past, unless it is related to the present or a source of strength; and (c) avoids punishing, criticizing, or arguing with clients. According to Wubbolding (2000), therapists invite excuses when they ask clients why. The therapist ignores clients' excuses and presses them to make a workable plan to do things differently. Rather than trying to punish clients for failing to complete plans, the clinician helps them make new plans that they will implement.

Encourager. The reality/choice clinician is an encourager and understands that change is not an easy thing to do. The therapist does not give up on clients when they have failed to implement their plans. It is the clinician's responsibility to convey that there is always hope, no matter how bad things seem. The reality/choice clinician seeks to teach clients how to fulfill their needs. The session usually begins with the therapist teaching clients the basic tenets of choice theory. It must be the client's choice to change and not that of the therapist.

Assessment. Reality therapists assess clients' total behaviors. They ask questions that reveal what clients are doing, thinking, feeling, and experiencing within their bodies (physiology). The clinician makes note of the choices that the client has made and listens for how the client attempts to control his or her environment. He or she does not get drawn into interpreting the client's symptoms. Symptoms persist because they are needed to help a client deal with unsatisfying relationships or the inability to satisfy basic needs.

Glasser (2003) maintains that clients who have mental symptoms think erroneously that they will find happiness once they become symptom free. When people are depressing or becoming anxious, Glasser suggests that they are refusing to accept the reality that their total behavior is causing their depression.

Focus on the Present Rather Than the Past. Another goal of reality/choice therapy is to focus on the present rather than on the past. The therapist only goes back into the past to learn about needs and how they were satisfied previously. The objective is to help clients satisfy their needs in the present. Although clients are viewed as partially the products of their past, they are not seen as the victims of it. They can change by doing something different. Moreover, reality therapists reject transference because they contend that it allows both the therapist and the client to avoid being who they really are. It is unacceptable for therapists to go along with the notion that they are anyone but themselves. If a client accuses a reality therapist of acting in the same way that his father acted, the therapist is likely to say, "I am not your father; I am me, and I would like to have you to respond to me as me."

Importance of Relationship in Client's Life. The revised reality/choice theory emphasizes that an unsatisfying relationship or the lack of a relationship causes problems in a client's life. A major goal of reality/choice theory is to assist clients in getting connected or reconnected with the people in their quality world. Reality therapists believe that poor relationships are at the heart of most unhappiness. If therapy is to be successful, the therapist must guide the client to a satisfying relationship and teach the client to behave in more effective ways. Clients discover that their problems are the way they have chosen to behave.

Role of the Client

The client's role in choice therapy is to develop a workable plan to get what he or she wants. The plan focuses on what clients can control and can implement on their own. The therapist empowers clients by emphasizing what is in their control. Clients' plans must be simple and contain doing very specific behaviors. A client may not be able to get his girlfriend to go back with him, but he can do other things that might help him to get over this experience, such as dating other girls. The client's detailed plan might involve becoming a member of an online dating service and committing to filling out the application, meeting three prospective dates, and so on. A client's plan may form a counseling contract.

In addition, clients must be willing to learn the basic axioms and language of reality/choice therapy. It is especially important that the client has a **commitment** to change that involves doing rather than just talking about a problem. Reality therapists assert that changing what a person does is the key to changing how he or she feels. Clients are asked to make value judgments about their behavior. By posing skillful questions, therapists help clients to self-evaluate.

Therapy Techniques

Reality/choice therapists emphasize choice and responsibility, reject transference, focus on the present in therapy, and avoid focusing on the client's symptoms. Wubbolding (2000) has created a specific model that describes the counseling process for reality/choice therapy. He calls the model WDEP, wherein W = wants and needs, D = direction and doing, E = evaluation, and P = planning. Each of these letters constitutes counseling activities. The **WDEP system** contains procedures that are used during the practice of choice therapy. Such strategies help clients identify their wants, determine direction behaviors to accomplish them, conduct self-evaluations, and design plans for change. The WDEP model was originally intended for working with juvenile offenders in detention facilities, but it can also be applied to all people with a wide range of behavioral problems. In the workplace, the WDEP model can be used for on-the-job performance and as a tool that provides informal or formal feedback.

W = wants and needs. Reality therapists seek to help clients discover what they want. A client's wants provide information on the person's underlying (unmet) needs. As a result of the therapist's skillful questioning, clients are assisted to recognize, define, and redefine their basic needs and how they would like to meet them. Each client has memories of need-fulfilling behaviors that pertain to his or her life experience. The therapist explores clients' picture quality world and asks questions about the goodness of fit between their current lives and the pictures in their head about how they most like to fulfill their basic needs.

Clients are encouraged to explore what they want from their family, friends, and work lives as well as what they want from the therapist. The therapist's exploration of clients' wants, needs, and perceptions takes place throughout the counseling sessions. Wubbolding (1988, pp. 50–56) suggests the following questions:

W = Questions Related to Wants and Needs

- Does your behavior help you or hurt you? This question encourages clients to evaluate the effectiveness of their actions in a number of situations.

- By doing what you are doing, are you getting what you want? Clients are helped to evaluate their behaviors and to see if they are satisfying their needs. Clients are encouraged to evaluate if their needs and wants are conflicting with those of others.
- Are you breaking the rules?
- Are your wants realistic and attainable?
- What would you be doing if you were living the life you would like to lead?
- Do you really want to change your life?
- What is it that you are not getting from life?
- What stops you from getting what you would like to get out of life?

D = direction and doing. Reality/choice theory raises clients' awareness of their current total behaviors. The reality/choice therapist's most frequent question is, "What are you doing?" During the initial stages of counseling, therapists discuss with clients the overall direction of their lives, especially where they are going and where their behavior appears to be taking them. Some questions during this phase of therapy are, "Where are you heading? What are your recent successes? Recent challenges? What have you tried so far?" Sometimes the reality therapist holds a mirror before the client and asks, "How do you see yourself now and in the future?"

Instead of just concentrating on what clients are feeling, clinicians encourage clients to change what they are doing and thinking. Glasser asserts that what clients are doing can be easily seen, and therefore, they are less likely to deny their actions. Therapy sessions that emphasize feelings without relating them to what clients are doing are considered unproductive.

E = evaluation. Therapy is directed toward getting clients to evaluate their behavior. Helping clients engage in an inner evaluation is at the core of reality/choice therapy techniques. This segment of counseling is based on the belief that people do not voluntarily change their behavior until they evaluate that what they are doing is not working. Therapists ask, "Does your current behavior help you to get what you want now, and will it take you in the direction that you desire?" Wubbolding (2000) suggests questions such as the following:

- Is what you are doing helping you?
- Is your behavior working for you?
- Is what you are doing in your best interests or in the best interests of those you care about?
- If nothing outside you changes—such as at work or within your family—what will you do?

P = planning. After clients decide what they want to change in their lives, they are in a position to formulate an action plan that contains possible replacement behaviors for ineffective ones. A plan helps clients focus their thoughts and behaviors. Wubbolding (1988, 2000) has asserted that to fail to plan is to plan to fail. He uses the acronym SAMIC to represent the elements of a good plan. The plan for change must be *s*imple, *a*ttainable, *m*easurable, *i*mmediate, *c*ontrolled by the planner, *c*onsistently practiced, and committed to by the client. Some qualities of a good change plan are as follows:

Inner Reflections

What are you doing?

Examine the direction in which your total behavior is taking you.

Where is the overall direction of your life leading you?

Are you getting closer to or farther away from your core goals?

Is your present behavior helping you get what you want out of life?

- Flexible and open to modification
- Stated positively in terms of what the client is willing to do (behave)
- Capable of being completed independently without the assistance of others
- Repetitive and performed daily
- Written down to help client commit to it

Reality/Choice Therapy and the Schools

Glasser has described reality therapy for schools in books such as *The Quality School* (1990, 1998b), *The Quality School Teachers* (1991), and *Choice Theory* (1998b). Quality schools are those that intentionally apply the concepts of choice theory, the practices of lead management, and the process of reality therapy within schools. Quality schools are run along the principles of lead management. Glasser uses the term *lead management* to describe a democratic style of management. As a lead manager, the teacher endeavors to involve students in decision making. Teachers engage students' intrinsic motivation rather than relying on external stimuli of rewards and punishments to keep control in the classroom. The underlying theory is that when students' needs are fulfilled at school, they behave better, learn more, and view education as valuable and significant to them. Glasser and Wubbolding (1997) discuss three principles of lead management in schools: (1) elicit students' input, (2) learn and use the WDEP system of reality/choice therapy, and (3) focus on meeting needs rather than controlling behavior.

Three Principles of Lead Management. First, teachers must elicit students' input regarding classroom organization or instruction. Students are seated in a circle, and they are asked what they consider quality work and how such work should be recognized. Students are encouraged to determine the following: What is their best effort? What rules should be established for their classroom? The teacher posts these rules in a conspicuous place on the blackboard or a flipchart, and all students are asked to sign the rules agreement. The lead management teacher conducts other meetings on classroom issues involving discipline (Glasser, 1990, 1991).

In addition, the lead management teacher asks students how they believe that they best learn the academic content of their classes (Glasser & Wubbolding, 1997). Students learn valuable lessons when they are asked to evaluate their suggestions for running their classroom. One major benefit of this process is that students feel that teachers listen to them and that they have some control over their own learning. Students' needs for power and freedom are met when teachers elicit their input about the running of the classroom and their instruction.

Learn to Use the WDEP System of Reality Therapy. In quality schools, students must learn the WDEP system. Students are encouraged to examine their wants and needs in areas such as academic achievement, personal/social adjustment, and career development. Teachers ask students if their present behavior stands a reasonable chance of getting them what they want and if they believe that it is allowing them to proceed in the direction they want to go (Wubbolding, 2000). Students are motivated to change when they believe that their present behavior is not getting them what they want and when they believe that they can choose other behaviors that will help them achieve what they want.

It is very important for teachers to have students evaluate their own behavior, effort, and school work. Is their behavior helping or hurting themselves and their classmates? Teachers ask students how hard they want to work to get what they believe they want. Furthermore, students are asked what they are doing when they misbehave. Teachers and therapists avoid asking why students are displaying certain behaviors because this question will only elicit excuses (Glasser & Wubbolding, 1997).

All students are asked to complete the Choice Theory Career Rating Scale, which is based on Glasser's Choice Theory Needs Rating Scale (see Mason & Duba, 2009). This brief scale requires students to rate the strength and need satisfaction for each of Glasser's five categories of needs. After students are asked to evaluate their behavior, they are helped to construct a plan of actions that will help them meet their needs and achieve in school. It is recommended that during each school year, therapists schedule at least one individual planning session with each student.

Focus on Meeting Needs Rather Than Controlling Behavior. Instead of trying to control students' behavior, teachers help them understand their basic needs and how they are meeting their needs (Glasser, 1990, 1991). Students are asked to evaluate why they are excited to learn and work hard in some areas but not in others. Faculty meetings focus on how the school can better meet students' needs. When teachers emphasize controlling students' behaviors rather than helping them meet their needs without hurting others, there are fewer discipline problems in the classroom (Glasser, 1998a).

To become a Glasser Quality School, a core group of staff must complete the Institute Certification process through an Advanced Practicum. A "core" group is defined by each school in consultation with the institute instructor. Quality schools must meet the following criteria:

- School relationships are based on trust and respect, and all discipline problems, not incidents, have been eliminated.
- Teachers emphasize students' total learning competency, and an evaluation that is below competence or what is now a B has been eliminated. All schooling as defined by William Glasser has been replaced by useful education.
- All students do some quality work each year that is significantly beyond competence. All

> **Inner Reflections**
>
> Do you believe that the quality school approach would work in your school district? If so, why? If not, why not?
>
> Should teachers provide students the information that Glasser suggested about themselves?

> **Inner Reflections**
>
> What, if any, parts of reality therapy would you integrate with your approach to psychotherapy?
>
> Is there a "goodness of fit" between your own value and reality/choice therapy?

such work receives an A grade or higher, such as an A+.

- Students and staff are taught to use choice theory in their lives and in their work in school. Parents are encouraged to participate in study groups to become familiar with Glasser's concepts.
- Teachers emphasize the importance of state proficiency and college entrance examination tests.
- Students, parents, and administrators view the school as a joyful place.

RESEARCH AND EVALUATION — Multicultural Positives

Reality/choice theory has made several contributions to multicultural counseling. Its theory respects differences in clients' worldviews and cultural values. Clients assess how they are meeting their needs within their particular culture. Likewise, therapists encourage clients to make plans that are consistent with their cultural values. Glasser asserts that reality therapy can be applied to all cultures because relationship problems exist in all cultures. Wubbolding and Associates (1998) have expanded reality therapy in the following countries: Japan, Taiwan, Hong Kong, Singapore, Korea, India, Kuwait, and numerous countries within Europe. Skillful questioning helps assess how ethnic minorities have acculturated or been integrated within a given society. Because reality therapy leaves it to the client to determine what he or she wants, ethnic minority clients can retain their ethnic identity. The fact that reality therapy is goal specific makes it less vulnerable to a therapist's cultural imposition of his or her values.

More recently, Wubbolding, Brickell, Imhof, Kim, and Al-Rashidi (2004) have reviewed studies that indicate the effectiveness of reality/choice therapy with members of various ethnic and cultural groups. The Okonji (1995) study investigated the level of satisfaction of African American clients after participating in either person-centered, Rogerian counseling or reality therapy. Okonji reported that African Americans gave statistically significant satisfaction responses to their participation in reality therapy. Similar findings were reported by Kim and Hwang (2001) and their work with Korea with delinquent adolescents. Chung (1994) also reported that there were significant improvements among Hong Kong delinquents in the areas of punctuality, problem solving, and communication skills.

Multicultural Blind Spots

Multicultural scholars have challenged the effectiveness of reality therapy when used with individuals from different ethnic, racial, and cultural backgrounds. One of the limitations in working with clients from diverse cultures is that reality therapy might not take into consideration environmental factors such as racism and sexism. These factors might limit the amount of actual control that clients have over their lives. However, Wubbolding (2008) maintains that reality therapy helps clients focus on the choices they do have. I believe that clients may need to talk about how their environment acts to restrict their choices and how they might respond positively to overcome such restrictions. A second limitation is that cultural norms might restrict clients' expression of their needs. Some Eastern cultures emphasize the group over Western cultures' emphasis primarily on individuals' attempt to fulfill their wants and needs. Cultural norms and values might hinder their expression of needs and wants. Moreover, the direct questioning in reality/choice theory needs to be softened when working with individuals from ethnic minority backgrounds. Finally, individuals from some cultures might be reluctant to state what they need.

Contributions and Criticisms of Reality/Choice Therapy

Some of the contributions of reality/choice therapy are as follows: (a) It is a short-term approach that has been found to be effective with a wide range of clients, including youthful offenders in detention facilities, individual and group counseling, marital and family counseling, the military, drug and alcohol clinics, social work, and crisis intervention; (b) it provides structure for clients and therapists; (c) it provides simple and clear concepts that can be used by therapists, teachers, and clients; and (d) it is a positive, action-oriented approach. Because the focus is on self-evaluation and planning, both the therapist and the client are in a good position to assess the client's progress in their plans. Reality therapy also provides a refreshing contrast with the pathology approaches to counseling.

Reality/choice therapy is gaining in popularity as a drug-free approach to treatment of children with an attention deficit disorder. Although many clients with attention-deficit/hyperactivity disorder are treated with prescription stimulants and other medications, reality therapists focus on the client behavior that may be deficient, such as their needs for belonging, fun, power, love, and a sense of survival. Choice therapy is also becoming the therapy of choice for military families who have members suffering from posttraumatic stress disorders.

Another contribution of reality therapy is its emphasis on schools. Reality therapy has been the only major theoretical approach that has advocated the development of a particular approach to working with youth in a school environment. Its quality schools and lead management approach have had a major impact on how schools are run throughout the world.

Some limitations of reality/choice therapy are that it overemphasizes the importance of observable client behavior while ignoring the unconscious, the importance of a client's past, the influence of traumatic life experiences, and the examination of client's dreams. Therapists also point out that Glasser's failure to deal with issues of transference is an additional weakness of his therapeutic approach.

Another limitation is the belief that people choose mental illness rather than acknowledging the recent developments regarding mental illness, genetics, and brain development. People suffering from schizophrenia and bipolar depression and other thought and mood disorders may not be simply choosing depression or schizophrenia. Moreover, it is an oversimplification to view all mental disorders as the result of unsatisfying present relationships.

A third potential weakness of reality/choice theory deals with the absolute power and influence of the therapist. Therapists stress the importance of clients developing a plan. Sometimes, therapists can force a client to develop a plan before the client has the necessary skills or strength to do so. There is a great deal of therapist teaching in the therapeutic setting. Clients must learn the language of reality/choice theory and the WDEP system.

Evidence-Based Research

At best, there is only limited evidence-based results for the efficacy of reality/choice therapy, even though a number of empirical studies have been conducted on this theoretical approach. On Wubbolding's website, this question was posed: Is reality therapy evidence based? Wubbolding responded by noting that research already exists that reality therapy is effective. The issue is do such studies satisfy the American Psychological Association's criteria for evidence-based established therapy? Wubbolding cited 55 research studies on reality therapy. He noted that Rose-Inza Kim, Director of the Korea Counseling Center, has facilitated more than 250 master's theses and doctoral dissertations on reality therapy (Center for Reality Therapy, www.realitytherapywub.com/index.php/ct-menu-item-10).

CASE ANALYSIS

Justin Working With a Reality/Choice Therapist

A key issue with Justin is that he has difficulty getting his needs met, both at home and at school. Justin has little awareness of his needs or how he attempts to meet such needs in his interactions with others. Little by little, the therapist and the guidance therapist must teach Justin the elements of reality/choice theory. He must be taught that his basic needs are those of love and belonging, survival, power, freedom, and fun. The overriding evidence is that Justin's behavior both at home and at school reflects inappropriate and inadequate ways to satisfy his basic needs. Justin uses anger and acting out, disruptive behavior to satisfy his internal need for attention, power, and control. His dominant need is for love and belonging, which he gets only sporadically at home. Justin needs to learn more prosocial ways of satisfying his basic needs.

Reality/choice therapy stresses the importance of the therapeutic relation as the basis for positive counseling outcomes. Therapists who have such personal characteristics of warmth, sincerity, congruence, understanding, acceptance, concern, openness, and respect for others are able to establish a therapeutic alliance with clients. Once the therapist establishes a relationship with Justin, he can assist him in gaining a deeper understanding of his basic needs and the consequences of his behavior. The therapist helps Justin understand that he is not a victim. Instead, he has a number of options to choose from to change his current life situation. Therapy is designed to help Justin not only take more effective control of his life but also make positive changes that would militate against his being placed in residential treatment.

The WDEP system is used as means for helping Justin take more effective control of his life. Each letter in this acronym describes the basic counseling procedures for reality/choice therapy. The first letter, *W*, refers to wants and needs. The therapist helps Justin explore his wants, needs, and perceptions in the areas of academic achievement, personal/social relationships, and career development. For instance, the therapist might say in a respectful tone, "Justin, I want you to think about this, and don't tell me if you don't want to. Is what you are doing helping you to get what you want?" The therapist avoids using the seven deadly habits of criticizing, blaming, complaining, nagging, threatening, punishing, and rewarding to control.

The therapist might begin by saying, "Tell me a little something about yourself so I can try to understand how I can be of help to you. What do you enjoy doing in school and out of school when you have complete freedom of choice? Tell me about the important people in your life." To get at Justin's wants and needs, the therapist asks, "What do you want? Can you tell me about something that you want for yourself right now?"

To build rapport with Justin, the therapist never asks why questions, which promote client excuses. Instead, the therapist asks Justin to describe his behavior. "Can you tell me what you are doing in school? What were you doing when the teacher said that you were disrupting the class?" Next, the therapist gets Justin to evaluate how effective he is in moving toward what he wants. According to reality/choice therapy, people are motivated to change when they become convinced that their current behavior is not getting them what they want and when they believe that they can choose behaviors that will achieve what they want. Justin is asked if his present behavior has a reasonable chance of getting him what he wants now and if he believes it is taking him in the direction he wants to go. Depending on Justin's response, the therapist asks Justin if he would like to change his behavior.

Assuming that Justin states that he wants to change his behavior, he and the therapist arrive at what behavior he wants to change. It is hoped that Justin will come to the conclusion that his anger is not helping him get what he wants. In fact, his fighting at school has caused him to get suspended from school and in trouble in family court so that he may be confined in a residential treatment center for juveniles. The goal is to help Justin assume responsibility for his behavior and its consequences.

Justin does not want to be separated from his mother and family. He cries at the thought of being taken from his mother. Moreover, deep down inside, Justin wants to be recognized for his artwork, and he wants to have a few friends at school. In helping Justin formulate a plan, the therapist works to ensure that the plan is simple,

(Continued)

(Continued)

attainable, measurable, immediate, committed to by Justin, and controlled by him. Two copies are made of Justin's plan, one of which is kept by him and the other by the therapist.

The therapist works with Justin to develop alternative ways of handling his attention-deficit/hyperactivity disorder issues. Justin can be taught how to self-regulate and to gain control over his thinking and his actions. The therapist helps Justin devise ways to focus his attention on his class lessons. Justin learns that a relaxed brain can learn more easily than a brain emotionally aroused from anger, fatigue, or anxiety.

The therapist works with Justin's mother, Sandy, in an effort to teach her about the five universal needs. Particular attention is placed on helping her with ways to respond positively to Justin's needs for love and belonging, survival, freedom, power, and fun. The therapist suggests that Sandy establish clear boundaries with Justin and that she does not attempt to become Justin's friend or use him as a confidant. Sandy has to learn to be consistent in her discipline (teaching) of Justin. She establishes house rules and gives Justin choices in completing various household tasks. Moreover, the therapist also asks Sandy if her coercive parenting techniques are helping her to achieve what she wants with Justin. The therapist teaches her other parenting techniques such as "take-up time," meaning she requests a behavior and then withdraws, allowing time for Justin's compliance.

Sandy works with the therapist and Justin to establish intrinsic and internal rewards that have meaning for him. Sandy also undergoes reality/choice counseling to determine if her needs are being met and what if any changes she would like to make in her life. Sandy's own self-evaluation is the key to both her growth and that of Justin. She can be helped to eliminate her poor parenting strategies, such as smoking pot at home, cursing at Justin when she becomes angry, and so on.

Justin's teachers also become involved in helping him develop more satisfying prosocial behavior. His teachers are given in-service training on reality/choice theory, with particular emphasis on lead management. Teachers are instructed how to use the WDEP system of reality therapy. They ask students what they want from the class, from the school, from themselves, and from the teacher. In addition, they ask students how hard they want to work to get what they want and what they are doing when they misbehave. Equally important, teachers encourage students to evaluate their behavior, their effort, and their school work. Is what they are doing hurting or helping themselves and the class? Both class plans and individual student plans are created.

Teachers focus on helping students meet their needs rather than just controlling their behavior. Some classroom exercises students might use to help Justin are the following:

- Divide the class into groups of four and ask students to identify their needs that are being fulfilled adequately on an ongoing basis. Then have them discuss basic needs that they believe could be more effectively satisfied.
- Divide the class into groups of four and ask them to discuss what they want in school, with friends and family, and in recreational life.
- In groups of four, have students discuss behaviors that they choose that are ineffective at school and at home. How might they change these behaviors?

To be effective in treating Justin, reality/choice theory must be used on both fronts: home and school. By working with Justin, his mother, Sandy, will not only learn more effective parenting behavior but also begin to focus on changes she might make in her life. Life for Justin becomes much easier when his classroom also adopts the philosophy and basic techniques of reality/choice therapy.

SUMMARY

Reality therapy is a method of counseling William Glasser developed in 1965. The theory has undergone several revisions, first with control theory and then with choice theory. Reality therapists help clients control their lives more effectively and make better choices. It is based on the foundation that all people have five basic needs: love and belonging, power, freedom (independence, autonomy), fun, and survival (food and shelter).

A core principle of reality therapy is that people act to meet these five basic needs. People fulfill the need to belong by loving, sharing, and cooperating with others. They fulfill their need for power by achieving, accomplishing, and being recognized and respected. They fulfill their need for freedom by making choices in their lives and by gaining independence and **autonomy**. Individuals fulfill their need for fun by participating in athletics and other activities that they enjoy. One goal of counseling is to help clients assess if they are succeeding in meeting their basic needs. Reality therapists ask three basic questions: (1) What do you want? (2) What are you doing to get what you want? (3) Is it working?

Individuals have memories of need-fulfilling behaviors that are unique to their life situations. Such pleasurable memories form their quality world. Quality worlds consist of pictures (or perceptions) representing what individuals have most enjoyed in life. Such perceptions form the basis for their life choices. People choose to behave in different ways to fulfill their needs because their quality worlds are different.

Choice theory explains how people behave. Individuals have what Glasser calls total behavior, which includes acting, thinking, feeling, and physiology. Total behavior consists of four parts. For instance, there is a doing part of a behavior (which might involve walking or talking). The thinking part of behavior includes reasoning and fantasizing. The feeling part of behavior might involve angering or depressing, while the physiology could be sweating or headache. Because people choose their total behaviors, they have the option of changing them.

The most direct method of changing a total behavior is to change the behavior's doing and thinking components. When clients change what they are doing, they will notice that their thoughts, feelings, and physiological responses also change.

A key reality therapist statement is

> There is no guarantee that life is fair. The only guarantee is that you are the only person whom you know you can change. While complaining may feel good for a while, it is a completely ineffective behavior. Complaining, blaming, and criticizing are self-defeating habits.

SUPPLEMENTAL AIDS

Discussion Questions

1. Reality/choice therapy maintains that while clients' feelings are important, therapy should not focus on their feelings alone. According to this theoretical perspective, therapy should not separate feelings from actions and thoughts. The therapist should take into account clients' total behavior. Discuss whether you believe that therapy should not focus on clients' feelings. Compare this approach with the psychoanalytic approach to therapy.

2. You are working with a family that has been referred to you by Child Protective Services because the children have been truant repeatedly from school. The children's grades are suffering and have dropped to near failing in almost every subject. The school blames the parents for not making their children go to school. Using the WDEP system, outline a treatment plan for working with this family.

3. Many clients come to therapy complaining of depression. Glasser says that people participate in depressing. A woman comes to you for help with depression. How would you work with the woman from a reality/choice therapy perspective?

4. Glasser has stated that reality/choice therapy is highly appropriate for culturally diverse clients. Currently, there are more than 20 international associations connected with reality/choice therapy. In your opinion, how might reality/choice

therapy work with clients in such diverse countries as Singapore, England, and Japan? What is it that attracts members of these countries to reality/choice therapy?

5. Using the WDEP model as developed by Wubbolding, apply some concepts described in this model to your own life. In a small group, each person is to write down on a sheet of paper or on a 5- by 8-inch index card.

W = What is it that you want out of life? Examine your wants, your basic needs, and your perceptual world. What are you doing now to get what you want out of life?

D = What are you doing? Is your total behavior moving you toward or away from what you want? How satisfied are you with how you are progressing toward what you want out of life?

E = Are you willing to make a self-evaluation of what you want and your total behavior—your actions, thinking, feelings, and physiology? What specific actions in your life would you like to retain because they are working for you? What specific behaviors in your life would you like to discard because they are not working for you?

P = What plans are you ready to make to meet your needs? Make your plan simple and determine if it is realistic and within your ability to accomplish. Make your plan specific and measurable so that you will know when you have achieved your goals. Outline the details of your plan.

Glossary of Key Terms

autonomy   A state that individuals experience when they accept responsibility for what they do and when they take control of their lives.

basic needs   Classified under five headings—power (which includes achievement and feeling worthwhile as well as winning); love and belonging (families, friends, loved ones); freedom (which includes independence, autonomy, and your own "space"); fun (which includes pleasure and enjoyment); and survival (nourishment, shelter). A central principle of reality therapy is that we are acting all the time to meet these needs.

choice theory   Theory that states that people are internally motivated and work to control their world based on some purpose within them. People are self-determining, and they create their own destiny.

commitment   Demonstrated by clients when they stick to their plan.

involvement   Term used to denote a therapist's interest in and caring for his or her clients.

paining behaviors   People choose misery by developing symptoms (headaching, depressing) because at the time they seem to be the best behaviors to manifest for survival.

perceived world   The reality we experience and interpret.

picture album   Perceptions and images we have of how we can best fulfill our basic psychological needs.

positive addiction   A pathway we have established to gain psychological strength, for instance, running and meditation.

quality world   The perceptions and images we have to fulfill our basic psychological needs.

responsibility   Occurs when we satisfy our personal needs while not interfering with other people's needs.

success identity   The state in which effective need-fulfilling behaviors are mastered.

total behavior   Integrated components of doing, thinking, feeling, and physiology.

WDEP system   Strategies that help clients identify their wants (W), figure out the direction (D) their behavior is taking them, make self-evaluations (E), and construct plans (P) for change.

Website Materials

Additional exercises, journals, annotated bibliography, and more are available on the open-access website at https://study.sagepub.com/jonessmith2e.

PART III

The Third Force in Psychotherapy
Existential and Humanistic Theories

THE EXISTENTIAL AND HUMANISTIC THEORIES

The term *third force* refers to a general categorization of several theoretical orientations within the field of psychotherapy and psychology. Although the third force encompasses almost anything that is not psychoanalysis or behaviorism, most researchers have maintained that the existential and humanistic theories constitute the "third force" in psychotherapy and psychology (Bugental, 1981; Deurzen, 2002; Schneider, 2008). Humanistic psychology may be defined as an orientation that rejects

both the quantitative reductionism of behaviorism and the psychoanalytic emphasis on unconscious forces in favor a view of man as uniquely creative and controlled by his own values and choices. Through experiential means, each person can develop his greatest potential, or self-actualization. Humanistic psychology is related to the human potential movement and its encounter groups, growth centers, sensitivity training, etc. (Campbell, 1989)

Similar to humanism, existentialism emphasizes personal responsibility, free will, and the striving toward personal growth and fulfillment. It posits that our major choices in life are marked by anxiety because we understand that we alone are responsible for the decisions that we make. This introduction to the third force in psychotherapy reviews briefly key contributors who laid the foundation for the development of existential and humanistic approaches to psychotherapy.

This introduction provides a brief overview of the existential-humanistic worldview in psychotherapy and describes some of its major tenets. It serves as an introduction to Chapter 7, which focuses on existentialism and the work of Rollo May and Viktor Frankl; Chapter 8, which describes the contributions of Carl Rogers and person-centered therapy; Chapter 9, which details the work of Fritz Perls and Gestalt therapy; Chapter 10, which presents motivational interviewing by William Miller and associates; and Chapter 11, which discusses the expressive arts therapies. I first begin with an overview of the existential worldview. Then I move to describe briefly the humanistic worldview. Next, I examine the merger of existentialism and humanism. Following this, similarities and differences between existentialism and humanism are presented.

THE EXISTENTIAL WORLDVIEW

Existential therapy originates from a branch of philosophy called existentialism, which explores the meaning of human existence.

Basically, existential therapy is an experiential approach that places a high value on clients' personal freedom in deciding their fate and on their awareness of their existence. Certain life themes are emphasized, including life and death, freedom of choice, responsibility to self and others, finding meaning and purpose in life, and dealing with anxiety and a sense of meaninglessness. Members of this school stress the importance of looking beyond our daily problems and developing honest, intimate relationships with significant others. The theory focuses on the essence of individuals' inner being—with *ontology*, the science of being.

According to Deurzen-Smith (1997), existential therapy is not designed to cure people in the same manner as the medical model. Instead, it asks profound questions about the nature of human existence. It maintains that all human beings face similar issues in life: finding meaning and purpose, death, and so on. Therapy becomes a process, whereby the therapist and the client search for meaning in life. The therapist's basic goal is for the client to discover and to create a meaningful life existence.

Existential Worldview

- People can choose what they become.
- People are responsible for the choices they make and for their life direction.
- Human experiences are extremely important, and every person seeks to understand his or her own personal life experience.
- Four existential problems form the core of the existential struggle and constitute the root of most psychological difficulties: (1) death, (2) freedom versus responsibility, (3) isolation, and (4) meaninglessness.
- The counseling relationship emphasizes genuine and authentic relationships between the therapist and the counselor.
- Counseling sessions focus on being in the moment and on the here-and-now.

THE HUMANISTIC WORLDVIEW

The existential movement in Europe gave rise to humanism in the United States. One way to understand the humanist contribution to psychotherapy is to view it in comparison with the other major schools of therapy presented thus far in this book. Both the first force (psychoanalytic tradition) and the second force (behavioral-cognitive) regard people who seek their help as patients who require the intervention of an experienced expert therapist to get better. The other two forces in psychotherapy follow the medical model in that they believe they are treating people for illnesses rather than for human issues in living. Because they conceptualize psychotherapy as a treatment for a disease that they diagnose, they conceptualize the everyday problems of living as illness states, and those who seek their assistance are treated as passive carriers of the illness. The goal of therapy is to diagnose and to remove the mental disease—the mental illness.

When humanism made its presence known and felt during the 1950s and 1960s, it stood in stark contrast to the medical model and the disease view of human problems. Humanists saw those who came seeking relief from their problems in living as clients rather than as patients. Rather than viewing clients as passive victims of their problems, humanists conceptualized people as powerful creators and maintainers of their own problems. The goal of humanistic therapy was to set up the conditions that would enable clients *to choose to help themselves* rather than to rely on the expert techniques of a doctor or therapist. Therapy became person centered rather than therapist centered, as therapists avowed that they respected the power of the person in therapy to choose to change or not. Humanists placed less attention on specific therapy intervention techniques and more emphasis on helping clients achieve an overall good state of mental health and wellness than on removing their "mental illness."

Humanists maintained that they wanted to empower clients to help themselves. Their developmental and secular view of human nature asserted that human problems and maladaptive behavior are caused by a faulty or interrupted developmental process and that most problems could be attributed to a basic immaturity in the person's psychological functioning. A major goal of humanistic therapy is to facilitate people's social and emotional maturity and growth, to help them get back on their feet, and to correct their derailed emotional development that caused them to be in pain and to cause pain in the lives of others—usually those whom they professed to love.

Abraham Maslow and the Humanist Tradition

The humanistic worldview in counseling and psychotherapy is influenced highly by the work of Abraham Maslow, who wrote about the human tendency toward self-actualization. As Maslow (1954) has stated, "A musician must make music, an artist must paint, a poet must write if he is to be ultimately at peace with himself" (p. 9). According to Maslow, human motivation is governed by much more than the need for drive reduction of id impulses. People have an inherent capacity for growth. This capacity may be suppressed when we experience a negative upbringing or environmental factors (racism, sexism) that function to delimit our potential. Our inherent actualizing tendency and growth potential can be activated or released under the right conditions, such as effective therapy or education.

Maslow explained the actualizing tendency in terms of a hierarchy of basic needs that he proposed was common to all people. The hierarchy of needs was conceptualized as a pyramid that contained levels that progressed from lower-ordered to higher-ordered needs. At the bottom rung of the pyramid were our basic physiological needs for air, water, food, shelter, sleep, and sex. The next ascending level of needs contained our needs for safety and security. The third level housed belongingness and love, and the fourth level consisted of our needs for self-esteem and respect. At the top of the hierarchy, Maslow placed our growth or self-actualization needs. As we take care of needs at the bottom of the pyramid, we then strive to satisfy those needs at the next higher level. Maslow (1954, 1968) asserted that all needs must be met if we are to evidence good mental health. If needs at each level of the hierarchy are not met, a deficiency condition results, and it may be manifested in a neurosis, personality disturbance, psychosis, and so on.

Carl Rogers: Client-Centered Therapy as a Clinical Framework for Humanistic Therapies

Despite his tremendous contributions to humanism, Maslow did not develop a humanistic theory of psychotherapy. That was left up to his colleague, Carl Rogers (1951, 1961), who first wrote about nondirective therapy, then client-centered therapy, and finally person-centered therapy. Carl Rogers (1902–1987) provided the crucial clinical framework for the humanistic therapies and critical leadership for three generations of humanistic clinicians. Rogers came into conflict with the behaviorists because he emphasized an empathic approach to clients. From his perspective, behaviorism treated people like animals or machines to be manipulated by stimulus and control and various reinforcement strategies.

Rogers spent his early career identifying the "necessary and sufficient conditions" that enable human beings to spontaneously grow and seek fulfillment, and he wrote about the conditions for therapy that are virtually accepted across most therapies: (a) two persons are in emotional contact; (b) one of them, the client is experiencing challenges in his or her life; (c) the other, called the therapist, shows genuineness and congruence in the therapeutic relationship; (d) the therapist experiences and displays unconditional positive regard for the client; (e) the therapist expresses an empathic understanding of the client; and (f) the client perceives the genuineness, positive regard, and empathy of the therapist. Rogers maintained that if the therapist could create these conditions during therapy, the client will self-actualize in his or her own self-defined directions (Moss, 1998, pp. 41–43; Rogers, 1957).

Inner Reflections

Who do you think actually won the debate between Carl Rogers and B. F. Skinner?

If you were given the opportunity, which of the theorists presented in this book would you like to see debate each other?

How about having your own debate between favorite theorists of psychotherapy in your class?

In 1957, Skinner and Rogers debated about the efficacy of their different approaches to therapy, especially Roger's emphasis on the use of empathy and the client's subjective inner experience. Rogers believed that the therapist could only help the client, if he or she understood the client's personal world and subjective self. Behaviorism did not accept the uniqueness of human beings and free will. Rogers and Skinner's debate is recorded in a book called *Carl Rogers-Dialogues: Conversations With Martin Buber, Paul Tillich, B. F. Skinner, Gregory Bateson, Michael Polanyi, Rollo May, and Others* (Kirschenbaum & Henderson, 1989a).

During the debate, Carl Rogers put forth the humanistic position and advocated for the reality of a person's inner experience, will, choice, freedom, feelings, growth, courage, and self-actualization. Debating from the perspective of behavioral psychology, B. F. Skinner emphasized behavioral principles such as the *outer* life, specifically external, observable behavior, modes of reinforcement, and the problems of shaping and control.

Skinner argued that "personality" and the inner life are fictions that humanistic psychologists use to account for a reality that is primarily external. According to him, humanistic psychologists mistake the ideas of our "selves," our own "will," and "innerness" as the first cause of our actions, when in reality, the real "cause" is, in fact, a history of external reinforcement from the past, in which our actions have been met with certain consequences, and thus, they have been shaped. Rogers and Skinner posed entirely different models of what a human being is and how psychologists should respond to them in therapy. Because Chapter 8 in this book presents an in-depth examination of Rogers and his contributions to humanistic therapy, I refer the reader to that chapter for a discussion of Rogers.

Frederick "Fritz" Perls: Gestalt Therapy

Trained as a psychoanalyst, Fritz Perls was one of the many striking and memorable individuals of the humanistic movement. Trained as a psychoanalyst, Perls is another major contributor in the humanistic psychotherapy movement (Perls, Hefferline, & Goodman, 1951). Perls developed Gestalt therapy, which drew from the holistic understandings of the German Gestalt psychologists and from his contact with Wilhelm Reich and Karen Horney. Perls was a colorful therapist who conducted live demonstrations of Gestalt therapy in workshops throughout the United States.

The Worldview of the Humanistic Therapist

- Humanism views people as basically good and growth oriented. People have a tendency toward self-actualization. They will instinctively move toward goals that are satisfying and socially responsible. Irresponsible behavior develops when individuals are alienated from their basic positive nature.
- Humanists emphasize the primacy of experience and seek to understand individuals' unique life experiences. Counseling should focus on exploring clients' feelings.
- The focus of humanistic psychotherapy approaches is on the self and the individual's view of his or her behavior.
- When people depart from their basic positive nature, they may experience maladaptive behavior or destructive acts.
- Relationships built on acceptance, caring, trust, and respect promote mental health.
- The major goal of counseling is to facilitate an individual's personal development.
- The therapeutic relationship should be characterized by a core group of necessary and sufficient conditions for therapy to take place. When therapists provide counseling relationships characterized by acceptance, empathy, caring, trust, and respect, a person can regain his or her emotional and spiritual equilibrium.
- The ideal therapist is genuine, congruent, transparent, nonjudgmental, and empathic. He or she uses open-ended questions, reflective listening, and tentative interpretations to promote client self-understanding, acceptance, and self-actualization.

MERGER OF EXISTENTIALISM AND HUMANISM

During the 1970s and 1980s, humanistic and existential psychology merged to become existential-humanistic psychology. This merger was created because of the many perceived similarities between existentialism and humanistic psychology. For instance, the existential-humanistic worldview sees people as capable of determining their own destinies. Both existentialism and humanism are phenomenological in orientation. Both value personal experience and individual subjectivity, and both decry the limitations of so-called objectivity.

Similarities Between Existentialism and Humanism

Both the existential and the humanistic theoretical worldview emphasize the "here-and-now" of human existence and stress the value of self-awareness. Although the past is important, advocates maintain that focus in psychotherapy should be on the present. Humanistic and existential worldviews collide with psychoanalysis, the first force in psychotherapy. While the psychoanalytic approaches view the therapeutic relationship as primarily a product of transference, humanistic and existential approaches *do not* emphasize transference issues. Although many psychoanalytic approaches to therapy view the therapy relationship as primarily a product of transference, existential and humanistic therapies focus on the real in the relationship. Moreover, existential-humanistic worldview concentrates on the self of the client rather than on the symptom that the client might be exhibiting. Both existential and humanistic therapy approaches are directed toward increasing client self-awareness and self-understanding. From the existential-humanistic worldview, clients experience psychological problems when they have an inhibited ability to make authentic, meaningful, and self-directed choices about how they want to live. Yet while the central words for humanistic therapy are *acceptance* and *growth*, the major themes of existential therapy are client *responsibility* and *freedom*. Existentialism and humanistic psychology are similar in that they are both concerned with how people can lead a meaningful life and how they handle the inevitability of death. Both psychological theories are phenomenological in nature in that they value personal experience and a person's subjectivity.

Differences Between Existentialism and Humanism

Despite the merger between the two theoretical schools, important differences exist between them. The humanistic school views human nature as basically good, with individuals having a potential to establish healthy, meaningful relationships and to make good choices. The goal is to help people free themselves from negative attitudes so that they can live happier lives. Therapists create a therapeutic relationship that facilitates client self-growth and self-actualization instead of curing mental illness. Moreover, humanists have emphasized the quality and conditions of the therapeutic relationship, as evidenced by Carl Rogers's "necessary and sufficient conditions" for psychotherapy (Rogers, 1961).

In contrast to the humanists, existential therapists are more concerned with helping clients find meaning in the face of anxiety by learning to think and act authentically and responsibly. From the existential perspective, the central problems people encounter are caused by anxiety over loneliness, isolation, despair, and death. All people suffer losses (family members die, relationships end), and these losses bring about anxiety because they point to our human limitations and to our inevitable death. Clients must learn to live authentically—that is, in accordance with their own ideals, priorities, and values. Authentic living means being true to oneself and continually creating one's own identity, despite having some uncertainty about the future (van Deurzen-Smith, 1997).

Differences also exist in who constitutes the major contributors for existential and humanistic psychology. Humanistic psychotherapy uses several major theoretical approaches, including the developmental theory of Abraham Maslow, which emphasizes a hierarchy of need motivations; Rollo May's existential therapy, which acknowledges human choice; Carl Rogers's client-centered therapy, which emphasizes the client's capacity for self-direction; and Fritz Perls's Gestalt therapy. Gestalt therapy is a phenomenological-existential therapy founded by Fritz Perls that teaches therapist and clients a method of awareness of what they are feeling, thinking, and doing. Gestalt therapy stresses what is being done, thought, and felt at any given moment in therapy rather than on what might be or what was. It uses focused awareness and experiments during therapy to help clients achieve insight.

NEW DEVELOPMENTS IN HUMANISM: MOTIVATIONAL INTERVIEWING, THE STAGES OF CHANGE THEORY, AND THE EXPRESSIVE ARTS THERAPIES

Motivational Interviewing can be conceptualized as one of the modern derivatives of person-centered counseling. William R. Miller first developed motivational interviewing during the early 1980s (Miller, 1983), and later he was joined by his frequent coauthor and subsequent codeveloper, Stephen Rollnick (Miller & Rollnick, 2002). Motivational interviewing has been conceptualized as "a directive, client centered counseling style for eliciting behavior change by helping clients to explore and resolve ambivalence" (Rollnick & Miller, 1995, p. 326). The motivational interviewing spirit draws heavily from person-centered therapy; however, it differs from his parent theory in that it is much more directive and structured. Motivational interviewing is designed to reduce client ambivalence about change. Both motivational interviewing and person-centered therapy emphasize unconditional positive regard for clients, and both use techniques such as reflective listening, responding to resistance in a nonconfrontative style, summarizing, and reinforcing positive change talk.

Motivational interviewing has been designated as an evidence-based therapy, and it has had well over 325 empirical studies under its belt (Miller & Rose, 2009). The therapy efficacy results for motivational interviewing rival and, in some instances, supersede those for cognitive-behavior therapy. Because of the many empirically based studies affirming the efficacy of motivational interviewing and because it has been endorsed by national organizations such as the National Institute of Mental Health and the National Institute of Drug Abuse, it merits its own chapter (Miller & Rose, 2009). Most agencies dealing with substance abuse require clinicians to become knowledgeable about motivational interviewing.

Chapter 10 of this book presents both motivational interviewing and the stages of change theory (Prochaska & Norcross, 2010). The stages of change model maintains that people pass through a series of changes when they are faced with making change during the counseling process. This model is often linked and sometimes even confused with motivational interviewing, and therefore, I have placed stages of change within the humanistic tradition.

Another new addition to this text is Chapter 11 on the expressive arts therapies. The expressive arts therapies are usually considered part of the humanistic tradition in literature and in psychology. There are many areas of expressive arts; however, I have chosen three expressive arts categories that I believe might help round out a therapist's clinical practice, and these are (1) art therapy, (2) music therapy, and (3) play therapy. Although a growing number of counseling theory texts have small sections on the expressive arts, few present an entire chapter on the expressive arts with a section on play therapy. I have chosen to include play therapy because toys and play are important parts of growing up and learning about the world. Moreover, increasingly play therapy is being used with all age groups, including children, adolescents, and adults. The focus of the section on play therapy in this book is primarily on children and adolescents. Play heals children, adolescents, and adults. In the coming years, I predict that play therapy will be used a great deal with adults because some of the techniques in play therapy can get to the heart of a problem very quickly (Schaefer, 2003a). Play is part of our developmental history. Most of us have a memory of our playing when we were younger. Reports have been provided in the literature of high-power

Inner Reflections

How many of you can recall playing games when you grew up?

I remember playing one-two-three red light, hopscotch, and double-dutch jump rope on warm summer evenings with my friends.

What do you remember? What game, toy, or play would help you get in touch with the child that still resides within you?

corporate executives participating in various play activities of their youth in an effort to get in touch with the inner part of themselves (Schaefer, 2003a).

CHOOSING EXISTENTIALISM OR HUMANISM AS A PSYCHOTHERAPEUTIC APPROACH

Both existentialism and humanism are important features of Western history and psychotherapy. Humanism is so firmly entrenched in American society that we seldom "notice" it; instead, we tend to take for granted many of the principles that early humanists fought so hard to have included within psychology and psychotherapy. The humanist worldview include its emphasis on the importance of human subjectivity and its phenomenological orientation. That is, if we want to understand a person, we must view the world from his or her perspective, not our own view. Humanist clinicians look beyond the medical model to work with clients, and they downplay the pathological features of a client's life in favor of the healthy aspects (Cain, 2002). Humanistic approaches to therapy are especially helpful when they are used as supportive psychotherapy for people who are grieving, needing to overcome shame and guilt, and getting in touch with their organismic valuing processes. Humanistic approaches to therapy may be less successful in treating problems that have been said to have a biological or physiological basis, such as schizophrenia or bipolar disorder.

The existential-humanistic school changed forever our views regarding the therapeutic relationship between the counselor and the client. Most theoretical schools of counseling and psychotherapy have adopted concepts popularized by the existential humanists—concepts such as empathy, positive regard for the client, and unconditional positive regard. Nevertheless, few practicing psychotherapists today would characterize their professional orientation as humanistic.

CHALLENGES FACING THE EXISTENTIAL-HUMANISTIC SCHOOL

Both existentialism and humanistic therapies are facing some real challenges about their very survival. While part of the problem may be attributed to the lack of clearly articulated theories (existentialism and Gestalt therapy), other issues relate to their failure to update their theories and likewise, the incorporation of their core tenets by newer psychotherapies. My review of articles cited in the individual chapters seems to suggest that existential humanists feel that the public and mental health insurance companies may be asking them to become more evidence-based. For example, Gestalt therapy has made a concerted effort to become more contemporary by adopting the label of relational Gestalt therapy. So many of Carl Rogers's core ideas about the sufficient conditions for therapy have simply been accepted and incorporated into most therapeutic approaches. Motivational interviewing is a modern-day offshoot of person-centered therapy that has been able to escape the fate of person-centered therapy. Because it has conducted so many empirical studies, it is listed as an evidence-based practice (Miller & Rose, 2009). The expressive arts therapies will most likely continue to flourish because they—art, music, and play—are so fundamental in the lives of most people. What is exciting about the expressive arts therapies is that many are conducting empirically based studies to establish the efficacy of its specific expressive modality. A number of individuals have contributed to the existential-humanistic school of psychotherapy. I have chosen to write about only a few of the actual people who contributed to this third force in psychotherapy.

CHAPTER 7

Existential Therapy

BRIEF OVERVIEW_____

The historical background of **existentialism** is traced to several philosophers: Søren Kierkegaard, Friedrich Nietzsche, Martin Heidegger, Jean-Paul Sartre, Martin Buber, and Ludwig Binswanger. The first part of this chapter provides a brief overview of each of these contributors of existentialism. The second part then focuses on the contributions of Rollo May and Viktor Frankl.

Søren Kierkegaard (1813–1855), a Danish philosopher, is called the father of existentialism. Born into a wealthy and prominent merchant family that had six children, Kierkegaard lived for only 42 years. He wrote books that dealt with the conflicts and problems of human existence. Two of his works include *The Concept of Dread* (1844/1957) and *Either/Or* (1843/1959). Kierkegaard asserted that the individual is solely responsible for giving his or her life meaning and must live with integrity, despite the existential distractions of despair, angst, alienation, and meaninglessness. Kierkegaard was especially concerned with *angst*—a word that has been translated to mean anxiety and dread. He believed that each person carves out his or her own destiny, and one's being is the product of action.

The German philosopher Friedrich Nietzsche (1844–1900) highlighted the importance of human subjectivity. From his perspective, too much emphasis was placed on the rationality of humans, and not enough attention was put on our irrationality. Nietzsche wrote about the dynamics of resentment, guilt, and hostility that people attempt to repress. He was skeptical of religion. In his book *Thus Spake Zarathustra*, Nietzsche (1916) argued that God is dead. He believed that religion had lost its effect on people and that it no longer served as a major reference point for individuals' moral values. From his perspective, individuals' values were based on fear and resentment. Nietzsche criticized Christianity in his book *The Antichrist* (1930/ 1972). He developed the concept of the superman and asserted that people who develop their "will to power" are creative and dynamic.

Søren Kierkegaard

Kierkegaard and Nietzsche helped bring existentialism to Western Europe. A number of philosophers followed in their footsteps, including the French writers Albert Camus and

Friedrich Nietzsche

Martin Heidegger

Jean-Paul Sartre

Martin Buber

Jean-Paul Sartre, the German philosopher Martin Heidegger, and Martin Buber, who had an important influence on American thought.

Being and Time (1927/1962), by Martin Heidegger (1889–1976), has assumed a prominent place in existential therapy because of its emphasis on the awareness of existence, which he labeled *Dasein* and is literally translated as "being there." (*Da* = there; *sein* = being. Being-in-the-world is a characteristic or phenomenon of *Dasein*.) **Dasein** is a term used to represent a person's attempt to reach high levels of consciousness and uniqueness by examining himself or herself. Heidegger called the opposite of such thinking *das Man*, which represents conventional thinking or simply going through the motions of life.

When we become aware that our existence is thrown on us, we sometimes experience a sense of dread and anguish in dealing with the world. We can respond to the world authentically or inauthentically. When we respond to our angst by conforming to conventional ways of acting and thinking, we are said to be inauthentic. Heidegger believed that we start life by being inauthentic; however, we become authentic through a process of accepting the inevitability of death and nothingness and by becoming aware of our moods and feelings. Being-in-the-world, a phenomenon of *Dasein*, applies to our consciousness and active awareness of our own life while still caring about the lives of others.

Jean-Paul Sartre (1905–1980) dealt with issues involving the meaning of human existence. He posited that individuals must find a reason to exist. Sartre believed that the failure to acknowledge our freedom and choices brings about emotional problems. He called excuses **bad faith**. Clients find it difficult to face the choices they have made in life. For instance, a person might say, "I am a failure because I had an overbearing mother and an alcoholic father." Sartre would respond, "You are a failure because of the choices you have made in life." Sartre stressed that we can change our lives. No matter what we have been, we can make choices in the present and become what we desire to be.

One of the most famous existentialist propositions is Sartre's dictum "Existence precedes essence," which is generally taken to mean that *there is no predefined essence to humanity except that which we make for ourselves*. Because Sartrean existentialism does not acknowledge the existence of a higher power or any other determining principle, people are free to do as they choose.

Martin Buber (1878–1965) is best known for his book *I and Thou*. In this book, Buber (1970) distinguishes between *I–Thou* and *I–It* relationships. Buber's major theme is that human existence can be seen in the way people engage in dialogue with each other, with the world, and with God. People may adopt two attitudes toward the world: I–Thou or I–It. The "I" is the person who is considered the agent. The other is conceptualized as the "thou." When the other person is reduced to the status of a mere object, the relationship becomes I–It. In the I–Thou relationship, people do not view each other as having specific qualities but engage in a dialogue involving each other's whole being. In contrast, in the I–It relationship, people perceive each other as having specific, isolated qualities and see themselves as part of a world that consists of things. I–Thou relationships are ones of mutuality and reciprocity, whereas I–It relationships are ones of separateness and detachment. In a famous exchange with Carl Rogers, Buber argued that the therapist and the client could never be truly equal because the client comes for therapeutic help.

According to Buber (1970), God is the eternal Thou who sustains the "I–Thou" relationship. The

I–Thou relationship between the individual and God is a universal relationship that is the foundation for all other relationships. If a person has a real I–Thou relationship with God, then his or her actions in the world must be guided by that I–Thou relationship.

Ludwig Binswanger (1881–1966), a Swiss psychiatrist and a pioneer in existential psychology, developed a holistic model of self that emphasized the relationship between the person and his or her environment. Binswanger was the first medical doctor to combine psychotherapy with existential ideas.

Binswanger adopted many of the terms that Martin Heidegger had introduced, and he believed that people have the ability to perceive meaning in their world and to go beyond specific life circumstances to deal with life issues. He called this universal ability to perceive meaning *existential a priori*. As a result of focusing on clients' perceptions of their world and their current experience, Binswanger helped them understand the meaning of their behavior and become their authentic selves. Binswanger asserted that crises in psychotherapy involve critical choice points for clients. Although many existential therapists drew on the clinical formulations of Binswanger, he did not dominate existentialism in the same way that Freud dominated psychoanalysis or Rogers towered over humanism.

MAJOR CONTRIBUTOR: ROLLO MAY (1904–1994): THE FIRST MAJOR AMERICAN EXISTENTIALIST

Bernard Gotfryd / Premium Archive / Getty Images.

Rollo May

Depression is the inability to construct a future.

Hate is not the opposite of love; apathy is.

If you do not express your own original ideas, if you do not listen to your own being, you will have betrayed yourself.

—Rollo May

Rollo May (1904–1994) is considered the father of American existential psychotherapy. He is the author of works such as *Love and Will* (1969), *The Courage to Create* (1975), and *Freedom and Destiny* (1981). May was the second of six children (three boys and three girls) and the eldest son of Earl and Matie May. May's childhood was not very pleasant. His family life was problematic; his parents divorced, and his sister had a psychotic breakdown. May's relationship with his father was closer than that with his mother, whom he said did not make him feel acceptable. May has described his early years as being lonely.

May initially attended Michigan State College but, after some difficult circumstances, left. Shortly thereafter, he attended Oberlin College in Ohio, where he earned his bachelor's degree. After a brief study abroad and a fellowship with Alfred Adler, he entered Union Theological Seminary in 1936 and befriended Paul Tillich, the existential theologian, who had a major influence on his thinking. From Union Theological Seminary, May entered the ministry.

May began his ministry in a congregational parish in Verona, New Jersey. For 2 years, his experience in Verona was filled with disappointments. As a result, he enrolled in Columbia University to major in clinical psychology. His studies were ended when he came down with tuberculosis. Given a 50–50 chance of surviving, May entered a sanatorium at Saranac Lake in Upstate New York where he stayed for 18 months. His struggle with death ignited his existential leanings, and he was especially interested in Kierkegaard's view that anxiety is the result of a threat to one's being. As he lay in the sanatorium, May came to the conclusion that he alone had to decide if he would live or die.

May earned his Ph.D. in 1949, and he was appointed an adjunct professor of clinical psychology at New York University. May's doctoral dissertation, *The Meaning of Anxiety*, was published in 1950. He argued that the free-floating anxiety experienced by most people is both normal and essential to the human condition. Self-realization takes place by confronting and coping with the tensions that develop with every new possibility and from the threats to being that all people encounter.

May contends that we fulfill our possibilities in the world only to the extent that we consciously choose and act on our goals (May, Angel, & Ellenberger, 1958). Furthermore, because we must make our choices in the face of doubt, loneliness, and anxiety, our strivings and choices are sometimes painful. Becoming is our self-conscious search for and the expression of our individual identities. In *Man's Search for Himself*, May (1953) deals with the anxiety and loneliness that confront people in modern society.

Although May is connected to humanist psychology, he differs from this school because he highlighted the tragic dimensions of human existence. In his book *Love and Will*, May (1969) wrote about the **daimonic**. The daimonic consists of the entire system of motives, which are different for each person. According to May, a daimon is anything that can take over the person, a situation that he referred to as daimonic possession. May viewed eros as one of the most important daimons. Eros is love (not sex) and, in Greek mythology, was a minor god portrayed as a young man. Eros is a good thing until it consumes the personality and until we become obsessed with it. Sometimes, the daimonic ends up being those parts of ourselves that we deny or repress; however, by repressing them, we give them power or strength. This concept is similar to Jung's idea of the shadow, but May felt a different term was necessary and used *daimonic* as a broader term that extends beyond Jung's conception.

Another important concept for May is **will**, which he conceptualized as the ability to organize oneself to achieve one's goals. Will is a person's conscious capacity to move toward his or her goals. It is part of one's intentionality. May conceptualized will as "the ability to make wishes come true." Wishes are manifestations of our daimons. They are our "playful imaginings of possibilities." We have to make our wishes come true. May has described three personality types associated with the will: The first one is called "neo-Puritan." The neo-Puritan will type has all will but no love. People fitting this type have amazing self-discipline and can "make things happen"; however, they do not have wishes to act on. As a consequence, they become perfectionistic but empty and "dried up." The second type May refers to is called "infantile." People in this category are all wishes but no will. These people are filled with dreams and desires, but they lack the self-discipline to make anything of them. Therefore, they end up becoming dependent and conformists. Although they love, their love means little. The last type that May described is the "creative" type. From May's perspective, we should cultivate a balance of these two aspects of our personalities. He stated, "Man's task is to unite love and will."

According to May (1961), the therapeutic process is a series of therapist–client encounters wherein the therapist helps clients free themselves from the limits of their existence. May stated, "There is no such thing as truth or reality for a living human being except as he participates in it, is conscious of it, has some relationship to it" (1961, p. 17). The real heart of the therapeutic situation exists between two people. Therapy consists of two persons existing in a world together at the therapist's office.

Instead of discussing stages of human development, May offers six essential characteristics that form the nature of an authentic person:

1. People are centered in themselves. Anxiety is just one method people use to protect their own center of existence.

2. People are usually in a state of anxiety, in a struggle against things that would destroy their being.

3. People are self-affirming. They seek to preserve their center, and the preservation of this center requires will.

4. People can move from centeredness to participation with other people, but such movement requires risk.

5. Awareness resides on the subjective side of centeredness. People are able to be subjectively aware of that which they are in contact.

6. Self-consciousness is a type of awareness, of knowledge of external dangers and threats, which is unique to human beings.

Viktor Frankl (1963) added a seventh characteristic to May's description of the existing person. According to Frankl, the primary force in our lives is a search for meaning. Each of us must find his or her unique meaning in life. When we strive toward existence, we exercise our will.

One limitation for May was that his experiential knowing was given priority over counseling technique. He does not provide a systematic presentation of procedure, methodology, or empirical validation. Practitioners must rely on their own spontaneity during therapy. They are free to borrow techniques from other psychotherapeutic approaches if they contribute to the personal encounter of the therapeutic relationship. Other major American existential therapists are James Bugental (1964, 1986, 1990) and Irving Yalom (1980).

KEY CONCEPTS OF EXISTENTIAL THERAPY _____

View of Human Nature

The main focus of existentialism deals with human existence and what it means to be alive. To be human means asking questions about our very existence. Existentialists assert that searching for meaning in life is a distinctly human characteristic, and that although people are basically alone in the world, they long to be connected with others (May & Yalom, 2005). Although we want to have meaning in one another's life, we must ultimately come to understand that we cannot depend on others for validation of ourselves. With this understanding, we begin to realize that each of us is essentially alone in this world. This revelation creates anxiety within us because we conclude that our validation must come from within rather than from others.

Existentialists contend that people face important and difficult decisions during their lives and that life is either fulfilled or restricted by the choices they make. Even in the worst situations, there is an opportunity to make important life-and-death decisions, such as whether or not one will struggle to live. People create their own values. People are free when they choose freely and when they accept the consequences of their actions.

The freedom to choose presents us with anxiety (Yalom, 1980, 1991). Sometimes, we pretend that we do not or cannot make choices about our lives. This illusion tricks us into believing that we are not responsible for our lives. Avoiding choices causes us not to reach our potential. Anxiety is associated with paralysis in making decisions. Awareness of our feelings and the finite nature of our human existence promotes healthy, life-enhancing choices.

Being isolated, alone, and free to choose means that we cannot assign blame for our problems to someone other than ourselves. We make the choices for our lives and therefore are responsible for the outcomes in our lives. At any point, we can make different decisions. Oftentimes, accepting responsibility for our lives becomes burdensome. Therefore, we pretend that we do not have a choice and are not responsible for what happens in our lives. Sartre (1943/1948) calls this situation living in bad faith. He maintained that it was almost impossible to live without such self-deceptions. We must summon the courage to choose what we want out of life and to hold fast to it.

Death or nonbeing assumes a central place in an existential understanding of human nature. Heidegger (1962) argued that we live on two levels: (1) in a state of forgetfulness of being and (2) in a state of mindfulness of being. In a state of forgetfulness of being, we live in continual distraction and are unaware of ourselves. We are preoccupied with things, diversions, and careers. When we live in a state that promotes a mindfulness of being, we are continually aware of our being and in touch with our existence. As we age or have threatening life experiences, we are inclined to live in a state of mindfulness of being.

From the existentialist perspective, it is human nature to deal with the issue of death because we are all mortal. We are afraid of death, and the thought of our death creates anxiety within us (May & Yalom, 2005). Although the knowledge that we are finite is frightening, it is also invigorating. Knowledge of our own finality creates tension and conflict during most of our lives. Existentialists believe that it is possible for us to face the anxieties of life and embrace our human condition of aloneness. Existentialists focus on the meaning of anxiety in human life. Clients who become aware of their feelings and the finite nature of human existence come to make healthy, life-enhancing choices.

The "I-Am" Experience

Existential psychotherapy highlights the importance of the "I-am" experience, which relates to a person's realization of his or her existence in a way perhaps not understood previously (May & Yalom, 2005). The I-am experience recognizes one's being-in-the-world. This experience can be contrasted with its opposite, which is not being or nothingness. People face the threat of nonbeing (death, severe incapacitating anxiety, and critical sickness) throughout their lives. In existential thought, the I-am experience or the experience of being is labeled the ontological experience, which is the science of being (May & Yalom, 2005). The I-am experience can be contrasted with the experience of not being or nothingness. The threat of nonbeing (death) is with people most of their lives.

Being-in-the-World: Four Forms of the World

Existential therapists avoid personality models that label people. On the contrary, they look for universals that can be observed cross-culturally. No existential theory of personality divides people into types. Instead, existentialists describe the different levels of experience and existence that confront people. The manner in which people exist in the world at a particular part of their journey reflects where they are on the chart of human existence (Yalom, 1980). From the existential perspective, existence is being-in-the-world. Existentialists reject a dualistic split between mind and body, or experience and environment. Being and the world are intertwined because we create our worlds.

May and Yalom (2005) state that the "human world is the structure of meaningful relationships in which a person exists and in the design of which he or she participates" (p. 272). Ludwig Binswanger (1963) suggested that to understand how existence feels, we need to comprehend our life experiences at three different levels. The conscious experience of being alive has three components: (1) *Ümwelt* (biological), (2) *Mitwelt* (social), and (3) *Eigenwelt* (inner or psychological experience). Frankl has added a fourth type of being-in-the-world: *Überwelt* (spiritual world; Figure 7.1).

The word *Ümwelt* is the biological world or the environment. All living things have an **Ümwelt**. The Ümwelt contains the living cycles of organisms, such as their sleep patterns, drives, instincts, and so on. The Ümwelt is the world into which people are thrown after their birth. To truly understand how existence feels, we need to be aware of our physical sensations, such as pain, pleasure, hunger, warmth, and so on. We must become aware of our Ümwelt, our being or existence in the world. Existential analysts acknowledge the reality of the natural world.

Mitwelt refers to existence as influenced by our social relationships. To comprehend how existence feels, we must become aware of our social relationships and what we feel and think as social beings who live in a world with other people. The unique quality of our human existence involves self-consciousness in relation to others. Deep

Figure 7.1   Levels of Being-in-the-World

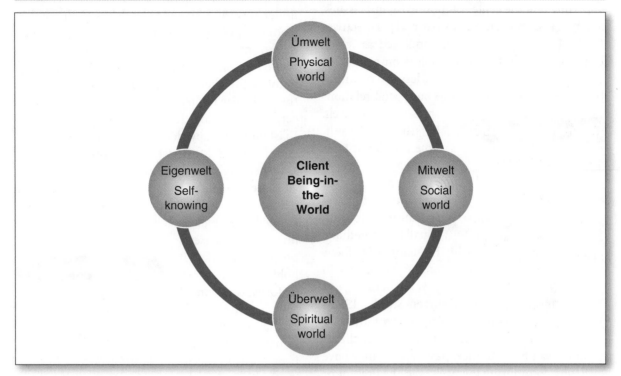

Source: © Elsie Jones-Smith (2012).

down inside of us, we desire an authentic rather than an inauthentic contact with significant others. Being in a relationship with others helps validate our existence on Earth; it affirms our being and contributes to our sense of meaning and purpose (Yalom, 1980).

When our social being-in-the-world is frustrated, we experience a sense of loneliness and a loss of self. We must decide if we have the courage to risk sharing our world with others or accept the invitation to enter another's world. Our decisions about how we will develop our social being-in-the-world (our Mitwelt) may have profound consequences on how happy we judge ourselves to be (van Deurzen-Smith, 1998).

Eigenwelt refers to our own individual world. Eigenwelt represents our attempt to understand ourselves. It consists of our awareness, introspection, and our self-knowing. A fairly substantial part of existential psychotherapy deals with clients'

"Eigenwelt," their efforts to reach self-understanding via examining their thoughts and feelings. Existentialists point out that life is difficult, but people can transcend their worlds. The physical world, Ümwelt, sometimes can give us pain as well as pleasure. Likewise, the social world, our Mitwelt, can be full of love and affection or heartbreak and loneliness. Our personal world may be fraught with anxiety and guilt.

Überwelt (van Deurzen-Smith, 2002) refers to the spiritual world of being. People relate to the unknown and create a sense of an ideal world, as well as a philosophical outlook on that world. The spiritual dimension helps people put all the pieces of the puzzle together. Some people satisfy this dimension by adhering to a religion or a formalized worldview. Still others discover their own personal meaning in life. The spiritual dimension often leads to people finding something for which they are willing to live or die.

The Importance of Existential Time

Time is at the center of most existential issues, and it can be understood from several perspectives. In the Ümwelt, time is conceptualized as "clock time" or according to space points on a clock or calendar (Sharf, 2004). Time has less of a quantitative quality when referring to our social relationships in the Mitwelt. In the Eigenwelt, time is also not typical clock time. Insight experiences or moments of great self-awareness are usually immediate. Existentialists' focus on the role of time in psychotherapy is highly significant (van Deurzen-Smith, 1998). When therapists emphasize a client's past, they are dealing with the area of Ümwelt. Sometimes clients talk incessantly about their past because they have difficulty committing themselves to the present or to the future. The therapeutic goal is to have clients focus on the present and the future because there is very little they can do about their past.

Keen (1970) has described several forms of time that take place in pathological situations: (a) a deteriorating future, (b) a status-driving future, and (c) a fantastic future. Individuals feel that they are locked in a deteriorating future when they believe that life and the world are on a downhill course. In contrast, individuals with a status-driving future promise themselves that someday they will really live. They save their money and their enjoyment of life for the future, which never quite comes for them. They live as if meaning will come from material possessions, degrees, or status positions rather than from their own free decisions that emerge from within. People who have a fantastic future sense of time spend their lives wishing that someday things will be different. They live for their prince in shining armor.

A major difference between the psychodynamic and the existential approach resides in its time orientation. Existential therapists conduct therapy in the present tense. Clients are to be understood and helped to understand themselves from the perspective of the here-and-now rather than from the past (May & Yalom, 2005). Whereas Freud interpreted deep client issues from the viewpoint of the client's early years, existentialists use the term *deep* to mean the most fundamental concerns confronting the client at a given moment. Existential therapy does not attempt to resurrect and understand the past. It explores the past only as it sheds light on the present.

Intentionality is a key concept contained within existentialists' approach to time and can be defined as people's capacity to have a conscious and unconscious sense of purpose in life. It holds that people can be forward moving if they act consciously on their world. Intentionality results when people create meaning. Individuals make an intentional decision to move toward that which is positive and possible in human relations. As Sartre (1967) has stated, man is what he makes of himself, and this is the first principle of existentialism. Our intentionality determines what we focus our attention on in life.

Meaninglessness

Most people ponder, "What is the meaning of life? Why was I ever born? What might be my purpose on Earth? What in my life gives me a sense of purpose?" Existential philosophy suggests that the universe is not designed to be purposeful or entirely coherent and understandable. The world does not come with a prepackaged bill of goods that says this is the meaning of life. Despite this observation, most people desire a sense of meaning in life; otherwise, they might experience a sense of hopelessness, discouragement, or emptiness.

Existentialists indicate that we must create meaning in our lives. We look for understanding and patterns in things that happen to ourselves and to others. We construct meaning from their existence. Finding meaning in life is important because it helps us interpret life events. May and Yalom (2005) state that our values provide us with a blueprint for life. Woven together within the life stories we create are our values.

Meaninglessness in life results in a type of emptiness or hollowness that existentialists call the **existential vacuum**. To avoid a sense of meaninglessness, we must do things that give us a sense of purpose in life. For instance, studies have shown repeatedly that aging seniors who have pets often live longer than those who are isolated or alone. Some have reported that taking care of their pets gives them meaning in life. Service to others provides many people with meaning in life and therefore helps them fill the existential vacuum.

Clients often come to therapy because their lives lack meaning. Some questions the therapist might ask the client are the following: Do you like the way you are living your life? Are you living your life in the direction that you value? How pleased are you with where you are right now in life? The therapist helps the client examine his or her internal value system to determine if his or her being-in-the-world is consistent with that system.

Existentialists contend that the major solution to meaningless is engagement. Finding meaning in life is a by-product of engagement, which is demonstrated by the client's commitment to creating, loving, working, and building. Engagement in life is viewed in opposition to alienation. To some extent, the alienated individual has disengaged from life. When we are actively engaged in life, we are being-in-the-world in accord with our own nature and of the world. Engagement involves actively constructing who we are and what we want to become, even in the face of anxiety or the threat that we may no longer be. Engagement helps us create a success rather than a failure identity. Existentialists caution that few of us are actively engaged in constructing who we are according to those things that we most value. Instead, many of us simply go through the motions of living. We live by deadly routines.

Existential Guilt

Also connected to the concept of existential meaninglessness is the notion of **existential guilt**, which emanates from a sense of incompleteness or the realization that we did not use our talents to the fullest or failed to reach our potential in life. Guilt can be defined as regret resulting from the impossibility of fulfilling all of one's innate potential (a denial of Eigenwelt), of relating perfectly to others (a denial of Mitwelt), and of always recognizing our communion with nature (a denial of Ümwelt). When the client expresses existential guilt, the therapist explores issues to see what can be learned about how the client has lived his or her life thus far. The therapist does not seek to have the client experience a sense of blame. Blame will get the therapist nowhere. Rather, the therapist helps the client come to terms with the existential guilt over not doing what he or she had intended to do in life and to focus on how he or she might do so with the remainder of life.

> **Inner Reflection**
>
> Many clients come to therapy because they are lonely and feel isolated. How might you deal with clients who come to therapy feeling lonely and isolated from the rest of the world?

Isolation and the Human Condition

Another major concept in existential therapy is isolation. Existential isolation differs from other types of isolation. May and Yalom (2005) identify three types of isolation: (1) interpersonal isolation, (2) intrapersonal isolation, and (3) existential isolation. Interpersonal isolation pertains to the chasm that exists between yourself and other people, primarily because of a deficiency in social skills and psychopathology in the area of intimacy. Intrapersonal isolation alludes to the situation wherein you are isolated from part of yourself. For instance, some feminists have accused men of being disconnected from their feminine side. In this situation, the goal of therapy is to have the client become aware of the split-off parts of the self.

Existential isolation is deeper than either interpersonal or intrapersonal isolation. It refers to the fact that no matter how close we feel to another, there is always a gap. Each of us enters this world alone and leaves it alone. As we age, we become aware that we can never fully share our consciousness with others. People who face imminent death have a greater understanding of existential isolation than do others.

Our fear of existential isolation forms the basis of a great deal of interpersonal psychopathology. We experience a basic conflict between the awareness of our fundamental isolation and our wish to be protected and to merge with others and be a part of some larger whole. When people become overwhelmed with the dread of isolation from others, they will use others to shield against that isolation, as sometimes is the situation with people suffering from sexual addiction. To prevent a sense of existential isolation, some people use sex to avoid such a feeling. Other people attempt to use fusion with key figures in their lives to deny their feelings of existential isolation. Fusion exists when individuals relax their ego boundaries and allow them to become merged with those of significant others. Essentially, they become a part of another individual or another group. People are willing to relax their ego boundaries to reduce their sense of existential isolation.

No relationship, no matter how close, can shield us from the pain of isolation. A healthy way to deal with existential isolation is to first acknowledge that it exists, then confront it, and finally turn lovingly toward others. The goal is not to use others in a distorted attempt to deal with existential isolation.

Theory of Personality

From the existentialist viewpoint, the way in which we choose to be in each of our three levels of being-in-the-world forms our personality. People differ in terms of existing at each of the three levels of being and, therefore, in terms of what many psychologists call their personalities. For some people, the emphasis might be on their Ümwelt being, that is, the biological and physical aspects of their world—their being-in-nature world. Other people might accentuate their being-for-others world. Individuals who emphasize their being-for-others world sometimes are said to be other directed. When people stress the importance of being-for-themselves, they are reflecting on or evaluating their own existence. People run away from or toward self-introspection. The goal is to have an integration of these three levels of being so that no one level is given more time or attention than any other.

> ### Inner Reflections
>
> Sometimes life can be so anxiety provoking that we live lives of distraction. We're on our cell phones constantly, and the television is usually on. We fill our lives with distractions to keep from looking inward.
>
> How might you get a client to look inward?

Theory of Healthy Psychological Development

As we try to create a healthy existence, we are confronted with the dilemma of choosing the best way to be "in nature," "with others," and "for ourselves." The behaviorists suggest that the best way to be in the world is to maximize our reinforcements and to minimize our punishments. Freudians suggest that we adapt our instinctual desires to the environment in which we find ourselves. Existentialists propose that the best way to be in the world is to be authentic. They maintain that authenticity is its own reward (Prochaska & Norcross, 2003).

When people have an authentic existence, they are open to nature, to others, and to themselves. To have an authentic existence, we make a decision to deal with the world forthrightly and honestly, without running away from it when life gets messy. Authentic people are those who are open because they have chosen not to hide things from themselves. Authentic people are spontaneous in their transactions with the three levels of being-in-the-world. When we establish authentic relationships with others, a high level of trust and intimacy exists.

An authentic existence is considered healthy because we have integrated the three levels of our being so that they are not in conflict with each other. We experience ourselves as an integrated whole. We do not wear facades. The way we are with nature is the same way we present ourselves to others and also the same way that we know who we are. Authentic individuals have a high level of awareness with each level of their being, without sacrificing one level for another (Prochaska & Norcross, 2003).

Theory of Maladaptive Behavior

The existential model of personality posits that humans' basic conflict is not with suppressed instinctual drives or with parental figures, as proposed by Freud, but rather the conflict of human life can be seen in the individual's issues dealing with death, freedom, isolation, and meaninglessness. In existential philosophy, death assumes a major place in one's internal life. Children become aware and afraid of death. As humans grow older, they erect defenses against death awareness. The majority of adults spend their 20s, 30s, and 40s largely ignoring or denying death. It is not until many years have passed that they begin to have a keen awareness that their days are numbered and that they have used up most of them. Existentialists believe that individuals' symptoms and maladaptive character structure have their origin in the individual terror of death (May & Yalom, 2005).

According to Heidegger (1962), death or nonbeing operates on two levels: (1) in a state of forgetfulness of being and (2) in a state of mindfulness of being. When we live in a state of forgetfulness of being, we are essentially living in a state of continual distraction and diversion to be wholly unaware of ourselves. We become preoccupied with things, abstractions, and diversions. For instance, one therapist described how his client was constantly on the cell phone because she could not stand to be alone with herself and the choices she was making in life.

When we live in a state of mindfulness of being, we are continually in touch with our existence and world of being. Despite the fact that awareness of death can create a sense of dread in individuals, it can also push some people to lead a creative life (May, 1981). For instance, death may not be viewed as a threat but as an urging for individuals to live their lives more fully and more meaningfully. Although this living in the awareness helps us live life authentically, we also feel anxiety when we think about our death or nonbeing.

The existential therapist subscribes to the notion that if we fail to live in a state of awareness of our being, we will eventually experience maladaptive behavior in our lives. Lying to ourselves about how we have constructed our lives or our responsibility in doing so leads to psychopathology because it helps us run from our sense of nonbeing. Lying to ourselves leads to neurotic anxiety (Prochaska & Norcross, 2003).

Existential philosophy also asserts that human freedom is terrifying and can produce maladaptive behavior. Individuals experience conflict when they become aware of their freedom and their deep need for structure. Individuals differ according to how much responsibility they are willing to accept for their life situations. Most people want to blame others for their life situations—their parents, their children—but rarely do they accept responsibility for their actions.

Existentialists view anxiety as a threat to our existence. Anxiety is viewed as a condition of our living that arises from our strivings to survive. Existentialists place anxiety into two major types: (1) neurotic anxiety and (2) existential anxiety. Normal anxiety is an appropriate response to an event being faced, neurotic anxiety consists of an inauthentic response to our being, and existential anxiety is an honest response to nonbeing. Oftentimes, **neurotic anxiety** gives us the feeling that we must act on that anxiety. As a consequence, we develop symptoms of mental disorder, such as a compulsion to wash our hands repeatedly. We experience ourselves as objects without a will. Moreover, neurotic relationships also are those in which we have fused our identities with others. In relationships that have become fused, we trade the security of dependence for the anxieties that are connected to choosing for ourselves. Fused relationships are based on someone else's definition of us. We look for confirmation for our identities from others rather than from ourselves.

In contrast, **existential anxiety** is a constructive form of the normal anxiety we experience as we become increasingly aware of our freedom and responsibility to live an authentic life. Existential anxiety is normal. It is an outcome of being confronted with the four **existential givens** of our existence: death, freedom, existential isolation, and meaninglessness. van Deurzen-Smith (1990) asserts that a basic goal of existential therapy is not to make life appear easier for clients but rather to encourage them to recognize and deal with the sources of their insecurity and anxiety. When people face existential anxiety, they view life as an adventure rather than lying to themselves about securities that appear to offer protection from anxiety. It is important for existential therapists to recognize anxiety in clients and to help them find ways to deal with it constructively.

For existentialists, psychological health is evidenced by an ability to navigate the complexities of one's life, the world, and one's relationship with the world. In contrast, psychological disturbance results when one avoids life's truths and works under the shadow of other people's expectations and values. Existential therapists maintain that psychological disturbance is an inevitable life experience for most people. The question is not so much about how we can avoid psychological disturbance in our lives but rather how we can face life challenges with openness and a willingness to engage with life rather than retreat from it.

THE THERAPEUTIC PROCESS

The therapist assumes that the client experiences anxiety that emanates from an existential conflict that may be partially unconscious and that the client is coping with these conflicts ineffectually. Therapy is designed to help the client begin a journey of self-investigation in which the goals are to understand the existential conflict, identify the maladaptive defense mechanisms he or she uses, and develop more effective ways of coping with anxiety. Existential therapy can be appropriate for clients who are confronting some boundary situation—such as a confrontation with death or a transitional or milestone development, such as retirement—or facing some important irreversible decision (May & Yalom, 2005).

The therapeutic process in existentialism entails encouraging clients to enter into an authentic relationship with a therapist that helps them become aware of themselves as people who can act on the world and who have free will to choose. Therapists use the technique of free experiencing to assist clients in actively choosing to become what they want (Yalom, 1980). Clients are encouraged to express freely and honestly whatever they are experiencing in the present. As clients engage in free experiencing, they become aware that they may be reluctant to explore parts of themselves and their world (e.g., relationships with children, spouses, jobs, etc.).

The Therapeutic Relationship

The existential therapist seeks to understand the client's being-in-the-world. To facilitate this understanding, the therapist works to establish with the client an "I–Thou" relationship—that is, a sharing and experiencing together that helps them understand the client's being, freedom, choices, and responsibilities. The therapeutic relationship is part of the change process. The client works toward becoming an authentic person. The therapeutic relationship provides an opportunity for clients to enter into an authentic relationship. When the client chooses to become an authentic person with the therapist, real change can take place.

The existential approach characterizes people as creatures of continual change and transformation. The therapeutic relationship illuminates the client's styles of being-in-the-world. For instance, clients may learn that their being-in-the-world is based on lies to themselves and others. Clients are encouraged to face their existential anxiety as well as their neurotic anxiety. Existential therapy explores the meaning clients have been able to achieve via their being-in-the-world. The authenticity of the therapeutic relationship helps clients become aware of the choices they are making in their daily lives. The therapist uses the counseling relationship to help clients assume responsibility for their life choices.

Goals of Therapy

The basic goal of existential therapy is to help individuals lead authentic lives and make choices that will help them become all they are capable of becoming (van Deurzen-Smith, 1998). In early writings, May explains that "the aim of therapy is that the patient experiences his existence as real" (May et al., 1958). May argues that therapy is concerned with something deeper than curing a client's symptoms. Clients must fully sense and experience their existence and confront their feelings of guilt and anxiety if they are to achieve a lasting cure of their symptoms.

Two additional general goals of existential therapy are to help clients (1) expand their self-awareness and (2) become aware of the freedom they have in making choices about their lives and the responsibility of owning up to their choices. Clients are encouraged to shift from an outward to an inward frame of reference. Their choices result from an internal evaluation of what seems right or best for them. Another basic goal of existential therapy is to help clients listen to their inner selves.

> **Inner Reflections**
>
> Can you see yourself working as an existential therapist?
>
> What do you like most about the role of an existential therapist? What makes you feel that there is not a goodness of fit with you and existentialism?

According to Bugental (1990), there are three fundamental goals of psychotherapy: (1) to help clients recognize that they are not fully in the present in the therapy encounter and to assist them in understanding that this situation hampers their success outside of therapy, (2) to support clients as they confront their anxieties that they have avoided thus far, and (3) to promote client change in the area of greater authenticity. The goals of existential therapy may be summarized as follows:

- Finding personal meaning: The client is encouraged to find his or her own personal meanings and truths about life.
- Taking responsibility for one's decisions about living
- Living in the present so that the client experiences life more fully each moment
- Increasing self-awareness and authentic living

Role of the Therapist

The role of the existential therapist is to facilitate clients' encounters with themselves. Existential therapists help clients encounter their "stuckness" in life (Vontress, Johnson, & Epp, 1999). The goal is to help clients become unstuck. Existential therapists focus on the issue of client responsibility. They assist clients in learning how to embrace responsibility rather than avoid it. The therapist assists clients by identifying methods and examples of responsibility avoidance and bringing them to clients' attention. Clients learn how they are responsible for their own distress. When clients complain about their life situations, the therapist might ask, "What was your role in creating this situation?" In fostering client self-awareness, the existential therapist must be self-aware of his or her values and biases.

The therapist assists clients in making choices, removing the obstacles that block their decision-making ability, and understanding the methods they use in arriving at decisions. Clients may be in therapy because of concerns about making an upcoming decision or about their avoidance of making a decision. Existential therapy deals with an active decision that clients have to make. Therapy ends when clients take responsibility for the decision that has been at the center of counseling. Clients learn not to be afraid of their own limitations and weaknesses, their uncertainties and doubts about life (van Deurzen-Smith, 1997).

Role of the Client

Clients are asked to be active rather than passive participants in existential therapy. They learn that they must confront their ultimate (death, meaning) concerns rather than just their immediate ones. They explore their own lives, especially the meaning and values they have found or would like to have, and they make a commitment to live authentically. Authentic living means being true to themselves and honest about their own possibilities and limitations. They accept the role of creating their own identity, even when they feel uncertain about the future.

Existential therapy is appropriate for clients who view their problems as challenges of living, rather than as symptoms of psychopathology, and who are concerned with increasing their self-awareness. The therapeutic approach is best suited for people attempting to clarify their own personal ideology and for those who feel at the very edge of their existence, including those who are facing terminal illnesses or even with those who are beginning a new phase of life.

Therapy Techniques

More so than other models of counseling, the existential approach has few psychotherapeutic techniques. As Frankl (1967) has stated, "Approaching human beings merely in terms of techniques necessarily implies manipulating them" (p. 139), which is the direct opposite of what existentialists would like to take place during therapy. Existentialists are free to use techniques across the broad schools of thought, including diverse techniques such as desensitization and free association.

The primary guideline is that practitioners' interventions address the uniqueness of each person. During the first part of therapy, the therapist helps clients identify and clarify their beliefs about their worlds. Clients are encouraged to explore the ways in which they make sense of their being. The middle phase of counseling examines clients' values and their sources. Clients are asked to think about the kind of life they consider worthwhile. The final phase of counseling focuses on helping clients take action regarding the kind of life they want.

MAJOR CONTRIBUTOR: VIKTOR FRANKL (1905–1997) AND LOGOTHERAPY

Photo courtesy of IMAGNO.

Viktor Frankl

A man can get used to anything, but do not ask us how.

Fundamentally, therefore, any man can, even under such circumstances, decide what shall become of him—mentally and spiritually. He may retain his human dignity even in a concentration camp.

We can discover this meaning in life in three different ways: (1) by creating a work or doing a deed, (2) by experiencing something or encountering someone, and (3) by the attitude we take toward unavoidable suffering.

—Viktor Frankl

Viktor Frankl, an Austrian neurologist and psychiatrist and a Holocaust survivor, was the founder of **logotherapy**, which is a form of existential analysis. Viktor Emil Frankl (M.D., Ph.D.) was born on March 26, 1905, in Vienna into a Jewish family of civil servants. He graduated from Gymnasium in 1923 and studied medicine at the University of Vienna, subsequently specializing in neurology and psychology. His early treatment was concentrated on depression and suicide. Although his early development was influenced by his contacts with Sigmund Freud and Alfred Adler, he later departed from their teachings (Frankl, 1978).

From 1933 to 1937, he was chief of the suicide pavilion of the general hospital in Vienna. Despite the fact that he treated more than 30,000 women prone to suicide, in 1938 he was prohibited from treating "Aryan" patients because of his Jewish identity. Because of Nazi restrictions on his work, Frankl moved into private practice in 1940 and worked as a brain surgeon at the Rothschild Hospital (the only hospital in Vienna where Jews were admitted) and headed its neurological department (Redsand, 2006).

On September 25, 1942, Viktor Frankl, his wife (Tilly Grosser, married 1941), and his parents were deported to the Theresienstadt concentration camp. At the camp, Frankl worked as a general practitioner in a clinic until his skill as a psychiatrist was noticed. Thereafter, he was asked to establish a special unit to help newcomers to the camp overcome shock and grief at their treatment. Frankl set up a suicide watch unit, and all hints of suicide were reported to him. Frankl was also assigned to ordinary labor details until the last few weeks of the war. Notwithstanding his own hard labor, Frankl tried to cure fellow prisoners from despondency and prevent suicide. Despite his psychiatric work with prisoners, Frankl was transported to Auschwitz concentration camp on October 19, 1944. Then he was moved to Turkheim, another Nazi concentration camp associated with Dachau, where he spent 7 months working as a slave laborer. His wife was transferred to the Bergen-Belsen concentration camp, where she was killed; his father and mother were killed at Auschwitz.

The Americans liberated Frankl on April 27, 1945. His sister was the only immediate relative who had survived the Nazi takeover, and she survived by immigrating to Australia. Because of the suffering he and others had experienced in the Nazi concentration camps, Frankl concluded that even in the most painful and dehumanized conditions, life still has meaning, and therefore, even suffering is meaningful. This conclusion served as the foundation for the therapeutic approach he developed called logotherapy. During the postwar years, Frankl published 32 books. He lectured throughout the world and was awarded 29 honorary degrees. On September 2, 1997, he died of heart failure in Vienna.

Frankl and the Search for Meaning

Viktor Frankl's most famous book, *Man's Search for Meaning* (1963), details his experiences as a Nazi concentration camp inmate and describes how he found a reason to live under such circumstances. Frankl has stated that his book was designed to answer the question, "How was everyday life in a concentration camp reflected in the mind of the average prisoner?" The first part of the book consists of Frankl's examination of his experiences in the concentration camps, and the second part contains his ideas of meaning and his theory of logotherapy.

According to Frankl, inmates had three psychological reactions to imprisonment in the concentration camps: (1) shock during the initial admission phase to the camp; (2) apathy, which took place after one had become adjusted to camp existence; and (3) reactions of depersonalization, moral deformity, bitterness, and disillusionment, if the inmate survived and was freed.

What was most striking about Frankl's (1963) work was his conclusion that meaning is found in every moment of living. Life never stops having meaning, even in suffering and death. Frankl proposed that a prisoner's psychological reactions are based partly on the freedom of choice he or she has, even while experiencing severe suffering.

A prisoner survives because he or she has a spiritual self that has faith in the future, but once an inmate loses faith, he or she is doomed. In writing about his concentration camp experiences, Frankl (1963) stated,

> A thought transfixed me: for the first time in my life I saw the truth as it is set into song by so many poets, proclaimed as the final wisdom by so many thinkers. The truth—that love is the ultimate and the highest goal to which man can aspire. Then I grasped the meaning of the greatest secret that human poetry and human thought and belief have to impart: *The salvation of man is through love and in love.* I understood how a man who has nothing left in this world still may know bliss, be it only for a brief moment, in the contemplation of his beloved. (p. 59)

The Basic Premises of Logotherapy

In *The Doctor and the Soul* (1955), Frankl put forth the theory of *logotherapy*, a term derived from the Greek words *logos* (word or meaning) and *therapeia* (healing). Frankl's theory grew out of his experiences in Nazi death camps. As he watched who survived and who did not, he concluded that the Friedrich Nietzsche had it right when he said, "He who has a why to live for can bear with almost any how." There are three basic assumptions of logotherapy:

1. Life has meaning under all circumstances.

2. People have a will to meaning.

3. People have the freedom under all circumstances to activate the will to meaning and to find meaning in life.

How do we as human beings find meaning in life? Frankl indicates three ways by which we can find meaning in life. The first way we can find meaning is from our experiential values, that is, by experiencing something or someone whom we value or love. Maslow's (1968) peak experiences and visiting the natural wonders of the world help us develop meaning. Love is the greatest experiential value that we have, especially the love that we have toward others. Frankl (1963) maintains that love "is the ultimate and the highest goal to which man can aspire" (pp. 58–59). Sex is not to be confused with love. Frankl advocated monogamous marriage as one of the greatest ways to experience love.

The second way that people can discover meaning in their lives is through creative values, by completing a deed. One provides oneself with meaning by becoming involved in projects or by being the architect of the project of one's life. Developing meaning in life by creative values involves creativity evidenced in art, music, writing, and invention.

The third way that people find meaning in life is by the attitudinal values that we adopt to guide our behavior and actions. Some attitudinal values are compassion for others, bravery, and a good sense of humor. However, Frankl's best-known example of attitudinal values is achieving meaning by suffering. People who have suffered various negative experiences, such as cancer or other illnesses, sometimes mention the benefit of their illness in helping them understand their lives. In *Man's Search for Meaning*, Frankl (1963) states, "Everything can be taken from a man but one thing: the last of the human freedoms—to choose one's attitude in any given set of circumstances, to choose one's own way" (p. 104).

Inner Reflections

Does life have meaning for you under all circumstances?

Can you imagine being as humiliated as Frankl was during his imprisonment in a Nazi concentration camp?

Frankl would say that we all live in various types of prisons—some of which are self-made and others that are imposed by outside forces (poverty) and governments.

What kind of attitude do we need to survive, regardless of the circumstances of our lives?

We can choose our attitudes toward a condition, even if we cannot change a situation or circumstance. Changing our attitudes is a self-transcending method of finding meaning, especially when unavoidable suffering takes place. When confronted with unavoidable suffering, we can often find meaning in the situation by looking at it in a different way. As humans, we can learn to transcend the conditions of our lives. Frankl believed that people could enrich their lives with spiritual meaning despite their individual circumstances. Reflecting on his experiences in the Nazi death camps, Frankl (1963) stated,

> In spite of all the enforced physical and mental primitiveness of the life in a concentration camp, it was possible for spiritual life to deepen. . . . They were able to retreat from their terrible surroundings to a life of inner riches and spiritual freedom. (p. 56)

A dominant theme in logotherapy is that we must accept that our life (meaning where we stand at any given moment) is a consequence of the choices we have made. Happiness ensues from making responsible, good choices. We all search for meaning in life until the day that we die. It is this search for meaning that makes us feel that life is worthwhile and that there is some purpose to our existence. We are free to achieve our goals and purposes.

Theory of Maladaptive Behavior

From Frankl's perspective, various anxiety neuroses are based on existential anxiety. The individual does not understand that his or her anxiety is due to a sense of unfulfilled responsibility and a lack of meaning. Therefore, he or she takes that anxiety and displaces it on some problematic area of his or her life. The various anxiety disorders are individuals' attempts to make sense of their existential anxiety or their existential vacuum. For example, Frankl notes that the obsessive-compulsive person lacks a sense of completion that most people have about a task or thing. While most of us are satisfied with a near certainty that we have

locked our doors at night, the obsessive-compulsive person demands a perfect certainty that is ultimately unattainable. He or she keeps checking and checking, washing and rewashing his or her hands to arrive at a perfect sense of completion. The obsessive-compulsive person focuses on some small area in life that has previously caused problems.

When people experience frustration of the existential need for meaningful goals, they may engage in behavior that gives rise to aggression, addiction, depression, and suicide. Logotherapy helps clients in perceiving and removing factors that prevent them from pursuing meaningful goals in their lives. Therapists guide clients to realize the meaningful possibilities they have detected in themselves. The therapist cannot give meaning in life; the client must discover it for himself or herself. The therapist helps the client realize that he or she is not a victim of his or her circumstances. Although the client might have symptoms, the client is not defined by his or her symptoms (Frankl, 1963).

Inner Reflection

Use the paradoxical intention technique on someone close to you to get that person to respond contrary to his or her intentions.

Therapy Techniques

Frankl's (1969) logotherapy uses the Socratic dialogue, as the therapist and the client attempt to find meaning in life. Socratic dialogue is a conversational method logotherapists use to raise clients' consciousness about their possibilities. The therapist asks specific questions to raise into consciousness the possibility to find, and the freedom to fulfill, meaning in one's life. Socrates used this type of questioning to promote self-understanding among his students. Certain attitudes and expectations may act as obstacles to clients obtaining meaning fulfillment. Negative attitudes can alienate a person from the meaning potentialities in his or her life. Client attitudes can also accentuate neurotic disorders or even produce them. It is important that the therapist refrain from imposing his or her own values or meaning perceptions on the client. Clients are guided to relinquish (if they desire) counterproductive attitudes.

Frankl is also famous for his development of the paradoxical intention technique. Paradoxical intention may be defined as a therapy technique that directs a client to do something contrary to one's actual intentions. The paradoxical intention involves doing the very thing that you say you fear. Generally, a client is told to do something that the therapist believes will result in noncompliance. If the goal is to get a client to get up from a table, the therapist might instruct the client to sit there for 3 hours. The therapist gets the client to do what was originally desired by creating a paradoxical intention.

The second technique Frankl used is labeled **dereflection**. Frankl proposed that people encounter problems because they put too much emphasis on themselves. When people shift their attention to others, their own personal problems seem to lessen. Service to others takes our minds off ourselves. Many schools have reported that service projects have a positive impact on students' attitudes in school and on improving their academic grades. On another level, sexologists have proposed that when too much emphasis is placed on sexual performance, individuals' performance may actually decline. Therefore, instead of stressing the importance of orgasms from a partner, sexologists might just encourage the couple to limit themselves to petting. Petting reduces orgasm anxiety. Moreover, when people are told to limit their sexual encounters, they usually increase them, resulting in orgasms.

Existentialism and the Schools

For the most part, one does not think of using existential theory with helping school students; however, L. Carlson (2003) has pointed out that existentialism provides a foundation for understanding and intervening with youth at risk for violent behavior. School therapists can understand potentially violent youth using the existential lens of meaninglessness, isolation, freedom, and anxiety. Violent perpetrators engage in violence because they may be struggling with issues of meaninglessness, isolation, and belonging.

School administrators need to take into account the extent to which the school climate helps create a sense of existential isolation and anxiety. Do students feel as if their school provides meaning for their lives? Is the relationship between teachers and students one of mutual respect and cooperation? To what extent are students encouraged to live an authentic life? Schools can help youth deal with making decisions/choices and with learning how to accept responsibility for their choices.

RESEARCH AND EVALUATION

Multicultural Positives

The existential view of being-in-the-world has particular significance for multicultural counseling. Vontress et al. (1999) emphasize being with another person (Mitwelt) in ways that respect cultural uniqueness (Ümwelt). They contend that counseling must use all four dimensions of existentialism— (1) Eigenwelt (the individual), (2) Mitwelt (social relations), (3) Ümwelt (which consists of the client's culture), and (4) Überwelt (spirituality). Spirituality or Überwelt is critical to understanding the person and his or her culture. For instance, Japanese culture is anchored in Buddhist and Shinto spiritual dimensions.

One advantage of the existential approach is that it provides a basis for examining how a client's culture and social relations have influenced his or her behavior. How does one's culture influence one's being-in-the-world? What are a clients' cultural views of death? Clients can examine to what extent their choices in life are affected by their culture and other group relations. They can explore culture influences on their being-in-the-world. Conversely, the existential approach can be criticized for being too individualistic.

Multicultural Blind Spots

One limitation of existential therapies is that they are highly individualistic. Cultures that have a group rather than an individualistic orientation may find that existentialism challenges the underpinnings of the culture. Cultures that have a group orientation may not experience existential aloneness. For cultures that are group-oriented, it may be appropriate to talk about self and self-determination apart from their membership groups. Moreover, existential therapies tend to ignore the social factors that cause human problems. Even if clients do decide to change internally, their environments may work to restrict their opportunities. Many clients from non-Western backgrounds might expect a structured and problem-oriented therapy instead of discussion and examination of philosophical questions as is the case with existential therapy.

Contributions and Criticisms of Existential Therapy

The strengths of existential theory are its emphasis on client self-determination and self-actualization, its positive and optimistic conception of human nature, its focus on interpersonal relationships, and its emphasis on the here-and-now of the therapist–client relationship. In contrast, the major criticisms of existential approaches center on the lack of critical research, with the exception of studies completed by client-centered therapists. The second criticism involves its lack of emphasis on a client's past history with regard to counseling treatment. The third limitation is the tendency of the existential counseling approach to ignore person–environment transactions. Sometimes, the intense focus on the individual and his or her free choice may be unrealistic because of environmental constraints. Fourth, existential therapies have been criticized as being vague and as using a too global approach to therapy. Existential concepts have been portrayed as lofty. Fifth, existential therapies tend to lack a systematic statement of the principles and practices of psychotherapy.

Evidence-Based Research on Existential Therapies

There are few empirical studies investigating existential therapy, and those that have been completed were done so many years ago. Part of the problem can be traced to the actual existential theories themselves. Researchers generally do not investigate whether a person has become a qualitatively new person or has developed a new appreciation of life. The empirical task of existential therapies deals with the question, "How does one measure desirable existential change?" Quantitative approaches measure the basic goals of existential therapy that have been lacking. Instead of using quantitative measures, as are generally required to be called an evidence-based therapy, researchers are beginning to develop qualitative measures to gauge the effectiveness of humanistic therapies. In the *Handbook of Humanistic Psychology*, Schneider, Bugental, and Pierson (2001) have summarized several qualitative approaches, including, Robert Elliott's "Hermeneutic Single Case Efficacy Design," David Rennie's Grounded Theory Method, Arthur Bohart's Adjudication Model, and Kirk Schneider's Multiple Case Depth Research.

Cleare-Hoffman, Hoffman, and Wilson (2013) have argued that there is a solid basis for existential therapy as an evidence-based therapy, although they claim that this basis has not been adequately articulated in the literature. They proposed two important aspects of the evidence-based foundation of existential therapy: therapist factors and implications for diversity/individual differences.

While behavioral therapies target measurable symptom change as an indicator of effective therapeutic outcomes, humanistic psychotherapies tend to value criteria that may not be as easily measured. The empirical challenge of both humanistic and existential therapies is to determine how one goes about measuring qualitative changes within people. Cleare-Hoffman et al. (2013) have proposed a common factor approach to establish the evidence-based practice of existential therapy. According to these researchers,

> Although there is a solid basis for existential therapy as an Evidence-Based Practice in psychotherapy (EBPP), this has not been adequately articulated in the scholarly literature. This paper advances two important aspects of the evidence-based foundation of existential therapy: therapist factors and implications for diversity/individual differences. (p. 1)

Wampold (2001) has reached a similar conclusion that one can use a common factor approach to determine the effectiveness of existential therapy. He has stated that existential-integrative therapy could "form the basis of all effective treatments" (Wampold, 2006). Cleare-Hoffman et al. (2013) have asserted that EBPP can be considered a good fit with existential therapy if EBPP does not gravitate toward a narrow, restrictive manner. "Hoffman et al. (2012) have argued that existential and humanistic therapists must become a part of the discussions about how EBPP is understood and defined, as well as working to demonstrate that existential and humanistic therapy meets the criteria for being EBPP in psychology." As Cleare-Hoffman et al. (2013) have stated,

> This paper builds upon previous arguments that assert that existential therapy can rightly be considered an evidence-based practice (Hoffman, 2009a, Hoffman, et al., 2012). However it should be cautioned that EBPP is not about establishing specific therapy modalities as evidence-based, but rather conceives of evidence-based practice as something that extends beyond a particular therapeutic approach to also consider factors about the individual therapist and their competencies. Thus, when saying that existential therapy can rightly be considered an evidence-based practice we are stating this within the provision that the therapist implementing this approach must have established a number of basic competencies relevant across therapy modalities. (p. 2)

CASE ANALYSIS

Justin Working With an Existential Therapist

Even though Justin is a middle school student, the existential therapist approaches him with the orientation that he has the ability to increase his self-awareness and to make decisions about the future direction of his life. Specifically, he must make decisions about whether he will change the direction of his life and choose behavior that will help him remain outside of residential treatment confinement. The therapist wants Justin to understand that even though he is still young, he has the individual power to establish meaning in his life and to choose to act positively on his life goals. Justin can free himself from the negative influences of the environment in which he lives. He does not have to follow in his brother's footsteps or in those of his friends who were caught stealing at Walmart.

The existential approach does not emphasize counseling techniques but rather highlights the importance of the therapist's understanding of Justin's world. The therapist seeks to establish an authentic therapeutic relationship with Justin to facilitate his positive exploration of issues in his life. The therapist is interested in understanding the meaning of life to Justin. How does Justin view himself? Does he see himself as a victim, unable to deal constructively with the circumstances of his home and community environment? Or does he see himself as capable of achieving his goals, irrespective of his current living circumstances? What is the meaning of life for Justin? Does life have the meaning he would like it to have for him?

The therapist might work with Justin using the existential lens of meaninglessness, isolation, freedom, and anxiety. Justin has gotten into fights with his classmates at school and has been suspended. The existential therapist would seek to discover if Justin's fighting stemmed from his struggling with issues of meaninglessness, isolation, and belonging. What prompts him to get involved in fights at school? How meaningful is school to Justin? Ideally, how would Justin like for things to be at school?

The therapist would explore the extent to which Justin's school climate helps create a sense of existential isolation and anxiety within him. As it stands now, Justin is alienated from school. He feels isolated and disliked. His classmates make fun of him when he reads aloud in class. Except for art class, other kids perform better than he does in the school's core subjects. Does Justin have any meaningful relationships with his teachers or classmates at school? If so, what can be done to make such relationships stronger? If not, what steps might be taken to establish meaningful school relationships?

The therapist might use Frankl's technique of dereflection. As noted in the section on logotherapy, Frankl suggested that people have problems because they place too much emphasis on themselves. When we shift our attention to others, our own personal problems appear to be reduced. Service to others takes our minds off ourselves. Many schools have reported that service projects have a positive impact on students' attitudes in school and on improving their academic grades. Therefore, instead of focusing exclusively on changing Justin via therapeutic talk, it might be beneficial to have him volunteer his services in an area that has meaning for him. For instance, he might become involved in helping seniors with art (drawing or painting) at a community center.

Another approach would be for Justin to help younger students with art at his present school or at an after-school program. Justin's involvement in such a service project would have a number of positive effects. First, he would be able to use his art talent. Second, he would provide a much-needed service to someone less fortunate than himself. Third, Justin could take the focus off himself for a brief while and place it on helping others. Fourth, Justin would probably benefit by establishing positive relationships with those he helps, thereby giving his life a sense of purpose and meaning. Fifth, the court or the judge would most likely look favorably on Justin volunteering to do something for someone other than himself.

The existential approach to working with Justin would also indicate the importance of relationships for meaningful living. As Frankl put it, loving another gives life meaning. Justin needs a positive role model, a mentor—preferably a male to help fill the void of his missing father. To build on his art talent, the therapist might help Justin obtain a mentor in the area of art. The art mentor would provide structure to Justin's development of his creative abilities. Justin would be assigned definite art assignments or projects that he had to complete on a designated time schedule. In this manner, he would learn to take his art talent seriously and would recognize that it is something that has to be nourished and developed.

The existential therapist would also work with Justin to help him develop a sense of responsibility about the choices that he makes in life. Justin has not accepted personal responsibility for his actions. He blames others, including his mother and his classmates at school. Justin is demonstrating what Sartre would label *bad faith* by not accepting responsibility. The therapist confronts Justin about the ways in which he has attempted to avoid responsibility for his actions. For instance, he confronts Justin about being late several times for court appearances. Likewise, he confronts Justin about his lack of responsibility at school and at home. The therapist points out that even though Justin is quite young, he is still responsible for the choices that he makes in life.

(Continued)

(Continued)

The existential therapist takes the position that Justin needs to think about being and nonbeing. How would he like to be in the world? Does his current being-in-the-world match with where he would like to be? The therapist deals specifically with the different levels of Justin's existence, including his (1) Eigenwelt, the world of his relationship with his own potential and values; (2) Mitwelt, the world of his relationship with other people; and (3) Ümwelt, the world that forms his physiological and physical environment. The therapist engages Justin to begin his thinking about what he would like his legacy to be to the world.

SUMMARY

Existential psychotherapy deals with issues that are central to human existence. The existential approach to psychotherapy views people as creatures of continual change and transformation. This theoretical school explores meaning and value and learning to live authentically in accordance with one's own values. Authentic living means being true to oneself and honest about one's potential and limitations; it means living deliberately rather than by default. Existentialists view human nature as having the capacity for self-awareness and involving a search for meaning and purpose. Personal identity is conceptualized as the courage to be. The concept of bad faith refers to leading an inauthentic existence. An example of a statement that illustrates "bad faith" is "I'm this way because I grew up in an alcoholic family."

We are all basically alone. Therefore, we must give a sense of meaning to life, decide how we will live, and establish a relationship with ourselves and others. Clients' search for meaning in life leads to therapy questions such as "What is the meaning or purpose of your life?" "What do you want from life?" "What is the source for meaning in life?" Meaninglessness in life leads to emptiness and an existential vacuum. Existentialists contend that the major solution to meaninglessness is engagement. Finding meaning in life is a by-product of engagement, which is demonstrated by the client's commitment to creating, loving, working, and building. Engagement has the possibility of leading one toward a success rather than a failure identity.

The central issue in therapy is client freedom and responsibility. Existentialists use the concept of freedom to refer to the fact that we are the authors of our own world. We construct who we are by the daily decisions that we make. The bridge that connects wishing and action is decision. Existential psychotherapy is basically an experiential approach.

SUPPLEMENTAL AIDS
Discussion Questions

1. What experiences have you had with anxiety? What are the sources of your anxiety? Does any of your anxiety result from the realization that you are alone and that you will eventually die? How do you deal with anxiety in your life? Existentialists maintain that one can never quite eliminate anxiety in one's life. What does your anxiety mean for you? What is it telling you about yourself?

2. To what extent does your life have an existential vacuum—meaning a condition of emptiness and meaninglessness? List two reasons for your existential vacuum. Conversely, to what extent does your life have meaning and purpose? List two things that give your life meaning and purpose.

3. Existentialists maintain that you can understand others by observing what they strive

for in life. What are you striving for in life? What would you like your legacy to be? How would you like to be remembered for your brief stay on Earth?

4. In small groups of four to five people, have each person list on a sheet of paper what his or her dreams are for life. Then list two steps that you are taking to achieve your goals. What is moving you toward your life goals? What is holding you back from achieving your goals?

5. Responsibility is an important concept in existential therapy. To what degree do you accept responsibility for the direction of your life? Do you blame others for your success or your failure? What would it take for you to assume more responsibility for your life?

Glossary of Key Terms

bad faith   In existentialist philosophy, bad faith is an escape from anxiety and despair into a false or inauthentic way of existence.

daimonic   Defined by Rollo May (1969) as "any natural function which has the power to take over the whole person." Often, the daimonic winds up being those aspects of ourselves that we deny or repress; by repressing them, we give them power or strength. This concept is similar to Jung's idea of the shadow.

Dasein   A conscious and unconscious sense of oneself as a distinct and autonomous person existing in a physical and psychological world. A strong sense of being-in-the-world (Dasein) is important for the development of a healthy personality.

dereflection   A technique developed by Frankl involving counteracting obsessive ideation or hyperreflection by getting the person to stop thinking about the problem.

Eigenwelt   One of three German terms, along with Ümwelt and Mitwelt, often used together in existential theory to represent different aspects of our existential reality. Eigenwelt refers to our relationship with our self or our *own-world*.

existential anxiety   Takes place as a result of being confronted with the four givens of existence: death, freedom, existential isolation, and meaninglessness. A person experiences existential anxiety when he or she experiences apprehension caused by a threat to some value deemed critical to the existence of one's being. Because death is an inevitable fact of living, we all experience a certain amount of anxiety as a result of being human.

existential givens   Existential realities or basic truths about existence. For instance, death is an existential given in that all people die. Yalom (1980) identified the four main existential givens as (1) death, (2) isolation (or relationship, the given that we are social creatures), (3) freedom, and (4) meaninglessness (or meaning).

existential guilt   Guilt that results from the impossibility of fulfilling all of our innate potentials.

existential vacuum   A condition of emptiness and hollowness that comes from meaninglessness in life.

existentialism   A philosophical and therapeutic movement emphasizing individual responsibility for creating one's ways of thinking, feeling, and behaving.

intentionality   The ability of people to have a conscious and unconscious sense of purpose and to behave with purpose.

logotherapy   Viktor Frankl's approach to psychotherapy that highlights one's search for meaning. This approach challenges clients to search for meaning in life.

Mitwelt   One of three German terms, along with Ümwelt and Eigenwelt, often used together in existential theory to represent different aspects of our existential reality. Mitwelt refers to the world of fellow people or relational context.

neurotic anxiety Involves feelings of despair and anxiety that come from inauthentic living, a failure to make choices, and the avoidance of responsibility.

Ümwelt One of three German terms, along with Mitwelt and Eigenwelt, often used together in existential theory to represent different aspects of our existential reality. Ümwelt refers to the *world-around* or our environment, particularly our biological environment (as opposed to the people in our environment, which is Mitwelt). It can also be thought of as referring to being-in-the-world.

will Our conscious capacity to move toward our self-selected goals. It represents part of our intentionality.

Website Materials

Additional exercises, journals, annotated bibliography, and more are available on the open-access website at https://study.sagepub.com/jonessmith2e.

CHAPTER 8

Person-Centered Therapy

Roger Ressmeyer/Corbis.

Carl Rogers

In my early professional years I was asking the question: How can I treat, or cure, or change this person? Now I would phrase the question in this way: How can I provide a relationship which this person may use for his own personal growth?

A second characteristic of the process which for me is the good life, is that it involves an increasing tendency to live fully in each moment. I believe it would be evident that for the person who was fully open to his new experience, *completely without defensiveness, each moment would be new.*

My garden supplies the same intriguing question I have been trying to meet all my professional life: What are the effective conditions for growth?

—Carl Rogers

BRIEF OVERVIEW

Of all the humanist theorists, Carl Rogers is the most dominant therapist (Schneider et al., 2001). In fact, Rogers has been praised as the most influential psychotherapist in American history. He developed the nondirective, client-centered, and **person-centered approach** to psychotherapy. Rogers proposed that within each of us is a self-actualizing tendency to develop our potentials.

Prior to his arrival on the psychotherapy scene, therapy was largely directive, consisting of diagnoses and interpretations of clients' behavior. The therapist was the unmistakable authority in the therapy relationship who diagnosed and interpreted even the most difficult client problems, without very much input from the client. Like a breath of fresh air, Rogers came on the scene determined to change this authority-ridden state of affairs in psychotherapy. Rogers advocated for a psychotherapy treatment without couches and without dream interpretations. He wrote books (Rogers, 1951, 1961) advocating that clients be treated as coequals with the therapist, and he talked passionately about the "necessary and sufficient conditions" of therapy that therapists should provide to their clients (Rogers, 1957).

Client-centered therapy caught on like wildfire because of its emphasis on clients' growth potential, their self-actualizing tendency, and their ability to heal themselves if certain conditions were provided in therapy. Rogers's concepts permeated American culture. The broad American public began talking about "getting in touch with their feelings," "tuning into themselves," and "letting it all hang out." Rogers's influence has been profound on counseling and psychotherapy. Currently, most therapies have incorporated some aspect of the positive, growth-oriented humanistic perspective on clients (Schneider et al., 2001).

Most of the information on Rogers's life has been taken from Howard Kirschenbaum and Valerie Henderson's book *The Carl Rogers Reader* (1989b) and from Carl Rogers's own statements about his upbringing and professional life in an article that explained how his theory of client-centered therapy developed (see Rogers, 1973). Several websites also have included a historical sketch of Rogers (www.nrogers.com/carlrogersbio.html and www.nrogers.com [Carl Rogers: A Daughter's Tribute]). The definitive biography on Carl Rogers is Howard Kirschenbaum's (2007) *The Life and Work of Carl Rogers*, which can be found at the following link: http://howardkirschenbaum.com.

MAJOR CONTRIBUTOR: CARL ROGERS (1902–1987)

Carl Ransom Rogers was born in Oak Park, Illinois, the fourth of six children. His father was a successful civil engineer, and his mother was a devout Christian and housewife. Rogers has described his early upbringing as one characterized by close family ties, a very strict religious atmosphere, and a strong emphasis on the value of hard work. Because he could already read before kindergarten, his education began in the second grade.

Rogers has written that he was a "pretty solitary boy" growing up. At age 12, his father bought a farm to keep his children from the temptations of suburban life. Rogers stated,

> When I was twelve my parents bought a farm and we made our home there. . . . My father was determined to operate his new farm on a scientific basis . . . my brothers and I . . . reared from infancy lambs. I became a student of scientific agriculture, and have only realized in recent years what a fundamental feeling for science I gained in that way. . . . I started in college at Wisconsin in the field of agriculture. (Kirschenbaum & Henderson, 1989a, p. 8)

Rogers grew up isolated, independent, and self-disciplined. During his later professional career, Rogers stated that his upbringing had caused him to feel constricted in his feelings toward others (Cain, 2002). Rogers (1973) has described his early years as follows:

> I knew my parents loved me, but it would never have occurred to me to share with them any of my personal or private thoughts or feelings because I knew these would have been judged and found wanting. . . . I could sum up these boyhood years by saying that anything I would today regard as a close and communicative interpersonal relationship with another was completely lacking during that period. My attitude toward others outside the home was characterized by the distance and the aloofness which I had taken over from my parents. I attended the same elementary school for seven years. From this point on, until I finished graduate work, I never attended any school for longer than two years, a fact which undoubtedly had its effects on me. Beginning with high school, I believe my hunger for companionship came a little more into my awareness. But any satisfaction of that hunger was blocked first by the already mentioned attitudes of my parents, and second by circumstances. (pp. 3–4)

Although Rogers initially went to the University of Wisconsin majoring in agriculture, he later switched to the study of religion and the ministry. A key development for Rogers took place when he was selected as one of 10 students to go to Beijing for the "World Student Christian Federation Conference" for 6 months. This experience led him to understand that there were great differences in religious doctrines, and he began to question the doctrines of his upbringing. Rogers earned a B.A. in history from the University of Wisconsin in 1924.

Following his graduation from the University of Wisconsin, Rogers married a childhood sweetheart, Helen Elliott, whom Rogers has described as the love of his life. Helen was a friend dating back to second grade. Also during this same year, Rogers enrolled in liberal Union Theological Seminary in New York City. During the summer of 1925, Rogers served as a visiting pastor in Dorset, Vermont. At Union Theological Seminary, a group of fellow students formed their own seminar in which they challenged the ideas presented to them at the seminary. As a result, Rogers and some of his classmates talked themselves out of religious work. As a consequence, Rogers enrolled in the clinical psychology program at Teachers College, Columbia University. On March 17, 1926, Rogers's son, David Elliott Rogers, was born.

On June 1, 1927, Rogers earned his M.A. degree from Columbia University, and in 1928, he accepted a position as a psychologist in the Child Study Department of the Society for the Prevention of Cruelty to Children in Rochester, New York. His starting salary was only $2,900, which was low even for that time in American history. On October 9, 1928, his daughter, Natalie Rogers, was born. By 1930, he had become the director of the department. In 1931, he received his Ph.D. degree from Columbia University. From 1928 to 1939, Rogers continued to work at the Rochester children's clinic, where he began to question the effectiveness of the prevailing directive, or "the therapist knows best" approach to psychotherapy. During this time, he was influenced by Otto Rank, one of Freud's former disciples.

In 1936, Rank published *Will Therapy*, which stated that each person is born with a will to fulfill each potential (Rank, 1936/1978). When people

express their will freely, they develop in a healthy manner. Suppressing one's will causes problems. Rank supported a more egalitarian relationship between the client and the therapist. Clearly, Rogers borrowed from Rank's emphasis on the here-and-now and the egalitarian client–therapist relationship. In fact, Rogers stated that he became infected by Rankian ideas.

From 1935 to 1940, Rogers lectured at the University of Rochester. According to him, the years in Rochester were valuable ones. Rogers moved on. From Rochester, he accepted an academic position as professor of psychology at Ohio State University in 1940.

By 1942, he published his second book, *Counseling and Psychotherapy: Newer Concepts in Practice*. This book contained his formal statement of his theoretical approach called nondirective counseling or psychotherapy. From Ohio State University, Rogers was to accept several appointments. In 1945, he went to the University of Chicago, where he accepted a position as professor of psychology and executive secretary of the University Counseling Center. From 1945 to 1957, thousands of students took his courses and spread his ideas about therapy. Sometimes students throughout the world came to study with him. While at Chicago, he wrote a major book *Client-Centered Therapy: Its Current Practice, Implications and Theory* (1951).

Toward the end of 1957, Rogers was appointed professor of psychology and of psychiatry at the University of Wisconsin, where he directed a study on clients hospitalized in a mental hospital. From this experience, he published *The Therapeutic Relationship and Its Impact: A Study of Psychotherapy With Schizophrenics* (Rogers, Gendlin, Kiesler, & Truax, 1967). Rogers said that he left the University of Wisconsin because he became disillusioned with the academic infighting (Kirschenbaum & Henderson, 1989a).

During the 1960s, Rogers became a leader in the **humanistic psychology** movement. One of his more famous books, *On Becoming a Person*, was published in 1961. This book attracted worldwide attention, and the following year, he collaborated with people such as Abraham Maslow, Virginia

Satir, Rollo May, and Charlotte Buhler to establish the Association for Humanistic Psychology. In 1964, Rogers left academia again and joined the staff of the Western Behavioral Studies Institute in La Jolla, Southern California. Just 4 years later, he and several associates established The Center for Studies of the Person, also located in La Jolla.

Subsequently, Rogers became interested in the group movement, and he extended his theory to the basic encounter group. In 1970, he published *Carl Rogers on Encounter Groups*. During this same time, Rogers extended his theory to education, and he published *Freedom to Learn* (1969). This book demonstrated how the "core conditions" for creating a good therapy relationship could be applied to education. These publications were followed by *Becoming Partners: Marriage and Its Alternatives* (1972) and *Carl Rogers on Personal Power: Inner Strength and Its Revolutionary Impact* (1977). During the 1970s, Rogers conducted person-centered workshops in Europe, South America, and Japan.

Rogers had an outstanding career as a theorist and a psychotherapist. He taught at some of the most prestigious universities in this nation. In 1956, he was among three psychologists awarded the first Distinguished Scientific Awards of the American Psychological Association (APA). He had been president of the APA (1946) and a fellow of several APA divisions.

Rogers was nominated for the Nobel Peace Prize because of his efforts to reduce racial conflict. He had facilitated a workshop for 50 leading figures—leaders, politicians, academics, and others from 17 nations—in Rust, Austria, and the topic was "The Central America Challenge." The workshop, called The Rust Peace Workshop, took place in 1985. Rogers continued his efforts by holding similar sessions in other troubled areas, such as Northern Ireland and South Africa.

Despite advancing age, Rogers continued to work. In 1987, at age 85, he fell and broke a hip. Although his hip operation was successful, he died a few days later of a heart attack on February 4, 1987 (Cain, 1987). Perhaps more so than any other therapist, Rogers has had a major impact on the therapeutic relationship across a number of theoretical approaches. Many of his basic tenets about what constitutes a good therapeutic relationship have become a part of generally accepted sound counseling. His necessary and sufficient conditions for therapy have been incorporated into the common factor approach to therapy. Throughout the years, Rogers's client-centered approach to counseling has gradually become known as *person-centered therapy*, and this term is used throughout this chapter to indicate the shift in how Rogers changed the terminology to refer to his work.

KEY CONCEPTS

View of Human Nature

Rogers's (1957) view of human nature is that people are basically good, and they are characteristically "positive, forward-moving, constructive, realistic, and trustworthy." Moreover, each one of us is aware, inner directed, and moving toward **self-actualization** from the date we are born onward. Rogers (1959) maintained that human infants have the following characteristics:

- Whatever an infant perceives becomes that infant's reality. An infant's perception is an internal process about which only he or she can be aware.
- All infants are born with a self-actualizing tendency that is satisfied by their subsequent goal-directed behavior.
- An infant's interaction with the environment is an organized whole, and everything he or she does is interrelated.
- An infant's experiences may be viewed as positive or negative depending on the extent to which they enhance his or her actualization tendency.
- Infants maintain experiences that are actualizing, and they avoid those that are not.

Rogers (1951) proposed that self-actualization is the most prevalent and motivating drive of human existence. He stated, "The organism has one basic tendency and striving—to actualize, maintain, and enhance the experiencing organism"

(p. 487). Rogers viewed individuals from a phenomenological perspective, which means what is important is individuals' perceptions of reality rather than objective reality itself. Although people are basically good, they can become aggressive and antisocial if their basic needs are threatened or frustrated. Rogers's positive view of human nature clashed with Freudian conceptions of id-dominated people.

Theory of Personality

Rogers's theory of personality revolves around several core concepts: (a) the organism, (b) the organism's phenomenal field, and (c) the self. **Organism** refers to the total individual, including his or her physical as well as psychological well-being. The second aspect of his theory, the **phenomenal field**, is the private world of each individual that becomes his or her source of internal reference for viewing life. It constitutes everything that the individual experiences, regardless of whether the individual consciously symbolizes experiences into awareness. Parts of our phenomenal field may be summoned into consciousness as it becomes associated with the satisfaction of certain needs we have established. Our phenomenal field constitutes our perception of reality. It is the perception of reality, rather than reality itself, that is of great importance in person-centered counseling. Rogers stated that the only reality he could possibly know was the world as he perceived and experienced it at any given moment.

Rogers (1951) points out that each person exists and reacts in a "continuing changing world of experience of which he or she is the center" (p. 483). As we react within our phenomenal field, we do so as an organized whole. By responding as an organized whole, Rogers means "that the organism is at all times a total system, in which alteration of any part may produce changes in another part" (p. 484). He maintains that an individual's personality and behavior are determined by the goal of actualization. Goal directedness is, therefore, the effort to satisfy our needs as experienced in our phenomenal field.

Each of us engages in what Rogers (1959) calls an **organismic valuing process**. The organismic valuing process is critical to our self-development. From interactions with others and from the total phenomenal field of experience, the infant gradually begins to differentiate a portion called the self. The **self-concept** is defined as the infant's differentiated elements of the experiential field that have the characteristics of the "I" or "me." As an infant becomes aware of a self, he or she develops a need for **positive regard** from others. Rogers maintains that there is a basic craving for affection within each of us, and he labeled this craving as a need for positive regard. To a large extent, Rogers conceptualized love from others as a learned need. As a result of a child's craving for affection, he or she now has two sources from which to evaluate his or her behavior: (1) an innate organismic valuing process and (2) the standards, feelings, and thoughts of others regarding the person.

In all societies, people learn to desire the positive regard of others. Essentially, the need for positive regard is the need to be valued, to be accepted, and to be loved. We all need positive regard from others to survive and to develop healthy personalities. From our interactions with others in the environment, we internalize certain values into our self-structure. This internalization of the values of others resembles Freud's notion of the superego. We learn what to do as well as what not to do to remain in the good graces of those dearest to us.

According to Rogers, all experiences that occur in our lives do not automatically become a part of our self-structure. We may respond by (a) ignoring some experiences because they do not appear to have any relationship to our perceived self-structure,

(b) denying them symbolization into awareness, or (c) distorting their symbolization because they seem to be inconsistent with our self-structure. When such distortions take place, there is incongruity between self and experience, or psychological maladjustment.

Our own self-regard also forms part of our self-structure. Rogers used the term *self-regard* almost interchangeably with *self-esteem*. Our self-regard is linked to the positive regard that others evidence toward us. Children can begin liking or disliking themselves based on whether they have or have not received positive regard from their parents and significant others. "My parents love me; therefore, I am valuable." "My parents always criticize; therefore, I am nobody, nothing." Self-regard is learned. It leads to children viewing themselves and their behavior in the same way that their parents or significant others saw them.

Self-regard can be distinguished from positive regard, even though the two are related. **Self-regard** refers to our own feelings about ourselves. Yet our self-regard does not just develop without outside influences. For a healthy self to emerge, we need positive regard—love, warmth, care, respect, and acceptance. When the significant people in our lives provide us with positive regard, our self-regard or self-esteem increases. At times, we may be more able to obtain the positive regard from others than we can from our own positive self-regard. Securing other people's approval is only part of the battle. According to Rogers, gaining one's own self-regard is the goal we really wish most to achieve. To paraphrase Mark Twain, we can secure other people's approval if we do right and try hard, but our own good opinion of ourselves is worth a hundred of it.

Children develop best if they receive unconditional positive regard from their parents and significant others. **Unconditional positive regard** takes place when parents and significant others accept and love a person for who he or she is. For instance, a parent does not withdraw his or her positive regard for a child if the child does something wrong. "I still love you, even though you broke my favorite piece of china." When individuals experience unconditional positive regard, they are more likely to feel free to try things out and to make mistakes, because they are not afraid of losing a significant person's positive regard for them. The unconditional positive regard of significant others helps people move toward self-actualization.

In contrast, **conditional positive regard** is where positive regard, praise and approval, depend on a person behaving in ways that others think is correct. A person is not loved for who he or she is but rather on condition that he or she behaves only in ways approved by the others, usually one's parents. Individuals who have extreme approval-seeking behavior are most likely those who experienced only conditional positive regard as a child.

Usually, positive regard or love from others comes when we do things that please them. Our parents and others put conditions on their love for us. As a result, most people receive primarily conditional positive regard from their parents, teachers, and friends. If we do not receive unconditional positive regard from significant others, we develop what Rogers called conditions of worth. **Conditions of worth** are established when our parents attach conditions under which they will love us. For instance, our parents love us if we achieve good grades in school or clean our rooms on a regular basis. If we experience only unconditional positive regard from our parents and significant others (friends, peers, teachers, etc.), then we develop our own positive self-regard. We experience what therapists would label positive mental health development.

In contrast, when our parents and significant others place conditions of worth on us, we tend to not to love ourselves or not to have positive self-regard for ourselves unless we meet their specified conditions. When our parents raise us with conditions of worth, we learn to discriminate the conditions under which we will or will not get their love or positive regard. We tend to spend a great deal of time trying to compromise with our parents' conditions for loving us and what we really want to do. For instance, a high school student walked into his middle-class, White suburban school and blew his head off with a shotgun. He had become tired of living up to his parents' expectations of him. Because his grades were a bit lower than what his parents thought would get him into college, they denied him the right to continue working as a volunteer for a local fire company—something that gave him a sense of purpose and made his life meaningful. The son's suicide was an extreme measure. Yet this case demonstrates what can happen when parents substitute their own organismic valuing process for those of their children.

We are governed by others' conditions of worth when we choose to act based on what others feel rather than what we feel. Thus, conditions of worth form a second regulatory system of behavior. If the conditions of worth that we have learned coincide with our organismic valuing system, we feel a sense of congruence, and healthy behavior is likely to develop. Most of the time, however, this situation does not occur; the two regulatory systems tend to be in conflict, paving the way for maladjustment.

Theory of Healthy Psychological Development

Rogers (1961) described healthy psychological development in terms of the fully functioning person. The **fully functioning person** displays no defensiveness and has established no conditions of worth; he or she experiences unconditional positive regard from key significant others. Moreover, this person experiences a state of congruency between his or her own concept of self and his or her life experiences. The ideal fully functioning person does not exist. Some clients can be observed as moving toward this goal in therapy. Some primary characteristics of the fully functioning person are the following:

1. *Openness to experience:* Having gained positive regard from significant others and positive self-regard, fully functioning individuals are relatively free from defensiveness and threat. They are open to all their experiences, and stimuli from the environment are received and processed by the nervous system without selectivity or distortion. They have not erected barriers or inhibitions to prevent the full experiencing of whatever is present in their phenomenal field.

2. *Organismic trusting:* The organismic valuing process is an ongoing process in which we rely primarily on evidence of our own senses for making value judgments about our lives (Raskin & Rogers, 2005). We permit ourselves to be guided by the organismic valuing process. We should trust ourselves, do what feels right, and do what comes naturally. Organismic trusting means you are in contact with your self-actualizing tendency. The organismic valuing process is in direct contrast to having a fixed system of introjected values characterized by "oughts" and "shoulds" and by what is supposed to be right or wrong.

3. *Behavior is constructive and trustworthy:* You do not have to worry about trusting the fully functioning person because his or her true, positive nature emerges.

4. *Experiential inner freedom:* This freedom is an attitude or realization of our ability to think our own thoughts and live our own lives, choosing what we want to be and being responsible for ourselves.

5. *Creativity:* A fully functioning person will feel obliged by his or her nature to contribute to the actualization of others and to life itself. A number of ways can be used to demonstrate creativity—including in the arts or sciences, through social concern and parental love, or by doing one's best in life.

Theory of Maladaptive Behavior or Psychopathology

Under Rogers's theory, one of the fundamental causes of maladjustment is the incongruency between one's self-concept and one's experiences. Because this state of inconsistency may be unconscious, an individual may experience tension and free-floating anxiety. Experiences perceived as threatening are denied into awareness. In an attempt to protect themselves from an onslaught of threatening emotions or ideas, individuals armor themselves so strongly that they create more rigid self-structure. They tend to shy away from new experiences and to enclose themselves in a self-made prison of fear.

Gross incongruence of self, meaning the existence of a large difference between the perceived self and the actual experience, indicates maladjustment. During such times, a person feels that he or she has very few, if any, conditions of worth or self-regard. In an effort to regain a sense of balance and congruence with the self, the maladjusted person perceives experiences selectively. This kind of selective perception fosters enactment of subception. Rogers (1951) described **subception** as a defensive reaction that prevents incongruent material from coming into consciousness. Where the inconsistent experience is strong, defense is unsuccessful, anxiety develops, and disorganized or inconsistent behavior takes place. Personality disorganization is now in process.

Human beings are characterized by a tendency to move from a state of maladjustment toward psychological adjustment. Good interpersonal relationships propel us toward adjustment. Personality reintegration occurs when others communicate unconditional positive regard and empathic understanding to us. Such communications strengthen our unconditional self-regard. The defensive process previously described is now capable of being reversed. Previously denied or distorted experiences are symbolized into awareness and incorporated into the self-concept. The person becomes more congruent; positive regard for others is increased, and the individual's organismic valuing process becomes the basis for regulating behavior.

THE THERAPEUTIC PROCESS

Rogers's approach to counseling has been labeled nondirective, self theory, client-centered therapy, and person-centered therapy. Each of these designations reflects the evolution of his theory. Therapy is viewed as a process of helping people release already existing positive forces. It is an attempt to make a person more self-directive. Person-centered therapy is founded on two basic hypotheses: (1) Each person has the capacity to understand the circumstances that cause unhappiness and to reorganize his or her life accordingly, and (2) a person's ability to deal with these circumstances is enhanced if the therapist establishes a warm, accepting, and understanding relationship (Rogers, 1951). Thus, from Rogers's point of view, the most important question a therapist can ask is, "How can I establish a relationship that will facilitate the personal growth of my client?" Once a facilitative relationship has been established, the client is in a better position to reorganize self-structure in accordance with reality and his or her own needs.

> ### Inner Reflections
>
> APA has stated that instead of spending a great deal of time teaching therapists various techniques, therapy training programs should spend time teaching trainees how to establish a therapeutic relationship.
>
> On a scale of 1 (*low*) to 10 (*high*), rate your ability to establish a relationship with other people.
>
> How do you go about establishing a relationship with another human being? What do you do?

The Therapeutic Relationship

To establish a therapeutic relationship, Rogers (1957) proposed that certain conditions of therapy must exist. If the counselor establishes and maintains these conditions, then successful therapy stands a greater chance of taking place. Rogers listed six necessary and sufficient conditions of therapy. He has stated, "I launch myself into the therapeutic relationship having a hypothesis, or a faith, that my liking, my confidence, and my understanding of the other person's inner world, will lead to a significant process of becoming" (Rogers, 1951, p. 267). Expanding on his famous "necessary and sufficient conditions" for therapy, Rogers (1961) has stated, "If I can provide a certain type of relationship, the other person will discover within himself or herself the capacity to use that relationship for growth and change, and personal development will occur" (p. 33).

1. *Psychological contact:* The first condition requires that the two people should be in a state of psychological contact. In his early writings, Rogers used the word *relationship* to express the notion of psychological contact between two people. Being in a state of psychological contact means that the client and the counselor see their experience together as a relationship.

2. *Incongruent client:* The second condition is that the client be incongruent. The state of incongruency on the part of the client refers to the client's prior unsuccessful attempts to cope with life's problems. Rogers (1961) has described this condition: "He is, in short, faced with a problem with which he has tried to cope, and found himself unsuccessful" (p. 282).

3. *Therapist congruency:* The third condition is that the therapist should be in a state of congruence. Facades and role-playing on the counselor's part tend to inhibit learning. The congruent therapist is one who is in touch with what he or she is experiencing. The congruent counselor can also communicate these feelings to the client when they are appropriate to the encounter. Rogers asserts that unless the therapist is genuine, the client will find it difficult to be himself or herself in the counseling relationship.

4. *Unconditional positive regard:* Unconditional positive regard is the fourth necessary condition for therapy. Unconditional positive regard means that the therapist experiences a warm, positive, acceptant attitude toward the client. Seeing each client as a separate entity, the counselor attaches no strings to the acceptance of the client. It is the therapist's acceptance of the client that promotes the client's acceptance of self. Rogers (1986) has stated,

> When the therapist is experiencing a positive, non-judgmental, acceptant attitude toward whatever the client *is* at that moment, therapeutic movement or change is more likely. It involves the therapist's willingness for the client to *be* whatever immediate feeling is going on—confusion, resentment, fear, anger, courage, love or pride. . . . When the therapist prizes the client in a total rather than a conditional way, forward movement is likely. (p. 198)

5. *Therapist empathy:* The fifth important condition necessary for the success of the relationship is therapist empathy. Rogers (1961) defined **empathy** as the counselor's ability to sense the client's private world as if it were his or her own but without ever losing the "as if" quality. The therapist demonstrates an interest in appreciating the client's world and offers such understanding with a willingness to stand corrected. According to Raskin and Rogers (2005),

> Person-centered therapists vary in their views of the empathic understanding process. Some aim to convey an understanding of just what the client wishes to communicate. For Rogers, it felt right not only to clarify meanings of which the client was aware, but also those just below the level of awareness. Rogers was especially passionate about empathy's not being exemplified by a technique such as "reflection of feeling," but by the therapist's sensitive immersion in the client's world of experience. (p. 145)

6. *Communication of empathy:* The final condition for therapy is that the client should recognize the therapist's congruence, acceptance, and empathy. Without perception of these qualities, the client will not feel free or believe that he or she is in a nonthreatening relationship. It is part of the therapist's responsibility to make sure that his or her intended behavior is perceived accurately.

Goals of Therapy

Rogers (1977) asserted that the goal of therapy is not simply to solve clients' presenting problems but rather to assist clients in their growth process so that they have a better chance of coping not only with current problems but also with potential future problems. The therapeutic goal that runs through much of person-centered counseling is to help the client become a more fully functioning person. The therapist does not choose specific goals for the client, but rather, the client is self-directing and chooses his or her own goals. Person-centered therapy goals include raising the consciousness of clients and using the therapeutic relationship to release the client's intense expression of feelings, thereby producing corrective emotional experiences for him or her.

The goals of person-centered counseling are to focus on the client as a person and not on his or her problem. A primary goal of person-centered therapy is to help a client become the self that he or she truly wants to be. The goals of person-centered therapy can be conceptualized as a two-step process: (1) movement away from the self that one is not and (2) movement toward one's true self. Initially, person-centered therapy seeks to help clients give up self-concealment and the masks they wear so that gradually they might dismantle their false selves. The therapist works to help clients free themselves from the "oughts" and "shoulds" that keep them living out the expectations of others, all the while denying themselves the right to choose and live out their best lives.

Many of the desired changes in person-centered therapy have been expressed in terms of the goals of counseling. The major behavioral change sought is a change in the person's self-concept. As this occurs, the client is inclined to become more receptive of others and more open to experiences and feelings both inside and outside the therapy relationship. Becoming more self-confident and self-directive, the individual gradually moves toward becoming the type of person he or she would like to be. Often, this will bring about a more realistic adoption of goals, a greater maturity in behavior, more flexibility in one's perception of reality, and a more subjective experience of the self in the present rather than in the past.

Person-centered therapy is designed partly to eliminate clients' unhealthy need to please others. Sometimes we live our entire lives trying to please our parents, mates, children, and colleagues. The self becomes lost when we focus on pleasing others rather than on being true to ourselves. This goal is not meant to suggest that person-centered therapy wants fully functioning clients to be selfish. Although clients may do things to please others, they will not do so at the expense of losing the core of who they are. Healthy people remain true to themselves.

> ### Inner Reflections
>
> Do you believe that you can give unconditional positive regard to most clients?
>
> Are there any clients for whom you would find it difficult to show unconditional positive regard?
>
> Is there anyone in your life to whom you give unconditional positive regard?

> ### Inner Reflections
>
> Can you see yourself as a person-centered therapist? Why or why not?
>
> What do you find most attractive and least attractive about the role of a person-centered therapist?

Role of the Therapist

The essential role of the person-centered therapist is in *being, not doing*, and hence, his or her major task is to provide a therapeutic climate of safety and trust that will motivate clients to reintegrate their self-actualizing and self-valuing processing (McLeod & McLeod, 1993). The therapist produces a climate of trust by providing the six necessary and sufficient conditions for therapy. Most important among these six conditions is what is called the therapeutic triad—of **accurate** empathic understanding, congruence, and unconditional positive regard. It is the clinician's belief in the client's inner resources that establishes a therapeutic climate for growth (Bozarth, Zimring, & Tausch, 2002).

Person-centered therapists maintain that qualities associated with the therapeutic triad are deeply rooted in the therapist's being (Levant & Shlien, 1984). Although such qualities can be learned as counseling skills during graduate training, they must come from a counselor's very being if they are to be used effectively. Person-centered counselors rarely give advice, interpret, or focus on transference relationships.

Rogerian, person-centered therapy appears to be much simpler and easier than it actually is in real practice. Early in his career, Rogers quoted a beginning therapist who complained about the illusion of simplicity (Kirschenbaum & Henderson, 1989b). To paraphrase the student, it all appears so easy until you really try to do it. Then, as you are faced with a real-life client, you find out how difficult it is not to interpret, not to take charge, not to dominate the therapy proceedings with advice.

Brodley (1997) asserts that therapists do not try to regulate or control the client. He states, "In more specific terms the client-centered therapist does not intend to diagnose, create treatment plans, strategize, employ treatment techniques, or take responsibility for the client in any way" (p. 25).

Person-centered therapists generally do not take a history; do not evaluate the client's ideas, feelings, or plans; avoid making deep interpretations of clients' behavior; and do not decide for the client the frequency of therapy visits. The person-centered therapist is nonauthoritarian and seldom does the therapist engage in formal assessment of the client's problems. Therapy's emphasis should not be on the therapist's brilliance in making interpretations but rather on the client's worldview and process of self-discovery. The therapist may restate or reflect what the client is saying so that the client can correct and clarify the therapist's understanding. Gendlin (1988) has provided insight into Rogers's views on interpretation by stating,

> Rogers eliminated all interpretation. Instead, he checked his understanding out loud, trying to grasp exactly what the patient wished to convey. When he did that, he discovered something: The patient would usually correct the first attempt. The second would be closer, but even so, the patient might refine it. Rogers would take in each correction until the patient indicated, "Yes, that's how it is. That's what I feel." Then there would be a characteristic silence. During such a silence, after something is fully received, the next thing comes in the client. Very often it is—something deeper.
>
> Rogers discovered that a self-propelled process arises from inside. When each thing is received utterly as intended, it makes new space inside. Then the steps go deeper and deeper. (p. 127)

The therapist's function is to be present and accessible to clients and to focus on their immediate experience in therapy. The therapist meets clients on a moment-to-moment experiential basis. Rogers believed that self-exploration, if conducted honestly, leads ultimately to a restructuring of the self. The self participates in its own exploration, its own healing. Changes in clients' self-discovery are experienced as joyful self-discovery—a letting go process, rather than a forcing of something to happen in therapy.

One common misperception of person-centered counseling is that the clinician is supposed to adopt a passive, laissez-faire attitude in counseling—stay out of the client's way and let the counseling session just evolve. Rogers declared that a laissez-faire approach to counseling comes across to the client as uncaring and rejecting because it does not convey an atmosphere of unconditional positive regard for the client. He suggested that clients are inclined to leave the therapist who takes a laissez-faire attitude because they become disappointed in their failure to receive help and disgusted with the counselor for having little to offer.

Role of the Client

Rogers did not call the people who came for counseling "patients" because this designation suggested an involuntary relationship that resembled the situation of a person who must go to a hospital (Cain, 1990). Rogers preferred the term *client* because a client is a person who voluntarily seeks out a therapeutic relationship. Near the end of his life, Rogers chose an even less restrictive term. He called people who came for help "persons," and the therapy that was previously called client centered became known as person-centered therapy (Cain, 1990).

The person-centered counselor views people who come to therapy as having problems of living rather than mental disorders. Rogers believed that everybody has the same problem—the problem of finding the right path in life, of living according to one's self-actualizing tendency. Below the level of the presenting problem, each client is asking, "Who am I, really? How can I get in touch with my real self, beneath all my surface behavior? How can I become myself?"

Clients arrive in counseling in a state of **incongruence** or with a discrepancy between their self-perception and their life experience. In person-centered counseling, clients learn that they are responsible for themselves in the therapeutic relationship and that they can learn to become themselves by using the therapeutic relationship to gain self-understanding. As the therapist provides a supportive climate, clients' self-healing capacities are activated. As clients let go of their masks and facades, they ignite the healing process.

Rogers (1951) believed that a client had the capacity to deal with any material that came forth in therapy. He labeled this belief the self-actualization process. According to him, "the counselor chooses to act consistently upon the hypothesis that the individual has a sufficient capacity to deal constructively with all those aspects of his life that can potentially come into conscious awareness" (p. 22). Likewise, Tallman and Bohart (1999) have asserted, "Clients then are the 'magicians' with the special healing powers. Therapists set the stage and serve as assistants who provide the conditions under which this magic can operate" (p. 95).

Rogers (1951) reported a consistent pattern in successful therapeutic change. Clients go through a phase of getting behind the mask or the persona that they present to the world. Another sign of successful therapy takes place when clients move toward appreciating life as a process rather than as a thing or an end product. As clients continue in therapy, they become "tolerant of their own complexity" and more receptive to change. They become more open to experience, including those elements of their personality that they might have previously hidden from public view. They discover that letting go of their false selves is nothing to be feared. In fact, it sets the stage for positive growth. As Rogers (1951) has stated,

> Clients are not disturbed to find they are not the same from day to day, that they do not always hold the same feelings toward a given experience or person, that they are not always consistent. They are in flux, and seem more content to continue in this flowing current. (p. 171)

Therapy Techniques

Rogers did not write very much about counseling techniques. Instead, he chose to emphasize therapeutic conditions. Despite this observation, it is very clear that Rogers did use counseling techniques, as evidenced by many of his published videotapes. One such therapy technique Rogers used is that of active listening.

Rogerian Active Listening

Active listening takes place when we "listen for meaning." The listener says very little but conveys empathy, acceptance, and **genuineness**. The listener only speaks to see if a statement has been correctly heard and understood. Rogers was excellent at active listening. He communicated warmth usually by smiling at the client. Active listening facilitates the therapy relationship. For one thing, the counselor's silence forces the client to talk. Also, counselor silence helps focus therapeutic responsibility on the client.

One of the most difficult tasks for beginning therapists to master is learning how to remain silent when the client wants to talk. In the training of therapists, I have found that it has been necessary to teach toleration of client silence without feeling embarrassed or uneasy. Beginning therapists have a tendency to interrupt a client's speaking because a minute of client silence seems so very long.

Active listening is hard work. There are important nonverbal dimensions of active listening that include the counselor's eye contact, body language, vocal tone and speech rate, and physical space. Cultural groups vary in their comfortableness with certain attending behavior. For instance, when Europeans listen to a person, direct eye contact is usually displayed. Some Asian and African American groups may feel uncomfortable with the counselors' persistent eye contact when listening.

Reflection of Feeling

Person-centered therapists demonstrate empathy and **warmth** toward clients when they use the **reflection** of feeling therapy technique. A reflection of feeling statement provides a mirroring of the feeling or emotion present in a client's statements. Reflecting feelings involves expressing in the therapist's words the client's essential feelings that were either stated or implied. One purpose of reflecting clients' feelings is to place the emphasis on feelings rather than on content and to help clients own their feelings. Usually, therapists begin a reflecting statement with the words "you feel" as an attempt to get a client to own a feeling. The steps in reflection of feeling are to ascertain what feeling the client is expressing, to describe this feeling clearly to the client, to observe the effect of the reflecting statement on the client, and to determine by the reactions of the client if the reflection was facilitative or obstructive.

Rogers maintained that even inaccurate reflections of clients' feelings could become helpful because clients will often correct the therapist and state their feelings more clearly. Some examples of reflecting statements are "You really hate her guts." "It really hurts when those you love most reject you." "You are uncomfortable being around him because he makes you feel guilty about your achievements." Clients experience the reflecting therapist as a person who understands what they are experiencing and as one who helps them understand and own their own feelings. There's the feeling "Gee, I am not so mixed up after all."

A common error in reflecting is using stereotypical counselor responses and providing too much depth of feeling. Two questions beginning therapists might ask themselves are (1) "Were you able to keep the conversation going using only encouraging body language and a word or two?" and (2) "Were you able to keep from interjecting your own thoughts and opinions into the counseling session?"

Paraphrasing

Rogers also used the technique of paraphrasing when working with clients. Paraphrasing is a technique for restating the client's fundamental message in similar but fewer words. A primary objective of paraphrasing is for therapists to test their understanding of what the client has said. A second objective is to communicate to your clients that you understand their basic message. The paraphrasing technique is helpful in clarifying a double or mixed message. A major difficulty in using paraphrasing and other listening skills is that if they are overused during counseling, some clients become annoyed. Therapists may say repeatedly, "I hear you saying . . ." Some clients respond, "Why do you keep repeating what I have just said?" An ultimate objective of paraphrased statements is to encourage the clients to go on and to gradually take off their masks. To make an effective paraphrasing intervention, the therapist should do the following:

- Listen for the client's basic message.
- Restate to the client a concise and simple summary of his or her basic message.

- Observe a client cue, or ask for a client response that confirms or denies the accuracy and helpfulness of the paraphrase for promoting client understanding.

Person-Centered Counseling and the Schools

Rogers outlined his feelings about person-centered counseling and education in the three editions of his book *Freedom to Learn* (Rogers, 1969, 1983; Rogers & Freiberg, 1994). Rogers's theory of education has as its goal the development of the whole and fully functioning person. Rogers (1969) conceptualized the facilitation of citizens as vital, without which education will "doom us to a deserved and universal destruction" (p. 125).

Rogers (1969) saw "the facilitation of learning as the function which may hold constructive, tentative, changing, process answers to some of the deepest perplexities which beset man today" (p. 105). Most likely, these perplexities prompted Rogers to lead international cross-cultural workshops that proposed a revolutionary educational style for real-world problems both in the classroom and at the diplomatic table.

Rogers (1969) believed that "certain attitudinal qualities which exist in the personal relationship between the facilitator and the learner" yield significant learning (p. 106). To facilitate a young person's learning, teachers must do three things. First, facilitation demands having an initial genuine trust in learners. Second, teachers must create an acceptant and empathic classroom climate. Acceptance is "prizing," "nonpossessive caring," and the "operational expression of his [the facilitator's] essential confidence and trust in the capacity of the human organism" (p. 109). Third, students must perceive that teachers care about them. Teacher empathy is another important quality in student-centered learning. Rogers defined empathy as "the attitude of standing in the other's shoes, of viewing the world through the student's eyes, [which] is almost unheard of in a classroom" (p. 112). Teachers must be flexible in teaching methods, and they must be transparent with students, parents, principals, and teachers.

The following are characteristics of person-centered teaching. Teachers must

- set a positive climate for learning in their classroom,
- clarify the purpose of learning, and
- balance the intellectual and emotional components of learning.

Rogers believed that students should have a significant say in what and how they learn in a class. In the second edition of *Freedom to Learn* (Rogers, 1983), Rogers commented on his teaching a course at the University of Chicago:

> This course has the title Personality Theory (or whatever). But what we do with this course is up to us. We can build it around the goals we want to achieve, within this very general area. We can conduct it the way we want to. We can decide mutually how we wish to handle these bugaboos of exams and grades. I have many resources on tap, and I can help you find others. . . . We are free to learn what we wish, as we wish. (p. 26)

RESEARCH AND EVALUATION
Multicultural Positives

More than 50 years ago, Rogers (1951) maintained that "the only way to understand a culture is to assume the frame of reference of that culture" (p. 494). The most important contribution of person-centered counseling has been its focus on compassionate multicultural exchanges and cross-cultural conflict resolution. In terms of multicultural issues, an important goal is to help individuals identify and pursue their most subjectively meaningful path toward multicultural maturity.

During the last 20 years of his life, Rogers (1977) applied person-centered philosophy to all cultures, as evidenced by a chapter titled "The Person-Centered Approach and the Oppressed." To promote cross-cultural communication and positive interracial communication, Rogers conducted large workshops in Northern Ireland, Poland, France, Mexico, the Philippines, Japan, the Soviet Union, and other countries.

Similarities exist between the underlying philosophy of person-centered therapy and Eastern thought. For instance, Miller (1996) has indicated that similar to person-centered therapy, Taoist philosophy emphasizes that people need to be tuned to their own being. Likewise, Buddhist philosophy shares with person-centered therapy the value of people being open to a wide range of experiences (Harman, 1997). Both Buddhist philosophy and Taoist philosophy see the self as a process rather than as a fixed being, much in the same way that Rogers conceptualized the fully functioning person as one who was open to experiences and moving toward self-actualization. Singh and Tudor (1997) have examined Rogers's six conditions for therapy from the viewpoint of culture, and they have provided examples of how person-centered concepts can be applied to Sikh and Moslem clients. Glauser and Bozarth (2001) have pointed out that person-centered counseling is appropriate for working with people from different cultures because it focuses on empathic listening. These authors have stated,

> What a counselor says or does in a session must be based on the counselor's experience of the client in the relationship and the client's perception of the experience, not on the counselor's perception of the racial identity or culture of the client. (p. 144)

Person-centered therapy has been used with impoverished, maltreated, and neglected children and adolescents in Brazil (Freire, Koller, Piason, & da Silva, 2005). The program in the study was staffed by volunteer therapists and has worked with over 100 children. The researchers concluded that person-centered therapy is

> an effective strategy for the promotion of children's and adolescents' resilience, even in the context of multiple adverse conditions such as socioeconomic disadvantage, neglect, maltreatment, and abandonment. We conclude that the multicultural feature of

person-centered therapy explains its effectiveness in the distinct population of Brazilian lower class and non-White children and adolescents. (Freire et al., 2005, p. 225)

Likewise, Cain (2008, 2010) has maintained that person-centered therapy is well suited for working with clients from a wide range of cultural backgrounds, primarily because the core conditions that Rogers outlined are universal. Bohart and Watson (2011) have agreed with Cain's position and asserted that person-centered therapy is open and accepting of the client's individual world.

A person-centered therapist does not assume that because one is working with a client who comes from a different culture, there will be differences between the client and the therapist. Cultural difference is important only to the extent that clients experience or see themselves as being different. The person-centered therapist adheres to the core conditions of therapy regardless of who the client is, and it is these core conditions that produce change in therapy.

Multicultural Blind Spots

The multicultural blind spots of person-centered therapy have to do with the enactment of therapist style in the therapeutic relationship. Some researchers have pointed out that when people from Latino and Asian cultures seek therapy, they tend to want direction or advice that will be immediate rather than gradual (Chu & Sue, 1984). Person-centered counseling may not be appropriate for cultures that are group oriented or oriented toward the family. Person-centered therapy stresses individual empowerment and individual decision making rather than group decision making, as is evident in some Latino, Native American, and Asian cultures.

Contributions and Criticisms of Person-Centered Therapy

The greatest contribution of person-centered therapy has been its emphasis on the therapeutic relationship and the necessary and sufficient conditions that Rogers proposed. Departing from other leading theorists of his day, Rogers stressed the importance of the client in therapy. Moreover, the concept of empathy is one of Rogers's greatest contributions. Person-centered therapy has demonstrated, perhaps more so than any other theoretical approach, that therapist empathy plays a critical role in bringing about constructive client change in therapy. Watson (2002) conducted an extensive review of the research literature on empathy and found the following:

- Studies have found consistently that therapist empathy is the most powerful predictor of client progress in therapy.
- Regardless of the treatment modality, empathy is a critical component of successful therapy.
- The best predictor of a positive client outcome for therapy is the client's perception of therapist empathy.
- Regardless of the counseling modality, successful counseling outcomes are characterized by a high proportion of counselor statements that express empathy components such as client understanding, attentive listening, and openness to the client's view of things.
- No study has found a negative relationship between empathy and client outcome.

Another major contribution of person-centered therapy is that most of the other theoretical approaches discussed in this book have incorporated some aspect of Rogers's conditions for therapy into their theoretical approach. Even cognitive-behavioral counselors maintain that it is important to have a trusting and empathic relationship with their clients. These therapists caution, however, that Rogers's necessary and sufficient conditions for therapy are not sufficient to produce change in clients. The therapeutic relationship is not sufficient to change client phobias, depression, or other behaviors. They contend that there must be change in clients' behavior.

Moreover, many therapists report that they have incorporated some measure of Rogers's theory into their private practice (Baradell, 1990;

Miller & Foxworth, 1992; Watkins, 1993). The person-centered approach has been applied to working with couples and families (Johnson & Greenberg, 1994). Keijsers, Schaap, and Hoogduin (2000) found that the core conditions are clearly associated with successful outcome in cognitive-behavioral therapy. Haaga, Rabois, and Brody (1999) also reported that cognitive-behavioral therapy works best for therapists who convey the core conditions for therapy. O'Hara (1997) concluded that there is no therapeutic relationship without an empathic counselor. A final contribution has been in the area of research. Rogers has been credited not only with conducting his own research but also with stimulating thousands of studies on conditions related to the therapeutic relationship.

Critics of Rogers's person-centered therapy have challenged his basic conception of human nature as being essentially good and healthy. In addition, critics of Rogers's person-centered therapy have voiced serious doubts that therapists can, or should, establish a relationship of unconditional positive regard in the case of dangerously violent persons. Another criticism of person-centered counseling is that it places too much emphasis on the client's real self and ideal self, and it tends to obscure broad environmental issues (Ivey, D'Andrea, Ivey, & Simek-Morgan, 2007). For instance, racism and sexism may place limits on what individuals can do or achieve. Because of these forces, individuals may not be able to self-actualize. There are environmental constraints on the extent to which individuals can self-actualize.

Rogers's challengers claim that his ideas may be applied only among a limited range of clients, specifically those suffering from the milder forms of neurosis. Moreover, Rogers has been criticized for placing too much emphasis on the client's self without examining the cultural context for self-development. Other criticisms of person-centered therapy include the following:

- It places too much responsibility on the client and not enough responsibility on the expertise of the therapist.

- It is unrealistic to expect the therapists to have unconditional positive regard for their clients because everything is ultimately conditional.
- The approach is not useful for clients who are in a crisis and who may require directive therapeutic interventions.
- Person-centered therapy is more useful for highly verbal clients and less appropriate for clients who have difficulty expressing themselves.

Challenges About the Viability of Person-Centered Therapy. There are some concerns about the survivability of person-centered therapy. Although in some parts of the world person-centered therapy is doing quite well (Eastern Europe, South America, Austria, and China), in other regions, person centered therapists have struggled to maintain and develop their identity within the contemporary health care landscape. As Cooper, O'Hara, Schmid, and Bohart (2013) have asserted,

> In the UK, for example, publicly funded person-centred therapy services are being decommissioned, and members of the person-centred community state that they feel that their profession, orientation and employment are under threat (Cooper, 2011). . . . In Germany, meanwhile, Hofmeister (2010, p. 7) reports that the person-centred approach is "gradually and increasingly disappearing from sight" in the field of psychotherapy, the approach being marginalized within academic institutions, and person-centred therapists only being able to be licensed within the system of health insurance companies "under the accepted labels of 'psychodynamic' or 'cognitive behavior therapy.'" Even in Japan, which has an otherwise thriving person-centred and person-focusing community, Shimizu (2010) reports pessimism over the future of the person-centred approach, and that young trainee and practicing therapists are being attracted towards cognitive-behavioural therapy (CBT). (pp. 3–4)

Another challenge that has led to the decline of person-centered therapy has been the dilution of person-centered values and practices in integrative approaches to psychotherapy. Most psychotherapeutic approaches either refer to or have adopted person-centered principles such as empathy, attentiveness, authenticity, and positive regard for clients— usually even without reference to Carl Rogers. These principles are now standard operating principles for most therapeutic approaches. They have either borrowed from or watered down the core idea of person-centered therapy—namely, that it is the therapist's engagement of the client within the therapeutic relationship that is the therapeutic approach of Carl Rogers. Both person-centered therapy and Adlerian therapy face similar challenges in that the concepts and techniques of both therapeutic approaches have been adopted and integrated with newer theoretical approaches to therapy.

Evidence-Based Research

Cooper et al. (2013) attribute the decline of person-centered therapy partly to the rising popularity of cognitive behavior therapy and partly to the new demands of the empirically supported therapies movement. Another reason for the decline of person-centered therapy is that health care agencies are requiring that therapists engage in empirically supported therapies, and person-centered therapy is not recognized as an empirically supported therapy. Thus, therapists who identify their approach as person-centered may not be able to secure reimbursement for their mental health services. The general idea behind the empirically supported therapies movement is that therapeutic practices are considered valid only to the degree that they have been "proven to work, usually established by experimental studies (preferably randomized clinical trials [RCTs])." According to Cooper et al.,

> This is the viewpoint held by many powerful political organizations, such as England's National Institute for Health and Clinical Excellence, whose recommendations on clinical treatments for specific psychological difficulties has directly informed the commissioning and funding of publicly available therapeutic services and training, most notably through recent Improving Access to Psychological Therapies programme. (p. 4)

Cooper et al. (2013) continue by pointing out that the problem with client-centered therapy is not that they have been proved ineffective or inefficient. Rather, in contrast to other orientations such as cognitive-behavioral therapy, there have simply not

been enough of the kinds of study that organizations like the National Institute for Health and Clinical Excellence endorse to *prove* their efficacy. And the reason for this touches a principle: "To a great extent, the research methods employed in these studies violate the fundamental beliefs and practices of person-centred theory and practice" (p. 4). The authors go on to state that the requirements of randomized clinical trials, including placing clients in certain diagnostic categories; the delivery of standardized, manualized therapies; and an analysis of data reduces clients' lives to de-individualized averages. To deal with the challenge of evidence-based therapy requirements, Cooper et al. suggest that person-centered therapists conduct more empirically oriented studies.

Some person-centered therapists have begun to engage in evidence-based research. Gibbard and Hanley (2008) have conducted an evidence-based study of person-centered therapy in England. Using the Core Outcome Measure (CORE-OM) at referral and at the beginning and end of therapy, the authors found that person-centered counseling was effective for 697 clients, who had common mental health problems such as anxiety and depression, over a 5-year period.

CASE ANALYSIS

Justin Working With a Person-Centered Therapist

The person-centered therapist does not need any detailed assessment information about Justin to accomplish effective therapy. Instead, the therapist believes that if he establishes an empathic, caring, and trusting atmosphere, Justin will respond positively and begin to deal with issues that brought him to therapy. Initially, the nondirective nature of person-centered therapy confused Justin and produced a strong response from him. Justin was accustomed to being interrogated by professionals, including his probation officer, the judge, his teachers, and the school principal. Justin was surprised at the nondirective therapy session and asked the therapist, "Aren't you going to ask me any questions?"

Justin's initial puzzled reaction to person-centered therapy suggests that he was not used to being allowed to experience autonomy and self-determination. He was not accustomed to experiencing his personal power within a relationship in a positive way. Soon Justin came to realize that his relationship with his therapist was different from what he had experienced with other adult figures who made sure he recognized their authority. With his new therapist, Justin could talk about his feelings. The therapist was forcing him to talk, and because of the trusting relationship they had established, he did not have to be afraid that the therapist was going to label him crazy.

Justin is all mixed up inside. He does not have a clear sense of self. He got into trouble stealing at the Walmart because he let his friends define who he was. According to them, he was supposed to be cool and tough, needing no one except his friends. But Justin did not feel cool when the police locked him up. He wanted to go home with his mom. Justin's difficulties suggest that he does not have a clear idea of what he wants for his life. At one moment, he is cursing at his mother, and a short time later, he is crying because he is afraid that the presiding judge will place him in the residential treatment center for boys, a center that is a couple of 100 miles away from his home, friends, and school.

Except for his friends, Justin has little positive regard from others. The kids at school don't like him, most of his teachers don't want him in their class, and the principal has threatened to expel him permanently from school if he gets into another fight in school. He does not perform well academically in most of his subjects, except for art class. School has become a place of negative regard for Justin, and he is aware that he is not wanted each time he climbs the school's steps. He feels so bad about school that sometimes he just doesn't want to attend it at all. So he became truant on a number of occasions.

Justin's relationship with his mother is deeply troubled, even though he believes that she loves him. He feels less than nothing when his mother, Sandy, curses at him in a fit of uncontrollable anger and rage at his latest misdeed. Rarely does she ever just hug and kiss him when he comes home from school, nor does she fix him cookies like some of the kids in his school say that their mothers fix for them.

Deep down inside, Justin does not know who he really is. Sometimes his mother mocks him: "Will the real Justin stand up?" "Am I going to get the cry baby today or the tough gang member?" He wants to do well in school. He wants kids to like him, but whenever he is around them in class, he plays it real cool. Justin feels as if he is always wearing a mask for somebody, even sometimes for himself and his friends.

The therapist who works with Justin must first establish a trusting and caring relationship with him. Despite all the trouble that Justin has gotten himself into, he believes that deep down inside Justin is a good person and that if he can establish a nurturing enough counseling relationship with him, Justin will begin to see the more positive sides of himself that he hides mostly from everyone. The therapist strives to establish a relationship with Justin that will make him feel safe and that will encourage him to explore the real Justin. The therapist indicates that he respects Justin for coming to counseling and trying to sort things out. He is genuine and transparent with Justin during the therapy session. The therapist tries to understand what Justin's life must be like—what it feels like to walk in his shoes. He conveys with his nonthreatening tone of voice and his relaxed and open posture that he is listening deeply to Justin. Instead of directing the counseling session, the therapist waits for Justin to speak and to indicate where he wants to go in the session.

The therapist listens to Justin without trying to impose his own agenda on the therapy session or on Justin. If Justin has questions, the therapist tries to recognize and to respond to whatever feelings are implicit in the question. For instance, Justin's question, "How am I ever going to get out this mess?" may cover up the feeling "my case seems hopeless." If Justin asks for advice, the therapist responds that he does not have the answers but he hopes to help Justin find the answers that are right for him. He reflects back some of Justin's key feelings that deal with his feelings about himself.

The therapist does not focus intently on Justin's problems. Otherwise, the therapy session will become problem oriented. The therapist asks Justin what he would like to accomplish from meeting with him. Therapy is focused

(Continued)

(Continued)

on helping Justin define who he is, to talk about the conditions of worth that have been placed on him by his mother, his friends, and students in the school.

A desired therapeutic outcome is to help Justin activate his positive self-actualizing tendency. Another desirable therapeutic outcome might be to help Justin reintegrate the different parts of himself. Only Justin knows who the real Justin is. The therapist believes that the nurturing relationship between Justin and the therapist will stimulate Justin's inner resources and his innate capacity to find the best way to survive and to enjoy his life—to get out of the mess in which he finds himself.

Therapy will be successful if Justin comes to see himself in a positive light and if he is able to find purpose and hope for his life. Justin's empathic counselor helps him really hear what is going on inside of him. It is hoped that Justin will begin to move toward developing his own self-regard and to depend less on gaining the positive regard of his friends, who often get him into trouble with the law. As Justin becomes more trusting of himself and the therapist, he begins to drop the various masks he has worn to hide himself from others.

SUMMARY

Rogers viewed people as basically good. He stressed that people have an inherent tendency to grow and to move in positive, healthy directions. Rogers labeled this tendency the self-actualizing tendency, and he maintained that it was the primary motivating force of every human being. The self-actualizing tendency is guided by the organismic valuing process, which may be defined as an inherent capacity to choose what will enhance us and what will not. While the self-actualizing tendency creates the inner drive for us to create and to move toward our potential and purpose in life, the organismic valuing process helps us choose what we will or will not do to achieve our purpose in life.

The overarching characteristic of Rogers's person-centered theory is its postulates about the development of the self. During the process of growing up, the infant's self becomes differentiated in his or her phenomenal field. As the infant's self emerges, he or she becomes aware of the opinions of significant others toward him or her. If the infant receives positive regard from significant others, this person grows to like himself or herself. Most people grow up experiencing conditions of worth from members of their family. They learn that their parents will love them if they do what pleases them— that is, if they meet their parents' conditions.

Problems in development occur when there are distortions in our self-concept or when our self-concept is contaminated by conditions of worth or the lack of positive regard from significant others. Mental health problems occur when we find it difficult to have our own positive self-regard. Problems are also created when we substitute the opinions of others for our own organismic valuing system. Incongruity within ourselves produces maladjustment.

A central theme in person-centered therapy is that we have enormous resources for self-understanding and for changing our self-concepts, behavior, and attitudes toward others. The primary focus in therapy is on the relationship between the therapist and client. The role of the person-centered therapist is to provide a therapeutic climate of safety and trust, which will encourage clients to reintegrate their self-actualizing tendency and their organismic valuing processes. The therapist is able to achieve this task by providing the client with accurate empathic understanding, congruence, and unconditional positive regard. Instead of seeking to solve clients' problems, the therapist facilitates a process in which clients can become fully functioning people.

Most psychotherapeutic approaches have adopted features of Rogers's necessary and sufficient conditions of therapy. These approaches disagree that establishing an empathic, trusting, and caring counseling relationship is sufficient to bring about client behavior change. Only a relatively small percentage of therapists state that their primary theoretical affiliation is person centered, even though most subscribe to the importance of therapist empathy.

SUPPLEMENTAL AIDS

Discussion Questions

1. Consider what you have learned in reading about Rogers's conceptualization of the fully functioning person. List the categories Rogers enumerated in the fully functioning person. Now examine yourself and where you are in life. State two reasons why you believe you are a fully functioning person. In a small group, share your response to this discussion question with each other. What would it take for you to become a fully functioning person?

2. One of the key concepts in person-centered therapy is empathy. In your small group, discuss the following questions: What is your understanding of empathy? How can you become empathic? What are some barriers to empathic understanding of clients? Does therapist self-disclosure play any part in the expression of empathy?

3. This exercise is designed to help you increase your empathy for difficult clients. Think about the type of client you are most inclined to have the most difficulty understanding or relating to during therapy. In your small group, discuss the type of client whom you might find hard to counsel. Have one member of your small group assume the identity of that difficult client, and you role-play the therapist. During the small group session, each member of the group plays first a difficult client and then a therapist. Were you able to give the client empathy? If not, what blocked you from providing empathy to the client? What did you learn from playing the role of a difficult client? What did you come to understand about yourself as you played the role of the therapist with this client?

4. Active listening and reflection are two therapy techniques associated with person-centered therapy. This exercise is designed to help you evaluate your strengths and challenges in listening. In your small groups, discuss if the following situations apply to each of you:

 a. Talking too much and too soon

 b. Being quick to give advice or to look for an easy solution

 c. Asking too many questions

 d. Listening only to confirm your preconceived notions about members

 e. Focusing too much attention on the client's content meaning and failing to understand or to note the emotional part of the message

5. In your small groups, have someone in the group play the role of a depressed college student who is unable to study because she misses home. She comes into counseling because she says she is afraid she is going to flunk out of college. Take turns in your group playing the role of either the client or the therapist. Focus on making basic reflective statements.

Glossary of Key Terms

accurate empathic understanding Refers to a therapist's act of perceiving the internal frame of reference for a person such that he or she understands the person, without losing one's own identity.

conditional positive regard What our conditioning leads us to have. We feel good about ourselves only when we meet the standards others have applied to us. Because we are not always able to meet the standards that others set for us, we fall short and, therefore, experience less self-esteem for ourselves. See also **unconditional positive regard**.

conditions of worth Established when our parents attach conditions under which they will love us. That is, our parents, teachers, and loved ones only give us what we need when we show that we are "worthy." We get love and attention when we do what our parents and teachers want us to do.

congruence   Forms one of Carl Rogers's necessary conditions for therapy. It refers to the agreement between the feelings that a therapist is experiencing and his or her outward demeanor. The term refers to the matching of the therapist's inner experiencing with his or her external expressions.

empathy   Refers to the therapist's accurate understanding of the client's world from the client's perspective. Rogers listed empathy as one of the conditions necessary for therapy effectiveness.

fully functioning person   Term that describes individuals who are using their abilities and talents and who are reaching their potential and moving toward a full awareness and understanding of themselves.

genuineness   Refers to the quality of realness of a therapist. A person who lives without pretenses.

humanistic psychology   A movement, often referred to as the "third force," that stresses freedom, choice, creativity, spontaneity, growth, self-actualization, and peak experiences.

incongruence   The gap between the real self and the ideal self, the "I am" and the "I should."

organism   Refers to the total individual—in terms of physical and psychological functioning.

organismic valuing process   Process that allows us to make individual judgments or assessments of the desirability of an action or choice based on one's own sensory and life experience. The term refers to our inherent capacity to choose that which will promote or enhance our well-being and to reject that which does not do so.

person-centered approach   Term that Carl Rogers used later in life to refer to his approach to therapy. Rogers had used two other terms to describe his therapeutic approach—*nondirective therapy* and *client-centered therapy*.

phenomenal field   The private world of each individual that becomes his or her source of internal reference for viewing life. It constitutes everything that is experienced by an individual. Rogers (1951) pointed out that each person exists and reacts in a "continuing changing world of experience of which he or she does so as an organized whole" (p. 483). Each person's phenomenal field constitutes his or her reality.

positive regard   A basic craving for affection that Rogers maintained is within each person. He labeled this craving the need for positive regard. In Rogers's view, the need for positive regard is universal and reciprocal; that is, as a person satisfies another person's need for positive regard, the person fulfills for himself or herself that same need.

reflection   The primary technique for which person-centered therapists are well known. Reflection is the mirroring back to the client that you have heard and understood what he or she has said. The client says, "I feel worthless." The therapist responds, "You are feeling down in the dumps." The therapist must respond both to the content of what the client has stated as well as to the emotional component of the client's statement.

self-actualization   A growth force within us that predisposes us to develop in terms of our full potential. It is a basic human drive toward growth, completeness, and fulfillment.

self-concept   Consists of the organized, consistent, conceptual Gestalt composed of perceptions of the characteristics of "I" or "me" and the perceptions of the relationships of the "I" or "me" to others and to various aspects of life, together with the values attached to these perceptions. It is a Gestalt that is available to awareness though not necessarily in awareness. It is fluid and changing.

self-regard   Another dimension of a person's self structure. It may be distinguished from positive regard, which refers to others' feelings about us. We may be able to obtain the positive regard of others, but it may be difficult to obtain our own positive self-regard.

subception   Subception is a term Rogers used to describe the process whereby a stimulus is experienced or responded to without being brought into awareness. According to Rogers, the mind uses unconscious strategies to protect a person from a negative stimulus before it enters consciousness. The term *subception* is short for subliminal perception.

unconditional positive regard   Refers to the nonjudgmental expression of a basic respect for the person as a human being. The term also refers to our acceptance of another person without placing on him or her conditions of worth—"I'll love you if you get all As." See also **conditional positive regard**.

warmth   Term used by Rogers to describe the nonverbal and verbal actions of a therapist that express the therapist's caring for the client. Some nonverbal expressions of warmth include our posture—leading toward a client, listening attentively to what the client is saying, smiling, and so on.

Website Materials

Additional exercises, journals, annotated bibliography, and more are available on the open-access website at https://study.sagepub.com/jonessmith2e.

CHAPTER

Gestalt Therapy

I am not in this world to live up to other people's expectations, nor do I feel that the world must live up to mine.

Nobody can stand truth if it is told to him. Truth can be tolerated only if you discover it yourself because then, the pride of discovery makes the truth palatable.

Our dependency makes slaves out of us, especially if this dependency is a dependency of our self-esteem. If you need encouragement, praise, pats on the back from everybody, then you make everybody your judge.

—Fritz Perls

BRIEF OVERVIEW

Gestalt therapy is an experiential therapy based on the underlying premise that people must be understood and examined within the context of their relationship with their environments. Gestalt therapists emphasize awareness, choice, and responsibility for one's behavior and actions. During therapy, the therapist seeks to expand the client's awareness of what he or she is experiencing in the moment. The emphasis is on the client's perceptions of reality and existence. Gestalt therapy focuses on the here-and-now, the what-and-how of one's feelings, and the connection between one's

feelings and behavior. For instance, if a Gestalt therapist sees a client repeatedly tapping on a chair, he might ask, "Tell me what the tapping is saying to you." Gestalt therapy views the therapeutic relationship as a vehicle for developing the client's awareness. It focuses on process (what is actually happening right now in therapy) over content (what is being talked about in therapy). The therapist creates a dialogic relationship in which he or she not only attends to his or her own presence and awareness during therapy but also creates the therapeutic space for the client to enter and to become present. Gestalt therapy contains a theory of consciousness called phenomenology. It is highly experiential and phenomenological, and it uses a scientific theory called field theory. Currently, Gestalt therapy is using a focus termed *relational Gestalt therapy*. This approach emphasizes the dialogic relationship between the therapist and the client during the therapeutic process.

MAJOR CONTRIBUTOR: FRITZ PERLS (1893–1970)

Frederick Salomon Perls, addressed affectionately as Fritz by friends and followers, is recognized as the primary originator (along with his wife, Laura) and master practitioner of Gestalt therapy. Perls gave Gestalt therapy its name, and he can be credited with popularizing this counseling approach. **Gestalt therapy** is existential (people are always in the process of rediscovering themselves) and phenomenological (emphasizes clients' perception of reality), and it is based on the premise that people must be understood within the context of their ongoing relationship with the environment.

Born in Berlin into a lower-middle-class Jewish family, Perls has described his mother as loving and ambitious and his father as loving the arts but hating most other things, including his wife. Perls was a middle child and the only son. School was a mixed bag of results for him. Perls attended the Mommsen Gymnasium, a new conservative high school that had a reputation for rigid discipline and anti-Semitism. He has described his experiences there as a nightmare (Perls, 1969a). Perls failed the seventh grade twice. After a brief stint as an apprentice to a soft goods merchant, he was dismissed because he pulled pranks. Perls passed the entrance examination to Askanishe Gymnasium, a more liberal and humanistic high school that seemed to fit his personality. He performed quite well at Askanishe.

In 1916, Perls joined the German army and served as a medic in World War I. Thereafter, he went to medical school, where he earned an M.D. degree from Friedrich-Willhelm University with a specialization in psychiatry. In 1925, Perls underwent psychoanalysis with several notable psychoanalysts, including Otto Fenichel, Wilhelm Reich, and Karen Horney. Reflecting back on this part of his life, Perls (n.d.) stated,

> In 1925, I started seven years of useless couch life. I felt stupid. Finally, Wilhelm Reich, then still sane, began to make some sense. Also, there was Karen Horney, whom I loved. The rest of them I considered opinionated, missing Freud's good intentions. Confusing.

In his famous book *In and Out of the Garbage Pail*, Perls (1969b) wrote, "From Fenichel I got confidence; from Reich, brazenness; from Horney, human involvement without terminology" (p. 38).

In 1926, Perls accepted a position at the Institute for Brain Injured Soldiers in Frankfurt, Germany, where he worked with Kurt Goldstein, who helped him view people not as the sum of their parts but rather as whole entities. Perls married Laura Posner in 1930. With his wife and child, Perls fled Hitler's persecution of Jews, fleeing to the German–Dutch border with only the clothes they could carry and 100 marks (about $25) hidden in his cigarette case. Staying in a small attic apartment in Amsterdam, Perls (1969b) described these days as "utter misery."

During 1934–1935, Perls migrated to South Africa, where he founded the South African Institute of Psychoanalysis in 1935. In 1936, Perls traveled to Czechoslovakia for the International Psychoanalytic Congress. He has described this year as the beginning of Gestalt therapy because it signaled his break with Sigmund Freud. Perls was excited about presenting a paper because he believed that Freud and others would see it as a significant contribution to psychoanalysis. His colleagues did not receive his ideas very well. Perls set up an appointment with Freud. His cherished meeting with Freud lasted for only about 4 minutes and took place entirely in the doorway to Freud's room (Freud was ill). Hoping to impress Freud with his dedication to him, Perls informed Freud that he had come all the way from South Africa to meet him. Freud responded, "Well, and when are you going back?"

Perls was absolutely crushed, devastated. He became angry and resolved to prove to Freud and the members of the Psychoanalytic Society that they had missed his great contributions. Perls never forgot Freud's rudeness, and some three decades later, he said that his relationship with Freud was one of the unfinished business situations of his life.

As a result of his professional rejection, Perls became convinced that he did not need anyone, not even Laura, his wife. Subsequently, he renounced Freudian analysis and began his theoretical work, which he first called concentration therapy and later renamed Gestalt therapy, despite his wife's protestations to the contrary.

In 1946, Perls immigrated to the United States. It was in the United States that he was to piece together the disparate parts of his life and develop Gestalt therapy, a task at which he had been at work for some time. In 1942, Perls published *Ego*,

Hunger, and Aggression, wherein he pointed out the significance of Gestalt psychology in psychotherapeutic procedures and leveled criticism at psychoanalysis. From 1948 to 1951, Perls, Laura, and Paul Goodman conducted workshops on Gestalt therapy. In 1951, they established the Gestalt Institute in New York City. That same year, Perls, Hefferline, and Goodman published *Gestalt Therapy*. Perls traveled throughout the world demonstrating Gestalt therapy to large audiences.

One of the key factors in Gestalt therapy's achievement of national recognition was Perls's move to California and his joining the staff of the Esalen Institute in 1966. It was at the Esalen Institute that Gestalt therapy became intimately connected with the human potential movement. The staff of Esalen wanted to release the "too well-adjusted," the too tightly controlled people for growth and greater integration. In 1969, Perls published *Gestalt Therapy Verbatim* (Perls, 1969a), a book of selected and edited audiotapes completed at weekend dreamwork seminars he conducted at Esalen from 1966 through 1968. After a brief illness, Perls died in 1970 (at age 76) in a Chicago hospital where large groups of his supporters had gathered.

Throughout his life, Perls exuded a certain mystique, an aura of honesty that most people praised because they lacked it in themselves. A biography of Fritz Perls, written by Martin Shepard (1975, 1976), paints a different view of Perls. According to Shepard (1976), Perls was a Bauhaus bohemian who was self-driving, doubting, but lovable and brilliant. In some fundamental ways, he was almost completely dishonest in his personal life and in his closest personal relationships. Shepard describes Perls as suffering from a "neediness paradox." He states, "Fritz Perls wanted, but wouldn't ask. And so he condemned the wantingness of others" (p. 120). To those who were emotionally attached to him, he manifested impenetrable defenses and was contradictory in nature. As a detached "taker," however, he displayed a brilliant genius in his professional life in ferreting out and helping others work on their defenses. Like Freud, Perls minimized contact with his clients. Whereas Freud sat behind his clients,

Perls hid behind the empty chair, across from his clients. Both men sought relief from their clients; both men were brilliant manipulators in that they got not only their clients but other therapists as well to buy into the correctness and efficacy of their own needs for detachment and distance from others. Commenting on Shepard's biography of Perls, Ryback (1975) stated,

> This holistic view of Fritz, his neurotic rootlessness, his chronic self-doubts and, above all, his driving destiny to become a great master in the world of psychotherapy, reveals a human, lovable person. It leaves me feeling glad that Fritz did his thing, and that Martin Shepard did his, too. (p. 76)

PHILOSOPHICAL ROOTS FOR GESTALT THERAPY

Influence of Gestalt Psychology

Although Perls borrowed heavily from Freud and others, much of the impetus for Gestalt therapy can be traced to Gestalt psychology (Woldt & Toman, 2005). Foremost among the contributions from Gestalt psychology were the concepts of figure and ground, unfinished situation, and Gestalt.

During the 1920s, Gestalt psychology found its origins in Germany and in Europe in general. The word **Gestalt** does not have an equivalent English translation (Bowman, 2005). It refers to a perceptual whole, a figure, a configuration, a totality, or a whole. Gestalt psychology focused on the dynamic organization of experience into patterns of configurations. This school came into existence as a reaction against structuralism, which analyzed complex behavior as basic conditioned reflexes. Three friends—Max Wertheimer, Wolfgang Kohler, and Kurt Koffka—were the leading proponents. From their research came three critical concepts: (1) principle of closure, which describes our need to complete unfinished figures; (2) the principle of proximity, which suggests that we organize visual stimuli based on their distance from one another; and (3) the principle of similarity, which causes us to group elements that appear similar (Bowman,

2005). Perls was later to incorporate some of these concepts into his theory of Gestalt therapy.

Gestalt psychologists assert that organisms instinctively perceive whole patterns and not bits and pieces (Lobb, 2005). Furthermore, whole patterns have characteristics that cannot be determined by examining their parts. Perception is an active process rather than a passively received stimulation of our senses. All situations, even those that appear to be chaotic, have an inherent organization. Organisms have the capacity for accurate perception, if they use their inherent ability of immediate experience in the here-and-now. Because people naturally perceive whole patterns as they take place, our actual awareness can be trusted more than therapist interpretation.

Gestalt psychologists posit that the whole is greater than the sum of its parts. In fact, the whole determines the part (Lobb, 2005). Gestalt psychology supplied Perls with the central organizing principle for Gestalt therapy as an integrating framework. Perls used the term *Gestalt* to connote the entire being or wholeness of an individual. Gestalt therapists posit, therefore, a holistic concept of human beings. They do not divide human beings into different parts, as do some theoretical schools.

Similar to the Gestalt psychologists, Perls emphasized the here-and-now and the moment-to-moment awareness that people manifested as they sat opposite him in therapy. Perls (1973) asserted that the first basic premise of Gestalt therapy is that "it is the organization of facts or perceptions and not the individual items of which they are composed, that defines them and gives them specific and particular meaning" (p. 3).

Gestalt Psychology's Concept of Figure–Ground

One of the most basic tenets of Gestalt psychology is that we are born with some basic organizing tendencies, such as the ability to distinguish an object from a background. It is called an inborn organizing tendency because we can distinguish figures from backgrounds from birth. Gestalt

psychologists maintain that during the process of perceiving objects, an individual tends to form figures and grounds. A **figure** is an object, element, or person who emerges (becomes foreground) and stands out against a background. In terms of perception, a figure is that which you are paying attention to; it constitutes your center of awareness (Bowman, 2005).

A ground is the context in which a figure appears and against which the figure stands out (Bowman, 2005). For instance, babies may reach toward an object placed in front of them, which indicates that they are able to distinguish that object from the background that surrounds it. Because no one teaches babies how to do that, their reaching for the object suggests that we are born with some inborn programming that allows us to explore and interact with the world.

Gestalt psychologists have used optical illusions to demonstrate how **figure–ground** perception can be both reversible and a construct of the mind (Figure 9.1). A very famous example is provided below. Look at the picture. What do you see?

Depending on how you look at this picture, you may see either two faces looking at each other or a vase. If you focus on the black areas, the two faces (figure) appear to stand out in front of the white (background). On the other hand, if you concentrate on the white area, a vase (figure) appears to stand out against a black background. You have just experienced how figure–ground perception can be reversed, which indicates that it is a construct of the mind. That is, your internal mental world can differ from your external physical world as a result of how you perceive it. In any situation, there may be two entirely different perceptions of the same event.

You can change figure–ground relationships with little or no effort. For example, you may look at a painting twice and comment each time that you saw something different. This situation exists because the first time you were paying attention only to certain objects in the painting—a woman's face, for instance. When you looked at the painting the second time, the importance of the original figure (the woman's face) receded into the background, and thus, you were able to pay attention

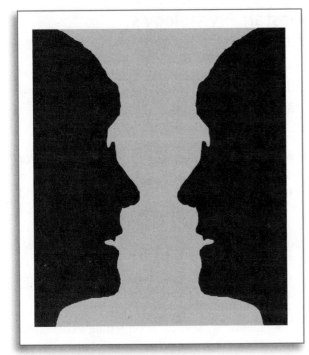

Source: © Can Stock Photo Inc./genenphotos.

to another object within the painting—the child next to the woman.

The fact that different objects may become the focus of your attention and then fade into the background is an important principle in Gestalt psychology (Bowman, 2005). This principle may be labeled the *principle of shifting attention or figure-ground formations*. That is, as a shift of emphasis occurs in what you are paying attention to, the figure and ground change positions, and a new Gestalt is formed.

Perls extended the Gestalt psychologists' concept of figure–ground as it relates to human visual perception of activities to other dimensions of people's lives. He affirmed that figure–ground relationships tend to occur in almost all aspects of human life. For example, your thoughts, feelings, and senses in general are governed by figure–ground relationships. You tend to hear, feel, and think certain thoughts because certain sounds or experiences have become figured in your life.

A mother might sleep through a loud thunderstorm but awakens when she hears the faint cry of her child. The child's cry became figured against the background of noise of the thunderstorm and whatever else was happening. The figure formation process indicates how people organize or manipulate their environment from moment to moment.

People feel certain ways about themselves because some events have become figured in their memory (Crocker, 2005). For instance, you might describe yourself as lazy because you have formed this type of rigid, figure–ground perception of yourself. Your life experiences, such as parents calling you lazy or your failure to complete specific tasks, constitute the background against which your view of yourself as lazy is figured.

Perls used the concept of figure–ground in Gestalt therapy in several important ways. First, he asserted that prior experiences constitute the background (ground) against which the individual figures a present experience. Second, a person's most pressing need becomes figured. For example, your immediate need of safety from a dangerous situation becomes more prominently figured than your need for love. People who have faced dangerous situations have usually been quoted as saying, "All I could think of was how to get out of there; I couldn't think about anything else." This statement illustrates Perls's belief that in a struggle for survival, your most pressing need not only becomes figured but also organizes your behavior until it (the need) is satisfied. As this need is satisfied, it recedes into the background, making room for the next most significant need. This change of need dominance, according to Perls, is necessary for an individual's survival and healthy development.

The destruction of Gestalts and the formation of new figure–ground relationships are important concepts in Gestalt therapy. According to Perls et al. (1951), the destruction of Gestalts is necessary for the healthy survival of a person. When you are unable to destroy old Gestalts and move on to new ones, you are living in the past. Moreover, interference with the formation and destruction of Gestalts may mean that you cling compulsively to the unfinished situation; this results in other needs going unmet.

One goal of Gestalt therapy is to help a person regain his or her former elastic figure–ground formation. Perls maintained that the healthy person experiences a continually emerging and receding interplay between figure and ground (Woldt & Toman, 2005). A person who is suffering from neurosis, for example, may manifest a rigidity of figure–ground formation. Part of the process of Gestalt therapy involves helping clients make contact with both the environment and the self so that they make less rigid or incomplete figure–ground relationships.

In addition, Perls used the concept of figure–ground to emphasize the importance of **awareness** (Bowman, 2005). In fact, what the Gestalt psychologists had designated as perception, Perls relabeled as awareness. People who have elastic figure–ground formations are generally more aware of themselves and of what is happening around them. This situation takes place because they are experiencing a dynamic, free-flowing relationship between figure and ground. For example, while walking to a car, the individual who has an elastic figure–ground relationship observes trees, birds, and people. Attention shifts spontaneously to whatever appears in the foreground. The individual is aware of the environment and of what he or she is doing. In contrast, the person who does not have an elastic figure–ground relationship is usually unaware of all the things going on. The level of awareness of environment and self is reduced.

One of the goals of Gestalt therapy is to help clients restore their awareness of themselves and their environment. In contrast to the psychoanalytic school, which stresses the importance of the unconscious, Gestalt therapists maintain that there is a free flow between a person's accessible and inaccessible awareness about the self. The most important information about us does not necessarily lie, as Freud asserted, in an unconscious realm that is largely inaccessible to the person without therapeutic assistance. Information in a client's unconscious may become accessible by his or her forming new figure–ground relationships and by staying in the here-and-now in therapy.

Gestalt Psychology's Concept of Closure

The Gestalt principle of **closure** means that our minds are able to derive meaning from objects or figures that are not perceived in full (Figure 9.2). People are inclined to organize their perceptions in a complete manner so as to reduce tensions that would arise from a sense of incompleteness. For instance, if you see an incomplete drawing of a familiar object—a house, for example—you tend to complete the drawing in your mind and to label it a house. This example illustrates the principle of closure, in which the person's mind acts to finish a figure and to perceive it as complete (Woldt & Toman, 2005). Some principles related to closure may be summarized as follows:

- Closure is the effect of suggesting a visual connection between sets of elements that do not actually touch each other in a composition.
- The principle of closure applies when we tend to see complete figures even when part of the information is missing.
- Closure occurs when elements in a composition are aligned in such a way that the viewer perceives that "the information could be connected."

Whereas Gestalt psychologists dealt with the principle of closure primarily in terms of visual perception, Perls extended its application to an individual's thoughts, feelings, and total senses

Figure 9.2   Gestalt Closure

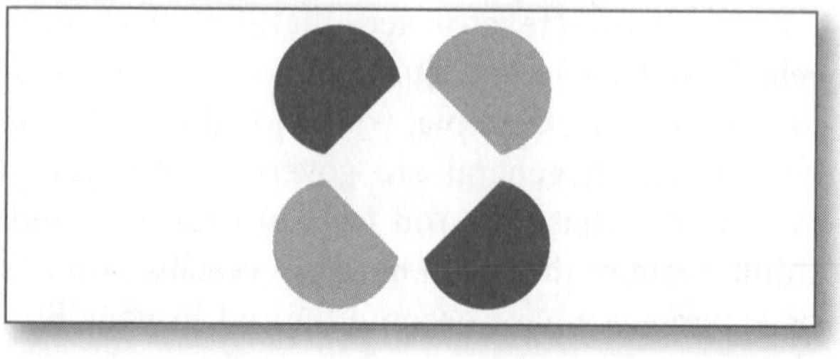

(Woldt & Toman, 2005). In Gestalt therapy, lack of closure represents almost all unfinished business or life experiences. If unfinished life experiences are powerful enough, they can cause maladaptive behavior. Clients achieve closure either through a return to the old business or by relating to parallel circumstances in the present (Clarkson, 2004). If a woman was never able to hug her father when she was a child, she might find closure by either hugging the father as an adult or hugging another fatherly figure in her life. Once the woman reaches closure over hugging her father by experiencing it in some form in the present (imagining it), her preoccupation with the old incompletion is resolved, and she can move on to current possibilities (Clarkson, 2004).

The contributions of Gestalt psychology to Gestalt therapy are as follows:

1. An individual's behavior is a Gestalt, a whole that is greater than the sum of its parts.

2. An individual experiences the world according to the principles of a figure–ground relationship.

3. An individual will seek closure of an incomplete Gestalt. An incomplete Gestalt draws an individual's attention until it is unified and stabilized.

4. An individual will complete Gestalts on the basis of his or her most prevalent need.

5. A person's behavior can be most meaningfully understood only in its immediate context.

INFLUENCE OF EXISTENTIALISM ON GESTALT THERAPY

Existentialism also exerted a considerable influence on Perls's development of Gestalt therapy (Kirchner, 2010). Perls adopted the existentialists' view that we must take responsibility for our own lives. Although Perls accepted the existential concept of personal responsibility, he felt that the major drawback of existentialism was that it needed some form of external conceptual support. According to Perls (1969a), "Gestalt therapy is the first existential philosophy to stand on its own two feet" (p. 16). Perls reproached the existentialist school for its failure to concretize its ideas and to develop an external conceptual support system. Commenting on existentialism and Gestalt therapy, Perls stated,

> Existentialism wants to do away with concepts, and to work on the awareness principle, on phenomenology. The setback with the present existentialist philosophies is that they need their support from somewhere else. If you look at the existentialists, they say that they are non-conceptual, but if you look at the people, they all borrow concepts from other sources. Buber from Judaism, Tillich from Protestantism, Sartre from Socialism, Heidegger from language, Binswanger from psychoanalysis, and so on. . . . Gestalt therapy has its support in its own formation because the Gestalt formation, the emergence of needs, is a primary biological phenomenon. (p. 16)

Despite Perls's criticism, Gestalt therapy does use some of the concepts with which existentialism has come to be identified. For example, Gestalt therapists emphasize one's being in terms of the present moment. They pay very little attention to past events. Moreover, Perls has posited that one of the goals of this approach is to create a "continuum of awareness." By creating a moment-to-moment awareness, the client becomes cognizant of the unfinished business of the past. Perls has also elaborated on the idea that unless one is asleep, one is always aware of something. When such awareness becomes unpleasant, an individual is inclined to interrupt it by intellectualizing, taking flight to the past, or "jumping like a grasshopper from experience to experience . . . just a kind of flash, which leaves all the available material unassimilated and unused" (Perls, 1969a, pp. 1, 51).

To help the client become more aware of what he or she is experiencing at any given moment, Gestalt therapists pay strict attention to bodily movements and voice intonations. As Perls (1969a) has stated, "A good therapist doesn't listen to the content of the bullshit the patient produces, but to the sound, to the music, to the hesitations"

Do the philosophical underpinnings of Gestalt therapy resonate with you?

What philosophical positions from Gestalt therapy might you choose to incorporate in your integrative counseling theory?

(p. 53). From observing the body cues, the Gestalt therapist points out inconsistencies in a client's verbal and nonverbal behavior. The therapist might say, for example, "You say that you are angry, but you are smiling," or "An angry person does not smile." These kinds of statements compel a person to make his or her own interpretation since discrepant behavior is brought to the present (Polster, 1987).

Emphasis on the Now

Gestalt therapists are more concerned with the *now* of behavior than with interpreting unconscious motivators of behavior. To focus on awareness of behavior, Perls asked *what* questions, such as "What are you doing now?" He avoids the why or cause questions. Similar to existential therapists, Gestalt counselors emphasize the Eigenwelt (the relations to one's self) rather than the past. To direct a client's attention to awareness of here-and-now behavior, Perls's famous dictum is "Lose your mind and come to your senses." In this instance, he is trying to get the person to become aware of the totality of experiences. Polster and Polster (1973), in their classic book, *Gestalt Therapy Integrated: Contours of Theory and Practice* devote only one paragraph to the contributions of existentialism to Gestalt therapy. They state,

> Existentialism's primary contribution to psychotherapy has been through the development of a new—and broadly inclusive—ethos. It has brought relativity into the social and behavioral sciences by defining fresh views of authority, truth, participant experience and the application of psychotherapy principles for personal growth. . . . Though the existentialists offer little in the way of practical prescriptions, their concepts of experience, authenticity,

confrontation . . . have encouraged psychotherapeutic inventiveness aimed at giving substance to these otherwise abstract goals. (p. 316)

KEY CONCEPTS

View of Human Nature

Unlike Carl Rogers's person-centered therapy, Gestalt therapy states that humans by nature are neither basically good nor evil. They do evidence a tendency toward growth, and they are inherently self-regulating. Gestalt therapy's view of human nature is founded on four major concepts: (1) biological field theory, (2) the entity of the organism, (3) the need for contact and relationship, and (4) the capacity for making wholes. The biological field theory proposes that all organisms exist in environmental contexts with reciprocal influences on each other. No organism, including people, can be reduced to separate components. People can only be understood in their organized, interactive, and interdependent totality. Every **field**—including experiential, social, cultural—is part of a unitary dynamic process (Kirchner, 2010). A person who is intrinsically self-regulating is an organized whole.

Human Nature and Contact

People have a need for contact. The essential character of human life is **contact**, which can be defined broadly as a meeting with various kinds of others. More specifically, contact may be defined as forming a figure of interest against a ground within the context of the organism–environment field. Contact is initiated by seeing, hearing, smelling, touching, and moving. Every organism (including humans) has the potentiality of forming effective and fulfilling contact with others in its environment and pursues ways of having contact with others so that the organism can survive and grow to maturity. Perls viewed all contact as creative and dynamic. Each experience takes place as a creative adjustment of the organism in the environment.

Polster and Polster (1973) describe contact as the "lifeblood of growth" and absolutely necessary for survival and change. As we have responsive meetings with others, we form a figure–ground relationship between ourselves and others. Such a figure–ground relationship allows us to have a concept of ourselves. Relationships with others are absolutely necessary to form a concept of ourselves as being distinct from those who surround us and become a part of our lives. Perls saw relationships as an indispensable part of our being and our relatedness to the world.

Inner Reflection

What, if any, features of Gestalt therapy's view of human nature would you incorporate into your integrative psychotherapy approach?

Meaning Making

Human beings synthesize a wide range of bodily, perceptual, cognitive, behavioral, and existential Gestalts (Crocker, 1999). Learning and change occur when we organize our experiences and assimilate novelty. Human beings are, then, meaning makers. We cannot refrain from meaning making, and we cannot stop from organizing and reorganizing ourselves as we have new experiences (Kirchner, 2010). We are wired to seek meaning from our experiences, and meaning making emerges both contextually and relationally. Gestalt therapists seek to understand their clients' meaning making. What meaning did the daughter make from her contact with her mother?

Meaning making takes place in small, everyday situations. A student perceives that a professor

Inner Reflections

To what extent is your life one of meaning making?

What meaning have you made out of your life or out of your life experiences?

frowns at him, and he doesn't know what to "make of the professor's frown." A boyfriend fails to buy a valentine gift for his girlfriend, and she wonders what meaning she should attach to his behavior. Is his failure just a case of forgetfulness or something more?

Human Nature and Holism

Gestalt therapists maintain that people function holistically. Bodily functions, emotions, thoughts, sensations, and perceptions of all kinds function interrelatedly. None of these parts can be understood adequately outside the context of the whole person. The principle of **holism** may be defined as the basic idea that everything is inevitably interrelated and mutually dependent on each other. The whole is more than, and different from, the sum of the individual parts. A holistic approach to human beings embraces and affirms complexity, inclusion, and diversity and resists reductionist approaches.

Moreover, people are a part of their environment, and they cannot be understood appropriately apart from their environment. This principle corresponds to the Gestalt view that an individual's behavior can only be meaningfully understood in context. People are capable of being fully aware of their sensations, thoughts, emotions, and perceptions. They are capable of making choices and are responsible for their behavior because of the process of self-awareness. People experience themselves primarily in the present. They are able to experience the past and the future in the here-and-now through the process of remembering and anticipating.

The Gestalt approach to human nature represents a deeply humanistic view of people; however, it should not be confused with the self-actualization theory of Rogers. Rogers posited that people are basically good, but he construed their self-actualization ability in terms of future satisfaction of goals. From Rogers's perspective, people are in the process of becoming; they strive to become. In contrast, Gestalt therapy emphasizes the now rather than the *process of becoming*.

The Phenomenological Perspective: Awareness

Phenomenology is an academic discipline that helps people stand back from their typical way of thinking so that they can discern the difference between what is actually being perceived and felt in the current situation and what is residue from the past (Woldt & Toman, 2005). A Gestalt therapist respects, uses, and clarifies immediate perceptions. Gestalt therapy treats both what the client subjectively feels in the present and what the therapist objectively observes as real and important data. This phenomenological approach to clients differs from approaches that treat what the client experiences as questionable and uses interpretation to find "real meaning" and "truth" in the client's life.

The goal of Gestalt phenomenological exploration is client awareness or insight. Insight is conceptualized as a patterning of a person's perceptual field in such a manner that the significant realities become apparent; it is the formation of a Gestalt in which the pertinent factors fall into place with regard to the whole. Gestalt therapy views insight as a type of clear understanding of the structure of the life situation being examined (Crocker, 2005). After a contact experience, people usually withdraw to integrate what has been learned. The principle of boundary is related to that of contact. A boundary has two functions: to connect and to separate. Contact and withdrawal are intimately connected to individuals' healthy psychological functioning.

Gestalt therapists use focused awareness and experimentation to attain client insight. The Gestalt therapist who holds a phenomenologist perspective studies not only the client's personal awareness but also the awareness process itself (Yontef, 1999). Clients need to learn how to become knowledgeable about their awareness.

Field Theory and Human Nature

According to Yontef and Jacobs (2005), Gestalt therapy is a radical ecological theory that contends that there is no meaningful way to consider any living organism apart from interactions with its environment, meaning apart from the organism–environment field of which it is a part. Yontef and Jacobs (2005) have stated,

> Psychologically, there is no meaningful way to consider a person apart from interpersonal relations, just as there is no meaningful way to perceive the environment except through someone's perspective. (p. 309)

Organismic Self-Regulation

Gestalt therapy theory presumes that people are inherently self-regulating and, therefore, capable of solving their own problems. **Organismic self-regulation** represents our creative adjustment to the environment. Our equilibrium with our environment is disturbed by the emergence of various needs or sensations. Organismic behavior is purposive and goal seeking rather than random. We organize our fields in terms of the principle of figure formation. For instance, we are hungry and we want to eat something. Our hunger is specific. We want pizza, and thus, what becomes figural (meaning comes to the forefront of our environment or field) will be related to our need/hunger for pizza. Once our need for pizza is met, the next need or interest becomes the center of our attention.

In healthy organismic self-regulation, we are aware of our shifting need states. Healthy functioning requires us to be in contact with what is actually taking place in our person–field environment. When we have made good contact with our environment, we are in touch with our experience in relation to the field. When we do not allow a figure to emerge or it is somehow interrupted or misdirected, there is disturbance in our awareness and contact,

Inner Reflections

What, if any, unfinished business exists in your life?

How does your unfinished business affect your relationships with others, including your spouse, partner, work associates, and so on?

Will any of your unfinished business affect your ability to become an effective therapist?

hence enhancing the chance of our developing maladaptive behavior (Yontef & Jacobs, 2005).

Unfinished Business

Although this concept is central to Gestalt therapy, its origins can be traced to the psychoanalytic school of thought. **Unfinished business** may be defined as the unexpressed feelings that are associated with distinct past memories and fantasies. Usually, these feelings may be resentment, rage, hatred, pain, anxiety, grief, guilt, and abandonment that are not fully figured into awareness (Polster, 1987). Instead, they exist in the background and affect present life behaviors by causing preoccupations, compulsive behaviors, and other self-defeating behaviors.

It is assumed that it is an inherent drive of an organism and of people to organize their perceptual and experiential field in a way that Gestalts reach closure. Each incomplete or unclosed experiential Gestalt represents an unfinished situation, which interferes with the formation of a new Gestalt (Polster & Polster, 1973). Thus, if a person has an incomplete Gestalt related to his father, that Gestalt will influence the formation of new Gestalts. Clients who have not achieved Gestalt closure experience an interference with free functioning. Instead of growth, one finds stagnation and regression to earlier stages in life (stuck points, or impasses). Unfinished business refers to the tendency of a person to relive in the present thoughts and feelings that belong more appropriately to the past—that is, those things that lie in the death of the past are still affecting one's behavior in the present.

Generally speaking, such unfinished business of the past is denied awareness and, therefore, never really becomes figured in one's continuum of awareness. It remains in the background, interfering with one's "contact functioning"—a present-oriented, reality-bound awareness of both oneself and others. Unfinished business can turn into unexpressed feelings of resentment, rage, hatred, and pain. It was Perls's belief that a person's unfinished business of the past should be dealt with to the extent that it is affecting present behavior.

When clients have unfinished business, they experience what Perls called a stuck point or an impasse. An **impasse** is felt when a person's usual supports are not available, and new supports have not yet been mobilized (Yontef & Jacobs, 2005). Clients in an impasse feel paralyzed. Their forward and backward energies are fighting each other. When clients experience an impasse, they feel real internal terror. They feel that they cannot go back, and they are unsure if they can survive going forward. To resolve the stuck point or impasse, clients usually need some support from others. When clients are unable to mobilize support to work through the impasse, they continue to repeat the same old maladaptive behavior.

The therapist's task is to be with (provide external support) clients in experiencing the impasse without rescuing or frustrating them (Polster & Polster, 1973). The therapist uses techniques designed to help clients fully experience their condition of being stuck. As clients completely experience the impasse, they are able to get into contact with their frustrations and to resolve the unfinished business.

The client's acknowledgment, acceptance, and owning of feelings are essential in resolving unfinished business. According to Gestalt therapy, once a feeling is owned in the present, it can become figured. Feelings that are figured by an individual no longer become the central organizers of behavior. Perls believed that unacknowledged grief, anger, or loss of a loved object constitutes the bulk of unfinished business. Therefore, very often he would ask a client to place a lost loved's object in an empty chair and to say good-bye to that person (Mackewn, 2004).

Authenticity

The development of **authenticity** pervades all Gestalt therapy modalities. Authenticity refers to a person's state of truly being himself or herself. To obtain this goal, your continuum of awareness must be systematically expanded and figured. Authenticity is linked to healthy psychological functioning. A person's life is not characterized by facades and layers of pretense. An authentic self is in direct contrast to a false self.

Theory of Personality

Unlike some of the other theorists discussed in this book, Perls does not present a systematic theory of personality development. This section presents briefly some of the key elements he stressed regarding the healthy functioning and growth of human beings. The terms *contact, ego boundary, self, organismic self-regulation, self-actualization,* and *need fulfillment* are central in Perls's description of human development.

As children develop, they discover that there is a difference between themselves and the rest of the world, recognizing that there is a place where they end and the rest of the world begins. This differentiation of the self from other human beings is an important element in Gestalt personality development. The moment that children begin to differentiate themselves from their surroundings, they have made contact with their environment and have begun what Perls called "ego boundary." In this instance, contact may be defined as children's awareness of and behavior toward assimilating the novelties in their environment and their rejection of the unassimilable novelties. As Perls et al. (1951) have stated, "The organism grows by assimilating from the environment what it needs for its very growth" (p. viii).

All contact between children and their environment is creative and dynamic because the novelty must be assimilated. Making contact is the way in which they grow. Through contact, children form figure–ground relationships. It is important that as children make contact with their environment, they make strong figures and grounds, for such relationships lead to strong Gestalts.

Gestalt theory postulates that there is no self separate from one's organism/environmental field; self does not exist without "other" or someone else (Yontef & Jacobs, 2005). Our human experience does not exist without contact. Our personalities cannot develop without contact. The contact we have with others dominates the formation of our personalities. Each of us establishes a boundary to protect ourselves from negative intrusion or overload.

Personality development involves, then, a process of contact and boundary line drawing. We grow as human beings from our contact and from our withdrawal from others. In our contact relationships, we identify with what is nourishing and reject what is harmful. Our differentiated contact promotes our growth as people. We can become enlarged by the nature of our contacts with others or feel diminished by our contacts with them.

Frustration is important in the development of the self. According to Perls (1969a), "Without frustrations there is no need, no reason, to mobilize your resources, to discover that you might be able to do something on your own" (p. 32). Frustration in life helps us become more self-supporting since the experiences that we undergo teach us that we can endure certain setbacks and achieve our goals.

When we maintain a self-image that is inconsistent with the self, we experience tension and internal conflict between what the self wants to

> **Inner Reflections**
>
> In your opinion, what constitutes healthy or normal psychological development for people?
>
> Would you adopt any of Perls's views on healthy development into your integrative psychotherapeutic approach?

do and what the self-image says should be done. According to Yontef and Jacobs (2005),

> Good health has the characteristics of a good gestalt. The good gestalt describes a perceptual field organized with clarity and good form. A well-formed figure clearly stands out against a broader and less distinct background. The relation between that which stands out (figure) and the context (ground) is meaning. In a good gestalt, meaning is clear. (p. 312)

Good mental health results from our creative adjustment that takes place within a context of environmental possibility. When we are functioning in a healthy manner, our Gestalt formation process is freely functioning. Figures and grounds shift based on our changing needs and field conditions. Perls decried what people called normal behavior. In his opinion, what people called normal behavior was in actuality *adjustment to the reality of others*. Perls et al. (1951) have summarized the functioning of the psychologically healthy person:

> The description of psychological health and disease is a simple one. It is a matter of the identifications and alienations of the self. If a man identifies with his forming self, he does not inhibit his own creative excitement; and conversely, if he alienates what is not organically his own and therefore cannot be vitally interesting, but rather disrupts the figure/ground, then he is psychologically healthy, for he is exercising his best power and will to do the best he can in the difficult circumstances of the world. But on the contrary, if he alienates himself and because of false identifications tries to conquer his own spontaneity, then he creates his life dull, confused, and painful. (p. 235)

Inner Reflections

How comfortable would you feel adopting Perls's views on maladaptive behavior into your own integrative theory of counseling?

Is there a match with your views on maladaptive behavior and Perls's theory?

Theory of Maladaptive Behavior or Psychopathology

Perls was much more explicit about maladaptive functioning than he was about normal personality development. People who are suffering from maladjustment experience a split between what they are and what they believe they should be. They alienate or disown large aspects of their personality. Such disowning results in their having personality "holes" that are usually covered over with identifications that were initially based on external demands.

In maladaptive functioning, the individual lives for the self-image rather than for the self. Instead of trying to actualize the self, the individual tries to actualize the self-image, which is usually distorted and unrealistic. The person who displays maladaptive behavior has lost or temporarily abandoned organismic self-regulation. He or she is regulated by the opinions of others and the external demands of the environment.

Because Gestalt therapists view forming contact important to healthy functioning, they have described resistances to contact as forces that create poor mental health. Each person develops styles of contact resistance. Polster and Polster (1973) have described five major channels of maladaptive development. Introjection, projection, retroflection, deflection, and confluence are the most common means we use to maintain maladaptive behavior. In each of these processes, a person disowns some part of himself or herself, and that part is not allowed to become figural or to organize and energize action (Yontef & Jacobs, 2005). **Introjection** takes place when we uncritically accept others' beliefs and standards without assimilating them to make them congruent with who we are. It can be defined as the swallowing whole of things that must be destroyed before they can be assimilated into a person's behavior repertoire. For instance, a person who meets someone whom he admires may adopt the other person's behavior, mannerisms, speech, and beliefs, becoming as much like the other person as possible. The individual becomes a phony because he has swallowed another person's behavior wholesale without transforming it to meet his own personality needs and self-actualization tendency. As a result, the introjected behavior stands out like a sore thumb.

Projection may be defined as our placing in the outside world those parts of our personality that we refuse to accept or with which we are unable to identify. The projecting person has difficulty distinguishing between the inside and the outside world. Those features of an individual's personality (e.g., attitudes, feelings, and actions) that are inconsistent with self-image are disowned and placed onto objects or persons in the environment. For example, if a neurotic person cannot love, she may place this unwillingness to love on others. Projecting an attribute allows the individual to avoid taking responsibility for her own feelings (Polster, 1987).

Retroflection may be defined as the means we use to give ourselves what we were unable to obtain from the environment. What was originally directed toward the world changes its course of direction and is bent backward toward us. For instance, a woman who wants to hurt another person kills herself. A narcissistic man falls in love with himself because he does not receive the love he sought from others. A person receives partial satisfaction from retroflective behavior by giving to himself or herself what the environment denied.

Clients use **deflection** when they use a process of distraction to make it difficult to maintain a sense of contact with another person. Clients who deflect try to diffuse contact by overusing humor, abstract generalizations, and questions rather than statements (Frew, 1986). Clients who deflect engage their environment on an inconsistent basis and hence are inclined to feel emotional depletion.

Confluence consists of blurring the differentiation between the self and the environment. Confluence may be defined as the loss of the experience of a separate identity. Confluence occurs when an individual's need to withdraw is blocked by someone or something. Clients are encouraged to become increasingly aware of their dominant style of blocking contact.

Gestaltists conceptualize mental illness as a person's inability to form clear figures of interest, identify with one's moment-to-moment experiences, and respond to what one becomes aware of (Clarkson, 2004). In unhealthy adjustment, neurotic self-regulation replaces organismic self-regulation. Organismic self-regulation is replaced by the tyranny of the "shoulds"—that is, by attempts to control and manage one's experience rather than by accepting one's experience. Gestalt therapy focuses on the process of anxiety rather than on the content of anxiety (Mackewn, 2004).

Perls tended not to use the term *psychopathology*. Instead, he preferred the term *growth disorders* to refer to the most common problems in living. When Perls (1969a) did hint at psychopathology, he used the term *neurosis*. For instance, he described maladaptive behavior in terms of five layers of neuroses. To become psychologically mature, we must peel off each of the five layers: (1) phony, (2) phobic, (3) impasse, (4) implosive, and (5) explosive. The removal of each layer improves the person's contact with the environment.

1. The phony layer refers to reacting to others in stereotypical or inauthentic ways. We play games and assume roles at the phony level. We act nice to a person to get his or her vote or money.

2. At the phobic layer of our pathology, we avoid and run from the emotional or psychological pain regarding how dissatisfied we are with ourselves and others. We find it difficult to admit to ourselves that we are better off if a relationship with a relative or friend is ended.

3. The impasse, which has already been touched on in this chapter, is the point at which we are stuck in our own maturation. When we are at an impasse, we feel little internal or external support. Fear related to the impasse often causes us to play helpless, stupid, or crazy to get others to take care of us.

4. At the implosive level, we experience the deadness associated with parts of ourselves we have disowned. The client is threatened with experiencing his or her own death for the purpose of being reborn.

5. The explosive layer of neurosis involves a release of life's energies. The size of the explosion depends on the amount of human energy bound up in the explosive layer. To become fully alive, the person must be able to explode into anger, grief, or joy (Ward & Rouzer, 1974). During his workshops, Perls informed participants that cathartic explosions could be reached only after they had increased their awareness of the games and roles they play and disown them (Woldt & Toman, 2005).

THE THERAPEUTIC PROCESS

Gestalt therapy is highly verbal and experiential. Therapy focuses on what is happening in the moment-to-moment therapeutic process rather than on what is being discussed (the content). The therapist is highly intuitive and can be compared to an artist (Clarkson, 2004). Clients become aware of what they are doing, how they are doing it, and what they need to do to bring about desired change. Clients learn about themselves in relationship to others.

Although Gestalt therapy has acquired a reputation for being conducted primarily in groups, its mainstay is actually individual treatment (Yontef & Jacobs, 2005). Gestalt therapy starts with the first contact with the client. Usually, assessment and screening are completed as a part of the ongoing therapy relationship, instead of in a separate time period designated for diagnostic testing and history taking. Areas of assessment include the client's willingness and support for therapy within the Gestalt framework, the match of the client and the therapist, decisions on the frequency of sessions, and the need for adjunctive treatment, including medical consultation. Sometimes individual work is combined with group therapy or family therapy (Yontef & Jacobs, 2005).

Gestalt therapy is designed for clients receptive to working on self-awareness and for those who desire mastery of their awareness process. Gestaltists maintain that although some people claim that they are interested in changing their behavior, the average person seeking psychotherapy simply wants relief from discomfort. Many people who engage a therapist believe that relief will come from their therapist doing the work; however, they soon find out that they must become deeply involved in their therapy and in delivering their own relief.

Consciousness raising in Gestalt therapy is designed to free people from *maya*—from the phony and fantasy layer of existence. Maya is primarily a mental world of concepts, ideals, and intellectual rehearsals. Perls asserted that to free ourselves from maya, we must lose our mind and come to our senses.

Gestalt therapy is most appropriate for people who create anxiety and depression by rejecting themselves, alienating aspects of themselves, and deceiving themselves. It is intended for people who do not know how they further their own unhappiness but who are open to awareness work, particularly that which deals with self-regulation. Clients who desire symptom relief without doing awareness work may be better suited for behavior modification, medication, and so on. Gestalt therapists help clients distinguish the differences between "I can't" and "I won't" (Clarkson, 2004). They work with clients to help them learn how their own internal barriers or resistance thwart awareness work. Therapists place a high value on clients' autonomy and their own self-determination (Mackewn, 2004).

Gestalt therapy is designed to promote a client's exploration of awareness issues in his or her life rather than to modify specific client behavior. Clinicians facilitate the growth process within clients. They do not attempt to cure clients. The method for Gestalt therapy is direct engagement, which is based on the Gestalt concept of contact (Clarkson, 2004). Clients receive honest feedback from clinicians. Clients are told in an authentic manner how they are experienced by the therapist. Therapy focuses on what the client does and on the interactions between the clinician and the client. Usually, therapy focuses on the **here-and-now** (Mackewn, 2004). Some of the principles of Gestalt therapy include the following:

- Live now; stay in the present.
- Live here; be with the present.
- Stop imagining; experience reality.
- Stop unnecessary thinking.
- Expressing rather than manipulating, explaining, justifying, or judging.
- Do not restrict your awareness; give in to your awareness of unpleasantness.
- Accept no "should" or "ought" other than your own.
- Take full responsibility for your own actions, feelings, and thoughts.
- Surrender to being who you are right now.

Perls (1969a) wrote the Gestalt Prayer to summarize his relationship between himself and the world as well as between himself and his clients:

The Gestalt Prayer

I do my thing and you do your thing.

I am not in this world to live up to your expectations,

And you are not in this world to live up to mine.

You are you, and I am I, and if by chance we find each other, it's beautiful.

If not, it can't be helped.

The Therapeutic Relationship

Gestaltists borrowed the concept of dialogues from Martin Buber (1958), the existentialist who proposed the concept of "I–Thou" relationships. Buber distinguished between genuine **dialogues** in which people truly hear and respond to each other ("I–Thou" dialogue) and apparent dialogues ("I–It" dialogue) in which they talk at each other, neither hearing nor understanding what the other has just communicated. "I–It" dialogues may, in fact, be a monologue rather than a dialogue. In relationships that are monologues, there is usually an oppressor and an oppressed. The more powerful person imposes a view on the less powerful.

In terms of the therapy relationship, dialogue refers to the character and the quality of spoken communication between practitioner and client. The therapist–client relationship in Gestalt counseling is often described as an "I–Thou," here-and-now relationship, a type of existential encounter that is authentic and nonjudgmental.

A dialogue in Gestalt counseling may take place along several dimensions. The first set of conditions is related to with whom the dialogue is taking place, where, and when. A man is angry with his father. He wants to have a dialogue with his father about an argument they had a couple of weeks ago.

The second dimension along which a dialogue can take place involves how the dialogue occurs. Gestalt practice describes one type of dialogue as a "life situation" or an "existential situation" dialogue. In this case, there is another person in your life with whom you are having a problem. A dialogue may also take place when the therapist deals with the client's "other person" *by imagination*. To promote a dialogue, clinicians often use the **empty chair**— that is, imagining that the other is sitting in an empty chair facing the client.

Another related kind of dialogue is one reenacted in the present, with someone or something from your past that involves unfinished business that keeps you from being fully present in the now. For instance, your brother died, and you had unresolved issues with him. The argument that you had with him just a few days before he died keeps playing and replaying in your head. The therapist asks you to talk to your brother in the empty chair about your relationship with him. You apologize to your brother for your role in the challenged relations; you cry, and the dialogue brings relief to you.

A third kind of imaginal dialogue is with a figure from your dreams or imagination. For instance, you keep dreaming about scary things. Someone is frightening you in your dream each night after you drift off to sleep. The therapist tells you to confront the scary thing, and you ask the figure in your dream to go away and not come back or else you will take definitive action. Essentially, the dialogue with the character in your dream has allowed you to take back your power and to assert yourself as a capable, strong person (Clarkson, 2004).

Sometimes children may not be ready to talk to an empty chair. Gestaltists who work with children have them draw pictures and have dialogues between figures they've drawn or between themselves and the picture. Children might also be asked to work with clay and to participate in a dialogue with their created figure (Lambert, 2003; Oaklander, 1988).

Finally, a fourth kind of dialogue is an internal one that takes place between various divided parts of yourself. There is the dialogue between your real self and your false self, between the self that wants to reach out to other people and the self that is afraid to do so. Dialogues can be very powerful in Gestalt counseling. A dialogue might help a client have cathartic release when it is done using the technique of the empty chair. A dialogue may help clients hear and see the other. Dialogue also results in some measure of increased awareness of clients' own life processes.

In addition to having a dialogue with other people in your life, the Gestalt therapeutic relationship can be conceptualized as a dialogue between the client and the counselor. Dialogue in the counseling relationship can be defined as a genuine, equal, and honest communication between two people in an "I–Thou" relationship. Gestalt therapy emphasizes four types of dialogue within the therapeutic relationship:

1. Inclusion, which occurs when therapists put themselves as much as possible into the experience of the client. In doing so, therapists do not judge, analyze, or interpret what they observe.

2. Presence refers to therapists expressing their observations, preferences, feelings, personal experience, and thoughts to the client.

3. Commitment to dialogue between the therapist and the client allows a feeling of connection (contact) between the two. Dialogue is something

that is done between the therapist and the client rather than just something that is said.

4. Dialogue is active and can be nonverbal as well as verbal. It can be any modality that expresses and moves the energy between therapist and client.

In Gestalt therapy, the interaction between the therapist and the client is an ever-changing dialogue characterized by the counselor's warmth and acceptance. A Gestalt therapist must bring a willingness and capability to be present as a person in the therapeutic encounter. Therapists maintain a dialogue with clients both verbally and nonverbally. Pointing out the nonverbal aspects of dialogue, Philippson (2001) has stated,

> Maintaining the dialogue does not mean that I need to do a lot of speaking, to answer the client's questions, or to say much about myself. I can uphold my side of the dialogue by my distance between me and the client, rather than by finding a verbal response each time. (pp. 149–150)

Mirroring (also labeled mimicry) can function as a powerful element in nonverbal dialogue. For instance, the therapist might say, "Here's what I see you doing" and then demonstrate nonverbally what the client is doing in therapy. An enactment can represent a dialogue. Clients with a begging, whining manner might be asked to get down and grovel on their hands and knees in front of the person to whom they're giving away their power. This type of enactment can result in clients' powerful recognition of the groveling position that they are assuming, and they might just decide to change and become more assertive.

Goals of Therapy

As pointed out throughout this chapter, a primary goal of Gestalt counseling is individual awareness. This goal includes greater awareness in specific areas and also greater ability for the client to bring automatic habits into awareness as desired. Client awareness includes knowing the environment, taking responsibility for choices, self-knowledge, self-acceptance, and the ability to contact. Gestalt therapy helps raise clients' awareness about how they are functioning in their environment (with family, at work, at school, and with friends). As noted earlier in this chapter, Perls affirmed that everything that happens to a person is grounded in awareness and that awareness is the only basis for knowledge and communication.

Awareness implies a state of individual consciousness that develops spontaneously whenever the individual pays attention to whatever becomes foreground. It suggests that the person is in touch with self and environment—with what he or she is doing, thinking, planning, and feeling. Gestalt therapists help clients recognize how they block and distort their awareness. Gestalt clinicians believe that when people become aware of what they are doing in the here-and-now, they are able to make more meaningful choices and to take direct action to solve problems (Mackewn, 2004). The shuttle technique is often used to enhance clients' awareness. The therapist repeatedly directs the client's attention from one activity or experience to another. It is possible to move the client back and forth between reality and fantasy and from the past to the present. Using this technique, clients learn the location of energy impasses.

Perls (1969a) asserted that awareness in and of itself can be curative. He stated,

> And I believe that this is the great thing to understand: that awareness per se—by and of itself—can be curative. Because with full awareness you become aware of this organismic self-regulation, you can let the organism take over without interfering, without interrupting; we can rely on the wisdom of the organism. (p. 17)

A second goal in Gestalt therapy that is closely related to awareness is the goal of contact. The contact cycle is a very important part of the Gestalt approach. The general notion is that all of our experiences progress through a sequence of stages called the contact cycle (Polster & Polster, 1973). These stages are as follows:

- In the beginning, we are at rest, and our field of consciousness is undifferentiated.
- A need or want emerges, such as physical, psychological, or spiritual want. Sometimes we may or may not seek to clarify exactly what this need is before doing anything. As we become aware of the need, we become aroused and our attention is focused on the possible sources of need satisfaction.
- Our energy has now been mobilized, and we scan the field for possible sources of satisfaction. Depending on the need, this might be a brief process.
- We choose one way of satisfying the need, and we move toward it to get it.
- We make contact with the object of choice and experience it.
- We judge it to be suitable or unsuitable and either continue with it or go back for further scanning.
- We experience satisfaction or dissatisfaction.
- We withdraw, and our energy now goes inward, fully digesting the experience. We are now ready for a new cycle to begin.

The point made by Gestalt therapy is that something can go wrong with each of these stages.

- Some people can never reach the point of rest.
- Some people are not unaware of their needs.
- Some people cannot mobilize their energy.
- Some people cannot fully experience anything.
- Some people cannot discriminate between what is good for them and what is not.
- Some people cannot or find it difficult to withdraw from the contact situation.

Each of these points on the contact cycle indicates a possible problem area. By understanding our contact cycle, we arrive at a better understanding regarding what the problem is.

A third goal in Gestalt therapy is to help people achieve integration or to re-own and integrate the parts of themselves that they have previously rejected. Integration means uniting the various parts of a person to form a complete

Inner Reflection

Do you believe that client awareness is a curative factor in and of itself?

whole (Mackewn, 2004). The Gestalt therapist stresses the importance of integrating opposing forces within a person—for example, love and hate, top dog and underdog, or one's "shoulds" and one's "wants." Perls cautioned against the idea that total integration is ever achieved. One can only approximate the achievement of these goals. He stated, "Now there is no such thing as total integration. Integration is never completed; maturation is never completed. It's an ongoing process forever and ever. . . . There's always something to be integrated, always something to be learned" (Perls, 1969a, p. 64).

A fourth goal of Gestalt therapy is to help clients mature and grow up. Commenting on this goal, Perls (1969a) asserted, "We have a very specific aim in Gestalt therapy, and this is the same aim that exists at least verbally in other forms of discovering life. The aim is to mature, to grow up" (p. 28). Gestalt practitioners promote client maturity by having clients take responsibility for their own lives. They push clients, at times almost relentlessly, to assume ownership of the feelings they have and the statements they make. Clients learn to own what they are and to disown what they are not.

Gestalt practitioners maintain that language is frequently used to disguise a person's unwillingness to assume responsibility. For example, the word *can't* is often used to disguise a person's unwillingness to assume responsibility. Similarly, Gestaltists view the statement "I feel guilty" as another example of how clients use language to avoid taking responsibility (Clarkson, 2004). The woman who says she feels guilty about working because it takes her away from her children too much might be concealing feelings of resentment toward either her children or the work that she does.

Inner Reflection

Do you ever say, "He made me so angry"? If so, you are placing responsibility for your anger on another person and not owning your anger.

Guilt feelings are usually a person's attempt to show good intentions or compliance with the mode of behavior society considers appropriate when, in reality, the person does not want to do what society deems acceptable. To get at the heart of guilt feelings, the Gestalt clinician may ask a client to experiment with substituting the words *I resent* or *I demand* for *I feel guilty*. As the client substitutes these words, the clinician asks if he or she feels more comfortable. The underlying belief is that unexpressed resentment prevents us from dealing adequately with a situation. We are inclined to hang on to feelings of resentment, thereby letting them interfere with our functioning.

Finally, another goal of Gestalt therapy is to help a person deal with and accept anxiety as part of the natural order of life. A client must be willing to take risks, to confront, and to try to assimilate experiences into a meaningful whole. Clients live their problems in therapy.

Role of the Therapist

Gestalt clinicians help clients develop their own awareness. They observe what has become figured in a client's life. The therapist is directive and serves as a major catalyst to bring about client change. According to Laura Perls (1976), "The therapist is a directive leader and orchestrates all aspects of the therapeutic interactions, with the advice and consent of the client who is working" (p. 222). One of the major roles of the therapist is to frustrate clients' demand for support and help so that they become more self-reliant. Perls labeled this a safe emergency (Clarkson, 2004). When clients become threatened by the fact that they must learn to rely on themselves, they become immobilized and experience what Perls labeled an impasse. When the client experiences an impasse, the therapist provides a "safe emergency," which allows the client to feel safe enough to continue working in therapy toward self-sufficiency or maturity.

Gestalt clinicians take the role of assisting clients to make important changes in their lives. They maintain that change takes place in clients when they fully own what they are doing and how they are doing it. Therapists help clarify the client's awareness of the self and the environment. They look for how and in what specific ways clients' self-support is strong or weak. They guide clients' developing awareness and contact with boundaries. Therapists pay attention to what their clients are doing moment to moment and what is happening between the clients and themselves. They work in the immediacy of the counseling session and under the assumption that the most pressing client need will emerge to figure. Therapists work on the symptom present in the counseling session, regardless of the symptom initially presented by the client.

In Gestalt therapy, clinicians are permitted and encouraged to disclose their personal experiences, both in the moment and in their lives (Yontef & Jacobs, 2005). Gestalt therapists must strive to be themselves during counseling sessions. To move toward this type of relationship, clinicians must be at peace with the differences between themselves and their clients. Gestalt counselors are inclined to use certain rules in helping clients become more aware of the now (Mackewn, 2004). Some of these rules are as follows:

- *The principle of now:* Gestalt therapists always use the present tense and deal with life in the present rather than in the past (Polster, 1987).
- *The use of* I *instead of* it: The therapist helps clients substitute personal pronouns (take responsibility for feelings) for impersonal ones. For instance, a person might say, "It's difficult to get a real date on campus." The therapist would ask the person to restate the sentiment by using *I*. "I have difficulty getting a real date on campus" (Polster, 1987).
- *Focusing on how and what rather than why:* Gestalt therapists maintain that when clinicians ask why questions, they are requesting a rationale/excuse from clients.
- *The conversion of questions to statements:* People sometimes hide behind their questions. Gestalt clinicians ask clients to change their questions into statements.
- *Paying attention to clients' language patterns:* A client's language can both describe and conceal. For instance, "I can" talk versus "I won't." The

therapist also looks for language that denies power—qualifiers and disclaimers such as "perhaps," "sort of," and "possibly."

- *Listening to clients' metaphors:* When therapists tune in to clients' metaphors, they learn about their internal and external struggles. Some metaphors are "I feel like a ton of bricks have been placed on my chest." "I feel as if I have been lynched." The therapist translates the meaning of these metaphors into manifest content so that it can be dealt with in therapy.

Role of the Client

Clients are active participants who make their own interpretations and therapeutic conclusions. Clients work toward re-owning unintegrated parts of themselves. Polster (1987) has presented a three-stage integration sequence that characterizes clients' growth in therapy. *Discovery* forms the first part of the sequence. During this sequence, clients arrive at a realization about themselves or come to a new understanding of an old situation. These discoveries might surprise them (Polster & Polster, 1973).

Accommodation is the second phase of the client integration sequence. Clients recognize that they have a choice in how they live their lives. Their awareness of self and others continues to expand. Clients gain in their coping skills. They may carry out therapist-directed homework assignments. *Assimilation* is the third phase of the clients' sequence toward reintegration. They learn how to influence their own environment. They develop confidence in their ability to take charge of their lives (Polster, 1987). The interaction between the therapist and the client is a continually changing dialogue marked by caring, acceptance, and self-responsibility.

Therapy Techniques

Gestaltists have developed therapeutic interventions called exercises and experiments. Exercises are defined as techniques used to elicit certain emotions in clients. Standard exercises have been developed in Gestalt therapy, such as the exercise

"May I feed you a sentence?" On the other hand, experiments emanate from the immediate interaction (dialogue) between the client and the therapist. **Experiments** are typically spontaneous, one-of-a-kind interventions that are related to a specific moment in therapy. They deal with an emerging issue such as clients' reports of a need, dream, fantasy, and/or body awareness. Experiments are conducted with clients' full participation, and they are constructed to broaden clients' awareness and to encourage them to try out new ways of behaving. Some examples of an experiment include assuming the identity of a parent, imagining a threatening event in the future, or reliving a painful event.

As clients participate in experiments, they actually experience the feelings associated with their conflicts or issues in the here-and-now. Experiments are tailored to each client, and they provide safety and support to clients while encouraging them to try out new behavior. Sometimes interventions are more appropriate in counseling groups than with clients in individual therapy. The following are interventions used in Gestalt therapy:

The Hot Seat. This technique is designed to bring about greater self-awareness among clients who are usually in a group setting. Typically, a session begins with the leader's explanation of the "hot-seat" concept (Polster & Polster, 1973). Members are told that anyone who wants to work may sit in a chair facing the leader. The person who decides to sit in the chair is told to begin by stating a specific life problem. All references to the problem must be made in terms of present feelings—the here-and-now. The group leader explains that other members may be asked to help in some sort of structured way, but that unless specifically asked to do so, they are not to interfere. The individual sits in the hot seat anywhere from 10 to 30 minutes or until both the individual and the leader feel closure has been reached. During a member's stay in the hot seat, the leader interacts directly and aggressively to get to the problem. If no one comes forward to work, the leader may decide to wait it out or to initiate warm-up exercises.

Now and How. Fritz Perls (1969a) once said that Gestalt therapy stands on two legs: now and how. Now refers to a person's immediate awareness of experiencing. How refers to a person's description of the manner in which certain feelings are experienced. A now statement brings the past and the present together. For instance, instead of talking about past experiences with significant others that caused unhappiness, a client might state, "Now I am feeling like a hopeless child, still clinging to my mother's apron strings." To get the client to deal with the how of this feeling, the therapist would ask the client to demonstrate behaviorally what this statement means. The therapist asks, "What are the sensations you experience when you feel like a child, clinging to your mother's apron strings?"

If the client responds by expressing anger when demonstrating the how, the therapist encourages him or her not to leave the feeling behind. This method is called "staying with it." The therapist might state, "Can you stay with this feeling?" The stay-with-it technique demonstrates Perls's belief that neurotic behavior is sustained by a person's phobic avoidance.

Top Dog and Underdog Introjections. Borrowing from the psychoanalytic tradition, Perls (1969a) used the concept of introjection to refer to the process by which people take into themselves aspects of other people, especially their parents. When individuals introject uncritically, they may fail to assimilate adequately that which they have introjected. There may be a split between what they want to do and what they feel they should do. Perls labeled "should" introjections as top dog. Top dog is roughly the equivalent of the psychoanalytic superego. Top dog operates on "shoulds" and has a righteous and authoritarian nature. "If you don't act like a good girl, then you'll be called cheap trash, and nobody will ever respect you."

In contrast, underdog attempts to control top dog by reacting defensively, apologizing and playing the role of "nobody likes me." Clients who operate from the underdog position are usually passive aggressive, make excuses for behavior, and have countless reasons for delay. The struggle between top dog and underdog often results in our having unfulfilled promises to ourselves. We are so busy trying to please top dog that we postpone doing what we would like to do with our lives. Those who play underdog have great resentment toward those whom they consider their top dog.

Dreamwork. Perls described dreamwork as "messages" that reflect a client's place at a certain time. Unlike psychoanalysts, Gestalt clinicians do not interpret clients' dreams. Instead, clients present dreams, and then the therapist directs them to experience what it is like to be each part of the dream. The goal is to bring dreams back to life and to relive them as if they were happening now. Working with clients' dreams means that the therapist makes a list of all the details of the dream, remembering each person and event. Next, the therapist asks clients to become each of these parts through role-playing and inventing dialogue. This technique helps clients get in touch with the multiple aspects of themselves. Clients with repetitive dreams are encouraged to understand that unfinished business is being brought into awareness and that there is a need to take care of the message the dream delivered.

Making the Rounds. This technique is used primarily in groups. In this warm-up exercise, confrontation is at its height. Frequently, making the rounds is precipitated by a person saying something that the therapist feels should be expressed to other members in the group. For instance, a participant might state, "I hate everyone in this room." The therapist might respond by saying, "Make that statement to each person here, and in doing so, express your feelings about each person." Making rounds may also take the form of asking a person, "Why are you in touch with in this group?"

Role Reversals. The role reversal technique may be used either in groups or in individual therapy. The therapist uses reversals to help clients understand that their overt behavior may represent the opposite of their latent impulses. A client might be asked to role-play a specific feeling or behavior that seems the opposite of what he or she wants. For instance, a woman may say that she suffers from extreme timidity. The therapist might ask her to play the role of an exhibitionist. By assuming an exhibitionist role, the woman may make contact with a part of herself that had been previously denied.

Homework. Sometimes Gestalt clinicians give homework assignments between therapy sessions. Homework might entail having clients write dialogues between parts of themselves or between the parts of their bodies. For instance, a therapist asks a client to have his heart write a letter to his mind. This technique is appropriate when the client's mind seems to be saying one thing but the heart is saying something else.

Rehearsal. From the rehearsal technique, clients can gain awareness of how much time they use preparing to play their social roles or the effort required when they are trying to be something other than what they are. For instance, using fantasy, clients can rehearse performing well on an important examination or asking their supervisor for a raise. Rehearsal permits practice and modeling of desirable behaviors, especially in situations that provoke in clients strong avoidance anxiety.

Exaggeration. This exercise requires clients to accentuate behavior or gestures of which they may only be mildly aware. Exaggeration of body language, including gestures, tone of voice, posture, and facial expressions, can promote clients' awareness of incongruences between their verbal messages and their nonverbal communications. For instance, some clients speak of fear while smiling or speak kindly of someone while clenching a fist, or they laugh at an accident in which a loved one was injured. The Gestalt therapist brings the client's behavior to awareness by copying or mimicking the client's posture or tone of voice or by asking the client to repeat or exaggerate a gesture or statement. The therapist may even ask the client to translate an emotion into motion—for instance, "Can you dance this emotion?"

Withdrawal. The Gestalt school emphasizes an individual's right to withdraw from contact and from therapy. Perls (1969b) suggests that just as there can be no left direction without a right, there can be no real contact without a withdrawal. Each individual must establish effective, personal contact boundaries so that his or her feelings may become fully figured. Likewise, each person must allow his or her withdrawal from a group to become fully figured. Withdrawal is significant because it symbolizes the organismic regulation of the person. People decide for themselves whether they want to be left alone or in contact with other people.

The Gestalt counselor helps a participant withdraw psychologically from a group if that individual indicates he or she wants to do so. Here the counselor takes into consideration the principle of saturation. That is, the participant may have become saturated with making contact with other group members. The technique can also be modified for individual counseling. If a person expresses a need to withdraw, a counselor might say, "Try to relax and imagine that you are going to leave this group. What are you experiencing now? Can you try to put yourself into what you are experiencing now?" Gradually, the participant breaks contact and withdraws into whatever he or she is experiencing in that moment. The client's own organismic self-regulating system determines when contact should be made again.

RESEARCH AND EVALUATION
Multicultural Positives

Gestalt therapy's basic tenets have been found to have a solid relationship with concepts of multicultural diversity. Counseling techniques can be tailored to accommodate the ways in which culturally diverse clients perceive and interpret their culture. Frew (2008) has pointed out that one of the cultural benefits of Gestalt therapy is that the Gestalt experiments can be tailored to each individual's interpretation of his or her culture. Similarly, Fernbacher and Plummer (2005) can be used to help clients develop their own cultural identity.

Gestalt therapy is especially helpful in getting clients to unite the various polarities in themselves; hence, this school might be highly effective in working with clients who have conflicting views about accommodation and assimilation into a particular culture. Clients can be encouraged to examine the sides of them that say, "I do not want to lose my native cultural identity," and "It is important that I change and accept the culture of my host." Using the empty-chair technique, therapist might help their clients deal with what it means to be a second- or third-generation Latino.

Enns (1987) has indicated that Gestalt therapy exercises can be useful for female clients in three ways: (1) assisting clients to become more aware of themselves as distinct people with their own special power, (2) promoting the expression of anger through the empty-chair and other exercises, and (3) helping women become more aware of the actual choices they are making in their lives. Gestalt therapy emphasizes the importance of individuals making their own choices.

Multicultural Blind Spots

The limitations of Gestalt therapy for working with culturally diverse clients are also sobering. Gestalt therapy produces intense client feelings that might be appropriate for European American cultures but less suitable for Eastern and Asian cultures—cultures that place high honor and respect on family and parents. Asian clients might find, for instance, that getting angry with their parents in a top dog–underdog experiment to be extremely upsetting.

Gestalt therapy has three primary cross-cultural limitations: (1) the confrontative role of

How do you evaluate the strengths and weaknesses of Gestalt therapy?

What, if any, parts of this theoretical approach would you include in your integrated theory of psychotherapy/counseling?

the counselor, (2) the intensity of the client's emotional experience in therapy, and (3) the therapy's highly individualistic philosophy. These limit the use of this approach for cultural groups that are more oriented toward the collective group than toward the individual. Gestalt therapy is focused on the individual. For instance, the Gestalt Prayer emphasizes that each person does his or her own thing. Some cultures are emotionally reserved, and the intensity of Gestalt therapy may result in cultural offense for some clients.

Contributions of Gestalt Therapy

The contributions of Gestalt therapy are several. For one thing, it has had a major impact on the field of counseling. The Gestalt approach is rich in counseling strategies to help the client and the counselor stay in the here-and-now and to work toward greater integration of the self's polarities. Another is that it is a highly creative approach that uses experiments to help clients focus on action rather than just talk. Gestalt experiments give the counselor a wide range of strategies to help clients discover different parts of themselves as well as different faces of the issues they bring to counseling. Because of the potential powerful impact of Gestalt techniques, beginning counselors should use such techniques with great caution and with sufficient close supervision. Additional strengths of Gestalt counseling may be summarized as follows:

- Gestalt counseling emphasizes helping people incorporate and accept all aspects of themselves. A person cannot be understood outside the context of the whole person choosing to act on the environment in the present.
- The Gestalt approach helps a client focus on taking action to resolve areas of unfinished business in his or her life.
- Gestalt counseling's primary focus on doing rather than talking helps clients experience what the process of change is all about.
- The Gestalt approach is flexible; counselors can use any strategy that helps clients become more integrative.

Current Development: Relational Gestalt Therapy

Relational Gestalt therapy is a contemporary development within that school that emphasizes dialogue and the relationship between the client and the therapist. During November 2009, the Gestalt therapy institutes in New York City convened a 1-day conference on "What is Relational About Gestalt Therapy?" (Bloom, 2011). This conference solidified what had been taking place within Gestalt therapy for some time, and that was the gradual movement from presenting Gestalt therapy to one that was relational. A skeptic might say that Gestalt therapy's movement to a relational emphasis is part of its effort to "simply survive and become relevant to new therapists". There are now two categories of Gestalt therapists: (1) originalists, who stress the individualistic work of Perls, and (2) the relationalists. To some extent, relational is a new thrust in psychotherapy as evidenced by the burgeoning subgroup of relational psychoanalysis. Adding the term *relational* makes the theoretical approach more contemporary and helps it survive among the new therapies.

What is relational Gestalt therapy? According to Yontef (2009), "Gestalt therapy is systematically relational in its underlying theory and methodology. A relational perspective is so central to the theory of Gestalt therapy that without it there is no coherent core of Gestalt therapy theory or practice" (p. 37). Subsequently, Yontef (2009) alludes to the shift from Perls's sometimes aggressive approach to clients with the contemporary relational stance. He states,

> Relational Gestalt therapy . . . functions in a world with another view of human nature. It 'emphasizes the importance in the therapy of compassion, kindness, wisdom, equanimity and humility'. . . . It is my opinion that these qualities are not given as much emphasis in talk about Gestalt therapy as is warranted by their impact. Centered on dialogue, relational Gestalt therapy pays attention to the patient's vulnerability, to the impact of the therapy on the patient and on others. This is a different normative image of human beings from that of non-relational Gestalt therapists. It is an image of an entirely different atmosphere in Gestalt therapy's clinical practice. (p. 49)

The shift to relational Gestalt therapy emphasizes the return to a psychotherapy of dialogue (Hycner & Jacobs, 1995). "The dialogical turn" represents a turn away from Gestalt psychotherapy "where the therapist is a stage director who proposes role-plays, and so on, to the patient. It is turn to a psychotherapy of engage conversation" (Bloom, 2011). In the original model of Gestalt therapy, therapists would abruptly challenge any client attempts considered to be manipulations and would refuse to answer their questions. In relational Gestalt therapy, the therapist is a partner in a give-and-take conversation. The question remains: Is Gestalt therapy's shift to relational Gestalt therapy sufficient to help this theoretical approach survive and thrive in the coming decade?

Inner Reflections

What are your thoughts on the survivability of Gestalt therapy?

Can the new emphasis on Relational Gestalt therapy serve to renew interest for this psychotherapeutic approach?

Does the emphasis on the therapy relationship attract you to this theory?

Limitations of Gestalt Therapy

Gestalt therapy comes with some concerns about the theory itself and therapist abuse. The popularity of Gestalt therapy has decreased significantly since the heyday of Fritz Perls. In a survey of a large sample of counseling psychologists, less than 5% of the participants chose Gestalt therapy as either their primary or secondary theoretical orientation (Watkins, Lopez, Campbell, & Himmel, 1986). Despite the declining popularity of Gestalt therapy, its techniques continue to influence the counseling profession. Therapists from a broad range of theoretical schools use Gestalt techniques for integrating different parts of the self.

Gestalt therapy has been criticized for its lack of a clearly articulated theory and its limited empirical studies. Some criticisms include the following:

- Gestalt therapy lacks a strong theoretical base; it is all experience and technique and very gimmicky.
- The theory puts major emphasis on the *now*-and-*how* of clients' experience. This two-pronged focus does not deal sufficiently with the past.
- The approach minimizes assessment and diagnosis. Even though Gestalt counselors do screen their clients for appropriateness for therapy, critics have argued that this process needs to be more formalized.
- Gestalt therapy is too concerned with individual development and is criticized for its self-centeredness. Contrast, for instance, Adler's statements about an individual's need for social interest with Perls's statement: "I am not in this world to please you." Although many counseling theories are based on self-discovery, Gestalt therapy is considered extreme in this regard.
- Gestalt therapy is effective with overly socialized, restrained people but may not be as helpful for severely disturbed clients.

Evidence-Based Research

Recently, there has been a concerted effort within Gestalt therapy to become an evidence-based research. In an interview, Philip Brownell, author of the book *Handbook for Theory, Research, and Practice in Gestalt Therapy* (2008), elaborates on the push for evidence-based research and Gestalt therapy. He alludes to several developments that have led to the demand for more research in this school, including potential denial of government funding for therapists who identified as Gestalt therapists and unfavorable comparisons with cognitive-behavior therapies. In a 2013 interview with Laurie Fitzpatrick, Brownell states,

> Well, Gestaltists had been lamenting that there was not much research support for Gestalt therapy, in a world that was just rushing toward building an evidence base. And then, the whole comparison with Cognitive Behavioral Therapy would always result in people saying CB people will have all kinds of research because it's easy to do with that approach and all kinds of excuses. Then one day people realized that in Germany the government had gone to regulating the practice of psychotherapy—and they had not accredited Gestalt therapy based on the fact that it didn't have a research base. And so in Germany, the people there had to re-certify as psychoanalysts in order to keep practicing and—everyone went "un-oh," and so then there began to be a little more urgency around the idea that we had to do something about research. (Brownell, Melnick, & Fitzpatrick, 2013, para. 2)

Much of the recent evidence-based research on Gestalt therapy has been completed in Germany and in England. Research has indicated that Gestalt therapy is appropriate for certain affective disorders, anxiety states, somatoform disorders, and adjustment disorders. Strumpfel and Goldman (2002) have reported that outcome studies have demonstrated Gestalt therapy to be equal to or greater than other therapies for various disorders. More recent studies have found that Gestalt therapy affects favorably on personality disturbances, psychosomatic problems, and substance addictions. Strumpfel and Goldman conclude, "Within the field of humanistic psychotherapy, research and development in Gestalt therapy have shown how powerful and effective therapy can be in helping people lead healthier and more fulfilling lives" (pp. 212–213).

In a review of a Gestalt therapy article, Wagner-Moore (2004) pointed out that orthodox Gestalt therapy was poorly articulated, and its techniques received only minimal empirical validation. However, recent empirical research suggests

> that the 2-chair technique is superior to other therapeutic interventions for conflict splits, decisional conflict, marital conflict, and unfinished business and that the 2-chair technique is as effective as Rogerian and cognitive-behavioral therapies. Although F. Perls's techniques may have been generated largely from his idiosyncratic personality, these techniques have some validity for very specific psychological dilemmas. (p. 180)

Clearly, the era of Perls's clinical showmanship is over. Recent empirical investigations have supported the use of some Gestalt techniques such as the two-chair dialogue. Despite this accomplishment, Gestalt therapy remains marginalized because it historically has failed to present a coherent theoretical model. As Wagner-Moore (2004) has pointed out, "Relatively few graduate-level institutions have a systematic method for teaching gestalt psychotherapy in their curriculum. Gestalt therapy remains, at its very best, marginalized in the eyes of practitioners of other theoretically eloquent and empirically validated treatment protocols" (p. 188).

CASE ANALYSIS

Justin Working With a Gestalt Therapist

Although Gestalt therapy is usually completed with adults, a number of clinicians have begun to use this therapy approach with children and adolescents (see Lampert, 2003; Oaklander, 1988). A Gestalt therapist might address several issues in working with Justin, including his anger, his feeling that he does not know who he really is, his low self-esteem as related to school, his involvement with the courts, and the threat that he may be placed in residential treatment for troubled boys.

From a Gestalt perspective, Justin's equilibrium has been destroyed with the intervention of the court in his life and in his family's life. His figure–ground contact relationships with his environment have been disturbed. The therapist begins by establishing a positive contact or therapeutic relationship with Justin. He engages Justin by asking him how he feels about coming for counseling. If Justin has a hard time explaining his feelings to the therapist, he might be asked to draw his feelings and to take on the role of his feelings. The therapist then asks Justin to act out the feelings that he drew on the paper regarding how he felt about coming to therapy.

Justin's drawing has three dominant feelings: anger, confusion, and resistance. Anger is shown by his placing large teeth in the therapist's mouth—much larger than what they really are and what one would expect them to be. The therapist asks Justin to give the therapist's teeth a voice. "What are those teeth saying, Justin?" Justin responds that the teeth are saying, "I'm going to get you. I'm going to eat you alive." The therapist asks Justin if the therapist's teeth are frightening to him. Justin responds yes—the therapist's teeth are frightening to him, and they would be frightening to the therapist, too, if he were in Justin's position.

The therapist uses the metaphor of the teeth to begin talking about their relationship together. He moves close to Justin and shows him his teeth. The therapist is deeply himself. He says, "Look at my teeth, Justin. Are they frightening to you? I've got my own teeth problems. Look, do you see a cavity there?" Justin peers cautiously into the therapist's mouth and says, "Wow, you've got more cavities than me." The therapist laughs and says, "Let me see." Then Justin opens his mouth, and the therapist looks in.

Justin begins laughing at the entire situation. He remarks that he did not think that he would be looking into his therapist's mouth for cavities. The entire situation breaks the ice. Contact has been made between Justin and his therapist—contact that the therapist hopes will lead to Justin trusting him enough to deal with his issues. Contact with Justin is established and evaluated at every session.

In subsequent sessions, the therapist deals with Justin's anger. He begins to wonder if Justin *deflects his true feelings by hitting, kicking, and striking out.* The therapist asks Justin to give his anger a voice. He asks Justin if he will participate in a little experiment that might help him better understand his anger. He directs Justin's attention to an empty chair in his office. He tells Justin to pick an animal from the display of stuffed animals located in "the animal corner" to represent his anger. Justin chooses a stuffed tiger rather than the stuffed lion sitting right next to the tiger. The therapist asks Justin why he chose the tiger instead of the lion, who is king of the jungle. Justin responds that his anger is strong but not as strong as the lion's anger. Besides, he does not feel as if he is king of anything.

Justin gives the tiger (his anger) a voice. The tiger is angry because the other animals in the jungle make fun of him. The other animals don't respect him because he has a black spot on his fur coat. The therapist helps Justin explore and express his feelings. Justin tells the therapist that when he gets angry at the kids in class for laughing at him, "It feels like some big giant is squeezing me so hard that none of my good feelings or good parts of me can get out. Only the bad parts of me can get out." The therapist assists Justin in getting in touch with his own aggressive energy and anger. Justin is helped to make contact with the many faces of anger in his life—his anger over his mixed racial/ethnic heritage, his anger over his family's poverty, and his anger over other kids in his class being smarter than he is.

Justin needs to learn how to take responsibility for his behavior and his emotions. The therapist has Justin first role-play the teacher. Next, he asks Justin to exaggerate what he does in the class. In Gestalt therapy, clients are encouraged to conclude all expressions of feelings or beliefs with, "And I take responsibility for it." Sometimes clients

(Continued)

are asked to assume responsibility for their behavior by making language changes, such as changing "I can't" to "I won't." Whenever Justin complains that the kids in his class make him so mad that they cause him to fight, the therapist asks him to say, "I take responsibility for my own anger."

One of Justin's problems in class is that he gets up out of his seat without his teacher's permission. To get Justin in touch with this feeling, he asks Justin to get out of his therapy chair every few seconds. Each time Justin gets out of his seat, the therapist asks him what "his getting out of his seat" is saying to him. Justin responds, "It's saying, I'm tired of sitting all day long. Look at me. Pay attention to me." Eventually, the exaggeration exercise has driven home a point. Justin tires of getting up out of his seat during the exercise. He's exhausted and asks the therapist, "Can we stop now?" Together the therapist and Justin work to figure out ways in which he can make the teacher and class pay attention to him in a positive way. He decides to volunteer to help clean up the classroom. Justin reaches closure with the need to receive negative attention from his classmates and the teacher. He makes positive contact with them.

Strengthening Justin's strong sense of self requires that the therapist be attuned to every nuance of his being. Even the way that Justin holds a crayon or grimaces while drawing reveals much about Justin's process and brings something that was hidden into the open where it can be worked on and completed. The therapist starts with a surface acceptance of Justin's child. When Justin develops a sense of readiness, the therapist moves into more difficult parts of Justin's self—parts that were initially difficult to bring into awareness and to share with others. During counseling, the therapist creates a number of experiments that help Justin become more self-accepting and actively nurturing to the self. The focus of this work is to help Justin reframe those negative introjects about the self that he has acquired. The therapist uses the technique of feeding Justin various sentences or lines about himself and having Justin to respond to them. He asks Justin to complete sentences such as "I resent," "I demand," and "I appreciate."

Young people *do not* come into therapy knowing what they want to do, work through, or discover about themselves. Justin's therapist is the one who needs to devise the means by which they can explore his inner world. The therapist designs experiments to improve Justin's sense of self. The therapist understands that negative beliefs that children develop about themselves can never be changed by an outside person, but they can be addressed in the therapeutic relationship by helping the child develop a stronger sense of self. The goal is to help Justin integrate the various polarities within himself—for instance, his desire to be independent of his mother, yet his crying at the very thought that he might have to leave her and be placed in residential treatment. Justin has to deal with other polarities, such as disciplined/impulsive, lazy/industrious, and family loyalty/peer loyalty.

The therapist works with Justin to help him make appropriate contact, withdrawal, and other boundary maintenance tasks. Violet Oaklander (1988) has a sequence of experiencing a ball of dough in her book *Windows to Our Children.* Using concepts from that book, the therapist finds some dough on the back activity table in his office and begins to knead it. He then asks Justin to knead the dough, pound it, caress it, poke it, smooth it, and touch it with his feet, elbows, wrist, tips of his fingers, and the top of his hand. The therapist has Justin concentrate on playing with the dough for at least 15 minutes. As Justin plays with the dough (and after the experiment is over), the therapist asks Justin what he felt and thought.

Justin will be helped to deal with his unfinished business, especially that involving his father. He is helped to make contact with his father via the therapist's use of the empty chair. Justin chooses a stuffed weasel to represent his father in the empty chair. Both he and the therapist discuss why he chose a weasel to represent his father. Did his father weasel out on him by leaving the family and never returning?

SUMMARY

Gestalt therapy traces its origin to Gestalt psychology, existentialism, and humanism. Fritz Perls is usually credited with developing and organizing Gestalt therapy. Clearly, the movement was strongly influenced by his style and behavior. From Gestalt psychology, Perls borrowed the concepts of figure and ground relations, boundary, and contact. A person's figure–ground formation is dynamic. What emerges in the foreground is the figure. The figure is contrasted against the background (ground), or that which does not become the focus. A figure and ground form a Gestalt.

The figure symbolizes the need in focus, while the ground symbolizes other needs. When a need is met, the new need that comes into focus becomes the figure. In a healthy, fully functioning organism, there is a natural, spontaneous relationship between figure formation and figure destruction. A client's history constitutes the background of his or her existence. When disturbances or problems occur in a client's background (ground relation), the need must come to the foreground to be dealt with therapy.

Gestalt psychologists embrace the concept of holism, which maintains that everything is ultimately interrelated and mutually dependent on each other. The whole is more than and different from the sum of its parts. Conceptualizing the person as a total organism, Perls believed that a client's full awareness could in and of itself be curative. Healthy people accept responsibility for their lives, and their figure–ground relationships function smoothly.

The influences of humanism can be seen in the school's emphasis on organismic self-regulation, which is a process in which the organism strives for the maintenance of an equilibrium that is continually disturbed by its needs and regained into a whole that encompasses the parts. Gestalt therapy focuses on the "what and the how" of behavior. It describes human existence in terms of awareness, and it is highly experiential. This school holds that therapists should focus on the client's thoughts and feelings as they are being experienced in the moment.

Gestalt theory asserts that healthy behavior takes place when people act as total organisms rather than when they fragment their lives. Healthy people focus on successfully meeting one need at a time, while neurotic people attend to many needs at once; as a consequence, they are not able to meet any needs. The psychologically healthy person is one whose organismic self-regulation is functioning properly. New Gestalts form with relatively little effort, and all parts of the self are integrated and available to the person. People who are psychologically healthy live in the present moment with awareness, even though they are aware of the past.

In contrast, maladaptive behavior takes place when people are unable to attend to one need at a time. Instead, they use their potential to manipulate others to do for them what they have not done for themselves. Perls proposed five layers of neuroses: (1) a phony layer, (2) a phobic layer, (3) an impasse layer, (4) an implosive layer, and (5) an explosive layer. Moreover, in maladaptive functioning, there is a loss of internal awareness and a lack of good contact relations. A person's self becomes fixed in inauthentic layers of existence. The person seeks excessive self-support from the environment using manipulative behavior.

Gestaltists assert that the self does not operate outside of relationships. Our self experience is connected to our relationships. There is no self that is independent of contact with others. The self is the product of relational experiences. Borrowing from field theory, the purpose of the self in Gestalt theory is to unify the whole field—the whole person.

The major goal of Gestalt therapy is to help clients restore (rediscover) their own natural ability to self-regulate as an organism, have fulfilling contact with others in the environment, and deal constructively with disowned parts of the self. The Gestalt therapist deals with how a person is creating his or her life in a certain way instead of why that person ended up being what he or she is. Gestalt therapy is about *doing* rather than *saying*. A therapist can choose from a number of counseling techniques, including the empty chair, dreamwork, making the rounds, exaggeration, rehearsal, reversal, and converting questions to statements.

SUPPLEMENTAL AIDS _____
Discussion Questions

1. A fundamental goal of Gestalt therapy is to increase a person's awareness. Which Gestalt therapy technique would you be most comfortable using to increase a client's awareness? Explain.

2. What are the pros and cons of using Perls's technique of the empty chair?

3. Gestalt therapy emphasizes the here-and-now and a present focus. Do you think this psychotherapeutic approach deals adequately with a client's past and his or her future?

4. Gestalt therapy maintains that the unfinished business of a person's past can affect his or her current functioning. What unfinished business from the past might be influencing your functioning as a therapist?

5. Gestalt therapy uses self-disclosure and confrontation to get a client to start experiencing what he or she is thinking about. In your opinion, what are the pros and cons of a therapist self-disclosing and using confrontation with clients?

Glossary of Key Terms

authenticity   Being aware and having genuine contact with self and others require authentic presence. We must honestly share our thoughts and feelings to make and experience contact (connection) with self and others.

awareness   The process of observing and attending to one's thoughts, feelings, and actions, including body sensations, as well as visual and auditory perceptions. Awareness refers to one's now experience. "Awareness is characterized by contact, by sensing, by excitement and by gestalt formation" (Perls et al., 1951, p. viii). "[It] is the spontaneous sensing of what arises in you of what you are doing, feeling, planning" (Perls et al., 1951, p. 75). In

Gestalt therapy, clients are encouraged to become aware of what they are doing and how they are doing it.

closure   A concept from Gestalt psychology that says that the mind perceives the missing parts of an image and closes the gap between the actual image and what is perceived. The principle of closure applies when we tend to see complete figures even when part of the information is missing—for instance, see three black circles covered by a white triangle, even though it could also be seen as three incomplete circles joined together. Our minds react to patterns that are familiar, even though we often receive incomplete information.

confluence   The condition of no contact. Instead of an "I" and a "you," there is a "we" or a vague, unclear experience of oneself. It can be conceptualized as a disturbance in which the boundary between the self and the environment is lost. *Confluence* is the blending of oneself into the background, for example, by "playing it safe" or by pleasing people. It is one of five resistances involving maladaptive behavior (along with introjection, projection, retroflection, and deflection) that is studied, addressed, and challenged in Gestalt therapy.

contact   The essence of human life, a meeting with various kinds of others. Every organism is capable of effective and fulfilling contact with others in their environment and pursues ways of having contact with others so that it can survive and grow to maturity. A contact boundary exists in each of us that limits how fully we experience ourselves, other people, and their world in general. Contact is made by seeing, hearing, touching, and feeling.

deflection   The avoidance of contact through means such as vagueness and verbosity.

dialogue   Dialogue between the therapist and the client that may include unconventional experiments and offbeat group techniques.

empty chair A technique in Gestalt therapy where the client imagines another person sitting. Usually, the client places his or her mother, father, and so on in the chair to deal with unfinished business.

experiment Procedures designed to encourage spontaneity and inventiveness in the therapeutic relationship. Clients try out activities (experiments) as a means to test out a new way of thinking, feeling, or behaving.

field The boundary that comes between the person and the environment. We can devote our attention to only one figure from the field at a time, but it is important that we experience that figure with full awareness, for if we fail to completely express our feelings in the present, the unexpressed emotions recede into the background as unfinished business, exerting a harmful influence on us.

figure May be defined as that which occupies the center of a person's awareness—that which commands a person's attention.

figure–ground Refers to that which occupies the center of a person's awareness. It becomes that which brings about one's attention. A ground is that part of a perceptual field that is not "figure." When combined, figure–ground forms a Gestalt.

Gestalt German word that means shape, figure, configuration, totality, or whole.

Gestalt therapy Deals with the interaction between the organism and its environment. In the healthy organism, many needs are present at any one time. People organize their needs into a hierarchy of importance. The most dominant need forms or becomes figure. To satisfy this need, the organism searches its environment for the desired object (sensory activity); when the object is found, the organism acts to assimilate it (motor activity). When the needed object has been assimilated, the Gestalt is closed, and a state of equilibrium is reached. The formerly dominant need recedes from awareness (becomes ground), and the energy thus freed is directed toward the next most dominant need.

here-and-now The focus on what is happening "now." Gestalt psychology points out that the present moment is a continuous transition from the past to the future, and the now is fleeting. Training our conscious awareness to focus on what is happening "right now" is the best way to fully experience contact. "What am I experiencing now . . . what am I thinking about and how does it make me feel . . . what do I want right now and what is stopping me from getting that?"

holism Term used by Gestaltists to indicate that they attend to a client's thoughts, feelings, behaviors, and body.

impasse Refers to the stuck point in a situation in which people believe they are unable to support themselves; therefore, they seek outside support.

introjection The process by which outside material is accepted uncritically and without discrimination. It refers to a person's uncritical acceptance of other people's thoughts, behavior, and values. The person who introjects repeatedly fails to develop his or her own personality.

organismic self-regulation A process in which the organism strives for the maintenance of an equilibrium that is continually disturbed by its needs and regained through their gratification and elimination. It leads to integrating parts with each other and into a whole that encompasses the parts.

projection The denial of something that is truly of the self; it is then reattributed to something outside.

retroflection Holding back an impulse (e.g., speech, expressing feelings, and/or behavior). The person's energetic flow is interrupted. Some outcomes of retroflection of our impulse may die naturally; the energy can be turned inward, causing bodily tensions, somatic illnesses, depression, or even self-harm.

unfinished business Unexpressed feelings that go back to one's childhood or focus on other primary relationships. An inherent drive of an organism is to organize the field in a way that Gestalts reach closure. Each incomplete (unclosed) Gestalt represents an unfinished situation, which interferes with the formation of any novel and vital Gestalt. Whenever closure has not been accomplished, the individual experiences difficulties in living. Instead of growth, one finds stagnation and regression (fixed gestate, stuck points, or impasses).

Website Materials

Additional exercises, journals, annotated bibliography, and more are available on the open-access website at https://study.sagepub.com/jonessmith2e.

CHAPTER 10

Motivational Interviewing and the Stages of Change Theory

Given a choice between changing and proving that it is not necessary, most people get busy with the proof.

—John Galbraith

Why do people change? If you treat an individual as he is, he will stay as he is, but if you treat him as if he were what he ought to be and could be, he will become what he ought to be and could be.

—Johann Wolfgang von Goethe

The proper question is not, "Why isn't this person motivated" but rather "For what is this person motivated."

—Miller and Rollnick (2002)

BRIEF OVERVIEW_____

Motivational interviewing (MI) and the transtheoretical model of behavioral change (TTM), (sometimes called the stages of change theory) are two new additions included in the revision of this book. These theories are relatively recent modifications of the humanistic approach to psychotherapy and counseling. In a September 24, 2013, e-mail communication with me, Miller stated, "MI belongs with the 'third force' humanistic group of

approaches. Some people mistakenly identify it as a cognitive-behavior therapy."

Both MI and TTM approaches originated with and have been used extensively with the treatment of substance abuse and addiction disorders, and the treatment of such disorders forms a significant proportion of psychotherapy (Miller & Rollnick, 2013; Prochaska & Norcross, 2010). MI and TTM are theories that have been supported by numerous empirical studies, and they are included in this book because of their widespread appeal across a number of academic disciplines. The principles underlying both MI and TTM have been adapted widely for dealing with health issues such as diabetes and the treatment of cancer, with the rehabilitation of individuals within the criminal justice system (Clark, 2005; Clark, Walters, Gingerich, & Meltzer, 2006), and with the treatment of eating disorders, gambling, smoking cessation, and sexual addiction (Arkowitz & Miller, 2008; Arkowitz & Westra, 2009; Miller, 2000; Miller & Rollnick, 2009; Prochaska, 2003; Prochaska & DiClemente, 1984; Prochaska, DiClemente, Velicer, & Rossi, 1993; Prochaska & Velicer, 1997). Both MI and TTM have gained international recognition. Addiction and substance abuse counseling provide a significant proportion of counseling jobs, and it is important to present counseling theories dealing with this topic in this revised text.

This chapter places a heavy emphasis on describing MI, and it provides a shortened presentation of the TTM because of MI's greater widespread national and international use in psychotherapy. A Delphi poll of distinguished mental health professionals and 30 editors of leading mental health journals predicted the relative increase or decrease of 38 therapy methods (Prochaska & Norcross, 2003). While cognitive-behavior therapy ranked number one, MI ranked significantly higher than transtheoretical therapy, client-centered/person-centered therapy, reality therapy, existential therapy, and a number of the other therapies presented in this text.

The TTM (or the stages of change theory) is presented in abbreviated form in the second half of this chapter because its principles are incorporated in MI as well as in many other theories. Both MI and change theory have tended to borrow from each other. Central to both theoretical approaches is the issue of change. For instance, MI includes stages of change as part of its treatment package, while change theory considers the motivation of clients during various stages of change. There has also been some cross-fertilization or collaboration with key individuals involved with both theories, and both theories were developed during the 1980s (Miller, 1983; Prochaska & DiClemente, 1984). Abbreviated biographical sketches are provided for both Prochaska and DiClemente.

MOTIVATIONAL INTERVIEWING _

Definitions of MI have evolved since 1983. As Miller and Rollnick (2009) have written, "We have sought to define clearly what MI is, and our descriptions have evolved over time" (p. 130). An early definition of motivational interviewing was as follows: MI is "a directive, client-centered counseling style for eliciting behavior change by helping clients to explore and resolve ambivalence" (Rollnick & Miller, 1995, p. 326). Their revised definition of MI is as follows: "Motivational interviewing is a collaborative, person-centered form of guiding to elicit and strengthen motivation for change" (Miller & Rollnick, 2009, p. 137). In a recent presentation in

Stockholm, Miller and Rollnick (2010) addressed the question, What makes it MI? According to them, MI is a conversation about change. Its purpose is to evoke and strengthen a client's personal motivation for change. Miller and Rollnick (2010) provided a pragmatic practitioner's definition, which is "Motivational interviewing is a person-centered counseling method for addressing the common problem of ambivalence about behavior change." The researchers also supplied a technical therapeutic definition of MI, which is as follows:

> Motivational interviewing is a collaborative, goal-oriented method of communication with particular attention to the language of change. It is intended to strengthen personal motivation for and commitment to a target behavior change by eliciting and exploring an individual's own arguments for change.

There are three essential elements in any definition of MI. First, MI is a particular kind of counseling or therapy conversation about change. Second, MI is a collaborative person-centered therapeutic partnership that honors the autonomy of the client. Third, MI is evocative in that it calls forth the person's own motivation and commitment (Miller & Rollnick, 2010). The basic assumption is clients both want to be healthy and want to make positive changes in their lives. MI posits that it will increase client change talk and diminish client resistance. It declares that the degree to which clients verbally defend status quo (resistance) will be inversely related to behavior change. In fact, the extent to which clients verbally argue for change or engage in change talk will be directly related to their behavior change (Miller, 2004).

Major Contributor: William R. Miller

William R. Miller

Photo courtesy of William R. Miller.

Brief Biography

William R. Miller was born on June 27, 1947, in Shamokin, Pennsylvania, a small Appalachian coal mining town to Ralph and Hazel Miller. His father worked for the Reading Railroad, in Pennsylvania, and in his September 24, 2013, e-mail to me, he provided a brief summary of his early childhood. He stated,

> I'm a Pennsylvania native, born and raised in Shamokin. My father worked for the Reading Railroad and we rode the line into the Market Street station in Philly. We followed the Phillies and ate Tastykakes, pickled eggs, and soft pretzels.

When the coal ran out and the railroad left Shamokin, the family moved to Reading, Pennsylvania. Miller had one sister who died at the age of 8 from complications of diabetes.

Miller went to Lycoming College in Williamsport, Pennsylvania, with the goal of becoming a pastoral minister. He majored in psychology because he thought psychology could be useful for a pastor and because he thought it would help him figure out "my own scrambled head." Miller has indicated that he experienced a crisis in faith while attending Lycoming College. His childhood Christian faith was no longer working for him, and he became an agnostic for a short period of time. Similar to Carl Rogers, Miller's goal of becoming a pastor was short-lived, with psychology becoming his subsequent area of professional interest.

During the late 1960s, music was an important part of Miller's life. He sang in coffeehouses, and according to him, "if I hadn't gone into psychology, music could have been another path." Miller still uses musical analogies in teaching and writing about MI. He plays guitar and piano and now in retirement has been composing choral music (some of it under Creative Writing on his website). In 1969, Miller graduated magna cum laude with a B.A. major in psychology and a minor in philosophy.

From 1969 to 1971, Miller attended graduate study in the department of psychology at the University of Wisconsin, Madison. Miller's number came up in the Vietnam War draft lottery, and he worked for two years at Mendota State Hospital in Madison. He married Kathleen Ann Jackson on December 9, 1972, and they adopted three children. From Wisconsin, Miller enrolled at the University of Oregon, earning an M.A. degree in psychology, with a minor in neurobiology and a Ph.D. degree in clinical psychology in 1976. Just by happenstance, he applied for a job at the University of New Mexico in 1976. During his interview reflecting on his life, Miller explained his early start at the University of New Mexico:

> I didn't really know what I wanted to do after internship or what I would apply for. I thought I might go into a clinical situation. Terry Wilson had a possible research job at Rutgers at the alcohol lab, but New Mexico had this faculty opening in October and so I got my resume together and sent it in. They interviewed me in November and offered me a job before Thanksgiving. Nobody else was even interviewing yet, so it was either a bird in hand or wait for someone else to maybe interview me, and I'm not a big risk taker, so I took it. I didn't know anything about New Mexico. Kathy had one college roommate here, so we knew one family in town and that was it. We came here and never left. I've loved New Mexico; it's been a wonderful place to work, and so happenstance, once again, affected the direction of my career. (see www.williamrmiller.net, "A Conversation with William R. Miller")

W. R. Miller: Founder of Motivational Interviewing

Although many textbooks credit both William Miller and Stephen Rollnick for developing MI, this book gives William R. Miller the distinction of being the "father" and the first major developer of this theory primarily because of his seminal 1983 article "Motivational Interviewing with Problem Drinkers." It was not until some 8 years later that Miller and Rollnick (1991) wrote the book *Motivational Interviewing: Preparing People to Change Addictive Behavior*. Miller (2004) and Miller and Rose (2009) have indicated that MI was originally based on principles derived from Miller's clinical practice with problem drinkers and that MI principles were enunciated prior to the actual development of the theory. Rollnick's significant contribution to MI came in 1991 when he added the concept of **ambivalence** as a central construct for change. Because Miller was the first one to write about MI, this book presents an in-depth description of his biography and the events that led to the theory's construction (Miller, 2004). Only a short biographical description is provided for Stephen Rollnick.

MI originated after Miller experienced an unanticipated finding regarding the impact of interpersonal processes on behavior change associated with problem drinking. During a clinical trial of behavior therapy for problem drinking (Miller, Taylor, & West, 1980), Miller trained nine counselors both in techniques of behavioral self-control training and in the client-centered skill of accurate **empathy** as proposed by Carl Rogers (1959). Much to Miller's surprise, therapist empathy during treatment predicted two thirds of the variance in client drinking 6 months later. Clients who worked with counselors using accurate empathy techniques had a lower rate of relapse (Miller, 1983; Miller & Baca, 1983; Miller & Rose, 2009).

During the 1980s, Miller went on sabbatical leave to Bergen, Norway, where he was asked to interact with a group of colleagues on behavioral treatment for alcohol problems. Miller's experiences in Norway helped him to crystallize his thinking. As a result, he wrote a conceptual model and some clinical guidelines for "Motivational interviewing." Describing the impact of the Norway experience on MI, Miller (1999) stated,

> As you know, MI did not evolve from a theory. It was drawn out of me. In a style much like that which I would be writing about, my Bergen colleagues had me demonstrate what my clients had taught me, and then helped me to unpack the unspoken assumptions and decision rules behind the method so that it could be communicated to others. (p. 2)

MI developed as an alternative to the existing theoretical paradigms that emphasized external controls, contingencies, and confrontation of clients by the clinician. Behavioral approaches and Alcohol Anonymous tended to advocate that clinicians should confront people with the strongest potential negative effects of their current drinking

---

Inner Reflections

Miller said that key decisions and developments in his life were governed by happenstance.

To what extent has your life been influenced by happenstance?

How do you feel about the events in your life that were caused by happenstance?

Were the happenstance events for your better or worse?

Inner Reflections

Imagine that you are older and you are looking back over that part of your life which you have already lived. How would you evaluate your life thus far?

Are you happy with what you have done with your life? How so?

Looking forward to the next 5 to 10 years, what do you see for you?

---

behavior. A relative newcomer on the block, rational emotive behavior therapy was advocating confronting clients with their irrational thoughts and nonproductive behavior. In contrast, Miller and others held that behavior change would be facilitated by causing clients to verbalize arguments for change ("**change talk**") (Miller & Rollnick, 2002). Moreover, relational factors (between the client and the clinician) and specifically the clinician's skill level of accurate empathy and positive client regard created critical therapeutic conditions that fostered an atmosphere of safety and self-acceptance, which helped clients to explore change.

According to Miller and Rose (2009), the MI model

> focused on responding differentially to client speech, within a generally empathic person-centered style. Special attention focused on evoking and strengthening the client's own verbalized motivations for change.... A guiding principle of MI was to have the client, rather than the counselor, voice the arguments for change. (p. 528)

Miller linked MI to Festinger's (1957) concept of cognitive dissonance, Daryl Bem's (1967, 1972) self-perception theory, Rogers's theory of the "necessary and sufficient" interpersonal conditions for promoting change (Rogers, 1959), and, subsequently, to the transtheoretical stages of change developed by Prochaska and DiClemente (1984). Miller and his colleagues conducted a series of studies and found that MI significantly increased client retention and abstinence from drinking (Miller & Rose, 2009).

While on sabbatical in Australia in 1989, Miller met Stephen Rollnick, who indicated that MI was a popular addiction treatment in the United Kingdom, and he encouraged Miller to publish more about MI. Miller and Rollnick coauthored the original MI book (Miller & Rollnick, 1991).

MI has come a long way since its early beginning in 1983. It has developed primarily from an empirical and inductive path rather than from rational deduction or theory. Reflecting on the development of MI, Miller asserted in our September 2013 e-mail communication,

> I look back over my life with astonishment and gratitude. I grew up in a poor family in Shamokin. We had relatives way out west in Ohio. In my most fantastic dreams I could never have imagined what has happened in my life and career, and indeed continues to happen. I have more invitations to travel the world, speak and teach than I can possibly accept. MI is being taught and practiced in at least 45 languages. Happily, Steve and I have trained so many trainers, and they in turn more trainers (more than 2000 have now been through MINT) that the future of MI no longer depends on us. We no longer serve as officers or on the Board of MINT (the MI Network of Trainers), and no longer do the training of trainers ourselves. We have stepped happily into the background as grandfathers, watching the next generations be creative and responsible.

One might ask, "After writing more than 400 articles and chapters and 40 books and developing a major theory that is used throughout the world for the treatment of a number of addictive and health issues, what remains important in Miller's life?" Miller officially retired from the University of Mexico in 2006. In many ways, he has come full circle from whence he began his career at Lycoming College. He is still very much interested in the spiritual part of his and others' living.

Currently, Dr. Miller is Emeritus Distinguished Professor of Psychology and Psychiatry at the University of New Mexico. During his tenure, he served as Director of Clinical Training for University of Mexico's doctoral program in clinical psychology and as Co-Director of the university's Center on Alcoholism, Substance Abuse and Addictions. Dr. Miller has been the principal investigator for numerous research grants, and he has served as a consultant to the U.S. Senate, the World Health Organization, the National Academy of Sciences, and the National Institutes of Health. He is a recipient of the international Jellinek Memorial Award. The Institute for Scientific Information lists Dr. Miller as one of the world's most cited scientists.

Major Contributor: Stephen Rollnick

Brief Biography

Stephen Rollnick grew up in Cape Town, South Africa, earned an undergraduate degree in psychology; and in 1978, he completed a masters training program in research methods in Strathclyde University in Glasgow, England (see www.stephen rollnick.com). Rollnick's contribution to MI was significant because, as noted earlier, he added the construct of ambivalence and provided greater delineation of change talk and resistance. In addition, Rollnick developed new applications of MI in health care (Rollnick, Mason, & Butler, 1999; Rollnick, Miller, & Butler, 2008). Currently, Rollnick is a clinical psychologist and professor of Health Care Communication in the Institute of Primary Care & Public Health, School of Medicine, at Cardiff University, Wales, in the United Kingdom.

Rollnick is one of the cofounders of the **MINT** network (Motivational Interviewing Network of Trainers—www.motivationalinterview.net/mint), which is a system for training trainees in the practice of MI for areas such as health care, social care, and criminal justice. He has conducted workshops on MI throughout the world. On his website, Rollnick summarize his private life.

> I have four children, Jacob, Stefan, Maya, and a baby boy. I live with my partner Nina in Cardiff. We spend as much time as possible in our small oak woodland in Mid-Wales, where we play, learn, chop wood and listen to the cricket on the radio. (see www.stephenrollnick.com)

KEY CONCEPTS OF MOTIVATIONAL INTERVIEWING

View of Human Nature

MI's view of human nature is similar to that of Carl Rogers, who believed that human nature is basically good. Miller (1999) has provided what he considers a concept of man (he uses the German word **Menschenbild**) or one's fundamental view of human nature (see www.fead.org.uk/docs/Glos sary_MI_Terms.pdf). Menschenbild makes positive assumptions about human nature. According to Miller (1999), "The efficacy of MI has something to do with communicating—even taking for granted—hope, profound respect, esteem, possibilities, and faith in the person, freedom to change. 'Other-efficacy,' perhaps." (p. 3).

Similar to Rogers, Miller (1999) espoused the importance of positive valuing of another human being, especially a client who may be experiencing low self-esteem. Miller maintained that a person's motivation to change is influenced by his or her self-esteem. He proposed that self-esteem has the potential to drain off a person's motivational juice:

> If I am doing myself in with my behavior, and there is something I could do about it, I still might not take action if I think I'm not worth saving. . . . Lacking self-esteem, our clients borrow our esteem for them. (p. 3)

For people to be motivated to change, they must experience some degree of acceptance from the therapist or service provider. Drawing parallels from Rogers's person-centered theory and his own theory, Miller has suggested that it is human nature to resist change in one's life if one feels unacceptable in one's present discrepant state. From Miller's (1999) perspective, "When one feels accepted or acceptable, then it becomes possible to change. . . . the motivational interviewer does not insist or even believe that a client must change" (p. 3).

MI has a set of metatheoretical beliefs that maintain people possess a powerful potential for change—people are active, growth-oriented organisms who have a natural tendency toward personal development and change—and that every client has strong inner resources to realize such change. The underlying belief is that clients desire to be healthy and want positive change in their lives. The clinician's job is to evoke and strengthen clients' inner resourcefulness and to facilitate the natural change process that is already inherent in each person, instead of trying to impose motivation on a client or trying to bring about a change process using externally controlling strategies.

Theory of Personality

MI developed from clinical practice instead of from a specific theoretical model. As such, MI has not developed a theory of personality. In fact, after more than 30 years of research, it was not until after 2000 that Miller and Rose (2009) began to develop a theory of MI. At best, MI relies on the personality constructs that Rogers (1959) created in his person-centered counseling. One area that future researchers might consider developing is the relationship between an individual's personality and his or her change orientation. Miller and Rollnick (1991) have stated that motivation should not be conceptualized as a personality problem or trait, but rather, it is connected to a state of readiness to change that may fluctuate and be influenced from one situation to another.

Inner Reflections

To what extent do you make positive or negative assumptions about the nature of people?

Are people basically good, evil, or a combination of the two?

The Spirit of Motivational Interviewing

MI is characterized by a particular kind of "spirit" or therapeutic "way of being" with a client. The **spirit of MI** is founded on three key components: (1) collaboration between the therapist and the client versus confrontation, (2) evocation (drawing out the client's thoughts about change instead of imposing ideas about change), and (3) emphasizing the client's autonomy versus the authority of the clinician. During MI, the therapist and the client establish a partnership (*collaboration*) based on the client's point of view and experiences. This stance can be contrasted with other approaches for treatment of substance abuse disorders that are based on the clinician assuming an "expert" role and confronting the client about his or her addictive behavior (Miller & Rollnick, 2013).

Evocation involves drawing out the client's thoughts and ideas, instead of imposing the therapist's ideas about change. The clinician's task is to "draw out" the client's motivations and skills for change. The belief is that lasting change takes place when a client discovers his or her own reasons and determination related to changing a specific behavior.

MI recognizes that in the final analysis the true power for change resides within the client. Clients must decide to make changes—*autonomy*. The MI clinician points out that there are many different ways in which change can take place. Clients develop a "menu of options" regarding how to achieve their desired change (Miller & Rollnick, 2013).

Five Principles of Motivational Interviewing

MI clinicians practice MI using five general principles: (1) express empathy using reflective listening, (2) develop discrepancy between clients' goals or values and their current behavior, (3) avoid argumentation and direct confrontation, (4) roll with resistance, and (5) support self-efficacy.

1. The *first principle* of MI is that the clinician practices empathy using reflective listening. Clinicians express empathy when they communicate respect for and acceptance of their clients and their feelings. Empathic MI creates a safe therapeutic environment that encourages clients to examine issues, including exploring their personal reasons and methods for change. An empathic counseling style communicates respect for and acceptance of clients and their feelings. It encourages a nonjudgmental, collaborative relationship. It listens rather than tells, gently persuades with the view that the

decision to change is the client's, and it provides support throughout the recovery process (Miller & Rollnick, 1991).

2. The *second principle* is that the clinician develops discrepancy between clients' goals or values and their current behavior. MI is based on a number of assumptions about client ambivalence, the therapist–client relationship, and the counseling style. Client ambivalence about substance use and change is normal and such ambivalence forms a part of the counseling process. People with addictive disorders are usually aware of the dangers of their addictive behaviors, but they continue to abuse drugs, medication, or engage in other self-destructive behaviors. Clients' lack of motivation to change is often related to their ambivalence. When clinicians interpret ambivalence as denial or resistance, tension occurs between them and their clients (Miller & Rollnick, 2009, 2013).

MI posits that a discrepancy between clients' present behavior and their important goals motivates their change. Clinicians develop discrepancy with clients when they make them aware of the consequences of their problem behavior. Clients' motivation for change is increased when they perceive discrepancies between their current situation and their hopes for the future. Clinicians help clients develop discrepancy when they raise their clients' awareness of the negative personal and familial consequences of their problem behavior. In creating discrepancy, the therapist works to separate the addictive behavior from the person and helps them explore how their personal, health, marital, family, and financial goals are being challenged by their current problem behavior.

Inner Reflections

Think about a time in your life when you wanted to change one of your behaviors.

What behavior did you want to change, and how did you go about trying to changing it?

Were you successful in making the desired change?

Clients should present the arguments for change (Miller & Rollnick, 2002).

One technique some MI clinicians use to increase client discrepancy is the **Columbo approach** (Kanfer & Schefft, 1988). Columbo was a famous detective on television who often asked his suspects to help him solve the murder mystery. The clues did not "add up" for Columbo. The Columbo clinician engages the client in solving the mystery of his or her continued problem behavior. The clinician might say, "Help me to understand what you do to continue this behavior." "How might you solve your addiction?"

3. The *third principle* guiding MI is that the clinician should avoid argument. MI maintains that arguments with clients about their addictive or problem behaviors are counterproductive. One area of argument sometimes centers on the client's unwillingness to accept a label such as "alcoholic" or "drug abuser" (Miller & Rollnick, 2013).

4. The *fourth principle* for MI is that the clinician "rolls with resistance." **Resistance** behaviors include making excuses, blaming others, minimizing the importance of the target behavior, challenging, using hostile language (verbal and nonverbal), and ignoring. MI clinicians agree that confronting clients can bring about resistance and, therefore, shut down a client during therapy. The provider does not confront resistance. Rolling with resistance refers to a clinician's ability to diminish client resistance, while still connecting with him or her. One way to roll with a client's resistance is to acknowledge his or her perception or disagreement. Examples of rolling with resistance include "You really enjoy smoking weed, and you have difficulty imagining giving it up." This type of reflection captures the client's

Inner Reflections

In making changes in your life, how important were your relationships with other people?

If you had to select two people whom you know to help you make a desired change in your life, who would that be and why?

reasons for not changing and helps them express their resistance without their feeling judged by the therapist. Reframing is another way to roll with resistance. A client says, "I tried to lose weight so many times and failed." The clinician reframes the client's statement: "It seems to me that you have given losing weight a lot of effort already. Every time you try you get closer."

5. The *fifth principle* for MI involves supporting clients' self-efficacy. **Self-efficacy** is what enables one to accomplish life's tasks. It is

- the belief that changing oneself is possible,
- the confidence and optimism that enables one to accomplish tasks,
- dynamic rather than static, and
- related to a client's estimation of his or her probability of success for change.

Some clients have a diminished sense of self-efficacy and believe that they cannot begin or maintain behavioral change in response to the problem behavior. Clinicians improve a client's self-efficacy when they elicit and support clients' hope, optimism, and the possibility of their achieving change. When clients believe that change is possible, they experience a reduced sense of discrepancy between their desire for change and their feelings of hopefulness about making such change. Because client self-efficacy is an important part of the behavior change process, it is important for the clinician to believe in the client's ability to achieve articulated goals. To increase clients' feelings of self-efficacy, the clinician engages in a process that involves breaking goals down into achievable small steps. Clients can have high self-efficacy in some areas and low self-efficacy in other areas (Miller & Rollnick, 2013).

Theory of Maladaptive Behavior or Psychopathology

MI does not present a description about how maladaptive behavior or psychopathology develops within a person. Instead, the focus is on treating the maladaptive behavior and helping clients change it to more satisfying and positive behavior. Miller (1983) adopted Carl Rogers's position about how unhealthy behavior develops within people.

Change Talk and Maladaptive Behaviors

MI asserts that people are more inclined to accept and to act on opinions about changing problematic behavior that they voice themselves. The more individuals argue for a change, the greater their commitment to it becomes. Therefore, in MI clients are encouraged to express their own reasons and plans for change (or the absence of such). Client expression of change talk appears to be a good predictor of future change of problematic behavior (Miller & Rose, 2009).

THE THERAPEUTIC PROCESS ___
The Therapeutic Relationship

To some extent, the MI therapeutic relationship has already been discussed in earlier sections of this chapter. The relational foundation is very similar to that described for person-centered therapy. The alliance between the therapist and the client is one of a collaborative partnership in which each has important expertise. The therapeutic relationship is empathic and supportive, while being directive. The MI clinician begins by developing trust, building, and guiding the client using empathic reflective listening (Miller & Rose, 2009).

The therapeutic relationship is goal directed, and the counselor seeks to reach clarity about the problem behavior being addressed and works to keep the therapeutic discussion focused on it. For instance, a client might discuss his or her historic or developmental issues involving the problematic behavior. After this discussion is completed, the clinician guides the client to discuss his or her relationship with the problem behavior and present goals.

Role of the Therapist

The role of the MI clinician is to uncover and help release a client's motivation to change problematic behavior. Another role is to develop discrepancy and roll with the client's resistance. The therapist listens for clients statements about discrepant parts of their behavior and their goals or values. For instance, a client might state that doing drugs interferes with her desire to be a good parent. The clinician reflects to clients the discrepancy between the addictive or problematic behavior and their goals or values.

Another therapist role is to elicit clients' change talk and self-motivational statements. The basic task of the MI therapist is to engage clients in the process of change. The therapist does not identify the problem or suggest ways to solve it. Instead, the therapist's job is to help the client recognize how life might be better and to choose ways to make it better. When MI is successful, clients argue for change and persuade themselves that they can make the changes they desire. Miller and Rollnick (1991) have identified four types of motivational statements:

- Cognitive recognition of the problem ("I'm beginning to see that this problem is more serious than I thought")
- Affective expression of concern about the problem ("I am worried about what is happening to my life")
- An implicit or explicit statement about the client's intention to change behavior ("I've really got to do something about this behavior or I am going to destroy myself")
- Optimism about one's ability to make the desire change ("I know that I have what it takes to change my life")

The provider reinforces clients' self-motivational statements by reflecting them, nodding, and affirming statements. Some strategies that tend to elicit clients' change talk involves using evocative open questions, such as "In what ways do your drinking concern you?" "What do you see as the problem with your cocaine use?" and "What might your life look like in the next couple of years if things remain the same?" Clients usually respond with statements such as "If I do nothing to change my situation, I might end up losing my children

and end up in jail." On the other hand, if I make changes in my drug use, I'll stay out of jail, and I will have a good relationship with my children.

Clients' resistance may occur because there is lack of client–clinician agreement toward a mutually agreed-on goal. Client resistance is often expressed by arguing, ignoring, and interrupting. The MI clinician identifies the source of dissonance in the therapeutic relationship and works to join with the client.

MI practitioners come from a broad spectrum of academic and professional disciplines, for example, they include psychologists, nurses, counselors, educators, correctional providers, social workers, doctors, and psychiatrists. Training seminars are available through the MINT (www.motivationalinterview.net/mint), which was started in 1997 by a small group of trainers trained by William Miller and Stephen Rollnick. A primary goal of MINT is to improve the quality and counseling with clients regarding behavior change. MINT encourages applications of MI across cultures.

> ## Inner Reflections
>
> Each one of us has his or her own change talk. Describe your change talk when you are ready to change things in your life.
>
> What are change words that you tend to use that signal your readiness for change?
>
> How do you know when you are not ready to make a change? Describe your sustain talk.

Four Fundamental Processes in Motivational Interviewing

Miller and Rollnick (2010) have claimed that there are four fundamental processes involved in MI: (1) engaging, (2) focusing, (3) evoking, and (4) planning. The process of **engaging** refers to the relational foundation of MI, which uses a person-centered counseling style that is characterized by listening to understand the client's dilemma and values. The second fundamental process is termed *focusing,* which is guiding the client to a target behavior that

How do you manifest resistance in your life? In your role as clinician?

How do you handle client resistance in the therapeutic relationships?

Evaluate your ability to roll with the resistance of those closest to you—your partner, family members.

How do you feel about rolling with your client's resistance?

is important to him or her. The focusing process entails agenda setting, asking the client what is important to him or her, and obtaining information. The third fundamental process is labeled **evoking**, and *it represents the transition to MI*. The clinician evokes the client's own motivations for change. During the evoking phase, the clinician engages in selective eliciting, selective responding, and selective summaries. The fourth fundamental process involves planning and constructing a bridge to client change. This process replaces the former Phase I and Phase II of MI. The clinician and the client negotiate a change plan and consolidate the client's commitment to change. Miller and Rollnick (2010) have affirmed that it cannot be MI without engaging, guiding, and evoking; however it can be MI without planning.

Client Goals, Planning, and Motivational Interviewing

The MI clinician helps clients reach their goals. Exploring clients' goals and values helps them to see what behaviors are inconsistent with what they say is important to them. This MI strategy helps clients determine what is important to them and how their values can help them during treatment. Some open-ended questions to assist clients in determining their goals and values might be as follows:

- List the most important values for you today.
- After the client has described his or her values ask, How are your most important values represented in your life today?

- If they are not the most important values, ask, "How might you adjust your life so that those values are more represented in your life today?"
- Ask the client to identify long- and short-term goals for him or her and his or her loved ones.
- How will you meet your goals and what are you doing today that will ensure that you will reach you goals for your future?

Planning involves helping clients negotiate change goals and plans, assisting clients in strengthening their commitment to change, and implementing the desired change and adjusting to it. In negotiating a change plan, clinicians and clients consider change options (see menu of options), and they arrive at a plan together (Miller & Rollnick, 2013).

Motivational Interviewing Techniques

From the outset, MI was designed to be a brief treatment intervention. It is typically delivered in two to four outpatient sessions. MI describes counseling techniques for displaying the "MI spirit," exhibiting the five MI principles, and guiding the therapeutic process toward eliciting client change talk and commitment for change. **OARS** (*O* for open-ended questions, *A* for affirmations, *R* for reflections, and *S* for summaries) is an acronym for remembering counseling techniques used in MI.

Open-ended questions are those that clients cannot easily answer with a yes/no or short response that contains only a limited piece of information. Such questions tend to encourage the client to elaborate and think more deeply about an issue. They encourage the client to do the majority of the talking, and they keep communication moving forward. In contrast, **closed questions** results in a limited answer from clients. Open-ended questions cause the client to explore his or her reasons for change. Examples of open-ended questions include the following:

- Would you tell me more about _____?
- How would you like things to be different for you?

- What would you lose if you stopped smoking weed?
- What have you tried before for stopping drinking?
- In what ways are you concerned about your use of meth?
- What would you like to do about your health?
- Tell me about the last time that you used heroin.

Affirmations are therapist statements about clients' strengths. Such statements build clients' confidence in their **ability** to change. It is not enough to make positive statements about clients. Affirmations must be congruent and genuine. Affirmations help build client–therapist rapport, and they assist in helping clients see themselves in a more positive light. Clinicians may use affirmations that **reframe** client behaviors, and they form a key way for promoting the MI principle of supporting client self-efficacy. Affirmations should acknowledge the difficulties clients have experienced. Affirmations emphasize clients' past experiences that demonstrate their strength, success, or power to change. The therapist might affirm the inner guiding spirit and faith for clients who have a strong spiritual foundation. Examples of affirming statements are as follows:

- You're a strong person to have lived with drinking for such a long time and not completely fall apart.
- I appreciate your efforts to deal with this problem.
- It wasn't easy for you to come here today seeking help.

Reflections form a core technique to guide the client toward change. **Reflective listening** helps the client by providing a therapeutic synthesis of the content and process of therapy. Reflections not only reduce client resistance but also encourage clients to keep talking. There are different levels of reflections. **Simple reflections** that repeat, rephrase, and stay close to clients' talking content. The therapist repeats the client's statement in a neutral form. Simple reflections acknowledge and validate what a client has said.

| Client: | I don't plan to stop smoking anytime soon. |
| Clinician: | You don't think that giving up smoking would work for you right now. |

An **amplified reflection** mirrors back what the person has said in an amplified or exaggerated form. Miller and Rollnick (2002, p. 101) provide an amplified reflection:

| Client: | I couldn't just give up drinking. What would my friends think? |
| Interviewer: | You couldn't handle your friends' reaction if you quit. |

Summaries constitute the S part of OARS techniques. Summaries indicate clinician interest, understanding, and focus attention on important elements of the client discussion. Sometimes summaries are used to shift attention or direction in MI and to help the client move on. A therapist might say, "Let me see if I understand what you have said thus far." Skillful summaries point out both sides of a client's ambivalence about change and encourage client development of discrepancy regarding the client's current behavior and goals. Summarizing can be used to begin and end each counseling session. "Summaries reinforce what has been said, show that you have been listening carefully, and prepare the client to move on" (Miller & Rollnick, 1991, p. 78). Clients should be

Inner Reflections

Our feelings of resistance sometimes sabotage our goals and prevent us from completing our tasks.

Before beginning any task, especially one that is onerous, remove your resistance to completing that task. We tend to fight our own resistance during the process of completing tasks. One student said that she had to remove her resistance to completing her "own personal theory of counseling paper" in order to complete it.

invited to correct therapist summaries. Summaries can be used to

- highlight important aspects of the discussion,
- shift the direction of discussions that have become "stuck,"
- highlight both sides of an individual's ambivalence toward change, and
- communicate interest and understanding of what a client has said.

Eliciting Client Change Talk

Another MI technique is to elicit change talk and self-motivational statements. Change talk consists of client statements that reveal a consideration of, motivation for, or commitment to change. MI maintains that the more clients talk about change, the more likely they are to change. The mnemonic device, DARN-CAT is used in MI to describe the different types of change talk. **Preparatory change talk** has been found to be predictive of positive MI outcome (Miller & Rollnick, 2002). **DARN** stands for the following: D—desire (I want to change), A—ability (I can change), R—reason (It's important for me to change), and N—need (I should change).

Implementing change talk (**CAT**) is an important part of the change process in MI. When clients implement change talk, they show C—commitment (I will make changes), A—activation (I am ready, prepared, and willing to change), and T—taking steps (I am taking specific actions to change). Some signs of clients' readiness for change include their decreased resistance, increased resolve to make changes, **self-motivational statements** that indicate they recognize the problem, are concerned about it, and are open to doing something about it.

Other important indicators of change readiness are that clients have increased questions about change, they begin envisioning life after the change, and they experiment with possible change approaches.

Another type of talk is **sustain talk**, which refers to the client's stated reasons not to make a change or to sustain the status quo. Interviewers are cautioned not to elicit sustain talk. The goal is to facilitate high level of change talk by clients and low levels of sustain talk. Some strategies to evoke change talk are provided in Table 10.1.

> ### Inner Reflections
>
> What MI techniques would you feel most and least comfortable using? Explain.
>
> To what extent could you see yourself working as a MI clinician?

Table 10.1	Eight Strategies for Evoking Change Talk

1. Ask **Evocative Questions**—Use Open-Ended Questions:
   - Why would you want to make this change? *(Desire)*
   - How might you go about it to achieve your goal? *(Ability)*
   - What are the three top reasons for you to make the change? *(Reasons)*
   - How important is it for you to make a change? *(Need)*
   - What do you believe you will actually do? *(Commitment)*

2. Ask for **elaboration** (When a change talk theme emerges, ask for details):
   - In what ways?
   - How do you think this will come about?
   - What have been your past experiences with making changes in your life?

3. Ask for examples (When a change theme emerges, ask for specific examples):
   - When was the last time you attempted to make a change?
   - Describe a specific example of how you make changes in your life.

4. Looking back (Ask about a time before the current concern developed):
   - Describe how things were better in your past.
   - Can you recall any past situations when things were different?

(Continued)

Table 10.1 (Continued)

> **Looking forward** (Ask about how the client views the future):
>
> - What might happen if things stay as they are (status quo)?
> - If you were 100% successful in making the changes you want, how would your life be different?
> - How would you like your life to be in the future?

5. Query extremes (Ask about the best and worst case scenarios):

   - What are the worst things that might happen if you don't make this change?
   - What are the best things that might happen if you do make this change?

6. Use Change Rulers (Ask open-ended questions about where clients see themselves on a scale from 1 to 10):

   - On a scale where 1 is *not at all important* and 10 is *extremely important*, how important (need) is it to you to change _____?
   - Explain why you are at a _____ and not a lower number.
   - What would have to happen for you to go to a higher number?
   - How much do you want this change (*Desire*)
   - How confident are you that you can achieve your desired change?(*Ability*)
   - How committed are you to _____ (*commitment*)?

7. Explore goals and values (Ask what the person's guiding values are):

   - What do you really want in life?
   - In what ways do your behavior conflict with your value system?

8. Come alongside (Explicitly side with the negative (status quo) side of ambivalence):

   - Maybe _____ (drinking) is so important to you that you won't give it up, no matter what the cost.

Source: This chart was adapted from "Ten Strategies for Evoking Change Talk" contained as a handout on the website www.motivationalinterviewing.org.

Menu of options is another MI technique. It refers to actions that a client and clinician identify collaboratively and agree to put in a behavior change plan. Clients and providers identify several actions versus one or two. The therapeutic encounter includes only actions that clients want to pursue, and each action is given a rating for potential success. Behavior change plans are fluid and can be changed; they become confidence builders for clients.

Ask permission to give advice or information. Before offering or giving advice, a MI practitioner first asks permission to do so. He or she might ask, "Would you be interested in hearing my ideas about what might be helpful for you?" If the client says yes, the clinician might recommend AA or getting a "buddy." Another question might be, "Would you be interested in learning more about this medication?" If the client responds yes, the clinician might provide written materials. The clinician should provide an opportunity for the client to reject his or her suggestions (Miller & Rollnick, 2013).

Sample Motivational Interviewing (MI) Session

1. *Set the agenda—determine the target behavior for client (e.g., using drugs, smoking, dieting).* The clinician clarifies the issues or agenda around a target behavior for which the client has ambivalence.

2. *Ask about the positive (good things) about the target behavior.* The clinician asks,

   - What are some of the good things about _____?
   - Usually people _____ (drink) because they feel it helps or benefits them in some way. How has _____ (e.g., drinking, using drugs) benefitted you?
   - What do you like about the effects of _____ (using drugs, eating)?

   ✓ The clinician summarizes the positive of the target behavior.

3. *Ask about the negative (harmful or less good things) about the target behavior.*

- Tell me something about the down side of _____ (e.g., using drugs, drinking).
- What bothers you about _____ (drinking, using drugs, not exercising)?
- If you could suddenly give up _____ (smoking), what are some of the things you would not miss?

  ✓ The clinician summarizes the negatives of the target behavior.

4. *The clinician explores the client's life goals and values.* Such goals become the fulcrum against which the client's cost and benefits of the target behavior is weighed.

- What kinds of things are important to you?
- What kind of person would you like to be?
- If things worked out in the best possible way for you, what would you be doing a year from now?
- The clinician uses affirmations to support the client's "positive" goals and values.

5. *Ask the client for a decision.*

- You were saying that you were trying to decide if you want to continue, cut down, or stop_____ (using drugs, smoking).
- After this discussion, do you feel clearer about what you would like to do?
- So, have you made a decision?
- The clinician restates the client's dilemma or ambivalence and then asks for a decision.

6. *Goal-setting—use smart goals (specific, meaningful, assessable, realist, timed). (If client decides to change behavior, resolves ambivalence, etc.)*

- What will be your next step?
- What will you do in the next 1 or 2 days?
- Have you ever done any of these things before to stop smoking, using drugs?
- Who will be helping and supporting you?

- On a scale of 1 to 10, what are the chances that you will do your next step? (anything under 7 and the client's goal may need to be restated to become more achievable)

7. *If the client does not reach a decision or decides to continue the behavior.*

- If no decision, empathize with the client's difficulty of ambivalence.
- Ask if there is something else that might help them make a decision.
- Ask if they have a plan to manage not making a decision.
- Ask if they are interested in reducing some of the problems while they are making a decision.
- If the client's decision is to continue the target behavior, the clinician goes back to explore the client's ambivalence.

Source: Adapted from website, motivationalinterviewing.org and Miller and Rollnick (2003).

Eight Stages in Learning MI

Miller and Moyers (2006) have delineated eight stages in learning for students:

1. The spirit of MI
2. OARS—client-centered counseling skills
3. Recognizing change talk
4. Eliciting and reinforcing change talk
5. Rolling with resistance
6. Developing a change plan
7. Consolidating client commitment
8. Integrating MI with other clinical methods

What Motivational Interviewing Is Not

Since MI was first introduced, it has become confused with other theoretical approaches to counseling and psychotherapy. In response to the confusion generated, Miller and Rollnick (2009) wrote an article "Ten Things That Motivational Interviewing Is Not."

The article discussed 10 things that MI is not (1) the TTM, (2) a way of tricking people into dong what you want them to do, (3) a technique, (4) decisional balance, (5) assessment feedback, (6) cognitive-behavior therapy, (7) client-centered therapy, (8) easy to learn, (9) practice as usual, and (10) a panacea.

According to Miller and Rollnick (2009), MI is not based on TTM (the stages of change theory). They are two distinct approaches, even though both models grew up together during the early 1980s:

> Nevertheless, MI was never based on the TTM. They are, in essence, kissing cousins who never married. TTM is intended to provide a comprehensive conceptual model of how and why changes occur, whereas MI is a specific clinical method to enhance personal motion for change. . . . It is neither essential nor important to explain the TTM stages of change when delivering MI. It is not necessary to assign people to a stage of change or as part of or in preparation for MI. (Miller & Rollnick, 2009, p. 130)

After you have read the section on TTM, do you believe that motivational interviewing is sufficiently distinct from TTM?

Do you feel that motivational interviewing is sufficiently distinct from person-centered therapy?

Likewise, Miller and Rollnick (2009) explained that MI is not person-centered therapy and that it departs from the latter by being consciously goal oriented and by having intentional direction for change. "In MI, the counselor strategically listens for, elicits, and responds selectively to certain forms of speech that are collectively termed 'change talk'" (p. 135). The authors indicated that such differential reinforcement of specific forms of client speech would have been considered an anathema by Carl Rogers.

CURRENT TRENDS IN MOTIVATIONAL INTERVIEWING _____

There are four dominant trends in MI. First, MI is increasingly being used around the world for a wide range of addictive disorders and health issues, including diabetes management, eating disorders, hypertension, gambling, dual diagnosis, and weight loss (Hodgins, Chin, & McEwen, 2009; Sciacca, 1997). Second, MI has entered its formal theory stage of development. As Miller and Rose (2009) have stated, "An emergent theory of MI is proposed, emphasizing two specific active components: a *relational* component focused on empathy and the interpersonal spirit of MI, and a technical component involving the differential evocation and reinforcement of client change talk" (p. 527). Third, the MINT component of MI, provides training for MI counselors, and such training is done worldwide, thereby broadening its multicultural base. Fourth, the effectiveness of MI appears to be amplified when MI is added to other active treatment methods. The addition of MI to other active treatments produced positive effects of greater size than MI alone (Miller & Rose, 2009).

RESEARCH AND EVALUATION OF MOTIVATIONAL INTERVIEWING _____

Multicultural Positives

MI is currently being used in nations throughout the world. One major reason for the theory's popularity in different cultures is that it focuses on change, a construct that is the concern of therapists worldwide. As Miller (2003) has stated,

> As MI has moved into new nations and subcultures, I've been waiting to encounter a cultural context in which it just doesn't seem to work. So far we've had good experience with the generalizability of MI to Hispanic, Native American, and Central and South American cultures. It also is faring well in European nations. In fact, MI took root in Scandinavia and the UK well before it became popular in the US. It has escaped the bounds of the English language with translations and applications in Dutch, French, German, Italian, Portuguese, and Spanish. . . . .The African and Arabic worlds are largely unexplored as contexts for MI, beyond Angelica Thevos' research in Zambia. (p. 1)

Miller (2003) did report that a few studies had indicated that MI had been less successful with African Americans; however, recent studies have indicated that MI is also effective with this cultural group. Ogedegbe et al. (2008) found that MI did work for African Americans dealing with poor medication adherence for hypertension. Miller (2003) surmised that different cultural styles of interacting with people may be one of the factors that suggested MI's less effectiveness with African Americans. Miller (2003) has raised questions about how different cultures might put their own particular slant on a culturally acceptable form of MI:

> If the communication norms of a culture require a rather different set of transactions, a different interpersonal style, in order to elicit commitment and change, is it still MI? Or is MI defined as the particular style of communication that Steve and I have described, even if it doesn't work across cultures? Does the overall spirit of MI—collaboration, evocation, and respect for autonomy—hold up across cultures, despite different ways of manifesting it? And who cares if it's called MI or not?

Contributions and Criticisms of Motivational Interviewing

MI has made a number of contributions to the literature by simply emphasizing the critical nature

of change during psychotherapy. Even though MI was originally developed to address substance abuse disorders, it has now been tested across a wide range of target behavior changes (Miller & Rose, 2009). Researchers have found that MI is effective both in reducing maladaptive behaviors (e.g., problem drinking, gambling, HIV risk behaviors) and in promoting adaptive health behavior change (e.g., exercise, diet, medication adherence) (Miller & Rose, 2009). Because the effectiveness of MI appears to be amplified when it is added to other active treatment methods, it shows promise as a "one clinical tool, to be integrated with other evidence-based methods, for use when client ambivalence and motivation appear to be obstacles to change" (Miller & Rose, 2009, p. 20).

Evidence-Based Research

More than 300 clinical trials of MI have been published, and a number of efficacy reviews and meta-analyses have been initiated (Burke, Arkowitz, & Menchola, 2003; Dunn, Deroo, & Rivara, 2001; Erickson, Gerstle, & Feldstein, 2005; Hettema, Steele, & Miller, 2005; Rubak, Sandbaek, Lauritzen, & Christensen, 2005) that have reported positive trials for a broad spectrum of target problems, including cardiovascular rehabilitation, diabetes management, dietary change, hypertension, illicit drug use, infection risk reduction, management of chronic mental disorders, problem drinking, problem gambling, smoking, and dual-occurring mental health and substance abuse disorders (Miller & Rose, 2009). The American Psychological Association has listed MI as an evidence-based practice (Miller & Rose, 2009).

THE TRANSTHEORETICAL MODEL OF CHANGE OR THE STAGES OF CHANGE THEORY ___

Similar to MI, the TTM (the stages of change theory) is an integrative theory that focuses on change. According to Prochaska and Norcross (2003), "In the committed integrative spirit, we set out to construct a model of psychotherapy and behavior change that can draw from the entire spectrum of the major theories—hence the name *transtheoretical*" (Prochaska & Norcross, 2003, p. 516).

Major Contributor: James O. Prochaska

Brief Biography

James O. Prochaska earned his bachelor's (1964), master's (1967), and doctoral (1969) degrees at Wayne State University. In recounting how he developed TTM, Prochaska has maintained that his father's death from alcoholism was pivotal in motivating him to create the transtheoretical model of behavior change (TTM). The model asserts that change isn't an event, it's a process—one that spans several stages of differing strategies. In addition, Dr. Prochaska has also noted that he was looking for a way to integrate the 300 different theories that made up psychotherapy during the 1980s (Prochaska & Norcross, 2003). Therefore, he and his research team went out and interviewed ordinary people who were struggling with quitting smoking. They asked people about the various processes they had gone through, and they responded something to the effect that "Early on I did this; later I did this." From his conversations with the smokers surveyed, Prochaska began to conceptualize that the participants were talking about stages of change. He realized that change was the missing link that could help him integrate different processes from different theories (Prochaska & Norcross, 2003).

Prochaska has been cited as one of the five most influential authors in psychology by the Institute for Scientific Information. He has authored more than 300 papers on behavior change for health promotion and disease prevention. He has received major awards from the American Psychological Association, the Society for Prospective Medicine, and Harvard University. He is the first psychologist to win a Medal of Honor for Clinical Research from the American Cancer Society. He is the Director of the Cancer Prevention Research Center and Professor of Clinical and Health Psychology at the University of Rhode Island.

Major Contributor: Carlo C. DiClemente

Brief Biography

Carlo C. DiClemente is the codeveloper of the TTM of behavior change. He earned his M.A. in psychology at the New School for Social Research and his Ph.D. in psychology at the University of Rhode Island. He is the author of numerous scientific articles and book chapters on motivation and behavior change and a coauthor of a self-help book based on this model of change, *Changing for Good*. He has written and coauthored several professional books, including *The Transtheoretical Model*, *Substance Abuse Treatment and the Stages of Change*, and *Group Treatment for Substance Abuse: A Stages of Change Therapy Manual*. Recently, Dr. DiClemente wrote *Addiction and Change: How Addictions Develop and Addicted People Recover*. Currently, he is professor and chair of the psychology department at the University of Maryland.

KEY CONCEPTS OF THE TRANSTHEORETICAL MODEL OF CHANGE ___

The transtheoretical model (TM), also known as the stages of change model, describes an individual's readiness to change behavior. The model suggests that to make a successful behavior change, people must go through a process of evaluating and increasing their readiness to change, finally making the change and maintaining the behavior. The TTM provides an explanation of how people can modify a problem behavior or acquire a positive behavior. It is constructed around three critical organizing dimensions: (1) the processes, (2) the stages, and (3) the levels of change.

Theory of Personality

Similar to many of the newer approaches to psychotherapy, the TTM does not provide a theory of personality. Prochaska and Norcross (2003) point out that more recent theorists (cognitive-behavior therapy, solution-focused therapy, and narrative therapy, etc.) are beginning to omit an explanation of how an individual develops a personality in their theories. Newer theories of psychotherapy focus on remedying a specific problem instead of trying to explain it by tracing it back to a client's personality.

Inner Reflection

In developing your own theory of counseling, list three principles that would form the foundation of your theory.

Processes of Change and TTM

Strategies that can help people make and maintain changes are called the processes of change. Different strategies become effective during the various stages of change. For instance, conscious raising and dramatic relief work best for individuals in the precontemplation stage, while counterconditioning and stimulus control seem to help people in the action and maintenance stages. Prochaska and DiClemente (1983) identified 10 processes of change:

1. *Consciousness raising* (awareness of a health or behavior issue): It involves a person's increased awareness about the causes, consequences, and remedies for a target behavior.

2. *Dramatic relief* (emotional arousal—taking action to decrease anxiety and other negative emotions): Experiences such as role playing, personal testimonies, and advertisements are examples of techniques that can have an emotional impact on people. "I respond emotionally to warnings about smoking cigarettes."

3. *Environmental reevaluation* (social reappraisal—learning how one's actions affect one's self and others): This change process involves one's awareness that one can serve as a negative or positive role model for others. Family interventions can produce reassessments of the target behavior. "I take into account that smoking can become harmful to my children, and they have asked me to stop smoking."

4. *Self-reevaluation* (self-evaluation): This change process involves both cognitive and affective assessments of a person's self-image with and without a specific target behavior. "My dependency on cigarettes makes me think less of myself."

5. *Social liberation* (environmental opportunities): Examples of this change process entail smoke-free zones, salad bars in school lunches, and access to contraceptives.

6. *Counterconditioning* (substituting—learning to substitute healthy behaviors for problem behaviors): An individual learns different or healthier behaviors that can be substituted for problem behaviors. For instance, nicotine replacement can substitute for cigarettes.

7. *Stimulus control* (reengineering—removing triggers for unhealthy behaviors): "I remove items from my home that remind me of smoking."

8. *Helping relationship* (therapy, supporting relationship—finding people who are supportive of change)—including a therapeutic alliance and buddy systems.

9. *Reinforcement management* (rewarding): Positive self-statements and contingency contracts; for example, "I reward myself when I don't drink."

10. *Self-liberation* (believing in one's ability to change and making commitments to act on that belief): "I have made commitments to my children not to smoke."

Stages of Change

Two major contributions of TTM are that it conceptualized change as a process instead of a one-time occurrence, and it deals with individuals' *readiness for change.* The model challenged earlier beliefs captured in the Nike trademark statement "just do it." When it comes to change, most people can't just do it—that is, before they are emotionally ready and properly prepared to make their desired life change. As Prochaska and DiClemente (1983) have pointed out, change is a complex and sometimes circuitous experience—one that may involve thinking about change, reconsidering making change, taking action, stumbling backward, and even starting all over again. TTM categorizes the change process into the following **stages of change**.

Stage 1: **Precontemplation stage** *(not ready to change).* It is the stage in which people have little intention of changing their behavior in the near future, typically measured as within the next 6 months. They defend their bad habits and do not feel they have a problem. Precontemplators are usually characterized as resistant or unmotivated (Prochaska & Norcross, 2010).

What holds people back in the precontemplation stage is the feeling that the necessary changes will take too much or bring about too much discomfort. The person may also experience a sense of hopelessness because of past failed attempts to make the behavior change, or he or she may have limiting beliefs about what is possible or permissible for him or her. In contrast, *what moves a person forward may be a positive or a negative life event* or developing a stronger sense of self-worth and confidence.

Stage 2: Contemplation (thinking of changing, getting ready, maybe soon). During this stage, people become aware of the personal consequences

of their bad habit or health issue (noncompliance with medication regimen), and they have spent time thinking about their problem. Yet they are still ambivalent about making change. Individuals weigh the pros and cons of quitting or changing their behavior. Generally, participants in this stage are intending to begin the healthy behavior within the next 6 months.

What can hold a person back in the **contemplation stage** is that he or she lacks a sense of urgency or motivation. What moves a person forward is the sense that change is possible "for me," or being inspired by role models or success stories about people who have made the change, or even feeling that one has reached the last straw of negative consequences of the target behaviors ("My drunken behavior has humiliated me in front of my children for the last time").

Stage 3: **Preparation/Determination** *(ready to change).* Individuals have made a commitment to make a change, and their motivation for changing may be captured in statements such as "I've got to make some changes in my life. I can't go on like this. I'm destroying myself and my family." Individuals at this stage may be ready to start taking action within the next 30 days. The number one concern of people in this stage is, Will they fail?

What can hold a person back in the preparation stage is one's underestimating what it takes to prepare, being afraid to ask for help or information, not knowing where to go for information and support, or trying to leap frog straight to the action phase without having first developed the requisite skills, knowledge, or confidence related to the desired change. Conversely, *what moves a person forward* are simple things, such as doing the necessary research about the change process, obtaining the proper equipment, becoming affiliated with a coach or mentor, or establishing a start date on the calendar.

Stage 4: Action/Willpower (making change, doing the healthy behavior, now it is time "to just do it"). During stage 4, people believe that they have the ability to make changes regarding the target behavior; hence, they use a variety of techniques to change their behavior. People rely on their willpower to make changes. Individuals are in the **action stage** if they are implementing a plan to change a target behavior. Because such clients are making overt efforts to change their behavior, they are at risk for relapse. One technique might be to have clients to post visual reminders on their refrigerator.

What can hold a person back in the action stage of change are unrealistic expectations regarding quick results, resistance to change, fear of failure, or the lack of social support. *What moves a person forward* includes developing good support systems, prioritizing activities, addressing and overcoming obstacles, and celebrating small successes.

Inner Reflections

If you could make one behavior change in your life, what would that be?

What's stopping you from making that change?

Using TTM, in what stage of change are you with regards to the behavior you want to modify?

Stage 5: Maintenance (staying on track; keep on "keeping on"). For individuals' behavior to be sustainable, it must enter a **maintenance** phase (usually 6 months or more of consistent action). Individuals are in the maintenance stage if for the past 6 months, they have been diligent and consistent in performing the actions they committed to as part of their desired behavior change. During the maintenance stage, individuals strive to continue their changed behavior, and they seek to avoid temptations that will lead them back to the old behavior of overeating, drinking, or smoking.

What can hold a person back in the maintenance stage of change are factors such as hitting a plateau (not being able to lose the last 30 pounds), getting bored, or feeling overwhelmed by life events. What move one forward are avoiding situations that might trigger a relapse and getting new friends who are changing or who don't abuse.

Stage 6: Termination (change fully integrated, not going back, "been there and did that."). Person has new image. When people in the maintenance stage are able to continue their changed behavior for at least 2 years, they enter into the **termination** stage. Individuals' behavior change is completely integrated into individuals' lifestyles.

Inner Reflections

Do you believe that there are six stages of change?

Consider a behavioral change that you have made in your own life. What stages did you go through?

What were the factors that helped you move from one stage to another?

In which of the five levels of change, would you like to make the most changes in your life?

Levels of Change

The levels of change refers to a hierarchical organization of five distinct but interrelated levels of psychological problems that can be addressed in psychotherapy. These levels are as follows:

1. Symptoms/situational problems
2. Maladaptive cognitions
3. Current interpersonal conflicts
4. Family/system conflicts
5. Intrapersonal conflicts

The Decisional Balance

People pass from one stage to another as a result of what TTM calls the decisional balance and their feelings of self-efficacy. The **decisional balance** reflects the individual's relative weighing of the pros and cons for changing a target behavior. The concept is borrowed from the model of decision making developed by Janis and Mann (1977) that included four categories of pros (instrumental gains for self and others and approval for self and others). After further testing of the decision balance construct, only two factors, the Pros and Cons, were found (Velicer, DiClemente, Prochaska, & Brandenberg, 1985). The Decisional Balance scale is related to the stages of change. For example, in the precontemplation stage, the pros of smoking far outweigh the cons of smoking. In contemplation stage, these two scales are more equal, whereas during the advanced stages, the cons outweigh the pros (Velicer, Prochaska, Fava, Norman, & Redding, 1998).

Self-Efficacy

Both MI and TTM use the concept of self-efficacy, a concept developed by Bandura. The self-efficacy construct represents the situation-specific confidence that people have that they can cope with high-risk situations without relapsing to their unhealthy or problem habit. This construct was adapted from Bandura's self-efficacy theory (Bandura, 1988, 1997). This construct is represented either by a temptation measure or a self-efficacy construct.

THE THERAPEUTIC PROCESS
Role of the Therapist

The transtheoretical clinician is viewed primarily as the expert on change—even though they should not be seen as having all the answers. Prochaska and Norcross posit that the role of the TTM therapist varies at different stages. With precontemplators, the role is similar to that of a nurturing parent with a resistant and defensive young person. With contemplators, the clinician's role is similar to that of a Socratic teacher who encourages clients to reach their own insights about their situation. With clients who are in the preparation stage, the clinician functions as an experienced coach who provide a good game plan. When clients are in the action and maintenance stage, the clinician functions similar to a consultant who is available to give expert advice and support.

RESEARCH AND EVALUATION OF TTM
Multicultural Positives

Although the website for the TTM states that there is a strong international following for the TTM, few studies could be found that examined this theory from a multicultural perspective. Is TTM appropriate for all cultures? Are the stages of change proposed in this model universal? It would appear that the issue of culture and spirituality might moderate a person's movement through the stages of change. For instance, cultures that have a high spiritual component might adhere to the belief that change can take place overnight—with the help of an all-powerful force.

Multicultural Blind Spots

Prochaska and Norcross (2014) have maintained that

> change as progress is so typically a Western and especially an American ideology. Transtheoretical therapists mainly assume that all they need to do is to help clients get unstuck and they will freely progress through the rest of the stages of change.... The 20th century raised profound challenges to the belief that historical change and cultural change inevitably represent progression. (p. 476)

Clearly, one limitation of the stages of change model is that it advocates a Western view of change—that is, change as progress.

Not all cultures view change in the manner that is described in the stages of change model. Some cultures see change as much more spiritual and as a continual movement backward and forward. The stages of change model suggests that there is always a struggle or a battle with making change in one's life. The Chinese perspective, for instance, is to let go of the battle for change—instead to allow oneself to flow with life's circumstances. The goal of change from a Native American perspective might be to

Do you think that the criticisms of the stages outlined in the transtheoretical are valid or overstated?

To what extent do you believe that the stages of the transtheoretical model of change are the same for all cultures? Explain.

move toward greater harmony with one's environment.

Criticisms of TTM

Although the TTM has been embraced in the United States, and to some extent in other parts of the world, there has been mounting criticism of this theoretical approach. A number of researchers have stated that there are flaws in the concept of stages of change as currently outlined in the TTM (Adams & White; 2004; Armitage, 2009; Armitage & Arden, 2002; Bandura, 1998; Brug et al., 2005). Sutton (2002) has stated,

> The notion that behavior change involves movement through a sequence of discrete stages is an important idea that deserves further consideration. Unfortunately, the TTM is a poor implementation of this idea. There are serious problems with the existing methods used to measure the central construct of stages of change. Staging algorithms are based on arbitrary time periods and some are logically flawed. In the case of multidimensional questionnaires (the URICA, the SOCRATES and the RCQ), the pattern of correlations among the subscales shows that they are not measuring discrete stages of change. . . . Even leaving aside these measurement problems, current evidence for the TTM as applied to substance use is meagre and inconsistent. (p. 183)

CASE ANALYSIS

Justin and MI and TTM

Justin sauntered into the counselor's office with his baseball hat cocked to the side of his head. He slid down in the chair facing the counselor as if to say "I've got to stay here and listen to you for 50 minutes, and I'll do that just to keep my probation officer off my back." The counselor introduced himself to Justin and shook Justin's limp hand. The counselor said, "Now that I have told you my name and something about me, tell me something about you Justin, what you want to do with the 50 minutes that you spend with me."

"Don't you know nothing?" Justin, responded impatiently and with little respect. "I thought you had all that information in the folder you got on your desk. Why are you asking me?"

"I do have some information about you in the folder, Justin. But I wanted to hear from you, get your take on why you are here and what you want to accomplish."

"I'm here because my probation officer told me that I had to see you and talk with you about my using weed and getting drunk a couple of times. I was at home lighting up with Mom and brother, so I don't know what everyone is so upset about. . . . I mean I wasn't out there in the streets trying to drive or to knock someone on his head with a pipe or something. . . . I was just smoking a little weed, but if you listen to my parole officer, you'd think I'd really done something really bad."

"You're here sitting in the chair across from me because your parole officer gave you an ultimatum . . . either go to counseling about your weed smoking and stop smoking . . . or you go to the residential center."

Justin looked at the counselor defiantly as if to say now we are getting closer to the truth, and said, "Now you've got it. I told you that you know why I am here. You're just trying to mess with my head . . . playing games with me."

(Continued)

(Continued)

"You feel that I am playing a kind of counseling game with you and that I am asking you what I already know. Maybe you're right. Maybe I was just trying to break the ice between us—give you a chance to kind of size me up a bit while at the same time hearing what you thought about your situation."

"Yeah," Justin acknowledged with the kind of sigh that seemed to say "now you're coming clean."

"OK," the counselor said, "let's see if we can be honest with each other. Let's say there was no probation officer telling you that you had to be here, would you want to stop smoking weed?"

"Probably not," Justin responded, "'Cause weed don't do nothing to you except to make you feel real good."

Feeling that he had broken the ice with Justin, the counselor seemed to move the session forward from where they were. "Tell me something about your smoking weed . . . like when do you smoke, who do you do it with, what do you feel like when you're high?"

Justin seemed to relax more, and he began to describe the last two times he had lit up with his Mom, his brother, and some friends at his home. Smoking weed was more than just smoking weed. Smoking weed was how they related to one another . . . it was being in each other's presence when they smoked—watching how each one responded when he or she got high . . . laughing with each other . . . passing around and sharing the blunt—getting the munchies. They had established an entire ritual around smoking weed that was satisfying and that made them feel like trusted family. Justin felt that he belonged when he was smoking. There was no arguing between him and his mother. Everyone just got along and felt good. Lighting up meant that things were going to be happy, OK, no problems—no complaints about Justin's not doing his homework or not washing the dishes. Why should he give up smoking—so he could be fighting with his Mom?

"You've told me about the good things about smoking weed—the fun times that you have with your mother, brother, and friends. You bond over sharing a blunt. You feel good because each one of you can do your own high, and no one criticizes. No one says, 'Don't do that,' or 'You look stupid doing that.'"

"Yeah," Justin said, surprised that the counselor really understood what he had been trying to say about smoking weed.

"You've told me something about the good things about smoking weed. Are there any bad things, anything that happens when you smoke that makes you think, 'Maybe, I should stop smoking . . . maybe there is a down side to weed?'"

"Yeah, like I saw on TV the other day that if you smoke a lot, you can damage your brain. People who smoke a lot can't remember some things. You might have trouble having children, but I'm not worried about that because I'm still young, and I don't want no kids. Sometimes when I smoke, I'm too high to do my homework or anything for school. Then I wonder, where is this all going to end? Am I going to be able to get a job when I grow up, or will I spend my time getting high and be on welfare for the rest of my life?"

"Although you like lighting up, there are times that you begin to wonder where it is all going to end? You're concerned that if you continue smoking, you might end up doing very little with your life. You don't won't to be 30 years old, still having weed parties, no job, and on welfare."

"Exactly," Justin said looking in amazement at the counselor. Finally, he met someone who understood the two parts of him—the part that liked smoking and the other side that wondered how his life would end up if he continued smoking weed.

From this point, the counselor and Justin explored more in depth what Justin liked about smoking and drinking. Justin shared that he smoked weed and drank alcohol because sometimes he just wanted to forget about his life. He wanted to forget about his failing in school, being seen as a problem to his mom and teachers, missing his father, wondering what his life would be like if his father and mom were together—being on welfare. All those things seem to disappear from his head when he smoked and drank. He had no worries. His headaches went away.

The counselor checked with Justin to make sure that he understood his reasons for continuing to smoke and drink as well as his reasons for wanting to stop doing these things. He summarized Justin's statements about the positive and the negatives about smoking weed and drinking alcohol. At this point, the counselor paused and asked Justin about his readiness for changing his behavior on a scale of 1 to 10. The counselor informally assessed Justin's confidence in making the changes and his readiness to make the change. "Let's just say that that part of Justin who may want to stop smoking weed and drinking decided to make those changes. How confident are you that you could make those changes in your life?"

"Not very confident, "Justin replied. "I haven't ever tried to stop before, so I don't know if I could do it." Justin acknowledged that this was the first time that he had thought seriously about making any changes regarding weed and drinking. He was concerned about his relationships with his mother, brother, and friends. How would they respond to him? Would they think that he was betraying them? What would he do when they lit up and he didn't? Would he feel that they looked stupid? He just wasn't ready to make changes right now or next week, but he was willing to talk about it with the counselor and his mother. He knew his brother would consider him a "chump," and so would his friends.

"Justin, you have some important decisions to make." The counselor explained that it was normal to feel both the need to change and the desire to continue the behavior. "Maybe if I asked you a couple of questions, they might help you to sort things out. What might be one positive reason for making a change in your smoking weed and in your drinking? Let's say you made a decision to stop smoking weed during the next month or so, how might your life be better?"

Justin asked the counselor what did the latter think he should do about the dilemma. "You probably think I should give it all up? Isn't that why I am coming here to see you so that you will convince me to stop smoking weed?" "No," the counselor said. "That's a decision that only you can make. You're the one who has to assume the responsibility for the decisions of your life—not me. I am not here to convince you of anything. If you want me to tell you what I think, I need your permission for that. I am not going to try to tell you what to do, but it's clear that any decision you make will have an impact on your being placed or not being placed in residential treatment. I am here to help you clarify the pros and cons of your behavior and your decision to change or not change it. Maybe, during the next session we can talk about your goals, Justin. Examining your goals might provide an important missing component in your decision-making process."

"What's my goals have to do with my stopping smoking weed?" Justin asked.

"If I asked you the top three things that are important in your life and that you really valued, what would you say, Justin?"

"That's easy," Justin answered. "My family and friends, school, and getting a decent job when I grow up."

The counselor paused for a few seconds, and Justin seemed surprised by the counselor's silence. "I didn't hear you say anything about weed or drinking being important to you, Justin. You didn't even mention them; yet these two things are having a serious impact on your life and might send you away for some time from the very things that you love—your family and friends. So, you see, I'm asking you about your goals and what's important to you because they might have a connection about what you want to do about weed and drinking."

"You're saying that I am messing up my life with something that's hurting me and that isn't even important to me."

(Continued)

"I didn't say that, Justin; you did. Deep down inside, you feel that you're messing up your life with weed and drinking, and they are not even really important to you."

"OK, that's cool. Maybe you're right. I'm not sure what my goals are. Right now, I am just not sure about a whole lot of things. But I've got to do something because I might be taken away from my home and placed in residential care a long distance from my home, and I know I don't want that."

"We'll talk about your thoughts about what's really important to you, what you value deep down inside and what you want to do with your life. Does that sound like something you might want to do? The counselor asked.

"Sure," Justin replied. "Sounds cool to me."

SUMMARY

The central issue in recovering from addiction is changing one's behavior. It is difficult to stop drinking alcohol, using heroin, overeating, and spending too much time sitting on the couch. Change in one's behavior is required. Two theories in this chapter tackled the issue of client behavioral change: MI and the TTM or the stages of change theory. MI has received widespread attention because it focuses on what produces change in a person's addictive and problematic behavior during counseling. The stages of change theory was included because it delineated the various stages people proceed through as they attempt to modify or recover from undesirable behavior. Both theories are related because they deal with different dimensions of behavior change.

MI is founded on five therapeutic guidelines: (1) clinician expression of empathy toward the client (**acceptance** of the client with the understanding that ambivalence about change is normal), (2) development of a discrepancy between the client's current behavior and his or her life goals and self-image, (3) clinician avoidance of argument and confrontation of the client, (4) rolling with the client's resistance, (5) support of the client's self-efficacy and ability to change (Miller & Rollnick, 2002).

Since Dr. Miller's early work, more than 200 clinical trials have been conducted on MI. These trials have reported positive findings for a wide spectrum of health issues that require a change in a client's behavior, such as cardiovascular rehabilitation, diabetes management, dietary change, illicit drug use, gambling, and management of chronic mental disorders (Miller & Rose, 2009). Overall, MI is a psychotherapeutic method that is evidence-based, applicable across a wide variety of target behavior areas, and complementary to other treatment methods. It has established a reliable system for training MI trainers, and a testable theory of its underlying precepts is emerging.

It has been found that MI influences change talk and that furthermore, MI can elicit clients' statements of desire and need to change. Even single sessions of MI have been found to produce effective client behavioral change. Therapist style of counseling delivery can either substantially improve or weaken client outcomes (Miller & Rose, 2009). The future of MI looks very promising as an evidence-based theoretical approach to counseling and psychotherapy.

The TTM was developed in an attempt to form an integrative theory based on a construct that cuts across theories of psychotherapy—namely, change. Prochaska and DiClemente (1983) developed initially a five-stage model and later a six-stage model of client behavioral change (Prochaska & Norcross, 2010). Although the stages of change model has been broadly included as part of a conceptual framework for health and substance abuse treatment, recent studies have questioned the actual existence of the underlying constructs of this integrative theory.

SUPPLEMENTAL AIDS

Discussion Questions

1. Discuss the main features of a motivational interviewing approach for counseling people with substance abuse disorders.

2. Compare and contrast motivational interviewing with one cognitive approach and one psychodynamic approach for counseling individuals with substance abuse disorders.

3. Discuss the core principles of motivational interviewing and state why each principle is important.

4. Discuss the components of the OARS approach as it relates to motivational interviewing and indicate how OARS is used to move a client forward by eliciting change talk, or self-motivational statements.

5. An important component of motivational interviewing is to learn to roll with a client's resistance. In small groups of three to five participants, discuss three ways you could roll with the resistance of a client who has some ambivalence about giving up drinking, even though he states he is an alcoholic.

Glossary of Key Terms

ability   A form of client preparatory change talk that indicates a client's perception of his or her perceived capability of making a change; typical words include can, could, and able.

acceptance   One of four central components of the underlying spirit of MI from which the interviewer communicates to the client a sense of the latter's absolute worth, accurate empathy, affirmation, and support.

action stage   Stage in TTM in which people have made specific overt changes in their lifestyles within the past 6 months.

affirmation   One of four aspects of acceptance as a component of the MI spirit, by which the counselor emphasizes the positive about a client—for instance, acknowledges the client's efforts in the past.

ambivalence   The simultaneous presence of competing motivations for and against change.

amplified reflection   A response in which the interviewer reflects back the client's content but with greater intensity than the client had expressed; one form of response to client sustain talk or discord.

CAT   An acronym for three subtypes of client mobilizing change talk: commitment, activation, and taking steps.

change talk   Any client speech that favors a client's movement toward a particular change goal.

closed question   A question that asks for a client's yes/no, or a short answer.

Columbo approach   an MI technique used to help a client perceive a discrepancy in what he or she says or does.

contemplation stage   A stage in TTM in which people are intending to change in the next 6 months. People who are thinking about change but aren't quite ready or don't know how to get started.

DARN   An acronym for four subtypes of client preparatory change talk: desire, ability, reason, and need.

decisional balance   A counseling technique that explores the pros and cons of change or of a specific plan.

elaboration   An interviewer response to client change talk that asks for additional detail, clarification, or example.

empathy   The degree to which an interviewer communicates accurate understanding of the client's perspectives and experience; most usually manifested as reflection.

engaging   The first of four fundamental processes in MI, the process of establishing a mutually trusting and respectful helping relationship to collaborate toward agreed-on goals.

evocation   One of four central components of the underlying spirit of MI by which the interviewer elicits the client's own perspectives and motivation.

evocative questions   Strategic open questions the natural answer to which is change talk.

evoking   The third of four fundamental processes of MI, which involves eliciting the person's own motivation for a particular change.

looking forward   A strategy for evoking client change talk that explores client talk about a possible better future.

maintenance   A stage in TTM in which people are working to prevent relapse—less tempted to relapse and increasingly more confident that they can sustain their change.

Menschenbild (German)   One's fundamental view of human nature.

MINT   The Motivational Interviewing Network of Trainers founded in 1997 and incorporated in 2008 (www.motivationalinterviewing.org).

OARS   An acronym for four basic client-centered communication skills: open questions, affirmation, reflection, and summary.

open-ended questions   Questions that clients cannot easily answer with a yes/no or short response that contains only a limited piece of information. Such questions tend to encourage the client to elaborate and think more deeply about an issue.

precontemplation stage   A stage in TTM in which a person wishes to change, but not in the immediate future (usually measured as the next 6 months).

preparation   A stage in TTM in which people are intending to take action in the immediate future, usually measured as the next month.

preparatory change talk   A subtype of client change talk that expresses motivations for change without stating or suggesting specific intent or commitment to do it; examples are desire, ability, reason, and need.

reflection   An interviewer statement designed to mirror the meaning of client's statement.

reflective listening   The skill of "active" listening that the interviewer uses to understand the client's subjective experience; interviewers offer reflections as guesses about a client's meaning.

reframe   An interviewer's statement that helps the client consider a different interpretation of what the client has just said.

resistance   In motivational interviewing to refer to a host of client behaviors such as arguing, avoiding. In MI, interviewers are taught to roll with a client's resistance. Client behaviors labeled as resistance serve as a signal that the interviewer might shift his or her approach.

self-efficacy   A client's perceived ability to achieve successfully a specific goal or perform a specific task; term first introduced by Albert Bandura.

self-motivational statements   The statements that indicate that the clients recognize the problem, are concerned about it, and are open to doing something about it.

simple reflection   A reflection that mirrors what the client has said but does not go beyond client's statements.

spirit of MI   The underlying mind-set within which MI is practiced.

stages of change   A sequence of stages outlined in the transtheoretical model of change through which people pass in the change process: precontemplation, contemplation, preparation, action, and maintenance.

summaries   Definition of summaries constitute the four part of OARS, which focus attention on key elements of a client's statements or issues. They are designed to shift attention during motivational interviewing and to help the client move forward.

sustain talk   Any client speech that supports the status quo rather than making a movement toward change.

termination   The final stage in TTM; when people in the maintenance stage continue their healthier behavior for at least 2 years, they enter into the termination stage.

Website Materials

Additional exercises, journals, annotated bibliography, and more are available on the open-access website at https://study.sagepub.com/jonessmith2e.

CHAPTER 11

The Expressive Arts Therapies

The arts are an even better barometer of what is happening in our world than the stock market or the debates in congress.

—Hendrik Willem Van Loon

The artist is the antenna of the race.

—Ezra Pound

Every artist dips his brush in his own soul, and paints his own nature into his pictures.

—Henry Ward Beecher

Play is . . . the free expression of what is in a child's soul.

—Friedrich Froebel

You can discover more about a person in an hour of play than in a year of conversation.

—Plato (Greek philosopher 427–347 BCE)

BRIEF OVERVIEW

Expressive arts therapy is placed in the humanistic tradition section of this text because that is where the arts are located—within the humanities. Expressive arts therapy is founded on the assumption that people can represent their own individual life experiences and recover from psychological hurts by using various forms of creative expression. While talk is still the dominant modus operandi for counseling and therapy, sometimes clients need methods other than talk to express their feelings. According to McNiff (1981, 1992), expressive therapies are those that provide action to psychotherapy.

A therapist's use of the expressive arts multiplies the ways in which a client can express himself or herself. Expressive arts therapy can bring light to areas of therapy that are blocked, inhibited, and stuck. The primary focus in this therapeutic approach is on the process, which allows a person to discover new insight and meaning that might not be achieved with traditional talk therapy. A client does not have to have great artistic ability to participate in expressive art therapy. This chapter begins with a definition of expressive arts therapies followed by a brief historical overview of expressive arts therapy that traces human beings' early use of the arts as a means for expressing themselves. It then proceeds to provide a delineation of key concepts and the general treatment process involved in expressive arts therapy. Three expressive arts therapeutic approaches are examined: (1) art therapy, (2) music therapy, and (3) play therapy.

Definition of Expressive Arts Therapies

Malchiodi (2005) has defined expressive therapies as

> the use of art, music, dance/movement, drama, poetry/creative writing, play, and sandtray within the context of psychotherapy, counseling, rehabilitation, or health care. . . . Additionally, expressive therapies are sometimes referred to as "integrative approaches" when purposively used in combination in treatment. (p. 2)

While there are a number of creative disciplines, this text examines (a) art therapy, (b) music therapy, (c) drama therapy, and (d) play therapy.

EXPRESSIVE ARTS: A HUMAN TRADITION

Throughout history, people have used the arts to reveal their emotions and to make sense out of life. People have painted their faces, their bodies, and their caves. They have danced and have sung around bright fires in praise of their God and to celebrate the harvest of good times. In small and in large groups, they have told the stories not only of their days but also of the days of their ancestors. Virtually every historical period dominated by upright humans has produced cultures in which the arts—singing, dancing, and telling stories—are celebrated in one form or another. For instance, the Egyptians encouraged people with mental illness to engage in artistic pursuits (Fleshman & Fryrear, 1981). It is well-known that the Greeks used drama and music for their curative properties (Malchiodi, 2005).

During the late 1800s to the early 1900s, people became interested in using the arts as an adjunct to medical treatment. Also during this same time period, Americans became more concerned about the humane treatment of individuals with mental illness. One product of the early 1900s was moral therapy, which mobilized the arts to treat clients with mental illness (Fleshman & Fryrear, 1981).

Art Therapy: Some Historical Markers

Although art expression has been used for healing throughout world history, art therapy did not emerge as a profession until the 1940s. Psychiatrists began to believe that art expression formed an important part of recovering from mental illness. Freud theorized that a patient's artwork consisted of productions of fantasy that revealed a significant amount of information about his or her unique inner world.

In England, Adrian Hill was one of the first persons to refer to the therapeutic benefit of clients' artwork. Hill's interest in art as a therapeutic medium rose as a result of his being treated in a sanatorium for tuberculosis. He suggested to his fellow patients that they participate in art projects. In his book *Art Versus Illness*, A. Hill (2004) discusses his work as an art therapist. Also in England, artist Edward Adamson, who worked with Hill, introduced art therapy to long-term British patients in mental hospitals, beginning with Netherne Hospital in Surrey. Adamson collected and displayed more than 100,000 pieces of art made by patients.

Margaret Naumburg and Edith Kramer were two pioneers of art therapy in the United States. During the mid-1940s, Naumburg's work was based on the idea of using art to release the unconscious by encouraging free association. A client's artwork was viewed as symbolic speech, which the therapist encouraged the client to interpret and analyze. Naumburg is viewed as the primary founder of American art therapy, and she is often described as the "Mother of Art Therapy" (Davis, 2004). After Naumburg's work, the term *art therapy* began to be used to refer to a form of psychotherapy that placed art interventions alongside talk as the primary modality of treatment. Naumburg viewed a client's artwork as symbolic communications of unconscious material in a direct, uncensored, and concrete form. Dr. Edith Kramer was an Austrian woman who immigrated to the United States and who became an American citizen. She founded the art therapy graduate program at New York

University and served as the adjunct professor of the program from 1973 to 2005.

The concept of artwork as projection led to a series of projective drawing assessments. Florence Goodenough (1975) analyzed children's drawings to measure their cognitive development. In 1926, Goodenough published her first book: *Measurement of Intelligence by Drawings*. Goodenough's most famous contribution was her development of the Draw-A-Man test (also known as the Goodenough Scale), which was the first instrument to test nonverbal IQ in preschool and older-children populations. These drawings were looked at as a window to see mental processes and organization playing off the concept that children draw what they know—not what they see (Goodenough, 1975).

Music Therapy: Some Historical Markers

The earliest American reference to music therapy appeared in 1789 in an unsigned article that appeared in *Columbian Magazine* titled "Music Physically Considered" (see http://www.musictherapy.org/about/history/). During the early 1800s, two medical dissertations were published—the first by Edwin Atlee (1804) and the second by Samuel Matthews (1806), both of whom were students of Dr. Benjamin Rush, a psychiatrist, who was a strong advocate of using music to treat medical diseases.

The two World Wars had a profound effect on using the expressive arts to help people heal emotionally. Music therapy was developed during World War II when physicians became aware that soldiers suffering from mental illness associated with combat responded positively to music. Music therapy was put into practice during and after World War I to treat mentally ill soldiers who were difficult to reach using talk therapy.

During the 1940s, three individuals emerged as leaders in the field of music therapy: (1) Ira Altshuler, a psychiatrist who promoted music therapy in Michigan for three decades; (2) Willem van de Wall, who pioneered the use of music therapy in state-funded institutions and who wrote the first "how to" music therapy text, *Music in Institutions*

(1936); and (3) E. Thayer Gaston, also known as the "father of music therapy," was key in pushing the profession to form a professional organization (see www.musictherapy.org/about/history/).

In 1944, Michigan State University established the first academic program in music therapy. Other universities soon followed suit, including the University of Kansas, the Chicago Musical College, and Alvemo College. In 1950, the National Association for Music Therapy was organized with the goal of standardizing training and promoting unity among those who were already serving as music volunteers (Pratt, 2004). By the 1950s, major psychiatric hospitals—Menninger Clinic in Kansas and St. Elizabeths in Washington, D.C.—included the arts alongside psychological treatment (see www.musictherapy.org/about/history/).

Drama and Play Therapy: Some Historical Markers

The contributions of Joseph Moreno (1889–1974), the founder of psychodrama, also had a significant impact on the expressive arts. Psychodrama makes use of elements of the theater, and it is sometimes conducted on a stage where props are used. As a result of recreating real-life situations and acting them out in the presents, clients are given a chance to evaluate their behavior. Psychodrama is typically used in a group setting so that each person in the group can become therapeutic agents for one another's drama scenes. For instance, during a session of psychodrama, one client within a group is asked to become the protagonist, and another might become an antagonist. Some psychodrama techniques include role reversal, positive creative imagery, and "monodrama" (in which a client enacts all parts of the self) to restore mental health to people.

Moreno reported in his autobiography an encounter with Sigmund Freud. After attending one of Freud's lectures in 1912, Freud stopped him to talk. Moreno (1985) has stated,

> As the students filed out, he singled me out from the crowd and asked me what I was doing. I responded,

"Well, Dr. Freud, I start where you leave off. You meet people in the artificial setting of your office, I meet them on the street and in their homes, in their natural surroundings. You analyze their dreams, I give them the courage to dream again. You analyze and tear them apart. I let them act out their conflicting roles and help them to put the parts back together again."

Psychodrama provided an early foundation for play therapy because both focus on clients acting out some aspect of their lives. During the 1920s, Margaret Lowenfeld (British pediatrician and child psychiatrist) began developing play therapy. During her work as a pediatrician, she made observations about children's play that led her to develop a method of using toys to understand children's feelings (Lowenfeld, 1969). Lowenfeld's first book, *Play in Childhood*, was published in 1935 in the United States. Lowenfeld (1935/1991) developed what has become known as her World Technique through which "direct contact could be made, without interference from the adult, with the mental and emotional life of a child" (p. 3).

There were also major theoretical influences on the development of play therapy. Anna Freud (1965) and Melanie Klein (1932) worked on a psychoanalytic approach to play therapy. Jungian analyst Dora Kalff (1980) extended Lowenfeld's technique by encouraging children to "make a world" in a tray filled one third with sand—sandtray therapy (Allan & Berry, 1987; Homeyer & Sweeney, 1998). The psychoanalytic influence shifted play therapy to a directed format. David Levy (1939) developed release play therapy, Gove Hambidge (1955) promoted structured play therapy, and J. Solomon (1938) developed active play therapy, which used specific toys to help children work through specific issues (Homeyer & DeFrance, 2005).

Using Carl Rogers's work on client-centered therapy, Virginia Axline (1969) constructed nondirective play therapy. Axline is best known for her classic case study of *Dibs* (1971), which is still one of the best-selling books on play therapy. Axline's nondirective approach became known as

child-centered play therapy (Landreth & Sweeney, 1997). Other important play therapists included Clark Moustakas (1953, 1966, 1992) who espoused play therapy from a humanistic framework. Terry Kottman (1987, 1995) developed Adlerian play therapy, and Susan Knell (1993) wrote about a cognitive-behavioral play therapy.

KEY CONCEPTS

Unique Characteristics of Expressive Arts Therapy

Expressive arts therapy has an impact on four major areas: (1) *self-expression*, (2) **imagination,** (3) *active participation*, and (4) **mind–body connection** (Malchiodi, 2005).

Self-Expression. All expressive therapies (as well as most therapies) encourage clients to engage in self-exploration. Expressive arts therapy is based on the underlying assumption that all people have the ability to be creative. It permits the client to express a wide range of emotions, such as fury, fear, sorrow, happiness, and anger. Art therapy activates the creative side of the brain. One discovers one's creative self during an expressive arts session. Creative self-expression is intrinsically curative and promotes a person's well-being and health.

Expressive arts therapists facilitate their client's own discovery of personal meaning and understanding in the expressive artwork. They help people communicate aspects of their lives that might not be readily apparent through conversation (Malchiodi, 2005). A therapist might ask a client to tell his or her story using different types of expressive arts. The therapist begins with asking the client a few questions to get at his or her concerns and then listens to the client's story. "Draw what you feel is your life, and color your life using the crayons I have provided to you." "When you think about your life thus far, what songs come to mind?" In short, talk therapy only provides one mode for exploring a client's life; the expressive therapist can use five or six different—dance, art/drawing/painting, writing, dance, drama, play therapy—modalities to assist a client.

Imagination. According to Levine (1999), "Imagination is the central concept which informs the understanding of the use of arts and play in therapy" (p. 259). Although clients in expressive therapy may not have perfected artistic skills, in most instances, their imagination is involved during the process of creating.

Action or Active Participation of Clients. In general, psychology has labeled the expressive arts therapies as "action therapies" (Weiner, 1999). Knill, Barba, and Fuchs (1995) have pointed out that all of the expressive therapies involve action; however, each form of expressive therapy has its unique properties and usefulness in therapeutic work. The practice of having clients make and do things actually may energize them.

Mind–Body Connection. The expressive arts foster a mind–body connection that capitalizes on clients' using their five senses. Malchiodi (2005) has reported that

> the advances made in the field of neuroscience and neurodevelopment have also drawn attention to the potential of expressive therapies in regard to mind-body intervention, particularly in the areas of mood disorders, stress disorders, and physical illness. . . . Music, art, and dance/movement may be helpful in tapping the body's relaxation response. (p. 12)

She has stated that expressive therapies can be helpful in reestablishing and encouraging healthy attachments through sensory experiences and hands-on activities (Malchiodi, 2003).

Curative Powers of Expressive Arts

The creative process involved in artistic self-expression helps clients resolve conflicts and problems, develop interpersonal skills, manage behavior, reduce stress, and achieve insight, while at the same time increase self-esteem and self-awareness. Each of the sections on art therapy, music therapy, and play therapy deals with the curative powers of that particular specialty. The underlying premise is that the act or painting, making music, and so forth involved in the expressive arts are therapeutic in and of themselves.

Expressive Arts Therapy Process

When a therapist combines the expressive arts with a psychotherapy method of choice, he or she increases the ways in which a client can seek to express emotions, seek meaning, clarify feelings, and obtain healing. The expressive arts therapy process recognizes that each client's pathway to recovery is different. While some clients can best express themselves using painting, another client might prefer journaling, or music. In expressive arts therapy, the emphasis is on *the process of creating rather than on artistic outcomes.*

Expressive Therapies and General Treatment Procedures

Typically, an expressive therapy session begins with a discussion of the client's, family's, or group's goals, concerns, or current problems. Whereas traditional therapists usually explore such issues by way of talking, expressive art therapists encourage clients to use art as a form of communication for exploring goals, concerns, and so forth. For instance, clients might be asked to draw an image of their emotion, role-play a dramatic situation, write a poem, play with toys, or use a musical instrument to express an idea. Expressive arts sessions can begin with a warm-up activity. For instance, an expressive art therapist can also begin a therapy session with warm-up activities, such as a quick scribble or doodle to reflect how a client's day has been proceeding (Malchiodi, 2005). The opening activity might be used to help clients relax or to help the therapist evaluate clients' beginning mood. Therapists can use more than one type of expressive arts therapy during a session. A client writes a poem, and the counselor asks him or her to act out the feelings contained therein or to utilize colors to convey the emotions contained in the poem. The therapy session becomes multimodal using writing, drama, and artwork.

THREE EXPRESSIVE ARTS THERAPEUTIC APPROACHES

This section presents three expressive arts—(1) art therapy, (2) music therapy, and (3) play therapy. Other expressive arts therapies such as dance therapy, drama therapy, and **sandplay therapy** could have easily been included; however, space limitations for coverage of the expressive arts in this book prevent discussion of these expressive art forms. The three chosen expressive art forms were selected because of their widespread use across a number of disciplines and

because of the relative ease with which they can be incorporated with other theoretical approaches to psychotherapy.

Art Therapy: Cathy A. Malchiodi, Art Therapist and Expressive Arts Therapy Writer

The Greek word ζωγραφιά or *zografia* for drawing summarizes the meaning of art therapy in a single word, because it is translated as "I draw my life." Experiences from an individual's past and present, dreams and fears for the future, thoughts, problems, ideas, anger, love, and confusion can all be put on a piece of paper, on the wall, or anywhere appropriate with the use of brushes, pens, pencils, or clays. **Art therapy** is a form of expressive arts therapy that uses the creative processes involved in art making to facilitate a person's mental, emotional, and physical well-being. According to the American Art Therapy Association,

> Art therapy is the therapeutic use of art making, within a professional relationship, by people who experience illness, trauma or challenges in living, and by people who seek personal development. Through creating art and reflecting on the art products and processes, people can increase awareness of self and others, cope with symptoms, stress and traumatic experiences; enhance cognitive abilities; and enjoy the life-affirming pleasures of making art. (www.arttherapy.org)

Art therapists are trained in both art and therapy; therefore, they are knowledgeable about human development, psychological theories, clinical practice, and multicultural artistic traditions. Art therapists work with people of all ages and backgrounds—from the very young to the old, with individuals as well as with groups, and families. They provide services in settings such as mental health clinics and private practice, rehabilitation agencies, medical and forensic institutions, schools, and nursing homes. People who seek out an art therapist need not have had previous experience in art or even be good at it. Art therapy is about

Inner Reflections

Of the three expressive art forms, art, music, and play therapy, which one do you think you would feel most comfortable using? Why?

Do you have special talents with any of the art form categories? Which one(s)?

Which art form would you be inclined to use with a client? Explain.

expressing feelings and emotions and not about mixing the right colors or painting a masterpiece.

The Therapeutic Process of Art Therapy

Role of the Expressive Art Therapist

The overall or general role of the expressive art therapist is to encourage the client's art making such that the two discover the client's deepest thoughts and experiences through the use of his or her art making and art experiencing. The therapist's role changes based on his or her underlying theoretical orientation—psychodynamic, humanistic, cognitive-behavioral, or social constructivist. Depending on which psychotherapeutic school forms the foundation for one's work as an art therapist, art therapists may differ on the amount of encouragement or directiveness they give to clients during the art-making process and the amount or degree of interpretation they provide regarding a client's art expressions. Art therapists work on a continuum of being nondirective to directive, from being action oriented to insight oriented, and from being interpretive to being noninterpretive. Because art therapists are trained to recognize the nonverbal symbols and metaphors that are communicated within the creative process, they can help clients understand what underlying thoughts and feelings are being communicated in the artwork under consideration.

Expressive art therapists understand the art processes, meaning the client's use of art material, the significance of the colors that the client chooses, the size of the artwork or figures within it, and relative position of the component parts of an artwork—including any missing parts. An expressive art therapist also provides a trusting and facilitating therapeutic environment that helps clients express themselves. The art therapist does not just wing it, but instead, he or she creates a treatment plan, with goals and measurable outcome objectives. When art therapy is utilized in a proper fashion, clients are helped to see things about themselves that were formerly imperceptible. Clients' recognition of their hurt is the first step in the healing process.

Inner Reflections

Have you ever had a spiritual experience or an epiphany in your life?

Draw, paint, or sculpture that spiritual experience.

What color(s) would you use to represent your spiritual experience?

Inner Reflections

If you were an art therapist, what would be your underlying psychotherapy theory guiding your work?

To what extent do you feel comfortable incorporating art expressions as part of your approach to psychotherapy?

Art Therapy and Models of Psychotherapy

The American Art Therapy Association conducted a survey that revealed that most art therapists practice art therapy from a psychodynamic perspective, which includes psychoanalytic, object relations, and Jungian approaches (Elkins & Stovall, 2000). Another high percentage of respondents stated that they were "eclectic" in their approach to art therapy, indicating that they incorporated several theoretical perspectives in their work, dependent on their clients' needs and treatment goals. Art therapy has been used from a solutions-focused perspective (Selekman, 1997), from a narrative viewpoint (Freeman, Epston, & Lobovits, 1997), and from a family therapy perspective (Riley, 2003). The following paragraphs discuss psychoanalytic and analytic approaches, humanistic models using art therapy, and cognitive-behavioral models.

Psychodynamic and Psychoanalytic Approaches to Art Therapy. As noted in the brief history section of this chapter, the psychoanalytic school has been influential in the development of art therapy. While Naumburg highlighted the importance of clients' spontaneous drawings as representations and projections of their unconscious thoughts and feelings, Edith Kramer (2001) maintained that art expression functioned as a source of sublimation of aggression and other negative feelings. Art therapy has also been influenced by Carl Jung's theories of archetypes and the collective unconscious. Jungian art therapists emphasize the content of dreams and fantasies, assisting the client to explore possible meanings.

The following psychoanalytic concepts have been incorporated into the psychodynamic approach to art therapy:

• *Transference:* An art therapist operating from a psychodynamic perspective maintains that a client's art expression may become the focus of transference, and a client may react to the process of art making and the therapist as a transference relationship. The content of a client's artwork may contain unspoken feelings about the therapist—anger, anxiety, or love. The therapist might appear in a drawing or painting, and a therapist can use the artwork to discuss his or her relationship with the client (Malchiodi, 2005).

• *Spontaneous expression:* A client's artwork can be viewed as a spontaneous expression that provides clues or access to his or her unconscious, and this process is similar to the process of free association. A familiar technique in art therapy is the scribble drawing in which the person is instructed to

> create a scribble and then look for images within the lines of the scribble. After images are found, the person might further articulate them with color and additional features and then make verbal associations to describe the figures or objects created. (Malchiodi, 2005, p. 24)

Winnicott's (1971) "squiggle game" is an example of a psychoanalytic technique used in art therapy.

• *Active imagination:* Jung used the technique of active imagination to release a person's creativity. The therapist encourages a client to observe his or her internal images and to permit them to change and emerge while paying attention to what the

client is experiencing. The therapist can continue to explore an art image by asking the client to relate additional images to the original one.

• *Transitional space and transitional objects:* Art therapists who operate from an object relations perspective use the concepts of transitional space and transitional object in examining a client's artwork. Both a client's artwork and play activity are viewed as transitional spaces because they are ways to link a client's subjective and objective realities as well as a method to practice attachment and relationship. A client's artwork or art expression is conceptualized as a "holding environment" within which object relations between a therapist and a client can develop. The client's art expressions are seen as transitional objects that are imbued with personal meaning. For example, a person may draw a picture of a woman to represent his mother. A client's artwork may also serve as a symbol or a transitional object representing the therapist between sessions.

Humanistic Approaches to Art Therapy. Humanistic psychology has also had a profound influence on art therapy. Humanistic approaches to art therapy emphasize using art as an authentic expression of one's feelings as opposed to eliminating or curing such feelings. Clients' art expressions provide a way for them to communicate nonverbally.

Although there are a number of humanistic approaches to art therapy, Natalie Rogers (1993), the daughter of Carl Rogers, is one of the most well-known expressive therapists. She has maintained that active and empathetic listening embody the person-centered approach. The therapist actively and empathetically sees what the person is drawing or painting. The person-centered therapist does not interpret a client's art expression but instead pays careful attention to what the person is communicating. The therapist reflects what clients have conveyed in their art expressions, and he or she asks for additional clarification to deepen clients' understanding of their feelings.

In the Gestalt approach to art therapy, the client, the artwork, and the therapist form part of the overall Gestalt. Gestalt art therapy is action oriented, and the therapist uses the client's art expression to activate the latter's sensory and motor responses. Gestalt art therapy is typically integrated with other art forms, such as music. A Gestalt art therapist might ask a client to draw a line or shape to represent a feeling and subsequently asks the client to make a sound that represents that feeling (Malchiodi, 2005). A Gestalt art therapist should be used for people who are capable of self-direction, because although the therapist directs the session, the client is ultimately responsible for making meaning out of the clinical experience.

Cognitive-Behavioral Approaches to Art Therapy. Therapists who use a cognitive-behavioral orientation often use homework assignments that involve drawing or other art activities mentioned during therapy sessions. A therapist might suggest a drawing journal in which a client draws images of his or her feelings between sessions. The therapist might also suggest drawing activities to relieve stress or to deal with the presenting problem. Artwork is also used to assist clients to reframe difficult situations or emotions. Working with adult clients, Rozum and Malchiodi (2003) have suggested the following cognitive-behavioral interventions for art therapy:

• *Make an image of a "stressor":* The cognitive-behavioral approach to art therapy identifies stressors that produce or trigger negative feelings. During a therapy session, the therapist might encourage the client to make an image of the stressful life event that produces negative self-talk, or he or she could ask the client to keep an art journal of negative triggers.

• *Make an image of "how I can prepare for a stressor":* The cognitive-behavioral art therapist might ask the client to create an image or art expression of what he or she will do to meet a challenging situation. For instance, if a client experiences anxiety about going outside in the marketplace, the therapist asks him or her to create positive art images of him or her going out in the marketplace—for instance, shopping for clothes or groceries.

• *Make an art image of step-by-step management of a problem situation:* The client is asked to make a series of pictures that show how a problem can be tackled by breaking it down into its component parts.

• *Create positive art imagery for stress reduction:* The therapist suggests that clients collect or create positive art images from magazines and other sources that produce positive thoughts to counteract negative thoughts. (p. 76)

Materials Used in Art Therapy

Art therapists use drawing, painting, sculpture, photography, and other types of visual art expression. The following is a list of materials used in art therapy, along with a brief statement regarding how and for what purpose they can be used.

• *Watercolors:* Therapists can have clients paint anything they desire using any color that they want. Water colors create a state of being calm and relaxed.

- *Acrylic paint:* This material allows clients to emulate most physical structures or things in nature. It promotes a connection to Mother Nature.
- *Colored pencils:* A therapist might use colored pencils to draw circles to help clients develop a sense of being self-assured and centered.
- *Markers:* A therapist might ask clients to draw pictures of the people in their lives whom they are having problems with and how they can coexist in harmony once again.
- *Photography:* The therapist asks the client to take a picture that conveys exactly how he or she is feeling at a moment in time. Such pictures will help clients recognize their actual emotions and feelings.
- *Pencils:* The therapist gives each family member a pencil to draw how each person sees his or her family. This technique will enable clients to look at their family differently, hopefully being able to see their positive and negative sides.
- *Collage:* The therapist suggests that the client gather any pictures that he or she can get from coloring books, magazines, or the newspaper to create an image of who he or she would like to be, how he or she would like to feel, and how he or she would like to look. This visual information will help clients see what they seek that exists in their environment as well as what they would like to have personally for themselves.
- *Clay:* Clients can create or use clay pots in which to place their anger or other types of feelings. By placing angry feelings in a pot, clients gain a sense of control over them.

Methods and Techniques for Expressive Art Therapy

An art therapist can use numerous techniques in working with clients. The following techniques are suggestions that have been gathered from a broad spectrum of resources.

- *Draw or paint your emotion technique:* The "draw or paint your emotion technique" can be used with clients individually or within groups. The expressive arts therapist asks an individual to focus entirely on what he or she is feeling and to paint that emotion or the therapist provides an emotion wheel and asks the client to color that wheel.
- *Paint your heart:* The therapist gives the client a blank picture of a heart. Using the heart as a pattern, the client is asked to fill in different parts of the heart with the emotions he or she is currently feeling and to color those emotions with crayons.
- *Create a sculpture of a client's hurt, love, or anger:* The client is asked to engage in the practice of making a sculpture that represents his hurt, anger, or frustration.
- *Draw your version of a happy day in your life:* Have the client think about a happy day in his or her life. Have the client draw that happy day, putting in the drawing the people and events that contributed to his or her happiness. This exercise helps a client focus on the good times in his or her life.
- *Create a body image sketch:* This technique can be used with clients who are experiencing difficulties with eating disorders or with individuals who have low self-esteem because of their weight.
- *Draw a portrait of someone who changed your life for the better:* Another version of this technique is to ask the client to bring in a picture of someone who changed his or her life for the better. This technique encourages clients to review the relationships in their lives and how such relationships have made their lives richer.
- *Create a future self-portrait of the client:* Ask a client to paint or draw a self-portrait of himself or herself in the future. This technique can be varied by having clients bring in self-portraits of themselves throughout critical periods of their lives. Clients are encouraged to consider change in their lives. To what extent have their outward appearance changes reflected their inward changes?

- *Taking pictures:* Use a camera to take pictures of things for which the client is grateful.

- *Draw a mountain and a valley:* The mountain can represent a time when the client was happy, and the valley, a time when he or she was sad. Color the mountain and the valley. Include specific events that should be placed on either the mountain or the valley.

Evidence-Based Research on Art Therapy

Although the practice of art therapy has existed for many decades, only relatively recently have scholars addressed the efficacy of this clinical approach. Reynolds, Nabors, and Quinlan (2000) conducted a review of the literature on the efficacy of art therapy and concluded that although art therapy seems to demonstrate efficacy, the results were mixed. This section on research for art therapy is not intended to be exhaustive, but rather to point to findings that either support or do not support this expressive modality for treatment of people.

Inner Reflections

How competent do you feel in using artwork with your clients?

Have you ever had training in the psychology of colors, lines, figures, and so forth?

Would you ever consider getting training in art therapy or in the expressive arts?

Eaton, Doherty, and Widrick (2007) conducted a review of research and methods on the efficacy of art therapy for traumatized children. The authors included published, peer-reviewed literature that focused exclusively on the use of art therapy for treating children who had experienced a traumatic event. Their review found that art therapy was used successfully in a variety of contexts for traumatized children. One limitation of the studies was that many were case studies without control groups.

In a response to the review of Reynolds et al. (2000), Slayton, D'Archer, and Kaplan (2010) conducted a review of studies that measured outcomes of art therapy effectiveness with all ages of clinical and nonclinical populations. Slayton et al.'s (2010) review led to the identification of four categories of art therapy outcome studies: (1) thorough and detailed qualitative studies, (2) single-subject pretest/posttest designs; (3) designs using control and treatment groups without random assignment, and (4) controlled clinical trials with randomized assignment to groups. The researchers concluded that "the results of these 35 studies provide varying degrees of support that art therapy does work" (p. 115). Slayton et al. also asserted,

> Even though much more research is needed, we found that a small body of studies now exists in which art therapy as a treatment modality has been isolated, measured, and shown to be statistically significant in improving a variety of symptoms for a variety of people with different ages. (p. 115)

Art therapy worked for elementary school children, adolescents, and the elderly.

Current Developments: Clinical Neuroscience and Digital Art Therapy

There are two major current developments in art therapy. The first major thrust is in the area of neuroscience. The first major development in art therapy has been aligned with clinical neuroscience (Hass-Cohen, 2003; Klorer, 2005; Malchiodi, 1999). Hass-Cohen (2012) has suggested that neuroscience might help art therapists understand better what makes art healing. Art therapy elicits certain responses in different parts of the brain. According to him, neuroscience can outline art-making processes in meaningful ways. For example, one can test if art therapy promotes electroencephalography rhythms to increase in alpha frequency, thereby decreasing behavior symptoms of anxiety. When art therapy goals are centered on neuroscience, it becomes possible to make therapy more concrete and outcome based.

Developments in neuroscience may assist researchers and therapists alike to pinpoint how art therapy produces emotion-centered images to promote brain activity in the limbic system and simultaneously to engage the hippocampus. An art therapist might systematically gear his or her practice toward positive, emotion-centered image making, and discussions can be focused on the development of positive, strengths-based statements to create new neural brain pathways. Two recent studies combined art therapy and neuroscience by using electroencephalography recordings to determine what takes place in the brain during and after art expression; however, more studies are needed in this area (Belkofer & Konopka, 2003; Kruk, 2004).

The second major development in expressive art therapy involves digital art and computer art therapy. Digital art is defined as any art that is made with the assistance of a computer. It can include drawings made on paper that are scanned in and changed in any way on the computer, photographs that are modified, 3D characters created using a computer, website designs, animation, computer-generated images, and games. Although some people have contended that digital art is not real art because it is computer generated with an infinite number of copies and no "original," it is now widely accepted as art because it involves creativity and the knowledge of art and design principles. Digital art represents the next major step in the evolution of art. Using a computer, artists can create something that was never possible. Digital art integrates art, technology, math, and science. It requires creativity as well as the knowledge of art, design, and computers. There are now computer apps that one can download on one's computer that deal with how children, adolescents, and adults are feeling.

> ### Inner Reflection
>
> You have changed over the years. No one stays the same. Create a transformational portrait series of yourself showing how you have changed since you were a child.

Art making can be used to help adult clients explore different aspects of their personalities and relationships and to relieve stress in their lives. For children, art therapy can provide an easier way for them to express themselves without the use of words.

Music Therapy: Michele Forinash, Music Therapist

Virtually every known culture on the earth has music. One of the basic actions of humans is music (Malchiodi, 2005). In fact, Daniel Levitin (2006) has called music a basic human instinct. No one knows for certain when human beings first started to use music. One hypothesis is that music preceded language as a means of communication, because the structures that respond to music in the brain evolved earlier than those that respond to language (Levitin, 2006).

Researchers have also traced people's ability to understand and respond to music to the neonatal period (Jourdain, 1997; Storr, 1992). During this time, the young child's vocalizations resemble musical responses. As the infant begins to grow, the musical qualities of rhythm and pitch are incorporated into the development of speech. Musical qualities are localized mainly in the left side of the brain, which undergoes significant growth between the ages of 2 and 4. An infant's brain seems to have an innate capacity to interpret musical information, suggesting that the musical process has some survival value.

Recently, neuropsychologists have proposed that musical experience changes the brain (Zatorre, 2003). As Zatorre (2003) has asserted, "I think there's enough evidence to say that musical experience, musical exposure, musical training, all of those things change your brain." Dr. Charles Limb, associate professor of otolaryngology and head and neck surgery at Johns Hopkins University, says, "It allows you to think in a way that you used to not think, and it also trains a lot of other cognitive facilities that have nothing to do with music" (cited in Landau, 2012).

Zatorre (2003) has found that music is strongly associated with the brain's reward system. It forms part of the brain that tells people if things are valuable or important or relevant to survival. Zatorre and colleagues conducted an experiment in which they used whatever music participants said gave them pleasure to examine dopamine release. Music with words or lyrics were excluded so that the focus would be primarily on the music itself and not on words. When participants experienced peak pleasure from the music, part of the brain called the ventral striatum released dopamine. Dopamine was also released from a different brain area (the dorsal striatum) about 10 to 15 seconds before the moment of peak pleasure. Zatorre concluded that people make predictions about the pleasure they are going to receive from hearing a certain point in the music. Information on music and the reward centers of the brain is important for therapists seeking to use music therapy with clients.

Music speaks to the soul of most people. Listening to music can predispose one to feel happy, sad, angry, loving, and a host of emotions. Because of its early presence in the development of humankind, music has been found to have healing and curative factors associated with it. For instance, music helped Thomas Jefferson write the Declaration of Independence for Americans (O'Donnell, 1999). According to O'Donnell (1999), "Music was the key that helped Albert Einstein become one of the smartest men who has ever lived. Einstein himself says that the reason he was so smart is because he played the violin."

Definition of Music Therapy

Music therapy can be defined as the prescribed use of music by a qualified music therapist to effect positive change in an individual's psychological, physical, cognitive, or social functioning (Forinash, 2005). Music therapy is used with clients of all age groups and with a variety of psychological disorders and medical problems, developmental disabilities, substance abuse, interpersonal problems, and aging. For example, research evidence suggests that music helps Alzheimer clients remember things better. Music with a beat appears to help clients with motor disorders such as Parkinson's disease walk better than in the absence of music. As Thaut and McIntosh (2010) have stated,

> Biomedical researchers have found that music is a highly structured auditory language involving complex perception, cognition, and motor control in the brain, and thus it can effectively be used to retrain and reeducate the injured brain. . . . Therapists and physicians use music now in rehabilitation in ways that are not only backed up by clinical research findings but also supported by an understanding of some of the mechanisms of music and brain function . . . the traditional public perception of music as a "soft" addition, a beautiful luxury that cannot really help heal the brain, has not caught up with these scientific developments. . . . Evidence-based models of music in therapy have moved from soft science—or no science—to hard science. Neurologic music therapy does meet the standards of evidence-based medicine, and it should be included in standard rehabilitation care.

Role of the Expressive Music Therapist

Music therapists use music to engage clients in reminiscence/orientation work with the elderly, processing and relaxation work from the young to the old, rhythmic entrainment for physical rehabilitation in stroke victims, and relationship building with self and others. After assessing the needs of each client, music therapists may use interventions such as creating music, singing, moving to, and/or listening to music. Music therapists formulate an individualized treatment plan, with goals and measurable outcome objectives.

An important consideration in music therapy is the role of music and words in the therapeutic process. Some music therapists put the music-making process at the forefront of therapy; they maintain that it is the experience of music that creates change in the client (Forinash, 2005). This approach emphasizes music as therapy because less emphasis is placed on the verbal processing of music. For other music therapists, the focus is on the verbal processing of the music experience that leads to insight and change.

The role of the music therapist is also influenced by what Wheeler (1983) has termed *the level of practice*. Wheeler has identified three levels of music practice that a therapist might assume: (1) supportive music therapy, (2) reeducative music therapy, and (3) reconstructive music therapy. The support level of music practice is designed to restore "individuals to an emotional equilibrium so that they can function as closely as possible to their normal levels" (p. 9). Reeducative music therapy helps clients become more aware of their clinical issues and gives them "sufficient command of their difficulties to enable them to keep acting out impulses in check" (p. 9). Reconstructive music therapy stresses changing the basic structure of a client's personality. Wheeler posited that reconstructive music therapy should be used with clients "whose egos are strong enough to change and who are interested enough and who are able to devote extensive time to the process" (p. 9). A therapist has to determine which level of music practice he or she will use with a client.

Music Therapy and Models of Psychotherapy

Bruscia (1998) has identified five internationally recognized models of music therapy that have a specific orientation in a theory of psychology. These are (1) behavioral music therapy (behavioral theoretical orientation), (2) Benenzon music therapy (psychodynamic orientation),

(3) Nordoff-Robbins music therapy (humanistic and transpersonal), (4) analytic music therapy (psychodynamic), and (5) the Bonny method of guided imagery and music (humanistic and transpersonal). This section collapses these categories into three areas.

Behavior Music Therapy. This theoretical model uses music to manage behavior. Bruscia (1998) has explained that "the therapist uses music to increase or modify adaptive (or inappropriate) behaviors and to extinguish maladaptive (or inappropriate) behaviors" (p. 184). Davis, Gfeller, and Thaut (1999) have maintained that behavior music therapy comprises traditional behavior modification techniques, including positive reinforcement and differential reinforcement. Positive reinforcement occurs during music therapy when the therapist can provide the client with a musical reward, such as a music CD or listening to the client's preferred music after he or she has demonstrated an appropriate response (Forinash, 2005). The desired response is usually a nonmusical goal, such as completing homework in a timely fashion.

Behavioral music therapy also uses the technique of differential reinforcement that involves positive reinforcement for appropriate behaviors while ignoring maladaptive behaviors and consequently extinguishing the undesirable behavior. The music therapist provides appropriate awards for the client's being on task, while ignoring acting-out behavior (Forinash, 2005). Behavior music therapy focuses on overt client behaviors. Behavioral music therapy is used to improve social skills, academic skills, and other adaptive behaviors.

Psychoanalytic and Psychodynamic Music Therapy. Analytic music therapy is characterized by psychodynamic principles. A Freudian-oriented music therapist would reflect and interpret the client's music. The therapist would have responsibilities of "identifying the issue, suggesting the appropriate action method, and leading the verbal process and integration after the improvisation" (Scheiby, 1999, p. 264). The Jungian music therapist uses the technique of improvisation. The Jungian music therapist focuses more on "ways of expression that can be related to as musical archetypes, such as projections of the animus/anima or identification of the musical shadow or personal, while at the same time focusing on facilitating a musical individuation process" (Scheiby, 1999, p. 265).

The music therapist working from an object relations orientation pays particular attention to the "client's developmental stage through the qualities of the client's music that reflect problems of symbiosis, separation and rapprochement" (Scheiby, 1999, p. 265). The object relations music therapist uses music as a transitional object (Winnicott, 1971).

Humanistic Music Therapy. The music therapist operating from a humanistic theoretical orientation helps clients achieve self-actualization and personal meaning. Nordoff and Robbins (1977) have been two pioneers of the humanistic tradition in music therapy. They attended what they described as the music child with severely disabled children. These clinicians have stated,

> The entity in every child, which responds to musical experience, finds it meaningful and engaging, remembers music, and enjoys some form of musical expression. The Music Child is therefore the individualized musicality inborn in each child: The term has reference to the universality of musical sensitivity . . . it also points to the distinctly personal significance of each child's musical responsiveness. (p. 1)

The humanistic musical therapist strives to make a connection with the client through music. "Once a connection is made in the music, the therapist works through the music to enhance that connection and bring the child into a musical relationship" (Forinash, 2005, p. 55). The Gestalt-oriented musical therapist participates in the client's musical improvisation and focuses on making contact with the client in the here-and-now.

Materials Used in Music Therapy

Music therapy uses a variety of materials, including musical instruments, recordings of songs, radio, CDs, and other listening devices. Clients can bring to therapy their own musical compositions or those of others. They may also bring their own recordings, CDs, or musical videos. Music therapists have their own arsenal of musicals, songs, instruments, or recordings.

Methods and Techniques of Expressive Music Therapy

Music therapy techniques include live music production, improvisation, guided imagery (i.e., the pairing of visualization with music), creative songwriting, and lyric analysis. A music therapist conducts a careful assessment of a client's needs to determine which music method or technique will be used. Some common music methods are provided in the following:

- *Improvisation* involves making up or constructing music either by oneself or with others. Musical improvisation provides a means of nonverbal communication during therapy. It enhances a client's self-expression and encourages creativity and spontaneity. Clients can improvise a musical piece during or before therapy.
- *Recreative experiences* take place when the client and therapist use precomposed music in treatment. Such experiences involve reproducing, performing, or interpreting musical selections.
- *Composition experiences* refer to the creation of a specific musical product. The therapist and client might write songs, lyrics, or instrumental pieces. This music technique helps clients improve their planning and organizing skills, encourage client self-responsibility, and assists them to create an organized, creative product.

Inner Reflections

Do any of the theoretical schools discussed in this section resonate with an approach that you might take with music therapy and your clients?

Using a concept from Nordoff (1977), describe your music child.

- *Receptive experiences* take place when the client listens to live or prerecorded music and responds either verbally or by using another art form, such as writing.

Receptive music experiences bring about various types of affective states.

Evidence-Based Research on Expressive Music Therapy

According to the American Music Therapy Association,

> Research in music therapy supports its effectiveness in many areas such as: overall physical rehabilitation and facilitating movement, increasing people's motivation to become engaged in their treatment, providing emotional support for clients and their families, and providing an outlet for expression of feelings. (www.musictherapy.org/about/quotes)

The American Music Therapy Association has made available a list of research exploring the benefits of music as treatment through publication of the *Journal of Music Therapy, Music Therapy Perspectives*, and other resources (www.musictherapy.org). The CD-ROM "Music Therapy Research— Quantitative and Qualitative Foundations" offers a complete collection of research published by the music therapy associations in the United States from 1964 through 2003. According to this association, the following outcomes are documented in music therapy research: (a) reduction of muscle tension in clients, (b) clients' improved self-image and self-esteem, (c) decreased anxiety/agitation, (d) increased verbalization, (e) enhanced interpersonal relationships, (f) improved group cohesiveness, (g) increased motivation, and (h) safe emotional release.

In general, research measuring the efficacy of music therapy has been more empirically oriented, more robust, and voluminous than the other expressive art categories. The research studies are voluminous, and therefore, only a brief sampling of some of the findings are provided here. Gold (2007) found that music therapy improves

symptoms in adults hospitalized with schizophrenia. In an earlier study, Gold, Heldal, Dahle, and Wigram (2005) found that when music therapy was added to the standard care, clients with schizophrenia improved their global and mental state, and functioning were improved if a sufficient number of music therapy sessions were provided. Silverman (2006) conducted a meta-analysis of 19 studies and concluded that music has proved to be significantly effective in suppressing and combating the symptoms of psychosis.

Music therapy with adolescents and children has also been found to be effective. Depressed adolescents listening to music experienced a significant reduction in stress hormone (cortisol) levels, and most adolescents shifted toward left frontal electroencephalography activation, which is associated with positive affect (Field et al., 1998). Moreover, adolescent music therapy clients improved significantly on the Aggression/Hostility scale of Achenbach's Teacher's Report Form, implying that group music therapy can promote self-expression and can provide a way for transforming frustration, anger, and aggression into the experience of creativity and self-mastery.

Music therapy with adults has also been efficacious. Leardi et al. (2007) examined the effect of music therapy in patients' stress response to day surgery. The authors concluded that perioperative music therapy change the neurohormonal and immune stress response to day surgery, especially when the patient selected the type of music. Another study conducted a meta-analytic review of research articles using music to decrease arousal due to stress. A total of 22 quantitative studies were included in the analysis. Results indicated that music alone and music-assisted relaxation techniques significantly decreased arousal. The studies in this section demonstrate that music therapy is effective for a broad range of clients and problems.

Current Developments: Neurologic Music Therapy

Thaut and McIntosh (2010) have pointed out that a new scientific model called neurologic music therapy has developed as a result of biomedical research in music that has produced clusters of scientific evidence that reveal the effectiveness of specific music interventions. According to them, neurologic music therapy may be defined as the therapeutic application of music to individuals' cognitive, sensory, and motor dysfunctions that emanate from human neurologic diseases. The designated neurological dysfunctions include stroke, traumatic brain injury, Parkinson's disease, Huntington's disease, cerebral palsy, Alzheimer's disease, autism, as well as other neurological disease affecting cognition and movement. Neurologic music therapy is defined as the therapeutic application of music to cognitive, sensory, and motor dysfunctions due to disease of the human nervous system. It is founded on neuroscience models of music perception and the affect that music has on changes in nonmusical brain functions and behavior. Practitioners are educated in the disciplines of neuroanatomy and physiology, brain pathologies, and medical terminology.

Play Therapy: Margaret Lowenfeld, Developer of Play Therapy; Linda Homeyer: Play Therapist

Play is part of the natural world of most children. Children learn about themselves, others, and the world through play. The importance of play as part of a child's normal healthy development is revealed in the Office of the United Nations High Commissioner for Human Rights' 1989 declaration that states that play is a human right for all children everywhere, and it is absolutely necessary for children to achieve optimum development. Furthermore, in 2007, the American Academy of Pediatrics issued a white paper emphasizing the significance of play for healthy child development (Gingsburg, 2007).

Most people have had the opportunity to watch a child play. If you have ever seen a child deliberately smashing a toy, you might be concerned that anger is lurking close to play. Or, on the other hand, maybe you have witnessed another child consoling her friend if he has lost during play. That child may have budding nurturing strengths and rank high on empathy because she is able to put herself in the "feeling place" of another person. Children use play to express themselves because their restricted level of cognitive development and their language competency does not permit their engaging the world in other ways. "Toys are children's words," and toys constitute children's predominant tools for expressing their feelings and their understanding of their world. Is children's play ever "just play" or is such way almost always purposeful?

Inner Reflections

When was the last time in your life that you engaged in play? What did you do—play a game, play basketball? Where were you, and who was with you?

As you reflect on your play experience, what feelings come to mind?

Definition of Play Therapy

The American Association for Play Therapy defines **play therapy** as "the systematic use of a theoretical model to establish an interpersonal process wherein trained play therapists use the therapeutic powers of play to help clients prevent or resolve psychosocial difficulties and achieve optimal growth and development" (www.a4pt .org). Researchers have defined play therapy as a structured approach that is theoretically based and one that uses the normal communicative and learning processes of children (Carmichael, 2006; Homeyer & DeFrance, 2005). Because the American Association for Play Therapy defines play therapy as the use of a systematic theoretical model to establish an interpersonal process through play, a subsequent section examines play therapy within the confines of three theoretical approaches: (1) child-centered play therapy, (2) Adlerian play therapy, and (3) Jungian play therapy (Homeyer & DeFrance, 2005).

Play therapists maintain that children's play has healing or curative powers (Carmichael, 2006; Landreth, 2002). According to Schaefer (2003a), play helps children overcome resistance to therapy. For involuntary clients, play promotes a working alliance with the therapist because the environment is nonthreatening. In addition, play functions as a developmentally appropriate means for children to communicate with therapists. The curative aspect of play therapy reveals itself in many different ways. During a therapy session, therapists provide a positive relationship that serves as a corrective healing experience. Play therapy builds on the natural way that children learn about themselves; it may provide the means of helping children gain insight about what is troubling them (Reddy, Files-Hall, & Schaefer, 2005). During play therapy, children use toys and other materials to experience feelings of cathartic release of emotions. They learn adaptive behaviors as a result of their guided play with a therapist (Pedro-Carroll & Reddy, 2005). Schaefer (2003b) has suggested that enjoying play is therapeutic for children because it is a pleasurable activity that contributes to their sense of well-being and that serves as an antidote to stressful living.

Play therapy differs from regular play in that play is used intentionally to help children address their problems as well as to assist them in learning new, more positive behaviors. Toys provide a way for children to *show* what has happened when they have been threatened, not to *tell* (Homeyer & DeFrance, 2005). They provide the means by which a child can obtain sufficient emotional and psychological distance to permit talk to continue while experiencing overwhelming and frightening

Inner Reflections

When was the last time that you spent time actually playing with a child? Who was that child, and what was his or her relationship to you?

Did you enjoy your play experience? What childhood memories surfaced for you as you played with the child?

feelings. According to the American Association for Play Therapy,

> Through play therapy, children learn to communicate with others, express feelings, modify behavior, develop problem-solving skills, and learn a variety of ways of relating to others. Play provides a safe psychological distance from their problems and allows expression of thoughts and feelings appropriate to their development. (www.a4pt.org)

Research studies have reported the effectiveness of play therapy with children experiencing learning and behavioral problems, as well as children having difficulty with problems related to life stressors, such as divorce, relocation, hospitalization, chronic illness, domestic violence, and sexual abuse. In terms of curative results, play therapy has been found to help children (Reddy et al., 2005):

- To become more responsible for their behaviors and to help them use successful strategies to resolve issues
- To develop different and creative solutions to problems
- To develop respect and acceptance of self and others
- To learn to experience and express their emotions
- To develop empathy and respect for others' thoughts and feelings
- To learn new relational skills within their families

Role of the Play Therapist

Play therapists are trained specifically in mental health programs to use children's play as the basis of therapeutic interaction. The primary role of the play therapist is to develop a positive, therapeutic relationship with the child and his or her family. The therapist structures play therapy so that it builds on a child's developmental communicative and learning processes (Carmichael, 2006; Landreth, 2002). Children become capable of imbuing symbolic meaning onto their play by the age of 2 to 3 years. During a play therapy session, a child may use a dinosaur to symbolize her aggressive father. She may add growls and emotional sounds and facial expressions as the dinosaur interacts with other play figures. The therapist understands that it might be frightening for the child to talk about her father's anger, so playing with the dinosaur gives her emotional distance from her father and her fears of revealing his anger to another person. Another child might draw a picture of her mother that is very large in relationship to other family members, suggesting the mother's dominance or oversize role in the family.

Therapists use play therapy to encourage children to express what is bothering them when they cannot do so with words. For example, abreaction, which is the reexperiencing of past life events, sometimes takes place during play therapy. During play, children play out negative life events by breaking them down into smaller slices of life. Therapists help children release those feelings that deal with each experience and assimilate each experience back into a perception that they hold of themselves (Homeyer & Morrison, 2008).

Families assume an important role in play therapy as well as in the healing processes for children. Play therapists communicate on a regular basis with children's caretakers. They discuss with parents the treatment plan for their child, and they work with parents to monitor a child's emotional progress. Play therapists may assist parents in modifying how they interact with the child at home. Play therapists determine the level of a parent's involvement. In some instances, the whole family may be involved in family play therapy (Guerney, 2001).

Although play therapy sessions vary in length, they typically last about 30 to 50 minutes on a weekly basis. Research suggests that it takes an average of 20 play therapy sessions to help children resolve the

problems that brought them to treatment. Whereas some children may improve much faster in their psychological and psychosocial functioning, those with more serious or ongoing problems may take longer to resolve (Carmichael, 2006; Landreth, 2002).

Play Therapy, Models of Psychotherapy: Methods and Techniques

The Association for Play Therapy states in its definition of play therapy that it is a type of therapy that operates from a given psychotherapeutic orientation. Within the field of play therapy, therapists use a variety of psychotherapeutic theoretical orientations. This section considers one major dimension on which play therapy theoretical approaches can be compared. Virginia Axline (1947), developer of child-centered play therapy, has asserted that approaches to play therapy may be placed on a nondirective to directive continuum. She has stated, "Play therapy may be directive in form—that is, the therapist may assume responsibility for guidance and interpretation, or it may be nondirective; the therapist may leave responsibility and direction to the child" (p. 9). Although play therapists may come from any of the forces of psychotherapy described in this text, many play therapists use (a) child-centered or (b) Adlerian play therapy.

Child-centered play therapy is at the extreme left of the nondirective play therapy continuum. This theoretical form of play therapy views children as the source of their own positive growth and therapeutic direction. The child-centered play therapist provides "the good growing ground" and the appropriate therapeutic climate for the child to experience his or her own potential for growth. The so-called good growing ground constitutes the basis for the therapist–child relationship and allows the child to feel safe

Inner Reflections

Could you see yourself becoming a play therapist?

If so, would your play therapy be with children or adults?

How would you propose to interact with parents of children with whom you might work?

Inner Reflection

Which model of psychotherapy would form the foundation for your approach to play therapy? Explain.

and secure. The child-centered therapeutic relationship is founded on Axline's (1947, pp. 66–67) eight basic principles. The therapist must do the following:

1. Develop a warm therapeutic relationship with the child

2. Accept each child as he or she is without attempting to change him or her in any way

3. Form an accepting therapeutic environment that allows the child to feel free to express all emotions

4. Acknowledge the child's feelings in such a way that the child acquires insight into his or her behavior

5. Communicate a deep respect for the child's ability to solve his or her own difficulties and permit the child to assume responsibility for choices and behavior change

6. Make no effort to direct the child's play or verbal expression

7. Follow the child's lead in the therapeutic process

8. Establish only those play therapy limits necessary to comply with safety, legal, and ethical standards

The child-centered therapist uses techniques that facilitate the child's "good growing ground" for therapy. Facilitative therapist techniques include reflection of the child's content and feeling and statements that indicate that the therapist is there for the child during the play therapy experience (Homeyer & DeFrance, 2005). The therapist keeps questions to a minimum such that they are used primarily to clarify the reality of the child's experiences. Another technique is that of structuring the therapy so that the child is provided with information about the logistics of therapy, including the length of the therapy sessions, where the sessions will take place, whether the parents will be involved in therapy, and how. If the child asks questions about specific activities, the child-centered therapist responds that "in here, you decide what toys you will play with." A third child-centered

technique involves the setting of limits so that the child has a stake in defining the areas in which he or she will function. Landreth (1991) has used the acronym *ACT* to conceptualize the process in limit setting:

A—Acknowledge the child's feelings, wishes, and behavior ("I see that you are angry and would like to hit me").

C—Communicate the limit broken by the behavior ("Although you are angry, I am not for hitting").

T—Target acceptable behavioral alternatives ("If you feel angry with me, you can hit the Bobo").

Adlerian Play Therapy. Adlerian play therapy is at the directive end of the nondirective/directive continuum—although it is not the most directive form of play therapy. Terry Kottman (1993) has articulated the following principles of Adlerian play therapy:

- Children are inherently social beings who have a strong need to belong, and each child uses his family as a way of deciding how he or she will fit in other settings.
- Children's behavior is purposeful and goal oriented, and counselors must understand the goal that a child's behavior is serving.
- Children are creative and are capable of making choices to achieve their goals.
- Children experience life from a subjective perspective, and it is the role of the therapist to understand their phenomenological world. (Please refer to Chapter 3 of this book.)

Kottman (1995) has also outlined some goals for Adlerian play therapy, which include the following:

- Understand the child's lifestyle based on his or her experiences within the family of origin
- Help the child change faulty, self-defeating perceptions of self, others, and the world and move from these faulty convictions (private logic) to common sense
- Work on positive goals of behavior
- Increase the child's social interest and sense of belonging

- Help the child learn new ways of dealing with life's disappointments instead of becoming discouraged
- Optimize the child's creativity

There are four nonlinear overlapping phases of Adlerian play therapy. The first phase focuses on building an egalitarian, caring relationship between the child and the therapist. Adlerian play therapy includes parents and teachers when appropriate in the therapy session. The primary goal during the first phase is to listen to the child and the parents and to encourage any positive aspect of their functioning.

During the second phase of Adlerian play therapy, the therapist engages in assessment and gathers information about the child's lifestyle from a variety of sources, including information from the child's parents and teachers, observations of the child's interactions with family members, and a number of assessment activities within the play sessions, including having the child complete the Kinetic Family Drawing, make a body outline, and using a dollhouse to get the child's sense of family members. In addition, the therapist evaluates the impact of the parents' priorities (their own personal issues and goals) on their ability to apply parenting skills. Therapists may engage in teaching positive-parenting skills. The experiential components of this session will involve the child drawing his or her family. The child will be asked to use the dollhouse and dolls to illustrate a typical night at home for him or her. If time permits, the child will also be asked to draw a picture of an early recollection. "Draw me a picture of something that happened when you were little."

The third phase of Adlerian play therapy involves helping the child and the parents gain insight into the child's lifestyle. The therapist shares his insights about the goals of the child's behavior, the child's faulty convictions, and he gains a sense of significance at home and at school. During Session 3, the therapist gathers information about the child's behavior in class and his or her interactions with classmates and teachers. The therapist may ask the child to draw a school picture that includes himself, his teacher, and a friend or two. The Adlerian play therapist makes extensive use of expressive arts material that will help children gain insight into their lifestyle, determine whether or not their goals are being met, and decide if their behaviors need to be changed. The therapist works to help children make connections between what happens in the playroom and in the outside world at home and at school. He or she may observe the child at school.

The fourth phase of Adlerian play therapy is called reorientation/reeducation, and this phase is geared to help children practice new behaviors. Adlerian therapists focus on the following skills with children: problem solving, learning socially appropriate behaviors, and developing positive alternative behaviors. They use role play with puppets, dollhouse figures, and psychodrama to reorient children to the outside world.

Materials Used in Play Therapy

The therapist chooses toys that allow for children's creative and emotional expression, children's testing of limits, and children's replay of their reality. Play therapists must have a sound theoretical rational for placing toys and materials in a play therapy playroom (Kottman, 1995; Landreth, 2002). Some types of play therapy toys include dolls and dollhouses, building blocks, farm and wild animals, toy knives and swords, musical instruments, puppets, dress-up costumes, and art supplies. The play room should have a large supply of expressive arts materials. The toys and expressive arts materials should be displayed in the playroom for the children to see and play with, and they should be consistently available so that the child returns each time to the same environment (Homeyer & DeFrance, 2005).

Therapists may also use games to promote children's social skills development. A play therapist's theoretical orientation will determine if a child's play with toys and games is child directed or therapist directed (Landreth, 2002). For older children, game play is a more developmentally appropriate form of play that requires them to focus and sustain their attention. Game play is quite useful for easily distractible youth. During the process of game play, young people learn how to play by the rules, take turns, and be a gracious winner or loser.

Evidence-Based Research on Play Therapy

Research studies have provided evidence of the effectiveness of play therapy with children experiencing a wide variety of social, emotional, behavioral, and learning problems, including children whose problems are related to life stressors, such as divorce, death, relocation, chronic illness, assimilate stressful experiences, physical and sexual abuse, domestic violence, and natural disasters (Reddy et al., 2005).

Leblanc and Ritchie (2001) and Bratton et al. (2005) conducted meta-analytic reviews of more than 100 play therapy outcome studies and found that the overall treatment effect of play therapy ranges from moderate to high positive effects. Play therapy has been proved equally effective across age, gender, and presenting problem. Researchers found that positive treatment effects were greatest when there was a parent actively involved in the child's treatment.

Current Developments in Play Therapy: Neuroscience

Play Therapy and Neuroscience: Trauma-Informed Play Therapy. One recent development in play therapy and in the other forms of expressive arts has a distinct neuroscience influence. Trauma-informed expressive arts integrate neuroscience, neurodevelopment, somatic approaches, mindfulness practices, and resilience enhancement, using art making as the fulcrum around which treatment is based. Trauma-informed expressive arts therapy is founded on the premise that a person's art expression can be used to reconnect implicit (sensory) and explicit (declarative) memories of trauma and in the treatment of post-traumatic stress disorder (Malchiodi, 2003, 2008, 2012). This new treatment approach improves the person's capacity to self-regulate affect and moderate the body's reactions to traumatic experiences for the purpose of eventual trauma integration and recovery.

RESEARCH AND EVALUATION
Multicultural Issues and Expressive Arts Therapy

Culture pervades the expressive arts. To become a multicultural competent expressive arts therapist, one has to understand the role and tools of creativity in the client's culture as well as in the culture created between the client and the therapist during therapy. One must view cultural issues from several different perspectives: (a) mental health counseling, (b) expressive arts, and (c) the culture of both the therapist and client. Culture defines what is and what is not appropriate in the creative arts; it both supports and constrains one's art expressions. Highlighting the difference between the connection between mental health counseling and the work of the expressive art therapist, David Johnson (1999) has stated,

> The creative moment begins with the representation of the void: the empty stage, the blank page, and the moment of silence. The artist pauses before creating the world again. And in creating the world, the self is again recast. For what fills the stage or page or silence is not a design, or prearranged model, it is the spontaneous expression of one's inner spirit. As the inner spirit emerges it is altered, and then, as it is understood and taken in, one's internal world is changed. . . . A successful artwork is so powerful

because it reassures us that significance and meaning can emerge from nothing. (p. 26)

Acton (2001) has commented on multicultural counseling competencies within the field of art therapy. The art therapist is aware of her or his "own culturally biased assumptions when viewing color, symbol, line, and shape" (p. 111). According to Acton, the art therapist expands his or her skills "by examining how art has been utilized within diverse cultures to promote psychological healing" (p. 111).

In a recent doctoral dissertation study, Donna Owens (2012) investigated the issue of multicultural counseling competency training in the creative arts therapies from three perspectives: (1) the governing association, (2) the training institution, and (3) the student/trainee. Owens used an online survey that included demographic questions, questions about multicultural coursework and internship experiences of current students, and the Multicultural Awareness, Knowledge, and Skills Survey Revised, which assesses three domains of multicultural counseling competency: awareness, knowledge, and skills.

The results showed that 43% of expressive arts therapies associations did not have specific requirements related to multicultural competencies, and that 6% of states did not require licensure applicants to meet a multicultural competency standard. Overall practitioners scored lower than did students on the individual subscales of the Multicultural Awareness, Knowledge, and Skills Survey Revised. Owens concluded that there is a need for the incorporation of the multicultural counseling competencies across the expressive arts curriculum and within faculty supervision.

Clearly, there is a need for the expressive arts to take into consideration the culture of the client and therapist when conducting expressive arts therapy. Paolo Knill (2005) has proposed that to motivate a client to engage in a meaningful art process, the expressive arts therapist must consider "the skill level of the client and find the culturally relevant manifestations of art which are best suited to the client and to the facilitator in terms of the situation at hand" (p. 97).

School Counseling and the Expressive Arts

In a recent article in *Counseling Today*, a publication of the American Counseling Association, Patricia Van Velsor (2013) called for the increased use of the expressive arts in schools. She proposed that "[t]he expressive arts—visual arts, movement, drama, music and writing—offer countless ways to promote the academic, career and personal/social development of students, which are goals of a comprehensive school counseling program" (http://ct.counseling.org/2013/02/thinking-creatively-expressive-arts-for-counseling-youth-in-the-schools/). Some of the suggestions made were to provide an underachieving student with old magazines to make a collage of things he or she does well and to have small groups of students create a rap song using information they have learned from class.

The results of two studies appear to support Van Velsor's call. Mason and Chuang (2001) found that students participating in an after-school arts program evidenced increases in self-esteem, social skills, and leadership. In Canada, Smithrim and Upitis (2005) used a sample of more than 6,000 Canadian students to investigate the 3-year effects of a Canadian schoolwide arts education program (Learning Through the Arts, LTTA) on student achievement and attitudes. At the conclusion of 3 years of LTTA, the Grade 6 LTTA students scored significantly higher on tests of computation than students in control schools.

Based on the preceding studies, it appears that the expressive arts do have a role in most

Inner Reflections

What are some multicultural challenges an expressive arts therapist might encounter?

Does any one of the art forms, music, art, or play present challenges for you in the multicultural realm?

schools. In many American schools, however, the expressive arts are the first programs to be cut in a budget crisis. Moreover, most public schools do not have programs that are linked to students' overall achievement in schools. Not every school counselor should think of himself or herself as an art therapist, a music therapist, or a play therapist. There are important training requirements for these specialties, which leads us to the limitations of expressive arts therapy.

Limitations of Expressive Arts Therapy

Not everyone can become an expressive arts therapist, and not every counselor or therapist should attempt to use some form of the expressive arts in mental health counseling. There are stringent educational and training guidelines for each of the different forms of the expressive arts. Therefore, a therapist must first be trained or receive some education in the specific creative art form chosen.

An activity is only one aspect of expressive arts therapy. When the expressive arts are oversimplified to a drawing or a collage and then offered as a quick solution, it's power to help clients is greatly reduced. A therapist can use the arts, but this doesn't necessarily mean that he or she is doing art therapy or music therapy. A therapist must have the training to facilitate the processes involved in professional art, music therapy, or play therapy. One should not just assume that one can ask a client to draw a picture, listen to music, and incorporate the results into effective mental health counseling. The expressive arts are more than just a set of techniques. All of the expressive arts therapies discussed within this chapter have developed within the context of theoretical constructs and also have credential and certification procedures. Most creative art forms have maintained that therapists be thoroughly grounded in one of the existing theoretical approaches to psychotherapy. Therapists must distinguish between using an art form to facilitate therapy and stepping outside their area of expertise.

CASE ANALYSIS

Justin Working With an Expressive Arts Therapist

Justin had been looking forward to this counseling session because the counselor had indicated that he was going to use the arts as part of their session. His counselor had also told him to bring a couple of his favorite music CDs, because if they had time, they would be listening to his music. Justin slipped into the chair eager to show the counselor his talent in art. At least once he would be able to show the counselor what he could actually do. "Hey, Doc, you want to see me draw today? I'm pretty good. Even my art teacher says so. I can draw you."

"I heard that you were quite good in both drawing and painting, Justin. Tell me how you got involved in art" the counselor responded in a very positive mood.

"I can't even remember, it's been so long ago. Ever since I was able to pick up a crayon or a pencil, I've been drawing or painting," Justin replied. "It's like my favorite thing to do, outside of listening to my music, and maybe smoking a little . . . well I won't go into that because you know . . . laughs—doing that got me in the trouble I'm in."

The counselor reflected Justin's feelings, "Art's a part of you. It is your way of communicating with the world. You can lose yourself drawing and painting . . . art represents the deepest part of you . . . "

Justin moved uncomfortably in his chair, wondering how the counselor knew how he felt about his artwork without his ever telling him so. There was a part of him that felt that the counselor was messing with his head and yet, another part that said, "Hey, I just might be able to talk with you about something that means a great deal to me."

Instead of saying what he was actually thinking, Justin asked, "Well, what are we going to do today? Do you want to see me draw?"

"Yeah, I do want you to show me what you got, Justin," the counselor said. "I've been looking forward to your coming today and showing me what you can do in artwork. I also want to use your artwork to explore some of the things we've been talking about during the last few sessions. If it's all right with you, I'd like for you to participate in a couple of art exercises that might help us get a better understanding about how you feel about certain things."

"Cool, I'm game," Justin responded.

"OK", the counselor said, agreeing. "I want you to participate in an exercise called '*Missing Pieces*.' I want you to think of a bad experience from your life that still affects you now. It can be the situation that you're facing now with the threat of being placed in the residential center or something else. Imagine that some part of you ran away because of the pain you experienced. I want you to draw what part of you that ran away and what feeling caused you to run away. After drawing that part of you that ran away, I want you to color it with the crayons or chalk or any of the other material you see on the table next to you. Now using a different sheet of paper, I also want you to draw that part of you that would like to stand up to the part of you that ran away. Color that part also with the colors of your choosing."

After you have drawn that part of you that ran away on one sheet of paper and that part of you that wants to stand up to the part that ran away, write a letter asking the ran away part to return. You can make up your own letter or use the one that I have just given you that states,

"Dear _____, I know you left because of _____. It is now safe for you to return because _____. I miss you and need you in my life because _____. Please return so that I can be whole again. Love, _____."

Justin spent about 20 minutes drawing and coloring the two parts of him, the part that ran away and the part that wanted him not to run from his issues. Watching the different expressions on his face while he was drawing and coloring was revealing. At one point, his eyes filled with tears, and at a later part, he smiled. Finally, he completed the letter using the form that the counselor had given him.

"Hey, what you asked me to do was no joke. So many things . . . so many different things I remembered that I thought I had forgotten. It seems like I'm always battling two parts of Justin—the part that wants to do right and the other part that wants to do . . . whatever . . . you know . . . take the easy way out . . . have fun . . . whatever. I guess you can say that I am running away from what happened at the mall—my arrest, the charge of stealing on my record. . . . I just want it all to be over. Forgotten. But nobody wants to forget. The only time that I can forget is when I am lighting up or playing my music, or watching TV with my mom."

"It's difficult dealing with all the pressures of not knowing what is going to happen to you, and it's frightening for you to think about leaving your home, your mother, and your friends for life in a residential center with other boys having problems," the counselor responded.

"Yeah," Justin said. "Sometimes I just can't handle it all. It's all too overwhelming. I feel I can't cope, and I become angry and get into trouble."

Justin and the counselor talked for a few minutes about what it felt like being overwhelmed, and then the counselor said, "It seems like we're back to our 'missing-pieces' exercise. Let's look at what you have drawn. Your art teacher is right. You are quite an artist. You have a talent, Justin, in art, and I want to encourage you to pursue that talent. Art seems to speak to that quieter, more reflective side of you. It's as if you are not only observing the world but you are also observing yourself as a participant in the world."

"You're right," Justin said. "You're exactly right. I drew my forehead as the part that ran away. My head tells me to run, lie; do whatever I've got to do, but get out of the situation I'm in."

The counselor asked, "So for you, fear is in your head, and that's why you drew a picture of your forehead"?

(Continued)

(Continued)

"Yes," Justin answered. "The fear keeps swirling around in my head and in my mind until I can't take it any longer, so I run away."

"It's interesting that you colored your forehead red, Justin, because the color red has been shown to increase blood pressure and stimulate the adrenal glands. Red is also a color that is associated with anger, and that can make a person irritable. You've seen on television how a red cape is put in front of a bull to make him angry. Red is also sometimes associated with sexuality. How does what I said relate to what you drew and colored in the part of you that ran away from a problem?"

"It's right on target," Justin interjected. "I'm scared, but I am also angry—angry with the situation, angry with myself, angry with the boys I went to the mall with, and angry with my mom and my dad. Just angry about a whole lot of stuff. So my head says run, Justin, run Justin, run. Maybe you can outrun your problems."

"But there is a missing part of you that does not want to run, that wants to stand up and face your situation the best way that you can."

"Yup, that's why I am coming here to you. I'm trying to make things right, to show that I do care and that I can become responsible, that I am not all bad."

"I agree with your assessment, Justin," the counselor said. "There is so much good in you—so much that is positive, so much that is talented. I would hate for you to throw it all away by running away. Tell me about the missing part of you that wants the runaway to return to you."

"The second picture is my heart. My heart wants me to stop being a problem, to take responsibility for me. It's telling the angry part that I don't have to run away or get into any more trouble. I painted my heart purple to sort of symbolize the royalty in me. I'm not just a piece of garbage from the hood. I'm not a throwaway kid. I'm worth something."

"You're worth a great deal, Justin, and I agree you're not a throwaway kid. Regardless of how the residential center situation turns out, I believe that you have the ability to turn it all around to your favor—that you will work your problems so that they become lemonade, so to speak. It's interesting that you chose the color purple to color in your heart in your drawing. The color purple is often associated with not only royalty but also with balancing the body. Purples have been used in caring for some mental disorders because they have been shown to help balance the mind and transform obsessions and fears. Purple is related to sensitivity to beauty, high ideals, creativity, and compassion. So, you see, Justin, your choice of colors says a great deal about what you are feeling."

The therapist asked Justin to put one of the songs he had brought with him in the CD player. At first Justin had the music turned up real loud, but then without anyone saying anything, he got up and turned the rap song down. "My music speaks to me," Justin said after a few moments of silent listening to the music. "It makes me feel mellow." The counselor smiled and nodded his head in agreement. The picture of the two of them listening to rap music seemed a bit incongruous—a middle-aged White male counselor and an African American boy from the inner city. Yet there they were listening and appreciating Justin's music—sharing each other's culture, reaching out across the ocean that divides ethnic, age, cultural, and socioeconomic groups.

"Now, what about your letter. Can you summarize what you said in your letter to the part of you that was running away?"

"Yeah," Justin answered. "My letter said that I am tired of running. I left because I was afraid. It is now safe for my head to return because for the first time I am getting help from you in dealing with my issues. When things go all crazy in my head, I can talk with you. I said in the letter that I missed my head because I needed it to do all sorts of things—like school."

"Hold onto that thought, Justin, for next time. We will work on setting up ways that we can talk and work things out when all else seem to be going haywire. See you next time," said the counselor.

SUMMARY

This chapter has examined expressive arts therapy. A brief history of the expressive arts was presented with an emphasis on the art forms of art, music, and play therapy. Clearly, many other art forms could have been included, such as dance movement, psychodrama, poetry or writing, and so forth. Key concepts in the expressive arts, such as self-expression, action or active participation of clients, imagination, and mind–body connection, were discussed. The expressive arts and general treatment procedures were examined. Each section on art, music, and play therapy contained a definition of the art form, the role of the expressive therapist, models of psychotherapy used in conjunction with, materials used, and methods and techniques, empirical research, and current developments in the field. The role of neuroscience was considered in the expressive arts. A brief section on the schools and the expressive arts looked at research using an after-school program and a national Canadian expressive arts program for 6,000 youth that resulted in the computational scores of children increasing significantly over a control group.

It was concluded that expressive arts activities alone are insufficient to make an expressive art therapist. Specific training and credentials are needed for one to call oneself an art therapist, music therapist, or play therapist. Expressive arts therapy involves more than the use of a series of activities. Expressive art therapy is usually done from one or more of the major theoretical perspectives. The expressive arts are multicultural in orientation in that all cultures use some form of the expressive arts. This profession is gradually moving toward having a neuroscience foundation, which may produce more empirical studies on the effectiveness of the various art forms and their psychotherapeutic treatment modalities.

SUPPLEMENTAL AIDS

Discussion Questions

1. *Using the expressive arts to strengthen a client's resilience:* Discuss in a circle with four to five classmates the topic of resilience and how therapy is designed to increase or strengthen a person's resilience. After a 10-minute discussion, have each group member draw a picture of an image in nature that has survived a harsh environment. It could be a flower in the crack of a sidewalk, a rose thriving among weeds. Now have each person draw a picture of his or her own resilience. How have you survived a tough environment? Have a client you are working with either draw or cut out pictures from a magazine that represent his or her resilience. Using the go-around technique, have each group member discuss one or two songs that he or she believes fortifies his or her resilience.

2. *Your inner child:* Therapy so often deals with the inner child within all of us—the child we try to hide from others—the hurt child, the hopeful child, and so on. In small groups of four to five class members, form a small circle and discuss one aspect of the inner child that lives within each person. Then hand each person a blank sheet of paper and ask the person to draw himself or herself as a child on the paper. Group participants are told to add images and words to give this child everything that it needs, including a supportive nurturing parent. Now think of a song that deals with the inner child within you. Each person in the group identifies and discusses how one song deals with some aspect of the child within him or her.

3. *Relationship needs, music and art:* In a small group, ask each group member to identify the three most important people in their lives. Next each person identifies a song that seems to epitomize one's relationship with that person. For instance, the song "Loving You Is a Battle" could be used to describe one relationship. Draw a line connecting each of the people to the picture of you in the center of a page. On the top of each line, write a word or phrase about what you need from that person and what you think that person needs from you.

4. *Your therapist compatibility quotient and the expressive arts:* In small groups of four or five members, discuss how comfortable you would feel in using the expressive art therapies to work

with clients. What expressive therapy art form would you be most comfortable using with clients?

5. *Training in the expressive arts therapies:* Discuss the kind of training you believe you need for using the expressive arts therapies for working with clients.

Glossary of Key Terms

art therapy   A method of psychological treatment that is based on using art as a form of communication and self-expression or as a form of visual language through which people express their thoughts and feelings.

expressive arts therapy   The use of art, music, dance/movement, drama, poetry/writing, and sandtray within the framework of psychotherapy, counseling, or health care.

imagination   The central concept that informs the understanding of the use of arts and play in therapy—the healing agent to all forms of self-expression.

mind–body connection   Those connections that are designed to promote the mind's capacity to influence bodily connections. Most of the expressive therapies are geared to make mind–body connections through the use of an art form.

music therapy   Music Therapy is an established form of treatment in which music is used within a therapeutic relationship to address physical, emotional, cognitive, and social needs of individuals. After assessing the strengths and needs of each client, a qualified music therapist provides treatment that might involve creating, singing, moving to, and/or listening to music. Through musical involvement in the therapeutic context, clients' abilities are strengthened and transferred to other areas of their lives.

play therapy   The Association for Play Therapy (2012) defines play therapy as "the systematic use of a theoretical model to establish an interpersonal process wherein trained play therapists use the therapeutic powers of play to help clients prevent or resolve psychosocial difficulties and achieve optimal growth and development." (www.a4pt.org)

sandplay therapy   Dora Kalff, a Jungian therapist, developed sandplay therapy in Switzerland in the 1950s and 1960s based on her studies at the C. G. Jung Institute, Zurich, in Tibetan Buddhism, and with Margaret Lowenfeld, in England. Sandplay therapy has been defined as a psychotherapeutic technique that helps clients arrange miniature figures in a sandbox or a sandtray to create a "sandworld" corresponding to various dimensions of his or her social reality.

Website Materials

Additional exercises, journals, annotated bibliography, and more are available on the open-access website at https://study.sagepub.com/jonessmith2e.

PART IV

The Fourth Force in Psychotherapy
Social Constructivism and Postmodernism

Theories of counseling and psychotherapy can be examined according to the dominant periods in human history. Sexton (1997) has divided human history into three eras: premodern, modern, and postmodern (also called "contructivist"). Each of these eras emphasizes a perspective that influenced how people dealt with events and problems and how they conceptualized solutions to problems. For instance, the premodern era, which was roughly from the 6th century BCE through the Middle Ages, focused on dualism, idealism, and rationalism. During this period, faith and religion assumed center stage roles, and "effective change efforts were prayer, faith, thinking, and/or reasoning" (p. 5). The modern era took place approximately from the Renaissance through the 1950s and 1960s. This time period emphasized empiricism, logical positivism, scientific methodology, the identification of objective truths, and validity (Raskin, 2002). According to Sexton (1997), the modern era solidified scientific and professional knowledge as "the legitimate source of understanding the world. Through the logical process of science we could discover that which was true. . . . Scientific knowledge was assumed to be a mirror image of objective reality" (p. 7).

Sexton (1997) has labeled the present time as the "third era" and has designated it as the postmodern/constructivist era (the fourth force in counseling theory). *Postmodern* means literally "after the modern." There are important distinctions between the dominant patterns of modern and postmodern thinking. Modernists subscribe to objective reality that can be observed and systematically investigated. They maintain that reality exists objectively or independently of any one person's observation of it. In the postmodern world, truth and reality are often presented as points of view influenced by history and context.

Postmodernism focuses on human participation in the construction of knowledge. Therefore, people who hold a postmodern view are often described as *constructivists*, and more specifically as *social constructivists*. Constructivists believe in subjective rather than objective realities. They maintain that reality does not exist independently of someone's observational processes. Constructivists assert that none of the ways of understanding that people have developed provide a purely objective view of the world. Instead, all theorists, psychotherapists, and people in general have constructed meanings that reflect a particular point of view.

POSTMODERNISM AND THE ROAD TO SOCIAL CONSTRUCTIVISM ____

George Kelly and Personal Construct Psychology

Historically speaking, George Kelly's (1955) personal construct psychology represents the first systematic use of constructivism within clinical psychology. Although an in depth description of Kelly's personal construct psychology has not been presented in this book, it is important to understand how Kelly's personal construct theory helped pave the way for social constructionism and for the development of an integrative psychotherapy approach.

Three terms have been associated with George Kelly: (1) personal constructivism, (2) personal construct psychology, and (3) personal construct theory. (*Personal construct theory* is the most frequently used term; however, the other two are contained in the literature.) Kelly theorized that people organize their experiences by developing bipolar dimensions of meaning or personal constructs. Individuals use the constructs they create about life to anticipate and to predict how the world and its inhabitants behave. Moreover, people continually test the robustness of their personal constructs by tracking how well they predict life events and by revising them when they lose their capability to explain or predict life events. Personal construct psychology uses the metaphor of the knowing individual as a personal scientist who repeatedly puts his or her constructions to the test (Raskin, 2002). At the heart of Kelly's theory is the view of *the person-as-scientist*, a perspective that stresses our human capacity for making meaning out of life and out of what happens to us. Life is conceptualized as an ongoing revision of personal systems of knowing. Like scientists, people formulate constructs or hypotheses about the apparent regularities of their lives in an attempt to make their lives more understandable and predictable. People are continually engaged in meaning making and in formulating constructs that will help them understand their lives.

Another important contribution of Kelly's personal construct theory is his idea of *constructive alternativism*, which postulates that there are infinite possibilities for conceptualizing life events (Kelly, 1955). When people discover that their prior sets of constructions prove to be unsatisfying, they may develop entirely new dimensions of meaning. From Kelly's perspective, the self is viewed as constructed, not discovered. It is influenced by the way a person successively construes himself or herself. Sometimes deeply embedded constructions of the self that were formed early in one's life become impermeable to self-reflection and alteration. Such self-constructs become what Kelly labeled *core constructs*. In the social constructivist paradigm, there is no such thing as a human personality. According to Burr (1995), "In order to account for the things you find yourself and other people doing . . . you have to come up with the idea that people have a thing called a personality that is responsible for this behavior" (p. 21).

Kelly's (1955) theory was eclectic, and he encouraged therapists to use a variety of clinical interventions. He used the technique of *fixed role therapy* to get the client to experiment and to act out in everyday life the role of someone psychologically different from himself or herself. As clients experiment with new ways of being in the world, they can then develop new constructs of themselves.

Some of Kelly's (1955) central theses have been incorporated into cognitive-behavioral therapy. For instance, a central task of the cognitive-behavioral therapist is to help clients understand how they construct and construe reality. Beck's (2005) theory of cognitive therapy assumes, as did Kelly's personal construct theory, that clients can examine themselves. Beck (1991) maintained that depressed clients were embedded in their own negative construction of the world and that they needed to be taught how to think about alternatives. The therapist's task is to help the client change his or her constructs of the world, with the hope that if one changes the way that one views the world, the way one acts in the world will also change.

Relativism

Social constructionism is *relativistic* because it stresses how *contextual*, *linguistic*, and *relational* factors combine to determine the kinds of people each of us will become and how our individual views of the world will develop. In the social constructionist paradigm, each of us has multiple, "multiphrenic" selves that are forged from the different messages we hear in our environment and that are socially constructed within the boundaries of culture, context, and language (Gergen, 1991). Social constructionist theorists downplay the notion of personality, which in many theories is presented as a static structure of the self. Instead, they point out that people construct various identities for themselves that are negotiated and defined within specific interpersonal relationships and cultural contexts (Gergen, 1994).

Psychology has given a lukewarm reception to social constructionism, partly because this perspective challenges some of the discipline's most cherished assumptions about the self and the importance of the intrapsychic. Historically, psychology and psychotherapists, in particular, have focused on the individual, often times ignoring or minimizing significant contextual and cultural factors. Some of psychology's studies have been designed to "control for" and to eliminate "extraneous variables"—the very contextual variables that intrigued social constructionists (D'Andrea, 2000).

Social constructionism is about relationships between people and between groups of people. It emphasizes what Shotter (1993) once termed *joint action*—meaning the cooperative development and implementation of shared functional meanings that take place when two or more people interact. From a postmodern perspective, counseling and psychotherapy are considered socially constructed practices. Sigmund Freud, Alfred Adler, and others did not discover ultimate realities. People like you and me have created each of the theories presented in this text; yet the counseling and psychotherapy profession has often treated these theories with such reverence that it would be easy to believe that there is some ultimate form of psychotherapy (Hoffman, 2005). There is not. Theories of psychotherapy are all socially constructed versions of reality.

Modern-day constructivism focuses on an individual's collaborative coconstruction of new meaning out of his or her experiences. Constructivists maintain that people create and construct their own realities and that they process new information for the purpose of adapting to environmental demand. A person's primary goal is to construct meaning and purpose from life.

Social constructionism emphasizes the client's reality without debating whether or not it is rational or accurate (Gergen, 1999). Using a social constructionist framework, the therapist disavows the role of an expert and substitutes a more collaborative or consultative position. Clients rather than therapists are viewed as the experts on their lives. Social constructivists maintain that language and the concepts we use to understand the world are culture bound.

Multiculturalism in Psychology

The *multicultural paradigm* in psychology is based on a concept of postmodern social constructionism. The multiculturalism school proposes a certain degree of relativity in viewing people and their life circumstances. Researchers from this school have emphasized the importance of understanding the worldviews of people from different cultures and the impact that culture has on our construal of reality (Ivey, D'Andrea, Ivey, & Simek-Morgan, 2007).

I take a different approach from some researchers who label multiculturalism as the fourth force in counseling (Pedersen, 1991). I view postmodern/social constructivism as the fourth force, with multiculturalism being a part of this school. By taking this approach, I acknowledge the tremendous impact that multiculturalism has had on the field without overstating its theoretical contributions.

American and Western approaches to multicultural therapy are still in their beginning stages. Such theoretical models have tended to emphasize therapist attitude states rather than specific counseling techniques that can be used with a broad spectrum of people. Almost none of the Western multicultural approaches have developed a theory of personality development or a theory of how ethnic identity develops from childhood throughout adulthood. I make this comment without trying to be unkind to any of the multicultural theories. For some time, I have worked on a theory of ethnic identity that cuts across ethnic/cultural/racial lines. My approach has been to present ethnic identity development as a group identity that is modified by our enculturation and other experiences.

DIFFERENCES BETWEEN MODERN AND POSTMODERN/CONSTRUCTIVIST PSYCHOTHERAPIES

A theory is a way of examining reality; it does not necessarily constitute reality itself. The theories in this book are different individuals' constructions of reality, their perspectives on how the world works, and their constructions of how people develop problems, resolve them, and so on. For the past 100 years, three traditional theoretical forces have dominated the human service, counseling, and psychology professions:

(1) the psychodynamic force (first force), (2) the cognitive-behavioral force (second force), and (3) the existential-humanistic force (third force). These therapy models focus on the internal frame of individuals rather than on their total existence within a society, locating the problem within the client rather than within the social or the political system. For instance, psychoanalytic theory describes the individual in terms of innate drives and defense mechanisms associated with anxiety. Humanistic theory is founded on an individual's striving to meet inner needs and to accomplish self-actualization. Cognitive-behavioral and rational-emotive therapists seek to correct irrational thinking and to change individuals' behavior by changing their thoughts. For each of these three major forces in psychotherapy, little attention is focused on environmental or societal factors.

A Strengths-Based Approach

The postmodern/constructivist period represents a paradigm shift—a change from a problem-focused therapy to a strengths-based approach. The strengths-based approach has grown tremendously across numerous fields, including psychology, social work, and psychiatry (Smith, 2006a). In the modern historical framework, therapists searched for diagnosable mental problems within clients. In contrast, using a postmodern perspective, therapists not only search for a client's strengths but also recognize the use of such strengths as a general intervention.

Recognizing a client's strengths early in the therapy relationship is especially important in cross-cultural relationships because it builds therapeutic rapport and solidifies the therapeutic alliance. Moreover, when therapists focus on clients' strengths, clients are inclined to reveal more about themselves, especially those areas of their functioning about which they feel good. Clients get better because therapists learn how to marshal clients' strengths to address their problems. In the modernistic framework, clients' perceptions of counseling led them to tell counselors what they believed counselors were interested in hearing: their problems. There was something of the implicit message: "I've come to counseling for you to tell me what's wrong with me." Yet people are motivated to change when they believe that they have the capacities and the resources to change. A strengths-based approach to counseling increases a client's sense of competence, power, and hope for the future (Saleebey, 2001; Smith, 2006a).

> **Inner Reflection**
>
> *Pathology or Strength Orientation of Traditional Counseling Theories*
>
> Where do you stand on the argument that traditional theories of psychotherapy are pathology oriented rather than strength oriented?

Therapists find clients' strengths when they are prepared to look for them. Yet most therapists and counselors have been trained in the medical model, which focuses on pathology and what's wrong rather than on what is right about clients (Smith, 2006a). New training models have to be developed that help therapists identify clients' strengths. Therapists in the postmodern age need training in human resiliency models, and they require knowledge about the strengths of cultural groups with which they work.

Challenge to Empiricism

There are other important distinctions between the modernist and the postmodern/constructivist perspectives in theories of psychotherapy. Critical issues revolve around the clinician's so-called objective and real assessment of clients' problems. Are the mental disorder categories that psychologists and psychiatrists have constructed for people really based on objective factors, or are these categories highly subjective and culturally based? Can researchers determine which therapy treatment is more effective?

Psychotherapy theories that take a modernistic perspective contend that therapy can be evaluated using objective scientific methods. From their perspectives, research can definitively determine how effective a particular therapy is for clients. Moreover, counseling theories that endorse modernism take the position that therapy treatment modalities that have empirical support are superior to those that lack such empirical support.

The postmodern perspective challenges the premise that says therapies that offer empirical support are better than those that lack such empirical documentation. This perspective takes exception to the capacity of empirical research to be truly objective. It raises the questions, "Objective from whose perspective?" "Were the research methods truly objective?" Hoffman (2005) maintains, for example, that different types of research are more appropriate for evaluating various theoretical approaches to therapy. Whatever measurement a researcher uses must be consistent with the theory; otherwise, epistemological problems threaten the very validity of the research.

Moreover, postmoderns/constructivists argue that another factor that delimits the appropriateness of modernism's emphasis on empirical studies is the fact that not all psychotherapies seek the same end. Although most psychotherapies share the goal to decrease clients' symptoms, they disagree on what this looks like (Hoffman, 2005). Differences in the end goals of the various therapeutic schools make it difficult to compare their comparative efficacy in empirical studies (Hoffman, 2005).

Postmodernism contends that it is unwise to engage in debates over which therapeutic approach is best because such a determination depends on too many client and therapist factors. One therapeutic approach may be appropriate for clients who have one value or cultural system and not another. Both client values and effectiveness need to be taken into account when making decisions about which psychotherapy is best.

Principles of Traditional Theories of Psychotherapy

- Dichotomize a person's psychological life into discrete parts (e.g., id, ego, and superego) from a psychodynamic perspective, irrational thoughts that sustain ineffective behaviors from a cognitive-behavioral perspective, and a hierarchy of needs from an existential-humanistic perspective (Pedersen, Draguns, Lonner, & Trimble, 2002).
- Emanate from culturally and gender-biased perceptions of psychological development that value the importance of individual autonomy and independence over interdependence and collectivity (Ivey et al., 2007; Pedersen et al., 2002).
- Either consider it inappropriate to intervene or undervalue interviewing in social forces that delimit the mental health and well-being of clients from diverse ethnic groups and backgrounds (Ivey et al., 2007).

Principles of Postmodern Therapy

- The client is the expert; the therapist assists in empowering the client.
- Client change involves considering choices and alternatives and accepting responsibility for one's actions.
- The therapist and client work collaboratively to deconstruct defeating core assumptions that block change.
- The client's strengths provide the basis for constructive change. The therapist's focus is on helping clients marshal their strengths to deal with issues. Therapy becomes strengths based rather than deficit based.

Criticisms of Postmodernism in Psychotherapy

Postmodernism in psychotherapy is not without its critics. A frequent criticism of postmodernism is that it promotes relativism. Those who hold this criticism maintain that there is no way to say that anything is wrong or immoral. Postmodern advocates maintain that some ultimate truths may exist; however, it is difficult to know these truths (Hoffman, 2005).

THE POSTMODERN PSYCHOTHERAPIES

A number of therapies can be placed into the postmodern category, including multicultural and feminist approaches to psychotherapy, solution-focused therapy, narrative therapy, motivational interviewing, strengths-based counseling, and mindfulness approaches (Wampold, 2001). Relational analysis, control theory, dialectical behavior therapy, and schema therapy are additional postmodern approaches.

In postmodern/constructivist versions of psychotherapy, therapists view people's lives as "stories" in the sense that they are narratives about their lives. They contend that it is arrogant to assume that the therapist's construction of reality (the therapist's narrative) is superior to or truer than the client's narrative. Therapists who hold a postmodern/constructivist perspective maintain that the therapist's views are just as culture bound as the client's; therefore, their conceptualization and interpretation of client behavior may be biased and dead wrong. Postmodern/constructivist therapists do not try to correct the client's narrative by comparing it with any standard of psychotherapeutic truth. Instead, the postmodern mindset argues for the acceptance of multiple culturally determined realities, all of equal validity. Postmodern/constructivist therapists endeavor to help clients rewrite their personal narratives and reframe their lives.

OUTLINE OF CHAPTERS IN PART IV

Part IV of this book, on postmodern counseling theories, is longer than the other parts because it represents the future. I remember teaching a course on counseling theory and the comments of one graduate student. Essentially, she stated that after reviewing the 10 major theories of psychotherapy, she felt that she was reviewing *what was* rather than *what is*. Her agency was using counseling approaches that were *not* discussed in our text or in any of the major texts. Moreover, it wasn't as if the counseling approaches used at her agency were brand new. The dominant approach her agency used could be traced to the 1980s. My goal in presenting some of the theoretical approaches contained in Part IV is to move from the modern age to the postmodern age in psychotherapy.

The first three chapters of Part IV focus on multiculturalism because it has been a dominant force within the helping professions since the 1970s. Chapter 12 provides a broad examination of multicultural therapy. The focus in this chapter is Western in orientation, and even more so, it presents American interpretations of multicultural issues in therapy. There is a world beyond our American interpretations of multicultural issues in therapy.

Chapter 13 examines Asian, African, and other approaches to psychotherapy that are considered multicultural in orientation. For instance, how do Asian, African, or Arab cultures view personality development and psychotherapy? Perhaps building a bridge between Eastern and Western approaches to psychotherapy might be the true integrative theory of psychotherapy. How might the classical teachings of Buddhism, Daoism, and Confucianism be used to inform and expand Western counseling and psychotherapy? Can you imagine being required to learn Japanese Naikan therapy (which sees introspection as a way of healing) in your counseling theory course? Do you have to be working with Japanese clients to want to learn Naikan therapy? Are there elements of Buddhist principles of mindfulness that can be used regardless of one's ethnic or cultural background?

Chapter 14 deals with feminists and gay and lesbian approaches to therapy. This chapter is conceptualized as social constructivist because both feminist and gay and lesbian approaches have constructed their approaches using parts of some of the theories described throughout this text.

Chapter 15 presents the contributions of solutions-focused therapy, and Chapter 16, narrative therapy. Solutions-focused therapy has integrated many Adlerian techniques; narrative therapy blends social constructivism with personal constructivism to create a different version of truth for therapy.

Chapter 17 deals with spiritual approaches to psychotherapy. Spirituality can have a profound impact on clients. I examine issues such as "How is spirituality connected to clients' mental health?" "How might therapists integrate spirituality into the clinical intake process?" "What would an approach to spiritual assessment in therapy look like?" "Should therapists even bother to integrate spirituality into the therapeutic process?" and "Should there be 'a separation of religion and spirituality' from the therapy hour?"

Chapter 18 presents strengths-based counseling theory. Strengths-based counseling has grown tremendously since 2005. More so than some of the other newer therapies, strengths-based counseling offers the potential of changing the pathology focus of much of psychology and therapy. In 2003, there were few references on the Internet regarding using a strengths-based approach. At the time of this writing, at least 10 new books have been published on this topic. Strengths-based counseling offers the possibility of incorporating multicultural counseling as one of its prominent legs.

Chapter 19 covers family approaches to psychotherapy. These approaches integrate several bodies of knowledge: (a) systems analysis, (b) group dynamics theory, and (c) theories of psychotherapy. In the broadest sense, family approaches to psychotherapy have been socially constructed.

CHAPTER 12

Multicultural Psychotherapy Theories

I've learned that people will forget what you said, people will forget what you did, but people will never forget how you made them feel.

—Maya Angelo

No man ever looks at the world through pristine eyes. He sees it edited by a definite set of customs and institutions and ways of knowing.

—Ruth Benedict

Never doubt that a small group of committed people can change the world. Indeed, it is the only thing that ever did.

—Margaret Mead

The hottest places in HELL are reserved for those, who in times of great moral crises, maintain their neutrality.

—Dante Alighieri

Assumed similarity and assumed dissimilarity are key factors that affect a multicultural counseling/psychotherapy relationship—from both a client and a therapist perspective.

—Elsie Jones-Smith

BRIEF OVERVIEW

A good argument that the counseling and psychology professions are moving toward social constructivism is found in the constructive underpinnings of the multicultural movement in counseling. Begun in the 1970s, the multicultural movement has gained in power and influence within the helping professions. It has continued to develop and change, insisting, in some respects, that all theories of psychotherapy should be examined for multicultural contributions and limitations. Multicultural counseling is considered socially constructive because it acknowledges each culture's perspective within the therapeutic process.

The postmodern/social constructivist philosophical framework complements the multicultural view because both emphasize the importance of conceptual relativity when working with clients. Multicultural therapists see clients' descriptions of their life stories as different ways of constructing meaning out of their life experiences. They also acknowledge that counseling theories have historically reflected a number of cultural biases, values, and beliefs about mental health that are largely Eurocentric in origin and therefore do not represent universal truths about psychological health.

The significance of the multicultural perspective in counseling and psychotherapy cannot be underestimated. Multicultural diversity has gone global. Most countries in the world are multicultural in some respect—religion, culture, or color/race. Iceland has an African and an Asian population. In general, Europe is multicultural and multiethnic/racial. England, France, Switzerland, and Germany have significant African, Asian, and Muslim populations. The global spreading of cultural and racial diversity has led some researchers to conclude that the worldwide multicultural phenomenon is leading to a paradigm shift across academic disciplines.

This shift in population diversity has resulted in a movement from a monocultural to a multicultural perspective in counseling and psychology. Increasingly, multicultural theories compete with established theories. This movement has come about because both clients and therapists have come to recognize that culture is often a "silent intruder" in the therapeutic relationship. Clients' cultural beliefs about the causes and solutions for their mental health issues affect what they believe to constitute appropriate treatment for the issues they bring to therapy (Smith, 1991). Traditional therapeutic approaches to assessment might be inappropriate and harmful when applied to culturally diverse clients. Counselors can no longer ethically treat clients if they do not understand the cultural influences in the therapeutic relationship. Developing and maintaining **multicultural competence** are ongoing tasks that requires clinical awareness, understanding, and skill development.

Because theories of psychotherapy are always influenced by the cultural background of the theorist, most current theories need to be expanded in terms of multicultural issues. A major issue is "Do we need separate multicultural theories for psychotherapy, or can the current major theoretical schools simply be modified to include multicultural perspectives?"

It is my view that multicultural counseling will continue to change over the years and that it will combine its emphasis with other theoretical approaches, such as cognitive-behavioral theory and relational theory.

EUROCENTRIC PSYCHOTHERAPY THEORIES AND WESTERN VALUES

Historically, psychologists and other mental health professionals have used **Eurocentric counseling theories** to formulate their thinking about client issues. Yet each of the Western theoretical formulations is value laden. How could they be otherwise? Whatever theory a person constructs is influenced by his or her cultural framework. Multiculturalists contend that traditional counseling theories fail to consider the ways in which culturally diverse persons construct their own meanings of mental health, psychological stress, and appropriate coping strategies (Ponterotto, Casas, Suzuki, & Alexander, 2001). They argue that no theory, however objective it appears on the surface, is value free.

In evaluating each theoretical approach for psychotherapy, it is important to know something about the Zeitgeist that was prevalent during the theorist's lifetime. What factors in the person's own life prompted him or her to develop a particular theory? For instance, Sigmund Freud's theory of penis envy was colored by his Austrian cultural upbringing that was patriarchal in nature (Jones, 1953). Alfred Adler's early illness as a child led to his theory of organ inferiority and superiority and inferiority complexes. Carl Rogers has indicated that his early strict upbringing was a significant factor that led him to stress the preeminence of the counseling relationship and positive, unconditional positive regard for people regardless of their life circumstances (Barrett-Lennard, 1998).

Yet just because a counseling approach has a Eurocentric, Western perspective does not mean that it does not have useful points. For instance, the behavioral contributions of B. F. Skinner and the cognitive-behavioral school of Albert Ellis and Aaron Beck can have relevance to most cultures. Every ethnic and cultural group establishes culturally relevant cognitions or thoughts that influence individuals' behavior. Likewise, most cultures use the principle of reinforcement to ensure that individuals' behavior will conform to that group's norms or values. Therapists must become aware of the dominant cultural cognitions within each ethnic group.

Even though there are benefits to adopting a cognitive behavioral framework, mental health professionals must examine how a Western perspective may hold certain cultural biases. For instance, most Western counseling theories assume that people are capable of change and that they should pick themselves up by their own bootstraps. Such theories maintain that the self is more important than the community, that an individual should have an internal rather than an external (group) locus of control, and that an individual's spirituality should be deemphasized in therapy. People who come from cultures that emphasize the importance of the group over the individual may find it offensive to stress the importance of the self. Clients may not value self-disclosure, especially when such disclosure deals with revealing family secrets.

Moreover, the therapeutic process is laden with certain beliefs, such as the value of talk therapy—the belief that establishing a relationship with another person skilled in psychological principles and intervention strategies can help that person deal with deep-seated personal issues. Counseling students frequently value client characteristics and behaviors that involve clients' making their own choices rather than those of their parents, being open and self-revealing, and gaining independence from their families and other groups.

Eurocentric counseling interventions may not work with clients from Eastern, Asian, and African cultures. Does this mean that only Asians should counsel other Asians, or that African Americans should treat only members of their ethnic group? Research shows that one does not have to be a member of the client's ethnic group to counsel a client. However, client-perceived similarity does have an influence on the rapidity with which one can establish a therapeutic alliance (Sue & Sue, 2003).

Inner Reflections

Do you believe there is a Eurocentric bias in counseling theories?

Is it possible for any theory of counseling or psychotherapy to be truly culture free?

What cultural biases might be included in your own integrative theory of psychotherapy?

WHAT IS MULTICULTURAL COUNSELING?

Multiculturalism is the doctrine that holds that several different cultures (rather than one national culture) can coexist peacefully and equitably in a single country. Aspects of multiculturalism include race/ethnicity, religion, age, gender, sexual orientation (gay, lesbian, bisexual, and transgender), language, geographic location, and socioeconomic status. **Multicultural counseling** refers to a counseling relationship in which a client and therapist are of different ethnicities, cultures, races, and/or backgrounds. The term *multiculturalism* is in direct contrast to the term *monocultural*. **Monocultural** means having familiarity with only one culture or sharing a common culture to the exclusion of others. Sometimes, therapists who are monocultural may apply their culture's values and norms to all clients, regardless of their cultural backgrounds. Such an approach may lead to misunderstandings in counseling when the client's and therapist's cultures are not the same.

Therapists who use a monocultural approach when working with a client from a different culture may encounter problems with diagnosis (overdiagnosing or underdiagnosing disorders), assessment, interpretation of symptoms, and chosen treatment methods (Fabrega, 1995). Therapists using divergent theoretical approaches such as psychodynamic, cognitive-behavioral, or existential-humanistic may use a multicultural framework to work with clients.

The Concept of Worldview

A *worldview* is a frame of reference that an individual holds about life. It includes the individual's assumptions, understandings, interpretations, and beliefs about his or her relationship to the people, institutions, and phenomena within his or her environment. Worldviews are the ways in which people construct meanings of their worlds. Individuals' worldviews develop as a result of their cultural and historical upbringings. Although all of us live in the same world, each of us constructs different meanings of what we experience and feel. Oppression and societal discrimination against an individual's class, gender, religion, sexual orientation, and other aspects of one's identity affect one's worldview.

A culturally sensitive therapist examines a client's problems and potential solutions within the context of worldview. Clinicians have worldviews that influence how they perceive clients' problems. A therapist's worldview is evident in how he or she makes sense of what he or she believes are the sources of a client's problems. One of the biggest challenges for therapists who are not cross-culturally aware is to learn how to view clients' issues apart from their own *ethnocentric* worldviews and to suspend their own cultural meaning temporarily when working with culturally diverse clients.

One major problem with ethnocentric counselors is that they falsely assume that their clients view the world in the same or a similar manner as they do. Such clinicians also tend to diagnose their clients inappropriately when clients present worldviews that differ from theirs. Oftentimes, if they don't receive multicultural training, ethnocentric clinicians may not even be aware of their own biases in viewing the world.

Culture: A Definition

Culture may be defined as the sum of intergenerationally transmitted lifestyles, behavior patterns, and products of a people that involve their language music, art, and artifacts, beliefs, values, history, eating preferences, customs, and social rules (Harper & McFadden, 2003). People learn their cultures through a process of enculturation; that is, they learn skills needed to function in a particular society. The family and the community are the major transmitters of culture.

The cultural rules each **ethnic group** adopts are not universally or consistently obeyed; yet all members recognize them, and individuals usually live by limiting the range within patterns of communication, beliefs, and social behavior found in cultures. Each culture produces (a) shared ways of behaving among ethnic members, (b) a basic motivational structure for behavior, and (c) psychological needs within its members.

According to Das (1995), "Culture is an inevitable silent participant in all counseling because counseling is a culture-specific human invention. Each form of counseling is a reflection of the culture that produces it" (p. 50). Culture guides our behavior and provides the framework for observing and identifying problems. Culture also teaches people problem-solving behaviors. Whitfied, McGrath, and Coleman (1992) have identified 11 variables that are conceptually useful in examining specific cultural patterns. These variables are presented in the following box:

Whitfied, McGrath, and Coleman's Variables in Cultural Patterning

Cultural patterning does the following:

1. Defines an individual's sense of self

2. Addresses and values the appearances of men and women

3. Holds specific beliefs and attitudes toward the world and others

4. Relates to family members, significant others, and peers

5. Makes use of leisure time or play

6. Learns and makes use of knowledge (cognitions)

7. Communicates and uses language

8. Maintains certain values and mores

9. Uses time and space

10. Eats and uses food in its customs

11. Works and applies its people to daily living issues

Inner Reflections

Do you believe that theories of psychotherapy have focused primarily on the individual level of identity as opposed to a group (ethnic/cultural) level of identity?

Why do you think theories of psychotherapy have deemphasized the importance of culture and ethnicity in a person's development?

What is your cultural, racial, or ethnic identity?

competition, and individuals' mastery and control over nature (Sue & Sue, 2003).

Both the therapist's and the client's backgrounds influence the counseling process. Counselors must comprehend how their own cultural worldviews determine how they observe, assess, define, and approach client problems (Ivey et al., 2007). For instance, studies have found that attending behavior (how we listen, sit, or respond nonverbally when working with a client) varies from culture to culture. Traditionally, for individuals from European North American backgrounds, conversation distance is an "arm's length" or more for comfort. In contrast, some Middle Eastern cultures use a 6- to 12-inch conversational distance, a point at which the European American becomes uncomfortable.

Studies have also revealed that culture influences the meaning that individuals give to their symptoms and to the causes and implications of the personal difficulties they experience in life (Flores & Carey, 2000; Ingoldsby & Smith, 1995; Okun, 1996). For example, in Italian and Jewish families, members may use emotional expressiveness to share personal suffering, while those from Scandinavian, Asian, and Native American backgrounds may be inclined to withdraw and not discuss their feelings. The European American worldview that dominates counseling holds the values and beliefs of rugged individualism,

Acculturation and Acculturative Stress

Issues of **acculturation** almost invariably involve cultural awareness and ethnic loyalty. *Cultural awareness* refers to a person's understanding and perception of native and host cultures. In contrast, *ethnic loyalty* reflects a person's preference for one culture over another, along with his or her level of pride and identity. Cuellar, Arnold, and Maldonado (1995) defined acculturation on the basis of changes at three different levels of functioning: behavioral, affective, and cognitive. At the *behavioral level* are customs, foods, and cultural expressions such as the music one chooses to listen to or dance to. The *affective level* consists of emotions that have cultural connections. For example, the meaning one attaches to flags and other symbols are all culturally based. The *cognitive level* contains beliefs about male and female roles, ideas and attitudes about illness, and fundamental values.

Sometimes clinicians deal with what Berry and Kim (1988) have labeled *client acculturative stress*. Stress occurs as individuals adapt to new values and a different culture. Sometimes members of ethnic/racial minorities experience threats to their cultural identities, feelings of powerlessness, inferiority, hostility, and discrimination. Other researchers have used the concept of *bicultural* to symbolize family adaptation and adjustment in a pluralistic society (Ivey et al., 2007). Intergenerational acculturation takes place when families are pulled in two different directions by the acculturative process. For instance, an adolescent may embrace the new culture, while older family members pull him or her to their culture of origin. Counselors need to take clients' levels of acculturation into consideration in therapy because it is closely related to the client's psychological functioning.

MULTICULTURAL COUNSELING: FIVE EMERGING THEORIES

A number of researchers—Coleman (1995, 1997); Gonzalez, Biever, and Gardner (1994); Hanna, Bemak, and Chung (1999); Ramirez (1999); Smith (1985); and Sue, Ivey, and Pedersen (1996)—have posed theories of multicultural counseling. Most theories of multicultural counseling use a Western cultural framework. Multiculturalism was defined primarily in terms of race/ethnicity or oppression. Many theories focused on Black/White racial identity development (Helms, 1984), or on Asian/White (Sue, 1972) or Latino/White relations (Christensen, 1979). Emerging theories of multicultural counseling have branched out to include a number of variables. This section briefly reviews five multicultural theories.

Sue, Ivey, and Pedersen's Multicultural Counseling Theory

Dr. Derald Wing Sue is a professor of psychology and education at Columbia University. He earned his doctorate at the University of Oregon. With more than 150 publications, he is the most cited multicultural scholar in this country. He has held numerous positions throughout the American Psychological Association (APA), including president of Division 45, Society for the Study of Ethnic Minority Issues. *Dr. Allen Ivey*, ED.D., ABPP (Diplomate of the American Board of Professional Psychology), earned his doctorate from Harvard University and his undergraduate degree from Stanford University. He is a distinguished university professor (emeritus) of the University of Massachusetts, Amherst, and the author or coauthor of 40 books and 200 articles and chapters. *Dr. Paul B. Pedersen* is professor emeritus in the Department of Counseling and Human Services in the school of education at Syracuse University. He is the recipient of the 2010 APA award for distinguished contributions to the APA, Society for International Advancement of Psychology. He has authored or edited 45 books, 100 articles, 82 chapters, and 22 monographs on aspects of multicultural cross counseling and international communities.

Sue et al. (1996) have provided a metatheory (i.e., a theory about theories) of multicultural counseling. The researchers propose six propositions that purport to describe a culture-based conceptualization of counseling. The propositions are listed in the following box:

Sue, Ivey, and Pedersen's Theory of Multicultural Counseling

1. Each Western and non-Western theory represents a different worldview.

2. The totality and interrelationships of client–counselor experiences and contexts must become the focus of treatment.

3. A counselor or client's racial/cultural identity influences how problems are defined and dictates or defines appropriate counseling goals or processes.

4. The ultimate goal of a culture-centered approach is to expand the repertoire of counseling responses available to counselors.

---

5. Conventional roles of counseling constitute only some of many alternative helping roles available from other cultural contexts.

6. The importance of expanding personal, family, group, and organizational consciousness in a contextual or relation-to-self-orientation is emphasized.

Sue et al.'s (1996) multicultural counseling theory (MCT) is not a theory; rather, it synthesizes the philosophical and spiritual essence of the multicultural movement in counseling. It is a treatise on multicultural counseling rather than a theory of it. The treatise has major limitations. For instance, it does not provide any theory about the personal development of individuals. It does not present elements of the counseling process, nor does it offer goals of counseling or counseling techniques or methods. The theory resembles very closely the multicultural competencies discussed later in the chapter.

The theory/treatise encourages us to see culture as embedded deeply in the consciousness of all human beings and basic to all human functioning. Both the counselor and the client are conceptualized as cultural beings, a view that is missing from most traditional theories of psychotherapy. Sue et al. (1996) acknowledge the value of traditional counseling theories as starting points for therapy. They also point to the importance of taking into account environmental factors such as racism, sexism, and homophobia. The researchers list the liberation of clients' consciousness and personal freedom as appropriate counseling goals or outcomes of therapy.

Casas and Mann (1996) have provided a critical examination of Sue et al.'s (1996) MCT. Casas and Mann (1996) point out that MCT attempts to present two theories as one, thereby creating a theoretical inconsistency. While on the one hand the theory claims to be a metatheory, on the other it claims to be a theory of counseling. Casas and Mann maintain that until Sue et al. (1996) resolve which of these two foci will constitute their theory, it will be difficult to use research methods to research the theory.

At the heart of Casas and Mann's (1996) critique of Sue et al.'s (1996) MCT is the issue of whether or not MCT meets the requirements for a theory. For instance, MCT does not provide a discussion of any of the underlying philosophical implications of the theory. Instead, the theory is based largely on an overarching concept of multiculturalism. MCT contains a number of references to racism and oppression. It does not indicate how culture is incorporated into a person's identity or related to one's mental health.

González, Biever, and Gardner's Social Constructionist Approach

Dr. Roberto Cortéz González is an associate professor in the department of Counselor Education, Educational Psychology, and Special Services at the University of Texas at El Paso. In 1990, he earned a Ph.D. degree in counseling psychology from Stanford University. His areas of research include models of multicultural development and career counseling models for diverse populations. *Dr. Joan L. Biever* is a professor of psychology at Our Lady of the Lake University in San Antonio, Texas. She earned her Ph.D. degree in counseling psychology from the University of Notre Dame. Her research areas include therapists' experiences of cross ethnic therapy with Spanish-speaking clients and a curriculum model for training competent therapists. *Dr. Terry Gardner* was a professor of psychology at Our Lady of the Lake University in San Antonio, Texas. He is deceased and no picture is available for him.

González et al. (1994) have drawn similarities between multicultural counseling and social constructionist views. They define *social constructionism* as a mechanism for the counselor to obtain racially or culturally based information from the client's situation to assist in comprehending the role of culture in the client's life. González et al. describe some of the basic tenets of social constructionism and multiculturalism. Seven propositions constitute their social constructionist model and are presented in the following box:

---

1. *Therapist as learner:* The therapist must become sensitive to the client's understandings of the impact of the client's culture on his or her behavior.

2. *Entertainment of all ideas:* The therapist should look for more than one answer to a client's problem and for different ways to arrive at a solution.

3. *Maintenance of curiosity:* The counselor endeavors to avoid learning too quickly or assuming he or she has an answer before asking a question. The therapist makes sure that the client's self-stated problem is the problem, and he or she avoids prematurely assuming that he or she knows the answer(s) to the client's presenting problem.

4. *Collaboration between the client and the therapist:* The therapist has confidence in the client's ability to incorporate different descriptions and explanations that might be useful in creating solutions to the client's problem.

5. *Therapist's understandings as "grist for the Mill":* The therapist introduces his or her understandings of a client's story as tentative hypotheses rather than as better stories, better descriptions, or better options.

6. *Creation of a space for the client's story:* Clients from an ethnic minority group sometimes understand and explain their world significantly differently than a person from a majority culture.

7. *Seeing opportunities rather than barriers:* The therapist emphasizes opportunities in the form of strengths, skills, and competencies rather than emphasizing barriers in the form of weaknesses, deficits, and incompetence.

González et al. (1994) note that therapists must relinquish their privileged "expert" position in therapy to one that accepts all understandings as potentially practical and valuable. They also note that therapists should not rely on socially constructed documents like the *Diagnostic and Statistical Manual of Mental Disorders* (4th edition, text rev; *DSM-IV-TR*; American Psychiatric Association, 2000). Clinicians should be more concerned about exploring clients' theories about the nature of their problems and less interested in fitting clients into their established or preferred theories of psychotherapy.

Although this model makes a number of good points, it assumes that clients are always articulate and self-aware. Another limitation is that the authors do not place an emphasis on macrosystem variables such as racism and sexism. In addition, the therapist appears to be more passive rather than directive, a stance that some clients might consider unhelpful.

Ramirez's Cognitive-Behavioral Multicultural Model

Manual Ramirez earned his Ph.D. from the University of Texas at Austin. He is currently a professor in the psychology department at the University of Texas at Austin. His current research interests include mental health in Latino families, acculturation, cultural democracy in education and multicultural development assessment, and psychotherapy. Dr. Ramirez's areas of expertise include ethnopsychology and cross-cultural psychology.

Ramirez's (1999) cognitive-behavioral model is designed to help clients develop a flexible, multicultural personality and to help clients express their cultural uniqueness. Therapists assist clients in identifying the self that they may have been suppressing earlier in life. Clients learn how pressures from others and from society may have impinged on their self-identities. Ramirez assumes that every client has the potential for multicultural development. Counselors have preferred cognitive and cultural styles, and they should be cognizant of these styles. Ramirez outlines seven major tasks for therapists, which are presented in the following box.

Ramirez's Multicultural Model of Psychotherapy

1. Match clients in an atmosphere of acceptance by providing a nonjudgmental, positive, and accepting atmosphere that has an absence of conformity or assimilation pressures.

2. Formally assess clients' preferred styles by administering three personality inventories that measure the clients' preferred cognitive and cultural styles.

3. Conduct a life history interview that identifies critical times in which the client was pressured to conform or to assimilate culturally.

4. Conduct a self-assessment to ascertain areas of match and mismatch with the client, allowing the therapist flexibility to better match with the client.

5. Introduce the client to the major concepts of both the flex theory of personality (a person's ability to modify his or her dominant personality style or type when confronted with others who have a different personality type) and the multicultural model of counseling and give homework assignments to clients based on that model.

6. Compare data gathered from the re-administration of the paper-and-pencil inventories and from the observation instruments with those obtained in the initial stage of therapy.

7. Encourage clients to become change agents committed to multiculturalism.

Coleman's Coping With Diversity Counseling Model

Dr. Hardin Coleman earned his doctorate in Counseling from Stanford University. He was appointed dean and professor at the Boston University School of Education in 2008. Dr. Coleman's primary area of research is the strategies adolescents use to cope with cultural diversity, particularly in how they affect school and job performance. He is also investigating the effect of cultural factors on the counseling process.

In contrast to some of the other multicultural theorists, Coleman (1995, 1997) emphasizes coping strategies people use when faced with cultural diversity. According to him, people deal with diversity in six possible ways: (1) **assimilation**, (2) acculturation, (3) alternation, (4) multiculturalism/integration/pluralism, (5) fusion, and (6) separation. Coleman uses these categories to form a 6 × 6 matrix between client and counselor. These six strategies lead to either convergence or divergence in the counseling relationship. Coleman discusses briefly the coping, adaptation, and social patterns of clients operating from each of these six diversity perspectives. Conflicts in multicultural counseling relationship are caused by the divergence in the strategies used by counselors and clients to cope with diversity.

Coleman bases his model on the belief that the nature and quality of the client's coping strategies have a significant impact on the nature and etiology of the presenting problem, the client's expectations of the counselor, the therapy relationship, and the outcome of counseling. The strength and type of therapeutic alliance between the counselor and the client are also influenced by how a client copes with cultural diversity and by the counselor's diversity strategy for dealing with members of a specific cultural/ethnic group. Coleman emphasizes the relationship between culture and behavior, and he helps us understand how a client's strategy for coping with cultural diversity affects various parts and stages of the counseling relationship.

Coleman (1995) also describes cultural behavior schemas, and he provides limited information on behavioral episode schemas as part of an individual's personality. A *behavioral episode schema* is defined as "a learned pattern of behavior that is stimulated within particular contexts" (p. 725). Coleman spends insufficient time on explaining behavioral episode schema, even though it is one of the core constructs in his model. His clinical examples throughout the model are excellent.

Elsie J. Smith's Theory of Ethnic Identity Development

During 1985, I published the "Smith Ethnic Identity Development Model"—one of the first theories of multicultural counseling to be published in *The Counseling Psychologist*, the official journal for Division 17, Counseling Psychology of the APA (Smith, 1985). I conceptualized multicultural theory from the perspective of ethnic identity rather than from racial identity. As I looked at the world, there was only one race, and that was the human race. We were all just variants on the general theme of the human race. What distinguished one group from another was their ethnicity, which could be measured in many different ways, including their ethnocultural heritage or their culture, their history, their values, sense of belonging, and so on. The theory conceptualized ethnic identity in terms of majority and minority status rather than in terms of one race dominating the other (Smith, 1989, 1991). I maintained that it was the minority or majority status that had a major impact on the privileges that an individual could experience in life, regardless of what country or culture one lived in (Smith, 1991). For instance, during the 1970s, women in America were in the majority, yet they were given a minority, undervalued status—despite their greater numbers.

Since 1985, I have revised my multicultural theory several different times, each time expanding my view that ethnicity was an important group-level identity, perhaps even as important as one's individual-level identity, which theorists often label as one's personality. Although scholars from ethnic minority backgrounds had begun the initial impetus to include multicultural counseling as a legitimate area within psychology, I contended that ethnicity influenced us all, regardless of whether we were African American, Asian American, Native American, or White. Instead of talking about personality, I focused on developing a tripartite level of identity—(1) the individual level (personality), (2) the group level (ethnicity), and (3) the universal or panhuman level (we are all human beings). My revision of the Smith Ethnic Identity Development Model is presented in ensuing sections.

The Smith (1991) model of **ethnic identity development** proposes that everyone has three levels of identity: (1) an *individual level* that refers to that person's unique personality development;

(2) a *group identity* that pertains to the person's culture, ethnicity, gender, and other group identities; and (3) a *universal identity* that refers to the person's perception of linkage to the rest of humanity. A person's cultural identity is a group-level identity that becomes influenced by factors such as acculturation, assimilation, and migration. Various group-level identities become shared *reference groups*.

These three levels of identify are everchanging, depending on a person's unique life circumstances. For instance, at one time, one's cultural identity may become more salient than one's ethnic or racial identity; at another time, one's gender identity may surge to the forefront. Traditional counseling tends to focus primarily on the individual level of identity and to minimize or ignore the client's multicultural reference group identities. The effective multicultural helping professional makes an effort to relate to all levels of client identity.

Ethnic identity development is a social construction that involves an interaction of contextual and developmental factors. Young children and adolescents who come from ethnic minority cultures may be challenged to develop positive ethnic identities because of prejudice, discrimination, immigration or replacement (loss of significant others, loss of country, uncertainty, and instability), socioeconomic reality, institutional barriers, acculturation (children's and parents') of personal issues, and developmental factors. Ethnic identity development entails change, construction, and reconstruction of one's ethnic identity.

Ethnic identity is a powerful identity and, perhaps, in the final analysis much more powerful than an individual identity or what we traditionally label as personality. It is often the source of interethnic conflict both within and between nations. Despite the power of ethnic identity on individuals' actions, psychology has focused primarily on the study of the individual level of identity—personality. Virtually, all of the *DSM-IV-TR* (American Psychiatric Association, 2000) deals with diagnoses of individual disorders, and scant emphasis is placed on disorders related to individuals' activities in groups. Psychologists would do well to focus more attention on healthy ethnic identity development and on disorders that might be related to our ethnic group identities.

The Smith (1991) model differs in significant ways from the extant racial/ethnic identity models in the psychological literature because the majority of the models (Cross, 1971, 1995; Helms, 1995; Kim, 1981) have focused on racial identity development of single ethnic groups (usually their own) and White mainstream society. The Smith model is designed to apply to all ethnic groups, and it is developmental, whereas the other models do not consider ethnicity across the life span.

Another difference is that most of the extant cited models focus on oppression or ethnic conflict in individuals' development of an ethnic identity (Atkinson, Morten, & Sue, 1998; Cross, 1971; Helms, 1995; Kim, 1981). They describe a conflict situation as the impetus that starts the exploratory process for developing an ethnic identity. In contrast, the Smith (1991) model asserts that ethnic identity development can take place without oppression; the most meaningful part of our ethnic identity development takes place outside of ethnic conflict situations. Furthermore, the racial identity models argue that an individual develops one ethnic identity, whereas the Smith model asserts that an individual may have multiple ethnic identities, with usually one salient ethnic identity.

Four concepts are central to the stage-wise component of the Smith model: (1) the concept of ethnic identity across the life span stages, (2) ethnic identity developmental tasks, (3) the ethnic self-schemas, and (4) ethnic identity maturity. Each stage has a major identity crisis that the individual must overcome (Smith, 2003).

Ethnic Identity: A Lifelong Process of Developmental Stages

Ethnic identity development is viewed as a lifelong process. Individuals socially and personally construct ethnic identity as they interact with the environment. Ethnic identity development begins in childhood and continues throughout old age. (Stages are discussed in more detail later in the chapter.) It involves a process of differentiation and integration that helps one move from a state of unawareness of ethnic differences to ethnic awareness, from nonethnic self-identification to ethnic self-identification, and from partial ethnic identifications to ethnic identity formation and integration. Individual differences in ethnic identity development occur within an ethnic group because individuals absorb culture differentially along a scale of acceptance to rejection (Smith, 1991). Different life experiences may cause one to recycle or to repeat parts of stages they have previously gone through.

Ethnic Identity Developmental Tasks

The process of ethnic identity development involves mastering developmental tasks associated with one's ethnicity and culture (Smith, 1985). A Mexican American child must learn what it means to be Mexican American, as does a White American child. Ethnic developmental tasks are largely unwritten. Social support from family and friends helps one achieve ethnic identity developmental tasks (Levine et al., 1994). The successful mastery of ethnic identity tasks leads to healthy development, while failure leads to ethnic identity conflict, confusion, or diffusion (Smith, 2003).

The Ethnic Self: Ethnicity as Schema

The ethnic self is part of an individual's overall self-schema (Smith, 2001). *Self-schemas* are organized views about the self, and they contain personally defining and important attributes (Montepare & Clements, 2001). For instance, Markus (1977) found that individuals for whom independence was a salient personal attribute were quicker to identify independence-related traits as self-descriptive than those for whom independence was not self-defining. Likewise, individuals highly schematic for gender react faster to information about their gender schema (Forbach, Evans, & Bodine, 1986).

Individuals are not schematic for all of the characteristics, traits, and skills that are true or observable about them (Markus, 1977). Rather, self-schemas indicate domains that are valued in one's social life (Oyserman & Markus, 1993). When a domain becomes self-schematic, it becomes important for the individual to maintain a specific view of the self within this domain (Oyserman & Markus, 1993). People are more inclined to refute, challenge, or dispute negative or disconfirming schema feedback.

The Smith model proposes that while some individuals organize themselves along their ethnicity self-schemas, others do not (Oyserman, Kemmelmeier, Fryberg, Brosh, & Hart-Johnson, 2003). Some members of ethnic groups may be aschematic with reference to their ethnicity. Individuals who are ethnic self-schematic are likely to state, "My ethnicity means the world to me; I'm glad of my ethnicity and would not want to be anything else." In contrast, individuals who are aschematic for ethnicity tend to state, "Really, my race does not matter to me. Ethnicity means nothing to me." Individuals who are schematic for their ethnicity make sense of who they are in terms of their ethnicity and their ethnic culture. Their ethnic culture is important to them.

Individuals vary in the contents of their ethnic self-schema. Whereas the content for some individuals contains only ethnic membership (in-group) values and issues, the ethnic self-schema for others may contain in-group and out-group material. Bicultural individuals' ethnic self-schema may have content from several ethnic groups.

Ethnic self-schema is not a thing but the fulcrum around which one organizes one's entire ethnic identity. It is a psychological structure that is responsible for the maintenance of one's ethnic identification, ethnic self-esteem, and affiliative behaviors. During the early stages of development, the ethnic self is more unconscious than conscious. Ethnic self-schemas undergo a continual process of differentiation, integration, and reintegration of old and new partial identifications based on one's contact experiences.

Ethnic self-schemas contain the following components:

1. An ethnically related concept of self that ranges on a continuum from positive to negative ethnic self-esteem

2. A worldview that conceptualizes their ethnic membership group's place or standing within a society (Romanucci-Ross & DeVos, 1995)

3. A view of the opportunity structure (either open or closed) within a given society for members of their ethnic group and nonmembership ethnic groups within a given society

4. Attitudes toward in-group and out-group ethnic members (Smith, 2001) that range on a continuum from positive to negative

5. Beliefs about what constitutes appropriate behavior for ethnic group members toward each other

6. Beliefs about what constitutes appropriate behavior toward nonmembership groups

7. A stance toward their own ethnic membership participation in their society—a stance that may be conceptualized as (a) oppositional—movement against the values of the greater society (Ogbu, 1992), (b) assimilative—movement toward the values of the greater society, and (c) disengagement from the greater society or nonmembership ethnic groups—movement away from societal values (Smith, 2001). In the last stance, individuals do not view mainstream institutions as self-defining or meaningful (Oyserman et al., 2003).

Individuals who are ethnic self-schematic may deal with negative ethnic stereotypes in two predominate ways. First, they may devalue the domains that define the out-group. Second, they may rely primarily on the feedback and reflected appraisal of close and trusted ethnic group members who use in-group rather than out-group definitions of success. When ethnic group members rely solely on the views of in-group ethnic members, they tend to perceive negative feedback as evidence of prejudice and disengage themselves from domains (school, work) that provide negative feedback.

Ethnic Identity Maturity

The concept of ethnic identity maturity is used to denote a person's process of developing with regard to ethnic matters (Smith, 2003). A mature ethnic identification is defined as one in which people (a) describe themselves accurately in terms of their ethnic group's culture and history, (b) have a realistic and secure identification such that they are able to take pride in their own ethnic groups and assume favorable attitudes toward other groups, and (c) have confidence in being an adequate performer in at least one ethnic identity (Romanucci-Ross & DeVos, 1995). People who are secure in their ethnic identities act with greater flexibility and openness to others of different ethnic and cultural backgrounds than do those who are insecure in their identities.

Inner Reflections

What is the content of your own ethnic schema?

Who helped develop what is contained in your ethnic schema?

What role, if any, did your family play in the development of your ethnic schema?

Do you believe that ethnic identity development is a lifelong process?

Why or why not? How would you describe the ethnic identity development stage or phase in which you find yourself?

What factors in your life have been critical in helping you arrive at your present stage of ethnic identity development?

How do you think your ethnic identity development will proceed as you grow older?

Stage 1: The Evolving Ethnic Self and Contact Stage: Learning Who We Are (Ages 0–4 years). The evolving ethnic self and contact stage focuses on several factors, including ethnic awareness, the development of ethnic attitudes, and the beginnings of ethnic self-identification. The dominant crisis of this stage is ethnic awareness. The first stage of ethnic identity development is learning who we are. Three types of learning take place during the ethnic socialization process: (1) imitative; (2) instructed learning from parents, adults, teachers, and community elders; and (3) collaborative learning that takes place as a result of within-group interaction among ethnic group members (Vygotsky, 1978).

Concepts have been borrowed from Tomasello's research (1999) to explain the cultural transmission process that occurs in helping an infant and young child develop an ethnic identity. Central to the cultural transmission process are the concepts of shared activity and cultural intentionality. Infants' understanding of others' intentions forms the basis of their learning about their own cultures and their initial development of an ethnic identity (Tomasello, Carpenter, Call, Behne, & Moll, 2005). Children learn about cultural intention and cultural goals from watching their parents and family members perform many daily tasks and rituals.

The ability to read others' goals and intentions is critical in cultural learning because sometimes it is necessary to do things the way others do—that is, when learning the use of cultural artifacts or communicative symbols (Tomasello, 1999). As children grow older, they become adept at understanding the cultural goals and intentions of members of their ethnic groups. It is this knowledge that gives young people a sense of ethnic cultural competence—that is, the belief that they are able to perform the tasks that other members of their ethnic group perform in a satisfactory manner (Tomasello, 1999).

In addition, ethnic identity development is a process of increasing cognitive development. Young children develop ethnic values, customs, language styles, and behavioral clues long before they become able to cognitively label and know them as ethnic. They develop an awareness of ethnicity, and subsequently they move toward ethnic self-identification and other ethnic group identification. They develop beliefs and attitudes about their own ethnic groups, as well as those toward nonmembership ethnic groups (Corsaro & Fingerson, 2003).

As children age, they learn that ethnic categories do not change, and they develop preferences for ethnic groups. Their cognitive ethnic group identities gradually become laden with affective layers. Culture and ethnicity become internally represented for the preschool child (Cosaro & Fingerson, 2003). The internal representation of one's culture and the association of one's culture with one's mother or parents cause ethnicity to be very emotionally laden.

Quintana's (1994) model of social perspective–taking ability has been modified for ethnic perspective taking (Quintana, Castaneda-English, & Ybarra, 1999). For Stage 1, children are in Level 1 ethnic perspective taking. This level helps them become increasingly capable in classifying ethnicities based on observable and some nonobservable characteristics. During the preschool years, children identify their own and other's racial or ethnic groups around the age of 3 or 4 years—earlier for members of racial minorities and for those in mixed-race settings. Children's ability to engage in ethnic identification begins earlier for those who have explicit (instructed) race socialization.

The essential developmental tasks of the evolving self and contact stage are as follows:

1. Children recognize themselves as being similar to and different from others in terms of their ethnicity (Aboud, 1987).

2. They engage in the process of boundary line drawing—that is, drawing the inner boundary lines of family members (Corsaro & Fingerson, 2003).

3. They exhibit an awareness of ethnic group members and nonmembers.

4. They develop a basic level of comfort with their ethnic group's food, music, dance, and rituals.

5. They recognize the basic physical features of their ethnic group (Smith, 2003).

Stage 2: The Inclusion and Defining the Inner Boundary Stage (Ages 5–8 years). In Stage 2, the child's sense of ethnic identity becomes more conscious than unconscious, partly because the people in the child's primary group (family) and secondary reference groups (community) may consciously teach her or him an ethnic identity. Moreover, the child becomes increasingly skillful in learning how to conceptualize differences in people and in behaviors observed (Aboud, 1987). The dominant crisis or developmental issue during this stage is ethnic self-identification.

Children gradually grow in their ethnic reasoning abilities. One cognitive skill young people develop is ethnic perspective taking, which is related to young people's ability to take a social perspective of themselves and their lives. As children age, their increased cognitive ability helps them understand how others perceive them in terms of their ethnic membership groups (Aboud, 1987). They also become more proficient in construing both overt and subtle indices of others' ethnicity.

During Stage 2, children move into Level 2 of ethnic perspective taking. They begin to understand the heritage or ancestry components of ethnicity. When children become aware of ethnic cues, they subsequently come to recognize themselves as members of one or more ethnic groups. *Ethnic self-identification* is a term used to describe children's accurate and consistent use of ethnic labels, based on their perceptions of themselves as belonging to an ethnic group. Three critical factors influence children's ethnic self-identification (Aboud, 1987):

1. Children describe themselves in terms of the ethnic group attributes (ancestry, national or religious background, language, skin color, and the group's label).

2. Children perceive their ethnic groups' attributes as being different from those of other ethnic groups.

3. Children perceive their ethnicity as constant and consistent across changes in context.

Initially, during the inclusion stage, children may believe that they have some choice in selecting their ethnic membership groups. They may say that they do not want to be African American or Asian American, and therefore, they are not members of those groups. Hence, in the early part of the inclusion stage, children may have little understanding of the permanence of ethnic membership.

Also during the inclusion stage, children develop an ethnic orientation (Aboud, 1987). They display strong social preferences with reasons for doing so by the age of 5 years (Bernal & Knight, 1993). Later (ages 5 to 8 years), children cognitively consolidate ethnic group concepts. Children manifest increasing competence in (a) perceiving the similarity of themselves to the group, (b) categorizing groups according to their visual cues (physical features), (c) labeling groups appropriately or in a manner consistent with that of adults, and (d) recognizing that one's ethnicity is largely unchangeable (Bernal & Knight, 1993).

During the inclusion stage, children must have contact with both ethnic membership and nonmembership groups. Without having some contact (even if it is only a result of television viewing), children do not develop a sense of being distinct from other ethnic groups. A feeling of ethnic distinctiveness is necessary for ethnic group identification to occur. Children's ethnic identity is modified according to their contact situations with ethnic membership and nonmembership groups.

The developmental tasks of the inclusion and of defining the inner boundary stage are as follows:

1. Children begin to engage in the process of inner boundary line drawing.

2. They exhibit an awareness of their own ethnic group members (Bernal & Knight, 1993).

3. They become familiar with some of their ethnic groups' basic rituals and religious ceremonies (Aboud, 1987).

4. They recognize the signs and symbols of their ethnic membership groups.

5. They label ethnic groups accurately and consistently.

6. They understand the constancy and the unchangeability of ethnicity and race.

7. They begin to show a preference for their own ethnic groups.

8. They start to define themselves in terms of appropriate ethnic and gender roles.

9. Ethnic peer groups become increasingly important for validating their own self-worth and identity.

10. They develop a sense of "we" and "they" (Searle, 1995).

Stage 3: Us and They/Exclusion: Defining the Outer Boundary Stage (Ages 9–12 years). Stage 3 is characterized by children's impressive cognitive development as a means to enlarge and to solidify their ethnic identities. Children enter Level 3 of cognitive ethnic perspective taking that focuses on a social perspective of ethnicity. They become aware of ethnic differences in friendship patterns, ethnic discrimination and prejudice, and their ethnic groups' shared cognitive orientations and beliefs (Searle, 1995). The greater the degree to which individuals subscribe to the shared cognitions of their ethnic membership groups, the stronger will be their level of ethnic group identification. Parents' ethnic socialization practices are important during this stage (Hughes et al., 2006).

During Stage 3, the emphasis is on defining the outer boundary groups—essentially the "they." It is a stage that begins the process of ethnic group exclusions, and children outline the groups with which they have the most salient conflicts in identification (Corsaro & Fingerson, 2003). Preadolescents' boundary line drawing promotes their later crystallization of personal ethnic group identities. During Stage 3, children are open to influence from other nonmembership ethnic groups. They begin to develop more formally attitudes and beliefs toward members of their own ethnic groups and nonmembership ethnic groups (Atkinson et al., 1998). Children's openness and lack of crystallization of inner and outer ethnic groups allow them to choose friends and playmates from a variety of ethnic groups. Thus, during this period, children stand a good chance of having in-group and out-group ethnic self-schemas.

The essential ethnic identity developmental tasks of the us-and-they boundary line drawing stage are as follows:

1. Young people develop a concept of "they" in terms of nonmembers' ethnic groups (Levine et al., 1994).

2. They begin drawing the outer boundary of ethnic group exclusiveness (Harwood, Miller, & Irizarry, 1995).

3. They develop stereotypes as a means of dealing with people from nonmembership ethnic groups.

4. They learn their appropriate gender roles for their ethnic groups (Corsaro & Fingerson, 2003).

5. They learn how to enact ethnic-related behavioral styles.

Stage 4: Adolescence: Ethnic Identity Formation: Boundaries (Ages 13–20 years). Adolescence is a critical period for ethnic identity formation (Phinney, 1990). The major task of adolescence is for the individual to integrate childhood ethnic identifications with ethnic contact experiences one has had throughout one's life with ethnic membership and nonmembership groups. On approaching adolescence, individuals attempt to reintegrate childhood identifications and to consolidate them into a meaningful whole. As this occurs, adolescents' meaning of ethnic identity changes.

Adolescents' enlarged cognitive development allows them to consolidate their ethnic identities (Romanucci-Ross & DeVos, 1995). Increasingly, adolescents recognize that they have some choice in picking the groups with which they will associate and identify. They come to understand that they can decide the extent to which being Italian, Jewish, Japanese, or African American is important to them and to their overall identities. Cognitively speaking, adolescents enter Level 4, which is the social perspective of ethnicity. Adolescents evidence a social understanding of ethnicity, and they comprehend the subtle aspects of ethnicity, such as socioeconomic status. They conclude that interpersonal interactions are based on individuals' ethnicity, and they formulate beliefs about how others respond to and treat members of different ethnic groups (Phinney, 1990).

During adolescence, one's peers, neighborhood community, and the ethnic makeup of one's school influence one's ethnic self-schemas, particularly the extent to which such schemas contain both in-group and out-group content. Adolescents' ethnic identity formation is affected by their majority or minority ethnic status (Quintana et al., 1999). Problems in ethnic identity formation occur when adolescents perceive that their membership in a specific ethnic group restricts their educational, occupational, and economic opportunities (Phinney, 1990).

Additionally, difficulties in ethnic identity formation may occur when members of ethnic minority groups experience a dual or bicultural socialization (Padilla, 2006). For instance, ethnic immigrants may be socialized with one set of values and cultural rules within their homes and quite another set of values and cultural rules in their schools. Moreover, for multiethnic adolescents, Hitlin, Scott Brown, and Elder (2007) found that a significant proportion of youth changed racial self-identification over time. Youth who reported being multiracial were four times as likely to switch self-identification instead of reporting consistent multiracial identities.

During adolescence, individuals work to achieve cultural competence in an ethnic identity (Smith, 2002). Largely, one's peers, family, and neighborhood residents define such cultural competence. The ethnic community contributes to adolescents' ethnic identity by providing a subculture in which their level of cultural competence is validated. Individuals who are deprived of sufficient contact with members of their own ethnic groups will display less proficiency in performing the behavioral style of the ethnic group and will be less able to read and send group-associated signals than will those who have had a great deal of ethnic membership contact.

Both majority and minority young people are aware of their ethnicity, but each may ascribe a different level of importance (salience) to the impact that ethnicity has on their lives (Kim-Ju & Liem, 2003). White Americans are dually socialized into ethnic groups: (a) a large White American ethnic group composed of individuals from various White ethnic groups and (b) their own White ethnic subgroups (McDermott & Samson, 2005).

Young people who have multiple strains on their ethnicity (multiple White identities) may evidence greater difficulty in ethnic identity formation than those who have one primary ethnic identification (McDermott & Samson, 2005). Individuals with bicultural ethnic identities are inclined to have a diffused ethnic identity, or they may forestall forming a core ethnic identity until they have resolved which aspects of their bicultural backgrounds they want to include as part of their core ethnic identity (Padilla, 2006). Interethnic conflict during this stage is likely to be related to issues such as school attendance, intermarriage, engaging in sports, and other social activities where one is competing for superiority in defined areas.

Adolescents sometimes experience conflicts in their ethnic self-schemas because they may be caught between their parents' ethnic beliefs and values, the beliefs of other ethnic groups, and those of the mainstream society. In the ever-changing global society, adolescents are moving gradually toward a multicultural identity that is composed

Inner Reflections

Think about your adolescence. Did you have ethnic identity have during adolescence?

If so, what kinds of ethnic identity experiences were they?

Would you characterize them as primarily positive, negative, or neutral ethnic identity development experiences?

What people or critical incidents affected your ethnic identity development?

of multicultural identifications based on their in-group and out-group ethnic self-schemas (Farley, 2002). The essential developmental tasks of adolescence are as follows:

1. Adolescents consolidate their partial ethnic identifications through the process of identity formation (Phinney & Tarver, 1988).

2. They achieve a satisfying and socially acceptable masculine or feminine role that is anchored in their cultures and ethnic groups (Bernal & Knight, 1993).

3. They are accepted by their peers as ethnic group members.

4. They develop positive ethnic selves (Phinney, 1990).

5. They deal with ethnic conflicts with membership and nonmembership groups.

6. They integrate their ethnic selves with their overall personal identities.

Stage 5: Young Adult and Cultural Transmittal Stage (Ages 21–40 years). Adult ethnic socialization is characterized by one's attempt to maintain a core of sufficiently consistent behavior that proclaims to others one's commitment and allegiance to one's membership ethnic group. During adulthood, the cognitive stage of ethnic identity development focuses on individuals' ability to take the perspective of other ethnic groups. Individuals may be able to identify with other oppressed groups or subgroups within ethnic groups. Ethnic conflict tends to be acted out in the work world, where one competes for promotions, merit increases, and so on.

The dominant issue in Stage 5 is *cultural transmittal*. One makes a decision about the kind of ethnic family one will have—traditional, nontraditional, or marginal—in its practice of ethnic and cultural traditions of one's membership group. Ethnic self-schemas become translated into ethnic family self-schemas. Some developmental tasks involved with young adult and cultural transmittal stages of ethnic identity development are as follows:

1. Young adults decide which aspects of the ethnic group they will pass on and which they will modify or discard.

2. They determine how to inform their offspring about their ethnic groups and culture—that is, teaching children, family members, and friends the cultural meanings associated with their ethnic rituals and ceremonies.

3. They decide on a level of family ethnic identification (Romanucci-Ross & DeVos, 1995; Searle, 1995).

Stage 6: Management of Ethnic Self-Schemas (Ages 40–59 years). The dominant issue in this stage is the management of one's ethnic self-schema, which is characterized by clarifying for oneself standards relating to ethnic in-groups and out-groups (Smith, 2001, 2003). Individuals tend to make carefully thought-out decisions about what will constitute the content of their in-group and out-group ethnic self-schemas. During this stage, ethnic self-schemas are related to achieving one's ultimate goals, resolving one's problems, and improving oneself. This stage is characterized by the resolution of inner conflicts related to one's inner and outer ethnic boundary groups, particularly with regard to cultural and social stereotypes.

People in this stage and age-group constitute the backbone of the ethnic group's political organizations; thus, there is typically a focus on the content of their in-group self-schemas. They maintain the ethnic group in the face of opposition from outside forces. People seek to join ethnic organizations as a means of strengthening their ties to the ethnic community. The ethnic friends one has at this stage of one's life are likely to be those who will see one through old age.

Ethnic identity conflicts that dominated one's earlier years are largely resolved in this stage (Sokolovsky, 1985). Individuals in the maintenance stage exhibit a crystallized maintenance of an enduring ethnic identity. The developmental task for this stage involves managing an authentic ethnic self-schema and resolving whatever remaining discrepancies exist in one's ethnic self.

Stage 7: The Integrated and Reflective Ethnic Self (Age 60+ or various ages). There are two primary developmental tasks at this stage of development: (1) integration and (2) the desire to pass on ethnic knowledge and place to members of the younger generation.

Varying ethnic and cultural lifestyles influence the way in which old age is encountered and experienced. Different ethnic groups provide differential familial support and differential status to the aged. For some aged people in ethnic groups, ethnic identity becomes a major source of continuity in their lives. Some individuals have a longing to return to their roots to put their lives in order (Sokolovsky, 1985). Individuals attempt to bring about an understanding of the role of ethnicity in their lives. They heal themselves by a process of ethnic perspective taking (Cuellar & Weeks, 1980). Ethnic conflicts are few because individuals have left the work world and situations that might generate conflict.

During the last stage, individuals make an attempt to integrate all discrepant parts of their ethnic selves and other role identities into an integrated self (Atkinson et al., 1998). The integrated self is an existential search for unity and meaning in life. The major ethnic identity crisis for this stage is identity integration. Individuals review the ethnic self-schemas that they have constructed throughout their lives, and they integrate all discrepant parts of their ethnic selves and other role identities, including painful memories of ethnic injustice and intolerance that they have experienced.

ETHNIC SELF-SCHEMAS AND MENTAL HEALTH ISSUES _____

Mental health is related to individuals' ethnic self-schemas. Across a variety of ethnic samples, researchers have documented positive links between ethnic identity and well-being (Brooks & Pahl, 2005; Gray-Little & Hafdahl, 2000; Greig, 2003; Kiang, Yip, Gonzales-Backen, & Witkow, 2006; Ryff, Keyes, & Hughes, 2003). The Smith model proposes two types of ethnic-related disorders. They are (1) **reactive ethnocentrism**, either in-group or out-group hatred (stigmatism) based on contact experiences that are generalized to the entire populations under consideration, and (2) **socialized or stigmatized ethnocentrism**, either in-group or out-group hatred and stigmatization due to socialization practices of parents, the media, or the mainstream society (Smith, 2001). Positive ethnic self-identification can be construed to be a strength, or at the very least a protective factor.

School Counseling Implications for Ethnic Identity Development

School counselors themselves must first become knowledgeable about the process of ethnic identity development for individuals from minority groups and majority groups. Second, counselors must help create school climates that embrace ethnic and cultural diversity and that empower students to explore their ethnic and cultural heritages. Third, counselors need to be aware of how ethnic self-schemas can affect children's, adolescents', and adults' daily lives.

There exists, for instance, a great deal of evidence to suggest that in the case of African American adolescents, negative ethnic self-schemas may function to help them construe academic achievement as "acting White" (Oyserman et al., 2003). Counselors might ask clients questions about their ethnic self-schemas. What are the ethnic self-schemas for their membership and their salient, nonmembership ethnic groups? How do ethnic self-schemas influence their views of the opportunity structure and their participation within the broader society? The stages of ethnic identity development provide a framework within which we can examine both the client's and the counselor's ethnic self-schemas. Can people be taught to change the content of their ethnic-self schemas so that they include other ethnic groups? How can parents promote children's positive ethnic socialization?

OTHER RACIAL IDENTITY MODELS _____

Multicultural theorists have worked to develop various racial and/or ethnic identity models. Racial and ethnic identity consists of (1) self-identification of the label individuals give themselves; (2) knowledge about one's culture, including its customs, values, beliefs, and traits; and (3) adoption of the feelings and attitudes of the group in question. African Americans have been in the forefront of constructing models of cultural/racial identity development (Cross, 1971, 1991, 1995; Helms, 1990, 1995; Jackson, 1990). In addition, cultural/racial/ethnic identity models have been constructed by Latinos (Casas & Pytluk, 1995) and about White persons (Helms, 1995; Ponterotto, Utsey, & Pedersen, 2006) and biracial and multiracial groups (Kerwin & Ponterotto, 1995). This section describes the first major model of racial identity development by William Cross, who may be conceptualized as the father of racial identity models. Of course, there are more individuals who have worked on such models than I can present in this brief section.

William E. Cross, Developer of the First Major Racial Identity Development Model

Dr. William E. Cross Jr. (Ph.D. from Princeton University) is an important leading theorist and researcher on African American identity development in particular and racial-ethnic identity development in general. His book *Shades of*

Black (1991) has become a classic in the field of racial identity development. Dr. Cross was a part of the Black Consciousness Movement of the 1960s and 1970s, and he later developed the "Psychology of Nigrescence" to explicate the psychological identity transition of African Americans based on the consciousness movement. The Cross Model became the template for scholars on Native American identity, women's identity, gay–lesbian identity, Asian American identity, and so forth.

Cross (1971, 1991) asserted that individuals experienced a process of forming a racial identity through a transformation of an existing identity (in this case, a non-Afrocentric identity) into one that was more Afrocentric and less based on the devalued conceptualizations of the dominant White culture. According to him, the process proceeded in stages, from pre-encounter, wherein individuals are inclined to view the world from a White frame of reference and when they thought, acted, and behaved in ways that devalued or denied their Blackness, to encounter, immersion–emersion, and finally to the internalization stage. The encounter or second stage is characterized by a person experiencing a personal or social event that causes him or her to realize the consequences of the dominant society's view. For instance, a person who has denied the significance of his or her race is suddenly denied the right to purchase a home in an exclusive White neighborhood. This experience signals the significance of his or her race within the society. The encounter stage has two phases: (1) a realization phase in which a person recognizes that his or her old frame of reference is inappropriate and (2) an exploration phase wherein the person decides to develop a new African American identity. The third stage called the immersion–emersion stage represents a turning point in a person's conversion to a new identity. The person tends to immerse himself or herself into African American culture and sometimes is inclined to denigrate White culture. The final, fourth stage is the internalization stage, which is characterized by a person achieving a sense of inner security and self-confidence with his or her new African American identity. The person moves toward a more pluralistic, nonethnocentric perspective. The significance of the Cross model is that it was the first one not only to develop a model for racial identity development but also to construct a template for a person's identity development within a society that had established oppressive conditions against one's ethnic or cultural group.

THE THERAPEUTIC PROCESS

Various authors have made suggestions for working with members of specific ethnic groups—for instance, counseling Hispanic Americans (Casas & Vasquez, 1996), African Americans (Carter, 1995; Helms, 1990; Smith, 1989), Asian Americans (Sue, 1997), and Native Americans (Sage, 1997; Trimble, 1990). In proposing guidelines for working with any racial/ethnic group, practitioners have to be careful of overgeneralizing and stereotyping the very clients they seek to help. Trust is a critical issue in working with members of ethnic minority groups. It is important that therapists discuss the client's preference or reaction to a therapist of a different ethnic/racial or cultural background. African American clients tend to show a preference for working with same-race practitioners, although studies also indicate that what is most important for them is to have a culturally competent counselor (Sue & Sue, 2003). During the first session or early sessions, a practitioner might ask, "Sometimes clients prefer working with a therapist of the same race or ethnic group. I am wondering how you might feel about working with me."

The clinician examines the worldviews of the client and explores his or her feelings about counseling. What does the client's culture say about mental health counseling? The clinician explores issues around racial/ethnic identity. Investigate whether external factors might be related to the client's presenting problem. What cultural values does the client maintain? What is the client's cultural identity? The extent to which a client places importance on an African American, Native American, or Asian American identity should be explored.

Does the client have feelings about oppression of his or her ethnic group?

Is the client experiencing acculturation conflicts with his or her parents or members of the extended family? For instance, youth of Asian descent may attribute psychological stress over the difference in their values and those of their parents. Recent immigrants may experience a type of cultural grief. *Cultural grief* refers to bereavement caused by an individual's forced adaptation to a new culture. When immigrants come to a country, they experience many losses, such as loss of identity, loss of loved ones, and loss of culture. Cultural grief also refers to the loss that immigrants encounter due to loss of social structures, cultural values, and self-identity. To work with such individuals, counselors need to understand the meaning that clients give to their multiple losses.

The Therapeutic Relationship in Culturally Diverse Settings

This book maintains that all counseling is inevitably multicultural counseling if one takes into account the broad factors in which people differ, such as race, socioeconomic status, sexual orientation, age, physical disability, and so on. Each person has different life experiences, even when they come from the same ethnic or cultural group and even when they come from the same family. Multicultural counseling is not just something that can be tacked onto so-called regular counseling. This situation occurs because for each individual, culture is an internalized object that becomes introjected into one's being.

Culture has both conscious and unconscious components that might have a bearing on the presenting issue that the client brings to therapy, or it might have an influence on how the client copes with or responds behaviorally and emotionally to the presenting issue. Therapists must comprehend how their cultural values and theoretical orientations provide a therapy worldview that determines how they observe, assess, define, and approach client problems.

Role of an Effective Multicultural Therapist

Each therapist has an internalized culture, which contains features such as his or her values, philosophy of life, ethnicity, sex, age, geographical roots, religion, and social and economic class (Smith, 1985, 1991). Each of these features exerts a differential pull, valence, or strength on the individual's overall makeup. Therapists are challenged to transcend their internalized cultures and to experience the client's culture almost as if it is the therapist's own.

To achieve an accurate understanding of the different ways in which people construct meaning in their lives, psychotherapists must have an understanding of both their clients' cultures and their own. Therapists endeavor to understand how their own cultural conditioning influences their work with clients. What cultural values have they adopted? How do their cultural values color the way in which they view clients' life challenges? Likewise, it is important that counselors understand how clients from different cultures view them as therapists as well as how they perceive the helping process.

The postmodern, social constructivist philosophical framework complements the multicultural view because both emphasize the importance of conceptual relativity when working with clients. The multicultural counselor sees clients' descriptions of their life stories as different ways of

> ### Inner Reflections
>
> What culture have you internalized? How do you know you have internalized your culture?
>
> What factors in your family, education, or the general society helped you internalize your culture?
>
> Identify one person in your life who helped you internalize your culture? Who was this person?
>
> What was his or her relationship to you? How important is this person in your life today?

constructing meaning out of their life experiences. Therapists incorporate a multicultural perspective when they maintain one or more of the following perspectives:

- Clients' life stories represent their ways of constructing meaning in the world.
- The theories that therapists have historically used contain cultural biases, values, and beliefs about individuals' mental health that are largely Eurocentric in nature and that may not agree with those from different cultures.
- Traditional theories do not represent universal truths about individuals' psychological wellness and mental health.

Role of the Client

There is no specific role for the client in multicultural counseling because so much depends on the cultural context within which therapy takes place. Clients' culture may influence the roles that they assume in the therapeutic relationship. Wampold (2001) has underscored the importance of choosing a therapist who shares one's worldview and who is sensitive to one's cultural issues. He recommends that clients choose the therapy that accords with their own worldviews. Given the pervasiveness of issues connected with race, ethnicity, and culture in American society, selecting a therapeutic approach that considers multiculturalism is important for all clients. Clients stand a chance of benefiting from therapists who understand the role of oppression and social and economic

Inner Reflections

What impact do you believe your current phase or stage of ethnic/racial/cultural development will have on your competence to counseling individuals different from your membership group?

Considering your ethnic identity stage of development, with which ethnic/racial/cultural groups would you feel most comfortable providing counseling or psychotherapy?

injustice in their lives. Therapists working with culturally different clients should be credible to them and be able to build an alliance with them. Moreover, therapists must understand that clients' beliefs about the causes of and solutions for mental health problems are embedded in their cultures.

Cultural and Racial/Ethnic Identity Development for Therapists

Although a great deal has been written about the cultural and racial identity development of clients, less has been published about these variables for counselor trainees. How can training programs help counselors, social workers, and psychologists to work effectively with multicultural clients? What are the stages trainees travel through as they confront their own ethnocultural histories as well as those of others? Ponterotto et al. (2006) have developed a four-stage cultural/racial/ethnic identity model for White counselor trainees. These researchers have posited that European North American White counselor trainees often go through (1) Stage 1, pre-exposure; (2) Stage 2, exposure; (3) Stage 3, zealotry or defensiveness; and (4) Stage 4, integration.

During Stage 1 (pre-exposure), White counselor trainees have typically not thought about counseling and psychotherapy as a multicultural experience. Usually they make statements such as "My ethnicity or race is not an important part

Inner Reflections

What is your cultural heritage? What is the culture of your parents and grandparents?

With what cultural groups do you identify?

What is the cultural relevance of your name? What values, beliefs, and attitudes do you subscribe to that are consistent with the dominant culture? Which are inconsistent? How did you learn these values and attitudes?

of me" or "People are just people." Because such individuals deny the influence of culture or race in their own daily lives, they unconsciously and unintentionally tend to perpetuate various forms of institutional racism, sexism, or other types of cultural oppression as they attempt to "treat all clients" in the same manner.

During Stage 2 (exposure), Ponterotto et al. (2006) proposed that as a result of their training, White therapists (or experienced professionals) learn about cultural differences, racial oppression, and institutional oppression of diverse groups. As a consequence of such multicultural training, they may come to the conclusion that their prior mental health training was insufficient concerning multicultural issues. Confronted by their new understanding that their prior training was deficient because it did not include multicultural issues, trainees may become confused and upset by the issues clients present in therapy.

The zealotry or defensiveness of Stage 3 is characterized by White trainees' either wholehearted acceptance of multicultural principles or retreat into quiet defensiveness. As criticisms are made of White European American culture, some trainees may feel personally attacked. Those who adopt multicultural principles may become strong advocates for cultural diversity.

During Stage 4 (integration), White trainees and practitioners not only develop a greater appreciation for the impact of culture and race on the counseling process, but they also learn more about their clients and their ethnocultural histories and how such histories may influence the manner in which they develop a treatment plan or deliver counseling services. These trainees embark on a lifetime commitment to learning about multicultural issues.

One limitation of the Ponterotto et al. (2006) model is that it is directed primarily toward White trainees and not toward members of other ethnic groups. Clearly, members of ethnic minority groups also experience change as they engage in multicultural training. Such individuals may begin to examine their group-level identities, how they were formed, and what they desire these identities to be in the present and near future. African American, Asian, and Latino trainees may confront both within-member group issues as well as outside-group issues. Members of ethnic minority groups confront their own prejudices toward members of their groups and other nonmembership groups.

Cultural Formulation in Understanding and Assessing Clients

Clinicians take into account that either overreliance or underreliance on the significance of culture in accounting for clients' presenting issues is problematic. The clinician must avoid oversimplistic assumptions about clients' culture. To avoid culturally stereotyping clients, counselors need to be careful about making overgeneralizations about the impact of their clients' cultural backgrounds (Sue & Sue, 2003). The APA's *Guidelines on Multicultural Education, Training, Research, Practice, and Organization Change for Psychologists* (2003a) provide some direction for assessing clients from diverse cultural backgrounds. The guidelines state,

Consistent with Standard 2.04 of the APA Ethics Code (APA, 1992), multiculturally sensitive practitioners are encouraged to be aware of the limitations of assessment practices, from intakes to the use of standardized assessment instruments . . . diagnostic methods . . . and instruments used for employment screening and personality assessments in work settings. . . . Culture-centered psychologists are also encouraged to have knowledge of a test's reference population and possible limitations of the instrument with other populations. Multiculturally sensitive practitioners are encouraged to attend to the effects on the validity of measures of issues related to test bias, test fairness, and cultural equivalence.

In Appendix I, the *DSM-IV-TR* presents an outline for cultural formulation and a glossary of culture-bound syndromes (APA, 2003a). The cultural outline is designed to supplement the multiaxial diagnostic assessment and to address issues that may be experienced in using *DSM-IV-TR* criteria in multicultural counseling relationships. The *DSM-IV-TR* suggests that the clinician provide a narrative summary for each of the categories presented in the following sections.

Cultural Identity of the Individual

The clinician notes the client's ethnic or cultural reference groups. For immigrants and members of ethnic minorities, the *DSM-IV-TR* recommends that the clinician note separately those individuals' degree of involvement with both the culture of origin and the host culture. The clinician also notes clients' language abilities, use, and preference (including multilingualism).

Cultural Explanations of the Individual's Illness

The effective multicultural clinician identifies the client's predominant ways by which he or she expresses symptoms of distress or the need for social support. For instance, some cultures are more inclined to produce individuals who express symptoms of distress by saying that they possess spirits, or they exhibit numerous somatic complaints. Additionally, the practitioner might examine if the client manifests any of the culture-bound syndromes displayed in the *DSM-IV-TR*'s glossary. What reference group does the client use to explain the illness and what are his or her preferred sources of healing? Are there any cultural explanations for the person's illness? Is the person in conflict with any cultural norms? What is the person's usual culturally based help-seeking behavior?

Cultural Factors Related to Psychosocial Environment and Levels of Functioning

The clinician takes note of the client's relevant interpretations of social stressors, available social supports, and levels of functioning and disability. Attention is directed toward examining stresses in the client's social environment, and the role of religion and kin networks in providing emotional, instrumental, and informational support. What is the influence of the client's family?

Cultural Elements of the Relationship Between the Individual and the Clinician

Are there cultural elements involved in the relationship between the client and the practitioner? What is the client's preference for his or her counselor's ethnicity? To what extent is there cultural similarity and dissimilarity between the client and the counselor? Is there any cultural mistrust between the therapist and the client? What are the roles of the client's and counselor's worldviews in the therapeutic relationship? The therapist should indicate differences in culture and social status between him or her and the client and should mention whether such differences may cause problems in diagnosis and treatment—for instance, difficulty in communicating in the client's first language or in understanding the cultural significance of the client's symptoms.

Overall Cultural Assessment for Diagnosis

The therapist concludes with a discussion of how cultural considerations specifically influence comprehensive diagnosis and care for the client.

The overall assessment might include factors such as the client's identified ethnicity, language, degree of acculturation, gender, age, sexual orientation, religion, or spirituality.

Multicultural Counseling Techniques

Multicultural theorists have presented few counseling techniques that can be used across a wide spectrum of individuals. Most counseling techniques have been specific to working with different ethnic groups. Paniagua (2001) among others has suggested that therapists use more directive techniques with members of ethnic minority groups. For instance, it might be helpful to explore religious and spiritual issues with African American clients. When working with Latino clients, he indicates that therapists might employ a more formal approach during the early stage of the helping process, followed by a gradual introduction of *personalismo*, a more personal helping style. Therapists should also assess Latino clients for spiritual and religious issues.

For working with Asian American clients, Paniagua (2001) recommends the use of a more formal therapeutic approach. He suggests that therapists provide information about their education to Asian clients, because members of this group place a high value on education. Personally, I hesitate to use such recommendations simply on the basis of a client's cultural background, because there is wide variation within groups depending on their assimilation.

Multicultural Competencies

The paradigm shift in psychology toward multiculturalism is evidenced by major professional associations' adoption of multicultural guidelines and competencies. The APA has acknowledged the importance of multicultural issues in psychology in its publication of *General Guidelines for Providers of Psychological Services*. Recently, it has endorsed a set of multicultural guidelines for psychologists (APA, 2003b). Moreover, the American Counseling Association (ACA) took an early stance on endorsing multicultural competencies (Sue, Arredondo, & McDavis, 1992). This professional organization has also adopted social justice advocacy competencies (Lewis, Arnold, House, & Toporek, 2003). Both these professional organizations are having a profound influence on the way that mental health professionals conceptualize their roles. They challenge therapists to analyze carefully how best to respond to clients from diverse populations.

The history of multicultural competencies dates back formally to the 1980s and early 1990s. During April 1991, the Association for Multicultural Counseling and Development approved a paper outlining the need and rationale for a multicultural perspective in counseling. Subsequently, this professional association proposed 31 multicultural competencies. These competencies were outlined in three broad categories: (1) counselor awareness of his or her own cultural values and beliefs, (2) counselor awareness of clients' worldviews, and (3) counselor learning of appropriate intervention strategies. Within each of these three categories, the association further delineated attitudes and beliefs, knowledge, and skills.

Not all counseling or mental health professionals are in favor of the multicultural competencies. Weinrach and Thomas (2002) criticized the multicultural competencies on the grounds that they focused primarily on four ethnic groups: (1) African, (2) Asian, (3) Hispanic, and (4) Native American. They contended that they were troubled by what seemed to be imprecise and contradictory definitions of multiculturalism and diversity as well as other terms used throughout the competencies. In addition, these researchers maintained that the competencies seemed to stereotype clients by suggesting that those who were members of a group should be treated as examples of groups rather than as individuals. The authors stated in their criticism,

> It is untenable to suggest that individuals are templates of any collectivity. Although they may each emerge from an identifiable community, they individually perceive the reality of that and other communities differently. . . . Instead of promoting a psychotherapeutic model that stereotypes people, we recommend strengthening current efforts to highlight the individual uniqueness of all clients, regardless of their cultural backgrounds. (p. 24)

Weinrach and Thomas (2002) were troubled by the undue emphasis placed on race, because race "does not provide an adequate explanation of the human condition" (p. 24). They objected to the multicultural movement on grounds that it advocated a social justice movement rather than therapy for clients. To a certain extent, this book agrees with the latter point in that race may not be the real problem; the problem may be the significance that individuals attach to race. In a reaction article, Vontress and Jackson (2004) agreed that the multicultural competencies might be considered out of date. They maintained that the competencies might be dated because the American society has changed a great deal since the 1960s and 1970s. American society is no longer as race oriented as it used to be. Dr. Martin Luther King Jr.'s dream is slowly coming true. Table 12.1 adapts and summarizes key

Table 12.1 Multicultural Competencies and Standards

Goal 1: Counselors Evidence Awareness of Their Own Cultural Values, Beliefs, and Biases

Attitude and Beliefs Competencies Related to Goal 1

Culturally competent mental health professionals are

1. Aware and sensitive to their own cultural heritage and value and respect cultural and ethnic differences among their clients
2. Aware of the impact of their own cultural backgrounds, life experiences, attitudes, values, and biases on the counseling process
3. Able to recognize the limits of their competencies and expertise in working with clients from different cultural backgrounds
4. Comfortable with differences that exist between themselves and clients in terms of race, ethnicity, culture, and beliefs

Knowledge Competencies Related to Goal 1

Culturally competent mental health professionals

5. Obtain specific knowledge about their own racial and cultural heritage and how these factors affect their definitions of normality/abnormality and the process of counseling
6. Have knowledge and understanding about how oppression, racism, discrimination, and stereotyping affect their personally as well as in their work; acknowledge their own racist attitudes, beliefs, and feelings
7. Secure knowledge about how their communication style differences may clash with or foster the counseling process with minority clients; learn how to anticipate the impact of their communication patterns on clients

(Continued)

Table 12.1   (Continued)

Goal 2: Counselor Awareness of Client's Worldview

Attitudes and Beliefs Competencies Related to Goal 2

Culturally competent mental health professionals are

1. Aware that their negative emotional reactions toward nonmembership ethnic and racial groups may prove detrimental to their clients in counseling; willing to examine their own beliefs and attitudes in relation to those of culturally diverse clients in a nonjudgmental fashion
2. Aware of stereotypes and preconceived notions they may have toward other racial and ethnic minority groups

Knowledge Competencies Related to Goal 2

Culturally competent mental health professions

3. Have specific knowledge and information about the particular group with which they are working. They are aware of the life experiences, cultural heritages, and historical backgrounds of their clients; competency is enhanced by reviewing the racial/ethnic/minority development models available in the literature
4. Understand how ethnicity/race, culture, gender, and other factors may affect personality formation, vocational choices, manifestation of psychological disorders, help-seeking behavior, and the appropriateness or inappropriateness of counseling approaches
5. Have knowledge about sociopolitical forces that affect the lives of ethnic minorities; gain knowledge about immigration issues, poverty, racism, stereotyping

Skills Competencies Related to Goal 2

Culturally competent mental health professionals

6. Familiarize themselves with the existing research regarding mental health and mental disorders of various ethnic/racial groups; actively seek out educational experiences that foster their knowledge and understanding of cross-cultural skills
7. Become actively involved with individuals from ethnic and cultural minority groups outside the counseling setting (via community events, social and political functions, celebrations, friendships, neighborhood groups, and so forth) to ensure that their perspectives of such individuals are more than an academic or professional helping exercise.

Goal 3: Culturally Appropriate Intervention Strategies

Attitude and Beliefs Competencies Related to Goal 3

Culturally competent mental health professionals

1. Respect clients' religious and/or spiritual beliefs and values, including their attributions and taboos because such traditions affect clients' worldview, psychosocial functioning, and expressions of distress
2. Respect indigenous helping practices, including clients' community help-giving networks
3. Value bilingualism and do not view clients' language as an impediment to counseling (monolingualism may be the culprit)

Knowledge Competencies Related to Goal 3

Culturally competent mental health professionals

4. Have a clear and explicit knowledge of the generic characteristics of counseling and how such characteristics may clash with the cultural values of some ethnic and religious groups
5. Understand the institutional barriers that prevent members of some ethnic groups from using mental health services
6. Possess knowledge of the potential bias in assessment instruments and use procedures and interpret findings taking into account clients' cultural and linguistic characteristics
7. Have knowledge of the family structures, hierarchies, values, and beliefs related to the ethnic groups that they serve
8. Exhibit knowledge of relevant discriminatory practices at the social and community level that may influence the psychological welfare of the populations they serve
9. Have knowledge of varying models of minority and majority identity development and understand how these models relate to the counseling relationship and the therapeutic process

Skill Competencies Related to Goal 3

Culturally competent mental health professionals

10. Participate in a number of verbal and nonverbal helping responses; are not bound to only one theoretical model or counseling approach but recognize that helping approaches may be culture bound; when they believe their counseling style is limited and potentially inappropriate, they ameliorate its negative effect
11. Use institutional intervention skills on behalf of their clients to determine whether a problem originates from racism or bias in others (e.g., the concept of healthy paranoia) so that clients do not inappropriately blame themselves
12. Consult with traditional healers or religious and spiritual leaders and practitioners in the treatment of culturally different clients when appropriate
13. Take responsibility for interacting in the language that the client requests; when the linguistic skills of the counselor do not match the language of the client, seek a translator with cultural knowledge or refer to a knowledgeable and competent bilingual counselor
14. Acquire training and expertise in the use of traditional assessment and testing instruments; are aware of the cultural limitations of the instruments they use
15. Work to eliminate biases, prejudices, and discriminatory practices; are cognizant of the sociopolitical contexts in conducting evaluations and providing interventions
16. Assume responsibility in educating their clients regarding the processes of psychological intervention, such as informing them about the goals and expectations in counseling and therapy, the client's legal rights, and the counselor's helping orientation
17. Adjust their relationship-building strategies, intervention plans, and referral considerations to the stage of their clients' cultural/racial identity development, while taking into account therapist's own level of identity development.
18. Participate in psychoeducational or systems intervention roles—such as consultant, advocate, adviser, teacher, facilitator of indigenous healing, and so on—in addition to their clinical roles

components of the Association for Multicultural Counseling and Development's 31 multicultural competencies. The multicultural competencies that have been developed deal with three broad areas of (1) counselor attitudes, (2) counselor knowledge, and (3) counselor skills.

The Social Justice Movement in Multicultural Counseling

Although the social justice movement in American society pervades several professions, counseling psychology has been at the forefront of this movement (Baluch, Pieterse, & Bolden, 2004). A social justice approach to counseling is founded on the acknowledgment of broad, systemic societal inequities and oppression within American society and within other global societies as well (Arredondo & Perez, 2003). The ACA supports the concept of social justice. The 2005 ACA *Code of Ethics*, Standard E.5.c ("Historical and Social Prejudices in the Diagnosis of Pathology") asks counselors to "recognize historical and social prejudices in the misdiagnosis and pathologizing of certain individuals and groups and the role of mental health in perpetuating these prejudices through diagnosis and treatment."

Social justice in counseling is a multifaceted approach that encourages counselors to strive to promote human development and the common good by addressing changes related to both individual and distributive justice. According to Crethar and Ratts (2009), counselors are asked to direct their attention to four critical principles that guide their work: (1) equity, (2) access, (3) participation, and (4) harmony. *Equity* is the fair distribution of resources, rights, and responsibilities to all people within a given society. *Access* involves notions of fairness for all people regarding their ability to access the resources, services, power, information, and understanding crucial to realizing a standard of living that allows for self-determination and human development. *Participation* involves the right of every person in a society to participate in and be consulted on decisions that influence their lives and those of others within the society. *Harmony* refers to the need to get along among different groups within a society.

A major driving force behind the social justice movement is the idea that social illnesses are caused by various forms of oppression. Mental illness and developmental delays take place as a response to various social illnesses rather than as a result of an internal derivative (e.g., biological substrate, trauma). The social justice movement represents an ideological shift in thinking from the historic roots of counseling and psychotherapy to an individual, to a sociological perspective. Such an approach represents a paradigm shift regarding client conceptualization, from counselors' identifying individual pathology and/or developmental issues to focusing on social illness as a major source of client problems and issues.

Critics of the social justice approach have indicated that the social justice movement is inappropriate for psychology. According to critics, the primary focus of social justice advocates is on social illness within the broader context of society. Social advocacy counseling goes beyond the traditional boundaries of individual and group counseling. As a result, counselors are held responsible for taking action against social injustices rather than for clients' mental disorders.

Ethical Issues and Multiculturalism

Counselors face a number of ethical issues when working with culturally different clients. Increasingly, multicultural counseling standards, ethical codes, guidelines, and competencies now pervade the counseling and helping profession. Currently, the Council for the Accreditation of Counseling and Related Programs requires that counseling programs include "Social and Cultural Issues" in their curricula. To meet the council's requirement, counselor training programs disperse multicultural perspectives throughout their counseling program and offer separate coursework in multicultural counseling.

Professional associations have also played significant roles in the movement toward multiculturalism. The ACA (2005) presents diversity as a central issue in the Preamble to their *Code of Ethics*: "Association members recognize diversity and embrace a cross-cultural approach in support of the worth, dignity, potential, and uniqueness of people within their social and cultural contexts" (p. 3). The American Mental Health Counseling Association *Code of Ethics* (2010) states that mental health counselors "will actively attempt to understand the diverse cultural backgrounds of the clients with whom they work" (p. 9).

The APA (2003b) maintains that psychologists have an ethical obligation to develop cross-cultural competencies when working with clients who are culturally different from them. The counselor's role is to help clients deal with life challenges that are consistent with their clients' worldviews.

Theories of psychotherapy are not value neutral and applicable to all people. Some of the underlying values existing in most counseling theories include an emphasis on individualism, individuation as the basis for adult maturity, and decision making and responsibility residing within the individual rather than the group. In contrast, some Eastern, Latino, and African cultures have values that emphasize the importance of the group over the individual. It is unethical for clinicians to provide therapeutic services to culturally diverse clients when they are not clinically competent to work with such clients.

Ethical practice requires that clinicians develop multicultural competencies in testing and assessment. Diagnosis using the *DSM-IV-TR* may present major ethical problems when working with some culturally diverse clients, if clinicians do not have the requisite multicultural competencies.

RESEARCH AND EVALUATION
Contributions and Limitations of Multiculturalism

The multicultural movement has had a tremendous impact on the fields of counseling and psychotherapy. It has made us look more closely at the various psychotherapy theories that have been developed. All counseling theories are now viewed as being influenced deeply by the historical period in which they were constructed as well as by the theorists' own cultural backgrounds. In general, the multicultural competencies have had a positive effect on the various helping professions.

As they stand now, multicultural counseling theories provide a perspective from which to use the traditional theories of psychotherapy. However, most multicultural counseling theories deal with platitudes and are not theories at all. I view them as treatises on different aspects of multicultural counseling. They restate what has become common knowledge as a result of the multicultural competencies. There are few descriptions of how culture or ethnicity or any other variable affects human development. What is the process of developing an ethnic identity that cuts across racial, cultural, or ethnic guidelines? What are the specific multicultural counseling techniques?

Although multiculturalism is a very powerful force, it is more appropriately viewed within the framework of the postmodern constructivist movement within psychotherapy. Much work needs to be accomplished before multiculturalism can rise to the level of a fourth force in psychotherapy and counseling.

This conclusion does not mean that such a theory could not be constructed, because it can. It just has not been developed as of the present time. Before a robust theory of multicultural counseling can be developed, researchers must first begin with a theory of ethnic identity development that cuts across ethnic, cultural, and racial lines. For it is within a theory of ethnic identity development that we can begin to examine just how an ethnic and cultural identity is formed.

My own assessment of multicultural therapy is that we need to move beyond a description of personality as merely an individual construct. Such an approach is clearly Western and definitely Eurocentric—without meaning any negative connotation of the label "Eurocentric." The greatest contribution of multicultural psychotherapy will rest not in the multicultural competencies that have dominated the profession of psychology for the past 30 years but rather on those researchers who will develop a theory of a group level of identity that applies to most ethnic and cultural groups.

Inner Reflections

Is the multicultural movement a fourth force in counseling?

Has the multicultural movement reached the stage of developing a new paradigm in counseling and psychotherapy?

Evidence-Based Research and Multiculturalism

A major criticism of multicultural approaches is that they are not evidence based. In response to this criticism, researchers have noted that the evidence-based practice (EBP) movement gives insufficient attention to cultural competence or existing culturally specific practices (Isaacs, Huang, Hernandez, & Echo-Hawk, 2005). The Hogg Foundation for Mental Health (2006) has pointed out that differences in cultural beliefs and values are important to consider in the mental health service delivery systems because such variables influence treatment preferences and outcomes. Culture affects how individuals receive mental health services: (a) identify and express or present distress, (b) explain the causes of mental illness, (c) view mental health clinicians, and (d) utilize treatment.

Despite the criticism of evidence-based research from some multiculturalists, studies of mental health treatment efficacy that have had significant representation of members of ethnic minority groups provide promising evidence that EBPs may be successful within diverse populations (National Alliance on Mental Illness [NAMI], 2008). A study by Miranda et al. (2005) has reported that evidence-based care may successfully generalize to both African American and Latino populations as effectively as with White American populations. Because of the lack of available information on the use of EBPs for Asian American or Native American populations, no similar conclusive statement could be made on the effect of EBPs with members of these ethnic groups. Kohn, Oden, Munoz, Robinson, and Leavitt (2002) found that EBPs that used culture-specific issues and concerns during the delivery of cognitive behavioral therapy for African American women with depression showed greater decreases in symptoms than did similar women who were treated with the culturally unadapted cognitive behavioral therapy.

A critical issue in EBP studies is the adequate sampling of ethnic/racial populations; however, this situation appears to be improving. The Child and Adolescent Mental Health Division of the Hawaii Department of Health (2007) gathered information from 26 efficacy trials of cognitive-behavioral therapy and deemed this EBP to be a "best support" treatment of anxious or avoidant behavior problems among Asian, African American, Caucasian, Hindu, Latino, and Indonesian Dutch, and multi-ethnic youth populations (NAMI, 2008).

Cultural adaptations of EBP are being used in both research and practice settings (Bernal & Jimenez-Chafey, 2008). For instance, the Indian Country Child Trauma Center at the University of Oklahoma Health Sciences Center was established to investigate cultural adaptation of EBP trauma-related protocols and service delivery guidelines for tribal communities (www.icctc.org). The center has developed four successful culturally adapted interventions for Native American children and their families, including trauma-focused cognitive-behavioral therapy and parent–child interaction therapy (NAMI, 2008).

Multiculturalists have moved to include practice-based evidence (PBE) in order to combat problems associated with EBP studies. PBE is defined as a set of unique and inherent cultural practices that have nontraditional evidence based on the consensus of a cultural community (Martinez, 2008). PBE is responsive to the therapeutic and healing needs of individuals and families within a culturally specific framework. The cultural foundation of PBE can be contrasted to the scientific basis of EBPs. EBPs are not the panacea of effective mental health treatment for all people. It is important that researchers and clinical providers recognize the value of cultural adaptation and community stakeholder involvement in EBP. The NAMI (2008) has developed the following recommendations at a 2005 Consensus Meeting on Evidence-Based Practices for Consumers and Families of Color:

- Communities of color must be included in the development of EBPs.
- Cultural competence must be defined and required for all EBPs.
- The process of developing and credentialing EBPs should be modified to include communities of color.
- The process of implementing EBPs in ethnic minority communities must be supported with adequate resources.

CASE ANALYSIS

Justin From a Multicultural Perspective

A multicultural framework can be used in counseling Justin. First the therapist must examine himself and his own worldview and values. Hence, the therapist would examine his racial views. Justin is of mixed racial/ethnic heritage—White mother and African American father. How does the therapist feel about Justin's ethnic and cultural background? The therapist begins to examine his own awareness as a racial/ethnic and cultural being. What kinds of cultural encounters has he had in the past? What meaning does he give to himself as a cultural being? Does he refer to himself as a White American, a White German, or an Italian American?

Awareness of self is an important component of learning to work with culturally different students whose backgrounds are different from that of the therapist. To work effectively with Justin, the counselor must be aware of his own sociocultural backgrounds, biases, and values. He must come to terms with issues such as racism, sexism, economic and social class, as well as other societal realties. A culturally sensitive counselor takes the time to become aware of his client's history and culture. The counselor should take the time to fully understand Justin's environmental concerns. How does Justin deal with the adversities in his environment? How does he feel similar to or different from those whom he hangs out with? What about his classmates? To what extent did race raise its head in the school fighting incident?

After a thorough examination of his own culture and the impact that it has on his daily functioning, the therapist begins to consider what it must feel like to be in Justin's shoes. The school that Justin attends in Utah is predominantly White. There are only about 10 African American students attending Justin's middle school, and there are 5 Native Americans, 9 Latinos or Hispanics, and 6 Asian Americans in a school that has a population of about 1,200 students. There are no African Americans in any of Justin's classes. Justin feels lonely because he does not feel comfortable with the White kids in his class. Usually, he feels that they look down on him because of his mixed racial heritage. All of Justin's teachers have been White since he has been enrolled in school in Utah.

(Continued)

(Continued)

One of Justin's core issues is his mixed racial background and the negative responses he has received from his classmates regarding his mixed ethnic/racial heritage. Justin does not know whether he should consider himself African American or African American and White. His color is a light brown. Some people think that he is Puerto Rican or Mexican. His hair is full of curls that he wears just above his shoulders.

For the most part, race has been the silent gorilla sitting in the middle of the counseling sessions with Justin. Justin only mentioned the issue of race during the first intake interview. Tears filled his eyes when he talked about his rejection from his classmates, but he refused to let one tear fall. While he was telling the therapist about one racial incident in class, he felt like saying, "You probably feel about me the same way as they do." But he just kept silent and let the thought pass. Still, he wasn't sure what the therapist felt about African Americans.

The therapist felt that he was tired of the silent gorilla sitting in the middle of his therapy room. He decided to approach Justin and to ask him about one of the incidents in class that Justin had said had caused the fight for which he was thrown out of school. Justin used the puppets and stuffed animals in the back of the room to reenact the dispute. He claimed that what caused him to strike the other student was that he had silently mouthed a racial slur. The teacher did not hear him, and neither did anyone else. That's what made it so bad. The student mouthed the slur because he did not want to get in trouble. All blame would be placed on Justin for hitting him.

Justin's reenactment of this racial incident provided the open door for the therapist to have an honest discussion about race and the meaning that race had in Justin's life. The therapist asked Justin to create a council of advisers. He could choose anyone to be on his council, including people who were deceased. For instance, he could choose Martin Luther King Jr., Sister Mary Terese, the president, Tom Brady, L. L. Cool J, Beyonce, his mom—anyone. Justin chose his council of advisers, and the therapist asked him to consult his council about how he might respond should a similar situation take place in his classroom.

Justin had chosen the rapper Jay-Z to be on his council. The therapist asked Justin, "How do you think Jay-Z is going to advise you, based on what you know about him? Where did Jay-Z grow up? Did he live with his father and his mother? What was it like for him to grow up extremely poor in New York City?" Justin began to point out similarities and differences between himself and Jay-Z. He concluded that Jay-Z, who earns about $80 million a year, would have been too smart to get in a fight in school. His focus would have been on his music, not on trying to "prove himself to some White kid." One conclusion that Justin reached was that he was going to consult his council of advisers before taking any drastic action or before making an important decision.

The therapist asked Justin how he felt about him. Justin laughingly responded, "You're OK for an old White guy." The two then began to discuss their own racial and cultural similarities and differences. The discussion seemed to clear the air between Justin and the therapist. The therapist suggested that Justin complete a cultural genogram. The genogram is fashioned most directly after a family genogram, and this technique was used to increase Justin's understanding of himself and his mother. Justin has had only limited contact with the White part of his ethnic identity. The cultural genogram was designed to help Justin figure out what his dominant ethnic makeup is from his mother and from his father. The therapist sought to draw out positive narratives about Justin's cultural background. "Could you tell me a positive story about the family activities in which you, your mother, and brother engage?" The genogram may also offer the potential for Justin to talk about his father.

Justin is intrigued about finding out about his heritage because he left most of it behind when his mother left Chicago. The therapist and Justin decide to work on the genogram together, and they even agreed to have Sandy, Justin's mother, come in to help them complete it. The therapist gives Justin several questions to ponder in constructing his genogram: What are three to six organizing principles for his family and three to six pride and shame issues for each of the dominant ethnicities? Justin is asked to consider how people grow up knowing what behavior is appropriate for males and females. Does he cause problems for his mom at home because he believes that she is the weaker of the two? There is some exploration of sex role stereotypes in Justin's behavior.

The therapist forms a therapeutic alliance with Justin that allows him to explore issues of race and culture. He listens empathically to Justin's descriptions of racism in the environment. The two work on strategies to cope with racism within his school and in the broader community. They also discuss the impact that the eternal realities of race have had on his self-concept as well as on his behavior.

The therapist teaches Justin the technique of perspective taking. He places a stuffed gorilla in the middle of the room, and he asks Justin to pretend that the gorilla represents all the racism that he experiences at his school and within the broader Utah community in which he lives. Justin is informed that the gorilla is blocking something that he wants—achievement in art, respect from his teachers and his mother, and so on. The issue is "What does Justin do to keep the gorilla (racism) from harming him?" Although the therapist leaves it up to Justin to devise coping strategies, he is given the instruction that he cannot touch or move the gorilla. Justin wants to outsmart the gorilla, so at first, he says that he'll just go around the gorilla. Then he jumps over the gorilla. Justin enjoys not letting the gorilla get next to him. In fact, he finds himself laughing at evading the potential negative effects of the gorilla. Justin learns that it is best not to spend too much time fighting the gorilla. Instead, he renders the gorilla ineffective.

This exercise becomes Justin's metaphor for dealing with racism and the unfair acts of others. He will find a way around the behavior. He will not permit the behavior or racism to deter him from achieving his goal. Racism is, after all, only a distraction. The exercise also gives Justin a sense of power—a feeling that ultimately he is in control of how he chooses to respond to the racism of others.

SUMMARY

This chapter examined theoretical and practice issues related to multicultural therapy. The first section of the chapter focused on multicultural development in counseling and reviewed the historical development of the postmodern/social constructivist movement and compared it with the modernist movement. The traditional theories of counseling were placed in the modernist category—the group that focuses on science, scientific theory, and location of psychological problems within clients. The postmodern movement is dominated by theorists who hold a social constructivist perspective. Multicultural therapy was placed within the postmodern, social constructivist category.

Next, five emerging multicultural theories were examined in terms of their major propositions and strengths and weaknesses. Racial identity development theory was discussed. I examined the therapeutic process in multicultural counseling, with special emphasis on the therapist's role, the client's role, and the culturally competent assessment. The multicultural competencies and ethical issues in multicultural therapy were reviewed.

An important issue in this chapter was "To what extent does multiculturalism represent a fourth force with regard to theories of counseling and psychotherapy?" I concluded that although multiculturalism has had a worldwide impact, it has not risen to the level of a new paradigm or a fourth force.

SUPPLEMENTAL AIDS

Discussion Questions

1. What culturally learned assumptions shape your counseling interviews with clients?

2. Identify a client with whom you have had a clinical relationship and interpret that client's behavior within his or her cultural context.

3. What cross-cultural barriers impede your counseling with clients?

4. Discuss your culture-centered skill development, for example, understanding oppression (social, economic, and political).

5. Do you feel that the multicultural competencies have gone too far in trying to work effective with members from diverse ethnic and cultural groups?

Glossary of Key Terms

acculturation   The multidimensional and multi-directional process of immigrant groups in adopting both overt and covert cultural characteristics of the dominant culture. Overt characteristics adopted include dress, language usage, eating habits, and celebrations.

assimilation   Process through which a person or a minority group comes to adopt or accept the beliefs, values, attitudes, and behaviors of the majority or dominant culture, such that the person/group no longer retains the specific characteristic of the native culture.

culture   An ethnic group's organized body of beliefs and rules about the ways in which persons should communicate with one another, think about themselves, and behave toward each other and objects in their environment. Acculturation is a process whereby people change aspects of their lives based on their contact with people from other cultures.

ethnic group   A reference group called on by people who share a common history and culture, who may be identifiable because they share similar physical features and values, and who, through the process of interacting with each other and establishing boundaries with others, identify themselves as being a member of that group.

ethnic identity   Awareness of one's membership in a particular group.

ethnic identity development   Model that proposes that everyone has three levels of identity: an individual identity, a group identity, and a universal identity.

Eurocentric counseling theories   Theories developed primarily by White males from European ancestry. Underlying the theories are Western cultural assumptions.

monocultural   May be defined as espousing the culture of only one group—something that is lacking in cultural diversity.

multicultural competence   A counselor's or therapist's appreciation of different cultures. Multicultural competence can be seen as an attribute of both individuals and organizations. It represents an individual's ability to provide therapy and other helping services to individuals who come from cultures and ethnic groups other than one's own.

multicultural counseling   Counseling in which the therapist and counselor come from different cultural, ethnic, and gender backgrounds. Because no two people come from the exact same background (due to differences in their experiences), all counseling is, in some respect, multicultural.

multiculturalism   Doctrine that holds that several different cultures (rather than one national culture) can coexist peacefully and equitably in a single country.

reactive ethnocentrism   Ethnic-related disorder characterized by in-group or out-group hatred and stigmatization based on contact experiences that are generalized to entire populations. See also **socialized or stigmatized ethnocentrism**.

socialized or stigmatized ethnocentrism   Ethnic-related disorder characterized by in-group or out-group hatred and stigmatization due to socialization practices of parents, the media, or the mainstream society. See also **reactive ethnocentrism**.

Website Materials

Additional exercises, journals, annotated bibliography, and more are available on the open-access website at https://study.sagepub.com/jonessmith2e.

CHAPTER 13

Transcultural Psychotherapy

Bridges to Asia, Africa, and the Middle East

BRIEF OVERVIEW

© iStock/tacojim.

Living life fully is a matter of building bridges between people.

Chapters 12, 13, and 14 form a trilogy of chapters dealing with psychotherapy with culturally diverse clients. A vacuum exists in Western multicultural counseling models. Currently, multicultural psychotherapy consists of applying multicultural competencies—beliefs, attitudes, and skills that do not themselves form a theory of human behavior and human psychological development—to theories that are clearly monocultural in outlook. I have maintained elsewhere in this book that the multicultural competencies cannot be substituted for a theory of multicultural psychology.

According to Moodley and West (2005), multicultural psychotherapy has

> failed to theorize early childhood development, conceptualizations of the multicultural self, or any analysis of cultural psychopathology. All we seem to have are the cultural competencies as therapeutic techniques, and much of this work has no "force" outside the theorizing and researching by a small constituency of dedicated scholars. (p. xvii)

While these competencies are a start toward examining the impact of culture on psychotherapy, they do not substitute for rigorous theorizing about how individuals develop or construct group-level identities. Instead of focusing on the multicultural competencies, multicultural theorists might consider integrating psychological constructs from different cultures and nations. Does culture have a significant impact on individuals' expression of mental health issues? Do certain cultures facilitate the development of psychosomatic illnesses, while others lay the groundwork for more expressive and acting-out disorders?

One problem with multicultural theorizing is that too many areas are included under the multicultural umbrella to formulate a comprehensive theory of psychotherapy. For instance, multicultural counseling includes diverse areas such as

417

ethnicity, culture, sexual orientations, disability, and aging. While I am not advocating eliminating these areas under the multicultural heading, I am proposing that the field of psychotherapy might benefit from focusing on developing a theory of psychotherapy that deals primarily with ethnicity and culture.

The dominant position of this book is that the current Western paradigm in counseling and psychotherapy is inadequate to meet the needs of a culturally diverse population. Because all Western psychotherapy approaches are Eurocentric in their cultural outlook, the real challenge is to find commonality between Western approaches to psychotherapy and non-Western approaches (Santee, 2007). Lee (1993) asserts that when psychology texts examine the history of psychology, they invariably report only the early Greek thinkers and the thinkers from Europe. Typically, no consideration is given to the contributions of early Chinese thought—namely, Confucianism and Daoism—on psychological thinking. When Western psychology ignores the contributions of Eastern and other nations throughout the world, the focus is culturally biased. If psychotherapy is to truly become multicultural, we must take into account psychotherapy models from non-Western cultures.

This chapter offers a theoretical bridge that could possibly unite psychotherapies around the world. It is called the *psychological healing bridge* across cultures from Western and Eastern cultures. As Santee (2007) has pointed out, all cultures deal with stress, stress management, and psychological healing. What could Western approaches to psychotherapy learn about stress management and psychological healing from Chinese, Japanese, African, and Arab approaches to stress and psychological healing? A psychotherapy healing bridge would allow psychotherapists from different countries and cultures to collaborate more effectively with each other. We might also learn something about the mind and about stress management from examining how others many miles away from our homelands have dealt with such issues within their culture.

A dominant theme of this book deals with the integration of theories of psychotherapy. We can approach such integration from primarily two perspectives. First, we can concentrate on integrating different Eurocentric theories of psychotherapy. Second, we can integrate Eurocentric approaches to psychotherapy with various cultural approaches to psychotherapy. One of my goals in this chapter is to nudge the reader to consider integrating non-Western approaches into his or her integrated theory of psychotherapy.

I deal with a number of non-Western psychotherapies. It was difficult to find a format for describing each theoretical approach; therefore, I did not try to force the description of the non-Western approaches so that they could fit neatly in my outline of the role of the therapist, client, and so on. I adopted the Buddhist doctrine of "go with the flow"—that is, describe the theory according to how the theorist described it. Moreover, none of the sections of the chapter provides an in-depth discussion of the specific transcultural approach. My goal is simply to introduce the reader to these approaches and to refer them to resources that provide a detailed analysis of each psychotherapy model.

The chapter begins first with Asian psychotherapies: Buddhism and the Japanese approaches of Naikan and Morita therapy. Then, I examine the Chinese approach of mindfulness, the African Ma'at model, and Dwairy's (2008) Arab Muslim approach to psychotherapy. As you read this chapter, imagine a fulcrum around which you might integrate any one of these approaches with Western models of psychotherapy. For instance, what is the role of meditation in developing your own integrative approach to therapy? Do you encourage your clients to meditate as a means of dealing with stress? I maintain that most mental health issues and disorders reflect individuals' stress response syndromes. How do you perceive stress and the role of psychotherapy in dealing with stress?

COMMONALITIES AMONG ASIAN THEORIES OF PERSONALITY AND PSYCHOTHERAPY

Before describing the individual Asian psychotherapies, I examine the commonalities among the various approaches. Reynolds (1982) has described the Asian psychotherapies as the "quiet therapies," primarily because clients spend so much time in isolation with their thoughts. The Asian perspective uses principles from Buddhist and Chinese meditation in its practice. Asian psychotherapies focus on clients' attention and awareness, use meditation, and stress the importance of enlightenment.

In general, Asian approaches to therapy focus on clients' engaging in the process of self- and other understanding. In this respect, Asian approaches are very similar to existential approaches to therapy. Moreover, Asian therapies tend to emphasize and respect social relationships. They de-emphasize the individual and stress the value of the whole of humanity. Individuals are viewed within the context of the families and the communities in which they live. Western family therapists are most similar to the Asian therapists in their emphasis on family rather than on individuals (Reynolds, 1982).

In addition, Asian therapies use meditation to achieve a number of levels of awareness (Wilber & Walsh, 2000). In most Western theories of psychotherapy, the focus is on two levels of awareness: the unconscious level and the conscious level. Clients can observe their own thoughts and feelings through the process of meditation (Walsh, 2000). As one meditates, one is able to reach a higher level of consciousness and therefore distance oneself from the hold of one's issues.

Asian approaches to therapy stress the importance of enlightenment and freedom from fears and anxieties (Reynolds, 1982). Buddhism maintains that it is important not to be controlled by fears, dependencies, and anxieties, and it is frequently used to fight alcoholism and drug addiction.

Influence of Buddha and Buddhist Principles of Living

Asian philosophers (Buddha, Confucius, and others) have had a profound influence on the psychological development of individuals across Asia. At the heart of most Asian approaches to therapy is the practice of Buddhist meditation, an integral part of the Buddhist philosophy. It is used as a way not only to get in touch with one's inner self but also to develop insight and wisdom. In *Buddhism: The Illustrated Guide*, Trainor (2004) points out that there are more than 350 such meditation centers in Britain, while Bauman (1999) estimated that in the mid-1990s, there were 3 to 4 million Buddhists and 500 to 600 Buddhist centers in the United States and more than 1,000 meditation centers throughout North America.

Siddhārtha Gautama was a spiritual teacher from ancient India who is considered to be the founder of Buddhism. In most Buddhist traditions, he is regarded as the Supreme Buddha. *Buddha* means "awakened one" or "enlightened one." The time of his birth and death are uncertain. Most

Bronze statue of Buddha

Medioimages/Photodisc/ThinkStock.

20th-century historians date his lifetime as ca. 563 BCE to ca. 483 BCE.

The Four Noble Truths and the Eightfold Path

Buddhist teachings focus on Four Noble Truths and the Eightfold Path. These truths and path were taught by the Buddha about 2,500 years ago. They are essentially the same through every sect and tradition of Buddhism. The Four Noble Truths are as follows:

1. *Life means suffering:* To live means to suffer, because both human nature and the world we live in are not perfect. Each of us will have to endure physical suffering such as pain, sickness, injury, tiredness, old age, and eventually death, and likewise, we have to endure psychological suffering like sadness, fear, frustration, disappointment, and depression.

2. *The origin of suffering is attachment:* We suffer because we become attached to transient things. Transient things include the physical objects that surround us, ideas, and all objects of our perception. Our minds are attached to impermanent things. The reasons for suffering are desire, passion, pursuit of wealth and prestige, and striving for fame and popularity, or, in short, *craving* and *clinging.*

3. *The cessation of suffering is attainable:* The cessation of suffering can be attained through *nirodha,* which means the unmaking of sensual craving and conceptual attachment. Suffering can be ended by attaining dispassion. Nirodha extinguishes all forms of clinging and attachment. Suffering can be overcome through human activity and by not wanting things and by perfecting dispassion. Attaining and perfecting dispassion is a process that ultimately results in the state of *Nirvana,* which means freedom from all worries, troubles, complexes, fabrications, and ideas.

4. *The path to the cessation of suffering involves a gradual path of self-improvement:* It is the middle point between the two extremes of excessive self-indulgence (hedonism) and excessive self-mortification (asceticism), and it leads to the end of the cycle of rebirth. The path to the end of suffering can extend over many lifetimes, throughout which every individual's rebirth is subject to karmic conditioning.

The principles of the Eightfold Path provide the way to end suffering (Walsh, 1999a):

1. *Right understanding:* Learning the nature of reality and the truth about life

2. *Right aspiration:* Making the commitment to living in such a way that our suffering can end

3. *Right effort:* Just doing it; no excuses

4. *Right speech:* Speaking the truth in a helpful and compassionate way

5. *Right conduct:* Living a life consistent with our values

6. *Right livelihood:* Earning a living in a way that doesn't hurt others

7. *Right mindfulness:* Recognizing the value of the moment; living where we are

8. *Right concentration:* Expanding our consciousness through meditation

These Buddhist teachings have influenced thinking in India, China, and Japan for more than 2,000 years (Reynolds, 1989a; Walsh, 2001). Although many people associate Buddha with China, Buddhism was brought from India to China. In China, Buddhist teachings were merged with Confucius's values and teachings. During the 6th century, the writings of Buddha and Confucius were introduced in Japan.

Buddhist Principles and Values

- The greatest achievement is selflessness.
- The greatest worth is self-mastery.
- The greatest quality is seeking to serve others.

- The greatest precept is continual awareness.
- The greatest medicine is the emptiness of everything.
- The greatest action is not conforming with the world's ways.
- The greatest magic is transmuting the passions.
- The greatest generosity is nonattachment.
- The greatest goodness is a peaceful mind.
- The greatest patience is humility.
- The greatest effort is not concerned with results.
- The greatest meditation is a mind that lets go.
- The greatest wisdom is seeing through appearances.

Example of Japanese art

JAPANESE APPROACHES TO PSYCHOTHERAPY

The Japanese have made a number of contributions to the development of psychotherapy. This section considers only two of the most popular and best-known Japanese approaches to psychotherapy: Naikan therapy and Morita therapy. If there is any overriding theme in Japanese psychotherapy, it is that life is a matter of attention—that is, what you place your attention on and what you withdraw your attention from. If you focus your attention on anxiety-provoking thoughts, you will become anxious. If you focus your attention on depressive thoughts, you will become depressed. As Shoma Morita, the founder of the Japanese school of Morita therapy said, "Neurosis is misdirected attention."

Zen Buddhism influenced Japanese approaches to psychotherapy because it emphasized the practice of meditation to gain wisdom and self-understanding. Zen Buddhism places a high value on experiential knowledge as opposed to theoretical knowledge. As a result of the influence of Zen Buddhism, Japanese approaches to psychotherapy increase individuals' gaining self-awareness through meditation and by examining their life experiences.

Naikan Psychotherapy

Ishin Yoshimoto, the founder of **Naikan therapy**, defined "the Naikan" as the way to explore your real self (Yoshimoto, 1983). In the Japanese language, *Nai* means "inner" or "inside," and *kan* means "looking." Therefore, another definition of *Naikan* is "to look within yourself." A more poetic translation of the word *Naikan* is "seeing oneself with the mind's eye." According to Ishii (2010), a master or an expert in practicing Naikan, Yoshimoto once said,

> I'm not the first person who placed emphasis on looking into oneself, which is an old human tradition. From ancient times, many sages such as Buddha and Socrates have emphasized the importance of looking into oneself. I have just given shape to one particular method of introspection.

Naikan psychotherapy is a structured method of self-reflection that helps individuals understand themselves, their relationships, and the fundamental nature of their human existence. One goal of Naikan therapy is to increase awareness of oneself and to accept life, oneself, and others without judgment. As a result of the Naikan process, individuals come to realize that they have responsibility for how they relate to other people and their environments. Individuals who practice Naikan therapy report that they are able to let go of guilt and self-defeating behaviors that accompany a self-centered life. The therapist's primary role is to guide the client during his or her introspection and recollections. Another goal of Naikan therapy is to help clients recognize their responsibility to the people in their lives.

Major Contributor: Ishin Yoshimoto (1916–1988)

Ishin (birth name Inobu) Yoshimoto was born as the third boy of five children in the Yamatokoriyama city, Nara Prefecture, on May 25, 1916 (Maeshiro, 2008). Ihachi, his father, was a fertilizer distributor. During his junior high days, Inobu studied calligraphy, and he used the name of Ishin as a pen name.

Yoshimoto was deeply religious and a follower of Jodo Shinshu Buddhism, which emphasized the love and self-sacrifice of Buddha. Followers could achieve happiness by accepting life the way it is and by giving joyously to others. Spiritual training involved introspective meditation and fasting. At age 21, and for most of his young adult years, Yoshimoto attempted a very difficult, somewhat secretive Buddhist practice called *mishirabe*, which entailed going into a cave and meditating on life for days without food, water, or sleep (Maeshiro, 2009).

Initially, Yoshimoto failed three times to effectuate the mishirabe approach. After the fourth attempt, he succeeded in mastering the art. The net result of Yoshimoto's experience was that he wanted to bring to the general public a method of self-reflection that would keep some of the characteristics of mishirabe but not be as dangerous or arduous. In 1941, Yoshimoto refined mishirabe and renamed it Naikan.

In 1953, Yoshimoto opened his first Naikan center in Nara (Maeshiro, 2009). Originally, the Naikan method was an ascetic method used to achieve enlightenment. It was not until 1965 that it began to attract attention throughout the world. In 1978, the first annual meeting of the Naikan Association was held in Nara. In 1980, the first Naikan seminar was held in Austria. In 1985, the Naikan Training Institute Association was established.

In 1988, Ishin Yoshimoto passed away at the age of 73. Since then, Naikan therapy has spread throughout the world and made its home within the United States. Currently, Naikan therapy is practiced by a small number of American psychotherapists. It has a universal appeal regarding individuals' relationships with each other.

Key Concepts of Naikan Therapy

For decades, Naikan therapy in Japan has been used as a therapeutic approach for dealing with conflict resolution in the workplace, in marriage counseling, in addiction counseling, and in prison therapy. It has been estimated that 60% of the prison facilities in Japan have used Naikan. Prison officials have stated that those inmates who received Naikan had a lower recidivism rate than those who received either another treatment or no treatment at all (Reynolds, 1982).

Similar to most Asian psychotherapies, Naikan focuses on the existential and transpersonal levels of human existence, with little attention directed toward the pathological. Buddhism teaches that it is a waste of time to be preoccupied with one's condition. When one focuses on a problem, one becomes attached to that problem. According to Buddha, life should be lived simply and practically, with an individual accepting events and circumstances as they take place. The Buddhist lesson is that people should live their lives like water, which always flows around objects and which does not try to fight rocks or other obstacles. "Live life simply" is the Buddhist mantra.

Japanese culture tends to hold that personal problems and dissatisfactions are often the result of the discrepancy between a person's actual self and his or her ideal self or the difference between what one is and what one wants to be. In contrast, Western approaches to psychotherapy tend to emphasize problem development.

Theoretical Basis of Naikan Therapy

Buddhism forms the theoretical basis of Naikan. Buddhism emphasizes self-discipline or self-control, especially control related to one's physical body. Naikan is also closely connected to meditation. It uses meditation to (a) give insight into self-defeating behaviors, (b) retrain the client's attention, and (c) produce positive feelings within the body.

Naikan therapy is practiced by both mentally healthy and mentally unhealthy people. For some individuals, the therapy is used as a spiritual practice, a practice designed to help a person acquire self-understanding or self-improvement. Other individuals use Naikan therapy to treat various human conditions, including marital conflict, alcohol dependence, juvenile delinquency, school truancy, neurosis, and a number of other problems. Clients assume responsibility for how they have polluted their relationships, their bodies, and the environment.

The Therapeutic Process of Naikan Therapy

During his life, Ishin Yoshimoto began a successful leather company. His experiences with the leather company, especially the principle of income and expenditure, led him to develop the three questions that have become the cornerstone of Naikan therapy.

The Naikan therapeutic process shares some similarities with psychoanalysis. In psychoanalysis, the therapist might say to a client, "Please talk freely during this 1-hour session. Don't try to edit whatever comes to your mind. Instead, mention anything that comes to your mind, even if seems silly." In Naikan therapy, the Naikan-sha (the Japanese terminology for a person undergoing this form of introspection) stays 6 or 7 nights at a center and reflects and examines himself or herself intensively. The therapeutic process involves having a client deal with Yoshimoto's three basic questions:

1. What has a specific person done for me?

2. What have I done for this person?

3. What troubles and difficulties have I caused this person?

Whereas a great deal of Western psychotherapy is intended to help people feel better about themselves, in Naikan, the goal is not necessarily to help the client feel better. The purpose of Naikan is to help clients see the truth of their lives—wherever that takes them.

Used creatively, the three questions can shed light on the hidden features of our relationship to all things. Naikan is ultimately dedicated to the truth. The three questions provide a foundation for reflection on our relationships with significant others in our lives, including our parents, partners, friends, teachers, siblings, children, work associates, and acquaintances. We can reflect on ourselves in relationship to our pets and our professions, or even objects that serve us such as cars, homes, and so on. In each of these cases, we search for a realistic rather than a self-centered view of our conduct and of the give-and-take that has taken place within the relationship.

Question 1: What has a specific person done for me? In general, we remember things we did not receive from our significant others. My mother worked, and she did not give me enough love. My father deserted us. We focus on those life events that did not conform to our expectations or the things that we lost. During the process of emphasizing what we missed, what was done wrong to us, and how we were mistreated, we do not pay sufficient attention to what we received or what we had. We become convinced that our world is mainly composed of what we did not get. This situation becomes particularly sensitive when we deal with our parents. More often than not, we blame our parents because they did not fulfill the expectations that we had projected onto them in our minds. Simply put, they failed to act in the manner that we desired or thought was appropriate for them to act toward us.

Ishii (2010) points out, for example, that mothers usually cook about 1,000 meals a year. A client once said to him, "My mother left us when I was 10 years old; therefore, she has done nothing for me." Ishii responded that the client's statement was not true if his mother had prepared three meals a day or 1,000 meals a year. If the mother stayed for 10 years, she most likely prepared 10,000 meals during that time. Clearly, the client had received

Some Naikan therapy requires participants to count all the diapers their caregivers changed for them.

Name the person who changed the most diapers for you. Then calculate the number of diapers this person most likely changed for you. What are your feelings toward this person? Do you have any feelings of gratitude toward this person?

something, even if his mother did not prepare 10,000 meals. By asking the first question regarding what the person has done for us, we get a more accurate and realistic picture of our lives.

The first question reminds us that we hurry through our day giving little attention to all the "little" things others are giving to us and that we are receiving (Krech, 2010). Very often, little things seem to be little because we are being supported, we take them for granted, and our attention is focused on other things. The Naikan approach raises the question, Which is a more appropriate way to live—to spend our lives with the mission of collecting what is owed to us or to go through life trying to repay our debt to others? As Krech (2010) has stated,

> As we list what we receive from another person we are grounded in the simple reality of how we have been supported and cared for. In many cases we may be surprised at the length or importance of such a list and a deeper sense of gratitude and appreciation may be naturally stimulated. Without such a conscious shift of attention to the myriad ways in which the world supports us, we risk our attention being trapped by only problems and obstacles, leaving us to linger in suffering and self-pity.

Question 2: What have I done for this person? This question is hard for some clients to answer. We may not recall immediately what we have done for our mother. A client might say, "I can remember making a sandwich for my mother," "I put my arm around her while she cried," "In second grade, I drew a picture for my mother," or "I saved up my money, and I bought my mother a Mother's Day card."

Question 3: What troubles and difficulties have I caused this person? This question concerns the hurt that we have caused others. Usually our hurtful memories are about things that others have done to us. Yet this Naikan question asks the client to consider the hurt he or she has caused others. It forces the client to accept responsibility for his or her actions. If we remember only the things that others have done to us, then we become entrapped victims. During Naikan, the therapist and the client examine their part in the relationship with a person from the past until the present or until the person has died.

The client or Naikan-sha is to answer these three questions about the significant people in his or her life, beginning with his or her mother, father, spouse, siblings, and continuing to others. The mother is usually the person with whom we form the closest relationship during our childhood. If the client did not live with his or her mother, he or she starts with the person who provided the most nurturing: a grandmother, a father, an older sister.

Naikan therapy is based on the underlying assumption that most of us practice looking outside at others. That is, we look through our value judgments; we engage in outer reflection. Because we engage in outer reflection, we cannot see ourselves. The process of inner reflection permits us to see ourselves. During the process of guided introspection, we examine relationships from which we suffer.

The Naikan process consists of two components: immersion and counseling.

Immersion

Immersion takes place in a temple or a center where the client can be isolated from others. They sleep and take meals alone; and they are required to undergo meditation training. Meditation is the primary therapeutic technique used, and it may last from 4:30 a.m. until 5:00 p.m. During the day, therapists visit clients at intervals of 1 to 2 hours to instruct them on meditation and to participate in dialogues with them. Therapists guide clients in introspection and dialogue by focusing on reoccurring life themes, such as dishonesty, negativity, or blaming.

Naikan therapists honor their clients' struggles by bowing to them when they enter the room and by continually reinforcing the clients' ability to solve their personal problems. For instance, the therapist opens the folding screen, bows his or her head to the floor before the client, and asks him or her the topic of the current meditation. This ritualized format symbolizes the therapist's humility as he or she prepares to listen to the client's confession.

The client's response is similarly in ritual form. He or she reports the person and time period of his or her recollections (Reynolds, 1982, p. 47). Typically, clients spend about 20% of their meditation on significant people who have given to them and on what they have returned to them. The vast majority of the time (60%) is spent on the trouble or inconveniences clients have caused their significant others.

The Naikan therapeutic process maintains that the traumas or failures of the past cannot be undone; however, clients' attitudes toward these traumas can be altered. Naikan therapy shares points of similarity with cognitive therapy in that the therapy process attempts to restructure clients' thinking, while at the same time providing a moral structure for living based on Buddha's ideal of giving (France, 2010).

If the Naikan therapy is scheduled for more than 1 week, clients discuss their ideas of past events, working from the earliest event to the present time. They discuss themes in their relationships while the therapists listen without comment, interpretation, or interruption. It is only after the therapists have gained an in-depth understanding of their clients' issues that they begin to interpret and to guide their clients' actions. Reynolds (1982) has stated that the therapist "directs the client away from abstract or vague descriptions of past events and personal suffering. The goal is [for clients to use] concrete statements about specific personal experiences" (p. 48).

Counseling

During the second phase, which is labeled *counseling*, clients come to see the therapist on a weekly or monthly basis and report on their activities and the progress of their meditation. Oftentimes, clients are asked to complete a journal to help structure the client–therapist interactions. The therapist may give homework assignments, which might consist of summaries of helping others and saying things that show appreciation to others. Naikan therapy can be as short as 1 day, 1 week, or several weeks.

Role of the Naikan Guide-Therapist

Naikan therapists function as guides. To become a Naikan guide, one must exemplify understanding, mindfulness, and deep respect. The role of guide is in direct contrast to the role assumed by many therapists who practice Western therapies. The two theoretical schools that tend to endorse the role of the therapist as a guide are existentialism and humanism (with an emphasis on person-centered counseling).

What are the tasks of a Naikan guide? First, Naikan guides are responsible for providing and maintaining a quiet setting that allows Naikan participants to engage in introspection undisturbed. The guides provide basic physical comforts necessary to engage in Naikan therapy—a room, a daily structure, meals, and anything else that may be needed during the stay, usually a week at the Naikan center. Second, Naikan guides give clients support during their process of introspection. Over the course of a day, a Naikan guide visits clients for a short interview about 8 or 10 times a day or about every 60 to 90 minutes. Interviews usually last for

> ### Inner Reflection
>
> When someone's had a traumatic experience and continually talks about and revisits that experience, it becomes the dominant event of his or her life. Naikan says that . . . it's *not* the dominant event of your life. It was one part of your life. (Krech, 2001, p. 7)

about 5 to 10 minutes. During a week or weekend retreat, Naikan guides are available for clients night and day. The Naikan guide asks, "What person and what period have you examined?" The Naikan participants answers, "I examined my relationship with _____ when I was _____ years old. One, I received _____ from her; two, I have done _____ for her; three, I caused her difficulties by _____." The Naikan guide responds, "Thank you very much. Next, please reflect on your relationship with _____ when you were _____ years old."

At the beginning, Naikan guides just listen with all their attention. They neither judge nor criticize. The guide accepts whatever comes up as it is presented. Because the Naikan guides merely listen politely and carefully to the findings of clients, clients discover only those things that they have really come to think of themselves. They have not learned from anyone how to analyze; therefore, the introspective process is truly owned by them. Ishii (2010) has summarized what he considers some of the benefits of Naikan therapy:

Inner Reflections
Could you see yourself working as a Naikan therapist?
What specifically do you like or dislike about the role of a Naikan therapist?

> By doing Naikan, we see ourselves so clearly, that we cannot destroy this realistic picture of ourselves anymore; consequently, the discrepancy between the realistic self and the ideal, which we take to be the ultimate goal, dissolves. Since this discrepancy is being dissolved, we lose our hatred for ourselves, our inferiority complexes, our negative feelings of guilt. . . . The more we discover in the course of Naikan how much we had, the happier we become.
>
> In the long run, we determine ourselves whether we are happy or not. The question is whether we feel happy right now or not. Collecting examples of what others have done for us means to collect proofs of happiness. Therefore, Naikan is the search for happiness. . . . To look for and find the cherry blossoms in one's own garden, that is Naikan. (p. 10)

Role of the Naikan Client

Traditionally, the Naikan client sits in the corner of the room, walled off by a folding screen (in Japanese, a *byobu* screen). Using a byobu makes it easier for clients to observe themselves because it cuts off visual stimulation from the outside. While sitting in a quiet place and remaining in a relaxed position, clients look inside themselves from 6:00 a.m. to 9:00 p.m. Clients examine carefully how they have lived and who they are. Practicing Naikan means pausing for a day or a week to make a stop in the flow of time and to see life from another side. This procedure helps clients let go of their worries. As clients get rid of their worries, they become happier, and so do the people around them.

Naikan Therapy Techniques

Naikan therapy requires that the guide-therapist have excellent interviewing skills. The golden skill for Naikan therapy is listening, listening, and listening, without commenting or interrupting the client to insert one's own thoughts or feelings about the client's life. The Naikan guide must also be skillful in the use of techniques such as rephrasing, recasting, and reflecting the client's ideas. The Naikan therapist must understand how to help a client focus on and clarify the three questions for his or her life.

Research and Evaluation of Naikan Therapy

Theory Integration With Naikan Therapy and Western Therapy Models

Naikan therapy offers potential points of theory integration with psychoanalysis, existentialism, behavior therapy, and cognitive therapy. Both psychoanalysis and Naikan emphasize the importance of early childhood and family relationships. The differences can be observed along issues such as transference and countertransference, neither of which is stressed in Naikan therapy. Existentialism and Naikan therapy are similar in that both theories deal with the spiritual aspects of people—coming to terms with themselves and their responsibilities in life.

In addition, Naikan therapy has points of commonalities with behavior therapy. Clients learn how to use meditation to gain more control over their anxieties and emotion. Both Naikan and behavior therapy have the goal of self-control, and both have the same objective of teaching clients new behaviors and reducing the gap between the real self and the ideal self. They differ in that behaviorism emphasizes using the technique of counterconditioning, while Naikan therapy stresses the importance of insight to behavior. In contrast to Western psychoanalytic psychotherapy, Naikan keeps transference issues simplified and positive, while resistance is dealt with procedurally rather than interpretively. Naikan shares similarities with cognitive therapy in that therapy is designed to help clients develop more realistic thoughts about their past and present living circumstances. Their lives may not be as horrible as they state. In reality, their lives have patches of blue.

Benefits and Limitations of Naikan Therapy

Naikan therapy has multidimensional effects on individuals. People choose Naikan because they want to understand themselves better, they want to understand others better, they desire to find a solution to a difficult situation (marital problems, addiction issues, or work issues), and they desire to change something in their lives in order to find happiness. Naikan is a method used to explore one's inner self. It helps individuals find peace with things that took place in the past and develop inner peace under any adverse circumstances. American psychotherapy has an "I" focus. Naikan therapy forces the therapist and the client to focus on others. Through Naikan, individuals get in touch with their spirituality. Even though Naikan has its roots in Buddhism, it has no religious content. Whatever your chosen religion, Naikan can be used to deepen your faith. Naikan shows you how your spirituality influences your everyday life. Naikan increases individuals' sense of gratitude toward others and life.

As a therapeutic approach, Naikan therapy has several strengths. First, it takes the focus away from "I" and places onto "you, it, they, them, environment." Instead of interpreting clients' issues for them, therapists permit clients to come to their own meanings. Second, the use of meditation can be carried over for nontherapy purposes. Third, Naikan is a short-term therapy and can be used for clients who have limited time and resources for therapy. On the other hand, a major limitation of Naikan therapy is the amount of time spent in immersion. Few people may have the resources to take off work or other responsibilities for a week at a Naikan retreat.

An Example of Naikan Therapy

France (2010) has provided a brief case example using Naikan within a Western context. The case example does not involve the immersion or retreat format for Naikan. A 35-year-old man came to her because he was having difficulty coming to grips with a relationship breakup with a woman. He engaged in counseling because he wanted to reduce stress and to overcome a blue feeling. He said that he was still angry even after expressing his anger. He felt stuck. The therapist explained Naikan to Mr. M. Shortly thereafter, Mr. M shared his feelings for more than an hour. The therapist listened and asked only clarifying questions. Mr. M reported difficulties with his work colleagues.

The Naikan guide taught Mr. M the skill of meditation. Mr. M practiced it for some time and subsequently mastered meditation. The guide then focused on significant relationships, both positive and negative, in his life. Mr. M chose to focus on a work colleague who had treated him unfairly. Instead of focusing on the negative aspects of their relationship, the Naikan guide asked Mr. M to focus on what he had learned in the encounter with that person. After two 1-hour sessions, Mr. M reported that he was surprised at what he had learned. He reported that he had become more aware of little kindnesses of acquaintances and he had become much closer to his family. The guide used the following format to explore the themes in Mr. M's life:

- Therapist guidance on exploring the life theme developed during meditation
- Mr. M's meditation for 1 hour on the topic, dialoguing the messages raised during meditation in a journal, and sharing of the messages with the therapist

Eventually, Mr. M reported greater happiness in his life as he became more aware of the many little things that others did for him on a daily basis.

Naikan challenges individuals to cultivate love through gratitude and an honest self-examination of their own conduct toward others. Gregg Krech (2010) uses Naikan to deal with relationships. According to him, his Naikan relationship program is not about "expressing feelings of anger," nor is it about "getting the love you want." It is about becoming the best partner you can be. Some of the tips he gives for fulfilling relationships are as follows:

- Stop focusing on how your partner needs to change and channel your energy into what you can do differently.
- Shift your attention away from how much you're giving and toward what you receive and the ways in which you cause trouble for your partner.
- Try to put yourself in your partner's shoes. What is it like for him or her to be in this relationship with you?

Morita Therapy

Morita therapy is a Japanese psychotherapy that was developed by the psychiatrist Shoma Morita during the late 1910s and 1920s (Morita, 1974). The therapeutic approach has its foundations in the Eastern philosophy of maintaining a balanced lifestyle (Chen, 2005). Originally, Morita therapy was developed for clients suffering from anxiety and nervousness—what is called *shinkeishitsu* in Japanese. Since the late 1970s,

Morita therapy has received considerable attention from Western therapists.

Major Contributor:
Shoma Morita (1874–1938)

Shoma Morita is perhaps Japan's most famous psychiatrist. Although his real first name was Masatake, he was nicknamed Shoma, and he used this nickname whenever he signed his name in English. Shoma was born in 1874 as the eldest son of a carpenter father. His father was quite strict, but his mother spoiled him, and Shoma became very attached to her. During his elementary years, Shoma was said to be very nervous. When he was a child, Shoma manifested a number of problems, including insomnia, enuresis, truancy, and failing at school. Shoma suffered from neurasthenia (neurosis or anxiety disorder) for most of his early and later childhood.

Morita's father taught him Chinese philosophy, and in high school, he became interested in Buddhism. Initially, Morita wanted to become a philosopher, but he changed his mind.

At the age of 25, Shoma entered the Tokyo Imperial University Medical School in 1899, where he specialized in psychiatry. Shoma experienced difficulties in college, and for a brief time, he felt that he was going to repeat the same year. A friend encouraged him. As a result, he studied hard despite his neurotic symptoms and did well on his final exams. After experiencing success with his final exams, Shoma realized that his symptoms had disappeared. This realization played a key role in his subsequent development of Morita therapy. On his graduation from medical school in 1902, Morita became actively involved in the treatment of neurasthenia.

From 1925 to 1937, Morita served as a professor of Jikei University School of Medicine. Because at the time there were no effective treatments for neurasthenia, Morita made trials and errors. While teaching at Jikei Medical School, Morita took several neurotic patients to live in his home. After living at Morita's home for a month in a highly structured manner, one of the patients, an acquaintance of Morita, recovered from his neurasthenia.

Morita suffered from neurotic symptoms throughout his life. He died in 1938 at the age of 65. Near his death, he is reported to have told his followers that he still desperately wanted to live, and he admonished them not to treat him as if he would not make it (Maruyama, 1991). Similar to the other theorists discussed in this book, Morita's approach developed partly out of his own creative desire to deal with his issues and problems.

Initially, Morita called his therapeutic approach "home therapy," "natural therapy," and "awareness therapy." As a result of publishing an article about his approach in a German medical journal, in 1937, the approach was termed *Morita therapy*. The residential treatment method that Morita had initiated became a standard clinical intervention format of Morita therapy. Today, instead of the residential treatment taking place in a therapist's home, Morita therapy is practiced in institutional settings such as hospital, therapeutic residences, and treatment centers (Fujita, 1986; Goto, 1988; Reynolds, 1976).

Morita therapy has gained much popularity in Japan, and it has been introduced gradually to the Western world (Watanabe, 1992). During the 1980s and 1990s, Morita therapy became one of the few well-recognized and well-respected and influential Eastern approaches recognized not only in North America but throughout the world (Chen, 2005). Morita's followers have extended the use of his approach to work with people who are terminally ill with cancer.

Key Concepts of Morita Therapy

Over the years, Morita therapy has continued to develop and become much more integrated than the original model (Chen, 1996). As with many Asian therapies, Morita therapy was influenced by Zen Buddhist and other Eastern perspectives on life (Kondo, 1992). The Chinese philosophy of yin and yang forms a significant part of Morita therapy. Yin/yang refers to the Chinese idea that to maintain a healthy mental state, we must adopt the right attitude and be in harmony with the world (Chen, 2005).

Arugamama

Morita's approach was not so much to get rid of the problem as it was to help people focus on living life fully. In most Western cultures, feelings drive most people's actions. In contrast, Morita believed that there was no need to try to change or fix clients' thoughts and feelings. Instead, we should accept reality as it is. **Arugamama** refers to the naturalness of feelings and to the acceptance of reality as it is. For instance, if we feel depressed, we should accept our feelings of depression. If we feel anxious, we accept our feelings of anxiety. How does one live with depression or anxiety? Morita believed that we should set goals and take steps to accomplish what is important, even as we coexist with unpleasant feelings such as depression or anxiety. For instance, if you are anxious about your final exams, Morita would interpret such anxiety as reflecting your *Seinoyokubou* (your desire to life fully). Morita would advise you to continue studying, even though you feel anxious. This position is based on the assumption that we cannot control our feelings, but we can control our behavior.

> **Inner Reflections**
>
> What do you feel anxious about?
>
> How do you deal with your feelings of anxiety?
>
> What does your anxiety about a situation tell you about how you feel about that situation?

Feelings Are Uncontrollable

An underlying assumption of many Western therapeutic methods is that it is necessary to change or modify our feeling state before we can take action. Western therapists tend to maintain that we must overcome fear, for instance, to ask a girl for a date. Morita asserted that it is not necessary to change our feelings in order to take action. On the contrary, our efforts to change our feelings make us feel worse about a situation. Take the necessary action, and our feelings will follow in the manner that we want. The Morita approach to feelings is in direct contrast to Western psychotherapy, which is founded on an assumption of the primary role and importance of feelings. Morita saw emotions and feelings as only a part of the human condition rather than the primary focus of life.

Self-Centeredness and Suffering

Morita therapy contends that we are overly preoccupied with ourselves. The more that we pay attention to our symptoms (anxiety, depression, etc.), the bigger the symptoms loom in our lives. We do not become cured by the alleviation of discomfort but rather by taking constructive action that helps us live life fully. Focus on the things that can be done in a given moment. In Morita therapy, clients learn to accept their emotions, to maintain fluid awareness, and to shift from a feelings-governed to an action-based and purpose-oriented life. Morita proposed the following three ideas about emotions:

1. *Accept your feelings because they are a natural part of life:* Although feelings can provide valuable information about our environment, they do not necessarily provide an accurate view of the world. Acceptance of the current condition is the first step that leads to positive changes in life. This position is in stark contrast to most Western therapies that focus on conquering a situation—for instance, conquering your fears. Morita therapy offers a therapeutic approach that is less about conquering and more about coexisting with your concern. If you are anxious about a job interview, Morita therapy suggests going to the interview and taking your anxiety with you. Morita therapy suggests that we accept the presence of our demons and move forward anyway. By doing this, the demons lose their power.

2. *Know your purpose:* Place your attention on the world about you and establish short- and long-term goals. Find out what needs doing to achieve your goals.

3. *Do what needs doing:* Regardless of your emotional state, you are responsible for your behavior. Your actions will either benefit your purpose or work against it. Do not try to fix your feelings.

The Therapeutic Process of Morita Therapy

The Morita therapeutic process is structured. It consists of four stages, during which time the therapist functions as a guide. Morita emphasizes a client's development of practical and concrete steps to reality instead of the search for ultimate perfection or idealism. Within each of the stages, the therapist works to help a client achieve self-awareness and social responsibility.

Stage 1: Absolute Bed Rest. The client usually is placed in a center or retreat or placed in an institutional setting. This period lasts from four to seven days, depending on each client's needs. Clients are isolated from any social contacts and activities, and they are required to stay in bed all the time except for basic living activities, meals, showers, and so on. The Morita therapist asks the client to encounter the psychological problem. According to Chen (2005), "the intense bed rest aims to help the client recover from exhaustion caused by the inner psychic conflicts, inducing the client's spontaneous desire for action" (p. 225).

Stage 2: Light Work. After the client has completed absolute bed rest, he or she must participate in some form of light work for three to seven days. The client is not allowed to socialize with other people, and his or her sleeping time is limited to 7 or 8 hours per day. The client is encouraged to stay outside and to become involved in light work such as sweeping, raking leaves, and washing clothes. The work is completed in silence. The therapist gives lectures three times a week to the client. The goal of the second stage is to provide a transition from absolute rest to spontaneous activity. During this stage, the client's attention is drawn to action rather than to his or her symptoms. The client is encouraged to endure his or her symptoms as they are when he or she experiences them. The client participates in journal writing. The therapist provides guidance via the client's journal writing.

Stage 3: Intensive Work. Clients are required to do more intensive work, such as gardening, carpentry, and farming. Morita called this stage the "chopping woods stage." Clients begin healing themselves through a strength-oriented physical therapy program. During this stage, clients are permitted to interact with others. The rationale behind the strenuous work is that the more time the client spends in these living tasks, the more confident he or she becomes that he or she can lead a productive life. The timeline varies for how long each person remains in Stage 3.

Stage 4: Preparation for Daily Living. The last stage of Morita therapy is a preparation for clients to return to society. Morita would send clients outside the hospital setting. Although the time for this stage varies, it usually lasts for about 10 days. One goal is to help clients reintegrate into their nontreatment worlds. Clients are permitted to go out of the hospital site to take care of practical issues, such as visiting friends or families so that they can gradually adjust to the real work situation again. They apply what they learned in the first three stages. The client learns to integrate a new lifestyle that consists of meditation, physical activity, more ordered living, and a renewed relationship with the natural world. Clients work on deciding their future steps, and they make arrangements to return to their world. By the time the client is discharged from the hospital or the retreat, he or she will be able to accept his symptoms as they are without resisting them.

Inner Reflections

What are your thoughts about the process of Morita therapy?

Would you host a retreat for your clients?

What ethical issues might surround Morita therapy in the United States?

An Example of Morita Therapy

In Reynolds's (1989b) edited book, Ishiyama provides a good case example of how outpatient Morita therapy works. Ms. V, a 40-year-old woman, is afraid to take her college exams. Ishiyama's description of the first half-hour is as follows:

> I explained her anxiety in terms of the desire for living fully: "Where there is a desire, there is anxiety about being unable to fulfill it. The intensity of your anxiety is an indication of the strength of your desire for meaningful academic accomplishment. Which would you choose, exhausting your energy trying to conquer anxiety or getting your studying done in spite of it?" She agreed that she would prefer to try the latter.
>
> At the end of the 30-minute session, I gave Ms. V the following set of instructions:
>
> 1. Accept fears and feelings as they come. Continue studying and abandon any attempts to change the feelings.
>
> 2. Acknowledge the anxiety when it appears and continue studying while experiencing it.
>
> 3. Notice the fine details of her anxiety. When she cannot get her mind off the anxiety, study it as she would any natural object. (p. 51)

Morita therapists use journal writing as a way to help clients keep track of the details of their progress. Ms. V was required to journal about her actions regarding test anxiety. In a subsequent interview, the active acceptance that the therapist had encouraged allowed her to stop the self-blame regarding

Inner Reflections

Could you see yourself functioning as a Moritist therapist?

To what extent do you agree or disagree with the Moritist view that we deal with anxiety and other feelings by working on another activity and by shifting our attention to our goals?

Are there any parts of this theoretical approach that you would integrate with your own approach to psychotherapy?

the exam. Gradually, she was able to shift her attention from critical self-evaluation and her search for perfectionism to objective self-observation.

CHINESE CONTRIBUTIONS TO PSYCHOTHERAPY: MINDFULNESS

Look deeply at life as it is in the very here and now.

—Samyutta Nikaya, cited in Bodhi (2002, p. 326)

Chinese contributions to mindfulness can be examined through the culture's involvement with Buddhism. Buddhism entered China from India during the first millennium. For the next 500 years, Buddhism became integrated into Chinese culture (Santee, 2007) and is considered one of the major cross-cultural events in recorded history. During a period of about 1,000 years, Chinese Buddhism was influenced by the philosophies of Daoism and Confucianism. According to Santee (2007),

> This cross-pollination, if you will, resulted in integrations that produced new schools of thought. . . . Daoism and Buddhism integrated to produce Chan Buddhism (6th–8th century CE). Chan Buddhism is probably better known by its Japanese counterpart and the pronunciation: Zen. (p. 9)

The Chinese built a cultural bridge that connected an Indian Buddhism perspective with the classical teachings of Daoism and Confucianism.

The Chinese character for mindfulness (Figure 13.1) consists of two idiograms: one is presence, and the other heart (Santorelli, 1999). The character means "bringing the heart into the present." Chinese culture emphasizes the importance of including heart qualities in the attentional part of mindfulness. Mindfulness is about waking up and connecting with your true self. According to Chinese Buddhism, Buddha taught that life is pain. The Chinese use mindfulness training to teach people the skills to be able to live and work well in spite of life's pain and frustration. They maintain that mindfulness is an awareness process that is guided by connecting with the present moment and detaching oneself from the pain of one's own thinking. Instead of struggling with our thoughts, we learn to hold them gently and to understand them for what they are—mere thoughts made up of words and physical pictures.

Moreover, Chinese mindfulness teaches acceptance—giving space to painful thoughts and feelings. We observe our thoughts from a space sometimes called our *observing self.* An important goal is to discover your values, what life means to you deep down inside. What are you living for, or what is your purpose in life?

Finally, Chinese mindfulness emphasizes committed action. Individuals adhere to the belief that nothing will work for us if we do not take committed action. For worthwhile changes to happen, you must make a concerted effort to produce the change (T'ai Shen Centre, n.d.).

Definition of Mindfulness

Mindfulness is one of the fastest-growing approaches to psychotherapy in the West. Within

Figure 13.1 Chinese Symbol for Mindfulness

Source: T'ai Shen Centre for Mindfulness, Happiness and Healing (n.d.).

the past 5 years, more than 40 books about it have been listed on Amazon.com. What is mindfulness? Should it be viewed as a new theory or as an *approach to being* that can be incorporated into many of the major theoretical approaches to psychotherapy?

Mindfulness has been described as a process of bringing a quality of attention to moment-by-moment experience (Kabat-Zinn, 2005). The technique for evoking mindfulness originates from Buddhist spiritual practices. However, as Shapiro and Carlson (2009) have noted,

> Although the concept of mindfulness is most often associated with Buddhism, its phenomenological nature is embedded in most religions and spiritual traditions as well as Western philosophical and psychological schools of thought. . . . In this work, we draw from the richness and wisdom of Buddhist teachings; however, our intention is to present mindfulness as universal human activity. (pp. 3–4)

Mindfulness is knowing the state of your mind at any given moment without judging it, trying to change it, or doing anything about it (Shapiro & Carlson, 2009). According to Buddha,

> Feelings are understood as they arise, understood as they remain present, understood as they pass away. Thoughts are understood as they arise, understood as they remain present, understood as they pass away. Perceptions are understood as they arise, understood as they remain present, understood as they pass away. (Samyutta Nikaya 47:35, as cited in Bodhi, 2002)

Mindfulness may be defined as a kind of nonelaborative, nonjudgmental, present-oriented awareness in which each thought, feeling, or sensation that arises in the attentional field is acknowledged and accepted as it is (Kabat-Zinn, 2005; Segal et al., 2002). When clients are in a state of mindfulness, their thoughts and feelings are observed as events in the mind, without overidentifying with them and without reacting to them. This dispassionate state of self-observation creates a "space" between one's perception and response.

Mindfulness begins with the breath. The breath relates to the Chinese Daoist teachings of simplicity, beginning points, commonalities, and endings. As Santee (2007) has stated,

> The act of breathing is quite simple. The breath, which is impermanent, nonsubstantial, and interdependent, is the very basis of life. At birth, life begins with the first breath. At death, life ends with the last breath. Breathing is common to all human beings. It is with the breath that mindfulness begins. (p. 106)

"Mindfulness has to be experienced to be known" (Germer, Siegel, & Fulton, 2005, p. 8). Mindfulness brings awareness to one's current experience—observing and attending to the changing field of thoughts, feelings, and sensations from moment to moment—by regulating the focus of attention (Segal et al., 2002). Initially, the client is aware only of his or her breathing. Such awareness leads to a feeling of being very alert to what is taking place in the here-and-now. Mindfulness is not a practice that advocates thought suppression. All thoughts or experiences are viewed as objects of observation, not as distractions. Yet once a thought is acknowledged, attention is directed back to the breath, thereby preventing further elaboration on the thought. Hence, mindfulness practices are associated with switching attention and with improvements in cognitive inhibition, especially at the level of stimulus selection. In essence, mindfulness involves the self-regulation of attention, which involves sustained attention, attention switching, and inhibition of elaborative processing. To participate in mindfulness breathing, find a comfortable place to sit quietly. Your sitting posture should be relaxed yet upright and alert. Focus your attention on your breath as the primary object of your attention. Feel your breathing in and breathing out, the rise and fall of your abdomen, and the gentle caress of air as you exhale from your nostrils. Whenever something other than the breath arises in your awareness, note it, and then gently bring your mind back to breathing. If you have any reactions, such as enjoying what arose in your mind, or feeling irritated by some thoughts, simply note the enjoyment or irritation with kindness and again return to your breathing. Can you tap into the awareness inside of you that is always present?

Mindfulness is said to consist of two components: (1) a person gives focused attention on whatever he or she is experiencing (i.e., thoughts, emotions, or physical sensations) during the present moment and (2) an individual assumes a nonjudgmental stance of acceptance toward what he or she is experiencing in the present moment (Vujanovic, Youngwirth, Johnson, & Zvolensky, 2009). In psychotherapy, mindfulness is an approach for relaxation and for dealing with psychological distress. The underlying premise of mindfulness is that pain, whether emotional or physical, becomes worse when we try to avoid it, ignore it, or fight it. We can reduce our pain when we take note of it with no attempt to do anything about it. Our acceptance of our being in the world provides some distance from our distress. Therefore, we are not in pain, but rather, we are in a state of observing our pain—being mindful about it. Mindfulness is a way of being—a way of living, moment by moment.

Inner Reflections

Think about your most recent clinical experience.

Were you truly present with the client? If yes, what did you do that permitted you to be fully present with your client?

If not, what stopped you from being fully present with your client?

Key Concepts of Mindfulness

Mindfulness practice has a number of concepts. For this brief summary, only a few are described.

Intention, Attention, and Attitude

Mindfulness practice consists of three components: (1) intention, (2) attention, and (3) attitude. Buddhist teachings highlight **intention** as an important core of mindfulness (Shapiro & Carlson, 2009). As Kabat-Zinn (1990) has stated, "Your intentions set the stage for what is possible. They remind you from moment to moment of why you are practicing in the first place" (p. 32). Kabat-Zinn (2005) recommends that the person use personal vision with intention. He continues,

> I used to think that meditation practice was so powerful . . . that as long as you did it all, you would see growth and change. But time has taught me that some kind of personal vision is also necessary. (p. 46)

In addition to intention, mindfulness philosophy states that it is necessary to reflect on whether one's intentions are wholesome or unwholesome—to detriment or benefit. Mindfulness practice helps therapists and clients (a) bring unconscious values to awareness, (b) determine if they are really the values they want to have, and (c) develop wholesome values while decreasing unwholesome ones. The American Psychological Association (2002), for instance, has articulated clear intentions and values in that the organization has stated that it is committed to relieve suffering, do no harm, and cultivate compassion. Intention itself is not a goal. Instead, it is a general direction that one wants to take.

Attention is the second major component of mindfulness (Shapiro & Carlson, 2009). It should be noted that attention is critical to most Asian therapies. Paying attention means that a person observes on a moment-to-moment basis his or her internal and external experiences. The mindfulness approach to psychotherapy views attention as critical to healing. Clients learn how to cultivate their attention so that it is discerning and nonreactive.

Inner Reflections

What is your intention right now as you read this chapter?

When you go home tonight, notice what your intention is.

Try to connect with your deeper intention for wanting to become a therapist.

Attitude is the third component of the mindfulness model of psychotherapy. You must bring certain qualities to attention—for instance, curiosity, openness, acceptance, and love. Sometimes a person might bring a critical attitude to attention. An appropriate attitude for mindfulness practice is one that is nonjudging, a kind of impartial witnessing; nonstriving, meaning remaining unattached to the outcome or achievement; accepting, meaning seeing and acknowledging things as they are in the present moment; patience, allowing things to unfold in their time; and trust, developing a basic trust in your experience. As Kabat-Zinn (1990) has stated, "The attitude with which you undertake the practice of paying attention . . . is crucial. . . . Keeping particular attitudes in mind is actually part of the training itself" (pp. 31–32). Clients are taught how to intentionally bring attitudes such as patience, compassion, and nonstriving to therapy.

The Therapeutic Process of Mindfulness

Shapiro and Carlson (2009) make the argument that mindfulness awareness is fundamental to all therapy and that cultivating mindfulness can help therapists better relate to their clients. According to Germer et al. (2005), mindfulness is "a crucial ingredient in the therapy relationship, and as a technology for psychotherapists to cultivate personal therapeutic qualities" (p. 9). The practitioners propose three ways that therapists can integrate mindfulness into psychotherapy. They label their approach *mindfulness-oriented psychotherapy*. First, a therapist can integrate mindfulness into his or her clinical practice through the personal practice of mindfulness meditation. This first way is termed *therapist mindfulness*. The second way in which mindfulness

> ### Inner Reflection
>
> When you go home tonight, notice how well you pay attention to those who talk with you.

can be incorporated into psychotherapy is through the application of a theoretical frame of reference that is informed by theories and research about mindfulness and Buddhist psychology. Germer et al. called this integration route *mindfulness-informed psychotherapy*. The third way to integrate mindfulness into your practice is to teach clients mindfulness skills and practices to increase their own mindfulness—a process Germer et al. labeled *mindfulness-based psychotherapy*.

Role of the Mindfulness Therapist

Several researchers have suggested that mindfulness is a common factor that cuts across all successful therapeutic encounters, regardless of the therapist's theoretical orientation (Germer et al., 2005; Martin, 1997). Anderson (2005) has recommended that therapists in training programs should be given meditation training so that they can develop core clinical skills. He believed that such training would equip beginning therapists with skills that would strengthen the therapeutic relationship. Shapiro and Carlson (2009) have suggested that the following therapist characteristics would be enhanced if training were provided in meditation: (a) therapist attention capacity, (b) therapist attitudes during therapy, (c) therapist self-attunement and self-compassion, (d) therapist empathy and attunement toward the client, and (e) therapist emotional regulation and handling of countertransference.

Attention and Therapist Presence. A therapist's ability to pay attention to and sustain attention is critical to effective therapeutic practice. For instance, Sigmund Freud advised clinicians to apply "an evenly hovering attention" to the therapy session, and Fritz Perls commented that "attention in and of itself is curative." If a therapist cannot sustain attention during therapy, it is difficult to develop a therapeutic relationship with a client. Many of us have had experiences when the person we were talking with was not listening attentively. Most of us have the capacity to be mindfully present with another person. For a therapist, it is important to deepen this capacity and to be able to do so reliably.

Research studies suggest that the ability to focus attention and to sustain this focus on a chosen object may develop with greater mindfulness practice (Shapiro & Carlson, 2009). Therefore, therapists can improve their mindfulness attention with sufficient practice. A qualitative interview study (McCartney, 2004) was conducted with experienced therapists who practiced mindfulness. Therapists were given the question, "How does having a personal mindfulness meditation practice influence the therapists' ability to be present with clients in the therapeutic relationship?" The therapists stated that being in the moment involved developing a still and quiet place within themselves where they felt centered, calm, and peaceful. In another qualitative study with counseling graduate students, Schure, Christopher, and Christopher (2008) found that students who had mindfulness training reported they were more attentive in the therapy session. Mindfulness meditation helped students develop skills in paying close attention to the client. Researchers in the studies concluded that mindfulness practice is one systemic approach for cultivating attention and presence in therapists.

Preliminary evidence seems to support the view that therapist mindfulness training has a positive impact on the therapeutic relationship. A series of studies by Grepmair and colleagues in Germany examined therapist training in mindfulness and client outcome. In the first study, Grepmair, Mitterlehner, Loew, and Nickel (2007) examined the outcomes of 196 patients treated by therapists in training who were or were not practicing Zen meditation. The researchers reported that those patients whose therapists were practicing meditation had better self-reported outcomes on measures of understanding of their own psychodynamics, difficulties, and goals. Those patients also reported making better progress in dealing with their difficulties.

A second study randomly assigned 18 therapists in training to either learn Zen meditation or to a control group that had training as usual (Grepmair, Mitterlehner, Loew, Bachler, et al.,

2007). The therapists in training in the Zen group practiced meditation with a Zen master daily on weekdays for 1 hour throughout the study. Patients were unaware of what type of training their therapists had. Overall, patients whose therapists trained in Zen meditation said they better understood their own psychodynamics and characteristics of their difficulties. Patients who were treated by therapists in the Zen meditation group evidenced greater improvement related to their symptoms. That is, they reported few symptoms of anxiety and depression, hostility, compulsions, and so on.

Therapist Attitudes and Mindfulness. The manner in which therapists pay attention can be critical to the success of therapy. Kabat-Zinn (1990) indicates that some of the most helpful mindfulness attitudes are nonattachment, acceptance, letting go, nonstriving, nonjudging, patience, warmth, and friendliness. These attitudes enhance the therapeutic environment so that clients can feel safe enough to disclose their shameful pasts and thoughts. Martin (1997) has described the application of mindfulness in therapy as achieving a state in which "such attitudes as being right, controlling the situation, or maintaining therapist self-esteem give way to a quiet, limber, nonbiased and non-reactive response" (p. 299). Mindfulness experiences and training strengthen specific qualities in the therapist that are essential for a healing relationship.

Empathy and Attunement With Others. A number of researchers have posited empathy as a necessary condition for therapy (Arkowitz, 2002; Bohart, Elliott, Greenberg, & Watson, 2002). Carl Rogers (1957) defined empathy as the ability "to sense the [client's] private world as if it were your own, but without losing the 'as if' quality" (p. 95). Studies indicate that meditation can significantly improve empathy in therapists. Lesh (1970) reported that counseling psychology students evidenced significant increases in empathy after a Zen meditation intervention compared with a wait-list control group. The study measured empathy according to a student's ability to accurately assess the emotions expressed by a videotaped client.

More recent studies in mindfulness training for medical and premedical students showed that there were significant increases in empathy for the group that participated in Zen meditation training (Shapiro, Schwartz, & Bonner, 1998). In a related study, Shapiro, Brown, and Biegel (2007) found that counseling psychology students who were exposed to 8 weeks of training in mindfulness-based stress reduction improved significantly in empathic concern for others. These studies suggest that students exposed to meditation training are inclined to show greater empathy than those who have not been given such training.

Research in neurobiology has shed some light regarding how meditation may help therapists develop empathy. There is a neurological underpinning of empathy (di Pellegrino, Fadiga, Fogassi, Gallese, & Rizzolatti, 1992). Meditation may promote *mirror neurons*, which allow for the ability to create an image of the internal state of another's mind. Mirror neurons "ensure that the moment someone sees an emotion expressed on your face, they will at once sense that same feeling within themselves" (Goleman, 2006, p. 4). Neuroscience has discovered that "the ability to imagine another person's perspective and to empathize correlates with mirror neuron activity" (Siegel, 2007, p. 137). For instance, if a client is feeling sad, a therapist may feel sad. A therapist who has been trained in mindfulness is open to accurately sensing his or her environment, including the emotions present in the therapeutic setting.

Emotional Regulation. During psychotherapy, a therapist becomes a vessel that can hold a great deal of emotional content. Mindfulness training increases a therapist's ability to regulate himself or herself. As therapists become more capable of regulating their own emotional reactions, they become more capable of dealing with their clients' emotional issues. Formal training in mindfulness practices can assist therapists across a broad range of theoretical orientations to establish better therapeutic relationships with their clients. Shapiro and

Carlson (2009) suggest that at the beginning of each therapy session, it might be helpful for therapists "to connect with the breath and the body and to consciously form an intention to informally practice mindfulness throughout the therapeutic encounter" (p. 29). Therapists ground themselves in the present moment and acknowledge whatever emotions or physical sensations they find in themselves prior to therapy. Throughout the therapy session, therapists use intentional attending to better relate with their clients. Mindfulness practice offers systematic training for critical therapist skills. Such practice also helps therapists maintain their health and well-being.

> **Inner Reflection**
>
> How might you use mindfulness techniques to get you ready for a therapy session with a client?

Mindfulness and Mental Health

Mindfulness treats mental health disorders and problems as a form of suffering. The mindfulness approach maintains that suffering comes from one's reactions to and judgments about what is present as opposed to what is actually present. Shapiro and Carlson (2009) report a story about a teacher, his students, and a boulder:

> A teacher walking with his students points to a very large boulder and says, "Students, do you see that boulder?" The students respond, "Yes, teacher, we see the boulder." The teacher asks, "And is the boulder heavy?" The students respond, "Oh yes, very heavy." And the teacher replies, "Not if you don't pick it up." (pp. 5–6)

According to Shapiro and Carlson (2009), people are constantly trying to move the boulders out of their lives into places they believe that the boulders should be. Our reactions to the boulders in our lives create a great deal of suffering. Mindfulness offers a different way of being in the world. You recognize that there is a boulder in this very moment, and you don't like it. How does your body react to the boulder? Using a mindfulness approach, there is no need to change one's experience. One simply understands one's experience. Despite the fact that one accepts the presence of the boulder, it does not mean that one accepts unnecessary injustice or suffering.

Buddhist philosophy teaches that suffering stems from wanting things to be different from what they are. People try to change reality to fit their expectations and their desires. The struggle that ensues causes even more suffering. As Shapiro and Carlson (2009) have stated,

> Mindfulness is an antidote to this suffering. It is a way of being with all of one's experience. It allows whatever arises to be here, which makes sense because it already *is* here. As noted earlier, this allowing is not a passive resignation but a clear seeing acceptance that simply says, "This is what is true, here, now." (p. 6)

Mindfulness Therapy Techniques

Mindfulness therapists have developed a number of techniques used in the practice of this approach. A few of these techniques are described in this section. Other mindfulness techniques are presented in Thomas Bien's *Mindful Therapy: A Guide for Therapists and Helping Professionals* (2006).

Sitting Meditation. Therapists may use this technique with clients and for their own well-being. The client begins this exercise by establishing an intention for this meditation practice. The intention can be whatever the person feels in the moment or it can be something on which the client would like to work. For instance, a person might say, "May I bring peace to each moment." Once you have determined your intention, say it silently to yourself, and then let it go as you consciously focus your attention on sitting. Become aware of your feet, your legs, your seat, spine, and torso. Become aware of your hands and arms as they rest in your lap.

Take notice that you are breathing. Do not try to change your breath, but simply become aware of it. Focus your attention on the sensations of each breath as it flows in and out of the body. Notice the rising and falling movement of the stomach, or the in and out of the air at the nostrils. Your awareness of your breathing should be accepting rather than controlling. Feel the sensations of each breath. Whereas sometimes the breath will be strong and clear, at other times, it may be soft or shallow.

As you attend to the breath, sounds may call your attention, but attend only to the experience of the sound rather than to the sound itself. Always bring your attention back to the breath. Keep your awareness anchored in the experience of breathing. As other things may call your attention away, return again and again to breathing. As you conclude your sitting meditation, thank yourself for taking time to cultivate your awareness.

Guided Mindfulness. Guided mindfulness helps you take back control of what is going on in your life. The basic technique is to become aware of what is taking place in your body and in your mind from moment to moment. You observe what is happening without making any value judgments about whether it is good or bad. By eliminating self-criticism, guided meditation allows you to create a compassionate relationship with yourself.

Walking Mindfully. Walking meditation involves mindfully noting sensations within your body as you walk. Find a quiet place in which you can walk back and forth. The room or place should at least be between 15 and 20 feet long. This technique can be used with a single client or with a small group of clients. Focus your attention on the experience of walking. You can mentally note the stepping or movement in your walking. Once you reach the end of your path, take a deep breath and reconnect with your breathing. Walk slowly back to your starting point. If your mind wanders off during your walking, refocus your attention on the physical sensations of your walking.

The Integration of Mindfulness With Other Psychotherapy Models

Currently, the mindfulness approach is being combined or integrated with four different approaches to psychotherapy (Baer & Huss, 2008; Turner, 2009). Such integration might suggest that mindfulness is more of a technique than a theory and is not strong enough to be called a theory. The theories that have integrated mindfulness techniques are (1) mindfulness-based stress reduction (MBSR), (2) mindfulness-based cognitive therapy (MBCT), (3) dialectical behavior therapy (DBT) and mindfulness; and (4) acceptance and commitment therapy (ACT).

Mindfulness-Based Stress Reduction

MBSR was developed by John Kabat-Zinn in 1979 at the University of Massachusetts Medical Center to be used as a pain reduction treatment for chronically ill patients. MBSR consists of an 8-week group program of up to 35 participants who meet weekly for 2 to 3 hours each week. Between classes 6 and 7, participants go on a 6-hour, weekend, silent retreat. Clients are engaged in an intensive training program in a number of mindfulness practices, such as yoga and meditation. Kabat-Zinn (1990) describes the MBSR approach in his book *Full Catastrophe Living: Using the Wisdom of Your Body and Mind to Face Pain, Stress, and Illness.* Kabat-Zinn's approach has been modified in cognitive-behavior therapy.

Mindfulness has been expanded to treat psychological pain as well as physical pain. Mindfulness approaches have been found to reduce the frequency of panic attacks and avoidance in panic disorder (Miller, Fletcher, & Kabat-Zinn, 1995) and binge-eating episodes associated with eating disorders (Kristheller & Hallett, 1999).

Interest in the clinical application of mindfulness has been created by the manualized treatment program called Mindfulness-Based Stress Reduction (see Kabat-Zinn, 2005). Recent research studies with controlled trials have reported impressive reductions in psychological morbidity associated with medical illness (Reibel, Greenson, Brainard, & Rosenzweig, 2001) and mitigation of stress and enhanced emotional well-being in nonclinical samples (Williams, Kolar, Reger, & Pearson, 2001). Mindfulness approaches are not considered to be relaxation nor mood management techniques. Instead, they are considered to be a form of mental training to reduce cognitive vulnerability to reactive modes of mind that might otherwise increase stress and emotional distress or that might continue psychopathology.

AFRICAN APPROACHES TO HEALING AND PSYCHOTHERAPY

There is no one universal African approach to psychotherapy. Instead, there are many African models of healing, models that are linked largely to specific tribal cultures. I focus here on the African worldview of healing to consider the different ways in which members of an entire continent conceptualize psychotherapy. This review does not delineate the role of the therapist, client, or specific counseling techniques, as other chapters in the book do, because methods vary from one region of Africa to another. According to Graham (2005), African-centered worldviews are founded on three principles or underlying assumptions:

1. There is a spiritual nature of all human beings.

2. All living things are interconnected.

3. There is a oneness of mind, body, and spirit.

Spirituality is central to African-centered worldviews. In this instance, *spirituality* is defined as a creative life force that connects all living beings and things together. All human beings share the experiences of a universal existence. Such an interconnected sense is expressed in the phrase *umuntu ngumuntu ngabantu*, which means "a person is person through other persons" (Holdstock, 2000).

Ma'at: African Philosophy

Ma'at is a fundamental feature of African approaches to mental health and to each other as individuals. The philosophy of Ma'at serves a similar role for Africans as Buddhism does for Asians. The goddess Ma'at was part of the ancient Egyptian/Kemetic system of spirituality. She was the female balance to the male god Tehuti. The declarations of Ma'at formed a moral code for the living, and they served as the standard by which the dead would be judged. The Kemites believed that when a person died, his or her heart would be weighed against the Ma'at principles of truth, justice, and righteousness (Karenga, 1994). After the heart was weighed, it would be judged whether the person's soul would receive a heavenly reward or not.

Ma'at is the divine order that sustains the universe and society. On an individual level, Ma'at can be best understood as the daily living of an ethical code that places responsibility on the individual for his or her actions. Ma'at seeks balance in individuals' lives. The virtues of Ma'at are truth, righteousness, harmony, balance, reciprocity, justice, and order. The principles of Ma'at are presented in the following box (Karenga, 1994). The second box lists the 42 declarations of Ma'at.

The Principles of Ma'at

- Control of thought
- Control of action
- Devotion to one's purpose
- Faith in a master's ability to teach truth
- Faith in oneself to wield the freedom from resentment under persecution
- Freedom from resentment under wrong
- Ability to distinguish right from wrong
- Ability to distinguish real from unrea

The 42 Declarations of Ma'at

1. I have not done iniquity.
2. I have not done violence.
3. I have not stolen.
4. I have done no murder or harm.
5. I have not stolen food.
6. I have not swindled offerings.
7. I have not acted deceitfully.
8. I have not told lies.
9. I have not wasted food.
10. I have not caused anyone or anything pain.
11. I have not closed my ears to the truth.
12. I have not committed adultery.
13. I have not caused anyone to shed tears.
14. I have not committed fornication.
15. I have not cursed.
16. I have not laid waste to the ploughed land.
17. I have not stolen anyone's land.
18. I have not been an eavesdropper.
19. I have not falsely accused anyone.
20. I have not committed a sin against my own purity.
21. I have not seduced anyone's wife.
22. I have not polluted myself.
23. I have not terrorized anyone.
24. I have not polluted the Earth.
25. I have not burned with rage.
26. I have not cursed God.
27. I have not worked grief.
28. I have not caused disruption of peace.
29. I have not acted hastily or without thought.

30. I have not overstepped my boundaries of concern.

31. I have not exaggerated my words when speaking.

32. I have not worked evil.

33. I have not used evil thoughts or deeds.

34. I have not polluted the water.

35. I have not spoken angrily or arrogantly.

36. I have not cursed anyone in thought, word, or deed.

37. I have not placed myself on a pedestal.

38. I have not spoken scornfully.

39. I have not stolen from or disrespected the deceased.

40. I have not taken food from a child.

41. I have not acted with insolence.

42. I have not slaughtered animals.

Ancestors assume an important role in African psychology. People are expected to abide by their ancestors' traditions (Diallo & Hall, 1989). The head of the family is supposed to keep watch over its members so that they do not offend members of the invisible community of ancestors. The family unites to chase off evil spirits. When a member of a family falls sick, the head of the family seeks to discover why an ancestor is displeased with the person's behavior. If the family member is unable to resolve the situation and to restore the sick member's health, he consults an indigenous doctor or healing person.

The Many Roles of African Healers and Indigenous Doctors

Traditional healers in Africa are known by many different names. Each tribal unit or ethnic group within Africa has a culture-specific understanding of healers and their roles. In small communities, one person may serve as the healer for the entire community. In a larger community, healers may specialize. This section describes one representative type of healer in Africa called *indigenous doctors* or *spiritual healers*.

Dickinson (1999) has pointed out that indigenous doctors have been used by Africans for thousands of years. In Francophone Africa, the indigenous healers are called *les guerisseurs* ("healers"). The Anglophone part of Africa calls such healers *juju men*. In Nigeria, the Edo people call such healers *obos*.

The spiritual healers or doctors relate to their clients as authority figures (Vontress, 2005). Sometimes the healing doctor might not even talk directly with the client who is suffering from a psychological problem but rather with the head of the person's family. There is some similarity between the early days of Japanese Morita therapy and African approaches to healing. In both cases, the healer may invite the client into his home for several days and weeks. Such a stay permits the healer to monitor the client's progress. Touch is permitted in African approaches to psychotherapy, and on some occasions, the healer may massage the client's body.

African people believe that their healers have contact with a universal force or a universal soul. To help their clients, healers may pray with their clients; give them direct advice, fetishes, or herbs; or consult the spiritual realm on their behalf (Vontress, 2005). If, for instance, a healer is dealing with a couple who has been infertile and desires a child, he may go to the couple's home and massage the couple with oil. Wives may consult a healer to get a love potion to put in a drink of a wayward, philandering husband. Indigenous doctors may also function as demon fighters, and they attempt to undo spells or hexes believed to have been placed on families or individuals.

Healers use many different types of diagnostic approaches and techniques for helping their clients. For instance, some traditional healers may throw lots (chips, sticks, stones, etc.) and "read" their landing configuration. Other healers consult plants and trees to diagnose a client's problem and to determine the best treatment for it (Vontress, 1999). Some healers claim that they can heal a person simply by touching a person's garment. An old diagnostic method involves observing the movement of caged mice to determine diagnostic information about the client. (Lest one should find this diagnostic approach strange, I point out that in the United States we use whether or not a groundhog sees his shadow as a means to determine how many more weeks of winter we will have. Most cultures use some form of animism to determine healing.)

Healing practices are deeply influenced by one's culture and worldview. Borrowing from existential therapy, one might say that each culture develops its own weltanschauung. Despite the increased interest in traditional healing and multicultural counseling, our lack of a shared reality with other cultures is a major reason that attempts toward forming a cross-cultural psychotherapy have not worked (Vontress, 2001). Initially, it appears that traditional and modern healers are radically different. Yet, as Torrey (1986) has pointed out, the techniques of therapy used throughout the world are quite similar. People prefer certain types of therapies because they are compatible with their cultural values and expectations. Culture operates at both the conscious and the unconscious levels. It is difficult sometimes for individuals to use cross-cultural approaches because they are unable to relate to the unconscious part of culture that has been absorbed at a very young age. In the final analysis, knowing another person's culture only cognitively may be insufficient to use psychotherapy techniques from that culture.

Inner Reflection

What similarities do you see between African healers and Western psychotherapists?

ARAB APPROACHES TO PSYCHOTHERAPY

Individuals within the Middle East constitute a significant proportion of the world's population. There is no such thing as a monolithic Middle Eastern culture, and there is no such thing as a homogeneous Arab culture. Important cultural differences exist within the Middle East, depending on religion and country of origin. Because there is insufficient information written on Arab approaches to psychotherapy, I rely heavily on Marwan Dwairy's "Counseling Arab and Muslim Clients" (2008).

Arabs are the descendants of Arabic tribes who live in what are now called the Saudi Peninsula, Iraq, and Syria. During the early 7 century (610 CE), Islam emerged in Mecca as a result of the efforts of the Prophet Mohammed, who wrote the Qur'an. Although the terms *Arabs* and *Muslims* are often used interchangeably, there are important differences between them. Currently, there are about 285 million Arabs who live in 22 countries in North Africa and the Middle East. The religion of Islam has been adopted by many Arabs; however, there are Arabs from each of the major religions, including Christianity.

By far, the majority of Muslims (people who follow the practices of Islam)—Indonesians, Malaysians, Iranians, Turks, and others—are not Arabs. As Dwairy (2008) has stated,

> Despite this, the Arabic language and history remain central to Muslims since Islam was revealed to an Arab prophet, Mohammad, who was a member of the biggest Arab tribe, Quraysh, in an Arab city in Arabia, Mecca, and its holy book, the Qur'an was written in Arabic. (p. 148)

Many non-Arab nations have adopted Islam, and it has been estimated that there are about 1.3 billion Muslims worldwide. Islam has established strict rule and laws (*Shari'aa*), based on the Qur'an and the Prophet's life (*Sunna*), and members of this faith must live their family, social, economic, and political lives based on these religious laws (Dwairy, 2006). Currently, there is anger and tension among Arabs and Muslims and members of the Western world around critical issues such as the attacks of September 11, 2001, in the United States and the Palestinian–Israeli conflict. One goal of this section of the chapter is to present as sensitively and as respectfully as possible the cultural underpinnings of Arab Muslim culture. At least some of the conflict between Arab Muslim and Western culture is generated because of major differences in the ways both populations view themselves and their relationship with the surrounding environment.

Arab Muslim: Collective Culture

The Arab Muslim culture has at its center tribal collectivism and Islamic values. It is a culture that is authoritarian in nature. Young people raised in such a culture are taught that the individual is submissive to the family and that the father is the patriarch and the authority within a family. Whereas in many Western countries the government intercedes on behalf of family members to provide money or health benefits for its people, this is not the case in Arab Muslim countries. The Arab Muslim family is on its own. Members must depend on each other for whatever financial, social, and emotional support they need. The individual is raised to serve the collective, meaning the family (Dwairy, 2006).

Nearly all choices in life are collective matters within a family; therefore, the family rather than the individual determines what kind of clothing a person will wear, what kind of career can be chosen, whom the person will marry, what kind of housing is appropriate, and so on. To get along and to maintain family cohesion, the individual learns to suppress all goal striving unless it is sanctioned by the family. Children are raised not to express their own opinions but rather to express what others anticipate. Communication between family members is based on the value of respect (*Ihtiram*), fulfilling social duties (*wajib*), and pleasing others and avoiding confrontations (*mosayara;* Dwairy, 2008).

Immigration of Arab Muslims to the United States and to other Western nations sometimes results in a clash of cultures. Arab Muslims raised in a collectivist culture with the values described

previously may find Western cultures to be too individualistic, too permissive, and therefore, threatening to traditional Arab Muslim values concerning family, women, and child rearing (Dwairy, 2008). Although some Arab Muslims desire to become part of the Western culture, others are afraid of losing their cultural identity. Intergenerational conflict sometimes erupts within Arab families over a difference in family members' attitudes toward traditional and Western values. Counselors may find themselves in a difficult situation. While on the one hand, they may be asked to help family members adapt to Western society, on the other, they may be asked to uphold traditional values.

Personality Development

There is a major disconnect between how Arab Muslim culture views a positive personality development and how the Western world perceives such development. For the most part, Western personality theorists emphasize the process of separation and individuation. According to Sigmund Freud, for instance, a young child possesses an independent personality structure after the age of 5. Erik Erikson conceptualized ego development with a stage called "identity development" during adolescence. Moreover, according to Western theorists, a healthy person is "one who is independent, autonomous, individuated, internally controlled, and responsible for himself with an inner sense of self" (Dwairy, 2008, p. 150). In collective and authoritarian societies, assuming autonomy and independency is inappropriate.

Timimi (1995) proposed that Arab youth do not experience identity crises in adolescence or achieve individual autonomy because their identities are enmeshed within their families. Studies by Dwairy and others found that Arab Palestinian adolescence was more foreclosed and diffused than that of American youth (Dwairy & Menshar, 2006). Racy (1970) has indicated that Arab youth are not expected to be self-centered or to participate in nonconforming behavior. Both adolescents and adults in Arab Muslim societies continue to be emotionally and socially dependent on their families.

Many Western therapists might interpret Arab Muslim lack of individuation from parents and family as a sign of psychopathology. Therapists must become aware of the value system of their clients prior to committing to counseling them. A substantial difference in client/therapist value systems might indicate that a client referral is in order.

There are other important differences between Arab Muslim and Western approaches to psychotherapy. Arab Muslims do not place a great deal of stock on personality as it is described by Western theorists. Western theorists describe personality as an intrapsychic construct that has an ego, self, trait, and drives. In contrast, in most collectivist societies, individuals are other focused rather than inner focused (Dwairy, 2006). There is little emphasis on the self and autonomy. As Dwairy (2006) has stated,

> In most collective societies, where the personality does not become autonomous but rather continues to be other focused (Markus & Kitayama, 1998), norms, values, rules, and familial authority, rather than personality explain the behavior of the individual. . . . The main dynamic in the personal life of the Arab/Muslim individual is in the interpersonal domain rather [than] in the intrapsychic one. . . . The main conflict is intrafamilial (personal needs vs. family control) rather than intrapsychic. (p. 151)

Muslim society subscribes to the concept of *Mosayara* (or *Mojamala*) and *Istighaba* (Dwairy, 2008). Mosayera refers to a person's ability to get along with others' needs and expectations by concealing one's feelings and attitudes (Dwairy, 2006). Conversely, Istighaba permits feelings, attitudes, and needs that were not expressed. Socially unacceptable behavior is expressed in solitude. Dwairy (2008) warns against using the typical instruments that measure the intrapsychic structures of personality. Instead, he recommends the "Multicultural Training Models and Person-in-Culture Interview" (Berg-Cross & Chinen, 1995).

Counseling Arab Muslims

It is recommended that a therapist who works with Arab Muslims should be thoroughly grounded in the latter's culture and history. He or she should be knowledgeable about Arab Muslim history and Islam. I can't emphasize enough that if the therapist is of a different religion or faith, he should have respect for Islam and honor it in the therapeutic setting. The belief system that underlies Islam is extremely critical to the issues Arab Muslim clients bring to therapy.

Dwairy (2008) suggests that therapists use indirect methods of counseling with Arab Muslim clients. Therapists should avoid helping such clients uncover unconscious material or reach self-actualization because the latter is a Western value. Because Arab Muslims do not feel comfortable discussing their family lives directly, therapists should consider using metaphoric language to express their distresses. Kopp (1995) uses a three-stage metaphor therapy that might be useful in working with Arab Muslims. First, he asks the client to select a metaphor that describes his or her presenting problem. A client might say, "I feel as if I have been run over by a truck." During the second stage, the therapist asks the client to change the metaphor so that it represents a solution to the problem. Near the end of therapy, the client is asked what he or she has learned from the metaphoric solution. Metaphor therapy is good when the therapist does not want to do a good deal of uncovering.

Another indirect method of therapy that works well with Arab Muslims has been provided by Bresler (1984), who asked his clients suffering from chronic pain to control the pain by controlling the images in their minds. First, he asks his clients to draw the pain. Next, he asks them to draw the state of no pain, and finally, the pleasure state. Bresler teaches clients to both manipulate the images in their minds and to retain the pictures of no pain.

Additional indirect therapies for working with Arab Muslims include metaphor therapy, art therapy, guided imagery, and bibliotherapy. These therapies help clients find solutions to their problems at the symbolic imaginative level.

RESEARCH AND EVALUATION OF TRANSCULTURAL PSYCHOTHERAPY

Impact of Transcultural and Asian Therapies on the Western World

A major revolution in American psychotherapy seems to be taking place. There is an increased integration of Eastern approaches in psychotherapy in dominant American therapies. Of the three new evidence-based psychotherapies presented in this book, all have made mindfulness a core component of their therapy. As mentioned earlier, mindfulness is a core component of DBT, ACT, and MBCT. Clearly, there is a decided Asian value influence in cognitive-behavioral therapies. Cognitive-behavioral therapies are beginning to understand that not all client behaviors can or should be changed and that a therapist's efforts to get a client to change certain behaviors may actually backfire and make matters worse. Therefore, acceptance is a key component of ACT, DBT, and MBCT.

The new cognitive-behavioral therapies bear a marked resemblance to Naikan therapy and Morita therapy—two Japanese approaches to psychotherapy. For instance, both ACT and Morita therapy suggest that people are overly preoccupied with themselves and that the general goals of therapy are to have clients accept their feelings. Meditation is a core component of Naikan therapy, Morita therapy, ACT, DBT, and MBCT. All of these therapies suggest that the more attention we pay to our symptoms, the bigger our systems and problems become.

Western and Eastern Conceptualizations of the Self and Relationships. Other changes involving the sense of self and relationships also seem to be occurring in American psychotherapy that reflect a decided Asian influence. For the most part, the East and the West have sharply differing views of human life. The Western view of the self is highly individualistic and focused on the uniqueness and will of individuals. Generally speaking, the Western view of selfhood has the self at center stage, and the world is perceived by and through it. The self belongs to the individual and to no one else. It possesses a sense of control and mastery over one's environment (Ho, 1995).

The Eastern perspective on the self is decentered and dethroned (Ho, 1999):

> The self is not the measure of all things. Humility rather than a sense of sovereignty is the hallmark of Eastern ideals. In Confucianism, the self is subdued: Mastery over impulse control is paramount; there is no place for unbridled self-expression because it threatens to disturb the social order. . . . The Confucian conception of selfhood and identity is not individualistic, but relational. This relational conception takes full recognition of the individual's embeddedness in the social network. . . . selfhood is realized through harmonizing one's relationships with others. (p. 99)

Relational conceptions of human existence, which have been long revered by Asians, now are in vogue among some contemporary Western theorists. For example, Gergen (1994), a social constructivist, asserts that relational realities must be taken into consideration. According to him, "A fundamental aspect of social life is the network of reciprocating identities. . . . Identities, in this sense, are never individual" (p. 209). As the poet John Donne once wrote,

> No man is an island,
>
> Entire of itself,
>
> Every man is a piece of the continent,
>
> A part of the main.
>
> If a clod be washed away by the sea,
>
> Europe is the less.
>
> As well as if a promontory were.
>
> As well as if a manor of thy friend's
>
> Or of thine own were:
>
> Any man's death diminishes me,

Because I am involved in mankind,

And therefore never send to know for whom the bell tolls;

It tolls for thee.

The Movement Toward Global Transcultural Psychotherapy. What does this all mean for psychotherapy and Eastern and Western conceptions of humankind? It appears that there is some kind of rapprochement, resonance, or even gradual intercultural convergence toward relational conceptions of human existence. I propose, along with Ho (1999), that there is an emerging paradigmatic shift from methodological individualism to a type of relationalism that places primary importance to relational contexts in which all actions in human society occur. The focus in Western psychology is gradually shifting from individualistic conceptions of the self to relational conceptions, and this paradigmatic shift is being stimulated by the integration of Asian and Western views of human life, what is important in life, and how one should face adversity. Emotional crisis and breakdowns should not be conceptualized as disturbances in individuals' minds but rather as disturbances in their relations with themselves and others. Psychotherapy is then above all a relationship that helps a person resolve relational disturbances in an individual's life. Partly as a result of the Asian influence, the focus in relational analysis, for instance, is now on the self with others instead of the self with autonomy as the ultimate stage of development (Ho, 1999). My crystal ball says that in the coming years there will be more of an Eastern influence on psychotherapy within relational contexts, as is the case with Morita therapy and Naikan therapy. The basic unit of analysis will not be the individual, as is currently the case, but rather the person in relationships and the person in different relational contexts (see, e.g., Curtis, 1991, and Duck, 1993).

The greatest movement is not so much the American version of multicultural therapy (which emphasizes fairness [social justice] for members of ethnic minority groups, women, gays, and other groups) but rather the current movement toward transcultural therapy and the development of new therapeutic approaches that attempt to adopt or to integrate value systems of other cultures that might prove helpful for individuals suffering from mental challenges or disorders. Americans and the Western world are adopting the Asian perspective on the value of acceptance of life to promote mental health and the view of self in relational contexts instead of the prizing of the autonomous, individual self.

Within the field of relational psychotherapy, there are a number of theories, including relational analysis (see Chapter 1, this book; Mitchell, 1988; Mitchell & Lewis, 1999; Safran, 2012, 2003) and relational-cultural therapy (refer to Chapter 14 on Feminist therapies; Baker & Stiver, 1998; Jordan, 2000). For instance, according to relational-cultural therapy, the goal of development is not forming a separate, independent self, but rather to develop and participate in relationships that promote the well-being of everyone involved—growth-fostering relationships. The relational-cultural model emphasizes the growth of relatedness and connectedness. These concepts can be traced to Buddhism and Confucianism as well as to other Asian approaches to life.

CASE ANALYSIS

Justin From a Transcultural Perspective

In working with Justin, the therapist uses an integrated approach involving mindfulness therapy, Naikan therapy, and Ma'at. Justin is anxious about his entire situation with the courts and at school. When he thinks about being placed in a residential treatment center hundreds of miles from home, he cries. He does not want to leave his mother, even though he doesn't get along with her and he talks back to her disrespectfully whenever she tries to get him to complete his chores. Justin has never quite accepted the role he played in getting himself in trouble with the law. Even if he is telling the truth that he did not steal anything at the mall, Justin has yet to deal with the fact that he went there with boys who had stolen from the mall on several different occasions. He sits in the therapist's office anxious and depressed.

The therapist's first goal is to help Justin deal with his anxiety and depression. He decides to begin with mindfulness techniques to help Justin get some immediate relief from the stress that he is experiencing in his life. The therapist asks Justin if he would like to feel better as they sat there talking together. Justin responds, "Yeah. Every day I keep thinking that my probation officer is going to tell me that the judge is sending me to the residential treatment center. I don't want to go."

The therapist responds, "If you could say anything you wanted to the judge, what would you say to him?"

"I'm sorry. I won't go to the mall again with my friend, but I didn't steal nothing. I was just there."

The therapist said to Justin, "Let's start with that feeling. I'm going to teach you a way to ease some of the stress that you are feeling. It has to do with your breathing." The therapist then went on to demonstrate and to describe the mindfulness sitting meditation to Justin. As Justin began to breathe in, the therapist suggested that he let go of all thoughts about being placed in the residential treatment center. Instead, Justin should focus on his breath. If Justin's thoughts should wander away from his breath, just gently bring his mind back to focusing on his breath.

"That's all I gotta do?" Justin asked. "Just breathe? I can do that. Watch me."

The therapist had Justin to participate in the mindfulness sitting meditation for 15 to 20 minutes, depending on Justin's ability to continue his breathing. The therapist engaged Justin in guided mindfulness. The therapist stated the following:

I want you to concentrate your attention on your breathing, Justin. Become aware of the sensations inside your air passages as the air enters your nose. Just become aware of the breathing sensations as your breath goes in and out. Do not try to influence or force your breathing. Just let it happen naturally. . . . Just allow yourself time to become aware of the air going in and out. . . . Keep your mind on your breathing.

When thoughts come into your mind, that's okay. Just examine the thoughts for what they are. When thoughts come into your mind, just allow them to wander off on their own. . . . When a thought or feeling arises, simply observe and acknowledge it. If you find yourself drifting away on a thought, then just return and refocus on your breathing.

The therapist cautioned Justin, "Don't try to force the thoughts about being placed in the residential treatment center to go away. Just focus on your breath, and let these concerns leave you naturally." As Justin participated in the meditation exercise, the anxiety that marred his face slowly left it, and for a brief moment, Justin smiled.

From the mindfulness sitting meditation exercise, the therapist moved to Naikan therapy, which is a structured method of reflecting on one's life, one's relationships with others, and one's individual impact on the world. This therapeutic approach helps clients develop a natural and profound sense of gratitude for blessings given to them by others. In addition, it helps clients find meaning in their lives and inspires them to contribute to the happiness and welfare of others.

The therapist's tentative, ongoing assessment of Justin was that he tended to react rather than to respond to the events and circumstances of his life. A thought would enter Justin's mind, and he would just react to it without little thinking about the situation in which he found himself. Moreover, Justin's life was almost totally self-centered.

(Continued)

(Continued)

Rarely did he do chores around the house without his mother having to nag him. Somehow (perhaps because he was the baby of the family) he felt that he was entitled to "things" without having to give back very much.

One of the therapist's goals was to get Justin to accept where he is, instead of being anxious about it. Naikan therapists believe that much suffering arises because one resists what is happening, wanting things to be different from how they actually are. Justin does not want to be under the jurisdiction of family court. He does not want to go to the residential juvenile detention center. He hates taking orders from his mother, and he would prefer going to another school with more kids who looked like him. So much of Justin's life is "wanting to be somewhere else."

The therapist introduces Justin to the three Naikan therapy questions:

1. What has a specific person (Sandy, Justin's mother) done for me?

2. What have I done for my mother?

3. What troubles and difficulties have I caused my mother?

Justin began to rattle off a few things that Sandy had done for him before he left for school. The therapist asked Justin, "Do you remember anything about when you were a baby?"

"A few things," Justin responded.

"Like what?"

"Like when I pooped in my pants after my mother had given me a bath and dressed me in a new suit. She was yelling and screaming that I did it on purpose."

"Did you?" the therapist asked.

"I dunno. I can't remember. I just remember her yelling and screaming."

"Let's just stay with the diapers for a moment. How many diapers do you think your mom changed for you when you were little?"

"How am I supposed to know that?" Justin responded.

"Let's just say your mother changed your diaper seven times a day—one after each meal, twice during the day, and once before you went to bed. There are usually 365 days in a year; so we can multiply it 365 by 7. Let's see I have a calculator right here. That would be about 2,555 diapers in 1 year. And you were toilet trained at about 3 years? Well, during a 3-year period, your Mom changed about 7,665 diapers for you."

Justin and the therapist begin to discuss other things Sandy did for him—like cooking him breakfast and dinner. As the two began to calculate the number of meals Sandy had cooked for Justin, he just said, "Wow. I guess she really does love me if she did all of that."

Next, the therapist dealt with the two remaining questions. Justin had a difficult time thinking what he had done for his mother yesterday. The next question brought a sheepish kind of look on Justin's face: What troubles and difficulties had he caused Sandy? He mentioned that he had refused to do his chores and the trouble with the police at the mall.

Justin began to get a sense of the many things that Sandy did for him on a daily basis—things that he had usually taken for granted. The therapist gave Justin the assignment of writing a gratitude journal. He was to make at least three entries a day and bring the journal to their next counseling session. In addition, the therapist asked Justin to keep a giving journal that would contain the many little things that he did for other people. Justin was told that it didn't matter how big his act of giving was but simply that each day he was to write one thing that he did for another person. In this manner, Justin would get a sense of empowerment. He was capable of giving to others. Justin was encouraged to examine what life was offering to him and what he was giving in return.

Before Justin left, the therapist asked him to look over the first 10 of the 42 declarations of Ma'at, as part of the African approach to counseling. Both the therapist and Justin alternated reading the 10 items and after each one how true the item was for him—from very true to not true at all. The two then discussed Justin's reaction to the 10 items.

Justin liked the therapist's approach because he did not feel that the therapist was placing any pressure on him and because the therapist was not treating him as if he were crazy. In addition to discussing the contents of Justin's journal, the therapist made a decision to work with him on the Buddhist quality of responding rather than acting.

SUMMARY

This chapter has discussed several transcultural approaches to psychotherapy, including Naikan therapy, Morita therapy, Mindfulness therapy, Ma'at therapy, and Arab Muslim therapy. A dominant theme has been the integration of primarily Eastern and collectivist cultural views into Western or American therapeutic approaches. The Asian influence on American and Western psychotherapy has taken place in three areas: (1) the widespread incorporation of mindfulness principles (acceptance) into Western therapies such as DBT, ACT, and MBCT; (2) the integration of Eastern views on the self; and (3) the integration of Eastern concepts of the relational self and the importance of relationships in an individual's life.

There appear to be two distinct multicultural movements in psychotherapy. The first movement is characterized by the multicultural competencies and the social justice movement for members of ethnic minority groups, women, and diverse cultural groups. This group is heavily influenced by American researchers who have become known as the multiculturalists. The second major movement is transcultural and involves the incorporation of mainly Eastern values and perspectives into Western cognitive-behavioral approaches to psychotherapy. In the introduction to this chapter, I spoke about psychological healing bridges between different cultures and their approaches to psychotherapy. It appears to me that we have partially arrived at building the first part of our healing bridge with the incorporation of mindfulness concepts and practices in Western cognitive-behavioral approaches such as DBT, ACT, and MBCT. This second movement in multicultural perspectives signals a global movement toward intercultural integration of psychotherapies. As we learn more about different cultures, it is anticipated that such integration will increase rather than decrease. No one culture has all the answers to life's challenges. We all can and will learn from each other.

SUPPLEMENTAL AIDS

Discussion Questions

1. If we resent it when people do not fulfill our expectations, we live as if we are entitled to get whatever we want. List the names of two people who are significant in your life and toward whom you have feelings of resentment. What is the source of your resentment? What expectations did you have for the two individuals in your life? To what extent did they fulfill your expectations? How might you resolve your feelings of resentment toward the individuals?

2. In your opinion, what are the key differences between Asian approaches to psychotherapy and Western approaches?

3. Several prominent theories (DBT, ACT, MBCT) have all incorporated mindfulness as part of their theoretical framework. Do you

think it is appropriate to incorporate Eastern perspectives into basically a Western approach to psychotherapy?

4. Discuss the similarities between Japanese approaches to psychotherapy and some of the new third-wave psychotherapies, such as ACT and MBCT.

5. Do you think that the world will ever have an agreed-on theory of psychotherapy that unites the features of two or more cultures? Explain your answer.

Glossary of Key Terms

arugamama   A Japanese word that deals with the concept of the naturalness of feelings. Arugamama means acceptance of reality as it is, accepting our feelings and thoughts without trying to change them or to work through them. Instead of directing our attention to our feeling state, we focus our efforts on taking constructive steps to live well.

attention   A core component of mindfulness. Paying attention means that a person observes on a moment-to-moment basis his or her internal and external experiences. See also **attitude** and **intention**.

attitude   A core component of mindfulness. An appropriate attitude includes curiosity, openness, acceptance, and love. See also **attention** and **intention**.

intention   A core component of mindfulness. One sets a general direction that one wants to take. See also **attention** and **attitude**.

mindfulness   Our abiding awareness and deep knowing of our mind. Mindfulness also refers to a practice wherein a person intentionally attends to life and the mind in a caring and discerning way. In its simplest form, mindfulness involves paying attention on purpose and with acceptance.

Morita therapy   Treatment approach developed by the Japanese psychiatrist Shoma Morita during the 1920s and 1930s as a treatment for a type of anxiety neurosis. In Morita therapy, we learn to accept our feelings without trying to change them and take action without changing our feeling state. When clients take realistic action, self-development takes place.

Naikan therapy   ("inside looking" or "introspection") A structured method of self-reflection developed by Ishin Yoshimoto (1916–1988). A goal of Naikan therapy is to increase awareness of oneself and to accept life, oneself, and others without judgment.

Website Materials

Additional exercises, journals, annotated bibliography, and more are available on the open-access website at https://study.sagepub.com/jonessmith2e.

CHAPTER 14

Feminist Therapy and Lesbian and Gay Therapy

This chapter explores feminist therapy and lesbian and gay therapy, also known as gender therapy. The first section of this chapter focuses on feminist therapy. Although feminist therapy has had a profound impact on gender therapy, the two movements in psychotherapy can be distinguished from one another. The second section examines the complexity of therapy with gay and lesbian individuals. I discuss the social, cultural, and historical context of sexual orientation as well as identity development for lesbian and gay individuals.

FEMINIST THERAPY
Brief Overview

There is no one major feminist therapeutic approach. There are, however, a number of key figures in feminist therapy; these include, in alphabetical order, Sandra Bem, Laura Brown, Bonnie Burstow, Lillian Comas-Diaz, Carolyn Enns, Olivia Espin, Carol Gilligan, Jean Baker Miller, Pam Remer, and Judith Worell. Photos of some of these women, with the titles of their works, appear in the chapter.

Major Contributors

Photo courtesy of Sandra Bem.

Sandra Bem, *The Lenses of Gender* (1993) and *Gender Schema Theory* (1981)

Photo courtesy of Laura S. Brown.

Laura S. Brown, *Feminist Therapy Code of Ethics* (2000) and *Subversive Dialogues: Theory in Feminist Therapy* (1994)

Photo courtesy of Carolyn Zerbe Enns.

Carolyn Zerbe Enns,
*Feminist Theories and
Feminist Psychotherapies:
Origins, Themes and
Diversity* (2004)

Photo courtesy of the Jean Baker Miller Training Institute.

Jean Baker Miller, coauthor
of *The Healing Connection*
(1997)

Feminist therapy is a school of thought that is basically a combination of the social constructivist and the social justice movements. It emphasizes both psychological and sociological factors that have an impact on the development and mental health of clients (Enns, 1993, 2004). Feminist therapy is concerned with the different ways in which men and women develop throughout the life span. Feminist therapists focus on helping men and women understand the impact of gender roles and power differentials in a given society (Brown, 2000).

Feminist therapy grew out of the women's movement during the 1970s. The movement has had a profound impact on psychology and on the helping professions. Women began to understand the common experiences and problems associated with the social roles that they were made to endure. During the 1970s, Phyllis Chesler (1972, 1997) asserted that the traditional therapeutic relationship was patriarchal. Chesler argued that women were often misdiagnosed in therapy because they did not conform to gender role stereotypes of male therapists. Female clients received higher rates of depressive diagnoses, and they were hospitalized more frequently than were men. In her book *Women and Madness* (1972), Chesler gave many examples of sexism in therapy. Some 20 years later, she wrote an article (Chesler, 1997) stating that much progress had been made with women clients in therapy.

The 1970s gave birth to a great deal of research on gender bias and to organizational development with an emphasis on women within the field of psychology. During this decade, the Association for Women in Psychology and the American Psychological Association's (APA) Division 35 (Society for the Psychology of Women) were created. Several organizations, including APA, established nonsexist guidelines for publication and for treatment of women clients (Enns, 1993).

The 1980s ushered in a concerted effort to define feminist therapy. Individual therapy was the most frequent modality used in working with women. Feminist therapists began to criticize the traditional systems of psychotherapy. They challenged the intrapsychic focus in psychotherapy. The overrepresentation of women within certain diagnostic categories, such as depression and eating disorders was another major issue addressed. Feminists also began to examine issues related to body image, abusive relationships, eating disorders, and sexual abuse (Enns, 1993, 2004).

Four Main Philosophies of Feminists

By the end of the 1980s, the feminist movement had changed considerably, and so had the feminist philosophies that guided the practice of therapy. Researchers have identified four major feminist philosophies, which are sometimes termed as the "second wave" of feminism. These philosophical positions are (1) liberal feminism, (2) cultural feminism, (3) radical feminism, and (4) socialist feminism. These philosophic views overlap; however, a point of commonality is their focus on equality.

Liberal feminism emphasizes helping individual women to transcend the limits of their gender socialization patterns. Individuals in this philosophical category contend that women deserve equality with men because they have the same abilities as men. The major goals of liberal feminist therapy are personal empowerment, dignity, self-fulfillment, and equality.

Cultural feminism asserts that oppression originates from society's devaluation of women's strengths. Feminists in this group stress the differences between women and men and contend that society would benefit from feminization of the culture so that it becomes more nurturing, intuitive, cooperative, and relational (Herlihy & Corey, 2005).

Radical feminism emphasizes that women are oppressed in patriarchal societies. Their goal is to change society by activism. Such therapists conceptualize therapy as a political enterprise. Radical feminists identify the ways in which patriarchy dominates a person's everyday life, including household chores, paid employment, violence, and parenting (Herlihy & Corey, 2005).

Enns (2004) made a distinction between radical and liberal feminist therapy. According to her, nonsexist therapy does not focus on social change, anger, or power issues but on the therapist's awareness of his or her own values and on an egalitarian approach when working with female clients. In contrast, radical and feminist therapists emphasize the political nature of the client and the role of social institutions. Radical feminists become involved in changing social issues, while liberal feminist therapists may or may not do so. Radical feminist therapists state that men should not be feminist therapists because they cannot serve as role models for women. Men can, however, be profeminist. Currently, feminists permit men to be clients.

Socialist feminism shares with radical feminism the goal of change in institutional and social relationships. Instead of focusing just on gender, social feminists emphasize multiple oppressions in a woman's life. The major goal is to change social relationships and institutions.

Since the 1980s, feminist women of color and postmodern feminists have challenged the underlying assumptions of traditional theories of psychotherapy. **Postmodern feminism** constitutes the "third wave" of feminist therapy. Postmodern feminists offer a framework for comparing and contrasting traditional therapies with feminist therapy. Several trends in postmodern feminism include an increasing role for women of color and inclusion of lesbian feminists, who share many commonalities with radical feminists, and global international feminists, who maintain that women throughout the world live under oppression.

Rationale for a Specialization in Therapy for Women

There are a number of factors that led to a specialization in a therapeutic approach for women. First, two epidemiological surveys of community samples (Brown, 1992, 1994) sponsored by the National Institute of Mental Health showed that a high proportion of people with signs of depression, anxiety, panic, simple phobia, and agoraphobia were women. In contrast, men are overrepresented in the categories of substance abuse and antisocial behaviors. These surveys also revealed that women had a higher utilization rate than men of health and community mental health agencies. Moreover, women were prescribed a disproportionate share of psychoactive drugs that had deleterious or unknown side effects (Brown, 1994, 2000). There was also concern about the increasing medicalization of women's psychological problems, including issues of diagnosis and prescriptive drugs (Worell & Remer, 2003).

Dissatisfaction With Existing Theories and the Low Representation of Women in Psychology

Feminists dissatisfied with existing theories, the psychological knowledge base, and the treatment approaches motivated a call for change (Worell & Remer, 2003). Discussion groups among women led to their awareness that the personal problems of individual women were rooted in their subordinate status in their families and society. These *consciousness-raising groups* were instrumental in the demand for an end to the sexist and oppressive social structures that characterized a male-dominated society (Enns, 2003). There was unhappiness with traditional theories of female and male development, which depicted stereotypical male traits as the norm and females as deficient because they differed from such norms. In addition, there was frustration with the continuing omission of women from the knowledge base of psychology (Brown, 2000). Women questioned the relevance of the existing therapy theories because they all located the problem within the mind of the woman (intrapsychic) instead of within broad societal injustices. Feminists argued that women's problems originated from external rather than internal sources. They demanded greater representation in the APA.

Dissatisfaction With Diagnostic Categories and Mother Blaming

Feminists claimed that psychological theories and treatment focused on "mother blaming" for children's pathology. Mothers were blamed for causing homosexuality among their children. In 1989, Pam Caplan wrote *Don't Blame Mother*, which focused on the difficult relationships between mother and daughter.

Ballou and West (2000) have discussed a number of ways in which gender issues and sexism are entrenched in therapy and psychotherapy. Just 30 years ago, most therapists were White males. Women's responses to inequitable power struggles were often viewed as aberrations and as failures in adopting a proper adult role. It was not so much that women were more insane than men; instead, it was a case that men had the naming power. They could label a woman as hysterical if she seemed emotional. Male therapists rarely took into consideration the societal injustices that may have led to a woman's depression. In contrast, feminist therapists consider how gender interacts with other diversity variables, including religion, race, ethnicity, and culture. Arab women may have different issues confronting them from those facing African American women. Gender is usually tempered with other social factors.

Traditional Theories Versus Feminist Therapies: Six Characteristics

Feminist therapists view traditional therapies as being fundamentally different in outlook and in underlying assumptions from feminist therapies. These critics point out that most of the extant theories of psychotherapy were developed during a time when women and men were seen as having different personality characteristics. Moreover, it was believed that the biological differences between males and females resulted in their different outlooks on life and work. Worell and Remer (2003) have outlined six characteristics of traditional theories that indicate obsolete ideas about the role of gender in people's lives:

1. An **androcentric theory** uses male-centered constructs to reach conclusions about human life.

2. **Gender-centric theories** articulate separate developmental paths for men and women.

3. *Ethnocentric theories* make the incorrect assumption that their view of human development and interactions are valid for all races, cultures, and countries.

4. *Heterosexist theories* conceptualize a heterosexual orientation as normative and desirable, while devaluing same-sex relationships.

5. An *intrapsychic orientation* emphasizes a client's impulses, ideas, conflicts, or other psychological phenomena that take place within his or her mind, as opposed to an interpersonal orientation, which sometimes results in blaming the victim.

6. *Determinist theories* maintain that personality patterns are fixed at an early stage of development.

KEY CONCEPTS OF FEMINIST THERAPY

View of Human Nature

The feminist perspective on the nature of human beings is quite different from that of the other theories presented in this book. Most of the traditional theories were written from a male perspective; therefore, development is described primarily in terms of males. Feminist therapists have challenged the masculine interpretation of human behavior. Feminist approaches to human nature present an androgynous view of human nature. Feminists argued that there are few truly biological differences between men and women. Most of the differences that we come to accept are socially constructed and influenced by culture. Human nature is neither male nor female.

Sex Role Stereotypes and Androgyny

In 1974, Sandra Bem constructed the Bem Sex Role Inventory, which is one of the most widely used gender measures. Based on their responses to this instrument, individuals are categorized as having one of four gender role orientations: masculine, feminine, androgynous, or undifferentiated. A *masculine* person is high on instrumental traits (person makes use of people for pleasure or profit or a person's attitude about an event or outcome depends on his perception of how that outcome is related [instrumental] to the occurrence of other desirable or undesirable consequences) but low on female expressive traits (showing and sharing one's emotions and feelings). A feminine individual is high on feminine (expressive) traits and low on masculine (instrumental) traits. *Androgyny* is a term derived from the Greek words *andras*, meaning "man," and *gyné*, meaning "woman" and refers to the mixing of masculine and feminine characteristics, a kind of hermaphroditism. An androgynous individual can be either a male or a female who has a high degree of both feminine (expressive) and masculine (instrumental) traits. An *undifferentiated* person is low on both feminine and masculine traits (Bem, 1974). The ideal therapist is **gender neutral** and **gender fair**.

Gender Schema Therapy

Based on her work on androgyny, Sandra Bem (1981, 1987) developed **gender schema** theory. A *schema* is an organized set of mental associations used to interpret what one sees. Gender schema examines people in terms of how likely they are to view a situation in terms of gender issues. Bem observed that children learn to apply gender schemas fairly early. For instance, girls wear nail polish, and boys do not. Boy are not supposed to cry, whereas girls can and do cry. Adults who are gender focused tend to see behaviors as unmanly or unfeminine. Gender schema is a very strong schema. Bem proposes that parents teach their children an *individual difference* approach. If one child calls another a sissy because he likes ballet, the mother might point out that both males and females engage in ballet. Clients need to become aware of their own gender schema, especially as such a schema relates to how they view themselves. What factors enter into how a person might view himself or herself as a man or as a woman?

Gender Role Stereotyping Across Cultures

Although research reveals that males and females do not differ significantly from each other on most variables, **gender role** ideology is rather consistent across the world, and it is patterned by cultural factors. Typically, Western and developed nations that have a higher number of educated women employed have more egalitarian beliefs than do less developed countries (Williams & Best, 1990). Despite these differences, there is remarkable agreement across cultures about what men and women are like; therefore, researchers have concluded that gender stereotyping may be universal (Berry, Poortinga, Segall, & Dasen, 1992).

Claude Steele's (2003) seminal research has demonstrated the effect of racial and gender stereotypes on a person's performance. Steele and his colleagues began investigating the underperformance of women in difficult math classes and the underperformance of African Americans in higher educational settings compared with classmates who were intellectually equal. The researchers asked the following question: If two people are equally prepared for a challenging task, what is getting in the way for those who are performing below their ability? Using a series of experiments, the researchers identified a factor they called *stereotype threat*. Stereotype threat could be "felt by anyone who cared about a performance and yet knew that any faltering at it could cause them to be reduced to a negative group stereotype" (p. 316). The researchers' subtle activation of a negative stereotype consistently resulted in the participants' decreased performance on difficult tasks.

> ### Inner Reflections
>
> What gender roles have you adopted for your life?
>
> Are the gender roles you have adopted working or not working for you?

Differences Between the Terms *Sex* and *Gender*

Feminists provide distinctions between the terms *sex* and *gender*. In general, the term *sex* refers to a biological variable that is used to distinguish between two categories of individuals: females or males. Besides certain physical and reproductive capabilities, few human characteristics can be explained by sex alone (Worell & Papendrick-Remer, 2001). In contrast, the term *gender* usually refers to culturally and socially constructed beliefs and attitudes about the traits and behaviors of females and males (Worell & Papendrick-Remer, 2001).

The Social Construction of Gender

We construct our own meanings about reality and about gender that represent culturally shared agreements about what behavior is appropriate for males and females. The personal characteristics typically attributed to gender are not "true" attributes of females and males but are socially constructed categories that help maintain female/male dichotomies and dominant-group power structures.

Gendered beliefs and practices vary across cultures and differ according to who makes the observations and judgments. In any given society, gender constructions vary within and across groups in a society. For example, White women in the United States might have different concepts of womanhood and femininity from those of Asian women, and African American women may have gender constructions different from those of Latina women. In each of these ethnic groups, subcultures retain their own distinctive gender expectations. Our social construction of gender intersects with other social status identities, thereby creating in each of us a self-image of who we are as females and males and how we should behave. The cognition "I am a woman" functions to activate a person's entire experience of femaleness in society and serves as a general schema or cognitive framework that shapes her actions (Bem, 1981, 1983, 1993). The cognition "I am a Latina American woman" generates alternative images as each person constructs her personal and social identities from the complex matrix of her culture and personal experience. Gender also influences the expectations and behaviors of those with whom we interact, and these expectations result in self-fulfilling prophecies. We change our gender behavior to meet the expectations of important others (Bem, 1993). Our social construction of gender influences the socialization practices we use with girls and boys. The social construction of gender assumes a major role in the definition and diagnosis of women's illness, in the expression of symptoms, in the treatment strategies, and in theoretical explanations. Thus, mental illness is both a social and a personal event.

Gender and Power Differentials

Feminine therapy has developed from the recognition that a great deal of human suffering takes place because of the unequal distribution of power in society that is based on factors such as race and ethnicity, class, disability, sexual orientation, and so on. These power differentials not only have resulted in physical assaults against individuals, but also the end product may be psychological and economical, including limited educational and professional options. Power differentials are also linked to gender role expectations. For instance, feminist therapists maintain that societal gender role expectations greatly affect a person's identity from birth onward. Such expectations become deeply ingrained in one's personality and persist throughout one's life. The practice of feminist therapy is politicized in its understanding of the causes of psychological injury. In addition, feminist therapy has influenced postmodern psychotherapy's concept of power (Enns, 2004).

Most feminist approaches to therapy share a core group of beliefs that influence therapeutic practice (Enns, 2000; Worell & Papendrick-Remer, 2001). They are presented in the box that follows.

> ### Core Feminist Beliefs
>
> 1. Males and females develop in different ways related to language, worldview, values, and perceptions, and such differences should be taken into consideration and respected in therapy.
>
> 2. Historically, women and minorities have been marginalized, and therefore dealing with issues related to power is an integral part of the therapeutic process for those who feel powerless.
>
> 3. Political, social, and cultural variables are at the core of many presenting complaints for women.
>
> 4. The current diagnostic system is biased against both nontraditional and traditional female behavior. Sometimes women's behavior is considered maladaptive when it might not be so. The *Diagnostic and Statistical Manual of Mental Disorders*, fourth edition, text revision (*DSM-IV-TR*; American Psychiatric Association, 2000) and its earlier versions were developed primarily by White male psychiatrists. This diagnostic manual focuses on psychological symptoms and not on the social factors that caused them. Some feminist therapists have acknowledged these weaknesses, but they use the *DSM-IV-TR* in working with clients and assessing the cultural context of clients' problems to prevent them from being blamed for their own problems.

Feminist Therapy Approaches

There are four major approaches that are specific to feminist therapy: (1) consciousness raising, (2) social and gender role analysis, (3) resocialization, and (4) social activism.

Consciousness Raising

Typically, consciousness raising is done in small groups in a leaderless manner; the group discusses women's individual and shared experiences. Women in these groups examine how oppression and socialization contribute to their personal distress and dysfunction. Consciousness raising helps women feel empowered to take steps against oppression by participating in social action. Consciousness-raising groups were held very effectively during the 1970s, 1980s, and 1990s.

Therapists frequently incorporate consciousness raising into their practices because it helps women realize that they are not the sole cause of their distress and that others share their problems. Consciousness raising has many similarities with traditional group psychotherapy, including provision of role models, sharing personal experience, imparting information, peer support, identifying commonalties, and instillation of hope. Clients examine how oppression of women contributes to personal distress and discuss solutions for creating individual and social change. Consciousness raising empowers women by making them feel able to take action against oppression through the mutual support of group members.

Social and Gender Role Analysis

In social and **gender role analysis**, the therapist helps the client to identify his or her own experiences in relation to social and gender role norms. Together, the therapist and the client analyze how implicit and explicit sex roles may have contributed to the client's problems. This helps the client explore the possible origins of psychological distress. Together, the therapist and the client come up with ways to bring about social change and gain self knowledge.

Some therapists ask clients to complete measures to assess gender role identity and beliefs (Worell & Remer, 2003). The therapist helps the client identify both explicit and implicit sex role messages that the client has internalized over her lifetime. Together, they develop a plan for implementing changes. Social and gender role analysis focuses on assisting the client in identifying the messages she has received across her life span and assessing their impact. For example, a client may learn how society teaches women to be submissive and self-sacrificing. Feminist therapists do not challenge a client's sex role beliefs as erroneous.

Women from ethnic minority backgrounds are often doubly oppressed by race/ethnicity and gender, which affect clients' role perceptions. The "deleterious effects of sexism, racism, and elitism" (Espin, 1994, p. 272) must be dealt with in sessions. When working with clients from ethnic minority backgrounds, Comas-Diaz (1994) recommends using "ethnocultural assessment" as outlined by Comas-Diaz and Jacobsen (1991), which is a diagnostic tool used to assess a client's level of ethnocultural identity. This social and gender role analysis should then be used during therapy to help clients find solutions to their problems.

Social and gender role analysis helps clients explore the impact of social expectations and cultural norms on their mental health. The extant research suggests that social and gender role analysis is likely to provide therapeutic benefit by providing clients with the opportunity to identify difficulties and to adopt different, more assertive, problem-solving roles. Knowledge gained through social and gender role analysis is helpful to clients.

Resocialization

Resocialization takes place after social and gender role analysis and involves reorganizing the client's belief system. Clients learn to view things differently and develop new coping skills and strategies. Methods are taught that increase self-esteem, assertiveness, and self-views. A main goal of resocialization is an overall increase in well-being.

Social Activism

Social activism is a fourth approach that some therapists use. This approach is founded on the premise that "the personal is political" and that the client's problems originate from the structural inequalities of a given society. The feminist therapist who adopts the philosophy of social activism advocates that clients speak out, organize protests, and engage in letter-writing campaigns. Feminists maintain that social change supports the mental health of all individuals.

THE THERAPEUTIC PROCESS IN FEMINIST THERAPY

The Therapeutic Relationship

The therapeutic relationship is based on empowerment of clients and equalizing of power between therapist and client. The therapeutic relationship is structured to help the client identify gender-delimiting schema. Therapists teach clients to recognize how they define themselves and how they relate to others (gender role expectations). The therapist demystifies the counseling process.

Goals of Feminist Therapy

Feminist therapists assert that the goals of therapy should include both changes in the client's own personal life as well as changes in society's institutions. Enns (2004) has proposed five goals for feminist therapy: (1) equality, (2) balancing independence and interdependence, (3) empowerment, (4) self-nurturance, and (5) valuing diversity. The final goal of feminist therapy is to work to eliminate sexism and oppression within the broad society (Worell & Remer, 2003).

Political awareness and social action are important goals in feminist therapy. Feminist theoretical approaches stress the need for women to become aware of gender role stereotyping, sexism, and discrimination (Ballou & West, 2000). Women are encouraged to become involved politically in organizations such as the National Organization for Women.

Whereas traditional theories of therapy and psychotherapy place little emphasis on the ways in which power affects the mental health of clients, feminist therapy considers the analysis of power differentials to be important to the therapeutic process (Hill & Ballou, 2005). Feminist therapists avoid fostering a sense of victimology among the clients they serve. *Victimology* refers to the belief that a person is a helpless victim of her environmental or contextual circumstances.

Feminist therapists stress the importance of intentionally using a strengths-based approach with women and men. Brown (2000) states that women should not be assessed primarily from a pathological perspective. Feminist therapy refers clients to women's support groups, community action work, and legal aid. Clinicians should help clients realize their strengths. Most feminist clinicians combine feminist concepts with the traditional models of therapy. Worell and Remer (2003) maintain that feminist therapists help clients

- become cognizant of their own gender role socialization process;
- identify their internalized messages and replace them with positive, self-enhancing messages;
- learn how sexist and oppressive societal beliefs and practices influence them in negative ways;
- develop the skills needed to effect changes in the environment;
- restructure institutions to eliminate discriminatory practices;
- assess the impact of social factors on their lives;
- construct a sense of personal and social power; and
- learn to trust their experience and intuition.

Role of the Therapist in Feminist Therapy

The therapist is an active participant in feminist therapy. Therapists are expected to integrate feminist analysis in all areas of their work. The feminist therapist must be able to recognize a client's socioeconomic and political circumstances as such factors relate to the client's mental health care. Feminist therapists are expected to be actively involved in ending oppression and empowering women and girls. They are committed to monitoring their own biases. They must be aware of their own gender schema. Feminist therapists accept and validate their client's experiences and feelings.

Feminist therapists establish an egalitarian role in the therapy session. They do not hide behind the expert role. They may also use self-disclosure to reduce the power differential between client and therapist. Therapists focus on the power that clients have in themselves. They demystify the counseling relationship and make the clients active partners in therapy. They use gender and power analyses to understand clients and their concerns.

Many feminist therapists do not use diagnostic labels, or they use them sparingly. Feminist therapists believe that diagnostic labels are limiting because they focus on the individual's symptoms and not on the social factors that cause dysfunctional behavior. Sometimes diagnostic labels may represent an instrument of oppression, and they have the potential to reduce the therapist's respect for the client.

Role of the Client in Feminist Therapy

The client is treated as an equal during therapy. Clients are expected to participate actively in their own therapy. They may be asked to attend workshops and to engage in reading that explicates their situation. Clients become empowered as a result of participating in the therapeutic process.

Role of Men in Feminist Therapy

Men can benefit from feminist therapy. Similar to women, men also deal with gender constraints, such as the demands for strength and autonomy. Moreover, men are limited by the notion that they should not express vulnerability, sensitivity, and empathy. Men can benefit from feminist therapy by working on these issues and by learning new relationship skills to help them understand and explore issues involved with emotions, intimacy, and self-disclosure.

Inner Reflections

How relevant is feminist therapy to your life?

What parts, if any, of feminist therapy would you incorporate into your integrative approach to psychotherapy?

Feminist therapists do treat men clients. Levant (2001) has pointed out that feminist therapy might be helpful for men who feel overwhelmed about society's demands for achievement and performance. Ganley (1988) has described several issues and techniques for counseling men from a feminist perspective. For instance, men might desire assistance with intimacy issues.

The jury is still out on the effectiveness of men as feminist therapists. There are some who maintain that men can be profeminist therapists when they embrace the principles and incorporate the practices of feminism in their therapy.

Feminist Therapy Techniques

Feminist therapists address a number of life issues, including family and marriage relations, reproduction, career concerns, physical and sexual abuse, body image disorders, self-esteem, and empowerment of women. According to Bohan (1992), feminist practitioners should follow six guidelines:

1. Therapists should be knowledgeable concerning gender role socialization and the impact these standards have on what it means to be a woman or a man.

2. Therapists should be cognizant of the impact of the distribution of power within the family and power differentials between men and women in terms of decision making, child rearing, career options, and division of labor.

3. Therapists must understand the sexist context of the social system in which men and women live and its impacts on both the individual and the family.

4. Therapists must be committed to promoting roles for both women and men that are not limited by cultural or gender stereotypes.

5. Therapists must acquire intervention skills that assist clients in their gender role journey.

6. Therapists must be committed to working toward the elimination of gender role bias as a source of pathology throughout society.

These principles are based on a gender-fair ideology for counseling that may be applicable to family therapists as well.

Worell and Remer (2003) have described feminist therapeutic techniques from a cognitive-behavioral framework. The techniques are gender role analysis, **gender role intervention**, assertiveness training, power analysis, and bibliotherapy.

Gender Role Analysis

Gender role analysis is used to help clients understand the influence of gender role expectations. The first step is to have the client identify various gender role messages that she has experienced during her lifetime. Second, the counselor helps the female client to identify the positive and negative consequences of gender-related messages. Third, the clinician and client identify the statements that the client makes to herself based on these gender role messages. Fourth, the clinician and the client decide which messages they want to change. Fifth, the clinician and the client construct a plan to implement the client's desired change and to have the client follow through. As a result of identifying and analyzing gender role messages, the client starts the process of freeing herself from such messages (Enns, 2004).

Gender Role Intervention

A counselor does not go through a detailed gender role analysis but instead helps the client to understand and deal with the impact of gender role and other social expectations on her or him (Enns, 2000). The therapist helps the client achieve insights about social role expectations. For instance, an older woman may feel that she is not qualified to obtain a job. The counselor works with the woman to understand the societal basis of such beliefs but keeps the focus on identifying positive worker abilities that the client possesses.

Assertiveness Training

Feminist therapists sometimes recommend assertiveness training for their clients. Therapists believe that teaching assertiveness skills helps reduce the sense of helplessness and depression among clients. Assertiveness training teaches people how to stand up for themselves without violating the rights of others. In contrast, aggressiveness involves insisting on one's rights while trampling on the rights of others.

Power Analysis

Throughout history, especially American history, White men have exercised more power than women in making and enforcing decisions about family life, work, laws, and interpersonal relationships. Worell and Remer (2003) assert that therapists can help women clients make changes where their lack of power has prevented change in the past. The first step in **power analysis** is to have the client provide a definition that fits her and to apply it to different kinds of power (Enns, 2004). For instance, if a woman wants the power to express herself to her partner without being interrupted, she and the therapist examine ways for her to demonstrate communication power in her relationship with her partner. Second, the therapist and the client discuss differential access to power—legal, financial, and interpersonal. Third, the therapist and client discuss different ways power can be used to bring about the desired change. Fourth, clients reexamine the gender role messages they have been raised with that deal with power. Finally, the client and the counselor develop power strategies to be used to obtain change.

Bibliotherapy

A therapist might refer clients to nonfiction books, autobiographies, self-help books, and movies. For instance, a therapist might give a reading assignment for a woman who is very concerned about being overweight. She might recommend reading some medical summaries involving obesity as well as autobiographies of women who successfully dealt with their weight issues. In addition, therapists give clients reading assignments that address issues such as coping skills, gender role stereotypes, power differentials between men and women, gender inequality, and society's obsession with thinness. Reading assignments may serve to bridge cultural gaps between the client and the therapist.

Relational-Cultural Theory: The New Feminist Psychotherapeutic Approach

Feminist therapy is still in the process of developing. **Relational-cultural theory (RCT)** is the most current form of feminist therapy. Comstock et al. (2008) trace the history of RCT to Jean Baker Miller's (1986) book *Toward a New Psychology of Women*. In that book, Miller noted the centrality of relationships in women's lives, while the traditional models of psychotherapy emphasized concepts dealing with individuation, separation, and autonomy as markers of emotional maturity and psychological health (Comstock et al., 2008). She suggested that mental health professionals' lack of understanding of the contextual and relational experiences of women, people of color, and marginalized men has led to their devaluing important factors that contributed to such clients' psychological well-being.

RCT complements the multicultural/social justice movement by (1) identifying how contextual and sociocultural challenges impede individuals' ability to create, sustain, and engage in growth-fostering relationships in therapy and life and (2) examining relational competencies over the life span. RCT complements the multicultural/social justice movement by functioning as an alternative theoretical framework from which mental health professionals can explore how issues related to sex role socialization, power, marginalization, and subordination influence the mental health and relational development of all people.

The RCT approach to therapy is founded on the idea that healing takes place within the context of mutually empathic, growth-fostering relationships. It identifies and deconstructs obstacles to mutuality that individuals encounter in diverse relational contexts and networks (Comstock, 2005; Comstock & Qin, 2005). Although people may want a connection with others, they often develop an entire repertoire of behavior that alienates them from such connections. For instance, instead of loving others, they withhold love and affection. They withdraw from others and criticize loved ones (Comstock, 2005). Negative interpersonal strategies keep individuals out of relationships, and they contribute to their maladjustment in living.

RCT therapists contend that the manner in which people navigate through their lifelong relational changes affects their mental health significantly. Comstock, Duffey, and St. George (2002) have asserted,

> According to this model, understanding one's relational capacities in a sociocultural context allows one to move out of a place of shame and frustration and into the possibility for more mutually empathic and authentic connections (Hartling et al., 2000; Walker, 2001). As such, the relational model can be used with both women and men from diverse backgrounds and in therapy settings that address a multitude of issues (Jordan & Dooley, 2000). (p. 256)

RCT is based on the belief that the experiences of isolation, shame, humiliation, oppression, and marginalization are relational violations and traumas that are at the heart of human suffering (Comstock et al., 2008). The theory asserts that therapy that is not founded on relational, multicultural, or social justice ideology has the potential to perpetuate oppression. Core RCT principles highlight the process of psychological growth and relational development.

Inner Reflection

To what extent, if any, does relational-cultural theory add to feminist theory in psychotherapy?

---

1. Throughout their life spans, people grow through and move toward relationships.

2. Mature functioning is marked by movement toward mutuality rather than separation.

3. Psychological growth is characterized by a person's ability to participate in increasingly complex and diversified relational networks.

4. Mutual empathy and mutual empowerment are at the core of growth-fostering relationships.

5. Authenticity is required for real engagement in growth-fostering relationships.

6. People grow as they contribute to the development of growth-fostering relationships.

7. The goal of development is an individual's realization of increased relational competence over the life span.

RESEARCH AND EVALUATION IN FEMINIST THERAPY

Multicultural Positives

Feminist therapy is sensitive to diversity and social contexts that may limit a client's life chances and happiness. Feminist therapists are especially attuned to uncovering sources of oppression, and they make an effort to understand client's experiences of racism, sexism, and culture in relationship to gender. Feminist therapy seeks to create change at both the individual and societal levels of life. They encourage clients to examine the interaction between their personal lives and the larger society in which they live.

The vast majority of all traditional approaches to psychotherapy have been developed by men, and they contain male assumptions about women's psychological development. Feminist therapy examines women's issues from the perspectives of women. It has elucidated the negative effects that traditional gender roles have on women and men. Some men, for instance, experience role strain in the demands they face at work and at home.

Feminist therapy has provided insight into the cultural demands and challenges facing men that may impede on their positive development. Feminist therapy approaches have been used to work with men in battering groups, modeling how to express emotions, including anger and love. McGregor, Tutty, Babins-Wagner, and Marlyn (2002) developed a program called Responsible Choices for Men, a feminist-based, 12-week group therapy program for abusive men using narrative interventions. The overall goal of the program was to help men express their concerns in a nonabusive way that respected the rights and feelings of others. Participants were assessed before and after the program for their levels of physical and nonphysical abuse, self-esteem, perceived stress, family relations, depression, assertiveness, and sex role beliefs. The program was deemed effective because participants showed improvement in all categories.

Both feminist therapy and multicultural therapy have focused attention on the negative effects of discrimination and oppression. In addition, culturally competent feminist therapists search for ways to work within clients' cultures. Many of the techniques feminist therapists have developed can easily be modified to work with a variety of ethnic and cultural groups. In recent years, these two approaches have worked on developing linkages between them. Both schools have called attention to the fact that therapy theories should be gender fair, multicultural in orientation, and life span oriented.

Multicultural Blind Spots

One criticism of feminist therapies is that they place too much blame on society, creating a victim mentality for women and members of ethnic minority groups. Individuals who make this criticism maintain that an overemphasis on society factors tends to contribute to clients' not taking personal responsibility for the situations that exist in their lives. Clients should be encouraged to make the changes that they desire in their lives—not blame society for their problems. Feminists have challenged this criticism by saying that they not only educate their clients about the impact of their oppressive environments but also offer empowerment strategies to help clients take control of their lives.

Another criticism of feminist theories is that they are skewed toward the political feminism of primarily White, middle-class, women oftentimes excluding the life situations of women of color. Women of color have maintained that race rather than gender is the appropriate category of analysis. In recent years, feminism has expanded to include more women of color.

One criticism of feminist therapy is that therapists may be too feminist and militant in their views, thereby influencing clients. Feminist therapists have been accused of advocating a certain way of looking at gender roles and appropriate behavior for men and women. Instead of trying to persuade a client to look at gender roles in a certain way, the therapist's task is to provide support and information to challenge the client to examine for herself which road to take. Another criticism is that feminist therapists do not take a neutral stance during therapy. Critics maintain that feminism originated and was developed by middle-class White women who were overly represented in the lesbian tradition.

Some critics have asserted that feminist approaches to psychotherapy have polarized males and females and that they have failed to acknowledge true differences between men and women, preferring to claim that all differences are socialized differences. For instance, consider the following recent research on sex differences:

- A 2013 University of Pennsylvania (Ingalhalikar et al., 2013) study showed "striking differences" in how the neural nets are wired in male versus female brains.
- A 2012 University of Turin study of 10,000 individuals (Del Giudice, Booth, & Irwing, 2012) that "using new and more accurate methods to measure and analyze personality differences" found differences that were "extremely large . . . by any psychological standard" and concluded that "the true extent of sex differences in human personality has been consistently underestimated. . . . The idea that there are only

minor differences between the personality profiles of males and females should be rejected as based on inadequate methodology."

- A 2008 Northwestern/University of Haifa study using functional magnetic resonance imaging to study language abilities:

For the first time and in unambiguous findings, researchers show both that brain areas associated with language work harder in girls during language tasks, and that boys and girls rely on very different parts of the brain when performing these tasks. Language processing is more abstract in girls, more sensory in boys (See http://www.eurekalert.org/pub_releases/2008-03/nu-gdi030308.php)

- Multiple studies documenting "robust" sex differences in spatial ability, including at least one, by University of California, Los Angeles (UCLA) in 2008, detected significant differences in children as young as 5 months of age.
- Men tend to perform better than women at tasks that require rotating an object mentally, studies have indicated. Now, developmental psychologists at Pitzer College and UCLA have discovered that this type of spatial skill is present in infancy and can be found in boys as young as 5 months old.

Although women tend to be stronger verbally than men, many studies have found that adult men have an advantage in the ability to imagine complex objects visually and to mentally rotate them, and that this advantage goes back to infancy according to Scott P. Johnson, a UCLA professor of psychology and an expert in infant perception, brain development, cognition and learning. "Infants as young as 5 months can perform the skill, but only boys—at least in our study." (See http://newsroom.ucla.edu/releases/psychologists-report-a-gender-72612)

Integration of Feminist Therapy With Other Approaches

There is a high potential for integrating feminist therapy principles with other therapeutic practices. Worell and Remer (2003) have indicated that before a theory of psychotherapy can be integrated with feminist therapy, feminists should look for sources of bias in the theory by analyzing its historical development, its key theoretical concepts, the use of sexist language, and bias in diagnosis and therapeutic techniques. They can work to eliminate sexist features of the theory to see whether the theory is compatible with feminist principles. That some principles of feminist therapy, such as gender equality, can be incorporated into other therapies is a strength because it can broaden the theoretical base of other models and therapies.

Feminist therapy has been integrated with behavior and cognitive therapies. To make cognitive and behavior therapies more consistent with feminist therapy, Worell and Remer (2003) have recommended changing diagnostic labels that emphasize the pathology of people, focusing instead on feelings and integrating concepts from gender role socialization. Enns (1997) has recommended that through the Gestalt emphasis on awareness and self and choices, women may expand their options in the world. The Gestalt emphasis on taking responsibility may not take into consideration the social and economic factors that also influence clients' choices—issues that are an important part of feminist therapy.

Contributions and Criticisms of Feminist Therapy

Feminist therapists have made a major contribution to therapy and psychotherapy by leading the way for gender-sensitive practice. Apart from the work of feminists, there is no other theory that places gender at the center of its theory. Another noteworthy contribution is that feminist therapists have increased public awareness of the impact of culture and multiple oppressions on people. They have also helped the therapy field to understand how important it is to become aware of the gender role messages under which therapists and clients have been raised. Feminist therapists should be credited with helping the world to understand power relationships in families and between men and women.

Feminist therapists have been an important voice in questioning the traditional therapy theories. Most therapy theories put the cause of problems within the individual rather than within the external circumstances that exist in the environment or society. As noted earlier, feminist therapists examine clients' problems in terms of the social context in which they live, and they have advocated an **egalitarian relationship** between the therapist and the client. They have worked to establish policies that reduce discrimination involving gender, race, culture, sexual orientation, and age. Feminist therapists have also demanded action in cases of sexual misconduct where male therapists abused the trust of female clients.

The following is a summary of the important contributions feminist approaches have to psychotherapy:

1. Feminist therapeutic approaches acknowledge the role of an oppressive environment and its forces on people, both females and males.

2. The feminist perspective has helped therapists understand the use of power in relationships and the role that power plays in racial and cultural contexts.

3. Feminist therapists encourage change and not just adjustment to one's circumstances.

Evidence-Based Research and Feminist Approaches to Psychotherapy

Although there have been a number of uncontrolled trials on the efficacy of feminist therapy, consciousness-raising groups, and gender-sensitive psychoeducational groups, the effectiveness of feminist therapy has not been rigorously evaluated (Beutler, Crago, & Arezmendi, 1986; Bowman, Scrogin, Floyd, & McKendree-Smith, 2001; Sue & Lam, 2002). This researcher did not find any controlled outcome research conducted on feminist therapy. Meta-analyses on the effectiveness of adult psychotherapy do not include any representative studies on feminist therapy. Studies and reports from workshops do suggest that it is important to have a therapist of the same gender and that such therapists should present a nonstereotypical gender perspective. The lack of outcome studies on the effectiveness of feminist theoretical approaches may be attributed in part to the fact that most research studies investigate a client's remission of psychological symptoms, which forms only part of the feminist agenda.

APA has developed a task force that is charged with describing the state of evidence-based practice research related to feminist interventions/practice and contributing to the larger dialogue within psychology about the form and nature of evidence-based practice (e.g., what it should look like using feminist, diversity, and social justice perspectives). The task force's goals are (1) to increase evidence-based practice research on feminist interventions and models and (2) to increase the presence of feminist psychologists by creating the future of evidence-based practice in psychology.

Despite a search of the literature, I could find few articles on evidence-based practice using feministic approaches to psychotherapy. Most of the articles put forth arguments to demonstrate that feminism works, but there were few empirical studies demonstrating such. In the article "Still Subversive After All These Years: The Relevance of Feminist Therapy in the Age of Evidence-Based Practice," Laura Brown (2006) addressed questions about the viability of feminist practice in the current zeitgeist of evidence-based practice. Using the framework of responding to questions raised by doctoral students about feminist therapy, Brown proposed that feminist diagnostic strategies enhance cultural competence for therapists, thus better preparing practitioners for the clients of the 21st century. She did provide limited empirical support that feminist therapy works. Feminist approaches to psychotherapy are, however, not listed as evidence based by the APA.

GAY AND LESBIAN THERAPY ___
Brief Overview

Feminist therapists have worked with lesbian clients and homosexual or gay men. In discussing feminist therapy approaches to homosexual people, Brown (1988) has touched on gender role socialization, coping with homophobia, and working with "coming out" issues with gay and lesbian clients. A gender role analysis helps lesbians and gay men to see the influence of societal influences on their development.

Counseling gay or lesbian individuals is a difficult process that requires that a therapist have strong multicultural counseling competencies (Barret & Logan, 2002; Hancock, 2000; Pope, 2008). Three important documents discuss the competence of therapists who work with lesbian and gay people: (1) the *Multicultural Counseling Competencies and Standards* (Sue, Arrendondo, & McDavis, 1992); (2) the Association for Gay, Lesbian, and Bisexual Issues in Counseling's *Competencies in Counseling Gay, Lesbian, Bisexual, and Transgendered Clients* (Terndrup, Ritter, Barret, Logan, & Mate, 1997); and (3) the APA's (2000) *Guidelines for Psychotherapy With Lesbian, Gay, and Bisexual Clients.*

KEY CONCEPTS OF GAY AND LESBIAN THERAPY _____

To counsel gays and lesbians effectively, therapists must have a basic understanding of the social, cultural, and historic context in which lesbian women and gay men live. Therapists should become aware of the history, language, traditions, and sense of community that make up the gay and lesbian cultures (Pope & Barret, 2002).

A Definition of Terms: *Gay, Lesbian, Bisexual, Transgender*

The term *gay* can be used to refer to men or women who are sexually and affectionally attracted to members of the same sex (Pope, 2008). Although some women identify with the word *gay*, many others prefer the term *lesbian*. Throughout this section, the term *gay* will be used to refer to men, while the term *lesbian* will be used for females.

> *Bisexual* is a term that refers to a person of one gender who is sexually attracted to individuals of both genders. *Transgender* refers to individuals who identify as one gender but have the physiology of the opposite gender. . . . Queer . . . is a political statement of difference from the majority culture. (Pope, 2008, p. 203)

Discrimination Against Gays and Lesbians

Just a few decades ago, gays and lesbians were subjected to widespread societal discrimination throughout the world. During the 1960s, law enforcement sometimes conducted raids on gay bars, and sometimes the police recorded the identities of those present at the raid and provided the information to newspapers for publication. Prior to the 1960s, many gay and lesbian individuals kept their true sexual orientation hidden from their families and work colleagues. Stonewall created a sense of solidarity and community for these individuals.

Did you know, for instance, that in 1969, gays and the New York City police engaged in what are known as the Stonewall Riots? The Stonewall Riots are considered a key and defining moment in gay and lesbian history. The riots consisted of a series of violent conflicts between gays (as they were called at that time) and New York City police officers that started on June 28, 1969. Police raided the Stonewall Inn, a bar in West Village, New York City (Cooper, 1989). The Stonewall conflicts lasted several days and drew a crowd of 400 gay protesters. Never before had gay people stood up for themselves publicly to resist police harassment that targeted their community.

Since the 1990s, many milestones have been reached. For instance, in some Western countries, gay men are permitted to serve in the armed forces. There was movement to get rid of the "Don't ask, don't tell" provision within the U.S. Armed Forces. In December 2010, President Obama signed a bill reversing the "Don't ask, don't tell" policy, so that gay men and lesbian women can serve openly and with honor within the armed forces.

During May 2004, Massachusetts became the first state in the nation to grant marriage licenses to same-sex couples (Human Rights Campaign, 2005). In addition to Massachusetts, gays and lesbians can now marry legally in New Hampshire, Connecticut, Iowa, and Vermont. New York, Rhode Island, New Mexico, and Washington, D.C., recognize marriages of same-sex couples legally performed elsewhere. In California, gay and lesbian couples could legally marry between June and November 2008, but with the passage of Proposition 8 in California in November 2008, same-sex marriage is prohibited by law. The gay and lesbian couples who were married in 2008 are still legally married, but no new legal marriages can be performed in California. The issue continues to make its way through the state courts.

> ### Inner Reflection
> Have you ever witnessed homophobia or gender discrimination against gays and lesbians?

Increasingly, countries throughout the world are giving gays and lesbians the right to marry: Canada, Europe, Norway, the Netherlands, Belgium, Spain, Portugal, Iceland, and South Africa. Despite these landmark developments, lesbian and gay discrimination continues to exist within the United States and throughout the world (Belge, 2010).

What Is Heterosexism?

Heterosexism is the belief that every person is heterosexual; therefore, it marginalizes or disregards persons who do not identify as heterosexual (Croteau, Lark, Lidderdale, & Chung, 2005). It is also the belief that heterosexuality is superior to homosexuality and other sexual orientations. Heterosexism pervades societal customs and institutions. When you first meet a person, do you naturally assume that the person is heterosexual? Why or why not? From my perspective, heterosexism exists because "normal" sexual development is thought to be heterosexual instead of homosexual. Stereotypes and negative attributions are at the heart of heterosexist attitudes.

What Is Homophobia?

Despite the progress that has been made in the treatment of gay men and lesbians, there is still much **homophobia**, which may be defined as a fear and hatred of **lesbian**, **gay**, **bisexual**, and **transgendered** (**LGBT**) individuals based on a lack of knowledge and cultural conditioning. Individuals who are experiencing conflicts in their own sexual identity may also manifest fears of being perceived as gay or fear their own attraction to members of the same sex. Gay and lesbian people sometimes experience *internalized homophobia*, which is defined as a process by which a member of the LGBT community comes to accept and live out inaccurate, disparaging myths and stereotypes about LGBT persons. Thus, the social and cultural context within which gays and lesbians live is extremely important. Environments, especially family environments, that view a same-sex or bisexual orientation as negative and as a disgrace produce individuals who experience internalized homophobia and sexual identity conflict. Homophobia can be summarized as containing the following elements:

- Irrational hatred for, fear of, and contempt for LGBT people
- Persecution of or violence against LGBT people
- Internalized hatred when one believes that one is a gay man or lesbian
- The belief that if LGBT people touch you, they are making sexual advances
- The belief that LGBT people are asking to be treated "special" because they demand basic civil rights

- Changing one's seat when an LGBT person sits next to you
- Repulsion by public displays of affection between LGBT people, while affection displayed between heterosexuals is acceptable

Sexual Orientation Development

Sexual orientation is an enduring emotional, romantic, or sexual attraction that a person feels toward men, toward women, or toward both. When one's attraction is toward the same sex, orientation is said to be homosexual; toward the opposite sex, it is heterosexual; and toward both sexes, it is bisexual. Research has not conclusively found sexual orientation to be determined by any particular factor or factors, and the timing of the emergence, recognition, and expression of one's sexual orientation differs across people (Just the Facts Coalition, 2008).

Sexual orientation cannot necessarily be used interchangeably with *sexual activity*. Some adolescents and adults identify themselves as lesbian, gay, or bisexual, but they do not have sexual encounters with a person of the same sex. Likewise, other individuals do have sexual experiences with persons of the same sex, but they do not consider themselves lesbian, gay, or bisexual. During adolescence, for instance, many young people participate in a period of sexual experimentation and discovery.

LGBT Youth and Schools

LGBT young people are becoming more visible in our schools. Recent studies have revealed that, on average, lesbian and gay youth first become aware of their same-sex attractions at an average of 9 to 10 years of age and first identify as lesbian or gay at an average of 14 to 16 years of age. LGBT students are subjected to many of the same problems experienced by adult gays and lesbians. According to a 2007 survey by the Gay, Lesbian and Straight Education Network, 86.2% of LGBT students reported being verbally harassed. More than half of the students surveyed stated that they felt unsafe in schools because of their sexual orientation, and a third said they felt unsafe due to their gender expression.

Lesbian, gay, and bisexual youth embark on developmental pathways that are both similar to and different from those of heterosexual adolescents (Just the Facts Coalition, 2008). The majority of LGBT youth are healthy persons who make significant contributions to their families and schools. LGBT youth face additional hurdles in that they may have to cope with prejudice, discrimination, and violence in both their families and within the general society. Such marginalization negatively affects their mental and physical health. In one study, for example, LGBT students were more likely than heterosexual students to report about missing school because of fear, being threatened by other students, and having their property damaged at school. "One result of the isolation and lack of support experienced by some lesbian, gay, and bisexual youth is higher rates of emotional distress, suicide attempts, and risky sexual behavior and substance use" (Just the Facts Coalition, 2008, p. 4).

To provide an open and safe school environment, school personnel must understand the nature of sexual orientation development and support the healthy development of all students. When school environments become more positive for LGBT youth, the youths' higher rates of depression, anxiety, and substance abuse will most likely decrease.

Top 10 Physical and Mental Health Concerns of LGBT College Students

Pace University's Westchester campus publishes the *Spotlight* newsletter. In its Fall 2008 issue, it identified the "top ten physical and emotional health concerns of LGBT students." The newsletter pointed out that LGBT students in college are facing numerous transitions in their lives—moving away from home, facing academic challenges, and making new friends, all the while exploring issues around their sexuality. These concerns were originally published in *The Advocate College Guide for*

LGBT Students (Windmeyer, 2006). D'Augelli (1991) has provided a scholarly foundation for preventing mental health problems among lesbian and gay college students. Following are the 10 concerns that LGBT college students face:

1. *Access, comfort, and trust:* LGBT students take notice and appreciate when college programming involves them and when the college has policies of nondiscrimination to protect their rights as members of the LGBT community.

2. *Coming out:* Many LGBT students "come out" while at college. They may contemplate coming out, accepting their sexual orientation, and revealing it to others. LGBT students consider the risks versus the benefits of publicly identifying oneself as lesbian, gay, bisexual, or transgender.

3. *Healing from oppression:* When LGBT students experience anti-LGBT discrimination, violence, and hatred, they may develop physical and mental health problems (D'Augelli, 1993).

4. *Coping with stress, anxiety, and depression:* Individuals who are LGBT are more likely to experience depression and anxiety than are their heterosexual counterparts. If they are isolated on college campuses, they might feel intense sadness, anxiety, loneliness, and discomfort in social situations.

5. *Surviving suicidal thoughts, plans, or attempts:* Decades of research have reported a link between LGBT young people and suicide. College students who report having gender characteristics usually associated with their opposite sex tend to be at greater risk for suicidal symptoms, regardless of their sexual orientation (D'Augelli, 1993).

6. *Sexual health concerns:* Sexually transmitted diseases have increased among members of the LGBT group. Although there is a myth that sex between women carries no risk, women can transmit HPV, herpes, hepatitis A, hepatitis B, gonorrhea, and Chlamydia when having sex with other women.

7. *HIV/AIDS:* After 13 years of declining rates of new HIV infection, studies have found that

rates of new HIV infection among men who have sex with men have recently increased.

8. *Smoking:* Approximately 43% of young gay men and lesbians of ages 18 to 24 smoke, in comparison with 17% of the rest of the population.

9. *Drinking and other drug use:* It has been estimated that 20% to 25% of gay men and lesbians are heavy alcohol users. Gay and bisexual men have a higher addiction rate than heterosexual men with drugs such as marijuana, cocaine, and ecstasy.

10. *Body image:* Both gay men and lesbians struggle with issues regarding their body images. Women in the gay community may become overweight, while gay men may struggle to achieve an exaggerated sense of male beauty.

Coming Out and Gender Identity Development for Gays and Lesbians

There have been some questions about whether or not gays and lesbians experience the same type of **gender identity** development as do individuals with heterosexual orientation. For the most part, identity development for gays and lesbians has focused on the process of **coming out**. When individuals have conflict about their sexual identity or they are forced to hide their true sexual identity because of fears of being ostracized, harmed, or demeaned in some way, their identity development is arrested or impaired.

Coming out is one of the most important developmental processes in the lives of LGBT people. Coming out *to others and to oneself* is a unique process that differentiates lesbians and gay men from other minority cultures. It can be defined as a process of recognizing, accepting, expressing, and sharing one's sexual orientation with oneself and others. The phrase *coming out* means to publicly affirm one's homosexual identity, sometimes to one person in conversation, sometimes by an act that puts one in the public eye. Coming out, however, is

never a single event but rather a lifelong process. Altman (1979) has defined coming out as

the whole process whereby a person comes to identify himself/herself as a homosexual, and recognizes his/her position as part of a stigmatized and semi-hidden minority. The development of a homosexual identity is a long process that usually begins during adolescence, though sometimes considerably later. Because of the fears and ignorance that surround our views of sex, children discover sexual feelings and behavior incompletely, and often accompanied by great pangs of guilt. [Many of us] manage to hide into our twenties a full realization that [we are] not like [them]. (pp. 15–16)

Part of the reason that individuals experience a coming-out process is that they have already been gender socialized or socialized into a male or a female role. Each culture provides a definition of what is masculine and what is feminine. The traditional definition of masculinity has implications throughout the life span for boys and men. Kindlon and Thompson (2000) have asserted that there is a rigid male gender role that is based on "emotional illiteracy" (p. 5) and a culture of cruelty among young boys. Teenage boys who agreed with traditional gender roles for men were more inclined to "drink beer, smoke pot, have unprotected sex, get suspended from school, and 'trick' or force someone into having sex" (p. 16). In contrast, a traditional female identity development for young girls is likely to focus on "sugar and spice and everything nice." It is assumed that the favorite color of young girls is pink and that they are submissive rather than assertive.

Coming out for a member of an ethnic/racial minority can be very challenging. Usually, there does not have to be a coming-out process about one's ethnicity. The client's skin color, hair texture, and other defining features have been with him or her throughout life. Research suggests that the coming-out process for a gay ethnic/cultural minority person may be especially difficult because the individual may have to face two sources of prejudice and oppression (Pope, 2008).

Coming out is a continuous process. Each time a gay man or lesbian woman meets a new person, he or she must make a decision to come out or not. Individuals use different strategies in the coming-out process, including using the correct gender-specific pronouns when mentioning love relationships or introducing themselves as a member of the LGBT community (Pope & Schecter, 1992). However, coming out has its costs. Gonsiorek (1993) has described some of the consequences of delaying accepting one's sexual orientation. It may cause a developmental domino effect such that other developmental tasks—choosing a mate, choosing a career—are delayed.

Coming Out to Parents, Relatives, and Straight Friends

The following was obtained from the website and is adapted from a pamphlet found on The Gay, Lesbian, Bisexual & Transsexual SIG of the National Capital Freenet, Ontario, Canada.

18 Things to Consider Before Coming Out

1. Understand your own feelings about being gay. If you are still dealing with a lot of guilt or depression, seek help in getting over that before coming out to parents or other non-gay people. If you are comfortable with your gayness, those to whom you come out to will often see that fact and be helped in their own renewed acceptance of you.

2. Timing can be very important in coming out. Be aware of the health, mood, priorities, and problems of those with whom you would like to share your sexuality. The midlife crises of parents, the relationship problems of friends, the business concerns of employers, and countless other factors over which you have no control can affect another's receptivity to your information.

3. Do not come out during an argument. Never use coming out as a weapon. Never encourage parents to feel guilty for having "caused" your sexual orientation—because they didn't.

4. When coming out to parents or family, try to affirm mutual caring and love before launching into your announcement about your gay or lesbian life.

5. Be prepared that your coming out may initially surprise, anger, or upset other people. Do not react angrily or defensively. Consider that the initial reaction will not likely be the long-term one. People who have really faced and dealt with their homophobia may be far more supportive than those who give an immediate but superficial expression of support.

6. Emphasize that you are still the same person. You were gay yesterday and will be gay tomorrow. If you were responsible and caring yesterday, likewise you will be responsible and caring tomorrow.

7. Keep lines of communication open with people after you come out to them—even if their response is negative. Respond to their questions, and remember that they are probably in the process of reexamining their myths and stereotypes about gay people.

8. Be sure that you are well informed about homosexuality. Read some good books about the subject, and share them with individuals to whom you have come out.

9. Encourage your parents or others to whom you come out to meet some of your lesbian and gay friends.

10. Understand that it takes many gay men and lesbians a very long time to come to terms with their own sexuality and even longer to decide to share the fact with others. When you come out to non-gay people, be prepared to give them time to adjust and to comprehend the new information about you. Don't expect immediate acceptance. Look for ongoing, caring dialogue.

(Continued)

(Continued)

11. If you are rejected by someone to whom you have come out, do not lose sight of your own self-worth. Your coming out was a gift of sharing an important part of yourself which that person has chosen to reject. If rejection does come, consider whether the relationship was really worthwhile. Is any relationship so important that it must continue in an atmosphere of dishonesty and hiding? Was the person really your friend or simply the friend of someone he or she imagined you to be?

12. If coming out means the loss of a friend, remember that the loss is not the end of the world. Coming-out decisions must be made cautiously but with integrity and self-respect.

13. A casual approach to coming out often works best with work colleagues and relatives. A formal statement can be avoided by being honest, in a conversational way, about whom you live with and date and how you spend your leisure time. The other person is given a chance to recognize the circumstances of your life and to admit to your homosexuality without being obliged to make some immediate response on this issue.

14. The decision to come out should be yours. Don't be guilt-tripped into it by people who think that everyone must come out or by snooping people who ask impertinent questions. You can usually decide when, where, how, and to whom you wish to come out. Complete public declarations about one's sexuality are not necessarily the best decision for most people.

15. Do not to let your family and close friends find out about your gayness from third parties, such as neighbors or the media. Try to tell them personally beforehand.

16. After you come out, reflect on the experience, and learn from it.

17. Do not let yourself be pressured into coming out before you are ready.

18. Coming out is one the most difficult things a person can do in his or her life. It won't always go well, but most of the time it is a very freeing experience.

Source: Retrieved from http://www.joekort.com/articles60.htm

Cass Gender Identity Development Model for Gays and Lesbians

Cass (1979) presented an early model for the gender identity development stages of gays and lesbians. Currently, there are no theories that describe the identity development of bisexual or transgender individuals. Cass's six stages of gender identity development help explain individuals' thoughts, feelings, and behaviors as they grapple with sexual orientation. These stages are listed below:

Stage 1—Identity confusion: "Could I be gay?" Individuals begin this stage because they become aware of gay or lesbian thoughts, feelings, and attractions and begin to label them as such. Typically, the individual feels confused and experiences inner turmoil because he or she has already been gender socialized. The person's major task is to ask the question "Who am I?" He or she then can accept, deny, or reject that he or she is gay or lesbian. During the identity confusion stage, the individual explores internally the positive and the negative associated with an LGBT identity. At this stage, individuals do not disclose their gender identity turmoil to others.

Stage 2—Identity comparison: This stage involves bargaining or rationalizing. The person begins to think, "I may be a homosexual, but then again I may be bisexual." "Perhaps this is just temporary." "My attractions are just for this one person and not for other people of my same sex." Individuals experience a heightened sense of not belonging anywhere and the sense that "I am the only one in the world like this."

Stage 3—Identity tolerance: This stage constitutes the "I probably am" stage. To counteract feelings of isolation and alienation, the person contacts other LGBT people. He or she tolerates instead of fully accepting a gay or lesbian identity. The person experiences a sense of not belonging with homosexuals.

Stage 4—Identity acceptance: As the person has greater contact with the LGBT community, friendships are forged. The individual begins to evaluate LGBT individuals more positively and accepts rather than merely tolerating a lesbian or gay self-image. He or she finally answers the questions posed in Stage 1: "Who am I?" "Where do I belong?"

Stage 5—Identity pride: The person becomes immersed in the LGBT community. Where initially, the individual perceived a large rift and difference between the LGBT and straight communities, he or she now comes to perceive less of a dichotomy. A gay or lesbian identity is integrated into the individual's personality structure. The individual identifies the gay culture as the sole source of support: all gay friends, business connections, and social connections.

Inner Reflections

Have you been taught gender identity development in college?

To what extent is gender identity development for homosexuals different from and similar to identity development for heterosexuals?

Stage 6—Identity synthesis: The intense anger at heterosexuals has subsided. The person integrates his or her gender identity with all other aspects of self. Gender orientation becomes only one part of the self rather than the entire identity.

Reparative Therapy and Sexual Orientation Conversion Therapy

The terms *reparative therapy* and *sexual orientation conversion therapy* refer to psychotherapy whose goal is to eliminate or suppress a person's homosexuality. Reparative therapy and sexual conversion therapists claim that they can change one's sexual orientation. Both these therapeutic approaches are founded on a view of homosexuality that has been rejected by all the major mental health professions.

For the most part, conversion therapy is rejected in most circles, except when clients have strong religious sanctions against homosexuality. The general consensus among mental health organizations and professions is that both heterosexuality and homosexuality are normal expressions of human sexuality. The *DSM* (American Psychiatric Association, 2000), which defines the standards of the mental health field, does not include homosexuality as a disease.

> Thus, the idea that homosexuality is a mental disorder or that the emergence of same-sex attraction and orientation among some adolescents is in any way abnormal or mentally unhealthy has no support among any mainstream health and mental health professional organizations. (Just the Facts Coalition, 2008, p. 5)

The nation's leading mental health organizations have issued statements indicating that they do not support efforts to change individuals' sexual orientation through therapy and that they have serious concerns about the potential harm from such efforts. The American Psychiatric Association, the APA, and the American Academy of Pediatrics have denounced conversion and reparative treatment because of the high number of negative outcomes and low, questionable success rate (Heffner, 2003).

The National Association of Social Workers (2006), in its policy statement on lesbian, gay, and bisexual issues, states that it endorses policies in both the public and private sectors that ensure nondiscrimination; that are sensitive to the health and mental health needs of lesbian, gay, and bisexual people; and that promote an understanding of lesbian, gay, and bisexual cultures. Social stigmatization of lesbian, gay, and bisexual people is widespread and is a primary motivating factor in leading some people to seek sexual orientation changes. Sexual orientation conversion therapies assume that homosexual orientation is both pathological and freely chosen. No data demonstrate that reparative or conversion therapies are effective, and in fact they may be harmful. NASW believes social workers have the responsibility to clients to explain the prevailing knowledge concerning sexual orientation and the lack of data reporting positive outcomes with reparative therapy. NASW discourages social workers from providing treatments designed to change sexual orientation or from referring practitioners or programs that claim to do so. NASW reaffirms its stance against reparative therapies and treatments designed to change sexual orientation or referrals to practitioners or programs that claim to do so.

Similarly, the American School Counselor Association (2007), in its position statement on professional school counselors and LGBT youth and youth who are **questioning gender identity**, states,

> Lesbian, gay, bisexual, transgendered and questioning (LGBTQ) youth often begin to experience self-identification during their pre-adolescent or adolescent years, as do heterosexual youth. These developmental processes are essential cognitive, emotional and social activities, and although they may have an impact on student development and achievement, they are not a sign of illness, mental disorder or emotional problems nor do they necessarily signify sexual activity. . . .
>
> It is not the role of the professional school counselor to attempt to change a student's sexual orientation/gender identity but instead to provide support to LGBTQ students to promote student achievement and personal well-being. . . .
>
> Recognizing that sexual orientation is not an illness and does not require treatment, professional school counselors may provide individual student

planning or responsive services to LGBTQ students to promote self-acceptance, deal with social acceptance, understand issues related to "coming out," including issues that families may face when a student goes through this process, and identify appropriate community resources.

THE THERAPEUTIC PROCESS IN GAY AND LESBIAN PSYCHOTHERAPY

Except for issues that emanate from the first five stages of the Cass gender identity model, treatment for gay men and lesbians is similar to that for heterosexuals. In terms of mood disorders, anxiety disorders, relationship concerns, stress, and sexual issues, gay men and lesbian women present at about the same rate as their heterosexual counterparts, and treatment should be the same for both groups (Heffner, 2003). For adolescents who are struggling with gender identity issues, depression is significantly higher, and the suicide rate is double that of their straight friends. Suicidal ideation, depression, and anxiety tend to be higher among clients who have not accepted their sexuality or who are struggling for sexual orientation acceptance from friends and family. Heffner points out that couples therapy for gays should be treated no differently than marital therapy for straights, except for the obvious legal and social issues.

Role of the Therapist in Working With Gay and Lesbian Clients

Therapists who work with gay and lesbian clients should first take a personal inventory of their own sexual orientation attitudes. How does the therapist feel about gays and lesbians? Are there any negative or positive feelings for members of these groups? Does the therapist have any religious beliefs that would suggest that it might be better that the therapist does not work with members of the LGBT community? If therapists have prejudices against members of the LGBT community, then they should refer the client to someone else.

Heffner (2003) also states, "If a therapist believes homosexuality is wrong, sinful, immoral, or a mental illness, he or she should NOT work with gay clients. Refer this client to someone who is able to provide the necessary components of a therapeutic relationship." (p. 1). Both the American Counseling Association (2005) and the APA (2002) have ethical codes that provide guidelines for working with clients around issues of their sexual orientation.

Second, before beginning treatment for a homosexual client, therapists are responsible for making sure that they are knowledgeable on issues related to sexuality and that they have the clinical skills needed to create a positive and nonjudgmental counseling relationship and will not feel uncomfortable discussing issues related to homosexuality (Heffner, 2003). It is usually unadvisable for a therapist to think that a person can change his or her sexual orientation (through conversion, reparative, or reorientation therapy).

Third, therapists should be knowledgeable about the gender identity development of gays and lesbians. When counseling gay or lesbian clients, it is important to understand where they are in terms of their own sexual identities. Clients who state that they are trying to convert to a "straight lifestyle" are most likely in stage 2 or 3 of the Cass sexual identity model. They have not accepted themselves as gay and most likely have not experienced strong love and acceptance from those who know their sexual orientation. Clients in stages 4 and 5 are usually trying to reinvent themselves with their newly found acceptance of their sexuality. They may be looking for gay friends. Although they have accepted their sexuality, they have not learned how to integrate their sexuality into their overall sense of self. Heffner (2003) has stated, "In treatment, the strength these individuals feel should be embraced and treatment should be focused on what they can do, not to make the world accept them, but to show the world that they are worthy of acceptance." Clients in stage 6 of the Cass gender identity model present as no different from most other clients in therapy. Because they have accepted their sexuality and have developed relationships, they don't see being gay as the issue in their lives. Instead, they view their gayness as just one of the many issues they must contend with. They may also see their gayness in a positive light.

Morgan and Brown (1991) found that age cannot be a predictor of lesbian or gay identity development because people discover their sexual orientation at different ages. To counsel gays and lesbians effectively, therapists must be aware of the stages of the clients' gender identity development in addition to their overall psychosocial development.

Fourth, therapists should be familiar with the gay and lesbian culture as well as the status of gays and lesbians within other cultural communities. Pope (2008) has pointed out that gays and lesbians have historically suffered discrimination and oppression. He stated,

> They are also a psychological minority in the sense that lesbians and gays were labeled as "diseased" by the psychological community until 1973 and the seventh printing of the third edition of the *Diagnostic and Statistical Manual of Mental Disorders* (American Psychiatric Association, 1980). (p. 205)

If therapists are lacking in knowledge regarding gay and lesbian issues, there are a number of sources that can provide the information. For instance, the American Counseling Association has the Association for Gay, Lesbian, and Bisexual Issues in Counseling, the APA has Division 44—The Society for the Psychological Study of Lesbian and Gay Issues.

The APA Council of Representatives adopted the following Guidelines for Psychological Practice With Lesbian, Gay, and Bisexual Clients on February 18 to 20, 2011, and replaced the original Guidelines for Psychotherapy With Lesbian, Gay, and Bisexual Clients adopted by the Council, February 26, 2000, which expired at the end of 2010. Each of the 21 new guidelines provide an update of the psychological literature supporting them, including a section on "Rationale" and "Application," and expand on the original guidelines to provide assistance to psychologists in areas such as religion and spirituality, the differentiation of gender identity and sexual orientation, socioeconomic and workplace issues, and the use and dissemination of research on lesbian, gay, and bisexual issues. The guidelines are designed to inform the practice of psychologists and to provide information for the education and training of psychologists regarding lesbian, gay, and bisexual issues. Below are 16 of the 21 guidelines that APA has adopted.

Attitudes Toward Homosexuality and Bisexuality

Guideline 1. Psychologists strive to understand the effects of stigma (i.e., prejudice, discrimination, and violence) and its various contextual manifestations in the lives of lesbian, gay, and bisexual people.

Guideline 2. Psychologists understand that lesbian, gay, and bisexual orientations are not mental illnesses.

Guideline 3. Psychologists understand that same-sex attractions, feelings, and behavior are normal variants of human sexuality and that efforts to change sexual orientation have not been shown to be effective or safe.

Guideline 4. Psychologists are encouraged to recognize how their attitudes and knowledge about lesbian, gay, and bisexual issues may be relevant to assessment and treatment and seek consultation or make appropriate referrals when indicated.

Guideline 5. Psychologists strive to recognize the unique experiences of bisexual individuals.

Guideline 6. Psychologists strive to distinguish issues of sexual orientation from those of gender identity when working with lesbian, gay, and bisexual clients.

Relationships and Families

Guideline 7. Psychologists strive to be knowledgeable about and respect the importance of lesbian, gay, and bisexual relationships.

Guideline 8. Psychologists strive to understand the experiences and challenges faced by lesbian, gay, and bisexual parents.

Guideline 9. Psychologists recognize that the families of lesbian, gay, and bisexual people may include people who are not legally or biologically related.

Guideline 10. Psychologists strive to understand the ways in which a person's lesbian, gay, or bisexual orientation may have an impact on his or her family of origin and the relationship with that family of origin.

Issues of Diversity

Guideline 11. Psychologists strive to recognize the challenges related to multiple and often conflicting norms, values, and beliefs faced by lesbian, gay, and bisexual members of racial and ethnic minority groups.

Guideline 12. Psychologists are encouraged to consider the influences of religion and spirituality in the lives of lesbian, gay, and bisexual persons.

Guideline 13. Psychologists strive to recognize cohort and age differences among lesbian, gay, and bisexual individuals.

Guideline 14. Psychologists strive to understand the unique problems and risks that exist for lesbian, gay, and bisexual youth.

Guideline 15. Psychologists are encouraged to recognize the particular challenges that lesbian, gay, and bisexual individuals with physical, sensory, and cognitive-emotional disabilities experience.

Guideline 16. Psychologists strive to understand the impact of HIV/AIDS on the lives of lesbian, gay, and bisexual individuals and communities.

Source: APA's Guidelines for Psychological Practice With Lesbian, Gay, and Bisexual Clients (2011).

Gay Affirmative Psychotherapy

A number of theoretical approaches can be used with gay men and lesbians as long as some of the principles enunciated in the APA guidelines are maintained. The critical issue is respect for gay rights and issues in psychotherapy. Since the 1980s, psychotherapists have begun to use **gay affirmative therapy**, which encourages gay and lesbian clients to accept their sexual orientation (Malyon, 1982). This practical approach does not attempt to change gay men or lesbians to eliminate or to reduce their same-sex desires and behaviors (Brown, 1989). Gay affirmative psychotherapy states that homosexuality or bisexuality is not a mental illness. In fact, it encourages psychotherapists to assist clients in overcoming the stigma of homosexuality rather than the orientation itself. Gay affirmative therapy recognizes that many gays and lesbians are rejected by their families and therefore must form their own families (Milton & Coyle, 1999). It states that embracing and affirming a gay identity can be a key component to recovery from a mental illness or substance abuse.

Gay affirmative therapy is viewed as the appropriate answer to conversion therapy, which focused on trying to change the client's sexual identity from homosexual to heterosexual. Psychotherapy for gays and lesbians appears to be still in the process of developing, as researchers, clinicians, and theorists learn more about homosexuality and identity development for gays and lesbians. Specific counseling techniques need to be identified for gay affirmative psychotherapy.

The therapist should work to create an accepting therapeutic environment. To achieve this goal, the following suggestions are offered (Buhrke & Douce, 1991):

- Do not assume that every client is heterosexual.
- Create an atmosphere of acceptance by using inclusive language during therapy. You might want to have magazines and brochures that are inclusive of gender orientation.
- Work at feeling comfortable talking about sex, gender, and sexual orientation.
- Do not assume that being LGBT is the cause of the client's problem.

- On the other hand, do not assume that being LGBT should not matter. It just might be part of the client's issue(s).

LGBT-Specific Psychotherapy Treatment

As was the case with feminist therapy and multicultural therapy, there is no one established model of psychotherapy for working with LGBT clients (Barret & Logan, 2002). In lieu of a specific therapy model with provisions for personality and individual development, gay and lesbian scholars have developed various approaches to psychotherapy—approaches that are primarily designed to sensitize the therapist to the issues that LGBT clients encounter in life. The absence of fully developed models for therapy for LGBT clients raises the question (Barret & Logan, 2002) "What is LGBT-specific treatment?" I describe one approach, the gay affirmative psychotherapy approach. While I do not consider myself to be an expert in this area, I offer the following suggestions. LGBT-specific treatment should do the following:

- Recognize *LGBT-specific issues* raised either explicitly or implicitly by the client during therapy. Such issues might include coming out, homophobia (internalized and externalized, it can lead to suicide, self-injury, and self-medication), leading a double life, drugs, alcohol, and HIV (Hancock, 2000)
- Have psychotherapy services that are geared to address LGBT issues as they arise during the therapeutic relationship
- Help a client to locate support within a given community to deal with LGBT issues, if necessary
- Deal with internalized and externalized homophobia

Barriers to Assessment of LGBT Clients

It is important to consider barriers to the assessment of LGBT clients. Such barriers include both attitudinal and knowledge issues as well as behavioral issues (Barret & Logan, 2002). Gay men and lesbians might feel hesitant to disclose their sexual orientation to the therapist. Therefore, the therapist must work to create a safe environment for an LGBT client to disclose (Pope, 2008).

Other barriers to accurate assessment of LGBT clients include the following:

- Personal biases of providers
- The client's own internalized homophobia
- The therapist's lack of information and knowledge about the LGBT population

Positive Clinical Assessment of LGBT Clients

To conduct a meaningful assessment of LGBT clients, the therapist assesses along several dimensions, including medical or physical health, mental health concerns, and LGBT concerns (Anderson, Croteau, Chung, & DiStefano, 2001). Medical assessments should include specific questions for LGBT clients. The client is informed of the limits of his or her confidentiality and his or her right to refuse to answer any question. Some sample assessment questions that a therapist might make about the client's LGBT status include the following (Barret & Logan, 2002):

- How do you feel about your sexual orientation?
- Are you currently sexually involved—with males, females, or both?
- Describe your past sexual involvements.
- Have you come out about your sexual orientation? If so, to whom?
- When did you come out?
- Why did you come out?
- What was the coming-out process like for you? Would you say that it was primarily positive or negative?
- How does your family respond to you about your sexual orientation?
- How would you describe the sexual orientation of your closest friends?
- What is your culture's response to LGBT individuals?
- To what extent are sex and drugs linked together in your life?

- To what degree have you experienced shame, depression, anxiety, and low self-image due to your sexual orientation?

Common Mental Health Concerns for LGBT Clients

LGBT clients are first of all individuals with their own stories about what it meant to grow up with their specific sexual orientation (Brown, 1989). They are both similar and different from heterosexual clients. Despite this observation, their group membership (LGBT) predisposes them to share some common mental health concerns. Clearly, there will be variation among LGBT clients, and not all will experience the following common mental health concerns (Brown, 1989):

- Posttraumatic stress disorder from living in an environment hostile to gay men and lesbian women
- Damaged self-image due to stigmatization, oppression, and the coming-out process
- Fragmented identity that comes from living a double life
- Developmental issues that result from a focus on sexual orientation and insufficient attention to other developmental tasks unrelated to sexual orientation

A Short Therapeutic Model for Working With Gays and Lesbians

In working with gay and lesbian clients, the therapist might consider a model based on the presenting problem. The presenting problem for counseling gays can be placed into three basic categories. The first group contains problems common to both gays and heterosexuals: anxiety and depression. The second group consists of presenting problems specific to the gay and lesbian population, such as coming out and internalized homophobia. The third group is composed of problems common to gays and heterosexuals but that require a different emphasis for this population. These problems include adoption and religious conflicts.

Justin From a Feminist Perspective

A feminist theoretical framework can be used in therapy with Justin. It is clear that Justin has issues—love and hate issues with his mother, Sandy. He treats Sandy with little respect. There has been the underlying feeling that Sandy can be ignored because she does not have any power. She's just a woman trying to do a man's job in taking care of her two sons, and Justin is giving her a low grade for her efforts.

Feminist therapy suggests that Justin is behaving disrespectfully toward his mother because of her status and power as a female and as a mother. "Women do not have real power; no one really listens to what women have to say. They only cry when they get upset." A tentative assessment also indicates that there are relational problems between Justin and his mother. The relationship between mother and son has been severely weakened and in some respects almost destroyed. Sandy, Justin's mother, is at her wits' end. She keeps asserting herself, but the truth is that when she tells Justin to go to his room, they are standing eye to eye. Sometimes Sandy looks at Justin and wonders whatever happened to her beautiful baby. On other occasions, she looks at him and thinks, "I deserve better treatment than this. I did my best. I don't deserve what's happening to me."

Deep down inside, Sandy is really scared, not just for Justin but also for herself. What will she do with herself if he is sent off to residential treatment? Her oldest son already left her a long time ago for the gangs. There's no getting him back. He's gone. He just lives in the house because it is convenient for him.

As the therapist sat in his office weighing whether he should see Justin with his mother or just him alone, he recalled the tears forming in Sandy's eyes as she talked about her fear of Justin going to residential treatment. Sandy could benefit from therapy. He needed her to be strong in order to help Justin through this difficult period in his life. He decided to see them separately for one more time before seeing them as a family.

During the next session with Justin, the therapist focused on Justin's feelings about boys and girls, men and women. He began by asking Justin about his relationship with his mother, Sandy. "Tell me about your relationship with your mother, Justin. Would you say that it is bad or good between the two of you?"

"Some good, some bad," Justin answered.

"Tell me about the times when the relationship between the two of you is good," the therapist continued. "When are times good between the two of you?"

"I dunno," Justin said looking down. "Usually, we're just sitting at the table eating dinner. She fixes my plate the way that I like, and she just places it right in front of me. She'll ask me if there is anything else that I want before she sits down."

"So what makes dinner time special is that she is paying attention to you and trying to fulfill your needs."

"Wow! I never thought about it like that. It's just like she knows what I like, and she tries to give it to me on my plate. You know like sometimes she'll fix one of my favorite dishes and then give me a big helping. She must really care about me to go through all that trouble."

"You feel she really cares about you when she cooks your favorite dish."

"Yeah, like kind of special because she fixed it just for me."

The therapist smiles at Justin and says, "I know what you mean. When I was growing up, my favorite was chocolate cake. Boy, my mother could cook chocolate cake. It's almost like I can smell it right now. I remember when I lost a swimming meet, and I came home all upset and depressed. My mother met me at the door, gave me a hug, and said she had a surprise for me. She didn't have to tell me what the surprise was. I could smell the chocolate cake. I put my arms around her and said, 'I lost. At the last tenth of a second,

(Continued)

(Continued)

I lost.' My mother said that she knew I had lost, and that was part of the reason she had baked my favorite chocolate cake.

"I know what it feels like when your Mom cooks something just special for you. It's a good feeling, a loving feeling. You feel safe and loved by her."

"Yeah," Justin responded. "It's kind of funny thinking about you as a little boy. But yeah, that's how I feel too when my mother cooks my favorite dish."

From this point, the therapist began to elicit other times when the relationship was good between Justin and his mother. The relationship was good when they weren't pressured to do anything, sharing food together, watching television—those kinds of things.

The relationship seemed to get bad when the issue of chores, homework, curfew hours, and other things came up between them. It became clear that Justin loved his mother as long as she was nurturing him, putting no demands on him. He resented her most when she tried to "act like a man." As the therapist probed Justin, he learned that Justin really resented her acting in any kind of authoritative role. He had pigeonholed Sandy in primarily one role—nurturer. When Sandy tried to assert her authority as a parent, Justin resisted. Deep down inside he did not want to act like a punk and be pushed around by his mom. His older brother mostly ignored her, and he did the same thing.

Sensing the gender typing and sex role typing that Justin had placed on Sandy, the therapist began to conduct an informal gender role analysis of Justin. He asked Justin to identify gender role messages he had heard while growing up from his friends, brother, teachers, and so on. Some of the messages Justin heard were that "women are weak; they cry at the drop of a hat. Mothers can't make you do anything. Only fathers can do that." It did not help that Sandy sometimes cried in front of Justin when she became really frustrated with his behavior.

The therapist asked Justin what kind of impact the messages that he had heard about men and women had on him. "I felt strong," Justin responded. "I knew that in a few years I would be bigger than her and that she could talk all she wanted. If I didn't want to do what she said, oh well. I just wouldn't do it." From that point on, Justin began to reveal a number of stereotypic messages about women—and mothers in particular.

The therapist reflected back to Justin. "So the message you heard in your head was 'Someday I am going to be stronger than you. So all I have to do is to wait my time.' You're just about as tall as your mom is right now."

The therapist decided to make an intervention on the spot. He said that he would play Sandy, and Justin would play himself. The role-play was about doing the dishes, one of Justin's least favorite chores. Although the therapist was playing Sandy, he utilized all the authority that is usually given to a male or a father. Justin backed down. The role-play provided an excellent opportunity for the therapist to point out that some of the messages that Justin had heard about women were negative. The therapist asked Justin to play the role of Sandy in the scenario about the unwashed dinner dishes. As he role-played his mother, he whined instead of asserting himself.

The therapist asked Justin to notice for 3 days how he was treating his mother in terms of sex roles. "Next to my brother," Justin offered, "I am the second man in the house." Justin had moved himself out of the role of child and into the role of man, even though he was only 12 years old. The absence of a male figure in the house who could serve as father meant that the role of "man" was up for grabs, and Justin was claiming it.

The therapist wanted Justin to understand several things. First, not all women were weak. Sandy had a number of strengths as a parent. He had Justin list some of Sandy's strengths as a parent and as a mother. Just because Sandy cried when she began to get very frustrated with Justin's repeated disrespect and failure to complete chores did not mean that she was weak. The therapist reminded Justin about the tears he had seen him shed over his fear of being sent to residential treatment. Was he a baby, a sissy, because he cried at the thought of leaving his mother? The therapist helped Justin to see that he was responding to his mother on the basis of negative stereotypes of her as a woman. Justin was helped to see that each one of us has both masculine and feminine traits and that tears did not just belong to women. Tears were meant to help cleanse strong emotions.

Justin agreed that his mother had both what he had called "manly" traits and feminine ones. After all, she was taking care of the family. She was the one who put food on the table and who provided a place for them to stay. When he got into trouble, she was the one who came to the police station to pick him up. She was the one who came to court with him, who took him to his probation officer, and who met with his teachers, the therapist, and the principal. One had to have some strength to manage all those things.

Therapy ended with the therapist giving Justin a homework assignment that would help him restore and build on his relationship with his mother. He could pick any day during the week and write his mother a thank you note that named three things that she did for him for which he was grateful. He was to bring in the impact of the thank you note on his relationship with his mother. He was also to list two ways in which he would no longer pigeonhole his mother into the "weak mother" role. Third, he was to describe two gender messages he had heard about "how to be a man." Those messages could come from other people he knew or from the radio or television.

SUMMARY

This chapter examined theoretical and practice issues related to feminist therapy and gay and lesbian therapy. The origins of feminist therapy can be traced to the women's movement in the 1960s and 1970s, when women first expressed dissatisfaction with their roles in society. Chesler's (1972) book *Women and Madness* was critical in bringing attention to the bias of White male therapists. Research on sex role stereotypes further supported Chesler's claims of discrimination in the therapy room.

The feminist perspective in therapy and psychotherapy has had a major impact on how people think women should be treated and what should be the proper role of therapists who counsel them. The feminist perspective has promoted women's development and power over the past 40 years. For instance, the feminist perspective has placed an emphasis on building egalitarian relationships between men and women and between client and therapist. The client is the expert on his or her life. This focus has resulted in the empowerment of women throughout the United States and the world.

Although there is no universal feminist view, the key construct of feminist therapy is that clients' problems are examined within a sociopolitical and cultural context. Whereas traditional psychotherapies focus on individual personality development, feelings, thoughts, or behaviors, feminist therapists emphasize the importance of societal variables such as power, sexism, and racism. Feminist therapy places gender and power issues at the center of the therapeutic process (Bem, 1981, 1993). These therapists maintain that it is critical to consider the social and cultural context that contributes to a person's problems prior to therapy. Understanding a client's problems means that a therapist must adopt a sociocultural perspective and that empowerment of the client is important. Clients are encouraged to take social action to change how society has socially constructed gender in a particular society.

In addition, feminist therapy deals with the psychological oppression of women and the constraints that a society puts on women. Many feminists have adopted a postmodern, social constructionist view of therapy.

Feminist therapists have developed techniques that they integrate with traditional approaches.

Their techniques have been developed to deal with societal issues such as social injustice, power and status, and gender/sex role stereotypes. RCT presents an exciting new framework for both multicultural therapy and feminist therapy.

Feminist therapies are largely gender free, and they are flexible enough so that they can be applied to individuals regardless of their age, race, culture, sex, or sexual orientation.

For too long, the issues that relate to gays, lesbians, and bisexuals have been ignored and silently omitted from theories of psychotherapy and counseling. This chapter reviewed some of the key concepts related to the LGBT population's well-being, especially homophobia and heterosexism. The Cass identity development model for LGBT individuals was examined. The topic of coming out was discussed. Eighteen things to consider before coming out were offered. Affirmative gay therapy was also discussed as holding potential for working with the LGBT population.

SUPPLEMENTAL AIDS _____
Discussion Questions

1. What does being a "feminist," gay person, or lesbian mean to you?

2. Do you believe that men can be feminists and counsel from a feminist perspective?

3. Has your gender put constraints on your life? Explain.

4. *Attitudes toward gender:* This is a good activity for closing a class session. Hand out a sheet of paper with the following information to each class member. Students are to complete each statement as they see fit, or they may abstain from answering two statements.

   - A person I admire of my sex is . . .
   - A person I admire of the other sex is . . .
   - Something I would like to change about the situation for young men/young women is . . .
   - I feel really happy when . . .
   - I think everybody should . . .
   - An occasion when I was proud to be a woman/man was . . .
   - An occasion when I wished I was of the other sex was . . .
   - If I were in power, I would . . .

5. What are your greatest concerns about working with male and female clients in therapy? How do you intend to deal with these concerns? Do you believe that feminist therapies can be used successfully with men? Explain

Glossary of Key Terms

androcentric theory   A theory that uses male-oriented constructs to reach conclusions about individuals' behavior.

bisexual   A term that refers to a person of one sex who is sexually attracted to individuals of both sexes.

coming out   The process of recognizing one's sexual orientation, gender identity, or sex and being open about it with oneself and with others.

cultural feminism   An approach that maintains that oppression comes from society's devaluation of women's strengths. This therapeutic approach emphasizes the differences between men and women. Advocates believe that the solution to oppression lies in the feminization of the culture. A major goal of this approach is the infusion of society with values based on cooperation.

egalitarian relationship   A relationship in which power is balanced. Feminist therapy acknowledges the voices of the oppressed.

feminist therapy   A type of therapy that maintains that women are in a disadvantaged position in the world due to their sex, gender, sexuality, race, ethnicity, religion, age, and other factors. The goal of therapy is to recognize these forces and to empower clients. The therapist and the client work as equals.

gay   Preferred synonym for *homosexual.*

gay affirmative therapy   Therapy that encourages gay and lesbian clients to accept their sexual orientation.

gender fair describes differences in men's and women's behavior in terms of socialization processes instead of differences in their innate nature.

gender identity One's understanding or feeling about whether one is emotionally or spiritually male or female or both or neither.

gender neutral refers to the idea or belief that our language, counseling theories, and governmental policies should avoid distinguishing roles or benefits according to people's sex or gender and should be fair in their treatment of males and females.

gender role One's gender expression and beliefs and feelings about the appropriate and/or comfortable expression of one's gender. To some degree, gender role is learned (socially constructed and culture specific). To some degree, people are probably biologically predisposed to be more feminine or masculine.

gender role analysis Therapeutic practice that helps clients understand the impact of gender role expectations on their lives.

gender role intervention Therapeutic practice that helps clients develop insight and understanding into the ways social issues influence their problems.

gender schemas Mental associations and interpretations that a person makes based on his or her perceptions about gender.

gender-centric theory A theory that holds that there are two separate paths of development for women and men.

heterosexism The presumption that heterosexuality is superior to homosexuality or bisexuality. Also, prejudice, bias, or discrimination based on that presumption.

homophobia In classic psychological terms, an irrational fear of homosexuality. Now usually bias against or dislike of gay, lesbian, bisexual, and transgender people or stereotypically gay or lesbian behavior, discomfort with one's own same-sex attractions, or fear of being perceived as gay or lesbian.

lesbian The preferred term for gay women. Many lesbians feel invisible when the term *gay* is used to refer to men *and* women.

LGBT Abbreviation for gay, lesbian, bisexual, and transgender.

liberal feminism An approach to psychotherapy that focuses on helping women overcome the limits and constraints of socialized patterns. Its major goals are the personal empowerment of women, dignity, self-fulfillment, and equality.

postmodern feminism A framework for comparing and contrasting traditional therapies with feminist therapy. Trends include an increasing role for women of color, inclusion of lesbian feminists, and global international feminism that maintains that women throughout the world live under oppression.

power analysis The emphasis on the power differences between men and women in any society. Therapists help clients to recognize the different kinds of power they possess and how they can use their own power.

questioning gender identity A term used to describe individuals who are contemplating their own sexual orientation and/or gender identity but who have not yet decided on their identity; often viewed as the beginning of an inner journey that may or may not result in an LGBTQ identity.

radical feminism A philosophy that states that the oppression of women is embedded in patriarchy. Therapy is viewed as a political enterprise, and the goal is to change society.

relational-cultural theory (RCT) A theory developed by Jean Baker Miller and Irene Stiver. The relational-cultural model focuses on the growth of relatedness and connectedness. It emphasizes belief in the importance and centrality of mutuality and connection in the lives of all people. The goal of development is to participate actively in relationships that foster the well-being of everyone involved (i.e., growth-fostering relationships) rather than to form a separated, independent self.

socialist feminism   A philosophy of feminism that emphasizes societal change. Therapists must work for solutions to problems of class, race, and other forms of discrimination to transform social relationships and institutions.

transgender   An umbrella term used to refer to anyone whose gender identity does not conform to society's expectations of gender role as determined by the sex assigned at birth. The term includes, but is not limited to, preoperative, postoperative, and nonoperative individuals who may or may not use hormones and individuals who exhibit gender characteristics or identities that are perceived to be incompatible with their birth or biological sex.

Website Materials

Additional exercises, journals, annotated bibliography, and more are available on the open-access website at https://study.sagepub.com/jonessmith2e.

CHAPTER 15

Solution-Focused Therapy

In the 1970s and in early 1980s, a startling discovery was made that almost every problem contains an element of solutions.

—Insoo Kim Berg

If it works, do more of it; if what you do does not work, do something different.

—Steve de Shazer

BRIEF OVERVIEW

Steve de Shazer, Insoo Kim Berg, and others developed solution-focused theory at the Brief Family Therapy Center in the 1980s. The historical development of solution-focused therapy reflects some of the dominant changes in the field of theories of psychotherapy. During the 1980s, researchers became increasingly dissatisfied with the traditional therapies. The prevailing view was that psychotherapy had to focus on problems and problem causes (Walter & Peller, 2000). Therapists believed that the causes of clients' problems could be traced to their unresolved childhood issues and that such problems were tucked away deep in clients' psyches.

According to de Shazer (1982), Milton Erickson, the famous hypnotist, had a profound influence on the development of solution-focused theory. Dr. Erickson's contribution was that he took the learning that clients already had and then helped them apply this knowledge to new situations. Dr. Erikson was an American psychiatrist who had unorthodox ideas about how effective therapy worked. Dr. Erickson did not believe in diagnostic labels, but he believed in people's ability to solve their own problems. From his perspective, therapy did not have to be long to be effective. A client's small change is often sufficient to set in motion a much larger change. It is not necessary to understand the root causes of a client's problems for change to take place. Learn the pattern of the client's problem, and then prescribe a small change in the problem.

Dr. Erickson employed paradoxical intention techniques, getting clients to do something while appearing to suggest something different. He also practiced a form of brief therapy. One of his more famous clients is the African Violet Lady of Baltimore, who was severely depressed. One could understand her depression because she had no friends and no family and lived alone. Rarely did she ever leave her house and associate with other people. This lady would not seek help from anyone. A concerned neighbor contacted Dr. Erickson, hoping that he would take on this depressed lady as a client. Dr. Erickson agreed to make just one visit to the lady's house. He was surprised at what he saw. The lady lived in squalor beyond anything he had ever imagined.

While walking around the house, Dr. Erickson found one wilting African violet, which was to be the turning point in the woman's life. Dr. Erickson advised the woman to grow the flower she loved so much and then send these flowers to everyone whom she found in the local paper advertising that they were having a birthday, a wedding, or any event that would be a cause of celebration. The African Violet Lady agreed to do it. Finally, she had found a purpose in life. The African Violet Lady continued to send out her precious flowers for years to come while receiving great joy from the endeavor. News spread quickly throughout the city about the mysterious lady who sent everyone African violets.

When she died, hundreds of people came out to mourn the famous lady known simply as the African Violet Lady, who was now loved by all. One simple change in behavior, and an exceptional psychiatrist who had insight about what really mattered in life, made a remarkable change in this woman's life. Although Dr. Erickson had provided the suggestion, the African Violet Lady had healed herself. She did not need drugs or intensive therapy; she reached down inside of herself and through connecting with something that she loved and extending kindness to others healed not only herself but many other people (Cade, 2007).

Dr. Erickson's treatment of the African Violet Lady was indicative of how he viewed life. He was totally paralyzed at age 17. Instead of allowing his physical condition to destroy him, Dr. Erickson saw his paralysis as an advantage. He became an excellent observer of people instead of a complainer. Dr. Erickson taught himself to walk again, but he also suffered from other afflictions: He was colorblind, dyslexic, tone deaf, and arrhythmic (Cade, 2007).

Dr. Erickson's work was based on three principles: (1) meet clients where they are, (2) help clients to gain control by changing their perspectives, and (3) allow for change that meets clients' needs (de Shazer, 1982). de Shazer and Berg incorporated Dr. Erickson's principles into solution-focused therapy.

Gregory Bateson is another important influence in the development of solution-focused therapy. Bateson was an English anthropologist who married Margaret Mead, another famous anthropologist. Bateson's research area was systems theory and cybernetics. He contributed to solution-focused therapy because of his premise that the social system in which people function is of great importance to the development and solution of problems (Visser, 2008).

Bateson's most direct contribution to solution-focused therapy was that he initiated the Bateson Project, a communications research project that featured researchers such as John Weakland, Jay Haley, and William Fry. These individuals would meet and analyze videotapes of famous therapists. The Bateson Project formed the basis of the Mental Research Institute, which was founded in Palo Alto, California, in 1958.

The Mental Research Institute was critical to the development of solution-focused counseling because it brought together a critical couple—Steve de Shazer and Insoo Kim Berg. In 1966, the therapists at this institute developed a briefer, more goal-oriented and pragmatic approach to therapy (Visser, 2008). Therapists focused on what the client said about his or her problem. The therapists maintained that it was not necessary to talk extensively about the client's childhood or about any underlying causes of the presenting problem. They asserted that the reasons for the client's current problem existed in the here-and-now and that solutions could be located in the present also. The goal of therapy was to discover what the client was doing currently to maintain a problem and to convince the client to replace the troublesome behavior with effective behavior.

Insoo Kim Berg went to the Mental Research Institute to work with John Weakland, who became a mentor to her. In 1977, she was introduced to Steve de Shazer, who worked at the institute, and the two began working together. Soon the two became a couple, and Berg convinced de Shazer to leave California and join her in Milwaukee. In 1978, de Shazer and Berg started their private practice and called it the Brief Family Therapy Center. The two observed that analyzing and diagnosing clients' problems could easily be removed from the therapeutic conversation.

Next, Berg and de Shazer began to focus on what works. Each time a therapist did something that worked, they discussed it and tried that technique again. Therapists at the Brief Family Therapy Center looked for counseling interventions that helped clients state more clearly what they wanted to achieve in therapy and that helped clients to identify the next steps forward. Gradually, Berg and de Shazer constructed solution-focused therapy.

In 1984, de Shazer had a major breakthrough when he and Alex Molnar, an associate at the Brief Family Therapy Center, wrote an article on four useful interventions in brief family therapy. This article introduced the **continuation question**, which went something like this: "Between now and the next time we meet, I want you to observe, so that you can tell me next time what happens in your life that you want to continue to happen?" The continuation question identifies that which does not have to change. A counselor might say, "What is taking place in your situation that you want to continue to happen?" "What doesn't have to change because it is already going well enough?" The continuation question acknowledges that the client does not have to change everything because there are things that are going well. Once clients have made a list of things that do not have to change, they usually find it easier to focus their attention on things that do need to change.

A second intervention technique that led to the development of solution-focused therapy was the "do something different technique." This intervention was influenced by Bateson's (1979) work on replacing existing behavioral patterns with new ones. As clients tried out new behaviors, they learned more effective patterns of behavior that were solutions to their problems.

The third counseling intervention was labeled the *overcoming-the-urge task*. de Shazer and Molnar (1984) tried to develop a technique that would help clients not fall back into the old, ineffective habits. They instructed their clients thus: "Pay attention to what you do when you overcome the temptation or urge to . . . (perform the symptom or some behavior associated with the complaint)." Therapists' use of this intervention assisted clients in becoming aware that they sometimes managed to successfully resist their temptations and of how

they accomplished this feat. The fourth intervention described in the article was called the *stability-as-change intervention*. Whenever clients said that they were stuck in a situation and were not able to make progress, the therapist responded by explaining that remaining stable requires many skills and that other people might have fallen back instead of remaining stable.

de Shazer and Berg continued to construct what became known as solution-focused therapy. In his book *Keys to Solutions in Brief Therapy*, de Shazer (1985) stressed the significance of creating an expectation of change in counseling. By asking questions that suggested that change was going to take place as a result of client participation in counseling, the therapist increased the client's hope that change was actually going to take place. One rather well-known question that the therapist asked was "How will you know things will be better?" In *Keys to Solutions in Brief Therapy*, de Shazer argued for the first time that obtaining detailed information about a client's presenting problem is not necessary for solving it.

From 1985 to 1987, de Shazer and Berg added a number of techniques to their brief therapy. By the end of 1987, Molnar and de Shazer (1987) had written an article, "Solution-Focused Therapy: Toward the Identification of Therapeutic Tasks." From that point on, the term *solution focused* was used more frequently in describing their therapeutic work, until it was the sole term used to describe de Shazer's and Berg's work. Solution-focused therapy began to take off during the 1990s, with a number of publications by de Shazer, Berg, and their colleagues (Cade, 2007).

After 2000, solution-focused techniques began to be used throughout the world. The solution-focused approach is now being used in therapy, in education, and in organizations. Solution-focused counseling techniques have become fairly widespread in schools across the nation. Managers are using solution-focused techniques, and the approach has spread to coaching. The approach continues to keep on developing and renewing itself, even after the deaths of de Shazer and Berg (Visser, 2008).

Solution-Focused Therapy and Social Constructivism

Solution-focused therapy is based on the principles of social constructionist philosophy, which emphasizes our awareness of how we communicate with one another, how we satisfy our needs, and how we organize ourselves to get up every day to live. Theorists from this school believe that the struggles in which we find ourselves can be seen as partly the result of our own social constructions. Solution-focused therapy is not in competition with traditional approaches to psychotherapy, even though it is often treated as a young upstart in psychotherapy. Solution-focused therapists do not emphasize an individual's personality as the proper unit of psychotherapy, as do many of the traditional psychotherapies. In their opinion, personality is a social construction created largely for the benefit of therapists. Solution-focused therapy is in agreement with and honors the four factors that research has found cause change in clients: (1) extratherapeutic factors (the client's environmental factors, e.g., social support), (2) the client's view of the therapeutic relationship, (3) the therapeutic technique, and (4) client expectancy, hope, and placebo factors (Hubble, Duncan, & Miller, 1999).

Solution-focused therapy does not challenge either the existence or the etiology of problems. Rather, it maintains that "problems are best understood in relation to their solutions" (de Shazer, 1985, p. 7). Solution-focused therapy is a practice-based model for helping people find solutions to life's challenges. This approach helps clients to explore life without the problem, and it asserts the belief that "what you expect to happen influences what you do" (de Shazer, 1985, p. 45). A major goal of therapy is to discover what future the client sees as worth striving for, because it is this vision that will influence the process of therapy. Solution-focused therapy is a way to get the client to a place in which the problem does not exist. It is a valuable approach to therapy for clients who are struggling to view life without the problem.

Although on the surface the ideas behind solution-focused therapy appear to be quite simple, therapists who use this theoretical approach often indicate that it is very difficult to implement because it requires that the therapist set aside his or her own agenda and truly listen to what the client wants. This theoretical approach trusts in the expertise of clients to choose what is important to them in life. Client goals rather than therapist goals guide the therapeutic process. By emphasizing how life will be once the problem is resolved, clients feel a renewed sense of hope that change is possible and that they can have life without the problematic behavior.

Moreover, solution-focused therapy asserts that "expertise lies in the manner in which the [therapy] conversation is conducted, not in the ability to convey a venerated body of information" (Bobele, Gardner, & Biever, 1995, p. 16). Solution-focused therapists are able to assist clients by maintaining a neutral position, which is called the "not-knowing position." DeJong and Berg (2002) have described learning to effectively take and maintain this stance as a lifelong process. The not-knowing position can be compared with the all-knowing position, which some therapists claim is evident in traditional psychotherapies.

MAJOR CONTRIBUTORS: INSOO KIM BERG AND STEVE DE SHAZER

Brief Biographies of Insoo Kim Berg and Steve de Shazer

There is no one creator of solution-focused therapy; however, two clinicians stand out from the group: Insoo Kim Berg and her husband, Steve de Shazer. Berg and de Shazer were the cofounders and executive directors of the Brief Family Therapy Center in Milwaukee, Wisconsin. Berg cowrote 10 books on solution-focused counseling, which included *Interviewing for Solutions*, *Tales of Solutions*, *Children's Solution Work*, *Brief Coaching for Lasting Solutions*, and, more recently, *More Than Miracles: The State of the Art of Solution-Focused Brief Therapies*. Berg served on the editorial boards of the *Journal of Marital and Family Therapy*, *Family Psychology and Counseling Series*, *Families in Society*, and *Family Process*. She was a founder of the Solution-Focused Brief Association. She conducted workshops on solution-focused brief therapy (SFBT) throughout the United States, Canada, South America, Asia, and Europe.

Berg was born and raised in Korea. She studied at Ewha Women's University in Seoul, South Korea, prior to coming to the United States to study in 1957. She earned B.S. and M.S.S.W. degrees at the University of Wisconsin–Milwaukee. After exercising at a local gym on January 10, 2007, Berg went into the steam room, where she died.

Originally trained as a classical musician, Steve de Shazer worked as a jazz saxophonist. He earned a bachelor's degree in fine arts and an M.S.C. in social work from the University of Wisconsin–Milwaukee. He is the author of several books on solution-focused therapy, including *Keys to Solutions in Brief Therapy* (1985), *Clues: Investigating Solutions in Brief Therapy* (1988), *Putting Difference to Work* (1991), and *Words Were Originally Magic* (1994). Initially, Steve wrote the major works on solution-focused theory; however, Insoo Kim soon became a major leader. Like his wife, Steve conducted many workshops throughout the world. Several days after having been admitted to a hospital in Vienna, Austria, he died on September 11, 2005.

Steve de Shazer (1940–2005)

KEY CONCEPTS

View of Human Nature

Solution-focused counseling has a positive, social constructivist view of human nature; it sees people as basically healthy and competent to deal with life. An absolute reality does not exist. Reality differs from one person to another and from one culture to another. We construct our reality based on our social interactions with others. Different cultures have divergent understandings of the world, and even the people within those cultures have different views.

Solution-focused counseling espouses a non-normative, client-determined view. The theory makes few assumptions about the "true" nature of a person. People are viewed as the experts on the solutions to their problems. People not only want to change, but they also have the capacity to change; they are doing their best to make change happen when they come for counseling (Walter & Peller, 2000).

Each one of us has the innate ability to construct solutions to our problems that will enhance our lives. We are always in the process of constructing ourselves, and out of our experiences we form our own realities, which become our stories. We are more likely to change when therapists focus on what we are doing right rather than on what we are doing wrong (Walter & Peller, 2000). Therefore, clients can be trusted in

Insoo Kim Berg (1934–2007)

Inner Reflections

Does Personality Actually Exist?

Both radical behaviorists and solution-focused therapists have questioned the existence of personality. They maintain that theorists have simply created the concept of personality— that it does not exist in reality.

What do you think? Do you have a personality? Do your clients have a personality?

their intention to resolve their own problems. Because each one of us is unique, there are no "right" solutions for individual issues. People who come to therapy have the capacity to live effectively, even though this ability may be blocked temporarily by current situations or by their negative cognitions.

Theory of Personality

Solution-focused therapists maintain that it is unnecessary to assert that something called personality actually exists. Adopting the social constructivist perspective, these theorists claim that the concept of personality is human created and, therefore, does not exist in reality. The solution-focused school alleges that theorists created the term *personality* to describe certain aspects of human functioning— that is, the id, ego, and superego. This position is in keeping with that of radical behaviorists, who have since long denied the true existence of a structure called personality.

Moreover, the concept of personality suggests that we know the causes of individuals' difficulties in living and that we can fix problems that develop in their personality. Solution-focused theorists assert that we can never know the real causes of clients' problems. The best we can do is to construct different interpretations of their problems. The therapist's interpretation of a client's problems may be no better than that of the client's. In fact, an underlying premise of solution-focused therapy is that the client is considered the expert on his or her problem.

Solution-focused theorists do not tend to use the concept of personality because this term is highly problem centered. For instance, Freud's theory of personality suggests that there are land mines lurking for each of us. Every psychosexual stage of development is fraught with problems that the individual must overcome. In contrast to such conceptualizations, solution-focused therapy is solution centered. Traditional therapies suggest that therapists and clients need to know the cause of clients' problems before they can find solutions for changing those behaviors. Using the social constructivist position, solution therapists assert that there is little evidence to indicate that constructing the causes of clients' behavior leads to better solutions.

SFBT represents a paradigm shift from traditional psychotherapy's focus on problem formation and problem resolution, which undergirds virtually all psychotherapy approaches since Freud. SFBT emphasizes clients' strengths and resiliencies. It examines previous client efforts to resolve difficulties and prior exceptions to the problem (i.e., instances when the problem did not take place). Solutions are defined as describing what life would be like when the problem is gone or resolved. Scales are used to measure the client's current level of progress toward finding a solution. The approach has a deep faith in clients' ability to know what is best for them and to plan effectively to achieve goals.

Helping as Solution Building Rather Than Problem Solving. Solution-focused therapists assert that the underlying structure of problem solving—first determining the nature of a problem and then intervening—affects negatively the therapeutic relationship between clinicians and clients (DeJong & Berg, 2002). The proper focus of therapy is on solution building rather than on problem solving. In traditional psychotherapy, clinicians search for a mental disorder that can explain a client's behavior. Yet if clinicians emphasize primarily problems or pathology, clients may become discouraged, lose hope, and wallow in their problems.

Problem-focused therapy prevents clients from recognizing the positive and effective ways by which they have dealt with their problems. In traditional therapy, much of the interaction between client and therapist focuses on a negative approach to problems.

Emphasis on Mental Health Rather Than Pathology. Solution-focused therapists do not spend a great deal of time theorizing about clients' maladaptive behavior. Focusing on maladaptive behavior does not help solve clients' problems. Moreover, such an approach implies that the therapist actually has the right technique for the client's problems. "You have a bipolar mental disorder, and I am going to rid you of this problem with my skill and expertise." In solution-focused sessions, emphasis is placed on successes, strengths, resources, and abilities (Berg & Miller, 1992). Clinicians in this school are more interested in finding out what works and what is right, rather than exploring what is wrong and then trying to fix it.

Simplicity and Parsimony. Solution-focused therapists search for the simplest and most direct means to a desired outcome. de Shazer often cited the 14th-century philosopher William of Ockham, who said, "What can be done in fewer means is done in vain with many" (Berg & Miller, 1992). The clinician keeps things simple and does not introduce various theories about clients' problems. He or she does not try to impress the client with academic credentials.

Problem-Free Talk. It is important to engage clients in **problem-free talk** at the beginning of and throughout a counseling session. The therapist talks to clients about things that are going well in their lives—things that are not immediately connected to a client's presenting problems. For instance, the therapist might say, "Before we discuss the problems that brought you here, I would like to find out a bit more about you as a person. What are your interests and hobbies? Tell me something good about you." There is a decided emphasis placed on the positive in SFBT.

Change is inevitable; problems change. Solution-focused brief therapists subscribe to the belief that a problem does not operate all the time. On the contrary, they maintain that problems increase or decrease in their severity. They are interested in finding out when a problem does not occur, presumably because they want to help the client devise more situations that are devoid of the problem. There are exceptions to every problem. When therapists and clients talk about the exceptions to the occurrence of problems, clients are empowered with the belief that they can gain control over the problem. The notion that problems change forms the basis for the **exception questions** discussed in the later section on techniques.

Present and Future Time Orientation. Solution-focused therapy is future focused and goal directed. It is not particularly interested in exploring the past, with the exception of reviewing and uncovering exceptions to the problem or past successes. The focus is on what is happening now in the client's life and what needs to happen for a satisfactory future adjustment.

Working What Works. SFBT has a *pragmatic* focus. It endorses the adage "If it is not broke, don't fix it." When clients understand or know what is working, they should do more of it. Likewise, this approach suggests that clients should do something different if things are not working. Solution-focused therapy encourages clinicians and clients to change techniques when things are not working (Berg, 1994).

Big problems may require only small changes. Solution-focused therapy is founded on the principle that one small change in any part of the problem system can have a ripple

Inner Reflections

Can a Small Change Really Help a Client?

Solution-focused therapy maintains that even a small change in a client's life can have a ripple effect on his or her presenting problem.

Do you agree or disagree with this statement?

effect throughout a person's life. This approach may be encouraging to school practitioners, who don't have the time or resources to become involved in long-term, time-consuming interventions.

Summary of Solution-Focused Therapy's Major Principles and Constructs

1. If it ain't broke, don't fix it.

2. Once you know what works, do more of it. Finding exceptions where the problem does not dominate the client's life is critical. The client needs to do more of the same, when the problem is not a problem—an exception. Find an exception, and do the exception.

3. If something doesn't work in therapy, don't do it again. Do something different.

THE THERAPEUTIC PROCESS

Solution-focused therapy has outlined stages of solution building. The underlying principle of solution-building stages is that clients can build solutions to their problems without clinicians' assessing or understanding the nature of the problems. There are five basic stages of solution building: (1) describing the problem, (2) developing well-formed goals, (3) exploring for exceptions, (4) end-of-session feedback, and (5) evaluating client progress (de Shazer, 1988).

In Stage 1, clients are given an opportunity to talk about their problems. The therapist asks, "How is this a problem for you?" The therapist gets a complete problem description. If clients have more than one problem, the therapist asks which problem is most important to work on first. Other questions used during this step include "What have you tried?" and "Was it helpful?"

During Stage 2, the therapist works with clients to develop well-formed goals. The question posed to clients is "What will be different in your life when your problems are solved?" An alternate way of

phrasing the same sentiment is "What would have to be different as a result of our meeting today for you to say that our talking was worthwhile?" (DeJong & Berg, 2002).

At the exploring stage (Stage 3), the therapist asks about those times in clients' lives when their problems were not taking place or were less severe. The therapist asks who did what to make the exceptions happen. Some typical statements and questions during Stage 3 are "Tell me about the times when this problem is a little bit better" and "What are you doing differently during those times when things are a little better?" (DeJong & Berg, 2002).

Stage 4 involves the end of each solution-building conversation. As an intervention technique, the therapist compliments the client. The therapist suggests what the client can do to further resolve his or her problems. This step of solution building usually emphasizes what clients need to do more of and to do differently to increase their chances of achieving their goals. In solution building, the feedback that the therapist gives to clients at the end of a session is designed to help them in their development of well-defined goals and to notice who is doing what to make exceptions to the problems possible. DeJong and Berg (2002) suggest the following guidelines for giving feedback to clients:

- Find the bottom line first. What tasks confront the client?
- Agree with what is important to the client and what the client wants.
- Compliment the client for what he or she is doing that is helpful for solution building.
- Use the client's words to stay within the client's frame of reference.

Formulating feedback for clients is not a simple task. To help clinicians with giving feedback, solution-focused therapy has developed cribsheets and protocols. It is recommended that clinicians take notes on the client's actual words used for their problems. Writing down clients' own words helps clinicians to see clients' shifting perceptions in the solution-building process and provides the information required to develop

Inner Reflections

Should Counselors Use Cribsheets or Protocols?

How comfortable would you be using cribsheets or a formal protocol for working with your clients?

end-of-session feedback (Berg & Dolan, 2001; de Shazer & Dolan, 2007).

Stage 5 consists of evaluating client progress. During this phase of therapy, the clinician asks clients to rate their progress on a scale of 0 to 10. Once the progress has been scaled, the therapist and the client examine what remains to be done. Most clients stabilize and make progress once they engage in the solution-building process. Clients improve by focusing on past successes and strengths. They also get better when they are asked to remember their successful coping strategies.

The Therapeutic Relationship and Therapists' Functions

Clinicians assume that clients want to cooperate in counseling sessions. They ask for clients' understanding of the situation that brought them to counseling, and they listen for who and what are important to clients. The therapeutic relationship is that of co-collaborators or equals (Bertolino & O'Hanlon, 2002). The clinician refuses to accept the role of the expert who has the answer to all the client's problems. The basic relational strategy is to promote the client's own self-healing and self-corrective powers. The solution-focused clinician is a consultant whose major task is to learn about the unique ways an individual or a family has

Inner Reflections

Solution Building or Problem Solving?

Do you believe that the focus in therapy should be solution building or problem solving?

Aren't counselors supposed to help clients solve their problems?

conceptualized its complaints (Berg & Miller, 1992).

DeJong and Berg (2002) assert that there are several different types of therapist–client relationships: (1) client in a visitor relationship, (2) client in a complainant relationship, and (3) client in a customer relationship. The *client in a visitor relationship* with the therapist really does not want anything from the therapist. Typically, he or she is there involuntarily. DeJong and Berg (2002) cite the case of a person who came to their institute for substance abuse. The person really did not want the clinicians' help to stop the substance abuse. In the visitor relationship, there is no joint definition of the problem, nor does the client state any real goals. The authors suggest that the clinician should give the client compliments for even bothering to come to therapy and say that he or she would be happy to meet with the client again. The authors state that this approach increases the likelihood that the client will return and possibly develop either a complainant-type or a customer-type relationship.

The *client in a complainant relationship* suggests that the therapist and the client have jointly defined a problem; however, the client cannot identify exceptions or minimizes them. In this relationship, clients are inclined to provide detailed descriptions about the severity of their problems, which they believe are externally created by other persons or organizations. Because these clients do not have a sense of what they might have contributed to the situation, they do not see anything they can do to solve the problem (DeJong & Berg, 2002). These clients tend to feel powerless about their problems, and they want others to be different so that they can get better.

The first message the therapist gives to the client is an authentic compliment for carefully observing the problem and its effects on his or her life. The clinician then creates a bridge by suggesting the following task: "Between now and the next time we meet, pay attention to what's happening in your life that tells you this problem can be solved." This task is labeled the *formula first-session task* because it was originally given in the first session to all clients to help them in goal development (de Shazer, 1985). The client is asked to think about what should be continued:

> Between now and the next time we meet, I would like you to observe, so that you can describe to me next time, what happens in your (pick one: family, life, marriage, relationship) that you want to continue to have happen. (de Shazer, 1985, p. 137)

The *client in a customer relationship* is the third type of therapeutic relationship clinicians establish with clients. In this instance, the therapist has developed a joint definition of the problem with the client, and the client accepts his or her role in the solution and seems motivated to work in therapy. The client has high motivation, but he or she has no well-formed goals. The client says, "Something has got to change." de Shazer (1985) and his colleagues have constructed a task that helps the clinician to put the focus squarely on the client and his or her resources. It is called the *do something different task*. This task gives the client permission to be spontaneous and creative in taking steps to resolve his or her problems (Table 15.1). First, the therapist compliments the client for his work on the problem, and then states,

> Because this is such a stubborn problem, I suggest that in between now and the next time we meet, when the problem happens, you do something different—no matter how strange, weird, or off-the-wall what you do might seem. Whatever you decided to do, the only important thing is that you need to do something different. (DeJong & Berg, 2002, p. 134)

Follow-Up Sessions and EARS. Because it is the therapist's task to help clients achieve a more satisfying life, follow-up therapy sessions will usually begin with the therapist asking, "What is better?" If clients have made any improvement, even for a short period of time, the therapist explores such improvements. The therapist asks, "What was different? What did you notice? How did it happen? What strengths or resources did you use to make the improvement? What would be the next sign that things are continuing to change for the better for you?" Sometimes, clients have made improvements that they have not noted as improvements.

Table 15.1 Summary of Four Key Therapist Tasks for Session 1

Therapist Task	Examples of Questions
Find out what the client is hoping to achieve from the session or from working together.	What do you hope will be the outcome of our working together? How will you know if counseling has been useful for you?
Find out what the client's life would be like if his or her hopes for counseling were realized. Have the client focus on the everyday details of his or her life if the problem were resolved.	If tonight, while you were asleep, a miracle happened and it resolved the problem that brought you to counseling, what would you be noticing different tomorrow? (Miracle question)
Find out what the client is already doing or has done in the past to reduce the problem. Have there been any exceptions to the problem taking place in the client's life?	Tell me about the times the problem does not occur. What were you or others doing to prevent the problem from taking place? (Exception question)
Find out what might be different if the client took one very small step toward achieving his or her goals or hopes regarding the problem.	What would your spouse, mother, friend, or colleague notice if you moved just one small step toward the life you would like to lead?

Follow-up sessions usually use the techniques described in the acronym **EARS**, which stands for (1) *E*licit exceptions, (2) *A*mplify exceptions, (3) *R*einforce client's successes, and (4) *S*tart again. During the eliciting of exceptions, the therapist asks questions such as "What have you been doing to make your situation better?" The goal here is to acknowledge the client's efforts. Clients learn from their own behaviors. In the next step, amplify, the therapist seeks to use questions to get more details about any positive efforts toward problem solving. The therapist uses *who*, *what*, *where*, *when*, and *how* questions—for example, "When did you decided to do that?" The therapist reinforces the client for his or her solution-finding efforts. The *S* in the EARS model stands for starting over or using the scaling technique.

Brief Therapy: Number of Sessions for Solution-Focused Therapy

Solution-focused therapy is intended to be brief, and therefore, the clinician assumes an active role in shifting as quickly as possible from client problems to client solutions. As clients enter therapy, they learn that therapy will be brief (Berg & Dolan, 2001; de Shazer & Dolan, 2007). Solution-focused therapists are highly trained in guiding the process and structure of therapy. Both the client and the clinician work toward a shared solution. From the very beginning, they establish criteria that will indicate when they have succeeded with their counseling goals and when counseling can be ended. The average number of sessions is between three and five.

Goals of Therapy

Goals vary in solution-focused therapy depending on the type of relationship that the client establishes with the therapist (e.g., visitor, complainant, or customer type). Solution-focused therapists recommend starting with small, realistic, and achievable goals that stand a good chance of resulting in positive outcomes. Walter and Peller

(1992) point out that **goals** should be (1) stated in the positive using the client's language or own words; (2) process or action oriented; (3) structured in the here-and-now; (4) attainable, concrete, and specific; and (5) controlled or presented by the client. Clinicians are cautioned to listen carefully to clients before trying to arrive at goals for counseling.

Goals that are stated within a negative framework are oftentimes discouraging goals because they focus on what the client does not want. If a person says that she wants to stop arguing with her husband over minor things, she is highlighting the negative. Such a goal statement feeds discouragement, produces low energy, and creates a situation in which the client feels trapped. It is usually better for a client to do something that he or she perceives as positive. In the example just provided, the client restates her goal by stating, "I am going to give my husband at least three compliments a day" instead of "I am going to stop being negative toward him." In helping clients develop goals, the solution-focused therapist uses language that suggests a positive outcome. For instance, the therapist asks positively,

- "How will you do that?" rather than "Why will you do that?"
- "When this happens, . . ." rather than "If this happens, . . ."
- "What will you be doing?" instead of "What would you be doing?"
- "What will be happening?" rather than "What won't be happening?"

The clinician helps clients identify clear goals by having them provide a clear description of their preferred future without the problem. Questioning centers around what life will be like without the problem or challenge. It is important for the counselor to concentrate on the details of the client's preferred future. Some questions the clinician might ask here are as follows:

- What will you notice when the problem is better?
- How will things be different when the problem is better?

- What will you be doing differently when things are better?
- What will you be doing instead?
- How will your family/parents/friends know when things are going better?
- How will others know when the problem is better? Tell me more about that. (To get as much detail as possible, the counselor asks, "What else?")

Well-Described Goals in Solution-Focused Brief Therapy

Well-described goals will be

- positive;
- described in terms of what is wanted rather than what is not wanted;
- broken down into small, achievable steps;
- specific and observable; and
- realistic.

Role of the Client

DeJong and Berg (2002) make it clear that the client problems are not puzzles to be solved by the clinician. The problems that clinicians encounter are different from puzzles. Frequently, clients' problems do not have a single correct solution. Because individuals' lives are so diverse, it is difficult to recommend the same solution for all clients. Whereas science and medicine use convergent thinking, the helping professions should use divergent thinking (de Shazer & Dolan, 2007). Problems should be examined in terms of the various discourses affecting the client.

Solution-focused therapy declares that clients can construct their own solutions to problems. As de Shazer (1988) has stated, "The client constructs his or her own solution based on his or her own resources and successes" (p. 50). Therapists do not see themselves as experts at scientifically assessing client problems and then intervening. On the contrary, the solution-focused clinician strives to be expert at exploring clients' frames of reference and

identifying whatever perceptions they have about living better lives (DeJong & Berg, 2002). Because the therapist is using the client's frame of reference, it becomes less useful to concentrate on resistance.

Therapy Techniques

Many of the techniques for solution-focused therapy have already been discussed in the sections on the role of the client, the role of the therapist, and the process of therapy. This section expands on some of the more popular techniques already discussed in this chapter. It provides actual statements that counselors can use with their clients during therapy.

Miracle Questions. This intervention is at the heart of solution-focused therapy. The miracle question was taken from both Adler's work on individual psychology and Milton Erickson's clinical work on hypnosis (de Shazer, 1988). The clinician states,

> Suppose you wake up in the morning and you discover that a miracle has taken place and all the problems that have brought you to counseling have disappeared. How are you going to start recognizing that the miracle has happened? What else will you notice?

Looking for Previous Solutions. Solution-focused therapists believe that most people have previously solved many problems and, therefore, have some ideas regarding how to solve their current problem. Previous solutions to one problem may be helpful in resolving the current situation. This technique can be compared with the exceptions (Jackson & McKergow, 2002).

Compliments. The therapist uses compliments to validate what clients are already doing well and to acknowledge how difficult their problems are, while at the same time giving the message that the therapist is listening and cares. During counseling sessions, clinicians give compliments to encourage clients to continue what is working (Jackson & McKergow, 2002). Therapist compliments are designed to have clients compliment themselves. Therapists can compliment with questions such as "How did you do that?" When clients respond with how they accomplished an activity, they are invited to self-compliment themselves.

In addition, compliments should be process oriented rather than trait oriented. With process praise, you compliment the client for his or her effort or strategy. For example, the clinician might tell the client, "You must have worked very hard to achieve this" or "You must have used a good strategy to solve the problem." With trait praise, you compliment the client for some fixed internal quality: "You are very intelligent."

Moreover, any compliment you make should be focused on client behaviors that are related to their achieving goals. The compliment should refer to what actually happened and what the client did in the situation. Some suggestions for complimenting include the following:

- Don't compliment people, only what they do.
- Make compliments as specific as possible.
- Avoid phony compliments.
- Avoid compliments that set up competition.
- Focus your compliments on clients' behavior instead of on their presumed traits (e.g., intelligence).
- Focus your compliment on something you know is important to the person.

Exceptions. Solution-focused clinicians maintain that no problem is absolute. Although the problem may be highly significant to the person or family, the times in which the problem happens are not 24/7. Some possible exception-building questions are as follows: "Tell me about the times when your family members were loving toward each other. What were you doing during these times as a family? What was different about the times in which your family responded lovingly toward each other?"

Coping Questions. These are designed to draw clients' attention away from the fear, loneliness, and misery and refocus it on what the clients are doing to survive their pain and circumstances (DeJong &

Berg, 2002). They are a form of solution talk that has been developed to help clients who are feeling overwhelmed by their problems. **Coping questions** help the client and clinician uncover those times in which clients have struggled with the problem. The clinician asks, "What have you found helpful thus far?" When clinicians focus on how clients are coping with a problem, the clients become more confident that they are not stuck in a situation. To build coping momentum, clinicians need to notice and compliment clients on their coping.

Coping questions are especially important when working with clients who may be suicidal. DeJong and Berg (2002) suggest that the typical clinician reaction to suicidal clients is to place the person in a hospital or on medication. However, a better way might be to focus on how the client has coped successfully with suicidal tendencies. For instance, the clinician might ask, "How did you get out of bed this morning?" A client who has gotten out of bed, gotten dressed, and driven to a therapist's office has done something that requires a great deal of energy for a discouraged person. The coping question is a good way to have the client recount microsuccesses in dealing with the presenting problem.

Coping Questions

- How do you cope when things are so difficult?
- Who is helping you to cope?
- Describe the changes you will notice as you move up each number on the scale.

Consultation Brand and Invitation to Add Further Information. Usually, solution-focused clinicians take a brief consultation break during the second half of each therapy session. During the break, the therapist (or therapist and team) reflects carefully on what has transpired in the first half of the session. The client is usually complimented and offered a therapeutic message based on his or her goal.

Scaling Questions. **Scaling questions** help a clinician identify movement regarding clients' problems or challenges (Jackson & McKergow, 2002). They are also useful for clients who are struggling to identify goals or exceptions to their problems. The clinician describes a scale from 0, which represents the worst the problem has ever been, to 10, the best things could ever possibly be. Clinicians ask clients to rate their current position on the scale, and then questions are used to assist the client in identifying resources (e.g., "What's stopping you from slipping one point lower down the scale?"). The clinician combines exceptions with the use of the scaling technique. "On a day when you are a point higher on the scale, what would tell you that it was a 'one-point-higher' day?" Scales can also be used to describe a preferred future: "Where on the scale would be good enough for you?" or "What would a day at that point on the scale look like?"

What do you do when the client says that his current point on the scale is 0? Usually, when a client says that he is at 0, he is trying to convey just how frustrating the situation is. When clients are at a current 0 on their scale, use a coping question. You might say, for example, "How do you manage to continue with times so difficult?" The coping question indicates that the client is working on dealing with the problem and that he or she does have strength. It can help clients find new energy to deal with their problems.

It is important for the client to define his or her scale anchors, especially the 10—the ideal situation. Scales are most useful when the 10 position is defined in realistic rather than idealistic terms. If the client makes the 10 too idealistic, the ideal situation may never be achieved. Few people live problem-free lives. Instead, the clinician helps clients to define a 10 position as a situation in which one would be most satisfied—not completely satisfied. Other ways of using the scaling techniques are as follows.

Scaling Technique

- Imagine a scale from 0 to 10, with 10 representing how you want things to be when the problem is solved and 0 is the opposite.

- What number are you on the scale right now?
- What number were you at when the problem was at its worst?
- What will you notice if you moved up one or two numbers toward your goal?

Scales can be used to distinguish various parts of the problem and their solutions. For instance, a client's problem might be with family and work colleagues. Moreover, when a client is experiencing multiple problems, each problem can be explored with its own scale. Sometimes when several scales are used, clients become aware of overlap between them. As a consequence, clients learn that improvement in one area can also lead to improvement in other areas.

A Solution-Focused Scale

Points to Mark on the Scale	What to Explore
10 The perfect solution	Use the miracle question to get at the perfect solution
7 A good but realistic outcome	A picture of the client getting on with life
5 I could live with this	With the problem reduced or mostly eliminated
4 Current position	Where is the client now on this scale?
3 What the client is doing to prevent things from getting worse	Coping questions—How is the client managing to cope with the situation? What worked well for the client?
0 The worst possible scenario	Acknowledge, but don't go into detail

---

Normalizing. The technique of normalizing is used with clients who have been struggling with emotionally charged issues and who have lost perspective for their particular situation. Sometimes, because their problems have been around for such a long time, clients talk about their problems as though they are completely out of control and not normal. For instance, a parent might be having difficulties because a teenager is hanging out with the wrong crowd or a husband discovers that his wife has been stepping out on him, and both talk about their problems as if they are outside the boundaries of normalcy. Clinicians can easily get so caught up in the intensity of these clients' problem talk that they lose perspective regarding the normal range of the problems discussed.

According to DeJong and Berg (2002),

> Normalizing involves responding to problem talk by wondering with clients about whether their difficulties are not within the range of ordinary problems of living. It is meant to counter a tendency to see deep-seated problems and personal pathology in life's unexpected challenges. (p. 42)

In response to the parent who feels a total failure as a parent, the clinician might state, "You say your son is a 16-year-old boy? Knowing what you do about teenagers, would you say that part of what he is doing is or is not normal for a teenager his age?"

In making a normalizing intervention, the clinician must be careful not to minimize the client's struggles. DeJong and Berg (2002) have suggested that for the beginning therapist it might be better to use a more tentative framework of asking for clients' views of the normalcy of their difficulties. In working with clients, the clinician listens carefully for clues about what they want to be different. As soon as the clinician moves the conversation around what the client wants, therapy will proceed in a productive manner.

Returning the Focus to the Client. When describing their problems and how they would like things to change, most clients state what they would like others to do differently. Such talk helps them to feel as if they are powerless in their circumstances and at the mercy of others. To move from a sense of powerlessness to a position of empowerment, clients will have to shift their focus. As DeJong and Berg (2002) have asserted,

> They will have to focus less on what they do not appreciate about other people and their current circumstances and more on what they want to have happen differently in the situation and how they see themselves participating in a solution. (p. 44)

For instance, if a woman has a husband who verbally abuses her, she would be asked to focus on what she could do to stop being abused: "What power do you have that might make you less of a target of verbal abuse from your husband?" The woman might say, "Each time when he begins his verbal abuse, I will just get up and leave the room to work on my artwork."

Noticing. When clients first come to therapy, they may be prone to giving countless, repetitive details about their problems. Such repetitive details are often discouraging and give rise to the feeling that it is impossible to find a solution to the presenting problem. One of the biggest challenges for the clinician is not to get caught up in detailed, repetitive descriptions of the client's problem. It is very important for clinicians to notice statements clients make that could mark the beginning of a solution to the presenting problem. The therapist listens alertly for anything the client says that hints of a solution. Did the client suggest that he or she might want something different? Or did the client indicate that he or she had a past success with the presenting issue? What did the client say to indicate that he or she has already tried to improve the situation? We rarely notice everything there is to notice. When we notice something as a clinician, what we notice reflects our interests, beliefs, and assumptions. Notice solutions rather than problems.

Single Successful Sessions

In general, SFBT takes about five sessions, each of which takes no more than 45 minutes

(Jackson & McKergow, 2002). Counseling rarely extends beyond eight sessions, and sometimes only one session is needed. In solution-focused therapy, single-session successes are sufficiently common, which is not surprising. Three possible explanations are given for the success of single sessions. First, some clients are stuck in the problem because they cannot see a way out of it. Second, some clients have actually taken real steps to resolve the problem, but they do not realize that they are moving toward solving the problem. Third, some clients come to the conclusion that their lives may not be perfect, but they are managing life. For instance, a young man was about to be expelled from school because of aggressive behavior. The family came to counseling and discovered that the boy actually wanted to change his behavior but did not know how.

RESEARCH AND EVALUATION __
Multicultural Positives

Social constructionist theories support the underlying premises of multiculturalism. These theories assert that people construct multiple realities that are connected to the values within their culture. Diverse views are welcomed within the solution-focused therapy school because the client is the expert on his or her life rather than the therapist. The solution-focused therapist does not try to impose his construction of reality on the client. This position can be contrasted with some of the traditional counseling theories that posit a given personality that every person has. Under the traditional counseling theory framework, it is the therapist's responsibility to help the client work toward optimum arrangement of the various components of the client's personality.

Solution-focused therapists work closely with clients to clarify their goals. Clients are encouraged to use their own cultural framework within which to construct goals. Instead of having a preconceived notion of what is culturally appropriate, the practitioner follows the lead of the client, who is considered the expert. The therapist functions primarily as a guide for the client. The solution-focused therapist respects clients' cultural differences. He or she honors clients' values in selecting goals. Pedersen and Carey (2003) emphasize the importance of establishing a collaborative, multicultural alliance by having clients participate in goal setting. Respecting and honoring the goals of clients is a hallmark of solution-focused therapy and culturally respectful practice. Likewise, solution-focused therapy's emphasis on strengths is consistent with the literature on culturally competent therapy. As Ridley (2005) points out, "While vigorously looking for psychopathology in minority clients, counselors often miss opportunities to help clients identify their assets and use these assets advantageously" (p. 103). The counseling interventions in solution-focused therapy are responsive to the current standards and recommendations for culturally competent practice.

Several studies have evaluated the use of SFBT with Asian and Asian American cultures and found that this theoretical approach can be helpful. For instance, Cheung (2001) reported that some Asian cultures place a high value on finding pragmatic solutions to problems and that they are less comfortable with focusing on emotions. Hsu and Wang (2011) integrated the Asian belief of filial piety with SFBT. Filial piety is a prevailing cultural belief in Taiwanese/Chinese societies and influences a wide range of individual and interpersonal behaviors, counseling, and psychotherapy; hence, this cultural belief would be most effective when this cultural norm is considered and incorporated in the SFBT treatment process.

SFBT has been used with clients from major cultural groups within this country and throughout the world. Kim's (2014) new book, *Solution-Focused Brief Therapy: A Multicultural Approach* examines the usefulness of this therapeutic approach with a number of ethnic and cultural groups, including African Americans, Latino Americans, Asian Americans, and Native Americans as well as LGBTQ (lesbian, gay, bisexual, transgender, and queer) clients and clients with disabilities.

Multicultural Blind Spots

From a multicultural perspective, solution-focused therapy also has its limitations. Cultures that place therapists in positions of power might find it a bit disconcerting to assume that the client is an expert. Therapists might inform clients that they have expertise in conducting therapy; however, they will work collaboratively toward helping clients achieve their goals.

Contributions of Solution-Focused Therapy

There are a number of benefits of using solution-focused therapy. The therapist seeks solutions to problems that the client has been facing. Another advantage is that solution-focused therapy is brief, and therefore, it may be less expensive than other forms of therapy that traditionally take more sessions over a longer period of time. A third benefit is that solution-focused therapy establishes clear goals early in the counseling process. Early goal identification allows clients and counselors to know what success will look like. As a consequence, both client and counselor can easily identify when therapy is no longer needed.

Solution-focused therapy is one of the most popular and widely used counseling approaches around the world. It has been applied to family therapy (McCollum, Lewis, Nelson, & Trepper, 2003), couples therapy (McCollum, Trepper, & Smock, 2003), treatment of sexual abuse (Dolan, 1991), treatment of substance abuse (Berg & Miller, 1992), counseling within the schools (Cook & Kaffenberger, 2003; Corcoran & Stephenson, 2000), and a host of self-help books (Bertolino & O'Hanlon, 2002).

The solution-focused model has had encouraging results when applied to substance-abusing clients. Miller and Berg (1995) have declared, "Our clinical experience suggests that clients want to and do recover from alcohol problems rather rapidly" (pp. 22–23). In addition, solution-focused therapy has been found to be effective with mental health clients (Beyeback, Morejon, Palenzuela, & Rodriguez-Arias, 1996) and clients within the prison system (Lindforss & Magnusson, 1997). For instance, the miracle question has been used with clients who have been referred by the legal system and whose only stated goal is to get off probation. The therapist asks,

> Suppose that a miracle happened while you are asleep tonight. And the miracle is that you have gained the ability to get out and stay out of the prison system. But since you were asleep, you don't know that the miracle has happened. What will you notice when you wake up that lets you know that this miracle actually happened?

Solution-focused therapy is used across a number of different areas, including social work, psychology, guidance counseling, addiction treatment, and counseling for inmates. Gingerich and Eisengrat (2000) reviewed solution-focused outcome research and found that studies offered preliminary support that SFBT could be beneficial to clients. Of the 15 outcome studies reviewed, 9 provided strong or moderately strong support for solution-focused therapy, while 6 supplied only weak support.

SFBT is currently being applied to school settings (Murphy, 1997). Studies have found that SFBT is effective in school counseling for elementary school (Murphy & Duncan, 1997), middle school, and high school children. On using SFBT, students showed improvement in their grades and in school attendance. Newsome (2004) used SFBT group work with at-risk junior high school students. He found that in comparison with the students who did not receive the treatment, the students in the solution therapy treatment group increased their grade point average from pretreatment to posttreatment. Newsome concluded that SFBT showed promise as a group intervention with at-risk students.

Franklin and Streeter (2003) have been involved in an exciting application of SFBT in the schools in Austin, Texas. A demonstration project is currently underway at an alternative high school comprising high-risk students (Franklin & Streeter, 2003). This school utilizes a solution-building model that was based on principles from SFBT and is designed to engage the students by using solution-focused philosophies and skills. A preliminary pilot study found that 62% of the high-risk sample students graduated on time, and of those who did not, more than one half were still at the school pursuing their degree. Moreover, 91% reported that they plan to attend college or some type of postsecondary educational program.

Also, results showed these students rating all three dimensions of the school domain (school satisfaction, teacher support, and school safety) as assets, while comparison group students rated these three dimensions as either a caution or a risk. Although in its early stages of research, this study lends support to the application of SFBT principles and practices to motivate high-risk students toward postsecondary education.

Empirical research documentation for solution-focused therapy is increasing as the therapeutic approach is being applied across a number of disciplines. Because of its emphasis on brief therapy, solution-focused therapy stands a good chance of being reimbursable.

Limitations and Criticisms of Solution-Focused Therapy

One criticism of solution-focused therapy is that it overlooks gender and power difference. Dermer, Hemesath, and Russell (1998) contend that solution-focused therapy neglects to deal with important gender differences. Another criticism of solution-focused psychotherapy is the precept that one does not have to know anything about how the problem developed and that even some of the more difficult problems, including trauma, neglect, and abuse, can be dealt with quickly, often in a single session. Such beliefs may be somewhat naive when one thinks of clients who have long-standing disorders. While some clients may be able to move on without an exploration of their past, others may not be able to do so.

Thus, a major concern about solution-focused therapy is its neglect of client history and broader assessment. According to de Shazer et al. (1986, p. 214), solution-focused therapists begin with limited information about the client to "minimize preset ideas." Seeking information about a client's past is seen as **problem talk**, which needs to be kept to a minimum. Insight into the history of a problem is not seen as useful, and the therapist does not even have to know the details of the complaint but only needs to know one thing: "How will we know when the problem is solved?" (p. 210). The therapist appears to minimize the client's problems.

Stalker, Levene, and Coady (1999) have provided a stinging criticism of the "naïveté" of the solution-focused approach. They have criticized the one-model-fits-all approach for solution-focused therapy. According to them,

> Berg and DeJong's (1996) account of the single-session "success" with a teen mother whose children were in child welfare care and who was dealing with a physically abusive partner is an example of naïveté. This case example illustrates SFBT's disregard of a gender-sensitive perspective and of large-systems factors such as "the legal system, child welfare, the extended family, and medical system" (McConkey, 1992, p. 4). de Shazer's (1991) account of doing marital work with a couple where the husband had been diagnosed with paranoid schizophrenia is at best naive. In discussing this case, de Shazer notes that "it is all too easy to join in the exploration of history," (p. 137) and instead he fosters a "progressive narrative" to help the husband control hallucinations and delusions. de Shazer's purposeful refusal to consider the micro-systemic (i.e., biological/genetic) components of mental illness and the usefulness of the medication that was prescribed by a psychiatrist raises ethical as well as clinical issues. We would argue that SFBT's neglect of broad-based assessment is in opposition to social work's person-in-environment perspective and to clinical wisdom.
>
> A third, more general limitation of SFBT is that it perpetuates the problematic tendency of earlier strategic/systemic models toward rigid adherence to narrow models and the belief that one model can be all things to all people. (pp. 474–475)

Evidence-Based Research

SFBT has had a large number of empirical studies and has been examined in two recent meta-analyses. It is now officially supported as evidenced-based therapy by numerous federal and state agencies and institutions, such as SAMHSA's National Registry of Evidence-Based Programs & Practices (NREPP). To briefly summarize the basis on which SFBT is evaluated as evidence based, consider the following facts:

- There have been 77 empirical studies on the effectiveness of SFBT.
- There have been two meta-analyses (Kim, 2008; Stams, Dekovic, Buist, & de Vries, 2006) and two systematic reviews.
- There is a combined effectiveness data from more than 2,800 cases.
- All research was done in "real-world" settings ("effectiveness" vs. "efficacy" studies), so the results are more generalizable.
- SFBT is equally effective for all social classes.

- Effect sizes are in the low to moderate range, the same that are found in meta-analyses for other evidence-based practices, such as cognitive-behavioral therapy and intermittent presumptive therapy.
- Overall success rate average 60% in three to five sessions.

The conclusion of the two meta-analyses and the two systematic reviews, and the overall conclusion of the most recent scholarly work on SFBT, is that SFBT is an effective approach for the treatment of psychological problems, with effect sizes similar to other evidenced-based approaches, such as cognitive-behavioral therapy and intermittent presumptive therapy, but that these effects are found in fewer average sessions and using an approach style that is more benign (Gingerich, Kim, & MacDonald, 2012; Trepper & Franklin, 2012). Based on its cost-effectiveness and shorter duration, SFBT is considered to be an excellent first-choice evidenced-based psychotherapy approach for most psychological, behavioral, and relational problems.

CASE ANALYSIS

Justin From a Solution-Focused Perspective

The therapist endorsed several solution-focused principles in working with Justin. He focused on Justin's strengths, his resources, and what was possible at the current time. The therapist began the session by complimenting Justin on the fact that he made the decision to come to therapy and that he was on time. He complimented Justin for his strength and for taking action to do something about his problem by coming to counseling. He talked about the courage and the endurance Justin had in coming to school and facing his issues.

During the first part of the session, the therapist wanted Justin to feel comfortable with him. Therefore, the first 5 to 10 minutes of the session were filled with a few minutes of problem-free talk about the school's basketball championship efforts.

He gave Justin an opportunity to talk about his issues. Justin informed the therapist that he was picked up by the police for stealing at the local mall but that he did not steal, his friend did. The stealing incident brought him into court, and that's when all hell broke loose. His school was contacted, and the principal said that Justin had gotten into trouble fighting on several different occasions. The judge threatened that if he got into any more trouble, he would be placed in a residential treatment program some 200 or 300 miles from his home. Justin said that he had several problems. First, he wanted to stay out of the residential treatment center. Second, he couldn't get into any more fights at school because the principal was going to expel him and the judge would say that he

(Continued)

(Continued)

had not learned his lesson and needed to be away. Third, he had a problem with anger. Sometimes he and his mother got into big arguments. His anger had caused the fights in school.

After Justin had finished telling his tale of woes, he looked at the therapist and said, "A big mess. I've gotten myself into a big mess." The therapist took this comment as a cue to ask Justin the miracle question. He said to Justin, "You kind of feel that you need a miracle to make it all go away." Justin responded, "You've got that right. I need a miracle, and I don't see one coming."

The therapist said, "Just suppose you could have a miracle.

"Suppose that while you are sleeping tonight, and the entire house is quiet, a miracle happens. The miracle is that the problem that brought you here is solved. However, because you are sleeping, you don't know that the miracle has happened. So when you wake up tomorrow morning, what will be different that will tell you that a miracle has happened and the problem that brought you here is solved?"

"That would be great," Justin laughed. "Could you make it happen tonight for me?"

Solution-focused therapists use the miracle question because it gives clients permission to think about an unlimited range of possibilities. Clients are asked to think big so that they can get started on identifying what changes they want to see. In addition, the future focus of the miracle question evokes a picture of time in which the client's problems are no longer problems. The miracle question requires the client to take a leap of faith and imagine how his or her life will be changed when the problem is solved. It requires the client to make a dramatic change from problem-saturated thinking to considering solutions to the problem.

The therapist continued. "Now I want you to close your eyes, Justin, for just a few seconds. Take a deep breath, and when you open your eyes, the miracle has taken place. What will you first notice that suggests that the miracle has taken place? What will be different?"

Justin replied that for the first time in three weeks, he would wake up smiling. His heart would not feel so heavy, and his mom wouldn't be angry with him anymore. He would feel good about himself, and he would be determined not to get into anymore trouble at school or at home. He wouldn't have to be so scared about what was going to happen to him. He said that others would notice that he was happier and not so cranky. His teachers would notice that he was handing his homework on time and that it was done correctly for a change. His teachers would also notice that he was doing better on his tests.

What struck the therapist was that Justin had begun describing a vision of a different life. He said that he would do better in school—maybe even get a few As. He would make new friends from outside of the gangs in his neighborhood (i.e., if his mom moved), and he would even go to Mass with his mother. He would not be so angry anymore because finally something would have gone his way for a change. "Sometimes I feel so mad inside that I want to just hit someone, anyone who could not beat me up. I wouldn't have to carry that feeling around inside of me anymore. I'd be free for the first time."

There was a lot of hope in Justin's vision for the future, and the therapist wanted to build on this hope that had lain dormant for a long time. For one thing, Justin's preferred future had his being the kind of young man that his mother and the school desired. There was a great deal of prosocial talk in Justin's vision for the future. He wanted to get As in school; he wanted to change his friends and move from his gang-ridden neighborhood.

The miracle question had brought out a vision that Justin had for himself and that was not readily apparent to others who did not know his heart or his dreams. The miracle question had elicited a number of possible goals for Justin to work toward. The therapist asked which issue Justin would like to work on first. To get at which issue Justin wanted to work on first, the therapist inquired, "What would have to be different as a result of our meeting today for you to say that our talking was worthwhile?"

Justin indicated that he would most like to work on his anger because that seemed to be connected to so many different problems in his life. The therapist agreed that the two would work on Justin's anger issues. The therapist followed up with another question about Justin's hopes from counseling. The therapist continued, "How will you know if our meeting has been useful with helping you deal successfully with your anger?" Justin indicated that he would not have the knock-down arguments with his mom every other night and that he would not get into another fight in school for the rest of the school year.

The therapist continued the counseling session by asking Justin exception questions. "Tell me about the times when your anger is less and when it doesn't get you into trouble. "Justin indicated that he did not get into arguments with his mom when he was drawing or painting on an art project. "When I am really involved with my artwork, I don't have time to argue with my mom. I just go to my room. Usually, we get into shouting matches when we're watching TV or when she tells me to do some chore I don't want to do."

The therapist searched for Justin's coping strategies for dealing with his anger across several environments, including his home and school. The therapist inquired, "How have you managed so far? What has prevented your anger from getting worse?" These questions drew Justin's attention away from the problems related to his anger and focused it on what he was doing to overcome his anger and his life circumstances. The focus was on finding Justin's strengths and adaptive capacity. The coping questions actually drew attention to some of the control within Justin and helped empower him and give him hope that he can control his anger.

Justin replied that sometimes he played basketball with his friends but his mother did not like his friends. On some occasions, he just fell asleep on his bed, or he went to his brother's room to talk. Justin indicated that he did not have a lot of opportunities to get out of his neighborhood or out of the house, except for going to the mall. Sometimes he would ride his bike just to avoid an argument with his mother. Most of the time, he just tuned his mother out by listening to the radio or to his CDs. One time, he even began cleaning his room just to stop her complaining about his dirty room.

The therapist asked Justin to use the scale to describe where he currently stood with the anger problem. The therapist inquired, "Suppose I have a scale of 0 to 10, and 0 on the scale represents the worst scenario and 10 the perfect solution to your anger. Where would you place yourself on the scale right now? What number would you choose, and why? Where would you like to be on the scale? What do you see yourself doing to get to the number that you want on the scale?" If Justin indicates that he is at 3 and says that he wants to be at 7, there is hope.

The therapist began to help Justin define some goals for himself based on his responses to the miracle question. The therapist talked about goals in terms of first small steps. He asked Justin, "What will be the first small steps that you will take toward dealing successfully with your anger?" The therapist collaborated with Justin to articulate concrete, behavioral, and measurable goals that will help the two determine when they are making progress toward satisfactory solutions. The therapist asked Justin to state one small, measurable step that would indicate he is in control of his anger rather than his anger being in control of him.

Justin stated that he will do one of his chores without his mother having to tell him to do it. He has the responsibility of washing the dishes and cleaning his room. Both he and his mother argue because Justin does not wash the dinner dishes on a daily basis. If he washes the dishes without his mother having to tell him to do so, he will eliminate a cause for his nightly argument with her. Justin decided that he will wash the dishes immediately after he cleans off his plate. He won't sit down and watch television and then wash the dishes an hour or so later. The therapist asked, "What will your mother notice about you this week?" Justin responded, "She'll notice that we don't have as many arguments as we used to. She'll notice I've done my chore."

SUMMARY

An overriding goal of solution-focused counseling is that clients learn how to solution talk rather than problem talk. Whereas talking about a problem only keeps the focus on the problem, talking about solutions will produce change. Clients learn how to speak in terms of their competencies and strengths—what they have already done that has worked. The therapist should complete four tasks by the end of the first session:

- Find out what the client is hoping to achieve from counseling. Goals are framed in positive terms with expectancy for change.
- Find out what the small, mundane, and everyday details of the client's life would be like if these hopes (miracle) were accomplished.
- Find out what the person is already doing or has done in the past that might help the client to realize his or her goals (hoped-for situation).
- Find out what might be different in the client's life if he or she made one very small step toward realizing his or her hopes (goals).

SUPPLEMENTAL AIDS
Discussion Questions

1. One goal of SFBT is to help clients reduce talking about their problems and focus on solutions to problems. Is it more comfortable for you to help clients talk about their problems or to construct solutions for them?

2. How difficult would it be for you to focus on constructing solutions for clients' problems?

3. What value do you see in asking clients the miracle question? As a therapist, how helpful is it for you to ask clients to imagine that their problems would vanish one night as they slept?

4. What are some strategies you might use to help clients think about the exceptions to their problems?

5. What solution-focused therapy techniques or interventions do you find most helpful to you as a therapist?

Glossary of Key Terms

continuation question Identifies that which does not have to change. The continuation question acknowledges that the client does not have to change everything because there are things that are going well.

coping questions Used to elicit examples of times when the client coped with even the most difficult of situations. The therapist asks, "How have you coped?" The client's response can be transformed into a more positive and solution-focused alternative. This transformation is supported by the utilization of *problem-free talk*.

EARS A mnemonic device in solution-focused therapy that stands for *Elicit, Amplify, Reinforce,* and *Start* again. A mnemonic for talking with clients who are able to describe instances of progress toward their goals of therapy or to report exceptions or unique outcomes (DeJong & Berg, 2002).

exception questions Questions in solution-focused therapy that ask about those times in clients' lives when the problems that brought them to therapy were not a problem. When clients explore the exceptions to their problems, they learn that their problems are not all powerful and have not existed forever. Some exception-finding questions include the following: "When would you say you do not have that problem?"; "Can you think of any other time, either in the past or in recent weeks, when you did not have the problem (with drinking)?"; and "Can you think of a time within the past month that you and your husband did not argue?"

goals Desired outcomes of projects or processes in therapy or elsewhere. In solution-focused brief therapy, therapists elicit goals for therapy, and they help the client to make them well formed. Goals are usually stated in the positive—that is, stated as the presence of something rather than the absence of something.

miracle question A term borrowed from Alfred Adler. The therapist asks, "Suppose one night there is a miracle (or suppose a fairy godmother came with a magic wand), and while you are sleeping the problem you described in therapy is solved; what will you notice different the next morning that will tell you that there has been a miracle?" The importance of the miracle question is that it gets clients to think about a time when their problem is over. In describing what they would notice that would be different, clients typically describe the solution in detailed, behavioral terms. The therapist's task is to get the client to initiate the miracle's actions.

problem talk Centers around the problem that brought the client to therapy. Sometimes a client cannot get beyond talking about his or her problem.

problem-free talk Focuses on areas outside of the problem and enables both therapist and client to establish an atmosphere in which the strengths and positive qualities of the client can be highlighted and used to help improve other areas of life.

scaling questions Useful in helping clients assess their own situations, track their own progress, or evaluate how others might rate them on a scale of 0 to 10. The therapist asks, "On a scale of 1 to 10, with 10 being high, . . . " One can ask about clients' motivation, hopefulness, depression, or confidence; the progress they have made; or a host of other topics that can be used to track their performance and plan what might be the next small steps.

solution-focused therapy Targets what works rather than what's wrong with a client. Originally developed by Steve de Shazer and Insoo Kim Berg and colleagues at the Brief Family Therapy Center in Milwaukee, Wisconsin, solution-focused therapy has found worldwide acceptance and has generated excitement and renewed optimism among providers everywhere in schools, in agencies that treat alcoholism and drug addiction, and in the penal system.

Website Materials

Additional exercises, journals, annotated bibliography, and more are available on the open-access website at https://study.sagepub.com/jonessmith2e.

CHAPTER 16

Narrative Therapy

Narrative therapy seeks to be a respectful, non-blaming approach to counselling and community work, which centres people as the experts in their own lives. It views problems as separate from people and assumes people have many skills, competencies, beliefs, values, commitments and abilities that will assist them to reduce the influence of problems in their lives.

—Alice Morgan,
Dulwich Centre, Australia

And it's just dawned on me that I might be the author of my own story, but so is everyone else the author of their own stories, and sometimes like now, there's no overlap.

—Jandy Nelson,
author of *The Sky Is Everywhere*

Once upon a time, everything was understood through stories. . . . Stories always deal with the "why" questions. The answers they give did not have to be literally true; they only had to satisfy people's curiosity by providing an answer. . . .

—Alan Parry and Robert E. Doan,
Narrative Therapy in the Post Modern World

BRIEF OVERVIEW

Similar to solution-focused counseling, narrative therapy is also based on principles of social constructionist philosophy. Originating from family therapy, **narrative therapy** stresses that we seek to make sense out of our lives by creating stories about ourselves and others. Our stories are more than just reflections of actual events that took place in our lives. They constitute who we are, and they shape our relationships with others. I remember one student describing to me how he went from counselor to counselor—telling his sad little story about abuse from his father and his addiction to marijuana. He said to me,

> I got tired of telling my little story over and over again; and worse yet, I no longer wanted to listen to my own sad story. I began to feel angry and frustrated with myself. Why didn't I have a better story to tell? I wanted to change my story from being a victim to being a survivor, but I didn't know how.

Photo courtesy of Jill Freedman.

Michael White
(1948–2008)

David Epston (1948–)

Photo courtesy of Narrative Approaches.

The student had become synonymous with his sad story. He was frustrated by the fact that the life story he had helped create for himself was so very negative and self-damaging. As I listened to him, I responded,

> You can change the story that you have in your head—the story that you tell about you but you say really isn't you. You can't go back in time and change the events that happened, but you can rewrite your story. Write a different story. You decide what your story will be.

Narrative therapy emerged out of several traditions—postmodernism, social constructionism, and family therapy. Michael White (1984, 1986, 1991) and David Epston (White & Epston, 1990) were two Australian family therapists. In developing their theory, they were influenced by the theory of Gregory Bateson (1972, 1979)—an anthropologist who also had an impact on the development of solution-focused therapy. Other researchers who influenced narrative therapy include Edward Bruner (1986), Jerome Bruner (1987), Clifford Geertz (1973), and Michel Foucault (1973, 1988, 1995).

Bateson's (1972, 1979) work focused on the interpretive method within the social sciences. The interpretive method states that it is not possible for people to have direct knowledge of the world and that an objective description of the world is not available for us. No one human being has a privileged access to the naming of reality. We may think that we are stating objective reality when we argue about various points with our family members, friends, and colleagues, but the truth of the matter is that what we know of the world, we know only through our experience of it. We can only know our experience of the world—nothing more. Although we can try to walk in another person's shoes, we cannot know another person's experience of the world. At best, we can only interpret the experience of others. Hence, when a person states that he or she knows what you are feeling or thinking, they are making interpretations about your life experiences. We interpret the expressions of other people's lived experiences.

Geertz (1986) helped clarify the interpretive method of living. He has stated, "Whatever sense we have of how things stand with someone else's inner life, we gain it through their expressions, not through some magical intrusion into their surfaces" (p. 373). People make expressions about their interpretation of life. To interpret the expressions of others, including those closest to us, we have to rely on our own lived experience and imagination. In essence, we identify our own experience as the similar experience expressed by others. Our interpretations of our own experiences allow us to understand the experiences of others.

Empathy is a very significant factor in the interpretation or understanding of the experience of others. For instance, we can have empathy for people who ask for forgiveness because most of us have needed, at one time or another, forgiveness for ourselves. According to Bateson (1972, 1979), none of us can know objective reality because all knowing requires an act of interpretation. What we have is our interpretation of a situation, and sometimes we label our interpretation of a situation as objective reality. Borrowing from Bateson, White, and Epston (1990), narrative therapy is based on our "lived experience" or our lived interpretation of our experiences. White and Epston (1990) have raised the questions, "How do persons organize their stock of lived experience?" "What do persons do with this experience to give it meaning and to make sense out of their lives?" and "How is lived experience given expression?" (p. 9).

White also borrowed concepts from Jerome Bruner (1987) and Geertz (1973) to flesh out his theory of narrative therapy. Geertz, an interpretive anthropologist, provided White with the concept of interpretation and the story-making process within culture. From this point, White and Epston (1990) asserted that we make sense of our lives through stories. They stated, "It is this storying that determines the meaning ascribed to experience" (p. 10). From Jerome Bruner (1986), White and Epston (1990) took the metaphor of stories providing a temporal landscape for understanding the meaning of events across time. Narrative therapy contains a type of reflexive questioning that connects people's actions (landscape of action) and their meaning or beliefs (landscape of meaning) within the broad context of relationships.

Narrative therapy is based on the concept of a discourse. A **discourse** is a system of words, actions, rules, beliefs, and institutions that share common values. Discourses tend to be invisible—taken for granted as part of the fabric of reality. When therapists locate clients' problems in specific discourses, clients can see themselves as distinct from their problems. Each society creates various discourses. At the societal level, a discourse refers to a cluster of ideas produced within the broad culture and communicated to the members of a society through a variety of media, including television, songs, books, and movies. Societies tend to coalesce around a favored view on issues such as sexuality, sex roles, civic duty, and education, and when this situation occurs, the society is said to have developed a dominant discourse. For instance, a dominant discourse in American society prior to the women's revolution was that women were homebodies who were responsible for taking care of their husbands' every need. Thus, there was the television commercial about "ring around the collar," which was designed to shame the woman who did such a poor job of washing that she left a ring around the collar when she washed "her man's" shirt. A discourse today this same issue might be "Wash your own shirt; I'm not your maid."

The narrative therapists used Foucault's (1987) sociocultural philosophy that holds that knowledge is constitutive and language based. Foucault suggested that individuals internalize thoughts and actions that are products of normalizing ideas informed by and embedded in cultural, political,

and social contexts. Foucault maintained that the dominant discourses in our society powerfully influence what gets storied and how it gets storied.

Narrative therapy borrows from postmodernism in its premise that there is no one reality, no objective reality. All knowledge is interpretative, value based, and mixed with power messages—even in the therapy hour. Therapy is a social construction with a given social agenda and role. As Brown and Augusta-Scott (2007) have stated,

> For postmodernists, there is no one truth, no one universal, discoverable truth that exists outside human existence. There is no stable, fixed, knowable, or essential self or identity, as self and identity can emerge only within linguistic, cultural and relational practices . . . . What we take for granted to be true, reasonable, and normative are in fact social constructions that emerge within social and historical contexts and cannot be separated from human meaning-making processes. Knowledge is never innocent, but always culture bound. (p. vx)

KEY CONCEPTS

Narrative therapy suggests that therapy itself is a social construction that has a definite social agenda and role (Brown & Augusta-Scott, 2007). According to Epstein (1994), "therapeutism" is a dominant form of discourse that deals with the difficulties and conflicts individuals experience in contemporary society. It consists of an ideological discourse that concentrates on individuals' emotional problems and promises to "do good," while performing the social roles of surveillance, regulation, and control of what constitutes appropriate behavior. Therapy is not scientifically objective or apolitical. There are roles assigned to the therapist and to the client, roles that contain within them expressions of power.

View of Human Nature

Narrative therapy maintains that human beings are essentially social constructionists. People are continually acting on the world and the world is acting on them. There is no true emancipated self. White (1997) writes that the self just is. He objected to the idea that therapy can free people to live according to their true natures or real, authentic selves. There is no fixed, immutable, authentic self that can be found with the right therapeutic approach. Narrative therapy views self stories as interpretations of lived events. The self is inevitably always involved in the process of constructing itself. Furthermore, the self can never be completely understood simply by looking inward (Brown & Augusta-Scott, 2007). The self is being acted on by the world, by the politics of the situation, and by external events. Our looking inward provides only part of the answer. We also must look outward at external events.

Human beings are continually involved in the process of self-surveillance in which they watch themselves through the eyes of others. Hence, self-surveillance is hardly ever private because it always involves the judgment of the imagined social audience. Our views about ourselves are influenced by professional and institutional discourses. Our relational conversations with ourselves are based on internal self-surveillance (looking, monitoring, and evaluation). Narrative therapy uses the techniques of counterviewing, therapeutic letter campaigns as a means of remembering alternative selves. We can reauthor our stories. An alternative story usually develops in counseling in contradiction to the dominant story that is embedded in a client's presenting problem.

The narrative therapy school maintains that it is human nature for people to seek meaning from living. We are inevitably meaning makers. We have an experience, and then we attach meaning to that experience. Most people search for the answer, "Why am I here? What is my purpose in life?" To give meaning to our experiences, we must organize it, frame it, or structure it in some way so that it forms a pattern. To understand an experience, say, for instance, our early childhood, we must be able to frame it within a pattern of other experiences known to us. The story provides the dominant frame for the organization and patterning of our lived experiences. People make sense out of their lives through stories that they form about their life experiences.

Story making or storying constitutes part of human nature. We interpret our lived experiences based on the stories we construct for ourselves. Narrative therapy does not take a stance regarding whether humans are basically good or evil. Humans just are.

Narrative therapy espouses an optimistic view of human nature that is based on the belief that we have the ability to construct meaning in our lives and that we have the capacity to reauthor the meaning that we give to our lived experiences. We are responsible for the realities that we create in our lives. Bruner (2004) observed, for instance, that in narrative therapy there is no such thing as a "fixed" sense of one's personhood that simply waits to be discovered. From his perspective, "We constantly construct and reconstruct ourselves to meet the needs of the situations we encounter, and we do so with the guidance of our memories of the past and our hopes and fears for the future" (p. 4).

Some of society's narrative can be reenacted during the therapy hour—for instance, society's narratives about the roles of men and women. A female therapist might bring into the therapy situation the narrative that says men are dogs controlled by their penis or that women need to be taken care of because they cannot take care of themselves. During therapy, a clinician who held this narrative discourse might use counseling interventions that reinforce the woman client's dependency.

Narrative therapists hold that people are not their problems, that we can separate people from their psychological problems, their marital issues, nor their careers. The problems that we encounter in life are outside of us, and therefore, left open to interpretation by us. As Monk (1997) has stated, the person is not the problem; the problem is the problem.

Theory of Personality

Narrative therapy does not propose that people have a personality. From White and Epston's (1990) perspective, the concept of personality is socially constructed, and it is deeply intertwined with our cultural background. The term *personality* is taken from traditional counseling theories; it suggests that there is some type of permanent, internal structure that everyone has, regardless of one's culture. Moreover, traditional theories have tended to suggest that the structure of a person's hypothesized personality is static and largely inflexible after our early years. Narrative therapists contend that human beings are continually socially constructing and deconstructing themselves, including their so-called personality.

Narrative therapists reject theories of personality and psychopathology because they maintain that it is professional arrogance for therapists to believe that they can tell people who they are. In their opinion, clients are the experts; they must tell us who they are and who they want to be. Personality theories are oppressive because they impose one formula or one perspective on all people. Theories of psychotherapy only masquerade as reality. In truth, the narrative therapists say, there is no reality; there are only stories we tell about reality. Our stories do not mirror our lives. Instead, they shape our lives. They guide us throughout our lives.

Whereas traditional counseling theories use personality as a central construct that organizes a person, narrative therapists declare that stories are major organizing forces. Narrative therapy focuses on the stories of individuals' lives and is founded on the idea that human problems are created in social, cultural, and political contexts. People produce meaning from the stories that they create about themselves and others. Our stories outline who we are, where we have come from, where we are going, and what we think about life. Our stories represent our experiences in the world. We become the stories that we tell about ourselves. Our stories can propel us to greatness or serve as a prison in which we lock ourselves.

Commenting on the importance of our stories, Madigan (n.d.) has stated,

> The internalized stories we tell to ourselves about ourselves, and the stories told about us are not insignificant. Stories become us—they live us—they are us. Our internal stories are at the same time responsible for hundreds of thousands of violent yearly suicides and millions of people falling in and out of love. Stories can inspire us toward greatness and act to completely undermine the fabric of our lives. (Retrieved from http://yaletownfamilytherapy.com)

The Story as the Basic Unit of Experience

Each type of psychotherapy indicates a different feature of life as the basic unit of experience. For instance, behavioral therapy emphasizes behavior as the unit of experience, cognitive therapy focuses on accurate thinking, while psychoanalytic therapy focuses on the unconscious and the id, ego, and superego as the basic unit. For narrative therapy, *the client's story is the basic unit of experience*. Stories or narratives refer to the stories that people tell about themselves. They represent what people remember and think about their lived experiences.

Morgan (2002) points out that we have stories about the past, present, and future. We have family stories, relationship stories, and community stories. A person might have stories about himself as being successful and competent as a businessman but failure stories in interpersonal relationships. Alternatively, a person may have stories about being poor at driving directions or poor at getting people to like him or her. Families create stories about themselves as being cold, distant, caring, dysfunctional, or close. Various communities create stories about themselves as being isolated, politically active, or financially strong.

We live more than one story at a time; and hence, we have stories about work, family, friends, and so on. White (1995) refers to the different stories that people have about their lives as *multiple* stories. Our multiple stories vary at any given time, and they are acted out within the broad context of our families, community, and culture. Furthermore, stories have a regulatory function in that they guide how we act, think, feel, and make sense of our lived experience. Figure 16.1 contains a schematic representation of our lived experiences in the world. Lived experiences lead to interpretation of events, which result in our stories.

Stories constitute a way of describing or communicating to both ourselves and others the meaning we find in our experiences. Narrative therapy is concerned with the stories we carry around with us about who we are and about what is most important to us. Our stories are necessarily a selection of our experiences. They do not include all that we have experienced. Our stories serve as filters for our life experiences. Based on our stories, we filter in or screen out certain information from our lives. For instance, if a person sees himself primarily as a winner, then he tells stories about his winning or succeeding. In contrast, if a person views himself as a loser, then his stories will contain information about losing and being a failure and a disappointment to himself and others. Each time the person has a losing event take place in his life, he embellishes his story with the new "losing experience."

Individuals whose stories focus on their losing or failing automatically screen out examples of their succeeding at a task. I once conducted a self-esteem workshop with young people who had committed nonviolent criminal acts—shoplifting, curfew violations, and so on. I asked the group to write down three positive things about

> **Inner Reflection**
>
> Analyze the parts of your story in terms of setting, characterization, and plot.

Figure 16.1   Our Experience of the World and Stories

Source: © Elsie Jones-Smith (2012).

themselves and to report them back to the group. One 16-year-old male participant became quite irate and stated that he did not have anything positive to write down. His entire family called him a loser. As I probed a bit longer, the young man revealed that he volunteered to work with developmentally disabled youngsters—teaching them how to play baseball. Everyone in the group clapped and told how this bit of information made him a winner rather than a loser.

Obviously, this young man needed to rewrite his **dominant life story**. Dominant stories are often problem saturated. Individuals' dominant stories usually have a major impact on their daily coping and living as well as on the life path they choose. Narrative therapy focuses on how our important life stories can get written and rewritten or reauthored. For instance, the student just mentioned needed to rewrite certain negative events that he had overemphasized in his story. A reauthored story would magnify the boy's positive behaviors, which he had minimized.

Narrative therapists concentrate on the dominant themes that have helped shape their lives. What experiences have had the most meaning for a person? What choices and relationships have been the most important? From the narrative perspective, only those experiences that are part of a larger story will have a significant influence on a person's lived experience. Hence, narrative therapy stresses the importance of building the plot that connects a person's life together.

White and Epston (1990) contend that **narrative stories** vary, depending on one's position within a given society. They are co-created by our relationships with others. No identity can exist without some input from a member of our audiences, especially our families, friends, teachers, and coworkers. Co-created identities are influenced by the dominant culture within a society.

Components of a Story or Narrative

Narrative therapists analyze their clients' stories by examining setting, characters, plot, and themes. *Setting* indicates where and when the story takes place. Some possible settings include a house, an outdoor setting, an image, or a dream. The setting supplies the background for the characters to act out the plot. The time of the setting can be just a few seconds or a number of years.

Characterization refers to the people contained in a client's story. Oftentimes, the client is the protagonist or the main character. Antagonists are those people within the client's story who are in conflict with him or her. Supporting characters are the other people in a client's story, and this group may vary greatly. It is important for the therapist to help clients describe the various people who are significant in their story.

Plot describes what happened in a client's story. A plot may be composed of several episodes or actions. Sometimes clients are encouraged to retell their stories from different perspectives; therefore, distinct plots may emerge. Narrative therapy stresses building the plot that connects a person's life into a meaningful whole. Therapists ask questions that focus on what have been the most meaningful developments in a client's life. Some areas of inquiry include client intentions, influential relationships, turning points, treasured memories, and discovering how these areas connect with each other to give meaning to the client's life. Stories will be interpreted based on the meaning (plot) that is dominant at that time.

Alternative and Preferred Stories

Our living involves a continual negotiation between the dominant and the alternative stories of our lives. **Alternative stories** refer to other versions of life as lived (White, 1995). They are different stories about the same lived experience, as told by the person whose life is being narrated. The importance of alternative stories is that they help a client recognize that there have been occasions when they have experienced themselves and events in ways different from the ones they are accustomed to. Alternative stories set the stage for the client's discussion of preferred stories about a client's hoped-for destination or status in life. A client's *preferred stories* can only become available for work in therapy once the client's alternative stories are recognized and identified as preferable to the original narrative (White, 1995).

Thin and Thick Descriptions of Stories

It is important for therapists to find alternative and preferred stories because the meanings that a client ascribes to in the first or original narrative (frequently meanings reached facing adversity) contain what White (2002) called thin description. **Thin descriptions** exist because although clients have permitted the description to become meaningful to themselves, they have not allowed space for the complexities and contradictions of life, including their own complexity (Morgan, 2002). Clients tend to think of their stories in negative or positive sound bites. Thin descriptions of one's story may involve blaming, criticizing, and labeling of oneself and others. They are inclined to be surface descriptions of complex human emotions and interactions. For instance, people might label themselves with such thin descriptions as "bad," "troublemaker," "loser," or "lazy." Sometimes thin descriptions may hide strengths and ignore a more thickly described account of our lives.

Often, other people create thin descriptions of people's actions and their identities. Generally speaking, individuals with the power of definition in particular circumstances (e.g., parents and teachers in the lives of children, health professionals in the lives of those who consult them) create thin descriptions. For instance, a young male is labeled as a troublemaker because he sought to defend himself from the attacks of his classmates. Sometimes kids who are bullied are considered a problem by their classmates and teachers. Thin descriptions frequently are expressed as truths about a person. Such descriptions are usually taken from problem-saturated stories that are based on a person's weaknesses, disabilities, dysfunctions, or inadequacies. Even families have thin descriptions, such as "cold family" or "dysfunctional family." Family members come to believe their own thin descriptions of the family.

Then, too, thin descriptions may obscure power relations. The young man who is portrayed as an attention-seeking person is being abused at home. It is relatively easy for people, especially those in power, to participate in gathering evidence to support their dominant problem-saturated stories. Thin conclusions produce more false conclusions, as individuals' skills, knowledge, abilities, and competencies become hidden or covered up by the problem story (Morgan, 2002). People are much more complex than their thin descriptions. Thin descriptions almost invariably focus on an individual's or a family's weaknesses rather than on their strengths.

When narrative therapists are confronted with overwhelming thin conclusions and problem stories about clients, they seek out alternative stories that are identified by the client as stories by which they would like to live their lives (Morgan, 2002). The therapist is interested in creating conversations (stories of identity) with clients that will help them break the influence of the problems confronting them. Whereas some thin descriptions support and sustain client problems, alternative stories work to reduce the influence of problems. They create new possibilities for the client. For instance, the therapist who works with a student given the thin description of attention seeker would explore alternative stories of the student's life that might create space for change. The therapist would ask the student to remember stories of determination throughout his or her life, or stories of how he or she overcame difficulties or showed strength in church or in athletics. In exploring alternative stories of the student's life, the therapist searches for stories that the student identifies as those by which he or she would like to guide his or her life.

One of the most significant contributions of narrative therapy is its emphasis that new or different stories are possible for clients (Brown & Augusta-Scott, 2007). Some important questions for narrative therapists are, How can I help my client break away from thin conclusions? How can I help my client reauthor new and preferred stories for his or her life and relationships? During the process of counseling, clients pack and unpack unhelpful stories. As Freedman and Combs (1996) have stated,

> Narrative therapists are interested in working with people to bring forth and thicken stories that do not support or sustain problems. As people begin to inhabit and live out the alternative stories, the results are beyond solving problems. Within the new stories, people live out new self images, new possibilities for relationships and new futures. (p. 16)

To help free clients from the influence of their problematic stories, therapists must do more than just have them reauthor an alternative story. They must help clients uncover ways in which their alternative stories can be "richly described," a process that is labeled as making **thick descriptions**. To obtain rich (thick) descriptions of a client's stories, the therapist extracts quite a lot of detail about the story line. The therapist may have to help the client in **coauthoring** a thick description. A therapist assists clients by asking questions that lead to a greater understanding of the richness of their lives. Thus, clients' stories become thickened or enriched by providing the details and particularities of the major and minor themes of their lives. New directions may come from creating alternative stories and from thick descriptions. Narrative therapists consider a rich or thick description of clients' lives and relations to be the opposite of a thin description.

Theory of Maladaptive Behavior or Psychopathology

Narrative therapists do not write about psychopathology. They raise the question, Psychopathology from whose perspective? Such therapists maintain that psychopathology is socially constructed. Professionals—psychiatrists, psychologists, and counselors—have gotten together to develop various stories about what constitutes mental illness. For instance, the social constructions of mental illness are based on the fact that professionals have shared their stories about what constitutes bipolar disorder, schizophrenia, depression, and so on. The shared narratives of psychiatrists and psychologists have been based on what is considered appropriate behavior within a given culture.

Moreover, narrative therapy speaks against the current binary view of healthy adjustment and mental disorder. When therapists use binaries such as healthy/unhealthy, normal/abnormal, and functional/dysfunctional, they are ignoring the complexities of peoples' lived experiences as well as the personal and cultural meanings that may be ascribed to their experiences in context. Few of us are totally maladjusted. Our lives concerning adjustment and maladaptive behavior occur on a continuum.

In narrative therapy, client problems are conceptualized as restraining narratives that are influenced by their culture and society (White & Epston, 1990). The clients' restraining narratives are usually viewed as dominant stories. Our realities about what constitutes mental health or maladaptive behavior are not the absolute truths we try to make them out to be. Mental health and mental illness are tied up in cultural and political issues for each society. Furthermore, each society creates its own narratives about what constitutes mental health and maladaptive behavior.

THE THERAPEUTIC PROCESS

The Therapeutic Relationship

Narrative therapists view therapy as a conversational art that concerns itself with the recording and careful expanding of clients' story accounts. It is a nonblaming approach to human problems. Clients try to arrive at a sense of identity from their stories. Narrative conversations are interactive and always in collaboration with the client. The therapist seeks to understand what is of interest to the client and how the therapeutic journey is suiting them.

- How is this conversation going for you?
- Should we keep talking about this or would you be more interested in . . . ?
- What should we spend our time talking about?
- I was wondering if you would be more interested in my asking you questions about . . .

Goals of Therapy

An important goal of narrative therapy is to help clients realize what forces are influencing their lives and focus on the positive aspects of the story. When clients analyze their lives as a story, they begin to understand the different forces and roles that are influencing their behavior. This recognition gives clients the flexibility to make the necessary changes in their lives. Clients learn that the meaning that they attach to the events of their lives can change. Once clients learn that they are the authors of meaning in their lives, they also come to understand that they can reauthor meanings for lived experiences.

Role of the Therapist

Narrative therapists are active facilitators. They demonstrate care, interest, respectful curiosity, openness, empathy, and contact. They adopt a *non-knowing position* that permits them to be guided by the client's story. They listen to clients with an open mind and encourage them to share their stories. The therapist listens to the client's problem-saturated story without getting stuck.

Narrative therapists collaborate with clients to arrive at a mutually acceptable name for the problem. They help clients restructure the problem story so that it brings forth their preferences, hopes, dreams, ideas, and values in relationship to the problem. As noted, they also help clients externalize and deconstruct the power of a narrative. They help clients develop a preferred, alternative story.

The narrative counselor assumes an investigative approach to therapy. Both the client and the therapist actively seek out support from individuals and groups to maintain the new preferred, alternative story. The counselor continually seeks to understand the client's experience.

Role of the Client

Clients are placed in both the protagonist and author roles. The client's life is criss-crossed by invisible story lines. These unseen story lines have great power in shaping the client's life. Narrative therapy consists of drawing out and amplifying these story lines. The therapist asks questions about what has been most meaningful in a person's life—influential relationships, turning points, treasured memories—and how these areas connect with each other. An important feature of narrative therapy is to empower the client.

Phases of Therapy

Epston and White (1992) view therapy as a process of "storying" and/or "restorying" the lives and the experiences of their clients. Narrative therapy helps people resolve problems by (a) helping them separate their lives and relationships from stories they believe limit and impoverish them, (b) assisting them to challenge the ways of their lives that they judge to be subjugating, and (c) encouraging them to reauthor their own lives based on alternative and preferred stories of identity. Narrative therapy usually consists of five stages. The *first stage* is labeled problem definition. The *second stage* is termed *mapping the influence* of the problem. The *third stage* consists of evaluating and justifying the effects of the problem. The *fourth stage* entails identifying unique outcomes. The *fifth stage* is *restorying*.

In defining the problem (Stage 1), the clinician obtains a client's description of the problem. Clinicians suggest that clients put a name on their problem (White & Epston, 1990). For instance, White and Epston (1990) described the case of a 6-year-old boy with a history of encopresis (involuntary defecation). The family described the accidents as sneaking up on the family, and therefore, the name for the accidents became "sneaky poo." Naming the problem implies power and authority for those who feel that they are disempowered by their present difficulties.

There are a number of ways to introduce the naming process. The clinician might ask, "What name would you give to what you are going through at the present time?" "What name would you like to give to what has happened to you?" Naming the problem constitutes the first step in the process of externalizing. It is important for the clinician to choose an appropriate name for the problem. The name should be related to words the client used in describing the problem. Sometimes it is difficult for the client and the counselor to come up with a name for the problem. If this happens, it might be better to proceed to the next stage, mapping the influences of the problem.

During Stage 2, the therapist helps clients map the influence of the problem. Mapping is a questioning process designed to help clients identify and heighten the experience of the problem's effects and subsequently to externalize the problem (White, 2004). During mapping the influence, it is important that therapists develop questions that examine the history, influence, and effects of the problem on the client. Some questions that help map the client's problem-saturated dominant story include the following:

- What brings you to therapy?
- What has been the effect of the problem on everyday life?
- How has the problem affected relationships with people to whom you are closest?
- How have you been recruited into this way of viewing yourself?
- When do you remember the first time the problem happened?
- How have those closest to you reinforced the problem?

Externalizing Clients' Problems. **Externalizing the problem** in narrative therapy runs counter to beliefs in traditional psychotherapy. Traditional therapies suggest that client problems are self-caused pathology. In narrative therapy, the therapist talks in such a manner that the problem is placed outside rather than inside of the client. Problems seem more manageable when they are externalized. In contrast with the humanist therapist who states, "You became depressed," the narrative therapist declares that "depression attacked your life." Instead of saying that the client is an alcoholic, the narrative therapist says, "Alcohol has had some success in taking over your life."

Externalizing the problem can lift a burden off clients because the problem is no longer located inside of them. Instead of making the person the problem, narrative therapy seeks to make the problem the problem. The therapist asks how the "fear," the "addiction," the "anger or guilt," or "depression" affect the daily life of a client. According to White and Epston (1990), externalizing the problem is "an approach . . . that encourages a person to objectify and, at times, to personify the problems that they experience as oppressive" (p. 38). The therapist then helps the client identify the many ways in which the problem has affected the client's life across several domains, including work, relationships, and daily functioning. Clients might state, "I am not my depression" or "I am not my addiction." Differences between traditional counseling theories' emphasis on internalized and externalized problems are summarized in Table 16.1.

A strong rationale for mapping the influences of the problem is to increase a client's sense of agency. As clients identify unique outcomes during the clinical process, they become more self-confident of their ability to solve the problem. Once the therapist has used the mapping process to indicate the various influences on the problem, he or she can go back to these influences and inquire about unique exceptions. For instance, if the client has an anger problem, the therapist might ask about unique exceptions to the client's angry responses with family members, with friends, or at work.

During the process of mapping the influences, the therapist helps clients increase the richness or thickness of their stories. Therapists can increase a story's thickness by using it as a metaphor. The

Table 16.1 Comparison of Internalizing and Externalizing Clients' Problems

Problem Internalized Within Client	Problem Externalized From Client
1. Person is the problem.	1. Problem is the problem.
2. Problem is what is wrong with the client.	2. Problem is external to the client's self-identity.
3. Experts are needed to explain the client's behaviors.	3. People are invited to give their own interpretations of self.
4. Therapist is an expert on the client.	4. Clients are experts over themselves.
5. The social context of the client's problems is minimized or downplayed. The therapist does not deal with racism or sexism.	5. Therapist examines the cultural, social-political contexts that affect client's story. Racism and sexism are dealt with.
6. In therapy sessions, a great deal of time is placed on the client's problem.	6. Focus is on enabling clients to separate themselves from their problem stories.
7. The therapist reorders the client's personality according to theory of personality.	7. Clients reauthor their own lives based on alternative and preferred stories of identity.

therapists may ask questions about the problem's tricks, tactics, methods of operating, intentions, and beliefs. What are the rules, desires, and motives of the problem? How has it managed to keep hanging around the client for so long? What deceits or lies does the problem use to sustain itself? After clients have done the naming and initial mapping process, they are ready to begin to challenge or restory the dominant story that has oppressed them.

Deconstructing clients' negative self-identities is aided by contextualizing the problem. This process reflects an empowerment process—a shift from being trapped by the story to active participation in reauthoring the story (Brown & Augusta-Scott, 2007). Clients explore what events have occurred that support the dominant problem story and what events have challenged this story. They examine events that have helped produce stories such as, "I am worthless," "I am a bad person," or "Nobody loves me." Deconstruction of clients' problem-saturated stories helps reduce client guilt, shame, and blaming. It also promotes a positive client–therapist working relationship as the two collaborate to resolve the problem story.

The third stage of narrative therapy involves evaluating and justifying the effects of the problem. During this stage, the clinician invites clients to evaluate their own position regarding the problem. The therapist asks questions about the extent to which clients themselves have been part of the problem. How has their behavior been self-defeating or self-freeing? For instance, the clinician might ask clients to state how the negative effects of the problem are or are not congruent with their stated goals and intentions.

Stage 4 in narrative therapy focuses on identifying unique outcomes. A unique outcome is any thought, behavior, feeling, or event that contradicts or provides an exception to the dominant story (White & Epston, 1990). The therapist looks for exceptions to the client's problem and inquires how the unique outcome came about. Some questions therapists might use to get at unique outcomes include "How were you able to not let the problem influence you at this moment in time?" and "What did you do to overcome the problem in this case?" Whatever influences the client identifies as producing unique outcomes can be used during the restorying stage, which is the next and final stage of therapy. Other unique outcome questions include the following:

- How have you kept the problem from becoming worse?
- Tell me about the times the problem is manageable.
- How do you cope when your life requires that the problem not get in the way?
- What things are more important to you than your problem?
- What was going on in your life when you let the problem get in your way?

Reconstruction or the **reauthoring** stage is the final stage of therapy. Therapy has reached a critical, culminating point. Clients are invited to decide to stay with the old story or rewrite another one. If the latter point is chosen, clients are requested to establish an alternative narrative. New possibilities are on the horizon when clients explore alternative stories. The alternative story must be rich with setting, actions, and consequences. Even resistances to the alternative story are explored. Alternative stories emphasize the following:

- Client desires, wishes, and preferences
- Personal values
- Relationship values
- Intentions and plans

Alternative stories are attached to every unique outcome. It only takes one unique outcome to begin the reauthoring or the reconstruction process, such as a fleeting thought—something that the client thought about but failed to mention during therapy. During therapy, the clinician helps clients make sense out of their unique experiences, turning points in their lives, and progress made in life. When therapists and clients identify unique outcomes, their efforts promote a history of struggle or protest against oppression by the problem. The process of restorying begins with the clinician posing questions such as "What does this unique outcome say about you and your ability to influence the problem?" or "What qualities have you found within you that help you deal with the problem?"

Brown and Augusta-Scott (2007) have suggested the following reauthoring questions:

- Tell me about the time you stood up and said "no" to your depression.
- Can you think of other times when you refused to let the problem control your life?
- What were you feeling when you said "no" to the anxiety problem?
- What does it say about your future that you faced the depression problem down?
- What does it say about you that you said enough is enough—that you were not going to let anxiety stop you from enjoying life?

Once clients have developed an alternative story, it should be named, for instance, "strength and survival" instead of "hopeless." In addition, the therapist engages the client in "thickening the plot," which entails asking the client for more details, more characters, and other perspectives that support the alternative story. During this time, the therapist helps the client name the counterplot. This step gives the plot greater definition. When a specific event takes place, the therapist asks which plot was associated with that event.

Reauthoring investigates how clients have had an influence on the problem instead of simply how they have been affected by the problem. It entails constructing a helpful story that lies outside of the problem. Such a story emphasizes expanding and opening up opportunities for the client. Previously, the client's dominant story had the effect of keeping invisible other more positive stories.

During the reauthoring stage, therapeutic documents are made that provide permanent records of what transpired during therapy. Such therapeutic documents may include notes of sessions, letters, questions, lists of achievements, unique outcomes, achievement certificates, and bravery awards. These documents are designed to memorialize the counterplot. Witnesses may be called from outside the counseling situation to listen, validate, and affirm the client's new or reauthored story. Witnesses will be significant people in the client's life who will be confirming of the client. Who would validate the new story by personal experience with the person? The client may even find a support group of individuals to help him or her sustain the alternative story.

Therapy Techniques

What techniques do exist in narrative counseling have already been discussed throughout the previous sections. The techniques include those of externalizing the problem and developing unique outcomes, deconstructing all stories, and constructing alternative narratives. In addition, therapists use certificates to mark improvement in therapy. For instance, one narrative therapist gave a client a certificate that read, "Certificate for Graduation From the Blues."

Therapeutic Letter Writing. A major narrative technique not discussed is that of *therapeutic letter writing.* Clients are encouraged to write therapeutic letters to significant others, including the therapist. To assist clients in their therapeutic letter writing, the therapist models such letter writing. White and Epston (1990) propose using letters to carry on therapeutic dialogues between counseling sessions. The therapist's letter may chronicle the process of the interview, the agreements reached, the naming of the problem, and the questions asked during the session.

Nylund and Thomas (1994) assert that narrative letters reinforce what has taken place during therapy. They report that the average worth of a letter is equal to more than three individual sessions. Likewise, McKenzie and Monk (1997) have declared, "Some narrative counselors have suggested that a well-composed letter following

a therapy session or preceding another can be equal to about five regular sessions" (p. 113).

Outsider Witnesses. The technique of *outsider witnesses* constitutes another technique used in narrative therapy. Outsider witnesses are used as invited listeners to a client's consultation. Usually outsider witnesses are friends of the consulting person or past clients of the therapist who possess intimate knowledge and lived experience about the client's presenting problems. The outsider witness listens without comment as the therapist conducts the interview with the client.

After the therapist conducts the interview with the client, he or she then interviews the outsider witnesses and instructs them not to evaluate or to make a statement about what they have just heard. Instead, they are to state what phrase or image stood out for them and to report any comparisons between their own life struggles and those witnessed regarding the client. Next, the outsider witnesses are asked in what ways they experienced a shift in how they experienced themselves as they listened to the therapy conversation.

The therapist then asks the client, who has been listening all the while, what words or phrases stood out in the conversation with the outside witnesses. Both the outsider witness and the client benefit from the consultation; however, the benefits are greatest for the client who learns that he or she is not the only one with the problem. Outsider witnesses also provide material for an alternative story. They can be used to document that the client is moving toward his or her preferred story and provide additional suggestions for reauthoring. They also provide support for the client as they relate their own **story deconstruction** and reauthoring process to the client.

RESEARCH AND EVALUATION ___

Multicultural Positives

Narrative therapy fits well with many of the multicultural principles. Each of us lives within what narrative therapists call a *dominant culture*, which becomes a major discourse within our lives. Dominant culture consists of the ideas that are generationally passed on and socially maintained such that they become prevalent in our thinking and being. The way that we make meaning about our lives is controlled by our dominant cultural beliefs. As Gergen (2000) states, "The very shape of our lives—the rough and perpetually changing draft of the autobiography we carry in our minds, is understandable to ourselves and to others only by virtue of cultural systems of interpretation" (p. 126).

In its smallest form, dominant culture breaks down into discourse dyads. A dyad consists of a two-person group that participates in face-to-face encounters. White (1995) has suggested that wherever two people communicate, a discourse is created in their dyad. The dyads form external discourses because they take place outside of the client as opposed to internal discourses—those that take place inside the client. When sufficient dyads share the same discourse, the discourse becomes dominant. Dominant discourses function at the simplest system level (e.g., the family) all the way to one of the greatest system levels—a society where the dominant discourse becomes part of the prevailing culture (White, 1995).

Epston and White (1992) have proposed that cultural stories determine the form that our individual life narratives take. Each of us is born into cultural narratives out of which we construct our personal narratives. Dominant cultural discourses have a major influence on the meaning that we make of our lives. The dominant cultural story attempts to marginalize other forms of meaning and keeps these discourses out of the mainstream.

Narrative therapy assesses the influence of culture on clients' narrative stories. Clients are invited to assess how culture has affected their narrative stories. The clinician and the client map the influence of cultural discourses on the problem. Such assessment permits a client to express the client's problem story via his or her own cultural lens. This process reduces the chances of cultural misunderstandings.

Narrative therapy provides a framework for culturally sensitive counseling. It helps create change in clients' lives by helping them deconstruct the old problem story, to revision and create a preferred story. The approach takes into account cultural themes, social injustices, history, gender issues, politics, acculturation issues, and the politics of therapy. Sometimes clients live with subjugating narratives revolving around gender, culture, ethnicity, or race. These subjugating narratives become incorporated in clients' narrative stories. Even psychotherapy can become a subjugating narrative if the therapist puts mental illness labels on the client's behavior—"I am the expert psychologist; you are the problem-saturated client who needs my expert service and evaluation."

During the process of deconstructing stories, clients become aware of the cultural premises on which their stories are built. For instance, a woman discovers that she has negative feelings about herself because within her culture women are treated as second-class citizens. A Latino or an Asian client who complains about racial discrimination finds that the narrative therapist just does not throw up her hands and say, "Racial considerations are outside the boundaries of my private practice. The problem is inside of you, not in the dominant culture."

Narrative therapy is culturally sensitive because it does not dismiss issues that ethnic minority groups experience (e.g., exclusion, harassment, and racism) as irrelevant to therapy. For instance, an African American college student complained to his counselor about racism from his dissertation advisor. He was so discouraged that he was ready to give up pursuit of his doctorate. The therapist was able to discuss the political and power discourses that were in existence at the student's university. Racism was not all in the student's head. In fact, it was very much a part of the dominant discourse and culture of the university.

The unspoken dominant discourse at the university suggested that the African American student had gotten into the university primarily because of the university's affirmative action policy rather than because of the student's talent or academic achievement. The therapist helped the student deconstruct the narrative that had the student portrayed as the inferior student. Calling the professor a racist was viewed as a "thin description." The student felt relieved that he could talk about how he felt about racism with his counselor who was White. Yet the counselor's acknowledgment of racism was just the beginning of counseling.

To assist the student in dealing with the "Black is inferior dominant discourse," the therapist began to question him about past times when he had dealt successfully with racism. The more the student remembered situations and events in which he had successfully dealt with racism, the more empowered he felt. The process of counseling had deconstructed the helpless, powerless victim story of a student having to leave his doctoral program because of racism. He now understood how to handle the professor successfully and would remain in the doctoral program with a renewed focus and energy.

Multicultural Blind Spots

Although narrative therapy has many positive multicultural features, it also has some multicultural blind spots. The assumption of an egalitarian relationship between the therapist and the client might not work well with clients who come from cultural backgrounds that emphasize the importance of power and respect for individuals in a position of authority. Furthermore, some clients may be more interested in problem solving rather than in telling the stories of their lives. In addition, there is only a small amount of research that suggests that narrative therapy is effective with individuals from diverse cultural backgrounds.

Contributions and Criticisms of Narrative Therapy

A major contribution of narrative therapy is that it has helped change (along with solution-focused therapy) the dominant paradigm in counseling and in the helping professions. Gradually, counselors and psychotherapists are moving from the paradigm of viewing clients as containing primarily deficits and problems toward the paradigm of strength development. Clients are not their disorders. Moreover, this paradigm change suggests a positive view of people. Therapists view clients as having the ability to move quickly to achieve their goals and to remedy problems. The nonpathologizing position of clinicians with a social constructionist perspective (solution-focused, narrative therapy, strength-based counseling) is an important contribution to the field of psychotherapy.

Narrative therapy has been criticized for being too closely linked to social constructivism. Critics have argued against the social constructionist premise that there are no absolute truths but rather only socially sanctioned points of view. In addition, opponents object to the conceptualizing psychotherapy as a discourse and to the notion that psychotherapy is a cultural narrative that locates problems within people.

Another criticism of narrative therapy is that the school has tended to produce "gurus." Guru-type psychotherapists present their own particular points of view, while not being very charitable to the founders of the traditional schools of psychotherapy. They also value clients' perspectives and expertise over those of the therapist. Criticisms of narrative therapy have also stressed its lack of clinical and empirical studies to validate its many claims. A study by Etchison and Kleist (2000) reported that research on the effectiveness of narrative therapy is still in its infancy. The theory lacks empirical, quantitatively oriented studies. It also has only few counseling techniques.

Narrative therapy has made major contributions to theories of psychotherapy. A broad cross-section of groups has responded favorably to this theoretical approach. Equally important, the narrative therapy model tends to be much less Eurocentric than the traditional models. Narrative therapy has brought therapy into the postmodern world, and it has revolutionized the role of the counselor and the process of treatment. Narrative therapy examines clients' cultural stories to discover how they view their lives.

Evidence-Based Research

My literature review revealed no randomized control studies involving narrative therapy that would result in it being considered an evidence-based therapy. The Dulwich Centre in Australia has developed a repository of studies that the center maintains establishes the effectiveness of narrative therapy. More than 50 studies are included in this repository. A retrospective audit of the therapy outcome of 108 children with soiling and their families showed that children who were treated with externalizing did better than the comparison group treated by the standard methods of family therapy (Silver, Williams, Worthington, and Phillips, 1998). Cashin, Browne, Bradbury, and Mulder (2013) investigated the effectiveness of narrative therapy with young people with autism. The researchers found significant improvement in psychological distress. Another study examined the effectiveness of group narrative therapy for improving the school behavior of a small sample of girls with attention-deficit/hyperactivity disorder (ADHD). Fourteen clinics referred girls between the ages of 9 and 11 with a clinical diagnosis of ADHD who were randomly assigned to treatment and wait-list control groups. Teachers' posttreatment ratings indicated that narrative therapy had a significant effect on reducing ADHD symptoms one week after completion of treatment and sustained such after 30 days.

Narrative therapy proponents assert that change takes place by paying close attention in therapy to "unique outcomes," which are narrative details outside the realm of the main story. Matos, Santos, Gonçalves, and Martins (2009) analyzed unique outcomes in five good-outcome and five poor-outcome psychotherapy cases using the Innovative Moments Coding System. Poor- and good-outcome groups evidenced a global difference in the salience of the innovative moments. The results suggested that two types of innovative moments are required in narrative therapy for therapeutic change to take place: (1) reconceptualization and (2) new experiences.

Clearly, a number of researchers have examined the effectiveness of narrative therapy in a variety of therapeutic and client populations. In most instances, narrative therapy has been found to be effective. I refer the reader to the Dulwich Centre's website and its research on narrative therapy (http://dulwichcentre.com.au/narrative-therapy-research.html).

CASE ANALYSIS

Justin Working With a Solution-Focused and Narrative Therapist

Justin's story is problem saturated with outbursts of anger, violence, abandonment by his father, difficulties in school and at home, and trouble with the police and courts. The current case analysis uses narrative therapy's five-stage process of counseling.

During the first stage of counseling Justin, the therapist guides the naming of Justin's problem. Several different names can be applied to Justin's narrative story, including "the problem kid," "the delinquent kid," and "the kid from a broken home." In naming the problem, the therapist obtains a description from Justin. The therapist uses the words that most closely approximate Justin's experience of the problem. Justin is encouraged to put a descriptive

(Continued)

name on the problem, and Justin decides that he has several dominant problems. He decides, however, that his anger tends to cross over into many of the other problems that he has.

The therapist invites Justin into a conversation with his externalized problems. In this conversation, Justin's problem comes to be regarded as a "thing" or "person" with which he has had a complex and changing relationship during his life. Justin names his problem "the Incredible Hulk" because he feels that his anger changes his entire personality from one of being kind and likeable (the mild-mannered doctor part of the Hulk) to the large green monster who rips off his shirt and attacks all who stand in his way. Justin is treated as the expert on his naming of the problem. The therapist invites Justin to comment further on his externalized anger problem. They talk about his anger. The two discuss what brings out the huge green monster. Who can cause the Incredible Hulk to appear? Can you show me what you look like when the Incredible Hulk appears? How does the Incredible Hulk act when he's at home with his mom?

The counselor enters into Stage 2 of narrative therapy, which is called mapping the problem. He tries to get Justin to describe to the best of his ability the history of the Incredible Hulk problem. The therapist inquires about Justin's intentions, what plans he has made, what thoughts he has, and what actions he has taken to reduce the influence of the externalized problem. The therapist asks, "What was the plan behind your last Incredible Hulk outburst at home? At school?"

The therapists summarizes Justin's understanding of the Incredible Hulk problem. After hearing the therapist's summation, Justin began to describe the Incredible Hulk as an annoying problem in his life that interfered with his freedom and with his work at school and at home. Justin began to understand that he had established a basis for evaluating and justifying the effects of the problem.

To help Justin focus on what life might be like without the Incredible Hulk, the therapist asks the miracle question of Justin, "Suppose that while you were sleeping tonight and the entire house is quiet, a miracle takes place. The miracle is that you are now able to control the Incredible Hulk, and the angry responses that used to get you in trouble in your classes and at home are no longer a problem for you. You are in control of your anger. You don't blame anyone for making you so angry. Your anger problem and the Incredible Hulk problem are solved. However, because you are sleeping, you don't know that the miracle has taken place. So when you wake up tomorrow morning, what will be different that will tell you that a miracle has happened and that the Incredible Hulk anger problem is solved?"

Justin responds that he would know the miracle had happened because he would not argue with his mother in the morning about getting up and getting ready for school. The kids in his class would like him and eat lunch with him, and his teachers would not turn away from him every time he raised his hand to say something. Justin indicated that he sure would like to have a miracle like that to actually take place. So many of his problems would go away if he did not get into trouble because of his anger. From Justin's responses to the miracle question, the therapist began to work on goals with Justin. The therapist stated, "Maybe we can't have a miracle that changes everything at once, but maybe you can take a small step toward making the miracle happen. What small step might you take toward achieving some part of your miracle?"

The therapist asked Justin about the times that he did not become angry—the unique outcomes as narrative therapists conceptualize such occasions. He described several occasions when he was provoked by his classmates, but he did not respond angrily. Justin stated, "It seemed like they were trying to provoke me last week so that I would be placed in the residential home, and they would not have to have me in class any more. I just said to myself, 'You're not going to let them put you in that home away from my family.'"

As the therapist and Justin discuss the exceptions to his anger, Justin began to get some sense of hope that he could change his life. He did not have to let the Incredible Hulk spoil everything for him. Deep down inside, he really did want to get along with his mother. He loved her. That's why he was crying about going to the residential center. He did not want to leave his mother. Also, he really wanted to get along with the students in his class, but so much had happened that he did not know how to change things around.

The therapist told Justin that he did not have an Incredible Hulk puppet, but that he would get one for their next session. In the meanwhile, he asked Justin to choose one of the stuffed animals or puppets in the back of the therapy room to represent the Incredible Hulk. Justin chose a large gorilla-like action figure that had muscles bulging out and an angry look on his face. The therapist asked Justin several questions about why he chose the gorilla action figure. He indicated that he had chosen the gorilla because that animal was almost like a human. He could be very loving, and he could also harm people—like King Kong loved the woman, but he terrorized the rest of the city.

The therapist asked Justin to take the gorilla home with him. Each time he became angry with his mother, Justin was asked to take out the gorilla and to talk with him. Ask the gorilla what he is feeling and what he is planning to do. Justin's role was to counsel the gorilla and to have the gorilla talk to Sandy, Justin's mother.

At the beginning of the second session, Justin reported that he had gotten along a lot better with his mother during the intervening week. "I had to talk to the gorilla about his anger several times." Justin told the therapist, "One time when he became very angry, I asked him what was wrong with him—what was going on in his head. He just blew me off. So I put him in my room to cool off, and later when he was calmed down, I came back to talk with him."

The stuffed animal—the gorilla—gave voice to Justin's anger problem. Justin was speaking for the gorilla. He was showing compassion and empathy by removing the gorilla from the scene of the argument. Justin was formulating a solution to his own anger problem. He could take steps to remove himself from the anger-provoking situation. He could chill out.

The therapist asked, "What did he say to you to help you understand him a little better?" Justin responded, "He said he was angry because nobody ever listened to him. Everybody just kind of talked while he was talking. Everybody talked over him. Nobody ever listened to him, and that's why he was so angry." "So what did you say to him after that?" Justin responded, "I told him to just chill for a while. Things would work out. All he had to do was to chill out. His world was not going to end because no one was listening to him."

The therapist thought that maybe he should ask the gorilla about how things have been in the past week. Justin spoke for the gorilla who said, "I'd like to hit those who hurt me. Deep down inside, I'm a good gorilla, but when I get mad, watch out. I didn't like it when Justin put me in the room to cool off because I wanted to scream at his mom."

The counselor then asked Justin, "You spoke for the gorilla, Justin. Does the gorilla ever speak for you?"

Justin responded, "Yes, sure, lots of times. That's how I get into trouble. That's how I get into fights."

An animated therapy conversation ensued about the influences that the gorilla had on Justin during the past week. Justin mentioned another situation in which he had to put the gorilla in his room to cool off because he (Justin) was experiencing anger toward his mom.

The counselor asked Justin, "How did you manage not to let the gorilla (his anger) to get the best of you?"

Justin explained, "I decided it wasn't worth it to get into a big fight with my mom over nothing. That's how fights usually happen between us. I try to prove my point. She talks over me, and she says that she's the mom and what she says goes."

(Continued)

The counselor continued, "You must feel really proud of yourself. You took control of your anger rather than it having control over you."

Justin paused for a moment, smiling, and said, "I guess I did, didn't I?"

The counselor continued. "How does it feel, Justin, knowing that you took control of your anger rather than having it control you?"

Justin said, "Good. I felt really good when I put the gorilla in the room all by himself. 'You're not going to get me grounded,' I said."

During the next few sessions, Justin identified other unique outcomes related to the anger problem. He continued to take the gorilla home in between sessions, and he reported being very successful in controlling the gorilla's anger. As counseling continued over the next few weeks, Justin entered into the restorying or reauthoring stage of counseling. The therapist worked with Justin to change the thin description of him as being an angry, out-of-control kid, to a thick description of him that included examples of his caring and concern for others. Justin's mother, Sandy, was invited to counseling sessions to provide outsider witness of Justin's changed behavior. She offered story lines about Justin's helping her out around the house and helping an elderly neighbor. Sandy's comments acknowledged Justin's improvement and provided examples of additional unique outcomes. Justin was able to ascribe new meanings to his behavior. He was able to see the many positive dimensions of himself.

SUMMARY

Narrative therapy is an approach that views people as the experts on their own lives. Narrative therapy maintains that the basic unit of experience for people is their story. Stories determine how people act, think, feel, and make sense of new experiences. They help organize information in a person's life. Narrative therapy focuses on how our important stories get written and rewritten. It provides a way to refocus a camera lens on the construction and destruction of our stories.

Our stories are necessarily a selection of our experiences. They cannot include all that we have experienced. Social constructivism asserts that cultural realities, including political, historical, religious, familial, and scientific knowledge, influence our experiences and how we construct stories about our lives. If narrative therapy has one motto, it is "The person is not the problem. The problem is the problem." Narrative therapists engage in a process called *externalizing the problem* so that it does not reside in and become synonymous with the individual. Thus, a person who is alleged to be suffering from a bipolar disorder is treated as if he or she *is* the bipolar disorder. We all have a dominant narrative that is inclined to be problem saturated. Narrative therapy involves a process of deconstructing the problem-saturated narrative to more self-empowering narratives.

Narrative therapy proceeds through five stages. *Stage 1* consists of naming or defining the problem. *Stage 2* is termed mapping the influence of the problem. *Stage 3* consists of evaluating and justifying the effects of the problem. *Stage 4* entails identifying unique outcomes. *Stage 5* is restorying or reauthoring the story. Narrative offers great promise for working effectively with a wide spectrum of clients, including children and young people, adolescents, and adults.

SUPPLEMENTAL AIDS
Discussion Questions

1. If you were asked to externalize a major problem that you have struggled with for the past year, what would that be like for you? How might you go about considering the problem as separate from who you are?

2. Narrative therapy maintains that it is important to find an appreciative audience to support you in the changes you are making in your life. Who would you include in the audience that would appreciate your new story?

3. Narrative therapy adopts the stance that a therapist should be able to listen to a client's problem-saturated story without getting stuck. How might you go about helping a client separate himself or herself from the problem?

4. Narrative therapists established a collaborative relationship with their clients. As a therapist, how might you go about establishing a collaborative relationship with your client.

5. What are some therapist attitudes and skills that you might use in helping clients tell their stories?

Glossary of Key Terms

alternative story   A story that develops in counseling that contradicts the dominant story that is contained within a client's problem.

coauthoring   Describes the process by which both the therapist and the client assume responsibility for the development of alternative stories.

discourse   A system of words, actions, rules, beliefs, and institutions that share common values.

dominant life story   Consists of a widely held belief in a society such that it comes to represent reality for most of its people. In any given culture, dominant stories shape reality in that they construct and form what people perceive and do.

externalizing the problem   Refers to the concept that the person is not his or her problem. Narrative therapy helps clients externalize the problem—separate the problem from the client.

narrative story   Subscribes to the view that every life story is characterized by a plot that contains the events in a person's life, and by examining the plot

carefully, the person may emerge a happier and more satisfied person.

narrative therapy   Provides options for the telling and the retelling of the preferred stories of people's lives. It is a specific set of therapy practices that are informed by postmodernist, social constructivist thinking. Michael White in Adelaide, Australia, and David Epson in New Zealand have contributed significantly to the development of these practices. A narrative approach to therapy maintains that stories are the stuff that forms people's lives. In narrative therapy, clients are guided by therapists who help them uncover themes that lend to connectedness to their life stories.

reauthoring   A process in narrative therapy in which both the therapist and the client create alternative stories.

story deconstruction   This takes place when the therapist or the client explores the meaning of a story by taking apart or unpacking the obvious parts of the theory. The process of deconstruction is used to be able to notice the effects of the story's construction on the person's identity.

thick descriptions   Descriptions in telling a narrative story that evoke clients' consciousness in explanations of why they do what they do—about the invocation of notions of desire, whim, mood, goal, hope, intention, purpose, and so on.

thin descriptions   Reveal the severity of a problem as experienced by the client. The word *thin* is used because the client is sketching a very poor image of himself or herself. The rich description of life and its complexities is missing from a thin description. Thin descriptions provide clues regarding how the individual perceives himself or herself and situations.

Website Materials

Additional exercises, journals, annotated bibliography, and more are available on the open-access website at https://study.sagepub.com/jonessmith2e.

CHAPTER 17

Integrating Spiritual/Religious Issues During Psychotherapy

We are not human beings on a spiritual journey. We are spiritual beings on a human journey.

—Stephen Covey

BRIEF OVERVIEW

Most books on theories of psychotherapy do not include a chapter on spirituality. This book maintains that spirituality is an important part of an individual's life. The purpose of this chapter is not to promote any one religion or spiritual approach to psychotherapy. I have no desire to have therapists become experts on the world's various religions. Instead, a major goal is to assist therapists in using spirituality concepts and the wisdom from religions to help their clients function more effectively in their everyday lives. A second major goal of this chapter is to provide some guidelines for you to consider for integrating spirituality and religion in your approach to therapy. Not dealing with underlying religious and spiritual issues in counseling may be a mistake for therapists. Effective therapists cannot say to their clients, "Park your religion at the door before you enter my office. My psychotherapeutic approach only deals with secular concerns." The lives of human beings can rarely be so compartmentalized. Oftentimes, the spiritual seeps over into the secular, and vice versa.

A true multicultural perspective in psychotherapy must take into account clients' spiritual and religious worldviews. Therapists need to learn how to assess clients' spirituality and religious perspectives to determine what impact such views might have on their clients' mental health and physical issues. In addition, therapists need to understand how their own spiritual and religious views influence their concepts of mental health. For instance, if a client said to you that he or she talked with God each day, would you believe that the client was having a thought disorder—a lack of contact with reality? Or would you accept the fact that your client might be perfectly normal in believing that God is, in fact, talking with him or her daily?

This chapter raises a number of questions. For instance, do our theories of psychotherapy have contained within them implicit spiritual and religious views? Most religions have stated that as a man thinketh, so he is. Yet cognitive therapists have claimed this concept as their contribution to psychotherapy. Existentialists have claimed that issues dealing with meaning and purpose in life are the domain of existentialism rather than the province of the spiritual or religious realm. Recently, scholars within the field of psychotherapy disagreed with the view that a search for meaning in life is existential rather than spiritual (Fukuyama & Sevig, 1999; Plante, 2009). They point out that people were looking for meaning and purpose in life long before the existentialists ever arrived on the scene. If anything, existentialists have borrowed heavily from religion and spirituality, without giving these fields sufficient credit for their contributions. My position is that thousands of years before psychotherapy ever graced the human scene, people used spiritual approaches to calm their minds, deal with anxiety and depression, and cope with feelings of inadequacy. Religion and spiritual approaches provide meaning, structure, and hope for people throughout the world.

What, then, is the relationship between theories of psychotherapy and spirituality/religion? Could it be that theorists in the field of psychotherapy have simply taken spiritual concepts and presented them in secular, so-called scientific language? Do our theories of psychotherapy implicitly and explicitly contain tenets or underlying assumptions that might be categorized as spiritual/religious? Is, for example, the Rogerian belief that people should work toward self-actualization a spiritual concept or a scientific, secular concept—or perhaps both? Have therapists, by their very adoption of certain theoretical perspectives, chosen a certain spiritual perspective in working with their clients? I encourage you to go back and examine each of the theories presented thus far in this book and analyze them from a spiritual perspective. What, if any, spiritual/religious concepts do the theories of therapy endorse either implicitly or explicitly?

> ### Inner Reflections
>
> Do you believe that theories of psychotherapy are free of spiritual or religious issues?
>
> Looking at the theories examined thus far in this text, which do you believe are the most/least free from spiritual and/or religious issues?

Integration of Spirituality/Religion in Psychotherapeutic Approaches

Increasingly, clinicians are reporting that clients are bringing spiritual issues to the therapeutic relationship (Aten & Leach, 2009; Fukuyama & Sevig, 1999; Plante, 2009). Many of these issues have to do with finding meaning and purpose in life—issues that deal with one's spirituality (Plante, 2009). While there is no single spiritual approach to psychotherapy that is acceptable to people from all religions, spirituality and religion may be integrated with secular theoretical approaches to psychotherapy. In this respect, Eastern approaches to psychotherapy may be far ahead of Western approaches because from the very beginning they have integrated spiritual forces into their psychotherapy. For instance, Japan's Naikan and Morita therapies incorporate principles from Buddhism in their psychotherapeutic approach. The foundation for Chinese mindfulness is also Buddhism. Hindu approaches to psychotherapy integrate the principles of yoga into psychotherapeutic treatment. Muslim approaches to psychotherapy use the Qur'an as the guidebook for providing psychotherapy.

The Western approach to psychotherapy has been to separate the spiritual from the secular. For instance, Western-style psychotherapy has established two fields, one dealing with pastoral (spiritual/religious) counseling and another that emphasizes nonreligious or secular approaches to psychotherapy. While the Western approach to psychotherapy has presented psychotherapy as the talking cure, Eastern approaches have stressed that the spiritual realm provides the cure. Perhaps a more critical issue is whether we can create a counseling theory without having the theorist's cultural or spiritual worldview intruding into that theory?

The truth regarding which perspective—Western or Eastern—is the more appropriate way of providing psychological healing for people may not be known for some time. Both psychotherapy and spirituality/religion provide a way of healing from psychological and physical pain. In some respects, the separation of spirituality and psychotherapy is an artificial one. Spiritual or religious forces are almost invariably sitting there silently in the therapy session, waiting to be called forth and used appropriately for healing. An important issue is this: How does one include a client's spiritual concerns within the therapeutic relationship? How can a therapist deal with spiritual issues without being intrusive and unethical? Can one provide adequate spiritual counseling to an individual if one does not share his or her spiritual faith?

National Data on Americans and the Importance of Spirituality

Additional support for including a chapter on spirituality and religion in this psychotherapy theory book is reflected in the recent national survey data on the average American. Such data have shown that spirituality and religion are important for most Americans. A recent online Harris Poll (conducted online within the United States between November 13 and 18, 2013, among 2,250 adults, of ages 18 and older) has reported that a strong majority (74%) of U.S. adults say that they believe in God, but that's down from the 82% who adhered to such a belief in earlier years. Approximately 72% of Americans believe in miracles, down from 79% in 2005 (Jones, 2013). Other findings dealt with those who have an "absolute certainty that there is a God"—down from 10 years ago (54% vs. 66% in 2003). Outside of specific religious samples, the groups most likely to be absolutely certain there is a God include African Americans (70%), Republicans (65%), and baby boomers (60%). Approximately 19% of Americans describe themselves as "very" religious, and an additional 4 in 10 (40%) describe themselves as "somewhat" religious (down from 49% in 2007). The poll data revealed that people state that spiritual and religious beliefs give meaning and purpose to their lives; they provide a framework that helps them cope with the stressors of life (Oman & Thoresen, 2003).

Compare, however, psychologists' and other helping professionals' responses to a similar question. Research has found that in contrast to the general American population, most psychologists do not describe themselves as spiritual or religious (Bilgrave & Deluty, 2002; Delaney, Miller, & Bisono, 2007). There is a disconnect between therapists and clients in their spiritual/religious orientations.

Delaney et al. (2007) have reported that "relative to the general population, psychologists [are] more than twice as likely to claim no religion, three times more likely to describe religion as unimportant in their lives, and five times more likely to deny belief in God" (p. 542). In a study by Shafranske (2000), approximately 33% of psychologists were affiliated with any religious faith tradition, 72% reported any belief in God or a higher power, and 51% stated that religion is not important to them. Plante (2009) has stated,

> Therefore, a significant disconnection exists between psychologists, who generally are nonreligious and nonspiritual, and their clients, who generally are religious and spiritual and are seeking professional mental health services about how best to live their lives and cope with various stressful and challenging life events. Furthermore, most psychologists have received essentially no training in how best to work with religious-spiritual clients or related themes during the course of their professional training. In fact, two thirds of psychologists report that they do not feel competent to integrate religious-spiritual matters into their clinical work (Shafranske & Malony, 1990). (p. 11)

Part of the chasm between therapists and clients in their orientation toward spiritual/religious issues can be traced to the actual training of psychotherapists. The vast majority of therapists have been trained to provide professional psychological services in a secular manner that purports to be primarily scientific and unaffected by spiritual and religious beliefs (Plante, 2009). Few universities offer courses that would help graduate students learn how to deal with spiritual/religious issues that arise during therapy. In fact, 68% of all training directors in clinical psychology internship training programs said that they "never foresee religious/spiritual training being offered in their program" (Russell & Yarhouse, 2006, p. 434). Yet Puchalski (2004) has reported that two thirds of medical schools do provide religious/spiritual diversity training, and some offer a model curriculum for psychiatry residency training programs (Larson, Lu, & Swyers, 1996).

Although this chapter emphasizes the connection between spirituality and counseling theory, it is important to remember that not all clients are spiritual. With some clients, spirituality may be irrelevant to treatment. I do not presume to suggest a spiritual identity for the atheist, secular humanist, or agnostic who does not profess a belief in the sacred or in God. "To do so would amount to the same questionable imposition of values and worldview as the atheist therapist who pathologizes all faiths and sacred traditions" (Zinnbauer & Barrett, 2009, p. 147).

Definitions of Important Terms: *Spiritual/Religious*

Definitions of **spirituality** and **religion** have varied in the literature. Plante (2009) has defined religion as "the organizational and community structure of wisdom traditions that generally include sacred scriptures or religious writings, an articulated doctrine of belief structure that describes the faith community's values and beliefs, and an identified leader or spiritual model to emulate" (p. 4). He lists the major religious traditions of the world as Christianity, Judaism, Buddhism, Hinduism, Islam, Taoism, and Confucianism, with each one having different subdivisions—for instance, within Christianity, there are Baptists, Methodists, Roman Catholics, and Eastern Orthodox. Moreover, religions form an organized community within which members submit themselves to specific rituals, traditions, beliefs, and activities (Plante, 2009).

Definitions of spirituality have generated much more debate than those offered for religion. The word *spirituality* is derived from the Latin *spiritus*, which means breath or life force (Hage, 2006). Zinnbauer and Pargament (2005) have defined spirituality as a "personal or group search for the sacred. Religiousness is defined as a personal or group search for the sacred that unfolds within a traditional sacred context" (p. 35). Frame (2003) has emphasized the various components of spirituality in her definition: "Spirituality includes one's values, beliefs, mission, awareness, subjectivity,

experience, sense of purpose and direction, and a kind of striving toward something greater than oneself. It may or may not include a deity" (p. 3).

Between 20% and 35% of Americans define themselves as "spiritual but not religious" (Fuller, 2001). Such individuals are usually not identified with a specific religious tradition or church; still, they consider themselves to be spiritual. Although they might feel connected to a higher power, nature, or the sacredness of human life, they do not self-identify with any established religious faith. Sometimes those who identify themselves as spiritual but not religious have been turned off by religious leaders and the scandals within the various religions.

Scholars have divided ways of being spiritual into *intrinsic* and *extrinsic* components (Salsman & Carlson, 2005). People for whom spirituality is an internal, guiding, and significant impact on their everyday lives were described as manifesting an intrinsic orientation. In contrast, individuals for whom spirituality was more peripheral to how they lived and conducted their lives were said to have an extrinsic spirituality. Their spirituality was often determined by external forces or need—such as the need to be a member of a community. Individuals who are still seeking their own spirituality have been described as having a quest orientation.

> **Inner Reflections**
>
> How do you define your own spirituality?
>
> To what extent is your spirituality related to an organized religion?

Brief Historical Overview of Spirituality and Religion in Psychotherapy

Prior to the advent of formal psychology and psychotherapy, spiritual and religious leaders took responsibility for the mental health of individuals (Sevensky, 1984). The relationship between religion and psychology has been marked by conflict and controversy. One of the first major conflicts between religion and psychotherapy in the United States took place during what is known as the Emmanuel Movement.

In 1906, Dr. James Jackson Putnam, a Harvard University medical school professor, and Dr. Elwood Worcester, an Episcopalian minister, convened Boston medical doctors and Episcopalian ministers (respectively) to provide for the poor in Boston (Caplan, 1998). Soon, the efforts of both groups developed into a national movement called the Emmanuel Movement. Participants in the Emmanuel Movement supplied health and religious education, including medical examinations and minister-employed psychotherapy. According to Caplan (1998), "More than any other single factor, the Emmanuel Movement not only raised the American public's awareness of psychotherapy but also compelled the American medical profession to enter a field that it had long neglected" (p. 118).

Freud and Other Psychology Theorists and Spirituality. Conflict arose between physicians and ministers over whether or not the ministers were qualified to provide psychotherapy services to people (Caplan, 1998). The physicians claimed that the ministers were not properly trained to provide such services and that, therefore, only physicians should provide such services. Just 3 years later, Sigmund Freud delivered a series of lectures at Clark University that officially brought psychoanalysis to the United States. Given the attack from physicians and Freud's introductory lectures, the Emmanuel Movement ended with the rise of psychoanalysis.

Freud delivered a series of teachings regarding the harmful effects of religion and spirituality—even though his own father was a highly religious and devout Jew (Caplan, 1998). He and his colleagues presented spirituality and religion as a universal neurosis, thereby influencing the way later generations of psychologists would view these issues. For instance, in *Future of an Illusion*, Freud (1927/1961) asserted that religious views "are illusions, fulfillments of the oldest, strongest and most urgent wishes of mankind" (p. 30). He also described religion as an "obsessional neurosis" (p. 43). Similarly, Watson (1924/1983) referred to religion as a "bulwark of medievalism" (p. 1). Freud, Watson, Ellis, Skinner, and other famous psychologists put forth the view that religious interest was a sign of pathology and not health (Plante, 2009).

Psychology's Effort to Be Seen as Scientific. Part of psychologists' opposition to spirituality and religion may be attributed to their desire to be seen as scientists. Pargament (2007) has pointed out that American psychologists who were interested in examining spiritual issues sometimes delayed doing so until after their award of tenure or promotion to full professor. According to him, academic psychologists who were interested in pursuing spiritual research were counseled to leave the profession or to pursue religious or seminary studies. As a result, only a few psychology training programs have embraced the integration of psychology and the spiritual, two of which are Eastern University and Fuller Theological Seminary.

Recent Developments and Research on Spirituality and Health. Despite the long history of psychology's eschewing of integrating spiritual issues and psychology, the American Psychological Association (APA) and other mental health associations have recently begun to legitimize research completed on spirituality and physical and mental health (Hage, 2006). From the 1990s to the present day, APA has published about a dozen books on spirituality and psychotherapy. The majority of the research on spirituality has found a relationship between faith and health (Koenig, McCullough, & Larson, 2001; Pargament, 1997; Plante & Thoresen, 2007; Richards & Bergin, 2005). By far, the research has shown that religion and spirituality are good for people's mental and physical health. On average, studies have found that religious/spiritual people live about 7 years longer than nonreligious and nonspiritual people and African Americans live a full 14 years longer than their nonspiritual counterparts (Miller & Thoresen, 2003).

Spiritual rituals, such as prayer and meditation, have been reported to improve participants' mental and physical health (Argyle, 2002). Spirituality influences the way people interpret their experiences and make meaning out of life. Researchers have reported that spiritual beliefs can promote individuals' healthy coping when they face a personal illness or loss (Pargament, Desai, & McConnell, 2006). After reviewing more than 500 studies from 1980 to 2000, Koenig (2004) found positive relationships between spirituality and general mental health, well-being, and a reduction in substance abuse. Getting involved in a spiritual community can also provide social support.

It is also noteworthy that negative conditions can result from individuals' religious affiliations. Spiritual and religious situations can also contribute to strain in individuals' lives. Religious strain, such as being angry with God, can cause depression in some people (Exline, Yali, & Sanderson, 2000). Individuals' spirituality and religious affiliations can produce excessive feelings of guilt, which in turn tends to lead to obsessive-compulsive behavior (Zuckerman, Austin, Fair, & Branchey, 1987). Individuals' religiosity can also lead to terrorism, as exemplified by the attacks on September 11, 2001, in New York City and Washington, D.C. Thus, individuals' spirituality and religious affiliations can have a number of negative effects on their mental health functioning and on the well-being of others.

Pastoral Counseling: A Specialized Type of Spiritual Counseling

Pastoral counseling is a specialized form of counseling that uses both a spiritual framework and psychological understanding to promote healing and growth within a client. Pastoral counselors are trained mental health providers who also have training in theology. A client in pastoral counseling can usually count on his or her values being part of the cornerstone of counseling. The pastoral counselor brings God's presence into the therapy room.

What distinguishes pastoral counseling from other forms of counseling and psychotherapy is the role and accountability of the counselor and his or her understanding and expression of the pastoral relationship. Pastoral counselors are representatives of the central images of life and its meaning affirmed by their religious communities. Thus pastoral counseling offers a relationship to that understanding of life and faith. Pastoral counseling uses both psychological and theological resources to deepen its understanding of the pastoral relationship. (Hunter, 2005)

The American Association of Pastoral Counselors has the following mission statement:

The mission of the American Association of Pastoral Counselors is to bring healing, hope, and wholeness to individuals, families, and communities by expanding and equipping spiritually grounded and psychological informed care, counseling, and psychotherapy. (Retrieved from http://www.aapc.org/home/mission-statement.aspx)

> **Inner Reflections**
>
> Do you believe that your spiritual practices have anything to do with your health and psychological well-being?
>
> What is the influence of prayer in your personal life?

KEY CONCEPTS

This section deals with a spiritual mindset, models of spiritual development, the therapist's awareness of spiritual matters, discrepancies between the therapist's and the client's beliefs, and spirituality and the therapeutic relationship. Therapists are trained to have a psychological mindset when working with clients. Such a mindset uses principles of psychology for viewing clients' thoughts, feelings, and behavior to assist them in therapy.

A Spiritual Mindset

Just as therapists learn how to develop a psychological mindset when working with clients, they must also learn how to develop a spiritual mindset.

A spiritual mindset means being aware of and thoughtful about taking into account the spiritual influences on clients' current or future behavior. Therapists who have a spiritual mindset develop an openness to exploring the religious/spiritual dimensions of their clients. Even though therapists might not consider themselves to be religious/spiritual, they are able to perceive and understand what their clients hold sacred.

Pargament (2007) has proposed specific qualities that therapists should strive for in developing a spiritual orientation or mindset during psychotherapy. The therapist might assume the attitude that religious/spiritual qualities in clients can be the source of clinical problems and the source of resistance to trying out solutions to problems. In addition, therapists should maintain a high degree of spiritual literacy, self-awareness, openness, tolerance, and authenticity in religious/spiritually oriented psychotherapy. Another quality is that the therapist perceives therapy as having a spiritual quality, even if discussions about religion/spirituality are not the focus in treatment. Finally, a therapist with a spiritual mindset understands that psychological interventions can influence a client's spiritual development, and in turn, spirituality can enhance the psychological interventions used during therapy.

Fowler's Theory of Faith Development

Spirituality is a comprehensive construct that involves practice, belief, and individual experience. Fowler (1981) has provided one of the most widely used theories of the **stages of faith** development. According to Fowler, faith can be defined as "a person's way of seeing him or herself in relation to others against the backdrop of shared meaning and purpose" (p. 4), and he proposed the idea of faith as a "human universal" (p. xiii). Faith is a part of the human experience. Fowler's model suggests that individuals' levels of spiritual development reveal the different ways in which they understand themselves, others, and social situations.

Spiritual development is a process that entails moving toward progressively more complex levels of understanding, integration, meaning making, and interpersonal relationships (Fowler, 1981; Miller, 2003). Fowler's stages of faith relate closely to Kohlberg's moral developmental stages.

Fowler's (1981) theory consists of six stages of faith development in which individuals move toward increased maturity and personalization of their spiritual "identity":

1. Intuitive–Projective faith (from birth to age 2)

2. Mythic–Literal faith (mostly seen in school children)

3. Synthetic–Conventional faith (this stage arises during adolescence)

4. Individuative–Projective faith (usually from midtwenties to late thirties)

5. Conjunctive faith (midlife crisis)

6. Universalizing faith

In the first three stages of faith development, individuals rely on some authority outside of themselves for spiritual beliefs. During the first stage of faith (*intuitive–projective*), young children follow the beliefs of their parents. They imagine or fantasize angels and other religious figures in stories as characters in fairy tales. In the second stage of faith (*mythical–literal*), children respond to religious stories and rituals literally instead of symbolically. As children pass on through adolescence to young adulthood, their religious beliefs are based on authority focused outside of themselves— their parents, the church, and so on. In this third stage of faith (*synthetic–conventional*), individuals exemplify a conformist acceptance of a faith belief, with little self-reflection or examination of these beliefs. Most people remain at this level (Fowler, 1981). People who move to the fourth stage of faith (*individuative–reflective*) begin a radical shift from dependence on others' spiritual beliefs to development of their own. Fowler (1981) says, "For a genuine move to Stage 4 to occur there must be an interruption of reliance on external sources of authority . . . . There must be . . . a relocation of authority within the self" (p. 179). People no longer define themselves by the groups to which they belong. Instead, they choose beliefs, values, and relationships that are critical to their self-fulfillment. During the fifth stage of faith (*conjunctive*), people still rely on their own views; however, they move from self-preoccupation or from dependence on fixed truths to acceptance of others' points of view. As they accept others' points of faith, they become more tolerant and begin to serve others.

People who move to the sixth and last stage of faith (*universalizing*) are rare. Usually, they are older adults who begin to search for universal values, such as unconditional love and justice. Self-preservation becomes irrelevant. Some examples of the sixth stage of development include Mother Theresa and Mahatma Gandhi (Fowler, 1981).

Clinebell (1995) has indicated that there are seven areas of spiritual needs. Therapists must become aware of their own spiritual needs as well as those of their clients. As you review Clinebell's list of spiritual needs, consider which ones are operating in your life. Clinebell's list of needs is as follows:

1. For a viable philosophy of life
2. For creative values
3. For a relationship with a loving God
4. For developing our higher selves;
5. For a sense of trustful belonging in the universe
6. For renewing moments of transcendence
7. For a caring community that nurtures spiritual growth

SPIRITUALITY AND THE THERAPEUTIC PROCESS _____

For therapy to be effective, therapists must establish a therapeutic alliance with their clients. The factors that build a strong therapeutic alliance are similar to the ones for integrating spiritual issues in therapy. Young, Dowdle, and Flowers (2009) have indicated that therapists should do the following to forge a relationship with their clients:

1. Adopt a position of curiosity when engaging clients in a discussion of their spirituality
2. Pay close attention to how clients perceive the therapist's view of their spiritual beliefs
3. Develop a deep understanding of clients' feelings and understanding of their spiritual or religious teachings
4. Give clients a number of opportunities to discuss their views of the therapeutic relationship
5. Evaluate carefully clients' statements regarding the therapist's lack of understanding of their spiritual views.

The Therapeutic Relationship

Spiritual issues have typically been a part of the psychotherapeutic relationship, even though, for the most part, there has been an effort to delineate carefully between spiritual and psychotherapeutic issues. Spiritual issues, such as making meaning, hope, suffering, and transcendence, are linked to most approaches to psychotherapy. As Fukuyama and Sevig (1999) have stated,

Therapy is a time for change and transformation to happen, that is, transformation of the self (self-awareness), coming in touch with something outside of one's self or a higher power (transcendence), and gaining meaning in one's life (meaning making). Part of the spiritual process in therapy involves removing blocks to awareness, gaining a sense of transcendence, and developing meaning making, thereby providing an environment in which transformations can naturally occur. (p. 142)

This section examines the clinical intake interview and spiritual issues. Next, I focus on issues involving assessment of spiritual issues. Following this, I examine discrepancies between therapists' beliefs and clients' beliefs. The goal is to present material that can be used within a number of theoretical approaches to psychotherapy.

Goals of Therapy

There is no one model for integrating spiritual issues into psychotherapy. As has been suggested throughout this chapter, therapists should first engage in a process of self-examination to help themselves become clear about their own spiritual and religious beliefs. After therapists have undergone this first step, they are in a better position to determine the extent to which the spiritual dimension will be integrated in their therapeutic process. Second, the degree to which spirituality is integrated into therapy will also be based on the therapist's religious/spiritual orientation.

Understanding the meaning of clients' faith and spirituality may become a part of the therapist's case conceptualization. Therapists endeavor to understand how their clients' spiritual/religious orientation may be intertwined with their presenting problems. Are the clients' spiritual/religious issues part of their distress and contributing to their presenting problems? Is their spirituality a source of strength that helps them cope and that can be used during therapy? Richards and Bergin (2005) suggest that a treatment plan may contain one or more of the following spiritual goals: helping clients to (1) affirm their spiritual identity, (2) live in harmony with their spiritual and religious values, (3) examine their visual images of God or a deity, (4) deal with and resolve spiritual and religious issues that are related to their presenting problems, and (5) discuss if their faith and spirituality can be a positive resource to help them during therapy.

When clients believe that their faith and spirituality are positive resources, the therapist can design interventions that help them use these resources. An integrated spiritual treatment plan might include recommending that clients engage in spiritual practices such as prayer, meditation and contemplation, spiritual writings, repentance and forgiveness, worship, and direct efforts to seek spiritual direction (Richards & Bergin, 2005). When using spiritual techniques during therapy, the therapist works to avoid potential ethical dangers such as creating dual relationships (religious and professional), displacing clients' religious authority, and imposing the therapist's religious values (O'Grady & Richards, 2009).

Role of the Therapist

As indicated in the preceding section, the role of the therapist is to be deeply respectful of clients' right to privacy regarding spiritual/religious issues. Using a narrative therapy approach, the therapist works to elicit the client's spiritual story. Many clients are not given an opportunity to talk about the importance of spiritual issues in their lives. The therapist may assist clients in uncovering or elucidating their spiritual journey. If a client gives a therapist permission to deal with such issues, the therapist may assist him or her by posing spiritually relevant, open-ended questions, such as those presented in the spiritual assessment section of this chapter. The therapist works to identify the purpose or meaning of the clients' behavior.

In addition, the therapist should be genuine and authentic in response to clients' expressions of spirituality. Usually, clients can detect when therapists are not authentic in their responses to clients' spiritual issues. Therapists are entitled to their own spiritual beliefs, and they are not required to agree with clients' spiritual beliefs or to participate in spiritual rituals with clients (Worthington & Sandage, 2002). Therapists can address the client's spiritual belief system by using reflection or restatement skills. For instance, the therapist can say, "From what you have shared with me, I can feel how important your beliefs are to you. You've indicated that your faith has been critical in helping you deal with the challenges you've faced in life." When differences occur between client and therapist, the therapist must make an ethical decision regarding whether or not he or she feels comfortable working with the client.

Therapists are authentic when they respect their clients' spiritual beliefs and delineate differences between them or when they attempt to find commonalities in the two spiritual belief systems.

For instance, most religions teach hope and forgiveness, and these commonalities can be used effectively in the therapeutic relationship. Are there any commonalities in the ways Christianity, Judaism, and Islam view hope? How does each group view an afterlife?

Therapist Awareness, Knowledge, and Skills Related to Spiritual Matters

Therapist Awareness of Spiritual Issues. The therapist's own spiritual awareness is the first step in the therapeutic process. Therapists must become aware of the spirituality within themselves and within their clients. In gaining spiritual self-awareness, therapists must determine how they view spirituality within a therapeutic framework. How does the therapist perceive his or her own spiritual development? How significant is spirituality to the therapist? Does the therapist accept spirituality as an important construct for psychotherapy? If the therapist believes that spirituality is an important construct for psychotherapy, then he or she should be attuned to the client's spiritual content (Plante, 2009). Therapists who believe that spirituality is a legitimate part of therapy must be careful not to make assumptions about spirituality until such issues have been explored with the client. In contrast, if the therapist rejects spirituality as an important part of the therapeutic process, then he or she must consider if there may be a spiritual component to the client's presenting problem. Therapists must make sure that they have a good understanding of the differences between spirituality and religion. Some behaviors that might be considered pathological are completely acceptable in certain religions.

Pargament (2007) has discussed several problematic attitudes that therapists can bring into counseling when they integrate religious/spiritual issues into therapy. Spiritual bias takes place when therapists harbor stereotyped and oftentimes negative perceptions of religious/spiritual concepts and people. This situation sometimes arises when a therapist has had infrequent contact with individuals of a different religious faith. Negative spiritual bias involves attributing negative characteristics to individuals from a religious/spiritual group—for instance, viewing all Muslims as sympathetic to terrorists. Therapists might also have a positive religious/spiritual bias when they attribute positive characteristics to a particular religious group.

Pargament (2007) defines *spiritual myopia* as perceiving religious/spiritual issues in a narrow, focused, and undifferentiated manner. Spiritual myopia can be conceptualized as a type of spiritual tunnel vision. For instance, a therapist might believe that Catholic clients will not consider the use of birth control or that Buddhist clients are all vegetarians.

Therapists display *spiritual timidity* when they avoid any client–therapist conversations that involve spiritual matters unless the client explicitly initiates such discussions. It might be helpful for therapists to have an intake form that specifically asks if clients are interested in dealing with spiritual matters in therapy.

To help therapists gain greater *awareness of their own spirituality*, it might be helpful for them to write a spiritual autobiography (Curtis & Glass, 2002). Therapists embark on a self-reflective process regarding spiritual issues. They examine their own values that influence their approach to psychotherapy. What religious/spiritual beliefs do they have, and how do these beliefs influence their views of therapy? Researchers have indicated that clients should have some understanding of their therapists' religious beliefs. Zinnbauer and Pargament (2000) state that when therapists provide some indication of their religious views, clients are in a better position to make informed statements. Similarly, Worthington and Sandage (2001) suggest that therapists engage in open and honest answers about their own faith.

Therapist Knowledge Base Related to Spiritual Issues. There is also a knowledge component of a therapist's spirituality. Therapists should assess their own knowledge of spirituality and its role in therapy. If therapists' knowledge about their own spirituality as well as that of others is lacking, it is unethical for them not to secure additional training. If the therapist has little understanding of Islam, for example, it might be unethical for him or her to work with a client from this faith if religious issues are part of the client's presenting issues. Does the therapist understand what it means to have been raised as an Orthodox Jew or as a fundamentalist Christian?

Therapist Skill Level Related to Spiritual Integration. In addition, therapists must be able to apply their own awareness and knowledge of spiritual issues to their clients in a skilled way. If therapists choose to integrate spiritual issues in their practices, what are the best ways to go about doing so? Therapists need to have a thorough understanding of how spirituality can influence the lives of their clients. Competent therapists also refer their clients to another therapist when they have exceeded their competence level. The following are APA's Division 36's preliminary practice guidelines for working with religious and spiritual issues (as cited in Hathaway & Ripley, 2009, pp. 46–49).

Religious/Spiritual Intervention Guidelines

1. Psychologists obtain appropriate informed consent from clients before incorporating religious/spiritual techniques and/or addressing religious/spiritual treatment goals in counseling.

2. Psychologists accurately represent to clients the nature, purposes, and known level of effectiveness for any religious/spiritual techniques or approaches they may propose using in treatment.

3. Psychologists do not use religious/spiritual treatment approaches/techniques of unknown effectiveness in lieu of other approaches/techniques with demonstrated effectiveness in treating specific disorders or clinical problems.

4. Psychologists attempt to accommodate a client's spiritual/religious tradition in congruent and helpful ways when working with clients for whom spirituality/religion is personally and clinically salient.

Religious/Spiritual Multicultural Practice and Diversity Guidelines

1. Psychologists make reasonable efforts to become familiar with the varieties of spiritually and religion present in their client population.

2. Psychologists strive to be self-aware of their own perspectives, attitudes, history, and self-understandings of religion and spirituality. Psychologists should be mindful of how their own background on religious/spiritual matters might bias their response and approach to clients of differing backgrounds.

Spiritual Assessment: Listening for Clients' Spiritual Language

Most therapists are trained how to conduct a psychological assessment. Few, however, receive any training in conducting a spiritual assessment. This section focuses on how to conduct a spiritual assessment within your chosen integrative approach to psychotherapy. According to Pargament and Krumrei (2009), spiritual assessment should be based on a clear understanding of spirituality, how it works, and how it may be part of a client's solution or part of his or her problems. The authors define spirituality as the search for the sacred, which can involve any aspect of a person's life. For instance, the sacred refers to not only God and the

> ### Inner Reflections
>
> What is your knowledge level of the religious/spiritual issues of ethnic/cultural groups other than your own membership group?
>
> Do you have high, medium, or low knowledge of the religious/spiritual beliefs and values of groups different from your membership group?

attributes of a divinity but also to relationships, nature, and so on. Spirituality is a search for what individuals consider sacred in their lives. As Pargament and Krumrei (2009) have stated,

> Spirituality refers to the effort to discover the sacred, conserve a relationship with the sacred once it has been discovered, and transform that relationship when necessary. A client's spirituality is positive when it is well integrated within his/her total being. It becomes negative when it is not well integrated into a person's life, when it clashes with the larger social system, and when it causes a person to pursue matters of limited spiritual value. (p. 94)

The first step in conducting a spiritual assessment entails listening for clients' implicit spiritual language (Pargament & Krumrei, 2009). Therapists examine where clients stand in relationship to spirituality. How central is spirituality to the client's life? What is his or her motivation for spirituality? Second, therapists should be cognizant of the fact that clients enter therapy at various phases in their spiritual journey. For instance, some clients seek therapy during a spiritual struggle or a transformation, while others choose therapy in a conservational mode—that is, when their spirituality has experienced long-term stability.

Third, therapists should explore the content of clients' spirituality. What do their clients consider to be sacred, and what are the roads they take to the sacred? Fourth, therapists should seek an understanding of how their clients' spirituality is related to their social living. Fifth, therapists should understand how to evaluate the efficacy of clients' spirituality by exploring the different ways in which spirituality affects their lives. Sixth, after all these steps have been completed, therapists weigh how spirituality might be addressed in treatment—whether clients' spirituality is well integrated or disintegrated and whether it is contributing to clients' problems or offers potential solutions (Pargament & Krumrei, 2009, p. 98).

Some clients enter therapy without an awareness of how spirituality is affecting their presenting problems. Therapists can begin a spiritual assessment by introducing spirituality as a topic for therapeutic discussion. It is important for the therapist to convey a sense of deep respect for clients' sense of spirituality and to leave the door open for discussion of spiritual issues. However, if clients are hesitant in discussing spiritual issues, the therapist should respect their wishes and discontinue such conversations. The therapist obtains consent from clients to discuss spiritual issues during therapy.

Pargament and Krumrei (2009) provide a three-stage process in spiritual assessment that can be useful for therapists wishing to integrate spiritual issues within an approach to psychotherapy. It is important that spiritual assessment continues throughout the therapeutic relationship. The three stages of assessment are (1) examining clients' past spirituality, (2) exploring clients' current spirituality, and (3) discussing clients' future spirituality. In each of these three stages, the therapist deals with how clients express and experience their spirituality. The questions begin with having clients reflect on their spirituality when they were young.

Clinical Assessment: Questions to Elicit Clients' Spiritual Life

1. Questions designed to elicit clients' past spirituality

   a. How did you express your spirituality in the environment in which you grew up?

   b. When did you first discover your spirituality?

   c. When you were young, how did you conceptualize your spiritual/religious self?

   d. How did you express your spirituality/religion in growing up?

   e. What, if any, spiritual milestones have you experienced in your life?

   f. Have you ever felt that the spiritual/religious was missing from your life?

2. Questions designed to elicit clients' present or current spirituality

2.1. Clients' views of spirituality/religion

   a. What do you believe is sacred in your life?

   b. Have your spiritual/religious beliefs changed over the years? How?

   c. What do you feel is God's purpose in your life?

   d. What does God or your religion want from you?

   e. How do you think God views the pain you are currently experiencing?

   f. Do you ever have mixed thoughts about your own spirituality and religion? How do you experience such mixed or conflicting thoughts?

2.2. Clients' expression and experience of spirituality

   a. How would you describe your present spiritual orientation?

   b. How do you experience the spiritual in your life?

   c. What in your environment has helped you nourish the spiritual in your life?

   d. When/where do you feel the most connected to the spiritual?

   e. When/where do you not experience the spiritual?

   f. What has been damaging to your spirituality?

   g. What spiritual practices are important to you?

   h. What spiritual beliefs do you find most comforting?

2.3. Spiritual efficacy

   a. How has your spiritual life changed for the better?

   b. How has your spiritual life changed for the worse?

   c. How has your spirituality given your life meaning or pleasure?

   d. How has your spirituality given you a sense of connection to others?

   e. How has your spirituality given you a feeling of being loved?

   f. To what extent, if any, has your spirituality/religion been a source of pain? Guilt? Anger? Confusion or doubt? Feelings of alienation from others?

   g. How has your spirituality/religion helped you understand or deal with the problems that brought you to therapy?

   h. Has your spirituality/religion been harmful in dealing with the issues that brought you to therapy?

   i. Who supports you spiritually?

   j. Who does not support you spiritually? How so?

3. Questions related to clients' future spirituality

   a. Do you see yourself changing spiritually in the future?

   b. In what ways do you want to grow spiritually in the future?

   c. Does your spirituality relate to your life goals?

Source: Adapted from Pargament and Krumrei (2009, pp. 93–120).

Client Intake Forms and Assessment of Religious/Spiritual Issues

The majority of clinicians use an intake form or a questionnaire related to their clinical practice. I recommend that you include in your intake form basic questions that assess religious/spiritual factors. Such an intake form might ask about clients' religious affiliation and about how important religious/spiritual issues are in their lives. Some religious/spiritual items that might be included in an intake form are given on the next page.

Spiritual Assessment Instruments

Researchers have developed a number of instruments to assess clients' religious and spiritual issues. The Spiritual Well-Being Scale (Paloutzian & Ellison, 1982) is a 20-item measure that assesses perceptions of spiritual quality of life. The measure has two subscales: (1) religious well-being ("I believe that God loves me and cares about me") and (2) existential well-being ("I feel good about my future"). Clinicians might find that to assess spiritual issues, the 10-item Religious Well-Being Scale is sufficient for therapeutic purposes.

The Revised Religious Orientation Scale (Gorsuch & McPherson, 1989) is a 14-item scale that measures intrinsic religious/spiritual values ("I enjoy reading about my religion") and extrinsic religious/spiritual values ("I go to church because it helps me make friends") and religious motivation.

The Religious Problem-Solving Scale (Pargament, Smith, Koenig, & Perez, 1998) is a 30-item scale that measures three religious approaches to solving problems. The scale assesses if the person assumes an active or a passive approach toward problem solving and if primary responsibility is attributed to self or to God. The three scales outlined can be helpful in assessing clients' religiosity/spirituality.

Spiritual Techniques

There are a number of techniques therapists can use to integrate spiritual issues into psychotherapy, which include a spiritual genogram, guided spiritual journaling, spiritual autobiographies, spiritual narratives, and spiritual life maps. These techniques can be used to foster spiritual understanding for both clients and therapists.

Spiritual Genogram

Genograms help therapists represent and analyze family composition and other demographics across several generations. A spiritual genogram helps a therapist gain insight into how clients' spiritual or religious legacies continue to influence their current beliefs and practices (Frame, 2009). Clients can be asked to draw a three-generation genogram. They should note significant family events and dates, such as births, marriages, divorces, remarriages, and deaths. The genogram should depict the gender of each family member, all adoptions, family members' sexual orientation, and family relationship quality (Frame, 2009).

The therapist might suggest that the religious/spiritual genogram be color coded to represent different religious and spiritual traditions. For instance, a client might color-code Jewish influences with the color blue, Buddhists with the color yellow, Roman Catholics with red, and Protestants with orange. Frame (2009) suggests not using any color when a family's religious or spiritual background is not known. As Frame (2009) has suggested, the color coding on the spiritual genogram shows a family's multiplicity of spiritual and religious backgrounds. A religious/spiritual genogram may reveal religious conflict, and it might help clients discover the sources of their beliefs, morals, values, and attitudes that might have an influence on therapy.

Clients record important events that took place in the family's spiritual or religious life. For instance, the client would indicate baptisms, first communions, confirmations, bar and bat mitzvahs, and other rites of spiritual passage. Brackets should be placed around individuals who have left a spiritual/religious community or who have converted to a different faith. Frame also suggests using symbols to represent a family's close religious/spiritual bond.

After constructing the spiritual genogram, therapists might ask clients to respond to the following questions—and give their own responses as well (Frame, 2003):

1. What role, if any, did your family of origin give to religion/spirituality when you were growing up?

2. What role does religion/spirituality currently assume for your family of origin?

3. What religious beliefs do you adhere to now, and how important are they for you? To what extent are these religious/spiritual beliefs a source of conflict between you and your family of origin and your current family?

4. How does your religion/spiritual tradition view gender and the roles of men and women? How does it view sexual orientation and ethnicity?

5. What, if any, patterns emerge as you study your spiritual genogram? Are you currently maintaining or digressing from those patterns?

6. Does your spiritual/religious history relate to your current presenting problem in therapy?

7. Based on what you have learned from this genogram, what new insights have occurred to you? How has spirituality/religion been a source of strength for your family? Has it interfered with your family's relationships?

Guided Spiritual Journaling

Guided spiritual journaling can be used as a technique to further a therapist's own spiritual awareness. It may also be used to help clients in therapy. Clients are asked to keep a journal of their spiritual beliefs and experiences. Krug (1982) has maintained that a spiritual journal should contain personal life events and individuals' responses to them as well as significant and meaningful conversations they have had. Clients can also use spiritual journaling to record questions they might have about life and how they are dealing with such questions on a daily basis. A spiritual journal might also contain clients' memories, passages from books, insights about their experiences, and their achievements and failures. Spiritual journaling should be scheduled on a regular basis. The journal is intended to help clients come to terms with their lives and their place within the universe.

Spiritual journaling for therapists themselves should help them deal with the difficult questions that clients might ask of them during therapy (Frame, 2009). For instance, a therapist might have to deal with questions such as these: Do people really have free will, or are their thoughts, feelings, and actions determined by God or some force within the universe? Why do bad things happen to good people? What happens to people after they die? What are the qualities of the Supreme Being in whom you believe?

Which types of clients or client problems involving religious/spiritual issues would challenge you the most? What is your comfort level in working with clients from different faiths or religious/spiritual groups?

Spiritual Autobiography

Therapists might also use the technique of having clients write a spiritual autobiography. This technique helps clients view their lives in terms of their spiritual journey and gain a perspective on their spiritual lives. A spiritual autobiography should begin with clients' earliest memories of spirituality or religion in their families of origin. Faiver, Ingersoll, O'Brien, and McNally (2001) have proposed that therapists might use five broad categories to help clients write their spiritual autobiographies.

Categories for Writing Spiritual Autobiographies

1. *Introductory statements:* In this category, clients are urged to use free association to consider their relationship with religious/spiritual issues. They examine how they view themselves as a religious or spiritual being.

2. *Spiritual themes:* Clients write about spiritual themes that have affected their lives. For instance, they might write about gratitude or forgiveness, humility, and so on.

3. *Spiritual influences:* Clients write about individuals who have nurtured them spiritually, who have helped them become spiritual or nonspiritual.

4. *Life's lessons:* Clients write what they have learned in their spiritual journey, and they ponder the lessons they have learned. They might also consider how they will pass on the lessons they learned to future generations.

5. *Personal conclusions:* In this section, clients write about their thoughts and feelings about the overall effect of spirituality on their lives. Clients also might consider what barriers prevent them from connecting with the sources of their spirituality.

The Exceptional Human Experience

Palmer (1999) has proposed using the exceptional human experience as another way of writing a spiritual autobiography. The term *exceptional human experience* was coined in 1990 by Rhea White to investigate what could be learned about all types of psychic, mystical, spiritual, death-related, peak, and other anomalous life experiences. White (1999) concluded that many types of exceptional experiences are very similar, even though there may be differences in how such events take place. The one characteristic that defined exceptional human experiences was their transformative influence on people's lives. Many people have described near-death exceptional human experiences. Usually, they state that they saw a white light in the sky.

Exceptional human experiences are usually discarded as mystical and unscientific. Therefore, they tend to be discounted or dismissed by scientists. In integrating spiritual issues in psychotherapy, therapists inquire if clients have had any exceptional human experiences. Clients may be asked to write an exceptional human experience autobiography or journal.

Spiritual Letters

Sometimes writing a spiritual autobiography might be too much for a client. Clients might be more amenable to writing spiritual letters. Blanton (2006) has recommended that clients' spiritual letters contain the following components: (a) descriptions of spiritual struggles, (b) descriptions of spiritual goals and progress toward those goals, (c) descriptions of recent encounters with the spiritual or religious realm, and (d) questions that they might have about the spiritual process.

Spiritual Life Maps

Hodge (2005) has suggested the use of spiritual life maps for clients who are visually oriented. A spiritual life map is a pictorial representation of the spiritual milestones clients have experienced in their lives. Clients are asked to either draw or use pictures cut out of magazines to symbolize key spiritual moments in their lives. Hodge offered a case study of a 42-year-old African American male whose spiritual life map demonstrated how his life experiences were linked to spiritual changes, such as crying out to God in pain, feeling spiritually dead, and experiencing a spiritual reawakening.

Bibliotherapy

Therapists should consider using bibliotherapy as a technique to engage clients on religious/spiritual issues. Clients are encouraged to read self-help literature as part of their treatment. For instance, a therapist might suggest a book that deals with how others have dealt successfully with stress.

Some religious/spiritual traditions recommend that clients read the Bible and other sacred religious books.

Forgiveness and Gratitude Exercises

Most religions emphasize that people should forgive others and that they should show gratitude for their lives. One benefit of forgiveness is that it reduces anger and bitterness. When people learn to forgive themselves, they learn to love themselves in healthy ways and release themselves from past mistakes. In addition, forgiveness helps move clients from using the present to focus on hurts in the past. Unforgiveness keeps people tied to the past. When clients fail to forgive themselves, they are continually being hurt by unresolved pain. As a consequence, they may experience low self-esteem, unnecessary guilt, and self-destructive behavior.

Self-Forgiveness Exercise. Have your clients write about an event for which they wish to seek forgiveness from themselves. Next ask them to identify the hurt they had caused others and themselves by their actions. Then, ask your clients to read over what they have written about that event. Ask them to indicate how long they have held on to those feelings. Does this area affect the way they live their life and interact with others? Have them let go of the pain and release the negative emotions associated with the incident. After this step, ask clients to shred or burn the written account as a visual symbol of letting go. If clients report that the pain has resurfaced, remind them that they have forgiven themselves and have chosen to move on with their lives without the pain of the incident.

Clients role-play forgiving significant others with the therapist, or they might write a letter of forgiveness to someone who has slighted them. Clients also need to forgive themselves; therefore, one technique is to have them write on a daily or weekly basis all the things for which they forgive themselves.

Therapists ask clients to keep daily gratitude journals. Clients write three things each day for which they are grateful. They are asked to construct their own meaningful gratitude ritual. To demonstrate their feelings of gratitude, therapists suggest that clients perform an act of kindness each day.

Manualized Treatment Approaches

Within the past two decades, a number of manualized or highly structured protocols have been constructed that integrate religious/spiritual and psychotherapy principles for various types of clinical problems. For instance, Worthington (1989) has developed *Marriage Counseling: A Christian Approach for Counseling Couple*s and, more recently, *Experiencing Forgiveness: Six Practical Sessions for Becoming a More Forgiving Christian* (Worthington, 2010). Other manualized programs for integration of spiritual issues include *Solace for the Soul: An Evaluation of a Psychospiritual Intervention for Female Survivors of Sexual Abuse* (Murray-Swank, 2003), *Lighting the Way: A Spiritual Journey to Wholeness* (Pargament et al., 2004), and *Spiritual Renewal: A Journal of Faith and Healing* (Richards, Hardman, & Berrett, 2000). Most of these manualized programs are Christian oriented. Treatment usually involves 4 to 10 sessions.

Some nondenominational programs include the *Spiritual Renewal Program*, a 10-session approach for women with eating disorders (Richards et al., 2000), and the *Re-Creating Your Life Program*, a six-session nondenominational group treatment approach for those experiencing a serious medical illness, such as cancer (Cole & Pargament, 1998). The latter program emphasizes spiritual

> ### Inner Reflections
>
> Of the therapy techniques described, which one would you feel most comfortable using in therapy? Why?
>
> Would you ever consider using a manualized treatment book for integrating spirituality in your private practice?

coping strategies, such as obtaining community support, meditation, spiritual visualization, and so on. The overall thrust of the *Re-Creating Your Life Program* is to use religious/spiritual principles of coping to adjust to medical illnesses. Research studies have found that these and other religious/spiritually integrated psychotherapy programs are effective relative to either no treatment or secular treatment approaches (Plante, 2009).

Ethical Issues in Integrating Spirituality and Psychotherapy

Most mental health associations have issued either an ethical code or practice guidelines regarding religious and spiritual issues. The APA Ethical Principles of Psychologists and Code of Conduct (2002) states that psychologists must take into consideration religious issues as they would other types of diversity, such as race, ethnicity, gender, and sexual orientation. More specifically, APA's (2002) ethics code states,

> Psychologists are aware of and respect, cultural, individual, and role differences, including those based on age, gender, gender identity, race, ethnicity, culture, national origin, religion, sexual orientation, disability, language, and socioeconomic status and consider these factors when working with members of such groups. (p. 1063, Principle E)

The American Counseling Association has its Association for Spiritual, Ethical, and Religious Values in Counseling. Members of this association have published a list of spiritual competencies for counseling (Cashwell & Young, 2005). The American Counseling Association's Code of Ethics (2005) states that "counselors do not condone or engage in discrimination based on ... religion/spirituality" (p. 10).

Ethical considerations are in order if therapists are considering integrating religious/spiritual issues into their approach to therapy. First, therapists must stay within their areas of competence.

It is important to remember that therapists are not theologians or trained clergy. Therefore, they must be careful not to overstep the boundaries of their competence. Even when therapists have obtained religious/spiritual training, they must *not* practice outside their area of expertise or promote their religious/spiritual views during therapy. The APA's (2002) Ethical Standard 2.01b, "Boundaries of Competence," states,

> Where scientific or professional knowledge in the discipline of psychology establishes that an understanding of factors associated with ... religion is essential for effective implementation of their services ... psychologists have or obtain the training, experience, consultation, or supervision necessary to ensure the competence of their services, or they make appropriate referrals. (pp. 4–5)

Second, therapists must avoid potential dual relationships, particularly when their clients are members of their own faith tradition. Dual relationships occur when therapists counsel clients who are members of their church, synagogue, or mosque. Although a client might request counseling from a therapist from the same faith, the therapist must be extremely careful not to engage in such relationships.

APA Division 36 (Psychology of Religion) has been developing guidelines for professional practice with spiritual and religious issues. In 2004, an ad hoc committee of APA Division 36 began exploring the development of practice guidelines for working with religious and spiritual issues (Hathaway, 2005). It is important to note that these guidelines are only preliminary and have not been formally adopted by APA Division 36 or by any other authoritative body within APA. Spiritual and religious issues are ubiquitous in the human tradition. A therapist's religious and spiritual bias can affect negatively the therapeutic relationship. Major professional associations have provided some guidelines for what constitutes ethical practice when dealing with religious and spiritual issues in therapy.

RESEARCH AND EVALUATION __
Evidence-Based Spirituality

One might question if there should be a requirement that spiritual approaches to counseling and psychotherapy be evidence based. After all, isn't the evidence spiritual and coming from a higher power? In an article on spirituality and evidence-based practices for addiction, Ringwald (2003) has made the case that spiritual approaches to counseling are evidence based. According to him, most of the 11,000 treatment programs in the United States expose their clients to some form of spirituality (Roman & Blum, 1997). Many programs offer spiritualities such as yoga, Islam, Native American religions, or Christianity. As Ringwald (2003) has stated,

> Publicly, professionals often downplay the spiritual roots of recovery, as if they are embarrassed by this seemingly non-scientific, old-fashioned notion. But take heart and be bold; spiritual interventions are quintessentially evidence-based. Second, these also appeal to many members of disadvantaged or minority groups, which satisfies the demand for cultural competence and diversity. Third, spiritual interventions are low-cost during treatment, and self-sustaining and community-based after treatment. It's the perfect aftercare. Finally, recovery offers the oldest and most established form of a faith-based solution, one that should be studied for lessons by proponents of faith-based services. (p. 32)

There is moderate to strong support for Ringwald's (2003) assertion that spirituality is crucial in the treatment of various forms of addiction. William R. Miller (the father of motivational interviewing) conducted in 1998 a review of studies and found that spiritual or religious involvement reduces the risk of substance abuse and that increased spiritual involvement was correlated with recovery. Miller concluded that a client's spirituality seemed to drive out his or her addiction to alcohol. In addition, Miller found that substance abusers who engaged in the 12 Steps to Islam for recovery were more inclined to remain abstinent than those treated with two other types of nonspiritual therapy (Miller, 1998).

Another review, sponsored by the National Institute on Alcoholism and Alcohol Abuse and the Fetzer Institute, found "strong support" for the protective nature of spirituality and religion (110 studies) and that it was significant with Alcoholics Anonymous involvement (51 studies). Spiritual methods are similar to cognitive-behavioral therapy, which encourages clients to restructure their thoughts and control their emotions. For instance, the Bible says, "For as he thinketh in his heart, so *is* he: Eat and drink, saith he to thee; but his heart *is* not with thee" (Proverbs 23:7). Well before cognitive-behavioral therapy ever existed, the Bible pointed out the importance of a person's thoughts and focused on helping people to change their thoughts.

Spirituality resonates with women and members of various ethnic and racial minority groups. Addiction programs coordinated by and for Native Americans have likewise embraced traditional spiritualities to help clients who have not recovered using mainstream treatment. At Desert Visions, a 24-bed treatment center located on the Gila River reservation that treats chemically dependent Native American youths, addicted youths attend sweat lodges, which detox them (Ringwald, 2003). Moreover, a network of groups called Jewish Alcoholics incorporate spirituality in their treatment. Zaid Imani has written a book *Milati Islami* (The Path of Peace), which reconciles the 12 Steps to Islam and the Qur'an. Other recovered substance abusers find comfort in Buddhism.

Summarizing the importance of spirituality in the treatment of substance abuse, Ringwald (2003) has stated,

> **Inner Reflection**
>
> Let's assume that you open up your own private practice next year. Would you integrate religious/spiritual issues in your practice? Explain.

Spirituality, practiced in thousands of ways and either by individuals or through groups, can provide the long-term help needed to persist in a new life. This is not to argue that society should stop treating addicts, but managed care and other changes have whittled down what's available. Today, many patients are referred directly to support groups, which have reported a surge in such newcomers. In a way, the situation returns the recovery movement to its roots, that of the last resort for those not helped elsewhere. Even in the best scenario, treatment invariably ends. Support groups can be there, down the block, for the long term. There or elsewhere, spirituality can be developed for a lifetime. (p. 36)

CASE ANALYSIS

Justin From a Spiritual Perspective

Justin's therapist had been considering integrating religious/spiritual issues into therapy for the past couple of weeks. The therapist's concern was prompted by something Justin had said when he had asked him how he was coping with the possibility of his being placed in a residential treatment setting. Justin had responded that he had been praying to God to give him just one more chance. It appeared that Justin did not believe that he could do something to keep himself out of the residential setting. He had conveyed the feeling that his situation was "so messed up" that only God could help him now.

Based on Justin's level of spirituality—meaning his belief that God could deliver him if he prayed hard and long enough—the therapist had decided to invite Justin's mother, Sandy, to come to a couple of therapy sessions to discuss the possibility of integrating religious/spiritual issues into therapy. The therapist sought Sandy's permission and support because of the sensitivity of religious/spiritual issues.

Sandy and Justin entered the therapy session looking apprehensive about what might take place during the 50-minute session. The therapist began with small talk about their trip to therapy, but he quickly began to indicate the purpose of inviting Sandy to participate in the day's therapy session. He stated that when he works with young people below the age of 16, he likes to get the parents' permission before delving into religious/spiritual matters. Soon the therapist mentioned what had taken place in an earlier session with Justin. The therapist stated, "At one of our earlier sessions, I asked Justin what he was doing to deal with the pressures associated with the possibility of his being placed in residential treatment. Justin responded, 'I've been doing a whole lot of praying and begging God to give me one more chance.' The fact that Justin mentioned God caused me to think about how his religious/spiritual beliefs and values might be of some assistance to him and to you during these difficult times. So I am wondering if you would like to explore the possibility of integrating religious/spiritual issues into Justin's treatment."

Sandy hesitated but said that it was okay to talk about spiritual issues with Justin. Sandy said, "Sure, it's okay with me as long as you don't try to change our faith. The only problem is that we don't go to church that much anymore. We're all so tired that we sleep in on Sundays. It's the only day that we can sleep late without having to do any chores around the house. We're usually running around on Saturdays."

With Sandy's permission, the therapist began exploring some religious/spiritual feelings that were part of Sandy's family. The therapist began by asking typical spiritual intake questions: "What is your religious-spiritual affiliation?" "How often do you attend religious services?" "How important are spiritual matters to you?" "How important are religious/spiritual issues for you when dealing with serious problems, such as those facing Justin regarding residential placement?"

For the most part, Sandy answered the questions, except when they dealt with the importance of religious/spiritual matters. The therapist asked for Justin's input for each of the "importance of religion to you" questions.

Sandy revealed that at one time religion had been extremely important to her. She had been raised a Methodist with fundamental beliefs in God's existence. It had been a long time since Sandy had thought about her relationship with God. She said that she had drifted away from God and from the Methodist Church, much in the same way that she had drifted from other things that she used to do—like having girlfriends her own age and friends she could visit and talk to about issues facing her family. Those conversations had ended. She still prayed to God, but her prayers were mainly habit. Somehow she had lost her previous belief that God would answer her prayers. It seemed that God did not stop at her family's house anymore. Like Santa Claus, he just moved on to the house next door.

The therapist sensed a note of sadness in Sandy's voice. He could almost hear her unspoken question: "How did I ever lose my relationship with God?" Sensing Sandy's feelings, the therapist reflected, "It's almost like what was supposed to be a positive move from the bad streets of Chicago has gradually changed. You left your husband and Justin's father. Although you took steps to leave and to end that relationship, it still left you feeling the loss of a relationship in your life . . . the loss of a man, someone who could comfort you and help you through things. You left your family of origin behind, your own mother and father. Now, somehow, gradually your relationship with God has slowly deteriorated such that you forget if you said your prayers or not before you hop into bed."

Sandy responded, "Yeah, that's it. It's like you're inside my head, and I'm a bit uncomfortable. I thought that this session was supposed to be about Justin and not about me."

The therapist responded that he understood Sandy's concerns and that he would back off for a moment so that she could catch her breath and thoughts.

Sandy replied, "No, no. It's good that you're getting me to think about these things—my losses, my relationship with God and all. You're making me think about things I haven't thought about in a long time. I usually don't get a chance to talk about my feelings. I'm usually taking care of Justin and his brother."

The therapist reassured Sandy that where she was at that very moment was okay and that he wanted to take a moment to get Justin's reactions to several of the questions. Both Sandy and Justin indicated that religion/spirituality was very important in their lives, even though they did not engage in many spiritual practices or attend church on a regular basis. Both said that religion gave them hope to keep on getting up each day and helped them cope with problems in their lives. The issue was "How could they get back to where they were when they first moved to Utah and used to attend church?" Both believed in the power of prayer, even though they seldom prayed as a family anymore.

The therapist asked Justin and Sandy, "Would you like to pray as a family again?" They both smiled and nodded their heads. "But how?" Sandy asked. "I have enough trouble getting him into bed at a reasonable hour on most school nights."

The therapist responded, "If you could say a prayer for Justin, Sandy, what would that prayer ask?" Without hesitating, Sandy said, "I would pray that he would be safe, that he would not be placed in that residential setting, that he would stop hanging out with the wrong people, and that our relationship would be better, more loving, more caring."

The therapist turned and asked the same question of Justin: "What would your prayer be for your mother? Could you say aloud what you would ask God to do for your mom?"

"I'd ask God," Justin began with a kind of earnestness suggesting that he had thought about some aspect of the question before, "if he would give my mom a life again. . . . That everything wouldn't be so tied up between my brother and me. . . . That we could become a real family instead of people living in the same house together. . . . That we would really love and care about each other. . . . And for myself, I'd ask God to give me a second chance and not to send me to residential treatment."

(Continued)

(Continued)

Struck by the sincerity of both Justin and Sandy, the therapist asked Sandy if she would hold hands with Justin and say her prayer for him to God aloud. Sandy began praying in the therapy session, and as she did, tears rolled down her cheeks. Suddenly, she got up from her chair and hugged Justin and said: "I love you, Justin. I just don't show it all the time."

The therapist asked Justin if he would say aloud his prayer to God about his mother. As he began to ask God to bring happiness into his mother's life, he, too, began to cry.

The therapist asked Justin, "What are those tears saying, Justin?"

"I dunno," Justin responded. "I guess they're saying I love her too. Things just get so crazy at our house. Everybody's shouting and yelling. Everybody's angry. It's hard to show love when things are like that at home."

The therapist felt that he had made a real breakthrough in Justin and Sandy's relationship. They had rediscovered their love for each other in their prayers to God. The therapist gave two assignments, one for Sandy and Justin to complete together and the other for Justin to work on alone. The latter would be Justin's own special project. The therapist asked Justin and Sandy to begin working on a spiritual genogram that they would complete over the next couple of weeks. First, they would trace the family's religious/spiritual affiliations over both sides of the family for three generations. For instance, they would go back as far as Sandy's grandmother and indicate her religion/spirituality, then Sandy's mother's religious affiliation, and finally Sandy's affiliation. The same procedures would be used for Justin's father's side of the family.

Justin was asked to make a spiritual life map using his outstanding artistic skills. He could draw pictures representing his spiritual journey as a young child. For instance, "What is his earliest memory of God? What did God look like to him? Was God kind, gentle, or what?" Justin was informed that he could cut out pictures from magazines that symbolized the kind of relationship he had with God and place these pictures on his spiritual life map.

The therapist ended the session by recommending that Justin and Sandy attend church on Sunday instead of sleeping in and that they go up to the pastor/minister and shake hands and reacquaint themselves with the minister. The goal of this assignment was to help Justin and Sandy reconnect with a spiritual community and develop a sense of belonging by giving their names and shaking hands. The therapist also asked the two to see if the church offered any special programs for Sandy (such as a single-mothers ministry) and for Justin (preteen or artistic ministry). When the therapist asked Justin and Sandy what went right in therapy today, both mentioned that for the first time in a long time they really felt their love for each other. They liked sharing their prayers, and both indicated that they would like to establish a way of praying together at home. "It's hard to be angry with my mother if I am praying to God for her," Justin said as he readied himself to leave the therapy session.

SUMMARY

This chapter examined ways in which a therapist might integrate religious/spiritual issues into psychotherapy. Including religious/spiritual issues in psychotherapy rounds out the multicultural perspective in therapy. National data on religious/spirituality issues were reviewed. Most of the people in the United States indicate that they are religious/spiritual. There is, however, a large chasm between clients who are very religious/spiritual and psychologists, who are less religious/spiritual. This disconnect between therapists and clients on the issue of religion/spirituality affects what is discussed in the therapeutic session.

Assessment of religious/spiritual issues was examined from a number of perspectives. For instance, the contents of a basic intake questionnaire were presented. Questions for clinical interviewing of clients for religious/spiritual issues were also provided. Brief summaries of instruments to assess these dimensions were given.

A number of spiritual therapy techniques were discussed, including spiritual journaling, spiritual autobiographies, spiritual life maps, and exceptional human experience journaling. Ethical considerations and guidelines for practice in integrating religious/spiritual issues into therapy were also presented.

SUPPLEMENTAL AIDS _____

Discussion Questions

Spirituality can be defined as that which gives meaning and purpose in life to people.

Although it can be achieved through participation in an organized religion, it also can be much broader than that. How do you define spirituality? How do the norms of your cultural or ethnic group affect your views on spirituality?

1. How have you used spirituality to cope with your problems?

2. We have all been hurt or slighted by another person, and even hurt by them. Have you ever forgiven another person for hurting or slighting you? What did you experience when you forgave that person?

3. Gratitude is an important element in viewing life. For what are you grateful in your life? Have you ever felt grateful for a negative event, such as an illness in your life? Explain.

4. Hope is important for people to go on with life. Yet during difficult times, people sometimes lose their hope. How has your own spirituality worked to keep hope alive in your life during difficult times? How has spirituality brought happiness into your life?

Glossary of Key Terms

religion   May be defined as "the organizational and community structure of wisdom traditions that generally include sacred scriptures or religious writings, an articulated doctrine of belief structure that describes the faith community's values and beliefs, and an identified leader or spiritual model to emulate" (Plante, 2009, p. 4).

spirituality   May be defined as a "personal or group search for the sacred. Religiousness is defined as a personal or group search for the sacred that unfolds within a traditional sacred context" (Zinnbauer & Pargament, 2005, p. 35). A person's spirituality includes his or her "values, beliefs, mission, awareness, subjectivity, experience, sense of purpose and direction, and a kind of striving toward something greater than oneself. It may or may not include a deity" (Frame, 2003, p. 3).

stages of faith   Developed by Professor James W. Fowler at the Chandler School of Theology. Fowler proposed six stages of faith development that are believed to take place across the life span.

Website Materials

Additional exercises, journals, annotated bibliography, and more are available on the open-access website at https://study.sagepub.com/jonessmith2e.

CHAPTER 18

Strengths-Based Therapy

Success is achieved by developing our strengths, not by eliminating our weaknesses.

—Marilyn vos Savant, billed as the person with the highest IQ (228) in the world

People develop strengths as part of their driving force to meet basic psychological needs, such as belonging and affiliation, competency, feeling safe, autonomy, and/or finding meaning and purpose in life.

—Richard M. Ryan and Edward L. Deci (2000)

The acid test for a strength is if you can fathom yourself doing it repeatedly, happily, and successfully.

—Marcus Buckingham and Donald O. Clifton

What does not kill me makes me stronger.

—Johann Wolfgang von Goethe

BRIEF OVERVIEW

Over the past couple of decades, psychology and social work have been moving toward a strengths perspective in both philosophy and in clinical practice (Aspinwall & Staudinger, 2003; Bingham & Saponaro, 2003; Clark, 1999; Desetta & Wolin, 2000; Epstein, 1998; Gelso & Woodhouse, 2004; Lopez & Snyder, 2003; Maton, Schellenback, Leadbetter, & Solarz, 2004; Saleebey, 1992, 1996, 2001; Seligman, 1998, 1999; Smith, 2006a; Snyder, 2000; Snyder & Lopez, 2002; Walsh, 2004). In 1998, Martin Seligman, the former president of the American Psychological Association, reminded psychologists that our field has become one sided and enamored of the dark side of human existence. He stated, "Psychology is not just the study of weakness and damage; it is also the study of strengths and virtue. Treatment is not just fixing what is broken; it is nurturing what is best within ourselves" (Seligman, 1999, p. 1).

Several professions and movements have formed the foundation for strengths-based therapy counseling psychology, with its critical role in helping create multicultural guidelines and competencies, prevention and positive psychology movements, social work and the writings of Dennis

Saleebey, solution-focused therapy, and the narrative movement.

The various contributory streams (positive psychology, social work, narrative therapy, etc.) led to the gradual development of Elsie J. Smith's (author of this text) core philosophical and theoretical concepts for the strengths-based counseling. In January 2006, *The Counseling Psychologist* published the article, "The Strengths-Based Counseling Model." The following brief sections examine the various contributions to the **strength perspective**. It should be pointed out that although there are a number of antecedents to the strengths perspective in therapy, social work has assumed a major role in presenting some of the key articles in this school of thought. In a benchmark article, Weick, Rapp, Sullivan, and Kisthardt (1989) coined the term *strengths perspective*. Dennis Saleebey (1992) identified the basic assumptions of the strengths perspective for social workers, and he challenged clinicians to change how they worked with clients so that they focused on learning how the individual has survived. Social workers have assumed a leadership role in identifying family strengths and in working with youth who face a number of challenges in life. This author acknowledges that her current strengths-based therapy stands on the foundation built by Saleebey (1992), Rapp (2008), and others in the social work profession. Those early contributors in the social work profession subscribed to what Saleebey called the strengths perspective rather than a theory of strengths.

A social work model that merits attention is the strengths-based case management model (social work) developed by Rapp and Goscha (2006). Used mainly in social work, strengths-base case management focuses on an individual's strengths with three other notions: (1) promoting the use of informal supportive networks, (2) offering assertive community involvement by case managers, and (3) highlighting the relationship between the client and the case manager. Strengths-based case management has been implemented in a variety of fields, such as substance abuse and outpatient mental health (Rapp, 2008).

The Jones-Smith (2014) approach to strengths-based therapy exists side by side with its cousin, positive psychology. Although the two are related, they are not the same. An important difference between the two is that there does not currently exist a theory of positive psychotherapy, even though many articles and a number of books have been written on positive psychology (Compton & Hoffman, 2012; Seligman, 2004; Snyder, Lopez, & Teramoto, 2010). Positive psychology focuses on the pursuit of happiness and flourishing (Seligman, 2004). Based on the work of Seligman (2004), positive psychology puts character strengths at center stage in its formulations. For this and other reasons, positive psychology is conceptualized as part of the wellness approach. Although concepts from positive psychology can relate to individuals from varied socioeconomic, ethnic, and cultural backgrounds, it has largely been used with people from the middle-class White. Moreover, positive psychology does not present a model of how strengths are developed within a person; it does not describe how strengths are involved in the development of healthy and maladaptive behavior and how a therapist might use a client's strengths during the therapeutic process. Notwithstanding these observations, positive psychology has made important discoveries involving the role of positive emotions in the broaden-and-build theory of positive emotions discussed later on in this chapter (Fredrickson, 2001).

Strengths-based therapy acknowledges the fact that studies in positive psychology are incorporated and made a part of its theoretical approach. Whereas positive psychology focuses on happiness and flourishing, strengths-based therapy is designed as a therapeutic approach for individuals' dealing with very real psychological difficulties and challenges in life. Both approaches are valuable for different reasons. Strengths-based therapy developed by this author is intended for the struggling young kid in distressed urban areas as well as for the youth living in well-manicured suburban communities—for the drug addict, as well as for the corporate executive who may be endeavoring to find real, honest meaning in his or her life. Moreover, the strengths-based therapy presented in this chapter has outlined stages or phases of therapeutic treatment and therapeutic techniques. The therapy applies to individuals in treatment as well as for families (family strengths) that may be experiencing problems. In the author's strengths-based therapy book (Jones-Smith, 2014), individual chapters deal with using a strengths-based approach with families, juvenile offenders, those suffering from alcohol and other drug addictions (recovery strengths), and members of the aging population. The Jones-Smith strengths-based therapy espouses a broader conceptualization of strengths other than just character strengths. It asserts that strengths are brain based and nurtured by significant relationships. A dominant theme is that only a person's strengths (inner and outer) will help him or her deal with psychological challenges. Most therapeutic approaches subscribed to the view that clients' strengths should be used during therapy (like "apple pie and motherhood"); yet most have not developed structured ways to achieve this goal. Focusing on a client's strengths should not be an add-on after a therapist has spent most of the therapy hour emphasizing what's wrong with the client.

MAJOR CONTRIBUTOR: ELSIE JONES-SMITH

Elsie Jones-Smith

Find your strengths and act on them with focused attention, and the world will beat a path to you.

Life is a matter of acting intentionally on your strengths and managing your weaknesses so that they don't trip you up.

—Elsie Jones-Smith

The strengths-based therapy presented in this chapter is based on the work of Elsie Jones-Smith. For a more in-depth description of the therapy, the reader is referred to Dr. Jones-Smith's recent book, *Strengths-Based Therapy: Connecting Theory, Practice and Skills* (2014). Dr. Jones-Smith is a licensed clinical psychologist, therapist educator, and president of the Strength-Based Institute, which provides consultation to organizations dealing with youth suffering from problems including drug and alcohol addiction. She is a fellow of two divisions of the American Psychological Association, Society of Counseling Psychology, and the division on Ethnic Minority Issues. She has been a professor at Temple University, Michigan State University, University of Buffalo, and Boston University. Dr. Jones-Smith has served on numerous editorial boards, including the *Journal of Counseling Psychology*, *The Counseling Psychologist*, and *Therapist Education and Supervision*. She served 18 years as an education consultant for violence prevention in New York schools.

She holds dual Ph.D. degrees—in clinical psychology and in counselor education—and she is a board-certified diplomate of the American Board of Professional Psychology. Recent books by this author include *Strengths-Based Therapy: Connecting Theory, Practice and Skills* (2014), *Spotlighting the Strengths of Every Single Student* (2011), and *Nurturing Nonviolent Children* (2008). Two of her articles have been presented as major contributions to the field of psychology by *The Counseling Psychologist*: "The Strength-Based Counseling Model" (2006a) and "Ethnic Minorities: Life Stress, Social Support, and Mental Health Issues" (1985). She has published extensively in the area of working with culturally diverse clients.

Dr. Smith's involvement with searching for a strengths-based approach began during the late 1980s when she focused on identifying the strengths of ethnic minority students. Over the past two decades (1990–2010), she has sought to expand her strengths-based therapy of working with at-risk youth to counseling individuals across the life span—from children to aging adults. Strengths-based therapy is the first attempt by a clinician or a researcher to provide an integrative theory of strengths.

KEY CONCEPTS

The various contributory streams (positive psychology, social work, narrative therapy, etc.) led to the gradual emergence of core philosophical and theoretical concepts for strengths-based counseling. The following section develops a definition of strength and the contextual process in which strengths develop; it also discusses strength characteristics.

Definition of Strength

Aspinwall and Staudinger (2003) have noted the difficulties involved in defining human strength. According to these researchers, one reason why psychology was entrenched in the predominant medical model of repair and healing was that defining the desired or adaptive direction of change would be easier if the goal of such a change were to return to a prior state of normality. **Strength** may be defined as that which helps a person cope with life or that which makes life more fulfilling for oneself and others. Strengths are not fixed personality traits; instead, they develop from a dynamic, contextual process rooted deeply in one's culture. Our strengths are the lenses we use to process information, to experience others, to view time and structure, to accommodate or to make change in our lives, and to communicate with others.

Clifton and Anderson (2002) have defined a strength as specific qualities that enable and empower an individual to do certain things quite well. Following is a list of strength characteristics.

Strength Characteristics

- You must be able to do it consistently.
- You must derive some intrinsic pleasure from the strength activity.
- Strengths consist of talents, knowledge, and skills.
- Knowledge consists of the facts and lessons learned.
- You excel only by maximizing your strengths, never by fixing your weaknesses.

Culturally Bound Strengths. Strengths are almost inevitably culturally expressed. Characteristics regarded as strengths in one culture may be viewed as weaknesses in another culture (Smith, 1985). Ethnic groups may be said to have particular **cultural strengths** (Chang, 2001). A strength for one culture may be its emphasis on the family, whereas the strength of another culture may be its ability to save and engage in profitable commerce. The importance of strengths differs among cultures. For example, in cultures labeled as individualistic, autonomy is highly valued (Smith, 1985). Conversely, in cultures described as collectivist, relational skills may be emphasized more. Helping professionals are faced with the challenge of learning and understanding both individual and cultural strengths so that they can address the needs of diverse clients.

Contextually Based Strengths. Human strengths have contextual dependencies (Aspinwall & Staudinger, 2003) as they involve interaction with a material environment or with human contexts (Staudinger, Marsiske, & Baltes, 1996; Staudinger & Pasupathi, 2000). Strengths are developed within a given situation containing certain contextual characteristics that may either promote or retard the human strength. During war, for example, certain character strengths, such as courage or cowardice, may be exemplified. Therapists must consider the contextual situation confronting clients. A client's behavior might be considered a strength in one setting and a liability in a different social context. For instance, studies have found that clients who evidence internal control beliefs and problem-focused coping may become highly dysfunctional under conditions of high constraints, such as poor health (Staudinger, Freund, Linden, & Maas, 1999). Furthermore, in some non-Western cultures (Chang, 2001), pessimism is adaptive rather than dysfunctional because it increases active problem solving.

Developmental and Life Span–Oriented Strengths. Strengths are developmental in that they require a certain level of cognitive, physical, and emotional maturity or experiential development (Lyons, Uziel-Miller, Reyes, & Sokol, 2000; Masten & Reed, 2002). Strengths are age related because young children's actions cannot be interpreted in terms of strengths such as courage (Benson, 1997). Strengths are both malleable and changeable. They can be learned or taught. An individual's strengths may unfold or blossom over his or her life span (Benson, Galbraith, & Espeland, 1995). Strengths are also incremental, so that one strength provides the foundation for achieving another.

Adaptability and Functionality. A person's ability to apply as many different resources and skills as necessary to solve a problem or to achieve a goal may be considered a human strength. Charles Darwin's (1859/1995) work on the origin of species first highlighted the importance of a person's ability to adapt to change. Darwin stated that individuals' ability to adapt to change equals their chances of survival. Strengths may be conceptualized as part of the human adaptational system (Masten & Reed, 2002). From this perspective, people are biologically prepared to develop strengths (Saleebey, 2001). Researchers have characterized human strengths as critical survival skills that allow people to right themselves (Masten & Coatsworth, 1998). Strength develops as individuals move toward external adaptation. Humans are self-righting organisms engaged in an ongoing adaptation to the environment (Bronfenbrenner, 1974; Masten &

Coatsworth, 1998). More recently, researchers have begun to study the critical significance of a person's ability to apply in a flexible manner as many different resources and skills as required to solve a problem or to work toward a goal (Staudinger et al., 1999; Staudinger & Pasupathi, 2000).

Normative Quality and Enabling Environments. Strengths also have a normative quality because they exist in comparison with other, often less developed, states. For example, the strength of courage exists in contrast to cowardice. Each society develops norms for what are considered human strengths. Individuals' violations of strength norms may cause societal sanctioning and rebuke. Moreover, each culture or environment contains enabling and limiting conditions that assist or thwart individuals in their progress along the strength hierarchy (Smith, 1985). Social class structures may prevent individuals from achieving particular strengths (McCubbin, McCubbin, & Thompson, 1993). Each society tends to establish situations, events, or structures to help individuals move from one strength level to another. Cultures provide role models and parables that indicate the desired strength (e.g., Jackie Robinson—patience and skill; George Washington—truth and honesty).

Each Environment Has Attributes That Affect Well-Being. Some social, cultural, economic, and political environments exert a negative effect on a person's strength development, while others have a positive influence. Studies have found that some environments have restorative qualities (a sense of getting away), which promote relaxation and alleviate stress (Kaplan, 1995; Korpela & Hartig, 1996). Other environments or places are imbued with symbolic meanings related to an individual's personal or group identity (Csikszentmihalyi & Rochberg-Halton, 1981). Such shared meanings of place historically represent the continuity of people's attachments to particular places and support their feelings of belonging to an ethnic group, thereby leading to a sense of "shared placed identity" (Proshansky, Fabian, & Kaminoff, 1983).

Poverty Environments Tend to Delimit the Strength of Individuals and Entire Communities. Hence, strength development is a process influenced by heredity, environment, and an interaction of these two forces. The social and economic attributes of environments can build strength if they have positive effects on individuals' lives.

Transcendence. Human strengths can also have qualities of transcendence, as they can be used to resist a force or attack, whether mental or physical (Aspinwall, 2001). Many studies on resilience emphasize the importance of a person's ability to transcend life circumstances. Strengths help one transcend and improve personal (e.g., being physically handicapped or learning disabled) and societal (e.g., living in poverty or having parents with substance addiction or mental illness) circumstances (Affleck & Tennen, 1996). Strengths may develop from a need to find meaning and purpose in our lives so that we seek people, places, and transformational experiences that help us feel a sense of connectedness with the world.

Polarities. Strengths often develop from polarities. Human existence is characterized by polarities such as happiness/sorrow, autonomy/dependency, and health/sickness (Riegel, 1976). Human strengths may develop from the coactivation of negative and positive human states. Youth, for instance, is a time of physical prowess; thus, young individuals work hard to compete athletically, but they are not typically wise. A shift in polarity occurs as we age, so that age is associated with a loss in physical functioning but a gain in wisdom. Developmental losses produce compensatory efforts that cause strengths.

Strength Estrangement

Strength estrangement may be defined as the lack of awareness of one's talents and strengths; or, if such awareness exists, the lack of direction (or floundering) in using one's strengths to achieve desired goals or to bring about happiness. It is also defined as an individual's alienation from his natural talents such that a disruption of the bond between these talents and the individual takes place. One goal of counseling is to help individuals locate the source of the strength alienation and help them restore it to a desired place in their lives to deal effectively with everyday life issues. One consequence of strength estrangement is that some people experience a state of unspecified unhappiness. They may ask themselves, "Why am I unhappy? I've got everything going for myself." Addiction to chemical substances can cause strength estrangement.

Managing Weaknesses

The mantra for strength development is to promote strengths and **manage weaknesses** that may sabotage our strengths. The goal is to learn how to use one's strengths to manage one's weaknesses. The strengths perspective maintains that spending most of one's time in one's area of **weakness** will only improve one's weakness to a level of average (Buckingham, 2007). It will not produce excellence. This position is supported by research conducted by the Gallup Organization, which conducted more than 30 years of research on top achievers. The highest achievers

- spend most of their time in their areas of strength,
- focus on developing and applying their strengths and managing their weaknesses,

---

Inner Reflections

Strength Indicators

Notice your yearnings.

What do you enjoy doing the most?

Describe a successful day in your life.

Describe key achievements in your life.

Look for rapid learning—what comes easily?

Watch for "strength flow" or a time you achieved excellence without conscious thought or trying hard to do so.

- use strengths to overcome obstacles,
- invent ways of capitalizing on their strengths in new situations, and
- have learned to partner with someone to tackle weaknesses.

Focusing on weaknesses rather than managing them reduces the effectiveness of our real strengths. Managing our weaknesses includes using our strengths to develop new ways of solving problems, partnering with others, delegating to others, learning the skills and/or knowledge required, and developing new techniques to use our strengths in positive ways.

We often focus on our weaknesses, as if fixing what is weak is actually going to help us become excellent. Instead of trying to make our weaknesses our strengths, we should bring the area of weakness to **functional competence**. We might not be good in math or science; however, we can bring our skills in these areas up to a level of functional competence. The concept of functional competence is similar to Winnicott's notion of the "good-enough mother" (Winnicott, 1953).

Theory of Strengths Development

Currently, there is no existing theory of strengths development. This section contains a modest proposal for such a possible theory. Strengths-based development is an emerging area that traces its roots to research in a number of areas including brain development theory, multiple intelligences (Gardner, 1983, 2000), positive psychology (Seligman, 1998, 1999), neuroscience (LeDoux, 2003), and the recent studies on strengths leadership and management (Buckingham & Clifton, 2001).

The Brain and Strength Development. Children learn and develop strengths in the areas that produce the most synaptic connections in the brain. This situation occurs because the brain is the biological organ of learning. It contains the basis of mental processes that underlie mental functioning, often referred to as thought or mind. Learning is a

function of the effectiveness of synapses to produce signals and initiate new signals along connecting neurons (Hinton, 1992). As the brain learns and masters new skills or content, it needs less energy. Moreover, the *brain looks for patterns* so that it does not have to work as hard when similar information is presented to it. Patterns constitute one of the brain's primary ways to process new information. A young person or an adult looks for information it already knows to make new information fit. As a child ages, the brain cells begin to specialize to complete different tasks. The brain eliminates a system or a neuron path if a particular skill or function is not used.

Individuals develop talents and strengths as a result of the repeated formation of synaptic connections in neural networks. As a child ages, stronger synapses within the network of brain connections continue to strengthen, whereas weaker connections tend to wither. After a young person reaches about age 15, his or her unique network of synaptic brain connections remain fairly stable and do not change. This scientific discovery about the brain provides scientific evidence for the belief that talents, recurring patterns of thoughts, feelings, or behavior do not change significantly over time.

The brain operates on a "use it or lose it" principle, meaning only those neural connections and neural pathways that are frequently activated are retained. Other brain connections that are not used consistently are pruned or discarded, thereby enabling the active connections to become stronger. According to Dr. Harry Chugani (1998), professor of pediatrics, neurology, and radiology at Wayne State University School of Medicine, the synaptic connections in the brain that are the most used become the strongest. Dr. Chugani has stated that the "road with the most traffic get widened. The ones that are rarely used fall into disrepair" (Coffman & Gonzalez-Molina, 2003, p. 21).

As pruning increases after 10 years of age, those synapses that have been reinforced because of repeated experience tend to become permanent. Conversely, the synapses that were not used often enough in the early years tend to become eliminated. The types of experiences children have influence how their brains will be wired as adults and accordingly what their talents, skills, and strengths will be.

During Stage 1, critical synaptic connections are formed within the brain. These connections are influenced highly by one's genetics. Stage 2 signals the significant influence of one's environment outside the womb. It consists of sensory inputs and interactions with one's parents, siblings, and family members. The infant makes repeated use of some synaptic connections. Some strengths grow stronger as we age (wisdom), while other strengths grow weaker, such as our physical strengths. Stage 3 entails repetition or repeated use of these synaptic connections to create neural pathways and networks, which provide hints or evidence of the child's strengths. Children who use certain neural networks or synaptic connections repeatedly develop knowledge and skills in those areas. Such knowledge and skills may later mature into talents and strengths.

Relational Component of Strength Development.

Although strength development is a process that is first begun in the brain, it is later continued as one interacts with caregivers and the environment. Strength development takes place most easily within the context of a trusted relationship where we express our intentions to grow in a particular area. For instance, a young girl tells her father that she wants to become an artist. The father buys his daughter numerous art supplies, comments positively on her paintings, and takes her to art shows. He arranges for art lessons and a mentor in the type of paintings that she likes painting the most. The girl's artwork becomes important to and a source of pride for both her and her father. Strength development is almost inevitable. Someone, somewhere along the line, encourages the development of the strength, expresses support for it, and assists the person while he or she is in the process of improving and perfecting the strength.

More often than not, our ability to develop our strengths lies in our perceived social support or relational support for our strengths. Parents can provide emotional and instrumental support for the development of their children's strengths. A young boy living in the inner city tested very high on a musical ability test. He was offered free piano lessons for a year, but his parents could not afford to buy a piano. After a year or so practicing on the school's piano, he gave up his goal to learn how to play the piano. Relational support provides positive reinforcement for the development of our strengths.

Differences in People's Strengths.

People differ in five dimensions of strengths: (1) their specific strengths or combinations of strengths, (2) the relative intensity of their strengths, (3) their unique combinations of strength, (4) the degree to which they have developed their strengths, and (5) the extent to which they apply their strengths to achieve their goals or to find life satisfaction (Clifton & Anderson, 2002).

Strength Awareness and Attention.

Strength development deals with the issue of attention and what we choose to focus on. As information-processing individuals, we choose what we will attend to. We can choose to focus on our strengths or our weaknesses. Oftentimes, what we focus on is guided by significant others in our environment, especially our parents. Individuals must come to recognize their talents and the value that accrues to them as they engage in activities involving their strengths. When people gain awareness of their strengths, some make a conscious effort to seek out opportunities to use them. Awareness of one's strengths usually is based on our own evaluation of our performance of certain activities or feedback that we gain from those in our inner and outer circles—parents, friends, and teachers. As people gain strength awareness, they sometimes share information about their strengths with family members, friends, classmates, or coworkers. To improve on their strengths, individuals may add relevant practice, knowledge, and other skills.

Strength development affects our relationships with others because it increases both our own self-awareness as well as our awareness of others. As we become aware of our strengths, we also begin to notice the strengths that others have. We all go through a strengths progression, which entails self-awareness of strengths, awareness of others' strengths, and self-management of our strengths.

Strengths Development and Self Theory. Strengths development theory also draws from self theory. Strengths are organized into our views of self. There is an interaction between your beliefs about your strengths and your views of the self. Self theory is the theory of attention. What distinguishes people is where their talents lie and to what extent their talents are nourished and viewed as meaningful as they grow up. Those young people who have had the good fortune to be provided with opportunities to express their talents and strengths in meaningful ways will grow up to be happy, productive adults. Notice how happy you are when you have been given an opportunity to show your strengths at work or how happy your children are when you have given them a chance to shine. As Mark Katz (1997) stated in his book, *On Playing a Poor Hand Well*:

> Being able to showcase our talents and to have them valued by important people in our lives helps us define our identities around that which we do best. This is how people develop a sense of mastery. The reverse is true as well. If you spend a disproportionate amount of your life doing things that you do poorly, and do these things around important people who see you only in this light, you're apt to define yourself in harsh and devaluing ways. (p. 76)

As young people engage in strength awareness, their feelings about themselves become more positive. They may feel proud of themselves and come to value themselves as worthwhile. Positive strength awareness promotes a positive self-concept and facilitates feelings of self-efficacy in the strength area (Buckingham & Clifton, 2001).

Cognitive Component of Strength Development. Strength development also has a cognitive component, in that we develop cognitive **strength schema** about that which we do well. Cognitive schema function as organizers of meaning regarding all aspects of our worldview, including our relational views toward self, our strengths, others, and the world in general. All of us develop strength and weakness cognitive schema that guide our actions. Cognitive schema, when triggered, can generate automatic thoughts, strong affect, and behavioral tendencies. Some people fear that they have no real strengths, and therefore, they become defensive when therapists try to help them discover their strengths. Others have been hurt and put down for their strengths by people who felt threatened by those strengths.

Therapists need to understand the cognitive schema that clients have developed about their strengths and their weaknesses. What automatic thoughts come to the forefront when a client thinks about his or her strengths and weaknesses? Is there pain or pleasure in the client's cognitive strength schema?

Capitalizing on Our Strengths. Our strengths usually lead to a flood of positive emotions. Research by Fredrickson (2001) has reported that positive emotions are worth cultivating because they help individuals achieve psychological growth and improved well-being over time. Positive emotions function as internal signals for a person to approach or continue an activity. Based on a large body of research on positive emotions, Fredrickson has offered the broaden-and-build theory, which states that "certain discrete positive emotions—including joy, interest, contentment, pride, and love—although phenomenologically distinct, all share the ability to broaden people's momentary thought–action repertoires and build their enduring personal resources, ranging from physical and intellectual resources to social and psychological resources" (p. 219). Fredrickson found that positive emotions can undo lingering negative emotions (e.g., depression). Positive emotions can also fuel individuals' psychological resiliency. "Individuals who experienced more positive emotions than others became more resilient to adversity over time, as indexed by increases in broad-minded coping. In turn, these enhanced coping skills predicted increased positive emotions over time" (p. 224).

Fredrickson (2001) found that although positive emotions were fleeting, they were the vehicle for individual growth and social connection: "By building people's personal and social resources, position emotions transform people for the better, giving them better lives in the future" (p. 224). The point of citing Fredrickson's research on positive emotions and her broaden-and-build theory is that strengths produce positive emotions in clients. Watch the face of your child, partner, or friend when you talk about their strengths as opposed to their weaknesses. Focusing on clients' strengths produces a flood of positive client emotions, which will lead to their overall better psychological functioning. This situation occurs even when the therapist's focus on client's strengths is fleeting. Based on Fredrickson's research findings, when a clinician uses a strengths approach to therapy, clients broaden and build to a higher level of functioning. They are not only more resilient to stress and adversity but also "bump" up to a higher level of psychological functioning.

Lifelong and Intentional Process. Strength development is a lifelong process that involves a dynamic interplay of a number of forces, including neural pathway development, instruction, observational learning, and culture. Strengths reflect individuals' dominant pattern of thought and feeling that they use in a productive manner to achieve their goals. It involves applying one's strengths rather than fixing one's weaknesses.

Strength development involves a process of self-examination, reflection, and self-discovery. To this extent, it is almost invariably focused and intentional in nature. To really know your strengths, you have to look inward, become introspective, and be deeply honest with yourself about who you are.

Strength development is an **intentional process**. It involves putting intentional energy into one of your strongest areas. To achieve the best results, choose one strength that you want to develop and then create a strategy to enhance it. For instance, a young boy who loves playing the drums chooses to practice 2 hours a day to get better. Larry Bird once said that to make a clutch basketball shot that won the game in the last few seconds, he had to practice shooting that shot a thousand times during that week. For strengths to truly exist, you must apply them in action; otherwise, you are talking about potential rather than strengths. Strengths involve practice, repetition, and more practice.

Strengths Development States

Human strengths development is a process that involves several states: (a) brain and neurological development of strong synapses related to a person's talents, (b) identification of one's talent(s) or things that one does with excellence, (c) naming and claiming one's talents as points of strength, (d) incorporation of talent and strengths into one's concept, (e) acquiring of necessary knowledge and skills to perfect one's strengths, (f) practice and repetition of already strong neurological synapses, and (g) application of strengths in several different settings.

Categories of Strength

The core concepts of strengths-based counseling provide the foundation for building strength categories and a rationale for counseling intervention. Categories of strengths suggest several attributes that contribute to positive or negative social and emotional functioning (Aspinwall & Staudinger, 2003). Strength categories are needed because they help the clinician identify a client's positive attributes, focus on what is going right in a person's life, and place such strengths within an overall framework of the client's psychological and social functioning (Peterson & Seligman, 2003). Moreover, once the characteristics of strength are understood, psychologists can better clarify the role of client strengths in psychotherapy (Peterson & Seligman, 2004).

Scholars are in the initial stage of defining, isolating, and categorizing the human strengths that cut across cultures. Ten categories of strengths that have emerged from the literature are described briefly next. These categories are presented to assist psychologists in working with clients and helping them. They are by no means exhaustive, and psychologists are encouraged to develop a universal classification of strengths that will apply in all cultures. The 10 strength categories are (1) wisdom, (2) emotional strengths, (3) character strengths (e.g., honesty, discipline, and courage), (4) creative strengths, (5) relational and nurturing strength, (6) educational strengths, (7) analytical and cognitive strengths, (8) economic and financial strengths, (9) social support strengths, and (10) survival strengths. Survival strengths help people provide for their basic physiological and safety needs, and survival often refers to health status (Masten & Coatsworth, 1998; Masten & Reed, 2002).

Individuals may possess strengths in several categories simultaneously. Few individuals possess strengths in all categories, simply because each individual has limitations and weaknesses. Researchers theorize that several factors may cause individuals to move from one strength category to another, including gender, life developmental stage, life experiences, exposure to and survival of adversity, and the ability to reflect on life experiences.

Individuals live in either strength-building or strength-limiting environments. Strength-building environments produce individuals who have a high sense of self-efficacy and self-esteem, while strength-limiting environments tend to produce individuals who have lower levels of self-efficacy and self-esteem. Risk factors interact with protective life factors, and the individual's successful maneuvering or negotiation of risk factors may lead to his or her development of resilience. Resilience, then, is a process of strength development.

Theoretical Framework for Strengths-Based Therapy

Strengths-based therapy constitutes a theoretical integration of several theories blended to produce a conceptual framework that synthesizes the best of several psychotherapy conceptual frameworks. Culled from a review of the literature on the strengths perspective, prevention movement, current positive psychology movement,

need and drive theory, and logotherapy (Aspinwall, 2001; Frankl, 1963; Maslow, 1954, 1971; Seligman, 1998, 1999), the theory represents an integrative approach that blends different theories, movements (positive psychology, prevention, resilience theory, and hope theory), and techniques that build client strength within a multicultural framework.

Strengths-based therapy also builds its foundation on the growing body of resilience literature and research. *Resilience* is defined as the process of struggling with hardship, characterized by the individual's accumulation of small successes that occur with intermittent failures, setbacks, and disappointments (Desetta & Wolin, 2000; Wolin & Wolin, 1993). Resiliency research establishes that individuals possess an innate capacity for bouncing back. Resiliency provides the process by which strength is developed. Moreover, a resiliency perspective maintains that an adaptational quality of resilience strengths exists. Resilience is not a fixed trait; it is instead a dynamic, contextual process developed as a result of the interactions between individuals and their environments.

Strengths-based therapy also draws on need theories. Maslow's (1954) need hierarchy provides part of the theoretical explanation for human motivation to build and express strengths. Maslow (1954, 1971) posited a hierarchy of needs based on two groupings: (1) deficiency needs and (2) growth needs.

Updating Maslow's (1954, 1971) theory, Deci and Ryan (2000) suggested three needs that are not necessarily ordered: (1) the need for autonomy, (2) the need for competence, and (3) the need for relatedness. By way of comparison, strengths-based theory proposes that individuals have an innate need to recognize their strengths. Their need to recognize strengths, however, is not necessarily premised on the complete satisfaction of their lower-ordered safety needs. Young people who are given opportunities for positive ways to develop their strengths have different life experiences than those who are not given such opportunities. The needs for competence and relatedness described by Deci and Ryan are partly addressed in the competency stage of strengths-based therapy.

People develop strengths as part of their driving force to meet basic psychological needs, such as belonging and affiliation, competency, feeling safe, autonomy, and/or finding meaning and purpose in life (Bandura, 1997; Baumeister & Leary, 1995; Maslow, 1954; Ryan & Deci, 2000). Our psychological need to feel competent motivates us to develop our cognitive, problem-solving strengths. Our need to find meaning in our lives motivates us to seek other people, places, and transformational experiences that give a sense of purpose. Our nurturing and **relational strengths** are developed out of our psychological need for belonging and out of our need to relate to and to connect with others (Maslow, 1971).

In addition, Frankl's (1963) logotherapy forms a cornerstone for strengths-based therapy, with its emphasis on the search to find meaning out of adversity. Greenstein and Breitbart (2000) described Frankl's belief in the importance of life meaning by noting, "Having a feeling of purpose and meaning can also help alleviate the distress caused by these painful facts of life [terminal illness] in the first place" (p. 487). Similarly, the strength perspective focuses on helping clients find meaning in their adverse life circumstances.

Furthermore, strengths-based therapy is founded on concepts within the multicultural counseling literature (Smith, 1985, 1991). All cultures have strengths, and some cultures value certain strengths more than others. In cultures described as individualistic, such as that of the mainstream United States, autonomy is a highly valued personal strength, whereas in collectivist cultures, such as parts of Asia, social competence and connectedness skills are valued. Cultural socialization may provide protective factors, which insulate or buffer individuals from the harmful effects of a racially discriminatory environment (Miller, 1999). Such socialization may also help the individual cope with and develop individual resiliency. For instance, one product of a racially hostile environment is that individuals may be motivated to overcome roadblocks, thereby providing evidence of their own resiliency.

Ten propositions outline the basic principles of strengths-based therapy. These propositions provide the theoretical framework within which therapists can conduct counseling.

Proposition 1. Humans are self-righting organisms who engage perpetually in an ongoing pattern of adaptation to their environment, a pattern that may be healthy or unhealthy (Benard, 1991; Bronfenbrenner, 1989; Darwin, 1859/1995). Strengths develop as people try to right themselves as they adapt to their environment (Masten & Coatsworth, 1998). All people engage in the self-righting mechanism, although some are more effective than others. The self-righting mechanism allows people to develop strengths for survival, which may be archetypal and encoded in their genetic makeup.

Proposition 2. People develop strengths as a result of internal and external forces and as part of their human driving force to meet basic psychological needs (e.g., safety, belonging and affiliation, autonomy, meaning and purpose in life) (Carver & Scheier, 1990; Maslow, 1954, 1971). For instance, our social competence strengths, including nurturing and relational strengths, are human efforts to satisfy the psychological need for belonging and our need to connect with others. Our needs to experience power and accomplishment are a function of our mastery motivational system (Bandura, 1997).

Proposition 3. Each individual has the capacity for strength development and for growth and change (Maslow, 1971; Rogers, 1961, 1964). Strength development is a lifelong process that is influenced by the interaction of individuals' heredity and the cultural, social, economic, and political environments in which they find themselves. People develop strengths through resiliency. Resilience strengths are critical survival skills that typically may be intrinsically motivated or biologically driven but culturally expressed. In part, survival needs drive healthy strength development.

All people also have a natural drive for positive growth and a natural tendency to seek the realization and/or expression of their strengths and competencies (Maluccio, 1981; Maslow, 1954, 1971; Rogers, 1961; Weick & Chamberlain, 2002). Strengths-based clinicians engage and support this natural drive when they help clients identify their strengths during counseling.

Proposition 4. Strength levels vary, ranging on a continuum from low to high (Epstein, 1998; Epstein & Sharma, 1998). Each person's level of strength is influenced by several contextual factors, including the environment in which they are raised, the people to whom they have been exposed, and the available role models in their lives. Individuals raised in resource-deprived environments may evidence different strengths than do those raised in environments that are rich in community, family, and individual resources. Strengths will vary even within families, because each person's contact with resources and others differs.

Proposition 5. Strength is the end product of a dialectical process involving a person's struggle with adversity. Riegel (1976) asserted that human existence appears to be influenced by basic dialectics (e.g., happiness and sorrow, autonomy and dependency). Growth may depend on the losses we experience during our lifetimes (Baltes, Lindenberger, & Staudinger, 1998). Thus, one goal of counseling is to intervene in such a manner that the therapist helps the client achieve an optimal balance between dialectical pairs (e.g., happiness and sorrow) with regard to any given circumstance. The strengths-based clinician assists clients to understand that strengths may be developed out of adversities. The goal is to help the client understand the paradox of adversity, as reflected in the client's past and present difficulties (Desetta & Wolin, 2000; Garbarino, 1991, 1994).

Proposition 6. Human strengths act as buffers against mental illness (Seligman, 1991; Seligman, Schulman, DeRubeis, & Hollon, 1999; Vailant, 2000). Through the process of resilience development, individuals become aware that they have internal resources permitting them to overcome or mitigate obstacles. Individuals gain what might be labeled "strength awareness," which has the net effect of giving a sense of self-efficacy or authentic self-esteem derived from observing their strength in action (Bandura, 1997). Individuals' strength awareness and authentic self-esteem serve as mediating forces or buffers when signs of mental disorder occur. For instance, individuals sense that something is wrong with them, and they seek remedy. Their strengths alert them that their mental health or survival is somehow threatened. Crisis counseling helps reduce, remove, or replace that which threatens individuals' mental health.

Proposition 7. People are motivated to change during counseling when practitioners focus on their strengths rather than on their deficits, weaknesses, or problems (Saleebey, 1992, 1996). As the psychologist focuses on a client's strengths, he or she provides an external verbal and relational reward (Weick et al., 1989). Good or effective psychotherapy builds strength.

Strengths built during psychotherapy may include courage, optimism, personal responsibility, interpersonal skills, perseverance, and purpose. Strength building during psychotherapy has healing effects on clients.

Proposition 8. Encouragement is a key source and form of positive regard that the therapist intentionally provides to effect behavioral change in the client. In psychotherapy, encouragement functions as the fulcrum for change. It provides the basis for the client to be willing to try or to consider change in behavior and self. The strengths-based therapist builds an arsenal of encouragement techniques, including the compliment (DeJong & Berg, 2002).

Proposition 9. In strengths-based therapy, the therapist consciously and intentionally honors the client's efforts and struggles to deal with his or her problems or presenting issues (Rogers, 1961, 1964). The therapist's strength-perspective philosophy creates an atmosphere that dignifies and respects clients (Goldstein, 1990; Rapp, 1998). Clients who feel that they have been intentionally validated are theorized to achieve their counseling goals at a higher rate than those who feel they have not been so validated by their therapists (Weick & Chamberlain, 2002).

Proposition 10. The strengths-based practitioner understands that people are motivated to change dysfunctional or self-defeating behavior because they hope that doing so will bring about the desired life changes and anticipated rewards. Hope mobilizes the individual (Snyder, 2000). Hope functions to create within clients a sense of anticipated or expected positive reinforcement for their behavioral or attitudinal changes. Hope for a better life or future sustains clients' positive participation or involvement in counseling. Clients who evidence a higher sense of hope are hypothesized to achieve their counseling goals at a higher rate than those who evidence pessimism (Snyder, McDermott, Cook, & Rapoff, 1997). Similarly, clients treated to strengths-based therapy will manifest less anxiety and depression both during the course of counseling and at its termination than will those given problem-centered counseling.

Adaptive Mental Health

Healthy psychological development takes place when individuals are not only aware of their strengths but also able to capitalize and use their strengths in a positive manner to achieve their goals. Individuals do not focus on their weaknesses. Instead, they learn how to manage their weaknesses. People who are working in areas of their strengths express the greatest happiness and life satisfaction.

Theory of Personality

Strengths-based counseling uses a postmodern approach to personality development. That is, it does not subscribe to the theory that personality actually exists. At best, personality consists of habitual traits and characteristics that individuals display on a consistent basis. Hence, what is labeled as personality is a socially constructed rather than a static part of individuals. Individuals' perceptions of their strengths and weaknesses form a part of what traditional theories label as personality.

Theory of Maladaptive Behavior

Strengths allow humans to function with or keep in check psychological disorders so that they can continue to function. Mental illness occurs when strengths are insufficient to deal with the threats to psychological well-being. The strengths-based therapy proposes that by identifying and focusing on a set of strengths that buffers at-risk individuals against mental disorder, we do effective prevention work (Beck et al., 1979; Peterson, 2000; Seligman, Reivich, Jaycox, & Gillham, 1995). To restore the individual to a state of mental equilibrium, the psychological treatment must focus on rebuilding his or her strengths. Human strengths keep mental disorders in check or under control.

THE THERAPEUTIC PROCESS ___
Role of the Therapist

The role of the strengths-based therapist is to help clients discover their strengths and marshal those strengths toward resolving the issues or challenges that brought them to therapy. Such therapists engage in strengths discovery with clients, and they help move clients through eight phases of strengths-based therapy. Strengths-based therapists gauge their clinical skills partly along the lines of a strengths-based competency continuum.

The Strengths-Based
Competence Continuum for Therapists

Strengths-based therapist competencies occur on a continuum of therapist skill from deficit-based destructiveness to strengths-based proficiency. Practitioners who focus entirely on a client's problems, weaknesses, and deficits represent the most negative end of the competence continuum (Berg, 1994; Epstein, 1998). When clients leave such practitioners' offices, many are left with feelings of being drained from the experience (Rapp, 1998). Their self-concepts and sense of self-efficacy may even be lowered because of the almost exclusive focus on their negative, presenting problems (Saleebey, 2001). Deficit-based clinicians believe that childhood trauma predicts adult pathology. They lack encouraging and hope-instilling counseling skills. He or she devalues or may not be aware of clients' strengths or their resiliency in coping.

The second level on the continuum deals with strengths-based precompetence. Practitioners begin to develop an awareness that traditional counseling approaches have focused on the deficit model. While practitioners have found some success with this therapy, they feel that its value is limited in working with youth and other individuals who are at risk in the broader society. Such practitioners are both consciously and unconsciously searching for a better and different way of working with clients, but their training may have provided few clues in this direction. Precompetent strengths-based practitioners realize the limitations of the psychiatric worldview for minority clients and at-risk clients (Smith, 2006a). Although they have modified their counseling practices to better serve members of these groups, they have been trained in only traditional counseling methods (Maluccio, 1981).

What distinguishes precompetent strengths-based helping professionals from their deficit-based counterparts is that they are beginning to desire to change their counseling practices to meet clients' needs more effectively. Precompetent strengths-based therapists actively seek to gain knowledge and training about positive ways to work with clients. They may have even noticed a difference in how clients respond; however, they can only articulate vague notions of strengths-based counseling, asset development, and so on.

The third level of the continuum involves the competent, strengths-based practitioner. Such practitioners have received some training in strengths-based therapy, asset development, and risk and protective factors. Such therapists understand that trauma, abuse, illness, and struggle may be injurious but that they may also be sources of challenge and opportunity. Competent strengths-based helping professionals are culturally aware. They understand both their own and their clients' culture (American Psychological Association, 2003b). While competent strengths-based helping professionals may have adopted part of the philosophy of the strength perspective, they cannot consistently obtain the results that they desire with clients (Rapp, 1998).

Competent strengths-based helping professionals have a limited knowledge of strengths-based assessment techniques. They have not yet mastered using strengths-based techniques, nor do they feel comfortable using them in counseling. The competent strengths-based practitioner vacillates between using a deficit model and a strengths-based therapy and has not mastered the phases of strength therapy.

Proficient strengths-based psychologists are thoroughly grounded in the tenets of positive psychology, risk factors, protective factors, resiliency, and hope (Saleebey, 2001). These practitioners are skilled in strengths assessment, and they have mastered a core body of strengths-based therapy techniques, such as encouraging, instilling hope, and reframing. Proficient strengths-based professionals know how to help their clients develop competencies related to their goals and strengths. Such therapists have learned how to listen, understand, and converse in the language of their clients as opposed to the language of theory. They can help clients change and achieve their goals. Proficient strengths-based therapists help clients build life competencies based on their strengths.

The Compassionate Therapeutic Communication

Strengths-based therapy has been revised to include a specific framework for *compassionate therapeutic communication* with clients. Compassionate therapeutic communication is adapted from Newberg and Waldman's (2012) 12 strategies for effective communication. When a therapist communicates with a client, a process of neural resonance should occur. Neural resonance is the process of mirroring the neural activity in another person's brain. That is, the more therapists can mirror the neural activity in a client's brain, the better able they will be to establish a therapeutic alliance. If a therapist closely observes a client's face, gestures, and tone of voice, the therapist's brain will begin to align with the client's brain (Newberg & Waldman, 2012). Neural resonance takes place when a therapist listens to and observes a client as deeply and fully as possible. Brain scan research has revealed that the more deeply we listen, the more our brain will mirror the activity in the client's brain. Deep listening helps therapists understand their clients and empathize with them. To create neural resonance between therapists and clients, it helps to have their belief systems in alignment or to have some measure of assumed similarity between the two. The strategies of compassionate therapeutic communication are designed to stimulate cooperation between the therapist and the client as they converse during the therapy hour. As Newberg and Waldman have stated,

> Effective communication depends upon neural resonance. As researchers at Princeton University demonstrated in an fMRI brain-scan experiment, neural coupling vanishes when participants communicated poorly. . . . The researchers also discovered that good listeners—the ones who paid the closest attention to what was being said—could actually anticipate what the speaker was going to say a moment before they said it. (p. 82)

Compassionate therapist communication is based on the principle of brain-based mirroring. Research has established that when two people like each other, they mirror each other's posture, facial gestures, and movements. Mirroring between a therapist and a client builds mutual rapport, and it communicates a desire to cooperate and to work together (Newberg & Waldman, 2012).

Compassionate therapeutic communication is designed to train a therapist's brain to connect with his or her client's brain. The process of therapist mirroring involves training one's brain to mentally visualize oneself in the situation that one's client describes. An article by Grèzes (2006) states when one imagines one is in the same situation as that of another, it allows one's brain to build a better understanding of the other person.

Newberg and Waldman (2012) identified the following 12 strategies of compassionate communication: (1) relax, (2) stay present, (3) cultivate inner silence, (4) increase positivity, (5) reflect on your deepest values, (6) access a pleasant memory, (7) observe nonverbal cues, (8) express appreciation, (9) speak warmly, (10) speak slowly, (11) speak briefly, and (12) listen deeply. Strengths-based therapy proposes the phrase PIPA Speaks WSB and Listens deeply.

- P = (*present*) The therapist stays *present* in the therapeutic relationship.
- I = (*inner silence*) The therapist nurtures *inner silence* to stop his or her continual inner speech. Our inner voices have different effects on the brain. Most people have positive and negative inner speech. The therapist calms his or her inner speech to be able to give the fullest attention and be present with the client during therapy.
- P = (*positivity*) The therapist increases his or her use of *positive words* and helps clients increase the use of positive words to describe their lives and circumstances. Remember the three to one ratio of positive to negative statements. If a therapist expresses fewer than three positive thoughts or behaviors for every negative one, the relationship is likely to fail. When therapists begin therapy with optimism, a client is more likely to respond positively. If a therapist wants the relationship with a client to succeed, he or she should generate at least five positive messages for every negative statement.
- A = (*appreciation*) The therapist *expresses appreciation* for the client's efforts and struggles with challenges. The therapist's appreciative compliments of the client's efforts enhance the therapeutic relationship. The appreciation must

be genuine. The therapist begins and ends the therapy session with an expression of appreciation of the client. To increase appreciation of clients, the therapist asks, "What do I really value about this person?" "Which attribute about the client do I value the most?"

Speaks: The therapist speaks (how the therapist speaks affects the client's brain).

- *Warmly:* The therapist speaks warmly and sincerely to convey compassion and sensitivity to the client and his or her situation. Using a warm voice will double the healing power of therapeutic treatment. A strengths-based therapist uses a warm, friendly voice; has a few seconds of thoughtful silence; and then communicates confidence and positive expectation to the client.
- *Slowly:* When a therapist speaks slowly, it increases a listener's ability to understand what is being said. A slow voice has a calming effect on a client who may be experiencing anxious feelings. Speaking slowly will also deepen a person's respect for you.
- *Briefly:* Whenever possible, the therapist should limit his or her speaking to 30 seconds or fewer. If a therapist is trying to communicate a critical piece of information to a client he or she should break down the information into smaller segments—a sentence or two—and then wait for the client to respond. Conscious minds can only retain 30 seconds or so of information.

And the strengths-based therapist

- *Listens deeply:* Therapists listen deeply when they observe a client's nonverbal cues and when they do not interrupt the client. Listening deeply means quieting the therapists' own inner speech and dialogues taking place in their heads.

Client Bill of Rights for Treatment

- I have a right to be treated with dignity and respect.
- I have a right to privacy and confidentiality.

- I have a right to be viewed as a person capable of changing, growing, and becoming positively connected to my neighborhood and community.
- I have a right to be considered a collaborative partner in the counseling process.
- I have a right to ask for services that build upon my strengths and teach me how to manage my weaknesses.
- I have a right to have my culture and ethnicity included as a strength and to request services that honor, respect, and take into consideration my cultural beliefs.
- I have a right to ask that all clinical assessment of me include my strengths in addition to my needs, limitations, and challenges.
- I have a right to learn from my past mistakes and not to be viewed only in terms of such mistakes.
- I have a right to have messages of hope infused throughout my counseling process.
- I have a right to have a therapist who knows how to help me build upon my competencies and strengths.
- I have a right to set my own treatment goals rather than to have them set for me.

Source: © Elsie Jones-Smith (2012).

Role of the Client

The strengths-based approach to counseling endorses a client bill of rights. These rights emphasize how a client is to be treated during the therapeutic encounter. Conversely, the client also has responsibilities, and he or she must commit to accepting partial responsibility for getting well or for solving difficult issues. The role of the client is to agree to actively participate in the therapeutic process, to adopt a framework of hope, to subscribe to the belief that change is possible for him or her, and that his or her individual strengths are key elements in getting well, recovering, or achieving goals in life. The client must disavow a "victim mentality" and agree not only to search for his or her strengths but also to use them to recover from psychological challenges. Where appropriate, the client must agree to participate in homework assignments related to strength development and other matters.

Capitalizing on Clients' Strengths as a Major Therapeutic Intervention. Focusing on a client's strengths can have a number of positive, therapeutic benefits. In general, clients are inclined to have higher levels of motivation, greater engagement in counseling, greater personal or life satisfaction, higher levels of productivity and performance, improvement in self-efficacy and confidence, and a deeper understanding of themselves and others (Clifton & Anderson, 2002;

McQuaide & Ehrenreich, 1997). Table 18.1 provides a comparison and contrast of the strength and deficit perspectives.

Why Use a Strengths-Based Approach to Therapy and Counseling?

There are a number of sound, research-driven reasons why clinicians should consider adopting a strengths-based approach to therapy. As pointed out several times in this chapter, the strengths approach is not all about "fluff and meaningless feel-good dribble." The work of scholars such as Fredrickson (2001) points to potentially long-lasting results of emphasizing positive emotions

Table 18.1   Comparison of Strength and Deficit Perspectives

Strengths	Pathology
Person is unique with talents and resources to be tapped for counseling.	Person is a "case" or a "diagnosis," such as bipolar, schizophrenic.
Counseling intervention is possibility focused.	Counseling intervention is problem focused.
The therapist comes to appreciate the person through personal narratives. Counseling is a collaborative process.	The therapist is the "expert" who interprets the individual's personal narrative for the purpose of arriving at a diagnosis.
Childhood trauma may contribute to a person's strengths or weaknesses.	Childhood trauma predicts later pathology.
The focus is on what is right about the person and on the person's strengths.	The medical model focuses on client's deficits and emphasizes what is wrong or abnormal.
Individuals, families, and communities are viewed as the experts and their input is valued.	The professional is the expert on clients' lives. Input from clients may not be sought.
A client's strengths, skills, and abilities are resources for the work to be accomplished.	The knowledge and skills of the professional are the resources for the work to be accomplished.
A person's behavior is viewed as the problem.	The person is viewed as the problem.
Therapy focuses on strength development and on finding one's place in the family and communities.	Therapy involves reducing symptoms and consequences of problems.

Source: © Elsie Jones-Smith (2012).

with people. Using Fredrickson's research as a foundation, strengths awareness contributes to positive human emotions, which in turn causes individuals to broaden their thinking, build enduring personal resources, and transform people to produce upward spirals in productivity.

When people become aware of their strengths and they learn how to apply them to goals and other aspects of their lives, they experience a personal sense of achievement and positive life achievement. As individuals recognize the strengths in others and how their strengths function in interpersonal relationships, they begin to acquire a sense of community and connectedness with others. When clients learn how to apply their strengths to new situations or challenges, they broaden their coping skills, and they are better able to resolve the problems that brought them to therapy in the first place. Clients stand a greater chance of success when they apply their strengths to areas needing improvement. Focusing on clients' strengths motivates them to excel, and it provides new pathways to hope and achieving positive goals.

There is a great deal to be gained by using a strengths-based rather than a pathology-based therapy approach. Even if the medical model is able to help clients eliminate their outward symptoms of a diagnosed disorder, there is little research to suggest that there will be positive carryover in other areas of a client's life. In contrast, research on positive emotions suggests that positive emotions correct or undo the after effects of negative emotions—what Fredrickson (2001) and her colleagues call the *undoing hypothesis*. Positive emotions result when clinicians emphasize clients' strengths. Positive emotions help people place the negative events in their lives in a broader context, thereby reducing the resonance of any given negative life event. Clinicians can help clients by cultivating within their clients positive emotions at opportune moments to cope with negative emotions.

Phases of Therapy

Strengths-based therapy (Smith, 2006a) provides a major therapeutic framework for working with clients. This therapy contains 8 phases (previously called stages; see Figure 18.1), which are designed to culminate in an individual's increased awareness of his or her own strengths, an increased ability to self-regulate, an increased ability to use strengths to deal with challenging life situations, and an enhanced sense of meaning and purpose in life. These phases represent a collapse of 2 of the previous 10 counseling phases outlined in the article that presented this model (Smith, 2006a). A major theme of the Smith strengths-based therapy is that therapists help clients not only to identify and build their strengths but also to manage their weaknesses.

Phase 1: Creating a Therapeutic Alliance

The strengths-based therapist gives the client a copy of the Client Bill of Rights to establish clearly that the client is respected as a human being, regardless of his or her presenting issues. The therapist asks the client to read over the Client Bill of Rights. If the client has known difficulty reading, then the therapist summarizes the content of this document. The therapist elicits the client's presenting problem and strengths story.

> *Purpose of Session One:*
> - To outline basic information about strengths-based therapy
> - To develop therapeutic rapport with the client (and family, if applicable)
> - To learn about the client's story—about his or her challenging life situation; the therapist elicits two stories—one about the problem and a second involving the client's strengths
> - To learn what the client wants from the clinician
> - To develop mirror neurons between the therapist and the client

Phase 2: Strengths Discovery

After the clinician takes steps to build on the therapeutic alliance, he or she proceeds with strength assessment, which takes place throughout the counseling relationship. It is, however, accentuated in the first three to four sessions. Typically,

Figure 18.1   Strengths-Based Therapy Model

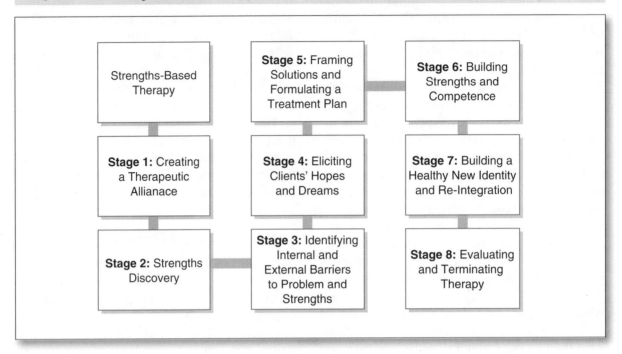

Source: © Elsie Jones-Smith (2012).

strength assessment begins in the first session as a means to establish a relationship with the client.

Clients sometimes have difficulty discussing strengths. Clinicians can help clients begin to identify their strengths by examining the following potential strength indicators.

1. *Category 1—Feelings:* Your feelings provide clues to your strengths.

    a. Your hopes, dreams, and longings

    b. Experiencing happiness and joy when you are engaged in the activity

    c. Experiencing a sense of destiny or "rightness"

    d. Being passionate about something

2. *Ability/acquisition of knowledge and skills can point to strengths*

    a. A deep sense of satisfaction about learning

    b. Places where your learning is rapid

    c. Instant insights and understandings

3. *Actual performance can point to strengths*

    a. Where you performed at levels of excellence

    b. Consistent patterns of success in a particular role, context, or set of tasks

    c. Doing something well almost effortlessly

The model for strength assessment revolves around two axes. The first axis is a horizontal continuum that measures clients' strengths from an internal (those things that reside within the individual) to an external (those things that reside in the environment, i.e., social support, friends, etc.) basis.

The second axis is a vertical continuum that ranges from internal barriers (those self-limiting barriers that reside within the individual, i.e., low self-esteem) to external barriers (obstacles within the environment) to harm reduction behavior, abstinence, or mental health. At the center of these two axes is the client's challenging life situation. The clinician helps the individual assess both internal and external strengths, as well as internal and external barriers to goal achievement.

Strengths-based therapy maintains that early problems should not define a person's total identity (Bretton, 1993; Goldstein, 1990; Rapp, 1998). A person's identity is primarily described in terms of his or her talents and assets. Strengths-based therapy shifts focus from problems to assets for overcoming adverse circumstances. Finding a client's strengths may not be easy because we may not be seeking what is working and because strengths may be obscured by symptoms or oppressive circumstances (Bretton, 1993). The clinician helps the client uncover strengths at the biological, psychological, social, cultural, environmental, economic, material, and political levels (DeJong & Miller, 1995). Biological strengths can include rest, nutrition, compliance with medication, health status, exercise, and adequate leisure time.

Psychological strengths might be subdivided into categories such as cognitive strengths (e.g., intelligence, problem-solving abilities, and knowledge), emotional strengths (e.g., self-esteem, stable mood, optimism, good coping skills, self-reliance, and self-discipline), social strengths (e.g., belonging and support, friends, family, and mentors), cultural strengths (e.g., beliefs, values, and traditions), economic strengths (e.g., being employed and having sufficient money and adequate housing), and political strengths (e.g., equal opportunity and having a voice in decisions).

The therapist helps identify client strengths by asking clients to describe what positives they would like to continue in their relationships (Durrant & Kowalski, 1992; Saleebey, 1992).

To help clarify a client's strengths, the clinician might ask questions such as the following: How have you managed to survive? What do you do well? What do other people look to you for? What are your outstanding qualities? How and with whom do you build alliances? How have you been able to adapt to change? What special characteristics or talents distinguish you from others?

A strengths-based assessment is one that evidences a balance between the difficult life situations or problems that people have and the strengths (internal and external) and barriers (internal and external) they have for dealing with their life situations. Some general guidelines for strength assessment are as follows:

Strength Assessment Procedures

- Honor the client's struggle with a problem. Strengths-based therapists honor the client's pains associated with the problem (e.g., addiction).
- Make assessment a collaborative activity between the clinician and the client, using language the client understands. Assess a client's strengths from a multidimensional framework: Consider the client's individual strengths (e.g., cognition, emotion, motivation, coping behavior, and interpersonal style).
- Focus on understanding how the client has managed to survive in spite of his or her troubles; what has he or she done or used to combat his or her misfortune?
- Make assessment of the barriers to a client's resolution of the presenting problem using the continuum from internal to external barriers: "When you have successfully faced barriers, and what did you do to face them?"
- Assess what internal and external strengths can be used to deal effectively with the barriers that prevent a client from dealing effectively with the presenting problem.
- Do not permit a mental disorder label to become the cornerstone of the client's emergent identity.

Source: © Elsie Jones-Smith (2012).

Therapist Statement for Strength Assessment. The therapist points out to the client that activating strengths-oriented self-concept is part of the treatment process. The therapist states,

We use strength assessment as a means of helping you identify what resources you have to deal with some of the challenges you're facing. Strengths-based assessment tends to be different from assessments that you may have had in the past. We have found that when people recognize their strengths, it provides the basis for helping them accomplish their goals. Tell me about your strengths, what you like doing, etc.

Ways to Ask Questions About a Client's Strengths

- What strengths do you have? Or, tell me something that you're good at doing.
- Is there anything that you were born with that has helped you deal with the current situation that brought you to counseling? (Elicitation of internal strength)
- What are you most proud of accomplishing in your life?
- What do you like most about yourself?
- What do others like most about you?
- How would you describe yourself?
- What do you still want to accomplish?

Source: © Elsie Jones-Smith (2012).

Relational Strengths. Strengths-based counseling takes into account the importance of relationships in clients' lives. Therefore, this part of counseling asks about the individual's relationships that provide a source of strength to him or her. Information gleaned from this area might be used to identify potential resources clients can enlist in dealing positively with their challenges and issues. The goal is to determine who has been there for the client. For young clients, the clinician might want to encourage movement toward prosocial relationships and away from relationships that are codependent. The strengths-based therapist understands that difficulties in interpersonal relationships are often at the core of clients' presenting problems. In strengths-based assessment, the therapist examines the client's relationship strengths.

Clinician Identification of Client Strengths. Sometimes clients are hesitant to talk about their strengths because they believe that they are bragging or because they feel that they lack

strengths. When this situation occurs, clinicians might identify client strengths by asking themselves questions such as these:

- What are the outstanding qualities of this person?
- What special or unique characteristics distinguish this person from others?
- How has this person been able to adapt to change?
- "This is what I have noticed is a strength for you." (e.g., friendliness, sense of humor)

Phase 3: Identifying Internal and External Barriers to Change—Treatment

Although strengths-based therapists focus on finding solutions, they must also take time to arrive at a clear understanding of clients' perceptions of their problems. If practitioners do not take sufficient time to explore what their clients view as the problem, and if they edit or disregard the client's story too early, the solutions generated are unlikely to work. Hence, the therapist must have clients reveal what they perceive their problems to be, why they believe the problems exist, what behaviors or situations cause them the most problems, and what are the consequences of their actions.

Change is difficult for most people because it requires them to adjust and because there is usually some element of loss in change—even when it is for the better. Many people have ambivalent feelings about change. Harm reduction requires change—how drugs are harming them and the pleasures that using drugs bring. Individuals have to examine both sides of change. Because people establish a relationship with drugs and alcohol, they have to decide how that relationship will change or remain the same. Change may mean eliminating drugs totally or limiting when they use or how they use drugs. Client ambivalence ("I'm not sure if I want to change or I'm not sure I can change") about change is an extremely important factor that will either impede or move the client forward in harm reduction counseling.

It is important that the therapist help clients deal effectively or resolve their ambivalence about change. Change is an ongoing process for most people. Change may be caused by either internal or external issues (see Figure 18.2). *Internal motivation* for change can be caused by factors such as being tired of the lifestyle, having found God or a new spiritual relationship, or hitting rock bottom. *External factors* that bring about a desire for change include criminal proceedings, Child Protective Services, threat of divorce proceedings, and safety issues. Usually, there is an interaction between internal and external factors that bring matters to a head. Internal barriers to change include the fears of clients. What fears will stand in the way of what the client desires? External barriers to change include factors such as a history of violence in the household, a lack of money and decent housing, and so on.

Phase 4: Eliciting Clients' Hopes and Dreams

Hopes and dreams keep people alive and motivated. Oftentimes, clients who are experiencing challenges in life have forgotten about their hopes and dreams. While the primary goal of this protocol is to engage the client in meaningful harm reduction for the substance abuse, a secondary goal is to help a client remember and reignite his or her hopes and dreams. It is important to understand the role of hope in the counseling relationship.

Definition of Hope. According to Jevne and Miller (1999), hope may be defined as "looking forward with both confidence and uncertainty to something good. When we hope, we anticipate that something we want to happen can indeed happen" (p. 10). Hope is typically experienced in relationship to

Figure 18.2 Model for Assessing Clients' Strengths and Barriers

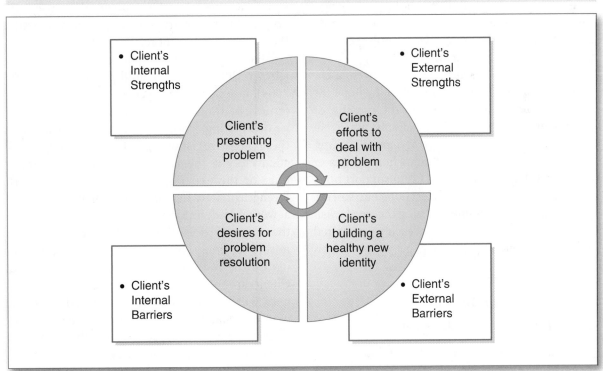

Source: © Elsie Jones-Smith (2012).

someone or something, and there are at least two levels of hope: a specific and a general hope. Snyder (2000) has defined hope as the process of thinking about one's goals and one's motivation (agency) and ways to achieve those goals.

The importance of hope in the therapeutic relationship has been well documented (Edey, Jevne, & Westra, 1998; Snyder, 2000). Hubble, Duncan, and Miller (1999) have referred to hope as an "expectancy effect" or a "placebo effect." That is, the curative effects of therapy are not specifically the result of a given treatment procedure, but rather they are the result of the client's positive and hopeful therapeutic expectations. Clients have been known to show some improvement in their presenting problem immediately after making an appointment for therapy. What allowed them to improve was their expectation of hope—that they were going to get the help they needed to deal with the problem or situation.

Edey et al. (1998) found that clients' high ratings of hopelessness predicted their risk for suicide. Therapists use hope intentionally in the counseling relationship to help motivate clients for change. They ask questions about the client's hope or ask clients to reframe their stories from a hope perspective using their particular strengths.

The strengths-based therapist uncovers a client's story while placing emphasis on the hope the client has for the future, feels in the present, or remembers from the past. The therapist uses what Edey (2000) calls *the language of hope in therapy.* She has identified three functions of hope language: (1) to draw hope from stories, (2) to support hope in clients' stories, and (3) to inject hope into stories. Moreover, Edey recommends using the word *when* to support hope (i.e., *when* you reach your desired harm reduction goal, *when* you get your children back, *when* you get a job).

Phase 5: Framing Solutions and Formulating a Treatment Plan

Phase 5 emphasizes framing solutions and formulating a treatment plan. The strengths-based therapist understands that you need not solve a problem to find a solution to a troubling situation (Walter & Peller, 1992). A useful counseling technique for this phase is the exception question. The therapist actively looks for exceptions to the occurrence of the problem and enlists clients' help in finding practical solutions to core or presenting issues. Practical solutions might be adopting a different schedule or finding a confidant (Berg & DeJong, 1996).

Strengths-based psychologists engage in solution-building conversations with their clients (de Shazer, 1985, 1994). They address how the client is addressing problems rather than the problems themselves (Berg & DeJong, 1996).

Strengths-based practitioners help identify and evaluate the client's past modes of coping and the current sources of support for confronting issues (Durrant & Kowalski, 1992). Clinicians seek information about what is working in a client's life and may ask questions such as "How have you been trying to solve this problem?" "What works for you, even for a little while?" "Was there ever a time you remember when the problem did not exist?" Together they construct a realistic plan of action that will help the client realize goals.

Forgiveness is an important part of healing (Brown, 2004; Brown & Phillips, 2005; Holeman, 2004). Often, clients are consumed by anger, bitterness, betrayal, and despair—emotions that may be debilitating. To help clients rid themselves of these negative emotions, therapists must have clients forgive the person they view as the wrongdoer or the persons responsible for their hurt. Strengths-based therapy helps clients formulate a workable definition of forgiveness within the therapeutic process. It helps clients confront their misconceptions about forgiveness and to recognize the roadblocks to achieving forgiveness. Clients are encouraged to create a circle of forgiveness, which includes those who helped create the pain or situation and themselves (Brown, 2004). As clients forgive themselves and others, they are asked to release the energies trapped in their previous lack of forgiveness.

Phase 6: Building Strength and Competence

People require competence and strength building across the developmental life span. Strengths that might be built during psychotherapy include courage, insight, optimism, perseverance, putting troubles in perspective, and finding purpose (F. Walsh, 1998). During the competence-building phase, therapists help clients realize that they are not powerless to effect change in their lives. This recognition contributes to a sense of autonomy as clients learn that they can find solutions (Dana, 2002; Wall, Klechner, Amendt, & Bryant, 1989). The competencies that clients desire may vary according to their presenting issues. Therapists can enlist the aid of community networks and resources to help build competencies for their clients or recommend they attend anger management classes, relaxation training, assertiveness training, or resiliency training to help build their competencies in these areas. Strength building for clients entail the following steps:

1. The *first step* in strength building is helping the client identify his or her strength themes. For instance, strength assessment might involve the client's taking the StrengthsFinder Profile (Buckingham & Clifton, 2001), VIA Signature Character Strengths, or the Strengths-Based Inventory (Smith, 2006a). As a result of taking these instruments and the therapist's clinical assessment, the therapist and the client collaboratively identify one to three strengths or strength themes for the client.

2. The *second step* involves having the client affirm those strengths with significant others, including family members, friends, teachers, and work colleagues.

3. In *Step 3*, the therapist and the client construct ways to develop the client's strengths by learning knowledge and by practicing sets of skills related to the identified strengths.

4. In *Step 4*, the client further develops his or his strengths by learning new knowledge and practicing new or related skills. He or she then applies the strengths to new or challenging situations.

5. *Step 5* consists of the client evaluating and obtaining feedback from self and others regarding the development of his or her strengths.

During the building strength and competencies phase, the therapist asks clients to complete a basic brief questionnaire to indicate their strength competency.

Strength Competency Questionnaire

Check either "Yes" or "No" if the following statements apply to you.

- I know my strengths, and I can name them. ___ Yes ___ No
- I know how to develop and nourish my strengths. ___ Yes ___ No
- I know how to use my strengths to deal effectively with my problems. ___ Yes ___ No
- I know my weaknesses, and I know how to manage them. ___ Yes ___ No
- I know how to focus on my strengths rather than on my weaknesses. ___ Yes ___ No
- I know how to manage weaknesses so that they do not interfere with my happiness. ___ Yes ___ No

Source: © Elsie Jones-Smith (2012).

Phase 7: Building a Healthy New Identity and Healthy New Connections

It is important for counseling to help clients build healthy new identities and healthy connections with their family members, their strengths, and their goals. Is the individual connected meaningfully to the community or marginalized? Strengths-based therapy maintains that many problems in living are caused by strength deficiencies in interpersonal relationships. People need opportunities to be of service to others.

Phase 8: Evaluating and Terminating

Collaborative treatment evaluation between the client and the therapist takes place at least 1 week prior to counseling termination. The therapist meets with the client to discuss the treatment he or she has received. During this phase, both the therapist and the client honor the progress that has been made (Weick & Chamberlain, 2002). They determine whether the client has accomplished goals, whether changes can be attributed to the intervention, and what client strengths and environmental resources were most significant in helping them achieve their goals. In addition, counseling deals with issues such as the critical points of treatment, what the client learned, what was meaningful, and what they wish had happened. During termination, strengths-based therapists seek to answer questions such as "Has the client accomplished what he or she contracted to do?" "What factors brought about the client change?" "Does the current situation suggest the need for further counseling?" Discussion is also focused on steps the client can take to maintain the successes they have achieved as a result of treatment.

It is important for the clinician to consider clients' reintegrative strengths, which are sometimes conceptualized as coping strengths. For instance, the client can establish boundaries between himself and other members of his family. Or, if the problem was one involving substance abuse, a reintegrative strength might be if the client understands the chain of events, including the small decisions that lead from drug triggers to drug use. Reintegrative strengths are those that demonstrate that the client has found a way to use successfully his strengths to deal with the presenting problem.

Therapy Techniques

> ### The Hope Chest Counseling Technique
>
> - A technique to instill hope during counseling is creating a hope chest.

> - Ask your client to imagine a hope chest that will permit all of their problems to disappear.
> - Ask your clients to describe the three hopes they would take out of the hope chest and how the granting of these hopes would change their present situation: "Let's suppose you could create a hope chest that would make your problems go away."
> - You can make a request to take out of the hope chest three wishes.
> - Although three hopes will be granted, you must make changes to ensure their continuation.
> - What three hopes would you take out of your hope chest?
> - How would the granting of these three hopes change your present situation?
> - What would you have to do to keep these three hopes alive?
> - What internal and external strengths do you have to bring about and sustain the three hopes that were granted to you in the hope chest?

Strength Journal. Beginning with Phase 3, the therapist asks the client to keep a strength journal, which records on a daily basis the specific strength the client used to deal with everyday life issues. The client is asked to identify the strength used, how it was used, and any other thoughts or developments that have occurred related to his or her strengths.

Hope Chest Technique. The hope chest counseling technique reveals what clients want to change about their lives and what they are willing to do to bring about those changes. The primary goal is to help clients reconnect with their dreams.

Creating Hope Symbols. Have the client create hope symbols that the client can refer to or carry with him or her. For instance, a client mentioned that a friend had given him a little elephant with his birthstone near the elephant's trunk. The client decided to use the elephant as his hope symbol. When he felt low in hope, he would take the elephant out and engage in positive self talk about his dreams.

Strength Memories. Ask clients to remember a time in their lives when they displayed good strength and to keep this image in mind while planning and working toward goals. For instance, one client had been an excellent swimmer during his youth, winning many medals. When he came to counseling and recounted swimming as one of his strengths, the therapist asked him to get a picture in his mind of him winning one of his prized swimming medals. Every time that he went for a job interview or took a step toward reaching one of his goals, he was asked to first take a few seconds to ready himself with his hope memory.

Circle of Support Technique. The circle of support technique requires therapists to assist clients in examining their current and needed levels of social support in several different areas. This technique encourages clients to examine their external strengths. The therapist asks clients to fill out the circle of support with the names of those individuals who provide a source of external strengths in their lives. Throughout counseling, the therapist asks clients to indicate any changes in their circle of support. Sometimes clients might be encouraged to widen their circles of support or to consider changing or eliminating individuals from the circle.

Managing Weaknesses and Barriers Exercise. The following exercise helps clients understand their weaknesses or barriers. Ask your client to draw a large circle. In the middle of the circle, have them draw their weakness or barrier to a goal. Around the circle, tell them to write how they will manage this weakness in concentric circles, until the weakness is surrounded by ways to manage it. Completion of this exercise gives clients a sense of power over the weakness or barrier.

The Forgiveness Appointment. According to Webster's *New World Dictionary*, "Forgiveness is the act of giving up resentment against another or the desire for punishment of another." The thought action of forgiving is a step that allows a client to stop being angry and/or judgmental toward another and to start feeling better. Forgiveness can be conceptualized as a mental and spiritual act that helps our bodies engage in mental and physical detoxification. The act of forgiveness encourages clients to release themselves and others from the past.

Ask your client to do the following: Write down on your calendar an appointment reminder for forgiving a person who has hurt you. As we place forgiveness reminders on our calendars, it becomes easier to say to a person, "I forgive you, and I forgive myself." Make a list of family members, friends, rude coworkers, or anyone you can think of, including yourself. Remember, you are not condoning or approving the person's actions. Rather, you are releasing them from your life so that you both can go your own separate ways. The forgiveness act allows you to move forward on your life journey without bringing them along with you. An example of a forgiveness statement might be

- "I forgive you and I release you from my mind. My forgiveness for you is total. I am free and you are free to go our separate ways. I forgive both you and myself."
- "I forgive you and I release myself from any anger or hurt in our relationship."

Strength Cards. Strength cards are used to remind clients of their strengths. The card is wallet sized, and it contains on it four affirmations about strengths.

1. I achieve the goals that I establish for myself, one by one, step by step.

2. I am a survivor, an achiever, not a victim.

3. I am confident in using my strengths to achieve my goals and to deal with challenges.

4. I manage my weaknesses in a successful manner.

Wheel of Life Exercise. This exercise is designed to deal with the issue of balance in life. Sometimes people fail to use their strengths because there is no balance in their lives. The happiest people are those who have found a balance in their lives, so that they can use their strengths. The Wheel of Life exercise helps clients determine if they are focusing too much on one part of their lives while neglecting other areas. Clients are asked to rank their level of satisfaction from 0 to 100 with each area of their lives—where 100 is totally happy.

The Wheel of Life is powerful because it gives clients a vivid visual representation of the way they are conducting their lives compared with the way they would ideally like to live. It is called the Wheel of Life because each area of a person's life is mapped on a circle, like the spokes of a wheel (see Figure 18.3).

Figure 18.3   Wheel of Life Exercises

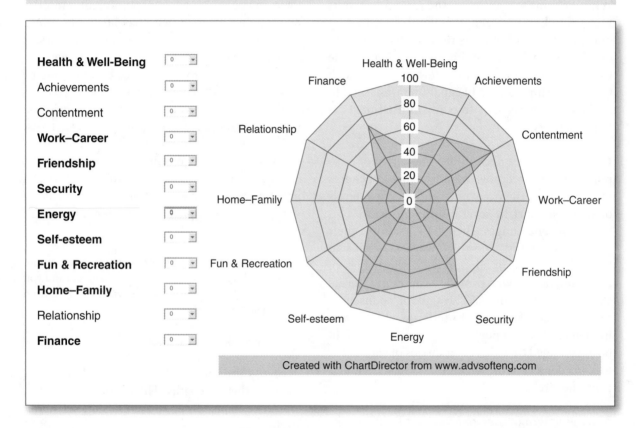

Created with ChartDirector from www.advsofteng.com

Strength Charts. The therapist can use strength charts to help clients better understand their strengths. Strength charts can vary, depending on the client's presenting issue, age, and other challenges. The case analysis of Justin provides an example of a strength chart that can be used with students in kindergarten through Grade 12. For instance, a strength chart can be created for college admissions. Developmental issues such as the client's level of development should be taken into consideration. Strength charts can be developed for clients dealing with issues of depression, anxiety, and so on. Parents can be asked to complete strength charts for their children. Table 18.2 provides a basic format for a strength chart.

Table 18.2   Strength Chart

Strength	High Strength	Medium Strength	Low Strength	Functional Competency	Weakness
Emotional strengths: Insight, optimism, perspective-taking, purpose in life, persistence, ability to endure, and coping					
Character strengths: Honesty, integrity, courage, and discipline					
Wisdom: Ability to reflect on one's actions and those of others					
Creative strengths: Art, music, dance, writing, and cooking					
Educational strengths: Academic degrees, level of academic achievement, and informal education					
Analytical and cognitive strengths: Problem solving, decision making, and ability to reason					
Financial and economic strengths: Work-related and provider strengths					
Social support and community strengths: Survival skill strengths					

Source: © Elsie Jones-Smith (2012).

RESEARCH AND EVALUATION —
Multicultural Positives

The strengths-based therapist assumes that race, class, and gender are organizing elements in every counseling interaction (Albee, 1994; American Psychological Association, 2003a; Baines, 2000; Betancourt & Lopez, 1993). The therapist analyzes the manner in which the larger social structures affect clients and the resources available to them (Katz, 1997; Smith, 1985, 1991). He or she takes into account how clients' opportunities, expectations, and choices are influenced by factors such as race, gender, and class relations. Furthermore, the therapist considers clients' ethnic group membership, cultural identifications, and the strengths of the ethnic and cultural community with which he or she identifies.

The strengths-based therapist is sensitive to issues regarding racism, sexism, ageism, and other areas that impinge on individuals' being able to use their strengths without interference from others or from the sociopolitical–economic system. Some questions the therapist might ask themselves are as follows: What roles do discriminatory practices, procedures, and policies have on the client's situation under review? What strengths did the client evidence in responding to experiences of discrimination and cultural insensitivity?

Strengths-based therapy maintains that culture is a human strength because it provides a patrimony of shared values among a group of people. Our psychological identification with a cultural group may be viewed as a strength in and of itself because cultural attachment and identification provide a sense of "we" rather than just "I." When we identify with a cultural group, we view ourselves as part of a community that shares certain beliefs, attitudes, holidays, and the like. We know who we are because we know where we belong and with whom. Choose almost any community in the world, and one will find that similar cultural groups tend to live in relative close proximity with each other. They do so partly because of the emotional strength they receive from ethnocultural bonding. Put another way, our ethnocultural bonding helps us satisfy what Maslow (1954) called our need for belonging.

Therapist cultural competence is an integral part of strengths-based therapy. A therapist's cultural competence refers to his or her clinical ability to work effectively with people from a variety of ethnic, cultural, political, economic, and religious backgrounds. Developing cultural competence in working with clients is a four-prong process that involves the following: (1) enhancing self-awareness of one's own culture, (2) increasing one's knowledge of cultural groups, (3) examining one's attitudes toward cultural groups, and (4) obtaining the necessary clinical skills to assess clients within a cultural framework and learning appropriate and culturally relevant interventions.

Multicultural Blind Spots

One limitation of strengths-based therapy is that different cultures respond differently to the issue of individual strengths. In some Eastern cultures, strengths are considered possessions of the collective group rather than of the individual. A culturally sensitive therapist should not adopt a Western, self-centered articulation of the client's strengths. Instead, the therapist should recognize that clients from Eastern cultures may choose to contribute their ability, talents, and strengths for the sake of family honor. Clients' strengths should be regarded as assets of the collectives to which the client belongs.

It may be insufficient and improper for a therapist to encourage clients from some cultures to demonstrate or show their strengths for themselves. In Eastern cultures, one must obtain approval to display one's strengths or talents at work. A company will not consider an employee's strengths to be beneficial to the organization if the demonstration of such talents is not approved first by supervisors. If an employee demonstrates his or her strengths without first seeking supervisor approval to do so, the organization will consider the employee to be a threat and adopt a policy of ignoring him or her. The Chinese value the strength of humility (Yip, 2008). Yip explains that to gain the approval of one's supervisors, one needs to be humble and to attribute one's strengths and talents to the graces and caring of supervisors. Moreover, the employee should let the supervisor take the glory and the benefits from his or her strengths. This cultural position is consonant with Confucian culture. In Western societies, individuals are encouraged to focus on asserting their individual strengths. Such societies stress the importance of making sure that others know your talent. Talents are used primarily for individual rather than for group benefit.

Evidence-Based Research

In 2003, President George W. Bush's New Freedom Commission on Mental Health called for a basic transformation of the nation's approach to mental health care. In the report, *Achieving the Promise: Transforming Mental Health Care in America* (2003), the commission outlined two principles for a successful transformation: Services and treatments must be consumer and family centered, building on strengths, and care must focus on coping with and building resilience to face life challenges. In the book *Investing in Children, Youth, Families, and Communities: Strengths-Based Research and Policy* (2004), coeditors Maton, Schellenback, Leadbetter, and Solarz state that there now exists an impressive body of research to support the hypotheses that strengths-based approaches to individuals, families, and communities are effective in fostering resiliency, improved physical health, and overall positive outcomes.

One of the criticisms of strengths-based therapy is that it is not evidence based. If one is using randomized control trials as the only or major measure for being considered evidence based, then strengths-based therapy is still working on meeting this criterion. Randomized control trials constitute only one measure of efficacy of a theoretical approach. Clinical evidence is also important in achieving the designation of being considered an evidence-based practice. As this author has pointed out elsewhere, randomized control trials are elevated to a high standard because they are valued by those who have adopted a Eurocentric worldview. Santee (2007), however, has pointed out that the Chinese did not have to have American randomized controls trials to establish that mindfulness worked. The Chinese have been using mindfulness for more than a thousand years because it worked.

There is one reported study that used the Jones-Smith strengths-based therapy. Scheel, Davis, and Henderson (2013) conducted a study of therapists who used some of the concepts and strengths put forth by Smith (2006).

> Therapists reported using client strengths to broaden client perspectives and create hope and motivation, to create positive meanings through reframing and metaphors, to identify strengths through the interpersonal therapeutic process, to match client contexts through strengths, and to amplify strengths through encouragement and exception finding. (p. 392)

Scheel et al. (2013) found support for Smith (2006) and stated, "Smith's strength-based model includes the creation of the therapeutic alliance, identification of strengths, instill[ing] hope, forming solutions, changing meanings, and empowering, each of which is represented in our findings" (p. 422).

Other studies point to the benefit of a strengths-based approach. Rapp (2006) used a strengths-based approach with successful outcomes for adults with substance abuse issues. A study has reported that the strengths-based case management model produced positive results in a study of grandparents with custody of their grandchildren. Strengths-based case management promoted a sense of independence and self-assurance among grandparents and enhanced levels of confidence to nurture and support their grandchildren (Whitley, White, Kelly, & Yorke, 1999).

Tehan and McDonald (2010) have found that using strengths-based approaches with parents increases program effectiveness and improves parental engagement with services. Price-Robertson (2010) has studied strengths-based approaches to work with young parents and at-risk children. When the strengths-based approach shifted from the "at-risk" approach, young parents were given an opportunity to identify their own strengths and to work toward achieving positive personal and parental outcomes. A strengths approach has been used successfully with parent education programs in preventing child maltreatment (Holzer, Bromfield, Richardson, & Higgins, 2006). Cox's (2006) investigation examined the impact of using a strengths-based assessment tool, the Behavioral and Emotional Rating Scale with children and adolescents with behavioral or emotional disorders. The findings indicated that child functioning outcomes were significantly better for those who received the Behavioral and Emotional Rating Scale assessment in comparison with those who were given a deficit-based assessment tool.

What empirical research exists on the strengths-based approach suggests that this approach has a positive psychological impact. In a pilot study of people with serious mental health issues, participants were asked to identify the factions they believed were critical to their recovery. The most import elements they identified were the ability to have hope and trust in their own thoughts and judgments (Ralph, Lambric, & Steele, 1996). Strengths-based approaches have been found to be effective for developing and maintaining hope in clients (Smock et al., 2008).

Evidence is beginning to develop concerning the use of strengths-based approaches with children, young people, and families. Several studies have found an association between personal strengths in young people and their academic success, self-determination, and life satisfaction (Arnold, Walsh, Oldman, & Rapp, 2007; Lounsbury, Fisher, Levy, & Welsh, 2009; Park & Peterson, 2006). Early and GlenMaye (2000) reported that the use of the strengths approach in working with families helped the family (a) identify resources for coping and (b) use their existing family strengths

to sustain hope and a sense of purpose by setting and achieving goals consonant with their personal aspirations, capabilities, and visions for a future possible life.

Providing a complete summary of research studies supporting a strengths-based approach is beyond the scope of this chapter. In reviewing other studies that examined using a strengths-based approach with various populations, it is clear that there is a lack of empirical support for strengths-based approaches. Evidence is limited primarily to descriptive case studies of successful applications (Gray, 2011). In terms of strengths-based therapy, I welcome empirical studies to test the efficacy of the therapy. Some research questions that researchers might consider are

- Do people who know and use their strengths on a regular basis experience less depression than those who do not know their strengths?
- Do students who know and use their strengths achieve higher academic levels than those who do not know their strengths?
- What is the relationship between life satisfaction and a person using his or her strengths?
- What is the relationship between therapist attitudes using the strengths-based therapy versus other theoretical approaches?

CASE ANALYSIS

Justin From a Strengths-Based Therapy Perspective

The strengths-based therapist works with Justin; his mother, Sandy; and school personnel in an effort to get Justin to use his strengths to overcome the obstacles that he is facing, especially the threat of the court placing him in residential treatment for boys. The first step the therapist takes is to establish a relationship with Justin. The strengths-based therapist engages in what Bisman (1993) calls "belief bonding"—that is, the therapist is competent and can help Justin deal with his issues as defined by the court: violence, stealing, fighting at school, and so on. Bonding between Justin and the therapist takes place when Justin accepts the therapist's interest in him—especially that he wants to help him deal positively with his challenges. The therapist does not establish a power differential with Justin. He begins the therapeutic relationship with the assumption that he is there to respect Justin.

The therapist presents Justin with a copy of the strengths-based *Client's Bill of Rights*, and he goes over them with Justin. The therapist takes the position that Justin has the right to know what is going to take place during therapy. The goal is to make sure that Justin understands how the therapist will be approaching the problem to avoid any unnecessary surprises during therapy. The focus of the work with Justin should not be on all the problems facing him but rather on his survival abilities and his ability to change to meet the challenges facing him.

Justin is pleasantly surprised to learn that the therapist believes that he has rights, even though he is a child, and that his rights will be honored. Justin is also encouraged when the therapist takes the time to explain his role and what Justin's role will be. To deepen the relationship, the therapist asks Justin to tell his version of his story—what actually happened as he sees it. Justin relates a story different from the one contained in the report that was given to the therapist.

Justin is informed that one function of therapy will be to learn about his strengths and how such strengths might be used to help him stay out of the residential treatment program. As a consequence, the therapist asks Justin to tell him about himself: "Tell me something good about you, Justin, something that maybe people outside of your family don't know about you. What are you good at? What do you like doing when you are not completing your homework, watching television, etc.?"

Justin responds by saying, "Don't you want to know some of the bad things that I do to get into trouble?" The therapist responds, "Oh, there will be time for me to learn about some of those behaviors, Justin." A smile comes over Justin's face, and initially, he wonders if the therapist is "for real." Despite being given the opportunity to say good things about himself, Justin just shrugs as if he does not know where to begin. He had not thought about any of his good points.

Believing that Justin is temporarily unable to say good things about himself, the therapist decides to help him out a bit. The therapist decides to use the three-category strength framework of (1) feelings—Justin's hopes, dreams, and longings, and things that he feels a sense of destiny or "rightness about"; (2) abilities or any knowledge and skills that can point to his strengths; and (3) actual performance—where Justin has performed at levels of excellence. He begins with Justin's hopes and dreams: "Let's say that the problem with the courts was over and the judge decided to let you stay at home with your mom. What would be your hopes for yourself? What do you dream about being?"

The therapist engages in strengths discovery with Justin. To help Justin out, he presents him with a chart of strengths, and he asks him to check the strengths that he believes he has. During the process of strength discovery, the therapist raises questions about Justin's internal and external strengths—family, friends, social support, and so on. He elicits a strength story from Justin about something that he has done well in the past. From there, the therapist asks about what holds Justin back—his internal barriers: "What's holding you back, Justin, from being what you want to be—apart from the fact that you're still a boy and in school?" Justin begins to consider the internal pressures that he has placed on himself and his own fears that "no matter how hard he tries, he is still going to lose" because kids from his neighborhood don't seem to get very far in life. The therapist talks about fear as an emotion that might be holding Justin back—the fear that he is not good enough.

Therapy with Justin takes place over a number of sessions. To help Justin become more aware of his strengths, the therapist asks Justin to keep a strength journal, where he writes down a specific strength that he used during the day. The strength could be ever so small or big—such as deciding to walk away from a fight. Justin describes how he used the strength as well as his thoughts and feelings about himself after using the strength. After the first two sessions, the therapist asks Justin to think about his best strength memory. What did he do? What were the results? As Justin reveals his strength memory, the therapist asks Justin to relax, and he has him participate in a brief relaxation exercise that teaches him how to call on the strength memory when he is feeling down or challenged. Justin's strength memory is about when he won an art prize at school. He recalled how when the teacher called his name, he stood up and the kids clapped as he went to receive his prize. Whenever Justin becomes afraid that he will be rejected or that he will not be able to keep his cool, he is asked to pull out this strength memory.

(Continued)

The therapist works with Justin to see how he might use his strengths to deal with his court issues. Gradually, Justin gains an understanding of the barriers in his life and how he has allowed some of his weaknesses to sabotage his strengths. For instance, Justin identifies his not going to bed early enough to be on time for court as a weakness. Whatever strengths he had wanted to show to the judge were sabotaged by being late for his appearance. The therapist asks Justin to participate in the managing weaknesses and barriers exercise. Justin is presented with a large circle. In the middle of the circle, he is asked to draw his weakness or strength barrier. Using concentric circles, Justin is asked to surround the weakness with a strength or a competent way to manage the weakness. Justin draws three concentric circles around his lateness barrier that will permit him to conquer it. For example, the first circle says that he goes to bed early; the second circle says that he sets his alarm clock; the third circle says that he gets his clothes ready for court the night before, and so on.

By getting in contact with his strengths and examining the barriers that he erects and those that are contained within the environment, Justin develops increased self-esteem. He adopts self-management strategies to prevent his weaknesses from sabotaging his goals, dreams, and hopes about life. Together, the therapist and Justin develop wallet-size strength cards that Justin can carry around with him to remind himself of his strengths and that he can work on to achieve his goals. For instance, one of his strength affirmations states, "I do not let others control my emotions. I control how I respond to others rather than reacting to their behavior." Another strength card says, "I, Justin, take today one small step toward achieving my goal to become a respected artist." Still another affirmation says: "I, Justin, do not permit my circumstances to affect my goals."

The therapist engages Justin in the circle of support technique. Justin is asked to write down the names of people in his inner and outer circles of support. Justin discovers that he has only a few people in his circle of support—his mother, his brother, and the friend with whom he got into difficulty at the mall.

The therapist and Justin work out a detailed treatment plan in which Justin outlines his goals, his strengths to help him achieve his goals, and the internal and external barriers to his goals. The therapist engages in competence building with Justin. He is encouraged to attend three sessions on anger management. The two work out strategies Justin might use in developing a healthy new identity that would allow him to be accepted at school and in the community.

SUMMARY

Strengths-based therapy provides a new framework that offers an opportunity for helping professionals modify the psychiatric worldview that still dominates so much of therapy. Strengths-based development involves the identification of strengths, the integration of these strengths into our views of ourselves, and the resulting changes in behavior. To move toward this therapy, clinicians must make a paradigm shift to a strength emphasis. The strength paradigm does not eliminate the need to address barriers in a client's life—barriers such as poverty, abuse, neglect, and other life challenges that can be devastating for people. Moreover, a strengths-based approach does not just focus on positives while ignoring real challenges or problems. Instead, it entails figuring out ways to recognize and use genuine strengths to allow building on existing client competencies. The strengths-based therapist understands that if multifaceted client needs are to be addressed effectively during counseling, clinical interventions must be based on strengths and what works for clients. What people need is a balanced paradigm in which deficit reduction efforts are matched with strength interventions.

Although research is still in its beginning stages, the evidence is beginning to mount that a strengths-based program leads to a number of positive outcomes, including better function of families, improved mental health, greater life satisfaction, and improved educational performance. Strengths are the building blocks for change and form the primary focus in therapy. Strengths-based therapy offers much to those professionals who desire to work from a positive psychological perspective.

SUPPLEMENTARY AIDS _____

Discussion Questions

1. Suppose you were planning to have a child. Discuss three strengths you would like your child to have.

2. Discuss two strengths you would like to have as a therapist and describe one strength you already possess as a therapist or counselor.

3. Identify and discuss three strengths that your cultural or ethnic membership group has. List one strength of another cultural group with whom you come into contact.

4. Think about your own family. What are two strengths of your family that help members deal with challenges.

5. Everyone is influenced by what researchers call the "negativity bias." How does the negativity bias operate in your own life? How might the negativity bias influence your relationship with a client?

Glossary of Key Terms

cultural strengths   Those that are produced by the people in a given group. For instance, cultures that appreciate autonomy value strengths dealing with independence, whereas cultures that focus on collectivist issues produce people who value relational strengths.

functional competence   Refers to a level of achievement people might strive for in working on their weaknesses.

intentional process   Involves acting with a sense of capability and deciding from among a number of alternative actions. The intentional person generates alternatives in a given situation.

manage weakness   A concept that says people develop the least in the area of their weakness; therefore, they should work only for functional competence in their area of weakness. In general, people spend too much time trying to improve their weaknesses rather than on developing their strengths.

pathology perspective   Refers to the view that clinicians focus on looking for what is wrong in the client.

relational strength   Those strengths that develop as individuals attempt to fulfill their belonging needs. Collectivist cultures tend to place a high value on relational strengths.

strength   May be defined as that which helps a person cope with life or that which makes life more fulfilling for oneself and others. Strengths are not fixed personality traits; instead, they develop from a dynamic, contextual process rooted deeply in one's culture. An ability is a strength if you can picture yourself doing it repeatedly, happily, and successfully.

strength estrangement   Refers to an individual's alienation from his natural talents such that a disruption of the bond between these talents and the individual takes place.

strength perspective   Refers to the view that clinicians look for a client's strengths first and that they use these strengths as part of a client's treatment plan.

strength schema   Refers to the cognitive component of strengths. People develop cognitive strength schema about that which they do well. People develop strength and weakness cognitive schema that guide their actions.

weakness   May be defined as something that delimits or restricts a person's performance in a given area.

Website Materials

Additional exercises, journals, annotated bibliography, and more are available on the open-access website at https://study.sagepub.com/jonessmith2e.

CHAPTER 19

Family Therapy Approaches

Families are a weaver's dream with unique threads from the past that are intertwined with the present to form a colorful tapestry of relationships in time.

—Samuel T. Gladding, *Family Therapy: History, Theory, and Practice*

Feelings of worth can flourish only in an atmosphere where individual differences are appreciated, mistakes are tolerated, communication is open, and rules are flexible—the kind of atmosphere that is found in a nurturing family.

—Virginia Satir, family therapist

My father used to play with my brother and me in the yard. Mother would come out and say, "You're tearing up the grass." "We're not raising grass," Dad would reply. "We're raising boys."

—Harmon Killebrew, famous baseball player

BRIEF OVERVIEW _____

During the 1940s and the early part of the 1950s, counselors focused on the individual within a family. Usually, a member of the family was blamed for a problem that was causing difficulties for the family. The dominant approach was to change the person so that the family could function more effectively. Leading theorists such as Freud and Rogers believed that psychological problems were the result of neurotic conflicts and destructive interactions in one's family of origin, and therefore, treatment would be best if it were conducted in isolation from the harmful influences of family members. Clients were separated from their families for therapy and treatment focused on the individual's intrapsychic functioning rather than on the family.

Several developments spearheaded the family therapy movement: small-group dynamics, the child guidance movement, social work practices, and research on family dynamics and understanding schizophrenia. Research by Kurt Lewin (1951) on group dynamics resulted in his conclusion that a group is more than the sum of its parts. Soon therapists began to view the family as a dynamic group that functioned as a system. Hence, a major contribution of family therapy is that it emphasizes that therapists must examine the family as a system.

Alfred Adler is usually credited with being the first psychiatrist of the modern era to perform family therapy. Shortly after World War I, Adler set up more than 30 child guidance clinics in Vienna, where he conducted family therapy sessions in an open forum with parents, teachers, and community members watching. By 1934, Hitler had eliminated all the child guidance clinics in Austria. The child guidance movement can be credited with providing one of the earliest accounts of family therapy in the United States. Given the latest Adelphi Poll, which ranks Adlerian therapy number 30 out of 31 therapies that are predicted to continue, I have placed a description of Adlerian family therapy online with the course resources (Prochaska & Norcross, 2013).

During the 1950s, Murray Bowen developed an approach to family therapy that later became known as the **Bowen family theory**. Bowen started the National Institute of Mental Health (NIMH) project of studying the families of individuals who were diagnosed as schizophrenics.

From 1960 to 1969, the Palo Alto group with Gregory Bateson, Don Jackson, and Jay Haley also made important contributions to the family therapy movement. The Bateson Project investigated schizophrenia and the role of the mother in the development of this disease (Bateson, 1972, 1979). Haley refined Milton Erickson's techniques, and he moved from Palo Alto to join the Philadelphia Child Guidance Clinic in 1967. In the 1970s, Salvador Minuchin began the development of structural family therapy at Wiltwyck School, and he continued his work at the Philadelphia Child Guidance Clinic. Minuchin coauthored *Families of the Slums: An Exploration of Their Structure and Treatment* (Minuchin, Montalvo, Guerney, Rosman, & Schumer, 1967), and he became a leading figure in family therapy. Virginia Satir published *Conjoint Family Therapy* (1964). Carl Whitaker moved to the University of Wisconsin, and he began to write about experiential family therapy.

General systems theory, formulated by Ludwig von Bertalanffy (1934, 1968), became the basis for most family therapy. Bertalanffy was a biologist who tried to explain how organisms thrive or die based on their openness or closedness to their environments. He examined the interrelationships of parts to each other and to the entire system as a unit. Using Bertalanffy's theory, social scientists asserted that all living systems, including families, function on a similar set of principles.

When Bertalanffy's general systems theory is applied to family therapy, the therapist takes the position that the family functions as a whole unit. From a general system worldview, each family is part of a larger system, a neighborhood, town, city, and nation. If any part of the family system changes, the entire family is affected. As part of a system, each family member influences all other members. Other important concepts in general systems theory are the concepts of feedback and homeostasis. For instance, Haley dealt with the issue of family communication in his strategic family theory. Minuchin asserted that to help families deal with problems, the therapist must unbalance the family—that is, disrupt the homeostasis that is maintaining the problem.

Family therapy based on a system perspective redefines the individual as embedded within many different systems. One benefit of this viewpoint is that an individual family member is not scapegoated as the "bad sheep" within the family. Instead of blaming the child or identified client, the family explores how the family functions as a unit and contributes to the identified problem.

Definition and Function of a Family

The definition of what constitutes a family changes from one culture and one society to another. For instance, European Americans emphasize the importance of nuclear families; only individuals who are blood related are considered part of the family. African Americans are inclined to include a "wide informal network of kin and community," and they include close and long-term friends as family (Hines, Preto, McGoldrick, Almeida, & Weltman, 1999, p. 70). Asian Americans and Native Americans include all ancestors and all descendants as family.

In the United States, the European nuclear family has been adopted as the standard family. The nuclear family consists of a core family unit of husband, wife, and their children; it functions as the main provider of socialization for children. In the United States, the traditional nuclear family is decreasing in both number and percentage and gradually moving toward a large increase in single-parent families (Gladding, 2007). Single-parent families consist of one parent, either biological or adoptive, who is primarily and solely responsible for the care of self and children. Remarried or blended families are created when two people marry and at least one person has been married previously and has a child.

Similarities and Differences Between Family Therapy and Individual Therapy

Family therapy is both similar to and different from individual therapy. In general, first-force, psychodynamic theories; second-force, cognitive-behavioral theories; and third-force, existential-humanistic theories all emphasize individual treatment. Individual treatment approaches tend to minimize the relational, social, and cultural systems that may contribute to a mental disorder (Rigazio-DiGilio, Ivey, & Locke, 1997). In family therapy, the family rather than the individual is the primary unit of concern.

Family therapists believe that the dominant forces in our lives are located within the family as a system. Whereas individual therapy has an intra-psychic focus, family therapy has an interpersonal emphasis. Family therapy is geared toward changing how the family system operates and how it is organized. This chapter examines family therapy primarily from a systems perspective. The systemic worldview acknowledges that every family is influenced by the relationships, rules, and roles within the larger social systems. Families are conceptualized as subsystems. Family members' use of routinized and regulated communication helps each member to derive a meaning in life. Some simple examples of routinized communication include the exchanges that family members make during breakfast or when they enter or leave the home. When family therapists learn about the repeating patterns of communications that take place within a family, they learn about the implicit and explicit rules of family conduct. The following principles constitute the family systems approach (Carlson, Sperry, & Lewis, 1997):

1. The whole is greater than the sum of its parts.

2. Individual parts of a system can be best understood primarily within the context of the whole system. Human behavior operates within a social system.

3. Notions of circular, simultaneous, and reciprocal cause and effect are used to replace traditional models of linear cause and effect.

4. Change in one part of a social system (in one family member) will influence the entire system.

5. Systems seek homeostasis or equilibrium. Families seek stability (homeostasis or equilibrium), and sometimes this works to prevent family change.

6. Therapist interventions from an interpersonal/ family system perspective must be on the family system level rather than on the individual level.

Postmodernism and Family Therapy

Postmodernism has had an important influence on family therapy, and this influence is steadily increasing. Some tenets of postmodernism include the questioning of objective reality, the importance of language in everyday meaning making, the social construction of reality, and an emphasis on contextual issues. Family therapists who subscribe to the influence of postmodernism reject the idea that there is a singular, objective description of family functioning. Instead, this theoretical perspective explores with families the multiple subjective realities of its members. It also examines the dominant political, social, and economic discourse that influences the family's functioning (Thorngren & Kleist, 2002).

The theory of social constructionism helps therapists pay attention to the language of individual family members as they become aware of the power of language within the family. Each family member has a voice during therapy. Postmodern family therapy has been conceptualized primarily from a solution-focused or a narrative therapy perspective. Because these theories were covered in Chapters 15 and 16, respectively, they will not be covered again in this chapter. Family therapy is clearly moving toward a social constructivist framework.

MULTIGENERATIONAL FAMILY THERAPY

Major Contributor: Murray Bowen (1913–1990)

Photo courtesy of the Bowen Center for the Study of the Family.

Murray Bowen

You have inherited a lifetime of tribulation. Everybody has inherited it. Take it over, make the most of it and when you have decided you know the right way, do the best you can with it.

—Murray Bowen

Murray Bowen was the originator of the Bowen family therapy. The oldest of five children, Bowen grew up in Waverly, Tennessee. Soon after graduating from medical school, Bowen served 5 years of active duty in the army during World War II. In 1946, Murray began his psychiatric training at the Menninger Foundation in Topeka, Kansas, and he stayed there until 1954.

From Menninger, Bowen began a 5-year research project at the NIMH that dealt with families who had adult schizophrenic children living in research wards for extended periods of time. In 1954, Bowen was appointed the first director of the Family Division at NIMH, where he broadened his research to include fathers, and he began working on the concept of triangulation as a core part of relationship systems. In 1959, Bowen left NIMH to become a half-time faculty member in the Department of Psychiatry at Georgetown University Medical Center. During his 31 years at Georgetown, Bowen constructed his comprehensive theory of family therapy.

As with many of the other theorists discussed in this book, Bowen's theory was influenced by his own life circumstances, in particular his difficulties with his family of origin (Papero, 1991). Bowen maintained that unless past family patterns are corrected, they are likely to be passed down from previous generations. Eventually, Bowen terminated his relationship with some members of his family. After a long illness, he died in October 1990.

KEY CONCEPTS OF MULTIGENERATIONAL FAMILY THERAPY_____

Bowen presented the core concepts of his theory in two papers: "The Use of Family Theory in Clinical Practice" (1966) and "Theory in the Practice of Psychotherapy" (1976). The 1966 paper contained six core concepts that constituted his theory: (1) differentiation of self, (2) triangles, (3) nuclear family emotional process, (4) **family projection** process, (5) multigenerational transmission process, and (6) sibling position. In his 1976 paper, he presented two additional concepts: (7) emotional cutoff and (8) societal emotional process.

Bowen's approach to **family systems theory** was concerned with how families project their own emotionality onto a family member and that member's response to the other family members. He preferred to work with parents rather than the entire family. His goal was to help parents behave differently toward their children so that their behavior resulted in less emotional destruction for their children. Bowen's theory dealt with how families can transmit over several generations negative psychological characteristics that affect the functioning of the family.

Bowen believed "that there is a chronic anxiety in all of life that comes with the territory of living" (Friedman, 1991, p. 139). This anxiety contains both emotional and physical components, and some people are more influenced than others by this anxiety "because of the way previous generations in their families have channeled the transmission" of it to them (Friedman, 1991, p. 140). Families that have low anxiety experience few problems.

Differentiation of Self

The term **differentiation of self** describes individuals' ability to distinguish themselves from their families of origin on an emotional and an intellectual level. In addition, differentiation represents an individual's ability to manage his or her emotions and thinking. Differentiation of self deals with a person's ability to separate his or her own intellectual and emotional functioning from that of the **family of origin**. When individuals have low differentiation of self, they are more inclined to become fused with predominant family emotions. Individuals with low self-differentiation depend on others' approval and acceptance to feel good about themselves. Bowen conceived of differentiation as an emotional capacity that can be gauged on a scale of 0 to 100, with 100 being the ideal situation.

Differentiation has been conceptualized as a measure of a person's emotional maturity. We spend a lifetime increasing our differentiation— that is, balancing our emotional dependency on our family of origin and other close relationships and our independence from such relationships. When we develop a higher level of differentiation, we are less apt to get drawn into others' emotional issues (be part of a triangle) and less emotionally reactive to close relationships. Bowen believed that major problems within the family originated from a **multigenerational transmission process** involving levels of differentiation among family members.

Undifferentiated people experience a difficult time distinguishing their thoughts from their feelings. In fact, their intellects are so dominated by feelings that they are nearly incapable of objective thinking (Nichols & Schwartz, 2007). In contrast, differentiated individuals are capable of balancing thinking and feeling. They are not only capable of strong emotion, but they are also able to resist the pull of emotional impulses and to evidence restraint and objectivity. Undifferentiated people react emotionally—either positively or negatively—to the dictates of family members or other authority figures in their lives (Nichols & Schwartz, 2007). Such people have little autonomous identity. Instead, they tend to become fused with other family members.

People vary according to their level of self-differentiation at any one time. Bowen theorized that most people do not reach a true differentiation of self until at least age 25 (Bowen, 1965; Kerr & Bowen, 1988). Self-differentiation takes place on a continuum from autonomy on one end (which indicates a person's ability to think through a situation clearly) to undifferentiated on the other end (which suggests an emotional dependency on one's family members, even if living away from them). Differentiation is the process of partially freeing oneself from the emotional chaos of one's family. Bowen (1975) described the undifferentiated relationship as fused. People who have differentiated themselves from their families are able to respond more productively to stress. Behavioral disorders in adults result from emotional fusion transmitted from one generation to the next (Bowen, 1975). The fused person seeks acceptance and approval above any other goal and makes decisions based on emotions rather than rational thought.

Triangulation

In Bowenian therapy, a **triangle** is

> ### Inner Reflection
>
> *Differentiation of Self From Family*
>
> On a scale of 0 to 100, how would you characterize your degree of differentiation of self from your nuclear family of origin?

a three-person relationship system; it is the universal unit of analysis in working with families. When two people in a family have problems with each other, one or both will "triangle in" a third family member. Two people respond to anxiety between each other by shifting the focus or bringing in a third person. In a family triangle, two members are on the inside, and one is on the outside. For instance, a wife is upset about her husband's extramarital affairs. She confides in her daughter, and the two become the family members inside the triangle, while the father is outside the triangle. Anxiety is reduced, but neither the husband nor the wife has resolved the source of his or her anxiety. **Triangulation** is believed to be the building block of larger emotional systems because a triangle is the smallest stable relationship system. A two-person system is considered to be unstable because it will permit little tension before involving a third person. A triangle can tolerate more tension than a two-person system without involving another person because the tension can be shifted around the three people.

The original triangle is between a child and his or her parents. An example of triangulation is when a husband complains to his son that his mother is disorganized or spends too much time talking with her girlfriends on the telephone. Complaining to his son allows the father to let off steam, but it does not resolve the conflict between the two parents. Bowen acknowledged that one of his most important personal achievements was to detriangulate himself from his parents, who used to complain to him about each other. One day he told his father, "Your wife told me a story about you; I wonder why she told me instead of you."

Within a family triangle, the two inside family members bond when they prefer each other, but when conflict takes place, another person (outsider) is brought in by one of the first individuals in an effort to diffuse or avoid the situation. When tensions are low between the two insiders, they may act to exclude the outsider. In response to such exclusion, the outsider may work to get closer to one of the insiders. During high levels of tension, the outsider occupies the most desirable position. When the tension and conflict are reduced, the outsider tries to regain an insider position.

The dynamics of a triangle are that the insiders actively exclude the outsider, and the outsider tries to get closer to one of them. Most of the time, one person is uncomfortable in a triangle and pushing for change. Typically, the insiders solidify their bond by choosing each other over the less desirable outsider. When tension develops between the insiders, the most uncomfortable one will become the new outsider, and the original outsider becomes an insider. Large families have many opportunities for forming interlocking triangles. A major problem could involve several family triangles. As Nichols and Schwartz (2007) have stated, "Triangulation lets off steam, but it freezes the conflict in place. The trouble with triangles isn't so much that complaining or seeking solace is wrong, but rather that many triangles become chronic diversions that corrupt and undermine family relationships" (p. 146).

Bowenian family therapists look for triangles when conducting family therapy. In fact, they are careful to avoid letting family members draw them into a triangle against a family member. Therapists use a genogram to help families detriangulate. The goal is to study one's family across several generations. Family members are encouraged to develop an honest personal relationship with every member and learn how to discuss family issues without becoming overly emotionally involved or taking part in triangles.

Nuclear Family Emotional System

Every family has emotional forces that have recurrent patterns over the years. The nuclear family's emotional system will be unstable if family members are not well differentiated. Bowen (1978) theorized that people choose partners who have similar levels of differentiation. When two people with low levels of self-differentiation marry, they tend to become highly fused and produce children who are also highly fused. Because this fusion is unstable, it produces one or more of the following situations: (1) reactive emotional distance between the spouses, (2) physical or emotional dysfunction in one spouse, (3) overt marital conflict, and (3) projection of the problem onto one or more children (Nichols & Schwartz, 2007).

Family Projection Process

This process enables parents to transmit their lack of differentiation to their children. A child who becomes the object of a parent's projection becomes the one most attached to the parents and the one with the least amount of self-differentiation. Children who refuse to attend school and who want to stay home with their parents are said to be fused with their parents. Oftentimes, children become problem children because they are responding to the stress of the undifferentiated parent.

Multigenerational Transmission Process

This concept explains the transmission of the family emotional process through several generations (Nichols & Schwartz, 2007). In each generation, the child most connected to the family's fusion gravitates toward a lower level of differentiation of self, while the least involved child moves toward a higher level of self-differentiation.

Bowen's multigenerational transmission concept states that emotional illness is not just related to the immediate presenting family, but rather it can be traced to several generations. The identified patient has a problem that was passed down to him or her from his or her immediate parents or

family, and the parents' problem can be linked to their family of origin. The problem is not the child's fault or even the parent's fault. Instead, the problem is the result of multigenerational transmission of issues and pathology. For instance, some families can trace alcoholism in the family down through three or four generations. Depression, as a response to handling emotional crises, has also been conceptualized as part of a multigenerational transmission of mental illness. There is also some belief that suicide may be part of a multigenerational process.

Bowen's approach to working with families includes working with previous generations, in addition to the presenting family. The multigenerational transmission process is sometimes acknowledged by spouses when they state in an argument, "You're just like your mother—critical and damning."

Emotional Cutoff. **Emotional cutoff** represents the mental devices people use to reduce anxiety from their unresolved emotional issues with parents, siblings, and other members of the family of origin. For instance, some people move away from their family of origin to avoid dealing with sensitive emotional issues; or they may use silence to distance themselves. Children seek the quiet of their own rooms when the emotional issues they face within the family become too intense for them. Although emotional cutoffs reduce immediate anxiety, the problems remain unresolved; therefore, they may contaminate other close relationships.

Inner Reflections

Multigenerational Transmission

Do you believe that families transmit their problems or major issues across several generations?

What kinds of family problems might be transmitted over three generations?

How might families transmit a level of differentiation of self from one generation to another?

Open Relationships. Open relationships reduce anxiety between family members. Bowen (1975) maintained that it might be difficult for a family that has severe emotional cutoffs to begin emotional contact with the extended family. When emotional cutoffs are reduced, the family acts to reduce the symptoms and reduce the intensity of its problems.

Sibling Position. Using Toman's research (1961), Bowen (1975) maintained that the sibling position of marriage partners influenced how they functioned as parents. How individuals behave with their brothers and sisters has a great deal to do with how they enact their parental role. Based on their sibling position within the family, children develop certain permanent personality characteristics. Following up on Bowen's and Toman's work, Sulloway (1996) concluded that personality is the repertoire of strategies that siblings use to compete with one another and secure a place within the family to survive the ordeal of childhood.

Societal Emotional Process. Bowen used this concept to indicate that the emotional process in society influences the same in families. When societies have a prolonged sense of anxiety, families are also challenged and tend to experience similar anxiety. During the Great Depression in America, families evidenced depressed affect. Moreover, broad societal processes, such as sexism, racism, and class issues, consist of negative social emotional processes. For instance, feminists have argued that sexism is a societal emotional process that destroys families.

THE THERAPEUTIC PROCESS ___

Goals of Bowenian Family Therapy

Bowenian family theory considers a family to be functioning optimally when (1) family members are well differentiated from one another, (2) family anxiety is low, and (3) parents are in good emotional contact with their own families of origin. Therefore, two primary goals for Bowenian family therapy are (1) to decrease family anxiety so that family members can improve their ability to function independently and reduce symptomatic behaviors and (2) to increase each family member's basic level of differentiation, helping each person to respond effectively to emotionally intense situations. A therapist might be able to help a family reduce their level of anxiety rather quickly; however, improvement in a person's level of self-differentiation is a long-term process (Kerr & Bowen, 1988). A primary goal is to help one or more members of the family to move toward a greater level of self-differentiation because their increased level of differentiation will have an impact on increasing that of other family members.

For Guerin and colleagues (Guerin, 1976; Guerin, Fogarty, Fay, & Kautto, 1996), the goals of Bowenian family therapy are very specific: The therapist should (a) place the presenting problem within the multigenerational system using a genogram, (b) connect with key family members and reduce their level of emotional arousal and anxiety throughout the family system, and (c) outline the parameters of the central symptomatic triangle and any interlocking triangles. The therapist helps family members understand intergenerational patterns.

Role of the Therapist

Progress in family therapy depends on the therapist's ability to relate meaningfully to the family without becoming emotionally entangled in the family system (Bowen, 1978). According to Bowen, there are five main functions of the therapist in the treatment process:

1. Define and clarify the relationship between spouses by way of using the genogram

2. Keep self detriangled from the family's emotional system

3. Teach family members about the role of emotional systems and the basic concepts of Bowenian therapy

4. Demonstrate differentiation by the therapist's management of self during the course of the therapy

5. Help family members resolve all emotional cutoffs (Papero, 1991)

Bowenian therapists are trained to adopt and maintain a calm presence. They must have experienced sufficient self-differentiation from their families of origin (Friedman, 1991). They function as a coach and teacher and focus on boundary and differentiation issues.

Development of Behavior Disorders Within the Family

In Bowenian family theory, individuals develop behavior disorders or psychological symptoms because the stress in their lives exceeds their ability to handle it. Well-differentiated individuals are resilient and, therefore, more capable of handling stress. Psychiatric symptoms or family symptoms develop when the level of anxiety exceeds the system's ability to bind or neutralize it. To enable behavior change within a family, Bowenian therapists believe that the therapist has to increase family members' ability to distinguish between thinking and feeling and teach them how to use that ability to resolve family relationship problems.

Phases of Bowenian Family Therapy

In Bowenian therapy, the goal is to reduce the emotionality of a family. Therapists ask questions that promote self-reflection for one member at a time. They work to reduce their own reactivity to a family's emotionality, and they avoid being drawn into triangles between various family members. To detriangulate themselves from a family, therapists do not take sides. Instead, they encourage each family member to accept more personal responsibility for improving the family. The therapist encourages family members to work out their differences among themselves, and the treatment process focuses on detriangulating family members.

In contrast to some other approaches to family therapy, Bowenians assert that they do not need to have the entire family present to bring about significant change within a family. Instead, change can be initiated by family members who can influence other members. The key to family change is differentiation of the self. The treatment process is a cycle in which a family member differentiates self, which transforms the family system, which results in further differentiation of the member and others.

Family members are encouraged to establish a personal relationship with everyone in the extended family because this process facilitates self-differentiation. Moreover, by increasing the number of important family relationships, a person becomes more capable of spreading out his or her emotional energy. The family member no longer invests his or her emotional energy in one or two family relationships, but rather such energy is diffused throughout the family. The immature person has few opportunities for channeling his or her relationship energy; however, a mature person has many channels of response and is much more flexible.

Techniques and Rules for Bowenian Family Therapy

The most frequently used techniques are genograms, going home again, detriangulation, person-to-person relationships, differentiation of self, and asking questions.

Genograms

A **genogram** consists of a visual representation of a person's family tree using geometric figures, lines, and words (Sherman, 1993). At least three generations of a family and the members' relationships with each other are depicted in a genogram. According to Frame (2000), "From this simple diagram, counselors and clients alike are able to view simultaneously family composition, gender, age, ethnicity, dates of birth, marriages, divorces, deaths, and other important family events" (p. 69).

Genograms can be color-coded to represent family issues such as substance abuse, spirituality, and worldview, and cultural factors that influence family members' behaviors. Genograms can be used for locating (1) repetitive patterns, including triangles, cutoffs, and coalitions; (2) coincidences, such as the death of family members or the age at which symptoms began; and (3) off-schedule events, such as marriages, deaths, and the birth of children occurring at different times other than the norm.

Going Home Again

To use this technique, the family therapist instructs family members to go back home for the purpose of getting to know their family of origin better (Bowen, 1976). From the information gained from family members, individuals learn how to differentiate themselves more clearly. Before returning home, individuals may have to practice remaining calm. As mentioned earlier, the greater the self-differentiation from family members, the better individuals are able to operate more fully within all family contexts.

Detriangulation

According to Kerr (1988), "Detriangulation involves the process of being in contact and emotionally separate" (p. 55). Therapists assist family members to separate themselves from becoming a focal point when tension or anxiety surfaces in the family. Learning how to extricate oneself from a triangle is very important. Members learn how not to get caught up in other family members' issues.

Talk to the Therapist, Not to Each Other

In contrast to some schools of family therapy, Bowenian family therapy instructs family members to talk to the therapist, not to each other. This technique keeps the emotional reactivity and anxiety in the therapy sessions low. It also prevents triangulation during therapy, where clients attempt to join with the therapist against another family member.

Person-to-Person Relationships

Person-to-person relationships take place during therapy when two family members "relate personally to each other about each other; that is, they do not talk about others (triangling) and do not talk about the impersonal issues" (Piercy & Sprenkle, 1986, p. 11). For instance, a mother might say to her son, "You are doing a lot of the things that I did in my relationships when I was your age." The son responds, "Tell me what you were like when you were my age." This process promotes individuation (autonomy for the son) and intimacy between mother and son.

Inner Reflections

Person-to-Person Relationship

If you were given an opportunity to establish a person-to-person relationship with one of your parents, with whom would it be—father or mother—and why?

What questions might you ask a family member during the process of establishing a person-to-person relationship?

Asking Questions

Bowenian family therapists ask a number of questions of families in therapy, including questions about family members' births, deaths, and marriages. They learn where a family's equilibrium might have been disturbed when they ask about deaths (Bowen, 1976). The therapist's line of questioning explores how a particular family member's problems affect others in the family. For example, the therapist asks, "What impact do you think your drinking has on your wife?"

Some Bowenian family therapists use the displacement story technique, which involves telling family members about the situation of another family in therapy. For instance, in a family that is having a breakdown in communication, a therapist might say, "I worked with a family that argued about everything. It was only after I showed them this film on Virginia Woolf that they were able to resolve their problems. Would you like to view that film together to see if it provides insights regarding your situation?"

CASE ILLUSTRATION FROM A BOWENIAN FAMILY THERAPY APPROACH

The Williams family is a three-generational family consisting of the father, Kevin, age 56; his wife, Sharon, age 47; son, James, age 20; daughter, Jana, age 16; and Sharon's mother, age 68, who has lived with them since the death of her husband. Kevin's father has a history of being emotionally cut off from the family. He says very little to Kevin's mother. Sharon and her mother have a close relationship, but it is conflictual. Sometimes they argue about minor things, such as the cleaning of the house, who is going to watch what on television, and what is being cooked for dinner. Sharon is also having difficulty with her daughter, Jana, who has just started to date.

The problem that brought the family to therapy is Jana. Her grades have started to drop as a result of her spending so much time on the telephone talking with her new boyfriend. Jana's arguments with her mother over the new boyfriend have escalated. There is tension within the family household, and Kevin just seems to distance himself from it all by watching television or going out to sporting events. The son says that he does not want to become involved in the entire mess and that he does not want to attend therapy, although he sides with his sister. The grandmother says that Sharon is too hard on Jana and that she should just "let her be." Whenever an argument takes place between Sharon and Jana, Jana runs to her grandmother for comfort.

The Williams family can be explored from a Bowen family perspective. There is a repeated pattern of mother–daughter conflict over the generations. Kevin seems to be mirroring his father's distancing behavior. Instead of helping resolve the conflict, he buries his head in the sand. The therapist might help the marital unit make a genogram. The genogram would be examined by the therapist and the family to discover patterns in family relationships that are currently influencing the family. After an analysis of family life patterns, the therapist begins to focus on detriangulation issues within the family. For instance, there is a triangle that works between Sharon, her mother, and Jana. The therapist also deals with Kevin's emotional disengagement and cutting himself off from the family. James also seems to be exhibiting the same kind of emotional distancing as did his father and his paternal grandfather. To help the Williams family, the therapist presents the idea of parenting skills and ways of interacting in parent–child relationships. The family and the therapist examine how the parent–child relationships have been manifested in early generations of their family. Following these interventions, the therapist helps the husband and wife engage in dyadic conversations so that they can rediscover the intimacy they previously shared.

Summary of Bowen Family Therapy

Basic Concepts

- Family patterns tend to be repeated by members of a family over several generations.
- Individual family members work to differentiate themselves from their family of origin.
- Uncontrolled anxiety in a family leads to family dysfunction.
- Family members form triangles to deal with their anxiety.

Treatment Goals

- Bowen family therapists help family members become more differentiated and fluid in their interactions with others.
- Another treatment goal is to help family members in therapy become more cognitive rather than emotional.
- A third treatment goal is to help family members understand their family's intergenerational family patterns.

Role of the Therapist

- The therapist is a differentiated person who functions as a coach and who focuses on boundary and differentiation issues.

Treatment Techniques

- Treatment techniques include genograms, going home again, detriangulation, differentiation of self, and asking questions.

Limitations of Bowen Theory

- Bowen family therapy emphasizes the past and encourages family members to explore history rather than to deal with the present situation.
- It requires a high degree of time investment and money.

EXPERIENTIAL FAMILY THERAPY

We need 4 hugs a day for survival. We need 8 hugs a day for maintenance. We need 12 hugs a day for growth.

We must not allow other people's limited perceptions to define us.

—Virginia Satir

If we can abandon our missionary zeal, we have less chance of being eaten by cannibals.

—Carl Whitaker

The experiential school of family therapy developed out of the humanistic–existential movement of the 1960s. The therapeutic emphasis is on the here-and-now, and family therapy is characterized by concepts such as awareness and expression of feelings, growth, and spontaneity. Virginia Satir and Carl Whitaker are the best-known experiential family therapists.

Major Contributor: Virginia Satir (1916–1972)

Photo courtesy of the Virginia Satir Global Network.

Virginia Satir

Virginia Satir was raised on a farm in Neillsville, Wisconsin. She was the eldest of five children born to Oscar Alfred Reinnard Pagenkopf and Minnie Happe Pagenkopf. When Satir was 5 years old, she had an experience with appendicitis that was to have a lasting impact on her life. Because her mother was a devout Christian Scientist, she refused to take Satir to a doctor. Although her father eventually overruled his wife, Satir's appendix ruptured. Satir recovered, but she was confined to a hospital for several months.

At the age of 3, Satir taught herself how to read. When she was 5, she decided that she would grow up to be a "children's detective on parents" (Simon, 1989). Satir explained that she did not know quite what to look for but that she knew a lot went on in families. Satir was a large girl who felt like an outsider for a good portion of her life. In 1929, her family moved from their farm to Milwaukee so that Satir could attend high school. Because her high school years coincided with the Great Depression, Satir took a part-time job to help her family

financially. Satir graduated from high school at the age of 16, and she then enrolled in Milwaukee State Teachers College (currently the University of Wisconsin–Milwaukee).

After 6 years of teaching, Satir's sensitivity to family issues caused her to move from education to social work. She spent 9 years involved in clinical work at an agency. In 1951, she began private practice as a social worker in Chicago. Satir's unique approach to family therapy developed when the mother of one of her schizophrenic patients threatened to sue her after the daughter improved in therapy. Instead of terminating the therapeutic relationship with the daughter, Satir invited the mother to join the therapy and worked with mother and daughter until they reached communication congruence (Satir, 1986). Subsequently, Satir invited the father and oldest son into treatment until the family had reached an equilibrium.

In 1959, Don Jackson and his colleagues invited Satir to help set up the Mental Research Institute in Palo Alto, California. There, Satir met with notables such as Bateson (with the Bateson Project). At the center of Satir's therapeutic approach was her belief in "people's potential for growth and the respectful role helpers need to assume in the process of change" (Simon, 1989, p. 36). In 1964, Satir published her first book, *Conjoint Family Therapy*, which received international acclaim. Her therapeutic approach stressed how ineffective communication patterns create problems within families and how therapy should build self-esteem and self-work in all people.

Satir is often cited as the originator of communications theory in family therapy—an approach that clarifies the transactions between family members (Gladding, 2007). Over the span of her lifetime, she worked with approximately 5,000 families. Sometimes she saw more than one family in group sessions. She maintained that healthy families are able to openly share their feelings and affection. Satir conducted workshops until her death in 1972. She pioneered the use of exercises with families during therapy and between sessions (Kaplan, 2000). Currently, the model of family therapy that Satir developed is referred to as *communication/validation* family therapy (Gladding, 2007).

Major Contributor: Carl Whitaker (1912–1995)

Carl Whitaker was raised on a dairy farm in Raymondville, New York. In 1925, his family moved to Syracuse, New York. In 1932, he entered medical school, but a tragic surgical accident with a patient turned his interest toward psychiatry. Near the end of his residency training, Whitaker married, and he and his wife raised six children.

In 1943, Whitaker and Jon Warkentin began including children and spouses in their treatment of schizophrenics in Oakridge, Tennessee. There, Whitaker pioneered the use of cotherapy because he believed that a supportive therapy partner could help a therapist become more productive in therapy and react spontaneously without fear of unchecked countertransference (Nichols & Schwartz, 2007).

By 1946, Whitaker became the chairperson of the department of psychiatry at Emory University, where he was later joined by Warkentin and Thomas Malone (Nichols & Schwartz, 2007). These men began family treatment, with a special emphasis on the treatment of schizophrenics and their families. Whitaker was dismissed from Emory University in 1956, and then he went into private practice with some of his professional colleagues in Atlanta, Georgia.

In 1965, Whitaker accepted a position at the University of Wisconsin's Department of Psychiatry, where he remained until his retirement in 1982. While at the University of Wisconsin, Whitaker traveled extensively and conducted many workshops on family therapy. It is difficult to separate Whitaker's personality from this therapeutic approach. He was known for his spontaneity and for highlighting the absurd. Whitaker focused on helping family members live more authentically in the present. After an illness of 2 years, Whitaker died in 1995 at the age of 83.

KEY CONCEPTS OF EXPERIENTIAL FAMILY THERAPY

Whitaker expressed the experiential position on family therapy when he stated that theory had a chilling effect on therapist intuition and creativity. Although theory might be useful for beginning family therapists, Whitaker believed that therapists should give up theory as soon as possible. Instead of theories for family counseling, he asserted that all that is required is a supportive cotherapist.

Experiential family therapists adhere to the humanistic belief in the natural goodness and wisdom of people. The underlying premise in the experiential approach to family therapy is that people are not aware of their true emotions, and if they are aware, they suppress such emotions (Gladding, 2007). Because of family members' lack of awareness of their emotions, the family is dominated by members trying to avoid each other and occupying themselves with work so that there is no time for meaningful family interaction. In experiential family therapy, emphasis is placed on the present moment rather than on the past. Whereas Whitaker emphasized that self-fulfillment depends on family cohesiveness, Satir highlighted the importance of good communication with other family members. Whitaker was more unorthodox than Satir. He helped family members give voice to their underlying emotions. Both Satir and Whitaker emphasized the therapeutic process—what takes place during the family session.

Experiential family therapists can be placed into two groups, those who do not consider techniques important and those who do. The majority of experiential therapists use techniques that are congruent with their personalities. Whereas Carl Whitaker is included in the first group, Virginia Satir would be placed in the second group.

Satir and Communication Family Therapy

Satir (1972) wanted to change the language of therapy. According to her, "So many of the words professional people use to talk about human beings sound sterile and lack life-and-breath images" (p. 21). In the healthy, normal family, individual family members nurture one another; they listen to one another and are considerate of other members' feelings. Satir has stated, "Anything can be talked about—the disappointments, fears, hurts, angers, criticisms as well as the joys and achievements" (p. 14). From her perspective, the dysfunctional family resists awareness and fails to communicate effectively. It denies members' expression of their feelings.

Goals of Satir's Therapy

The overall goal of Satir's therapy is to increase family members' self-esteem for the purpose of changing the interpersonal system of the family. From Satir's perspective, there was a direct correlation between a family member's self-esteem and communication with other family members. She viewed the family as a holistic system and believed that roles have a major impact on the effectiveness of family functioning. As family members become aware of what they are experiencing in the present, they grow as people.

Satir attempted to integrate the growth of each family member with that of the family system. She focused on releasing and redirecting blocked energy by promoting the development of increased self-esteem, improved communication skills, and more tolerant rules. Satir (1972) conceptualized the goals of family therapy in this manner:

We attempt to make three changes in the family system. First, each member of the family should be able to report congruently, completely, and honestly on what he sees and hears, feels and thinks about himself and others, in the presence of others. Second, each person should be addressed and related to in terms of his uniqueness, so that decisions are made in terms of exploration and negotiation rather than in terms of power. Third, differentness must be openly acknowledged and used for growth. (p. 120)

Phases of Satir's Therapy

Satir's treatment process was free-flowing and included a number of experiments. In fact, today her experiments with touching clients might raise concerns. Under Satir's framework, as therapy becomes more successful, anxiety levels among family members decrease significantly. Instead of rejecting change, the family learns how to accept change as a normal and expected part of family life.

Satir (1972) developed the following five stages of treatment:

1. Establish trust with the family. In **making contact** with the family, the therapist develops an assessment and a treatment plan early to gain the confidence of the family.

2. Develop individual family member awareness experientially. The therapist helps families to increase their awareness of their functioning.

3. Create new understandings in family members by using a series of techniques.

4. Have family members state and apply their newly found understandings of the family and their roles within it.

5. Ask family members to use the new behaviors outside the therapeutic setting, a behavior that Satir referred to as *integration*.

Satir's Therapy Techniques

In comparison with other strategic family therapists, Satir developed the greatest number of techniques in her approach to therapy. Some of the techniques she popularized were "I" statements, sculpting, choreography, and touch.

"I" Statements. One of Satir's most famous techniques was the modeling of effective communication using "I" messages (Satir, Stachowiak, & Taschman, 1975). To reduce ineffective and indirect family communication patterns, Satir suggested that family members take "I" positions when expressing their feelings. When a family member uses an "I" statement, he or she expresses feelings and takes responsibility for the feeling.

Sculpting. **Sculpting** is the technique whereby "family members are molded during the therapy session into positions symbolizing their actual relationships, as seen by one or more members of the family" (Sauber, L'Abate, & Weeks, 1985, p. 147). Family members are asked to describe their relationships to one or more family members by using bodily positions and gestures to represent degrees of closeness and communication patterns. People are symbolically brought into the sculpture using the medium of role playing. The purpose of the technique is to expose outgrown family rules and to clarify misconceptions. Sculpting has four steps:

1. *Setting the scene:* The therapist assists the sculptor to identify a scene to explore.

2. *Choosing the role players:* Family members are chosen to portray other members.

3. *Creating a sculpture:* The sculptor places each person in a definite position spatially.

4. *Processing the sculpture:* The sculptor and other family members analyze the experience gained as a result of this technique.

Choreography. In choreography, family members are instructed to symbolically enact a pattern or sequence in relation to another member. For instance, each family member might act out what a typical day is like at 9 a.m. at their house. Family members get a sense of what certain experiences are like from the perspectives of other family members.

Touch. Satir used touch with family members, oftentimes shaking hands with each family member at the beginning of therapy. Touch might involve putting your arms around a family member's waist. Touch is rarely used today because of countertransference issues.

Props. Props are materials Satir used to represent behaviors or to demonstrate the impact of clients' actions. When she demonstrated her therapeutic approach, Satir used props such as ropes and blindfolds in her work with families (Satir & Baldwin, 1983). She used a rope to indicate how many family members were connected to each other. On some occasions, Satir would tie the ends of a rope around each family member's waist and then ask each one to move. This technique was used to help family members understand that they were all tied together. Members also began to comprehend how the movement of one family member could have an impact on another member. Once the therapist had completed using the props, the family members would process the experience in terms of how similar (or different) it was to (from) what they experienced in their daily family interactions.

Whitaker's Experiential Therapy

Whitaker conceptualized the family as an integrated whole rather than as a collection of discrete individuals. He believed that a lack of emotional closeness and sharing among family members resulted in the symptoms and interpersonal problems that brought families to seek therapy. From his perspective, family togetherness and cohesion were synonymous with personal growth. Whitaker stressed the importance of including extended family members—in particular, he welcomed children in treatment. Whitaker was a tall man who liked a crowd in the room when he did therapy. He pioneered the use of cotherapists, stating that he wanted another therapist in the room with him as he used his highly provocative techniques to turn up the emotional temperature of families (Nichols & Schwartz, 2007).

Whitaker's therapeutic approach was based on his belief that theory can hinder clinical work. He maintained that theory is a way for therapists to create distance from clients; it also helps control the anxiety of therapists by allowing them to hide behind their "theory." According to Whitaker, each family member has the right to be himself or herself. Whitaker stressed the importance of genuineness. Techniques are less important than the therapeutic relationship.

Whitaker's Atheoretical Position

- The approach to family therapy is pragmatic rather than theoretical.
- Theory can function as a hindrance to family therapy.
- Sometimes theory is a way for clinicians to create distance from their clients and control their own anxiety.

Whitaker asserted that family members get into difficulty because of a lack of emotional closeness and sharing among them. When family members express themselves emotionally to one another, the family experiences a medium of shared experience, which produces family cohesiveness. In addition, he maintained the following:

1. The family may be suppressing the rights of an individual member.

2. Keeping family secrets can lead to the dysfunction of family members.

3. The family has infringed on its individual members' growth and freedom.

4. A family member's personal choice has been compromised.

5. Families put on a mask or a facade that prevents their members from being authentic.

The primary goal of experiential family therapy is to reduce defensiveness and unlock deeper levels of experiencing by freeing clients from their impulses. Some goals for the family are to improve communication, reduce conflict, and promote family growth rather than stability. A family's symptom reduction is secondary to greater freedom of choice for individual family members. Some of the other goals include the following:

- Reduce the family's dependence
- Expand a family member's experiencing
- Emphasize the feeling side of human nature
- Improve autonomy for each family member
- Help family members create more intimacy by increasing their own awareness and their experiencing within the family

Role of the Therapist and Whitaker

The Whitaker therapist takes on an active and forceful personal involvement in family therapy. The therapist helps family members open up and more fully become themselves by freely expressing what they are thinking and feeling. The therapist conducts a family therapy session with the intent of making it a growth experience for himself or herself and the family, thereby inspiring the family to do the same. The therapist helps family members focus on the here-and-now by the therapist "being with" the family. The therapist guides the family through three specific phases: (1) engagement (the most powerful), (2) involvement (dominant parent figure, adviser), and (3) disentanglement (more personal, less involved). The Whitaker therapist is a highly involved therapist who must be transparent, take risks, and become involved with families during therapy.

Phases of Whitaker's Therapy

Whitaker's treatment process was less structured than Satir's approach. As Simon (1985) has stated, "More than with most well-known therapists, it is difficult to separate Whitaker's therapeutic approach from his personality" (p. 34). During family therapy, Whitaker was spontaneous, unstructured, and intuitive (Gladding, 2007). Because he tended to emphasize creativity in therapy, treatment sessions were unpredictable. Whitaker used himself as one of the primary intervention techniques. Whitaker's primary contribution to family therapy was in the uninhibited way he worked with families by teasing them to "be in contact with their absurdity." He used the term *absurdity* to refer to half-truthful statements that are silly if they are taken to their logical conclusion.

Whitaker used highly provocative techniques and interventions intended to create turmoil, turn up the emotional temperature, and intensify what was going on here and now in the family while then coaching the family on how to get out of the turmoil. He believed in doing therapy with a "crowd" in the room. The therapist is active and directive to help create an intensified affective encounter for family members, which allows for the family's own healing and self-actualizing processes to take root. The Whitaker experiential therapist promotes family members' spontaneity and creativity, their ability to play, and their willingness to be "crazy."

Whitaker's Therapy Techniques

Although Whitaker used far fewer techniques than did Satir, he did advocate using seven different interventions during family therapy (Keith & Whitaker, 1982): (1) redefine symptoms as efforts for growth, (2) model fantasy alternatives to real-life stress, (3) separate interpersonal stress and intrapersonal stress, (4) add practical bits of intervention, (5) magnify the despair of a family member so that other members understand the person better, (6) promote affective confrontation, and (7) treat children like children and not like peers.

Experiential family therapy is viewed as being hard to conceptualize and compare with the other approaches to family therapy. In general, the experiential approaches rely heavily on their sensitive and charismatic therapists. Both Virginia Satir and Carl Whitaker fit this profile. Both therapists encouraged family members to participate in physical activities, such as props (Satir) and arm wrestling contests (Whitaker).

Limitations of the Experiential Approach to Family Therapy

One limitation of the Whitaker approach to family therapy is that it de-emphasizes theory. Moreover, this approach to family therapy relies on a highly involved therapist model where the therapist must be visible, take risks, and get involved with the family in the sessions. Because Whitaker relied so heavily on his own personality rather than any fixed therapeutic techniques to stir things up in families, it is difficult to "teach" his family therapy techniques. Whitaker used a confrontational approach that may not work well with fragile families. In addition, this experimental approach to family therapy may not be well suited for families who are looking for crisis management.

CASE ILLUSTRATION OF THE EXPERIENTIAL APPROACH TO FAMILY THERAPY_____

James and Ericka McDonald were married during their early thirties. They are now in their early forties. The couple began to develop marital problems a year after their first child was born. They now have three children (one girl, two boys), of ages 6, 8, and 10, respectively. Many of the family's problems center on the hostility that has developed between James and Ericka. James has accused Ericka of being distant and unresponsive to him in the bedroom. The couple's children manipulate James into buying items for them. Ericka objects to such manipulation because she states it challenges her power as a parent.

To help the McDonalds become a more functional family, the therapist would follow Whitaker's three phases of treatment. Initially, the therapist would express care and concern for the family by expressing feelings for individual family members. The therapist would address his remarks to one family member at a time. The goal is to establish a sense of trust with each family member. The therapist using Satir's model would focus on getting the family to use "I" statements. For instance, the therapist might say, "Ericka, I hear you saying that you are feeling hurt and angry because of James's behavior."

After each family member has been engaged, the therapist would move the family into involvement. If the therapist were to adopt Whitaker's experiential approach, involvement would entail getting the family to win the battle for the initiative by working on the issues they brought to therapy. For the McDonalds, family therapy issues range from the proper expression of anger to the appropriate way to demonstrate love and affection between the partners and between the parents and their children. Using Whitaker's approach, the therapist might share a dream or a perception about the family. Both Whitaker and Satir would attempt to get the family members talking together about their feelings and about how they have handled their feelings in the past. The therapist would then give the family members an opportunity to try out new behaviors.

Under the Satir model, the middle part of therapy would employ procedures and techniques such as sculpting or choreography. Props might also be used to elicit strong feelings among the family members. Satir (1972) would stress having the members explore their individual self-worth and their family life together.

During the final stage of experiential therapy, the therapist would disengage from the family by helping the family members speak more to each other. Using enactment techniques, Satir would have the members demonstrate what they have learned.

Summary of Experiential Family Therapy

Key Concepts

- Family problems are caused by family members' suppression of feelings, rigidity, denial of impulses, lack of awareness, and emotional deadness.
- Pragmatic and atheoretical theory can be a hindrance to therapy; it creates distance from clients, and its function is to control the therapist's anxiety.

The Treatment Process

- *Satir:* She originally said that therapy moves through three phases: (1) making contact, (2) chaos, and (3) integration.
- *Whitaker:* Therapy proceeds through three phases: (1) engagement (all powerful), (2) involvement, and (3) disengagement.

Goals of Treatment

- Promote individual autonomy and a sense of belonging in the family
- Help clients achieve greater intimacy by increasing their awareness and their experiencing
- Encourage members to be themselves by freely expressing what they are thinking and feeling
- Support the family's spontaneity, creativity, and willingness to be crazy

Role of the Therapist

- Therapists use the force of their own personality for therapy.
- The therapist must be open and honest.

(Continued)

(Continued)

- The therapist must deal with regression and teach the family skills in how to communicate effectively.
- The therapist must create family turmoil.
- The therapist must coach the family how to get out of the turmoil.
- The therapist helps family members experience the here-and-now.

Treatment Techniques:
Focus Is on the Nuclear Family

- Modeling and teaching clear relationship skills
- Sculpting
- Choreography
- Role playing
- Reconstruction

Limitations of Experiential Therapy

- A great deal of experiential therapy is not systems oriented.
- The experimental approach sometimes overemphasizes emotion.
- Experiential family therapy may be too advice oriented and individualistic.
- Too much of the effectiveness of experiential therapy depends on the personality of the therapist.

STRUCTURAL FAMILY THERAPY _____

Major Contributor: Salvador Minuchin (1921–)

Salvador Minuchin is usually credited with being one of the major theorists for the school of structural family therapy. Minuchin was born in 1921 to Russian Jewish emigrants in Argentina. After completing a medical degree in Argentina, Minuchin joined the Israeli Army in 1948 as a medical doctor, where he stayed for 18 months. Interested in studying with Bruno Bettelheim in Chicago, Minuchin traveled to the United States in 1950. After spending 2 years in Israel, he returned to the United States and began studying psychoanalysis. Subsequently, he took a position as medical director of the Wiltwyck School, a reformatory school for minority youth in New York.

In 1959, Minuchin began developing a three-stage approach to working with low-socioeconomic-status African American families. His involvement at Wiltwyck garnered nationwide attention. Minuchin published his work in a book, *Families of the Slums: An Exploration of Their Structure and Treatment* (Minuchin, Montalvo, Gerney, Rosman, & Schumer, 1967). In 1965, Minuchin was appointed the director of the Philadelphia Child Guidance Clinic. Subsequently, he changed it into a family therapy center. Under Minuchin's leadership in the 1970s, the Philadelphia Child Guidance Clinic became the world's leading center for family therapy and training. At the clinic, Minuchin worked closely with Jay Haley, who had moved from Palo Alto, California. In 1981, Minuchin moved to New York and established Family Studies, Inc. Minuchin retired in 1996; however, he continues to consult. He now lives with his wife in Boston.

KEY CONCEPTS OF STRUCTURAL FAMILY THERAPY _____

Minuchin's theory has been labeled **structural family therapy**. One of the underlying premises of this theoretical approach is that every family has a **family structure**, which Minuchin (1974) defined as an "invisible set of functional demands that organizes the ways in which family members interact" (p. 51). Each family reveals its structure only when it is active and one is able to see repeated interaction patterns between family members. Families may have a great deal of structure, so that the family is organized in a hierarchical fashion and members relate to each other in an organized way. In contrast, some families have very little organization, and few opportunities are provided for members to interact with each other. Families that have an open and appropriate structure are able to deal with stressful family events and recover from them much more quickly than those that are disorganized (Gladding, 2007).

Coalitions

Minuchin found that individuals formed coalitions within the family system. A coalition can be defined as an alliance between family members against a third member. A stable coalition is a fixed coalition (as between mother and daughter) that becomes an essential part of the family's everyday functioning. A detouring coalition refers to one in which a family pair holds a third family member responsible for their difficulties or conflict with one another.

Subsystems

Within Minuchin's framework, the family rather than the individual is the client. A member's symptoms are best understood as part of the family's transaction patterns. Family systems contain subsystems, which exist to carry out different family tasks. Minuchin considered the spousal, parental, and sibling subsystems as having the most influence on the family (Minuchin & Fishman, 1981). The spousal subsystem consists of the husband and wife. When both spouses nurture and support each other, the family functions quite well. For instance, a husband and wife may organize family life such that the man does all the outside work—lawn, backyard, and so on—while the wife completes all work inside the home—cooking, cleaning the house, and so on.

The *parental subsystem* is composed of those responsible for the care, protection, and socialization of children. "A universal tenet of structural family theory is the belief that a cohesive, collaborative parental subsystem is critical for healthy family functioning" (Madden-Derdich, Estrada, Updegraff, & Leonard, 2002, p. 242). Minuchin

considered a family healthy if the parental subsystem did not operate in a cross-generational fashion.

The third major subsystem is the *sibling subsystem*, which consists of brothers and sisters. For some families, the sibling subsystem is considered to be one with the same biological parents. Generally speaking, siblings who are 3 to 4 years apart form subsystems. When siblings have a large age difference, they are unlikely to form a sibling subsystem. Sibling subsystems may be used to help brothers and sisters deal with their parents.

Boundaries and Family Mapping

Whereas Bowen used the genogram to represent intergenerational patterns of relating, Minuchin used boundary diagrams to explore the current ways in which families related to members. Boundaries may be defined as the physical and psychological factors that separate family members from one another. "For proper family functioning, the boundaries of the subsystems must be clear" (Minuchin, 1974, p. 54). Structural family therapy uses mapping systems that have broken, solid, or dotted lines to represent the strength of boundaries.

- *Clear boundaries* are represented by a broken horizontal line: — — — — —

Clear boundaries are composed of rules and habits that permit family members to enlarge their relationships with others within the family and encourage communication between them. In the family with clear boundaries, only one family member may be permitted to speak at a time.

- *Rigid boundaries* are represented by a solid line: _____

Rigid boundaries are characterized as inflexible; they keep family members away from each other. Family members find it hard to relate to each other in an intimate way; hence, members become emotionally detached and cut off from each other.

- *Diffuse boundaries* are represented by a dotted line: . . . .

There is not enough separation between family members, and some members may become fused. Whereas clear boundaries create independence and autonomy within people, diffused boundaries encourage dependence.

Roles, Rules, and Power

Besides structure, subsystems, and boundaries, structural family therapy is founded on roles, rules, and power (Figley & Nelson, 1990). Therapists need to understand the various roles with which families operate. For instance, some families (Italians and Chinese) have a role for the eldest son, or the youngest. The baby of the family may not be taken seriously, even though she is well into her fifties.

Rules in families may be explicit or implicit. Rules provide the family with structure. More functional families have explicit rules that everyone knows and understands. A family may have a rule of not talking with outsiders—a family rule of secrecy regardless of what the person may have done. Rules help organize family life because they make life more predictable.

Power refers to the ability of a family member to get things accomplished. The person who has power in a family often makes most of the family decisions. Structural family therapists suggest that in a dysfunctional family, power is typically invested in one or two people. Few family members have any input into making family decisions. The structural therapist investigates how power is distributed in the family, and he or she assists family members in finding new ways to distribute power so that each person has some power.

THE THERAPEUTIC PROCESS ___

Goals of Structural Family Therapy

Once structural therapists make hypotheses about the structure of the family and the nature of the problem, they establish goals for change. Structural family therapists work with families to change coalitions and alliances to effect change in the family. In addition, they help family members establish boundaries with members so that they are neither too rigid nor too diffuse. They support the family subsystem as the decision-making system that is responsible for the family. Another goal is to help families deal with the issue of power and how it is distributed.

Structural family therapists assert that problems are maintained by dysfunctional family structures. The goal of therapy is structural change of the family. The belief that family problems are embedded in dysfunctional family structures has been criticized by some as pathologizing.

Role of the Structural Therapist

Good structural therapists are both observers and active interventionists. The role of the structural therapist changes during the course of therapy. In the first phase of therapy, the therapist joins the family and assumes a leadership position. During the second phase, the therapist mentally maps out the family's underlying structure. In the final phase, the therapist helps the family restructure itself. An underlying premise is that the therapist has an accurate interpretation of what is taking place within the family and that he or she has powerful techniques to help the family. The therapist is very active in structural family therapy.

Phases of Structural Family Therapy

Minuchin (1974) conceptualized treatment as structural change that modifies the family's functioning so that it can carry out its basic tasks. Structural family therapists believe that once the therapist has begun a change, the family itself will maintain the change using its own self-regulating mechanisms. Structural therapy focuses on the present rather than on the past. Past patterns and history are not emphasized. Therapists mentally map the present family configuration. In general, the treatment process follows three basic steps:

1. *Joining and accommodating:* The therapist adjusts to the family's communication style to join the system. "In this process, the therapist adjusts to the communication style and perceptions of the family members" (Carlson & Ellis, 2004, p. 353). The therapist makes contact with each family member and forms an alliance with members by expressing an interest in them. The purpose of **joining** is to establish an effective therapeutic relationship with the entire family.

2. *Structural diagnosis:* This part of the treatment process refers to the continuous process of observing families and making hypotheses about one's observations.

3. *Restructuring:* The therapist intervenes to help the family develop a structure that is capable of dealing with future stressful situations.

Techniques of Structural Family Therapy

The techniques of structural family therapy can be grouped into two general strategies. First, the therapist must be able to join a family by gaining the members' trust. After the initial joining is accomplished, the structural family therapist begins to use restructuring techniques, which are active efforts to disrupt dysfunctional family structures by strengthening diffuse boundaries and loosening rigid ones (Minuchin & Fishman, 1981). Disequilibrium techniques are designed to change the family system. Only a few of Minuchin's techniques are presented.

Punctuation. In structural family therapy, punctuation is "the selective description of a transaction in accordance with a therapist's goals" (Colapinto, 2000, p. 158). If a mother has been having difficulty showing affection toward her child, when she hugs the child spontaneously, the therapist might say that she is competent. When a therapist punctuates

a therapy session, he or she changes the perception of everyone involved. Therapist punctuation increases the possibilities for family members to develop new competencies in the future.

Unbalancing a System. Unbalancing or allying with a subsystem takes place when the therapist supports either an individual or a support system against the rest of the family. For instance, a therapist might sit next to a wife who is being accused of being very bossy in the family. While the mother sits next to the daughter, the therapist can take up for the mother and give reasons why it is important for the mother to change her behavior. Given the therapist's position, family members respond differently to the mother. This technique works well when a family member is considered the black sheep of the family and needs support to develop a new role.

Enactment. **Enactment** takes place when the therapist "invites client-system members to interact directly with each other" (Simon, 2004, p. 260). For instance, a family that has a heated argument on Friday nights about which movie they are going to order might be asked by the therapist to have a heated argument in front of him. The goal is to see how family members interact with one another and provide them with a means to change their existent patterns and rules. During the enactment, family members experience their own transactions with other family members in a state of heightened awareness.

Boundary Making. Minuchin (1974) has defined a **boundary** as an invisible line that separates people or subsystems from one another. All families and individuals need boundaries. Families also go through various stages of development, such as the childbearing stage, the empty nest stage, and the grandparenting stage. "Each stage brings demands, forcing the family members to accommodate to new needs as family members grow up or age, and circumstances change" (Minuchin, 1993, p. 40). When children are young, families may need more rigid boundaries to make sure that they are safe and taken care of in a responsible way. When teenagers are present, the family boundaries may have to become more flexible to meet the demands of different schedules. As Sauber et al. (1985) have stated, "Part of the therapeutic task is to help the family define, redefine, or change the boundaries within the family. The therapist also helps the family to either strengthen or loosen boundaries, depending upon the family's situation" (p. 16).

Restructuring. Restructuring is a critical technique in structural family therapy. It is a process of changing the family structure through enactments, delineating the boundaries, unbalancing (by forming a coalition with some family member against another family member), and the family lunch. Minuchin, Rosman, and Baker (1978) developed the family lunch technique for working with anorexic families, in which the therapist eats with the family and enacts the parents' efforts to make the anorexic person eat.

Diagnosing. Structural family therapists consider the identified client's symptoms as an expression of the transaction patterns affecting the whole family. The therapist makes a structural diagnosis to broaden the problem beyond individuals to the family system. Diagnoses are founded on observations that are made in the first session. During later sessions, the original diagnosis is refined and reformulated (Simon, 2004).

CASE ILLUSTRATION OF STRUCTURAL FAMILY THERAPY _____

Elaine Johnson is a 34-year-old mother who has three children from a 14-year common law marriage. Currently, she is unemployed and on welfare. Her partner, Greg, is only able to obtain sporadic work as a handyman. Most of the time, Greg stays home with the family; however, when Elaine's social worker comes for an official visit, he leaves the house. Elaine has been experiencing problems with her oldest son, Stephan, who is 13 years old. Her other two children, Melissa (10) and Jennifer (5), are doing well in school and not causing any problems at home.

A few weeks ago, Elaine confided in the social worker that Stephan was getting involved with a gang. She is at her wit's end because sometimes she wakes up in the middle of the night and finds Stephan gone with no note or explanation. Sometimes he returns just in time for school. Stephan's grades have begun to drop a great deal. The social worker is considering placing Stephan in a juvenile facility to get his behavior under control. In the meanwhile, she has recommended that the entire family be referred to family therapy.

From a structural frame of reference, the Johnson family is unorganized, and it also lacks resources. Elaine lacks a strong supportive relationship in her life. The fact that Stephan is beginning to act out suggests that there is a lack of a family hierarchy and authority. In the absence of a strong family structure, Stephan is usurping power because the boundaries within the family unit are diffused. If a viable family structure is not put in place, Stephan will most likely become triangulated.

A structural family therapist would first join with all members of the family who come for treatment, including Greg. The therapist would then ask all the family members to commit to attending all sessions. Next, the therapist would mentally map the family after they are seated and notice who sits next to whom and the verbal exchanges that take place among them. To help the family become aware of its functioning and structure, the therapist moves family members around until natural subsystems form—such as parents and children.

Once the therapist joins the family, he or she would begin to take on a leadership role within the family. First, he or she would unbalance the family by allying with the parent subsystem. In this way, the therapist stresses the importance of a strong parent subsystem. Attention would then be focused on Stephan and his role within the family. As treatment continues, less attention will be directed toward Stephan, and he would lose his status as the identified patient. A primary goal during treatment would be to establish appropriate boundaries in the family so that the parent subsystem has the acknowledged power within the family. The therapist shares with Elaine and Greg some family rules and structure that would lead to more healthy family functioning.

Summary of Structural Family Therapy

Key Concepts

- The family is treated as a system or a subsystem, but individual family members are not ignored.
- Family functioning involves family structure, subsystems, and boundaries.
- Family structure is an invisible set of functional demands or rules that organize the manner in which family members relate to one another.
- Observe family members to see the family structure.
- Focus is on family interactions to understand the family structure or family organization.
- A family member's symptoms are a result of structural failings in the family.
- Structural changes must take place in a family before a family member's symptoms can be reduced or addressed successfully.
- Focus on how, when, and to whom family members relate. Who says what to whom? In what manner? With what outcome?
- Family subsystems include the parental subsystem (husband and wife, mother and father); the sibling subsystem (children, usually brothers and sisters); and the extended subsystem (grandparents, other relatives).
- Family members play a different role in each of the subsystems to which they belong.

- Structural difficulties or problems occur when one subsystem takes over or intrudes on another subsystem.
- Boundaries are emotional barriers that protect and enhance the integrity of individuals, subsystems, and families.
- There are extremes in boundary setting.
- Problematic family structures have boundaries that are rigid or diffuse—subsystems that have adopted inappropriate tasks and functions.
- Enmeshment is where one family member becomes overly involved in another family member's life. Enmeshment promotes dependency on parents.
- Clear, healthy boundaries help individuals attain a sense of personal identity while still retaining a sense of belonging in a family system.

The Treatment Process

- Engage the family as a unit, and effect structural change by (1) joining the family in a position of leadership, (2) mapping its underlying structure, and (3) intervening in ways that change or transform an ineffective family structure.
- The treatment process challenges rigid family transaction patterns. Therapy consists of the therapist's pushing for clearer family boundaries and increasing the amount of flexibility in family interactions.

Goals of Treatment

- One goal of treatment is to bring out into the open problematic behavior so the therapist can see and help change such behavior—reduce symptoms of dysfunction.
- Another goal is to bring about change in a family structure that has supported family members' dysfunction or disordered behavior.

(Continued)

(Continued)

Role of the Therapist

- Therapists mentally "map" their families and work actively in therapy sessions. They instruct families to interact through enactments. Therapists function as directors and coaches.
- The therapist brings about structural change in families by (1) modifying the family's transactional rules, (2) developing more appropriate boundaries, and (3) creating an effective hierarchical structure.

Treatment Techniques

- *Joining*: Build and sustain a positive therapeutic alliance with family members.
- *Family map:* Draw a map to identify family boundaries and interpersonal transaction styles.
- *Enactments:* The family participates in a conflict situation that would take place at home so the therapist can understand the problem.
- *Restructuring:* Change the structure of the family to make the family more functional.
- *Unbalancing:* Therapeutically ally with a subsystem within the family. The therapist supports a subsystem, and this support unbalances the family
- *Making boundaries:* These are the physical and psychological factors that separate people from one another.

Limitations of Structural Family Therapy

- Structural family therapy was initially developed for low-socioeconomic-status families.
- Feminists have claimed that the theory promotes gender stereotypes by emphasizing traditional paternal roles.
- The theory is weak in explaining family dynamics and development.
- The distinctions between structural family therapy and strategic family therapy have become blurred.

STRATEGIC FAMILY THERAPY ___

Strategic therapy isn't a particular approach or theory, but a name for the types of therapy where the therapist takes responsibility for directly influencing people.

—Jay Haley

Major Contributor: Jay Haley (1923–2007)

Jay Haley was born in Wyoming on July 19, 1923. When he was 4 years old, his family moved to Berkeley, California. During World War II, he served in the U.S. Air Force. Subsequently, he earned a B.A. in theater arts at the University of California at Los Angeles. Although Haley pursued briefly a career as a playwright, he returned to continue his education and earned a bachelor of library science degree from the University of California at Berkeley and then a master's degree in communications from Stanford University. In 1950, he married and had three children.

During his tenure at Stanford, he met the anthropologist Gregory Bateson, who asked him to join a communications research project that became known as the Bateson Project, which focused on schizophrenia in families and was important in the development of Kim Berg, Steve de Shazer, and Salvador Minuchin, and virtually every major family theorist discussed in this chapter. Haley met with patients and their families to observe the communicative style of schizophrenics. Members of the Bateson Project (Gregory Bateson, Jay Haley, Donald Jackson, and John Weakland) published what has been termed the most important paper in the history of family therapy, "Toward a Theory of Schizophrenia."

From 1954 to 1960, Haley developed his family counseling skills under the supervision of the master hypnotist Milton Erickson. During those years, Haley began to develop a brief therapy model that highlighted the context and possible function of the client's symptoms. Haley used therapeutic directives to instruct clients to behave in ways that were counterproductive to their maladaptive behavior.

In 1962, Haley worked at the Mental Research Institute in Palo Alto, California. There he became the founding editor of the family therapy journal *Family Process*. In 1967, Haley left the Mental Research Institute and joined Minuchin and Braulio Montalvo at the Philadelphia Child Guidance Clinic, where he was director of family research for a number of years. Both Minuchin and Haley have reported that the relationship was beneficial for both of them.

Sometime in 1974, Haley moved to Washington, D.C., to establish the Family Therapy Institute with Cloé Madanes, his second wife. During this time, Haley published two of his most well-known books, *Problem Solving Therapy* (1976) and *Leaving Home* (1980). After leaving the Family Therapy Institute in the 1990s, Haley moved to the San Diego, California, area, where he was the scholar in residence at Alliant International University. In 2007, he died while working at Alliant University.

Haley claimed not to have a theory of family therapy. Instead, his approach uses provocative instructions to which clients are to respond. Despite his rejection of his approach as a theory of family counseling, Haley is usually credited with being the father of strategic family therapy. There is much cross-fertilization of strategic family therapy with structural family therapy—most likely because Haley and Minuchin worked closely together at the Philadelphia Child Guidance Clinic. To eliminate repetition of ideas from these two theoretical approaches, I have chosen to give only a very abbreviated summary of strategic family therapy.

KEY CONCEPTS OF STRATEGIC FAMILY THERAPY

In general, strategic family therapists have adopted many of Milton Erickson's principles. These therapists pride themselves on using a brief approach to therapy that is focused on providing solutions and facilitating client behavioral change rather than providing insight and giving interpretations (Goldenberg & Goldenberg, 2002). Therapy usually consists of short-term treatment of about 10 sessions. Haley (1976, 1984) was deeply concerned with power issues within the family—especially how family members attempt to take control of relationships. For instance, a therapist who meets a family for the first time might ask, "What is the problem that should be addressed within the family?" A family member—the mother, for instance—might say, "Every day there is shouting and a verbal fight that I have to intervene in before the punches start flying between my two boys, my husband, and sometimes my daughter."

The therapist would first determine who was involved in the problem and then construct a plan of action for changing the dysfunctional family situation. Emphasis would be placed on the communication patterns established between the two boys and then between each boy and the father. The therapist would point out how the two boys and their father are communicating (angrily) and the role each person is assuming within the family with respect to power.

In addition, the therapist would investigate the solutions that have been tried in the past and the type of success or failure the family experienced with them. The mother and the role that she plays in the situation would also be examined. The therapist might give the two sons and the father a paradoxical intervention—that is, to argue for 30 minutes without hitting or harming one another.

Strategic family therapy is founded on the belief that families are rule-governed systems and that they can be best understood within this framework. In addition, the presenting problem serves a function in the family that must be acknowledged. Family members' symptoms are system maintained. Strategists concentrate on the following dimensions of family life:

- *Family rules:* The implicit and explicit rules families use to govern themselves, such as "We don't talk about or show our feelings"
- *Family homeostasis:* A family's tendency to stay in the same pattern of its members relating to

one another unless they are challenged to do something different

- *Redundancy principle:* The principle that says a family has a limited range of repetitive behavioral responses and sequences
- *Circular causality:* The belief that one event does not "cause" another but rather that family events are interconnected (therefore, there are multiple factors that surround a parent's yelling at a child or a spouse's slap)

THE THERAPEUTIC PROCESS

Goals of Strategic Family Therapy

Strategic family therapists are interested in changing behavior rather than in trying to understand it. The hallmark of **strategic therapy** is creating novel strategies for solving problems (Nichols & Schwartz, 2007). Strategic family therapists treat "presenting symptoms as a solution to a problem (rather than an expression of some hidden, underlying 'real' problem) and go about designing a plan for its extinction" (Goldenberg & Goldenberg, 2002, p. 93). The therapist works to help the family achieve its next **family developmental life cycle**.

Inner Reflection

Rules in Family Therapy

If you were a family therapist, what rules would you establish for families during therapy?

Phases of Strategic Family Therapy

Haley (1976) maintained that the therapeutic process should be simple, practical, brief, and therapist led. The treatment process is designed to interrupt behavioral sequences that interfere with the family's functioning. Haley (1976) has outlined five stages of therapy:

1. *Social stage:* The therapist speaks with each person, making personal contact to establish a relationship. As the family sits in the therapy room, the therapist notices the seating arrangement that the family has chosen, and he or she makes hypotheses about the mood of the family based on its communication patterns.

2. *Problem stage:* The therapist asks questions about the family's problem.

3. *Interaction stage:* The therapist asks family members to talk with one another about the presenting problem. As the family is so engaged, the therapist notices who talks to whom, who remains silent, and who interrupts whom, but he or she does not share this information with the family members.

4. *Goal-setting stage:* The therapist and the family work out goals to be attained as a result of being in therapy.

5. *Task-setting stage:* The therapist gives the family a task to be completed, usually in between sessions.

The therapist repeats these stages until the presenting problem is resolved. It is the therapist's responsibility to plan strategies to resolve family problems. Techniques in strategic therapy are usually quite similar to those used in structural therapy.

Haley and Working With Children

Family therapists frequently look at the behavior of the disruptive member as helpful or constructive in some way to the family system. For instance, a child's disruptive behavior continues because it is unconsciously or consciously supported and maintained by others within the family system.

According to Haley (1984), family therapists should consider viewing a child's disruptive behavior as serving to stabilize the family structure. The child's behavior may serve to hold two parents together who might otherwise be in a divorce court. They unite in sharing their pain over their child's disruptive school behavior. Haley has indicated that when working with disruptive children, it is important to assume that (1) the client's symptoms are serving a protective function; (2) the client has the capacity to assume responsibility for disruptive behavior; (3) the power hierarchy of the family is confused, with the "little" people controlling the "bigger" people; (4) the real problem is the family communication problem, not the child; and (5) power should be restored to the parents, and the child should not be indulged. If the inconsistencies and conflicts in the family communication system are clarified, then the child will adopt appropriate behavior or behave without destabilizing the family.

Inner Reflection

Haley said that a child's acting-out behavior can be a solution to a family problem—that is, his parents' poor relationship. Can you think of any other examples in which a problem might be a solution to a family situation?

Once the child's disruptive behavior is no longer needed to keep the family together, the child's problems can be resolved. Haley referred to this situation as the *problem being the solution*. The child's destructive acting-out behavior is diagnosed as the solution to the problem of poor communication between the parents. Family counseling is then directed toward helping the parents resolve their conflicts or communication issues.

Summary of Strategic Family Therapy

Key Concepts

- Symptoms are viewed as serving a purpose, and they are accepted in therapy.
- Treatment should be pragmatic and short term.
- Focus is on solving problems in the present.

The Treatment Process

- The family is helped to resolve and remove the problem that brought them to therapy.

- Family members experience how they are interconnected.
- Therapeutic change focuses on breaking up negative styles of interaction and replacing them with more positive, virtuous cycles.

Role of the Therapist

- The therapist is a consultant, expert, and stage director.
- The therapist uses directives and circular questioning to change the family system. He or she gives advice, suggestions, and therapy homework assignments.
- The therapist designs strategies to resolve the family's problems.
- Help is given to family members to develop alternative ways of being, behaving, knowing, and living.

Treatment Techniques

- Reframing
- Using directives
- Circular questioning

Limitations of Strategic Family Therapy

- Historical family patterns are largely ignored.
- Families can change as a result of treatment but without understanding why.
- Confusion exists about the differences between strategic and structural family therapy.

RESEARCH AND EVALUATION
Multicultural Positives

Race, ethnicity, and culture affect families and the experience of family life. Ethnicity influences the way families and individuals give meaning to their symptoms. Even within families, there may be issues of acculturation and differential socialization. Therapists who work with families must acquire knowledge about different family types and develop skills in working with them.

Different cultural groups deal with health, mental health, and counseling in various ways. In working with culturally diverse families, therapists should be sensitive to how different cultures instill different values in family members, as reflected in their attitudes and actions, and how these values play out in their daily lives. When therapists do not understand the values and characteristics of families and their cultures, they are likely to pathologize and undervalue those characteristics.

Culturally diverse families give different levels of importance to the extended family and kinship ties. Therapists need to take into account culturally diverse families' "definition of family, as well as the timing of life cycle phases. They must come to understand the importance of different transitions, that vary depending on a family's cultural background" (Carter & McGoldrick, 1988, p. 25). If therapists hope to work therapeutically with individuals, they must learn how people function within their family system.

Multicultural Blind Spots

Therapists who do not examine family issues fail to take into account an important dimension of their clients' development. Focusing on the family as a system helps therapists understand better the functioning of their clients. Therapists search for ways in which families' culture can inform their work with them. Breunlin, Schwartz, and Mackune-Karrer (1992) have identified 10 areas of assessment that are critical in helping family therapists to bring a multicultural perspective to their therapy:

- Membership as an immigrant in a dominant society
- Level of economic privilege or poverty
- Ethnicity
- Religion
- Gender
- Age

- Race, discrimination, and oppression
- Minority versus majority status
- Regional background
- Stage of acculturation

Using a multicultural framework in family counseling means that the therapist understands that discrimination and oppression shape the experiences and symptoms families report. In any given society, the dominant culture organizes itself in terms of the issue of power. That is, each dominant culture (1) reinforces itself and its values and (2) acts to reduce the power and influence of those who are in the minority (Smith, 1991). From the dominant group's power base, discrimination and oppression are enacted on members of minority groups.

The dominant power group within the United States is Anglo-Saxon White males 35 to 65 years of age. Although members of this group include males from every socioeconomic level, those who exercise the most power tend to be educated, rich property and business owners. Individuals in this group exercise White privilege.

McIntosh (1989), a White woman, has delineated some of the characteristics of White privilege. First, there is the fundamental belief in the superiority of the dominant group's cultural heritage, meaning the superiority of its history, values, language, traditions, and arts/crafts. In American society, White, European American cultures tend to be viewed not only as normative but also as the desirable goal to which one should aspire. According to McIntosh (1989), White privilege refers to an invisible package of unearned assets that can be used each day to cash in on advantages not given to those who are not included in the dominant group. Some of the advantages that she lists are as follows:

- I can turn on the television each day and see people of my ethnic, racial, or cultural group represented positively on television.
- I can go shopping in a store without having store detectives assume that I am going to steal and, based on this misconception, follow me everywhere I go.

- When the American flag is shown, most people know that it refers to members of my ethnic group and that people of my ethnic cultural group have made the United States what it is today.

Family therapists must be finely attuned to their own cultural value system so that they do not become judgmental and negative in working with families from different ethnic backgrounds. Family therapists need to examine closely the therapeutic system they are using to determine if it is biased in favor of or against certain ethnic groups. When designing exercises for families to participate in, clinicians should take precautions to ensure that such exercises do not violate the values and standards of the family's ethnic membership group.

When family theorists say that they are using a systems approach, they must also take into account the American system that gives privileges to citizens based on their majority or minority status. Families in this country and throughout the world structure their family systems partially in response to power distributions within the broad society. Therapists are in error when they fail to consider the impact of racism. Some families are afforded greater privileges and advantages than others. Therefore, family therapists must ensure before labeling a family as disorganized that they comprehend the broad societal forces that may have led to this adaptive response. Feminists, for example, have criticized system family therapists on the ground that they only analyze the family system rather than the total system within which the family lives.

Inner Reflection

Which of the family therapy approaches would you feel most comfortable using? Why?

Evidence-Based Research and Family Therapy

Family therapy approaches emanated from clinical practice. Most of the family therapists who labeled themselves as communication/strategic therapists have not conducted controlled assessments of their treatment approach. Although Satir (Satir & Baldwin, 1983) reported that she had treated almost 5,000 families, she indicated that she had not completed any formal research on her effectiveness. Several evaluations using Satir's approach to family therapy have produced small, and in some instances nonsignificant, effect sizes (Shadish et al., 1993). Studies have found that strategic therapy is robust for treating substance abusers; its effectiveness is unclear with schizophrenic, anxiety, and psychosomatic disorders, disorders it claims to treat successfully (Sandberg et al., 1997). More evaluations are needed to determine the absolute effectiveness of communication/strategic family therapy in psychotherapy.

Structural family therapy has been evaluated in the family treatment of substance abuse, psychosomatic disorders, and conduct disorders. The findings of studies indicate that structural therapy is probably effective but clearly superior to no treatment at all (Stanton & Shadish, 1997). Shadish and Baldwin (2003) have reported that the effectiveness of structural family therapy is untested in relation to schizophrenia, mood disorders, anxiety disorders, and most childhood disorders. Similar untested results have been found for Bowen family theory (Nichols, 2003).

Contributions of Family System Approaches to Therapy

Family system therapy has made several important contributions to psychotherapy. One important contribution of these approaches is that individuals are not blamed for a problem. A systems perspective emphasizes that individuals are influenced by external forces and systems. A second contribution of family system theory is that the theories examine system factors that influence a person's development. Most of the other theories in this text restrict investigation of the influence of external factors on a person's development.

Limitations of Family System Approaches to Therapy

Family therapy has evolved over the years. Critics of family therapy have indicated that such therapy often reinforces stereotypical roles for women and men, and parents and their children. Distinctions between the various family theoretical approaches have become blurred. For instance, as practiced today, structural family therapy and strategic family therapy are quite similar. Much of the early influence of family therapy can be attributed to its charismatic leaders, who are no longer with us.

CASE ANALYSIS

Justin and Family Therapy

The case of Justin presents some important challenges for family therapy primarily because of its single-parent structure. This case analysis examines Justin from the perspective of two therapies reviewed in this chapter: (1) Bowen's intergenerational approach and (2) Minuchin's structural view of family therapy. It is important to remember that the court system has decreed that Justin would be required to attend counseling sessions. Justin's mother, Sandy, is required to assist in any way she can; however, there is no mandate that she attend counseling sessions with or without Justin. Justin's brother is desperately needed in family counseling. He is involved in a gang, and he has considerable influence over Justin; but he has declined to participate in family counseling.

In working with Justin, the therapist asks Justin's mother and brother to attend the therapy session. At the start of the counseling session, the therapist meets with Justin and Sandy to explore the issues they will address during therapy. The therapist makes an effort to join with Justin and Sandy. The therapist urges the two to attend all therapy sessions.

As a Bowenian, the therapist mentally maps the family after they are seated. He notices where Justin sits in relationship to his mother, and he notes the verbal interactions between the two. The therapist attempts to match the family's mood and avoids forming a triangle with Justin and Sandy.

After the therapist joins in and accommodates the family, he begins to take a leadership role during therapy. First, the therapist unbalances the family by allying with the parent subsystem—essentially Sandy. By allying with the parent subsystem, the therapist emphasizes the importance of a strong parental system. Once an alliance with the parent system has been formed, the therapist then allies with Justin, or the children subsystem. Thus, both Sandy and Justin come to understand that the therapist has the flexibility to align himself with either system to achieve therapeutic goals.

Next, the therapist inquires of Justin and Sandy what goals they would like to commit themselves to. The therapist examines the family rules to improve their flexible adaptation to the environment. The goal is to release both Justin and Sandy from the rigidly defined positions they occupy within the family system. This restructuring process frees Justin and Sandy to enhance their ability to cope with stress and conflict, especially between themselves.

Using the structural theory proposed by Minuchin, the therapist examines the boundaries within the family, especially those between Justin and his mother. In addition, the therapist explores the types of boundaries the family may need to protect itself from the surrounding community. The therapist seeks to have Justin and Sandy open up their boundaries between each other to facilitate communication between the two. The boundaries between Justin and his mother are enmeshed such that at times it appears that it is Justin who is ruling the house. The fact that Sandy holds "pot" parties at her house (which some of her two sons' friends attend) indicates that the boundaries between the mother and son have become blurred. In many respects, Sandy has abdicated her boundary as parent by holding an illegal pot party with her sons' friends.

In many respects, the initial part of counseling Justin and Sandy has focused on listening carefully to their different perspectives and reframing or placing Justin's problem in the structural framework of the family's system. The therapist's goal is to help the family establish a firm but clear boundary between Justin and Sandy. Minuchin described this boundary as a clear or healthy boundary. A clearly defined boundary between Justin and Sandy will help the parent and child subsystems maintain a degree of separateness, while also stressing the importance of belongingness.

The basic treatment goal of the structural approach is to restructure the family's system of rules and interactional patterns to improve its flexible adaptation to the demands of their environment and the requirements of the family court. In doing so, the therapist uses three types of structural inventions with the family. First, the therapist uses the technique of relabeling and reframing. The therapist works to help change the negative connotation of Justin's behavior so that it is represented more positively. For instance, Justin's frequent angry outbursts and violence are conceptualized as his signal that he is hurting inside. The therapist teaches Justin and Sandy that anger and violence occur when a person feels he has been hurt or violated in some significant manner. Moreover, anger is often an attempt to protect the self from a physical or psychological intrusion that challenges one's very being.

A similar situation takes place with Sandy. Her angry tirades and yelling at Justin for violating his curfew or not being on time for a court appearance are not intended to hurt Justin, but rather they are protective attempts to place a fence around him that shields him from danger and problems that could get him into further trouble with the law. Hopefully, instead of yelling at Justin and cursing, she will learn to express her deep concerns for his safety. The therapist also gives Justin and Sandy the directive that whenever they find that they are beginning to get angry with each other (e.g., by raising their voices and other means), they will each go to their respective bedrooms and ask themselves (engage in the reframing process), "Where am I hurt? What might be a better way of dealing with my hurt other than by yelling and screaming?"

The therapist might also give Justin and his mother some homework—to begin the work of creating a family genogram. The genogram should be a family picture or map of their family of origin. In this genogram, we might learn that Justin's father and other male members within his father's family have had issues with violence. There might be evidence of multigenerational issues in Justin's current identified problem. The genogram will help shed light on this idea. Sandy's part of the genogram also encourages her to get in touch once again with members of the family that she left behind when she moved to Utah from Chicago. The goal of the genogram is to help map family history and family processes.

Bowen (1978) believed that multigenerational patterns and influences are critical determinants of current family difficulties. Family themes tend to emerge that shed light on how the family's current problems may be connected to family patterns extending back over several generations. It is important that the genogram for Justin and Sandy examine not only ages and dates of birth and death of key family members but also birth order, sibling positions, family roles, family rituals and traditions, and persistent family beliefs.

Sandy's generational background might indicate that she, too, has a problem with anger because, as noted, she loses it and swears at Justin over his inappropriate behavior. Moreover, the genogram might help Justin connect with his father, whose absence has left a big hole in Justin's life. Justin needs to find positive examples of men in his family's history. He has to connect with something bigger than himself, and contact with his extended family could be very beneficial.

As a result of constructing the genogram, Sandy decides to make contact again with some of her family members. She invites her mother down for a week to get to know her two boys, and Sandy herself begins to call home on a regular basis so that she does not feel so isolated from the rest of the world. Clearly, Sandy might profit from

(Continued)

(Continued)

reconnecting with the women in her family. Right now she feels all alone, isolated from the rest of the world, and afraid that she might be the root cause of Justin's current situation with the law.

Having a one-parent subsystem is extremely difficult. Sandy needs help and support from others. The fact that she socializes with her young sons and their friends shows that she has become enmeshed with her children. Future family counseling situations will be devoted to helping Sandy build on her immediate family structure with Justin. Clearly, Sandy needs to be taught how to organize and effectuate a solid parental subsystem that will provide guidelines for how Justin is to act within the family and the outside world.

In typical structural family counseling style, the therapist is honest and upfront with Sandy. He challenges her and tells her that she needs to engage in rewriting her story as a parent. The therapist's emphasis is first on how Sandy is responding to Justin and then on Justin's behavior. Does Sandy make excuses for Justin's behavior, or does she simply ignore it until the law steps in and tells her Justin has to change or be locked up? The therapist has to help Sandy talk about the pain she is experiencing with regard to Justin, the court, and her life in general. For instance, the therapist might confront Sandy with the statement "Your life is so empty and pathetic that you have taken to hanging around and smoking pot with 12- and 16-year-olds. Whatever happened to the parent in you, the adult in you?"

Future sessions with Justin and Sandy will be focused on (a) restructuring the family system so that there is a competent parental subsystem and sufficient external support for it to carry out its functions, (b) working to unmesh the relationships between Sandy and her sons, (c) examining the genogram for intergenerational issues that are being acted out between Sandy and Justin, (d) helping Sandy make intergenerational contact with family members again, and (e) helping Justin to both understand and change his behavior, especially his relationship with his mother and his tendency to become violent when his needs are not being met.

SUMMARY

Many of the individual psychotherapies in this book have an intrapsychic focus rather than a system one. Family therapy is important because it places a person within the system that might have contributed to the problematic behavior. One of the central contributions of systemic family therapy approaches is that the theories do not blame the family for its problems. Instead of blaming the identified client, the therapist has an opportunity to examine the system from which the individual came. One limitation of family therapy models is that it may be hard for therapists to examine the family as a system while they are still focused on the intrapsychic world of individual family members.

Four groups of family therapists were reviewed in this chapter. Bowen's intergenerational theory deals with issues such as the multigenerational transmission process involving problems and roles,

differentiation of self versus fusion, and triangles. In contrast, Minuchin's structural approach to family therapy stresses the importance of family roles, boundaries, subsystems, coalitions, **enmeshment**, and **disengagement. Experiential therapy** stresses the significance of open and honest communication between family members. Strategic family counseling emphasizes communication patterns and paradox.

Although each school of family therapy emphasizes different points, they also have certain common points. For instance, most family therapists highlight the importance of "joining the family" or building rapport with the family. Most family therapists think in terms of the family system. On average, family counselors are more flexible, more active, and more structuring than practitioners of other treatment modalities. This happens because counseling sessions can become highly emotionally charged. In addition, family therapists tend to be more integrative in their counseling style, adopting whatever strategy seems to work with each family. Counselors should become skillful in structurally diagnosing, analyzing, and testing boundaries and rules within families.

It is important for every counselor to understand the singular importance of the family to either healthy or maladaptive functioning of individuals. An important thrust in family research is on developing family strengths in the areas of communication, boundaries, and family relationships.

SUPPLEMENTAL AIDS _____
Discussion Questions

Each family member tends to play a distinctive role, contributing to the continuation of either helpful or harmful family patterns. Describe your role in your family with whatever words pop into your mind. For instance, your first thought might be harmonizer or rebel or the one in the middle.

1. Families are important in developing members' sense of self-worth. Discuss in your group answers to the following questions: When you were growing up, who in your family had high self-worth? Whose self-worth was low? Discuss any memory that comes through strongly about self-worth themes in your family, noting both positive and negative influences by family members.

2. Every family has both spoken and unspoken rules. Make a list of three rules, spoken or unspoken, that you remember from your childhood and adolescence. Discuss your responses to the following questions, giving examples or recounting incidents: Who made the rules in your family? How were the rules enforced? How were you affected by your family's rules as a child? How have you either retained or changed your family's rules as an adult?

3. Family patterns exist in every family. Discuss three helpful family patterns that you experienced in the family you grew up with. These can be qualities that nurtured you, habits that assisted you, or actions that modeled healthy behavior.

4. Discuss what your family taught you about trust in your family and with the outside world.

5. Do you think that the identified client for family therapy usually represents a family problem?

Glossary of Key Terms

boundary   A concept in structural family therapy to describe emotional barriers that protect and enhance the integrity of individuals, subsystems, and families.

Bowen family theory   Views the family as an emotional unit and uses systems thinking to describe the complex interactions in the unit.

coalition   An alliance between two specific family members against a third member.

differentiation of self   The psychological separation of a person's emotions and intellect from another. It leads to the independence of self from others and is the opposite of fusion. In Bowen's theory, it is the separation of one's intellectual and emotional functioning; the greater the differentiation, the better the person is able to resist being overwhelmed by his or her family's emotional reactivity and the less prone the person is to dysfunction.

disengagement   Minuchin's term for psychological isolation that stems from overly rigid boundaries around individuals and subsystems in a family.

emotional cutoff   The term Bowen used for flight from an unresolved emotional attachment. Bowen used the concept to describe a family in which the members avoid each other, either physically or psychologically, because of an unresolved emotional attachment.

enactment   An interaction simulated in structural family therapy for the purpose of observing and then changing transactions that make up the family structure.

enmeshment   Refers to a family process in which boundaries become blurred and members become overconcerned about and overinvolved in one another's lives, limiting the autonomy of the individual family members. Minuchin's term that describes a family structure in which there is a blurring of psychological boundaries, making autonomy very difficult to achieve.

experiential therapy   The name of the approach (sometimes also referred to as symbolic experiential therapy) used by Carl Whitaker's theory of working with families.

family developmental life cycle   A term used to describe the developmental trends within a family over time. It consists of the stages of family life from separation from one's parents to marriage, having children, growing older, retirement, and finally death.

family dysfunction   Refers to the inability of a family to achieve harmonious relationships and interdependence.

family of origin   The family a person was either born into or adopted into.

family projection   The term Bowen used to indicate when couples produce offspring at the same level of differentiation as themselves.

family structure   The term Minuchin (1974) used to describe "the invisible set of functional demands that organizes the ways in which family members interact" (p. 51).

family systems theory   A concept used by Bowen to indicate the theoretical model that emphasizes the family as an emotional unit or network of interlocking relationships best understood from a transgenerational or a historical perspective.

genogram   A schematic device of a family's relationship system in the form of a genetic tree, usually including at least three family generations. It is used to trace patterns of recurring behavior within a family.

joining   The process of "coupling" that takes place between the therapist and the family, leading to the development of the therapeutic system. A family therapist meets and forms a bond with family members during the first session in a rapid but authentic manner.

making contact   The first stage in Satir's human validation process model, where attention is focused on each member of the family in an effort to raise the level of the person's self-esteem.

multigenerational transmission process   The process that takes place over several generations in which poorly differentiated individuals marry similarly differentiated mates, who then have children who suffer from severe mental disorders.

sculpting   An experimental family therapy technique in which family members are molded during therapy into positions symbolizing their actual relationships to each other as seen by one or more family members.

strategic therapy   A therapeutic approach in which the therapist develops a plan or strategy and then designs interventions directed at solving a specific presenting problem.

structural family therapy   A therapeutic approach that is designed to change or to realign the family organization or structure in order to change dysfunctional transactions and clarify family system boundaries.

triangle   A three-person relationship, which Bowen states is the smallest stable unit of human relations.

triangulation   Takes place when the conflict between two people is avoided or detoured by involving a third person who stabilizes the original relationship.

Website Materials

Additional exercises, journals, annotated bibliography, and more are available on the open-access website at https://study.sagepub.com/jonessmith2e.

PART V

The Fifth Force in Psychotherapy

Neuroscience and Theories of Psychotherapy

INTRODUCTION_____

During the past two decades, the world has experienced an explosion of knowledge in the field of neuroscience (Wolpe, 2002). Neuroscience has made major developments that offer the prospects of revolutionizing our knowledge about the human brain, mind, nervous system, and even psychotherapy (Kandel, 1998, 2001, 2005; Siegel, 2010). Some researchers have labeled these developments as the *neuroscience revolution*. For instance, Wolpe (2002) has stated,

> Neuroimaging and psychopharmaceuticals are only the tip of the neuroscience iceberg. Implantable computer "brain chips" are allowing the blind to see, the deaf to hear, and monkeys to control cursors on computer screens entirely with their minds. Trans-cranial magnetic stimulation can temporarily turn specific areas of the brain off by sending electric charges through the skull. (p. 8)

Moreover, neuroimaging studies are beginning to show neuroscientists' capacity to correlate mental states and traits to detectable brain patterns or structures (Linden, 2006). Clearly, we are just beginning to understand the awesome power and influence of the brain. Grawe (2007) has stated, "All that we think, know, believe, hope, suffer, decide or do, is ultimately linked to . . . the structures of the neurons, synapses and the processes among them" (p. 2). The brain scientist LeDoux (2002) expressed the same sentiment in a different way in his book *The Synaptic Self: How Our Brains Become Who We Are*. In the last sentence of this book, he stated, "You are your synapses. They are who they are" (p. 324).

The phenomenal growth in neuroscience can be attributed partly to the fact that in 1990, the U.S. Congress designated the 1990s as the "Decade of the Brain." Support for neuroscience becoming the new paradigm is provided by the fact that neuroscientists were awarded 23 Nobel Prizes during the 20th century. Commenting on the neuroscience paradigm, Grawe (2007) has also asserted,

> The current neuroscientific paradigm is not linked to a single person. The decade of the brain accelerated the rate of progress in the neurosciences. The main reason for this acceleration has been the availability of new research tools, in particular, the newly available capacity to observe the brain in action. . . . The only other scientific domain that can perhaps rival the dynamism and impact of the current neuroscientific knowledge is genetics. (p. 1)

What is neuroscience? Neuroscience may be defined as the scientific study of the nervous system. It involves understanding how the brain functions. According to the Society for Neuroscience, "Neuroscientists investigate the molecular and cellular levels of the nervous system; the neuronal systems responsible for sensory and motor function; and the basis of higher order processes, such as cognition and emotion" (www.sfn.org).

It is probably more accurate to speak of the neurosciences because there is more than one specialty within this broad discipline. Although historically, neuroscience was viewed as a branch of biology (neurobiology), it is now seen as an interdisciplinary science that collaborates with fields such as medicine, anatomy, chemistry, computer science, engineering, mathematics, and psychology. The term *neuroscience* encompasses professional specialties such as experimental neuroscientists, developmental neurobiologists, computational neuroscientists (those who use mathematics and computers to develop models of brain functions), and a growing body of individuals who consider themselves neuropsychotherapists (Farmer, 2009).

What is neuroscience's connection with psychology and theories of psychotherapy? The connection between neuroscience and psychotherapy is that at center stage for both fields is the study of the brain and the mind. The brain controls all body activities, including one's heart rate, sexual functions, emotions, learning, and memory (Grawe, 2007).

> The brain is even thought to influence the immune system's response to disease and to determine, in part, how well people respond to medical treatments. Ultimately, it shapes our thoughts, hopes, dreams, and imaginations. In short, the brain is what makes us human. (www.sfn.org, *Brain Facts*)

There can be no psychotherapy without engaging a person's brain and mind (LeDoux, 2002).

Developments in neuroscience may assist us in understanding how people learn and benefit from psychotherapy as well as how the therapeutic relationship functions to bring about desired changes within a client (LeDoux, 2002). Information about clients' neurological functioning may enable therapists and counselors to understand the challenges and issues that bring people to therapy. Neuroscience is clarifying for psychologists how their "therapeutic talk" and therapeutic relationships affect their clients' brains.

In addition, neuroscience is helping scientists and practitioners understand the human motivational system (LeDoux, 2002; Siegel, 2013). The Greek philosopher Democritus (460–370 BCE) was one of the first to propose that the two basic human motivations are to approach rewards and to avoid pain. Some 2,000 years later, neuroscience has identified some of the brain systems involved in approach and avoidance motivation. Neuroscience is even helping psychologists, anthropologists, and others to unravel the mysteries of love and romantic relationships. Discovering one causes one person to love another and to feel that one does not want to go on without that

Inner Reflections

Can you remember your first real love?

How would you describe your brain when you are in love?

What are your love neural pathways?

person is highly significant research. Consider, if you will, that on any given day in the United States, and indeed throughout the world, one person kills another "because of love." As Helen Fisher (2004) has stated, "Everywhere people sing for love, work for love, live for love, kill for love, and die for love. . . . Nothing will extinguish the human drive to love" (p. 107).

Neuroscientists maintain that human emotions and motivations arise from distinct systems of neural activity—networks that can be traced to their mammalian precursors (Bartels & Zeki, 2000, 2004). For instance, Fisher, Aron, Mashek, Li, Strong, and Brown (2002) conducted a study investigating the neural mechanisms of mate or partner choice and concluded that courtship attractions is associated with elevated levels of central dopamine and norepinephrine and decreased levels of central serotonin in the reward pathways of the brain. Courtship attraction is part of a triune brain system formatting, reproduction, and parenting. According to Fisher, love is not an emotion but rather a motivational system—a drive that is part of the reward system of the brain. Psychologists, counselors, and helping professionals in general need to understand the neurobiology of love—how loving someone affects the same areas of the brain involved in addiction. Love is a product of both the heart and the brain. As Popova (2010) has stated, love is "a combination of neurochemistry and storytelling, the hormones, and neurotransmitters that makes us feel certain emotions, and the stories we choose to tell ourselves about those emotions."

The purpose of this introduction is to present the rationale for conceptualizing neuroscience as the fifth major "force" in psychology and psychotherapy and to summarize the developments in neuroscience that offer the potentiality for changing—indeed, for revolutionizing—all major approaches to psychotherapy. This book has described four major forces in psychotherapy: (1) psychoanalytic and psychodynamic forces, (2) the behavioral and the cognitive-behavioral forces, (3) the humanistic and the existential forces, and (4) the social constructivist force. What makes a force in psychotherapy? A force in psychology may be likened to what the Germans called a Weltanschauung, a comprehensive world view, from a specified standpoint or perspective (*The American Heritage Dictionary*, 2010). The following is a diagram of the forces in psychotherapy.

Major Forces in Psychotherapy

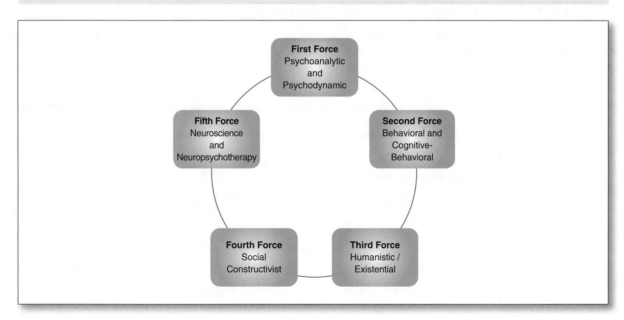

THE PROMISE OF NEUROSCIENCE

Why should knowing and learning neuroscience matter to psychologists and helping professionals? According to Cozolino (2010),

> On a practical level, adding a neuroscientific perspective to our clinical thinking allows us to talk with clients about the shortcomings of *our* brains instead of the problems with theirs. The truth appears to be that many human struggles, from phobias to obesity, are consequences of brain evolution and not deficiencies of character. (p. 356)

Cappas, Andres-Hyman, and Davidson (2005) have noted that

> neuroscience can be useful to psychotherapy in at least two ways: through validation of existing psychotherapeutic theories and interventions, on the one hand, and, alternatively, by suggesting directions to enhance current clinical practice on the other. (p. 374)

In essence, neuroscience is focused on two broad goals: (1) to understand human behavior better—why we love, fight, work, and why we are motivated to do or achieve certain things in life; and (2) to discover ways to prevent or cure a number of brain disorders. Neuroscience research holds the promise of helping millions of people who suffer from mental illness and brain disorders. According to the Society of Neuroscience,

> The more than 1,000 disorders of the brain and nervous system result in more hospitalizations than any other disease group, including heart disease and cancer. Neurological illnesses affect more than 50 million Americans annually, at costs exceeding 400 billion. In addition, mental disorders, excluding drug and alcohol problems, strike 44 million adults a year at a cost of some $148 billion. (www.sfn.org, *Brain Facts*)

CRITERIA FOR NEUROSCIENCE TO BE THE FIFTH FORCE IN PSYCHOTHERAPY

There are several criteria that determine if a new development in psychotherapy is a force, and these include that the newly proposed theoretical school of psychotherapy (Ilardi & Feldman, 2001; Verschuuren, 2012)

1. offers a *new paradigm* for viewing the field of psychology, the mental health professions, and psychotherapy,

2. has expanded significantly the professional and scientific knowledge base for psychology and psychotherapy,

3. has a *pervasive impact* on the field of psychotherapy such that it cuts across theories of psychotherapy as well as various other academic disciplines,

4. adds significantly new methods and techniques for the conduct of psychotherapy or for the study of its efficacy,

5. must be *heuristic* or must offer the possibility of testing its efficacy and generating a new body of research, and

6. has a strong *following of reputable individuals* within psychology and within the mental health profession in general—interdisciplinary nature of the new school.

Criterion 1: A New Paradigm

In his book *The Structure of Scientific Revolutions* (1962), Thomas Kuhn defined a paradigm shift as a change in the basic assumptions underlying or a profound change within a fundamental model. Kuhn maintained that scientific advancement is not evolutionary but rather a "series of peaceful interludes punctuated by intellectually violent revolutions," and in those revolutions "one conceptual world view is replaced by another." A paradigm shift is a change from one way of viewing the world.

Neuroscience is a new paradigm in psychotherapy because it is changing our understanding of much of human behavior and emotions. It is causing psychology, psychiatry, and the helping professions in general to review and revise how we conceptualize major constructs in the field, including how we classify mental disorders. Neuroscience offers a new conceptual framework for clinicians' understanding of what takes place during therapy. Within this framework, the structure and the processes of the brain assume center stage.

Neuroscience has brought order out of what one might consider the Tower of Babel for Psychotherapy. It has supplied a common language for the world of psychotherapy. For instance, whether we are talking about psychodynamic, cognitive-behavioral, humanistic/existential, or social constructivist approaches to depression, for instance, it is reasonable to ask how each of these theoretical approaches affects the serotonin system in the brain. Moreover, neuroscience can be used to evaluate the efficacy of each of these treatment approaches by measuring a client's serotonin metabolism. As Hanson (2010) has stated,

> Nonetheless, neuroscience has given us a common tongue in the Babel-like world of psychotherapy. For instance, whether we describe our work with depression as helping the client grieve the lost part-object, dispute depressogenic thoughts, face existential fears of death, heal disruptions of empathic attunement in early childhood or access their luminous core of being, it is reasonable to ask how each of these approaches affects the serotonic system in the brain. Similarly, brain science offers common metrics for evaluating efficacy, such as the difference a treatment modality makes in serotonin metabolism. (p. 5)

Criterion 2: Significantly Expand the Knowledge Base

Neuroscience is a fifth force in psychology and in psychotherapy because it is rapidly increasing our knowledge of the functioning and the malfunctioning of the human brain. Whenever science expands our understanding of a part of the human body that is so central to our existence, these advances will inevitably cause changes in our society and in psychology, thereby making the source of such change—neuroscience—a major force.

A major contribution of neuroscience is that it has helped researchers and practitioners *unite the mind, body, and emotion.* For many years, researchers did not understand the biology of emotions—that is, where emotions were in the brain, what caused them, how they influenced individuals' behavior. Therapists focused on the unconscious processes of emotions, and there was little effort to connect the biology of these emotions with their behavioral manifestation. The neuroscience paradigm helped practitioners connect the functioning of the brain with relationships—primarily the early attachment relationship with a primary caregiver, thereby creating an emotional revolution in psychotherapy (Schore, 1994, 2002). Neuroscience has brought about an intense, research-driven interdisciplinary study of emotion, psychobiology development, and relationship (attachment theory). Instead of viewing people in terms of the age-old divide between mind and body, research scientists and practitioners alike are now bringing mind, brain, and body together in one whole and complete human organism (Siegel, 2010). Within this revolution, psychotherapists assume a prominent role based on their ability to establish a specialized relationship that helps change the physical function and structure of their clients' brains. A major task will be to translate the findings about attachment, emotion, bioregulation, and right- and left-brain specialization into effective therapeutic methods and interventions (Grawe, 2007).

For instance, neurobiology has given important information about brain structures and the impact of the social environment on these structures. It has also helped us understand how different brain structures "behave" as a result of external or environmental triggers (LeDoux, 2002). It has been established that emotional trauma causes structural changes and damage to certain brain areas. Survivors of early childhood trauma have an increase in cortical blood flow in the right prefrontal cortex that manifests itself in negative thought loops, inability to regulate the stress response thereby causing panic attacks, generalized anxiety, and depression (Frodl et al., 2010).

Other neurobiological studies have focused on John Bowlby's (1969, 1988) attachment theory and have reported that maternal separation has a negative impact on an infant's brain in that such separation results in increased neuronal and glial cells death in the brain (Champagne et al., 2008). Neurons and glial cells make up the central nervous system, with neurons constituting about half the volume of the central nervous system, and glial cells making up the rest. Another important finding is that major depression and anxiety affects both neural functioning and neural structure. Studies have indicated a reduction of hippocampal volume as a result of severe depression (Fernandes, Pinto-Duarte, Ribeiro, & Sebastião, 2008; Warner-Schmidt & Duman, 2006).

Criterion 3: Pervasiveness

Pervasiveness of an idea, theoretical approach to psychotherapy, or a specialty is an important criterion used to determine if an idea, a profession, or an approach to psychotherapy has reached Zeitgeist-like status. The pervasiveness of neuroscience can be examined on several fronts, including the extent to which the profession of neuroscience and, in this instance, neuropsychology is growing and represented within the field of psychology. Neuroscience is the fastest growing area or subspecialty in psychology. In fact, it is the largest division within the American Psychological Association (http://www.div40.org).

Neuroscience as a Broad Spectrum of Academic Disciplines. The neurosciences include specialties such as experimental neuroscientists, developmental neurobiologists (who study the development and the maturation of the brain), neuroanatomists (who study the structure of the nervous system), neuroethologists, neurosurgeons (who perform surgery on the brain and the spinal cord), neuropathologists (who study diseases of the nervous system), and psychiatrists (Farmer, 2009).

Criterion 4: New Methods and Technology

Neuroscience offers new technology that will allow researchers to test the efficacy of therapy—especially, the nature of the therapeutic relationship established between the therapist and the client (Kandel, 1998, 2005). Some 60 years ago, when Carl Rogers (1951, 1957) was writing about the importance of the therapeutic relationship and the necessary conditions for therapy, we really did not have either the technology or the equipment to measure brain imaging as a therapist attempted to establish a therapeutic relationship with a client. Now we have brain-imaging equipment that will light up when the therapist strikes an emotional chord that registers in a client's brain (Siegel, 2010). Kandel (1998, 2005) has suggested that brain imaging might help evaluate the progress of psychotherapy. Kandel (1998) has stated, "We face the interesting possibility that as brain imaging techniques improve, these techniques might be useful not only for diagnosing various neurotic illnesses but also for monitoring the progress of psychotherapy."

Criterion 5: Heuristic

To become a major force in psychotherapy, the theory or approach must engender additional research, especially research that measures or evaluates different aspects of psychotherapy. The studies cited in Criteria 2 of this section demonstrate clearly that neuroscience has created a new wealth of studies. Based on research developments in neuroscience, recent treatment efforts have used movement, breathing, music, and sensory activities, yoga, tai chi, and mind–body centering with autistic children (van der Kolk, 2006; Perry, 2004). Neuroscience has supplied explanations of autism's neurological underpinnings and has given hope that once counselors understand how the autistic child's brain is functioning, they may be better equipped with appropriate clinical interventions.

Criterion 6: Interdisciplinary Nature of the Newly Proposed School of Psychotherapy

A sixth criterion to determine if a newly proposed school of psychotherapy has reached the status of a force is the degree to which it cuts across academic disciplines and professional fields or is interdisciplinary. The *neuroscience worldview is both integrative and interdisciplinary in nature.* Neuroscience cuts across academic disciplines and the various branches of psychotherapy—from cognitive-behavioral neuroscience to play therapy. It involves the fields of medicine, rehabilitation (brain injury clients), art therapy, and neuroleptic music therapy for young people to senior citizens (Belkofer & Konopka, 2003; Kruk, 2004; Pekna & Pekny, 2012; Thaut & McIntosh, 2010).

It seems clear to this author that psychotherapy is moving away from the medical model to a recovery model and from a recovery model to a neuroscience model that is based on the principle that psychotherapy produces long-term changes in behavior by producing changes in gene expression that change the strength of clients' synaptic connections as well as other brain changes. The emerging paradigm will be one of neuropsychotherapy (Etkin, Pittenger, Polan, & Kandel, 2005). According to LeDoux (2002), "Psychotherapy is fundamentally a learning process for its patients, and as such is a way to rewire the brain. In this sense, psychotherapy ultimately uses biological mechanisms to treat mental illness" (p. 299). When therapy does not change a client's brain, it cannot be effective.

The ensuing Chapter 20, "Neuroscience, Psychotherapy, and Neuropsychotherapy," is designed to pull together the diverse strands of key findings in neuroscience as they relate to psychotherapy. It is predicted that neuroscience will move psychotherapy forward, as therapists begin to truly understand what is going on in their clients' brains. Moreover, as researchers learn more about the impact of the environment on the brains of people, especially children and young people, my crystal ball predicts that neuroscience will increasingly assume a social justice stance. A framework is provided that might encourage others to develop a theory of neuropsychotherapy. In addition, a brief summary is provided for one published approach to neuropsychotherapy. Several different psychotherapy approaches that use core components of neuroscience include brainspotting (Grand, 2013), eye movement desensitization and reprocessing (Shapiro, 2001), and coherence theory (Ecker, Ticic, & Hulley, 2012). In addition, the neuropsychotherapeutic approaches of Daniel Siegel (2010) and Rich Hanson (2013) are also discussed briefly. We are living in an exciting time period for psychology and psychotherapy. We have moved from the medical model to the humanistic model, then to the social constructivist model, and now to the paradigm of neuroscience. Psychotherapy

In your opinion, what criteria should be used to determine what constitutes a "force" in psychotherapy?

From your perspective, should neuroscience be considered the "fifth" force in psychotherapy?

is gradually moving from focusing on clients' deficits and problems to focusing on their strengths. Even in the neuroscience paradigm, theorists emphasize the power of relationships, an Eastern and Asian influence. Psychologists are learning that the practice of mindfulness can change the brain. Therefore, it is little wonder that three cognitive-behavioral theories have incorporated mindfulness as a core component of their theories. Can a focus on the Asian views of harmony be far off from being incorporated in American approaches to psychotherapy? I incorporated the movement toward harmony in strengths-based therapy.

Many theories covered in this book are touched by recent developments in neuroscience that clarify and explain what was only guessed at during prior time periods. Neuroscience places primacy on attachment and the formation of neural pathways that occur in a baby's brain as a result of attachment. Strengths-based therapy maintains that strengths are well-traveled neural pathways in the brain that are influenced by our relationships with others. We understand that the brain has a negativity bias that causes us to see the negative in life more so than we see the positive and that it takes a number of positives to overcome just one negative experience. We now have information on which parts of the brain store negative information and sometimes traumatic experiences. Instead of believing that a person's brain is totally formed and unmalleable by the age of 7, we know that the brain engages in neuroplasticity until death. Therapists' encounter with their clients can change their clients' brains for better or worse, and during the therapy hour, mirror neurons are created between the therapist and the client. It may very well be that developments in neuroscience, especially the creation of new neuroscience theories, might make it so that in future decades some of the theories presented and developed during the 1950s and 1960s will be only historical footnotes in books on theories of counseling and psychotherapy.

CHAPTER 20

Neuroscience, Psychotherapy, and Neuropsychotherapy

It is difficult to overstate the importance of understanding mirror neurons and their function. They may well be central to social learning, imitation, and the cultural transmission of skills and attitudes—perhaps even of the pressed together clusters we call words.

—V. S. Ramachandran, *The Tell-Tale Brain: A Neuroscientist's Quest for What Makes Us Human*

Early experience shapes the structure and function of the brain. This reveals the fundamental way in which gene expression is determined by experience.

—Daniel Siegel, *The Developing Mind: How Relationships and the Brain Interact to Shape Who We Are*

The problem is, when you depend on a substitute for love, you never get enough.

—Louis Cozolino, *The Neuroscience of Human Relationship: Attachment and the Developing Social Brain*

BRIEF OVERVIEW

During the past two decades, major advances in neuroscience have changed our knowledge of the brain and the role it has in mental health and mental illness (Andreasen, 2001). A paradigm shift has taken place from the four previous forces in psychotherapy to one involving the use of neuroscience to inform psychotherapy (Arden, 2010; Rossouw, 2013). It is essentially a paradigm shift from focusing primarily on the so-called talking therapy to emphasizing the therapeutic relationship as an engagement with the whole person, his or her brain/mind, genetics/body, environment, and spirit.

This chapter is written to empower clinicians to use neurobiological information as a psychotherapeutic tool in their armamentarium of interventions. It is designed to shed light on how their work in psychotherapy might change their clients' very brains. Neuroscience provides either a new framework or an additional way for conceptualizing clients' problems and presenting issues. It has the capacity and the tools to reveal what is happening in a client's brain as he or she works with a therapist (Cozolino, 2010). Previously, therapists could only theorize about what might be happening in a client's brain. Moreover, neuroscience emphasizes holistic treatment of individuals, treatment that involves not only their mental health issues but also other factors in their environment that might be impinging on their mental health, such as the effects of poverty on the brains of young children and the influence of trauma in their homes and neighborhood on their being able to learn in school (Grawe, 2007).

This chapter has four basic goals, the first of which is to present a detailed examination of the connection between neuroscience and psychotherapy. Brief historical sketches are provided for several key figures who have connected neuroscience with psychotherapy. These are not the only major contributors to neuroscience and psychotherapy; however, to write a factual account of historical figures in neuroscience and psychotherapy is beyond the scope of this chapter.

A second goal is to provide a framework for neuropsychotherapy based on the principles that have already been established in the broad fields of neuroscience and neuropsychology. This chapter does not attempt to provide a full-blown theory of neuropsychotherapy, primarily because I am not a neuroscientist. Instead, throughout this chapter, the reader will be introduced (a) to various psychologists and medical doctors who are using neuroscientific principles and findings and infusing these findings within their already established psychotherapy frameworks and (b) to psychotherapists who are working on developing a theory of neuropsychotherapy. For the first category of psychotherapists, who infuse neuroscientific principles in their psychotherapy, I refer the reader to consider the work of Eric Kandel (1998, 2005), Louis Cozolino (2010), Daniel Siegel (1999, 2010, 2013), and Rick Hanson (2013). These writers have incorporated neuroscientific principles within their already established psychodynamic approach to therapy.

Additionally, this chapter discusses the work of several individuals who have developed what is termed in the neuroscience literature as brain-based therapies. For example, I present in summary form the work of Bruce Ecker and his colleagues (2012) on **coherence therapy**, a new

theory for psychotherapy that puts recent findings on memory reconsolidation at center stage (Tucker, Hully, & Ticic, 2012). Two other brain-based theories introduced in this chapter are eye movement desensitization and reprocessing (EMDR), developed by Francine Shapiro (2001), and **brainspotting**, developed by David Grand (2013). "Brainspotting is based on the profound attunement of the therapist with the patient, finding a somatic cue and extinguishing it by down-regulating the amygdala. It isn't just PNS (Parasympathetic Nervous System) activation that is facilitated, it is homeostasis" (Robert Scaer, MD, "The Trauma Spectrum," cited on the What Is Brain Spotting website https://brainspotting.pro/page/what-brainspotting).

- Brainspotting is a powerful, focused treatment method that works by identifying, processing and releasing core neurophysiological sources of emotional/body pain, trauma, dissociation and a variety of other challenging symptoms.
- A "Brainspot" is the eye position which is related to the energetic/emotional activation of a traumatic/emotionally charged issue within the brain, most likely in the amygdala, the hippocampus, or the orbitofrontal cortex of the limbic system. Located by eye position, paired with externally observed and internally experienced reflexive responses, a Brainspot is actually a physiological subsystem holding emotional experience in memory form. (https://brainspotting.pro/page/what-brainspotting)

The developers of these new brain-based approaches had the fascinating idea that there are brain-based procedures therapists can use to assist clients in actually erasing—not just coping with—painful memories. One does not have to spend the rest of one's life grappling with the issue of a rejecting parent, sexual abuse, and other traumatic events in one's life. These authors believe that they have uncovered how the brain circuitry works in memory consolidation as well as in memory reconsolidation and have developed a process of activating a distressing memory, destabilizing it, and reconsolidating a new memory in its place so that the terrifying memory no longer has its power to create problems for the person.

In presenting a beginning framework for developing a theory of neuropsychotherapy, I consider key concepts such as neuroplasticity, implicit memory, explicit memory, memory reconsolidation, mirror neurons, and right-brain to right-brain therapy. The chapter also examines mental health and illness from a neuroscientific perspective, the role of the neuropsychotherapist, and therapeutic techniques that some neuroscientists use in their clinical practice.

A third goal of this chapter is to explore the concept of cultural neuroscience. What is the impact of our culture on our brains? Are the brains of people raised in an Eastern culture different from those reared in a Western culture? Do cultural values condition people to prefer using the right-brain hemisphere over the left?

Finally, Goal 4 is to present the case study of Justin from a neuropsychotherapy perspective. Because the neuroscientific perspective emphasizes holistic counseling, factors such as Justin's wellness, his diet, the environment in which he lives, and his level of brain development are considered in this case study. Two implicit questions raised in the case study are "What might be helpful for the counselor to know about Justin's developing young brain?" and "What might be the relationship between Justin's impulsive behavior and his adolescent brain development?"

This chapter raises some ethical issues for therapists and helping professionals in general. For instance, does a therapist have an ethical responsibility to learn about brain development? What ethical issues does the neuroscience paradigm have for practicing therapists and counselors? Should psychology, social work, and counseling programs introduce their students to the developments in the neuroscientific revolution, or should they just continue to ignore it and focus primarily on theories of psychotherapy that were created during the 1940s, 1950s, 1960s, and 1970s? Should our professional organizations that credential individuals in the helping professions require that new entrants have competency in neuroscience?

A disclaimer should be made regarding the content of this chapter. For instance, the chapter does not pretend to be an exhaustive examination of the field of neuroscience, and it does not deal with rehabilitation of the brain due to traumatic injury or neurologic injury. It does, however, present a fairly readable introduction to neuroscientific thinking that holds the promise of revolutionizing how psychotherapy is conducted and tested for its efficacy.

MAJOR CONTRIBUTORS

The current neuroscientific paradigm is not connected to a single person, and therefore, this section presents three key individuals who have a link with neuroscience and psychotherapy: Sigmund Freud, Donald Hebb, and Eric Kandel. Only a brief description of their contributions is provided.

Sigmund Freud (1856–1939)

When most people think of Sigmund Freud (1856–1939), they think about him as the founder of psychoanalysis and as the person who created a theory of personality development—the id, ego, and superego. Few people know that Freud was a neuroscientist before he became a psychotherapist. He is included as one of the historical figures in neuroscience because of his early work in neurology and because he represents a major link between neuroscience and psychoanalytic psychotherapy. He is also represented as a major contributor because of his work on the unconscious, an important construct in the neuroscientific view of implicit memory.

Freud began his career investigating the central nervous system (Zillmer, Spiers, & Culbertson, 2008). In 1883, Freud worked under Meynert, a neurosurgeon and psychiatrist, and he confined himself to to studying the nervous system. For 2 years, Freud concentrated on the medulla of the **brain stem**, and he published three articles. From 1885 to February 1886, Freud studied with Jean-Martin Charcot, the famous neurologist. In 1891, he published his first book, *An Understanding of Aphasia*, which got only a tepid reception from scholars (Zillmer et al., 2008).

Freud's psychoanalytic model for personality is loosely related to brain processes (Zillmer et al., 2008) that are at the center of neuroscientific research. For instance, Freud's id, which is based on the pleasure principle, can be conceptualized as developing out of the reptilian brain. The superego is linked with the prefrontal lobe processes that are involved in forming abstract concepts such as morality, guilt, planning, and **inhibition**. The ego, which is based on the reality principle, can be associated with the complex brain processes in the cortex (Zillmer et al., 2008). In his book *On Narcissism* (1959), Freud proposed that all ideas in psychology would one day be explained by organic substrates. Freud actually coined the term *agnosia*, which came from the Ancient Greek word Γνωσία (meaning "ignorance" or "absence of knowledge") and refers to a loss of ability to recognize objects, persons, and sounds, usually associated with brain injury or neurological illness.

Neuroscience has given psychoanalysis and the psychodynamic perspective in psychotherapy a new resurgence. Regina Palley (2000), a psychiatrist and psychoanalyst, maintains that both the neuroscience of emotion and psychoanalysis center on unconscious mechanisms. While neuroscience emphasizes what one might consider *a biological unconscious governed by the rules and constraints of neural circuitry and neuropsychology*, psychoanalysis focuses on a psychological unconscious. Both psychoanalysis and neuroscience assert that conscious feelings form only the tip of the iceberg of human experience. The truly meaningful information for most people's lives resides beneath the tip of the iceberg—in the unconscious. Both neuroscience and psychoanalysis emphasize the importance of attachment and the mother–infant feedback loop in which mother and child regulate each other's minds and bodies.

Donald Hebb (1904–1985)

Hebb's Law: Neurons That Fire Together Wire Together

Donald Hebb was born in Chester, Nova Scotia, Canada, and was raised by parents who were physicians. Although he graduated in 1925 from Dalhousie University with a desire to be a novelist, he decided to choose the more practical field of education and, shortly after graduation, accepted a position as a school principal in the province of Quebec (Brown & Milner, 2003). In 1936, he earned a Ph.D. degree from Harvard in the area of the effects of early visual deprivation on size and brightness perception in the rat. Donald Hebb's contribution was that he made critical discoveries about the brain's wiring. In 1942, Hebb accepted a position at the Yerkes Laboratory of Primate Biology, where he began working on a book that was later published in 1949, *The Organization of Behavior: A Neuropsychological Theory* (Hebb, 1949). In this book, Hebb presented a theory that became known as Hebb's law: Neurons that fire together wire together. Hebb's law explains associative learning in which a simultaneous activation of neuron cells leads to an increase in the synaptic strength

> ### Inner Reflections
>
> Reflecting on Hebb's discovery that neurons that fire together wire together, what neurons in your brain have fired and wired together?
>
> Consider, for a moment, your basic values related to family, friends, and work, what neurons fired together such they have created strong neural pathways in your thinking?

between these neurons. The more the neurons fire in a given sequence, the stronger the neural connections become.

Eric Kandel (1929–)

Eric Richard Kandel was born on November 7, 1929, in Vienna, Austria, the younger of the two sons of Herman Kandel and Charlotte Zimels, who owned a toy store where both worked. In 1939, the Kandels left Austria and moved to Brooklyn, New York, to live with Charlotte's parents. Kandel attended Erasmus Hall High School in Brooklyn. He entered Harvard, majored in 19th- and 20th-century European history and literature, and graduated in 1952. In 1956, he earned his medical degree from New York University's medical school, and in 1956, he married Denise Bystryn. In 2000, Kandel was awarded the Nobel Prize in Physiology or Medicine for his groundbreaking research revealing what happens to the brain when memories are formed. Kandel had conducted studies on the single-cell sea slug *Aplysia* to learn how nerve cells (neurons) change during learning (Kandel, 2000). His research on the sea slug *Aplysia* revealed the basis of **short-term memory** and **long-term memory**. For more information on Kandel, his history, and the basis for the Nobel Prize, refer to http://www.nobelprize.org/nobel_prizes/medicine/laureates/2000/kandel-bio.html. The following is a brief paraphrasing of the five principles Kandel mentioned in his 1998 article on neuroscience and psychotherapy.

Kandel's Principles for Neuroscience and Psychotherapy

Principle 1: All mental processes, even the most complex psychological processes, come from operations of the brain. The mind is a range of functions carried out by the brain. Behavioral disorders that characterize psychiatric illness involve disturbances of brain function.

Principle 2: Genes are important determinants of the interconnections between neurons in the brain and the details of their functioning. A person's genetics contributes to the development of major mental illnesses.

Principle 3: Social or developmental factors can exert actions on the brain to produce mental disorder. Learning-dysfunctional behavior produces alterations in gene expression.

Principle 4: Alterations in gene expression brought on by learning leads to changes in the patterns of neuronal connections.

Principle 5: When psychotherapy is effective, it does so through learning, by producing changes in gene expression that change the strength of synaptic connections and structural changes that change the anatomical pattern of interconnections between nerve cells of the brain.

Kandel's principles sent shock waves through the leaders in the field, who were trying to infuse neuroscientific principles about the brain in their psychotherapy practices. His principles emphasized the neuroplasticity of the human brain and that a central component of psychotherapy was that it affected clients' brains.

> **Inner Reflections**
>
> Eric Kandel was awarded the Nobel Prize because of his work on memory and the brain.
>
> Could you ever see yourself as a Nobel Prize recipient? For what accomplishment might you be awarded the Nobel Prize?
>
> Do you agree or disagree with Kandel that all psychiatric illnesses are disorders of the brain?

TOWARD A THEORETICAL FRAMEWORK FOR NEUROPSYCHOTHERAPY

This section provides a framework that might be used to formulate a theory of neuropsychotherapy. The term **neuropsychotherapy** has been used in various ways throughout the literature (Grawe, 2007). One definition is that

neuropsychotherapy is an integrative approach to therapy that takes into account the dynamic interplay between the mind, body, social interaction, and the environment on a person's well-being with a focus on neuroscientific research. By understanding the mechanisms of our biology (an in particular our neurology), the processes of our psychology, and the influences of social interaction, it is believed a holistic therapeutic practice can be formulated. (*Neuropsychotherapy, Changing Minds*. Retrieved from http://www.neuropsychotherapist .com/about/neuropsychotherapy)

In addition, the term *neuropsychotherapy* has been used to refer to any psychotherapeutic approach that has been informed by neuroscience (Grawe, 2007).

For the most part, however, information about neuropsychotherapy is scattered in diverse books and articles. There is no standard theory of neuropsychotherapy that is generally accepted in the field of psychotherapy—although Klaus Grawe (2007) proposed the beginnings of one such theory before his death. Essentially, neuropsychotherapy advocates promoting therapists' greater in-depth knowledge of the workings of the brain as well as other features of the human biology to enhance their therapeutic practice, regardless of their theoretical orientation. Neuropsychotherapy seeks to change the brain. As Grawe (2007) has stated,

> Neuropsychotherapy aims to change the brain, but it does not directly target primarily the brain but focuses on the life experiences encountered by the person. The brain specializes in the processing of life experiences. Life experiences are meaningful with regard to the needs that are embedded within the brain structures of each human being. Neuropsychotherapy strives to shift the brain into a state that enables these basic needs to be fully satisfied. The best method for improving the health of the brain, then, is to ensure basic need satisfaction. (p. 424)

KEY CONCEPTS

Most of the important concepts in neuropsychotherapy are related to the brain, its structures, and its functions. It is important that therapists begin to

develop the language of neuroscience and acquire a beginning level of competency in understanding the impact of their words and behaviors on their clients' brains. This section discusses a number of key concepts that might be included in either a theory of neuropsychotherapy or a practice that uses neuroscientific principles within an established theoretical framework, such as psychodynamic or cognitive-behavioral approaches.

The Brain

The **brain** is a three-pound mass of tissue composed of gray and white matter. It used to be routine to say that the brain consists of 100 billion cells (Zillmer et al., 2008). However, a recent study by Azevedo et al. (2009) has found that an adult male human brain contains "on average 86.1 ± 8.1 billion NeuN-positive cells ('neurons') and 84.6 ± 9.8 billion NeuN-negative ('nonneuronal') cells" (p. 532), or approximately only 86 billion cells. The brain is the receiver of information from both inside and outside a person. Current neuroscience conceptualizes the brain as a dynamic structure that shapes and can be shaped, that changes and can be changed, and that gets mired down in neural firing patterns but can heal or repair itself to become unstuck.

The brain is a social organ. Our human interpersonal interactions basically shape the construction of our brains (Cozolino, 2010). A person's brain is fundamentally shaped during the attachment process with a primary caregiver. Cozolino (2010) maintains that "there are no single brains" (p. 6), and in making this assertion, he puts attachment constructs and relationships at the heart of the development of both adaptive and maladaptive behaviors in children and adults. The brain is also an organ of adaptation, and its structures are built in interaction with other people and with the environment (Figure 20.1). Recent advances in brain imaging have found that the brain is an organ that continually builds and rebuilds itself by one's life experiences.

Characteristics of the Brain. The brain has a number of characteristics, only a few of which are

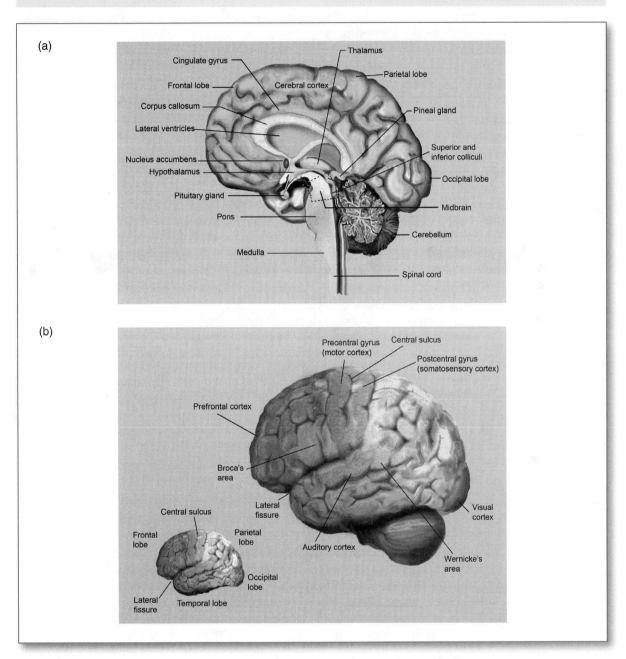

discussed herein. First, a neuroscientific view of the brain is that people are emotional beings who think, rather than thinking beings who have emotions (LeDoux, 1996). Second, the brain conducts many actions automatically and below the level of conscious control. Third, automatic functions that occur within the brain are located primarily in the occipital, parietal, and temporal lobes—the back, top, and side of the brain, respectively. In contrast, conscious control actions take place in the **cerebral cortex** (e.g., the **forebrain**—the front of the brain; Restak, 2006). Fourth, the brain is plastic; the brain changes due to influences from the environment. Because of the influence of the environment on the brain, no two people are identical in the neural wiring of their brains. Fifth, not all brains are alike, even though they are basically similar. Tancredi (2005) has pointed out the neurobiology of the differences between female and male brains (e.g., females evidence greater empathy). Sixth, human brains differ from nonhuman brains. Seventh, research has found that the construction of meaning is very different from the processing of information. According to Modell (2003), the metaphor is the brain's primary way of understanding and remembering the world (Table 20.1).

Neurons

Neurons may be defined as the electrically excitable cells that process and transmit information within the brain by electrical–chemical signaling. A **synapse** is the structural space between neurons in the nervous system. The word *synapse*

Table 20.1 The Brain and Its Four Lobes

Brain Lobe	Function	Results of Improper Functioning
Frontal lobe	The emotional control center of the brain responsible for forming one's personality and for making decisions. It is located at the front of the central sulcus where it receives information from other lobes of the brain. Most functions of the frontal lobe focus on regulating social behavior. The following are some important functions of the frontal lobe: • Cognition, problem solving, and reasoning • Impulse control • Regulating emotions • Regulating sexual urges • Planning • Motor skill development • Parts of speech	It is more common to injure the frontal lobe than any of the other lobes of the brain because it is located at the front of the skull or brain. Damage to the frontal lobe often results in personality changes, difficulty controlling sexual urges, and other impulsive and risk-taking behaviors.
Parietal lobe	Parietal lobe has several functions including sensation, perception and spatial reasoning. This lobe processes sensory information from various parts of the body. Some specific functions of the parietal lobe include: • Sensing pain, pressure, and touch • Regulating and processing the body's five senses • Movement and visual orientation • Speech • Cognition and information processing.	Damage to the parietal lobe may result in problems with spatial reasoning, reading, writing, understanding symbols and language. Right-side damage to the parietal area can impact a person's ability to dress himself or herself. Left-side damage to the parietal lobe can result in language disorders and disorders with perception.

Brain Lobe	Function	Results of Improper Functioning
Temporal lobe: There are two temporal lobes located on both sides of the brain that are located near the ears.	• The main function of the temporal lobes is to process auditory sounds. Other functions include: • The temporal lobe contains the hippocampus, the part of the brain responsible for transferring short-term memories into long-term one. Therefore the temporal lobe helps to form long-term memories and process new information. • It helps to form visual and verbal memories. • It is involved in the interpretation of smells and sounds.	• The type of impairment that result from damage to the temporal lobe varies according to where the damage took place. • Temporal lobe damage can result in difficulty processing auditory sensations and visual perceptions, problems concentrating on visual auditory stimuli, long-term memory problems, changes in personality, and changes in sexual behavior.

Occipital lobe: This lobe is the smallest of the four lobes of the brain. It is located near the posterior region of the cerebral cortex near the back of the skull.	• The occipital lobe is the primary visual processing center of the brain. Other functions include:
	  o Visual-spatial processing
	  o Movement and color recognition
		• Damage to the occipital lobe is less likely to occur than damage to the other lobes because the skull protects the occipital lobe.
		• Severe damage to the occipital lobe can result in loss of color recognition, visual hallucinations or illusions, and problems recognizing objects.

comes from the Greek and means "point of contact." Synapses, or specialized connections between neurons, allow signaling from one neuron to another to take place (Zillmer et al., 2008). Neurons communicate with each other within the brain and down the spinal cord. Neurons are interconnected into networks that have chemical and electrical communication systems. The brain functions as a complex system of neuronal circuits (Figure 20.2).

Three primary types of specialized neurons exist within the nervous system: (1) sensory neurons, which respond to touch, light, sound, and other stimuli; (2) motor neurons, which cause muscle contractions, influence glands within the body, and receive signals from the brain and the spinal cord; and (3) interneurons, which connect neurons in the same region of the brain or spinal cord (Zillmer et al., 2008).

Neurotransmitter

A **neurotransmitter** is a chemical that is released from a nerve cell that transmits an impulse from one nerve cell to another nerve, muscle, organ, or other tissue. It is essentially a messenger of neurologic information from one cell to another (Zillmer et al., 2008). Neurotransmitters contribute to a person's cognitive, emotional, psychological, and behavioral responses or patterns in life (Table 20.2). A person's production of neurotransmitters has been linked to environmental stressors and his or her lifestyle (including diet, coping strategies, and leisure time). Many of the problems that clients mention during therapy and counseling can be traced to their brain chemistry and to either overproduction or underproduction of specific neurotransmitters (Zillmer et al., 2008).

Figure 20.2　Neuron

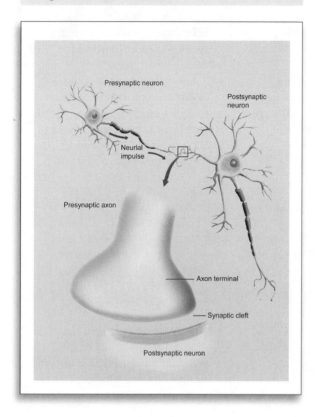

Presynaptic neuron

Postsynaptic neuron

Neurial impulse

Presynaptic axon

Axon terminal

Synaptic cleft

Postsynaptic neuron

Although there are more than 100 neurotransmitters, 4 are directly connected to problem behaviors that often bring people to therapy: (1) **acetylcholine**, a neurotransmitter that is critical for learning, optimal cognitive functioning, and emotional balance and control (deficiency causes deterioration of memory, increased forgetfulness, lack of emotional control, and increased aggression); (2) **serotonin**, a person's natural mood stabilizer and sleep promoter (deficiency of serotonin causes depression, difficulty sleeping, a sense of being disconnected, lack of joy); (3) **dopamine**, a person's natural energizer; and (4) **gamma-amino butyric acid (GABA)**, which helps reduce anxiety and induces sleep (deficiency causes the feeling that it is hard to relax) (Farmer, 2009).

Therapy and counseling strategies that tend to release acetylcholine include exercising and using meditation on a consistent basis. Because serotonin deficiencies are associated with depression, therapists can help clients by assisting them to develop action-based strategies that produce new meaning in their lives. Dopamine production may be increased within a person via massages. Studies have reported that when patients with cancer and other medical disorders receive massage therapy, they experience increased levels of dopamine, serotonin, oxytocin, **endorphins**, and natural

Table 20.2　Neurotransmitters and Their Functions

Neurotransmitter	Function	Imbalances
Acetylcholine	Important for memory, learning, optimal cognitive functioning, emotional balance and control. Affects attention, alertness, and voluntary muscle movement.	A deficiency produces a deterioration of memory, increased confusion, forgetfulness, cognitive disorganization and eventually as one ages leads to Alzheimer's disease.
Dopamine	Regulates movement, emotional wellness, and pleasurable feelings.	An oversupply of dopamine has been linked to schizophrenia and an undersupply has been associated with Parkinson's disease.

Neurotransmitter	Function	Imbalances
Serotonin	Influences how a person thinks, behaves, and feels, and is vital to sleep and anxiety control. It is a "feel good" chemical that affects sleep, mood, appetite, and impulsiveness.	An undersupply of serotonin is linked to depression and obsessive compulsive disorder.
		Antidepressant drugs raise serotonin levels.
		High levels of it, or sensitivity to it, are associated with serenity and optimism.
Norepinephrine	Affects alertness, sleep, and learning	Undersupply of norepinephrine can depress one's mood.
		Too much norepinephrine can produce an agitated state.
GABA (gamma-amino butyric acid)	Helps reduce anxiety and induces relaxation and sleep	Too little GABA is associated with anxiety disorders.
Inhibitory neurotransmitter	Inhibits excitation and anxiety	
Endorphins	Pleasurable sensations and control of pain	Undersupply can cause stress, pain, oversupply can cause euphoria or dependence (opiate addiction).
Glutamate		Glutamate supply has been linked to neurological disorders.
		Oversupply can stimulate brain, producing migraines or seizures (which is why some people need to avoid MSG, mono sodium glutamate, in food)

killer cells (Goodfellow, 2003; Hernandez-Reif et al., 2004).

Mind

The mind emerges from the brain, and it is shaped by interpersonal relationships. The mind can be defined as a process that regulates the flow of energy and information. Human relationships shape the neural connections from which a person mind emerges. According to Siegel (1999), "1. The human mind emerges from patterns in the flow of energy and information within the brain and between brains. 2. The mind is created within the interaction of internal neuro-physiological processes and interpersonal experiences" (p. 2).

Neuroplasticity

The term *neuroplasticity* refers to the brain's ability to change and adapt as a result of life experiences (Butz, Worgotter, & van Ooyen, 2009;

It has been said that the mind is formed by the relationships that we have.

How would you describe your mind?

What relationships were critical in forming your mind?

What mindsets have you formed?

Holtmaat & Svoboda, 2009). Research has demonstrated that the brain continues to create new neural pathways throughout one's life and that it modifies existing neural pathways to adapt to new experiences, learn new information, and create new memories (Siegel, 1999, 2010).

Neuroplasticity is moderated by genetic factors and by dynamic epigenetic changes that influence the expression of genes without changing the DNA sequence. Psychologists and other helping professionals are interested in epigenetic processes because their external triggers (e.g., parental care, attachment, diet, drug abuse, and stress) can influence a person's vulnerability to many diseases, including mental or psychiatric disorders (Volkow, 2010). In future decades, researchers will most likely gain additional insights about what forms the basis of neuroplasticity.

Two Cerebral Hemispheres: Right-Brain and Left-Brain Development

The human brain consists of two **cerebral hemispheres**—a right and a left brain. The brain works as a unified system, even though it has different structures and two hemispheres. Each brain hemisphere is associated with different functioning in the cortex. For instance, the left hemisphere controls the four Ls of functioning in the cortex: language (speech and reasoning), logic (stepwise reasoning and analysis), literality (facts and details), and linearity ("straight-line" thinking) (Siegel, 2012). The left hemisphere of the brain (the cerebral cortex and the structures of the midbrain) conducts what has been described as left-mode processing (Badnoch, 2008), meaning the management of information and information processing. The left side of the brain is good at tasks that involve logic, language, and analytical thinking. It is better at factual/semantic memory, critical thinking, numbers, and reasoning.

The right hemisphere, which is involved in right-mode processing, controls sensory input (auditory and visual awareness) processing, creative abilities, and spatial and temporal awareness. The right brain manages a person's creative abilities and emotional responses. In the majority of mental processes, there is usually a bipartisan participation of the two hemispheres. Whereas the left hemisphere deals with externally focused attention and action, the right hemisphere concentrates on internally focused attention and action. Studies have reported that the right hemisphere is primarily responsible for reading social and emotional cues from other people. The right hemisphere of the brain seems to be more capable than the left hemisphere of regulating states of bodily arousal.

Both the right and the left hemispheres of the brain are involved in different ways of knowing the world. The right hemisphere seems to be able to perceive patterns within a holistic framework, observing spatial arrangements that the left hemisphere cannot sense. The right brain construes the overall meaning of events. Some abilities associated with the right hemisphere include the following: recognizing faces, expressing emotions, music, reading emotions, intuition, and creativity. It develops earlier, sees the world holistically, is largely

Inner Reflections

Although research says that the two brain hemispheres work as an integral unit, some people believe that people are more right- or left-brain oriented.

Would you describe yourself as being more right- or left-brain oriented in your daily dealings with people?

Are the things you really like to do more associated with the right- or left-brain hemispheres?

nonverbal, uses metaphors, contains autobiographical memory, recognizes faces, expresses emotions, likes music, reads emotions, recognizes color and images, is intuitive, and is creative.

Memory

Explicit Memory

All therapists deal with some form of client memory. Information that a person has to consciously remember is known as explicit memory. When an individual is trying to intentionally remember something (e.g., an algebraic formula), this information is stored in explicit memory. We use explicit memory on a daily basis, for example, to recall the time of a dinner date or a doctor's appointment. Explicit memory is also known as *declarative* memory. There are two types of explicit memory: (1) episodic memory, which contains a person's long-term memories of specific events and a person's internal sense of "I am remembering," and (2) semantic memory, which consists of memories of facts, concepts, names, and other general knowledge information. Episodic memory is autobiographic. A woman may recall a sense of self as a high school student, as a new mother, and as a mother of teenage children.

Episodic memories are often communicated to therapists as stories about oneself. Siegel (1999) describes a 35-year-old woman who began to recount her experiences of having been raised by a violent, alcoholic father. He states,

> When she began to tell her story, her eyes became filled with tears, her hands began to tremble, and she turned away from her therapist. She stopped speaking and seemed to become frozen, with a look of terror on her face. For the therapist, the feeling in the room was intense and consuming. The patient began to speak again, but this time she spoke of her father's "positive attributes." (p. 43)

Implicit Memory

Implicit memory consists of things that a person does not purposely try to remember; it is both *unconscious and unintentional*. This type of memory is also called *nondeclarative* memory because a person is usually not able to consciously bring it into awareness. Implicit memories are often termed procedural memories, like hitting a baseball. A person does not have to recall consciously how to perform procedural memories. Although procedural memories are not recalled specifically, a person can still perform an activity after a break—such as riding a bicycle again, even though one has not ridden one in 20 years.

Memory Consolidation

During the process of psychotherapy, clinicians work with a client's memory. Clinicians want to know how clients remember the things that have happened to them because such memories indicate how they have constructed an interpretation of their lives. **Memory consolidation** is a neurological process that involves gradually converting information from short-term into long-term memory (Zillmer et al., 2008). A person's short-term memories are stored for only about 20 to 30 seconds. If information is to be retained so that it can be retrieved and used later, the contents of short-term memory must be moved into long-term memory (Kandel, 2005).

The memory consolidation process starts at the synaptic level as the brain begins to form new pathways to the information that comes to its attention. This process can take place over a period of days, weeks, months, or even years. Memories are spread out throughout the entire brain. The brain creates a neural map of the information so that memories can be retrieved at a later point. Memory consolidation is the process involved in coding a memory so that it can be retrieved at a later moment (Kandel, 2005). Without memory consolidation, there would be no way for a person to store information in the brain.

The **hippocampus** appears to assume an important role in memory formation and storage. Rapid eye movement sleep also seems to assist with the process of memory consolidation, and sleep overall is thought to help the brain refresh itself.

Although memory consolidation usually occurs over an extended period of time, studies of people involved in learning tasks have found that the brain can consolidate a memory successfully in less than an hour (Kandel, 2005). Rehearsal and memorization strategies are techniques that can promote faster memory consolidation. Repeating the same information over and over can cause synaptic changes in the brain that lead to rapid consolidation of memory. It is important that counselors understand the process of memory consolidation for clients. The process involved in memory consolidation is also important in a number of the newer brain therapies, including EMDR (Shapiro, 1995, 2001).

Memory Reconsolidation

Just as there is memory consolidation, there is also a process called *memory reconsolidation*. Imagine that all of the precious memories that you painstakingly made were suddenly erased? That thought is frightening to most people. Yet recent studies have revealed that every time you recall a specific memory, you make it necessary for that memory to be reestablished (Kandel, 2005). The term used to describe this memory process is *reconsolidation*—a term that recognizes the characteristic that long-term memories, when formed initially, are labile and subject to disruption over a period of hours. The good news for people who have experienced trauma in their lives is that previously long-established memories are also subject to disruption specifically during that period immediately after each time they are recollected. Reactivated memories must be put back into long-term storage by a process similar to that involved in the initial consolidation period—hence, the term *reconsolidation*.

Studies related to memory reconsolidation (Nader, Schafe, & LeDoux, 2000; Sara & Hars, 2006; Sara, 2000) have shown that a consolidated memory could again become susceptible to impairment for a discrete period of time after retrieval. The memory reconsolidation hypothesis overturned the belief that emotional learnings and acquired responses stored in long-term implicit memory are indelible—unerasable and permanent during a person's lifetime. The existence of reconsolidation implies that the brain's built-in neurodynamics allow a person to experience freedom from negative emotional learnings formed early in life. The reconsolidation hypothesis has important implications for psychotherapy. Memory research supports a nonpathologizing model of analyzing a person's symptom production that is caused by a person's unconscious emotional learning contained in one's emotional memory. Ecker and Toomey (2008) have provided evidence of such a clinical process, named *coherence therapy* (Ecker et al., 2012). The basic tenets of coherence theory and eliminating symptoms of psychological issues using memory reconsolidation are discussed in the section on new brain-based therapies.

Mirror Neurons

Neuroscientific knowledge of mirror neurons is based on the work of the Italian researcher Gallese, who in 1995 studied macaque monkeys and found that a certain neuron fired when one monkey observed another monkey performing an action, which in this case was reaching for a peanut (Gallese, Fadiga, Fogassi, Rizzolatti, 1996). Mirror neurons may be summarized as follows:

> **Inner Reflections**
>
> Think about an event you have experienced in your life that you would like to erase or reconsolidate.
>
> What is this memory?
>
> Do you have any symptoms connected to this memory? If so, what are they?
>
> Repeatedly pair the negative memory with a meaningful positive one, such that each time the negative memory comes forth, you activate a positive one alongside it. Has the negative memory become destabilized or changed in any way? How?

When a person observes another person engaging in a behavior, certain brain areas are activated, and these are the same brain areas that are activated whenever the first person performs the same behavior (Rizzolatti & Sinigaglia, 2008).

Mirror neurons connect visual and motor experiences and are involved in social functions such as learning, the development of gestures and verbal language, and empathic attunement. Commenting on the impact of observing another person's hand gestures and speech, Newberg and Waldman (2012) have asserted,

> A recent neuroimaging study showed that hand gestures and speech originate in the same language-related area of the brain. This overlap between words and gestures appears to be associated with a rare cluster of brain cells called "mirror neurons." The neurons that fire in someone's brain when they make a specific gesture also fire in your brain as you observe them. (p. 45)

Mirror neurons in the human brain help us understand the actions and intentions of other people (Gallese & Goldman, 1998). Both clients and therapists experience neural activation when clients talk about their problems during therapy. When clients describe in detail their challenges or problems, mirror neurons are activated in the therapist's brain as he or she is engaged in deep listening and close observation of clients' behaviors. Schulte-Ruther, Markowitsch, Shah, Fink, and Piefke (2007) have pointed out that the "same neuronal activity patterns occur in the same areas of an observer's brain as in the brain of a closely observed and felt other person" (p. 1362). Neurological mirroring is facilitated when the interpersonal interactions between therapist and client are experienced as being nonjudgmental, positive regarding, respectful, accepting, and empathic in nature (Schulte-Ruther et al., 2007).

The better therapists can mirror the neural activity in their clients' brain, the more likely that they will be able to understand them (Newberg & Waldman, 2013). When therapists are able to accurately mirror their clients' feelings, they create neural resonance between them. As Newberg and Waldman (2013) have stated,

> If you really want to understand what the other person is saying, you have to listen and observe the other person as deeply and fully as possible. Otherwise your brains won't mirror each other. If we can't simulate in our own brains what another person is thinking and feeling, we won't be able to cooperate with them. (p. 81)

Neuroscience and the Environment

Neuroscience provides an enlarged role for the influence of the environment on people. Brain development in humans is influenced by both heredity (genes) and environment. Environment is conceptualized in two fundamental ways: first, one's early environment that shaped one's initial brain development and patterns of thinking, feeling, and behavior and, second, the current environment in which the client finds himself or herself. A client's current environment includes housing arrangements, relational affiliations, work situation, financial status, and any other significant environment variable.

Therapists can no longer ignore the impact of the environment on individuals' behaviors, including their mental disorders. Most likely the emphasis on environment will strike a responsive chord for clinicians who perceive themselves to be multiculturalists and social justice counselors. Clinicians need to understand that the neuroplasticity of the brain suggests the possibility of change, even for mental illnesses that have strong hereditary links; for example, individuals suffering from schizophrenia can recover and lead productive lives. They, too, can hope for a positive future. While medication may be part of the treatment equation, it is only part of it.

Neuroscience and Social Justice

Neuroscience may contribute to a greater emphasis on social justice as more and more studies are conducted on the effects of the environment on children's and adults' brains. Krugman (2008) has asserted that poverty poisons the brains of children. Neuroscientists are beginning to point out that children who grow up in poverty experience unhealthy levels of stress hormones, which hinders their neural development. Racism, sexism, and cultural oppression emit damaging cortisol in the brain. Ivey, Ivey, Zalaquett, and Quirk (2009) have maintained that clients need to be informed about how social systems affect their personal grown. These researchers have stated:

Inner Reflections

To what extent do you believe that therapists should be involved in social justice issues related to their clients?

How might school counselors work in their schools to include principles established by neuroscientific studies?

As counselors, we can help clients understand that the issue does not lie in them, but in oppressive systems. They should avoid self-blame and self-pity. We can build strengths through a wellness approach and a focus on positive gender and cultural identity. Neuroscientists have found that the brain fires most when seeing faces that resemble one's own. This is an important component of antiracism training. . . . A social justice approach includes helping clients find outlets to prevent oppression and work with schools, community action groups and others for change. (para. 24)

Psychotherapy Changes Your Brain

Neuroscience has uncovered a number of aspects about our human life that may revolutionize how we conduct psychotherapy (LeDoux, 1998, 2003; Siegel, 1999, 2010). As Eric Kandel (1998) has stated in his landmark, Nobel Prize–winning article, "A New Intellectual Framework for Psychiatry,"

> We are in the midst of a remarkable scientific revolution, a revolution that is transforming our understanding of life's processes—the nature of disease and of medical therapeutics. . . . [it] will have a profound impact on our understanding of mind. (para. 79)

Kandel (1998) has commented on how therapy affects clients' brains:

> [W]hen a therapist speaks to a patient and the patient listens, the therapist is not only making eye contact and voice contact, but the action of neuronal machinery in the therapist's brain is having an indirect and one hopes, long lasting effect on the neuronal machinery in the patient's brain; and quite likely vice versa. Insofar as our words produce changes in our patient's mind, it is likely that these psychotherapeutic interventions produce change in the patient's brain. From this perspective the biological and sociopsychological approaches are joined. (para. 76)

Neuroscience research has shown how psychotherapy or "talking therapies" change the behavior of the brain, its chemical operations, and its structure (Linden, 2006; Rossouw, 2013). For instance, Arthur Brody and his colleagues (2001) have reported metabolic brain changes in clients with depression treated with interpersonal therapy. They found that subjects treated with interpersonal psychotherapy experienced a 38% decrease in their scores on the Hamilton Depression rating scale, while those treated with the drug paroxetine had a greater mean decrease in their scores. Both subgroups "showed decreases in normalized prefrontal cortex (paroxetine-treated bilaterally and interpersonal psychotherapy-treated on the right) and left anterior cingulate gyrus metabolism, and increases in normalized left temporal lobe metabolism" (p. 631). Similar findings supporting psychotherapy's impact on a client's brain were reported by Stephen Martin (2001) and his colleagues, who identified blood flow changes in depressed clients treated with interpersonal psychotherapy. The investigation that showed interpersonal psychotherapy resulted in both limbic blood flow increase and basal ganglia blood flow.

In addition, other studies have also found support for the assertion that psychotherapy changes clients' brains. Thomas Furmark and colleagues (2002) reported that social phobic patients who underwent psychotherapy showed significantly reduced blood flow in amygdala-limbic circuits. Goldapple's (2004) team of researchers showed the effect of cognitive-behavioral therapy on cortical-limbic brain pathways for clients with major depression. Schnell and Herpertz (2007) conducted functional magnetic resonance imaging (fMRI) studies on clients diagnosed with borderline disorders and found that dialectical behavioral therapy produced significant changes in the right prefrontal cortical regions. Beutel (2010) and his team of researchers found that short-term psychodynamic inpatient therapy produced changes in brain activation in frontal-limbic patterns. Radu et al. (2011) used cognitive-behavioral therapy to help obsessive-compulsive clients reduce their compulsivity.

Findings that support the belief that psychotherapy changes clients' brains present certain ethical and professional responsibilities for therapists and helping professionals. What are the fundamental basics that every ethical practicing therapist should know about neuroscience and clients' brains during therapy? How might practicing clinicians incorporate knowledge gained from neuroscience about the human brain in their everyday clinical practice? Therapists have tended to approach neuroscience from two perspectives. First, some have begun to incorporate basic neuroscience findings into established practices that are framed in psychoanalysis and in cognitive-behavioral, humanistic, or social constructivist theoretical approaches (Cozolino, 2010; Davidson & Begley, 2012). Second, some

Inner Reflections

How comfortable do you feel about incorporating neuroscience in your work with clients?

Would you ever see yourself using a theory of neuropsychotherapy?

researchers are calling for a form of psychotherapy that is based primarily on neuroscience.

Mental Health From a Neuroscientific Perspective

Neuropsychotherapists present mental health in a manner different from the traditional Western way of thinking. One way to view mental illness is that one or more systems of the brain did not develop adequately and/or there is an absence of integration between various systems in the brain. To have a balanced mood, both right and left hemispheres have to be actively involved in an equal or democratic way and reciprocally balance each other (Cozolino, 20103). For instance, if a person has too much activation of the right side of the prefrontal cortex, he or she will experience depression and shame. If a person has too much activation of the left side of the prefrontal cortex, he or she will tend to have euphoria or mania.

The environment assumes a prominent role in activation of both right and left hemispheres of the brain—especially a person's attachment pattern formed with a primary caretaker. Attachment with a primary caregiver establishes one's emotional regulation and one's feelings about oneself and others. If during the attachment process, a child gets the message that he or she is not valued, shame and negativity will predominate in the right hemisphere.

Moreover, a key component of mental health is the integration of **cognition** (left-hemisphere activity) and emotion (right-hemisphere activity). For instance, some individuals might react emotionally to most things, while others respond intellectually to emotional events. To achieve mental health, there must be a balance between one's emotional and cognitive expressions and approaches to life.

Cozolino (2010) uses the concept of the social brain to challenge the Western value of individualism. Instead of saying that healthy "people are those who are autonomous and independent," he contends that because one's social brain is basically shaped in interaction with other people, healthy people are those who rely on others throughout their lives for strength and development of their abilities. This interdependent view of healthy personality development resembles closely that of some Eastern cultures that emphasize the role of the group and the subordination of the individual to the group. Cozolino's (2010) view of the healthy personality is consistent with several psychological theories, including relational theory (Mitchell, 1988, 1997) and attachment theory (Schore, 2000). Healthy relationships between people produce mentally healthy people. In contrast, disturbed relationships lead to mentally unhealthy individuals. Poor interpersonal relationships produce disorders of the social brain. Because the brain is an organ that adapts to its environment, one can change brain circuitry through relationships.

Cozolino (2010) asserts that optimal sculpting of the prefrontal cortex shapes our sense of ourselves, our trust in others, our intellectual and emotional intelligence, and our ability to regulate our emotions. He also maintains that the "Polyvagal Theory of Social Engagement" permits people to seek closeness to others without activating their fight-or-flight responses. When a person has good vagal regulation, one may become angry, upset, or anxious with a loved one without withdrawing or becoming physically aggressive toward them.

Inner Reflection

In your opinion, does labeling a mental illness as a brain disorder increase or decrease its stigmatizing effect?

Maladaptive Mental Behavior and Mental Disorders as Brain Disorders

The *Decade of the Brain* redefined mental disorders as brain disorders. During this historical renaissance, neuroscientists focused on uncovering the brain processes involved in such disorders, and neuroimaging became the dominant tool in such investigations (Brockman, 2002). Neuroimaging technology has found that specific brain pathways, mostly located in the prefrontal cortex, are implicated in major mental disorders (Davidson & Begley, 2012). As a result of neuroimaging breakthroughs, researchers have begun to study mental disorders as brain circuit disorders, with an emphasis on normal and abnormal conduction between brain areas and circuits (LeDoux, 2003). Mental illness is characterized by thwarted neural growth.

What causes circuit disorder in the brain? Some scientists and practitioners trace the damaged circuit wiring in the brain to early attachment issues and parenting and to the individual's contact with his or her surrounding environment (Arden, 2010; Cozolino, 2010; LeDoux, 2003; Siegel, 2010). Even though these early relationship issues are highly significant, most neuroscientists contend that the faulty circuit wiring in the brain can be changed with the appropriate psychotherapy interventions (Arden, 2010; Davidson & Begley, 2012). Neuroscientists assert that only human beings can help heal other humans. As Cozolino (2010) has stated, "Human brains have vulnerabilities and weaknesses that only other brains are capable of mending" (p. 307). An individual's mental health is then connected to the quality of human relationships that he or she experiences. The emerging paradigm of neuropsychotherapy explains scientifically individuals' behavior, which was previously only "guessed about" in other schools of psychotherapy.

THE THERAPEUTIC PROCESS

The Therapeutic Relationship From a Neuroscientific Perspective

Neuroscience offers a new conceptual framework for clinicians' understanding of what takes place during the therapy hour. Therapy involves a clinician's assisting clients to restructure old neural pathways and to build new ones to help them deal with their challenges and to lead a more satisfying life. When one uses the neuroscience conceptual framework, talk within the therapy hour becomes much more purposeful and intentional rather than hit or miss. The therapist is intentionally helping clients to engage in the process of neuroplasticity. Therapy may be considered successful to the extent that therapists are able to help create a therapeutic experience that results in creating neuroplasticity for clients (Cozolino, 2010).

Neuroscience can be used to help a therapist conceptualize what is happening in a client's brain. From the *neuroscience worldview*, psychotherapy is an interaction between two human brains and the neural pathways that therapist and client have created for themselves as a result of the interaction between their genetics and their life experiences. Additional support for this conceptualization is provided by Beitman and Viamontes (2006), who described the therapeutic relationship as "a relationship between two brains and their bodies" (p. 214). Both neuroscientists and clinicians have maintained that therapists can help a client develop new neural pathways as a result of establishing a caring and safe therapeutic relationship that communicates that they understand and accept him or her unconditionally (Hanson, 2013; Kandel, 1998, 2007; Siegel, 2010).

The therapeutic relationship can "enhance or replace an attachment relationship, based on how the right brain develops (the hemisphere that controls emotions) and continues to function in adulthood" (Farmer, 2009, p. 122). Therapeutic attachment facilitates neural restructuring in the right brain of clients (Farmer, 2009). In working with clients, therapists deal with more than just negative emotions, self-imposed limits, and bad memories. When therapists are engaged during the therapy hour, they deal with the very strategies that their clients use to encounter and cope with life. Clients generate neurological pathways of behavior in their brains. They even become addicted to their own brain chemicals as they repeat again and again life strategies that may not have been working for a long period of time. In essence, clients become addicted to their behavioral strategies that they use for living. Neural restructuring can change a person's habitual neurological pattern of behavior.

The first step in helping clients change their neural networks is to identify them. To achieve this goal, clinicians must engage in deep listening to what their clients are saying about their life situations, and especially what they are saying about themselves, such as their difficulty trusting others, problems in establishing and

maintaining relationships, low self-esteem, or poor anger management. Helping professionals must understand that the already established neural networks in their clients' brains are based on their own life experiences. If clients do not have an established network for something, then they do not have a reference point for change. As clinicians identify clients' neural networks, they can then begin to consider experiences that might help them build new neural networks that are more satisfying and less problematic. Clinicians might consider experimenting with brain sensory inputs such as art therapy, music therapy, therapeutic stories, and psychodrama. Sensory inputs tend to engage clients' neural networks to become active and open to learning new information. It is important that clients feel that they are in control of changing the neural networks in their brains.

How might a therapist help clients see a connection between their own brains and what they are working on in therapy? Both Cozolino (2010) and Hanson (2010) have pointed out that when a therapist translates psychological issues into neural terms, such issues become demystified, normalized, and de-stigmatized. The client is taught to recognize how the neural networks associated with the amygdala, for instance, bring about states of fear and anger. It is not that the client is crazy or weird but rather that the client might have to deliberately and intentionally change the wiring of his or her neural networks by having new affirming life experiences not built on fear (Arden, 2010).

Goals of Neuropsychotherapy

The neuroscience perspective maintains that therapy is a matter of helping clients to build new positive neural pathways that emphasize clients' strengths and to repair or extinguish neural pathways that impair clients' functioning in their inner and outer worlds (LeDoux, 2002). An important goal is to activate positive emotions and deactivate negative ones.

Another goal of neuropsychotherapy is to help clients integrate their brains, especially the two cerebral hemispheres, the neural circuits, and their functioning. According to Siegel (1999), neural integration is basic to self-organization and to the ability of the brain to create a sense of self. Tucker, Luu, and Pribram (1995) have suggested that integration within the brain may deal with specific anatomic circuits: (1) vertical, (2) dorsal–ventral, and (3) lateral.

A client's autobiographical narrative can reveal integration or incoherence. A client evidences a coherent autobiographical narrative when his or her narrative reflects a blending of left- and right-hemisphere processes. When a client has limited access to the right hemisphere's representational processes, his or her autobiographical narrative may be incoherent. In contrast, when an individual is able to draw on the right hemisphere, the left brain is able to make sense by integrating a coherent life story. Integration of left- and right-hemisphere processes produces coherent client narratives (Siegel, 1999).

Role of the Neuropsychotherapist

Who Is a Neuropsychotherapist?

A **neuropsychotherapist** may be defined as a psychotherapist (who may be eclectic or prepared educationally in a specific theoretical school of psychotherapy) who uses neuroscience to enhance his or her psychotherapeutic interventions. A neuropsychotherapist has a solid knowledge of the neurobiological foundation of individuals' mental states and behavior. The ideal neuropsychotherapist has substantial insight into the activity of a specific neural network involved with, for example, a client's fear, as well as a cultural and environmental understanding of the impact of

clients' interpersonal relationships on their emotions and behavior (Grawe, 2007). A neuropsychotherapist uses a multidisciplinary approach to

Inner Reflection

Could you ever see yourself becoming a neuropsychotherapist?

working with clients. A neuropsychotherapist is one who understands the different levels of a person's being and conducts therapy within a neuro-biopsychosocial framework.

Kandel (2006) has suggested that client care is the therapist's most important responsibility. Therapists must develop an understanding of the neuropsychological principles that govern not only their own behavior but also that of their clients. Therapists whose practice is informed by neuroscience learn how to cultivate their client's neuroplasticity. They must also be conscious of creating mirror neurons when working with clients. Therapy should produce new pathways of neural firing through the creation of a safe therapeutic environment and a corrective emotional experience (Allison & Rossouw, 2013). One role for a therapist is to help a client down-regulate his or her stress response so that new patterns of neural activation can take place. The therapist provides an environment in which a client's basic needs for safety and control are met so that a shift can take place from client patterns of avoidance and protection to patterns of approach. As Allison and Rossouw (2013) have stated,

> New neural patterns can be activated by down regulating the stress response and enhancing the basic needs of attachment and control. Safety is thereby facilitated through the development of new neural pathways that shift unhelpful patterns of thinking, feeling, and behaving. (p. 22)

Cozolino (2010) has maintained that a therapist can use neuroscientific principles to improve therapy by (a) using multiple means to influence the brain, (b) choosing and combining different treatments for clients, (c) educating clients about brain functions, (d) encouraging the rewriting of self-narrative by honoring the malleability of memory, and (e) emphasizing optimism and growth as possible outcomes of satisfying relationships.

What Happens If a Therapist Focuses on a Client's Negative Life Events?

For decades, therapists have focused on their clients' problems and negative life events. The belief was that it was therapeutic for therapists to spend hours talking about a client's negative reactions to his or her father or about a client's feelings of being left out and ridiculed as a child and as an adolescent. Yet recent research in neuroscience has indicated that such a focus may harm rather than help clients (Seligman, Steen, Park, & Peterson, 2005). The very moment a person or a therapist expresses even the slightest degree of negativity, a sense of negativity is increased in both the speaker's and the listener's brains (Fredrickson, 2009).

Negative words or even repeatedly uncovering or analyzing the negative events in a client's life may only serve to remind clients of their failures and inadequacies. Clients become mired down in the therapeutic quicksand of "My mother never loved me," "No one on both sides of my family liked me," or "I was always considered a problem child." When therapists have clients continually rehearse the negative circumstances of their lives, they send alarm messages to the client's brain—the **amygdala**. The quicker therapists are able to stop talking about the client's negative life events, the more readily they are able to generate a sense of safety and well-being within the therapy hour. Newberg and Waldman (2013) have explained that if you focus on a word such as peace or love, the emotional centers in the brain become calm. Even though the outside world has not changed, you feel safe and secure just by focusing on these words. This illustration demonstrates the neurological power of positive thinking, which has been supported by hundreds of well-designed studies.

When therapists work with clients to reframe negative thoughts and worries into positive affirmations, the therapeutic process improves, and the client regains self-control and confidence (Fossati et al., 2003). Therapists' interpretations that emphasize the negative circumstances of a client's life stimulate anxiety, while positive statements stimulate relaxation. Put in an alternate way, if a therapist focuses on a client's strengths (strengths-based therapy), the client will begin to experience a sense of peacefulness in herself or himself as well as toward others. The client's thalamus responds to the therapist's incoming message of strength instead of weakness, and it then relays this message to the rest of the brain. As a consequence of the strength message, the client is likely to experience the release of pleasurable brain chemicals such as dopamine, the reward system of the brain will be stimulated, and client anxiety and self-doubts are likely to dissipate (Brassen, Gamer, & Buchel, 2011; Fredrickson, 2009).

Concentrating on a client's strengths to deal with life challenges causes a client's body to relax. Strengths-based therapy stimulates a client's neocortex. Repeated highlighting of client's strengths may even increase the thickness of the neocortex and shrink the size of the client's amygdala, the fight-or-flight response mechanism in the brain (Newberg & Waldman, 2013).

Role of the Client

The role of the client in neuropsychotherapy is similar to that for the other theoretical perspectives discussed in this book. A major difference may lie in the tools that a neuropsychotherapist might use, such as neuroimaging. Clients may also be asked to be open to using the expressive arts and other sensory techniques to engage the right hemisphere of their brains. In addition, therapists who actively use neuroscience techniques also recommend that clients engage in the practice of mindfulness (Hanson, 2013).

Therapy as Right-Brain to Right-Brain Interaction

Neuroscience has helped reconceptualize therapy as partly a process that involves both left-brain to right-brain and right-brain to right-brain interaction between the therapist and the client. Therapists have changed not only what they think about therapy but also what they believe happens during therapy and how they can influence the therapeutic process. For instance, from the early days of Freud, psychotherapy has been primarily about using words—a left-brain process—designed to effect changes in a client's emotions and way of viewing the world and what has happened to him or her. For several decades, especially after the cognitive force in psychotherapy, the major focus in therapy was designed to help clients think about their irrational ideas, their negative emotions.

Therapists now understand the biology of emotions and feelings (Schore, 2003). From brain-based studies, they have uncovered what feelings are located in what parts of the brain, as well as what neural substrates continue to support such feelings. The left hemisphere primarily engages in logical thinking, whereas the right hemisphere deals with one's emotions.

Neuroscience provides a framework for right-brain to right-brain therapy. It points out that whatever we turn our attention to will cause a neuron to fire. When the therapeutic relationship becomes a point of a client's and a therapist's focal attention, brain change within the client becomes possible. When the therapist and client are engaged in moment-to-moment relational-emotional experience, this process will help the client's brain to build new implicit and explicit memory patterns regarding the experience (Siegel, 2010). For instance, the client develops a visual image of his therapist smiling at him with respect, appreciation, and compassion. This relational experience becomes real, is encoded into implicit memory, and, if repeated a sufficient number of times, replaces the old, disordered patterns of relationships.

Right-brain to right-brain therapy refers to therapy that is attachment based. The therapist uses emotion-focused techniques to activate and rewire the early unconscious patterns processed and stored in the right hemisphere of the brain when such patterns are unhealthy. In reality, a therapist has to use left-brain to right-brain as well

as right-brain to right-brain therapy because he or she has to be able to conceptualize and label what is taking place within the client and during therapy. Schore (2003) has emphasized right-brain to right-brain therapy because it serves as a counterbalance to the dominance of the left brain in therapists' usual dealings with clients. The focus is on the client's feelings and emotions and on the therapist's becoming an adoptive attachment figure for the client. The therapist relates to the client so as to foster the development of a secure attachment. The belief is that what heals a client who has negative attachment experiences is the relationship with the therapist.

Schore (2003) has used right-brain to right-brain therapy to describe a therapist's dealing with deep emotional issues—especially early-attachment issues. According to him, the right hemisphere of the brain stores the 3 *R*s, *r*ationality, *r*egulation of affect, and *r*esilience—factors that become the foundation of a person's sometimes lifelong exploration, learning, and growth. Neural patterns of these 3 *R*s are created by the time a child is 18 months old, and they remain fairly unchanged well into a person's early adulthood (Schore, 2003). Using research from neuroscience, Schore (2003) has asserted that the experiences that we have with early significant caregivers are important because they establish subsequent behavioral patterns. From these early experiences, we learn that our needs and feelings are either important or not—that we should approach or avoid people and the challenges of life.

When early attachment experiences are repeated over and over again, they cause neurons to fire and neural pathways to develop—thereby making it more likely that with similar or even new experiences these same neurons will fire once again in the same patterns that strengthen the old neural circuits and networks of the three *R*s—relationality (relationship issues), regulation of affect, and resilience. That is, the brain stabilizes our experiences into patterns of neural firing that determine how we respond to future new experiences.

Essentially, right-brain to right-brain therapy creates new experiences and installs them as new thought and behavior patterns. The therapist can use techniques from the four other forces of psychotherapy to engage in right-brain to right-brain therapy. Using a psychodynamic framework, the therapist can use clients' dreams, which typically have deep relational, emotional, and meaning content for them, coming from primary processing. The therapist can use the Gestalt technique of the empty chair to gain entry to early implicit memory and later explicit memory. In right-brain to right-brain therapy, it is important that the therapist remembers that imagining a thing, for instance, imagining food or a chair or someone loving the client, in one's visual cortex fires the same neurons as experiencing it, that is, seeing food or having someone love one. Using knowledge gathered from the findings on neuroplasticity, the therapist helps the client to rewrite his or her life and to rewire his or her brain. Right-brain therapeutic experiences help clients to rewire the patterns found in the inner experiences of the self.

Methods and Techniques for Neuropsychotherapy

There are few established methods and techniques that have been designed specifically for neuropsychotherapy. Typically, researchers borrow techniques from the other four forces of psychotherapy. This author asserts that one can glean neuroscientific methods of psychotherapy from the existing literature. Two such exceptions to this statement are Mindsight by Siegel (2010) and Hanson's HEAL approach to neuropsychotherapy. Therapy techniques for neuropsychotherapy can be grouped into the following categories:

1. *Techniques related to the brain*—techniques designed to increase mirror neurons and neural resonance, create new neural pathways, and reduce/eliminate old neural pathways: These are essentially techniques that are designed to make changes in the brain—thought stopping, positive reinforcement for new behavior, and so on—and are already broadly in use.

2. *Techniques related to the therapeutic relationship:* This involves the model of compassionate communication (Newberg & Waldman, 2013).

3. *Techniques that involve the integration of the right and left hemispheres of the brain*, the wheel of emotional awareness: This helps clients to build their attention strength and stimulates neuronal activation and growth to promote linkages (what Siegel, 2010, called Mindsight techniques).

4. *Techniques related to the client's emotional state*—increasing balance, harmony, and hope. Hope is always critical. Strengths-based techniques are also important to lower a client's defenses and to increase his or her motivation to produce the desired change.

Mindsight Techniques

To develop neural resonance with clients, Siegel (2010) suggests that therapists use an exercise called the "wheel of awareness" (p. 94), which is a metaphor for how a person can become aware of any element in his or her inner or outer worlds. The goal is to increase the therapist's awareness of where he or she is with the client at any given moment during therapy. "The therapist can then focus attention (the spokes) on any element of the rim. After the therapist reaches a point of inner peace (using mindfulness techniques associated with the wheel of awareness), he or she can then work with the client on 'SNAGging' the brain—stimulating neuronal activation and growth—to promote differentiation and then linkage" (p. 98).

HEAL Strategy

"Taking in the good" is a strategy that helps clients focus on the positivity in their lives. To assist clients with taking in the good in their lives, Hanson (2013) has developed the acronym HEAL, where H = positive experience, E = enrich it, A = absorb, and L = link it with positive and negative experiences. Step 1 activates a positive mental state in the client, while Steps 2 to 4 help install taking in the good in a client's brain. The therapist asks the client to notice a positive experience in his or her life. For instance, the therapist might ask the client to think about something for which he or she is grateful or to think about a job that was performed well. In Step 2, the therapist requests that the client stay with that experience for 5 to 10 seconds so that positive feeling is felt throughout the client's body. As the client thinks about the experience and enriches it, neurons begin firing together so that they will wire together. Step 3 involves absorbing that experience. In Step 4, the client is asked to link the positive and negative material. Hanson (2010) states,

> For example, when you feel included and liked these days, you could sense this experience making contact with feelings of loneliness from your past. If the negative material hijacks your attention, drop it and focus only on the positive. . . . Whenever you want, let go of all negative material and rest only in the positive. (p. 63)

The pairing of the positive and the negative helps uproot the neural pathways that have been wired together because of repeated negative life experiences.

RECENT BRAIN-BASED THERAPIES: EMDR, COHERENCE THERAPY, AND BRAINSPOTTING

Although there is no universally recognized theory of neuropsychotherapy, several new brain-based therapies have emerged that could be included under the neuropsychotherapy paradigm, including EMDR, coherence therapy by Bruce Ecker and colleagues (2012), and brainspotting therapy by David Grand (2013).

Eye Movement Desensitization and Reprocessing

EMDR is a neurologically based therapy approach that Francine Shapiro (1995, 2001) developed to resolve traumatic events, such as rape, and negative experiences in combat, as well as other disturbing, unresolved life issues. It is an integrative approach that includes elements of psychodynamic, cognitive-behavioral, interpersonal, experiential, and body-centered therapies. EMDR psychotherapy is an information-processing therapy that uses eight phases to address various mental health problems (see www.emdr.com/general-information/what-is-emdr.html).

The eight phases of treatment using EMDR are as follows:

Phase 1—History-taking sessions: The therapist assesses the client's readiness for EMDR and develops a treatment plan. The treatment plan deals with recent distressing events, current situations that elicit emotional disturbance, related historical incidents, and the development of specific skills and behaviors that will be needed by the client in future situations.

Phase 2: The therapist makes sure the client has sufficient methods for handling emotional distress and that the client is in a relatively stable emotional state.

Phases 3 to 6: A target is identified and processed using EMDR techniques that involve the client identifying the most vivid visual image related to the memory, a negative belief about the self, related emotions, and body sensations. The client identifies a positive belief, which is rated, and so is the intensity of the negative emotions.

Following this, the client is asked to focus on the image, negative thought, and body sensations while at the same time moving his or her eyes back and forth, following the therapist's fingers as they move across his or her field of vision for 2 to 30 seconds or more, based on the client's needs. In addition to using eye movements, the therapist can also use auditory tones, tapping, or other types of tactile stimulation. The therapist tells the client to notice whatever happens and then to let his or her mind go blank and to notice whatever thought, feeling, image, memory, or sensation comes to mind.

> When the client reports no distress related to the targeted memory, the clinician asks him/her to think of the preferred belief that was identified at the beginning of the session . . . while simultaneously engaging in the eye movements. After several sets, clients generally report increased confidence in this positive belief. (Shapiro, 2001)

Phase 7—Closure: The therapist requests that the client keep a journal during the week to document any related material that may arise and suggests that he or she use the self-calming techniques taught during Phase 2.

Phase 8: It involves reevaluation of the prior work and progress. After EMDR therapy, clients have said that the emotional distress related to the memory has been eliminated or greatly reduced.

EMDR has been supported in clinical trials for the treatment of posttraumatic stress disorder. Because of its positive clinical findings, EMDR is listed as an evidence-supported therapy by the American Psychiatric Association (2004). In 1995, a professional association—the EMDR International Association, independent from Shapiro—was founded, and it established standards for training and practice.

Coherence Therapy

Coherence therapy is an experiential system of psychotherapy that gives memory reconsolidation a central role. In fact, the steps of coherence therapy follow closely those outlined for the memory reconsolidation process by brain researchers. The therapeutic process for coherence therapy is experiential rather than analytic (Ecker et al., 2012). The goal of this form of brain-based therapy is to have the client experience during therapy personal constructs that underlie the unwanted symptom and to undergo a natural process of revising or dissolving those constructs, thereby terminating the existence of the

symptom. Usually, 12 sessions are necessary for the client to obtain complete relief from the symptom (Ecker & Hulley, 2006).

Ecker et al. (2012) maintain that memory reconsolidation is the brain's only known process capable of erasing an emotional learning. This theoretical approach guides clients to retrieve implicit, emotional learnings into awareness. One benefit of coherence therapy is that it does not pathologize a person's presenting symptoms. They are just implicit memories that need to be reactivated and, immediately after the reactivation, taken through a process of memory reconsolidation. Ecker and colleagues contend that our knowledge of memory reconsolidation will create transformational change for therapy and could serve as a unifying framework for psychotherapy integration. The authors call for brain imaging studies to provide empirical evidence for coherence therapy and memory reconsolidation.

Brainspotting

According to David Grand (2013), brainspotting therapy evolved from his work using EMDR in his private practice. It is a focused treatment that works by

> identifying, then processing, and releasing core neurophysiological sources of emotional/body pain. It is believed that brainspotting taps into and harnesses the body's innate self-scanning capacity to process and release focused areas (systems) which are in a maladaptive homeostasis (frozen primitive survival modes). (See https://www/brainspotting .pro/page/what-brainspotting)

A brainspot is the eye position connected to the emotional activation of a traumatic/emotionally charged issue within the brain, most likely in the amygdala, the hippocampus, or the orbitofrontal cortex of the **limbic system**. A brainspot is "actually a physiological subsystem holding emotional experience in memory form. When a brainspot is stimulated, the deep brain reflexively signals the therapist that an area of significance has been located" (see https://www/brainspotting.pro/page/what-brainspotting). Although brainspotting typically takes place outside of a client's awareness, there are a number of reflexive responses that indicate a brainspot has been located. These reflexive responses include eye twitches, blinks, pupil dilation, facial tics, yawns, foot moving, and body shifting. The brainspot can be accessed and stimulated by holding the client's eye position while the client is focused on the problem being addressed in therapy. Therapy is directed to activating, locating, and processing the brainspot. Oftentimes, clinicians use biolateral sound CDs because biolateral sound enhances the brain's processing abilities.

There are more than 5,000 people who have been trained in brainspotting. According to the *Brainspotting* website,

> Brainspotting is a "body to body" approach. The distress is activated and located in the body, which then leads to the locating of the brainspot based on eye position. As opposed to EMDR where the traumatic memory is the target, in Brainspotting, the brainspot is the target or "focus or activation point. Everything is aimed at activating, locating, or processing the brainspot. (See https://www/brainspotting.pro/page/what-brainspotting)

NEUROSCIENCE AND THE *DSM-5*

Neuroscience and Challenges to Diagnosing Mental Disorders—the *DSM*

The pervasiveness of neuroscience can be seen in the implicit challenges it is posing for the entire diagnosis of mental disorders. For instance, in May 2013, the American Psychiatric Association (2013) published its newest revision of the *Diagnostic and Statistical Manual of Mental Disorders* (fifth edition, *DSM-5*), the major manual for diagnosis in the world, which replaced the *DSM-IV-TR* (fourth edition, text revision, 2000). The *DSM-5* is based on the same principles that the American Psychiatric Association has followed for a number of editions of this manual. The *DSM* system has limited validity because it is supported by few studies verifying its diagnostic categories. The *DSM* system uses consensus by groups of clinicians to establish validity rather than clinical research data. It lacks neurobiological data to support its diagnostic categories.

Just prior to the release of the *DSM-5*, the National Institute of Mental Health (NIMH—the world's largest funding agency for research into mental health) withdrew its support from the manual. Thomas Insel, the director of NIMH, stated that the institute will no longer fund any research projects that rely on *DSM* criteria and that the institute will be "re-orienting its research away from DSM categories" (see NIMH, http://www.nimh.nih.gov). The official statement from NIMH (2013) was that the *DSM-5* only offers "fumbles and errors" and that "symptom-based diagnosis once common in other areas of medicine has been largely replaced in the past half century as we have understood that symptoms alone rarely indicate the best choice of treatment."

The NIMH (2013) suggested an approach based on developments in neuroscience and on brain-based research that was founded on the following assumptions:

- A diagnostic approach should be based on the biology, and symptoms must not be limited by the current *DSM* categories.
- Mental disorders are biological disorders involving brain circuits that implicate specific domains of cognition, emotion, and behavior.
- Each level of analysis should be understood across a dimension of function.
- Mapping the cognitive, brain circuit and genetic features of mental disorders will produce new and better targets for treatment.

RESEARCH AND EVALUATION ___

Cultural Neuroscience and Multiculturalism

Cultural neuroscience is an interdisciplinary field of study that investigates the relationship of culture, biology, brain functioning, and psychology as well as other social science areas. Cultural neuroscience is beginning to challenge the long-held belief that biological processes that take place in the brain are the same for all people regardless of their culture. Blanding (2010), however, has reviewed studies that seem to suggest that the results of brain imaging results (fMRIs) for American and Indian students who listened to classical music varied. The brain imaging results for this group revealed different patterns of neural activation in different parts of the brains of the American students versus their Indian counterparts.

An examination of brain imaging results for subjects from Japan and the United States revealed that the fMRI results of persons from the United States reflected significantly higher activation in the analytical brain regions while the Japanese subjects showed lower neural activation in this part of the brain. Citing a number of studies, Blanding (2010) concluded that cultural interactions produce certain patterns of neurological responsivity that are reflected in brain imaging procedures.

Moreover, neuroscience has provided some insight into how one's race influences perceived racial group trustworthiness (Stanley et al., 2012). Within the brain, the striatum and amygdala are the regions of the brain involved in trust decisions and trustworthiness estimation. The investigators used BOLD, blood oxygenation level–dependent activity, while individuals completed a series of single-shot trust game interactions with real partners of varying races. They found that White/White and Black/Black groups produced greater levels of trust while Black/White groups produced far less trust. Black-versus-White partner combinations produced greater activity in the amygdala, the emotional alarm center of our brains.

Clearly it would seem reasonable to expect that culture does have an impact on the brand. The verdict is out regarding whether or not individuals from Western cultures have a brain organization pattern that favors the left as opposed to the right hemisphere, whereas just the reverse is held true for individuals from Eastern cultures. Some Eastern cultures emphasize meditation and yoga, practices that function to calm the brain and, specifically, the amygdala. Could the greater emphasis on individualism, for instance, explain Western societies' high rate of violent crimes?

Inner Reflections

In your opinion, should the *DSM-5* be discarded or simply revised?

How useful is the *DSM-5* for working with clients?

CASE ANALYSIS

Justin and Neuropsychotherapy

Justin greeted his counselor with his familiar "Hi Doc, what are we going to do today?" "Didn't you tell me that we were going to be working on my brain? It's all messed up, Doc," Justin laughed. "We can go on to something else."

"I don't think that your brain is messed up, Justin. You've got a good brain. You're smart; you can draw; you can do a lot of different things with your brain, Justin. What I want us to work on today is increasing your knowledge of what is happening in your brain when it is functioning well and what's happening when it's not working so well.

(Continued)

(Continued)

So I brought in two things that I want to share with you. The first thing I want to do is to show you a brief video by Dr. Daniel Siegel on the teenage brain, even though you're not quite 13 yet. The video is about 7 minutes long, and in it, Dr. Siegel uses his hand in a useful way to think about the brain. He also talks about what goes on in the brain of teenagers, why they make what seems like some crazy choices—doing things that if they had a moment to think about the situation, they might not do. Then the second thing I'd like for us to do is to look at the model of the brain that I have on my desk and maybe engage in an exercise or two, depending on the time that we have left. How does that sound to you? Do you think you would like to do these things today?"

"Sure, I'm game. You know, Doc, I don't mind looking at a video and talking about it."

"Ok. But before we look at the video, I would like to get your thoughts about why there is sometimes friction and conflict between teenagers and their parents and teenagers and other aspects of our society—like school," the counselor said.

"Oh, that's easy," Justin replied. "It's like . . . it's like they're always telling us what to do—like do your homework, wash the dishes, stop watching so much TV, get up early enough so that you're not late for school, and so on and so on. It never stops. It's like we don't have a mind of our own. They don't trust us to do the right thing."

"So you feel as if you are not given an opportunity to make up your own mind about things, that adults don't trust you to make the right decisions," the counselor interjected.

"Exactly," Justin said, shaking his head. "I know that my mom doesn't trust me. I can look at her eyes and see that she is probably thinking, 'You're not going where you said you were going. You tell me anything just to get out of the house.' And sometimes she's right. I want to be with my friends. I don't want to be treated like some kind of a 'Momma's boy.'"

"Well, Justin, the video raises some of the same issues that you just mentioned. Let's watch it for 7 minutes and get your reaction to it," the counselor said.

The video showed Dr. Siegel putting his hand in the way to simulate the brain. He described how certain parts of the brain dealt with strong emotions, such as anger and fear. The amygdala was implicated for fear and angry responses to events. The video raised the question about why young people sometimes make such poor decisions. The video pointed out that during adolescence, the brain is experiencing a massive and necessary integration of functions that will have a long-term effect, that a young man's solidarity with his peers was evolutionary insofar as young people banded together because they understood that down the line, they would be living in a world with their friends and peers. The shared experiences that adolescents have with each other enables their generation to become leaders. Adolescents are at the peak of their creative powers and courageousness. Furthermore, Siegel mentioned the four qualities of the adolescent mind: novelty seeking, social engagement, increased emotional intensity, and creative exploration.

After viewing the video, Justin said, "Wow, I didn't know that's why I do some of the crazy things that I do."

The counselor responded, "What do you mean, Justin? Can you elaborate a little more about 'why you do the crazy things that you do'?"

"Well, things like what got me in trouble with the law and got me sent to you. My friends came by my house, and they wanted to go to the mall. I wanted to be with them. I didn't want to stay at home with my mom. We were going to go out and have some fun. I had no idea that that fun would land me in jail; otherwise, I would have stayed at home."

"We were in Walmart, and one of my friends said, 'Let's see if we can steal something and get away with it.' None of us had any money. At first, I thought that it was crazy. I could see the cop standing near the exit of the store, and I thought, 'Are you crazy? We could get caught.'"

"Then my friend said, 'Chick, chick, chick; you're just chicken, Justin.' So he stole something. I'm not even sure what he stole; and a store detective told him to put it back. He didn't, and we all ran out of the store. The cop ran after us, and we were caught and put in jail."

"How are you connecting what happened to you at the mall and the video, Justin?"

"Well just like the video said, young people like to be with their friends, and sometimes they will do things in groups that they wouldn't do if they were by themselves. I wanted my friends to like me. It was exciting that they invited me to go to the mall with them. I felt that I was finally doing something different from what I usually do at home." Justin sighed, remembering the sequence of events that had landed him in trouble. "Maybe if I hadn't run," Justin said. "Maybe I should have told my friend that I was leaving because I didn't want any part of the stealing. . . . It all happened so fast."

"What you're saying to me is that if you had been alone, what happened would never have happened. You wanted your friends to like you, and you made the poor choice of sticking with them when you knew that one of them was going to steal something on a dare."

"You've got it, Doc. I should have never gone out with them that night. I knew that Darren had been caught stealing at the mall a year ago. Still, I went with them."

"Choices," the counselor responded. "We all make some bad choices in our lives that we wish we had never made. You can't undo any of the choices you've already made. You have to move forward, Justin."

"We're running out of time, and I want to make sure that you get an opportunity to look at the brain model on my desk. Remember, Dr. Siegel spoke about where fear is located in the brain? Well here's where the amygdala is located, and when it is stimulated in fear or anger, our emotions can get out of control. This is the part of the brain that Dr. Siegel called our older brain, the reptilian brain. Here, put your hand on the reptilian brain. Sometimes when our emotions are out of control, it's because the reptilian brain has hijacked the front part of our brain—the prefrontal cortex. The next time you find yourself becoming so angry that you just want to hit someone, say to yourself, 'I'm not going to let my old brain hijack my thinking.'"

Justin said back in his chair and put his hands behind his head, as if he had just received a new insight. "Before, I thought that I couldn't do anything about my anger. Next time I get real angry, I am going to put my hand on the back of my brain and say, 'You're not going to hijack me, not today.'"

SUMMARY

A dominant theme throughout this chapter is that the human brain is a social brain that depends on the quality of its relationships with people and the surrounding environment. The neuroscience approach to psychotherapy has a strong environmental emphasis, and it is one that encourages a wellness orientation for helping professionals and their clients.

Neuroscience has provided scientific explanations of therapist and client interventions that were previously not well understood. Neuroscience is clearly the fifth force in psychotherapy because of its scientific findings regarding the brain, its functioning, and what happens during the therapy hour when therapists and clients work together to change old, default, and oftentimes destructive patterns of behavior.

The chapter began with a brief overview of key contributors who linked neuroscience and psychotherapy. Therapists tend to use two patterns for incorporating neuroscientific knowledge into their practice: (1) they may retain their usual theoretical framework (psychoanalysis, cognitive-behavioral, social constructivist, etc.) or (2) they may turn to developing a new approach that can best be labeled neuropsychotherapy. This chapter first identified key concepts and terms used in neuropsychotherapy. The rest of the chapter was dedicated to providing a framework for neuropsychotherapy that examined factors such as the therapeutic alliance, the role of the therapist, right-brain to right-brain therapy, and the techniques and methods that prominent neuroscientists have proposed in their therapeutic practice. The topic of cultural neuroscience was discussed to help practitioners think about the relevance of brain science for working with culturally diverse clients.

Mental health specialists are experiencing an exciting period after the Decade of the Brain. Research has indicated that the so-called talking therapies are more important than was thought previously. When therapy is provided in an enriched environment, new patterns of neural activation can be promoted within clients' brain functioning. Studies have found that the therapeutic alliance, limbic mirror neuron effect, and therapist facilitation of safety and client control are critical to promote positive neural change in clients. The process of positive brain change in clients via therapy or counseling is facilitated by the therapist's activation of the mirror neuron system, enhancing cortical blood flow to enable good solutions to problems and strengthening new activation of neural patterns to enhance long-term patterns and reduce risk of relapse into default neural protective patterns that may be destructive in clients' lives.

Neuroscience research on mirror neurons provides one of the most profound indicators of the interconnectedness of human beings. We are all connected together in some way through the mirror neuron process. The talking therapies provide a safe environment that encourages the building of healthy new neural pathways in clients. However, these new neural networks are usually fragile. To prevent a client from returning to destructive or negative default neural patterns, therapists must promote sufficient neural activation toward new patterns of firing so that the default patterns are changed. The therapist's interventions are guided by Hebb's finding that neurons that fire together sufficiently wire together.

Studies have found that a variety of talking therapies can be effective in promoting neural change within clients. Grawe's (2007) meta-analysis demonstrates that the single common denominator to promote change via talking therapies is the therapist's use of the basic principles of neuroanatomy. These key principles are the therapist's (a) activation of the client's limbic mirror neuron system, (b) promotion of safety (down regulation of client distress), (c) enhancement of cortical blood flow, (d) strengthening positive neural activation networks, and (e) encouraging healthy social relationships and interactions with one's environment.

SUPPLEMENTAL AIDS _____

Discussion Questions

1. In your opinion, what impact, if any, might present and future findings in neuroscience have on the social justice movement in counseling and psychotherapy? Do you believe that neuroscience findings might highlight the adverse effects of being routinely exposed to increased levels of family violence, poor attachment, and lack of social support?

2. Neuroscience findings are being considered in dealing with attention deficit disorders in children and adolescents. Discuss the pros and cons of such research.

3. Let's suppose that you have just completed your master's degree in counseling or social work. What neuroscientific principles or intervention techniques would you consider using in your new private practice?

4. To what extent do you think the value of neuroscience for psychotherapy is overstated or understated?

5. If you had to choose only one of the neuroscientific approaches to psychotherapy, which one would that be and why?

Glossary of Key Terms

(Please note that the terms listed below are paraphrased from *Brain Facts: A Primer on the Brain and Nervous System*, on the website for the Society of Neuroscience: http://www.sfn.org.)

acetylcholine   A neurotransmitter that is active in the brain, where it regulates memory, and in the peripheral nervous system, where it influences the actions of skeletal and smooth muscle.

amygdala   A structure in the forebrain that is part of the limbic system and that plays a critical role in emotional learning, especially within the context of fear.

brain   The human brain is the most complex organ of the human body. It contains an estimated 50 to 100 billion neurons. The scientific study of the brain and the nervous system is called neurobiology or neuroscience. The brain is part of the central nervous system, along with the spinal cord and the peripheral nervous system.

brain stem   The stem-like part of the base of the brain that is connected to the spinal cord. The brain stem controls the flow of messages between the brain and the rest of the body, and it also controls basic body functions such as breathing, swallowing, heart rate, blood pressure, consciousness, and whether one is awake or sleepy. The brain stem consists of the midbrain, pons, and medulla oblongata (MedicineNet.com, http://www.medterms.com/script/main/art.asp?articlekey=2517).

cerebral cortex   This is the outermost layer of the cerebral hemispheres of the brain and is primarily responsible for all forms of conscious experience, including perception, emotion, thought, and executive planning.

cerebral hemispheres   The two specialized halves of the brain that control different brain functions. For instance, in right-handed people, the left hemisphere is specialized for speech, writing, language, and math calculations. The right hemisphere is specialized for visual face recognition, music perception, and spatial abilities.

cognition   The process that allows a person to gain knowledge of or become aware of objects in his or her environment; the person then uses that knowledge for comprehension and problem solving.

coherence therapy   Formerly known as depth oriented brief therapy, was developed by Bruce Tucker and Laura Hulley. It is a system of experiential, empathic psychotherapy that uses memory reconsolidation techniques, permitting therapists to consistently promote deep shifts, dispelling clients' symptoms at their emotional roots often in a small number of sessions. The steps of coherence therapy correspond closely to the steps of the memory reconsolidation process brain researchers have identified.

dopamine   A catecholamine neurotransmitter that assumes various functions depending on where it acts. Dopamine is believed to regulate key emotional responses, such as reward, in the brain, and it plays a role in schizophrenia and drug abuse.

endorphins   Neurotransmitters produced in the brain that have cellular and behavioral effects similar to those of morphine.

forebrain   The largest part of the human brain; it contains the cerebral cortex and basal ganglia. The forebrain is responsible for the highest intellectual functions a human can perform.

frontal lobe   Contains our cognitive thinking, and this process shapes an individual's personality. The frontal lobe is made up of the anterior portion (prefrontal cortex) and the posterior portion, and it is separated from the parietal lobe by the central sulcus. Functions of the frontal lobe include reasoning, planning, organizing thoughts, behavior, sexual urges, emotions, problem solving, and judging.

gamma-amino butyric acid (GABA)   An amino acid transmitter in the brain whose major function is to inhibit the firing of nerve cells.

glutamate   An amino acid neurotransmitter that functions to excite neurons.

hippocampus   A sea horse-shaped brain structure that is considered an important part of the limbic system. It is one of the most studied areas of the brain; it functions in learning, memory, and emotion.

inhibition   A synaptic message that prevents a neuron from firing.

limbic system   A group of structures within the brain (including the amygdala, hippocampus, septum, basal ganglia, etc.) that help regulate the expression of emotion and emotional memory.

long-term memory   The last phase of memory; it allows information to be stored that may last from hours to a lifetime.

memory consolidation   The physical and psychological changes that occur when the brain organizes and restructures information to make it a permanent part of memory.

neuron   May be defined as the electrically excitable cells that process and transmit information by electrical-chemical signaling.

neuropsychotherapist   A psychotherapist who is thoroughly grounded in the knowledge of the neurobiological workings of the brain and other aspects of human biology and who uses this information in working therapeutically with clients.

neuropsychotherapy   A psychotherapy practice that is informed by neuroscience and that is built on using a multidisciplinary approach that takes into account the whole individual.

neurotransmitter   A chemical that is released from a nerve cell that transmits an impulse from one nerve cell to another.

occipital lobe   The smallest of the four brain lobes. It is located in the rearmost portion of the skull and contains the primary visual cortex. Functions of the occipital lobe include visual reception, visual-spatial processing, movement, and color recognition. Disorders of the occipital lobe can cause visual illusions.

parietal lobe   Responsible for integrating sensory information from various parts of the body. The optic nerve passes through the parietal lobe to the occipital lobe. Functions of the parietal lobe include information processing, movement, spatial orientation, speech, visual perception, pain, and touch sensation.

serotonin   A monoamine neurotransmitter that plays a role in temperature regulation, sensory perception, and the onset of sleep. Neurons using serotonin are located in the brain and in the gut. Several antidepressant drugs are targeted to brain serotonin systems.

short-term memory   A phase of memory in which a limited amount of information is held for several seconds or minutes.

synapse   The structural space between neurons in the nervous system.

temporal lobe   There are two temporal lobes, located at about the level of the ears on either side of the brain. The temporal lobes are responsible for auditory processing and are involved in hearing, speech, and memory.

Website Materials

Additional exercises, journals, annotated bibliography, and more are available on the open-access website at https://study.sagepub.com/jonessmith2e.

CHAPTER 21

Comparing and Contrasting the Theories of Psychotherapy

Psychotherapy is characterized by a diversity of theories and methods, each the province of a particular school. But all psychotherapeutic techniques are attempts to heal through persuasion.

—Jerome Frank, *Persuasion and Healing: A Comparative Study of Psychotherapy*

BRIEF OVERVIEW

To develop into a mature, professional therapist or counselor, we must make difficult choices about which counseling approaches are most suitable to our personality, interpersonal style, work setting, and client needs. Each of the theoretical approaches presented provides a framework for understanding the client's world. It can, however, be overwhelming to study so many different conceptualizations of how to best perform counseling. Typically, graduate students ask themselves, "Which theory should I choose? How do I know which theory best suits me given that I have never counseled anyone? Which theory is the best one?"

Each of the theories presented in this book represents an approximation of the truth as one theorist or group of theorists viewed "the truth" (Norcross, 2005a). These theories are imperfect working hypotheses about human functioning. As such, they may still be evolving. Ellis, for instance,

revised his theory of rational emotive therapy several times until it became rational emotive behavior therapy (REBT). Carl Rogers's theory was initially client-centered therapy, and then it became person-centered therapy. Psychoanalytic therapy has been revised several times—first by ego psychologists, then by object relationists, followed by self psychologists, and now by relational psychoanalysts.

No one theory has a complete stronghold on all there is to know about human functioning and psychotherapy. As we learn more about human emotions and the brain, theories of psychotherapy are likely to be revised. Focus on the basic terms and language of the theory. Does the theory seem to fit with who you are as a person? What is your level of comfort in working within the theoretical framework? Could you assume the role of the therapist that is described in the theoretical school?

It is important to keep in mind that most of the popular theories of counseling were created by White, upper-middle-class older men, and therefore, the biases of people from this group are reflected. Most counseling theories evidence a Western rather than an Eastern perspective. Yet just because a counseling theory has a Western perspective and was developed by a White male does not in and of itself limit its effectiveness. Nevertheless, a Western male perspective may hold certain covert rather than overt biases. For instance, most counseling approaches assume that the individual or the self is more important than the community, that an individual should have internal versus an external locus of control, and that a person's spirituality should be deemphasized. Notable exceptions to this statement are practitioners of feminist theory, multicultural counseling, relational theory, strengths-based theory, and other indigenous theories.

Whereas some researchers have predicted that multicultural counseling is the fourth force in the counseling profession (Pedersen, 1991), I take a slightly different position. Although I predict that multicultural issues in counseling will continue to dominate the counseling profession, it will not become the fourth force in counseling because the theories emphasize too heavily the issue of oppression and do not put sufficient stress on the importance of a cultural identity for all people. Members of White ethnic groups may not consider themselves "oppressed," yet ethnic identity development may be very important to them.

With new visions and perspectives, there is a good chance that multicultural counseling theories will become much more rigorous in their design and may focus on issues other than ethnic, racial, or cultural oppression of a minority. I recommend that theories of multicultural counseling focus on relational issues, for the power of culture lies in the group-level identity that many people share with each other. The cultural-level relational identity is strong such that people place great value on having an Italian wedding, having a Jewish Passover, or an Irish funeral. During the time that we are waiting for a multicultural theory to describe the process of ethnic or cultural identity development, most counselors and therapists will do their best to incorporate multicultural principles in their practice. A later section of this chapter presents a multicultural framework that can be used to integrate cultural diversity issues into your integrative approach.

In developing your own integrative approach to psychotherapy, it is important to be able to compare and contrast the major theories presented in this book. Twenty-two different systems of psychotherapy have been examined. Comparing and contrasting the theories could be extremely valuable in developing your overall multitheoretical framework. I have reviewed the 22 theories presented in terms of the worldview or underlying philosophy, key concepts, therapeutic goals, the therapeutic relationship between the therapist and the client, the therapist's role, the client's role, counseling techniques, settings for the theory, view on multicultural counseling, and contributions of the approaches. Comparative tables are presented for each of the seven areas that are being compared. A few brief paragraphs introduce the area being compared. Examples of how specific theories approach goals and the role of the therapist are given as illustrations.

WORLDVIEWS OF THEORIES OF PSYCHOTHERAPY

Each theory espouses a worldview or underlying philosophy that reflects how the theorists see life and people. For instance, some theorists emphasize that life is determined by forces and early experiences (psychoanalytic and psychodynamic approaches), while other theorists assert that people are always in the process of constructing themselves and reality. I have lumped together psychoanalytic and psychodynamic theories, even though there are important differences within this category. When counselors understand their own worldview and its influence on them as therapists, they stand a better chance of being able to avoid letting their own personal views encroach on the client's issues.

All psychotherapists have a worldview based on their family, culture, and life experiences. Therapists should examine their worldview when they have strong reactions to clients, feel uneasy about certain clients, or experience conflicting cultural values or cultural countertransference. Therapists who explore their own worldview are in a better position to change how they interact with their clients. According to Pedersen (2000), counselors who are unaware of their own worldview are encapsulated. They have a tendency to focus on one truth—usually their truth or the truth that the theory they are using espouses. Table 21.1 presents

Table 21.1 Worldview/Underlying Philosophy of the Theoretical Approaches

Theoretical Approach	Worldview
Psychoanalytic/ psychodynamic therapy	We understand our present by examining our past. We understand people by exploring their family histories. Emphasizes early childhood and psychosexual development. Theories focus on biological and deterministic features of behavior.
Adlerian therapy	People are motivated by social interest. Each person establishes goals in life, some of which are fictional. The focus is on people's ability to live positively and cooperatively in society. During early childhood, each person creates a style of life, which is inclined to remain fairly stable throughout his or her life.
Behavioral therapy (exposure therapies)	Although we are the products of our environment, we are also the producers of our lives. Individuals' behavior is the product of their learning. Old behaviors can be extinguished while new ones can be established.
Cognitive (rational-emotive therapy, Beck's cognitive therapy)	Individuals' thoughts are the primary causes of mental health issues. Therapy focuses on the thought patterns that individuals have that are causing difficulties. The cognitive approach to therapy is essentially a psychoeducational model, which views therapy as a learning process. Clients learn new ways of thinking, and they develop effective coping skills to deal with problems.
Reality therapy	Reality assumes that people need quality relationships to have a satisfying life. People create psychological problems when they try to gain control. Problems also take place when people do not take responsibility for their behavior.
Existential therapy	Existentialism stresses a belief in human freedom and choice. The primary philosophy deals with the nature of the human condition, self-awareness, the search for meaning, anxiety, and death.
Person-centered therapy	Person-centered therapy emphasizes a positive view of human beings. People experience a growth and self-actualizing tendency in life. Clients progress toward increased awareness and inner directedness.
Gestalt therapy	Individuals move toward wholeness and integration of thinking, feeling, and behaving. This approach is strongly grounded in the here-and-now.
Multicultural therapy	Multicultural counseling can help individuals adapt to new cultures and respond to oppressive cultural contexts. Multicultural counseling can be used to help immigrants adapt to new cultural environments while not losing touch with the homeland cultures.
Feminist therapy	Feminist therapy emphasizes an egalitarian relationship between the therapist and the client and the recognition of the influence of external forces such as discrimination on women. The personal problems that women encounter are connected to the political and the social climate in which they live.
Gay and lesbian therapy	The right to choose one's own sexual orientation is a basic human right. When therapists assume unconsciously that a person is heterosexual rather than homosexual, they are unconsciously adopting the worldview of heterosexism.

(Continued)

Table 21.1 (Continued)

Theoretical Approach	Worldview
Transcultural therapies	
Naikan and Morita therapies	Both Naikan and Morita Therapy maintain that life is a matter of attention—that is, what you place your attention on and what you withdraw your attention from. "Neurosis is misdirected attention" (Morita).
Mindfulness therapy	The mindfulness worldview says that mindfulness awareness is a way of being, a way of living within one's own body, one's own mind in a moment-by-moment experience. The mindfulness worldview focuses on attention, sometimes called *bare attention*. It involves knowing what is arising as it is taking place—without adding anything to it.
Ma'at African therapy	African-centered worldviews are founded on three principals or underlying assumptions: (1) there is a spiritual nature of all human beings, (2) all living things are interconnected, and (3) there is a oneness of mind, body, and spirit.
Arab Muslim therapy	The Arab and the Muslim worlds share the ethos of tribal collectivism and Islamic values. Choices in life are collectivist matters, and all major decisions in life are determined by one's family.
Postmodern therapies	
Solution-focused therapy	The underlying philosophy is that we socially construct our personal meaning. Counseling should focus on solutions to problems and not on problems.
Narrative therapy	Clients construct stories about their lives that reveal the sources of their difficulties. Narrative therapists say that people can improve their lives by making different stories. Clients learn how to externalize a problem.
Strengths-based therapy	Strengths-based counseling is intended to bring out positive consequences in clients' lives. Strengths-based counseling uses clients' strengths as a means to deal with presenting problems. Therapy changes from a problem focus to a strength focus.
Family systems therapy	The family is viewed from a system perspective. Clients are connected to a family system. A change in any part of the system will result in a change in other parts. The family supplies the context within which individuals are examined. A client's dysfunctional behavior stems from the family and the community within which he or she lives.
Dialectical behavioral therapy (DBT)	The DBT worldview is one that does not try to stop or prevent thoughts, as with cognitive-behavioral therapy, but instead this therapy believes in the acceptance and validation of clients' current thoughts. The dialectical emphasis comes from Eastern and Western perspectives in that it involves a synthesis of acceptance and change.
Acceptance and commitment therapy (ACT)	ACT also has as its core the acceptance of both positive and negative occurrences in life. The worldview is an integration of Eastern and Western perspectives on how one should approach life.

Theoretical Approach	Worldview
Mindfulness-based cognitive therapy (MBCT)	The worldview of MBCT is similar to that of both DBT and ACT: accepting both the good and the bad in life and the power of just observing our thoughts without experiencing a great deal of emotional involvement.
Motivational interviewing therapy	The worldview of motivational interviewing is that people are capable of making beneficial change; however, many people may have ambivalence about making change and may need outside support.
Expressive arts therapies	
Art and music therapies	Most people have some kind of creative ability, and some people can heal through the use of imagination and various forms of creative expression.
Play therapy	Play is a natural part of growing up, and play therapy uses the healing aspects of play to help children, adolescents, and adults.
Neuroscience and neuropsychotherapy	The neuropsychotherapy worldview involves focusing on the dynamic interplay between the mind, the body, social interaction, and environment on a person's well-being. It emphasizes a holistic view of people.

a brief summary of the worldviews and underlying philosophy of the major psychotherapy theories discussed in this book.

KEY CONCEPTS OF THEORIES OF PSYCHOTHERAPY

This section compares the key concepts of the major theories reviewed in this book. Theories are examined in terms of the major theoretical school with which they are affiliated: psychodynamic, cognitive-behavioral, existential-humanistic, and postmodern.

Key Concepts of Psychoanalytic and Psychodynamic Approaches

Freud's most central concept that pervades his entire theory is his idea of the unconscious. The human psyche can be placed into levels of awareness—unconscious, preconscious, and conscious. The psychoanalytic and psychodynamic perspective maintains that a great deal of human behavior is unconsciously motivated or out of our awareness. We are motivated by either biological drives and instincts or derivatives from psychological structures formed early in our childhood. The unconscious level of awareness contains much conflict between it and the other parts of the human psyche. Human nature is considered much more irrational than rational. An important premise of the psychodynamic school is that the crucial formative period of development is early childhood. I have come to believe that as powerful as the unconscious is, it is far more accessible to clients than what most people think. It might be better to use the term *out of immediate awareness* than to use the term *unconscious*.

During the past 50 years, psychoanalysis has begun to emphasize interpersonal relationships. The work of Freud's daughter, Anna Freud, on ego defense mechanisms focused on people's capacity to adapt to reality as well as the coping strategies or defense mechanisms they use to defend against anxiety. Object relations theory presented the idea that people are as motivated by their need for others as they are by their biological drives. Winnicott's "the good-enough mother" concept talks about the kinds of relationships we need with others.

Key Concepts of Cognitive-Behavioral Perspective

It is erroneous to talk of the cognitive-behavioral perspective because the two components were developed initially as two separate therapy movements. Both behavioral and cognitive approaches are designed to deal with particular symptoms and psychiatric disorders. Behavioral approaches are based on learning theory. Their position is that personality is malleable and shaped by environmental forces. Human motivation is conceptualized in terms of anticipated consequences that people hope to obtain or fear obtaining (rewards or punishment) rather than in terms of intrapsychic needs.

Problem behavior takes place as a result of faulty learning. An individual is viewed as a complex constellation of specific stimulus–response patterns that have been learned over a long period of time. For instance, John Wolpe found that neurosis takes place when anxiety becomes conditioned to a specific environmental stimulus. Psychiatric disorders are viewed as persistent maladaptive habits learned in a fear-generating environment. The individual is reconditioned through a reordering of the stimuli to which he or she was exposed so that more adaptive responses can be instituted.

During the 1960s, it became clear that the application of behavioral techniques alone was insufficient. For clients to be helped, they needed to process information cognitively. For instance, a client has to make a cognitive appraisal to deal with his or her phobia. Cognitive therapists broadened the area of concern to include clients' thoughts, assumptions, and beliefs, in addition to their behavior. Cognitive structures determine how we perceive our life experiences. As Hamlet stated in the play, "There is nothing either good or bad, but thinking makes it so."

In contrast to the psychodynamic school, cognitive therapists are interested in clients' conscious processes, and they see people as basically rational. Cognitive-behavioral concepts have a significant impact on the field of psychotherapy. Practitioners tend to adopt cognitive-behavioral techniques in therapy because such techniques are straightforward.

The third-wave cognitive theories (dialectical behavioral therapy, acceptance and commitment therapy, and mindfulness-based cognitive therapy) challenge the second cognitive theories in that these theories do not encourage clients to interrupt, stop, or block their unwanted thoughts but rather to accept them simply as thoughts that have no real power over them. The third-wave theories also incorporate mindfulness as a core component of the respective theory.

Key Concepts of the Existential-Humanistic School

Existential therapists are interested in the meaning of our being-in-the-world. People are in constant search of finding meaning in the world. They are responsible for their own destiny, and they can choose to be authentic or inauthentic. The American humanists, notably Abraham Maslow and Carl Rogers, emphasized the experiential nature of psychotherapy. They proposed that people have an inherent need for self-fulfillment.

Key Concepts of the Social Constructivist/Postmodern School of Psychotherapy

The postmodern approach to psychotherapy emphasizes the social construction of reality. A problem exists when people agree that it exists. Social constructionism maintains that the language and concepts we use to generally understand the world are culturally specific. Our knowledge is time and culture bound. Theories that reflect a postmodern perspective include solution-focused therapy, narrative therapy, and strengths-based counseling. The postmodern perspective can be compared with the modern view, which emphasizes that clients are seen as experts on their own lives. People are healthy, creative, and have strengths that they can use to deal with their life challenges.

Key Concepts of the Neuroscience and Neuropsychotherapy School

Neuroscience emphasizes a holistic view of human beings. The brain is a social organ in addition to being a biological organ. Many of the key concepts in neuropsychotherapy involve the brain, the concept of neuroplasticity, neurotransmitters, right brain and left brain development, mirror neurons, and so forth. Table 21.2 presents the key concepts of the major psychotherapy theories discussed within this book.

Table 21.2 Key Concepts of Theories

Theoretical Approach	Key Concept
Psychoanalytic/ psychodynamic therapy	Unconscious, id, ego, superego, defense mechanisms, drive theory, and psychosexual stages; ego psychology: ego defense mechanisms; object relations: childhood relationship with the mother, individuation, transitional object, good-enough mother, and true and false self; self psychology: narcissism, self object, idealized parent; and relational psychoanalysis: perception of relationships and intersubjectivity.
Adlerian therapy	Style of life, social interest, inferiority and superiority complex, and birth order. All behavior is goal directed.
Behavioral therapy	Classical and operant conditioning, positive reinforcement, generalization, extinction, discrimination, and shaping; Observational learning and self-efficacy.
Cognitive therapy	Albert Ellis: irrational beliefs, A-B-C theory of personality, and catastrophizing; Aaron Beck: automatic thoughts, cognitive schemas, cognitive distortions, all-or-nothing thinking, mind reading, and magnification or minimization.
Reality therapy	Responsibility, choice theory, psychological needs of belonging, power, freedom, and fun; choosing, doing, thinking, and feeling.
Existential therapy	Being-in-the-world; four ways of being: *Umwelt, Mitwelt, Eigenwelt, Uberwelt*; freedom and responsibility; isolation and loving; meaning and meaninglessness; and striving for authenticity.
Person-centered therapy	Positive regard, positive self-regard, conditions of worth, and fully actualized person. The principal mark of Rogers' person-centered therapy is his postulation of a self-concept.
Gestalt therapy	Figure and ground relationships, contact with self and others, introjection, projection, retroflection, deflection, and unfinished business.
Multicultural therapy	There is no one theory of multicultural counseling, but rather there are theorists who have offered a series of stages clients encounter when they enter a new culture or when they are members of a minority within a dominant culture. Culture, multicultural competencies, and stages of ethnic identity development.

(Continued)

Table 21.2 (Continued)

Theoretical Approach	Key Concept
Feminist therapy	There is no single feminist theory, but therapists emphasize gender differences, gender schema theory, gender equality, and dealing with oppression. Gender and culture are the central organizing forces of a person's life.
Gay and lesbian therapy	Key concepts involve sexual orientation identity development, Cass identity development model, coming out, and homophobia.
Transcultural therapies	
Naikan and Morita therapies	Both Naikan and Morita therapy use meditation and focus on self-control. Morita therapy emphasizes Arugamama. The theories maintain that we become what we focus our attention on. Most people are too preoccupied with themselves. The more attention we pay to our symptoms, the bigger our symptoms and problems become.
Mindfulness therapy	Mindfulness practice consists of three components: (1) intention, (2) attention, and (3) attitude. A person's attention sets the stage for what is possible. A core value of mindfulness is acceptance.
Ma'at African therapy	Ma'at seeks balance and control in one's life. Some key concepts include control of thought, control of action, and devotion to one's purpose. Ma'at has 42 declarations—I have not done any act of violence, stolen, etc.
Arab Muslim therapy	Communication between family members is based on the value of respect (*ihtiram*), fulfilling social duties (*wajib*), and pleasing others and avoiding confrontations (*mosayara*).
Postmodern therapies	
Solution-focused therapy	Focus on the present rather than on the past, on solutions rather than on problems; therapy is a collaborative dialogue. Identify time when the problem did not exist so that the client can create new meanings.
Narrative therapy	People's lives consist of stories, which they tell and retell. Each story has a setting, plot, characterization, theme, etc.
Strengths-based therapy	Strengths perspective, strengths transactions, managing weaknesses, cultural and contextual strengths, strength categories, and strength estrangement. Strength developmental states—begins early in life in the brain and continues in the various relationships that people form. Strengths are relational in that they are nurtured in relationships with others.
Family systems therapy	The individual is embedded in a larger relational system. The larger relational system includes many subsystems, such as the individual, the nuclear family, the extended family, and the community. Family systems theory consists of systems theory, feedback, and homeostasis: *Bowen's intergenerational model:* differentiation of self, triangulation, family projection process, emotional cutoff, and multigenerational transmission process. Intergenerational therapies emphasize a multigenerational process of symptom development.

Theoretical Approach	Key Concept
	Minuchin's structural approach: alignments and coalitions
	Haley's strategic approach: power in relationships, communication, and symptom focus—an appropriately organized family will have clearly marked boundaries or rules defining who participates, and how, in each system. There will be boundaries between the marital system and parental system, etc.
Dialectical behavioral therapy	Self-monitoring, dialectical, mixed and shifting nature of human emotion; self-regulation; and mindfulness.
Acceptance and commitment therapy	Acceptance, cognitive fusion, being present, self as context, values, committed action, and mindfulness.
Mindfulness-based cognitive therapy	Mindfulness meditation, stress reduction, depression, and separate person from thoughts.
Motivational interviewing therapy	The spirit of motivational interviewing, evocation, autonomy, reflective listening, and develop discrepancy.
Expressive arts therapies	
Art and music therapies	Self-expression, imagination, active participation, and mind–body connection.
Play therapy	Acknowledge child's feelings, communicate limits, target acceptable behavior, imagination, creativity, and play.
Neuroscience and neuropsychotherapy	Holistic, brain, mind, neurotransmitters, mirror neurons, right brain, left brain, attachment, implicit memory, explicit memory, and memory consolidation.

THE THERAPEUTIC PROCESS

Goals of Therapy

Every psychotherapy approach establishes goals. The question that the therapist raises in terms of goals is "What should or needs to be changed?" It is important that the goals of therapy are primarily determined by the kinds of problems that clients bring to therapy. Establishing the goals of therapy has much to do with the particular orientation with which the therapist identifies. It is extremely significant, then, that the therapist understands how a given theoretical model defines the goals of therapy. Once a goal is set, counselors develop strategies to help the client reach the goal and thereby solve the problem presented initially in counseling.

The goals of therapy will differ depending on which aspect of psychological functioning the therapist considers the most significant. By examining therapy goals, one can get an understanding of the hoped-for consequences of therapy. A primary goal in most psychoanalysis sessions is to help the client become more aware of the unconscious features of his or her personality. A second major goal is to assist a client in working through a developmental stage not previously resolved. If this goal is accomplished, clients become unstuck, and they are able to live more productive lives. A final goal is to help strengthen a client's ego so that his or her views and life goals are more reality oriented. The goals of Adlerian counseling entail helping clients develop healthy lifestyles. This usually involves an analysis of a client's lifestyle, which if done appropriately produces insight.

In experiential therapy (Gestalt therapy, existential therapy), clients may be unaware of their own feelings and ignore or suppress them. One goal of therapy would be to help clients explore their feelings during therapy. When the therapist explores clients' feelings, they assess to determine if their feelings serve an adaptive or a maladaptive focus. If therapists encourage awareness and expression of feelings, then the goal is to have clients gain insight from their emotional experience.

The goals of the behaviorist are to help clients make good life adjustments, modify or eliminate maladaptive behavior, and help clients acquire healthy, constructive ways of behaving. The counselor and the client work to achieve mutually agreed-on goals. Usually four steps are involved. The client and the counselor define the problem in terms of when, where, how, and with whom the problem arises. Next, he or she takes a developmental history of the client. Third, the two break down specific goals into small, achievable units. Finally, the therapist determines the best methods for change.

The primary goals of REBT are to assist people in realizing that they can live more rational and productive lives. Another goal of REBT is to help clients in changing any self-defeating habits of thought or behavior. One way in which this goal is accomplished is to teach clients the ABCDE (*A*ctivating event, *B*elief system, emotional *C*onsequences of A and B, *D*isputing irrational thoughts and beliefs, and cognitive and *E*motional effects of revised beliefs) of REBT.

In cognitive therapy, a counseling goal might be to reinforce adaptive cognitions and to extinguish dysfunctional ones. In this school, thoughts are viewed as behaviors that are in response to operant conditioning. Clients learn to participate in their own internal reinforcement. When a therapist reinforces adaptive cognitions, the desired goal is that clients will work to develop and strengthen new beliefs and will give up the old ways of thinking. Reinforcement will be stronger if the therapist and the client can establish real-life experiences that reward the new way of thinking (Brooks-Harris, 2008). Table 21.3 presents an outline of the therapy goals for the major psychotherapy approaches discussed in this book.

Table 21.3   Therapy Goals of the Theoretical Approaches

Theoretical Approach	Therapy Goals
Psychoanalytic/psychodynamic therapy	Primary goals are to make the unconscious conscious and have clients work through unresolved developmental psychosexual stages. Another goal is to reinterpret early childhood experiences and to restructure clients' personalities. The goal in object relations theory is to explore and resolve separation and individuation issues. A major goal in self psychology is to resolve issues dealing with self-absorption or idealized parents.
Adlerian therapy	Adlerian goals include helping clients develop social interests, correcting clients' faulty assumptions and mistaken goals, and effecting behavioral change by clients' acting "as if."
Behavioral therapy	To extinguish or eliminate learned maladaptive behaviors and to replace them with more adaptive behavior. Clients are encouraged to help set treatment goals. The therapist is active.
Cognitive therapy	The goal of cognitive therapy (Ellis) is to eliminate irrational thoughts and replace them with more adaptive thoughts. Faulty beliefs cause the client's dysfunction. Beck's goals include helping clients deal with automatic thoughts and cognitive schema.

Theoretical Approach	Therapy Goals
Reality therapy	To teach clients choice theory so that they will have a framework for getting reconnected with the people most important in their quality worlds.
Existential therapy	To help people become free and to live responsibly. Goal is to help clients determine what is keeping them from living authentically.
Person-centered therapy	Self-exploration, openness to self and others; to encourage clients to move toward positive growth in their lives; and to help clients trust themselves and their self-actualizing tendency.
Gestalt therapy	To help clients become aware of their moment-to-moment life experiences. Gestalt therapy is a process that helps clients live more full lives by increasing their awareness.
Multicultural therapy	To assist clients with understanding how their cultural messages, cultural identity development, and worldview influence their lives.
Feminist therapy	General therapy goals are to work with clients so that they understand the impact of gender and culture on their own life issues and identity development. The therapist helps clients work toward self-esteem and to accept one's own body.
Gay and lesbian therapy	Help clients deal with internalized and externalized homophobia and heterosexism. Recognize LGBT (lesbian, gay, bisexual, transgender)—specific issues raised either explicitly or implicitly by the client during therapy.
Transcultural therapies	
Naikan therapy	The purpose of Naikan therapy is to help clients see the truth of their lives. Three questions are proposed in Naikan therapy: (1) What has a specific person done for me? (2) What have I done for this person? (3) What troubles and difficulties have I caused this person?
Morita therapy	Morita therapy contends that people are overly preoccupied with themselves. Some general goals of therapy are to help clients focus on the things that can be done in a given moment and accept their feelings.
Mindfulness therapy	To help clients learn how to manage their attention to deal with a myriad issues, including pain, alcoholism, parenting, etc.
Ma'at African therapy	To help clients become one with the universe and to live a life of integrity.
Arab Muslim therapy	An important goal is to help restore the intrafamilial order. The therapist gives special attention to understanding the relationship dynamics of the family and the status of the client within the family.
Postmodern therapies	
Solution-focused therapy	To help clients find their own solutions to their problems.
Narrative therapy	To have clients tell their stories and to rewrite them so that the problem is dealt with adequately. To help clients learn how to externalize their problems so that they can distance themselves from the negative stories.

(Continued)

Table 21.3 (Continued)

Theoretical Approach	Therapy Goals
Strengths-based therapy	To help clients reconnect and use their strengths in dealing with life issues that brought them to therapy.
Family systems therapy	To work with clients so that they become more aware of the patterns of interrelationships that they have established within their families.
Dialectical behavioral therapy	To help clients create and maintain consistent, stable, personal environments in which they are comfortable with change. Another goal is to help clients deal with the dialectical tensions—to bring out the opposites in the therapeutic situation and in the client's life so as to provide the client with the conditions for synthesis. To get the client's behavior under control.
Acceptance and commitment therapy	To increase psychological flexibility, to help a client accept what is out of his or her personal control, and to commit to act in a way that improves and enriches a client's life. To help people realize their potential for a rich and meaningful life by teaching them mindfulness skills, to help them clarify what is really important and meaningful to them, and to use that knowledge to change their lives.
Mindfulness-based cognitive therapy	To prevent a relapse in depression for individuals diagnosed with a major depressive disorder. To teach clients to decenter their thoughts and to prevent an escalation of negative thoughts.
Motivational interviewing therapy	To strengthen a client's own verbalized motivations for change and to have the client rather than the counselor voice the arguments for change.
Expressive arts therapies	
Art and music therapies	To use art or music expression and imagination to promote a client's healing process.
Play therapy	To use play as a means to help clients deal with their issues, to use play to promote client healing.
Neuroscience and neuropsychotherapy	To promote holistic balance in a client's life by helping him or her examine brain issues, attachment, and so forth. To help clients build new, positive neural pathways in the brain to help them achieve their goals.

Role of the Therapist

Theories of psychotherapy can also be compared and contrasted in terms of the role that the therapist assumes. For instance, therapists who practice classical psychoanalysis play the role of the expert. They encourage clients to talk about whatever comes to mind—free association. The analyst's role is to assist clients in gaining insight by reliving and working through unresolved conflicts that surface during counseling. In contrast to other approaches, the psychoanalytically oriented therapist interprets for the client. The therapist may use projective tests to get at unconscious conflicts. The role of the Adlerian counselor is primarily that of psycho-educator. Adlerians are oftentimes active in sharing hunches or guesses with clients.

In the REBT approach to therapy, therapists are active and directive. They correct the client's cognitions. The primary assessment tool REBT therapists use is to evaluate clients' thinking. Table 21.4 summarizes the role of the therapist in different therapeutic approaches.

Table 21.4 Role of the Therapist and the Theoretical Approaches

Theoretical Approach	Role of the Therapist
Psychoanalytic/ psychodynamic therapy	Therapist, as expert, encourages transference and exploration of the unconscious; uses interpretation.
Adlerian therapy	Counselor models, teaches, and assesses client's situation; shares hunches; assigns homework; and encourages.
Behavioral therapy	Counselor as teacher, expert: active in sessions, assists client in clarifying goals and modifying behavior.
Cognitive therapy	Helps clients to stop thinking irrationally. Emphasizes elimination of shoulds, oughts, and musts—that is, making wants into demands, elimination of self-defeating habits.
Reality therapy	Helps clients take responsibility for their own lives.
Existential therapy	Helps clients realize their responsibility, increase awareness, freedom, and being-in-the-world.
Person-centered therapy	Emphasis on the counseling relationship—personal warmth, empathy, acceptance, concreteness, and genuineness.
Gestalt therapy	Counselor must be authentic, must emphasize the now and also the nonverbal and verbal messages.
Multicultural therapy	Counselor is respectful and knowledgeable about the client's culture and moves the client through several stages of cultural identity development.
Feminist therapy	Therapist is active, helps client examine the sociopolitical structure that may contribute to gender issues, and examines gender roles.
Gay and lesbian therapy	Therapist must be knowledgeable about gay and lesbian issues and must understand the multiple identities of such clients. The therapist engages in social engineering to help reduce homophobia.
Transcultural therapies	
Naikan therapy	Naikan guides (therapists) are responsible for providing and maintaining a quiet setting that allows participants to engage in introspection undisturbed. The guides provide basic physical comforts necessary to engage in Naikan therapy—a room, a daily structure, and meals at the Naikan center. Therapists listen and guide clients in introspection and dialogue by focusing on reoccurring life themes, such as dishonesty, negativity, or blaming.

(Continued)

Table 21.4 (Continued)

Theoretical Approach	Role of the Therapist
Morita therapy	The Morita therapist functions to guide clients through four stages: (1) absolute bed rest, (2) light work, (3) intensive work, and (4) preparation for daily living.
Mindfulness therapy	The role of the therapist is to use mindful practices during therapy—listening, sitting in silence, and being present. The mindful therapist uses practices such as nonattachment, acceptance, letting go, nonstriving, nonjudging, and patience.
Ma'at African therapy	The role of the therapist is to provide knowledge and wisdom to the client.
Arab Muslim therapy	Therapist is knowledgeable about collectivist Arab Muslim culture and uses the techniques associated with metaphor therapy, guided imagery, art therapy, and bibliotherapy.
Postmodern therapies	
Solution-focused therapy	Therapist is a co-equal, helps clients focus on solutions rather than on problems.
Narrative therapy	Therapist is a co-equal, helps clients tell their stories and revise them.
Strengths-based therapy	Therapist is a co-equal, actively involved in examining strengths and in giving homework and other experiential activities that will help clients understand and build on strengths, helps clients learn how to manage their weaknesses.
Family systems therapy	Therapist helps build strong, healthy families, since unhealthy systems resist change; the role of the family therapist is to help clients bring about the change process by first making small changes. *Bowen's intergenerational model:* reduce family stress level and assist family members in becoming more differentiated. *Minuchin's structural approach:* change coalitions and alliances in the family to effect family changes. *Haley's strategic approach:* focus on family communication patterns, boundaries.
Dialectical behavioral therapy	To guide the client through various stages, to conduct individual and group therapy sessions, to educate client in mindfulness skills, distress tolerance, and interpersonal effectiveness.
Acceptance and commitment therapy	To teach clients mindfulness and acceptance skills and to guide the client through six core processes.
Mindfulness-based cognitive therapy	To conduct individual and eight group sessions with clients that help them distance themselves from negative thoughts, to conduct one to four 2-hour follow-up reinforcement sessions, and to help clients improve their mindfulness skills.
Motivational interviewing therapy	To help clients move toward desired change in target behavior.

Theoretical Approach	Role of the Therapist
Expressive arts therapies	
Art and music therapies	To have clients increase or use their creative imagination and talents to deal with psychological issues.
Play therapy	To have clients use play to resolve or deal with psychological problems.
Neuroscience and neuropsychotherapy	To help clients build positive, new neural pathways and to rebuild or repair neural pathways that hinder a client from enjoying and having a meaningful life.

Therapy Techniques

Schools of psychotherapy also vary according to the techniques they use. This section reviews the techniques of the major theories discussed in this text. Only a representative sampling of techniques is presented. It is important to remember that some techniques may overlap the various schools, and that other techniques have been incorporated into many of the schools of therapy. The less active techniques of free association and interpretation have been associated with long-term psychoanalytic therapy. The primary techniques associated with each therapy school are listed in Table 21.5.

Table 21.5 Techniques of Therapy and the Theoretical Approaches

Theoretical Approach	Therapy Techniques
Psychoanalytic/psychodynamic therapy	Free association, analyzing resistance, interpretation of dreams and free association, analysis of transference.
Adlerian therapy	Spitting in one's soup, catching oneself, acting "as if," push-button techniques, and the questions.
Behavioral therapy	Systematic desensitization, imaginal flooding, in vivo techniques, modeling, self-instructional training, stress inoculation, relaxation techniques, assertiveness training, exposure, and activity homework.
Cognitive therapy	Disputing irrational beliefs, affirmations, and coping self statements.
Reality therapy	Friendly involvement, exploring total behavior, planning to do better, humor, and paradoxical intentions.
Existential therapy	Techniques are generally not used, instead, conditions are emphasized.
Person-centered therapy	Therapist provides the necessary and sufficient conditions for therapy. Therapy uses few techniques, active listening, reflection of feeling, and clarification.
Gestalt therapy	Use of exercises and experiments, empty chair, making the rounds, exaggeration, and I take responsibility.

(Continued)

Table 21.5 (Continued)

Theoretical Approach	Therapy Techniques
Multicultural therapy	Analyze cultural messages, cultural identity development, and client's values and worldviews.
Feminist therapy	Uses consciousness-raising techniques, gender role analysis, journal writing, reframing, and bibliotherapy.
Gay and lesbian therapy	Interventions include providing information on national lesbian and gay networks of professionals and community people and publishing a list of "out" gay/lesbian individuals who would be available for informational interviews with clients.
Transcultural therapies	
Naikan therapy	Naikan uses techniques of immersion and counseling; instruct clients on meditation.
Morita therapy	Techniques of Morita therapy include meditation, bed rest, and dialogues with therapist/guide.
Mindfulness therapy	Clients are trained in mindfulness techniques, including meditation, body scan, walking meditation, and guided mindfulness.
Ma'at African therapy	Healers consult plants and trees, and observe the movement of caged mice to diagnose a client's problem.
Arab Muslim therapy	Therapist uses the techniques associated with metaphor therapy, guided imagery, art therapy, and bibliotherapy.
Postmodern therapies	
Solution-focused therapy	Therapist uses change talk, miracle question, and scaling questions.
Narrative therapy	Externalizing and naming the problem; narrative therapist writes letters to clients, and they assist them in finding an audience to support their desired change.
Strengths-based therapy	Strength wheel, Wheel of Life exercise, strength charts, strength cards, strength memories, managing weaknesses and barriers exercise, and the hope chest technique.
Family systems therapy	Genograms, joining the family, enactments, and family mapping.
Dialectical behavioral therapy	Entering the paradox, dialectical assessment, wise mind, devil's advocate, mindfulness, and distress tolerance.
Acceptance and commitment therapy	Mindfulness, acceptance, cognitive diffusion, contact with the present moment, the observing self, and committed action.
Mindfulness-based cognitive therapy	To help clients identify negative thoughts, to teach breathing and mindfulness techniques, and to decenter thoughts.

Theoretical Approach	Therapy Techniques
Motivational interviewing therapy	OARS (*Open-ended questions, Affirmations, Reflections, Summaries*)—client-centered counseling skills, rolling with resistance; eliciting client change talk.
Expressive arts therapies	
Art and music therapies	Use of client's or others' art and music expressions and encourage client's imagination.
Play therapy	Encourage client play, sand tray, and doll houses.
Neuroscience and neuropsychotherapy	HEAL strategy (*healthy eating, active living*), mindsight techniques, memory reconsolidation, brainspotting, compassionate communication, mirror imaging, and brain mapping.

RESEARCH AND EVALUATION —
Multicultural Positives and Multicultural Blind Spots

Therapists should consider making a multicultural conceptualization when culture becomes a focal point or an important dimension in therapy. A multicultural conceptualization emphasizes the way in which cultural contexts influence individuals' thoughts, feelings, and behaviors. The American Psychological Association (APA, 2003a) has defined culture as "the belief systems and value orientations that influence customs, norms, practices, and social institutions, including psychological processes (language, caretaking processes) and organizations (media, educational systems)" (p. 380).

During psychotherapy, cultural contexts may affect clients' ethnic identity, gender roles, and religious beliefs. Whereas some clients will recognize their issues related to culture, other clients may not see initially that their presenting issues have a cultural context. When therapists believe that a client's presenting problems may be related to cultural contexts, the therapist examines the following: (a) cultural messages, (b) cultural and cultural identity development, and (c) the client's worldview and cultural values (Brooks-Harris & Savage, 2008).

Cultural messages may be defined as the lessons individuals learn from being raised within

a specific culture. The therapist listens for and identifies obvious and subtle cultural messages that may influence clients' concerns. Cultural identity development can be viewed as an ongoing way in which individuals view themselves within their group-level identity of ethnicity, religion, or culture. Individuals construct a worldview based on their cultural values and the way they perceive the world. Therefore, a multicultural conceptualization explores the manner in which different cultural contexts create messages that help form individuals' cultural identity development that culminates in their worldview and cultural values. The therapist uses a number of probing questions to form a multicultural conceptualization, which are represented in the box below (Brooks-Harris & Savage, 2008). The therapist seeks to discover what the client has been taught in his or her culture.

Cultural Messages

- What family or cultural values did your family transmit to you while growing up?
- What behaviors did you learn that were maintained or reinforced by members of your ethnic, cultural, or religious group?

(Continued)

(Continued)

- What messages did your cultural group give you regarding appropriate behavior for you as a male or as a female?
- How receptive were you to the cultural messages that your family and members of your cultural group attempted to impress on you?
- As you have developed in life, to what extent have you modified or maintained your early views of the cultural messages that your family and community group sent to you?
- What were the cultural messages your ethnic/religious group gave you about seeking counseling?

Cultural Identity Development/Acculturation

- With what culture do you feel the most bonded?
- Have you adopted the cultural values of any other group?
- To what extent do you identify with the cultural values of the country in which you live?
- Do you identify more so with the cultural group into which you were born or a different culture that you have chosen to accept as your own?

Worldview/Cultural Values

- To what degree has your cultural background influenced the way in which you see the world?
- Have you experienced any conflict between your worldview and the society in which you live?
- What cultural goals and values are important to you now?
- To what extent, if any, has a conflict in cultural issues brought you to counseling?
- Do you think our cultural differences as client and therapist will influence our working together in a productive fashion? Do you believe that I will understand you?

Forming a Multicultural Conceptualization of Clients

Table 21.6 displays how different counseling theories take into consideration multicultural issues. A critical issue here is whether you need a separate theory or approach to clients' multicultural issues or whether multicultural concerns can be introduced as part of each theoretical framework.

Future Outlook of Theoretical Approaches

Movement Toward Psychotherapy Integration. No one really knows the outlook for the theoretical approaches presented in this book. We can only make intelligent guesses what the future will be like based on where things now seem headed. Prediction number one is that the movement toward psychotherapy integration will continue and become even more heightened than it is now. The movement toward psychotherapy theories integration does not mean that graduate students will no longer have to study the theories presented herein, because they will be required to do so. Whereas previously graduate students could select one counseling theory as their theoretical framework, they will now be required to select two to three counseling theories and integrate them in some sort of meaningful way. Over the next decade, graduate programs will begin to adopt a multitheoretical framework. More will be outlined about the movement toward psychotherapy integration in Chapter 22.

Evidence-Based Movement. The second clear trend in theories of psychotherapy will be influenced by the evidence-based movement. From Lightner Witmer's early conceptions of applied psychology and the first psychological clinic in 1896, psychologists have been associated with an evidence-based approach to client care (McReynolds, 1997). After conducting an exhaustive review of evidence-based development in

Table 21.6 Multicultural Issues and the Theoretical Approaches

Theoretical Approach	Multicultural Issues
Psychoanalytic/ psychodynamic therapy	The focus on ego defense mechanisms can be useful in helping members of minority groups deal with oppression and discrimination.
Adlerian therapy	The Adlerian focus on social interest, importance of family, and belonging resonates with many different cultures.
Behavioral therapy	Behavioral counseling fits well with most cultures because it emphasizes clients' behaviors rather than their feelings. The educational and collaborative focus might be helpful to multicultural groups.
Cognitive therapy	The emphasis on thinking rather than feeling may be acceptable to members of some minority groups.
Reality therapy	Cultures that emphasize responsibility and choice might be attracted to reality therapy.
Existential therapy	This approach is useful for dealing with clients' being-in-the-world. People across cultures experience anxiety, dread, and fear of dying.
Person-centered therapy	Person-centered therapy stresses breaking cultural barriers.
Gestalt therapy	Gestalt therapy's focus on nonverbal expressions might be attractive to individuals from cultures that stress importance of nonverbal behavior.
Multicultural therapy	
Feminist therapy	This theoretical approach calls attention to discrimination.
Gay and lesbian therapy	Clients across various cultures might find gay and lesbian therapy helpful to deal with issues of sexual orientation identity development.
Transcultural therapies	
Naikan, Morita, and mindfulness therapies	Naikan, Morita, and mindfulness therapies have been accepted throughout the world.
Ma'at African therapy	Ma'at African therapy is limited to Africa.
Arab Muslim therapy	Arab Muslim therapy is limited to clients born of this ethnic/cultural/religious background.
Postmodern therapies	
Solution-focused therapy	The social and cultural context of behavior is emphasized.

(Continued)

Table 21.6 (Continued)

Theoretical Approach	Multicultural Issues
Narrative therapy	Clients' lives are socially constructed.
Strengths-based therapy	All people have strengths. The therapist might examine the cultural context of strengths.
Family systems therapy	Most members of ethnic minorities place a value on the family and the extended kinship system.
Dialectical behavioral therapy	Most people encounter dialectical situations in life and therefore, they must learn to choose behaviors that promote their mental health.
Acceptance and commitment therapy	Every culture teaches some aspect of acceptance of life. Some cultures are more oriented toward the "struggle" with negative life situations than are others. It is the struggle that often produces pain in an individual's life.
Mindfulness-based cognitive therapy	Meditation is a key component of many cultures. All people meditate or think about some aspect of life. Much depends on what we choose to meditate and the consequences of such meditations on one's mental health. Meditation on loss and negative events leads to depression.
Motivational interviewing therapy	All people are motivated to perform some behavior. Culture moderates or influences a person's motivation to perform or refrain from a given behavior.
Expressive arts therapies	
Art and music therapies	All cultures use the expressive arts in one way or another. All cultures use music and art to express emotions.
Play therapy	Children in every culture play, and their play is invariably symbolic.
Neuroscience and neuropsychotherapy	Neuropsychotherapy offers the possibility of a true transcultural and integrative theory of human functioning that has similarities and differences between and among the various cultures. Human behavior are direct projections of the neural mechanisms that caused them. Knowledge of the brain puts limits on psychotherapeutic theorizing. Proof of a theory's mental processes may now be generated by correlating its higher-order constructs with underlying brain phenomena. In the future, with the new findings in neurobiology, psychotherapists will be able to visualize the brain processes that underlie both psychopathology and psychotherapeutic change.

psychology, an APA Presidential Task Force on Evidence-Based Practice (2006) agreed on the following definition: "Evidence-based practice in psychology (EBPP) is the integration of the best available research with clinical expertise in the context of patient characteristics, culture, and preferences" (p. 273). Within this same article, the task force delineated the components of clinical expertise. These components have a great deal to do with a clinician's knowledge of counseling theories and treatment approaches. Even if we reject a counseling theory, we must understand the basis for our rejection. The task force stated,

Clinical expertise encompasses a number of competencies that promote positive therapeutic outcomes. These include (a) assessment, diagnostic judgment, systematic case formulation, and treatment planning; (b) clinical decision making, treatment implementation, and monitoring of patient progress; (c) interpersonal expertise; (d) continual self-reflection and acquisition of skills; (e) appropriate evaluation and use of research evidence in both basic and applied psychological science; (f) understating the influence of individual and cultural differences on treatment; (g) seeking available resources (e.g., consultation, adjunctive, or alternative services) as needed; and (h) having a cogent rationale for clinical strategies. (p. 276)

Theories of psychotherapy help us engage in diagnostic assessment, systematic case formulation, clinical decision making, and case formulation. Helping professionals must have a knowledge base from which to conduct their practice. Clinical expertise develops from "clinical and scientific training, theoretical understanding, experience, self-reflection, knowledge of research, and continuing professional education and training" (APA Presidential Task Force on Evidence-Based Practice, 2006, p. 276).

The cognitive-behavioral counseling theories have generated the most evidence-based research (Norcross, 2005a). Therefore, knowledge of cognitive-behavioral approaches for the treatment of specific disorders would seem to be essential to beginning and seasoned practitioners. Perhaps one might even say that a practitioner's lack of knowledge of what the research evidence says about the efficacy of specific treatment approaches could result in unethical practice (Norcross, Karpiak, & Lister, 2005).

We cannot just dismiss the contributions of psychotherapy theories that emphasize the importance of feelings and of establishing a therapeutic alliance. For instance, two major criticisms of existential-humanistic theories have been that they place too much emphasis on the therapy relationship as a curative factor and that such theories lack hard scientific data to demonstrate their efficacy in generating client change. Recent research in new brain-imaging technologies like magnetic resonance imaging and positron emission topography have highlighted the importance

of forming a therapeutic alliance during therapy (Siegel, 2007).

Siegel's research has found that brain-imaging studies show that representations of our life experiences, including our earliest experiences, are stored in different parts of the brain, in the form of connections between neurons (Siegel, 2007). What we learn from experience can be explained as a particular pattern of neurons firing throughout the brain's different structures so that we form a neural network. To demonstrate the importance of a neural network, Siegel (1999) gives the example of a traveler to Paris who sees the Eiffel Tower while also feeling hungry. When the person later recalled this experience, neurons in both the visual and sensory components of the brain fired, helping the person remember both the image of the Eiffel Tower and the hunger pangs associated with the memory.

Siegel (1999) points out that neural networks are plastic and are continually being changed as people engage in new life experiences. Hence, even the hard-wired networks formed during early childhood related to nurturing and expectations of love can be changed with new loving experiences. Oftentimes, clients come to counseling because they carry around within them issues related to abandonment and fears of emotional closeness. Clients' problematic behaviors may be held intact by networks of neurons that connect feelings of intimacy to memories of abandonment and emotional rejection. According to Siegel, a therapist's empathic, nonjudgmental interpersonal therapeutic relationship between the therapist and the client actually generates biological changes in the brain, rewiring it so that neurons associated with intimacy now link to the positive experiences of the therapeutic relationship between the client and the counselor. Such refiguring of the neuron network dealing with intimacy contributes to a resolution of the client's interpersonal difficulties (Atkinson, 2005; Fosha, Siegel, & Solomon, 2009; Siegel, 1999, 2007).

The critical point is that if Siegel's (2007) ideas continue to be validated by brain-imaging technology, existential-humanistic and other counseling theories that emphasize the importance of the therapeutic relationship will have the kind of evidence-based support that rivals that of the cognitive-behavioral school of therapy. The potential implications of Siegel's research could become very significant. What causes changes in a person's neuronal network related to his or her feelings and emotions may have much more to do with the quality of the therapeutic relationship established between the therapist and the client rather than due to any particular counseling technique or strategy. Perhaps every counseling training program should emphasize how to establish a therapeutic alliance with a client more so than training them with specific intervention techniques. Siegel's (2007) research suggests that all therapists should take time to form a solid therapeutic relationship before moving on to any problem resolution. It is the therapeutic relationship that heals.

I remember some time ago when a colleague asked me to work with a young boy who was having difficulty learning to read. As the boy entered my office, I could see the apprehension in his eyes. I asked him to sit next to me because we were going to have fun reading together. The young boy started to cry. We spent the rest of the hour playing hide-and-seek and all kinds of fun games. After my first blunder, I closed the book and focused on establishing a relationship with the boy. At the end of our session, I was exhausted, wondering whatever had gotten into me. Much to my surprise, the boy asked me if he could come back next week. As if to entice me, he said, "Maybe we could even read a little."

I believe that all learning is relational. Teachers who try to teach without first having created a positive relationship with their students may only be wasting much of their great knowledge. Establish an encouraging relationship with a child, and you can teach him or her almost anything. Establish a strong therapeutic alliance with your client, and he or she might even be willing to build new neuronal pathways that indicate that trust, love, and unconditional worth are possible for him or her too.

Movement Toward Incorporation of Mindfulness and Eastern Approaches to Psychotherapy.

The influence of Eastern cultural values on Western conceptualizations of psychotherapy is predicted to continue. The influence of the Chinese cultural approach of mindfulness has been far-reaching in its influence on Western theories of psychotherapy. Consider, for instance, that three of the new cognitive-behavioral theories—dialectical behavior therapy, acceptance and commitment therapy, and mindfulness-based cognitive therapy—have all adopted some form of mindfulness as part of their treatment approach. The dominant Western view that there must always be struggle against a life situation is gradually being replaced by the Eastern or Asian view of acceptance. Maybe we don't have to encourage clients to conquer all of their "demons" because that approach produces a struggle. This book did not even deal with contributions from India—especially using yoga to deal with the everyday problems of living. A third edition of this book will seek to include Indian approaches to psychotherapy and mental health. The greatest multicultural development is not then the fact that we are encouraging nonhomophobic ways of working with gays and lesbians or non-racist ways of dealing with minorities and other groups, but rather that we are bridging Eastern and Western cultures—hopefully, including the best of both cultures in our approaches to psychotherapy.

Movement Toward Strengths-Based Approaches to Psychotherapy. I predict that in the future there will be a greater movement toward strengths-based approaches to psychotherapy. The old approach of focusing on what's wrong with clients will gradually fall into disfavor as we learn more about the brain and how our words affect a person's brain and neural system. Psychotherapists are now trained to diagnose clients in a manner that emphasizes pathology rather than strengths. Improved research studies are predicted to show that a client's adaptive strategies aroused during psychotherapy are based primarily on the activation of preexisting but underused strengths. Although therapy can sometimes help clients develop adaptive behavioral patterns, more frequently than not psychotherapists are simply helping clients disinhibit the expression of adaptive patterns that have already been developed. Focusing on a client's pathology never helped a client to change. Brain imaging studies conducted during psychotherapy are expected to show the superiority of strengths-based approaches in working with clients. Approaches that increase a client's resistance will gradually fall into disuse. Strengths-based therapy will become more and more linked with neuroscience. The next wave of progress in psychotherapy will be based on neurobiology and strengths-based therapy approaches and what happens in the brain when a psychotherapist uses a strengths-based rather than a pathology-based theoretical framework.

TOP FIVE WAYS TO DETERMINE YOUR THEORETICAL ORIENTATION TO PSYCHOTHERAPY

There is nothing so practical as a good theory.

—Kurt Lewin

Having a theory of counseling is fundamental to your success as a therapist. Despite this observation, choosing your own theoretical orientation to counseling is not an easy task. You will want to choose a theoretical orientation that matches your views about people, your values, and your preferred way of relating to others. Your theoretical orientation consists of a set of assumptions that provide a framework for formulating hypotheses about treatment for your clients, for guiding your counseling interventions, and for conceptualizing the counseling process. Poznanski and McLennan (1995) have maintained that theoretical orientation consists of four elements:

1. The therapist's theoretical affiliation
2. The therapist's espoused theory—the theory the therapist states he or she adheres to
3. The theory inferred from observations of therapy sessions—what the therapist does in therapy

4. The therapist's personal therapeutic belief system

My top five ways for choosing a theoretical orientation for beginning therapists or students attending graduate school are as follows:

1. It should be intentional rather than haphazard.
2. It should resonate with your own personality characteristics.
3. It should be in agreement with your scores on the Theoretical Orientation Scale.
4. It should embody your basic concepts about human development, including the basis for mental health, adaptive behavior, and maladaptive behavior.
5. It should be in agreement with your personal values and should reflect your own preferred helping style of relating to others.

Make an Intentional Theoretical Choice

The concept of intentionality as related to counseling refers to the process of making decisions about what course of action to take. Ivey and Ivey (2001) have defined intentionality in this manner: "Intentionality is acting with a sense of capability and deciding from among a range of alternative actions. The intentional individual has more than one action, thought, or behavior to choose from in responding to changing life situations" (p. 220). Ivey, D'Andrea, Ivey, and Simek-Morgan (2007) have pointed out that few people would want a counselor or therapist who acted haphazardly. According to them, effective therapists should demonstrate professional intentionality that is based on a thorough understanding of counseling and therapy theories and accompanied by a broad range of intervention skills. Intentionality will be mentioned again in Chapter 22 in the section on how to choose an integrative approach to psychotherapy.

In his book *Intentional Helping: A Philosophy for Proficient Caring Relationships*, John Schmidt (2002) indicated that intentionality should be part of the underlying philosophy of any helping relationship. Schmidt defined intentional helping in this way: "Intentionality enables helpers to establish a consistent direction with a careful purpose and a dependable posture for assisting people who seek their help" (p. 25). Schmidt clarifies that *direction* means knowing what to do in a helping situation. *Purpose* entails knowing why you are choosing a specific action. An intentional practitioner knows what actions to take and why he or she is taking those actions. Some examples of intentional counseling statements might be as follows:

- "I am choosing a cognitive-behavioral perspective in working with this client because his problems are caused by irrational thoughts."
- "I am choosing to use a psychodynamic approach with my client because her primary issues lie in her early years."

Know Your Own Personality Characteristics

Worthington and Dillon (2003) have pointed out that there is "substantial evidence that counselors of different theoretical orientations exhibit different epistemic beliefs, verbal response behavior, and specific therapeutic techniques" (p. 95). These investigators have developed the Theoretical Orientation Profile Scale-Revised. This instrument uses a face-validity approach and contains items such as "I identify myself as psychodynamic" and "I utilize psychodynamic techniques" (p. 99).

Most scales of therapist theoretical orientation are constructed to get theoretical beliefs that may not be fully formed or articulated. For instance, Coleman's (2007) Theoretical Evaluation Self-Test is designed to tap helping professionals' orientation toward the major psychotherapy theories (cognitive-behavioral, family, humanistic, and psychodynamic). It also contains ecosystemic and pragmatic approaches and a cultural competency orientation. In a study of 146 social work students and 32 practicing clinicians, Coleman found that the six-factor solution, with its traditional theoretical divisions, is recommended for

use as a self-scoring educational tool; however, he recommended using the four-factor approach for statistical research purposes.

Ogunfowora and Drapeau (2007) explored the relationship between personality and theoretical orientation preferences in two separate samples of psychotherapy practitioners and students. A total of 493 participants (274 practitioners and 219 students) completed a web-based survey that assessed preference for theoretical orientation. The researchers found that after controlling for the effects of gender, profession, and degree type, personality was found to predict participants' preference for the humanistic-existential, cognitive-behavioral, psychodynamic, and feminist theoretical orientations across both samples. Ogunfowora and Drapeau also reported that personality predicted preference for the multicultural, family systems, and neuropsychological orientations, although these findings were applicable to only one sample. Similarly, Murdock, Banta, Stromseth, Viene, and Brown (1998) found that therapists' personality style is associated with their theoretical orientation.

Varlami and Bayne (2007) investigated if 210 British counselor trainees' psychological types were associated with their theoretical orientation. Using the Kersey Temperament Sorter II and a short demographic questionnaire, the investigators found that trainees who preferred the sensing–judging personality were more likely to choose the cognitive-behavioral orientation, those who preferred the intuition–feeling–judging personality chose the psychodynamic model, and those who preferred the intuition–feeling–perceiving personality selected the person-centered theoretical model. Participants who preferred the sensing–judging personality were more likely to choose the cognitive-behavioral therapy model, intuition–feeling–judging personality types chose the psychodynamic model, and intuition–feeling–perceiving personality types favored the person-centered model.

After administering the Millon Index of Personality Styles (MIPS), Arthur (2000) found significant personality differences between cognitive-behavioral and psychoanalytic therapists.

Therapists who preferred a behavioral orientation were characterized by rationality, extraversion, realism, assertiveness, and dominance. In contrast, those who preferred psychoanalysis were more introverted, intuitive, imaginative, and less assertive.

In a follow-up study, Arthur (2001) conducted a review of research describing variables believed to determine a therapist's choice of theoretical orientation. He found two types of variables: (1) the influence of training, colleagues, supervisors, and initial clinical experience and (2) the effects of personality traits and epistemological values, beliefs, and philosophy. Arthur concluded that personality and epistemological traits are significantly involved in counseling theoretical choice.

Overall, studies have found that either a counselor trainee's or a practicing therapist's personality variables contribute significantly to his or her choice of a psychotherapy theoretical orientation. Therefore, in choosing your theoretical orientation, it is important for you to consider your personality characteristics. You might consider taking the MIPS (Millon, 2003), which is designed to assess normal personality styles. The updated MIPS Revised helps address the need for a theoretically grounded instrument that may be administered to a broad range of professionals, including human resource specialists, social workers, and private practice clinicians. The MIPS Revised instrument measures three key dimensions of normal personalities: (1) motivating styles, which is anchored to evolution and psychoanalytic theories, helps assess the person's emotional style of relating to his or her environment; (2) thinking styles, anchored to Jungian theories, helps examine the person's mode of cognitive processing; and (3) behaving styles, anchored to interpersonal and social theories, helps assess the person's way of working with and relating to others.

So if you are still not sure about what your counseling theoretical orientation is, you might consider taking one of the above-described instruments. You might take the MIPS Revised to get an idea of your personality type as it is related to your theoretical orientation. Another approach would be to take Coleman's (2007) Theoretical Evaluation Self-Test. A third option might be to take Worthington and Dillon's (2003) Theoretical Orientation Profile Scale-Revised. Each of these measures has been found to be useful in revealing both counselor trainees' and practicing counselors' theoretical psychotherapy orientations.

Take the Theoretical Orientation Scale

I devised the Theoretical Orientation Scale to help you determine your theoretical orientation in counseling theories. This scale is not scientific, and I am not claiming any psychometric properties attached to this survey. The primary purpose of this scale is designed for your own self-discovery. The scale can be found in the online resources associated with this book.

Know at Least One Theory of Human Development

It is important for you as a counselor to know at least one human developmental theory. Human development is a branch of study that is designed to help us understand constancy and change throughout our life span. Although the field is characterized by great diversity in the interests and concerns of investigators, all share a single goal: to identify those factors that influence us from birth to death. How do we go about describing the differences and capacities between infants, children, adolescents, and adults? Is our development continuous or discontinuous? A continuous view of development suggests that we develop gradually and that we increase the skills that we had in the beginning.

In contrast, a discontinuous developmental view says that we develop new and different ways of understanding and responding to the world that emerge at specific times. Theories that accept the discontinuous perspective see development as taking place in stages. There are qualitative changes in thinking, feeling, and behaving that characterize specific periods in life. Two dominant stage-wise developmental models of human development were presented within this textbook: (1) Freud's

(1974) psychosexual stages of development and (2) Erikson's (1950) psychosocial stages of development. It is understandable that psychodynamic counseling theories would present a stage-wise, developmental approach to counseling.

Behavioral counseling approaches have not posited stages of human development. Their focus has been on learning and reinforcement. The existential-humanistic theories have tended to use Abraham Maslow's (1954) basic needs theory to conceptualize the process of human development. To what extent do you believe that development is lifelong? The life span development perspective maintains that no age period is supreme in its impact on the life course. Within each period, change takes place in three broad domains: (1) physical, (2) cognitive, and (3) emotional/social. Every age period has its own issues and its unique demands and opportunities that provide similarities in development across many people.

Understand what you believe about human development and how your chosen counseling theories support or do not support such views. My own particular bias is that it is difficult to counsel individuals without some beliefs in human development. Begin to articulate your views on human development. You might want to consider some of the following areas:

- I believe (or do not believe) that human development is continuous.
- I believe (or do not believe) that human development takes place in discrete stages.
- I believe (or do not believe) that human development is multidimensional.
- I believe (or do not believe) that human development is plastic. People can change at all stages in life.
- I believe that development is lifelong.
- I believe that genetic factors (environmental factors) are more important in a person's development.

Know what you believe about human development because such beliefs are correlated with your choice of a theory for psychotherapy. If you find yourself subscribing to Erikson's psychosocial

stages of development, then you might lean toward tapping some part of the psychodynamic approach for your approach to psychotherapy. If you find an affinity with the life span perspective of human development, then you might subscribe to the view that development is lifelong, multidimensional (affected by biological, psychological, and social forces), multidirectional (meaning a joint expression of growth and decline), and malleable or plastic (open to change through new experiences), as research on resilience indicates. The life span view of human development includes the role of culture on human development. A number of counseling theories could potentially mesh with the life span perspective of human development, including the postmodern approaches (solution-focused therapy, narrative therapy, and strengths-based therapy), the cognitive-behavioral school, and the existential-humanistic school (existential, person-centered counseling, and Gestalt therapy).

Know Your Personal Values and Your Preferred Helping Style of Relating to Others

Psychotherapy is not a value-free profession. Therapeutic models of psychotherapy are value laden. The values that counselors bring to the counseling relationship have been found to be highly significant (Richmond, 1996). Clients encounter the dilemma of finding a therapist whose theoretical orientation agrees with his or her values or risk having their values challenged. Jensen and Bergin (1988) conducted a national survey of practitioners and found that practitioners agreed on certain basic values for maintaining mental health. Among the values practitioners mentioned were assuming responsibility for one's actions, developing effective strategies for coping with stress, having a sense of identity, finding satisfaction in one's work, and being skilled in interpersonal relationships.

In its ethical code, the American Counseling Association (2005) states clearly that "counselors are aware of their own values, attitudes, beliefs, and behaviors and avoid imposing values that are inconsistent with counseling goals" (A.4.b.). From an ethical perspective, therapists must understand the influence that their values have on the manner in which they work with clients. Therapy is a value-laden process, and all counselors communicate their values to clients, either intentionally or not (Richards & Bergin, 2005). Therefore, it is very important that practitioners understand how their adoption of a theoretical model influences or communicates their values in the helping relationship.

Some therapists who advertise on the World Wide Web or Internet are beginning to state their values on their own websites. For instance, one counseling service that provided marriage and value counseling stated that it valued and believed in saving marriages and in the restoration of relationships. Another counseling service advertised that they believe in the value and sanctity of human life. Counseling services that offer pastoral counseling sometimes state that the Bible or Christianity forms the cornerstone of their counseling approach. Most practitioners value caring for themselves and others. Underlying this value is a belief in the dignity and worth of each person. Practitioners also tend to believe that people are capable of making positive changes in their lives. Most counselors believe that taking a stand on an issue is important (Richmond, 1996). It is important for counselors to examine their theory of choice for the purpose of understanding the theory's underlying or implicit values.

SUMMARY

This chapter has compared the theories presented in this book along several dimensions, including the theory's worldview, key concepts, goals, roles of therapists, and techniques. Comparing the theories is a starting point that helps beginning counselors/therapists formulate their own integrative approaches to counseling and psychotherapy. Future directions for the field of counseling were considered. I have presented my top five ways of deciding your theoretical orientation in psychotherapy. The Theoretical Orientation Scale was presented to help beginning counselors choose a counseling model. Both evidence-based research and mindfulness therapy were seen as important developments that will continue to make their mark on psychotherapy. Finally, questions are presented at the end of this chapter to help you decide what parts or components of the theories presented are attractive to you for building an integrative approach to therapy.

SUPPLEMENTAL AIDS
Discussion Questions

This section is designed to help you review the various approaches to psychotherapy. In reviewing each of the theories presented in this book, compare your views with those of the theorist. This approach may assist you in narrowing down the theories with which you have the greatest affinity.

1. Which features of each theory are most attractive to you? Why?

2. Suppose you were required to choose one theory that comes closest to your view about how counseling should be conducted, which theory would you choose and why?

3. Does your theory of choice take into consideration multicultural issues, such as clients' culture, gender, sexual orientation, and so on? How relevant do you think your theory of choice will be for working with culturally diverse individuals?

4. To what extent does your theory of choice lend itself to brief formats? Remember that insurance companies are increasingly demanding brief therapy for clients.

5. Which of the theories that you have studied in this book represent views that are the most different from those which you hold?

Website Materials

Additional exercises, journals, annotated bibliography, and more are available on the open-access website at https://study.sagepub.com/jonessmith2e.

CHAPTER 22

Integrative Psychotherapy

Constructing Your Own Integrative Approach to Therapy

The challenge is to find commonality between Western counseling and psychotherapy, on the one hand, and the non-Western approaches on the other hand. Once the commonality is established, theory and practice from non-Western approaches can be integrated for the purpose of informing, enhancing, and expanding the Western paradigm of counseling and psychotherapy.

—Robert G. Santee, *An Integrative Approach to Counseling*

Overall it looks as if there is little evidence to recommend one type of therapy over another. This surprising result has become known as the dodo effect: "Everybody has won and all must have prizes," as the Dodo proclaimed in Alice in Wonderland. This has led to a new focus in trying to identify just what it is in therapy that produces change.

—Maja O'Brien and Gaie Houston, *Integrative Therapy: A Practitioner's Guide*

BRIEF OVERVIEW

A major emphasis of this book has been on helping you construct your own integrated approach to psychotherapy. Research has indicated that psychotherapy is moving toward an integrated approach to therapy (Norcross, 2005b). Throughout the world, when you ask a psychologist or counselor what his or her theoretical orientation is, the most frequently given response is integrative or eclectic. It is highly likely that on graduation from your training program, you will integrate one or more of the theories presented in this book. In fact, my own professional journey has resulted in my adoption of an integrated psychotherapy framework. This chapter explores in detail the integrative approach to therapy.

The first part of this chapter traces psychology's historical development from emphasizing a single approach to therapy to the current integrative psychotherapy movement. In particular, I direct your attention toward multitheoretical approaches to psychotherapy integration. Jeff Brooks-Harris's (2008) **multitheoretical psychotherapy** framework is presented as a potential framework that you might consider either using or modifying to develop your own integrated approach to therapy.

After providing a foundation for an integrative approach that is multitheoretical, I move toward helping you construct your own personal integrative approach to therapy. After studying each of the various theories of psychotherapy presented in this book, it may be difficult for you to decide which approach seems to match best with your own personality, therapeutic style, and your methods of conceptualizing the many different types of life challenges people bring to therapy. How do you go about integrating or combining the best of several counseling theories? To help you with this task, I present a number of questions that you might ask yourself in constructing your own integrated counseling approach.

While constructing your own integrative approach to therapy is a very important professional step, you must also get a vision of what you have to do to become an effective therapist. I believe that every therapist who becomes an effective professional has to learn how to reflect on his or her therapy experiences. It's when we are alone in our offices thinking about a client with whom we have been working who appears to be struggling with therapy and himself that we begin to grow and mature as therapists. We reflect on what we did or did not do and what we might do in the next session.

The final section of this chapter contains an integrative psychotherapy plan for Justin, the young student who has served as a case study at the end of each theory chapter. In writing the integrative treatment plan, I use Jeff Brooks-Harris's (2008) multitheoretical framework.

The Integrative Movement in Psychotherapy

The movement toward integration of the various schools of psychotherapy has been in the making for decades. On the whole, however, psychotherapy integration has been traditionally hampered by rivalry and competition among the various schools. Such rivalry can be traced to as far back as Freud and the differences that arose between him and his disciples over what

was the appropriate framework for conceptualizing clients' problems. From Freud's Wednesday evening meetings on psychoanalysis, a number of theories were created, including Adler's individual psychology. As each therapist claimed that he had found the one best treatment approach, heated battles arose between various therapy systems. When behaviorism was introduced to the field, clashes took place between psychoanalysts and behaviorists.

During the 1940s, 1950s, and 1960s, therapists tended to operate within primarily one theoretical school. Dollard and Miller's (1950) book, *Personality and Therapy*, was one of the first attempts to combine learning theory with psychoanalysis. In 1977, Paul Wachtel published *Psychoanalysis and Behavior Therapy: Toward an Integration*. In 1979, James Prochaska offered a transtheoretical approach to psychotherapy, which was the first attempt to create a broad theoretical framework.

In 1979, Marvin Goldfried, Paul Wachtel, and Hans Strupp (Strupp & Binder, 1984) organized an association, the Society for the Exploration of Psychotherapy Integration, for clinicians and academicians interested in integration in psychotherapy (Goldfried, Pachankis, & Bell, 2005). Shortly thereafter, in 1982, *The International Journal of Eclectic Psychotherapy* was published, and it later changed its name to the *Journal of Integrative and Eclectic Psychotherapy*. By 1991, it began publishing the *Journal of Psychotherapy Integration*. As the field of psychotherapy has developed over the past several decades, there has been a decline in the ideological cold war among the various schools of psychotherapy (Goldfried et al., 2005).

Norcross and Newman (1992) have summarized the integrative movement in psychology by identifying eight different variables that promoted the growth of the psychotherapy integration trend in counseling and psychotherapy. First, they point out that there was simply a proliferation of separate counseling theories and approaches. The integrative psychotherapy movement represented a shift away from what was the prevailing atmosphere of factionalism and competition among the psychotherapies and a step toward dialogue and cooperation. Second, they note that practitioners increasingly recognized the inadequacy of a single theory that is responsive to all clients and their varying problems. No single therapy or group of therapies had demonstrated remarkable superior efficacy in comparison with any other theory. Third, there was the correlated lack of success of any one theory to explain adequately and predict pathology, personality, or behavioral change.

Fourth, the growth in number and importance of shorter-term, focused psychotherapies was another factor spearheading the integrative psychotherapy movement. Fifth, both clinicians and academicians began to engage in greater communication with each other that had the net effect of increasing their willingness to conduct collaborative experiments (Norcross & Newman, 1992). Sixth, clinicians had to come to terms with the intrusion into therapy with the realities of limited socioeconomic support by third parties for traditional, long-term psychotherapies. Increasingly, there was a demand for therapist accountability and documentation of the effectiveness of all medical and psychological therapies. Hence, the integration trend in psychotherapy has also been fueled by external realities, such as insurance reimbursement and the popularity of short-term, prescriptive, and problem-focused therapists.

Seventh, researchers' identification of common factors related to successful therapy outcome influenced clinicians' tendency toward psychotherapy integration. Increasingly, therapists began to recognize that there were common factors that cut across the various therapeutic schools. Eighth, the development of professional organizations such as the Society for the Exploration of Psychotherapy Integration, professional network developments, conferences, and journals dedicated to the discussion and study of psychotherapy integration also contributed to the growth of the movement. The helping profession has definitely moved in the direction of theoretical integration rather than allegiance to a single therapeutic approach. There has been a concerted movement toward integration of the various theories (Prochaska & Norcross, 2010).

Definition of Integrative Psychotherapy

As noted in Chapter 1, integrative psychotherapy is an attempt to combine concepts and counseling interventions from more than one theoretical psychotherapy approach (Stricker, 2001). It is not a particular combination of counseling theories, but rather, it consists of a framework for developing an integration of theories that you find most appealing and useful for working with clients. According to Norcross (2005b),

> Psychotherapy integration is characterized by dissatisfaction with single-school approaches and a concomitant desire to look across school boundaries to see what can be learned from other ways of conducting psychotherapy. The ultimate outcome of doing so is to enhance the efficacy, efficiency, and applicability of psychotherapy. (pp. 3–4)

PATHWAYS TO PSYCHOTHERAPY INTEGRATION

This section provides an overview of how theorists and practitioners have tried to integrate the various theoretical approaches to therapy. Perhaps in examining how others have integrated their therapy with different concepts and techniques, you might feel more comfortable in thinking about how you might pursue this same avenue. Clinicians have used a number of ways to integrate the various counseling theories or psychotherapy, including eclecticism, theoretical integration, assimilative integration, common factors, multitheoretical psychotherapy, and helping skills integration (Norcross & Goldfried, 2005).

The Pathway of Eclecticism

Eclecticism may be defined as an approach to thought that does not hold rigidly to any single paradigm or any single set of assumptions but rather draws on multiple theories to gain insight into phenomena. Eclectics are sometimes criticized for lack of consistency in their thinking. For instance, many

Key Points in the Integrative Movement

What key developments stand out in your mind about the integrative movement in psychotherapy?

Thoughts about theory integration date back to the 1930s and 1940s. In your opinion, what took so long for the movement to reach its current status?

psychologists accept some features of behaviorism, yet they do not attempt to use the theory to explain all aspects of client behavior. Eclecticism in psychology has been caused by the belief that many factors influence human behavior; therefore, it is important to examine a client from a number of theoretical perspectives (Goldfried et al., 2005).

What are some differences between eclecticism and psychotherapy integration? Typically, eclectic therapists do not need or have a theoretical basis for either understanding or using a specific technique. They chose a counseling technique because of its efficacy, because it works. For instance, an eclectic therapist might experience a positive change in a client after using a specified counseling technique, yet not investigate any further why the positive change occurred. In contrast, an integrative therapist would investigate the how and why of client change. Did the client change because she was trying to please the therapist or was she instead becoming more self-directed and empowered?

Integrative and eclectic therapists also differ in the extent to which they adhere to a set of guiding, theoretical principles and view therapy change. Practitioners who call themselves eclectic appear to have little in common, and they do not seem to subscribe to any common set of principles. In contrast, integrationists are concerned not only with what works but why it works. Moreover, clinicians who say that they are eclectic tend to be older and more experienced than those who describe themselves as integrationists. This difference is fast disappearing

because some graduate schools are beginning to train psychologists to be integrationists (Norcross & Goldfried, 2005). It is noteworthy, however, that practitioners ascribe to eclecticism/integration more frequently than academic and training faculty do (Norcross & Goldfried, 2005). Hence, it may take a while for therapist training programs to move toward integration of theory.

The Pathway of Theoretical Integration

The pathway of **theoretical integration** is perhaps the most difficult and sophisticated of the three types of psychotherapy integration because it involves bringing together theoretical concepts from disparate theoretical approaches, some of which may present contrasting worldviews. The goal is to integrate not just therapy techniques but also the psychotherapeutic theories involved as Dollard and Miller (1950) did with psychoanalysis and behavior therapy. Proponents of theoretical integration maintain that it offers new perspectives at the levels of theory and practice because it entails a synthesis of different models of personality functioning, psychopathology, and psychological change.

The Pathway of Assimilative Integration

The **assimilative integration** approach to psychotherapy involves grounding oneself in one system of psychotherapy but with a view toward selectively incorporating (assimilating) practices and views from other systems. Assimilative integrationists use a single, coherent theoretical system as its core, but they borrow from a broad range of technical interventions from multiple systems. Practitioners who have labeled themselves as assimilative integrationists are as follows: (a) Gold (1996), who proposed assimilative psychodynamic therapy; (b) Castonguay et al. (2004), who have advocated cognitive-behavioral assimilative therapy; and (c) Safran, who has proposed inter-personal and cognitive assimilative therapy (Safran & Segal, 1990/1996).

Assimilative integrationists believe that integration should take place at the practice level rather than at the theory level. Most therapists have been trained in a single theoretical approach, and over time, many gradually incorporate techniques and methods of other approaches (Dryden & Spurling, 1989; Goldfried, 2001). Typically, therapists do not totally eliminate the theoretical framework in which they were trained. Instead, they tend to add techniques and different ways of viewing individuals.

The Pathway of the Helping Skills Approach and Psychotherapy Integration

Clara Hill (2004) has provided a helping skills model to therapy integration. Her model describes three stages of the helping process that are based on different therapy schools. For instance, the first stage of helping is labeled *exploration*. Using Rogers's client-centered therapy as the therapy school of choice, C. Hill (2004) emphasizes the counseling skills of attending, listening, and reflection of feelings. The second stage is termed *insight*, and this stage is based on psychoanalytic theory; therefore, skills such as interpreting and dealing with transference are stressed. The third stage is termed the *action stage*, and this stage is based largely on cognitive-behavioral techniques. Using the helping skills model, training would focus on teaching graduate students techniques associated with each of these three therapeutic schools.

The Pathway of the Common Factors Approach

The common factors approach has been influenced by the research and scholarships of renowned leaders in psychotherapy such as Jerome Frank (1973, 1974) and Carl Rogers (1951, 1957). Clearly, Rogers's contributions to common factors research has become so accepted by clinicians throughout the world that his core conditions (or necessary and sufficient conditions to effect change in clients) have become part of the early training of most helping professionals (Rogers, 1951). Researchers and theorists have transformed Rogers's necessary and sufficient conditions into a broader concept that has become known as "therapeutic alliance" (Hubble, Duncan, & Miller, 1999). The therapeutic alliance is important across the various counseling theory schools; it is the glue that keeps the person coming to therapy week after week. Currently, more than 1,000 studies have been reported on the therapeutic alliance (Hubble et al., 1999). In describing the common factor approach, Norcross (2005b) has stated,

> The common factors approach seeks to determine the core ingredients that different therapies share in common, with the eventual goal of creating more parsimonious and efficacious treatments based on their commonalities. This search is predicated on the belief that commonalities are more important in accounting for therapy outcome than the unique factors that differentiate among them. (p. 9)

> **Inner Reflections**
>
> *Pathways to psychotherapy integration*
>
> Which pathway to psychotherapy integration do you choose—eclecticism, assimilative integration, theoretical integration, or multitheoretical framework?
>
> Do you have any particular reasons for choosing your designated pathway to psychotherapy integration?

MULTITHEORETICAL PSYCHOTHERAPY

This book uses the multitheoretical framework developed by Jeff E. Harris (Brooks-Harris, 2008).

Jeff E. Harris's Multitheoretical Model

Jeff E. Harris

Dr. Jeff E. Harris, Ph.D., ABPP, is an associate professor in the Department of Psychology and Philosophy at Texas Woman's University. He earned his doctorate from Ohio State University, and he is the author of *Integrative Multitheoretical Psychotherapy*. Dr. Harris has written extensively about psychotherapy integration, psychotherapy training, and multicultural counseling.

The most recent multitheoretical model for psychotherapy comes from Jeff Harris, who provides a framework that describes how different psychotherapy systems come together. Brooks-Harris (2008) begins with the premise that thoughts, actions, and feelings interact with one another and that they are influenced by biological, interpersonal, systemic, and cultural contexts. Given this overarching premise, he integrates the following theoretical approaches: (a) cognitive, (b) behavioral, (c) experiential, (d) biopsychosocial, (e) psychodynamic, (f) systemic, and (g) multicultural. A brief explanation of each of these areas is provided below. His framework emphasizes at what point a therapist might consider using elements of psychodynamic theory or multicultural theory. A major umbrella in multicultural psychotherapy consists of the focal dimensions for therapy and key strategies.

Multitheoretical Psychotherapy

- Cognitive strategies deal with the focal dimension of clients' functional and dysfunctional thoughts.
- Behavioral skills' focal dimension of actions encourage effective client actions to deal with challenges.

- Experiential interventions result in adaptive feelings.
- Biopsychosocial strategies emphasize biology and adaptive health practices.
- Psychodynamic-interpersonal skills are used to explore clients' interpersonal patterns and promote undistorted perceptions.
- Systemic-constructivist interventions examine the impact of social systems and support adaptive personal narratives.
- Multicultural-feminist strategies explore the cultural contexts of clients' issues.

Brooks-Harris (2008) presents five principles for psychotherapy integration: (1) intentional integration, (2) multidimensional integration, (3) multitheoretical integration, (4) strategy-based integration, and (5) relational integration. The first principle says that psychotherapy integration should be based on intentional choices. The therapist's intentionality guides his or her focus, conceptualization, and intervention strategies. The second principle (multidimensional) proposes that therapists should recognize the rich interaction between multiple dimensions.

The third principle asserts that therapists take into consideration diverse theories to understand their clients and guide their interventions. The fourth strategy-based principle states that therapists combine specific strategies from different theories. Strategy-based integration uses a pragmatic philosophy. Underlying theories do not have to be reconciled. The fifth or relational principle proposes that the first four principles be enacted within an effective therapeutic relationship.

Brooks-Harris's (2008) model offers a good plan for therapists seeking to implement an integrative multitheoretical approach. He outlines strategies for each of the seven core areas. For instance, cognitive strategies should encourage functional thoughts that are rational and that promote healthy adaptation to the environment. In addition, he enumerates a catalog of 15 key cognitive strategies, which include identifying thoughts, clarifying the impact of thoughts, challenging irrational thoughts, providing psychoeducation, and supporting bibliotherapy. To integrate behavioral therapy into one's practice, he suggests some of the following catalog of key strategies: (a) assigning homework, (b) constructing a hierarchy, (c) providing training and rehearsal, (d) determining baselines, and (e) maintaining schedules of reinforcement.

Integrative Treatment Planning. The multitheoretical psychotherapy model offers a step-by-step method to engage in integrative treatment planning. The first three steps emphasize using the multidimensional manner and the therapist's need to make intentional choices about the use of multitheoretical strategies. The last two steps emphasize using the catalog of key strategies during the psychotherapy process. *Step 1* involves watching for multidimensional focus markers. As clients tell their stories and describe their concerns, therapists listen for markers that reveal clients' areas of concerns. The therapist uses the Focus Marker Checklist, which is available on the Multitheoretical Therapy website (http://www.multitheoretical.com) in the treatment resources section.

Step 2 involves conducting a multidimensional survey to explore the seven dimensions in a structured manner: (1) thoughts, (2) actions, (3) feelings, (4) biology, (5) interpersonal patterns, (6) social systems, and (7) cultural contexts. Brooks-Harris (2008) suggests that the therapist conduct a multidimensional survey (examine the seven areas to determine which area is of most concern to the client). *Step 3* emphasizes establishing an interactive focus on two or three dimensions. After the therapist surveys the client's problems in terms of all seven dimensions, the therapist and client collaboratively identify two or three salient dimensions that will form the initial focus of therapy. *Step 4* entails formulating a multitheoretical conceptualization of the client's problem. A summary of multitheoretical conceptualization is provided on the web in the treatment resources section of the website. *Step 5* involves choosing interventions from a catalog of key strategies for each of the seven areas of client functioning. A summary of the catalog of key strategies is also found on the theory's website.

The multitheoretical model of psychotherapy gives the example of Claire, a Japanese American female in her 50s who is experiencing symptoms of depression after the death of her mother, a little over a year ago. The client is the oldest of three daughters; she has never married, lived with her mother, and was the primary caretaker while her mother was dying. Claire's multidimensional survey will examine the seven core areas Brooks-Harris outlines. Claire's

1. *Thoughts:* "I am having difficulty going on without my mother."

2. *Actions:* Claire displayed withdrawal and social isolation from family and friends.

3. *Feelings:* Claire experienced despair, hopelessness, and numbing sense of being.

4. *Biology:* Claire had decreased appetite and trouble sleeping.

5. *Interpersonal:* Claire's focused on being her mother's favorite child.

6. *Social:* Claire competed with her sisters growing up. Her father was emotionally distant.

7. *Cultural:* In the Japanese American tradition, the eldest takes care of her parents.

After surveying all seven dimensions of the multitheoretical model, the therapist selects two or three that will function as the initial focus for psychotherapy. He or she consults with Claire to determine the two dimensions on which she would like to work. Claire chooses her feelings of hopelessness and despair and her interpersonal patterns—the fact that her close relationship with her mother got in the way of her developing other sources of social support. For each focal dimension, the therapist chooses an existing theoretical school. For instance, to deal with the feeling conceptualization of Claire's issue, the therapist selects emotion-focused therapy. The therapeutic goal is to help Claire explore and express her sadness in more adaptive ways. To deal with her core conflictual relationship theme, the therapist uses psychodynamic conceptualizations. The therapist identifies relationship themes with Claire by exploring childhood experiences and her adaptations to interpersonal losses. The therapist uses the Key Strategies information provided on the website mentioned earlier.

RESEARCH AND EVALUATION —
Evidence-Based Research and Integrative Psychotherapy

Regardless of whether a therapist uses an integrative approach or one based on a single therapy school, he or she will have to take into consideration whether or not empirical support exists for a chosen treatment approach (American Psychological Association, 2006). Evidence-based practice (EBP) is a combination of learning what treatments work based on the best available research and taking into account clients' culture and treatment issues. The American Psychological Association (2006) conceptualizes EBP as "the integration of the best available research with clinical expertise in the context of patient characteristics, culture and preferences" (p. 273). EBP emphasizes the results of experimental comparisons to document the efficacy of treatments against untreated control groups, against other treatments, or both.

The arguments in favor of EBP are reasonable. First, clients have a right to treatments that have been proven to be effective (Gibbs, 2003). Second, managed care requires counselor accountability in choosing a method of treatment. Increasingly, counselors may have to consult with research studies to determine which approach is the most efficacious with what mental health disorder (Gibbs, 2003). Helping professionals may be required to answer for using a therapeutic approach with a specific disorder.

Twenty years ago, few therapists would have been concerned about whether or not their theoretical approach had accumulated much research evidence to support treatment of a particular disorder. However, conditions have changed in the world of therapy. Now not only must therapists be able to articulate a psychotherapeutic orientation but also ethical issues are being raised about one's choice of orientation for specific mental disorders.

Evidence-based treatment presents several ethical issues to clinicians. First, do you know what evidence exists to support your psychotherapeutic treatment of clients? What research evidence exists to demonstrate that your theoretical perspective and interventions actually do work and help clients recover from their disorders? Are you familiar with the treatments that have been found to be empirically supported in the psychotherapeutic literature? Or, do you use the same theoretical approach, regardless of the client's presenting problem or disorder? How ethical is it for you to use your theoretical approach when one examines it in terms of its treatment efficacy?

How does a therapist implement EBP in practice? The therapist must gather research that informs him or her about what works in psychotherapy. Such information should be obtained *before treatment begins*. There are several major resources for EBP. For instance, the Cochrane Collaboration (http://www.cochrane.org) sets standards for reviews of medical, health, and mental health treatments and provides "systematic reviews" of related research by disorder. The Cochrane Collaboration is an international, independent, not-for-profit organization of more than 28,000 contributors from more than 100 countries, dedicated to making up-to-date, accurate information about the effects of health care readily available worldwide. The Cochrane Reviews contain systematic health care interventions that are published online in The Cochrane Library. Cochrane Reviews are designed to help providers, practitioners, and patients make informed decisions about health care and are the most comprehensive, reliable, and relevant source of evidence on which to base these decisions. Moreover, the U.S. government also offers treatment guidelines based on EBP principles at the National Guideline Clearinghouse (http://www.guideline.gov/). This site contains very good information on medication.

Other online resources for EBP and treatment guidelines include the American Psychiatric Association (APA), which offers practice guidelines for mental health (http://www.psych.org/psych_pract/treatg/pg.prac_guide.cfm). Another way of accessing practice guidelines is to go to the APA website and select "Practice." This page links to the complete text of all APA practice guidelines published on Psychiatry Online, which gives additional resources for each guideline. EBP guidelines are available for the following mental health disorders: acute stress disorder and posttraumatic stress disorder, Alzheimer's disease and other dementias, bipolar disorder, borderline personality disorder, eating disorders, major depressive disorder, obsessive-compulsive disorder, panic disorder, and suicidal behaviors. Part A of every APA practice guideline is initially published as a supplement to the *American Journal of Psychiatry*. For the treatment of children and adolescents with mental health disorders, practice parameters may be obtained from the American Academy of Child and Adolescent Psychiatry.

The Outlook for Psychotherapy Schools and Integrative Psychotherapy

What does the future look like for psychotherapy schools that have been presented in this book? Norcross, Hedges, and Prochaska (2002) and Norcross, Hedges, and Castle (2002) used a Delphi poll to predict the future of psychotherapy over the next decade. The experts who served as participants in the poll predicted that the

following theoretical schools would increase the most: (a) cognitive-behavior therapy, (b) culture-sensitive multicultural counseling, (c) Beck's cognitive therapy, (d) interpersonal therapy, (e) family systems therapy, (f) behavior therapy, technical eclecticism, (g) solution-focused therapy, and (h) exposure therapies. Therapy orientations that were predicted to decrease the most included (a) classical psychoanalysis, (b) implosive therapy, (c) Jungian therapy, (d) transactional analysis, (e) humanistic therapies, and (f) Adlerian therapy. The poll also showed how psychotherapy is changing:

> The consensus is that psychotherapy will become more directive, psychoeducational, technological, problem-focused, and briefer in the next decade. Concomitantly, relatively unstructured, historically oriented, and long-term approaches are predicted to decrease. . . . Short term is in, and long term on its way out. (Prochaska & Norcross, 2003, p. 545)

The movement toward short-term therapy is one that was fairly easy to predict. Insurance companies will not pay for long-term treatment. Therefore, therapists have had to change their treatment focus and their estimate of the amount of time necessary to bring about client improvement. Moreover, long-term therapy focuses on fundamental change in a person's overall functioning. In contrast, short-term therapy seeks small change that is pragmatic to help clients deal with a presenting issue—it does not focus on "curing" a client. Whereas long-term therapy views the presenting problem as reflecting more basic client pathology, short-term therapy emphasizes clients' strengths and resources. Insurance companies are not interested in having a therapist to be there for clients while they make significant changes in their lives. On the contrary, they accept the reality that many changes will take place after therapy and will not be observable to the therapist.

In addition, insurance companies' demand for EBP is likely to increase, and therapeutic approaches that lack a sufficient evidence-based record will not be reimbursed. Psychoanalytically oriented and existential-humanistic approaches have a very limited evidence-based record on which to build. I predict that there will increasingly be a focus on manualized therapy. Therapists will be able to purchase books or manuals that describe the steps to take for a specific problem, life challenge, or disorder. **Manualized treatment** will most likely be evidence-based or empirically supported treatment. Therefore, it is important for beginning therapists to become aware of evidence-based, manualized treatment for specific mental disorders. A failure to use such treatment approaches could possibly lead to law suits centering on "failure to provide a basic standard of care."

I disagree that there will be an increasing emphasis on problem-focused therapy. Both strengths-based and positive psychology have spread throughout the world. Many federally supported programs for youth and their families are requiring a strengths-based rather than a problem-focused orientation. Much of this shift is being caused by recent empirical studies showing the value and importance of positive emotions. If researchers develop a diagnostic manual that is based on positive client emotions, there will most likely be a decrease in clinicians' emphasis on problem-focused disorders. It is clear, however, that psychotherapy integration will become the most frequently cited approach to therapy. The cognitive-behavioral school will continue to be the most dominant because it has provided the most empirically supported evidence for its effectiveness.

TOWARD DEVELOPING YOUR OWN APPROACH TO INTEGRATIVE PSYCHOTHERAPY

Yalom (1989) has pointed out that theories of psychotherapy are developed to reduce the counselor's anxiety in dealing with the complexities and the uncertainties of the therapeutic process. The theories discussed in this book are designed to help you view how others have conceptualized the therapeutic situation. Only you can decide how you will go about constructing your own personal, integrative approach to therapy.

Constructing your own approach to psychotherapy is a lifelong process, one that is begun in graduate school and continued throughout your professional career. It is my strong belief that graduate training is only the first step in becoming a therapist. It takes a certain amount of experience for you to truly develop your own integrative approach to therapy.

You begin the journey toward developing your own integrative therapy approach in graduate school when you are faced with trying to read and understand the various major systems of psychotherapy. As Yalom (1989) so aptly pointed out, having a theory helps quiet our own anxiety. I also believe that having our own integrated theory of therapy helps the client who seeks our assistance.

For the most part, I concur with Harris's multitheoretical framework for developing an integrative approach to therapy. Movement toward your own integrative theory should be intentional rather than haphazard—guided by forethought and completed with client consultation. Your integrative approach to therapy should be informed by your training, clinical experience, and research. In contrast to the multitheoretical therapy framework, I propose five additional categories: (1) spiritual, (2) relational (similar to Brooks-Harris's interpersonal), (3) strengths—internal and external, (4) evidence-based research, and (5) change process. More specifically, my own personal multitheoretical framework takes into account the following conceptual areas to form an integrative therapy approach.

Another Multitheoretical Framework for Integrative Treatment

- Cognitive conceptualizations or the role of cognitions with clients
- Affect or the influence of clients' feelings on issues
- Body—energy and health issues—holistic nature of mind and body
- Relational—all living is relational and most problems have a relational component

- Spiritual—we do not live by bread alone, influence of religion. There is increasing empirical evidence that our spiritual values and behaviors can promote physical and psychological well-being (Richards & Bergin, 1997; Richards, Rector, & Tjelveit, 1999)
- Multicultural—we live within a cultural context
- Systemic influences (political system, economic system, racism, sexism)
- Evidence-based research or empirical support for counseling interventions
- Change process—how clients are motivated to change and the change process

Guideline Questions to Help You in Choosing a Psychotherapy Orientation

What are some guidelines for constructing an integrative theory of counseling and psychotherapy? First, you should be able to have a working knowledge of the particular theories from which you will draw and a basic description of why each theory is important and relevant to you as a mental health counselor or therapist. It helps to write out your own integrated approach to counseling. You should demonstrate a balance between your knowledge of the particular theories from which you select and a genuine description of why each theory is important and relevant to you as a clinician or therapist. It is important that you examine in depth your reasons for choosing each theory. The following questions are designed to help you think about the core counseling theory that you are initially adopting.

Your Knowledge of Psychotherapy Theories

1. What are four basic concepts from the theory you are adopting as your core or base theory?
2. What constitutes a problem in your core counseling theory?

3. What are the goals of counseling for the theoretical approach you have chosen?
4. Who establishes the goals in counseling?
5. What is the nature of the relationship between you and the client?
6. What competencies must you have to carry out your role as therapist/counselor?
7. What are the responsibilities of clients during counseling? What is expected of clients?
8. What can the client expect from the therapist—from you?
9. What is your position on therapist self-disclosure?
10. What are some of the main values held by a counselor with your theoretical approach?
11. Using the theories you have selected to be integrated in your therapy approach, how do you want to be as a clinician?
12. How comfortable are you in expressing your emotions during counseling?
13. What is it about your personality and your personal history that leads you to believe that a particular theory or group of theories form a goodness of fit for you?
14. How have your personal ground, personal attributes, and life experiences affected your choice of a personal theory of counseling?
15. What techniques will you use from your chosen theory or group of theories?
16. How does your theory take into account diverse cultural groups?
17. How does your theory take into consideration political, social, and economic factors that lie outside the client—external factors?

Source: © Elsie Jones-Smith (2012).

Second, after you have developed a working knowledge of the particular counseling theories from which you will select, take into account your worldview or your basic way of understanding the world. Figure 22.1 is a beginning framework (Smith, 2010) for incorporating your worldview, personal values, and therapeutic intervention skills into your personal, integrative approach to counseling.

Figure 22.1   Framework for Choosing Your Own Theory of Integrative Psychotherapy

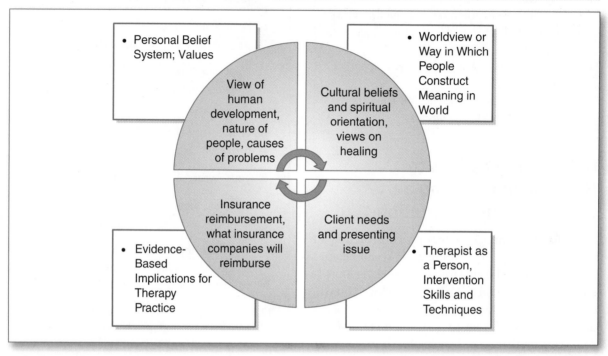

Source: © Elsie Jones-Smith (2012).

Your worldview will have a significant impact on how you conduct counseling. The following box contains some questions to help you sort out your worldview.

Worldview or Way of Understanding Clients and the World

18. What is your view of human nature? Which counseling theory best suits your view of human nature?

19. In the area of free will/determinism, to what extent do people direct their own actions, or are we governed by other forces outside of our awareness or control?

20. Nature/nurture: To what degree are people influenced by heredity (nature) and/or by their environment (nurture)?

21. Past/present orientation: To what degree are people controlled by early events in their lives and/or affected by later life experiences? What is the significance of the past, present, and future in governing human behaviors? Are we prisoners of our past, or can we work to free ourselves from our past?

22. What are some of the basic assumptions you have about people, and what theoretical approach to therapy best deals with your views on this topic?

Therapy deals with clients' thoughts, feelings, and behaviors. The next group of questions you might ask yourself in formulating an integrative approach to therapy deals with the relationship between cognition, affect, and behavior. Which counseling theory has a goodness of fit with your views on the role of cognition, affect, and behavior? This group of questions also focuses on change, especially as it relates to the therapeutic process. How is behavior changed in the therapy session? Some questions that deal with these issues are presented in the box below.

Cognition, Affect, and Behavior

23. How do people's thoughts (cognitions) and affect (feelings) influence their behavior? Which counseling theories best reflect your views on the role of cognitions and feelings on clients' behavior?

24. How are these three dimensions interrelated?

25. What motivates people?

26. What cognitive strategies do you use to encourage functional or positive thoughts with your clients?

27. What kinds of experiential interventions do you feel comfortable in using with clients to explore their feelings?

28. Where do clients' maladaptive thoughts, feelings, or behaviors come from?

29. What are some basic assumptions/beliefs about change underlying your approach?

Another set of variables includes personality development, maladaptive and adaptive behavior, and mental disorders. What counseling theories support your ideas regarding these variables? It might be helpful for you to write out simple statements. "I believe that maladaptive behavior is caused by ———, and I choose ——— theory as my frame of reference on personality development or maladaptive behavior."

Views of Developmental Periods, Adaptive and Maladaptive Behavior

30. Are there critical periods in a person's life development? If so, what are they?

31. How do individuals develop mental or emotional disorders?

32. What causes mental or emotional disorders and healthy development?

33. Using your current theoretical approach, what constitutes a problem for clients?

Stages in Developing an Integrative Theory of Psychotherapy

The questions presented in the foregoing section are not exhaustive. Rather, they represent a beginning point for you to think about yourself as a therapist. Becoming a therapist is not an easy journey. There is a great deal of work involved, including much self-introspection, experience, and training. Sometimes it is helpful to understand what the journey might look like in becoming a therapist or a counselor. Therefore, I have outlined the following stages that the typical therapist goes through in developing his or her own integrated approach to therapy (see Figure 22.2).

The Reflective Practitioner and Therapist Effectiveness

One of the goals of this chapter is to help you start the process of becoming a reflective practitioner. I maintain that an effective therapist is essentially a reflective therapist in the tradition described by Schön (1983, 1987). In his seminal work, Schön (1983) emphasized the role of self-reflection in the training of professional practitioners. He proposed that the knowledge needed for competence in the professions is twofold:

Figure 22.2 Stages of Professional Development as a Therapist

Person Enters Counseling Training Program With Orientation Toward Self and Others, Cultural Worldview, and Personal Belief System

Clinical Training Emphasizes Certain Counseling Skills and Techniques

<u>Single Therapy Adoption</u>

Counseling/Therapy Trainee Largely Adopts Orientation of Training Program

<u>Assimilative Integration: Phase 1 of the Reflective Practitioner</u>

Counselor/therapist engages in real-world counseling/therapy experience, which causes him or her to adopt techniques outside of orientation of graduate training program.

<u>Most therapists seek a firm grounding in one system of therapy but evidence a willingness to incorporate or assimilate practices from other therapy schools.</u>

<u>Pathway Toward Psychotherapy Integration</u>

Phase 2 of the Reflective Practitioner: Therapist revises theoretical orientation based on (1) real-world therapy experiences and (2) evidence-based studies of what works in therapy.

<u>The pathway toward psychotherapy integration is designed to improve the therapist's ability to select the best treatment for a client and his or her problem. Therapist uses diverse strategies without being hindered by theoretical differences.</u>

<u>Continued Pathway Toward Psychotherapy Integration</u>

Phase 3 of the Reflective Practitioner: Therapist seeks to comply with continuing education training requirements, which leads to a broadening of counseling techniques and further psychotherapy integration.

Phase 4 of the Reflective Practitioner: Therapist engages in practical theory integration based on what works, evidence-based reports, additional training, increased clinical experience, and revised beliefs.

Reflective Practitioner: Continual Stage of Professional Development

The clinician adopts the view that his approach to therapy has evolved into a personal style of counseling and psychotherapy about which he or she feels comfortable. Although the clinician is open to changes, psychotherapy integration is consolidated and only minor changes are made after this point—usually as a result of attending workshops for continuing education credit.

(1) technical-rational knowledge (e.g., the learning of counseling theories and the learning of treatment protocols) and (2) professional artistry (e.g., sensitivity to the dynamics of the therapeutic relationship, timing of interventions, and the instillation of hope). Schön maintained that while technical-rational knowledge can be (and typically is) conveyed by didactic procedures, the knowledge required for professional artistry is often tacit, the product of experience, and is best assessed by practitioner self-reflection. Schön's ideas regarding the value of self-reflection have been used in a number of fields, including medicine, social work, counseling, and teaching (Fook, 1996; Kressel, 1997; Niemi, 1997; Schön, 1987).

Schön's reflective practitioner model presents a framework for decision making and problem solving. A Harvard-educated man, Schön was critical of the traditional teaching methods adopted in many universities. From his perspective, universities used the technical-rational approach, in which students first studied basic science, then the relevant applied science, before finally applying their learning to real-life problems. Schön believed that this approach bore little resemblance to reality and did not equip professionals with the training needed to solve the practical problems they encountered in their daily practice.

In contrast to the rationality approach, Schön discovered that when effective practitioners were confronted with a problem in their practice, they instinctively worked through it, drawing on previous similar experiences. Using a mixture of knowing and doing, practitioners tended to try out various solutions until they resolved the issue. Schön labeled this process *reflection in action* and coined the term *theory in use* to describe the nature of the reflective activity in which the practitioner was engaged. According to Schön (1983, 1987), this type of practitioner problem solving was an intuitive rejection of the textbook that effective practitioners had been taught during their professional training. Schön labeled this formalized approach *the practitioner's espoused theory*. He argued that it was the practitioner's ability to reflect, both in and

on action, that separated the effective practitioner from less effective professionals.

Undoubtedly, Schön left an enduring legacy that has had a major impact on professional education and training programs. One of his accomplishments was that he highlighted the importance of the practical experience in the learning process. Another major contribution was that he challenged the view that theory is a privileged form of knowledge. Each one of us constructs on a daily basis our theories of the world and of the people with whom we work. Each therapist goes through a process of continually constructing his or her own theory of counseling or psychotherapy, and perhaps that is one reason a number of studies have reported that the average American therapist is an eclectic or an integrative therapist rather than a therapist of a single theoretical school. A third major contribution of Schön was that he recognized the difference between a practitioner's formal theory and his espoused theory. Much more will be said about this point in an ensuing section.

Schön's reflective practitioner model has implications for both therapist training and practice. Self-reflection produces a deeper sense of knowing than traditional didactic teaching. I recommend that practicum and training courses for counselors and psychologists contain a self-reflection component to increase therapists' therapeutic artistry. Training programs that do not include a self-reflection component tend to be more logical, evidential, and analytical. Training from such programs appeals predominantly to students' rational systems, and information learned may be less deeply embedded than experiential learning.

Conversely, if programs include a self-reflection component, students may be exposed to greater emotion (both within themselves and from other students undergoing the same training) that triggers their experiential system, and hence, a deeper level of encoding and realization. Self-reflective practitioners are usually effective therapists because they take time to integrate their knowledge with therapeutic experiences. Their self-reflection allows them to weed out techniques and approaches that have not worked for them and include those that have.

The Therapist's Implicit Theory as Opposed to Explicit or Formal Theory

Schön's (1983, 1987) work on formal and espoused theory has helped pave the way for current conceptualizations in psychology involving a therapist's implicit and explicit theory (Najavits, 1997). Lambert (1989) has pointed out that although the single most predominant way to define therapists is by their theoretical orientation, such orientations have been found unusually limited in their capacity to predict outcomes of treatment for clients. This finding is further supported by studies that show that therapists of the same orientation differ widely in their processes and impact on clients (Luborsky et al., 1986; Najavits & Strupp, 1994), while on the other hand, therapists of different theoretical orientations have been found to be highly similar in their therapeutic styles and outcomes (Smith, Glass, & Miller, 1980).

The concept of therapists' "implicit theories of psychotherapy" is important to consider in a course on theories of psychotherapy, because as pointed out in the section on the reflective practitioner, therapists construct their own theories of counseling as they develop their clinical skills and practices. Researchers have observed many times that therapists develop implicit theories in addition to the explicit theories to which they subscribe (Burrell, 1987; Kottler, 1986; Schön, 1983). An explicit theory usually represents a theoretical orientation of some school of thought.

Therapists' implicit theories may be conscious, preconscious, or unconscious. Implicit theories refer to the therapist's tacit assumptions. They can be distinguished from the formal propositions of the various psychotherapy schools—psychoanalytic, Gestalt, psychodynamic, and cognitive-behaviorist. According to Sternberg (1985), "Implicit theories are constructions by people . . . that reside in the minds of these individuals. Such theories need to be discovered rather than invented because they already exist in some form, in people's heads" (p. 608).

Scholars have offered various definitions of implicit theories. Najavits (1997) has defined a therapist's implicit theory "as therapists' private assumptions or 'working model' about how to conduct psychotherapy that is distinct from, but coexists with, formal theoretical orientations" (p. 4). Moreover, a therapist's implicit theory might consist of his or her views on what to do or what not to do in therapy.

Clearly, therapists do develop an implicit theory, perhaps beginning as early as their days of graduate training. The question remains, however: Can the implicit theory concept be used to improve a therapist's effectiveness or create research that would help us understand the variability among therapists? It would seem that understanding the therapist's implicit theory is important from several standpoints. First, implicit theories are not simply noise getting in the way of the real, formal or explicit theory. The study of implicit therapist theories may shed some light on therapist variability that may exist either independently of theoretical orientation or alongside it. There may be great similarity between therapists regardless of their theoretical orientation because all share a common implicit theory system that interacts with the explicit theory. In terms of a research study, therapists might be assessed (or they might engage in a process of self-reflection) on what is required to build an alliance with clients and what benchmarks they personally use to monitor their level of alliance with a client. How are their implicit theories of psychotherapy different from their espoused or explicit theory?

Training programs might consider developing more formal models of examining therapists' implicit beliefs as well as creating methods to assess them. To what extent, for example, do implicit theories of psychotherapy interfere with the material that training programs seek to elucidate? It might be helpful for counselor and therapist trainees to examine their implicit theories about forming relationships and therapeutic alliances and about the role of hope in therapy. Studies might also investigate the relationship of therapists' implicit theories to their counseling outcomes. In other words, the journey toward psychotherapy integration should encompass integrating both therapists' implicit and explicit theories into a coherent framework and not just integrating their explicit psychotherapy theories that they have learned through didactic methods.

CASE ANALYSIS

Justin and Integrative Treatment Planning

This section provides a general outline of integrative treatment planning with Justin. An in-depth treatment plan is not provided because Justin has already been examined from the perspective of each of the major counseling theories. In most private practices, Justin and his mother would be given an intake form, a professional disclosure statement for his mother, Sandy, to sign because Justin is a minor, and an intake form for Sandy to complete. This section is designed to give you a realistic view of the information that would be required in an intake or initial interview with Justin and his mother. Below is a copy of such an intake form that might be used with Justin.

CHILD AND ADOLESCENT INTAKE FORM

To be filled out by parent or guardian requesting services for a minor child. This information will help your therapist understand your child. This statement will be kept confidential to the extent to which state law permits.

BACKGROUND INFORMATION

Child's name _____ Date of Birth _____/_____/_____ Age _____

School attending and grade level (if applicable): _____

Child lives with (check one): both biological parents_____ mother_____ father_____ other_____

If parents are divorced, describe custody arrangements: _____

_____

_____

_____

Child's address _____

_____

Emergency contact person (other than parent) _____

Phone number _____-_____-_____

Custodial parent's contact information:

Phone _____ (Home) _____ (Cell) _____ (Work) _____ E-mail:_____

INFORMATION ABOUT CHILD'S MOTHER

Mother's name _____ Age_____ Race_____

(Continued)

(Continued)

Employer _____

Occupation _____

Hrs./wk. _____ Can you be contacted at work by phone? Yes No

Circle the best way to contact you:

Phone: _____ / (Home) _____ (Cell) _____ (Work) _____

E-mail _____

Denomination _____ Church _____ Active? Yes No

INFORMATION ABOUT CHILD'S FATHER

Father's name _____ Age _____

Race _____

Employer _____

Occupation _____

Hrs./wk. _____ Can you be contacted at work by phone? Yes No

Circle the best way to contact:

Phone _____

(Home) (Cell) (Work)

E-mail _____

Denomination _____ Church _____ Active? Yes No

Please list others living in custodian parent's home, including names, ages, and relationship to child:

_____

_____

Legal Issues

Is there any legal involvement with your child? Yes _____ No _____ If so, please describe: _____

_____

_____

Please bring copies of any court orders that are related to your child to our next session.

Has the court ordered that your child seek counseling?

Presenting Problem: Describe the issue your child is having.

Briefly state the problem that brought you here:

_____

_____

_____

_____

How long has this situation been in existence?

_____

_____

Problem Areas: From the following list, please prioritize each item that identifies an area of concern to you that you have for your child. For example, the number 1 would be placed by the item that concerns you the most today.

_____Anger   _____Shyness

_____Depression   _____Feels hopeless

_____Grades, academic performance   _____Fidgety, unable to sit still

_____Court trouble, legal issues   _____Daydreams too much

_____ Inability to get along with other children   _____Takes unnecessary risk

_____Bullying—being bullied by other children   _____Blames others for his or her troubles

_____Bullying, threatening other children   _____Takes things that do not belong to him or her

_____Religious/spiritual concerns   _____School grades dropping

_____Developmental issues   _____Distracted easily

_____Fights with other children in school   _____Has trouble with his teacher(s)

How were you referred? _____

_____

What are your reason(s) for seeking therapy? _____

_____

What goals do you have for therapy for your child? _____

_____

Have you sought mental health treatment before for your child? _____ Yes _____ No _____

(Continued)

(Continued)

If so, when and with whom? _____

_____

_____

Current medical doctor/family physician: _____ Phone number: _____

Is your child under medical care for any ailment? Is he or she on any medications? If so, please indicate current medications (type and dosage): _____

_____

_____

Have there been any suicide attempts? (If so, explain) _____

In case of emergency, please notify :

Name: _____ Phone: _____ Relationship: _____

Insurance (The following questions are about the policyholder.)

Policyholder's name: _____ SSN: _____ DOB: _____

Address: _____ City: _____ State: _____ ZIP: _____

Home phone: _____ Cell: _____ Work: _____

Insurance company: _____

Authorization #: _____ Number of sessions authorized: _____ Co-pay: _____

Employer: _____

Job title: _____

Form completed by: _____ Date: _____

Signature: _____

Source: © Elsie Jones-Smith (2012).

Information gathered from this form is typically reviewed prior to meeting with clients, although some therapists prefer to see clients immediately after they have completed an intake form. Typically, Sandy would be required to attend the initial counseling session in order to obtain informed consent. The initial counseling session would be used to focus on Justin's presenting problem from an integrative perspective.

Using the Multitheoretical Framework With Justin

After talking with Sandy and Justin, the therapist would use Brooks-Harris's Multitheoretical Dimensional Survey to explore the various dimensions of Justin's issues. For instance, the therapist would search the following seven dimensions to determine where his presenting issue(s) are located: (1) thoughts, (2) actions, and (3) feelings, and the contextual dimensions of (4) biology, (5) interpersonal patterns, (6) social systems, and (7) cultural contexts. Justin's multidimensional survey might reveal that his presenting problem has concurrent dimensions:

Thoughts: "I don't want to be placed in the residential treatment home, 100 or so miles from my mother and brother." (The therapist uses cognitive therapy to conceptualize one dimension of his current issue.)

"It's not my fault I get into fights at school. Kids make smart remarks about me so that I can hear them."

Actions: Social isolation at school because of fighting and inability to control his anger. (Behavior techniques might be appropriate—anger management training.)

Feelings: Low self-esteem. When the therapist asked Justin how he felt about the kids making fun of him in school, Justin responded, "sad," "angry," and "hurt." The therapist might consider using concepts from existential-humanistic therapy.

The therapist would also examine the contextual dimensions of Justin's presenting problem, meaning the role of biology, interpersonal relations, systemic issues, and cultural issues. Justin's mother is on welfare, and the family lives in a neighborhood that has a great deal of crime (i.e., gangs, etc.).

Biology: Justin has complained of headaches and trouble sleeping because of his fears of being placed in residential treatment. Because he has trouble sleeping, he overslept twice and was late for his court appointment. It also might be wise to have Justin examined for an attention deficit disorder because he frequently gets out of his seat in school and has difficulty concentrating.

Interpersonal: Justin has made a poor choice of friends outside of school. He hangs around boys much older than he and boys who have gotten into trouble with the law. Justin's brother is in a gang. (Psychodynamic therapy concepts could possibly shed light on Justin's development, especially Erickson's work on psychosocial stages of development.)

Social: Justin tries to hide his feelings of low self-esteem that are fueled by his family's poverty and his feelings that his father abandoned him. (Perhaps concepts from psychodynamic therapy might be useful to deal with issues regarding his mother, Sandy [the "good-enough" mother?].)

Cultural: Justin has experienced difficulty with his mixed racial/ethnic heritage—White mother and African American father. (Multicultural counseling theory might prove useful in helping him resolve his personal identity and his ethnic identity in predominantly White Utah.)

After surveying all seven dimensions described above, the therapist chooses two to three areas that will serve as the initial focus for psychotherapy with Justin. The therapist selects the focal dimensions in collaboration with Justin. The therapist asks Justin to notice what takes place in his life regarding the two to three focal dimensions selected for psychotherapy. In addition, the therapist writes down initial hypotheses that are taken from the corresponding theoretical school.

The next step involves choosing interventions from a catalog of key strategies from theories that address the selected focal dimensions. For instance, to address Justin's feelings about his situation, the therapist chooses experiential strategies from the Multitheoretical Therapy website (http://www.multitheoretical.com). The Catalog of

(Continued)

Key Strategies under the experiential theoretical school lists strategies such as EXP-10, creating experiments, and EXP-11, accepting freedom and responsibility. The therapist and Justin collaborate on the effectiveness of therapy and then move to the next focal dimension for work in psychotherapy. The Multitheoretical Therapy Model offers a useful method for treatment planning from an integrative perspective.

SUMMARY

A major theme was that counseling and psychotherapy are moving toward an integrative approach to psychotherapy. The days of adopting one singular therapy approach and using it for the rest of one's professional development seem to be coming to an end. Psychotherapy integration has become intertwined with the evidence-based movement in stressing that various client problems necessitate that the therapist use different solutions. Moreover, increasingly these solutions can be chosen on the basis of empirical outcome research—what is known as evidence-based studies. One advantage of integrative therapies is that they allow therapists the flexibility to meet the needs of clients who have different presenting issues and who come from a range of cultural contexts.

Psychotherapy integration can take several different paths, including assimilative integration, technical eclecticism, common factors integration, and theoretical integration. Clearly, over the past four to five decades, therapists and researchers have stressed therapy that goes beyond the limited confines of one theoretical school. The movement toward psychotherapy integration encourages therapists to take into consideration the benefits of individual therapeutic approaches. Integrative psychotherapy posits that many treatment methods can be helpful in working with different clients. It is predicted that evidence-based studies will have an important influence on psychotherapy theory integration.

Therapists must understand not only the individual theories so that they can decide for themselves what they feel is appropriate for them, but they also need to establish a multitheoretical or integrative framework from which they can integrate the theories they choose. The framework by Brooks-Harris (2008) offers the simplest route to developing one's own integrative approach. My own preference is to modify his framework to include the spiritual area as well as several mind–body approaches.

Currently, there are few graduate schools that offer an integrative approach to counseling and psychotherapy. Within the next couple of decades, it is predicted that graduate schools will adopt an integrative approach to psychotherapy training because such programs themselves will come under increasing pressure to equip their graduates with therapeutic skills that cross theoretical lines. Ethical guidelines for counselors and psychologists appear to be headed in the direction of requiring therapists to know evidence-based research (what techniques actually work with what clients with what problems) if they are to exercise an appropriate standard of care for their clients.

The effective therapist is a reflective practitioner—one who looks inward to discover who he or she is becoming as a therapist. Theories should guide one's therapy practice. Good luck on your journey to becoming a professional counselor/therapist/social worker or mental health worker.

SUPPLEMENTAL AIDS

Discussion Questions

1. *Number of theories to integrate into your theoretical approach:* How many theories do you feel comfortable using to conceptualize clients' issues or to guide your therapeutic interventions?

2. *The reflective practitioner:* Reflect back on your own life, with an emphasis on reviewing the various issues and difficulties that you have had throughout your life. How might you present yourself as a client? What would you be looking for in your therapist? What therapeutic goals might you establish if you were a client? For what issues might you consider personal counseling prior to engaging in the formal practice of psychotherapy?

3. *Disagreements between the various theories of psychotherapy:* In your opinion, what are the various schools of therapy really disagreeing about? Are they describing different features of the same phenomena, disagreeing about the very nature of those phenomena, or discussing completely different phenomena? Are the disagreements in psychotherapy approaches mainly differences in terminology? Choose a theory of psychotherapy with which you disagree. Role-play your arguing for the basic tenets of a theory with which you disagree.

4. *Reflection on therapist qualities:* The purpose of this exercise is to help you identify and assess your own strengths and weaknesses as future therapists and encourage self-reflection and openness in your group. Identify three things about yourself that you believe will assist you in becoming a good therapist. Record these things in your journal.

5. *Create a timeline for your own professional development:* Indicate on this timeline what you want (hope to achieve) and when, throughout your expected lifetime. What do you see yourself doing 10 years from now in the helping professions? If you could be the type of person that you wish you could be, what kind of person would you be?

What might you be doing if you were living as you dreamed or wanted to live?

Glossary of Key Terms

assimilative integration An approach to psychotherapy integration that involves having a strong grounding in one system of psychotherapy and a willingness to select (assimilate) practices and views from other systems.

eclecticism An integrative approach that advocates using multiple procedures taken from various therapeutic approaches without specific concern from which theories they come.

manualized treatment Involves the use of standardized, manual-based treatments. Proponents of evidence-based treatments often advocate the use of manual-based treatments.

multitheoretical psychotherapy Maintains that thoughts, actions, and feelings interact with one another and are shaped by biological, interpersonal, systemic, and cultural contexts. This simple foundation is used to organize seven theoretical models that can be used to conceptualize clients and guide interventions, resulting in a sophisticated and integrated approach to psychotherapy.

theoretical integration Involves the integration of two or more therapies with an emphasis on integrating the underlying constructs associated with each therapeutic system.

Website Materials

Additional exercises, journals, annotated bibliography, and more are available on the open-access website at https://study.sagepub.com/jonessmith2e.

REFERENCES

Aanstoos, C., Serlin, I., & Greening, T. (2000). History of Division 32 (Humanistic Psychology) of the American Psychological Association. In D. Dewsbury (Ed.), *Unification through division: Histories of the divisions of the American Psychological Association* (Vol. V). Washington, DC: American Psychological Association.

Abbass, A. A., Hancock, J. T., Henderson, J., & Kisely, S. (2006). Short-term psychodynamic psychotherapies for common mental disorders. *Cochrane Database of Systematic Reviews*, 4(CD004687). doi:10.1002/14651858. CD004687.pub3

Abbass, A., Kisely, S., & Kroenke, K. (2009). Short-term psychodynamic psychotherapy for somatic disorders: Systematic review and meta-analysis of clinical trials. *Psychotherapy and Psychosomatics, 78*, 265–274. doi:10.1159/000228247

Aboud, F. E. (1987). The development of ethnic self-identification and attitudes. In J. S. Phinney & M. J. Rotherham (Eds.), *Children's ethnic socialization* (pp. 32–55). Newbury Park, CA: Sage.

Abraham, K. (1927). The influence of oral eroticism on character formation. In K. Abramson (Ed.), *Selected papers*. London: Institute for Psychoanalysis and Hogarth Press.

Abrams, D. M. (1992). The dream's mirror of reality. *Contemporary Psychoanalysis, 28*, 50–71.

Acton, D. (2001). The "color blind" therapist. *Art therapy: Journal of the American Art Therapy Association, 18*(2), 109–112. doi:10.1080/07421656.2001.10129749

Adams, J., & White, M. (2004, July 14). Why don't stage-based activity promotion interventions work? *Health Education Research*, 10.1093/her/cyg105.

Adler, A. (1917). *Study of organ inferiority and psychical compensation: A contribution to clinical medicine* (Monograph, no. 24). New York: Nervous and Mental Disease Publishing Co.

Adler, A. (1929). Position in family influences lifestyle. *International Journal of Individual Psychology, 3*, 211–227.

Adler, A. (1930a). *The education of children*. New York: Greenberg.

Adler, A. (1930b). *Guiding the child*. New York: Greenberg.

Adler, A. (1931). *What life should mean to you*. New York: Blue Ribbon Books.

Adler, A. (1937). Position in family constellation influences life style. *International Journal of Individual Psychology, 3*, 211–227.

Adler, A. (1938). *Social interest: A challenge to mankind* (J. Linton & R. Vaughan, Trans.). London: Faber & Faber.

Adler, A. (1958a). *Social interest: A challenge to mankind.* New York: Capricorn.

Adler, A. (1958b). *What life should mean to you.* New York: Capricorn.

Adler, A. (1959a). *Individual psychology.* Paterson, NJ: Littlefield, Adams, & Company.

Adler, A. (1959b). *What life should mean to you.* Boston: Little, Brown. (Original work published 1931)

Adler, A. (1963). *The problem child.* New York: Putnam.

Adler, A. (1964). Organ inferiority and its compensation. In H. L. Ansbacher & R. R. Ansbacher (Eds.), *The individual psychology of Alfred Adler.* New York: Harper. (Originally published 1926)

Adler, A. (1972). *The neurotic constitution.* Freeport: Books for Libraries Press. (Originally published 1926)

Adler, A. (2005–2006). *The collected clinical works of Alfred Adler* (12 vols.). Various locations: Adler Institute of San Francisco & Northwestern Washington. (Originally published 1898–1937)

Adler, A., & Deutsch, D. (Eds.). (1959). *Essays in individual psychology.* New York: Ronald Press.

Affleck, G., & Tennen, H. (1996). Construing benefits from adversity: Adaptational significance and dispositional underpinnings. *Journal of Personality, 64*, 899–922.

Ainsworth, M. (1969). Object relations, dependency, and attachment: A theoretical review of the infant–mother relationship. *Child Development, 40*, 969–1025.

Ainsworth, M. (1979). Infant–mother attachment. *American Psychologist, 34*, 932–937.

Ajir, K., Smith, M., Lin, D. M., Fleishaker, J. C., Chambers, J. H., Anderson, D., . . . Poland, R. E. (1997). The pharmacokinetics and pharmacodynamics of adinazolam: Multiethnic comparisons. *Psychopharmacology, 129*, 265–270.

Albee, G.W. (1994). The sins of the fathers: Sexism, racism and ethnocentrism in psychology. *International Psychologist, 35*, 22–26.

Alcoholics Anonymous World Services, Inc. (1984). *Pass it on: The story of Bill Wilson and how the A.A. message reached the world* (pp. 376–381). New York: Alcoholics Anonymous World Services, Inc.

Allan, J., & Berry, P. (1987). Sandplay. *Elementary School Guidance and Counseling, 21*(4), 300–306.

Allison, K. L., & Rossouw, P. J. (2013). The therapeutic alliance: Exploring the concept of "safety" from a neuropsychotherapeutic perspective. *International Journal of Neuropsychotherapy, 1,* 21–29. doi:10.12744/ijnpt.2013.0021-0029

Altman, D. (1979). *Coming out in the seventies.* Sydney, New South Wales, Australia: Wild & Wooley.

American Counseling Association. (2005). *ACA code of ethics and standards of practice.* Alexandria, VA: Author.

American Mental Health Counseling Association. (2010). *American Mental Health Counseling Association code of ethics.* Alexandria, VA: Author.

American Psychiatric Association. (2000). *Diagnostic and statistical manual of mental disorders* (4th ed.). Washington, DC: Author.

American Psychiatric Association. (2004). *Practice guidelines for the treatment of patients with acute stress disorder and posttraumatic stress disorder.* Arlington, VA: Author.

American Psychiatric Association. (2006). *Practice guidelines.* http://www.psych.org/psych_pract/treatg/pg/prac_guide.cfm

American Psychiatric Association. (2013). *Diagnostic and statistical manual of mental disorders* (5th ed.). Arlington, VA: Author.

American Psychological Association Presidential Task Force on Evidence-Based Practice. (2006). *Evidence-based practice in psychology* (pp. 271–285). Retrieved February 16, 2011, from http://www.sonoma.edu/users/s/smithh/methods/evidence.pdf

American Psychological Association. (2000). *Guidelines for psychotherapy with lesbian, gay, and bisexual clients* (Adopted by the American Psychological Association Council of Representatives on February 26, 2000). Washington, DC: Author.

American Psychological Association. (2002). Ethical principles of psychologists and code of conduct. *American Psychologist, 57,* 1060–1073.

American Psychological Association. (2003a). Guidelines on multicultural education, training, research, practice, and organizational change for psychologists. *American Psychologist, 58,* 377–404.

American Psychological Association. (2003b). *APA ethical principles of psychologists and code of conduct.* Washington, DC: Author.

American Psychological Association. (2008, February). At least one in 10 Americans are prescribed psychotropics. *Monitor, 39*(2), 52. Retrieved from http://www.apa.org/monitor/feb08/atleastone.aspx

American Psychological Association. (2011). APA's *Guidelines for psychological practice with lesbian, gay, and bisexual clients.* Washington, DC: Author.

American School Counselor Association. (2007). *Position statement: Gay, lesbian, transgendered, and questioning youth* (Adopted 1995, revised 2000, 2005, 2007). Available at http://www.schoolcounselor.org/content.asp?contenid=217

Anderson, D. T. (2005). Empathy, psychotherapy integration, and meditation: A Buddhist contribution to the common factors movement. *Journal of Humanistic Psychology, 45,* 483–502.

Anderson, M. Z., Croteau, J. M., Chung, B., & DiStefano, T. M. (2001). Developing an assessment of sexual identity management for lesbian and gay workers. *Journal of Career Assessment, 9,* 243–260.

Andreasen, N. C. (2001). *Brave new brain.* New York: Oxford University Press.

Ansbacher, H. L. (1968). The concept of social interest. *Journal of Individual Psychology, 24,* 131–144.

Ansbacher, H. L. (1992). Alfred Adler, pioneer in the prevention of mental disorders. *Individual Psychology: Journal of Adlerian Theory, Research, and Practice, 48,* 3–34.

Ansbacher, H. L., & Ansbacher, R. R. (1956). *The individual psychology of Alfred Adler.* New York: Basic Books.

Ansbacher, H. L., & Ansbacher, R. R. (1964). *The individual psychology of Alfred Adler.* New York: Harper & Row Torchbooks.

Ansbacher, H. L., & Ansbacher, R. R. (Eds.). (1979). *Superiority and social interest: Alfred Adler, a collection of his later writings* (3rd rev. ed.). New York: Norton.

Arciniega, G. M., & Newlon, B. J. (1999). Counseling and psychotherapy: Multi-cultural considerations. In D. Capuzzi & D. F. Gross (Eds.), *Counseling and psychotherapy: Theories and interventions* (2nd ed., pp. 435–458). Upper Saddle River, NJ: Merrill/Prentice-Hall.

Arden, J. B. (2010). *Rewire your brain: Think your brain to a better life.* New York: Wiley.

Argyle, M. (2002). State of the art: Religion. *Psychologist, 1,* 22–26.

Arkowitz, H. (2002). Toward an integrative perspective on resistance to change. *Psychotherapy in Practice, 58,* 219–227.

Arkowitz, H., & Miller, W. R. (2008). Learning, applying, and extending motivational interviewing. In H. Arkowitz, H. A. Westra, W. R. Miller, & S. Rollnick (Eds.), *Motivational interviewing in the treatment of psychological disorders* (pp. 1–25). New York: Guilford Press.

Arkowitz, H., & Westra, H. A. (2009). Introduction to the special series on motivational interviewing and psychotherapy. *Journal of Clinical Psychology, 65*(11), 1149–1155.

Arlow, J. A., & Brenner, C. (1990). The psychoanalytic process. *Psychoanalytic Quarterly, 59*(4), 678–692.

Armitage, C. J. (2009). Is there utility in the transtheoretical model? *British Journal of Health Psychology, 14,*

195–210. Retrieved from http://onlinelibrary.wiley.com/doi/10.1348/135910708X36899/abstract

Armitage, C. J., & Arden, M. A. (2002). Exploring discontinuity patterns in the transtheoretical model: An application of the theory of planned behavior. *British Journal of Health Psychology, 7,* 89–103.

Arnold, E. M., Walsh, A. K., Oldham, M. S., & Rapp, C. A. (2007). Strengths-based case management: Implementation with high-risk youth. *Families in Society: The Journal of Contemporary Human Services, 88*(1), 83–94.

Arredondo, P., & Perez, P. (2003). Expanding multicultural competence through social justice leadership. *The Counseling Psychologist, 31*(3), 282–289.

Arthur, R. A. (2000). The personality and cognitive-epistemological traits of cognitive-behavioral and psychoanalytic psychotherapists. *British Journal of Medical Psychology, 73,* 243–257.

Arthur, R. A. (2001). Personality, epistemology, and psychotherapists' choice of theoretical model. A review and analysis. *European Journal of Psychotherapy, Counseling and Health, 4,* 45–54.

Aspinwall, L. G. (2001). Dealing with adversity: Self-regulation, coping, adaptation, and health. In A. Teaser & N. Schwarz (Eds.), *Handbook of social psychology: Intraindividual processes* (pp. 591–614). Malden, MA: Blackwell.

Aspinwall, L. G., & Staudinger, U. M. (2003). *A psychology of human strengths: Fundamental questions and future directions for a positive psychology.* Washington, DC: American Psychological Association.

Aten, J. D., & Leach, M. M. (2009). *Spirituality and the therapeutic process: A comprehensive resource from intake to termination.* Washington, DC: American Psychological Association.

Atkinson, B. (2005). *Emotional intelligence in couples therapy: Advances from neurobiology and the science of intimate relationships.* New York: Norton.

Atkinson, D., Morten, G., & Sue, D. (1998). *Counseling American minorities* (5th ed.). Boston: McGraw-Hill.

Axline, V. (1947). *Play therapy: The inner dynamics of childhood.* Boston: Houghton Mifflin.

Axline, V. (1969). *Play therapy.* New York: Ballantine Books.

Axline, V. (1971). *Dibs: In search of self.* New York: Ballantine Books.

Azevedo, F. A., Carvalho, L. R., Grinberg, L. T., Farfel, J. M., Ferretti, R. E., Leite, R. E., . . . Herculano-Houzel, S. (2009). Equal numbers of neuronal and nonneuronal cells make the human brain an isometrically scaled-up primate brain. *Journal of Comparative Neurology, 513*(5), 532–541. doi:10.1002/cne.21974

Bach, P., & Hayes, S. C. (2002). The use of acceptance and commitment therapy to prevent the rehospitalization of psychotic patients: A randomized control trial. *Journal of Consulting and Clinical Psychology, 70*(5), 1129–1139.

Badenoch, B. (2008). *Being a brain-wise therapist: A practical guide to interpersonal neurobiology.* New York: W. W. Norton.

Baer, R. A., & Huss, D. B. (2008). Mindfulness- and acceptance-based therapy. In J. L. Lebow (Ed.), *Twenty-first century psychotherapies: Contemporary approaches to theory and practice* (pp. 123–166). Hoboken, NJ: Wiley.

Baines, D. (2000). Everyday practices of race, class, and gender: Struggles, skills, and radical social work. *Journal of Progressive Human Services, 11,* 5–7.

Ballou, M., & West, C. (2000). Feminist therapy approaches. In M. Biaggio & M. Hersen (Eds.), *Issues in the psychology of women* (pp. 273–297). New York: Kluwer Academic/Plenum.

Baltes, P. B., Lindenberger, U., & Staudinger, U. M. (1998). Life-span theory in developmental psychology. In R. M. Lerner (Ed.), *Handbook of child psychology: Vol. 1. Theoretical models of human development* (5th ed., pp. 1029–1143). New York: John Wiley.

Baluch, S. P., Pieterse, A. L., & Bolden, M. A. (2004). Counseling psychology and social justice: Houston . . . We have a problem. *The Counseling Psychologist, 32*(1), 89–98.

Balzac, H. (1901). *The magic skin: The works of Honore de Balzac* (Vol. 1, E. Marriage, Trans.). Philadelphia: Avil. (Originally published 1831)

Bandura, A. (1969). *Principles of behavior modification.* New York: Holt, Rinehart & Winston.

Bandura, A. (1977). *Social learning theory.* New York: General Learning Press.

Bandura, A. (1986). *Social foundations of thought and action.* Englewood Cliffs, NJ: Prentice Hall.

Bandura, A. (1988). Self-efficacy conception of anxiety. *Anxiety Research, 1*(2), 77–98.

Bandura, A. (1997). *Self-efficacy: The exercise of control.* New York: Freeman.

Bandura, A. (1998). Health promotion from the perspective of social cognitive theory. *Psychology and Health, 13,* 623–649.

Bandura, A., & Perloff, B. (1967). Relative efficacy of self-monitored and externally imposed reinforcement systems. *Journal of Personality and Social Psychology, 7,* 111–116.

Bandura, A., & Walters, R. H. (1959). *Adolescent aggression.* New York: Ronald.

Bandura, A., Ross, D., & Ross, S. A. (1961). Transmission of aggression through imitation of aggressive models. *Journal of Abnormal and Social Psychology, 63,* 575–582.

Bandura, A., Ross, D., & Ross, S. A. (1963). Imitation of film-mediated aggressive models. *Journal of Abnormal and Social Psychology, 66,* 3–11.

Baradell, J. G. (1990). Client-centered case consultation and single-case research design: Application to case management. *Archives of Psychiatric Nursing, 4,* 12–17.

Barnard, P. J., & Teasdale, J. D. (1991). Interacting cognitive subsystems: A systematic approach to cognition affective interaction and change. *Cognition and Emotions, 5*(1), 1–39.

Barret, B., & Logan, C. (2002). *Counseling gay men and lesbians: A practice primer.* Belmont, CA: Brooks/Cole.

Barrett-Lennard, G. T. (1998). *Carl Rogers helping system: Journey and substance.* London: Sage.

Bartels, A., & Zeki, S. (2000). The neural basis of romantic love. *NeuroReport, 11,* 3829–3834.

Bartels, A., & Zeki, S. (2004). The neural correlates of maternal and romantic love. *NeuroImage, 21,* 1156–1166.

Bassin, A. (1993). The reality therapy paradigm. *Journal of Reality Therapy, 4,* 28–32.

Bateson, G. (1972). *Steps to ecology of mind.* New York: Ballantine Books.

Bateson, G. (1979). *Mind and nature: A necessary unity.* New York: Duncan.

Bateson, G., Jackson, D. D., Haley, J., & Weakland, J. (1956). Toward a theory of schizophrenia. *Behavioral Sciences, 1,* 251–264.

Bauman, M. (1997). *The Dharma has come west: A survey of recent studies and sources.* Retrieved February 20, 2010, from http://www.urbandharma.org/udharma/survey.html

Baumeister, F. F., & Leary, M. R. (1995). The need to belong: Desire for interpersonal attachments as a fundamental human motivation. *Psychological Bulletin, 117,* 497–539.

Baxter, L. R., Schwartz, J. M., Bergman, K. S., Szuba, M. P., Guze, B. H., Mazziotta, J. C., . . . Phelps, M. (1992). Caudate glucose metabolic rate changes with both drug and behavior therapy for obsessive-compulsive disorder. *Archives of General Psychiatry, 49,* 681–689.

Beauregard, M. (2007). Mind does really matter: Evidence from neuroimaging studies of emotional self-regulation, psychotherapy, and placebo effect. *Progress in Neurobiology, 81,* 218–236.

Beck, A. T. (1963). Thinking and depression: 1. Idiosyncratic content and cognitive distortions. *Archives of General Psychiatry, 9,* 324–333.

Beck, A. T. (1964). Thinking and depression: 2. Theory and therapy. *Archives of General Psychiatry, 10,* 561–571.

Beck, A. T. (1967). *Depression: Clinical, experimental, and theoretical aspects.* New York: Hoeber.

Beck, A. T. (1976). *Cognitive therapy and the emotional disorders.* New York: International Universities Press.

Beck, A. T. (1987). Cognitive therapy. In J. K. Zeig (Ed.), *The evolution of psychotherapy* (pp. 149–178). New York: Brunner/Mazel.

Beck, A. T. (1991). Cognitive therapy: A 30-year retrospective. *American Psychologist, 46,* 368–375.

Beck, A. T. (1997). The past and future of cognitive therapy. *Journal of Psychotherapy Practice and Research, 6,* 276–284.

Beck, A. T. (2005). The current state of cognitive therapy. *Archives of General Psychiatry, 62,* 953–959.

Beck, A. T. (2005). The current state of cognitive therapy: A 40 year retrospective. *Archives of General Psychiatry, 62*(9), 953–959.

Beck, A. T. (2010). The evolution of the cognitive model of depression and its neurobiological correlates. *American Journal of Psychiatry, 165,* 969–977. doi:10.1176/appi/ajp.2008.08050721

Beck, A. T., & Emery, G. (1979). *Anxiety disorders and phobias: A cognitive perspective.* New York: Basic Books.

Beck, A. T., & Steer, R. A. (1990). *Beck anxiety inventory manual.* San Antonio, TX: The Psychological Corporation.

Beck, A. T., & Weishaar, M. E. (2005). Cognitive therapy. In R. J. Corsini & D. Wedding (Eds.), *Current psychotherapies* (7th ed., pp. 238–268). Itasca, IL: Peacock.

Beck, A. T., & Young, J. E. (1985). Cognitive therapy of depression. In D. Barlow (Ed.), *Clinical handbook of psychological disorders: A step-by-step treatment manual* (pp. 206–244). New York: Guilford.

Beck, A. T., Brown, G., Berchick, R. J., Stewart, B. L., & Steer, R. A. (1990). Relationship between hopelessness and ultimate suicide: A replication with psychiatric outpatients. *American Journal of Psychiatry, 147*(2), 190–195.

Beck, A. T., Freeman, A., & Associates. (1990). *Cognitive therapy of the personality disorders.* New York: Guilford.

Beck, A. T., Freeman, A., & Davis, D. D. (2003). *Cognitive therapy of personality disorders.* New York: Plenum.

Beck, A. T., Rush, A. J., Shaw, B. F., & Emery, G. (1979). *Cognitive therapy of depression.* New York: Guilford.

Beck, A. T., Rush, A. J., Shaw, B. F., & Emery, G. (1979). *Cognitive therapy of depression.* New York: Guilford.

Beck, A. T., Steer, R. A., & Brown, G. K. (1996). *The Beck Depression Inventory manual* (2nd ed.). San Antonio, TX: The Psychological Corporation.

Beck, A. T., Steer, R. A., Brown, G. K., & Epstein, N. (1990). The Beck Self-Concept Test. *Psychological Assessment: A Journal of Consulting and Clinical Psychology, 2,* 191–197.

Beck, A. T., Steer, R. A., Kovacs, M., & Garrison, B. (1985). Hopelessness and eventual suicide: A 10-year study of patients hospitalized with suicidal ideation. *American Journal of Psychiatry, 4,* 561–571.

Beck, J. S. (1995). *Cognitive therapy: Basics and beyond.* New York: Guilford.

Beers, M. F. (2007). *Physician's drug handbook* (12th ed.). Philadelphia: Lippincott Williams & Wilkins.

Beitman, B. D., & Viamontes, G. I. (2006). The neurobiology of psychotherapy. *Psychiatric Annals, 36*(4), 214–220.

Belkofer, C., & Konopka, L. (2003, November). *A new kind of wonder: EEG and art therapy research.* Paper presented at the annual meeting of the American Art Therapy Association, Chicago.

Belmont, L., & Marolla, E. A. (1973). Birth order, family size, and intelligence. *Science, 182,* 1096–1101.

Bem, D. J. (1967). Self-perception: An alternative interpretation of cognitive dissonance phenomena. *Psychological Review, 74,* 183–200.

Bem, D. J. (1972). Self-perception theory. In I. Berkowitz (Ed.), *Advances in experimental social psychology* (Vol. 6, pp. 1–62). New York: Academic Press.

Bem, S. L. (1974). The measurement of psychological androgyny. *Journal of Consulting and Clinical Psychology, 42,* 155–162.

Bem, S. L. (1981). Gender schema theory: A cognitive account of sex typing. *Psychological Review, 88,* 354–364.

Bem, S. L. (1983). Gender schema theory and its implications for child development. *Signs, 8,* 598–616.

Bem, S. L. (1993). *The lenses of gender.* New Haven, CT: Yale University Press.

Benard, B. (1991). *Fostering resiliency in kids: Protective factors in the family, school, and community.* San Francisco: Far West Laboratory for Educational Research and Development. (ERIC Document Reproduction Service No. ED335781)

Benson, P. L. (1997). *All kids are our kids: What communities must do to raise caring and responsible children and adolescents.* San Francisco: Jossey-Bass.

Benson, P. L., Galbraith, J., & Espeland, P. (1995). *What kids need to succeed: Practical ways to raise good kids.* Minneapolis, MN: Free Spirit.

Berg, I., & DeJong, P. (1996). Solution-building conversations: Co-constructing a sense of competence with clients. *Families in Society, 77,* 376–391.

Berg, I. K. (1994). *Family based services: A solution-focused approach.* New York: Norton.

Berg, I. K., & Dolan, Y. (2001). *Tales of solutions: A collection of hope-inspiring stories.* New York: W. W. Norton.

Berg, I. K., & Miller, S. D. (1992). *Working with the problem drinker: A solution-focused approach.* New York: Norton.

Berg-Cross, L., & Chinen, R. T. (1995). Multicultural training models and person-in-culture interview. In J. G. Ponterotto, J. M. Casa, L. A. Suzuki, & C. M. Alexander (Eds.), *Handbook of multicultural counseling* (pp. 333–356). Thousand Oaks, CA: Sage.

Bergin, A. E., & Garfield, S. L. (Eds.). (1994). *Handbook of psychotherapy and behavior change* (4th ed.). New York: Wiley.

Bernal, G., & Jimenez-Chafey, M. I. (2008). Cultural adaptation of psychotherapy for ethnic-minority youth: Beyond one-size-fits-all. *Child and Family Policy and Practice Review, 4*(1), 3–5.

Bernal, M. E., & Knight, G. P. (1993). *Ethnic identity: Formation and transmission among Hispanics and other minorities.* Albany: State University of New York Press.

Berne, E. (1964). *Games people play: The basic handbook of transactional analysis.* New York: Ballantine.

Berry, J. W., & Kim, U. (1988). Acculturation and mental health. In P. R. Dasen, J. W. Berry, & N. Sartorius (Eds.), *Health and cross-cultural psychology: Toward applications* (pp. 207–236). Newbury Park, CA: Sage.

Berry, J. W., Poortinga, Y. H., Segall, M. H., & Dasen, P. R. (1992). *Cross-cultural psychology: Research and applications.* New York: Cambridge University Press.

Bertalanffy, L. von (1934). *Modern theories of development: An introduction to theoretical biology.* London: Oxford University Press.

Bertalanffy, L. von (1968). *General systems theory: Foundation, development, and application.* New York: Braziller.

Bertolino, B., & O'Hanlon, B. (2002). *Collaborative, competency-based counseling and therapy.* Boston: Allyn & Bacon.

Betancourt, H., & Lopez, S. R. (1993). The study of culture, ethnicity, race in American psychology. *American Psychologist, 48,* 629–637.

Beutler, L. E., Crago, M., & Arezmendi, T. G. (1986). Therapist values in psychotherapy. In S. L. Garfield & A. E. Bergin (Eds.), *Handbook of psychotherapy and behavior change* (3rd ed.). New York: Wiley.

Beyebach, M., Morejon, A. R., Palenzuela, D. L., & Rodriguez-Arias, J. L. (1996). Research on the process of solution-focused brief therapy. In S. D. Miller, M. A. Hubble, & B. L. Duncan (Eds.), *Handbook of solution-focused brief therapy* (pp. 299–334). San Francisco: Jossey-Bass.

Bien, T. (2006). *Mindful therapy: A guide for therapists and helping professionals.* Boston: Wisdom Publications.

Bilgrave, D. P., & Deluty, R. H. (2002). Religious beliefs and political ideologies as predictors of psychotherapeutic orientations of clinical and counseling psychologists. *Psychotherapy, 39,* 245–260.

Billinsky, J. M. (1969). Jung and Freud: The end of a romance. *Andover Newton Quarterly, 10,* 39–43.

Bingham, R. P., & Saponaro, L. (2003, August). *Social change for 2025 and the role of counseling psychology.* Paper presented at the annual convention of the American Psychological Association, Toronto, Ontario, Canada.

Binswanger, L. (1963). *Being-in-the-world.* New York: Basic Books.

Bisman, C. (1993). *Social work practice: Cases and principles.* Belmont, CA: Brooks/Cole.

Bitter, J. R. (2004). Two approaches to counseling a parent alone: Toward a Gestalt-Adlerian integration. *The Family Journal: Counseling and Therapy for Couples and Families, 12,* 358–367.

Bitter, J. R. (2009). *Theory and practice of family therapy and counseling.* Belmont, CA: Thomson-Brooks/Cole.

Bitter, J. R., & Nicoll, W. G. (2005). Case approach to Adlerian therapy: An Adlerian therapist's perspective on Ruth. In G. Corey (Ed.), *Case approaches to counseling and psychotherapy* (6th ed., pp. 57–81). Pacific Grove, CA: Brooks/Cole.

Bitter, J. R., Roberts, A., & Sonstegard, M. A. (2002). Adlerian family therapy. In J. Carlson & D. Kjos (Eds.), *Theories and strategies of family therapy* (pp. 41–79). Boston: Allyn & Bacon.

Blanck, R., & Blanck, G. (1986). *Beyond ego psychology: Developmental object relations theory.* New York: Columbia University Press.

Blanding, M. (2010, Winter). The brain in the world: A burgeoning science explores the deep imprint of culture. *Tufts.* Retrieved from www.tufts.edu/alumni/magazine/winter2010/features/the-brain.html

Blanton, P. G. (2006). Introducing letter writing into Christian psychotherapy. *Journal of Psychology and Christianity, 25,* 77–86.

Bloom, D. (2011). One good turn deserves another...and another . . . and another: Personal reflections [Review of the book *Relational approaches in Gestalt therapy,* edited by L. Jacobs and R. Hycner]. *Gestalt Review, 15*(3), 296–311.

Blum, G. S. (1949). A study of the psychoanalytic theory of psychosexual development. *Genetic Psychology Monographs, 39,* 3–99.

Bobele, M., Gardner, G., & Biever, J. (1995). Supervision as social construction. *Journal of Systemic Therapies, 14*(2), 14–25.

Bodhi, B. (2002). *The connected discourses of the Buddha: A translation of the Samyutta Nikaya* (2nd ed.). Boston: Wisdom Publications.

Bohan, J. S. (1992). *Replacing women in psychology: Readings toward a more inclusive history.* Dubuque, IA: Kendall Hunt.

Bohart, A. C., & Watson, J. C. (2011). Person-centered psychotherapy and related experiential approaches. In S. B. Messer & A. S. Gurman (Eds.), *Essential psychotherapies: Theory and practice* (3rd ed., pp. 223–260). New York: Guilford Press.

Bohart. A. C., Elliott, R., Greenberg, L. S., & Watson, J. C. (2002). Empathy. In J. C. Norcross (Ed.), *Psychotherapy relationships that work: Therapist contributions and responsiveness to patients* (pp. 89–108). New York: Oxford University Press.

Boldt, R. M., & Mosak, H. H. (1997). Characterological resistance in psychotherapy: The getter. *Individual Psychology, 53,* 67–80.

Bond, F. W., & Bunce, D. (2000). Mediators of change in emotion-focused and problem-focused worksite stress management interventions. *Journal of Occupational Health Psychology, 5,* 156–163.

Bornstein, R. F. (1993). *The dependent personality.* New York: Guilford.

Bowen, M. (1965). Family psychotherapy with schizophrenia in the hospital and in private practice. In I. Boszormenyi-Nagy & J. T. Framo (Eds.), *Intensive family therapy* (pp. 213–243). Hagerstown, MD: Harper & Row.

Bowen, M. (1966). The use of family theory in clinical practice. *Comprehensive Psychiatry, 7,* 345–374.

Bowen, M. (1975). Family therapy after 25 years. In S. Arieti, D. X. Freedman, & J. E. Dyrud (Eds.), *American handbook of psychiatry V: Treatment* (2nd ed.). New York: Basic Books.

Bowen, M. (1976). Theory in the practice of psychotherapy. In P. J. Guerin (Ed.), *Family therapy: Theory and practice* (pp. 42–90). New York: Gardner Press.

Bowen, M. (1978). *Family therapy in clinical practice.* New York: Jason Aronson.

Bowlby, J. (1969). *Attachment and loss. Vol. 1: Attachment.* New York: Basic Books.

Bowlby, J. (1988). *A secure base: Parent–child attachment and healthy human development.* New York: Basic Books.

Bowman, C. E. (2005). The history and development of Gestalt therapy. In A. L. Woldt & S. M. Toman (Eds.), *Gestalt therapy: History, theory, and practice* (pp. 3–20). Thousand Oaks, CA: Sage.

Bowman, D., Scrogin, F., Floyd, M., & McKendree-Smith, N. (2001). Psychotherapy length of stay and outcome: A meta-analysis of the effect of therapist sex. *Psychotherapy, 38,* 142–150.

Bozarth, J. D., Zimring, F. M., & Tausch, R. (2002). Client-centered therapy: The evolution of a revolution. In D. J. Cain & J. Seeman (Eds.), *Humanistic psychotherapies: Handbook of research and practice* (pp. 147–188). Washington, DC: American Psychological Association.

Branch, R., Salih, S., & Homeida, M. (1978). Racial differences in drug metabolizing ability: A study with antipyrine in the Sudan. *Clinical Pharmacology and Therapeutics, 24,* 283–286.

Brantley, J. (2003). *Calming your anxious mind: How mindfulness and compassion can free you from anxiety, fear, and panic.* Oakland, CA: New Harbinger.

Brantley, J. (2007). *Calming your anxious mind: How mindfulness and compassion can free you from anxiety, fear, and panic* (2nd ed.). Oakland, CA: New Harbinger.

Brassen, S., Gamer, M., & Buchel, C. (2011). Anterior cingulate activation is related to a positivity bias and emotional stability in successful aging. *Biological Psychiatry, 70*(2), 131–137.

Bratton, S. C., Ray, D., Rhine, T., & Jones, L. (2005). The efficacy of play therapy with children: A meta-analytic review of treatment outcomes. *Professional Psychology: Research and Practice, 36,* 376–390.

Brecher, E. M. (1972). *Licit and illicit drugs.* New York: Consumers Union.

Brenman-Gibson, M. (1997). The legacy of Erik Homburger Erikson. *Psychoanalytic Review, 84,* 329–335.

Bretton, M. (1993). Relating competence-promotion and empowerment. *Journal of Progressive Human Services, 5,* 27–44.

Breuer, J., & Freud, S. (1955). *Studies on hysteria* (Standard edition, Vol. 2.). London: Hogarth Press. (Originally published 1885)

Breunlin, D. C., Schwartz, R. C., & Mackune-Karrer, B. (1992). *Metaframeworks: Transcending the models of family therapy.* San Francisco: Jossey-Bass.

Briesmeister, J. M., & Schaefer, C. E. (1998). *Handbook of parent training: Parents as co-therapists for children's behavior problems* (2nd ed.). New York: John Wiley & Sons.

Brockman, J. (2002). *The next fifty years: Science in the first half of the twenty-first century.* New York: Knopf Doubleday.

Brodley, B. T. (1997). The non-directive attitude in client-centered therapy. *Person-Centered Journal, 4*(1), 18–30.

Brody, A. L., Saxena, G., Stoessel, P., Gillies, L. A., Fairbanks, L. A., Alborzian, S., ... Baxter, L. R., Jr. (2001). Regional brain metabolic changes in patients with major depression treated with either paroxetine or interpersonal therapy: Preliminary findings. *Archives of General Psychiatry, 58*(7), 631–640.

Bronfenbrenner, U. (1974). *A report on longitudinal evaluations of preschool programs, Vol. II: Is early intervention effective?* Washington, DC: Office of Development, Department of Health, Education and Welfare. (ERIC Document Reproduction Service No. ED093501)

Bronfenbrenner, U. (1989). Ecological systems theory. *Annals of Child Development, 6,* 185–246.

Brooks, J. S., & Pahl, K. (2005). The protective role of ethnic and racial identity and aspects of an Afrocentric orientation against drug use among African American young adults. *Journal of Genetic Psychology, 166,* 329–345.

Brooks-Harris, J. E. (2008). *Integrative multitheoretical psychotherapy.* New York: Houghton Mifflin.

Brooks-Harris, J., & Savage, S. (2008). Multicultural-feminist psychotherapy: Adapting to cultural contexts. In J. Brooks-Harris (Ed.), *Integrative multitheoretical psychotherapy* (pp. 370–412). Boston: Lahaska Press.

Brown, C., & Augusta-Scott, T. (Eds.). (2007). *Narrative therapy: Making meaning, making lives.* Thousand Oaks, CA: Sage.

Brown, L. S. (1988). Feminist therapy with lesbians and gay men. In M. Dutton-Douglas & L. E. Walker (Eds.), *Feminist psychotherapies: Integration of therapeutic and feminist systems* (pp. 206–227). Norwood, NJ: Ablex.

Brown, L. S. (1989). Lesbians, gay men, and their families: Common clinical issues. *Journal of Gay and Lesbian Psychotherapy, 15,* 323–336.

Brown, L. S. (1992). A feminist critique of the personality disorders. In L. S. Brown & M. Ballou (Eds.), *Personality and psychopathology: Feminist reappraisals* (pp. 206–228). New York: Guilford.

Brown, L. S. (1994). *Subversive dialogues: Theory in feminist therapy.* New York: Basic Books.

Brown, L. S. (2000). Discomforts of the powerless: Feminist constructions of distress. In R. Neimeyer & J. Raskin (Eds.), *Constructions of disorder* (pp. 287–308). Washington, DC: American Psychological Association.

Brown, L. S. (2006). Still subversive after all these years: The relevance of feminist therapy in the age of evidence-based practice. *Psychology of Women Quarterly, 30,* 15–24.

Brown, R. P. (2004). Vengeance is mine: Narcissism, vengeance, and the tendency to forgive. *Journal of Research in Personality, 38,* 576–584.

Brown, R. P., & Phillips, A. (2005). Letting bygones be bygones: Further evidence for the Validity of the Tendency to Forgive scale. *Personality and Individual Differences, 38,* 627–638.

Brownell, P. (Ed.). (2008). *Handbook for theory, research, and practice in Gestalt therapy.* South Wellfleet, MA: Gestalt International Study Center. Retrieved from http://www.gisc.org/giscblog/?tag=evidence-based-practice

Brownell, P., Melnick, J., & Fitzpatrick, L. (2013, Jan. 24). The evolving role of research in Gestalt therapy: An interview with Philip Brownell and Joseph Melnick. Gestalt International Study Center. Retrieved from http://www.gisc.org/giscblog/?tag=gestalt-therapy

Brug, J., Conner, M., Harre, N., Kremers, S., McKellar, S., & Whitelaw, S. (2005). The transtheoretical model and stages of change: A critique: Observations by five commentators on the paper by Adams, J. and White, M. (2004) Why don't stage-based activity promotion interventions work? *Health Education Research, 20*(2), 244–258.

Bruner, E. M. (1986). Ethnography as narrative. In V. Turner & E. Bruner (Eds.), *The anthropology of experience* (pp. 139–155). Urbana: University of Illinois Press.

Bruner, J. (1987). Life as narrative. *Social Research, 54,* 1–17.

Bruner, J. (2004). The narrative creation of self. In L. E. Angus & J. McLeond (Eds.). *The handbook of narrative and psychotherapy: Practice, theory, and research* (pp. 3–14). Thousand Oaks, CA: Sage.

Bruscia, K. (1998). *Defining music therapy.* Gilsum, NH: Barcelona.

Brussat, F., & Brussat, M. A. (n.d.). *Spirituality and practice: Resources for spiritual journeys.* Retrieved August 25, 2010, from http://www.spiritualityandpractice.com

Buber, M. (1958). *I and thou* (2nd ed.). New York: Scribner.

Buber, M. (1970). *I and thou* (W. Kaufmann, Trans.). New York: Scribner.

Buckingham, M. (2007). *Go put your strengths to work: 6 powerful steps to achieving outstanding performance.* New York: Free Press.

Buckingham, M., & Clifton, D. O. (2001). *Now, discover your strengths.* New York: Simon & Schuster.

Buckley, K.W. (1989). *Mechanical man: John Broadus Watson and the beginnings of behaviorism.* New York: Guilford.

Bugental, J. F. T. (1964). The third force in psychology. *Journal of Humanistic Psychology, 4,* 25.

Bugental, J. F. T. (1981). *The search for authenticity: An existential-analytic approach to psychotherapy* (Rev. ed.). New York: Holt, Rinehart & Winston.

Bugental, J. F. T. (1986). Existential-humanistic psychotherapy. In I. L. Kutash & A. Wolf (Eds.), *Psychotherapist's casebook* (pp. 222–236). San Francisco: Jossey-Bass.

Bugental, J. F. T. (1990). Existential-humanistic psychotherapy. In J. K. Zeig & W. M. Munion (Eds.), *What is psychotherapy? Contemporary perspectives* (pp. 189–193). San Francisco: Jossey-Bass.

Buhrke, R. A., & Douce, L. A. (1991). Training issues for counseling psychologists in working with lesbians and gay men. *The Counseling Psychologist, 19,* 216–234.

Burke, B. L., Arkowitz, H., & Menchola, M. (2003). The efficacy of motivational interviewing: A meta-analysis of controlled clinical trials. *Journal of Consulting and Clinical Psychology, 71,* 843–861.

Burr, V. (1995). *An introduction to social constructionism.* London: Routledge.

Burrell, M. J. (1987). Cognitive psychology, epistemology, and psychotherapy: A motor-evolutionary perspective. *Psychotherapy, 24,* 225–231.

Butler, A. C., Chapman, J. E., Forman, E. M., & Beck, A. T. (2006). The empirical status of cognitive behavioral therapy: A review of meta-analyses. *Clinical Psychology Review, 26,* 17–31. doi:10.1016/j.cpr.2005.07.003

Butz, M., Worgotter, F., & van Ooyen, A. (2009). Activity-dependent structural plasticity. *Brain Research Reviews, 60*(2), 287–305.

Cade, B. (2007). A history of the brief, solution-focused approach. In T. Nelson & F. Thomas (Eds.), *Handbook of solution-focused brief therapy: Clinical applications* (pp. 25–64). Binghamton, NY: The Haworth Press.

Cain, D. J. (1987). Carl R. Rogers: The man, his vision, his impact. *Person-Centered Review, 2*(3), 283–288.

Cain, D. J. (1990). Fifty years of client-centered therapy and the person-centered approach. *Person-Centered Review, 5*(1), 3–7.

Cain, D. J. (2002). Defining characteristics, history, and evolution of humanistic psychotherapies. In D. J. Cain & J. Seeman (Eds.), *Humanistic psychotherapies: Handbook of research and practice* (pp. 3–54). Washington, DC: American Psychological Association.

Campbell, R. J. (1989). *Campbell's psychiatric dictionary.* New York: Oxford University Press.

Cain, D. J. (2008). Person-centered therapy. In J. Frew & M. D. Spiegler (Eds.), *Contemporary psychotherapies for a diverse world* (pp. 177–227). Boston: Lahaska Press.

Cain, D. J. (2010). *Person-centered psychotherapy.* Washington, DC: American Psychological Association.

Campbell, R. J. (1989). *Campbell's psychiatric dictionary.* New York: Oxford University Press.

Caplan, E. (1998). *Mind games: American culture and the birth of psychotherapy.* Los Angeles: University of California Press.

Caplan, P. J. (1989). *Don't blame mother.* New York: Harper & Row.

Cappas, N., Andres-Hyman, R., & Davidson, L. (2005). What psychotherapists can begin to learn from neuroscience: Seven principles of a brain-based psychotherapy. *Psychotherapy: Theory, Research, Practice, Training, 42*(3), 374–383.

Carette, B., Anseel, A., & Van Yperen, N. (2011). Born to learn or born to win? Birth order effects on achievement goals. *Journal of Research in Personality, 45*(5), 500–503. doi:10.1016/j.jrp.2011.06.008

Carl G. Jung. (2011). In *Wikipedia.* Retrieved July 1, 2010, from http://en.wikipedia.org/wiki/Carl_Jung

Carlson, J., & Ellis, C. M. (2004). Treatment agreement and relapse prevention strategies in couple and family therapy. *The Family Journal: Counseling and Therapy for Couples and Families, 12,* 352–357.

Carlson, J., & Sperry, L. (1998). Adlerian psychotherapy as a constructivist psychotherapy. In M. F. Hoyt (Ed.), *The handbook of constructive therapies: Innovative approaches from leading practitioners* (pp. 68–82). San Francisco: Jossey-Bass.

Carlson, J., Sperry, L., & Lewis, J. A. (1997). *Family therapy: Ensuring treatment efficacy.* Belmont, CA: Thompson Brooks/Cole.

Carlson, J., Watts, R. E., & Maniacci, M. (2005). *Adlerian therapy: Theory and practice.* Washington, DC: American Psychological Association.

Carlson, L. (2003). Existential theory: Helping school counselors attend to youth at risk for violence. *Professional School Counseling, 6*(5), 310–315.

Carmichael, K. D. (2006). *Play therapy: An introduction.* Glenview, IL: Prentice Hall.

Carroll, L. (1865). *Alice in Wonderland.* London, Macmillan.

Carter, B., & McGoldrick, M. (1988). Overview: The changing life cycle—a framework for family therapy. In B. Carter & M. McGoldrick (Eds.), *The changing family life cycle* (3rd ed., pp. 3–28). New York: Gardner.

Carter, R. T. (1995). *The influence of race and racial identity in psychotherapy*. New York: Wiley.

Carver, C. S., & Scheier, M. F. (1990). Principles of self-regulation: Action and emotion. In E. T. Higgins & R. M. Sorrentino (Eds.), *Handbook of motivation and cognition: Vol. 2* (pp. 3–52). New York: Guilford.

Casas, J. M., & Mann, D. (1996). MCT theory and implications for research. In D. W. Sue, A. E. Ivey, & P. B. Pedersen (Eds.), *A theory of multicultural counseling and therapy*. Pacific Grove, CA: Brooks/Cole.

Casas, M., & Pytluk, S. (1995). Hispanic identity development: Implications for research and practice. In J. Ponterotto, M. Casas, L. Suzuki, & C. Alexander (Eds.), *Handbook of multicultural counseling* (pp. 155–180). Thousand Oaks, CA: Sage.

Casas, M., & Vasquez, M. J. T. (1996). Counseling the Hispanic. In P. B. Pedersen, J. G. Draguns, W. J. Lonner, & J. E. Trimble (Eds.), *Counseling across cultures* (4th ed., pp. 146–176). Thousand Oaks, CA: Sage.

Casement, A. (2001). *Carl Gustav Jung*. Thousand Oaks, CA: Sage.

Cashin, A., Browne, G., Bradbury, J., & Mulder, A. M. (2013). The effectiveness of narrative therapy with young people with autism. *Journal of Child and Adolescent Mental Health Nursing, 26*(1), 32–41. doi:10.1111/jcap.12020

Cashwell, C. S., & Young, J. S. (Eds.). (2005). *Integrating spirituality and religion into counseling*. Alexandria, VA: American Counseling Association.

Cass, V. C. (1979). Homosexual identity formation: A theoretical model. *Journal of Homosexuality, 4,* 219–235.

Castonguay, L. G., Schut, A. J., Aikins, D., Constantino, M. J., Laurenceau, J. P., Bologh, L., et al. (2004). Integrative cognitive therapy: A preliminary investigation. *Journal of Integrative and Eclectic Psychotherapy, 6,* 184–194.

Champagne, D. L., Bagot, R. C., van Hasselt, F., Ramakers, G., Meaney, M. J., de Kloet, E. R., . . . Drugers, H. (2008). Maternal care and hippocampal plasticity: Evidence for experience-dependent structural plasticity, altered synaptic functioning, and differential responsiveness to glucocorticoids and stress. *Journal of Neuroscience, 28*(23), 6037–6045.

Chang, E. C. (2001). Cultural influences on optimism and pessimism: Differences in Western and Eastern conceptualizations of the self. In E. C. Chang (Ed.), *Optimism and pessimism: Theory, research, and practice* (pp. 257–280). Washington, DC: American Psychological Association.

Charat, F. X. (2000). Understanding Jung: Recent biographies and scholarship. *Journal of Analytic Psychology, 45,* 195–216.

Chen, C. P. (1996). Positive living with anxiety: A Morita perspective of human agency. *Counseling Psychology Quarterly, 9,* 5–14.

Chen, C. P. (2005). Morita therapy: A philosophy of Yin/Yang coexistence. In R. Moodley & W. West (Eds.), *Integrating traditional healing practices into counseling and psychotherapy* (pp. 221–232). Thousand Oaks, CA: Sage.

Chen, M. J., & Davis, N. (Eds.). (2001). *Mental health: Culture, race, and ethnicity* (A Supplement to Mental Health: A Report of the Surgeon General). Rockville, MD: U.S. Department of Health and Human Services, Substance Abuse and Mental Health Services Administration, National Institute of Mental Health.

Chesler, P. (1972). *Women and madness*. New York: Doubleday.

Chesler, P. (1997, November/December). Women and madness: A feminist diagnosis. *MS,* 36–42.

Cheung, S. (2001). Problem-solving and solution-focused therapy for Chinese: Recent developments. *Asian Journal of Counseling, 8,* 111–128.

Christensen, E. W. (1979). Counseling Puerto Ricans: Some cultural considerations. In D. R. Atkinson, G. Morten, & D. W. Sue (Eds.), *Counseling American minorities* (3rd ed.). Dubuque, IA: Wm. C. Brown.

Christensen, O. C. (2004). *Adlerian family counseling* (3rd ed.). Minneapolis, MN: Educational Media Corp.

Chu, J., & Sue, S. (1984). Asian/Pacific Americans and group practice. In L. E. Davis (Ed.), *Ethnicity in social group work practice* (pp. 23–36). New York: Haworth.

Chu, S. H. (1999). Multicultural counseling: An Asian American perspective. In D. S. Sandhu (Ed.), *Asian and Pacific Islander Americans: Issues and concerns for counseling and psychotherapy* (pp. 21–30). New York: Nova Science.

Chugani, H. T. (1998). *Human behavior and the developing brain*. New York: Guilford.

Chung, M. (1994). Can reality therapy help juvenile delinquents in Hong Kong? *Journal of Reality Therapy, 14,* 68–80.

Clark, D. A., & Beck, A. T. (2010). Cognitive theory and therapy of anxiety and depression: Convergence with neurobiological findings. *Trends in Cognitive Sciences, 14,* 418–424.

Clark, D. A., Beck, A. T., & Alfrod, B. A. (1999). *Scientific foundations of cognitive theory and therapy of depression*. New York: John Wiley.

Clark, M. D. (1999). Strength-based practice: The ABC's of working with adolescents who don't want to work with you. Retrieved February 28, 2001, from http://www.drugs.indiana.edu/prevention/assets/asset2.html

Clark, M. D. (2005). Motivational interviewing for probation staff: Increasing the readiness to change. *Federal Probation, 69*(2), 22–28.

Clark, M. D., Walters, S. T., Gingerich, R., & Meltzer, M. (2006). Motivational interviewing for probation officers: Tipping the balance towards change. *Federal Probation, 70*(1), 38–40.

Clarkin, J. F., Levy, K. N., Lenzenweger, M. F., & Kernberg, O. F. (2007). Evaluating three treatments for borderline personality disorder: A multiwave study. *American Journal of Psychiatry, 164,* 922–928. doi:10.1176/appi.ajp.164.6.922

Clarkson, P. (2004). *Gestalt counseling in action.* London: Sage.

Cleare-Hoffman, H. P., Hoffman, L., & Wilson, S. (2013, August). Existential therapy, culture, and therapist factors in evidence-based practice. In K. Keenan (Chair), *Evidence in support of existential-humanistic psychotherapy: Revitalizing the third force.* Paper presented at the 121st Annual Convention of the American Psychological Association held in Honolulu, HI.

Clifton, D. O., & Anderson, C. E. (2002). StrengthsQuest: Discover and develop your strengths in academics, career, and beyond. Washington, DC: The Gallup Organization.

Clinebell, H. (1995). *Counseling for spiritually empowered wholeness: A hope-centered approach.* New York: Haworth Pastoral Press.

Coffman, C., & Gonzalez-Molina, G. (2003). *Follow this path: How the world's greatest organizations drive growth by unleashing human potential.* New York: The Gallup Organization.

Colapinto, J. (2000). Structural family therapy. In A. M. Horne (Ed.), *Family counseling and therapy* (3rd ed., pp. 140–169). Itasca, IL: F. E. Peacock.

Cole, B. S., & Pargament, K. I. (1998). Re-creating your life: A spiritual/psychotherapeutic intervention for people diagnosed with cancer. *Psycho-Oncology, 8,* 395–407.

Coleman, D. (2007). Further factorial validity of a scale of therapist theoretical orientation. *Research on Social Work Practice.* Advanced online publication. 10.1177/1049731506295406

Coleman, H. L. K. (1995). Strategies for coping with cultural diversity. *The Counseling Psychologist, 23,* 722–741.

Coleman, H. L. K. (1997). Conflict in multicultural counseling relationships: Source and resolution. *Journal of Multicultural Counseling and Development, 25,* 195–200.

Coles, R. (1970). *Erik H. Erikson: The growth of his work.* Boston: Little, Brown.

Coles, R. (Ed.). (2000). *The Erik Erikson reader.* New York: Norton.

Comas-Diaz, L. (Ed) (1994). *Women of color: Integrating ethnic and gender identities in psychotherapy.* New York: Guilford.

Comas-Diaz, L., & Jacobsen, F. M. (1991). Ethnocultural transference and countertransference in the therapeutic dyad. *American Journal of Orthopsychiatry 61,* 392–402.

Comas-Diaz, L., & Minrath, M. (1985). Psychotherapy with ethnic minority borderline clients. *Psychotherapy, 22,* 418–426.

Compton, W. C., & Hoffman, E. (2012). *Positive psychology: The science of happiness and flourishing.* Belmont, CA: Cengage Learning.

Comstock, D. L. (Ed.). (2005). *Diversity and development: Critical contexts that shape our lives and relationships.* Belmont, CA: Brooks/Cole-Thomas Learning.

Comstock, D. L., Duffey, T. H., & St. George, H. (2002). The relational-cultural model: A framework for group process. *Journal for Specialists in Group Work, 23,* 254–272.

Comstock, D. L., Hammer, T. R., Strentzsch, J., Cannon, K., Parsons, J., & Salazar, G., II. (2008). Relational-cultural theory: A framework for bridging relational, multicultural, and social justice competencies. *Journal of Therapy and Development.* Retrieved March 17, 2010, from http://www.highbeam.com/doc/1g1–180861154.html

Comstock, D. L., & Qin, D. (2005). Relational-cultural theory: A framework for relational development across the lifespan. In D. L. Comstock (Ed.), *Diversity and development: Critical contexts that shape our lives and relationships* (pp. 25–46). Belmont, CA: Brooks/Cole-Thomson Learning.

Comstock, G. A., & Rubinstein, E. A. (Eds.). (1972). *Television and social behavior: Vol. 3. Television and adolescent aggressiveness.* Washington, DC: Government Printing Office.

Cook, J. B., & Kaffenberger, C. J. (2003). Solution shop: A solution-focused counseling and study skills program for middle school. *Professional School Counseling, 6,* 116–124.

Cooper, C. (1989, April). Social oppressions experienced by gays and lesbians. In P. Griffin & J. Genasce (Eds.), *Strategies for addressing homophobia in physical education, sports, and dance* (pp. 212–223). Workshop presented at the annual convention of the American Alliance for Health, Physical Education, Recreation, and Dance, Boston, MA.

Cooper, M., O'Hara, M., Schmid, P. F., & Bohart, A. (2013). *The handbook of person-centred psychotherapy and counselling* (2nd ed.). Hampshire, UK: Palgrave Macmillan.

Corcoran, J., & Stephenson, M. (2000). The effectiveness of solution-focused therapy with child behavior problems: A preliminary report. *Families in Society, 81,* 468–474.

Cormier, S., & Nurius, P. S. (2003). *Interviewing and change strategies for helpers: Fundamental skills and cognitive behavioral interventions* (5th ed.). Pacific Grove, CA: Brooks/Cole.

Cormier, S., Nurius, P. S., & Osborn, C. J. (2013). *Interviewing and change strategies for helpers: Fundamental skills and cognitive behavioral interventions* (7th ed.). Belmont, CA: Brooks/Cole-Cengage Learning.

Corsaro, W. A., & Fingerson, L. (2003). Development and socialization in childhood. In J. Delamater (Ed.), *Handbook of social psychology* (pp. 125–155). New York: Kluwer.

Council on the Accreditation of Counseling and Related Educational Programs (CACREP). (2009). *CACREP Standards*. Alexandria, VA: Author.

Courtiol, A., Raymond, M., & Faurie, C. (2009). Birth order affects behavior in the investment game: Firstborns are less trustful and reciprocate less. *Animal Behaviour, 78*(6), 1405–1411. doi:10.1016/j.anbehav.2009.09.016

Cox, K. F. (2006). Investigating the impact of strengths-based assessment on youth with emotional or behavioral disorders. *Journal of Child and Family Studies, 15*(3), 287–301.

Cozolino, L. (2010). *The neuroscience of psychotherapy: Healing the social brain* (2nd ed.). New York: W. W. Norton.

Cramer, P. (2004). *Storytelling, narrative, and the Thematic Apperception Test*. New York: Guilford.

Crandall, J. (1981). *Theory and measurement of social interest: Empirical tests of Alfred Adler's concept*. New York: Columbia University Press.

Crethar, H. C., & Ratts, M. J. (2009). *Why social justice is a counseling concern*. Statement taken from Counselors for Social Justice. Retrieved January 28, 2011, from http://www.txca.org/images/tca/Template/txcsj/Why_social_justice_is_a_counseling_concern.pdf.../

Crocker, S. F. (1999). A well-lived life. In *Essays in Gestalt therapy*. Cleveland, OH: Gestalt Institute of Cleveland Press.

Crocker, S. F. (2005). Phenomenology, existentialism and Eastern thought in Gestalt therapy. In A. L. Woldt & S. M. Toman (Eds.), *Gestalt therapy: History, theory, and practice* (pp. 65–80). Thousand Oaks, CA: Sage.

Cross, W. (1971). The Negro to Black conversion experience. *Black World, 20*, 13–25.

Cross, W. (1991). *Shades of Black*. Philadelphia: Temple University Press.

Cross, W. (1995). The psychology of Nigrescence: Revising the Cross model. In J. Ponterotto, M. Casas, L. Suzuki, & C. Alexander (Eds.), *Handbook of multicultural counseling* (pp. 93–122). Thousand Oaks, CA: Sage.

Croteau, J., Lark, J., Lidderdale, & Chung, Y. B. (Eds.). (2005). *Deconstructing heterosexism in the counseling professions*. Thousand Oaks, CA: Sage.

Csikszentmihalyi, M., & Rochberg-Halton, E. (1981). *The meaning of things: Domestic symbols and the self*. New York: Cambridge University Press.

Cuellar, I., Arnold, B., & Maldonado, R. (1995). Acculturation rating scale for Mexican Americans-II: A revision of the original ARSMA scale. *Hispanic Journal of Behavioral Sciences, 17*, 275–304.

Cuellar, J., & Weeks, J. (1980). Minority elderly Americans: A prototype for area agencies on aging. *Executive Summary*. San Diego, CA: Allied Health Association.

Cummings, N. A. (2002). Evidence-based therapies and the future of mental health care. *Milton H. Erickson Foundation Newsletter, 22*, 4.

Cummings, N. A., & Lucchese, G. (1978). Adoption of a psychological orientation: The role of the inadvertent. *Psychotherapy: Theory, Research and Practice, 15*, 323–328.

Curtis, R. C. (Ed.). (1991). *The relational self: Theoretical convergences in psychoanalysis and social psychology*. New York: Guilford.

Curtis, R. C., & Glass, J. S. (2002). Spirituality and counseling class: A teaching model. *Counseling and Values, 47*, 3–12.

D'Andrea, M. (2000). Postmodernism, social constructionism and multiculturalism: Three forces that are shaping and expanding our thoughts about counseling. *Journal of Mental Health Counseling, 22*, 1–16.

D'Augelli, A. R. (1991). Lesbians and gay men on campus: Visibility, empowerment, and educational leadership. *Peabody Journal of Education, 66*, 124–142.

D'Augelli, A. R. (1993). Preventing mental health problems among lesbian and gay college students. *Journal of Primary Prevention, 13*(4), 1–17.

Dana, G. (2002). Friends of the children. *Reclaiming Children and Youth, 10*, 209–212.

Darwin, C. (1995). *The origin of species*. New York: Gramercy. (Original work published 1859)

Das, A. K. (1995). Rethinking multicultural counseling: Implications for counselor education. *Journal of Counseling and Development, 74*, 45–52.

Das, A. S. (1996). *Vedic stories from Ancient India*. Borehamwood, Hertfordshire, UK: Ahimsa.

Dattilio, F. M. (2000). Cognitive-behavioral strategies. In J. Carlson & L. Sperry (Eds.), *Brief therapy with individuals and couples* (pp. 33–70). Phoenix, AZ: Zeig, Tucker, & Theisen.

Dattilio, F. M. (2002). Cognitive-behaviorism comes of age: Grounding symptomatic treatment in an existential approach. *The Psychotherapy Networker, 26*, 75–78.

Dattilio, F. M., & Norcross, J. C. (2006). Psychotherapy integration and the emergence of instinctual territoriality. *Archives of Psychiatry and Psychotherapy, 8*(1), 5–16.

Dattilio, F. M., & Padesky, C. A. (1990). *Cognitive therapy with couples*. Sarasota, FL: Professional Resources Exchange.

Davidson, A. I. (1987). How to do the history of psychoanalysis: A reading of Freud's three essays on the theory of sexuality. *Critical Inquiry, 13*(2), 252–277.

Davidson, R. J., Putnam, K. M., & Larson, C. L. (2000). Dysfunction in the neural circuitry of emotion regulation—a possible prelude to violence. *Science, 289,* 591–594.

Davis, W. B., Gfeller, K. E., & Thaut, M. H. (1999). *An introduction to music therapy: Theory and practice.* Boston: McGraw-Hill.

De Luca, R. V., & Holborn, S. W. (1992). Effects of a variable-ratio reinforcement schedule with changing criteria on exercise in obese and nonobese boys. *Journal of Applied Behavior Analysis, 25*(3), 671–79. doi:10.1901/jaba.1992.25–671

de Shazer, S. (1982). *Patterns of brief family therapy.* New York: Guilford.

de Shazer, S. (1985). *Keys to solutions in brief therapy.* New York: Norton.

de Shazer, S. (1988). *Clues: Investigating solutions in brief therapy.* New York: Norton.

de Shazer, S. (1994). *Words were originally magic.* New York: Norton.

de Shazer, S., Berg, I., Lipchik, E., Nunnaly, E., Molnar, A., Gingerich, W., & Weiner-Davis, M. (1986). Brief therapy: Focused solution development. *Family Process, 25,* 207–222.

de Shazer, S., & Dolan, Y., with Korman, H., Trepper, T. S., McCollom, E., & Berg, I. K. (2007). *More than miracles: The state of the art of solution-focused brief therapy.* Binghamton, NY: Haworth Press.

de Shazer, S., & Molnar, A. (1984). Four useful interventions in brief family therapy. *Journal of Marital and Family Therapy, 10*(3), 297–304.

Deci, E. L., & Ryan, R. M. (2000). The "what" and "why" of goal pursuits: Human needs and the self-determination of behavior. *Psychological Inquiry, 11,* 227–268.

DeJong, P., & Berg, I. K. (2002). *Interviewing for solutions.* (2nd ed.). Pacific Grove, CA: Brooks/Cole.

DeJong, P., & Miller, S. D. (1995). Interviewing for client strengths. *Social Work, 40,* 729–736.

Del Giudice, M., Booth, T., & Irwing, P. (2012). The distance between Mars and Venus: Measuring global sex differences in personality. *PLoS ONE, 7*(1), e29265. doi:10.1371/journal.pone.0029265

Delaney, H. D., Miller, W. R., & Bisono, A. M. (2007). Religiosity and spirituality among psychologists: A survey of clinician members of the American Psychological Association. *Professional Psychology: Research and Practice, 38,* 538–546.

Dermer, S. B., Hemesath, C., & Russell, C. S. (1998). A feminist critique of solution-focused therapy. *Journal of Family Counseling, 26,* 239–250.

DeRubeis, R. J., & Beck, A. T. (1988). Cognitive therapy. In K. S. Dobson (Ed.), *Handbook of cognitive-behavioral therapies* (pp. 273–306). New York: Guilford.

DeRubeis, R. J., Tang, T. Z., & Beck, A.T. (2001). Cognitive therapy. In K. S. Dobson (Ed.), *Handbook of cognitive-behavioral therapies* (2nd ed., pp. 349–392). New York: Guilford.

Desetta, A., & Wolin, S. (2000). *The struggle to be strong: True stories by teens about overcoming tough times.* Minneapolis, MN: Free Spirit Press.

Deurzen, E., van. (2002). Existential therapy. In W. Dryden (Ed.), *Handbook of individual therapy* (4th ed., pp. 179–208). London: Sage.

Deurzen-Smith, E. (1997). *Everyday mysteries: Existential dimensions of psychotherapy.* London: Routledge.

Deutsch, C. J. (1984). Self-reported sources of stress among psychotherapists. *Professional Psychology: Research and Practice, 15,* 833–845.

Di Pellegrino, G., Fadiga, L., Fogassi, L., Gallese, V., & Rizzolatti, G. (1992). Understanding motor events: A neurophysiological study. *Experimental Brain Research, 91,* 176–180.

Diallo, Y., & Hall, M. (1989). *The healing drum: African wisdom teachings.* Rochester, VT: Destiny Books.

Dickinson, G. (1999). Traditional healers face off with science. *Canadian Medical Association Journal, 160,* 629.

Dinkmeyer, D. C., Dinkmeyer, D. Jr., & Sperry, L. (1990). *Adlerian counseling and psychotherapy* (2nd ed.). Englewood Cliffs, NJ: Prentice Hall.

Dinkmeyer, D. C., Dinkmeyer, D. C., Jr., & Sperry, L. (2000). *Adlerian counseling and psychotherapy* (3rd ed.). Upper Saddle River, NJ: Merrill/Prentice Hall.

Dinkmeyer, D. Sr., & Dreikurs, R. (2000). *Encouraging children to learn.* Philadelphia: Brunner-Routledge.

Dinkmeyer, D. Sr., McKay, G., & Dinkmeyer, D. Jr. (1997). *Systematic training for effective parenting* (2nd ed.). Circle Pines, MN: American Guidance Service, Publishers.

Dinkmeyer, D., McKay, G., Dinkmeyer, D. Jr., & McKay, J. (1997). *The parent handbook.* Circle Pines, MN: American Guidance Service.

Dinkmeyer, D., & Sperry, L. (2000). *Counseling and psychotherapy: An integrated, individual psychology approach.* Upper Saddle River, NJ: Merrill/Prentice Hall.

Disque, J. G., & Bitter, J. R. (1998). Integrating narrative therapy with Adlerian lifestyle assessment: A case study. *Journal of Individual Psychology, 54,* 431–450.

Division of Educational Studies, Emory. (2004 , July/August). Albert Bandura receives APA's Award for Outstanding Lifetime Contribution to Psychology. APA Conference, Honolulu, Hawaii, Retrieved from http://www.des.emory.edu/mfp/BanduraAPA2004.html

Division of Educational Studies, Emory. (2006, July). Professor Bandura honored with the Career Achievement Award for Outstanding Contributions in Self-Concept Research at the meeting of the Self Centre. University of Michigan, Ann Arbor. Retrieved from http://www.des.emory.edu/mfp/BanduraSelfCentre2006.html

Dixon, M. M., Reyes, C. J., Leppert, M. F., & Pappas, L. M. (2008). Personality and birth order in large families. *Personality and Individual Differences, 44*(1), 119–128. doi:10.1016/j.paid.2007.07.015

Dobson, K. S. (Ed.). (2001). *Handbook of cognitive-behavioral therapies* (2nd ed.). New York: Guilford.

Dobson, K. S., & Dozois, D. J. A. (2010). Historical and philosophical bases of the cognitive-behavioral therapies. In K. S. Dobson (Ed.), *Handbook of cognitive-behavioral therapies* (3rd ed., pp. 3–38). New York: Guilford Press.

Dolan, Y. (1991). *Resolving sexual abuse: Solution-focused therapy and Ericksonian hypnosis for survivors.* New York: Norton.

Dollard, J., & Miller, N. E. (1950). *Personality and psychotherapy: An analysis in terms of learning, thinking, and culture.* New York: McGraw-Hill.

Dolliver, R. H. (1991). The eighteen ideas which most influence my therapy. *Psychotherapy, 28,* 507–514.

Douglas, C. (2011). Analytical psychotherapy. In R. Corsini & D. Wedding (Eds.), *Current psychotherapies* (pp. 96–129). Belmont, CA: Brooks/Cole.

Dreikurs, R. (1948). *The challenge of parenthood.* New York: Hawthorn.

Dreikurs, R. (1949). The four goals of children's misbehavior. *Nervous Child, 6,* 3–11.

Dreikurs, R. (1957). *Psychology in the classroom.* New York: Harper.

Dreikurs, R. (1961). The Adlerian approach to therapy. In M. L. Stein (Ed.), *Contemporary psychotherapies* (pp. 80–94). Glencoe, IL: The Free Press.

Dryden, W., & Spurling, L. (Eds.). (1989). *On becoming a therapist.* London: Tavistock/Routledge.

Duck, S. (Ed.). (1993). *Individuals in relationships.* Thousand Oaks, CA: Sage.

Dufresne, T. (2003). *Killing Freud: Critics talk back: Twentieth-century culture and the death of psychoanalysis.* New York: Continuum.

Dufresne, T. (Ed.). (2007). *Against Freud: Critics talk back.* Stanford, CA: Stanford University Press.

Dunn, C., Deroo, L., & Rivara, F. P. (2001). The use of brief interventions adapted from motivational interviewing across behavior domains: A systematic review. *Addiction, 96,* 1725–1742.

Dunne, C. (2002). *Carl Jung: Wounded healer of the soul.* London: Continuum.

Durrant, M., & Kowalski, K. (1992). Enhancing views of competence. In S. Friedman (Ed.), *The new language of change* (pp. 107–137). New York: Guilford.

Dwairy, M. (2006). *Counseling and psychotherapy with Arabs and Muslims: A culturally sensitive approach.* New York: Columbia University, Teachers College Press.

Dwairy, M. (2008). Counseling Arab and Muslim clients. In P. B. Pedersen, J. G. Draguns, W. J. Lonner, & J. E. Trimble (Eds.), *Counseling across cultures* (6th ed., pp. 147–160). Thousand Oaks, CA: Sage.

Dwairy, M., & Menshar, K. E. (2006). Parenting style, individuation, and mental health of Egyptian adolescents. *Journal of Adolescence, 29,* 103–117.

Eagle, M. (1997). Contributions of Erik Erikson. *Psychoanalytic Review, 84,* 337–347.

Early, T. J., & GlenMaye, L. F. (2000). Valuing families: Social work practice with families from a strengths perspective. *Social Work, 45*(2), 118–130.

Eaton, L. G., Doherty, K. L., & Widrick, R. M. (2007). A review of research and methods used to establish art therapy as an effective treatment method for traumatized children. *Arts in Psychotherapy, 34,* 256–262.

Ecker, B., & Hulley, L. (2006). *Coherence therapy practice manual and training guide.* Oakland, CA: Pacific Seminars.

Ecker, B., Ticic, R., & Hulley, L. (2012). *Unlocking the emotional brain: Eliminating symptoms at their roots using memory reconsolidation.* New York: Routledge.

Ecker, B., & Toomey, B. (2008). Depotentiation of symptom-producing implicit memory in coherence therapy. *Journal of Constructivist Psychology, 21,* 87–150.

Eckstein, D. J., & Kern, R. M. (2002). *Psychological fingerprints: Lifestyle interventions.* Dubuque, IA: Kendall-Hunt.

Edey, W. (2000). *The language of hope.* Unpublished manuscript.

Edey, W., Jevne, R. F., & Westra, K. (1998). Hope-focused counseling. Edmonton, AB: The Hope Foundation of Alberta.

Edwards, D. (2004). *Art therapy.* London: Sage.

Egan, G. (2002). *The skilled helper: A problem management and opportunity development approach to helping* (7th ed.). Pacific Grove, CA: Brooks/Cole.

Elkins, D., & Stovall, K. (2000). American Art Therapy Association, Inc.: 1998–1999 Membership Survey Report. *Art Therapy: Journal of the American Art Therapy Association, 17,* 41–46.

Ellenberger, H. (1970). *The discovery of the unconscious: The history and evolution of dynamic psychiatry.* New York: Basic Books.

Ellis, A. (1951). *The folklore of sex.* Oxford, England: Charles Boni.

Ellis, A. (1954). *The American sexual tragedy.* New York: Twayne.

Ellis, A. (1957). How to live with a neurotic. Oxford, England: Crown Publishers.

Ellis, A. (1958). *Sex without guilt.* New York: Hillman.

Ellis, A. (1962). *Reason and emotion in psychotherapy.* New York: Lyle Stewart.

Ellis, A. (1970). Humanism, values, rationality. *Journal of Individual Psychology, 26,* 37–38.

Ellis, A. (1974). *Humanistic psychotherapy: The rational-emotive approach.* New York: Julian.

Ellis, A. (1976). The biological basis of human irrationality. *Journal of Individual Psychology, 32,* 145–168.

Ellis, A. (1994). *Reason and emotion in psychotherapy* (Rev. ed.). New York: Citadel.

Ellis, A. (1996). *Better, deeper, and more enduring brief therapy: The rational emotive behavior approach.* New York: Brunner/Mazel.

Ellis, A. (1998). *How to control your anxiety before it controls you.* New York: Citadel.

Ellis, A. (1999). *How to make yourself happy and remarkably less disturbable.* San Luis Obispo, CA: Impact.

Ellis, A. (2000a). Rational emotive behavior therapy. In R. Corsini & D. Wedding (Eds.), *Current psychotherapies* (6th ed., pp. 168–204). Itasca, IL: Peacock.

Ellis, A. (2000b). The importance of cognitive processes in facilitating accepting in psychotherapy. *Cognitive and Behavioral Practice, 7,* 288–299.

Ellis, A. (2001a). *Feeling better, getting better, and staying better.* Atascadero, CA: Impact.

Ellis, A. (2001b). *Overcoming destructive beliefs, feelings, and behaviors.* Amherst, NY: Prometheus.

Ellis, A. (2002). *Overcoming resistance: A rational emotive behavior therapy integrative approach.* New York: Springer.

Ellis, A. (2004). *Rational emotive behavior therapy: It works for me—it can work for you.* Amherst, NY: Prometheus.

Ellis, A. (2005). Rational emotive behavior therapy. In R. J. Corsini & D. Wedding (Eds.), *Current psychotherapies* (7th rev. ed., pp. 166–201). Belmont, CA: Brooks/Cole.

Ellis, A., & Dryden, W. (1997). *The practice of rational-emotive therapy* (Rev. ed.). New York: Springer.

Ellis, A., Gordon, J., Neenah, M., & Palmer, S. (1997). *Stress counseling: A rational emotive behavior approach.* New York: Springer.

Ellis, A., & Harper, R. A. (1975). *A new guide to rational living* (Rev. ed.). Hollywood, CA: Wilshire Books.

Ellis, A., & Harper, R. A. (1997). *A guide to rational living.* North Hollywood, CA: Melvin Powers.

Ellis, D. J., & Ellis, A. (2011). *Rationale emotive behavior therapy.* Washington, DC: American Psychological Association.

Enns, C. (1987). Gestalt therapy and feminist therapy: A proposed integration. *Journal of Counseling and Development, 66,* 93–95.

Enns, C. Z. (1993). Twenty years of feminist therapy and therapy: From naming biases to implementing multifaceted practice. *Therapy Psychologist, 21,* 3–87.

Enns, C. Z. (2000). Gender issues in therapy. In S. D. Brown & R. W. Lent (Eds.), *Handbook of therapy psychology* (3rd ed., pp. 601–638). New York: Wiley.

Enns, C. Z. (2004). *Feminist theories and feminist psychotherapies: Origins, themes, and diversity* (2nd ed.). New York: Haworth.

Enns, J., & Remer, P. (2003). *Feminist perspectives in therapy: Empowering diverse women.* New York: Wiley.

Epstein, L. (1994). *The therapeutic idea in contemporary society.* Unpublished paper presented at University of Toronto, School of Social Work Postmodernism Workshop, Toronto, Canada.

Epstein, M. (1995). *Thoughts without a thinker.* New York: Basic Books.

Epstein, M. J. (1998). Assessing the emotional and behavioral strengths of children. *Reclaiming Children and Youth, 6,* 250–252.

Epstein, M. J., & Sharma, J. (1998). *Behavioral and Emotional Rating Scale: A strength-based approach to assessment.* Austin, TX: Pro-Ed.

Epstein, R. (1997). Skinner as self-manager. *Journal of Applied Behavior Analysis, 30,* 545–569. Retrieved June 2, 2005, from http://seab.envmed.rochester.edu/jaba/articles/1997/jaba-30-03-0545.pdf

Epston, D., & White, M. (1992a). Consulting your consultants: The documentation of alternative knowledges. In *Experience, contradiction, narrative and imagination: Selected papers of David Epston and Michael White, 1989–1991* (pp. 11–26). Adelaide, Australia: Dulwich Centre.

Epston, D., & White, M. (1992b). *Experience, contradiction, narrative and imagination.* Adelaide, Australia: Dulwich Centre.

Erickson, S. J., Gerstle, M., & Feldstein, S. W. (2005). Brief interventions and motivational interviewing with children, adolescents, and their parents in pediatric health settings: A review. *Archives of Pediatrics and Adolescent Medicine, 1959,* 1173–1180.

Erikson, E. H. (1950). *Childhood and society.* New York: Norton.

Erikson, E. H. (1958). *Young man Luther.* New York: Norton.

Erikson, E. H. (1968). *Identity: Youth and crisis.* New York: Norton.

Erikson, E. H. (1969). *Gandhi's truth: On the origin of militant nonviolence.* New York: Norton.

Espin, O. (1994). *Latina realities: Essays on healing, migration and sexuality.* New York: Dover.

Etchison, M., & Kleist, D. M. (2000). Review of narrative therapy: Research and utility. *The Family Journal, 8*(1), 61–66.

Etkin, A., Pittenger, C., Polan, H. J., & Kandel, E. R. (2005). Toward a neurobiology of psychotherapy: Basic science and clinical applications. *Journal of Neuropsychiatry and Clinical Neuroscience, 17*(2), 145–158.

Exline, J. J., Yali, A. M., & Sanderson, W. C. (2000). Guilt, discord, and alienation: The role of religious strain in depression and suicidality. *Journal of Clinical Psychology, 56,* 1481–1496.

Fabrega, H. (1995). Hispanic mental health research: A case for cultural psychiatry. In A. Padilla (Ed.), *Hispanic psychology: Critical issues in theory and research* (pp. 107–130). Thousand Oaks, CA: Sage.

Fairburn, C. G., Cooper, Z., & Shafran, R. (2008). Enhanced cognitive behavior therapy for eating disorders ("CBT-E"): An overview. In C. G. Fairburn (Ed.), *Cognitive behavior therapy and eating disorders* (pp. 23–34). New York: Guilford Press.

Faiver, C., Ingersoll, R., O'Brien, E., & McNally, C. (2001). *Explorations of counseling and spirituality: Philosophical, practical, and personal reflections.* Pacific Grove, CA: Brooks/Cole.

Farley, R. (2002). Racial identities in 2000: The response to the multiple-race response option. In J. Pearlman & M. C. Waters (Eds.), *The new race question: How the census counts multiracial individuals* (pp. 33–61). New York: Russell Sage.

Farmer, R. L. (2009). *Neuroscience and social work practice: The missing link.* Thousand Oaks, CA: Sage.

Feltham, C. (1997). *Which psychotherapy?* London: Sage.

Feminist Therapy Institute. (2000). *Feminist therapy code of ethics.* San Francisco: Author.

Fenichel, O. (1945). *The psychoanalytic theory of neurosis.* New York: Norton.

Fernandes, C. C., Pinto-Duarte, A., Ribeiro, J. A., & Sebastião, A. M. (2008). Postsynaptic action of brain-derived neurotrophic factor attenuates alpha7 nicotinic acetylcholine receptor mediated responses in hippocampal interneurons. *Journal of Neuroscience, 28*(21), 5611–5618.

Fernbacher, S., & Plummer, D. (2005). Cultural influences and considerations in Gestalt therapy. In A. Woldt & S. Toman (Eds.), *Gestalt therapy: History, theory, and practice* (pp. 117–132). Thousand Oaks, CA: Sage.

Festinger, L. (1957). *A theory of cognitive dissonance.* Stanford, CA: Stanford University Press.

Fiedler, F. E. (1950). The concept of an ideal therapeutic relationship. *Journal of Consulting Psychology, 14,* 239–245.

Fiedler, F. E. (1951). Factor analysis of psychoanalytic, nondirective, and Adlerian therapeutic relationships. *Journal of Consulting Psychology, 156,* 32–38.

Field, T., Martinez, A., Nawrocki, T., Pickens, J., Fox, N. A., & Schanberg, S. (1998). Music shifts frontal EEG in depressed adolescents. *Adolescence, 33*(129), 109–116.

Figley, C. R., & Nelson, T. S. (1990). Basic family therapy skills. II: Structural family therapy. *Journal of Marital and Family Therapy, 16,* 68–70.

Fine, R. (1979). *A history of psychoanalysis.* New York: Columbia University Press.

Fisher, H. E. (2004). *Why we love: The nature and chemistry of love.* New York: Henry Holt.

Fisher, H. E., Aron, A., Mashek, D., Strong, G., Li, H., & Brown, L. L. (2002). The neural mechanisms of mate choice: A hypothesis. *Neuroendocrinology Letters, 23*(Suppl. 4), 92–97.

Fleshman, B., & Fryrear, J. (1981). *The arts in therapy.* Chicago: Nelson-Hall.

Flores, M. T., & Carey, G. (Eds.). (2000). *Family therapy with Hispanics: Toward appreciating diversity.* Needham Heights, MA: Allyn & Bacon.

Foa, E. B., & Kozak, M. J. (1986). Emotional processing of fear: Exposure to corrective information. *Psychological Bulletin, 99,* 20–35.

Foa, E. B., & Meadows, E. A. (1997). Psychosocial treatments for post-traumatic stress disorder: A critical review. *Annual Review of Psychology, 48,* 449–480.

Fook, J. (Ed.). (1996). *The reflective researcher.* Sydney, Australia: Allen & Unwin.

Forbach, G. B., Evans, R. G., & Bodine, S. M. (1986). Gender-based schematic processing of self-descriptive information. *Journal of Research in Personality, 49,* 459–468.

Fordham, M. (1996). *Analyst-patient interaction: Collected papers on technique.* New York: Routledge.

Forinash, M. (2005). Music therapy. In C. A. Malchiodi (Ed.), *Expressive therapies* (pp. 46–67). New York: Guilford Press.

Fosha, D., Siegel, D., & Solomon, M. (2009). *The healing power of emotion: Affective neuroscience, development and practice.* New York: W. W. Norton.

Fossati, P., Hevenor, S. J., Graham, S. J., Grady, C., Keightley, M. L., Craik, F., & Mayberg, H. (2003). In search of the emotional self: An fMRI study using positive and negative motional words. *American Journal of Psychiatry, 160*(11), 1938–1945.

Foucault, M. (1973). *The archaeology of knowledge and the discourse on language* (A. Sheridan, Trans.). New York: Pantheon Books.

Foucault, M. (1988). *Madness and civilization: A history of insanity in the age of reason.* New York: Vintage.

Foucault, M. (1995). *Discipline and punish: The birth of the prison.* New York: Vintage.

Fowler, J. W. (1981). *Stages of faith.* San Francisco: Harper & Row.

Frame, M. W. (2000). Constructing religious/spiritual genograms. In R. E. Watts (Ed.), *Techniques in marriage and family counseling* (pp. 69–74). Alexandria, VA: American Counseling Association.

Frame, M. W. (2003). *Integrating religion and spirituality in counseling: A comprehensive approach.* Pacific Grove, CA: Brooks/Cole.

Frame, M. W. (2009). Therapist self-awareness of spirituality. In J. D. Aten & M. M. Leach (Eds.), *Spirituality and the therapeutic process* (pp. 53–74). Washington, DC: American Psychological Association.

France, M. H. (2010). *Naikan: A Buddhist approach to psychotherapy*. Retrieved August 4, 2010, from http://www.educ.uvic.ca/faculty/hfrance/naikan.htm

Frank, J. D. (1973). *Persuasion and healing: A comparative study of psychotherapy*. Baltimore: Johns Hopkins University Press.

Frank, J. D. (1974). Psychotherapy: The restoration of morale. *American Journal of Psychiatry, 131,* 271–274.

Frankl, V. (1955). *The doctor and the soul: An introduction to logotherapy*. New York: Knopf.

Frankl, V. (1963). *Man's search for meaning*. Boston: Beacon.

Frankl, V. (1967). Logotherapy and existentialism. *Psychotherapy, Theory, Research, and Practice, 4,* 138–142.

Frankl, V. (1969). *The will to meaning: Foundations and applications of logotherapy*. New York: New American Library.

Frankl, V. (1978). *The unheard cry for meaning*. New York: Simon & Schuster.

Frankl, V. E. (1970). Fore-runner to existential psychiatry. *Journal of Individual Psychology, 33,* 122–141.

Franklin, C., & Streeter, C. L. (2003). *Solution-focused accountability schools for the twenty-first century: A training manual for Gonzalo Garza High School*. Austin, TX: The Hogg Foundation for Mental Health.

Fredrickson, B. (2009). *Positivity*. New York: Three Rivers Press.

Fredrickson, B. L. (2001). The role of positive emotions in positive psychology: The broaden-and-build theory of positive emotions. *American Psychologist, 56,* 218–226.

Freedman, J., & Combs, G. (1996). *Narrative therapy: The social construction of preferred realities*. New York: Norton.

Freeman, A., & Simon, K. M. (1989). Cognitive therapy of anxiety. In A. Freeman, K. M. Simon, H. Arkowitz, & L. Beutler (Eds.), *Handbook of cognitive therapy* (pp. 347–365). New York: Plenum.

Freeman, J., Epston, D., & Lobovits, D. (1997). *Playful approaches to serious problems: Narrative therapy with children and their families*. New York: W. W. Norton.

Freire, E., Koller, S. H., Piason, A., & da Silva, R. B. (2005). Person-centered therapy with impoverished, maltreated, and neglected children and adolescents in Brazil. *Journal of Mental Health Counseling, 27*(3), 225–237.

Fresco, D. M., Flynn, J. J., Mennin, D. S., & Haigh, A. P. (2011). Mindfulness-based cognitive therapy. In J. D. Hebert & E. M. Forman (Eds.), *Acceptance and mindfulness in cognitive behavior therapy: Understanding and applying the new therapies* (pp. 57–82). Hoboken, NJ: Wiley.

Freud, S. (1900). *The interpretation of dreams* (Vol. 4). In J. Strachey (Ed.), (1974), *Standard edition of the complete psychological works of Sigmund Freud* (Vols. 1–24). London: Hogarth.

Freud, S. (1901). *The psychopathology of everyday life.* (Vol. 6). In J. Strachey (Ed.), (1974), *Standard edition of the complete psychological works of Sigmund Freud* (Vols. 1–24). London: Hogarth.

Freud, S. (1905a). *Jokes and their relation to the unconscious.* (Vols. 8 and 16). In J. Strachey (Ed.), (1974), *Standard edition of the complete psychological works of Sigmund Freud* (Vols. 1–24). London: Hogarth.

Freud, S. (1905b). *Three essays on sexuality* (Vol. 7). In J. Strachey (Ed.), (1974), *Standard edition of the complete psychological works of Sigmund Freud* (Vols. 1–24). London: Hogarth.

Freud, S. (1917). *Introductory lectures on psychoanalysis* (Vols. 15 & 16). In J. Strachey (Ed.), (1974), *Standard edition of the complete psychological works of Sigmund Freud* (Vols. 1–24). London: Hogarth.

Freud, S. (1919). Turnings in the ways of psychoanalytic therapy. *Collected papers* (Vol. 2). London: Hogarth.

Freud, S. (1920). *Beyond the pleasure principle* (Vol. 19). In J. Strachey (Ed.), (1974), *Standard edition of the complete psychological works of Sigmund Freud* (Vols. 1–24). London: Hogarth.

Freud, S. (1923). *The ego and id* (Vol. 19). In J. Strachey (Ed.), (1974), *Standard edition of the complete psychological works of Sigmund Freud* (Vols. 1–24). London: Hogarth.

Freud, S. (1925). Character and anal eroticism. *Collected papers*. London: Hogarth.

Freud, S. (1926). *Inhibitions, symptoms, and anxiety* (Vol. 20). In J. Strachey (Ed.), (1974), *Standard edition of the complete psychological works of Sigmund Freud* (Vols. 1–24). London: Hogarth.

Freud, S. (1933). *New introductory lectures on psychoanalysis*. London: Institute of Psychoanalysis and Hogarth Press.

Freud, A. (1936). *The ego and the mechanisms of defense*. New York: International Universities Press.

Freud, S. (1949). *An outline of psychoanalysis*. New York: Norton.

Freud, S. (1953a). *The interpretation of dreams* (Vols. 4 & 5). In J. Strachey (Ed.), (1974), *Standard edition of the complete psychological works of Sigmund Freud* (Vols. 1–24). London: Hogarth. (Originally published 1900)

Freud, S. (1953b). *Standard edition of the complete psychological works of Sigmund Freud* (Vols. 1–24). London: Hogarth.

Freud, S. (1954). *The origins of psychoanalysis*. New York: Basic Books.

Freud, S. (1961). *The future of an illusion.* (J. Strachey, Ed. & Trans.). New York: Norton. (Original work published in 1927)

Freud, S. (1963). Uber Coca [On Coca]. *The cocaine papers.* Vienna and Zurich. (Originally published 1884)

Freud, A. (1965). *The psycho-analytic treatment of children.* New York: International Universities Press.

Freud, S. (1974). *The ego and the id.* London: Hogarth. (Original work published 1923)

Freud, S. (1984). *The neuro-psychoses of defence.* (Standard Edition, Vol. 3), 41–61.

Frew, J. (2008). Gestalt therapy. In J. Frew & M. D. Spiegler (Eds.), *Contemporary psychotherapies for a diverse world* (pp. 228–274). Boston: Lahaska Press.

Frew, J. E. (1986). The functions and patterns of occurrence of individual contact styles during the development phase of the Gestalt group. *The Gestalt Journal, 9*(1), 55–70.

Frewen, P. A., Dozois, D. J., & Lanius, R. A. (2008). Neuroimaging studies of psychological interventions for mood and anxiety disorders: Empirical and methodological review. *Clinical Psychology Review, 28,* 228–246.

Friedman, E. H. (1991). Bowen theory and therapy. In A. S. Gurman & D. P. Kniskern (Eds.), *Handbook of family therapy* (Vol. II, pp. 134–170). New York: Brunner/Mazel.

Friedman, L. J. (1999). *Identity's architect: A biography of Erik Erikson.* New York: Scribner.

Frodl, T., Reinhold, E., Koutsouleris, N., Donohue, G., Bondy, B., Reiser, M., . . . Meisenzahl, E. N. (2010). Childhood stress, serotonin, transporter gene and brain structures in major depression. *Neuropsychopharmacology, 35*(6), 1383–1390.

Fuchs, T. (2004). Neurobiology and psychotherapy: An emerging dialogue. *Current Opinion in Psychiatry, 17,* 479–485.

Fujita, C. (1986). *Morita therapy: Psychotherapeutic system for neurosis.* Tokyo: Igaku-Shoin.

Fukuyama, M. A., & Sevig, T. D. (1999). *Integrating spirituality into multicultural counseling.* Thousand Oaks, CA: Sage.

Fuller, R. C. (2001). *Spiritual but not religious.* New York: Oxford University Press.

Furmark, T., Tillfors, M., Marteindottir, I., Fischer, H., Pissiota, A., Långström, B., & Fredrikson, M. (2002). Common changes in cerebral blood flow in patients with social phobia treated with citalopram or cognitive behavioral therapy. *Archives of General Psychiatry, 59,* 425–433. doi:10.1001/archpsyc.59.5.425

Gallup, G., Jr. (2002). *The Gallup poll: Public opinion 2001.* Wilmington, DE: Scholarly Resources.

Gallup. G., Jr., & Lindsay, D. M. (1999). *Surveying the religious landscape: Trends in U.S. beliefs.* Harrisburg, PA: Morehouse.

Ganley, A. L. (1988). Feminist therapy with male clients. In M. A. Dutton-Douglas & L. E. Walker (Eds.), *Feminist psychotherapies: Integration of therapeutic and feminist systems* (pp. 91–117). Norwood, NJ: Ablex.

Garbarino, J. (1991). The human ecology in early risk. In S. J. Meisels & J. Shankoff (Eds.), *Handbook of early childhood intervention* (pp. 78–96). New York: Cambridge University Press.

Garbarino, J. (1994). *Raising children in a socially toxic environment.* San Francisco: Jossey-Bass.

Gardner, H. E. (1983). *Frames of mind: The theory of multiple intelligences.* New York: Basic Books.

Gardner, H. E. (2000). *Intelligence reframed: Multiple intelligences for the twenty-first century.* New York: Basic Books.

Garfield, S. (1987). Toward a scientifically oriented eclecticism. *Scandinavian Journal of Behavior Therapy, 16,* 95–109.

Gaudiano, B. A., & Herbert, J. D. (2006). Acute treatment of inpatients with psychotic symptoms using acceptance and commitment therapy: Pilot results. *Behaviour Research and Therapy, 44,* 415–437.

Gay, P. (1988). *Freud: A life for our time.* New Haven, CT: Yale University Press.

Gazzaniga, M. S. (2004). *The cognitive neurosciences III.* Cambridge, MA: MIT Press.

Gazzaniga, M. S., Ivry, R. B., & Mangun, G. R. (2002). *Cognitive neuroscience: The biology of the mind* (2nd ed.). New York: Norton.

Geertz, C. (1973). *Thick description: Toward an interpretive culture.* New York: Basic Books.

Geertz, C. (1986). Making experiences, authoring selves. In V. W. Turner & E. Bruner, *The anthropology of experience* (pp. 373–380). Chicago: University of Chicago Press.

Gellner, E. (1985). *The psychoanalytic movement.* London: Paladen Books.

Gelso, C. G., & Woodhouse, S. (2004). Toward a positive psychology: Focus on human strength. In W. B. Walsh (Ed.), *Counseling psychology and human strengths* (pp. 344–369). New York: Lawrence Erlbaum.

Gelso, C. J., & Carter, J. A. (1985). The relationship in counseling and psychotherapy: Components, consequences, and theoretical antecedents. *The Counseling Psychologist, 13,* 155–244.

Gendlin, E. T. (1988). Carl Rogers (1902–1987). *American Psychologist, 43,* 127–128.

Gergen, K. J. (1991). *The saturated self: Dilemmas of identity in contemporary life.* New York: Basic Books.

Gergen, K. J. (1994). *Realities and relationships: Soundings in social construction.* Cambridge, MA: Harvard University Press.

Gergen, K. J. (1999). *An invitation to social construction.* Thousand Oaks, CA: Sage.

Gergen, K. J. (2000). The self: Transfiguration by technology. In D. Fee (Ed.), *Pathology and the postmodern.* London: Sage.

Germer, C. K., Siegel, R. D., & Fulton, P. R. (2005). *Mindfulness and psychotherapy.* New York: Guilford.

Gibbard, I., & Hanley, T. (2008). A five-year evaluation of the effectiveness of person-centred counselling in routine clinical practice in primary care. *Counselling and Psychotherapy Research, 8,* 215–222. doi:10.1080/14733140802305440

Gibbs. L. (2003). *Evidence-based practice for the helping professions.* New York: Wadsworth.

Gibson, D. G. (1999). *A monograph: Summary of the research related to the use and efficacy of the systematic training for effective parenting program 1976–1999.* Circle Pines, MN: American Guidance Services.

Gilliland, B. E., & James, R. K. (1998). *Theories and strategies in counseling and psychotherapy* (4th ed.). Needham Heights, MA: Allyn & Bacon.

Gingerich, W., & Eisengrat, S. (2000). Solution-focused brief therapy: A review of the outcome research. *Family Process, 39,* 477–498.

Gingerich, W. J., Kim, J. S., & MacDonald, A. J. (2012). Solution-focused brief therapy outcome research. In C. Franklin, T. S. Trepper, W. J. Gingerich, & E. E. McCollum (Eds.), *Solution-focused brief therapy: A handbook of evidence-based practice* (pp. 95–111). New York: Oxford University Press.

Gingsburg, K. R. (2007). The importance of play in promoting healthy child development and maintaining strong parent-child bonds. *Pediatrics, 119*(1), 182–191.

Gladding, S. T. (2007). *Family therapy: History, theory, and practice* (4th ed.). Upper Saddle River, NJ: Pearson.

Glasser, N. (1989). *Control theory in the practice of reality therapy: Case studies.* New York: Harper Perennial.

Glasser, W. (1961). *Mental health or mental illness?* New York: Harper & Row.

Glasser, W. (1965). *Reality therapy: A new approach to psychiatry.* New York: Harper & Row.

Glasser, W. (1969). *Schools without failure.* New York: Harper & Row.

Glasser, W. (1976). *Positive addiction.* New York: HarperCollins.

Glasser, W. (1981). *Stations of the mind.* New York: Harper & Row.

Glasser, W. (1984). *Take effective control of your life.* New York: Harper & Row.

Glasser, W. (1985). *Control theory: A new explanation of how we control our lives.* New York: Harper & Row.

Glasser, W. (1986). *Control theory in the classroom.* New York: Harper & Row.

Glasser, W. (1990). *The quality school.* New York: HarperCollins.

Glasser, W. (1991). *The quality school teachers.* New York: HarperCollins.

Glasser, W. (1992). *The quality school: Managing students without coercion.* New York: Harper Perennial.

Glasser, W. (1998a). *Choice theory: A new psychology for personal freedom.* New York: HarperCollins.

Glasser, W. (1998b). *The quality school* (Rev. ed.). New York: Harper & Row.

Glasser, W. (2000a). *Counseling with choice theory.* New York: HarperCollins.

Glasser, W. (2000b). *Every student can succeed.* Chatsworth, CA: William Glasser Institute.

Glasser, W. (2003). *Warning: Psychiatry can be hazardous to your mental health.* New York: HarperCollins.

Glasser, W., & Glasser, C. (1999). *The language of choice theory.* New York: HarperCollins.

Glasser, W., & Glasser, C. (2000). *Getting together and staying together.* New York: HarperCollins.

Glasser, W., & Wubbolding, R. (1997). Beyond blame: A lead management approach. *Reaching Today's Youth, 1*(4), 40–42.

Glauser, A. S., & Bozarth, J. D. (2001). Person-centered counseling: The culture within. *Journal of Counseling and Development, 79,* 142–147.

Gold, C. (2007). Music therapy improves symptoms in adults hospitalised with schizophrenia. *Evidence-Based Mental Health, 10*(3), 77.

Gold, C., Heldal, T. O., Dahle, T., & Wigram, T. (2005). Music therapy for schizophrenia or schizophrenia-like illnesses. *Cochrane Database of Systematic Reviews,* CD004025. Retrieved from http://onlinelibrary.wiley.com/doi/10.1002/14651858.CD004025.pub2/pdf/standard

Gold, J. (1996*). Key concepts in psychotherapy integration.* New York: Plenum Press.

Goldenberg, H., & Goldenberg, I. (2002). *Counseling today's families.* Pacific Grove, CA: Brooks/Cole.

Goldfried, M. R. (2001). *How therapists change: Personal and professional reflections.* Washington, DC: American Psychological Association.

Goldfried, M. R., Pachankis, & Bell, A. C. (2005). A history of psychotherapy integration. In J. C. Norcross & M. R. Goldfried (Eds.), *Handbook of psychotherapy integration* (2nd ed., pp. 24–66). New York: Oxford University Press.

Goldstein, H. (1990). Strength or pathology: Ethical and rhetorical contrasts in approaches to practice. *Families in Society, 71,* 267–275.

Goleman, D. (2006). *Emotional intelligence: Why it can matter more than IQ* (10th ed.). New York: Bantam Books.

Gonsiorek, J. C. (1993). Threat, stress, and adjustment: Mental health and the workplace for gay and lesbian individuals. In L. Diamont (Ed.), *Homosexual issues in the workplace* (pp. 243–264). Washington, DC: Taylor & Francis.

González, R., Biever, J. L., & Gardner, G. T. (1994). The multicultural perspective in therapy: A social constructionist approach. *Psychotherapy, 31,* 515–524.

González-Prendes, A., Hindo, C., & Pardo, Y. F. (2011). Cultural values integration in cognitive-behavioral therapy for a Latino with depression. *Clinical Case Studies, 10*(5), 376–394.

Goodenough, F. (1926). *Measurement of intelligence by drawings.* New York: World Book.

Goodenough, F. (1975). *Measures of intelligence by drawings.* New York: Arno Press.

Goodfellow, L. M. (2003). The effects of therapeutic back massage on psychophysiologic variables and immune function in spouses of patients with cancer. *Nursing Research, 52,* 318–328.

Gorsuch, R. L., & McPherson, S. E. (1989). Intrinsic/extrinsic measurement: II/E-Revised and single-item scales. *Journal of the Scientific Study of Religion, 28*, 348–354.

Goto, K. (1988). Shinkeishitsu treatment by Morita therapy in its original form. *International Bulletin of Morita Therapy, 1*(2), 37–42.

Graham, M. (2005). An African-centered paradigm for psychological and spiritual healing. In R. Moodley & W. West (Eds.), *Traditional healing practices into counseling and psychotherapy* (pp. 210–220). Thousand Oaks, CA: Sage.

Grand, D. (2013). *Brainspotting: The revolutionary new therapy for rapid and effective change.* Boulder, CO: Sounds True.

Grawe, K. (2007). *Neuropsychotherapy: How the neurosciences inform effective psychotherapy.* New York: Psychology Press.

Grawe. L., Donati, R., & Bernauer, F. (1998). *Psychotherapy in transition.* Seattle: Hogrefe & Huber.

Gray, M. (2011). Back to basics: A critique of the strengths perspective in social work. *Families in Society, 92*(1), 5–11.

Gray-Little, B., & Hafdahl, A. R. (2000). Factors influencing racial comparisons of self-esteem: A quantitative review. *Psychological Bulletin, 126*, 26–54.

Grayson, P., Schwartz, V., & Commerford, M. (1997). Brave new world? Drug therapy and college mental health. *Journal of College Student Psychotherapy, 11*, 23–32.

Greenson, R. R. (1967). *The technique and practice of psychoanalysis* (Vol. 1). New York: International Universities Press.

Greenstein, M., & Breitbart, W. (2000). Cancer and the experience of meaning: A group psychotherapy program for people with cancer. *American Journal of Psychotherapy, 54*, 486–500.

Greever, K. B., Tseng, M. S., & Friedland, B. U. (1973). Development of the Social Interest Index. *Journal of Consulting and Clinical Psychology, 41*, 454–458.

Greig, R. (2003). Ethnic identity development: Implications for mental health in African American and Hispanic adolescents. *Issues in Mental Health Nursing, 24*, 317–331.

Grepmair, L., Mitterlehner, F., Loew, T., & Nickel, M. (2007). Promotion of mindfulness in psychotherapists in training: Preliminary study. *European Psychiatry, 22*, 485–489.

Grepmair, L., Mitterlehner, F., Loew, T., Bachler, E., Rother, W., & Nickel, M. (2007). Promoting mindfulness in psychotherapists in training influences the treatment results of their patients: A randomized, double-blind, controlled study. *Psychotherapy and Psychosomatics, 76*, 332–338.

Guerin, P. J. (1976). *Family therapy: Theory and practice.* New York: Gardner Press.

Guerin, P. J., Fogarty, T. F., Fay, L. F., & Kautto, J. G. (1996). *Working with relationship triangles: The one-two-three of psychotherapy.* New York: Guilford.

Guerney, L. (2001). Child centered play therapy. *International Journal of Play Therapy, 10*(2), 13–31.

Haaga, D. A., Rabois, D., & Brody, C. (1999). Cognitive behavior therapy. In M. Hersen & A. Bellack (Eds.), *Handbook of comparative interventions for adult disorders* (2nd ed., pp. 48–61). New York: John Wiley.

Hage, S. M. (2006). A closer look at the role of spirituality in psychology training. *Professional Psychology: Research and Practice, 37*, 303–310.

Haley, J. (1976). *Problem-solving therapy.* San Francisco: Jossey-Bass.

Haley, J. (1980). *Leaving home: The therapy of disturbed young people.* New York: McGraw-Hill.

Haley, J. (1984) *Ordeal therapy: Unusual ways to change behavior.* San Francisco: Jossey-Bass.

Hambidge, G. (1955). Structured play therapy. *American Journal of Orthopsychiatry, 25*, 601–607.

Hancock, K. A. (2000). Lesbian, gay, and bisexual lives: Basic issues in psychotherapy training and practice. In B. Greene & G. L. Croom (Eds.), *Education, research, and practice in lesbian, gay, bisexual, and transgendered psychology: A resource manual* (pp. 91–130). Thousand Oaks, CA: Sage.

Hanna, F. J., Bemak, F., & Chi-Ying Chung, R. (1999). Toward a new paradigm for multicultural counseling. *Journal of Counseling and Development, 77*, 125–134.

Hanson, R. (2010). The brain: So what? The benefits and pitfalls of applying neuroscience to psychotherapy. *Wise Brain Bulletin, 4*(2), 1–12.

Hanson, R. (2013). *Hardwiring happiness: The new brain science of contentment, calm, and confidence.* New York: Harmony Books.

Harman, J. L. (1997). Rogers' late conceptualization of the fully functioning individual: Correspondence and contrasts with Buddhist psychology. *The Person-Centered Journal, 4*, 423–431.

Harper, F., & McFadden, J. (2003). *Culture and counseling: New Approaches.* Boston, MA: Allyn & Bacon.

Harris, D. B. (1963). *Children's drawings as measures of intellectual maturity.* New York: Harcourt, Brace & World.

Harris, J. E. (2007). *Integrative multitheoretical psychotherapy.* Boston: Lahaska Press.

Harris, R. (2006). Embracing your demons: An overview of acceptance and commitment therapy. *Psychotherapy in Australia, 12*(4), 70–76.

Hartocollis, P. (2005). Origins and evolution of the Oedipus complex as conceptualized by Freud. *Psychoanalytic Review, 92*(3), 315–335.

Harwood, R. L., Miller, J. G., & Irizarry, N. L. (1995). *Culture and attachment: Perceptions of the child in context.* New York: Guilford.

Hass-Cohen, N. (2003). Art therapy mind body approaches. *Progress Family Systems Research and Therapy, 12*, 24–38.

Hass-Cohen, N. (2012). *Neuroscience in art therapy.* Retrieved January 2, 2014, from http://neuroarththerapy.blogspot.com/

Hathaway, W. L. (2005, August). *Preliminary practice guidelines for religious/spiritual issues.* Paper presented at the 113th Annual Convention of the American Psychological Association, New Orleans, LA.

Hathaway, W. L., & Ripley, J. S. (2009). Ethical concerns around spirituality and religion in clinical practice. In J. D. Aten & M. M. Leach (Eds.), *Spirituality and the therapeutic process* (pp. 25–52). Washington, DC: American Psychological Association.

Hawaii Department of Health, Child and Adolescent Mental Health Division. (2007). *2007 biennial report: Effective psychosocial interventions for youth with behavioral and emotional needs.* Honolulu, HI: Author.

Hayes, S. C. (2004). Acceptance and commitment therapy, relational frame theory, and the third wave of behavioral and cognitive therapies. *Behavior Therapy, 35,* 639–665.

Hayes, S. C., Barnes-Holmes, D., & Roche, B. (2001). *Relational frame theory: A post-Skinnerian account of human language and cognition.* New York: Kluwer Academic/Plenum.

Hayes, S. C., Bissett, R., Korn, S., Zettle, R. D., Rosenfarb, I., Cooper, L., & Grundt, A. (1999). The impact of acceptance versus control rationales on pain tolerance. *Psychological Record, 49*(1), 33–47.

Hayes, S. C., Follette, V. M., & Linehan, M. M. (Eds.). (2004). *Mindfulness and acceptance: Expanding the cognitive-behavioral tradition.* New York: Guilford Press.

Hayes, S. C., Luoma, J. B., Bond, F. W., Masuda, A., & Lillis, J. (2006). Acceptance and commitment therapy: Model, processes and outcomes. *Behaviour Research and Therapy, 44*(1), 1–25.

Hayes, S. C., Masuda, A., & De Mey, H. (2003). Acceptance and commitment therapy and the third wave of behavior therapy. *Gedragstherapie, 2,* 69–96.

Hayes, S. C., & Smith, S. (2005). *Get out of your mind and into your life.* Oakland, CA: New Harbinger.

Hayes, S. C., Strosahl, K. D., & Houts, A. (Eds.). (2005). *A practical guide to acceptance and commitment therapy.* New York: Springer.

Hayes, S. C., Strosahl, K. D., & Wilson, K. G. (1999). *Acceptance and commitment therapy: An experiential approach to behavior change.* New York: Guilford.

Hayes, S. C., Strosahl, K. D., & Wilson, K. G. (2011). *Acceptance and commitment therapy: The process and practice of mindful change* (2nd ed.). New York: Guilford.

Hays, P. A. (1995). Multicultural applications of cognitive-behavior therapy. *Professional Psychology: Research and Practice, 26*(3), 309–315.

Hays, P. A. (2009). Integrating evidence-based practice, cognitive-behavioral therapy and multicultural therapy: Ten steps for culturally competent practice. *Professional Psychology: Research and Practice, 40*(4), 354–360.

Hebb, D. O. (1949). *The organization of behavior: A neuropsychological theory.* New York: Wiley.

Heffner, C. L. (2003, August 12). Counseling the gay and lesbian client: Treatment issues and conversion therapy. *AllPsych.* Available at http://allpsych.com/journal/counselinggay.html

Heidegger, M. (1962). *Being and time.* New York: Harper & Row.

Heidenreich. T., Tuin, I., Pflug, B., Michal, M., & Michalak, J. (2006). Mindfulness-based cognitive therapy for persistent insomnia: A pilot study. *Psychotherapy and Psychosomatics, 75,* 188–189.

Hellweg, P. (2010). *The American heritage college dictionary* (4th ed.). Boston: Houghton Mifflin Harcourt.

Helms, J. E. (1984). Toward a theoretical model of the effects of race on counseling: A Black and White model. *The Counseling Psychologist, 12,* 153–165.

Helms, J. E. (1990). *Black and White racial identity.* Westport, CT: Greenwood.

Helms, J. E. (1995). An update of Helm's White and people of color of racial identity models. In J. G. Ponterotto, J. M. Casas, L. A. Suzuki, & C.M. Alexander (Eds.), *Handbook of multicultural counseling* (pp. 181–191). Thousand Oaks, CA: Sage.

Heppner, R. R., Rogers, M. E., & Lee, L. A. (1984). Carl Rogers: Reflections on his life. *Journal of Counseling and Development, 63*(1), 14–20.

Hergenhahn, B. R. (1994). Psychology's cognitive revolution. *American Psychologist, 49,* 816–817.

Herlihy, B., & Corey, G. (2005). Feminine therapy. In G. Corey (Ed.), *Theory and practice of counseling and psychotherapy* (7th ed.). Belmont, CA: Brooks/Cole.

Hernandez-Reif, M., Ironson, G., Field, T., Hurley, J., Katz, G., & Diego, M. (2004). Breast cancer patients have improved immune and neuroendocrine functions following massage therapy. *Journal of Psychosomatic Research, 57,* 45–52.

Herring, R. D. (1999). *Counseling with Native Americans and Alaska Natives.* Thousand Oaks, CA: Sage.

Hettema, J., Steele, J., & Miller, W. R. (2005). Motivational interviewing. *Annual Review of Clinical Psychology, 1,* 91–111.

Heward, W. L., Heron, T. E., Neef, N. A., Peterson, S. M., Sainato, D. M., Cartledge, G. Y., . . . Dardig, J. C. (2005). *Focus on behavior analysis in education: Achievements, challenges, and opportunities.* Upper Saddle River, NJ: Prentice Hall/Merrill.

Hill, A. (2004). Art therapy. In D. Edwards (Ed.), *Art versus illness.* London: Sage.

Hill, C. (2004). *Helping skills: Facilitating exploration, insight, and action* (2nd ed.). Washington, DC: American Psychological Association.

Hill, M., & Ballou, M. (2005). *The foundation and future of feminist therapy.* New York: Haworth.

Hines, P. M., Preto, N. G., McGoldrick, M., Almeida, R. & Weltman, S. (1999). Culture and the family life cycle. In B. Carter & M. McGoldrick (Eds.), *The expanded family life cycle* (3rd ed., pp. 69–87). Boston: Allyn & Bacon.

Hinton, G. (1992). How neural networks learn from experience. *Scientific American, 267*(3), 144–151.

Hitlin, S., Scott Brown, J., & Elder, G. H. Jr. (2007). Measuring Latinos: Racial classification and self-understandings. *Social Forces, 86*(2), 587–611.

Ho, D. Y. F. (1995a). Internalized culture, culturocentrism, and transcendence. *The Counseling Psychologist, 23*, 4–25.

Ho, D. Y. F. (1995b). Selfhood and identity in Confucianism, Taoism, Buddhism, and Hinduism: Contrasts with the West. *Journal for the Theory of Social Behavior, 25*(2), 115–139.

Ho, D. Y. F. (1999). Relational counseling: An Asian perspective on therapeutic intervention. *Psychologische Beitrage, 41*, 98–112. (Originally published in R. Roth (Ed.), *Psychologists facing the challenge of a global culture with human rights and mental health*, pp. 281–297. Lengerich, Germany: Pabst Science Publishers, 1999)

Hodge, D. R. (2005). Spiritual lifemaps: A client-centered pictorial instrument for spiritual assessment, planning, and intervention. *Social Work, 46*, 203–214.

Hodgins, D. C., Ching, L. E., & McEwen, J. (2009). Strength of commitment language in motivational interviewing and gambling outcomes. *Psychology of Addictive Behaviors, 23*, 122–130.

Hoffman, E. (1994). *The drive for self: Alfred Adler and the founding of individual psychology.* Reading, MA: Addison-Wesley.

Hoffman, L. (2005). *Depth psychotherapy and the empirically supported movement: Critical issues.* Retrieved February 15, 2011, from http//:www.depth-psychotherapy-network.com/Professional-Section/Empirically/Hoffman_EST_1.htm

Hoffman, L., Dias, J., & Sohom, H. C. (2012, August). Existential-humanistic therapy as a model for evidence-based practice. In S. Rubin (Chair), *Evidence in support of existential-humanistic psychology: Revitalizing the "third force."* Symposium presented at the 120th Annual Convention of the American Psychological Association, Orlando, FL.

Hofmann, S. G., Sawyer, A. T., Witt, A. A., & Oh, D. (2010). The effect of mindfulness-based therapy on anxiety and depression: A meta-analytic review. *Journal of Consulting and Clinical Psychology, 78*(2), 169–183. doi:10.1037/a0018555

Hogg Foundation for Mental Health. (2006). *Cultural adaptation: Providing evidence-based practices to populations of color.* Retrieved May 22, 2008, from http://www.hogg.utexas.edu/programs_cc.html

Holdstock, L. (2000). *Re-examining psychology: Critical perspectives and African insights.* London: Routledge.

Holeman, V. T. (2004). *Reconcilable differences: Hope and healing for troubled marriages.* Downers Grove, IL: InterVarsity Press.

Hollon, S. D., & Beck, A. T. (1994). Cognitive and cognitive-behavioral therapies. In A. E. Bergin & S. L. Garfield (Eds.), *Handbook of psychotherapy and behavior change* (4th ed., pp. 428–466).

Holzer, P. J., Bromfield, L. M., & Richardson, N., & Higgins, D. J. (2006). Child abuse prevention: What works? The effectiveness of parent education programs for preventing child maltreatment. *Australian Institute of Family Studies* (Research Brief No. 1). Retrieved from http://www.aifs.gov.au/nch/pubs/brief/rb1/rb1.html

Homeyer, L. E., & DeFrance, E. (2005). Play therapy. In C. A. Malchiodi (Ed.), *Expressive therapies.* New York: Guilford.

Homeyer, L. E., & Morrison, M. O. (2008). *Play therapy: Practice, issues, and trends.* Urbana: Board of Trustees of the University of Illinois.

Homeyer, L. E., & Sweeney, D. S. (1998). *Sandtray: A practical manual.* Canyon Lake, TX: Lindan Press.

Hopcke, R. (1999). *A guided tour of the collected works of C. G. Jung.* Boston: Shambhala.

Horney, K. (1926). The flight from womanhood: The masculinity complex in women as viewed by men and by women. *International Journal of Psychoanalysis, 7*, 324–329.

Horney, K. (1937). *The neurotic personality of our time.* New York: Norton.

Hsu, W-S., & Wang, C. (2011). Integrating Asian clients' filial piety beliefs in solution-focused brief therapy. *International Journal for the Advancement of Counseling, 33*(4), 322–334.

Hubble, M. A., Duncan, B. L., & Miller, S. D. (Eds.). (1999). *The heart and soul of change: What works in therapy.* Washington, DC: American Psychological Association.

Hughes, D., Rodriguez, J., Smith, E. P., Johnson, D. J., Stevenson, H. C., & Spicer, P. (2006). Parents' ethnic-racial socialization practices: A review of research and directions for future study. *Developmental Psychology, 42*, 747–770.

Human Rights Campaign. (2006). *The state of the workplace for lesbian, gay, bisexual, and transgender Americans—2004.* Retrieved January 15, 2006, from http://www.hrc.orgh

Hunter, R. J. (2005). Pastoral counseling. *Dictionary of pastoral care and counseling.* Nashville, TN: Abingdon Press.

Hycner, R., & Jacobs, L. (1995). *The healing relationship in Gestalt therapy: A dialogic/self psychology approach.* Highland, NY: Gestalt Journal Press.

Ilardi, S., & Feldman, D. (2001). The cognitive neuroscience paradigm: A unifying metatheoretical framework for the science and practice of clinical psychology. *Journal of Clinical Psychology, 57*, 1067–1088.

Ingalhalikar, M., Smith, A., Parker, D., Satterthwaite, T. D., Elliott, M. A., Ruparel, K., . . . Verma, R. (2013). Sex differences in the structural connectome of the human brain. *Proceedings of the National Academy of Sciences, 111*(2), 823–828. doi:10.1073/pnas.1316909110

Ingersoll, R. E., & Brennan, C. (2001). Positivism-plus: A constructivist approach to teaching psychopharmacology to counselors. In K. Eriksen & G. McAuliffe (Eds.), *Teaching counselors and therapists: Constructivist and developmental course design* (pp. 335–354). Westport, CT: Bergin & Garvey.

Ingoldsby, B., & Smith, S. (1995). *Families in multicultural perspective.* New York: Guilford.

Isaacs, M. R., Huang, L. N., Hernandez, M., & Echo-Hawk, H. (2005). *The road to evidence: The intersection of evidence-based practices and cultural competence in children's mental health.* Washington, DC: National Alliance of Multi-Ethnic Behavioral Health Associations.

Ishii, H. (2000). *The Naikan therapy: Personal history.* Toki, Japan: The Yasuda Life Social Work Foundation.

Ivey, A. E., D'Andrea, M., Ivey, M. B., & Simek-Morgan, L. (2002). *Theories of counseling and psychotherapy: A multicultural perspective* (5th ed.). Boston: Allyn & Bacon.

Ivey, A., D'Andrea, M., Ivey, M. B., & Simek-Morgan, L. (2007). *Theories of counseling and psychotherapy: A multicultural perspective* (6th ed.). Boston: Allyn & Bacon.

Ivey, A., & Ivey, M. B. (2001). Developmental counseling and therapy and multicultural counseling and therapy: Metatheory, contextual consciousness, and action. In D. C. Locke, J. Myers, & E. Herr (Eds.), *The handbook of counseling* (pp. 219–238). Newbury Park, CA: Sage.

Ivey, A. E., Ivey, M. B., Zalaquett, C., & Quirk, K. (2009. December). Counseling and neuroscience: The cutting edge of the coming decade. *Counseling Today, 53,* 44–48. Retrieved from http://ct.counseling.org/2009/12/reader-viewpoint-counseling-and-neuroscience-the-cutting-edge-of-the-coming-decade

Iwamasa, G. Y. (1997). Behavior therapy and a culturally diverse society: Forging an alliance. *Behavior Therapy, 28*(3), 347–358.

Jackson, B. (1990, September). *Building a multicultural school.* Paper presented to the Amherst Regional School System, Amherst, MA.

Jackson, P. Z., & McKergow, M. (2002). *The solutions focus: The SIMPLE way to positive change.* Clerkenwell, London: Nicholas Brealey Publishing.

Jacobson, E. (1938). *Progressive relaxation.* Chicago: University of Chicago Press.

Jacobson, N. S., & Christensen, A. (1996). *Acceptance and change in couple therapy: A therapist's guide to transforming relationship.* New York: Norton.

Janis, I. L. & Mann, L. (1977). *Decision making: A psychological analysis of conflict, choice, and commitment.* New York: Free Press.

Jensen, J. P., & Bergin, A. E. (1988). Mental health values of professional therapists: A national interdisciplinary survey. *Professional Psychology: Research and Practice, 19*(3), 290–297.

Jevne, R. F., & Miller, J. E. (1999). *Finding hope: Ways to see life in a brighter hope.* Fort Wayne, Indiana: Willowgreen Publishing.

Johnson, D. R. (1999). *Essays on the creative arts therapies: Imagining the birth of a profession.* Springfield, IL: Charles C Thomas.

Johnson, S. M., & Greenberg, L. S. (1994). *The heart of the matter: Perspectives on emotions in marital therapy.* New York: Brunner/Mazel.

Jokić-Begić, N. (2010). Cognitive-behavioral therapy and neuroscience: Towards closer integration. *Psychological Topics, 19*(2), 235–254.

Jones, E. L. (1953). *The life and work of Sigmund Freud.* New York: Basic Books.

Jones, E. L. (1955). *The life and works of Sigmund Freud* (Vol. 2). New York: Basic Books.

Jones-Smith, E. (2008). *Nurturing nonviolent children.* Santa Barbara, CA: Praeger.

Jones-Smith, E. (2011). *Spotlighting the strengths of every single student: Why schools need a strengths-based approach.* Santa Barbara, CA: Praeger.

Jones-Smith, E. (2014). *Strengths-based therapy: Connecting, theory, and skills.* Thousand Oaks, CA: Sage.

Jourdain, R. (1997). *Music, the brain and ecstasy.* New York: William Morrow.

Julien, R. M. (2001). *A primer of drug action* (9th ed.). New York: Worth.

Julien, R. M., & Lange, D. E. (2001). Integration of drugs and psychological therapies in treating mental and behavioral disorders. In R. M. Julien (Ed.), *A primer of drug action* (9th ed., pp. 543–578). New York: Worth.

Jung, C. G. (1904–1907). *Studies in word association. Collected works* (Vol. 2). London: Routledge & K. Paul.

Jung, C. G. (1911/1956). *Symbols of transformation. Collected works* (Vol. 5). Princeton, NJ: Princeton University Press. (Original work published 1911)

Jung, C. G. (1912). *Psychology of the unconscious: A study of the transformations and symbolisms of the libido.* Authorized transl. by Beatrice M. Hinkle, 1916. New York: Moffat, Yard and Company.

Jung, C. G. (1921/1971). *Psychological types. Collected works* (Vol. 6). Princeton, NJ: Princeton University Press. (Original work published 1912)

Jung, C. G. (1953). *Two essays on analytic psychology.* Princeton, NJ: Princeton University Press.

Jung, C. G. (1954). *Analytical psychology and education. The development of personality. Collected works* (Vol. 17, pp. 63–132). Princeton, NJ: Princeton University Press. (Original work published 1926)

Jung, C. G. (1961). *Memories, dreams, reflections.* Ed. Aniela Jaffe. New York: Random House.

Jung, C. G. (1965). *Memories, dreams, reflections.* New Jersey: Princeton University Press.

Jung, C. G. (1970). Symbols and the interpretation of dreams. In *The symbolic life. Collected works* (Vol. 18, pp. 185–266). Princeton, NJ: Princeton University Press. (Original work published 1950)

Jung, C. G. (2007). *Red book*. New York: Norton.

Just the Facts Coalition. (2008*). Just the facts about sexual orientation and youth: A primer for principals, educators, and school personnel*. Washington, DC: American Psychological Association. Retrieved August 16, 2010, from http://www.apa.org/pi/lgbc/publications/justthefactsd.html

Kabat-Zinn, J. (1990). *Full catastrophe living: Using the wisdom of your body and mind to face stress, pain, and illness*. New York: Delacorte.

Kabat-Zinn, J. (1994). *Wherever you go there you are: Mindfulness meditation in everyday life*. New York: Hyperion.

Kabat-Zinn, J. (2005). *Wherever you go, there you are: Mindfulness meditation in everyday life* (10th ed.). New York: Hyperion.

Kalff, D. (1980). *Sandplay: A psychotherapeutic approach to the psyche*. San Francisco: Browser.

Kandel, E. R. (1998). A new intellectual framework for psychiatry. *American Journal of Psychiatry, 155,* 457–469. Retrieved from http://ajp.psychiatryonline.org/article.aspx?articleid=172780

Kandel, E. R. (2000). *The molecular biology of memory storage: A dialog between genes and synapses*. Nobel Lecture, December 8, 2000, Stockholm.

Kandel, E. R. (2001). Psychotherapy and the single synapse: The impact of psychiatric thought on neurobiological research. *Journal of Neuropsychiatry and Clinical Neurosciences, 13,* 290–300.

Kandel, E. R. (2005). *Psychiatry, psychoanalysis, and the new biology of mind*. Washington, DC: American Psychiatric.

Kanfer, F. H., & Schefft, B. K. (1988). *Guiding the process of therapeutic change*. Champaign, IL: Research Press.

Kantrowitz, R. E., & Ballou, M. (1992). A feminist critique of cognitive-behavioral therapy. In L. S. Brown & M. Ballou (Eds.), *Personality and psychopathology: Feminist appraisals* (pp. 13–51). Oxford, UK: Oxford University Press.

Kaplan, D. M. (2000). Where are our giants? *The Family Digest, 12,* 4, 1,6.

Kaplan, S. (1995). The restorative benefits of nature: Toward an integrative framework. *Journal of Environmental Psychology, 15,* 169–182.

Karenga, M. (1994). *Maat: The moral ideal in ancient Egypt: A study of classical African ethics* (Vol. 1). Unpublished doctoral dissertation. University of Southern California, Los Angeles.

Katz, M. (1997). *On playing a poor hand well*. New York: Norton.

Kaut, K. P., & Dickinson, J. A. (2007). The mental health practitioner and psychopharmacology. *Journal of Mental Health Counseling, 29*(3), 204–225.

Kazdin, A. E. (2001). *Behavior modification in applied settings* (6th ed.). Pacific Grove, CA: Brooks/Cole.

Keen, E. (1970). *Three faces of being: Toward an existential psychology*. New York: Irvington.

Keijsers, G. P. J., Schaap, C. P. D., & Hoogduin, C. A. L. (2000). The impact of interpersonal patient and therapist behavior on outcome in cognitive-behavioral therapy: A review of empirical studies. *Behavior Modification, 24,* 264–297.

Keith, D. V., & Whitaker, C. A. (1982). Experiential/symbolic family therapy. In A. M. Horne & M. M. Ohlsen (Eds.), *Family counseling and therapy* (pp. 43–74). Itasca, IL: F. E. Peacock.

Kelly, G. (1955). *The psychology of personal constructs* (Vols. 1 and 2). New York: Norton.

Kelly, S. (2006). Cognitive-behavioral therapy with African Americans. In G. Y. Iwamasa & P. A. Hayes (Eds.), *Culturally responsive cognitive-behavioral therapy: Assessment, practice, and supervision* (pp. 97–116). Washington, DC: American Psychological Association.

Kern, R. M. (1982, 1990, 1997). *Lifestyle scale*. Bowling Green, KY: CMTI Press.

Kerr, M. (1988). Chronic anxiety and defining a self. *The Atlantic Monthly, 262,* 35–37, 40–44.

Kerr, M., & Bowen, M. (1988). *Family evaluation*. New York: Norton.

Kerwin, C., & Ponterotto, J. (1995). Biracial identity development. In J. Ponterotto, M. Casas, L. Suzuki, & C. Alexander (Eds.), *Handbook of multicultural counseling* (pp. 199–217). Thousand Oaks, CA: Sage.

Kiang, L., Yip, T., Gonzales-Backen, M., & Witko, M. (2006). Ethnic identity and the daily psychological well-being of adolescents from Mexican and Chinese backgrounds. *Child Development, 77,* 1338–1350.

Kierkegaard, S. (1957). *The concept of dread* (W. Lowrie, Trans.). Princeton, NJ: Princeton University Press. (Original work published 1844)

Kierkegaard, S. (1959). *Either/or* (D. F. Swenson & L. M. Swenson, Trans.; Vol. 1). Princeton, NJ: Princeton University Press. (Original work published 1843)

Kim, J. (1981). *The process of Asian-American identity development: A study of Japanese American women's perceptions of their struggles to achieve positive identities*. Doctoral dissertation. University of Massachusetts, Amherst.

Kim, J. S. (2008). Examining the effectiveness of solution-focused brief therapy: A meta-analysis. *Research in Social Work Practice, 18,* 107–116.

Kim, J. S. (Ed.). (2014). *Solution-focused brief therapy: A multicultural approach*. Los Angeles: Sage.

Kim, K. I., & Hwang, M. G. (2001). The effects of internal control and achievement motivation in group counseling based on reality therapy. *International Journal of Reality Therapy, 20,* 12–15.

Kim, Y. W., Lee, S. H., Choi, T. K., Suh, S. Y., Kim, B., Kim, C. M., . . . Yook, K. H. (2009). Effectiveness of mindfulness-based cognitive therapy as an adjuvant to pharmacotherapy in patients with panic disorder or generalized anxiety disorder. *Depression and Anxiety, 26*, 601–606.

Kim-Ju, G. M., & Liem, R. (2003). Ethnic self-awareness as a function of ethnic group status, group composition and ethnic identity orientation. *Cultural Diversity and Ethnic Minority Psychology, 9*(3), 289–302.

Kindlon, D. J., & Thompson, M. (2000). *Raising Cain: Protecting the emotional life of boys.* New York: Ballantine Books.

King, J. H., & Anderson, S. M. (2004). Therapeutic implications of pharmacotherapy: Current trends and ethical issues. *Journal of Counseling and Development, 82*, 329–336.

Kirchner, M. (2010). *Gestalt therapy theory: An overview.* Retrieved March 12, 2010, from http://www.g-gej .org/4–3/theoryoverview.html

Kirschenbaum, H. (2007). *The life and work of Carl Rogers.* Ross-on-Wye, England: PCCS Book.

Kirschenbaum, H., & Henderson, V. (1989a). *Carl Rogers-dialogues: Conversations with Martin Buber, Paul Tillich, B. F. Skinner, Gregory Bateson, Michael Polanyi, Rollo May, and others.* Boston: Houghton Mifflin.

Kirschenbaum, H., & Henderson, V. (Eds.). (1989b). *The Carl Rogers reader.* Boston: Houghton Mifflin.

Klein, M. (1932). *The psycho-analysis of children.* London: Hogarth.

Kline, P. (1999). *The handbook of psychological testing.* New York: Routledge.

Klorer, P. G. (2005). Expressive therapy with severely maltreated children: Neuroscience contributions. *Art Therapy: Journal of the American Art Therapy Association, 22*(4), 213–220.

Knell, S. (1993). *Cognitive-behavioral play therapy.* Northvale, NJ: Aronson.

Knill, P. J. (2005). Foundations for a theory of practice. In P. J. Knill, E. G. Levine, & S. K. Levine (Eds.), *Principles and practice of expressive arts therapy* (pp. 75–170). Philadelphia: Jessica Kingsley.

Knill, P. J., Barba, H., & Fuchs, M. (1995). *Minstrels of the soul: Intermodal Expressive Therapy.* Toronto, Ontario, Canada: Palmerston Press.

Koenig, H. G. (2004). Religion, spirituality and medicine. Research findings and implications for clinical practice. *Southern Medical Journal, 97*, 1194–1200.

Koenig, H. G., McCullough, M. E., & Larson, D. B. (2001). *Handbook of religion and health.* New York: Oxford University Press.

Kohn, L. P., Oden, T., Munoz, R. F., Robinson, A., & Leavitt, D. (2002). Adapted cognitive behavioral group for depressed low-income African American women. *Community Mental Health Journal, 38*(6), 497–504.

Kohut, H. (1971). *The analysis of the self.* New York: International Universities Press.

Kohut, H. (1977). *The restoration of the self.* New York: International Universities Press.

Kohut, H. (1978). The disorders of the self and their treatment: An outline. In H. Kohut (Ed.), *The search for the self: Selected writings of Heinz Kohut: 1978–1981* (pp. 359–385). Madison, WI: International Universities Press.

Kohut, H. (1984). *How does analysis cure?* Chicago: University of Chicago Press.

Kohut, H., & Wolf, E. S. (1978). The disorders of the self and their treatment: An outline. *International Journal of Psycho-Analysis, 59*, 413–425.

Kondo, A. (1992). A Zen perspective on the concept of self and human nature. *International Bulletin of Morita Therapy, 5*(1–2), 46–49.

Koons, C. R., Robins, C. J., Tweed, J. L., Lynch, T. R., Gonzales, A. M., Morse, J. Q., . . . Bastian, L. A. (2001). Efficacy of dialectical behavior therapy in women veterans with borderline personality disorder, Behavior Therapy, 32, 371–390.

Kopp, R. R. (1995). *Metaphor therapy: Using client-generated metaphors for psychotherapy.* New York: Brunner/Mazel.

Korpela, K., & Hartig, T. (1996). Restorative qualities of favorite places. *Journal of Environmental Psychology, 16*, 221–233.

Kort, J. (2010). *18 things to consider before coming out.* Available at http://www.joekort.com/articles60

Kottler, J. A. (1986). *On being a therapist.* San Francisco: Jossey-Bass.

Kottman, T. (1987). An ethnographic study of an Adlerian play therapy training program. *Dissertation Abstracts International, A49*(01).

Kottman, T. (1995). *Partners in play: An Adlerian approach to play therapy.* Alexandria, VA: American Counseling Association.

Kramer, E. (2001). *Art as therapy: Collected papers.* London: Kingsley.

Kramer, P. D. (2006). *Freud: Inventor of the modern mind.* New York: Eminent Lives.

Krech, G. (2001). *Naikan: Gratitude, grace and the Japanese art of self-reflection.* Berkeley, CA: Stone Bridge Press.

Krech, G. (2010). *How to practice Naikan reflection.* Available at http://www.todoinstitute.org/naikan3.html

Kressel, K. (1997). Practice-relevant research in mediation: Toward a reflective research paradigm. *Negotiation Journal, 2*, 143–160.

Kristheller, J. L., & Hallett, C. B. (1999). An exploratory study of a meditation-based intervention for binge eating disorder. *Journal of Health Psychology, 4*, 357–363.

Krug, R. (1982). *How to keep a spiritual journal.* Nashville, TN: Thomas Nelson.

Krugman, P. (2008, February 18). Poverty is poison. *New York Times.* Retrieved from http://www.nytimes .com/2008/02/18/opinion/18krugman.html

Kruk, K. (2004, November). *EEG and art therapy: Brain activity during art-making.* Paper presented at the annual meeting of the American Art Therapy Association, San Diego, CA.

Krumboltz, J. D., & Thoresen, C. E. (1976). *Counseling methods.* New York: Holt, Rinehart, and Winston.

Krysan, M., Moore, K. A., & Zill, N. (1990). *Identifying successful families: An overview of constructs and selected measures.* Washington, DC: Child Trends.

Kuhn, S. A. C., Lerman, D. C., & Vorndran, C. M. (2003). Pyramidal training for families of children with problem behavior. *Journal of Applied Behavior Analysis, 36*(1), 77–88. doi:10.1901/jaba.2003.36–77

Kuhn, T. (1962). *The structure of scientific revolutions.* Chicago: University of Chicago Press.

Lambert, M. J. (1989). The individual therapist's contribution to psychotherapy process and outcome. *Clinical Psychology Review, 9,* 469–485.

Lambert, M. J. (1992). Implications of outcome research for psychotherapy integration. In C. Norcross & M. R. Goldfried (Eds.), *Handbook of psychotherapy integration* (pp. 94–129). New York: Basic Books.

Lambert, R. (2003). *A child's eye view: Gestalt therapy with children, adolescents, and their families.* Highland, NY: Gestalt Journal Press.

Landau, E. (2012, May 28). *Music: It's in your head, changing your brain.* Retrieved December 28, 2013, from http://edition.cnn.com/2012/05/26/health/mental-health/music-brain-science/

Landreth, G. (1991). *Play therapy: Art of the relationship.* Muncie, IN: Accelerated Development.

Landreth, G. L. (2002). *Play therapy: The art of the relationship.* New York: Brunner-Rutledge. (Original work published 1991)

Landreth, G. L., & Sweeney, D. (1997). Child-centered play therapy. In K. O'Connor & L. M. Braverman (Eds.), *Play therapy theory and practice: A comparative presentation* (pp. 17–45). New York: Wiley.

Larson, D. B., Lu, F. G., & Swyers, J. P. (1996). *Model curriculum for psychiatry residency training programs: Religion and spirituality in clinical practice.* Rockville, MD: National Institute for Healthcare Research.

Lazarus, A. A. (1989). *The practice of multimodal therapy.* Baltimore: Johns Hopkins University Press.

Lazarus, A. A. (1997). *Brief but comprehensive psychotherapy: The multimodal way.* New York: Springer.

Lazarus, A. A. (2000). Multimodal therapy. In R. J. Corsini & D. Wedding (Eds.), *Current psychotherapies.* Itasca, IL: Peacock.

Leahy, R. I. (2002). Cognitive therapy: Current problems and future directions. In R. L. Leahy & E. T. Dowd (Eds.), *Clinical advances in cognitive psychotherapy: Theory and application* (pp. 418–434). New York: Springer.

Leak, G. K. (1992). Religiousness and social interest: An empirical assessment. *Individual Psychology, 48,* 288–301.

Leak, G. K., & Leak, K. C. (2006). Adlerian social interest and positive psychology: A conceptual and empirical integration. *Journal of Individual Psychology, 62,* 207–223.

Leak, G. K., Millard, R. J., Perry, N. W., & Williams, D. (1985). An investigation of the nomological network of social interest. *Journal of Research in Personality, 19,* 197–207.

Leardi, S., Pietroletti, R., Angeloni, G., Necozione, S., Ranalletta, G., & Del Gusto, B. (2007). Randomized clinical trial examining the effect of music therapy in stress response to day surgery. *British Journal of Surgery, 94,* 943–947.

LeBlanc, M., & Ritchie, M. (2001). A meta-analysis of play therapy outcomes. *Counseling Psychology Quarterly, 14,* 149–163.

LeDoux, J. (1996). *The emotional brain: The mysterious underpinnings of emotional life.* New York: Simon & Schuster.

LeDoux, J. (2002). *Synaptic self: How our brains become who we are.* New York: Penguin Books.

Lee, J. (2006). *Mindfulness-based cognitive therapy for children: Feasibility, acceptability, and effectiveness of a controlled clinical trial.* Unpublished doctoral dissertation. Columbia University, New York.

Lee, Y. T. (1993). Psychology needs no prejudice but the diversity of cultures. *American Psychologist, 48,* 1090–1091.

Leichsenring, F. (2005). Are psychodynamic and psychoanalytic therapies effective? *International Journal of Psychoanalysis, 86,* 841–868.

Leichsenring, F., Rabung, S., & Leibing, E. (2004). The efficacy of short-term psychodynamic psychotherapy in specific psychiatric disorders: A meta-analysis. *Archives of General Psychiatry, 61,* 1208–1216.

Leong, F. T. L., Wagner, N. S., & Tata, S. P. (1995). Racial and ethnic variations in help-seeking attitudes. In J. G. Ponterotto, J. M. Casas, L. A. Suzuki, & C. M. Alexander (Eds.), *Handbook of multicultural counseling* (pp. 415–438). Thousand Oaks, CA: Sage.

Lesh, T. V. (1970). Zen meditation and the development of empathy in counselors. *Journal of Humanistic Psychology, 10,* 39–74.

Levant, R. F. (2001). Context and gender in early adult relationships. *Prevention and Treatment, 4,* art. 14.

Levant, R., & Shlien, J. M. (Eds.). (1984). *Client-centered therapy and the person-centered approach: New directions in theory, research, and practice.* New York: Praeger.

Levine, E. (1999). On the playground: Child psychotherapy and expressive arts therapy. In S. Levine & E. Levine (Eds.), *Foundations of expressive arts therapy: Theoretical and clinical perspectives* (pp. 257–273). London: Kingsley.

Levine, R. A., Dixon, S., Levine, S., Richman, A., Leiderman, P. H., Keefer, C. H., & Brazelton, T. B. (1994). *Child care and culture: Lessons from Africa.* New York: Cambridge University Press.

Levitin, D. J. (2006). *This is your brain on music: Understanding a human obsession.* New York: Dutton.

Levy, D. (1939). "Release therapy" in young children. *Psychiatry, 1,* 387–390.

Lewin, K. (1951). *Field theory in social science.* New York: Harper.

Lewis, J., Arnold, M., House, R., & Toporek, R. (2003). *Advocacy competencies*. Retrieved October 12, 2005, from http://www.counseling.org/Resources

Lewis, P., Rack, P. H., Vaddadi, K. S., & Allen, J. J. (1980). Ethnic differences in drug response. *Journal of Postgraduate Medicine, 56,* 46–49.

Liebert, R. M., & Liebert, L. L. (1998). *Liebert and Spiegler's personality: Strategies and issues* (8th ed.). Belmont, CA: Wadsworth.

Liese, B. S. (1993). Coping with AIDS: A cognitive therapy perspective. *Kansas Medicine, 94,* 80–84.

Lin, K. M. (2010). Cultural and ethnic issues in psychopharmacology. *Psychiatric Times.* Retrieved from http://www.psychiatrictimes.com/articles/cultura-and-ethnic-issues-psychopharmacology

Linden, D. E. J. (2006). How psychotherapy changes the brain—the contribution of neuroimaging. *Molecular Psychiatry, 11,* 528–538. doi:10.1038/sj.mp.40001816

Lindforss, L., & Magnusson, D. (1997). Solution-focused therapy in prison. *Contemporary Family Therapy, 19,* 89–104.

Linehan, M. M. (1993). *Cognitive-behavioral treatment of borderline personality disorder*. New York: Guilford.

Linehan, M. M. (1995). *Treating borderline personality disorder: The dialectical approach: Program manual*. New York: Guilford.

Linehan, M. M., Armstrong, H. E., Suarez, A., Allmon, D., & Heard, H. L. (1991). Cognitive-behavioral treatment of chronically parasuicidal borderline patients. *Archives of General Psychiatry, 48,* 1060–1064.

Lobb, M. S. (2005). Classical Gestalt therapy. In A. L. Woldt & S. M. Toman (Eds.), *Gestalt therapy: History, theory, and practice* (pp. 21–40). Thousand Oaks, CA: Sage.

Lopez, S. J., & Snyder, C. R. (Eds.). (2003). *Positive psychological assessment: A handbook of models and measures*. Washington, DC: American Psychological Association.

Lounsbury, J. W., Fisher, L. A., Levy, J. J., & Welsh, D. P. (2009). Investigation of character strengths in relation to the academic success of college students. *Individual Differences Research, 7*(1), 52–69.

Lowenfeld, M. (1969). *The world technique*. London: Allen & Unwin.

Lowenfeld, M. (1991). *Play in childhood*. London: Cambridge University Press. (Original work published 1935)

Luborsky, L. L., Crits-Christoph, P., McLellan, A. T., Woody, G., Piper, W., Liberman, B., Imber, S., & Pilkonis, P. (1986). Do therapists vary much in their success? Findings from four outcome studies. *American Journal of Orthopsychiatry, 56,* 501–512.

Luborsky, L., Crits-Christoph, P., Mintz, J., & Auerbach, A. (1988). *Who will benefit from psychotherapy? Predicting therapeutic outcomes*. New York: Basic Books.

Lynch, T. R., Chapman, A. L., Rosenthal, M. Z., Kuo, J. R., & Linehan, M. M. (2006). Mechanisms of change in dialectical behavior therapy: Theoretical and empirical observations. *Journal of Clinical Psychology, 62,* 459–480.

Lyons, J. S., Uziel-Miller, N. D., Reyes, F., & Sokol, P. T. (2000). Strengths of children and adolescents in residential settings: Prevalence and associations with psychopathology and discharge placement. *Journal of the American Academy of Child & Adolescent Psychiatry, 39,* 176–181.

Mackewn, J. (2004). *Developing Gestalt counseling*. Thousand Oaks, CA: Sage.

Madden-Derdich, D. A., Estrada, U., Updegraff, K. A., & Leonard, S. A. (2002). The boundary violations scale: An empirical measure of intergenerational boundary violations in families. *Journal of Marital and Family Therapy, 28,* 241–254.

Maddi, S. R. (1996). *Personality theories: A comparative analysis* (6th ed.). Pacific Grove, CA: Brooks/Cole.

Madigan, S. (n.d.). *The language of our lives: Therapeutic conversations with internalized problem dialogues*. Retrieved from http://yaletownfamilytherapy.com

Maeshiro, T. (2005). *The Naikan method as psychotherapy*. Toki, Japan: Shobo.

Maeshiro, T. (2009, January). Naikan therapy in Japan: Introspection as a way of healing. *World Cultural Psychiatry Research Review, 33*–38.

Mahler, M. (1968). *On human symbiosis and the vicissitudes of individuation*. New York: International Universities Press.

Mahoney, M. J., & Craine, M. H. (1991). The changing beliefs of psychotherapy experts. *Journal of Psychotherapy Integration, 1,* 207–221.

Mahoney, M. J., & Lyddon, W. (1988). Recent developments in cognitive approaches to counseling and psychotherapy. *Counseling Psychology, 16,* 190–234.

Malchiodi, C. (1999). *Medical art therapy with adults*. London: Kingsley.

Malchiodi, C. (2012). Art therapy: There's an app for that. *Psychology Today.* Retrieved January 2, 2014, from http://www.psychologytoday.com/blog/the-healing-arts/201202/art-therapy-there-s-app-1

Malchiodi, C. (Ed.). (2003). *Handbook of art therapy*. New York: Guilford Press.

Malchiodi, C. (Ed.). (2005). *Expressive therapies*. New York: Guilford Press.

Malchiodi, C. (Ed.). (2008). *Handbook of art therapy*. New York: Guilford Press.

Malcolm, J. (1980). *Psychoanalysis: The impossible profession*. New York: Picador.

Maluccio, A. N. (1981). Competence-oriented social work practice: An ecological practice. In A. N. Maluccio (Ed.), *Promoting competence in clients: A new/old approach to social work practice* (pp. 1–24). New York: Free Press.

Malyon, A. K. (1982). Psychotherapeutic implications of internalized homophobia in gay men. *Journal of Homosexuality, 7,* 59–69.

Manaster, G. (1989). Clinical issues in brief psychotherapy: A summary and conclusion. *Individual Psychology, 45,* 243–247.

Manicavasgar, V., Parker, G., & Perich, T. (2011). Mindfulness-based cognitive therapy vs. cognitive behaviour therapy as a treatment for non-melancholic depression. *Journal of Affective Disorders, 130,* 138–144. doi:10.1016/j.jad.2010.09.027

Mantell, E. O., Ortiz, S. O., & Planthara, P. M. (2004). What price prescribing? A commentary on the effect of prescription authority on psychological practice. *Professional Psychology: Research and Practice, 35,* 164–169.

Markowski, E., & Greenwood, P. (1984). Marital adjustment as a correlate of social interest. *Individual Psychology, 40,* 300–308.

Markus, H. R. (1977). Self-schemata and processing information about the self. *Journal of Personality and Social Psychology, 35,* 63–78.

Martin, J. R. (1997). Mindfulness: A proposed common factor. *Journal of Psychotherapy Integration, 7,* 291–312.

Martinez, K. (2008, June 16). *Evidence based practices, practice based evidence and community defined evidence in multicultural mental health.* Paper presented at the 2008 NAMI Annual Convention in Orlando, FL.

Maruyama, S. (1991). Shoma Morita, founder of Morita therapy, and haiku poet, Shiki: Origin of Morita therapy. *Psychiatry and Clinical Neurosciences, 45,* 787–796.

Maslow, A. (1970a). Holistic emphasis. *Journal of Individual Psychology, 26,* 39.

Maslow, A. (1970b). Tribute to Alfred Adler. *Journal of Individual Psychology, 26,* 13.

Maslow, A. (1971). *The farther reaches of human nature.* New York: Penguin.

Maslow, A. H. (1954). *Motivation and personality.* New York: Harper & Row.

Maslow, A. H. (1968). *Toward a psychology of being* (2nd ed.). Princeton, NJ: Van Nostrand.

Mason, C., & Duba, J. D. (2009). Using reality therapy in schools: The potential impact of the effectiveness. *International Journal of Reality Therapy, 29*(1), 5–12.

Mason, M., & Chuang, S. (2001). Culturally-based after-school arts programming for low-income urban children: Adaptive and preventive effects. *Journal of Primary Prevention, 22*(1), 45–54.

Masten, A., & Coatsworth, J. (1998). The development of competence in favorable and unfavorable environments: Lessons from research on successful children. *American Psychologist, 53,* 205–220.

Masten, A., & Reed, M. (2002). Resilience in development. In C. Snyder & S. Lopez (Eds.), *Handbook of positive psychology* (pp. 74–88). New York: Oxford University Press.

Maton, K. I., Schellenback, C. J., Leadbetter, B. J., & Solarz, A. L. (Eds.). (2004). *Investing in children, youth, families, and communities: Strengths-based research and policy.* Washington, DC: American Psychological Association.

Matos, M., Santos, A., Gonçalves, M., & Martins, C. (2009). Innovative moments and change in narrative therapy. *Psychotherapy Research, 19*(1), 68–80. doi:10.1080/10503300802430657

May, R. (1950). *The meaning of anxiety.* New York: Ronald Press.

May, R. (1953). *Man's search for himself.* New York: NAL.

May, R. (1961). *Existential psychology.* New York: Random House.

May, R. (1969). *Love and will.* New York: Norton.

May, R. (1970). Myth and guiding fiction. *Journal of Individual Psychology, 14,* 153–157.

May, R. (1975). *The courage to create.* New York: Norton.

May, R. (1981). *Freedom and destiny.* London: Norton.

May, R., Angel, E., & Ellenberger, H. (Eds.). (1958). *Existence.* New York: Simon & Schuster.

May, R., & Yalom, I. (2005). Existential psychotherapy. In R. J. Corsini & D. Wedding (Eds.), *Current psychotherapies* (pp. 269–298). Belmont, CA: Brooks/Cole.

Mayne, T. J., & Sayette, M. A. (1990). *Insider's guide to graduate programs in clinical psychology.* New York: Guilford Press.

McCartney, L. (2004). *Counselors' perspectives on how mindfulness meditation influences counselor presence within the therapeutic relationship.* Unpublished master's thesis. University of Victoria, British Columbia, Canada.

McCollum, E. E., Trepper, T. S., & Smock, S. (2003). Solution-focused group therapy for substance abuse: Expanding competency-based models. *Journal of Family Psychotherapy, 14*(4), 27–42.

McConkey, N. (1992). Working with adults to overcome the effects of sexual abuse: Integrating solution-focused therapy, systems thinking, and gender issues. *Journal of Strategic and Systemic Therapies, 11,* 4–18.

McCoy, C. W. (1996). Reexamining models of healthy families. *Contemporary Family Therapy, 18,* 243–256.

McCubbin, H. I., McCubbin, M. A., & Thompson, A. I. (1993). Resiliency in families: The role of family schema and appraisal in family adaptation to crisis. In T. T. H. Brubaker (Ed.), *Family relations: Challenges for the future.* Beverly Hills, CA: Sage.

McDermott, M., & Samson, F. L. (2005). White racial and ethnic identity in the United States. *Annual Review of Sociology, 31,* 246–261.

McGregor, M., Tutty, L. M., Babins-Wagner, R., & Marlyn, G. (2002). The long term impacts of group treatment for partner abuse. *Canadian Journal of Community Mental Health, 21*(1), 67–84.

McGuire, W. (Ed.). (1974). *The Freud/Jung letters.* Princeton, NJ: Princeton University Press.

McIntosh, P. (1989, July/August).White privilege: Unpacking the invisible Knapsack. *Peace and Freedom,* pp. 8–10.

McKenzie, W., & Monk, G. (1997). Learning and teaching narrative ideas. In G. Monk, J. Winslade, K. Crocket, & D. Epston (Eds.), *Narrative therapy in practice:*

The archaeology of hope (pp. 82–117). San Francisco: Jossey-Bass.

McLean, J. (2007). Psychotherapy with a narcissistic patient using Kohut's self psychology model. *Psychiatry, 4*(10), 40–47.

McLeod, J., & McLeod, J. (1993). The relationship between personal philosophy and effectiveness in counselors. *Counseling Psychology Quarterly, 6,* 121–129.

McNair, L. D. (1996). African American women and behavior therapy: Integrating theory, culture, and clinical practice. *Cognitive and Behavioral Practice, 3*(2), 337–349.

McNiff, S. (1981). *The arts and psychotherapy.* Springfield, IL: Charles C Thomas.

McNiff, S. (1992). *Art and medicine.* Boston: Shambhala.

McQuaid, J. R., & Carmona, P. E. (2004). *Peaceful mind: Using mindfulness and cognitive behavioral psychology to overcome depression.* Oakland, CA: New Harbinger.

McQuaide, S., & Ehrenreich, J. H. (1997). Assessing client strengths. *Families in Society, 78,* 201–202.

McReynolds, P. (1997). *Lightner Witmer: His life and times.* Washington, DC: American Psychological Association.

Mead, M. (1974). On Freud's view of female psychology. In J. Strouse (Ed.), *Women and analysis: Dialogues on psychoanalytic views of femininity* (pp. 95–106). New York: Grossman.

Meichenbaum, D. (1985). *Stress inoculation training.* New York: Pergamon.

Meichenbaum, D. (1991). Evolution of cognitive behavior therapy. In J. Zeig (Ed.), *The evolution of psychology, II.* New York: Brunner/Mazel.

Meichenbaum, D. (1993). Stress inoculation training: A twenty-year update. In R. Wolfolk & P. Lehrer (Eds.), *Principles and practices of stress management.* New York: Guilford.

Meichenbaum, D. (1994). *A clinical handbook/practical therapy manual for assessing and treating adults with post-traumatic stress disorder (PTSD).* Waterloo, Ontario, Canada: Institute Press.

Meichenbaum, D. (1996). Stress inoculation training for coping with stressors. *The Clinical Psychologist, 49,* 4–10.

Meichenbaum, D. (2003). *Treatment with individuals with anger-control problems and aggressive behavior.* New York: Crown House.

Messer, S. B., & Warren, C. S. (2001). Brief psychodynamic therapy. In R. J. Corsini (Ed.), *Handbook of innovative therapies* (2nd ed., pp. 67–85). New York: Wiley.

Mikulas, W. L. (2002). *The integrative helper: Convergence of Eastern and Western traditions.* Pacific Grove, CA: Brooks/Cole.

Miller, D. B. (1999). Racial socialization and racial identity: Can they promote resiliency for African American adolescents? *Adolescence, 34,* 493–501.

Miller, G. (2003). *Incorporating spirituality in counseling and psychotherapy: Theory and technique.* New York: Wiley.

Miller, J. B. (1986). *Toward a new psychology of women* (2nd ed.). Boston: Beacon Press.

Miller, J. B., & Stiver, I. P. (1997). *The healing connection: How women form relationships in therapy and in life.* Boston: Beacon Press.

Miller, J. J., Fletcher, K., & Kabat-Zinn, J. (1995). Three-year follow-up and clinical implications of a mindfulness meditation-based stress reduction intervention in the treatment of anxiety disorders. *General Hospital Psychiatry, 17,* 192–200.

Miller, M. J. (1996). Some comparisons between Taoism and person-centered therapy. *The Person-Centered Journal, 3,* 12–14.

Miller, M. J., & Foxworth, C. L. (1992). Validating a subscale for assessing aspects of the person. *College Student Journal, 26,* 436–439.

Miller, S. D., & Berg, I. K. (1995). *The miracle method: A radically new approach to problem drinking.* New York: Norton.

Miller, S. D., Duncan, B. L., & Hubble, M. A. (1997). *Escape from Babel: Toward a unifying language for psychotherapy practice.* New York: Norton.

Miller, W. E., & Thoresen, C. E. (2003). *Spirituality, religion, and health: An emerging research field. American Psychologist, 58,* 24–35.

Miller, W. R. (1983). Motivational interviewing with problem drinkers. *Behavioural Psychotherapy, 11,* 147–172.

Miller, W. R. (1998). Researching the spiritual dimensions of alcohol and other drug problems. *Addiction, 94,* 979–990.

Miller, W. R. (1999). Pros and cons: Reflections on motivational interviewing in correctional settings. *Motivational Interviewing Newsletter for Trainers, 6*(1), 2–3.

Miller, W. R. (2000). Motivational interviewing: IV. Some parallels with horse whispering. *Behavioural and Cognitive Psychotherapy, 28,* 285–292.

Miller, W. R. (2003, October). Crossing cultures from the desert. *Motivational Interviewing Newsletter: Updates, Education and Training, 10*(3), 1–5.

Miller, W. R. (2004). *Toward a theory of motivational interviewing.* Retrieved December 7, 2013, from http://www.motivationalinterview.net/library/MItheory_files/frame.htm

Miller, W. R., & Baca, L. M. (1983). Two-year follow-up of bibliotherapy and therapist-directed controlled drinking training for problem drinkers. *Behavior Therapy, 14,* 441–448.

Miller, W. R., & Moyers, T. B. (2006). Eight stages in learning motivational interviewing. *Journal of Teaching in the Addictions, 5*(1), 13–17.

Miller, W. R., & Rollnick, S. (1991). *Motivational interviewing: Preparing people to change addictive behavior.* New York: Guilford Press.

Miller, W. R., & Rollnick, S. (2002). *Motivational interviewing: Preparing people or change* (2nd ed.). New York: Guilford Press.

Miller, W. R., & Rollnick, S. (2009). Ten things that motivational interviewing is not. *Behavioural and Cognitive Psychotherapy, 37,* 129–140.

Miller, W. R., & Rollnick, S. (2010, June). *What makes it motivational interviewing?* Presentation at the International Conference on Motivational Interviewing (ICMI), Stockholm. Retrieved June 7, 2010, from http://www.fhi .se/Documents/ICMI/Dokumentation/June-7/Plenary/ Miller-june7-plenary.pdf

Miller, W. R., & Rollnick, S. (2013). *Motivational interviewing: Helping people change* (3rd ed.). New York: Guilford Press.

Miller, W. R., & Rose, G. S. (2009). Toward a theory of motivational interviewing. *American Psychologist, 64*(6), 527–537.

Miller, W. R., Taylor, C. A., & West, J. C. (1980). Focused versus broad spectrum behavior therapy for problem drinkers. *Journal of Consulting and Clinical Psychology, 48,* 590–601.

Millon, T. (2003). *Millon Index of Personality Styles: Revised.* San Antonio, TX: The Psychological Corporation.

Milrod, B., Leon, A. C., Busch, F., Rudden, M., Schwalberg, M., Clarkin, J., . . . Shear, M. K. (2007). A randomized control trial of psychoanalytic psychotherapy for panic disorder. *American Journal of Psychiatry, 164,* 265–272. doi:10.1176/appi.ajp.164.2.265

Miltenberger, R. G. (2004). *Behavior modification: Principles and procedures* (3rd ed.). Pacific Grove, CA: Brooks/ Cole.

Milton, M., & Coyle, A. (1999). Lesbian and gay affirmative psychotherapy: Issues in theory and practice. *Sexual and Relationship Therapy, 14,* 43–59.

Minuchin, S. (1974). *Families and family therapy.* Cambridge, MA: Harvard University Press.

Minuchin, S. (1993). *Family healing: Tales of hope and renewal from family therapy.* New York: Free Press.

Minuchin, S., & Fishman, H. C. (1981). *Family therapy techniques.* Cambridge, MA: Harvard University Press.

Minuchin, S., Montalvo, B., Guerney, B. G., Rosman, B. L., & Schumer, F. (1967). *Families of the slums: An exploration of their structure and treatment.* New York: Basic Books.

Minuchin, S., Rosman, B., & Baker, L. (1978). *Psychosomatic families: Anorexia nervosa in context.* Cambridge, MA: Harvard University Press.

Miranda, J., Bernal, G., Lau, A., Kohn, L., Hwang, W., & LaFromboise, T. (2005). State of the science on psychosocial interventions for ethnic minorities. *Annual Review of Clinical Psychology, 1,* 113–142.

Mishne, J. M. (1993). *The evolution and application of clinical theory: Perspectives from four psychologies.* New York: Free Press.

Mitchell, S. (1988). *Relational concepts in psychoanalysis.* Cambridge, MA: Harvard University Press.

Mitchell, S. (1997). *Influence and autonomy in psychoanalysis.* Hillsdale, NJ: Analytic Press.

Mitchell, S. A. (1988). *Relational concepts in psychoanalysis: An integration.* Cambridge, MA: Harvard University Press.

Mitchell, S. A., & Lewis, A. (1999). *Relational psychoanalysis: The emergence of a tradition.* Hillsdale, NJ: Analytic Press.

Modell, A. H. (2003). *Imagination and the meaningful brain.* Cambridge: MIT Press.

Molnar, A., & de Shazer, S. (1987). Solution-focused therapy: Toward the identification of therapeutic tasks. *Journal of Marital and Family Therapy, 13*(4), 349–358.

Monk, G. (1997). How narrative therapy works. In G. Monk, J. Winslade, K. Crocket & D. Epston (Eds.), *Narrative therapy in practice* (pp. 3–31). San Francisco: Jossey-Bass.

Montepare, J. M., & Clements, A. E. (2001). Age schemas: Guides to processing information about the self. *Journal of Adult Development, 8,* 99–108.

Moodley, R., & West, W. (Eds.). (2005). *Integrating traditional healing practices into counseling and psychotherapy.* Thousand Oaks, CA: Sage.

Moreno, J. L. (1985). *The autobiography of J. L. Moreno, M.D.* (Abridged). Cambridge, MA: Harvard University Press.

Morgan, A. (2002). *What is narrative therapy?* Adelaide, Australia: Dulwich Centre.

Morgan, K. S., & Brown, L. S. (1991). Lesbian career development, work behavior, and vocational counseling. *The Counseling Psychologist, 19,* 273–279.

Morita, S. (1974). Shinkeishitsu-no Hontai-to ryoho [Nature and treatment of nervosity]. In S. Aizawa & S. Maruyama (Eds.), *Shoma Morita collected works* (pp. 279–442). Albany, NY: SUNY Press.

Mosak, H. H. (2005). Adlerian psychotherapy. In R. J. Corsini & D. Wedding (Eds.), *Current psychotherapies* (7th ed., pp. 52–95). Belmont, CA: Brooks/Cole.

Mosak, H. H., & DiPietro, R. (2006). *Early recollections: Interpreting method and application.* New York: Routledge.

Moss, D. (1998). *Humanistic and transpersonal psychology: An historical and biographical sourcebook.* Westport, CT: Greenwood Press.

Moustakas, C. (1953). *Children in play therapy: A key to understanding normal and disturbed emotions.* New York: McGraw-Hill.

Moustakas, C. (1966). *Existential child therapy: The child's discovery of himself.* New York: Basic Books.

Moustakas, C. (1992). *Psychotherapy with children: The living relationships.* Greeley, CO: Carron.

Mosak, H. H., & Maniacci, M. (2011). Adlerian psychotherapy. In R. J. Corsini & D. Wedding (Eds.), Current psychotherapies (9th ed., pp. 67–112). Belmont, CA: Brooks/Cole.

Mowrer, O. H., & Mowrer, W. M. (1938). Enuresis: A method for its study and treatment. *American Journal of Orthopsychiatry, 8,* 436–459.

Murdock, N. L., Banta, J., Stromseth, J., Viene, D., & Brown, T. M. (1998). Joining the club: Factors related to choice of theoretical orientation. *Counseling Psychology Quarterly, 11,* 63–77.

Murphy, J. J. (1997). *Solution-focused counseling in middle and high schools.* Columbus, OH: Merrill/Prentice Hall.

Murphy, J. J., & Duncan, B. L. (1997). *Brief intervention for school problems: Collaborating for practical solutions.* New York: Guilford.

Murray-Swank, N. A. (2003). *Solace for the soul: An evaluation of a psychospiritual intervention for female survivors of sexual abuse.* Unpublished doctoral dissertation. Bowling Green State University, Bowling Green, OH.

Myers, J. B., McCaulley, M. H., Quenk, N. L., & Hammer, A. L. (1998). *MBTI manual: A guide to the development and use of the Myers-Briggs Type Indicator* (3rd ed.). Palo Alto, CA: Consulting Psychologists Press.

Nader, K., Schafe, G. E., & LeDoux, J. E. (2000). Fear memories require protein synthesis in the amygdala for recon-solidation after retrieval. *Nature, 4046,* 722–726.

Naikan therapy. (n.d.). Retrieved August 4, 2010, from http://www.uproad.ne.jp/rengein/english/e-naikan.1.html

Nainis, M., Paice, J. A., Ratner, J., Wirth, J. H., Lai, J., & Shott, S. (2006). Relieving symptoms in cancer: Innovative use of art therapy. *Journal of Pain and Symptom Management, 31*(2), 162–169.

Najavits, L. M. (1997). Therapists' implicit theories of psychotherapy. *Journal of Psychotherapy Integration, 7,* 1–16.

Najavits, L. M., & Strupp, H. H. (1994). How do psychodynamic therapists differ in their effectiveness with patients? A process-outcome study. *Psychotherapy, 31,* 114–123.

Nathan, P. E., & Gorman, J. M. (Eds.). (2002). *A guide to treatments that work* (2nd ed.). New York: Oxford University Press.

National Alliance on Mental Illness. (2008). *Evidence-based practices and multicultural mental health.* Retrieved from http://www.nami.org/Template.cfm?Section=Newsletters3&Template=/ContentManagement/ContentDisplay.cfm&ContentID=71078

National Association of Social Workers. (2006). *Lesbian, gay, and bisexual issues.* Available at http://www.naswdc.org/resources/abstracts/lesbian.asp

National Institute for Clinical Excellence. (2004). *Eating disorders: Core interventions in the treatment and management of anorexia nervosa, bulimia nervosa, and related eating disorders* (NICE Clinical Guideline No. 9). London: Author.

Neal-Barnett, A. M., & Smith, J. M. (1996). African American children and behavior therapy: Considering the Afrocentric approach. *Cognitive and Behavioral Practice, 3*(2), 351–369.

Nelson, J. (2006). *Positive discipline.* New York: Ballantine Books.

New Freedom Commission on Mental Health. (2003). *Achieving the promise: Transforming mental health care in America. Executive summary.* Rockville, MD: Department of Health and Human Services.

Newberg, A., & Waldman, M. R. (2012). *Words can change your brain.* New York: Plume.

Newsome, W. S. (2004). Solution-focused brief therapy groupwork with at-risk junior high students: Enhancing the bottom line. *Research on Social Work Practice, 14*(5), 336–343.

Nichols, M. P., & Schwartz, R. C. (2007). *Family therapy: Concepts and methods* (8th ed.). Boston: Allyn & Bacon.

Nichols, W. C. (2003). Family of origin treatment. In T. L. Sexton, G. R. Weeks, & M. S. Robbins (Eds.), *Handbook of family therapy.* New York: Brunner-Routledge.

Niemi, P. M. (1997). Medical students' professional identity: Self-reflection during the pre-clinical years. *Medical Education, 31,* 408–415.

Nietzsche, F. (1916). *Thus spake Zarathustra: A book for all and none.* New York: Macmillan.

Nietzsche, F. (1972). *The antichrist.* Salem, NH: Ayer. (Original work published 1930)

Nikelly, A. G. (2005). Positive health outcomes of social interest. *Journal of Individual Psychology, 61,* 329–342.

Norcross, J. C. (1987). A rational and empirical analysis of existential psychotherapy. *Journal of Humanistic Psychology, 27,* 41–68.

Norcross, J. C. (2005a). The psychotherapist's own psychotherapy: Educating and developing psychologists. *American Psychologist, 60,* 840–850.

Norcross, J. C. (2005b). A primer on psychotherapy integration. In J. C. Norcross, & M. R. Goldfried (Eds.), *Handbook of psychotherapy integration* (2nd ed.) (pp. 3–23). New York: Oxford University Press.

Norcross, J. C., & Goldfried, M. R. (2005). *Handbook of psychotherapy integration* (2nd ed.). New York: Oxford University Press.

Norcross, J. C., Hedges, M., & Castle, P. H. (2002). Psychologists conducting psychotherapy in 2001: A study of the Division 29 membership. *Psychotherapy, 39,* 97–102.

Norcross, J. C., Hedges, M., & Prochaska, J. O. (2002). *The face of 2010: A Delphi Poll on the future of psychotherapy* (Module 8). Washington, DC: Council for the National Register of Health Service Providers in Psychology.

Norcross, J., Karpiak, C. P., & Lister, M. (2005). What's an integrationist? Self-identified integrative and (occasionally) eclectic psychologists. *Journal of Clinical Psychology, 61,* 1587–1594.

Norcross, J. C., & Newman, C. F. (1992). Psychotherapy integration: Setting the context. In J. C. Norcross & M. R. Goldfried (Eds.), *Handbook of psychotherapy integration* (pp. 3–45). New York: Basic Books.

Nordoff, P., & Robbins, C. (1977). *Creative music therapy.* New York: John Day.

Nye, R. D. (1992). *The legacy of B. F. Skinner.* Pacific Grove, CA: Brooks/Cole.

Nylund, D., & Thomas, J. (1994). The economics of narrative. *The Family Therapy Networker, 18*(6), 19–26, 28–29.

O'Connor, P. A. (1985). *Understanding Jung, understanding yourself.* New York: Paulist Press.

O'Donnell, L. (1999). *Music and the brain.* Retrieved December 28, 2013, from http://www.cerebromente.org.br/n15/mente/musica.html

O'Grady, K. A., & Richards, P. S. (2009). Case study showing inclusion of spirituality in the therapeutic process. In J. D. Aten & M. M. Leach (Eds.), *Spirituality and the therapeutic process* (pp. 241–266). Washington, DC: American Psychological Association.

O'Hanlon, W. H. (2000). *Do one thing different: Ten simple ways to change your life.* New York: Harper Collins.

O'Hara, M. (1997). Relational empathy: Beyond modernist egocentrism to post-modern contextualism. In A. C. Bohart & L. S. Greenberg (Eds.), *Empathy reconsidered: New directions in psychotherapy* (pp. 295–329). Washington, DC: American Psychological Association.

Oaklander, V. (1988). *Windows to our children.* Highland, NY: Gestalt Journal Press.

Oberst, U. E., & Steward, A. E. (2003). *Adlerian psychotherapy: An advanced approach to individual psychology.* New York: Brunner-Routledge.

Office of the United Nations High Commissioner for Human Rights. (1989). *Convention on the rights of the child.* Geneva, Switzerland: Author. Retrieved from http://www.ohchr.org/en/professionalinterest/pages/crc.aspx

Ogbu, J. U. (1992). Understanding cultural diversity and learning. *Educational Researcher, 21,* 5–14.

Ogedegbe, G., Chaplin, W., Schoenthaler, A., Statman, D., Berger, D., Richardson, T., . . . Allegrante, J. P. (2008). A practice-based trial of motivational interviewing and adherence in hypertensive African Americans. *American Journal of Hypertension, 23,* 1137–1143.

Ogles, B. M., Anderson, T., & Lunnen, K. M. (1999). The contribution of models and techniques: Contradictions between professional trends and clinical research. In M. Hubble, B. Duncan, & S. Miller (Eds.), *The heart and soul of change: What works in therapy* (pp. 201–228). Washington, DC: American Psychological Association.

Ogunfowora, B., & Drapeau, M. (2007). A study on the relationship between psychotherapists' personality and theoretical orientation. *Counseling and Psychotherapy Research, 8*(3), 151–159.

Okonji, J. (1995). Counseling style preference and perception of counselors by African-American male students. *Dissertation Abstracts International: Section B. Sciences and Engineering, 55*(9), 3811.

Okun, B. F. (1996). *Understanding diverse families: What practitioners need to know.* New York: Guilford.

Oman, D., & Thoresen, C. E. (2003). Spiritual modeling: A key to spiritual and religious growth? *The International Journal for the Psychology of Religion, 13,* 149–165.

Owens, D. (2012, May 19). *Examining multicultural competency education in the creative arts therapies.* Unpublished doctoral dissertation. Lesley University, Cambridge, MA. Retrieved January 10, 2014, from http://ir.flo.org/lesley/institutionalPublicationPublicView.action;jsessionid=394E0ADA0D7105D4A6DAC6E053D6BB75?institutionalItemId=124

Oyserman, D., Kemmelmeier, M., Fryberg, S., Brosh, H., & Hart-Johnson, T. (2003). Racial-ethnic self-schemas. *Social Psychology Quarterly, 66,* 333–347.

Oyserman, D., & Markus, H. R. (1993). The sociocultural self. In J. Suls (Ed.), *The self in social perspective* (Vol. 4, pp. 187–220). Hillsdale, NJ: Erlbaum.

Padilla, A. (2006). Bicultural social development. *Hispanic Journal of Behavioral Sciences, 28,* 467–495.

Pajares, F. (2004). *Albert Bandura: Biographical sketch.* Retrieved November 3, 2009, from http://des.emory.edu/mfp/bandurabio.html

Palley, R. (2000). The mind-brain relationship. *International Journal of Psychoanalysis Key Paper Series.* London: H. Karnac Books.

Palmer, G. T. (1999). Disclosure and assimilation of exceptional human experience: Meaningful, transformative, and spiritual aspects. *Dissertation Abstracts International, 60*(5), 2358B.

Paloutzian, R. F., & Ellison, C. W. (1982). Loneliness, spiritual well-being, and quality of life. In L. A. Peplau & D. Perlman (Eds.), *Loneliness: A sourcebook of current theory, research, and therapy* (pp. 224–237). New York: Wiley Interscience.

Paniagua, F. A. (2001). *Diagnosis in a multicultural context.* Thousand Oaks, CA: Sage.

Papero, D. V. (1991). *Bowen family systems theory.* Boston: Allyn & Bacon.

Paquette, V., Levesque, J., Mensour, B., Leroux, J. M., Beaudoin, G., Bourgouin, P., & Beauregard, M. (2003). Change the mind and you change the brain: Effects of cognitive-behavioral therapy on the neural correlates of spider phobia. *Neuroimage, 18*(2), 401–409.

Pargament, K. I. (1997). *The psychology of religious coping: Theory, research, practice.* New York: Guilford Press.

Pargament, K. I. (2007). *Spiritually integrated psychotherapy: Understanding and addressing the sacred.* New York: Guilford Press.

Pargament, K. I., Desai, K. M., & McConnell, K. M. (2006). Spirituality: A pathway to posttraumatic growth or decline? In L. G. Calhoun & R. G. Tedeschi (Eds.), *Handbook of posttraumatic growth: Research and practice* (pp. 121–137). Mahwah, NJ: Erlbaum.

Pargament, K. I., & Krumrei, E. (2009). Clinical assessment of clients' spirituality. In J. D. Aten and M. M. Leach (Eds.), *Spirituality and the therapeutic process* (pp. 93–120). Washington, DC: American Psychological Association.

Pargament, K. I., McCarthy, S., Shah, P., Ano, G., Tarakeshwar, N., Wachholtz, A. B., et al. (2004). Religion and HIV: A review of the literature and clinical implications. *Southern Medical Journal, 97,* 1201–1209.

Pargament, K. I., Smith, B. W., Koenig, H. G., & Perez, L. (1998). Patterns of positive and negative religious coping with major life stressors. *Journal for the Scientific Study of Religion, 37,* 711–725.

Park, N., & Peterson, C. (2006). Moral competence and character strengths among adolescents: The development and validation of the Values in Action Inventory of Strengths for Youth. *Journal of Adolescence, 29,* 891–910.

Parloff, M. B. (1976, February 21). Shopping for the right therapy. *Saturday Review,* 14–16.

PDR Network. (2014). *Physician's desk reference.* Montavale, NJ: Author. Retrieved from www.nxtbook.com/nxtbooks/pdr/physiciansdeskreference2014

Pedersen, P. (1991). Introduction to the special issue on multiculturalism as a fourth force in counseling. *Journal of Counseling and Development, 70,* 4.

Pedersen, P. (2000). *Hidden messages in culture-centered counseling: A triad training model.* Thousand Oaks, CA: Sage.

Pedersen, P. (2003). Culturally biased assumptions in therapy psychology. *Therapy Psychologist, 31*(4), 396–403.

Pedersen, P. (2008). Ethics, competence, and professional issues in cross cultural therapy. In P. B. Pedersen, J. G. Draguns, W. J. Lonner, & J. E. Trimble (Eds.), *Therapy across cultures* (6th ed., pp. 5–20). Thousand Oaks, CA: Sage.

Pedersen, P. B., & Carey, J. C. (2003). *Multicultural counseling in schools: A practical handbook.* Needham Heights, MA: Allyn & Bacon.

Pedersen, P. B., Draguns, J. G., Lonner, W. J., & Trimble, J. E. (Eds.). (2002). *Counseling across cultures* (5th ed.). Thousand Oaks, CA: Sage.

Pedersen, P. B., Draguns, J. G., Lonner, W. J., & Trimble, J. E. (Eds.). (2008). *Counseling across cultures* (6th ed.). Thousand Oaks, CA: Sage.

Pedro-Carroll, J., & Reddy, L. (2005). A preventive play intervention to foster children's resilience in the aftermath of divorce. In L. Reddy, T. Flies-Hall, & C. Schaefer (Eds.), *Empirically based interventions for children* (pp. 51–75). Washington, DC: American Psychological Association.

Pekna, M., & Pekny, M. (2012, July 30). *The neurobiology of brain injury.* Retrieved February 21, 2014, from http://dana.org/Cerebrum/Default.aspx?id=39479

Perls, F. S. (1969a). *Gestalt therapy verbatim.* Lafayette, CA: Real People Press.

Perls, F. S. (1969b). *In and out of the garbage pail.* New York: Bantam.

Perls, F. S. (1973). *The Gestalt approach and eye witness to therapy.* Palo Alto, CA: Science and Behavior Books.

Perls, F. S. (1992). *Ego, hunger, and aggression.* New York: Gestalt Journal Press. (Original work published 1942)

Perls, F. S. (n.d.). *An autobiography.* Retrieved March 11, 2010, from http://fritzperls.com/autobiography

Perls, F. S., Hefferline, R., & Goodman, P. (1951). *Gestalt therapy.* New York: Julian Press.

Perls, L. (1976). Comments on new directions. In E. W. L. Smith (Ed.), *The growing edge of Gestalt therapy* (pp. 221–226). New York: Brunner/Mazel.

Perry, B. D. (2004). *The impact of abuse and neglect on the developing brain.* Retrieved June 19, 2004, from http://www.teacher.scholastic.com/professional/bruceperry/abuse_neglect.htm

Peterson, C. (2000). The future of optimism. *American Psychologist, 55,* 79–88.

Peterson, C., & Seligman, M. E. P. (2003). *Values in Action (VIA) classification of strengths manual.* Retrieved from http://www.positivepsychology.org/taxonomy.htm

Peterson, C., & Seligman, M. E. P. (2004). *Character strengths and virtues: A handbook and classification.* Washington, DC: American Psychological Association.

Philippson, P. (2001). *Self in relation.* London: Karnac Books.

Phinney, J. S. (1990). Ethnic identity in adolescents and adults: Review of research. *Psychological Bulletin, 108,* 449–514.

Phinney, J. S., & Tarver, S. (1988). Ethnic identity search and commitment in Black and White eighth graders. *Journal of Early Adolescence, 8,* 265–277.

Piercy, F. P., & Sprenkle, D. H. (1986). *Family therapy sourcebook.* New York: Guilford.

Plante, T. G. (2009). *Spiritual practices in psychotherapy: Thirteen tools for enhancing psychological health.* Washington, DC: American Psychological Association.

Plante, T. G., & Thoresen, C. E. (Eds.). (2007). *Science, spirit, and health: How the spiritual mind fuels physical wellness.* Westport, CT: Praeger/Greenwood.

Pollet, T. V., Dijkstra, P., Barelds, D. P. H., & Buunk, A. P. (2010). Birth order and the dominance aspect of extraversion: Are firstborns more extraverted, in the sense of being dominant, than laterborns? *Journal of Research in Personality, 44*(6), 742–745. doi:10.1016/j.jrp.2010.10.002

Polster, E. (1987). Escape from the present: Transition and storyline. In J. K. Zeig (Ed.), *The evolution of psychotherapy* (pp. 326–340). New York: Brunner/Mazel.

Polster, E., & Polster, M. (1973). *Gestalt therapy integrated: Contours of theory and practice.* New York: Brunner/Mazel.

Pompili, M., Girardi, P., & Ruberto, A. (2005). Suicide in borderline personality disorder: A meta-analysis. *Norwegian Journal of Psychiatry, 59,* 319–324.

Ponterotto, J. G., Casas, J. M., Suzuki, L. A., & Alexander, C. M. (2001). *Handbook of multicultural counseling.* Thousand Oaks, CA. Sage.

Ponterotto, J. G., Utsey, S. O., & Pedersen, P. B. (2006). *Preventing prejudice: A guide for counselors, educators, and parents* (2nd ed.). Thousand Oaks, CA: Sage.

Pope, M. (2008). Culturally appropriate counseling considerations for lesbian and gay clients. In P. Pedersen, J. G. Draguns, W. J. Lonner, & J. E. Trimble (Eds.), *Counseling across cultures* (6th ed., pp. 201–222). Thousand Oaks, CA: Sage.

Pope, M., & Barret, B. (2002). Counseling gay men toward an integrated sexuality. In L. D. Burlew & D. Capuzzi (Eds.), *Sexuality counseling* (pp. 149–176), Hauppauge, NY: Nova Science.

Pope, M., & Schecter, E. (1992, October). *Career strategies: Career suicide or career success.* Paper presented at the Second Annual Lesbian and Gay Workplace Issues Conference, Stanford, CA.

Popkin, M. (1993). *Active parenting today.* Atlanta: Active Parenting.

Popova, M. (2010). *This is your brain on love.* Retrieved February 20, 2014, from http://www.brainpickings.org/index.php/2010/06/11/your-brain-on-love

Powers, W. T. (1973). *Behavior: The control of perception.* Hawthorne, NY: Aldine.

Poznanski, J. J., & McLennan, J. (1995). Afterthoughts on counselor theoretical orientation. Reply to Arnkoff (1995) and Gelso (1995). *Journal of Counseling Psychology, 42,* 428–430.

Poznanski, J. J., & McLennan, J. (1995). Conceptualizing and measuring counselors' theoretical orientations. *Journal of Counseling Psychology, 42,* 411–422.

Prasko, J., Horacek, J., Zalesky, R., Kopecek, M., Novak, T., Paskova, B., . . . Höschl, C. (2004). The change of regional brain metabolism (18FDG PET) in panic disorder during the treatment with cognitive behavioral therapy or antidepressants. *Neuro Endocrinology Letters, 25,* 340–348.

Pratt, R. R. (2004). Art, dance, and music therapy. *Physical Medicine and Rehabilitation Clinics of North America, 15,* 827–841.

Preston, J., & Johnson, J. (2014). *Clinical psychopharmacology made ridiculously simple.* Miami, FL: MedMaster.

Price-Robertson, R. (2010, December). Supporting young parents. *Australian Institute of Family Studies* (CAFCA Practice Sheet). Retrieved from http://www.aifs.gov.au/cafca/pubs/sheets/ps/ps3.pdf

Prochaska, J. O. (1979). *Systems of psychotherapy: A transtheoretical analysis.* Chicago: Dorsey.

Prochaska, J. O. (2003). Enhancing motivation to change. In B. B. Wilford, A. W. Graham, & T. K. Schultz (Eds.), *Principles of addiction medicine* (3rd ed., pp. 825–838). Chevy Chase, MD: American Society of Addiction Medicine.

Prochaska, J. O., & DiClemente, C. C. (1984). *The transtheoretical approach: Crossing traditional boundaries of therapy.* Homewood, IL: Dow/Jones Irwin.

Prochaska, J. O., & DiClemente, C. C. (2005). The transtheoretical approach. In J. C. Norcross & M. R. Goldfried (Eds.), *Handbook of psychotherapy* (2nd ed.) (pp. 147–171). New York: Oxford.

Prochaska, J. O., DiClemente, C. C., Velicer, W. F., & Rossi, J. S. (1993). Standardized, individualized, interactive and personalized self-help programs for smoking cessation. *Health Psychology, 12,* 399–405.

Prochaska, J. O., & Norcross, J. C. (1999). *Systems of psychotherapy: A transtheoretical analysis* (4th ed.). Pacific Grove, CA: Brooks/Cole.

Prochaska, J. O., & Norcross, J. C. (2003). *Systems of psychotherapy: A transtheoretical analysis* (5th ed.). Pacific Grove, CA: Brooks/Cole.

Prochaska, J. O., & Norcross, J. C. (2010). *Systems of psychotherapy: A transtheoretical analysis* (7th ed.). Belmont, CA: Brooks/Cole.

Prochaska J. O., & Norcross, J. C. (2014). *Systems of psychotherapy: A transtheoretical analysis.* Stamford, CT: Cengage Learning.

Prochaska, J. O., & Velicer, W. F. (1997). The transtheoretical model of health behavior change. *American Journal of Health Promotion, 12,* 38–48.

Pronko, N. H. (1980). *Psychology from the standpoint of a behaviorist.* Monterey, CA: Brooks/Cole.

Proshansky, H. M., Fabian, A. K., & Kaminoff, R. (1983). Place identity: Physical world socialization of the self. *Journal of Environmental Psychology, 3,* 57–83.

Puchalski, C. (2004). Spirituality in health: The role of spirituality in critical care. *Critical Care Clinics, 20,* 487–504.

Quenk, N. L., & Quenk, A. T. (1996). Counseling and psychotherapy. In A. L. Hammer (Ed.), *MBTI Applications: A decade of research on the Myers-Briggs Type Indicator.* Palo Alto, CA: Consulting Psychologists Press.

Quintana, S. M. (1994). A model of ethnic perspective-taking ability applied to Mexican American children and youth. *International Journal of Intercultural Relations, 18,* 419–448.

Quintana, S. M., Castaneda-English, P., & Ybarra, V. (1999). Role of perspective-taking abilities and ethnic socialization in development of adolescent identity. *Journal of Research on Adolescence, 9,* 161–184.

Racy, J. (1970). Psychiatry in Arab East. *Acta Psychiatrica Scandinavica, 221,* 160–171.

Ralph, R. O., Lambric, T. M., & Steele, R. B. (1996, February). *Recovery issues in a consumer developed evaluation of the mental health system.* Presentation at the 6th annual Mental Health Services Research and Evaluation Conference, Arlington, VA.

Ramirez, M., III. (1999). *Multicultural psychotherapy: An approach to individual and cultural differences* (2nd ed.). Boston: Allyn & Bacon.

Rank, O. (1978). *Will therapy: An analysis of the therapeutic process in terms of relationship* (J. Taft, Trans.). New York: Norton. (Original work published 1936)

Rapp, C. A. (1998). *The strengths model: Case management with people suffering from severe and persistent mental illness.* New York: Oxford University Press.

Rapp, C. A., & Goscha, R. J. (2006). *The strengths model: Case management with people with psychiatric disabilities.* New York: Oxford University Press.

Rareshide, M., & Kern, R. (1991). Social interest: The haves and have nots. *Individual psychology, 47,* 464–476.

Raskin, J. D. (2002). Constructivism in psychology: Personal construct psychology, radical constructivism, and social constructionism. In J. D. Raskin & S. K. Bridges (Eds.), *Studies in meaning: Exploring constructivist psychology* (pp. 1–25). New York: Pace University Press.

Raskin, N. J., & Rogers, C. (2005). Person-centered therapy. In R. J. Corsini & D. Wedding (Eds.), *Current psychotherapies* (7th ed., pp. 130–165). Belmont, CA: Brooks/Cole.

Rathod, S., Phiri, P., Harris, S., Underwood, C., Thagadur, M., Padmanabi, U., & Kingdon, D. (2013). Cognitive behaviour therapy for psychosis can be adapted for minority ethnic groups: A randomised controlled trial. *Schizophrenia, 143,* 319–326.

REBT Network. (2006). *Dr. Albert Ellis.* Retrieved November 3, 2009, from http://www.rebtnetwork.org/whois.html

Reddy, L. A., Files-Hall, T., & Schaefer, C. A. (2005). *Empirically based play interventions for children.* Washington, DC: American Psychological Association.

Redsand, A. (2006). *Viktor Frankl: A life worth living.* Boston, MA: Houghton Mifflin.

Reibel, D. K., Greeson, J. M., Brainard, G. C., & Rosenzweig, S. (2001). Mindfulness-based stress reduction and health-related quality of life in a heterogeneous patient population. *General Hospital Psychiatry, 23*(4), 183–192.

Reik, T. (1956). *Listening with the third ear: The inner experience of a psychoanalyst.* New York: Grove.

Restak, R. (2006). *The naked brain: How the emerging neurosociety is changing how we live, work, and love.* New York: Harmon Books.

Reynolds, D. (1976). *Morita psychotherapy.* Berkeley: University of California Press.

Reynolds, D. (1982). *Quiet therapies.* Honolulu: University of Hawaii Press; Tokyo: Hakuyosha.

Reynolds, D. (1989a). On being natural: Two Japanese approaches to healing. In A. Sheikh & S. Sheikh (Eds.), *Eastern and Western approaches to healing: Ancient wisdom and modern approaches.* New York: Wiley.

Reynolds, D. L. (1989b). *Flowing bridges, quiet waters: Japanese psychotherapies, Morita and Naikan.* Albany: State University of New York Press.

Reynolds, M. W., Nabors, L. A., & Quinlan, A. (2000). The effectiveness of art therapy: Does it work? *Art Therapy: Journal of the American Art Therapy Association, 17,* 207–213.

Richards, P. S., & Bergin, A. E. (1997). *A spiritual strategy for counseling and psychotherapy.* Washington, DC: American Psychological Association.

Richards, P. S., & Bergin, A. E. (2005). *A spiritual strategy for counseling and psychotherapy.* (2nd ed.). Washington, DC: American Psychological Association.

Richards, P. S., Hardman, R. K., & Berrett, M. E. (2000). *Spiritual renewal: A journal of faith and healing.* Orem, UT: Center for Change.

Richards, P. S., Rector, J. M., & Tjelveit, A. C. (1999). Values, spirituality, and psychotherapy. In W. R. Miller (Ed.), *Integrating spirituality into treatment: Resources for practitioners* (pp. 133–160). Washington, DC: American Psychological Association.

Richmond, L. J. (1996). Counseling models and their impact on how therapists handle value issues. *International Journal of Value-Based Management, 9,* 29–43.

Ridley, C. R. (2005). *Overcoming unintentional racism* (2nd ed.). Thousand Oaks, CA: Sage.

Riegel, K. F. (1976).The dialectics of human development. *American Psychologist, 31,* 689–700.

Rigazio-DiGilio, S. A., Ivey, A., & Locke, D. (1997). Continuing the post-modern dialogue: Enhancing and contextualizing multiple voices. *Journal of Mental Health Counseling, 19,* 233–255.

Riley, S. (2003). Art therapy with couples. In C. A. Malchiodi (Ed.), *Handbook of art therapy* (pp. 387–398). New York: Guilford Press.

Ringwald, C. D. (2003). Spirituality: An evidence-based practice for treatment and recovery. *Counselor: The Magazine for Addiction Professional, 4*(3), 32–37.

Rodman, R. F. (2003). *Winnicott: Life and work.* New York: Perseus.

Rogers, C. (1939). *The clinical treatment of the problem child.* Boston: Houghton Mifflin.

Rogers, C. (1942). *Counseling and psychotherapy: Newer concepts in practice.* Boston: Houghton Mifflin.

Rogers, C. (1961). *On becoming a person.* Boston: Houghton Mifflin.

Rogers, C. (1964). The concept of the fully functioning person. *Psychotherapy Theory, Research and Practice, 1,* 17–26.

Rogers, C. (1969). *Freedom to learn.* Columbus, OH: Merrill.

Rogers, C. (1970). *Carl Rogers on encounter groups.* New York: Harper & Row.

Rogers, C. (1972). *Becoming partners: Marriage and its alternatives.* New York: Delacorte Press.

Rogers, C. (1973). My philosophy of interpersonal relationships and how it grew. *Journal of Humanistic Psychology, 13,* 3–15.

Rogers, C. (1977). *Carl Rogers on personal power: Inner strength and its revolutionary impact*. New York: Delacorte Press.

Rogers, C. (1983). *Freedom to learn for the 80's*. Columbus, OH: Merrill.

Rogers, C. (1986). Client-centered therapy. In I. L. Kutash & A. Wolf (Eds.), *Psychotherapist's casebook: Therapy and technique in practice* (pp. 197–208). San Francisco: Jossey-Bass.

Rogers, C., & Freiberg, H. (1994). *Freedom to learn* (3rd ed.). New York: Merrill.

Rogers, C., Gendlin, E., Kiesler, D., & Truax, C. (1967). *The therapeutic relationship and its impact: A study of psychotherapy with schizophrenics*. Madison: University of Wisconsin Press.

Rogers, N. (1993). *The creative connection: Expressive arts as healing*. Palo Alto, CA: Science and Behavior Books.

Rollnick, S., & Miller, W. R. (1995). What is motivational interviewing? *Behavioural and Cognitive Psychotherapy, 23,* 325–334.

Rollnick, S., Mason, P., & Butler, C. C. (1999). *Health behavioral change: A guide for practitioners*. New York: Churchill Livingstone.

Rollnick, S., Miller, W. R., & Butler, C. C. (2008). *Motivational interviewing in health care*. New York: Guilford Press.

Roman, P., & Blum, T. (1997). *National Treatment Center study six and 12 month follow-up summary Report*. Athens, GA: Institute for Behavioral Research.

Romanucci-Ross, L., & DeVos, G. (Eds.). (1995). *Ethnic identity, creation, conflict, and accommodation*. Walnut Creek, CA: Altamira.

Rozum, A. L., & Malchiodi, C. (2003). Cognitive-behavioral approaches. In C. A. Malchiodi (Ed.), *Handbook of art therapy: Theory and techniques* (pp. 72–81). New York: Guilford Press.

Rubak, S., Sandbaek, A., Lauritzen, T., & Christensen, B. (2005). Motivational interviewing: A systematic review and meta-analysis. *British Journal of General Practice, 55,* 305–312.

Ruiz, F. J. (2010). A review of acceptance and commitment therapy (ACT) empirical evidence: Correlational, experimental psychopathology, component and outcome studies. *International Journal of Psychology and Psychological Therapy, 10*(1), 125–162.

Rule, W. R., & Bishop, M. (2006). *Adlerian lifestyle counseling: Practice and research*. New York: Taylor & Francis.

Rush, A. J., & Beck, A. T. (2000). Cognitive therapy. In H. I. Kaplan & B. J. Sadock (Eds.), *Comprehensive textbook of psychiatry* (7th ed.). Baltimore: Williams & Wilkins.

Russell, S. R., & Yarhouse, M. A. (2006). Religion/spirituality within APA-accredited psychology predoctoral internships. *Professional Psychology: Research and Practice, 37,* 430–436.

Ryan, R. M., & Deci, E. L. (2000). Self-determination theory and the facilitation of intrinsic motivation, social development, and well-being. *American Psychologist, 55,* 68–78.

Ryback, D. (1975). Books: The Fritz Perls mystique. *Psychology Today, 9,* 75–76.

Ryff, C. D., Keyes, C. L. M., & Hughes, D. L. (2003). Status inequalities, perceived discrimination, and eudaimonic well-being. Do the challenges of minority life hone purpose and growth? *Journal of Health and Social Behavior, 44,* 275–290.

Safran, J. D. (2003). *Psychoanalysis and Buddhism: An unfolding dialogue*. Boston: Wisdom.

Safran, J. D. (2012). *Psychotherapy and psychoanalytic therapies*. Washington, DC: American Psychological Association.

Safran, J. D., & Segal, Z. V. (1990/1996). *Interpersonal process in cognitive therapy* (2nd ed.). New York: Basic Books. Northvale, NJ: Aronson.

Sage, G. P. (1997). Counseling American Indian adults. In C. C. Lee (Ed.), *Multicultural issues in counseling* (2nd ed., pp. 35–52). Alexandria, VA: American Counseling Association.

Saleebey, D. (1992). *The strengths perspective in social work practice*. New York: Longman.

Saleebey, D. (1996). The strengths perspective in social work practice: Extensions and cautions. *Social Work, 41,* 296–305.

Saleebey, D. (2001). The diagnostic strengths manual. *Social Work, 46,* 183–187.

Salsman, J. M., & Carlson, C. R. (2005). Religious orientation, mature faith, and psychological distress: Elements of positive and negative associations. *Journal for the Scientific Study of Religion, 44,* 201–209.

Sandler, J. (1983). Reflections on some relations between psychoanalytic concepts and psychoanalytic practice. *International Journal of Psychoanalysis, 64,* 35–45.

Santee, R. G. (2007). *An integrative approach to counseling: Bridging Chinese thought, evolutionary theory, and stress management*. Thousand Oaks, CA: Sage.

Santorelli, S. (1999). *Heal thyself: Lessons on mindfulness in medicine*. New York: Random House.

Sapp, M. (2010). School counseling for African American adolescents: The Alfred Adler approach. *Multicultural Learning and Teaching, 5*(2), 60–72.

Sara, S. J. (2000). Retrieval and reconsolidation: Toward a neurobiology of remembering. *Learning & Memory, 7,* 773–784.

Sara, S. J., & Hars, B. (2006). In memory of consolidation. *Learning & Memory, 12,* 515–521.

Sartre, J. P. (1948). *Being and nothingness* (H. E. Barnes, Trans.). New York: Philosophical Library. (Original work published 1943)

Sartre, J. P. (1967). *Existential psychoanalysis*. Chicago: Henry Regnery.

Satir, V. M. (1964). *Conjoint family therapy*. Palo Alto, CA: Science and Behavior.

Satir, V. M. (1972). *Peoplemaking*. Palo Alto, CA: Science and Behavior.

Satir, V. M. (1986). A partial portrait of a family therapist in process. In H. C. Fishman & B. L. Rosman (Eds.), *Evolving models for family change: A volume in honor of Salvador Minuchin* (pp. 278–293). New York: Guilford.

Satir, V. M., & Baldwin, M. (1983). *Satir step by step.* Palo Alto, CA: Science and Behavior.

Satir, V. M., Stachowiak, J., & Taschman, H. A. (1975). *Helping families to change.* New York: Aronson.

Sauber, S. R., L'Abate, L., & Weeks, G. R. (1985). *Family therapy: Basic concepts and terms.* Rockville, MD: Aspen.

Sayers, S. L., & Heyman, R. E. (2003). Behavioral couples therapy. In G. P. Sholevar (Ed.), *Textbook of family and couples therapy: Clinical applications* (pp. 462–500). Washington, DC: American Psychiatric Association.

Schaefer, C. E. (2003a). *Play therapy with adults.* Hoboken, NJ: Wiley.

Schaefer, C. E. (2003b). Prescriptive play therapy. In C. E. Schaefer (Ed.), *Foundations of play therapy* (pp. 306–320). New York: Wiley.

Schedit, J. (1973). Sigmund Freud and cocaine. *Psyche,* 385–430.

Scheel, M. J., Davis, C. K., & Henderson, J. D. (2013). Therapist use of client strengths: A qualitative study of positive processes. *The Counseling Psychologist, 4*(3), 392–427.

Scheiby, B. B. (1999). Music as symbolic expression: Analytic music therapy. In D. J. Weiner (Ed.), *Beyond talk therapy: Using movement and expressive techniques in clinical practice* (pp. 261–273). Washington, DC: American Psychological Association.

Schmidt, J. (2002). *Intentional helping: A philosophy for proficient caring relationships.* Upper Saddle River, NJ: Merrill Prentice Hall.

Schneider, K. J. (2008). *Existential-integrative psychotherapy: Guideposts to the core of practice.* New York: Routledge.

Schneider, K., Bugental, J. F. T., & Pierson, J. F. (Eds.). (2001). *The handbook of humanistic psychology.* Thousand Oaks, CA: Sage.

Schön, D. A. (1983). *The reflective practitioner.* New York: Basic Books.

Schön, D. A. (1987). *Educating the reflective practitioner.* San Francisco: Jossey-Bass.

Schore, A. N. (1994). *Affect regulation and the origin of the self: The neurobiology of emotional development.* Hillsdale, NJ: Lawrence Erlbaum.

Schore, A. N. (2000). Attachment and the regulation of the right brain. *Attachment and Human Development, 2*(1), 23–47.

Schore, A. N. (2002). Advances in neuropsychoanalysis, attachment theory, and trauma research: Implications for self-psychology. *Psychoanalysis Inquiry, 22,* 433–484.

Schore, A. N. (2003). *Affect dysregulation and disorders of the self.* New York: W. W. Norton.

Schulte-Ruther, M., Markowitsch, H. J., Shah, N. J., Fink, G. R., & Piefke, M. (2007). Gender differences in brain networks supporting empathy. *Neuroimage, 42,* 393–403.

Schultz, D., & Schultz, S. E. (2001). *Theories of personality* (7th ed.). Belmont, CA: Wadsworth.

Schure, M. B., Christopher, J., & Christopher, S. (2008). Mind-body medicine and the art of self-care: Teaching mindfulness to counseling students through yoga, meditation, and qigong. *Journal of Counseling & Development, 86*(1), 47–56.

Schwartz, J. M., & Begley, S. (2002). *The mind and the brain: Neuroplasticity and the power of mental force.* New York: Regan Books.

Sciacca, K. (1997). Removing barriers: Dual diagnosis treatment and motivational interviewing. *Professional Counselor, 12*(1), 41–46.

Scovel, K. A., Christensen, O. J., & England, J. T. (2002). Mental health counselors' perceptions regarding psychopharmacological prescriptive privileges. *Journal of Mental Health Counseling, 24,* 36–50.

Searle, J. R. (1995). *The construction of social reality.* New York: Free Press.

Segal, Z. V., Williams, J. M. G., & Teasdale, J. D. (2002). *Mindfulness-based cognitive therapy for depression: A new approach to preventing relapse.* New York: Guilford Press.

Segal, Z. V., Williams, M. G., & Teasdale, J. D. (2002). *Mindfulness-based cognitive therapy for depression: A new approach to preventing relapse.* New York: Guilford.

Selekman, M. D. (1997). *Solution-focused therapy with children.* New York: Guilford Press.

Seligman, M. E. (1991). *Learned optimism.* New York: Knopf.

Seligman, M. E. (1998, July–August). The president's address. *American Psychologist, 54,* 559–562.

Seligman, M. E. (1999, July–August). Teaching positive psychology. *APA Monitor on Psychology, 30*(7). Available from http://www.apa.org

Seligman, M. E. P. (2004). *Authentic happiness: Using the new positive psychology to realize your potential for lasting fulfillment.* New York: Free Press.

Seligman, M. E., Reivich, K., Jaycox, L., & Gillham, J. (1995). *The optimistic child.* New York: Houghton Mifflin.

Seligman, M., Schulman, P., DeRubeis, R. J., & Hollon, S. D. (1999). The prevention of depression and anxiety. *Prevention and Treatment, 2,* Article 0008a. Retrieved from http://journals.apa.org/prevention/volume2/prev0020008a.html

Semple, R. J., Lee, J., & Miller, L. F. (2006). Mindfulness-based cognitive therapy for children. In R. A. Baer (Ed.), *Mindfulness-based treatment approaches* (pp. 143–166). New York: Academic Press.

Sevensky, R. L. (1984). Religion, psychology, and mental health. *American Journal of Psychotherapy, 38,* 73–86.

Sexton, T. L. (1997). Constructivist thinking within the history of ideas: The challenge of a new paradigm. In

E. L. Sexton & B. L. Griffin (Eds.), *Constructivist thinking in counseling practice, research and training* (pp. 3–18). New York: Teachers College Press.

Shadish, W. R., & Baldwin, S. A. (2003). Meta-analysis of MFT interventions. *Journal of Marital and Family Therapy, 29,* 547–570.

Shadish, W. R., Montgomery, L. M., Wilson, P., Wilson, M. R., Bright, I., & Okwumabua, T. (1993). The effects of family and marital psychotherapies: A meta-analysis. *Journal of Consulting and Clinical Psychology, 61,* 992–1002.

Shafranske, E.P. (2000). Religious involvement and professional practices of psychiatrists and other mental health professionals. *Psychiatric Annals, 30,* 525–532.

Shafranske, E. P., & Malony, H. N. (1990). Clinical psychologists' religious and spiritual orientations and their practice of psychotherapy. *Psychotherapy, 27,* 72–78.

Shapiro, D. H., & Astin, J. (1998). *Control therapy: An integrated approach to psychotherapy, health, and healing.* New York: John Wiley.

Shapiro, F. (1995). *Eye movement desensitization and reprocessing (EMDR): Basic principles, protocols, and procedures.* New York: Guilford Press.

Shapiro, F. (2001). *Eye movement desensitization and reprocessing (EMDR): Basic principles, protocols, and procedures* (2nd ed.). New York: Guilford Press. Retrieved from https://www.emdr.com/general-information/what-is-emdr/what-is-emdr.html

Shapiro, S. L., Brown, K. W., & Biegel, G. M. (2007). Teaching self-care to caregivers: Effects of mindfulness-based stress reduction on the mental health of therapists in training. *Training and Education in Professional Psychology, 1,* 105–115.

Shapiro, S. L., & Carlson, L. E. (2009). *The art and science of mindfulness: Integrating mindfulness into psychology and the helping professions.* Washington, DC: American Psychological Corporation.

Shapiro, S. L., Schwartz, G. E., & Bonner, G. (1998). Effects of mindfulness-based stress reduction on medical and premedical students. *Journal of Behavioral Medicine, 21,* 581–599.

Sharf, R. S. (2004). *Theories of psychotherapy and counseling: Concepts and cases* (3rd ed.). Pacific Grove, CA: Brooks/Cole.

Shedler, J. (2010). The efficacy of psychodynamic psychotherapy. *American Psychologist, 65*(2), 98–109.

Shepard, M. (1975). *Fritz: An intimate portrait of Fritz Perls and Gestalt therapy.* New York: Saturday Review Press.

Shepard, M. (1976). *Fritz.* New York: Bantam.

Sherman, R. (1993). The intimacy genogram. *The Family Journal: Counseling and Therapy of Couples and Families, 1,* 91–93.

Sherman, R., & Dinkmeyer, D. (1987). *Systems of family therapy: An Adlerian integration.* New York: Brunner/Mazel.

Shoben, E. J. (1962). The counselor's theory as a personal trait. *Personnel and Guidance Journal, 40,* 617–621.

Shotter, J. (1993). *Cultural politics of everyday life: Social constructionism, rhetoric and knowing of the third kind.* Toronto: University of Toronto Press.

Shueman, S. A., Troy, W. G., & Mayhugh, S. L. (Eds.). *Managed behavioral health care.* Springfield, IL: Charles C Thomas.

Siegel, D. J. (1999). *The developing mind: Toward a neurobiology of interpersonal experience.* New York: Guilford.

Siegel, D. J. (2007). *The mindful brain: Reflection and attunement in the cultivation of well-being.* New York: W. W. Norton.

Siegel, D. J. (2010). *The mindful therapist: A clinician's guide to mindsight and neural integration.* New York: W. W. Norton.

Siegel, D. J. (2012). *The developing mind: How relationships and the brain interact to shape who we are.* New York: Guilford Press.

Siegel, D. J. (2013). *Brainstorm: The power and purpose of the teen brain.* New York: Jeremy P. Tarcher/Penguin.

Silva, J. M. (2007). Mindfulness-based cognitive therapy for the reduction of anger in married men. *Dissertation Abstracts International: Section B: The Sciences and Engineering, 68*(3-B), 1945.

Silver, E., Williams, A., Worthington, F., & Phillips, M. (1998). Family therapy and soiling: An audit of externalizing and other approaches. *Journal of Family Therapy, 20,* 413–422.

Silverman, M. J. (2006). Psychiatric patients' perception of music therapy and other psychoeducational programming. *Journal of Music Therapy, 43*(2), 111–22.

Simms, W. (1999). The Native American Indian client: A tale of two cultures. In Y. Jenkins (Ed.), *Diversity in college settings: Directives for helping professionals* (pp. 21–35). New York: Routledge.

Simon, G. M. (2004). An examination of the integrative nature of emotionally focused therapy. *The Family Journal: Counseling and Therapy for Couples and Families, 12,* 254–262.

Simon, R. (1985, September/October). Take it or leave it: An interview with Carl Whitaker. *Family Therapy Networker, 9,* 27–34.

Simon, R. (1989, January/February). Reaching out to life: An interview with Virginia Satir. *Family Therapy Networker, 13,* 36–43.

Singh, J., & Tudor, K. (1997). Cultural conditions of therapy. *The Person-Centered Journal, 4,* 32–46.

Skinner, B. F. (1948). *Walden two.* Indianapolis, IN: Hackett.

Skinner, B. F. (1971). *Beyond freedom and dignity.* New York: Knopf.

Skinner, B. F. (1974). *About behaviorism.* New York: Vintage.

Skinner, B. F. (1976). *Particulars of my life.* New York: New York University Press.

Skinner, N. F., & Fox-Francoeur, C. A. (2010). Personality implications of adaption-innovation: V. Birth order as a determinant of cognitive style. *Social Behavior and Personality, 38*(2), 237–240. doi:10.2224/sbp.2010.38.2.237

Sklare, G. B., Taylor, J., & Hyland, S. (1985). An emotion control card for rational emotive imagery. *Journal of Counseling and Development, 64*(2), 145–146.

Slavik, S., & King, R. (2007). Adlerian therapeutic strategy. *Canadian Journal of Adlerian Psychology, 37*(1), 3–16.

Slayton, S. C., D'Archer, J. D., & Kaplan, F. (2010). Outcome studies on the efficacy of art therapy: A review of findings. *Art Therapy: Journal of the American Art Therapy Association, 27*(3), 108–118.

Sloane, R. B., Staples, E. R., Cristol, A. H., Yorkston, N. J., & Whipple, K. (1975). *Psychotherapy versus behavior therapy.* Cambridge, MA: Harvard University Press.

Smith, E. J. (1985). Ethnic minorities: Life stress, social support, and mental health issues. *The Counseling Psychologist, 13,* 537–579.

Smith, E. J. (1989). Black racial identity development: Issues and concerns. *The Counseling Psychologist, 17,* 277–289.

Smith, E. J. (1991). Ethnic identity development: Toward the development of a theory within the context of majority/minority status. *Journal of Counseling & Development, 70,* 181–188.

Smith, E. J. (2001). *Ethnic self-schemas and ethnic identity development.* Unpublished manuscript.

Smith, E. J. (2002). *Ethnic identity maturity and developmental tasks.* Unpublished manuscript.

Smith, E. J. (2003). *Ethnic identity development: Proposal for a theory.* Unpublished manuscript.

Smith, E. J. (2006a). The strength-based counseling model (Major contribution). *The Counseling Psychologist, 34,* 13–79.

Smith, E. J. (2006b). The strength-based counseling model: A paradigm shift in psychology. *The Counseling Psychologist, 34,* 134–144.

Smith, E. J. (2008). *Nurturing nonviolent children: A guide for parents, educators, and counselors.* Westport, CT: Greenwood Press.

Smith, M. L., Glass, G. V., & Miller, T. I. (1980). *The benefits of psychotherapy.* Baltimore: Johns Hopkins University Press.

Smithrim, K., & Upitis, R. (2005). Learning through the arts: Lessons of engagement. *Canadian Journal of Education, 28,* 109–127.

Smock, S. A., Trepper, T. S., Weltchler, J. L., McCollum, E. E., Ray, R., & Pierce, K. (2008). Solution-focused group therapy for Level 1 substance abusers. *Journal of Marital and Family Therapy, 34*(1), 107–120.

Snyder, C. R. (Ed.). (2000). *Handbook of hope: Theory, measures, and applications.* San Diego, CA: Academic Press.

Snyder, C. R., & Lopez, S. (Eds.). (2002). *Handbook of positive psychology.* New York: Oxford University Press.

Snyder, C. R., Lopez, S. J., & Teramoto, J. T. (2010). *Positive psychology: The scientific and practical explorations of human strengths.* Thousand Oaks, CA: Sage.

Snyder, C. R., McDermott, D., Cook, W., & Rapoff, M. A. (1997). *Hope for the journey: Helping children through good times and bad.* Boulder, CO: Westview.

Sokolovsky, J. (1985). Ethnicity, culture, and aging: Do differences really make a difference? *Journal of Applied Gerontology, 4,* 6–7.

Solomon, J. (1938). Active play therapy. *American Journal of Orthopsychiatry, 8*(3), 763–781.

Sperry, R. W. (1993). The impact and promise of the cognitive revolution. *American Psychologist, 48*(8), 878–885.

Spiegler, M. D., & Guevremont, D. C. (2003). *Contemporary behavior therapy* (4th ed.). Pacific Grove, CA: Brooks/Cole.

Spiegler, M. D., & Guevremont, D. C. (2010). *Contemporary behavior therapy* (5th ed.). Belmont, CA: Wadsworth, Cengage Learning.

St. Clair, M. (1996). *Object relations and self psychology: An introduction* (2nd ed.). Pacific Grove: Brooks/Cole Publishing Co.

St. Clair, M. (2000). *Object relations and self psychology: An introduction* (3rd ed.). Belmont, CA: Wadsworth.

Staats, A.W. (1993). Personality theory, abnormal psychology, and psychological measurement: A psychological behaviorism. *Behavior Modification, 17,* 8–42.

Stalker, C. A., Levene, J. E., & Coady, N. F. (1999). Solution-focused brief therapy—one model fits all? *The Journal of Contemporary Human Services, 80,* 468–477.

Stampfl, T. G. (1970). Implosive therapy: An emphasis on covert stimulation. In J. D. Leavis (Ed.), *Learning approaches to therapeutic behavior change* (pp. 182–204). Chicago: Aldine.

Stams, G. J., Dekovic, M., Buist, K., & de Vries, L. (2006). Effectiviteit van oplossingsgerichte korte therapie: Een meta-analyse [Efficacy of solution-focused brief therapy: A meta-analysis]. *Gedragstherapie, 39,* 81–94.

Stanley, D. A., Sokol-Hessner, P., Fareri, D. S., Perino, M. T., Delgado, M. R., Banaji, M. R., & Phelps, E. A. (2012). Race and reputation: Perceived racial group trustworthiness influences the neural correlates of trust decisions. *Philosophical Transactions of the Royal Society, 367*(1589), 744–753. doi:10.1098/rstb.2011.0300

Stanton, M. D., & Shadish, W. R. (1997). Outcome, attrition, and family-couples treatment for drug abuse: A meta-analysis and review of the controlled, comparative studies. *Psychological Bulletin, 122,* 170–191.

Staudinger, U. M., & Baltes, P. B. (1996). Interactive minds: A facilitative setting for wisdom related performance? *Journal of Personality and Social Psychology, 71,* 746–762.

Staudinger, U. M., & Pasupathi, M. (2000). Lifespan perspectives on self, personality and social cognition. In T. Salthouse & F. Craik (Eds.), *Handbook of cognition and aging* (p. 688). Hillsdale, NJ: Lawrence Erlbaum.

Staudinger, U. M., Freund, A., Linden, M., & Maas, I. (1999). Self, personality, and life regulation: Facets of psychological resilience in old age. In P. B. Baltes & K. U. Mayer (Eds.), *The Berlin Aging Study: Aging from 70 to 100* (pp. 302–328). New York: Cambridge University Press.

Staudinger, U. M., Marsiske, M., & Baltes, P. B. (1996). Resilience and reserve capacity in later adulthood: Potentials and limits of development across the lifespan. In D. Ciccjetti & D. Cohen (Eds.), *Development psychopathology: Vol. 2 Risk, disorder, and adaptation* (pp. 801–847). New York: John Wiley.

Steele, C. M. (2003). Through the back door to theory. *Psychological Inquiry, 14,* 314–317.

Stein, H. T., & Edwards, M. E. (1998). Alfred Adler: Classical theory and practice. *In P. Marcus & A. Rosenberg (Ed.), Psychoanalytic versions of the human condition: Philosophies of life and their impact on practice (pp. 64–93). New York: New York University Press.*

Sternberg, R. J. (1985). Implicit theories of intelligence, creativity, and wisdom. *Journal of Personality and Social Psychology, 49,* 607–627.

Stevens, A. (1994). *Jung: A very short introduction.* Oxford, UK: Oxford University Press.

Stevens, R. (2008). *Erik H. Erikson: Explorer of identity and the life cycle.* New York: Palgrave MacMillan.

Stiles, W. B., Shapiro, D. A., & Elliott, R. (1986). Are all psychotherapies equivalent? *American Psychologist, 41,* 165–180.

Stokes, D. (1986, June 11). It's no time to shun psychologists, Bandura says. *Campus Report,* pp. 1–3.

Stone, M. (1993). Balancing the self with the marital system. *Individual Psychology: Journal of Adlerian Theory, Research and Practice, 49,* 392–398.

Storaasli, R. D., Kraushaar, B., & Emrick, C. (2007). Convention, tradition, and the new wave: Assessing clinician identity in behavior therapy. *The Behavior Therapist, 30*(7), 149–155.

Storr, A. (1992). *Music and the mind.* New York: Free Press.

Stricker, G. (2001). An introduction to psychotherapy integration. *Psychiatric Times,* xviii, 7. Available at http://www.psychiatrictimes.com/p010755.html

Strumpfel, U., & Goldman, R. (2002). Contacting Gestalt therapy. In D. J. Cain & J. Seeman (Eds.), *Humanistic psychotherapies: Handbook of research and practice* (pp. 189–219). Washington, DC: American Psychological Association.

Strupp, H. H., & Binder, J. L. (1984). *Psychotherapy in a new key.* New York: Basic Books.

Sue, D. W. (1972). Counseling Chinese-Americans. *Personnel and Guidance Journal, 50,* 637–644.

Sue, D. W. (1997). Multiculturalism and discomfort. *Spectrum, 57*(3), 7–9.

Sue, D. W., Arredondo, P., & McDavis, R. J. (1992). Multicultural competencies/standards: A call to the profession. *Journal of Counseling and Development, 70*(4), 477–486.

Sue, D. W., Ivey, A. E., & Pedersen, P. B. (Eds.). (1996). *A theory of multicultural counseling and therapy.* Pacific Grove: CA: Brooks/Cole.

Sue, S., & Lam, A. G. (2002). Cultural and demographic diversity. In J. C. Norcross (Ed.), *Psychotherapy relationships that work* (pp. 401–422). New York: Oxford University Press.

Sue, D. W., & Sue, D. (1999). *Counseling the culturally different: Theory and practice.* (3rd ed.). New York: Wiley.

Sue, D. W., & Sue, D. (2003). *Counseling the culturally diverse: Theory and practice* (4th ed.). New York: Wiley.

Sue, D. W., & Sue, D. (2008). *Counseling the culturally diverse: Theory and practice* (5th ed.). New York: Wiley.

Sulliman, J. (1973). The development of a scale for the measurement of social interest. *Dissertation Abstracts International, 34,* 6.

Sulloway, F. (1996). *Born to rebel.* New York: Pantheon.

Sulloway, F. (1997). *Born to rebel: Birth order, family dynamics, and creative lives.* New York: Pantheon.

Sundland, D. M., & Barker, E. N. (1962). The orientation of psychotherapists. *Journal of Counseling Psychology, 26,* 201–212.

Sutton, S. (2002). Back to the drawing board? A review of the transtheoretical model to substance use. *Addiction, 96*(1), 175–186.

Suzuki, L. A., Ponterotto, J. G., Casas, J. M., & Alexander, C. M. (2010). *Handbook of multicultural counseling* (3rd ed.). Thousand Oaks, CA: Sage.

T'ai Shen Centre for Mindfulness, Happiness and Healing. (n.d.) Retrieved on February 8, 2011, from http://www.taishendo.com/Mindfulness-training.html

Tallman, K., & Bohart, A. C. (1999). The client as a common factor: Clients as self-healers. In M. A. Hubble, B. L. Duncan, & S. D. Miller (Eds.), *The heart and soul of change: What works in therapy* (pp. 91–131). Washington, DC: American Psychological Association.

Tanaka-Matsumi, J., & Higginbotham, H. N. (1989). Behavioral approaches to counseling across cultures. In P. B. Pedersen, J. G. Draguns, W. J. Lonner, & J. E. Trimble (Eds.), *Counseling across cultures* (pp. 269–298). Honolulu: University of Hawaii Press.

Tanaka-Matsumi, J., Higginbotham, H. N., & Chang, R. (2002). Cognitive-behavioral approaches to counseling across cultures: A functional analytic approach for clinical applications. In P. B. Pedersen, J. G. Draguns, W. J. Lonner, & J. E. Trimble (Eds.), *Counseling across cultures* (5th ed., pp. 337–379). Thousand Oaks, CA: Sage.

Tancredi, L. (2005). *Hardwired behavior: What neuroscience reveals about morality.* New York: Cambridge University Press.

Taub-Bynum, E. B. (1999). *The African unconscious: Roots of ancient mysticism and modern psychology.* New York: Teachers College Press.

Teasdale, J. D., Segal, Z. V., Williams, J. M. G., Ridgeway, V. A., Soulsby, J. M., & Lau, M. (2000). Prevention of relapse/recurrence in major depression by mindfulness-based cognitive therapy. *Journal of Consulting and Clinical Psychology, 68*(4), 615–623.

Tehan, B., & McDonald, M. (2010). Engaging fathers in child and family services (CAFCA Practice Sheet). *Australian Institute of Family Studies.* Retrieved from http://www.aifs.gov.au/cafca/pubs/sheets/ps/ps2.pdf

Ter Laack, J., de Goede, M., & Aleva, A. (2005). The Draw-a-Person Test: An indicator of children's cognitive and socioemotional adaptation. *Journal of Genetic Psychology, 166,* 77–93.

Terndrup, A., Ritter, K., Barret, B., Logan, C., & Mate, R. (1997). *Competencies in counseling gay, lesbian, bisexual, and transgendered clients.* Retrieved January 15, 2004, from http://www.aglbic.org/competencies.html

Thaut, M., & McIntosh, G. (2010, March 24). *How music helps to heal the injured brain.* New York: Dana Foundation. Retrieved December 28, 2010, from http://www.dana.org/news/cerebrum/detail.aspx?=26122

Thorndike, E. L. (1911). *Animal intelligence.* New York: Macmillan.

Thorngren, J. M., & Kleist, D. M. (2002). Multiple family group therapy: An interpersonal/postmodern approach. *The Family Journal: Counseling and Therapy for Couples and Families, 10*(2), 167–176.

Timimi, S. B. (1995). Adolescence in immigrant Arab families. *Psychotherapy, 32,* 141–149.

Toman, W. (1961). *Family constellation: Its effects on personality and social behavior.* New York: Springer.

Tomasello, M. (1999). *The cultural origins of human cognition.* Cambridge, MA: Harvard University Press.

Tomasello, M., Carpenter, M., Call, J., Behne, T., & Moll, H. (2005). Understanding and sharing intentions: The ontogeny and phylogeny of cultural cognition. *Behavioral and Brain Sciences, 28,* 675–735.

Torrey, E. F. (1986). *Witchdoctors and psychiatrists: The common roots of psychotherapy and its future.* New York: Harper & Row.

Trainor, K. (2004). *Buddhism: The illustrated guide.* New York: Oxford University Press.

Trepper, T. S., & Franklin, C. (2012). Epilogue: The future of research in solution-focused brief therapy. In C. Franklin, T. S. Trepper, W. J. Gingerich, & E. E. McCollum (Eds.), *Solution-focused brief therapy: A handbook of evidence-based practice* (pp. 405–412). New York: Oxford University Press.

Trimble, J. E. (1990). Application of psychological knowledge for American Indians and Alaska Natives. *Journal of Training and Practice in Professional Psychology, 4,* 45–63.

Tucker, B., Hully, L., & Ticic, R. (2012). *Unlocking the emotional brain.* New York: Taylor & Francis.

Tucker, D. M., Luu, P., & Pribram, K. H. (1995). Social and emotional self-regulation. *Annals of the New York Academy of Sciences, 769,* 213–239.

Turner, K. (2009). Mindfulness: The present moment in clinical social work. *Journal of Clinical Social Work, 37,* 95–103.

Twohig, M. P., Hayes, S. C., & Masuda, A. (2006). Increasing willingness to experience obsessions: Acceptance and commitment therapy as a treatment for obsessive-compulsive disorder. *Behavior Therapy, 37*(1), 3–13.

U.S. Census Bureau. (2005). Available at http://www.census.gov/

Vaihinger, H. (1924). *Philoslophie des als ob* (First published in England by Routledge and Kegan Paul, Ltd., 1924)

Vaihinger, H. (1968). *The philosophy of "as if": A system of the theoretical, practical and religious fictions of mankind* (C. K. Ogden, Trans.). New York: Barnes & Noble. (Original work published 1911)

Vailant, G. (2000). The mature defenses: Antecedents of joy. *American Psychologist, 55,* 89–98.

Van de Wall, W. (1936). *Music in institutions.* New York: Russell Sage Foundation.

van der Kolk, B. A. (2006). The neurobiology of childhood trauma and abuse. *Child and Adolescent Psychiatric Clinics of North America, 12,* 293–317.

van Deurzen-Smith, E. (1990). *Existential therapy.* London: Society for Existential Analysis Publications.

van Deurzen-Smith, E. (1997). *Everyday mysteries: Existential dimensions of psychotherapy.* London: Routledge.

van Deurzen-Smith, E. (1998). *Paradox and passion in psychotherapy: An existential approach to therapy and counseling.* Chichester, UK: Wiley.

van Deurzen-Smith, E. (2002). *Existential counseling and psychotherapy in practice.* London: Sage.

Van Velsor, P. (2013, February 1). Thinking creatively: Expressive arts for counseling youth in the schools. *Counseling Today: A Publication of the American Counseling Association.* Retrieved from http://ct.counseling.org/2013/02/thinking-creatively-expressive-arts-for-counseling-youth-in-the-schools/

Varlami, E., & Bayne, R. (2007). Psychological type and counseling psychology trainee's choice of counseling orientation. *Counseling Psychology Quarterly, 12,* 263–271.

Velicer, W. F., DiClemente, C. C., Prochaska, J. O., & Brandenburg, N. (1985). Decisional balance measure for assessing and predicting smoking status. *Journal of Personality and Social Psychology, 48,* 1279–1289.

Velicer, W. F., Prochaska, J. O., Fava, J. L., Norman, G. J., & Redding, C. A. (1998). Smoking cessation and stress management: Applications of the transtheoretical model of behavior change. *Homeostasis, 38,* 216–233.

Verschuuren, G. (2012). *What makes you tick? A new paradigm for neuroscience.* Antioch, CA: Solas Press.

Visser, C. (2008). A brief history of the solution-focused approach. Retrieved March 26, 2010, from http://articlescoertvisser.blogspot.com/2008/02/brief-history-of-solution-focused.html

Vontress, C. E. (1999). Interview with a traditional African healer. *Journal of Mental Health Counseling, 21,* 326–336.

Vontress, C. E. (2001). Cross-cultural counseling in the 21st century. *International Journal for the Advancement of Counseling, 23*(2), 83–97.

Vontress, C. E. (2005). Animism: Foundations of healing in sub-Saharan Africa. In R. Moodley & W. West (Eds.),

Integrating traditional healing practices into counseling and psychotherapy (pp. 124–137). Thousand Oaks, CA: Sage.

Vontress, C. E., & Jackson, M. L. (2004). Reactions to the multicultural counseling competencies debate. *Journal of Mental Health, 26*(1), 74–80.

Vontress, C. E., Johnson, J. A., & Epp, L. R. (1999). *Cross-cultural counseling: A casebook.* Alexandria, VA: American Counseling Association.

Vujanovic, A. A., Youngwirth, N. E., Johnson, K. E., & Zvolensky, M. J. (2009). Mindfulness-based acceptance and posttraumatic stress symptoms among trauma-exposed adults without axis 1 psychopathology. *Journal of Anxiety Disorders, 23*, 297–303.

Vygotsky, L. S. (1978). *Mind in society: The development of higher psychological processes.* Cambridge, MA: Harvard University Press.

Wachtel, P. (1977). *Psychoanalysis and behavior therapy: Toward an integration.* New York: Basic books.

Wachtel, P. L. (1977). *Psychoanalysis and behavior therapy: Toward integration.* New York: Basic Books.

Wagner-Moore, L. E. (2004). Gestalt therapy: Past, present, theory, and research. *Psychotherapy, Theory, Research, Practice, Training, 41*(2), 180–189.

Wall, M. D., Kleckner, T., Amendt, J. H., & Bryant, R. D. (1989). Therapeutic compliments: Setting the stage for successful therapy. *Journal of Marriage and Family Therapy.* New York: Brunner/Mazel.

Walsh, F. (1998). *Strengthening family resilience.* New York: Guilford.

Walsh, R. (1999a). Asian contemplative disciplines: Common practices, clinical applications, and research findings. *Journal of Transpersonal Psychology, 31*, 83–107.

Walsh, R. (1999b). *Essential spirituality: The seven central practices.* New York: Wiley.

Walsh, R. (2001). Meditation. In R. J. Corsini (Ed.), *Handbook of innovative psychotherapies* (2nd ed., pp. 368–380). New York: Wiley.

Walsh, R. A., & McElwain, B. (2002). Existential psychotherapies. In D. J. Cain & J. Seeman (Eds.), *Humanistic psychotherapies: Handbook of research and practice* (pp. 253–278). Washington, DC: American Psychological Association.

Walsh, W. B. (2004). *Counseling psychology and optimal human functioning.* New York: Lawrence Erlbaum.

Walsh, W. M., & McGraw, J. A. (2002). *Essentials of family therapy* (2nd ed.). Denver, CO: Love.

Walter, J. L., & Peller, J. E. (1992). *Becoming solution-focused in brief therapy.* New York: Brunner/Mazel.

Walter, J. L., & Peller, J. E. (2000). *Recreating brief therapy.* New York: W. W. Norton.

Wampold, B. E. (2001). *The great psychotherapy debate: Models, methods, and findings.* Mahwah, NJ: Lawrence Erlbaum.

Wampold, B. E. (2006). The psychotherapist. In J. C. Norcross, L. E. Beutler, & R. F. Levant (Eds.), *Evidence-based practices in mental health: Debate and dialogues on the fundamental questions* (pp. 200–208). Washington, DC: American Psychological Association.

Ward, P., & Rouzer, D. L. (1974). The nature of pathological functioning from a Gestalt perspective. *The Counseling Psychologist, 4*, 24–26.

Warner-Schmidt, J. L., & Duman, R. S. (2006). Hippocampal neurogenesis: Opposing effects of stress and antidepressant treatment. *Hippocampus, 16*(3), 239–249.

Watanabe, N. (1992). The expansion of Morita therapy. *International Bulletin of Morita Therapy, 5*(1–2), 50–55.

Watkins, C. E. (1993). Person-centered theory and the contemporary practice of psychological testing. *Counseling Psychology Quarterly, 6*, 59–67.

Watkins C. E. (1994). Measuring social interest. *Individual Psychology, 50*, 69–96.

Watkins, C. E., Lopez, F. G., Campbell, V. L., & Himmell, C. D. (1986). Contemporary counseling psychology: The results of a national survey. *Journal of Counseling Psychology, 33*, 301–309.

Watson, J. B. (1913). Psychology as the behaviorist views it. *Psychological Review, 20*, 158–177.

Watson, J. B. (1914). *Behavior: An introduction to comparative psychology.* New York: Holt.

Watson, J. B. (1924/1925). *Behaviorism.* New York: People's Institute Publishing Company.

Watson, J. B. (1983). Psychology from the standpoint of a behaviorist. Dover, NH: Frances Pinter. (Original work published 1924)

Watson, J. B., & Rayner, R. (1920). Conditioned emotional reactions. *Journal of Experimental Psychology, 3*(1), 1–14.

Watson, J. C. (2002). Re-visioning empathy. In D. J. Cain & J. Seeman (Eds.), *Humanistic psychotherapies: Handbook of research and practice* (pp. 445–471). Washington, DC: American Psychological Association.

Watts, R. E. (1993). Developing a personal theory of counseling. *Tennessee Counseling Association Journal, 21*, 85–95.

Watts, R. E. (2003a). *Adlerian, cognitive, and constructivist therapies: An integrative psychotherapy.* New York: Accelerated Development/Routledge.

Watts, R. E. (2003b). Adlerian therapy as a relational constructivist approach. *The Family Journal: Counseling and Therapy for Couples and Families, 11*(2), 139–147.

Wedding, D., & Corsini, R. J. (1989). Applied psychophysiology: A bridge between the biomedical model and the biopsychosocial model in family medicine. *Professional Psychology: Research and Practice, 27*, 221–233.

Weick, A., & Chamberlain, R. (2002). Putting problems in their place: Further explorations in the strengths perspective. In D. Saleebey (Ed.), *The strengths perspective in social work practice* (3rd ed., pp. 95–105). Boston: Allyn & Bacon.

Weick, A., Rapp, C., Sullivan, W. P., & Kisthardt, S. (1989). A strengths perspective for social work practice. *Social Work, 34,* 350–354.

Weiner, D. (1999). *Beyond talk therapy: Using movement and expressive techniques in clinical practice.* Washington, DC: American Psychological Association.

Weinrach, S. G., & Thomas, K. R. (2002). A critical analysis of the multicultural counseling competencies: Implications for the practice of mental health counseling. *Journal of Mental Health Counseling, 24,* 20–35.

Weinrach, S. G., & Thomas, K. R. (2004). The AMCD Multicultural Counseling Competencies: A critically flawed initiative. *Journal of Mental Health Counseling, 7,* 81–93.

Weishaar, M. E. (1993). *Aaron T. Beck.* London: Sage.

Weisz, J. R., Weiss, B., Han, S. S., Granger, D. A., & Morton, T. (1995). Effects of psychotherapy with children and adolescents revisited: A meta-analysis of treatment outcome studies. *Psychological Bulletin, 117,* 450–468.

Wheeler, B. (1983). A psychotherapeutic classification of music therapy practices: A continuum of procedures. *Music Therapy Perspectives, 1,* 8–12.

White, M. (1984). Pseudo-encopresis: From avalanche to victory, from vicious to virtuous cycles. *Family Systems Medicine, 2*(2), 150–160.

White, M. (1986). Negative explanation, restraint, and double description: A template for family therapy. *Family Process, 25*(2), 169–184.

White, M. (1991). Deconstruction and therapy. *Dulwich Centre Newsletter, 3,* 21–46.

White, M. (1995). *Re-authoring lives: Interviews & essays.* Adelaide, Australia: Dulwich Centre.

White, M. (1997). *Narrative of therapists' lives.* Adelaide, Australia: Dulwich Centre.

White, M. (2004). *Narrative practice and exotic lives: Resurrecting diversity in everyday life.* Adelaide, Australia: Dulwich Centre.

White, M., & Epston, D. (1990). *Narrative means to therapeutic ends.* New York: Norton.

White, R. (1999). *What are exceptional human experiences?* The Exceptional Human Experience Network. Retrieved August 29, 2009, from http://ehe.org/display/ehe-page3439.html?ID=6

Whitfield, W., McGrath, P., & Coleman, V. (1992, October). *Increasing multicultural sensitivity and awareness.* Symposium presented at the Annual Conference of the National Organization for Human Service Education, Alexandria, VA.

Whitley, D. M., White, K. R., Kelley, S. J., & Yorke, B. (1999). Strengths-based case management: The application to grandparents raising grandchildren. *Families in Society, 80*(2), 110–119.

Whitman, J. S., & Boyd, C. J. (2003). *The therapist notebook for lesbian, gay, and bisexual clients.* Binghamton, NY: Haworth.

Wilber, K., & Walsh, R. (2000). An integral approach to consciousness research. A proposal for integrating first, second, and third approaches to consciousness. In M. Velmans (Ed.), *Investigating phenomenal consciousness: New methodologies and maps. Advances in consciousness research* (Vol. 13. pp. 301–331). Amsterdam, Netherlands: John Benjamins.

Williams, J. E., & Best, D. L. (1990). *Sex and psyche: Gender and self viewed cross-culturally.* Newbury Park, CA: Sage.

Williams, K. A., Kolar, M. M., Reger, B. E., & Pearson, J. C. (2001). Evaluation of a wellness-based mindfulness stress reduction intervention: A controlled trial. *American Journal of Health Promotion, 15*(6), 422–432.

Williams, M. W., Foo, K. H., & Haarhoff, B. (2006). Cultural considerations in using cognitive behaviour therapy with Chinese people: A case study of an elderly Chinese woman with generalized anxiety disorder. *New Zealand Journal of Psychology, 35*(3). Retrieved April 8, 2014, from http://www.biomedseasrch.com/article/Cultural-considerations-in-using-cognitive/15852302

Wilson, G. T. (2005). Behavior therapy. In R. Corsini & D. Wedding (Eds.), *Current psychotherapies* (7th ed., pp. 202–237). Belmont, CA: Brooks/Cole.

Wilson, G. T. (2011). Behavior therapy. In R. Corsini & D. Welding (Eds.), *Current psychotherapies* (9th ed., pp. 235–272). Belmont, CA: Brooks/Cole-Cengage Learning.

Wilson, K. G., Follette, V. M., Hayes, S. C., & Batten, S. V. (1996). Acceptance theory and the treatment of survivors of childhood sexual abuse. *National Center for PTSD Clinical Quarterly, 6*(2), 34–37.

Windmeyer, S. L. (2006). *The advocate college guide for LGBT students.* Boston: Alyson.

Winnicott, D. (1971). *Playing and reality.* New York: Routledge.

Winnicott, D. W. (1953). Transitional objects and transitional phenomena: A study of the first not-me possession. *International Journal of Psychoanalysis, 34,* 89–97.

Winnicott, D. W. (1969). The use of an object. *International Journal of Psychoanalysis, 50,* 711–716.

Winston, D. (2003). *Wide awake: A Buddhist guide for teens.* New York: Berkeley Publishing Group.

Winter, A. (2004, December). Many thanks: Gregg Krech on the revolutionary practice of gratitude. *The Sun,* 1–13. Retrieved August 4, 2010, from http://www.todoinstitute.org/naikan3.html

Wittels, F. (1939). The neo-Adlerians. *American Journal of Sociology, 45,* 433–445.

Woldt, A. L., & Toman, S. M. (2005). *Gestalt therapy: History, theory, and practice.* Thousand Oaks, CA: Sage.

Wolin, S. J., & Wolin, S. (1993). *The resilient self: How survivors of troubled families rise above adversity.* New York: Villard.

Wolpe, J. (1958). *Psychotherapy by reciprocal inhibition.* Stanford, CA: Stanford University Press.

Wolpe, J. (1969). *The practice of behavior therapy.* Elmsford, NY: Pergamon.

Wolpe, J. (1973). *The practice of behavior therapy* (2nd ed.). Elmsford, NY: Pergamon.

Wolpe, J. (1982). *The practice of behavior therapy* (3rd ed.). Oxford, UK: Pergamon.

Wolpe, J. (1990). *The practice of psychotherapy* (4th ed.). New York: Pergamon.

Wolpe, J., & Lazarus, A. A. (1966). *Behavior therapy techniques.* New York: Pergamon.

Wolpe, J., & Rachman, S. (1960). Psychoanalytic evidence: A critique based on Freud's case of Little Hans. *Journal of Nervous and Mental Disorders, 131,* 135–145.

Wolpe, P. R. (2002, July–August). The neuroscience revolution. *Hastings Center Report, 32*(4), 8.

Wong, P. T. P., & Wong, L. C. J. (2006). *Handbook of multicultural perspectives on stress and coping.* New York: Springer.

Wong, S. E., Martinez-Diaz, J. A., Massel, H. K., Edelstein, B. A., Wiegand, W., Bowen, L., & Liberman, R. P. (1993). Conversational skills training with schizophrenic inpatients: A study of generalization across settings and conversants. *Behavior Therapy, 24*(2), 285–304. doi:10.1016/S0005-7894(05)80270-9

Woody, S. R., Weisz, J., & McLean, C. (2005). Empirically supported treatments: 10 years later. *The Clinical Psychologist, 58,* 5–11.

Worell, J., & Papendrick-Remer, P. (2001). *Feminist perspectives in therapy.* New York: Wiley.

Worell, J., & Remer, P. (2003). *Feminist perspectives in therapy: Empowering diverse women* (2nd ed.). Hoboken, NJ: Wiley.

Worthington, E. L., Jr. (1989). *Marriage counseling: A Christian approach to counseling couples.* Downers Grove, IL: InterVarsity Press.

Worthington, E. L., Jr. (1990). *Counseling before marriage.* Dallas, TX: Word Publishers.

Worthington, E. L., Jr. (2004). *Experiencing forgiveness: Six practical sessions for becoming a more forgiving Christian.* Unpublished manuscript, Virginia Commonwealth University, Richmond.

Worthington, E. L., Jr. (2005). *The power of forgiveness.* Philadelphia, PA: Templeton Foundation Press.

Worthington, E. L., Jr. (2006). *The power of forgiveness.* Philadelphia, PA: Templeton Foundation Press. (CD, books on tape)

Worthington, E. L., Jr. (2010). *Experiencing forgiveness: Six practical sessions for becoming a more forgiving Christian.* Retrieved from http://www.people.vcu.edu/~eworth/manuals/participant_manual_christian.doc

Worthington, E. L, Jr., & Sandage, S. J. (2001). Religion and spirituality. *Psychotherapy: Theory, Research, Practice, Training, 38,* 473–478.

Worthington, E. L., & Sandage, S. J. (2002). Religion and spirituality. In J. C. Norcross (Ed.), *Psychotherapy relationships that work* (pp. 371–387). New York: Oxford University Press.

Worthington, R. L., & Dillon, F. R. (2003). The theoretical orientation profile scale-revised: A validation study. *Measurement and Evaluation in Counseling and Development, 38,* 95–105.

Wubbolding, R. E. (1988). *Using reality therapy.* New York: HarperCollins.

Wubbolding, R. E. (2000). *Reality therapy for the 21st century.* Philadelphia: Brunner-Routledge.

Wubbolding, R. E. (2008). Reality therapy. In J. Frew & M.D. Spiegler (Eds.), *Contemporary psychotherapies for a diverse world* (pp. 360–396). Boston: Houghton Mifflin.

Wubbolding, R. E., & Associates. (1998). Multicultural awareness: Implications for reality therapy and choice theory. *International Journal of Reality Therapy, 17*(2), 4–6.

Wubbolding, R. E., Brickell, J., Imhof, L., Kim, R. I., & Al-Rashidi, B. (2004). Reality therapy: A global perspective. *International Journal for the Advancement of Counseling, 26,* 219–228.

Yalom, I. (1989). *Love's executioner and other tales of psychotherapy.* New York: Basic Books.

Yalom, I. D. (1980). *Existential psychotherapy.* New York: Basic Books.

Yalom, I. D. (1991). *When Nietzsche wept.* New York: Basic Books.

Yip, K. S. (2005). Chinese concepts of mental health: Cultural implications for social work practice. *International Social Work, 48,* 391–407.

Yip, K. S. (2008). Searching the Chinese cultural roots of the strengths perspective. In K. S. Yip (Ed.), *Strength-based perspective in working with clients with mental illness: A Chinese cultural articulation* (pp. 21–36). Hauppauge, NY: Nova Science.

Yontef, G. (1999). *Awareness, dialogue, and process.* Thousand Oaks, CA: Sage.

Yontef, G. (2009). The relational attitude in Gestalt theory and practice. In L. Jacobs & R. Hycner (Eds.), *The relational approach in Gestalt therapy* (pp. 37–59). New York: GestaltPress.

Yontef, G., & Jacobs, L. (2005). Gestalt therapy. In R. J. Corsini & D. Wedding (Eds.), *Current psychotherapies* (7th ed., pp. 299–336). Belmont, CA: Brooks/Cole.

Yoshimoto, I. (1983). *The invitation to Naikan method.* Osara, Japan: Toki Shobou.

Young, J. E., Klosko, J. S., & Weishaar, M. (2003). *Schema therapy: A practitioner's guide.* Guilford Publications: New York.

Young, J. S., Dowdle, S., & Flowers, L. (2009). How spirituality can affect the therapeutic alliance. In J. D. Aten & M. M. Leach (Eds.), *Spirituality and the therapeutic process* (pp. 167–192). Washington, DC: American Psychological Association.

Zane, N., Sue, S., Chang, J., Huang, L., Huang, J., Lowe, S., . . . Lee, E. (2005). Beyond ethnic match: Effects of client–therapist cognitive match in problem perception, coping orientation, and therapy goals on treatment outcomes. *Journal of Community Psychology, 33,* 569–585.

Zatorre, R. J. (2003). Music and the brain. *Annals of the New York Academy Sciences, 999,* 4–14.

Zettle, R. D. (2005). The evolution of a contextual approach to therapy: From comprehensive distancing to ACT. *International Journal of Behavioral Consultation and Therapy, 1*(2), 77–89.

Zettle, R. D., & Hayes, S. C. (1987). Dysfunctional control by client verbal behavior: The context of reason giving. *Analysis of Verbal Behavior, 4,* 30–38.

Zillmer, E. A., Spiers, M. V., & Culbertson, W. C. (2008). *Principles of neuropsychology.* Belmont, CA: Thomson Wadsworth.

Zimmerman, B. J., & Bandura, A. (1994). Impact of self-regulatory influences on writing course attainment. *American Educational Research Journal, 31,* 845–862.

Zinnbauer, B. J., & Barrett, J. J. (2009). Integrating spirituality with clinical practice through treatment planning. In J. D. Aten & M. M. Leach (Eds.), *Spirituality and the therapeutic process* (pp. 143–166). Washington, DC: American Psychological Association.

Zinnbauer, B. J., & Pargament, K. I. (2000). Working with the sacred: Four approaches to religious and spiritual issues in counseling. *Journal of Counseling and Development, 78,* 162–171.

Zinnbauer, B. J., & Pargament, K. I. (2005). Religiousness and spirituality. In R. F. Paloutzian & C. L. Park (Eds.), *Handbook of the psychology of religion and spirituality* (pp. 21–42). New York: Guilford Press.

Zuckerman, D. M., Austin, F., Fair, A., & Branchey, L. (1987). Associations between patient religiosity and alcohol attitudes and knowledge in an alcohol treatment program. *International Journal of Addictions, 22,* 47–53.

Zweigenhaft, R. L. (1975). Birth order, approval seeking, and membership in Congress. *Journal of Individual Psychology, 31,* 205–210.

INDEX

Simple reflections, 328, 344

Sitting meditation, 438

Skinner, B. F., 120–121, 124, 153, 232, 382

Skinner box, 121

Smith, Elsie J., 390–399, 556. *See also* Jones-Smith, Elsie

Smith Ethnic Identity Development Model, 390–399

Social activism, 458

Social and gender role analysis, 458

Social constructionist approach (Gonzalez, Biever, and Gardner), 387–388

Social constructivism, 374–375, 387–388, 488, 672. *See also* Family therapy; Feminist therapy; Lesbian and gay therapy; Multicultural psychotherapy theories; Narrative therapy; Postmodernism; Solution-focused therapy; Spiritual/religious issues therapy; Strengths-based therapy; Transcultural psychotherapy

Social constructivists, 374

Social interest, 84–85, 112

Social Interest (Adler), 95–96

Social justice
  movement, in multicultural counseling, 410
  neuroscience and, 650

Social liberation, 335

Social modeling, observational learning, and self-efficacy, 171–175

Socialist feminism, 453, 483

Socialized or stigmatized ethnocentrism, 400, 416

Socially useful type, 86–87

Societal emotional process, 598

Socratic questioning, 100

Socratic technique, in cognitive therapy, 181–182

Solace for the Soul (Murray-Swank), 547

Solomon, J., 348

Solution building, stages of, 492–493

Solution-Focused Brief Therapy (Kim), 500

Solution-focused scale, 498

Solution-focused therapy, 485–507
  Berg and, 488–489
  contributions of, 501–502
  definition, 507
  de Shazer and, 488–489
  goals of, 495–496
  Justin and, 503–505 (case study)
  key concepts, 489–492
  limitations and criticisms of, 502
  brief, 495, 496
  overview, 485–488
  principles and constructs, 492
  research and evaluation, 500–503
  single successful sessions, 499–500
  social constructivism and, 488
  summary, 506
  techniques, 496–499

therapeutic process, 492–500
  therapeutic relationship, 493–495
  See also Psychotherapy theories

Spiritual, definition of, 534. *See also* Spiritual/religious issues therapy

Spiritual assessment, 541–543, 544

Spiritual autobiography, 545–546

Spiritual genogram, 544–545

Spiritual letters, 546

Spiritual life maps, 546

Spiritual mindset, 536–537

Spiritual myopia, 540

Spiritual needs (Clinebell), 538

Spiritual Renewal (Richards, Hardman, and Berrett), 547

Spiritual Renewal Program (Richards, Hardman, and Berrett), 547

Spiritual self, 69

Spiritual timidity, 540

Spiritual Well-Being Scale, 544

Spirituality, 533, 534, 553. *See also* Spiritual/religious issues therapy

Spiritual/religious issues therapy, 531–553
  definitions, 534
  ethical issues in, 548
  Fowler's theory of faith development, 537–538
  Freud and, 535
  goals of, 539
  Justin and, 550–552 (case study)
  key concepts, 536–538
  manualized treatment approaches, 547–548
  overview, 531–536
  pastoral counseling, 536
  research and evaluation, 535–536, 549–550
  science and, 535
  spiritual assessment, 541–543, 544
  spiritual mindset, 536–537
  summary, 552
  techniques, 544–547
  therapeutic process, 538–548
  therapeutic relationship, 538–539
  See also Psychotherapy theories

Spontaneous expression, 352

Spotlighting the Strengths of Every Single Student (Jones-Smith), 557

Stages of change model/theory, 235, 336, 344. *See also* Transtheoretical model of change (TTM)

Stages of faith, 537, 553

Stations of the Mind (Glasser), 210

Steele, Claude, 456

Stereotype threat, 456

"Still Subversive after All These Years" (Brown), 466

Stimulants, 145

Stimulus control, 335

Stonewall Riots, 467

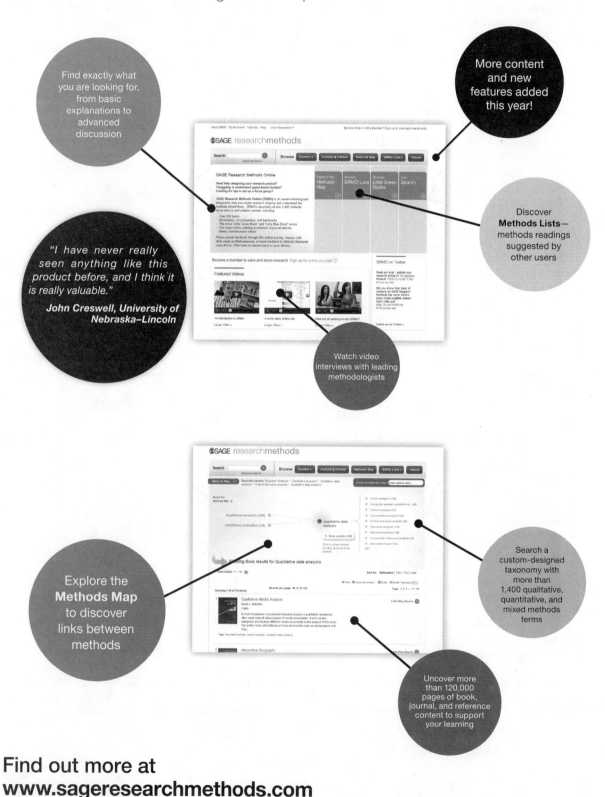

⊛SAGE researchmethods

The essential online tool for researchers from the world's leading methods publisher

Find exactly what you are looking for, from basic explanations to advanced discussion

More content and new features added this year!

"I have never really seen anything like this product before, and I think it is really valuable."

John Creswell, University of Nebraska–Lincoln

Discover **Methods Lists**— methods readings suggested by other users

Watch video interviews with leading methodologists

Explore the **Methods Map** to discover links between methods

Search a custom-designed taxonomy with more than 1,400 qualitative, quantitative, and mixed methods terms

Uncover more than 120,000 pages of book, journal, and reference content to support your learning

Find out more at
www.sageresearchmethods.com

1415

076693